Hypochondriasis

Body Dysmorphic Disorder

Pain Disorder

Factitious Disorders

Factitious Disorder

Dissociative Disorders

Dissociative Amnesia

Dissociative Fugue

Dissociative Identity Disorder (Multiple Personality Disorder)

Depersonalization Disorder

Sexual and Gender Identity Disorders

Sexual Dysfunctions
Sexual Desire Disorders: Hypoactive Sexual Desire Disorder; Sexual Aversion Disorder / Sexual Arousal Disorders: Female Sexual Arousal Disorder; Male Erectile Disorder / Orgasmic Disorders: Female Orgasmic Disorder (Inhibited Female Orgasm); Male Orgasmic Disorder (Inhibited Male Orgasm); Premature Ejaculation / Sexual Pain Disorders: Dyspareunia; Vaginismus / Sexual Dysfunction Due to a General Medical Condition / Substance-induced Sexual Dysfunction

Paraphilias
Exhibitionism / Fetishism / Frotteurism / Pedophilia / Sexual Masochism / Sexual Sadism / Voyeurism / Transvestic Fetishism

Gender Identity Disorders
Gender Identity Disorder: in Children; in Adolescents or Adults (Transsexualism)

Eating Disorders

Anorexia Nervosa

Bulimia Nervosa

Sleep Disorders

Primary Sleep Disorders
Dyssomnias: Primary Insomnia; Primary Hypersomnia; Narcolepsy; Breathing-related Sleep Disorder; Circadian Rhythm Sleep Disorder (Sleep-Wake Schedule Disorder) / Parasomnias; Nightmare Disorder (Dream Anxiety Disorder); Sleep Terror Disorder; Sleepwalking Disorder / Sleep Disorders Related to Another Mental Disorder

Sleep Disorder Due to a General Medical Condition
Substance-induced Sleep Disorder

Impulse Control Disorders Not Elsewhere Classified

Intermittent Explosive Disorder

Kleptomania

Pyromania

Pathological Gambling

Trichotillomania

Adjustment Disorders

Adjustment Disorders
with Anxiety / with Depressed Mood / with Disturbance of Conduct / with Mixed Disturbance of Emotions and Conduct / with Mixed Anxiety and Depressed Mood

Axis II

Mental Retardation
Mild Mental Retardation / Moderate Mental Retardation / Severe Mental Retardation / Profound Mental Retardation

Personality Disorders

Paranoid Personality Disorder

Schizoid Personality Disorder

Schizotypal Personality Disorder

Antisocial Personality Disorder

Borderline Personality Disorder

Histrionic Personality Disorder

Narcissistic Personality Disorder

Avoidant Personality Disorder

Dependent Personality Disorder

Obsessive-Compulsive Personality Disorder

Other Conditions That May Be a Focus of Clinical Attention

Psychological Factors Affecting Medical Condition

Medication-induced Movement Disorders

Relational Problems
Relational Problem Related to a Mental Disorder or General Medical Condition / Parent-Child Relational Problem / Partner Relational Problem / Sibling Relational Problem

Problems Related to Abuse or Neglect
Physical Abuse of Child / Sexual Abuse of Child / Neglect of Child / Physical Abuse of Adult / Sexual Abuse of Adult

Additional Conditions That May Be a Focus of Clinical Attention
Bereavement / Borderline Intellectual Functioning / Academic Problem / Occupational Problem / Child or Adolescent Antisocial Behaviour / Adult Antisocial Behaviour / Malingering / Phase of Life Problem / Noncompliance with Treatment / Identity Problem / Religious or Spiritual Problem / Acculturation Problem / Age-related Cognitive Decline

abnormal psychology

perspectives

EDITED BY   **William L. Marshall**   **Philip Firestone**
Queen's University   *University of Ottawa*

Prentice Hall Allyn and Bacon Canada
Scarborough, Ontario

Canadian Cataloguing in Publication Data

Main entry under title:

Abnormal psychology : perspectives

Includes bibliographical references and index.
ISBN 0-13-589748-3

1. Psychology, Pathological. I. Marshall, W. L. (William Lamont), 1935– .
II. Firestone, Philip.

RC454.A266 1999   616.89   C99-930673-1

Prentice-Hall, Inc., Upper Saddle River, New Jersey
Prentice-Hall International (UK) Limited, London
Prentice-Hall of Australia, Pty. Limited, Sydney
Prentice-Hall Hispanoamericana, S.A., Mexico City
Prentice-Hall of India Private Limited, New Delhi
Prentice-Hall of Japan, Inc., Tokyo
Simon & Schuster Southeast Asia Private Limited, Singapore
Editora Prentice-Hall do Brasil, Ltda., Rio de Janeiro

ISBN 0-13-589748-3

Vice President, Editorial Director: Laura Pearson
Acquisitions Editor: Nicole Lukach
Developmental Editor: Dawn du Quesnay
Marketing Manager: Kathleen McGill
Production Editor: Avivah Wargon
Substantive Editor: Gilda Mekler
Copy Editor: Rodney Rawlings
Production Coordinator: Peggy Brown
Photo Research: Susan Wallace-Cox
Permissions: Jean Ferrier
Art Director: Mary Opper
Cover and interior design: Monica Kompter
Cover image: Daniel Quirion
Page layout: Phyllis Seto and Joan Wilson

1 2 3 4 5   04 03 02 01 00

Printed and bound in the U.S.A.

Visit the Prentice Hall Canada Web site! Send us your comments,
browse our catalogues, and more at **www.phcanada.com**. Or reach us
through e-mail at **phabinfo_pubcanada@prenhall.com**.

Brief Contents

Contents

Chapter 5

Behaviour and Emotional Disorders of Childhood and Adolescence 97

Philip Firestone

Chapter 6

Developmental Disorders 119

Patricia M. Minnes

Chapter 7

Anxiety Disorders 151

Stéphane Bouchard

Steven Taylor

Brian J. Cox

Janel G. Gauthier

Chapter 8

Dissociative and Somatoform Disorders 181

Philip Firestone

Chapter 9

Eating Disorders 203

Fred J. Boland

Chapter 12

Sexual and Gender Identity Disorders 285

Myles Genest

William L. Marshall

Chapter 13

Mood Disorders and Suicide 315

Zindel V. Segal

H. Bruce Ferguson

Chapter 16

Therapies 397

John Hunsley

Catherine M. Lee

Chapter 17

Mental Disorders and Aging 421

V. Jane Knox

William L. Gekoski

Chapter 18

Mental Health Law and Ethics 445

James R. P. Ogloff

Maureen C. Olley

Lindsey A. Jack

Chapter 19

Prevention and Mental Health Promotion in the Community 461

Geoffrey Nelson

Isaac Prilleltensky

Ray DeV. Peters

Focus and ViewPoint Boxes

Preface

When we chose the subtitle "Perspectives" for this text, we felt it expressed the essence of the text's approach. First, this is a contributed volume, so there will necessarily be a number of individual perspectives. Second, we have taken care to present a balance of the various psychological perspectives. For each disorder, all of the relevant paradigms are discussed, and then, at the end of the chapter, the Panorama feature gives the "big picture." It synthesizes the perspectives, highlighting those that currently give us the most useful understanding of the etiology or treatment of the disorder. Finally, this text is written by Canadian experts: While it does pay tribute to the best of international research, it does not ignore the world-class scholarship happening in our own country, giving the book its uniquely Canadian perspective.

Why publish another introductory abnormal psychology text, when there are many fine texts out there already? We feel that *Abnormal Psychology: Perspectives* offers a difference:

- *Canadian content, from the ground up*: Not just an adaptation of an American text, *Abnormal Psychology: Perspectives* was written entirely with the Canadian student in mind. Our universal health care system and relatively high level of secondary education in Canada have resulted in mental health issues that are unique in North America, and are reflected in this text. As well, legal cases, laws governing therapists, ethical issues, prevention programs, ground-breaking research happening here, even the history of abnormal psychology in this country — all these important issues are considered from the perspective of people who will be studying, living, and working in Canada. (The chapter on Mental Health Law and Ethics in Canada is one of the ones most requested by Canadian instructors, tired of having to supplement texts that discuss only the American situation.)

- *Expert Contributors*: One of the advantages of a contributed abnormal psychology text is that each disorder chapter can be written by experts in that field, ensuring that the research discussed and the approach taken in each chapter are as accurate and up-to-date as possible. The panoply of well-known and highly respected contributors to this volume speaks for itself.

- *A Different Approach*: We have fine-tuned the organization of the text to reflect our views on the emerging importance of several areas of abnormal psychology. For example, you will find a whole chapter devoted to Eating Disorders, a topic gaining prominence because the disorders are so widespread and so insidious. We have also devoted an entire chapter to Prevention and Mental Health Promotion in the Community, because we recognize that no matter how adept we become at diagnosing and treating mental illnesses, their *incidence* will never decrease without programs designed to prevent them from occurring in the first place.

We have also changed the traditional placement of the childhood and aging chapters. Usually, these chapters follow one another in a "lifespan" arrangement. We have chosen to introduce childhood disorders early on the text, because childhood is the time when so many disorders begin to manifest themselves. Students will be able to understand this chapter without a full presentation of the other chapters. Mental Disorders and Aging, however, really requires an understanding of the disorders in their pure form, and so we have placed this chapter after all the conventional disorders have been discussed.

Although the book is multi-authored, we have striven at all times for consistency of level, depth, and format across the chapters. Each follows, where applicable, this pattern:

- Opening case
- Overview / introduction of the disorder
- Discussion of diagnostic issues (with DSM-IV criteria)
- Historical perspective
- Full description of the disorder
- Etiology (from all perspectives)
- Treatment (from all perspectives)
- "Panorama" (final integration of perspectives)
- Summary and Key Terms list
- Weblinks

We hope that students and instructors alike will benefit from this collaboration of many individuals who, no doubt like them, will always find the study of abnormal psychology endlessly challenging and utterly absorbing.

Features

Cases. Cases are, without a doubt, what students find most fascinating about abnormal psychology. Each chapter of this text opens with a case or cases designed to engage student interest. Subsequent cases or clinical examples appear throughout the remainder of the chapter, highlighted in the design by a tabbed box, to illustrate nuances between related disorders. Clinical examples are used to illustrate the discussion wherever possible.

Focus Boxes. These feature boxes present interesting topical information such as

- Chapter 1   Treatment and Mistreatment: The History of Mental Asylums
- Chapter 4   The MMPI: A Sample Profile

- Chapter 7   Cultural Differences in Dealing with Anxiety
- Chapter 17   Older Adults: The Missing Clients

ViewPoint Boxes. These engaging boxes present controversial issues in abnormal psychology. Critical Thinking Questions appear at the end of the box, designed to get students considering both sides of the argument. Examples of Viewpoint boxes in the text are

- Chapter 6   Who Should Be Parents?
- Chapter 8   Multiple Identities—Disorder or Role-Playing?
- Chapter 9   Are Eating Disorders Addictions?
- Chapter 11   Motivation for Treatment: The Client's or the Therapist's Responsibility?

Coverage of DSM-IV. A discussion of the DSM-IV, its strengths and its limitations first appears in Chapter 3, Classification and Diagnosis. Thereafter, explanations of the various disorders are always accompanied by tables listing DSM-IV criteria for the disorder. The DSM-IV endpapers at the front and back of the book are another useful reference for the student.

Key Terms. These are bolded and clearly defined where they are first discussed in the chapter. These definitions also appear in the Glossary at the end of the book.

Panorama. This section appears at the end of each disorder chapter. It is essentially a look at the "big picture": a concise summary synthesizing the various perspectives discussed in the chapter, showing what weight researchers currently place on the various paradigms and presenting the student with the most current thinking on how best to understand the etiology and treatment of the disorder.

Summary and Key Terms. Each chapter ends with a concise summary of the important points of the chapter in paragraph form. A list of the key terms for that chapter, with page references, follows.

Weblinks. We recognize the growing presence of the Internet in almost every aspect of our lives, and welcome the chance to use it as an additional learning and research resource. Relevant sites are listed in the Additional Resources section at the end of each chapter.

Supplements

Abnormal Psychology: Perspectives is accompanied by the following supplements:

For the Instructor

Instructor's Manual. Contains chapter summaries, key points, key terms, important names, supplementary lecture material, and questions to provoke class discussion.

Test Item File. This file is available in both printed and computerized formats (for Windows and Macintosh platforms), and contains over 1900 items in multiple-choice and essay formats. The answers to all questions are page-referenced to the text. Prentice Hall Test Manager II is a test generator and classroom management system designed to provide maximum flexibility in producing and grading tests and quizzes.

For the Student

Study Guide. A useful supplement to the text, this guide will help students organize and learn the course material. Includes chapter outlines, learning outcomes, key words, and factual and conceptual fill-in-the-blanks and multiple choice questions, with answers.

Acknowledgments

First, we would like to thank various people at Prentice Hall who provided the initial encouragement to undertake this project and who helped so much in the process of generating the final result. In particular Dawn du Quesnay's patience and guidance was always given with a smile and was vital to the completion of our task. The editorial feedback from Gilda Mekler and Rodney Rawlings was invaluable and we thank them for their efforts. Also deserving of our thanks are Kathleen McGill, who encouraged our initial interest, Rebecca Bersagel, who got us started in the right direction, and Avivah Wargon, our production editor.

In addition, we would like to thank our families (Jean, Liam, Allana, Patrick, and Quinn for Bill; Suzie, Zak, and Noah for Phil) for their support and patience throughout this task. Several undergraduate and graduate students also provided invaluable assistance, often working late into the night digging up references, proofreading, and providing important comments. The students were Geris Seran, Michel Larose, Tara Brun-Hayne, Kevin Nunes, and Ian Broom. Most importantly, we are extremely grateful to our chapter authors for their persistence and for their excellent contributions.

The research of Kenneth M. Prkachin and Glenda C. Prkachin used in Chapter 15, Psychophysiologic Disorders, was supported by grants from the Heart and Stroke Foundations of Canada. The authors would like to express their thanks for the assistance of Julie Orlando and the helpful commentary on earlier drafts of this chapter by Dana Edge and Cindy Hardy.

Finally, we gratefully acknowledge the comments and suggestions of the many knowledgeable colleagues who reviewed the manuscript at various stages:

Martin Anthony, University of Toronto

David Bernhardt, Carleton University

Gary Brooks, St. Francis Xavier University

Leanne Campbell, Malaspina University College

Michael Coles, Simon Fraser University

John Conklin, Camosun College

Enrico DiTomasso, University of New Brunswick

Linda Hatt, Okanagan College

Jack Hirschberg, Concordia University

Charlotte Johnston, University of British Columbia

R.J. Konopasky, St. Mary's University

Scott McCabe, University of Waterloo

Bill McLoughlin, Kwantlen University College

Shawn Mosher, York University

Robert Muller, York University

Demetrios Papageorgis, University of British Columbia

James Parker, Trent University

Ed Pomeroy, Brock University

Wendy Pullin, Concordia University College of Alberta

Jane Silvius, Kwantlen University College

Sherry Stewart, Dalhousie University

Douglas Wardell, University of Alberta

Ian Whishaw, University of Lethbridge

William Marshall, Kingston, 1999
Philip Firestone, Ottawa, 1999

About the Editors

William L. Marshall

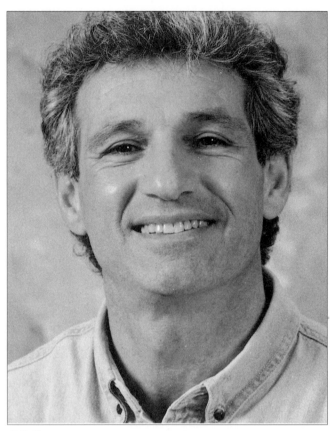

Philip Firestone

William Marshall was born in Western Australia, where he completed his Bachelor of Psychology. After completing his M.Sc. at the University of London, Bill went to Queen's University for his doctorate and stayed on as a staff member. He is currently a Professor in both Psychology and Psychiatry and an Associate Professor in Urology. Bill has over 200 publications and has been on the editorial board of 14 international scientific journals. He also directs treatment programs for sexual offenders in four federal penitentiaries and remains an active clinician. In 1993 he was given the Lifetime Achievement Award of the Association for the Treatment of Sexual Abusers. He is the 1999 recipient of the Santiago Grisolia Prize, given annually to the person who is judged to have made the most significant contribution to the reduction of violence worldwide. Bill is married and has a son and two grandsons. His leisure time is spent primarily with his family, swimming, canoeing, kayaking, and hiking.

Philip Firestone is a Professor in the School of Psychology and the Department of Psychiatry at the University of Ottawa. He has published extensively in the areas of attention deficit hyperactivity disorder, impulse control disorders, and the effects of childhood sexual abuse. His current research interests are related primarily to the assessment, treatment, and long-term outcome of individuals convicted of sexual offences. He is a consultant to the Forensic Program of the Royal Ottawa Hospital. In addition, he runs a clinic that provides psychological services to men on parole for violent and sexual offences. His primary teaching areas are abnormal psychology and developmental psychology. In his spare time Dr. Firestone enjoys playing a number of sports, particularly squash and tennis.

About the Contributors

Developmental Disorders

Patricia M. Minnes, Ph.D., C. Psych, is currently the Associate Professor and Chair of the Clinical Training Program in the Department of Psychology at Queen's University in Kingston. Her research presently focuses upon persons with developmental disabilities, and persons with acquired or traumatic brain injuries, their families, and caregivers. Her recent studies have included attitudes toward persons with disabilities, coping with stress associated with caring for a person with disabilities, and factors contributing to successful community integration of persons with disabilities. She also maintains a private practice where she works primarily with persons with disabilities and their families.

Anxiety Disorders

Stéphane Bouchard is a Professor at the Université du Québec à Hull. His main research interests are anxiety, panic disorder, cognitive-behavior therapy, and multivariate time-series analyses. In 1997 he received the Canadian Psychological Association award for Best Young Researcher.

Steven Taylor, Ph.D., is an Associate Professor in the Department of Psychiatry at the University of British Columbia. His research and clinical interests include cognitive-behavioural mechanisms and treatments of anxiety disorders, particularly panic disorder, obsessive-compulsive disorder, and posttraumatic stress disorder.

Brian J. Cox is an Associate Professor in the Department of Psychiatry at the University of Manitoba. His research on anxiety disorders has been recognized by awards from the Anxiety Disorders Association of America, the Association for Advancement of Behavior Therapy, and the Canadian Psychological Association.

Janel G. Gauthier is a full Professor at Laval University. His main areas of interest are anxiety disorders and biofeedback. He was the president of the Canadian Psychological Association in 1997 and 1998.

Eating Disorders

Fred J. Boland received his B.A. (1971) and M.Sc. (1973) from Memorial University and his Ph.D. (1978) in Psychology (Clinical) from McGill University. He was appointed to Queen's University Psychology Department in 1977 where he has served as Chair of Clinical Training and Chair of Undergraduate Studies. For the past 20 years his research has focused on theoretical and treatment aspects of substance abuse and eating disorders. He is cross-appointed to the Department of Psychiatry and is associated with the Eating Disorder Program at Hotel Dieu Hospital in Kingston.

Substance-Related Disorders

Marilyn Keyes obtained her M.A. in psychology from Carleton University and is presently a doctoral student in clinical psychology at the University of Ottawa. She is the recipient of a Social Science and Humanities Research Doctoral Fellowship and her doctoral research is in the area of self-regulation as it relates to problem gambling in particular.

Yolanda Korneluk received her B. A. from the University of Ottawa and is currently a doctoral student in Clinical Psychology there. Her primary area of interest is health psychology, with a focus on adolescent health issues and the impact of illness on the family.

Personality Disorders

Ralph C. Serin is a Senior Research Manager with Correctional Services of Canada. He has held various positions within the service since 1975, and currently manages programs research within the Research Branch. Ralph received his Ph.D. from Queen's University and maintains adjunct appointments in the Department of Psychiatry at Queen's and the University of Toronto, and in the Department of Psychology at Carleton University. He has published in the areas of psychopathy, risk assessment, sexual offending, and the assessment and treatment of violent offenders. Currently Ralph is pursuing research on treatment readiness and responsivity, measurement of program effectiveness, typologies in sexual and violent offenders, and systematic assessment protocols and clinical decision-making.

Sexual and Gender Identity Disorders

Myles Genest is Professor of Psychology at Acadia University in Wolfville, Nova Scotia. He maintains a private practice in Halifax and has served as President of the Association of Psychologists of Nova Scotia. His research has been in the area of cognitive-behavioural assessment and treatment of pain and other problems.

Mood Disorders and Suicide

Zindel V. Segal is Head of the Cognitive Behaviour Therapy Unit at the Centre for Addiction and Mental Health, Clarke Division, and is Professor in the Departments of Psychiatry and Psychology at the University of Toronto. He is also the Head of Psychotherapy Research for the Psychotherapy Program in the Department of Psychiatry.

H. Bruce Ferguson is affiliated with Queen's University in Kingston, Ontario, and Monash University in Melbourne, Australia. He taught psychology at Carleton University in Ottawa for nearly two decades before moving to the health care system. His published research is in the area of developmental psychopathology with a focus on the disruptive disorders of childhood. He holds appointments as a Professor of Psychiatry and Psychology at the University of Toronto, and is now the Head, Community Systems and Interventions in the Community Health/Mental Health Program at the Hospital for Sick Children in Toronto, where he is working to build networks and improve systems of care and support for children and families.

Schizophrenia

Richard W. J. Neufeld teaches introductory abnormal psychology at the University of Western Ontario. His areas of specialty are schizophrenia, stress, and cognitive efficiency. He received the Joey and Toby Tannenbaum Schizophrenia Research Distinguished Scientist Award in 1992, the Ontario Mental Health Foundation Senior Research Fellowship in 1995, and is presently the Associate Editor of *Psychological Assessment*.

Jeffrey R. Carter's research at the University of Western Ontario integrates mathematical and biological models of cognitive deficits in schizophrenia, especially concerning the perception of emotion. His clinical work at the London Health Sciences Centre focuses on children and adolescents.

Ian R. Nicholson is the Psychology Professional Practice Leader at the London Health Sciences Centre and an Associate Professor of Psychiatry at the University of Western Ontario. His research interests are in the assessment and classification of psychopathology.

David Vollick is affiliated with the University College of the Caribou in Kamloops, B.C. His research is concerned with stochastic modeling of information-processing deficits in schizophrenia. He has five years' experience conducting psychotherapy with individuals with schizophrenia.

Psychophysiologic Disorders

Kenneth M. Prkachin received his Ph.D. in clinical psychology from the University of British Columbia in 1978. Subsequently he taught in the Department of Psychology at the University of British Columbia, and the Department of Health Studies at the University of Waterloo. He is currently Chair of Psychology and Community Health, University of Northern British Columbia. His research is in the area of measurement of emotion, psychological determinants of cardiovascular reactivity, and psychological risk factors for heart disease.

Glenda C. Prkachin received her Ph.D. in biopsychology from the University of British Columbia in 1978. Subsequently she was a Killam Postdoctoral Fellow in the Department of Neuroanatomy at the University of Washington and a Natural Sciences and Engineering Council of Canada University Research Fellow. She has taught at the University of Western Ontario, Mt. Allison University, Wilfrid Laurier University, and the Universities of Guelph and Waterloo. She is currently Associate Professor in the Psychology Program, University of Northern British Columbia. Her current research is in the area of neuropsychological models of emotion recognition.

Therapies

John Hunsley is a Professor of Psychology in the School of Psychology, University of Ottawa, and is the Director of the Centre for Psychological Services, which is the clinical training unit of the School of Psychology. Dr. Hunsley is a registered psychologist who provides psychological services for the treatment of anxiety and mood disorders and for the treatment of relationship difficulties. He conducts research on psychological assessment, the impact of psychological services, and marital functioning.

Catherine M. Lee is an Associate Professor and Director of the Clinical Psychology Program at the University of Ottawa. Her work focuses on family members' adjustment to various stressors and on the delivery of psychological services.

Mental Disorders and Aging

V. Jane Knox, Ph.D., C. Psych. is a Professor and Acting Head of the Department of Psychology at Queen's University. Her research interests are attitudes toward and stereotypes of aging individuals, as well as the factors influencing mental health service underutilization by elderly Canadians.

William L. Gekoski is a member of the Department of Psychology at Queen's University in Kingston, Ontario. Trained in life-span developmental psychology at the University of Michigan in Ann Arbor, he specialized in gerontological psychology, doing post-graduate work at the Ardrus Gerontological Center at the University of Southern California in Los Angeles. Bill has been collaborating with Jane Knox for more than fifteen years on a program of research that addresses the questions of how aging and older people are perceived, what factors are important to positive adjustment of aging, and identifying the attitudes of people of different ages toward community care versus institutional care for older adults. Bill is a member of the Canadian Association on Gerontology, the Gerontological Society of America, and the Canadian Psychological Association, having served as Chair of its section on Adult Development and Aging.

Mental Health Law and Ethics

James R. P. Ogloff, J.D., Ph.D. is a Professor of Psychology at Simon Fraser University, and Adjunct Professor of Law at the University of British Columbia. Dr. Ogloff works in the law and psychology area and is President of the American Psychology Law Society. He also is Chair of the Committee on Ethics of the Canadian Psychological Association. He has been elected President of CPA and will take office in 2000.

Maureen C. Olley, Ph.D. is a clinical and forensic psychologist in British Columbia. She works as a psychologist in the Correctional Service of Canada and also works with children and adolescents with eating disorders.

Lindsey A. Jack, M.A. is a doctoral candidate in the Graduate Program in Law and Psychology at Simon Fraser University, specializing in clinical-forensic psychology. Her area of interest focuses on adolescent offenders.

Prevention and Mental Health Promotion in the Community

Geoffrey Nelson is Professor of Psychology and director of the M. A. Program in community psychology at Wilfrid Laurier University. He has served as the Senior Editor of the *Canadian Journal of Community Mental Health*, and currently is conducting research on the Better Beginnings, Better Futures prevention program in the Highfield community in Toronto, and on a national project on best practices in promoting family wellness and preventing child maltreatment.

Isaac Prilleltensky, a fellow of the Division of Community Psychology of the American Psychological Association, is a faculty member in the community psychology graduate program at Wilfrid Laurier University. He has an interest in the prevention of psychological problems and is currently the Principal Investigator of a large research and policy project on the promotion of family wellness and the prevention of child maltreatment.

Ray DeV. Peters, Ph.D., is Professor of Psychology at Queen's University in Kingston, Ontario, and is Research Director of the Better Beginnings, Better Futures project mentioned above, a large, multisite longitudinal study in Ontario on the prevention of social, emotional, health, and cognitive problems in young children from birth to 8 years of age.

Chapter 1

Concepts of Abnormality Throughout History

William L. Marshall

Paul had, since childhood, been sexually aroused by the sight of women's underwear. This had caused him considerable concern as a teenager and young adult because he felt different from others and was afraid they would find out about his secret desires and ridicule him. When Paul was 26 years old, after years of secrecy, he decided to consult a therapist in an attempt to deal with his unusual desires.

*   *   *

Lisa appeared at a clinic saying that her husband and two teenage children had persuaded her to seek treatment for what they saw as dysfunctional behaviour. She told the clinician that after she took a shower (which she did at least three times a day), she felt she had to wash the floor and walls of the bathroom in order to ensure that no dirt or bacteria had splashed off her body and contaminated the room. Lisa also insisted that her family not touch the faucets in the bathroom with their naked hands because she was sure that they would leave germs. The family members agreed to use a tissue to turn the taps on and off. Visits to the house by friends and relatives were not allowed because Lisa felt she could not ask visitors to follow these instructions and even if she could bring herself to ask them, she did not believe they would go along with her request. This, of course, meant that her husband and children could never invite friends to their house, and no doubt this, and various other restrictions Lisa imposed upon them, led the family to send her for treatment. Lisa did not herself consider her problems to be quite as bad as her family saw them.

*   *   *

Arnold had begun to develop odd ways of perceiving the world and had begun to have unusual thoughts shortly after he entered university at age 32. He had successfully graduated from high school and immediately joined his father's engineering business. Over the years Arnold's hard work and obvious skills gained him promotions and a good salary. After he turned 30, his father and his wife put pressure on him to enroll in an engineering degree program at university so he could take more responsible jobs at higher pay. Arnold resisted this pressure for some time, but finally gave in and took up the program. However, he was afraid he would fail and let everyone down. He was afraid they would find out he was really not competent. The pressures from his family, the threat of failure, the heavy workload of studies and his responsibilities to his family soon became too much for Arnold and he began to break down. He began to develop odd interpretations of world events and of his role in them, and he began to perceive personally relevant messages on the nightly television newscasts. These unusual thoughts and perceptions quickly escalated until finally Arnold went to the local police station requesting a meeting with Canada's prime minister and the American president so he could give them directions to solve the world's problems. Not surprisingly, Arnold's grades dropped and he had to leave school. He was placed in hospital.

Clearly, Paul, Lisa, and Arnold all have abnormalities of behaviour and thought, but they are also clearly very different from one another. There is no doubt, however, that most people would agree each of them displayed very unusual, if not bizarre, behaviour. Arnold's problems obviously seriously interfered with his life and his ambitions. Lisa was not as concerned about her problems as her family was, but they nevertheless markedly restricted her social life and interfered with other aspects of her functioning. Paul, on the other hand, found a partner who could share in his unusual sexual activities and his life was happy and apparently fulfilled.

What these three cases have in common is that each meets the criteria outlined in current diagnostic manuals for one or another psychological disorder. The current edition of the *Diagnostic and Statistical Manual* (DSM-IV) of the American Psychiatric Association (1994) is the most broadly accepted system for identifying particular types of disorders, although the *International Classification of Mental and Behavioral Disorders* (ICD-10), issued by the World Health Organization (1992), is also used by practitioners primarily outside North America. Both these diagnostic manuals would classify the three cases described above as disordered: Paul would be classified as having a paraphilia (in this case, a fetish), Lisa as manifesting obsessive-compulsive disorder, and Arnold as suffering from schizophrenia.

However, there are many people who engage in behaviours or express thoughts that most of us consider to be strange or deviant, and who may cause distress to others, yet who are not identified in diagnostic systems as disordered. Consider the following cases.

Eileen is a 19-year-old female whose religious beliefs forbid her to wear makeup or colourful clothes, or to listen to the radio or watch television. She will only go out with potential boyfriends in the company of her parents, and she will not attend dances or parties. Eileen believes, along with the rest of the people who attend her church, that the world will end in the year 2000 and she has been peacefully preparing herself for that day. In addition, and somewhat contrary to her religious teachings, Eileen believes that the planets and stars control our destiny, and she subscribes to a monthly astrology magazine and consults the daily astrological forecasts. Eileen also believes that she can communicate with the spirits of the dead and occasionally participates in seances with her family and their friends.

Roger is a professor at a large university. At age 46, he has never married and lives alone in a house whose windows he has painted black to shut out, as he says, "the views of his nosy neighbours." Roger wears the same worn and tattered suit he has worn for years and a rather dirty baseball cap that he says is a family heirloom. He often wears heavy coats in the summer, and sandals in the winter. His office is cluttered and he never seems able to find things; in fact, he has, on several occasions, lost students' essays. In the classroom, Roger wanders about among the desks as he lectures, and his lessons are rambling and difficult for the students to follow. He often introduces odd ideas that seem to have little to do with the topic on which he is lecturing. However, his research is greatly admired and his colleagues do their best to make up for his teaching inadequacies.

James has been a career criminal since he was an early teenager. He has broken into many homes and stolen property; he has been convicted of selling marijuana on several occasions; and he has stolen and then sold numerous bicycles and cars. James had, not surprisingly, spent some of his 42 years in prison. Recently, James was living with a woman whom he had met at a bar one week prior to moving in with her and her three children. This was the most recent in a series of relatively short-lived common-law relationships that James had been involved in throughout his adult life. He did not have a job and, despite his promises to his partner, James made little effort to get one. He stayed home watching television and drinking beer. This led to numerous arguments with his partner and, over time, these arguments became more physical, with each partner hitting the other. Finally, during one of these clashes, James lost his temper and beat the woman with his fists so severely that she lapsed into a coma and died.

Eileen and Roger would both be considered eccentric by most people and, indeed, some students found Roger scary, although he never did anything that would suggest he was dan-

gerous. But, neither he nor Eileen has ever been diagnosed as having a psychological disorder. Many people think that anyone who murders is insane, at least temporarily. However, careful examination of James by three independent psychiatrists led them to conclude that while he had a personality disorder, James was otherwise normal and the killing resulted from the persistent antagonistic relationship he had with the victim. James was, therefore, held to be responsible for his actions and duly convicted and imprisoned.

These cases illustrate two problems with defining abnormality. First, eccentric and unusual behaviour or beliefs are not necessarily abnormal according to diagnostic criteria, although the boundary between eccentricity and abnormality is not always clear. Arnold was clearly eccentric but also obviously disturbed. Both Eileen and Roger were eccentric but not so obviously disturbed. Second, behaviours that are repugnant and threatening to others, such as aggression and murder, are not always signs of an underlying psychological disorder. James has acted very badly and in a damaging way to others throughout his life, yet he is not considered to be seriously psychologically disordered. Neither Paul nor Lisa caused distress to other people, but they are judged to be suffering from a disorder.

This book describes our present understanding of the nature of psychological abnormality, the different forms such abnormality takes, how people become abnormal and what, if anything, can be done to make their functioning normal. A fundamental issue we will have to consider from the outset, then, is just what it is we mean when we say that someone (or a particular behaviour of that person) is psychologically abnormal.

Our notions about abnormality have a long history. Humans have, from the time of the earliest written records, and no doubt long before that, identified some of their fellow humans as abnormal and offered various explanations and treatments for the behaviours. It is also clear that, over time, definitions of what constitutes abnormal functioning have changed, as have the explanations and treatments. In this opening chapter of the book, we will first consider the various ways in which abnormality has been defined, and then we will examine the historical developments in the explanations and treatment of abnormality.

First, let us clarify some terms. **Psychological abnormality** refers to behaviour, speech, or thought that impairs the ability of a person to function in a way that is generally expected of them, in the context where the unusual functioning occurs. **Mental illness** is a term often used to convey the same meaning as psychological abnormality, but it implies a medical rather than psychological cause. A **psychological disorder** is a specific manifestation of this impairment of functioning as described by some set of criteria that have been established by a panel of experts. In this book we will use the term **psychopathology** to mean both the scientific study of psychological abnormality and the problems faced by people who suffer from such disorders. Psychological disorders occur in all societies and have been apparent at all times in history. However, just what is considered a disorder varies across time and place.

ATTEMPTS AT DEFINING ABNORMALITY

Why is there such confusion about normality and abnormality, and is it possible to resolve the issue? Perhaps the answer to the last part of the question is no, because the concept of abnormality changes with time and differs across cultures and subcultures. However, it is also possible that we cannot easily resolve these problems because the concepts of normality and abnormality are so vague, despite the attempts of many writers to provide clear criteria.

Several principles are commonly considered in attempts to establish criteria for abnormality. As will become evident, however, no one principle can be considered sufficient to define this elusive concept. Rather, depending on circumstances, the contribution of several criteria may be necessary. The following principles, either alone or in combination, have at one time or another been used to define abnormality.

Statistical Concept

According to this view, behaviour is judged as abnormal if it occurs infrequently in the population. It would, of course, make little sense to describe as abnormal ways of functioning that characterize the majority of people. Relative infrequency, then, ought to be one defining feature of abnormality. However, not all infrequent behaviour or thoughts should be judged abnormal. For instance, innovative ideas are necessarily scarce or they would hardly be innovative, but most people would not consider the person who had such ideas as displaying abnormality, at least not in its usual pejorative sense. The same is true of athletic prowess. Very few people can run 100 metres in ten seconds or less, but we admire those who can. They are, it is true, abnormal in the sense of

being rare, but we would usually describe such people as exceptional, a term that has no derogatory overtones.

Perhaps a more telling example concerns those people who fall at the extremes of the intellectual spectrum. Psychologists have developed tests to measure what they call intelligence. These tests produce a score called the intelligence quotient, or IQ. Measures of IQ are standardized on large samples of people that are meant to represent every aspect of the total population. The scores of this normative sample are then converted statistically so that the average score is equal to 100. This average score is arbitrary, however, and is set at 100 entirely for convenience. The array of scores around 100 is also arbitrarily distributed according to what is called a "normative distribution," meaning that there are an equal number of persons from the sample population who score at equal intervals above and below the arbitrary average. This normative distribution is often called a *bell curve* because of its shape, and Figure 1.1 illustrates this IQ distribution derived from the most commonly used intelligence test, the Wechsler Adult Intelligence Scale. (See Chapter 4 for further discussion of intelligence testing.)

Note that the scores of 68 percent of the population fall between 85 and 115. A smaller proportion (just over 2 percent) of the population scores 30 points above the average of 100 and a similarly small proportion 30 points below. According to diagnostic practices, based entirely on the statistical approach, those who score 70 or lower on IQ tests are said to be mentally retarded (that is, abnormal). An IQ score this low certainly indicates that a person will have considerable difficulty functioning independently in mainstream society, and will likely display behaviours that are inappropriate although not necessarily offensive or upsetting to others. However, those who score 30 points or more above the average (that is, who have an IQ of 130 or higher) are not considered to

Figure 1.1 The Distribution of IQ Scores

	−3δ	−2δ	−1δ		+1δ	+2δ	+3δ

Below average   Average   Above average

Percentage of scores in interval	0.13%	2.14%	13.59%	34.13%	34.13%	13.59%	2.14%	0.13%
Wechsler IQ		55	70	85	100	115	130	145

δ: the standard deviation which is the average of the variability about the mean.

be abnormal; indeed, they are admired if not envied. Again, we see that being unusual is not a sufficient reason for someone to be declared abnormal.

An additional problem with the statistical criterion is that it is not clear how unusual a behaviour has to be to be considered abnormal. For example, Robins, Locke, and Regier (1991) report that major depression, a clearly identified psychological disorder, affects one in twenty women and alcoholism occurs in one in ten men. Given these frequencies, neither depression nor alcoholism can be said to be statistically infrequent—yet both are thought to reflect a disorder in need of treatment.

Personal Distress

Many people who are considered to have a psychological disorder report being distressed. Someone who has an anxiety disorder, for example, will report feeling afraid or apprehensive most of the time. Depressed patients are obviously distressed. Yet distress is not present for all people identified as abnormal. An elderly manic patient who was evaluated at a local hospital would persistently pace rapidly around the ward, frequently bumping into people in his rush, despite having no obvious destination. While striding about at speed, he would keep up a constant conversation with no one in particular and he would leap from topic to unrelated topic. He seemed to be in exuberant spirits and he described himself as being extremely happy. Obviously he was not personally distressed and yet, just as obviously, he was not normal.

Some people who, to outward signs, appear happy and successful may reveal to intimate friends that they feel a vague sense of dissatisfaction. They may complain that despite their apparent success they feel unfulfilled. There may even be an associated sense of despair at not having achieved something significant, and such a person may seek professional help. It is unlikely, however, that they would be labelled abnormal.

In fact, all of us are distressed, or even depressed, at times. When someone we love dies, it is normal to be distressed; indeed, if we were not, we might be judged to be displaying an abnormal response. If this distress passes within a reasonable amount of time, our response would be considered normal. However, if our grief did not abate with time, and our depression deepened and persisted for several years, we would be described as suffering from pathological grief and, therefore, as abnormal. Distress, then, appears to be a frequent, but not an essential, feature of abnormality.

Personal Dysfunction

When behaviour is clearly maladaptive (that is, it interferes with appropriate functioning), it is typically said to be abnormal. Yet the definition of dysfunction itself is not clear-cut. What is appropriate functioning? What is appropriate functioning in a given context? Consider some of the behaviours of people interred in Nazi concentration camps during World War II. A number of them became extremely socially withdrawn; others displayed dissociative behaviour; and some became exaggeratedly dependent on others, even though they had previously been quite independent. Such behaviours would be considered inappropriate in the typical circumstances of peacetime life,

and would disrupt a person's ability to function. Yet in response to torture, degradation, and the imminent fear of death, such behaviours may be seen as understandable and expected; moreover, they may have helped people survive and have thus been highly functional. Wakefield (1992) has concluded that harmful dysfunction is the key notion—harmful to the individual or to others. Unless there are dysfunctional consequences to the individual, he suggests, it makes little sense to call behaviour abnormal. Indeed, most abnormal behaviours disadvantage the person, but again, it is a matter of degree. A person who hears voices, believes that others are trying to kill him, and speaks in unintelligible babble, for example, experiences disruption of functioning in all aspects of his life, but a person with an extreme phobia of snakes who lives in the city may rarely, if ever, be disadvantaged by her fear. People with snake phobia typically live full and well-functioning lives with only small inconveniences caused by their problem, but they would, nevertheless, be diagnosed as having a disorder. Thus, Wakefield's criterion is not always followed.

Wakefield (1992) has also considered the possibility that mental disorders may affect the reproductive capacity of persons so afflicted. Reproduction is of considerable importance to most people and has obvious relevance for survival, so any dysfunction that interferes with reproductive ability may be construed as reflecting abnormal processes. Some serious psychological disorders do reduce reproductive possibilities. For example, someone who is continually deeply depressed is unlikely to succeed in securing a sexual partner and may very well not wish to have the burden of children to care for. Other serious mental disorders such as schizophrenia or some of the developmental disabilities are also likely to interfere with reproduction; yet most psychological abnormalities do not reduce reproductive success. According to this criterion, homosexuality would be abnormal, since obviously an exclusive homosexual will not be reproductively effective. Yet there seems otherwise no obvious reason to consider such people to be abnormal, and homosexuality has gone from being a clear sign of abnormality in DSM-II (American Psychiatric Association, 1968) to not being considered a problem at all in DSM-IV.

Violation of Norms

The behaviour and thoughts of many psychologically disordered individuals run counter to what we might consider appropriate behaviour. The thoughts expressed by paranoid schizophrenics, for example, are often so bizarre that observers do not hesitate to declare the ideas irrational and as reflecting an extreme departure from what would be expected in the context. Similarly, a man who dresses in women's clothing in order to generate sexual arousal would be judged by most people to be displaying behaviours that are contrary to socially acceptable ideas. On the other hand, criminals clearly engage in behaviours that violate social norms, but few of them meet the criteria for any disorder. No doubt their criminal acts upset others but discomfort in an observer cannot alone count as the basis for judging someone's behaviour to be disordered. For example, the lyrics of gangsta rap music make many people uncomfortable, as indeed they are intended to, but that would not justify classifying these lyricists as psychologically abnormal, although that is a characteristic response people often make to ideas and behaviours they find personally repulsive.

Related to the notion of violating norms is the idea that psychologically abnormal people are unpredictable and somehow dangerous. In fact, very few people suffering from a psychiatric disorder are at all dangerous to others. Even psychotic patients, who are the most bizarre of all disordered people, rarely attempt to hurt anyone. Most psychologically disordered people are no more dangerous, and no more unpredictable, than are the rest of the population. Conversely, while television and movies like to portray all killers and rapists as mad, most are not. Apparently, it comforts us to think that someone who would do something so repugnant as to kill or maim another person must be insane.

Perhaps the most serious flaw in this criterion is that social norms vary over time and place. Thirty years ago, when homosexuality was classified as abnormal, it was also considered to violate social norms. Is it a reflection of changing norms that psychologists no longer consider homosexuality abnormal? To take a more extreme example, in Germany in the 1930s, Jews, homosexuals, gypsies, retarded people, and others were persecuted, tortured, or killed on the basis that they represented inferior specimens of human beings. These views, which are repugnant to our society, were apparently sufficiently acceptable to the German populace at the time to allow the Nazis to carry out their so-called ethnic cleansing. Do we conclude that 1930s Germany was an abnormal society—and if so, what does it mean to say that a whole population is abnormal?

Diagnosis by an Expert

Before we consider this issue, it is an opportune time to identify the professionals involved in the mental health field. **Psychiatrists** are trained in medicine prior to doing specialized training in dealing with mental illness. This specialized training focusses on diagnosis and medical treatment that emphasize the use of pharmacological agents in managing mental disorders. Not surprisingly, most psychiatrists attend to the medical aspects and biological foundations of these disorders, although they usually also consider psychological and environmental influences. **Clinical psychologists** are initially trained in general psychology and then receive graduate training in the application of this knowledge to the understanding and amelioration of disorders of thinking and behaviour. Psychologists have a thorough grounding in research methods, and some of them spend their careers doing research on abnormal functioning, although many also provide treatment. The treatment methods of clinical psychologists primarily involve psychological interventions of one kind or another. **Psychiatric nurses** have received formal training in nursing before completing a specialization in psychiatric problems. These professionals typically work in hospital settings where they manage the day-to-day care of mentally disordered patients. In addition to these professionals, **psychiatric social workers** attend to the influence of the social environment on disordered clients. Psychiatric social workers usually have a graduate degree in social work and

they provide assistance to clients in adjusting to life within their families and the community.

The fact is that the identification of a psychological disorder in any specific individual is ultimately left to a professional to judge. In the final analysis, it is the actions of particular mental health workers (usually psychiatrists) that determine whether a person is said to suffer from a psychological abnormality. In this sense, the DSM-IV (or ICD-10) provides the operational criteria for the various disorders and thereby defines abnormality. This, of course, does not clarify the criteria by which such judgements are made and an examination of the various criteria for the different disorders suggests that different aspects of the notions outlined above serve to define different disorders. It is hard to discern any clear common thread to the different criteria.

Thomas Szasz (1960), in an article entitled "The myth of mental illness," suggested that the idea of mental disorders was invented by psychiatry to give control to its practitioners to the exclusion of other people, such as clergymen, who in the past had greater power over the psychologically disordered. Such criticisms, while perhaps overstating the case, do serve a valuable function by encouraging the generation of evidence to support the existence of mental disorders. There seems little doubt today that there is overwhelming evidence of the reality of various disorders. Nevertheless, the power held by mental health professionals remains an issue.

Somewhat related to Szasz' idea that psychological abnormality is a social construction are the views first expressed over 30 years ago by the anthropologist Oscar Lewis (1961, 1969). He claimed a culture of poverty existed in the United States that kept people living in poor circumstances. Lewis suggested the features of poverty, such as violence and overcrowding, and the associated feelings of being excluded from the American dream, led to despair and helplessness which in turn set the stage for the development of abnormal behaviour. Studies of people living in urban settings in the United States offer some support for the ideas expressed by Lewis. In a study of midtown Manhattan residents during the period 1952–1960, it was found that the poor were much more likely to be identified as disordered than were the middle- or upper-middle-class residents (Srole, Langner, Michael, Opler, & Rennie, 1962). These findings have been essentially replicated in other large-scale epidemiological studies of city dwellers in the United States (Eaton, Anthony, Tepper, & Dryman, 1992; Regier et al., 1984).

Summary of Definitions

As we have seen, no one of the various criteria that have been offered for defining abnormality seems satisfactory on its own. There are many ways to approach defining a person's functioning as normal or abnormal, and the criteria discussed above do not exhaust all possible approaches. Nevertheless, together they represent the core defining features of abnormality. To identify a person or a behaviour as abnormal, no single criterion is either necessary (that is, must be present) or sufficient (enough on its own). Typically some combination of these criteria is used, with one or more features having greater relevance depending upon the specific circumstances or features of the client. Our purpose in discussing various criteria for abnormal psychological functioning has been to alert the reader to the rather elusive nature of the concept and to suggest that, while such a notion may have some general value, it has little practical application. In practice, most diagnosticians avoid the use of the term "abnormality" and simply prefer to match their clients' symptoms to a set of criteria appearing in the latest edition of the diagnostic manual. While this approach does not clarify the nature of abnormality, it works effectively in practice. Defining specific behaviours, thoughts, and feelings as representing particular disorders, as does the *Diagnostic and Statistical Manual of Mental Disorders* (DSM), is useful because then we can plan the management and treatment of the person displaying such problems. Searching for criteria that will define any and all instances of disordered functioning (or abnormality), however, may be pointless. Nevertheless, throughout the ages people have held quite different views not only about what abnormality is, but also about its causes.

HISTORICAL CONCEPTS OF ABNORMALITY

We now turn to an examination of the different notions that have, over time, guided approaches to dealing with abnormality. Looking at changes in the conceptualization of abnormal psychological functioning can provide a basis for understanding how we arrived at our current formulations and responses to abnormality. An understanding of history ought to help us avoid the errors of the past. As George Santayana, the Spanish-born American philosopher, once said, "Those who cannot remember the past are condemned to repeat it." Second, when we examine the way in which societies in the past have viewed and treated abnormality, we will see that their concepts are shaped by the prevailing views of the time concerning all manner of phenomena. Indeed, as the historian of psychiatry, Erwin Ackerknect, has suggested, "The criterion by which a person in any society is judged to be mentally ill is not primarily the presence of certain unvarying and universally occurring symptoms. It depends rather on whether the affected individual is capable of some minimum of adaptation and social functioning within his society" (Ackerknect, 1968).

Revolutions in philosophy and science generally, such as the Renaissance and the Enlightenment, had profound effects on all aspects of society, including a change in the way mad people were seen. For example, Darwin's radical conceptualization of the mechanism of evolution, which he called "natural selection," had an immediate influence not only on all the biological sciences but also on psychology, politics, and economics. Modern evolutionary biologists have since rejected the implications that were drawn from his theory by the eugenicists (Gould, 1985). Proponents of this view, who included Darwin's cousin, Sir Francis Galton (1822–1911), interpreted Darwin's work to mean that those whose intellectual, social, or economic functioning was seen as inferior were defective, or maladaptive. Many further argued that because

society now protected these deficiencies from the forces of natural selection, they ought to be selected by society for sterilization in order to eliminate their defective genes. Eugenics led, in the hands of the Nazis, to the extermination of millions of people.

An examination of the historical development of our ideas about abnormality, then, will reveal that such ideas are simply one aspect of the general views of the time. This is important for another reason. When we consider some of the notions of the past about abnormality, we might tend to scoff and treat them as absurd, and so they may be from the perspective of the present. However, they must have seemed obviously correct at the time because they matched the more general ideas of the day. Reflecting on this may help us to recognize that perhaps our own conceptualization of abnormality seems so right to us only because it fits with our current beliefs about all manner of other phenomena and about our place in the world. Note, too, that earlier ideas about abnormality were accepted not only by those who made decisions about the insane, but also by many of the sufferers and their families. Treatments that seem bizarre or even cruel to us today may have helped sufferers because they believed the procedures would be effective. Perhaps the same is true to some degree of our current ideas and treatments.

Throughout recorded history, and no doubt long before that, people have been concerned with identifying and treating psychological dysfunction. What has been seen as evidence of madness or of other disturbed thinking or behaving, however, has changed over the course of evolving societies. For many years people who claimed to be able to foretell the future were revered and frequently given jobs in royal courts to assist kings and queens in their decision-making. Today, most people regard with skepticism the claims of soothsayers and may even doubt the sanity of someone who repeatedly says they can foresee future events. Similarly, the ancient Hebrews thought people who had the "gift of tongues" (that is, speaking unknown words in extended talks) were inspired by God, and they were revered. Today, clinicians might be inclined to consider such a person to be suffering from schizophrenia, although some religious groups continue to consider such speech to be divinely inspired.

Not only have the notions about what constitute abnormality changed over time, so also have explanations for the causes of such behaviour. According to Shakespeare, Ophelia was made mad by Hamlet's cold indifference, obviously suggesting a social cause for her malady. During the same period in Elizabethan England, however, many similarly mad women were thought to be possessed by the devil. Likewise, treatments have also differed across time. They have ranged from compassionate care to brutal torture, depending upon the type of abnormality and the accepted account of its origin.

All of these changes in the acceptability, treatment, and theories of etiology of abnormal behaviour have reflected, and continue to reflect, the values of society at a particular time. A society that explains everyday events (weather, seasons, war, etc.) as resulting from **supernatural causes**—

causes beyond the understanding of ordinary mortals, such as the influence of gods, demons, or magic—will similarly view madness. Psychological dysfunction in various historical periods was thought to result from either possession by demons or the witchcraft of evil people. Treatment involved ridding the mad person of these influences by exorcism or other magical or spiritual means. When worldly events are seen to have **natural causes** (that is, causes that can be observed and examined), so too are mental afflictions, and they are treated in a way that addresses these presumed natural causes.

Although a belief in supernatural causes for madness has all too often been associated both with blaming the sufferers and with cruel treatment, there is no necessary connection between such explanations and harsh treatment. For example, when ancient Egyptian priests were given the responsibility for treating the insane, they provided the patients with the comforts and protection of their temples, despite the fact that they believed these mad people to be possessed by demons. Conversely, while natural and scientific explanations have predominated over the past hundred years, the custody and treatment of people suffering from mental disorders has sometimes been characterized by cruel and unfounded procedures. For example, until the late 1970s, aversive therapy involving the administration of a noxious stimulus (for example, an electric shock, or a nausea-inducing medication) was used to treat various addictive behaviours, although Quinsey and Marshall (1983) could find no evidence of the value of any form of aversive therapy. In addition, all manner of restraints (for example, the straitjacket or the padded room) have been employed until quite recently in the treatment of the mentally ill. Ken Kesey's book *One Flew Over the Cuckoo's Nest* illustrates very clearly that during a scientific era, the humane and respectful treatment of vulnerable individuals is not guaranteed. It is as well to keep this in mind when reading the following historical account of ideas regarding psychological abnormality.

Evidence from Prehistory

Paleoanthropologists have discovered human remains from the Stone Age that were originally interpreted as providing evidence of supernatural beliefs as early as half a million years ago. Skulls have been found with circular sections cut out of them. Since there are clear signs of bone regeneration around these holes, it was concluded that the operations (called **trephination**) were done while the person was still alive. Apparently a stone tool was used to cut the holes and it was originally presumed that this was done to let out evil spirits that were causing the victim to engage in severely abnormal behaviour. There may, however, be simpler explanations. Maher and Maher (1985), for example, suggest that trephination may have been intended to remove bone splinters or blood clots caused by blows to the head during warfare. Whatever the explanation for these neat circular holes in the skulls of Stone Age people, we know from early written records that demonic possession was popularly accepted in early human societies as

Trephination, the prehistoric practice of chipping a hole into a person's skull, was an early form of surgery possibly intended to let out evil spirits.

the cause of madness. Egyptian papyri from almost 4000 years ago describe supernatural explanations for various disorders and the use of magic and incantations as treatment procedures. These early Egyptians recognized that the brain was the site of mental activities, although they believed its functioning was disrupted in mad people by a demon having taken possession of the afflicted person. Thus their beliefs were something of a mixture of natural and supernatural assumptions.

Hunter-gatherer societies that have been examined over the past 100 years may provide clues to how our own prehistoric ancestors viewed madness. These societies characteristically do not distinguish mental from physical disorders; both are seen as having supernatural causes. As Ackerknect (1968) points out, so long as one believes in spirits, an explanation of mental illness in terms of demonic possession may not only be convincing, it may facilitate effective treatment. Furthermore, since the treatments these hunter-gatherers employ typically invoke some form of emotional release, often through induced trances, we might expect the procedures to be effective even if the theory guiding them is not correct.

Greek and Roman Thought

With the rise of Pericles (461–429 B.C.) to the leadership of Athens, the Golden Age of Greece began. Temples of healing were soon established that emphasized natural causes for

Hippocrates (430–367 B.C.).

mental disorders and that developed a greater understanding of the causes and treatment of these problems. The great physician Hippocrates (460–367 B.C.), who has been called the father of modern medicine, denied the popular belief of the time that psychological problems were caused by the intervention of gods or demons. This represented the first recorded instance of a rejection of supernatural causes for mental illness. Hippocrates, like the hunter-gatherers of this century, did not distinguish mental from physical diseases. Unlike hunter-gatherers, however, Hippocrates thought that all disorders had natural causes. Although he emphasized the primacy of brain dysfunctions, Hippocrates also allowed that stress could influence mental functioning. He also thought that dreams were important in understanding why a person was suffering from a mental disorder and in this he predated Freud and the psychoanalysts of the twentieth century. As for treatment, Hippocrates advocated a quiet life, a vegetarian diet, healthful exercise, and abstinence from alcohol. If these procedures did not work, and sometimes as a supplement to them, Hippocrates considered induced bleeding or vomiting to be of value.

This latter claim for the value of vomiting or bleeding arose primarily as a result of Hippocrates' idea that psychological functioning resulted from disturbances of bodily fluids or **humours**, as they were then called. Both vomiting and bleeding were thought to reduce excesses of one or another of the humours. Cheerfulness, so Hippocrates thought, was caused by an excess of blood; ill-temper by an excess of yellow bile; gloom by an excess of black bile; and listlessness by an excess of phlegm. Hippocrates was the first to describe what he called hysteria, which is now known as *conversion disorder*: psychologically induced blindness, deafness, or other apparent defects in perceptual or bodily processes. Hippocrates claimed that hysteria occurred only in women and was due to a "wandering" uterus. While Hippocrates' ideas seem absurd to us, at the time they represented a significant advance because they pointed to natural causes rather than demonic possession and other supernatural events. As a consequence, Hippocrates' theories encouraged the beginnings of a scientific understanding of disordered behaviour and thought.

Many of Hippocrates' ideas were taken up by the Greek philosophers Plato (427–347 B.C.) and Aristotle (384–322 B.C.). However, Plato placed more emphasis on sociocultural influences on thought and behaviour. Elaborating on Hippocrates' notions about dreams, Plato suggested that they served to satisfy desires because the inhibiting influences of the higher faculties were not present during sleep. This view foreshadows Freud's theory of dreams. Plato declared that mentally disturbed people who commit crimes should not be held responsible since they could not be said to understand what they had done. In this respect, he anticipated modern notions of legal insanity, which exempt afflicted people from responsibility for their crimes. Plato also suggested treatment responses that presaged current approaches. For example, he said that most cases of mental illness should be cared for at the home of relatives, anticipating the present trend toward community care. For those who must be hospitalized, Plato said their thinking must be rationally challenged in a conversational style of therapy that was remarkably like some forms of present-day psychotherapy.

Aristotle wrote extensively on mental disorders and on other aspects of psychological functioning. He accepted Hippocrates' bodily fluids theory and denied the influence of psychological factors in the etiology of dysfunctional thinking and behaving. In keeping with Greek tradition, Aristotle advocated the humane treatment of mental patients.

After Alexander the Great founded Alexandria in Egypt in 332 B.C., the Egyptians adopted and expanded the medical and psychological ideas of the Greeks. They established temples to Saturn, which came to be sanatoriums for people who were psychologically unwell. These temples provided pleasant and peaceful surroundings, the opportunity for interesting and calming activities, healthful diets, soothing massages, and education. The priests who attended these disturbed clients also employed bleeding, purges, and restraints, but only when all other attempts had failed.

After 300 B.C., there emerged in ancient Greece various schools of thought that rejected Hippocrates' theories of mental illness. The most important and best known of these was Methodism, its principal advocate being Soranus of Ephesus (circa A.D. 100). Methodism regarded mental illness as a disorder that resulted either from a constriction of body tissue or as a relaxation of these tissues due to exhaustion. The head was seen as the primary site of this affliction. Mania, Soranus said, resulted from overexertion, licentiousness, or alcoholism.

Ordinarily, so Soranus thought, natural bloodletting (for example, by hemorrhoids or menstruation) would provide an avoidance of the disorder, but in cases where this did not happen, mania or some other mental illness would result. Soranus rejected the mind-body distinction so common among Greek thinkers and maintained instead that there was no difference between mental and physical disorders; they all arose from problems in the body. The Greek physician Aretaeus (A.D. 50–130), however, considered emotional factors to be primary in causing disturbances of mental functioning and advocated using psychological, rather than strictly medical, methods.

The Greeks were first and foremost empirical. They provided the first clinical observations of disorders and made the first attempts at classification. Treatment, for the Greeks, was primarily physical, but some psychological and social components were typically included. Even though their theories were rarely accurate, and their treatments were sometimes unsuccessful, the Greeks remained devoted to naturalistic explanations and responsive to the world as they saw it.

After the Romans assumed control of the ancient world, their physicians carried on the work of the Greeks. Galen (A.D. 129–198), a Greek physician living in Rome, continued the work of Hippocrates. He thought there were two sources of mental disorder: physical and mental. Physical causes included head injuries, the abuse of alcohol, and menstrual disturbances, while psychological factors included stress, loss of love, and fear. The Romans thought it was necessary for effective treatment to provide comfortable surroundings for patients; and even when they employed physical treatments, they did not use any stressful procedures, preferring things like warm baths. Galen suggested that having people talk about their problems to a sympathetic listener had value in treating the mentally disordered. This was, apparently, an early form of what we now call psychotherapy.

The Arab World

With Galen's death in A.D. 198, the enlightened period of mental health research and treatment that began with Hippocrates in the fifth century B.C. came to an end in Europe, but it was carried on by the Arab world. While the Dark Ages descended on Europe, the Arabs continued the Greco-Roman traditions of investigation and humane treatment of the mentally ill. In Egypt, the gentle methods used in the temples of Saturn persisted into the Mohammedan period. These generally supportive and kindly approaches to the mentally ill continued to characterize the Arab world's approach throughout the period in Europe during which the writings of the Greek scholars were lost to Europeans. The Koran itself reflects compassionate attitudes toward the mentally ill, and it is interesting that, despite Western assumptions to the contrary, Arab societies in general continue to this day to hold to these admirable views and practices. The mentally ill are today treated with sympathy in the Arab world, as they were in the period beginning in the eighth century

A.D. Units for the mentally ill within the great Arab hospitals were established in Baghdad in A.D. 800 and asylums were created in other Arab cities in the years thereafter—some 500 years before Europeans built their first asylums. In these Arab **asylums** (a word meaning place of refuge and protection) treatment followed the tradition of care, support, and compassion (Polvan, 1969).

The Islamic physician Avicenna (A.D. 980–1037) developed an astonishing understanding of medicine and psychological functioning, which he described in his remarkable volume *The Canon of Medicine.* This book has been said to be the most widely read medical book ever written (Campbell, 1926). Avicenna's analyses of mental disorders reflect a practical approach characterized by an emphasis on natural causes, particularly environmental and psychological factors. His treatment recommendations followed the Greco-Roman emphasis on care and compassion, but he also employed procedures not unlike early behaviour therapy methods of the present century. For example, Browne (1921) describes Avicenna's way of dealing with a prince who believed himself to be a cow and repeatedly asked to be killed and made into a stew. When Avicenna first examined the case, the young man had stopped eating altogether and this was, of course, cause for great concern. Avicenna began by sending a message to the prince telling him that a butcher would arrive soon to slaughter him. Shortly after Avicenna appeared brandishing a knife saying, "Where is this cow that I may kill it?" He then felt the patient's body all over and declared, "He is too lean, and not ready to be killed; he must be fattened." The attendants then offered the prince food which he enthusiastically took and, as he gradually regained his strength, his delusion disappeared.

Europe in the Middle Ages

After the fall of the Roman Empire at the end of the fifth century, Europe entered a period from approximately A.D. 500–1500 when the teachings of the Greeks and Romans were either lost or suppressed. It is often claimed that the natural theories of Greco-Roman times were entirely replaced during this period by supernatural explanations, while the compassionate and practical treatment of the mentally disturbed was supplanted by quite unpleasant procedures meant to free the afflicted person of possession by the devil or his minions. However, this is not entirely true and, in fact, some of the theories of Galen survived and were expressed in naturalistic approaches to treatment (Schoenman, 1984). Whereas demonological theories of insanity attributed disorders to sin on the part of the sufferer, Kroll and Bachrach (1984), in an examination of cases recorded in the fifteenth and sixteenth centuries, note that in very few cases was sin considered to be an etiological factor. Kroll and Bachrach point out that the notion of "possession" so popular in the writings of authors of the Middle Ages may have meant much the same as our own current expression, "nervous breakdown." It may simply have been a colloquial descriptor applied to a vague and general set of problems without necessarily implying, in all

This medieval woodcut illustrates the practice of exorcism, which was used to expel evil spirits that had possessed people.

cases, that the afflicted person had been taken over by the devil or some other supernatural force.

Perhaps the issue to which earlier historians most frequently misapplied these demonological ideas was witchcraft (Zilboorg & Henry, 1941). Until the 1980s, it was generally held that people identified as witches during the late Middle Ages were mad and that their madness was considered to result from possession by the devil. There was some truth to this notion. For example, some of the most eminent physicians of the early sixteenth century firmly believed that mad people were possessed and in need of exorcism. Furthermore, Martin Luther (1483–1566) claimed that when people sinned in particularly bad ways, God would deliver them over to Satan, who could possess them either corporally (that is, bodily) or spiritually. According to Luther, if the devil possessed them corporally, they would become mad, but if he possessed them spiritually, they should be considered witches. Luther, then, made a clear distinction between madness and witchcraft. Despite earlier historical interpretations that the many thousands of so-called witches who were tortured or killed during the fifteenth and sixteenth centuries were insane, in fact it appears that most were not, nor were they considered at the time to be insane. The majority of these unfortunate victims were innocently accused of exercising evil powers over others by people who simply wanted to be rid of them, and the accusations were all too often eagerly accepted by those who were appointed to seek out witches for punishment.

Throughout the Middle Ages in Europe, people suffering from psychological disorders for the most part received treatment and care from the clergy, as they were the only ones with sufficient concern and resources to provide assistance. For a long time the insane were provided refuge from the world in monasteries and pilgrimages. The treatment they were given was typically mild, and emphasized prayer and a generally caring approach. Over time, treatments evolved toward more vigorous methods, perhaps because spiritual approaches involving prayer and the laying on of hands did not reduce the suffering of the more extreme cases. As the idea of possession by the devil became more popular, exorcism replaced these gentle approaches. Exorcism, meant to drive out the evil forces that possessed the afflicted, was itself initially mild, but over time became more and more vigorous. To rid the person of the possession, exorcists would curse and insult the devil. If this did not succeed, they would attempt to make the body uncomfortable for him by subjecting the disordered individual to all manner of bodily insults. In some cases, these bodily insults amounted to torture, becoming progressively more severe until the person was either cured or died—which was also considered a cure.

Such approaches to mental illness were not without critics, who also opposed the idea of witchcraft and vigorously protested the torture and killing of those identified as witches. This opposition grew with the onset of the Renaissance, when Greco-Roman thought was rediscovered and passed into the hands of secular scholars. Paracelsus, a famous Swiss alchemist and physician (1493–1541), was one of the first to attack the beliefs about supernatural possession. He was determined to develop a new approach to mental disorders and attempted to create a new system of classification. Paracelsus rejected the four-humours theory of the Greeks and Romans and instead claimed that all mental illness resulted from disturbances of the *spiritus vitae* (breath of life). In some cases, the *spiritus vitae* was upset by the stars, in others it was disturbed by vapours arising in various parts of the body. Although we would today consider these ideas false, they do represent an attempt to offer naturalistic rather than magical or demonic origins to madness.

During the waning years of the Middle Ages, there arose in Europe what came to be known as **St. Vitus' Dance**. This was an epidemic of mass hysteria, where groups of people would suddenly be seized by an irresistible urge to leap about, jumping and dancing, and sometimes convulsing. Some of these dancers claimed to have been bitten by tarantula spiders, apparently in order to excuse their behaviour so it would not be attributed to possession by evil spirits. Thus the behaviour was originally called the Tarantella, which subsequently became the name of a dance. However, the more general explanation at the time was that these people were possessed. Paracelsus denied this assertion and instead declared the problem to be a disease; in fact, he was among the first to suggest that psychic conflicts might cause mental illness and he treated disordered people with what appears to have been an early version of hypnotism.

This fifteenth-century engraving shows peasant women overcome by St. Vitus' Dance.

The Beginnings of a Scientific Approach

While Paracelsus' analysis of St. Vitus' Dance represents a far more scientific view of mental disorders than had existed in Europe for centuries, he also enthusiastically held that the moon influenced emotional and mental processes and he burned the works of Galen (Mora, 1967). Accordingly, Paracelsus did not have the influence on scientific thinking he might otherwise have done. This was left to others, the most significant of whom was Teresa of Avila in Spain, the head of a group of nuns at the time of the Spanish Inquisition (sixteenth century). When her charges began to display hysterical behaviours, and were in danger of being accused of possession by the devil, St. Teresa (she was later canonized) defended them by claiming they were sick (actually, "as if sick," *comas enfermas*) and her argument was so convincing that not only did she save them from the Inquisition, but her position came to be accepted as true by subsequent scholars (Sarbin & Juhasz, 1967).

Another eminent religious teacher, St. Vincent de Paul (1576–1660), who is today widely recognized for his compassion, also challenged heterodoxy by claiming that mental disease and bodily disease are not different. He advocated the protection of people suffering from mental disorders and declared that it was the responsibility of society to develop means to relieve such individuals of their suffering. St. Vincent was, therefore, arguing for the development of a scientific and humane approach to dealing with the problems of the insane.

The efforts of Paracelsus were followed by Johannes Weyer (1515–1588) who, despite still accepting that the devil was the cause of some cases of mental illness, advocated natural and physical treatments while rejecting exorcism. Weyer also observed that mental illness could arise from natural causes. For instance, he claimed that "fantasies" (he probably meant delusions or hallucinations) could be traced in some patients to their use of belladonna ointments. He based this claim on both clinical observation and experiments carried out by two earlier physicians, Cardona and Della Porta. Weyer's views are quite interesting because they reflect a characteristic of Renaissance thought—that is, the mixture of traditional ideas (such as possession by the devil), theological concerns, and original observations. His views represented a significant move toward a more scientific and naturalistic attitude about the insane.

This new humane attitude was most apparent in Spain due to the influence of the Moors. The Moors, Muslims from North Africa, had conquered the Iberian peninsula in the eighth century and had brought with them the knowledge and attitudes of the Arab world. Although the Moors were finally expelled from Spain in 1502, their influence remained. During the Renaissance, Spain enjoyed a golden era of medicine. Mental institutions were established in Valencia in 1409, in Seville in 1436, and in Toledo in 1430. In fact, the first mental institution in North America was built by the Spaniards at San Hippolyto in Mexico.

Teresa of Avila (1515–1582).

As a result of this movement toward a more caring and naturalistic way of construing psychological dysfunctions, asylums began to be established in Europe. While the intentions of those who created these institutions may have been compassionate, the reality was that most were places where the residents were treated cruelly and lived in appalling conditions. Perhaps the most famous of these early European asylums was the one established by Henry VIII in 1547 when he had the monastery of St. Mary of Bethlehem in London converted to a place where the mentally ill could be housed. Although it has been moved to several locations since, the Bethlem Royal Hospital (as it is now known) still exists, although it is now an exemplary mental hospital in the pleasant countryside south of London. While Henry VIII provided the institutional setting, he did not satisfactorily fund the asylum. In order to operate the place, those in charge had to raise funds by whatever means they could. One procedure was to invite the public to visit and charge them a small sum. The fee provided the tourists the opportunity to tease and poke with sticks the hapless residents who, not surprisingly, screamed and moaned, much to the pleasure of the tourists. This noise and disruption among the residents prompted the use of the word **bedlam** (the local corruption of "Bethlem") to describe any form of rowdy, chaotic behaviour.

Other asylums in Europe followed a form similar to that of Bethlem with the treatment of the insane being much the same. La Bicêtre in Paris was one of the most notorious. In this place patients were shackled to the walls in unlit cells, unable to lie down even for sleep. Their food was inadequate, they were not permitted to wash regularly, and they were essentially treated like animals. In North America, the conditions of mental asylums were no better and the treatments offered were harsh, including electric shocks, bleeding, and plunging the patients into ice-cold water (see the Focus box on asylums). Bennett (1947) examined historical records from these institutions in the United States dating from the early 1800s. These records revealed that patients were placed in unlit cells, had their heads shaved, and were given a restricted diet, often accompanied by purgatives. They were often isolated from all other patients, apparently to "cure" their frenzied behaviour. Not surprisingly, success rates from these procedures were quite low.

In the midst of these otherwise dreadful approaches there was at least one shining example of a distinctly humanitarian attempt to deal more effectively with these unfortunate people. A legendary tale, dating from the thirteenth century, tells of the flight of a young princess who had escaped from her incestuous father and fled to Belgium. Her father caught up with her just outside the town of Gheel, whereupon he killed her. She was said to have attended to the insane prior to her escape from her father. Some years after her death, five lunatics slept one night under the tree where she was slain. When they awoke in the morning, their insanity had disappeared; thereafter the place became a shrine visited by the mentally ill seeking a cure. These pilgrims frequently stayed on in Gheel, where the townsfolk took them into their houses and allowed them to live comfortably, which seems to have produced remarkably beneficial results (Karnesh & Zucker, 1945). In fact, the tradition lives on today, with as many as 1000 patients living with families in Gheel and working in local community centres. Although this unusual program is effective, it receives little recognition and has had little influence on the general approach to dealing with the mentally ill.

While there was significant progress toward a more humane and rational approach to understanding and managing the mentally ill during the sixteenth century, the trend did not continue in the following century. The large number of poor was seen as a serious social problem that the absolutist governments of the day wanted to get rid of. Their solution was to establish what the English called "workhouses," where the poor, the old, orphans, and others, including the insane, were incarcerated in dreadful conditions. Mad people were chained to the walls, flogged regularly, and given only the bare minimum of care; physicians were rarely if ever consulted. In Paris, the men were sent to the Bicêtre and the women to the Salpêtrière.

As a result of the European philosophical movement known as the Enlightenment, the eighteenth century saw radical changes in the way in which abnormal behaviour was conceptualized. The basic ideas of the Enlightenment concerned the superiority of reason in the analysis of problems, the idea that progress was an inevitable and desirable feature of human society, and that it was both appropriate and necessary to challenge traditional ideas, including religious doctrine. One of the many consequences of such thinking was a reexamination of the ways in which society dealt with the insane. One of the leaders of this movement was Philippe Pinel (1745–1826), who was appointed by the French revolutionary government as director of the Bicêtre in 1792.

In response to seeing the appalling conditions at Bicêtre, Pinel ordered the inmates' chains to be removed. He had the institution cleaned and the windows replaced to let in full sunlight, encouraged healthful exercise on the grounds, and instructed staff to treat the patients with kindness rather than giving them regular beatings. Although recent evidence (Weiner, 1979) indicates that it was the institution's manager, Jean-Baptiste Pussin, who had in fact begun these reforms, Pinel carried on these dramatic changes at a time when it was clear that, had the experiment failed, he would likely have been led off to the guillotine along with other failed revolutionaries. Pinel's actions were, then, those of a courageous and compassionate human being and he is properly remembered as one of the leaders of the humanitarian reforms that swept Europe in the late eighteenth and early nineteenth centuries. What brought an end to this approach was not its failure, for it was in fact quite effective; it was the remarkable increase in mental patients, primarily as a result of the increase in patients suffering from general paresis of the insane and those affected by alcoholism. This overcrowding of mental institutions made it all but impossible to treat every patient in the way that Pinel recommended.

Pinel should be remembered for his humanity but also for the influence he exerted on psychiatry as a whole. He developed a systematic and statistically based approach to the clas-

Focus   *Treatment and Mistreatment: The History of Mental Asylums*

Mental asylums were established throughout the world in the nineteenth century in response to the deplorable conditions in which the mentally ill were kept. All too often these unfortunates were forced to wander from town to town or to fend for themselves in the countryside. Turned out of their homes, they became part of the cavalcade of beggars across Europe. As King Lear observed:

> *Poor naked wretches, wheresoe'er you are,*
> *That bide the pelting of this pitiless storm,*
> *How shall your houseless heads and unfed sides,*
> *Your loop'd and window'd raggedness, defend you*
> *From seasons such as these?*

(William Shakespeare, King Lear, Act III, Scene IV)

Conditions were no better for those allowed to stay at home. Letchworth (1889) reports the description of home care given by a member of Ireland's House of Commons in 1817:

> *When a strong man or woman gets the complaint [madness], the only way they have to manage is by making a hole in the floor of the cabin, not high enough for the person to stand up in, with a crib over it to prevent his getting up. This hole is about five feet deep and they give the wretched being his food there, and there he generally dies.*

In the poorhouses, the mentally ill were commonly shackled and often taunted by other paupers or by passersby. The director of a rest home in Kent, England was summoned in 1776 to a workhouse to see a maniacal man. This poor man "was secured to the floor by means of a staple and an iron ring, which was fastened to a pair of fetters about his legs, and he was handcuffed." Visitors were frequently seen to be "ridiculing and irritating the patient, who was then made a spectacle of public sport" (Perfect, 1787).

Observations such as these led many reformers to demand that proper hospitals be established to care for the mentally ill. Dorothea Dix (1802–1877), a Boston schoolteacher who taught at the local prison, was shocked by what she saw there and became a crusader for better conditions for offenders. Her concern quickly spread to mental patients, and she launched an effective nationwide campaign to improve the lot of the mentally ill. Her campaign resulted directly in the opening of 32 state hospitals, including 2 in Canada, and indirectly to many more.

These efforts came to be known as the **mental hygiene movement**, which was characterized by a desire to protect and provide humane treatment for the mentally ill. Despite these noble aims, the movement of enormous numbers of mentally ill people into large asylums did not, in fact, improve their lot. The asylums were overcrowded and the staff had no time to do more than warehouse them. Restraints such as straitjackets were more refined than the old fetters but no less cruel (Bockhoven, 1972).

In addition, because physicians were put in charge, psychosocial treatments such as moral therapy were replaced by physical treatments, which were often quite unpleasant. Clifford Beers (1908) described his experience as a mental patient in one of these large institutions. Here is Beers' account of being placed in a straitjacket:

> *No one incident in my whole life has ever impressed itself more indelibly on my memory. Within one hour's time I was suffering pain as intense as any I ever endured ... My right hand was so held that the tip of one of my fingers was all but cut by the nail of another ... after four or five hours the excess pain rendered me partially insensible ... and not until the twelfth hour ... did an attendant so much as loosen a cord. (Beers, 1908, pp. 127–128)*

Beers described many other atrocious things done to him in the name of treatment. Although his insistence on reforms garnered support from eminent people such as the philosopher William James and the dean of American psychiatry, Adolf Meyer, it was years before significant changes were made. In *The Shame of the States,* journalist Albert Deutsch reported on a 1946 tour of U.S. mental institutions. He described "hundreds of patients sleeping in damp, bug-ridden basements." One doctor complained to Deutsch, "I know I should see many more patients individually. But how can I when I have five hundred patients under my care?"

The furor that resulted from Deutsch's book—along with the advent of antipsychotic drugs in 1954—led, finally, to a massive deinstitutionalization of mental patients. ▲

sification, management, and treatment of disorders. Pinel emphasized the role of psychological and social factors in the development of mental illness, and he elaborated clear descriptions of the symptomatology of the various disorders. He saw the asylum as therapeutic, a place where patients could be separated from their families and from the stresses of their everyday lives. Patients were to be treated respectfully so as to inspire their confidence and they were given activities to stimulate them. Pinel did not discard physical approaches to treatment, but rather saw the humane management of patients as the basis on which physical treatments could have their effects. Pinel was thoroughly scientific and looked only to natural ex-

The Homewood Retreat: A Canadian Venture

In 1853, the legislature of Upper Canada passed the Private Lunatic Asylums Act, instituted to care for the middle- and upper-class mentally ill who, it was considered, should not be housed with the destitute and feeble-minded inmates of public asylums. W. T. O'Reilly, the inspector of prisons and public charities, in his annual report of 1885, pointed out that "as regards the insane persons of the wealthy class, it is manifest that our public Asylums … cannot afford such persons the partial seclusion and special personal attention which they desire and are prepared to pay for … " (cited in Warsh, 1989, p. 9). Accordingly, in 1883 the Homewood Retreat, a privately owned and profit-oriented institution, was opened in Guelph.

Having a private institution funded by wealthy patients and their relatives allowed Homewood an independence from the administration of the public asylums and provided the finances for the latest treatment and assessment methods. It also attracted staff, or at least superintendents, who were interested in introducing ideal interventions. Indeed, the history of Homewood reflects the changes throughout the English-speaking world in the perceived exemplary approach to managing and treating insane people.

Stephen Lett, the first medical superintendent of Homewood, did not believe that mental illness could be cured, but he thought that patients should be cared for humanely and adopted the approach called *moral therapy*. Moral therapy, advocated by Philippe Pinel and his followers and widely adopted in Europe and North America during the early part of the nineteenth century, held that the insane could be controlled without the use of physical or chemical restraints. Patients were to be treated with respect and given quiet and peaceful surroundings, plenty of rest, a good diet, moderate exercise, and activities to keep them occupied and amused. Note the similarity to the treatments provided by the ancient Greeks and by the Arabs during Europe's Dark Ages. Despite Lett's belief, most moral managers did think they could cure patients by these methods, and Lett himself believed it would alleviate their symptoms. Moral management certainly did a lot to relieve some of the worst aspects of the institutional care of the insane and an examination of the records revealed that as many as 75 percent of patients receiving such treatments were apparently cured (Bockhoven, 1963).

The prevailing view in the 1880s, a view that Lett fully accepted, was that the body was an interrelated set of parts such that anything that affected one part correspondingly affected all other parts, including the mind. A healthy mind could not exist without a healthy body and vice versa, a view that has seen a more recent revival with the advent of holistic medicine.

When Alfred Hobbs, Lett's successor, assumed direction of Homewood in 1905, he shifted the emphasis to a somatic model. Hobbs accepted that the recent developments in medicine (for example, the discovery that general paresis of the insane was the long-term result of infection by the syphilis spirochete) indicated that eventually a biological (that is, disease) basis would be discovered for all mental disorders. Accordingly, he introduced physical treatments such as electrotherapy (a mild electric current applied to the body to "recharge" the lost nervous energy that in healthy people was generated by the brain), hydrotherapy (prolonged immersion in baths, thought to stimulate the nervous system), and chemotherapy. While Lett had used tonics (usually iron supplements) or stimulants (such as cocaine) to complement moral management, Hobbs, a forerunner of the research-oriented, biological psychiatrists of the later twentieth century, employed the latest in chemotherapy. Salvarsan (an arsenical) was used in the tertiary stage of syphilis, despite little evidence of efficacy. Few patients at Homewood improved as a result of its use and some died.

One obstacle was the fact that, since Homewood's patients paid for their own care, they could refuse his treatment recommendations, and many did. Most women patients, for example, refused sexual surgery. Hobbs believed, along with many other Victorians, that a woman's mental health was directly related to the proper functioning of her reproductive organs, and that insanity could be cured by surgical correction of a malfunctioning system. This notion has a long history, dating from Hippocrates' idea that hysteria was the result of a "wandering uterus." Similar ideas have reappeared in the latter half of this century, when all manner of psychological problems in women have been ascribed by clinicians to the fluctuations of the menstrual cycle (Fausto-Sterling, 1985). Warsh (1989) claims that these procedures resulted not only from the rise of the somatic paradigm but also partly in response to the perceived threat of the beginnings of women's political and economic emancipation.

In fairness to Hobbs, it should be noted that his methods were at the forefront of knowledge at the time. He also continued to employ aspects of moral management, which remained the basis for the management of patients at Homewood at least until 1934. In that year, the retreat's prospectus offered "normal sleep, freedom from worry, cheerful surroundings, quiet and intelligent nursing attention, and some occupation that will interest but not irritate" (*Homewood Retreat Prospectus of 1934* by Harvey Clare, M.D., Medical Superintendent, reproduced in Appendix 5, Warsh, 1989).

VIEWPOINT *continued*

Moral therapy in Canada, and in the rest of the English-speaking world, was largely replaced toward the turn of the century by physical and chemical restraints and somatic treatments. Public institutions became larger, and it became clear that moral management was possible only when an asylum housed fewer than 200 residents. Also, the increasingly popular biological approaches suggested that one need only identify the specific site of the problem or the infective agent and intervene surgically or chemically, and all would be well. Present-day milieu therapy can be seen as something of a revival of moral therapy, but it does not always match the latter's devotedly humane and compassionate approach. It is a pity that a remarkably effective approach has not been emulated in today's Canadian mental health services.

Critical Thinking Questions

1. Was it appropriate for the Upper Canada legislature to establish with public funds an asylum for middle- and upper-class people who were mentally ill?

2. Why do you think "moral therapy," which appeared to be quite effective, was abandoned throughout the world at the turn of the century?

3. There was great hope for biological therapies in the early 1900s and there has been a recent revival in the application of these interventions, particularly drug treatments. Is this because the evidence about their effectiveness is convincing or is it because they offer an easy, but limited, solution to problems?

planations for the origins of mental disorders. In Britain, Tuke (1732–1822) followed Pinel's example by establishing similar approaches in psychiatric hospitals, and Benjamin Rush (1756–1813) brought **moral therapy** (see the ViewPoint box on Homewood) to North America.

DEVELOPMENT OF MODERN VIEWS

Biological Approaches

Toward the end of the eighteenth century, theorists had abandoned the notions of Hippocrates and Galen that disruptions in the four humours cause people to become mentally ill. As a result of anatomical examinations of the cadavers of mad patients, and the concurrent discoveries regarding the functioning of the nervous system, mental disorders came to be viewed as disruptions in nervous system functioning. The culmination of this line of thought was expressed most clearly by Cabanis (1757–1808), who combined psychological and somatic factors in his account of mental disorders. His theories were particularly influential and encouraged the development of psychological approaches to treatment. Cabanis provided the first clear theoretical basis for moral therapy. The eighteenth century can be seen as the first flowering of what later became known as psychotherapy, and it more generally set the stage for a move toward a thoroughly rational and scientific approach to abnormal behaviour.

Heredity

Benedict Augustin Morel (1809–1873), a Viennese physician, was the first to introduce "degeneration" theory. This idea proposed that deviations from normal functioning are transmitted by hereditary processes and that these deviations progressively degenerate over generations. Morel's final version of this theory appeared in 1857, just one year before the publication of Charles Darwin's remarkable *Origin of Species*. Darwin's notion of the inheritance of advantageous features and the disappearance of disadvantageous features by natural selection lent support to theories like Morel's that proposed an inherited basis for human functioning. The possibility that human behaviour (both normal and abnormal) could be seen as being passed on genetically from generation to generation inspired many theorists to suggest that it might be possible to identify people as potential madmen or criminals before they developed such problems. Cesare Lombroso (1836–1909) concluded from his observations that criminality was inherited and could be identified by the shape of a person's skull. While phrenology (as this study was called) enjoyed a good deal of popularity for a time, it did not withstand more careful scrutiny. However, the idea that disorders of functioning could be passed on genetically not only survived, it now enjoys widespread acceptance in psychiatry and psychology.

Syndromes and the Beginning of Classification

Perhaps the most influential person in the latter part of the nineteenth century, however, was Emil Kraepelin. He published in 1883 a very important textbook, *Clinical Psychiatry*, that attempted to classify mental illness. Classification is, as we will see in Chapter 3, the fundamental basis on which research is generated. It also attempts to guide the selection of treatment, and to indicate the likely course and outcome of the disorder. In any case, without some form of classification, research would be markedly restricted, since it would be impossible to group people according to their common disorder. Kraepelin, however, was not interested in treatment, because he believed all mental disorders were the result of biological problems for which, at that time, there were no treatments available. Accordingly, he focussed on diagnosis and classification as ends in themselves. Kraepelin noted that certain groups of symptoms tended to occur together, and he called these groupings **syndromes**. These different syndromes,

Kraepelin observed, could serve as a way of grouping patients who shared certain features into categories that identified specific disorders. He was the first to recognize that the different disorders not only had distinct features, but also differed in terms of the age of onset of the disorder and their typical course over time. As a result, Kraepelin suggested that the different disorders probably had different causes, although he thought that these different causes were all biological of one sort or another.

Kraepelin's efforts led to an interest in classification that lives on in the current versions of DSM-IV and ICD-10. Although these more recent classification systems owe much to Kraepelin's innovative work, they have evolved to a considerably different, far more detailed and research-driven system of classifying mental disorders.

Infection as a Cause of Mental Disorder

Following Kraepelin's view that mental disorders were the result of biological processes, Richard von Krafft-Ebing (1840–1902) became interested in the possibility that patients with **general paresis of the insane (GPI)** might have acquired this disorder by an infection. GPI (or neurosyphilis) is now known to result from untreated infections by the syphilis spirochete. Initial infection results in a sore on the genitals and sometimes swollen lymph glands of the groin. Untreated, the spirochete does not disappear but remains in the bloodstream and, after about one year, it enters the meningeal lining of the brain and spinal cord, although it does not affect functioning at this stage. The immune system sometimes overcomes the infection at this point, but if it does not, then a decade or so later the affected person becomes symptomatic. Mania, euphoria, and grandiosity are the first marked features of this delayed response, followed by a progressive deterioration of brain functioning (called *dementia*) and paralysis. In the latter part of the nineteenth and the early part of the present century, GPI patients filled most of the beds in psychiatric hospitals (Shorter, 1997).

Louis Pasteur had established the germ theory of disease in the 1860s, and Krafft-Ebing noted that it had been observed that some patients with general paresis previously had had syphilis. His guess was that general paresis was a long-term consequence of syphilis. To test this theory, Krafft-Ebing infected GPI patients with syphilitic material. If his theory was correct, then his injected patients would not develop syphilis since they had already been infected. Although the ethics of his procedures are repugnant to modern readers, Krafft-Ebing's guess turned out to be correct. Subsequently, the spirochete that causes syphilis was discovered and it was shown that there was a link between infection and later destruction of particular areas of the brain that produced the mental and physical deterioration shown by GPI patients.

This confirmation of the idea that such a widespread and serious mental disorder as GPI was the result of an infectious agent encouraged confidence in the view that all mental disorders would soon be found to be caused by either other infections or by some other biological factor. **Somatogenesis** (the idea that psychopathology is caused by biological factors—*soma* meaning "body" in Latin) not only gained prominence as a result of the success in identifying the cause of general paresis, it also followed quite logically from the remarkable successes that occurred in the middle and latter half of the nineteenth century in science in general and in medicine more specifically. It seemed at the time that all disorders (physical as well as psychological) would be solved quite soon as a result of applying biological science. While such optimism proved unfounded, these views did encourage a scientific approach to abnormal functioning that became progressively more sophisticated.

The discovery that GPI had an organic cause not only led to a search for the somatic bases of other mental illnesses, it also encouraged trials of various physical approaches to treatment. Because GPI was now known to result from an infection, it was thought that deliberately inducing a fever in such patients would cause the increased body temperature to kill the infectious agent. Julius von Wagner-Jauregg in 1890 injected GPI patients with a vaccine in order to induce a fever. Shorter (1997) says it was tuberculin, a vaccine for tuberculosis, while Ackerknect (1968) says it was typhus vaccine. Whichever it was, Wagner-Jauregg got reasonably good results, but the unreliability of the approach encouraged him to try infecting these patients with malaria to reliably induce a fever. This actually worked to kill off the syphilitic spirochete and prevent further progress of the disease. In fact it proved so successful that he was awarded the Nobel Prize in 1927.

Shock Therapy

Since antiquity, it has been known that shocks could produce recovery from mental illness. For example, sudden submersion in water had been shown to alleviate the symptoms of some people suffering from disturbances of mental functioning (Ackerknect, 1968). It occurred to Manfred Sakel, a German physician, that shock treatments might, therefore, be effective in treating the insane. He had used insulin in the late 1920s to manage the withdrawal symptoms of morphine addicts. When insulin was occasionally given in an accidentally high dose, it induced a coma in the patient. Sakel observed that after the coma passed, the patient's desire for morphine disappeared and patients who were previously agitated became tranquil. Soon after these observations, Sakel began examining the value of insulin-induced comas with schizophrenics. He reported that 70 percent of these cases fully recovered and a further 18 percent were able to at least function well. Sakel's procedure was taken up enthusiastically by others and by 1944, Eliot Slater and William Sargant's influential English psychiatric textbook listed insulin-coma as the first choice in treating the mentally ill. This physical procedure was appealing not only for its effectiveness, but also because it allowed asylum psychiatrists to become more than just custodians and it aligned them with medicine (Shorter, 1997).

Insulin administrations not only induced a coma, they also occasionally produced convulsions and some theorists thought these might be the main active feature of the treatment. Ladislas von Meduna in 1934 suggested that deliberately provoking convulsions, by the administration of Metrazol (a drug similar to camphor), might ameliorate the symptoms of schizophrenia. Meduna noted that the brains of epileptic patients (that is, patients who suffered from chronic convulsions or seizures) were quite different (or so he thought) from those of schizophrenics, and it was also reported about the same time that epileptics who developed schizophrenia thereafter experienced fewer seizures. Meduna deduced from this that producing seizures in schizophrenics might eliminate their disorder. He tried his procedure with 110 patients and 50 percent completely recovered from their illness. As a result, a series of Metrazol-induced convulsions became reasonably popular in the treatment of psychotic patients. However, there were undesirable side-effects, including a terror of dying, such that many patients refused a second injection. With the discovery that electricity applied to the head could induce convulsions, other forms of coma or convulsive therapy disappeared.

The first to employ electricity to induce a seizure in mental patients was Ugo Cerletti in 1938. After a series of animal studies had established the difference between a convulsive and lethal shock intensity, and the optimal placement of electrodes on the skull, Cerletti and his assistants began to use the procedure with human patients. The device they developed delivered a shock of 80 to 100 volts to the temples for a fraction of a second. After 11 treatments, Cerletti's first patient, a severe schizophrenic, was able to be discharged, although he did return one year later. **Electroconvulsive therapy (ECT)**, as this treatment was called, was enthusiastically welcomed by psychiatry throughout the world and very soon replaced most other physical treatments. While ECT was initially used only with schizophrenics, it was found to be most effective with patients suffering from major depression, with whom it is still used to this day.

One problem with the initial uses of ECT was that during the bodily convulsion produced by the brain seizure, some patients suffered broken limbs or cracked vertebrae. These were obviously very undesirable side-effects. However, the finding that curare (a poison extracted from a South American vine *Strychnos toxifera* and applied by natives to the tip of their arrows) in very small doses produced relaxation of the limbs of spastic children, suggested that it may be useful in preventing the bodily reactions to ETC. It proved effective, but it was risky so it was replaced by the less dangerous drug succinylcholine which, when combined with a fast-acting barbiturate, allowed patients getting ECT to avoid pretreatment anxiety and within-treatment risks of fractures. By 1959, ECT was the treatment of choice for depression.

The Beginnings of Psychopharmacology

In the 1950s, pharmacological agents for the treatment of psychiatric disorders became widely available and began what the Canadian psychiatric historian Edward Shorter (1997) calls "the second biological psychiatry." The view of this period, which continues to the present, was that mental illness results from disordered brain chemistry. The widespread acceptance of this view led to the rejection by much of psychiatry of psychological perspectives, including psychoanalysis. Interestingly, this point in time corresponds to the revival, among psychologists, of the application of behaviourism to the amelioration of psychological disorders.

The first neurotransmitter was isolated in 1926 by Otto Loewi at the University of Graz in Austria. He identified the action of acetylcholine (the neurotransmitter) as mediating the transmission of nerve impulses within the brain. (See Chapter 2 for a discussion of neurotransmission.) Although this might have suggested a possible way to change brain functioning in mental patients by introducing an *agonist* (something that facilitates the production of acetylcholine) or an *antagonist* (something that inhibits its production), such approaches did not develop until the 1950s. Some of the early work on the effects of drugs derived from these ideas was done by Heinz Lehmann at Montreal's Verdun Protestant Hospital. His experiments, while unsuccessful, nevertheless paved the way for further research.

In an attempt to calm soldiers before surgery, Henri Laborit in 1949 examined the value of some recently developed antihistamines of the phenothiazine group of drugs. He found these drugs to be very effective in inducing a calm and relaxed state in his patients. Following this, Laborit obtained the latest drug in this series, called chlorpromazine, and persuaded some psychiatrist friends to try it with their patients. It virtually eliminated one manic patient's problems. Subsequently it was evaluated in more systematic trials and chlorpromazine soon enjoyed widespread popularity. In her book on the history of psychopharmacology, Anne Caldwell (1978) provides a dramatic description of the benefits and changes resulting from the adoption of this drug as a treatment for mentally ill patients.

The atmosphere in the disturbed wards of mental hospitals in Paris was transformed: straitjackets, psychohydraulic packs and noise were a thing of the past! Once more Paris psychiatrists, who long ago unchained the chained, became pioneers in liberating their patients, this time from inner torments, and with a drug: chlorpromazine. It accomplished the pharmacological revolution of psychiatry. (p. 30)

Chlorpromazine had remarkable advantages over other forms of treatment and management. Not only did it do away with physical restraints and make psychiatric management an easier task, it was less dangerous than ECT and more easily tolerated by patients.

Thereafter the pharmaceutical industry began to produce a plethora of neurotransmitter-affecting drugs to treat schizophrenic, manic, and depressed patients. The era of psychopharmacology had arrived. However, psychological or environmental explanations of mental disorders did not simply disappear throughout the twentieth century. Indeed, it has been one of the strongest periods for such theorizing. Somatic and psychological explanations and treatments of psychiatric patients, often seen by their proponents as antithetical to one another, proceeded to develop somewhat independently. It has only been in recent years that they have been seen by many as complementary and interactive.

Psychological Approaches

Psychological accounts of the etiology of mental disorders had been popular throughout history, and obtained some eminence in the latter part of the eighteenth century. An increased interest in psychological explanations was sparked by the work of Anton Mesmer (1734–1815) with hysteria (see Chapter 8 for a description of this disorder, now called *conversion disorder*), although Mesmer's explanation was physiological. Mesmer thought that hysteria was the result of a disturbed distribution of the magnetic fluid present in all bodies. Mesmer's procedure involved a good deal of mystery and required the patients to be touched by Mesmer with various rods that were said to transmit, from Mesmer directly to the patients, a magnetic force he called "animal magnetism" that would rearrange their fluids and cure the disorder. These procedures obviously required Mesmer to present his treatment very convincingly, using various tactics to strongly suggest to his patients that they would recover. Today we view Mesmer's approach as a predecessor of hypnotism and, in fact, it was called this by James Braid, a British surgeon of the mid-1800s, who saw great promise in the technique.

Hypnotism and the Birth of Psychoanalysis

While Mesmer was generally viewed by his contemporaries as a charlatan, the popularity of this procedure and his numerous apparent successes prompted an interest in the powers of suggestion. The Parisian neurologist Jean Charcot (1825–1893), in particular, came to believe that hypnotism might have value in treating hysterics and, accordingly, he revised his earlier somatogenic view to suggest that psychological factors caused hysteria. One of his students, Pierre Janet (1859–1947), elaborated this view into an account that claimed hysteria resulted from a break in the organized system of thought and emotion. Hysteria, in fact, became a focus of interest in itself, particularly among Viennese physicians. Josef Breuer (1842–1925) and his younger colleague Sigmund Freud (1856–1939) not only elaborated complex psychological conceptualizations of mental disorders (see Chapter 2 for an account of Freud's approach), they also developed specific treatment methods. Breuer's approach employed hypnosis in order to have the patient talk freely about, and relive, unpleasant past events that he believed caused the hysteria. He thought that vividly reliving these past experiences would somehow exhaust the emotional problems that resulted from them. Breuer called this treatment the *cathartic method*. Freud's approach was similar, although he also used procedures other than hypnosis and his treatment came to be called *psychoanalysis*.

Behaviourism

Another psychological approach to understanding abnormal behaviour emerged in the early part of the twentieth century. John B. Watson (1878–1958) produced a revolution in psychological thought (and, for that matter, in philosophical thought also) with the publication in 1913 of a provocative article entitled "Psychology as the behaviorist views it." This,

and subsequent work by Watson, established what became known as **behaviourism**. This viewpoint declared that if psychology were to become a science, it must be restricted to the study of observable features; namely, the behaviour of organisms. From this perspective, Watson considered abnormal functioning to be learned and, consequently, he believed it could be unlearned. His model for learning was derived from Ivan Pavlov's (1849–1936) studies of classical conditioning. All problem functioning, Watson claimed, was the result of unfortunate conditioning experiences. While this theory had a profound impact on thinking about mental disorders, it has not quite lived up to Watson's rather grand expectations. Nevertheless, behavioural approaches to the understanding and treatment of psychological disorders were reintroduced in the late 1950s and early 1960s and enjoyed considerable success and acceptance. In various forms they have become established parts of the overall approach to dealing with mental illness.

Throughout the present century, conceptualizing and theorizing about abnormal behaviour have followed one of the paths initiated by the earlier thinkers outlined above. Somatogenic theories remain very popular and have enjoyed better success in the analysis of some problems than others, although it is fair to say that the research generated by such views has contributed to a better understanding of all mental disorders. Similarly, psychogenic theories (Freudian, behavioural, and numerous others) and the research their advocates have produced have expanded our knowledge and treatment of all disorders—although, again, psychological approaches have proven to be more valuable with some disorders than with others. The various models derived from these two views are the subject of the next chapter.

THE GROWTH OF MENTAL HEALTH SERVICES IN CANADA

The history of the development of proper places of care for the mentally ill in Canada is well documented in a very detailed account by Hurd et al. (1916). It reveals a reluctance on the part of the various provinces (except for Quebec) to deal with the issue during the early days of settlement. The early British, and then provincial, leaders were content to place the insane in prisons along with criminals. Of course, they offered little or no treatment to these unfortunate citizens.

The Hôtel Dieu in Quebec was the first asylum anywhere in what was to become Canada to house the mentally ill. This institution was founded by the Duchess d'Aiguillon, niece of the powerful Cardinal Richelieu, who was at that time First Minister of France and the effective ruler of the country. The Hôtel Dieu housed not only so-called "idiots," who included patients suffering from all types of mental disabilities and dysfunctions, but also indigents and cripples. Similar hospitals were built in Quebec throughout the latter part of the seventeenth century. However, it was not until the nineteenth century that asylums were established in other parts of Canada.

The delay in the establishment of proper housing for the insane in places outside Quebec was not simply because Quebec was the first area to be extensively settled. After all, the British were well entrenched in North America in the seventeenth century. The area that became known as Ontario was a British territory by the middle of the eighteenth century, and Upper Canada was officially constituted in 1791. Yet it was not until 1841 that a mental asylum in Toronto first took in patients. This was followed shortly thereafter by the opening of the Rockwood asylum in Kingston, which was directed by Dr. J. P. Litchfield, an Australian who had at best minimal experience with the mentally ill. A tardy and rather careless approach, with little real concern for how these institutions were operated, characterized the early efforts of various Canadian provincial governments to provide care for the insane. In the latter part of the nineteenth century, the Dominion government began to pressure provinces to remove lunatics from their prisons; this was made an order in 1884. Some provinces had already done so and others followed. Asylums were first established in the various provinces in the following years: New Brunswick, 1835; Prince Edward Island, 1840; Manitoba, 1871; British Columbia, 1872; Alberta, 1907; and Saskatchewan, 1913. Nova Scotia finally made provision for housing the mentally ill only after the legislature had been won over by the eloquent pleadings of the redoubtable American reformer Dorothea Dix.

The first textbook printed in Canada dealing with the care and housing of the mentally ill was published in 1840 under the authorship of J. F. Lehman. Lehman's views were harsh and certainly did not reflect the approach called moral therapy in other countries. He strongly advocated a regimen of severe discipline in order to rid the afflicted of their disorder and he suggested that recalcitrant individuals should be flogged. Lehman deplored indulgence toward the insane, believing it simply worsened their problems. Fortunately, his views did not receive popular support, although later treatments employed in Canada were equally harsh.

For example, psychosurgery was widely used in Canada from the mid-1940s until the mid-to-late 1960s. During this time, tens of thousands of Canadians had **lobotomies** (surgical removal, or disconnection, of the frontal lobes of the brain) intended to relieve all manner of mental and emotional disorders (Simmons, 1987). Fortunately, in the early 1970s legislation was enacted requiring review boards to be established in all mental hospitals with the responsibility to decide in each individual case whether psychosurgery was justified. Thereafter psychosurgery was rarely done. According to Simmons (1987), prior to 1970 archival evidence reveals that most of the early lobotomies were performed primarily to alleviate hospital management problems or to advance research, rather than out of a concern to benefit the patient. It is also interesting to note (Simmons, 1987) that in Ontario during this period, the majority of lobotomies were performed on women (well over 60 percent of all psychosurgery patients were women).

Perhaps the worst instance of abuse of psychiatric power in Canada is the well-documented story of Dr. Ewen Cameron's brainwashing experiments at Montreal's Allen Memorial Hospital during the late 1950s and early 1960s (Collins, 1988). Cameron's work was, at least in part, funded by the American Central Intelligence Agency (CIA), which apparently hoped to discover ways both to overcome the effects of brainwashing by their enemies and to brainwash captured enemies. None of the unfortunate subjects in these studies, most of whom were mental patients seeking Cameron's help, were ever informed that they were part of a research project, let alone that such research was funded by the CIA. Cameron subjected his patients, under the guise of therapy, to massive and repeated doses of electroconvulsive therapy, prolonged sensory deprivation, and chemically induced sleep. This latter procedure was employed for days on end, during which audiotapes, telling the patients how awful they were and how they must change, were played under their pillows. Patients were also repeatedly injected with lysergic acid diethylamide (LSD), a hallucinogenic drug, without ever being told what it was or how it would affect them. Of course, most of them experienced terror.

By no means all mental health care in Canada has been reprehensible. Canada has had its share of dedicated, helping professionals, including some on the cutting edge of research. For example, Dr. Ruth Kajander, who now practises in Thunder Bay, Ontario, was one of the first psychiatrists in North America to recognize the potential value of a major tranquillizer in the treatment of schizophrenia (Griffin, December 1993). Dr. Kajander came to Canada from her native Finland in 1953 to train in Oshawa General Hospital. During her time at Oshawa, Kajander observed an anesthesiologist using a recently introduced drug to prepare patients for surgery, and she recognized it as the same drug (chlorpromazine) that was used in Europe to reduce anxiety in patients prior to surgery. When Kajander later in the same year moved to London Psychiatric Hospital as a resident psychiatrist, it occurred to her that chlorpromazine might be useful in the treatment of overactive schizophrenics in her care. Kajander's ideas, apparently formed quite independently and without knowledge of the developments in Europe at the same time, nevertheless matched Laborit's similar steps in discovering the value of chlorpromazine. Kajander obtained permission from the hospital superintendent to run a trial with the drug on 25 patients over a period of several months. The results were very encouraging: it calmed the patients' restlessness, reduced their activity, allowed them to discuss their problems, and made them able to eat and sleep without the difficulties they had previously shown. Kajander's subsequent presentation of the results at the Ontario Neuropsychiatric Association's conference in late 1953 represents what appears to be the first scientific report of the use of chlorpromazine with psychiatric patients in North America. At about the same time, Heinz Lehmann in Montreal began using it with his patients.

Over the years, many other Canadians have made significant contributions, in terms of both theory and new treatment approaches. Albert Bandura, who now lives and works in the United States but was raised in Canada, developed one of the most influential theories of human functioning to emerge in recent times. Social learning theory (see Chapter 2) was originally developed by Bandura and Richard Walters (who taught at the University of Waterloo, Ontario) to explain how aggressive behaviour was acquired as part of the learning process that occurs mostly in childhood (Bandura, 1973; Bandura & Walters, 1963). Bandura's analysis of aggression was so successful that he subsequently extended it to human behaviour in general (Bandura, 1969, 1977) and generated a variety of very effective treatment techniques for numerous disorders.

One of the most significant treatment developments of the 1970s was the extension of behavioural approaches to include the modification of cognitions (for example, thoughts, feelings, beliefs, and attitudes). This approach, which came to be called *cognitive-behavioural therapy* (see Chapter 16),

was led by a handful of researchers, prominent among them Canadian psychologist Donald Meichenbaum. Meichenbaum's early work provided a significant impetus to the growth of cognitive behaviour therapy (Meichenbaum, 1974), and his subsequent efforts have led to the development of very effective treatments for various problems including impulsivity (Meichenbaum & Goodman, 1971), pain, anxiety, and anger (Meichenbaum & Turk, 1976), stress (Meichenbaum, 1985), and post-traumatic stress disorder (Meichenbaum, 1994).

A number of other Canadian researchers who have made significant contributions will be mentioned throughout this book. Despite periodic "brain drains" to the United States and elsewhere, and despite cuts in research funds, Canadian scientists are still at the forefront of developments in the mental health field, where we are confident they will remain for the foreseeable future.

SUMMARY

Initially in this chapter, we considered the various criteria that have been suggested to define abnormality. In fact, none seems satisfactory on its own; it is only some combination of these criteria that seems to result in a reasonably satisfactory definition, although all attempts at defining such a general notion as abnormality seem doomed. It is only by a consideration of the specific disorders that we can come to fully appreciate what is meant by abnormal psychological functioning.

We then traced the development of the conceptualization and treatment of abnormal behaviour throughout the ages. The history of these ideas does not offer a clear evolution with a straightforward path from ignorance to enlightenment. Indeed, the early Greeks, Romans, and Arabs held many ideas that seem remarkably modern, although perhaps to think of it in those terms suggests the view that current approaches represent the ideal. In fact, the treatment and management of mad people in ancient times seems to have been kinder and more humane than many current practices.

Throughout what have been called the Middle Ages in Europe, there was a division between supernatural explanations of mental disorders and more naturalistic accounts. Similarly, treatments varied from humane and compassionate to torture in the guise of exorcism. However, humane approaches were not always synonymous with scientific or natural explanations, nor were cruel treatments always derived from supernatural views.

From the middle of the nineteenth century, with the rise of a scientific approach to all aspects of knowledge, the study and treatment of the mentally disordered has been placed on a more rigorous and constantly evaluated basis. However, there is still a long way to go in developing a more complete understanding of these problems, and in designing adequate treatment methods. The rest of this book describes what we presently know and how clinicians presently conceptualize and treat psychological abnormality.

KEY TERMS

psychological abnormality (p. 3)
mental illness (p. 3)
psychological disorder (p. 3)
psychopathology (p. 3)
psychiatrist (p. 6)
clinical psychologist (p. 6)
psychiatric nurse (p. 6)
psychiatric social worker (p. 6)

supernatural causes (p. 7)
natural causes (p. 8)
trephination (p. 8)
humours (p. 9)
asylums (p. 10)
St. Vitus' Dance (p. 11)
bedlam (p. 13)
mental hygiene movement (p. 14)
moral therapy (p. 16)
syndromes (p. 16)

general paresis of the insane (GPI) (p. 17)
somatogenesis (p. 17)
electroconvulsive therapy (ECT) (p. 18)
behaviourism (p. 19)
lobotomies (p. 20)

ADDITIONAL RESOURCES

Clarke Institute of Psychiatry
250 College Street
Toronto, ON
M5T 1R8
(416) 595-6878
(416) 595-6881 fax
hendryc@cs.clarke-inst.on.ca

Canadian Psychological Association
151 Slater Street
Suite 205
Ottawa, ON
K1P 5H3
(613) 237-2144
(613) 237-1674 fax
iparisien@cpa.ca

www.yorku.ca/faculty/academic/rmuller/
A searchable database with links to numerous sites related to abnormal psychology.

http://www.mk.net/~mcf/cbc1.htm
Transcription of an interview conducted by the CBC's Fifth Estate with victims and others involved in Canadian researcher Ewen Cameron's brainwashing experiments.

http://cpa.ca
The web site of the Canadian Psychological Association (CPA) provides information about research on mental illnesses and their causes, various treatments for disorders and education for professionals.

http://www.clarke-inst.on.ca
The Clarke Institute of Psychiatry is a Canadian-based psychiatric research institute. This site provides information about mental illnesses as well as details about the Institute's clinical programs and services and research endeavours. It also provides detailed information and statistics about a wide range of mental illnesses, from attention deficit disorders to phobias.

Chapter 2

Theoretical Perspectives on Abnormal Behaviour

William L. Marshall

Corey was a young man diagnosed by his therapist as suffering from panic disorder with agoraphobia. As an infant, Corey appeared to be overresponsive to changes in the environment. His parents described Corey as a nervous child and he showed all the signs of separation anxiety when he first began school. He was afraid of the dark and timid in physical play. Both Corey's father and his uncle had been diagnosed at one time with an anxiety disorder.

As a teenager, Corey was shy and kept to himself. He never hung out with a group, but made a few special friends. Afraid of rejection, he never had a girlfriend until the age of 19.

Corey became interested in music and played with friends. One of these friends convinced him to try marijuana, saying it would help him relax and express himself through his music. Unfortunately, Corey reacted to the drug by becoming hypersensitive to his physiological state and experienced a panic attack. He was shaken, and took weeks to overcome his fear of having flashbacks.

Corey was now 24; he was still going out with his first girlfriend, and planned to marry her the next year. But a few months after the dope incident, she broke up with him and refused to see him again. Devastated, Corey got into his car and drove aimlessly, trying to cope with his feelings of hurt and loneliness. When he finally began to pay attention to what he was doing, he realized he was lost, and immediately fell into a full-blown panic. In the weeks that followed, Corey experienced repeated attacks of panic that seemed to come out of the blue. As they increased in intensity and frequency, he began to withdraw from the world until, finally, he became unable to go to work. By the time he came for treatment, he was completely housebound, except for brief ventures out with his mother, who had had to bring him to the clinic.

The General Nature of Theories

Chapter 1 traced the development of ideas about abnormal behaviour from the ancient Greeks to this century. From early in the present century, there have been two main streams of thought concerning mental disorders. One focusses on the biological and the other on the environmental, roughly following the nature/nurture distinction that is made in so many areas of human functioning. Within each of these approaches there are many variations, but essentially biological approaches tend to dismiss or downplay the influence of experience, whereas psychological approaches emphasize environmental factors in the development of disorders. Indeed, some behavioural theories (for example, Skinner, 1953) attribute no effects at all to biology, assuming that, as British philosopher John Locke (1632–1704) put it, humans are born *tabula rasa* (a blank slate upon which experience writes all that is meaningful in thought and behaviour).

Biological and psychodynamic formulations view dysfunctional behaviour as the product of forces beyond the individual's control, while humanistic and existential approaches lay the responsibility for action and choices squarely on the shoulders of the individual. In some forms, behavioural and cognitive theories imply a mixture of external and internal factors as producing dysfunctions.

The perspective taken determines many things. It directs research, guides diagnostic decisions, and defines treatment responses. The acceptance of the biological model, for example, encourages researchers to seek a physical basis for disorders, leads to the formulation of a diagnostic system that classifies people as disordered, and implies that physical interventions should be the treatments of choice. The behavioural perspective, on the other hand, leads researchers to seek environmental events that shape specific dysfunctional responses and emphasizes the classification of behaviours rather than of people. Treatment, from the behavioural perspective, involves either manipulating the environment or (for those who adopt a cognitive-behavioural perspective) modifying the people's perceptions of their experiences.

For an example of how different perspectives would shed light on a disorder, consider the case of Corey with which we started the chapter. Corey's early infancy and childhood sensitivity to stimulation suggest that he may have been innately anxiety-prone. As a biologically oriented theorist would point out, the fact that two close relatives had anxiety disorders supports a genetic basis for Corey's problem. On the other hand, environmental factors—Corey's bad experience with marijuana and the breakup of his romance—also seem to be important. A Freudian would want to examine Corey's childhood relationships with his anxious father. A behaviourist would point to the role of learning processes in Corey's case. A cognitive theorist would emphasize that it was Corey's interpretation of what happened to him that caused him to panic. Someone who took an integrative perspective would look at the interaction among all these factors.

In the rest of this chapter, we will look more closely at the various theoretical approaches. In fact, throughout this book we will see confirmation of the theme illustrated by Corey's case: that the origins of psychological disorder are complex, with no one factor providing a complete explanation.

As we saw in the previous chapter, the view that enjoys most popular acceptance has changed over time and will no doubt change again in the future, and this influences how the majority of researchers and theorists think. For example, the view that biology largely determines human behaviour has become far more popular in the 1990s than was true in the late 1960s or early 1970s. Almost every week we read in the popular press of a newly discovered genetic, hormonal, or central nervous system defect underlying a particular human behaviour that was previously thought to be psychologically determined.

Interestingly, the adoption of a perspective is influenced far less by the weight of evidence than by the prevailing social belief system and by an individual's disposition to see human behaviour as determined by factors beyond or within the control of the individual. Indeed, theoreticians often stubbornly hold to a view in spite of evidence to the contrary. This tenacious clinging to a specific theory is not necessarily a bad thing, since it allows that theory to be fully explored. A theory is useful not so much because it is true, but because it generates research that leads to an increase in knowledge. A theory should be abandoned only when there is a better one available (that is, one that does a better job of integrating current knowledge and that generates more research). Thus, the scientific theories of the past should be judged not by how well they match current information, but rather, by how much new information they generated.

Biological and psychological perspectives to understanding abnormal behaviour represent overall models of construing such problems and are not, in this sense, theories. The biological model suggests that psychological disorders are analogous to physical disorders or diseases. This, in turn, implies that disrupted physical processes or structures cause the psychological abnormalities. Thus, these problems are called *disorders* and are classified in the same way as physical diseases; they are seen as amenable to physical treatments such as drugs, surgery, and the like.

Levels of Theories

When biological or psychological perspectives are applied to specific problems, they may become theories that detail the supposed causal chain leading to the emergence of the dysfunctional behaviour. In **single-factor explanations**, one factor is said to cause the disorder: for example, a genetic defect or a single traumatic experience. Human behaviour, in all its complexity, is unlikely to be a product of a single defect or experience. **Interactionist explanations**, which view behaviour as the product of the interaction of a variety of factors, generally make more satisfactory theories. In a theory of the etiology of sexual offending, for example, my colleague and I (Marshall & Barbaree, 1990) construe behaviour as a product of biological endowment and childhood, adolescent, and adult experiences interacting with transitory states (for example, upsetting mood states, intoxication, loss of self-confidence) occurring in conjunction with opportunities to offend. As knowledge of any single disorder increases, so, characteristically, does the complexity of theories offered to account for its development and maintenance. Single-factor theories, then, often simply reflect the lack of current comprehensive knowledge of disorders. Complex theories, particularly when they attempt to explain a group of problem behaviours (for example, all anxiety disorders) rather than a single problem (for example, snake phobia), generally identify risk factors rather than specific causes.

Theories may, in fact, be classified according to their level of explanation (Marshall, 1982). Some theories try to explain all human behaviour (for example, Maslow's [1954] theory of self-actualization), some try to explain all abnormal behaviour (for example, Freud, 1917), while others try to account for all disorders within a particular category, such as all types of personality disorders (for example, Millon, 1981). Even more specifically there are theories that endeavour to reveal the causes of a particular problem such as panic disorder (for example, Klein, 1993). Finally, there are theories that attempt to elucidate the influence of a single factor within a more general theory. An example of this latter type of theory is my own work (Marshall, 1989) on the role of lack of intimacy within a broader account of sexual offending.

Single-factor theories, however, should not be seen as valueless simply because they may later be discarded for more complex explanations. The history of science is replete with the rejection of theories that at one time were broadly accepted and seemed to explain phenomena. To expand on an earlier point, scientific theories are judged to be valuable not because they describe the enduring truth about an issue, but rather because they embody three essential features:

1. they integrate most of what is presently known about the phenomena;

2. they make predictions about aspects of the phenomena that were not previously thought of; and

3. they make it possible to specify what evidence would deny the theory

Testing Theories: The Null Hypothesis

Theories get replaced in science not because the evidence against them is significant (although that is a good reason to search for alternatives), but rather because a better theory comes along; that is, one that does a better job of integrating knowledge and generating novel predictions, and is open to disproof.

This latter notion often puzzles students; however, it is the cornerstone of science. Experiments (and other research strategies) are set up *not to prove the worth of a theory* but rather to reject (or fail to reject) what is called the null hypothesis. The null hypothesis essentially proposes that the prediction made from the theory is false. Let us look at a simple example. Suppose I claim that low self-esteem causes and maintains depression. A prediction from this claim would be that depressed psychiatric patients should have lower self-esteem than non-depressed psychiatric patients. If I compare these two groups of patients and find that the depressed group scores significantly lower than the non-depressed group, I may have offered some support for the theory, but I have not proved it to be true: some other, as yet unknown, factor may produce both depression and low self-esteem. However, these results allow us to reject the null hypothesis which, in this case, says there are no differences in self-esteem between the depressed and non-depressed groups. This at least eliminates an alternative possible theory; namely, that low self-esteem is characteristic of all psychiatric disorders.

Theories gain in strength not just because the evidence supports their predictions, but primarily because alternative explanations are rejected. Despite popular belief to the contrary, scientists do not set out to prove their theories to be true and, in fact, no amount of evidence can ever prove the truth of a theory. Theories are not facts, they are simply the best approximation we have at any moment, so that current theories are almost inevitably going to be replaced as knowledge accumulates. It is the very process of trying to prove our theories wrong that generates the new knowledge that will one day lead to their rejection.

Some accounts of abnormal behaviour, or indeed of psychological functioning more generally, do not in fact meet the criteria of scientific theories because they are essentially immune to disproof. Many critics have maintained that the theories of Sigmund Freud are not open to disproof. For example, Freud thought that paranoia (an overly suspicious view of others associated with the idea that other people can read your thoughts) resulted from repressed homosexual feelings. Presumably people who repress such feelings do not wish others to know about these desires, and this makes them worry that somehow other people will detect their homosexual tendencies. Such worries may lead them to become progressively more suspicious of others, and to begin to think that other people are reading their minds. Now this theory may seem reasonable, but how can it be tested? If an investigation reveals that all paranoid patients deny any homosexual thoughts or experiences, then this is just what Freud would expect. According to Freud, they are either keeping such desires to themselves or are, in fact, not even aware of such desires which are operating at an unconscious but nevertheless influential level. Thus, confirming the null hypothesis in this case (that is, that there are no differences between paranoid patients and others in the frequency of reported homosexual thoughts and behaviours) does not deny the theory. Indeed, the information necessary to confirm or deny the theory is not accessible to researchers (because the paranoid patient will deny homosexual tendencies) and presumably not even accessible to the patients themselves (because such tendencies are unconscious and beyond the patent's awareness).

Despite the dubious scientific status of Freud's theories, his ideas have had an enormous impact on psychological theorizing and on society and culture more generally. That is because Freud's work made the study of unconscious processes popular and he emphasized motivational processes (for example, sexual) that had previously been taboo. Freud opened the door to the study of influential processes of which we may only be marginally, if at all, aware. We will come to a more detailed examination of Freud's theories shortly.

THE SEARCH FOR CAUSES

Why do we seek to find the causes or **etiology** of abnormal behaviour? Perhaps the most obvious answer to this is that humans seem unable to avoid speculating about almost all the phenomena that life presents to us. We have to make sense of our world in order to function, and this is true also of our interactions with others. If someone has been particularly kind and supportive in the past, we will turn to that person in times of crisis because our guess (or hypothesis or theory) is that he or she will be kind and supportive now. We do not seek out certain other people because our expectations (that is, hypotheses or theories) about them, based on past experience, are that they will not be sympathetic. These are examples of quite limited theories but some accounts of human relationships see all behaviour as a product of such interpersonal hypotheses (Kelly, 1955).

The general aims of theories about mental disorders are to: (1) explain the etiology (that is, origins) of the problem behaviour; (2) identify the factors that maintain the behaviour; (3) predict the course of the disorder; and (4) design effective treatments. Of course, theories of abnormal behaviour are chosen also presumably because they fit with the theorists' more general sentiments about human nature. Some people feel uncomfortable attributing causes of behaviour to factors over which the person has little or no control (for example, biological causes or unconscious processes). Such theorists are likely to be attracted to accounts of human dysfunction that attribute causation to environmental influences. These theorists are, therefore, optimistic about the potential for environmental manipulations to produce behaviour change. If experience produces problem behaviours, then presumably different experiences can eliminate these difficulties. Other people are more attracted to biological explanations because they hold similar hopes for effective medical treatment.

It is important to note that factors in the etiology of a problem may not be relevant to its maintenance. For example, many young people may initially begin to drink alcohol, smoke cigarettes, or use drugs to impress others or to appear mature. Once entrenched, however, habitual use of alcohol, cigarettes, or drugs is maintained by the direct effects of the substance, the distress induced by withdrawal, and environmental cues such as being at a party with friends who drink, smoke, or use drugs. Similarly, the factors that determine the course of a disorder may have more to do with the lifestyle of the sufferer (or the deleterious effects of the substance in the case of drug use) than with the factors that caused the disorder in the first place. For example, a frightening experience with a dog may cause a person to become phobic, but subsequent careful avoidance of all dogs will maintain the disorder in some while others may force themselves to interact with the animals and thereby overcome their irrational fears.

Even in disorders where there is a clear biological cause, environmental manipulations may alleviate or even avoid the development of the most serious symptoms. For example, phenylketonuria (PKU) is an inborn metabolic defect that causes the body to be unable to metabolize phenylalanine, a substance present in many foods. This metabolic problem is genetically transmitted as a recessive autosomal trait, meaning that both parents must have the gene that carries the disorder for the child to develop PKU. The effects of untreated

PKU are to markedly raise blood levels of phenylalanine, resulting in a decrease in various neurotransmitters in the brain, thereby producing severe mental retardation. However, when PKU is detected in newborns (screening tests for PKU are now routine), and the infant is given a diet low in phenylalanine, most of the disastrous consequences are avoided and the child can live a relatively normal life.

An even more pertinent observation derives from a study by Baxter and his colleagues of patients suffering from obsessive-compulsive disorder (Baxter et al., 1992). Prior to treatment, Baxter's team completed a series of brain imaging studies, which revealed a defective brain circuit (dysfunctional caudate glucose metabolic rate) related to the patients' symptoms. After treatment with strictly psychological procedures (exposure and response prevention, described more fully in the Chapter 7, the chapter on anxiety disorders), Baxter et al. found that the defective brain circuit had been normalized in the treated patients. Obviously environmental manipulations can affect biological functioning quite dramatically: no doubt the converse is also true.

Many different theories have been advanced regarding the etiology of mental disorders. We limit ourselves here to a description of the most popular, grouped by the primary proposed cause: (1) biological; (2) psychodynamic (derived from the theories of Freud or his followers); (3) learning (behavioural or cognitive-behavioural theories); (4) dysfunctional thoughts or beliefs (cognitive theories); (5) intrapersonal processes (humanistic or existential theories); and (6) sociocultural influences. Of course, it is reasonable to assume that these various influences (the biological, psychological, intrapersonal, and cultural) interact to produce mental disorders. Even within each of these models various causes are seen as primary by one or another theorist. For example, within the biological category, some theories emphasize abnormal brain functioning, while others place the site of the problem in the autonomic nervous system, in genetic endowment, or in a dysfunctioning endocrine system.

In fact, all these systems (that is, biological, psychological, etc.) work in concert and it is well-nigh impossible (if not meaningless) to distinguish their influence. Indeed, the moral therapists of the nineteenth century (like those taking a holistic approach today) were quite correct in claiming that all aspects of functioning—biological, behavioural, and environmental—operate as a whole system, whose division is arbitrary. Dividing this whole system into its presumed component parts all too often has the effect of convincing some theorists that one or another aspect is causally more important than all other features. This type of thinking, which may attribute primary causation to biological problems (biological determinism), or to sociocultural, or environmental influences (cultural or environmental determinism), is a form of reductionism (sometimes called *elementarism*), in that the actions of the whole are said to be caused by (that is, reduced to the influence of) one or other of the component parts. This is akin to saying that body temperature is entirely determined by our internal thermal regulatory system, or alternatively by our external environment, when, of course, it is a product of

the dynamic interaction of the two, each of which is complexly determined. Reductionist thinking ignores the rather obvious possibility that human behaviour in all its forms is a product of a whole array of features (biological, environmental, personal choice, cultural, etc.) interacting. Being able to run a marathon in world-record time not only requires a biologically appropriate body (actually a broad range of body shapes seem suitable, although being born with only one leg would probably rule you out), but also a devoted training schedule and the right footwear (environmental features), and a culture that allows or encourages such long-distance running (cultural or social influences). Why, for example, is there a seemingly endless supply of great athletes from Kenya and Ethiopia? Is it because of the genetic constitution of people from these countries, or because they live at high elevations that promote maximum oxygen utilization, or simply because they grow up in a culture that requires them to run many miles from a young age? More likely, it is the interaction among all these factors, and perhaps others as well. Why so many theorists pit nurture against nature as opposing explanatory notions, in the face of such obvious mutually facilitating influences, is hard to understand.

Strict biological determinism all too often leads to the dismal conclusion that psychological or environmental interventions will do no good. When it comes to criminal behaviour, such arguments appeal to many people who wish to simply punish offenders while ignoring the possible social factors related to a higher incidence of crime (for example, unemployment, poverty, overcrowding). Similarly, with disorders that are very difficult to treat (for example, schizophrenia), well-intentioned clinicians discouraged with psychological treatments may readily accept that such disorders are biologically caused and, therefore, untreatable. However, Terry Fox clearly, and heroically, demonstrated to all Canadians and to the rest of the world, that even the absence of a leg and the presence of debilitating cancer do not prevent a determined person from performing at a physical level well beyond that of the majority of healthy people.

Similarly, cultural or environmental determinists often feel obliged to deny the influence of biological disadvantages. However, no amount of devoted training, expert guidance, Air Nikes, or determination would ever make a person who is 1.5 metres tall into a world-class high jumper. Lifestyle and education may ease the life of someone who inherits the defective gene that causes Huntington's disease but will not prevent the development of dementia, jerky body movements, depression, and psychosis.

In order to understand the various theoretical approaches to abnormal behaviour, we will have to consider them separately, as that is the way they have always been described. This separation, however, should not be taken to mean that we agree with any one model that assumes the prior causal control of behaviour. We view behaviour and thinking (whether normal or disordered) as arising out of the integrated dynamic and essentially inseparable interactions between biology and environmental experience.

BIOLOGICAL MODELS

Norman Endler, a distinguished Canadian psychologist, was stricken suddenly with severe, recurrent episodes of depression so debilitating he could not maintain his position as department chair. Overwhelmed by despair, he felt sure dreadful things were going to happen to him. By his own description, Endler's behaviour in the depths of depression became "bizarre and paranoid." For example, when his doctor asked for a urine sample, the only container Endler's wife could find was the bottle his daughter's antibiotics had come in. "I was reluctant to use it because for some reason it was impossible to remove the label completely. It was possible, however, to remove all identifying information. This was not good enough for me. For some reason I was convinced, irrationally, that if I left a sample in that container, Dr. P. would think that it was not my urine sample and would put me in the hospital for lying." Endler became desperate for a cure. Although he had been fiercely opposed to electroconvulsive therapy (ECT—see Chapter 13), when various other approaches had failed, he was persuaded to accept a course of ECT. Seven ECT treatments over a course of six weeks led to what Endler called "a miracle ... I had gone from feeling like an emotional cripple to feeling well" (Endler, 1982, pp. 50–51, 72–73, 81–83).

Responses like Endler's have encouraged many theoreticians to look for biological causes for abnormal behaviour. Biological theorists of human behaviour typically not only borrow their model from medicine, but also co-opt the language of medicine, calling clients "patients" and their problems "symptoms" or "syndromes," and describing the response to these problems as "treatment." Thus, adopting a biological model has implications for the way in which people with problems are dealt with. The same, of course, is true for all theoretical perspectives, and it is necessary to consider the ramifications of these often unnoticed implications when deciding on a particular point of view about abnormal behaviour. A model may be appealing because it fits with current thinking, but it may have less obvious features that may not be so attractive.

To appreciate the meaning of the various biological explanations of disordered behaviour or thinking, it is necessary to have some understanding of relevant aspects of bodily functioning. Biological theories have primarily implicated dysfunctions in or damage to the brain (the central nervous system or CNS), problems of dyscontrol of one or another aspect of the peripheral nervous system (that is, the autonomic nervous system or the somatic nervous system), or malfunctioning of the endocrine system.

The nervous system is, for purposes of exposition, divided into the CNS and the peripheral nervous system, although in normal functioning the activities of these two complex systems are integrated, and their actions are further coordinated with activity in the endocrine system.

The Role of the Central Nervous System

The brain is estimated (Fishbach, 1992) to have some 100 billion neurons (that is, nerve cells) and thousands of billions of glia cells (presumed to be support cells, although recent evidence suggests they exert a more active role in neuronal functioning). These cells group together into anatomically distinct areas, which appear to have somewhat distinctive functions, although active interconnections throughout the brain indicate that no one area exclusively performs any one function. It is perhaps better to think of brain activity related to particular functions or actions not as *located* in a single area of the brain but as *concentrated* in one or more areas.

Figure 2.1 describes the anatomical areas of the brain. The hindbrain primarily directs the functioning of the autonomic nervous system, which in turn controls primarily internal activities such as digestion, cardiovascular functioning, and breathing. The midbrain is the centre of the reticular activating system, which controls arousal levels (often called the "sleep-wake" centre) and thereby attentional processes. The forebrain controls thought, speech, perception, memory, learning, and planning—indeed, all the processes that make us sentient, self-conscious beings. Obviously damage to any of these parts of the brain will cause proportionate dysfunctioning in many areas, including psychological functioning. Some disorders (for example, general paresis of the insane, GPI, discussed in Chapter 1) have been shown to be directly linked to brain damage (in the case of GPI to the destruction of brain cells as a result of syphilis). The **dementia**

Figure 2.1 The Human Brain (side view)

Corpus callosum

Forebrain

Cerebral hemisphere

Midbrain

Thalamus

Hypothalamus

Hindbrain

Cerebellum

Pituitary

Reticular formation

Pons

Medulla

Spinal cord

Source: From Baron, *Psychology 3/e.* Copyright © 1995 by Allyn & Bacon. Reprinted by permission.

(a deterioration in all cognitive processes, particularly memory and learning, that occurs in disorders such as Parkinson's or Alzheimer's) is linked to the loss or ineffective functioning of brain cells. These losses of brain cell functioning can be transitory, but in many cases they are irreversible and may result from various sources such as direct head injuries, diseases, or toxins. Sophisticated methods are now available for detecting even quite small areas of damage or dysfunction in the brain. Various imaging techniques, such as computerized axial tomography (CAT scans), magnetic resonance imaging (MRI), and positron emission tomography (PET scans) have all enabled the detailed, although expensive, examination of brain functioning. However, current theories about the brain bases of abnormal behaviour have given more weight to the role of neurotransmitters than to actual neuronal damage.

Neurotransmitters are the chemical substances that carry the messages from one neuron to the next in the complex pathways of nervous activity within the brain. Nerve cells are not connected to one another, so activity in one neuron does not directly stimulate activity in other neurons. There is a gap (called a synapse or synaptic cleft) between the axons (which carry the nerve impulse to the synapse) of one neuron and the dendrites (which pick up the activity from the first neuron) of neighbouring neurons. The transmission of the electrical activity in the axon to the neighbouring dendrites occurs as a result of the release of chemicals called neurotransmitters (see Focus box). There are numerous neurotransmitters, but to date the majority of research attention has been given to the role of dopamine, serotonin, norepinephrine, and, more recently, gamma aminobutyric acid (or GABA). These neurotransmitters act either on their own, or more likely in concert with others, in the spread of nerve impulses throughout the brain. Different types seem to be concentrated in different areas of the brain and are, therefore, thought to play a role in different functions. For example, pleasure-seeking and exploratory behaviours seem to be

Focus — *Neurotransmission*

Anatomy of a Neuron

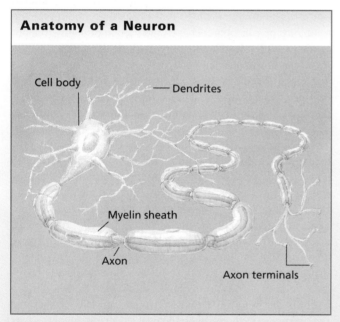

Transmission of Neural Impulses Across the Synapse

Source: From Baron, *Psychology 3/e.* Copyright © 1995 by Allyn & Bacon. Reprinted by permission.

Nerve impulses are electrochemical discharges that are received by the dendrites of one neuron, thereby activating (or inhibiting) that neuron, and then travel down the axons of that neuron to activate (or inhibit) the electrochemical activity in the dendrites of another neuron. At the point of contact between the axon of the neuron propagating the nerve impulse (called the presynaptic neuron) and the dendrite of the receiving neuron (called the postsynaptic neuron), is the synapse. This is a minute space through which strictly chemical messengers (the neurotransmitters) pass from the axon terminals to the receiving dendrites, where they either activate or inhibit electrochemically generated impulses.

The neurotransmitters (of which there are several kinds, all serving apparently different activating or inhibiting functions) are held in vesicles within the axon terminals. When these vesicles are stimulated by the neural impulse travelling down the axon, they move to the releasing site and emit the neurotransmitters into the synapse. Some of the released transmitters are reabsorbed (a process called *reuptake*) by the axon, some are deactivated by substances in the synapse, and the remainder are taken up at receptor sites on the dendrites of the postsynaptic neuron. These receptor sites are highly specialized and can only take up transmitters whose structure exactly fits into the structure of the receptor so that each receptor can only absorb particular neurotransmitters. This makes it possible to create drugs whose chemical structure is an exact match for particular transmitters so that when they are released into the synapse these drugs block the action of the transmitters by taking their place in the receptors. Other drugs can be made to accelerate or inhibit the action of the deactivators, again specifically affecting particular neurotransmitters, or they can stimulate or reduce the release of particular neurotransmitters. ▲

associated with dopamine activity, while serotonin activity appears to be related to the constraint or inhibition of behaviour; these two neurotransmitters, then, seem to act to create a balance in behaviour (Depue, in press).

Certain neurons seem to be more sensitive to one or another type of neurotransmitter and these neurons seem to cluster together, forming particular brain circuits. There appear to be as many as tens of thousands of such pathways or brain circuits that overlap one another, although they may finally separate into specific pathways (Dean, Kelsey, Heller, & Ciarenello, 1993).

When neurotransmitters are released into the synapse, some will be taken up at the receptor sites on the dendrites and thereby activate or inhibit (depending upon the action of the transmitter) an impulse in the post-synaptic neuron. However, within the synaptic cleft there are also substances that deactivate neurotransmitters, so some of the released transmitters will be destroyed before they can act on the dendrites. Furthermore, many of the released neurotransmitters are quickly drawn back into the releasing axon by a process called reuptake. Thus, abnormal behaviour can result from disturbances in neurotransmitter systems in various ways: (1) there may be too much or too little of the neurotransmitter produced or released into the synapse; (2) there may be too few or too many receptors on the dendrites; (3) there may be an excess or a deficit in the amount of the transmitter-deactivating substance in the synapse; or (4) the reuptake process may be too rapid or too slow. Any or all of these problems can cause either too much excitation or too much inhibition in the particular brain circuits and this excessive or reduced activity may result in abnormal functioning. Schizophrenia, for example, is thought by some theorists to result from too much activity in the brain circuits (the dopamine system) that mediate the importance we attach to stimuli in our environment so that the patient experiences his or her world as overwhelming; everything seems important and relevant. However, most researchers now believe that brain functioning is much more complex than this. Disturbances in neurotransmitter systems are now thought to more likely have general rather than specific effects and it is the interaction of various neurotransmitters that is related to behaviour (Depue & Spoont,

1986; Depue & Zald, 1993). Research now seems more concentrated on detecting the role that neurotransmitter pathways have in specific disorders, particularly in the interaction between various pathways.

The logic involved in inferring a causal relationship between disturbances in neurotransmitter functioning and abnormal behaviour depends to some extent on the methods used in examining this claim. For example, it is now known (with reasonable certainty) that drugs that ameliorate the symptoms of schizophrenia exert their action primarily (but not exclusively) by decreasing activity in the dopaminergic system. This is taken as supportive evidence for the hypothesis that schizophrenia is caused by excessive dopamine, but this may be a false inference. For example, the administration of quinine relieves the symptoms of malaria, but it is not the absence of quinine that causes malaria; it is the bite of the *Anopheles* mosquito, which introduces the *Plasmodium* protozoa into the body. At a more basic level, it is important to note that the processes connecting behaviour and the neurochemical bases of brain activity do not represent a one-way street. No doubt neurotransmitter activity affects behaviour, but behaviour also affects neurotransmitter activity. At present, it remains a possibility, although not one supported by many theorists, that environmental events cause schizophrenia and that the behavioural response to these events results in increased activity in neurotransmitter systems. Much more likely is the possibility that environmental events, the person's response to them, and biological substrates, all play a part in causing abnormal functioning.

The Role of the Peripheral Nervous System

The peripheral nervous system includes the somatic nervous system, which controls the muscles, and the autonomic nervous system (ANS). The ANS has two parts: the sympathetic nervous system and the parasympathetic nervous system (see Figure 2.2). These two systems typically function cooperatively to produce homeostatic (that is, balanced) activity in a variety of bodily functions such as heart rate, digestive and eliminatory processes, sexual arousal, breathing, perspiration, etc. In times of stress, however, they function antagonistically. During stress, or when the person feels threatened, the sympathetic nervous system readies the body for action (fight or flight) by, for example, increasing heart rate, pupil size (making vision more acute), and breathing (which becomes faster and deeper to take in more oxygen). At the same time, the parasympathetic nervous system shuts down digestive processes, since energy given to this function would be wasted in a time of emergency.

Since humans display variability in all other response systems, it would not be surprising to find that, in some people, the ANS response to stress or threat is either exaggeratedly strong or remarkably weak. Canadian physician Hans Selye studied responses to stress, beginning in 1936 and continuing until his death in 1983. Selye's work established the area of study now known as "stress physiology." It has become clear that individuals differ in both the strength and the duration of their response to threat and this variability has been related to the person's propensity to develop psychophysiological disorders (Friedman & Booth-Kewley, 1987). The ANS (more particularly, the sympathetic nervous system) is involved in fear and anxiety reactions. Thus, an overreactive ANS may increase readiness to acquire phobias or other anxiety disorders. For example, it is assumed by some behavioural therapists that conditioning processes are the basis for acquiring anxiety disorders. The strength of an individual's

ANS response to a "frightening experience" may determine whether he or she acquires a conditioned phobic reaction, and it has been found that there is a heritable component to the level of emotionality (Lader & Wing, 1964). Such differences in responsivity may explain why one person exposed to a traumatic experience develops a severe and enduring conditioned emotional response while another person exposed to exactly the same experience does not (Schnurr, Friedman, & Rosenberg, 1993).

The somatic nervous system also appears to display differential responsivity. This differential responsivity may or may not be tied to the response of the ANS, but it still may play a part in disordered behaviour. For example, patients suffering from generalized anxiety disorder (GAD) are described as *autonomic restrictors*, because they consistently show less responsivity on ANS measures of arousal, such as heart rate, blood pressure, sweat response, and breathing rates (Hoehn-Saric & Masek, 1981; Hoehn-Saric, McLeod, & Zimmerli, 1989). However, these same patients display chronic muscle tension (Marten et al., in press). Just exactly why GAD patients are autonomic restrictors, while at the same time being muscularly tense, is not completely clear, but obviously their muscle tension plays some part in their disorder.

However, no evidence has been produced indicating that these responses play a part in the development of any disorder. It has not been shown that phobic patients have higher ANS arousal prior to the onset of their disorder, nor that GAD patients have chronic muscle tension preceding their disorder. Perhaps the development of these disorders brings with them increased ANS or somatic nervous system responses. Becoming afraid or anxious may simply make people more sensitive to the possibility of threat and this greater sensitivity may produce elevations in ANS or muscle activity to prepare the person for the perceived threats.

The Role of the Endocrine System

Aspects of the central nervous system interact with the endocrine system in a feedback loop that maintains appropriate levels of hormones circulating in the bloodstream. Hormones are chemical messengers that are secreted by various glands. These secretions maintain adequate bodily functioning and play an important role in the development of the organism; they also appear to be involved in the activation of some behaviours.

The relationship of the endocrine glands both to each other and to the CNS is complex. For example, in response to feedback indicating that the circulating levels of sex hormones (or sex steroids) are low, the CNS activates the hypothalamus (a small CNS structure located in the lower central part of the forebrain), which secretes what are called "releasing" hormones that, in turn, activate the pituitary gland. Increased levels of circulating sex steroids alert the hypothalamus and pituitary to shut down this activity. The hormones secreted by the pituitary influence hormonal production in the adrenal gland and the testes (in males) and the ovaries (in females). The pituitary (which is often called

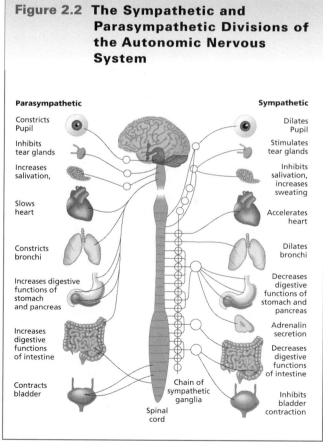

Figure 2.2   The Sympathetic and Parasympathetic Divisions of the Autonomic Nervous System

Parasympathetic

Constricts Pupil
Inhibits tear glands
Increases salivation,
Slows heart
Constricts bronchi
Increases digestive functions of stomach and pancreas
Increases digestive functions of intestine
Contracts bladder

Sympathetic

Dilates Pupil
Stimulates tear glands
Inhibits salivation, increases sweating
Accelerates heart
Dilates bronchi
Decreases digestive functions of stomach and pancreas
Adrenalin secretion
Decreases digestive functions of intestine
Inhibits bladder contraction

Chain of sympathetic ganglia

Spinal cord

Source: From Baron, *Psychology 3/e.* Copyright © 1995 by Allyn & Bacon. Reprinted by permission.

the "master gland" because it plays such a controlling role in activating the other endocrine glands) releases many different hormones, some of which, as we have seen, activate other glands while others have a more direct action. Growth hormone promotes and regulates muscle, bone and other tissue growth; prolactin stimulates milk production in women; and adrenocorticotrophic hormone helps the body handle stress. Obviously, the endocrine system has many and complex effects on behaviour.

Two disorders are known to be related to malfunctioning endocrine glands. Cretinism, a disorder involving a dwarflike appearance and mental retardation, is a result of a defective thyroid gland. Hypoglycemia, which results from the pancreas failing to produce balanced levels of insulin or glycogen, produces experiences that mimic anxiety, and some patients who report to anxiety disorder clinics are in fact suffering from hypoglycemia. Similarly, low levels of thyroid activity produce anxiety symptoms (Morley & Krahn, 1988), as do high levels of adrenaline secreted from the adrenal gland (Schachter & Latane, 1964).

Some theorists have proposed that disturbances in the sex steroid system may underlie various disorders of sexual behaviour in males, particularly the paraphilias (such as fetishes). While testosterone (which is primarily secreted by the testes) is perhaps the most important and certainly the most thoroughly studied of the male sex steroids, the other hormones involved in this complex system also play a role in regulating sexual desire and behaviour (Hucker & Bain, 1990). It has been suggested that elevated testosterone levels drive excessive or deviant sexual behaviour (Berlin & Meinecke, 1981), but the evidence in support of this is not strong (Hucker & Bain, 1990) and it appears that firmly established sexual response patterns function independently of circulating testosterone levels (Cooper, 1987).

Genetics and Behaviour

The idea that human behaviour is inherited has a long history. This idea is part of the more general concept of biological determinism: that what a person is is determined largely by inherited characteristics. Thomas Hobbes, a seventeenth-century English philosopher, thought that aggression and self-interest were inborn features of all humans and it was the business of political systems to restrain and usefully channel these impulses. By the nineteenth century, it was widely believed that all people took their biologically allotted place in society (that is, the destitute were condemned by their inherited characteristics to be poor, while the wealthy and the aristocracy were simply displaying their hereditary advantages). Cesare Lombroso (1836–1909) declared that criminals could be identified by the physiological features they had inherited from their degenerate parents. The eminent neuroanatomist Paul Broca (1824–1880) claimed that males were born with brains superior to those of females. Similar claims were made with respect to racial differences—with Europeans, of course, being seen as the supreme race. Some of these hereditary arguments about the superiority of one race (that is, whites)

over another (that is, blacks) live on today in the writings of Arthur Jensen (1969) and Hans Eysenck (1973) about presumed IQ differences.

It is well to keep in mind that claims about the inheritance of defective features can easily be used by those who would treat the supposed defectives in a prejudicial manner. For those who wish to read further on the controversies surrounding the genetic bases of behaviour, Leon Kamin, a Princeton psychologist, has written extensively and critically regarding the idea of inherited differences between races in IQ (Kamin, 1974). More general criticisms of genetic determinism are provided by Lewontin, Rose, and Kamin (1984) and by Hubbard and Wald (1993).

While these criticisms should make us cautious, they should not blind us to the possibility of genetic contributions to psychological disorders. Rejecting the idea that genes completely determine behaviour does not require us to accept that society, culture, or personal experience wholly account for human thought and action. It seems more reasonable to expect that most, if not all, behaviours are the product of an interaction between these sources of influence. **Behavioural genetics** offer us an insight into the biological bases of abnormal functioning, although, unfortunately, most researchers make little more than a token effort to spell out the way in which inherited features interact with the environment to produce behaviour.

Behavioural research into the genetic bases of psychiatric disorders typically takes one of three forms: family (or pedigree) studies, twin studies, and adoption studies. In all such studies, a person with a disorder is identified (called the index case or proband) and other people (family or nonfamily members) are examined to see if there is a match for the disorder. When the problem that characterizes the index case also occurs in the comparison person, the two are said to be *concordant* (or to display **concordance** for the problem). The degree of concordance is thought to reveal the influence of genetics. However, this assumption is not altogether accurate, since concordance can, depending on the circumstances, reveal environmental influences.

More recent techniques for studying genetic influences include **genetic linkage studies** and research methods in **molecular biology**. In genetic linkage studies, researchers examine families that have a high incidence of a particular psychiatric disorder. Within these extended families the researchers look for the presence of particular traits (called genetic markers) that can be linked to the occurrence of the disorder. Common among these genetic markers are features like hair or eye colour, colour blindness, and the presence of medical disorders that have a known genetic basis. If all members of the family who have the mental disorder also have the genetic marker, but the normal family members do not, then the conclusion is that the mental disorder has a genetic origin. These sorts of genetic linkage studies have provided strong evidence of a genetic basis for disorders characterized by episodes of both mania and depression (Stine et al., 1995).

Researchers in molecular biology have been able to compare specific DNA segments and identify the genes that determine individual characteristics. These are the methods underlying the attempt to map the entire human genome and researchers have been able to pinpoint the defective genes that cause various medical and psychological disorders (Glausiusz, 1997). In most of these cases, multiple gene defects appear to produce the disorder.

A detailed description of the research strategies involved in attempting to determine genetic influences in psychopathology, and the potential interpretations of the data derived from these studies, is outlined in detail in Chapter 4.

PSYCHOSOCIAL THEORIES

"Little Hans" was a five-year-old boy whose father brought him to Sigmund Freud's attention (1905). The boy was so fearful of being bitten by a horse that he would not leave the house. The father told Freud that one day he and Hans had boarded a streetcar (pulled, in those days, by horses). At some point in the trip the horses, frightened by a loud noise, reared up, pushing the streetcar backwards, and then bolted, dragging the careening car after them. When they finally stopped, the boy was very frightened and distressed, and his father took him home. Freud apparently analyzed this case without ever seeing Hans. He dismissed the experience with the bolting horses as a cause, considering the fear to have hidden unconscious origins.

Many theorists have ignored, or relegated to a lesser role, the influence of biological processes on behaviour and thought. Psychodynamic theorists, like Freud, have suggested that behaviour is motivated by inner, unconscious processes acquired during the formative years of life. In the case above, Hans' phobia was seen as a symbol of underlying psychic conflict. Hans' apparent fear of being bitten by a horse, Freud said, was a symbolic representation of his dread of being castrated by his father. Freud cast the story in terms of his famous Oedipus complex (explained later in this chapter). Other theorists believe behaviours are learned responses to environmental stimuli. This belief characterizes behavioural, cognitive-behavioural, and social learning theorists. For example, Little Hans' case has been seen as clear evidence for a behavioural or conditioning explanation for phobias. Strictly cognitive theorists claim it is the way people think about or perceive their world that causes them to develop disorders. (No doubt they would argue that it was the way Little Hans viewed and remembered the experience that caused him to become fearful.) Humanists and existentialists suggest that personal experience provides the basis for the development of self-directed behaviour. Finally, sociocultural theorists suggest that the surrounding society or culture exerts powerful influences on people; that such influences may cause a disorder to occur; and, moreover, that a particular society may define a person as abnormal because it suits the ends of society. What all these different theories have in common is that they stress experience.

Psychodynamic Theories

Sigmund Freud (1856–1939), a Viennese neurologist, was the founder of the **psychodynamic** school of thought. Psychodynamic theories claim that behaviour is controlled by unconscious forces of which the person is unaware. In this sense, psychodynamic theories, like biological theories, see the person as having little control over his or her actions. However, psychodynamic theorists consider the origins of unconscious controls to reside in the individual's personal experience (albeit during the very early formative years).

Freud's analysis of a patient known as "Anna O" provided the insights he needed to develop his theory. Anna O had quite complex symptoms, including paralysis, deafness, and disturbances of vision, which apparently were psychologically induced rather than a result of physical damage. During hypnosis, Anna O revealed traumatic past experiences associated with deep emotional responses. Memories of these experiences were apparently repressed, since the patient could not recall them during her waking state, but after she had expressed them during hypnosis, Freud and his mentor, Josef Breuer (1842–1925), judged Anna O to have improved. This led Freud to conclude that traumatic experiences early in life become repressed (that is, inaccessible to awareness) because they are too distressing to contemplate. Freud further assumed that these repressed or unconscious memories influence current functioning. Discharging the emotional responses attached to these unconscious memories, by identifying the original traumatic experiences during hypnosis, was called *catharsis* by Breuer and Freud, and they saw this as the effective element in treating such problems.

Sigmund Freud (1856–1939), founder of the psychoanalytic movement.

Interestingly, Anna O (whose real name was Bertha Pappenheim) continued to suffer from intermittent recurrence of her problems for some years after being discharged as effectively treated by Breuer, and she subsequently became quite hostile toward what she called "the talking cure" (what Freud came to call psychoanalysis). Pappenheim finally recovered completely and became not only Germany's first social worker, but also a leading feminist. She would not allow any of the girls in the home she ran to be psychoanalyzed despite their often considerable problems.

In Freud's theory, four features together determine current behaviour and thinking, both normal and abnormal. The different levels of consciousness determine the accessibility of thoughts and desires; the structures of personality represent the embodiment of the various controlling forces; the stages of psychosexual development indicate the points in experience where problems can arise; and, finally, defence mechanisms are the means by which people channel their psychic energy in functional or dysfunctional ways.

Levels of Consciousness

Freud distinguished what he believed to be three levels of awareness:

- the **conscious**, which contains information of which we are currently aware;
- the **preconscious**, which holds information not presently within our awareness but that can readily be brought into awareness; and
- the **unconscious**, which, according to Freud, contains the majority of our memories and drives—which, unfortunately can only be raised to awareness with great difficulty and typically only in response to particular techniques (that is, by psychoanalytic procedures)

The unconscious, for Freud, was the most important level of the mind. All our biological drives, particularly sexual and aggressive drives, reside at this level, as do our traumatic memories. Freud thought that sexual and aggressive drives, which he considered to be instinctual, upset people so much that they could not face the fact that they had such urges. (Freud did, after all, live in Vienna at a time when Victorian morality ruled the lives of those who inhabited his level of society.) These unacceptable drives and the traumatic memories were kept out of awareness by what Freud called *defence mechanisms*, of which we will have more to say in a moment.

Structures of Personality

According to Freud, there are three structures of personality (see Figure 2.3), which are in constant conflict. Whether Freud really meant these to be understood as actual structures or as metaphors for different psychic forces is not altogether clear, but there is no doubt he thought they represented the sources that determined personality.

The **id** is the structure present at birth and contains, or represents, the biological or instinctual drives. These drives are

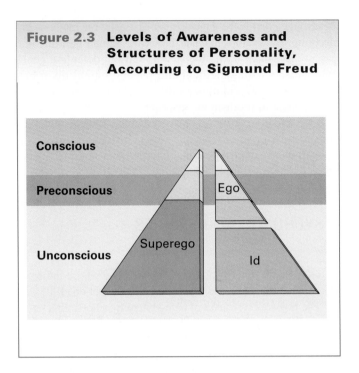

Figure 2.3   Levels of Awareness and Structures of Personality, According to Sigmund Freud

not constrained at birth, demanding as they do instant gratification without concern for the consequences either to the self or to others. In this sense the id acts according to what Freud called the *pleasure principle*. Fantasizing the achievement of these forbidden desires represents one way of obtaining gratification without having to enact the actual behaviours; Freud called this *primary process thinking*.

In the first year of life and thereafter, the infant becomes aware that his or her instinctual demands are not always immediately met and must learn to cope with this delay of gratification. It is in response to these experiences that the **ego** begins to develop. The ego develops to curb the desires of id so that the individual does not suffer any unpleasant consequences. There is no concern here for what is right or wrong, but only the avoidance of pain or discomfort and the maximization of unpunished pleasure. As the individual learns what expressions of desires are practical and possible, the ego comes to be governed by the reality principle. The compromise it strikes between the desires of the id and reality is called *secondary process thinking*. Early in life, then, there is a constant clash between the id and the ego, which is reduced over time so long as the ego develops normally. However, the development of the ego is affected by progress through the psychosexual stages of development, which we will consider in a moment.

Finally, as the child gets older, the **superego** begins to develop. The superego is the internalization of the moral standards of society inculcated by the child's parents. The operating guide of the superego is the moral principle, and it serves as the person's conscience by monitoring the ego. The ego, therefore, attempts to satisfy the id while not offending the principles of the superego. The more strongly developed the ego, the better able it is to handle these often opposing pressures.

Psychosexual Stages of Development

Freud thought that sexual drives were the most important determinants of behaviour, and that even the most innocent actions might be driven by sexual desires. Sexual drives were seen as the major life instinct, which Freud called *eros*, the energy for which was **libido**. Sexual pleasure, or the expression of libidinal energy, was focussed on different body parts, which Freud called *erogenous zones*, and the focus of these zones differed at different stages of psychosexual development. Failure to resolve a stage would result in a fixation on the erogenous zone associated with that stage.

The first year of life for an infant is characterized by oral activity. One of the child's strongest and most constant needs is for food, primarily from the mother's breasts or a bottle. In addition, infants typically engage in a lot of other oral behaviour. Anyone who has observed infants notices that they place everything they can handle into their mouths. Freud called this the **oral stage**. According to Freud, the sucking and biting that characterized this stage produced sexual gratification. It was, of course, quite shocking to Freud's contemporaries that he considered the seemingly innocent oral activities of infants to be associated with sexual gratification.

During the oral stage the child fears that the mother, who is the primary provider of the child's oral gratification, will leave and not return. Freud called this the fear of *object loss*, and *object relations* (the relationship between the child and its primary caregiver) has become an area of focus for some post-Freudian psychoanalysts. A failure to resolve the oral stage (that is, failure to have the libidinal desires focussed on oral activity fully satisfied) was thought by Freud to produce later behaviours that are either directly oral (for example, alcoholism or overeating) or symbolically so (for example, constantly talking).

From 18 months to 3 years the child is in the **anal stage** of development. Here the focus of libidinal pleasure shifts to the anus, with gratification coming from retaining feces (anal retention) or eliminating feces (anal expression). When the parents' efforts to toilet-train their child begin before the child is able to learn the necessary behaviours, or when the parents use toilet training methods that involve withdrawal of love for failures, anal fixation may result. The child may deliberately withhold a bowel movement, or deliberately soil his or her pants, to resist the parents' excessive demands. According to Freud a person who is anally fixated will display stubbornness, or be overcontrolling, or hoard things, all of which he saw as behaviours used by the child to combat the parents' severe training techniques.

Between the third and fourth years the child enters the **phallic stage**. This is a stage that has received a great deal of attention from psychoanalysts and the consequences of its disruption have featured in numerous books and films derived from psychoanalytic theory. In this stage, according to Freud, boys become focussed on their penis and girls become aware that they do not have one. In fact, girls are said to develop *penis envy* (that is, they desire to have a penis and feel cheated). Exactly why Freud thought that girls would envy boys for hav-

ing a penis is not clear but it is obviously a male-centred view of children and a phallic-centred view of sexuality.

During the phallic stage boys are presumed to develop sexual desires for their mother and see their father as a competitor for their mother's love. This is described as the **Oedipal complex**, in reference to the character of Oedipus in the play by the Greek tragedian Sophocles. In Sophocles' play, Oedipus unwittingly kills his father and marries his mother, Jocasta. At the same time as a boy recognizes his father as a threat to the fulfillment of his desire for his mother, he also fears reprisal from his father. In Freud's view, the boy fears that his father will mutilate the boy's genitals to prevent any union with the mother. This fear is called *castration anxiety*—an odd choice of term, since castration denotes removal of the testicles, not the penis, and would therefore not prevent intercourse. Because this fear is not consciously recognized, it can manifest itself as fear of something apparently unrelated, as in the case of Little Hans.

Similarly, girls are thought to desire their fathers—not to win their father's love, but rather by seducing him to gain what they truly desire: a penis. In girls, this desire for the father is called the **Electra complex**, again by analogy to a character in several Greek tragedies. (Electra, in fact, did not desire her father, but rather helped her brother, Orestes, kill their mother, who had murdered their father.)

For children to successfully resolve the Oedipal or Electra conflict, they need to identify with their same-sex parent. This can be achieved if parents are tolerant of the child's sexuality but at the same time gently discourage their desire for the mother or father. When parents are punitive about expressions of sexuality in their phallic-stage children, or subtly incite the child's inappropriate desires, then disturbances in sexual development will occur, resulting, so Freud thought, in some sort of sexual disorder. Thus, adults who display problems in sexual relations (being either sexually dysfunctional or promiscuous), or who are sexually deviant, are seen by psychoanalysts as having failed to resolve the phallic stage of their development.

From age 6 to 12 years children enter what Freud called the **latency stage**, a period of relative sexual quiescence, during which the child focusses on developing intellectual and motor skills. In this stage, children typically associate with same-sex friends, are embarrassed by sexual matters, and begin in earnest the process of socialization. It is a stage that has not had much attention from psychoanalysts, presumably because it is thought to be a time when sex is not particularly relevant. Somewhat contrary to this idea, some sexual offenders report high rates of masturbation, sexual involvement with others, and extensive use of pornography during the so-called latency years (Dhawan & Marshall, 1996; Goldstein, Kant, & Hartman, 1973). Similarly, evidence from non-European, pre-Victorian European, and even from current Western societies, indicates that sexual expression is common among children of this age (Ford & Beech, 1951; Kinsey, Pomeroy, & Martin, 1948; Kinsey, Pomeroy, Martin, & Gebhard, 1953; Langfeldt, 1981). There is no doubt, however, that sexual expression by latency-aged children was severely repressed during the Victorian period in Europe and still is by many parents today (Martinson, 1976). Oddly enough, although Freud contradicted prevailing sentiments of the time by recognizing early childhood sexuality, he seems to have accepted the attitudes of his day regarding latency-stage sexuality. Perhaps this simply reveals a dominant feature of Freud's theorizing: despite his brilliance as a theorist and his training as a scientist, Freud did not conduct any systematic research either to test his beliefs or to provide a basis for developing his views.

Finally, after age 12, children enter what Freud termed the **genital stage**. Sexual desires during this stage are directed toward involvement with others. Freud emphasized heterosexual relations, apparently because he believed homosexuality to be an aberration resulting from a failure to resolve the Oedipal or Electra complex. The genital stage involves the early adolescent shedding the narcissistic qualities of the earlier stages and developing the capacity to become involved in affectionate and romantic relationships with peers.

Table 2.1 summarizes the psychosexual stages of development.

Defence Mechanisms

Remember that the function of the ego is to restrain the direct expression of the libidinal desires of the id. It does so by employing, at an unconscious level, a kind of censoring system. Using what are called **defence mechanisms**, the ego allows the expression of libidinal desires in a distorted or symbolic form. The id, however, does its best to break through these defences, so that psychic energy is used up in this almost constant psychic conflict between the ego and the id. The

Table 2.1   Summary of Psychosexual Stages of Development

Stage	Duration	Manifestations
Oral	Birth–18 months	Focus on oral activities (for example, eating and sucking)
Anal	18 months–3 years	Toilet training—child may cooperate or resist by soiling or withholding
Phallic	3–6 years	Oedipal or Electra complexes
Latency	6–12 years	Consolidation of behavioural skills and attitudes—relatively quiescent stage
Genital	Adolescence to death	Achievement of personal and sexual maturity

Table 2.2   Some Typical Defence Mechanisms

Defence Mechanism	Description	Examples
Repression	Burying in the unconscious the unacceptable impulses of the id	Inability to recall being sexually abused as a child
Regression	Employing behaviours typical of an earlier stage of development	Petulance or tantrums in response to frustration
Projection	Attributing one's own desires to others	Someone, who cheats on an exam or is tempted to cheat, claiming everyone cheats
Intellectualization	Hiding the real issues behind a screen of abstract analyses	A criminal appealing his conviction, despite admitting guilt, on the grounds of improper trial procedures
Denial	Refusal to acknowledge an unpleasant reality	A person, told she has two months to live, planning a holiday in a year's time
Displacement	The transfer of feelings from one person to another, less threatening person	A person humiliated by her employer directing her anger toward her spouse
Reaction formation	Repressing unacceptable desires by expressing the opposite viewpoint	A man who has strong sexual desires toward most women berating people who are promiscuous
Sublimation	Transformation of sexual or aggressive energy into some more acceptable activity	Freud thought that artists who painted nudes were sublimating their sexual desires

weaker the ego (that is, the less resolved are the individual's psychosexual stages) the greater the conflict and, thereby, the greater is the exhaustion of psychic energy. It is this exhaustion of psychic energy that leads to a breakdown of psychological functioning, with the particular symptoms of this breakdown reflecting the unresolved stage of psychosexual development.

Table 2.2 describes some of the more commonly identified defence mechanisms. This aspect of Freud's theory has enjoyed the greatest acceptance among clinicians of any of his ideas. All of us, for example, engage in rationalization. If we do not win a tennis match that we tried hard to win, we might subsequently convince ourselves that we were just playing for fun and that winning against a friend is not important. In fact, if we did not engage in such defences we would probably be rather unhappy.

Repression is the most fundamental of these defences, according to Freud. After concluding that some people reject from consciousness their unacceptable impulses, Freud claimed that this repression did not mean the impulses went away; they simply reappeared in symbolic form. The rest of the defence mechanisms essentially serve to provide alternative symbolic expressions of these repressed urges. Thus, the notion of repression served as the basis for the idea, so crucial to psychoanalytic theory and to the practice of psychoanalysis, that the symptoms of psychopathology were symbolic representations of basic libidinal instincts.

Freud thought that sexual desires were often unwelcome to the ego or superego (for example, a desire for sex with a forbidden partner or for an unusual sex act) and were, accordingly, repressed or channelled into other activities. This repression, however, frequently led to problems for the person, although these problems would not be manifestly sexual and would be disguised from the person's own awareness by unconscious defences. When the ego was not strong enough to contain or rechannel the libidinal desires of the id, it was because one or another of the stages of psychosexual development had not been satisfactorily resolved. Failure to resolve one or another stage would result in the failure to appropriately channel the libido and this would ultimately lead to a breakdown that would produce symptoms associated with the unresolved stage. Thus, the psychoanalyst, by interpreting the symbolic nature of the symptoms, could focus on the particular period of the person's formative years (that is, the particular psychosexual stage) in order to reveal to the patient the origin of his or her problem. The patient's acceptance of the analyst's account of the origin of the problem was called *insight* and it was expected that this would result in an alleviation of the problem.

Freud's Influence

Freudian theory is largely speculative and has little empirical support. As we have seen, attempts to test Freud's ideas experimentally have run into the problem that no matter what the results are, they can be explained within the theory. Yet some aspects of Freud's thinking have been valuable to psychology. He legitimized discussion and research on sexual matters; he encouraged a concern with processes beyond our awareness; and he recognized that the motives for human behaviour were not always the obvious ones. In short, no single psychological theorist has been more influential than Freud, even though psychoanalysis (his method of treatment) is much less popular today than it was in the early and middle parts of this century. Some of his followers, however, have developed or modified Freud's theories and treatment approach, and these versions of psychoanalytic theory have enjoyed greater acceptance in recent years.

Later Psychodynamic Theories

Like Freud, later psychodynamic theorists think that unconscious processes direct behaviour. As we have seen, these processes operate through motivations arising in the id that clash with the ego's controls, thereby producing psychic conflict, which is symbolically transformed by defence mechanisms into behaviour (Watchtel, 1982).

Jung and the Collective Unconscious

Two members of Freud's inner circle broke away when their development of psychoanalytic theory came into conflict with his ideas. Carl Jung (1875–1961) came to believe that people not only have a personal unconscious, but also inherit what he called the *collective unconscious*. This collective unconscious is said to be the repository of all accumulated human experience and is passed on genetically. The images contained in this collective unconscious are primitive archetypes that include the notion of an all-powerful God, the fertile mother, the wise old man, and so on. Although these archetypes remain unconscious, they emerge in dreams and permit us to readily recognize such themes in art and literature.

Adler and the Quest for Power

Alfred Adler (1970–1937) developed the idea that people are driven by what he called an **inferiority complex** rather than by sexual desires. As children we all learn, Adler claimed, that because we are smaller and less powerful than adults, we are necessarily inferior, and the rest of our life then becomes a struggle to assert our superiority. The quest for power, then, becomes the primary drive, which in healthy people is moderated by a concern for others.

Object Relations and Self-Theory

Current theorizing in psychodynamic psychology emphasizes both object relations and self-theory. Margaret Mahler (1897–1985) followed the earlier work of British psychoanalyst Melanie Klein (1882–1960), who was among the first to develop object-relations theory. Mahler identified a process she called **separation-individuation** by which the child learns to distinguish the self from others. During development, according to object-relations theory, children *introject* (that is, incorporate internally) a symbolic representation of the powerful people in their lives. They then have to learn to separate their internal representation of the self from the introjected objects (that is, the symbolic representations of others). The more successful a person is in achieving this goal, the more likely he or she is to attain personal maturity. When the attitudes and beliefs of the introjected object clash with the person's own attitudes, internal conflict will occur and result in psychopathology. Since the internalization of others is symbolic, the person will not be aware of the cause of this conflict, so again it becomes the task of the psychoanalyst to uncover this unconscious conflict.

Otto Kernberg (1985) has applied object-relations theory to personality disorders by suggesting that people suffering from these problems have been unable to integrate introjected objects that are pathological. This would arise if the child's parents were, for example, abusive, or criminal, or in some other way dysfunctional. The child takes in these antisocial or disturbed representations of the parents but is unable to reconcile these pathological attitudes with those of other introjected people, including himself or herself. Consequently, the person remains controlled by alternating and often extreme attitudes.

In creating his self-theory, Heinz Kohut (1990) suggested that everyone has narcissistic needs in childhood; when these needs are not fulfilled, pathological self-centredness results. Problems occur, says Kohut, when the child becomes fixated on a parent and terrified of losing the parent (called *object loss*). The child perceives that he or she has a defect or character flaw that could cause the parent to reject the child. For Kohut, then, the relationship between the therapist and patient is critical: the therapist can take on the role of the parent (this relationship, which sometimes develops inadvertently in therapy, is called *transference*), allowing the fulfillment of the patient's unresolved narcissistic needs. For object-relations therapists, all disorders have their origin in parent-child relations.

Attachment Theory

John Bowlby (1973) also focussed on such relationships in his development of the psychoanalytic approach into what has become known as **attachment theory**. According to this view, children form attachments with their parents and the nature of these early attachments (that is, the primary experience of a relationship) becomes the child's internalized model for all subsequent relationships. If the parent is ambivalent toward the child, sometimes being loving and sometimes rejecting, then the child will become anxious about relationships, having learned to expect rejection. If the parent is hostile, the child will come to fear all relationships and grow up to be a lonely adult. Such difficulties form the basis for later problems (Ainsworth & Bowlby, 1991; Marshall, 1989), according to attachment theory.

These more recent developments in psychoanalytic theory (that is, object relations, self-theory, and attachment theory) are not only popular, they have generated considerable and quite productive research. Unlike Freud's original theory, these newer perspectives in psychodynamic thought generate testable hypotheses and have led to novel and apparently effective treatments.

Behavioural Theories

Conditioning Accounts

As noted in the last chapter, behaviourism was first introduced as a perspective on human behaviour by John B. Watson. Early behaviourists such as Watson were environmentalists in that they assumed all (or almost all) human behaviour, including abnormal behaviour, was learned. Watson

(1913) took the view that **classical conditioning**, as described by the Russian physiologist Ivan Pavlov (1849–1936), was the basis for this learning. Pavlov demonstrated classical conditioning in his famous experiment with dogs, bells, and food. Every time the dogs were fed, a bell was rung. At first the dogs salivated when they saw and smelled the meat. After a number of "conditioning trials," they would salivate at the sound of the bell alone. To put it in Pavlov's terms, initially, a bell (that is, the conditioned stimulus, or CS) elicited an orienting response; that is, the dog looked toward the sound and listened. The meat (unconditioned stimulus or UCS) elicited an unconditioned response, salivation. Repeated pairings of the CS and the unconditioned stimulus (UCS) result in the CS eliciting some degree of salivation (conditioned response, or CR). What is learned in classical conditioning, then, is the transfer of a response (that is, the UCR or its practical replication, the CR) from one stimulus (UCS) to another (CS). This process is called *stimulus-stimulus learning*.

Watson's most famous application of this type of analysis was to the acquisition of phobias: unrealistic fears of usually harmless things, like cats or dogs. According to Watson, people with a phobia about dogs must have had at one time a frightening experience with a dog; the dog may have rushed at them growling or may have bitten them. The case of Little Hans' horse phobia, described at the beginning of this section, has been interpreted as an example of classical conditioning (Wolpe & Rachman, 1960). Prior to the frightening experience, a horse was a neutral stimulus (that is, a CS) in that it did not elicit fear. The bolting horses and careening streetcar represent the UCS, and automatically elicited a fear response (the UCR). Watson believed that an unconditioned response to pain or threat was inborn, and served, along with other similar inborn UCS-UCR connections, as the basis for all subsequently acquired responses (CRs). The frightening experience with the horses invoked the conditioning processes that would instill a fear response (CR) to the sight, or even the thought, of a horse (CS).

Watson and his graduate student Rosalie Rayner (Watson & Rayner, 1920) demonstrated that classical conditioning could instill a fear of a white rat in an 11-month-old boy identified as Little Albert. This young boy was first shown a white rat, to which he displayed no fear; in fact, he appeared to enjoy trying to play with it. After several presentations like this to ensure that Little Albert was not fearful of the rat, Watson and Rayner followed the rat's appearance by making a sudden loud noise (distress at loud noise being another of Watson's presumed innate responses) close behind the boy. This loud noise startled and upset Little Albert. After seven presentations of the rat (the CS) paired with the sudden loud noise (the UCS), Little Albert displayed a conditioned fear response to the rat. Watson and Rayner had indeed demonstrated that conditioning procedures could instill a phobic response to a harmless animal. On the basis of this single demonstration, Watson concluded that all phobias resulted from classical conditioning experiences. This, of course, was an overgeneralization.

However, this study has served as a model for demonstrating conditioning possibilities in humans, and was for a long time taken as the basis for a conditioning account of human fears. As we will see in the chapter on anxiety disorders, classical conditioning accounts of the acquisition of phobias are no longer popular. In fact, classical conditioning alone cannot explain many of the facets of phobias, most particularly their persistence. For instance, when the UCS is removed from classical conditioning studies, extinction (that is, the loss of response to the CS) occurs quite rapidly. In Pavlov's study, for example, withdrawal of the meat followed by repeated presentations of the bell causes the bell to cease eliciting salivation. Most people with phobias repeatedly encounter their phobic stimulus without any dreadful consequences occurring (for example, see dogs that make no attempt to attack them and, indeed, are often quite friendly). Under these conditions (that is, the CS occurs repeatedly in the absence of the UCS) they should lose their fears (that is, CRs should cease to occur when the CS is presented). Yet, in fact, phobias display remarkable persistence.

Faced with this problem, O. Hobart Mowrer (1947) developed what came to be known as the *two-factor* theory of conditioning. He suggested there are two types of learning taking place in the acquisition and maintenance of phobias: (1) classical conditioning establishes the aversive response to a previously neutral stimulus (the CS) and (2) thereafter the organism avoids the CS in order to prevent feeling afraid. Avoiding the CS, of course, effectively prevents extinction from occurring. This latter component of Mowrer's theory is derived from the work of Burrhus F. Skinner (1904–1990), who developed the ideas involved in **operant conditioning**. In Skinner's operant conditioning, it is the consequences of behaviour that are important. All actions are followed by consequences of one kind or another. Some consequences encourage the repetition of the behaviour that produces them, while other consequences result in the opposite effect. When a behaviour increases in frequency as a result of consistent consequences, **reinforcement** is said to occur; when a behaviour decreases in frequency as a result of its consequences, this is described as **punishment**. Some behaviours (for example, opening a refrigerator door) lead to pleasant consequences or rewards (for example, eating ice cream) and the behaviour of going to the refrigerator increases; this is called *positive reinforcement*. Other behaviours (for example, taking an aspirin) result in a reduction of distress (that is, the headache goes away); this is called *negative reinforcement*. When a behaviour is reduced by the consequent occurrence of an unpleasant experience, it is called *positive punishment*, and when the behaviour is reduced by being followed by the removal of something desirable, *negative punishment* is said to have occurred. (Note that "positive" and "negative" are not used to mean good and bad; rather, positive refers simply to the presence of something and negative to the absence of something.) Table 2.3 summarizes these consequences and their effects.

Table 2.3 Operant Conditioning: Consequences and Their Effects

Examples	Condition	Effects
Reinforcement		
(a) Rat presses lever and gets food	Positive	Lever pressing increases
(b) Child imitates mother's speech and mother smiles		Imitation increases
(a) Rat escapes from white side of box to black side and shock terminates	Negative	Escape behaviour increases
(b) Student quits seminar course and feels relief from speech anxiety		Avoidance of seminar courses increases
Punishment		
(a) Rat gets shocked for exploratory behaviour	Positive	Exploratory behaviour decreases
(b) Bully starts a fight and is badly beaten		Attempts to start fights decrease
(a) Food tray is removed when a pigeon pecks a red key	Negative	Pecking red key decreases
(b) Child is rude and is not allowed to have ice cream		Rudeness decreases

Two-factor theory explains the persistence of phobias, in a way that simple classical conditioning cannot, by adding a negative reinforcement component to the process. Once a person has acquired a classically conditioned fear of a harmless stimulus, he or she begins to escape from the stimulus whenever it appears. Escape behaviour is negatively reinforced by the consequent reduction in fear and the person soon learns that avoiding the stimulus altogether eliminates the distress. Thus, the person never experiences the CS (that is, phobic stimulus) in the absence of the UCS (for example, an attack by a dog), and therefore extinction cannot occur.

Various other elaborations on basic learning paradigms have been developed to explain a variety of pathological behaviours, and behaviour therapists have had significant successes in treating numerous problems with procedures derived from learning principles. Perhaps the most influential of these more recent learning-based approaches is **social learning theory**, which was initially developed in Canada by Albert Bandura and Richard Walters.

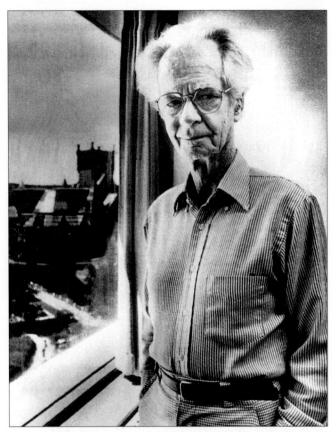

Burrhus F. Skinner (1904–1990) developed the ideas involved in operant conditioning.

Social Learning Theory

As originally outlined by Bandura and Walters (1959), social learning theory suggested that while classical and operant conditioning experiences are important, the majority of such experiences occur within a social context and are primarily acquired vicariously—that is, by observation of others rather than by direct personal experience. Accordingly, it was shown that children could learn to be aggressive by observing others being rewarded for aggression (Bandura, Ross, & Ross, 1961, 1963), or they could learn to be fearful by watching their phobic parents (Bandura & Menlove, 1968). Subsequently, this theory has been extended to include not only direct observation of others but also information derived from books, movies, and television.

Because Bandura's (1976) theory emphasizes the importance of cognitive processes, such as perceiving the behaviour of others and storing such information in memory, it gave rise to the notion that other mediational processes (for example, thoughts and feelings) play a part in learning. Eventually this led to the development of what became known as cognitive-behavioural theory.

Cognitive-behavioural theory reflects the view that both thinking and behaviour are learned and can, therefore, be changed. This approach assumes that the way people view the world, including their beliefs and attitudes toward the world, themselves, and others, arises out of their experience

and that these patterns of thinking and perceiving are maintained by consequences in the same way that overt behaviour is maintained. While this treatment approach incorporates some procedures derived from strictly cognitive therapy, it essentially follows the views expressed by Bandura's social learning theory.

Two of Bandura's key concepts (1977) that had a significant impact on theorizing were the notion of self-control and what Bandura called self-efficacy. Bandura recognized that much of behaviour was not simply the result of direct conditioning experiences. He soon realized that even indirect conditioning could not explain all behaviour. People, Bandura said, learn to regulate their own behaviour. They make choices between available alternative actions, evaluate the chosen action to see if it measures up to self-set standards, and then reward or punish themselves accordingly. Unlike earlier behavioural analyses, Bandura included the notion, which matches our personal experience, that people play an active role in monitoring or regulating their own behaviour.

Self-efficacy concerns the set of beliefs people have "about their capabilities to exercise control over events that affect their lives" (Bandura, 1989, p. 1175). When people exercising self-control make a choice between alternative actions, they must believe they are capable of enacting the behaviour (that is, they have the necessary skills) and that the enactment of the behaviour will lead to the desired results. Ongoing monitoring of behaviour results in ongoing changes in perceived self-efficacy: success increases self-efficacy and failures decrease it. In order to avoid failure, or at least minimize its possible occurrence, it may be best to initially attempt to enact a behaviour that is relatively easy. As our confidence grows, we can gradually enact more difficult behaviours, thereby allowing our sense of self-efficacy to gradually increase, which ought to make behaviour change more resilient.

Both these concepts (that is, self-control and self-efficacy), and various other cognitive processes, have been incorporated into the overall cognitive-behavioural approach to understanding and treating disorders. This more general approach, as we noted, derived many of its concepts from cognitive psychology more generally and also from strictly cognitive approaches to disorders.

Cognitive Theories

Two preeminent cognitive theorists have offered accounts of the etiology and treatment of abnormal behaviours: Albert Ellis and Aaron Beck.

Rational-Emotive Therapy

Ellis (Ellis & Grieger, 1977) developed **rational-emotive therapy**, which is concerned with how people interpret events and how these interpretations influence their responses. These interpretations, or mediating processes, are cognitive and result from the person's belief systems. Irrational beliefs, so Ellis claims, distort responding, making the person's behaviour dysfunctional. These irrational beliefs cause the person to catastrophize by magnifying unpleasant consequences and

Table 2.4   Irrational Beliefs That, According to Ellis (1962), Underlie Dysfunctional Behaviour

1. I must be loved and approved of at all times.
2. Things must always go right.
3. I must be competent at everything.
4. Life should always treat me fairly.
5. All problems should have ready and easy solutions.
6. I should never make mistakes.
7. I am presently, and will always be, as I always have been.
8. Unhappiness is externally caused and I have no control over it.

thereby increasing feelings of worthlessness and hopelessness. Some of the supposed irrational beliefs that Ellis says dysfunctional people hold are listed in Table 2.4. When these irrational beliefs are not supported by experience, as they rarely are, the person catastrophizes and becomes dissatisfied and unhappy. This unhappiness or dissatisfaction may become manifest as one or another psychiatric disorder.

Cognitive Schemata

Beck (1967, 1976) says that people with disorders have underlying cognitive schemata (organized ways of viewing themselves, their world, and their past and future) that inappropriately direct their processing of information, resulting in distortions of attention, memory, and comprehension. All people employ schemata to guide their thoughts and behaviour (Neisser, 1982) and these schemata are learned. Children whose early experiences are unhappy will incorporate disturbed schemata, which will subsequently lead them to think and act in ways that are dysfunctional. The cognitive errors that result from these disturbed schemata are, according to Beck, at the base of psychological disorders.

Both Ellis and Beck see the job of the cognitive therapist as helping the client recognize and correct distorted cognitions. Once this is achieved, the disorder, so it is assumed, will disappear. As we will see in later chapters, cognitive therapy has enjoyed success in the treatment of many disorders, most particularly with anxiety and mood disorders.

Humanistic and Existential Theories

Humanistic and existential theories can be considered to be variants on the phenomenological approach to understanding human behaviour. Phenomenology as a philosophical position had many antecedents, but Edmund Husserl (1859–1938) is generally considered the first to clearly formulate this viewpoint. Husserl's account was subsequently elaborated by French philosopher Maurice Merleau-Ponty (1908–1961). According to this view, it is through experience that people form their sense of themselves and of the world. However, experience is not the objective observation of external events, but rather, the accumulation of perceptions of the world. The way in which the world is perceived by an individual is a product of the personal experiences that have produced his or her sense of self. It is this sense of self that guides, and is formed by, the person's perception of his or her experiences. Life is said to involve a continuous synthesis of experience that progressively refines our sense of self and develops our values. This sense of self, along with our values and our accumulated experience, provides the basis for our choices of action. Behaviour is not determined by experience alone, since experience simply provides the basis for choice. These choices represent the expression of our free will.

From this perspective of human experience, phenomenologists developed theories about all manner of psychological functioning, including, of course, perception, but also the development of human values; and, most importantly, they generated accounts of personal development.

Humanistic Views

The two most eminent advocates of humanistic psychology were Carl Rogers (1902–1987) and Abraham Maslow (1908–1970). Both emphasized the dignity and potential of humans, and saw experience (as perceived by the individual) as providing the basis for improving oneself. Rogers' position has been called a *person-centred* theory of personality because he considered the person to be of central importance in understanding behaviour. According to Rogers, self-fulfillment is achieved by accepting oneself, being honest in all interactions, trusting experience (which he says is the highest authority), and relying on oneself for personal evaluations. People who can do so will be able to accept others for who they are, thus encouraging both them and others to be more honest, and such honesty will help accumulate experiences that will lead them to realize their potential.

Abnormal behaviour, according to Rogers (1961), results from a person's distorted view of himself or herself, which in turn arises from an inability to trust experience. Such lack of trust is said to result from distressing life events (or the perception of these events as distressing), which distort the person's perception of all subsequent experience. Thus, distorted perceptions misshape the person's sense of self, which provides the basis for choices of action. These choices will, accordingly, be detrimental to personal development and further entrench the distorted views of self and experience, thereby perpetuating dysfunctional behaviour.

Maslow (1954) essentially believed that people are good and that they only behave dysfunctionally or nastily as a result of experience (or their interpretation of it) that has diverted them from the path of **self-actualization**. He described a hierarchy of needs which, when fully satisfied, result in the actualization of the person's potential. It is toward this realization of personal potential that all persons should strive. Maslow's hierarchy of needs can be visualized as a pyramid (see Figure 2.4). At the base are biological or survival needs, including food, water, and shelter; safety occupies the next level. Unless these are met, the person will not survive, and if they are

Figure 2.4 Maslow's Hierarchy of Needs

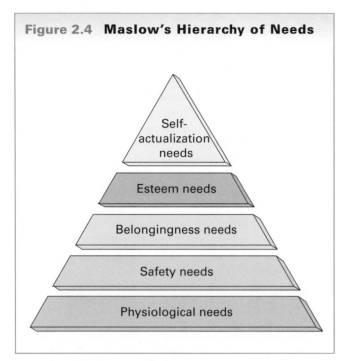

Source: From MOTIVATION AND PERSONALITY 3rd. ed. by Abraham H. Maslow. Copyright 1954, 1987 by Harper & Row Publishers, Inc. Copyright 1970 by Abraham H. Maslow. Reprinted by permission of Addison-Wesley Educational Publishers Inc.

Abraham Maslow (1908–1970), who developed the theory of self-actualization.

unsatisfactorily met, the person will not be able to move up the hierarchy toward self-actualization. The need to belong represents the next step up in the hierarchy and refers to needs for friendship and affiliation. When these are met, the individual seeks an assurance of self-worth, which comes from giving and receiving love and from an internalized sense of

self-esteem derived from experience. From this base of self-confidence, self-actualization becomes possible. In Maslow's view, abnormal or dysfunctional behaviour results from a failure to attain the self-esteem necessary to achieve self-actualization.

Both these humanists have an optimistic view of people and consider human behaviour to result from personal decisions and perceptions of their experience and of themselves. Thus, they hold the individual to be responsible, rather than forces beyond the individual's control (for example, biological determinants, unconscious processes, or actual external events). Obviously, then, if dysfunctional behaviour is derived from people's view of themselves and their experience, they can be helped to change their perspective and, thereby, overcome their problems.

Existential Views

Existentialists see the individual's awareness of his or her own existence as a critical feature of human functioning. This awareness brings with it the realization that we could, and obviously eventually will, cease to exist. However, it is not just the possibility of death that existentialists consider to be a threat, but also the loss of direction and meaning in our lives. Existentialists also stress our responsibility for our choices and, therefore, for our actions. We make free choices and must necessarily take responsibility for them.

This awareness of the possibility of nonbeing (whether death or the emptiness of no meaning) and the acceptance of responsibility for our actions makes us, according to the existentialist point of view, anxious. It is this existential *angst* (a German word that means something more than the English "anxiety" and conveys a sense of more severe distress) which causes people problems, so life becomes a search for meaning. Making the effort to seek meaning is said to reflect the "courage to be" (Tillich, 1952), whereas the alternative is to give up the struggle and become full of despair. This is a somewhat gloomier view of the human condition than the humanistic view, since the struggle to "be" is very difficult and few actually display the necessary courage. However, like humanistic psychology, existentialism sees the individual as responsible and as potentially capable of dealing effectively with life.

The leading exponents of the existential view, as applied to human problem behaviour, have been Rollo May (1961) and Viktor Frankl (1962). Both these theorists see the struggle to find meaning in our lives and our acceptance, or not, of responsibility for our choices as critical in understanding human behaviour. Treatment, therefore, is directed at confronting clients with their responsibility for their actions and assisting them in finding meaning in their lives. Very little research, however, has evaluated either this interesting approach or the humanistic approach to understanding and treating human problems.

Sociocultural Influences

Various theorists and researchers have considered the role that society or culture plays in the etiology and maintenance of dysfunctional behaviours. For example, one school of thought, described as **labelling theory** (Rosenhan, 1973), suggests that at least some important aspects of psychopathology result from the expectations instilled when an expert labels a person as having a particular disorder.

Labelling Theory

Labelling theory suggests that having been identified as having a disorder results in other people, particularly mental health workers, perceiving the person as dysfunctional and different. This perception, which tends to persist even after recovery, results in these people being treated disadvantageously and even disrespectfully.

To illustrate this, Rosenhan had eight normal people attend a psychiatric hospital and complain of hearing voices that said simply "empty," "hollow," and "thud." The on-duty psychiatrists, on the basis of these complaints, diagnosed each of the patients as suffering from schizophrenia, a very serious psychotic disorder, and admitted them to hospital. Once in hospital these pseudo-patients behaved in their normal way, but their behaviour was not seen as normal by hospital staff. For example, walking about the ward was described as "pacing" and was taken as an indication of nervousness. When these pseudo-patients asked staff (nurses, ward attendants, and psychiatrists) legitimate questions such as "When will I be eligible for ground privileges?" or "Can you tell me when I am likely to be discharged?" they were rarely answered. Staff, however, stopped what they were doing to respond only 2 to 4 percent of the time; on 71 percent of the occasions when they were asked reasonable questions by the pseudo-patients, psychiatrists turned away and did not respond. If, of course, the patients had behaved in the same way as the staff, it would have been taken as a sign of their illness.

VIEWPOINT *A Case of Mistaken Labelling*

A woman who was referred to a Canadian psychiatric hospital by her family doctor illustrates the effects of mistaken labelling in a genuine case. This woman was known in her small town as an extremely generous and good-willed person whose religious faith was unquestionable. She did many good deeds for her neighbours and friends despite the fact that she had five children of her own and received no help at all from her alcoholic husband. When her drunken husband would finally come home on payday and fall asleep on the sofa, she would take what remained of his pay package and buy the family's food before he awoke. He was so angry about this that he repeatedly complained to their family doctor that his wife was mad and should be locked up because she talked to God. Finally the family physician relented and referred the unfortunate woman to the hospital with his referral note indicating that she had conversations with God.

When the admitting psychiatrist asked her if God spoke to her the woman acknowledged that he did. The psychiatrist then asked if God spoke in a human voice like his, to which the woman replied, "Yes, he does." On the basis of this, and little else, he diagnosed her as schizophrenic and admitted her to hospital. Upon admission, she was so distressed at being separated from her children, and so despairing about her husband's capacity to care for them, that she cried almost constantly. This was taken by staff as a clear confirmation of psychological disturbance, although it almost certainly would not have been had she not been diagnosed as schizophrenic.

Nobody, unfortunately, took the trouble to examine this woman's remarkable strengths: she had single-handedly looked after her five children despite her alcoholic and verbally abusive husband; she had managed to devise ways of getting enough money to feed the family; she had tirelessly done many things for other people; and she had maintained through all of this a deeply affectionate and caring relationship with her children. Fortunately, another clinician intervened and assessed the woman. He discovered that what she meant by God speaking to her was simply that God put the idea to do good deeds into her head. She was advised by this clinician to tell her psychiatrist that she no longer heard God's voice but that he still inspired her to kind actions, and she was told to try to stop crying for a week. Shortly thereafter, she was discharged as "cured." She subsequently functioned very well after ridding herself of her husband.

Critical Thinking Questions

1. Was this woman really psychiatrically disturbed, or was she simply the product of a system that all too easily labelled her as psychotic? (Of course, this was an unusual case; but it draws attention to the potentially damaging effects of diagnosis.)

2. What presenting symptoms led the admitting psychiatrist to conclude that this woman was suffering from schizophrenia? Was this a sound decision on the basis of the evidence available to him?

3. What aspects of this woman's behaviours on the ward encouraged the staff to continue to see the woman as psychologically disturbed? What relevance does this have for the notion of labelling effects?

For the most part, the staff in mental hospitals are caring people who would never dream of responding like this to people outside hospitals. It was the label of being psychiatrically ill, so Rosenhan claimed, that allowed otherwise compassionate staff to treat these pseudo-patients as objects rather than as human beings. These pseudo-patients (that is, normal people) were kept in hospital, presumably for their own good, for up to 52 days. Rosenhan took these observations to mean that the psychiatric labelling of people as disordered causes other people (not only psychiatric staff) to thereafter interpret everything they do as abnormal.

Identifying people as having a psychiatric disorder (particularly a serious disorder such as schizophrenia) can have serious implications, not only for the way in which others respond to them, but also for other aspects of their lives. For instance, many countries refuse to grant immigration status to anyone who has ever been labelled as schizophrenic. Similarly, many employers refuse jobs to applicants who have, at sometime in their past, been identified as psychiatrically disordered.

Rosenhan's study was a somewhat artificial demonstration and may have depended on how good the pseudo-patients were as actors. The diagnosing psychiatrist may well have doubted the authenticity of the "symptoms," but may have concluded either that it would be best to err on the side of caution by admitting the patient, or that someone who is faking symptoms at a psychiatric evaluation must have a serious problem in need of care.

Obviously, though, there is some truth to Rosenhan's contention that psychiatric labels can at times be more damaging than beneficial to the people who receive a diagnosis of mental illness. Thus, *false positives* (that is, identifying someone as disordered who is not) can cause serious problems. On the other hand, labelling theorists like Rosenhan appear to neglect the possibility of *false negatives* (that is, failing to identify someone who actually does have a disorder). Perhaps this issue is most serious when it comes to identifying someone who may cause injury to others. While very few psychiatrically disturbed individuals constitute a threat to others, a small number do, and mental health professionals have a responsibility to ensure that the greatest care is taken to identify these people. Psychiatrists and psychologists who work in prisons, or in institutions that care for mentally disordered offenders, have a particularly onerous task in attempting to predict dangerousness. In the case of both psychiatric patients and criminals, mental health professionals tend to become excessively conservative (erring on the side of minimizing risk) and identify people as dangerous who, in fact, do not constitute a threat to others. These people represent false positives. The label "dangerous" typically has serious consequences. A dangerous person is likely to be kept confined to a prison or hospital for years longer than they would otherwise be. On the other hand, false negatives in this area (identifying as safe a person who is, in fact, dangerous) can have very serious consequences for innocent people in the community where the individual is released.

Social Support

Other social and cultural processes have also been identified as influential in mental disorders. There is clear evidence that support by others is a significant factor in preventing, or reducing the intensity of, psychological problems and that the absence of such support is a factor in the causal chain leading to dysfunction (Cohen & Wills, 1985). When children have a relationship with an adult outside the family whom they can trust and who supports them, they are protected from the otherwise upsetting consequences of a disruptive or violent household (Werner, 1992). People who experience a severe trauma (for example, a terrorist attack, sexual abuse, or a natural disaster such as an earthquake) may subsequently suffer from post-traumatic stress disorder (PTSD), a debilitating problem that will be discussed in more detail in Chapter 7. However, not all people who are exposed to such traumas develop PTSD. Among the factors that reduce the probability of suffering from PTSD after a traumatic experience is support from friends and family (Foy, 1992).

Gender

The influence of society's stereotypes and people's consequent reaction to specific groups also seem to play a part in the development of disorders, as do poverty and social class. The traditional role of women, which emphasizes and fosters dependency, lack of assertiveness, and submissiveness, is thought by some theorists to account, for example, for the higher rates of depression among females (Nolen-Hoeksema, 1990). There are very obvious differences in male and female rates of several disorders (Robins et al., 1984), and it may be that gender-specific socialization processes render males and females differentially likely to acquire one or another disorder. *Anorexia nervosa*, for example, is a disorder involving a refusal to eat properly in order to excessively lose weight or to maintain an already unhealthy low body weight. This disorder occurs predominantly in young women (Garner, Shafer, & Rosen, 1991) who believe that in order to be attractive they must be very thin (Heilbrun & Witt, 1990). It has been suggested that the frequency of this disorder is the result of a cultural ideal, promulgated in advertising and in other media, that female beauty is synonymous with a lean body (Pate, Pumariega, Hester, & Garner, 1992) and that this ideal body shape has progressively moved toward the thinner end of the spectrum (Williamson, Kahn, Remington, & Anda, 1990). This, it is suggested, accounts for the dramatic increase in anorexia over the past several years.

In addition, Canadian psychologists Pantony and Caplan (1991) point out that certain personality disorders appear to reflect exaggerated features of either female or male stereotyped behaviours. For example, dependent personality disorder is characterized by dependency and submissiveness, whereas antisocial personality disorder involves aggressiveness and self-interest. Very few men are diagnosed with dependent personality disorder and very few women are considered to have antisocial personality disorder. Is this sharp difference due to bias in the diagnostic criteria or in the clinicians doing the diagnosis, or is it simply that the men and women so diagnosed are displaying exaggerated features of the gender role that has been reinforced from their childhood on?

Clearly, gender roles have an influence on the identification of disorders, but it is not clear yet exactly what form this influence takes. For example, in conducting research on irrational fears of snakes, we initially called for volunteers who described themselves as phobic. Over 90 percent of the respondents were female. In a subsequent study, we asked volunteers to assist us in determining the value of a particular measure of snake phobia. In that study we told potential volunteers that we needed all types of subjects: those who were unafraid of snakes, those who were somewhat apprehensive, and those who were genuinely phobic. When we tested these volunteers, we found no differences between males and females in their ability to approach a live snake, nor were there any differences in their self-reports of fear (Marshall, 1996). According to these measures, then, males and females were equally likely to be phobic. We subsequently replicated these results with height phobia. These data suggest that, rather than being more likely to acquire a phobia as a result of gender training or of some biological defect, females may simply be more ready to acknowledge phobias than males.

Race and Poverty

Race and poverty have also been linked to the prevalence of psychiatric disorders, although, because ethnic minorities tend to be concentrated in the poor, it has proved difficult to disentangle these two influences. Members of ethnic minorities are the victims of various forms of prejudice that exclude them from many opportunities available to the dominant group, and they are treated as inferior and subjected to denigrating jokes. These prejudices, and lack of opportunities, create stress in the lives of minorities in the same way that poverty does. When minority ethnicity and poverty go together, as they so often do, we can expect all manner of psychological and social problems.

Poverty itself has been examined as a factor in mental illness. Hollingshead and Redlich (1958) found that particular disorders typified particular social classes. People who were aggressive or psychotic (that is, suffering from a severe mental disorder) were far more likely to be identified among the poor than among the middle class. Severe psychological problems have been found to be three times higher among the lowest income groups (Dohrenwend et al., 1992). These findings may reflect similar effects noted for racial prejudice. The resentment at being poor, in an otherwise reasonably wealthy society, may generate behaviours that are seen by others as antisocial or dysfunctional (Myers & Bean, 1968). Of course, it may be that because being poor produces such high levels of stress (Adler et al., 1994), higher rates of psychological dysfunction are to be expected. However, it might also be that dysfunctional people gravitate to the lower end of the socioeconomic spectrum (Turner & Wagonfield, 1967). Finally, it may be that professionals from the privileged classes are more apt to apply denigrating diagnoses (for example,

antisocial personality disorder or schizophrenia) to patients from the lower classes, while reserving more acceptable diagnoses (for example, chronic fatigue syndrome) for the upper classes.

....

INTEGRATIVE THEORIES

Throughout this book, we will see evidence for the influence of various biological factors in the onset of many psychological disorders. We will also find that environmental influences (psychological as well as sociocultural) have an important role to play. In fact, it is only through the interaction of all these various influences that disorders emerge. Two models have been proposed that attempt to integrate these diverse influences.

The Diathesis-Stress Perspective

According to the **diathesis-stress perspective**, a predisposition to develop a disorder (the diathesis) interacting with the experience of stress, causes mental disorders. According to this view, this interaction underlies the onset of all disorders, although either the predisposition or the stress may be more important in a particular disorder, or in a particular person.

Note that this perspective cannot be categorized as either a biological or a psychological model. A diathesis may be either biological or psychological—as may a stress. An example of a biological diathesis would be the role played by genetics in schizophrenia, mood disorders, and alcoholism. Dysfunctions of the central or peripheral nervous system or of the endocrine system may have a genetic basis or may be caused by events such as problems of gestation or birth, but would in either case be seen as a biological diathesis. Disturbed brain amines may predispose to anxiety disorders (Shear, 1988) and hormonal imbalance may predispose a person to some sexual disorders (Grubin & Mason, 1997).

Psychological diatheses may arise as a result of childhood abuse, or inappropriate parenting, or social or cultural pressures. For example, a readiness to acquire dissociative identity disorder (formerly called "multiple personality disorder") appears to come from childhood sexual abuse. A series of unpredictable and unpleasant events may produce a sense of resignation that predisposes a person to depression (Abramson, Metalsky, & Alloy, 1989). Sociocultural standards of an attractive body shape seem to create a diathesis for eating disorders (Brownell & Fairburn, 1995).

However, a predisposition will not produce a disorder without the trigger of some stress, whether biological (such as physical illness), psychological (such as breakdown of a relationship), or social (such as perceived pressure from others to meet certain standards). In the case of Corey, described at the beginning of the chapter, a "difficult" temperament, probably present from birth (see Chapter 5) could be considered the diathesis; the marijuana use and the breakup with his girlfriend were the stresses that triggered the disorder, agoraphobia.

The advantage of this perspective is that it encourages us to look at a range of possible influences rather than fixing on a single factor. Within this framework we cannot ignore biological, experiential, or sociocultural factors. It is more a matter of giving weight to one or another factor. In schizophrenia, for example, a biological diathesis appears to be important, and the stress may be either biological or psychological. In panic disorders, while there may be a role for neurochemical diathesis, psychological and social stress seems to be the critical factor in onset. Even within the same disorder, this perspective allows the possibility that different individuals may develop their disorders through the influence of different diatheses and different stressors.

The Biopsychosocial Model

Like the diathesis-stress perspective, the biopsychosocial model declares that disorders cannot be understood as resulting from the influence of one factor, be it biological, psychological, or social. Each of these factors must be taken into account, again with differing emphases depending on the disorder in question.

Several lines of research indicate the significance for human functioning of the interaction between biological and environmental processes. For example, Plomin and Neiderhiser (1992) have integrated research findings to strongly suggest that genetics and environment interact to determine human behaviour. Brain functions have been shown both to influence and to be influenced by psychological and social processes; the relationship is reciprocal (Cacioppo & Berntson, 1992). Medical researchers (for example, Anderson, Kiecolt-Glaser, & Glaser, 1994) have demonstrated quite clearly that environmental experiences markedly influence the course of physical diseases such as cancer.

Taking note of these and other observations, Cloninger and his colleagues (Cloninger, Svrakic, & Przybeck, in press) have outlined a biopsychosocial model of the origin and maintenance of alcoholism. This model suggests there are two types of alcoholics, based on family history and the symptoms of the disorder. Cloninger has shown that these two groups differ in terms of biological, psychological, and social features and develop their disorder as a result of different patterns of interaction among factors. Cloninger and his colleagues have extended this line of reasoning to other problems such as antisocial behaviour (Cloninger & Gottesman, 1987) and personality disorders (Svracik et al., in press).

Both the diathesis-stress model and the biopsychosocial models, or some variant thereon, have become more popular in recent years as evidence accumulates that various influences contribute to the development of mental disorders.

PANORAMA

While, at present, biological accounts of disorders are popular and much current research is focussed on searching for such causes, there has been a consistent move toward viewing the etiology of problems from an integrative perspective. Part of the surge in interest in biological explanations over the past few years has been due to the development of more sophisticated procedures for examining these hypotheses. Imaging techniques have become available for the investigation of brain functioning, assay methods allow greater accuracy in detecting changes in hormonal systems, and procedures for evaluating genetic contributions have been markedly improved. The availability of sophisticated technology understandably attracts researchers to examine the theories that the technologies can evaluate. Progress in the appraisal of environmentalist theories has not been so dramatic.

However, a consensus does appear to be emerging that influences from all areas (biological, psychological, and sociocultural) interact in complex ways to produce psychiatric disorders. One or another of these influences may be more important in specific disorders, but that does not deny the relevance of the other factors. Single-factor theories, as we suggested at the beginning of this chapter, are unlikely to explain the etiology of any disorder, and are gradually falling into disuse. The challenge for theorists in the future will be to develop ways of tracking the various influences within any one problem behaviour.

SUMMARY

Theoretical views of abnormal behaviour range from emphases on biological foundations, psychodynamic processes, learning experiences, cognitive distortions, and intrapersonal processes, to the influence of society and culture.

Biological views propose that brain dysfunction, hormonal or peripheral nervous system problems, or genetic errors cause psychological problems. While it is clear that these biological factors play a part in the etiology of mental disorders, it is also clear that what is important is the interaction between these factors and environmental experiences. The same is true for theories based on conditioning or social learning. For some problems these learning-based models seem helpful in understanding the disorder but biological influences cannot be discounted. Cognitive theorists consider problems to stem from dysfunctional beliefs, attitudes, or ways of thinking, while humanistic or existential views suggest that problems result from a failure to realize one's potential or to find meaning in life. All of these various influences, and their interaction, appear relevant to understanding psychiatric disorders.

Psychodynamic theories have evolved from Freud's original conceptualizations with current theories focussing on object relations and self-theories, and a consideration of the effects of parent-child attachment bonds. These more recent psychoanalytic perspectives have generated more research than did the earlier models, and permit the integration of psychodynamic theory with other influences.

Social and cultural factors have been shown to be related to disturbed functioning, although at times it has been hard to tell whether some of these influences (for example, poverty) directly produce, or are a consequence of, dysfunction.

Finally, integrative perspectives emphasize the combined influence of biology, experience, and social factors. The diathesis-stress perspective suggests that disorders arise from a combination of a predisposition and a triggering stress. Both the diathesis and the stress may be either biological or psychological. The biopsychosocial model emphasizes the interaction between biological and environmental processes.

KEY TERMS

single-factor explanations (p. 25)
interactionist explanations (p. 25)
etiology (p. 26)
dementia (p. 28)
neurotransmitters (p. 29)
behavioural genetics (p. 32)
concordance (p. 32)
genetic linkage studies (p. 32)
molecular biology (p. 32)
psychodynamic (p. 33)
conscious (p. 34)
preconscious (p. 34)

unconscious (p. 34)
id (p. 34)
ego (p. 34)
superego (p. 34)
libido (p. 35)
oral stage (p. 35)
anal stage (p. 35)
phallic stage (p. 35)
Oedipal complex (p. 35)
Electra complex (p. 35)
latency stage (p. 35)
genital stage (p. 36)
defence mechanisms (p. 36)
inferiority complex (p. 37)

separation-individuation (p. 37)
attachment theory (p. 38)
classical conditioning (p. 38)
operant conditioning (p. 39)
reinforcement (p. 39)
punishment (p. 39)
social learning theory (p. 39)
cognitive-behavioural theory (p. 40)
self-efficacy (p. 40)
rational-emotive therapy (p. 40)
self-actualization (p. 41)
labelling theory (p. 43)
diathesis-stress perspective (p. 45)

ADDITIONAL RESOURCES

Institute for Behavioral Genetics
University of Colorado at Boulder
Boulder, CO 80309
(303) 492-7362
(303) 492-8063 fax
info@ibg.colorado.edu

www.glaxowellcome.co.uk/science/phguide/chap7.html
Glaxo Wellcome's pharmacology guide presents detailed information about neurotransmitters and other chemical signalling agents.

ibgwww.colorado.edu/index.html
The web site of the Institute for Behavioral Genetics, which conducts and facilitates research on the genetic and environmental bases of individual differences in behaviour, provides information on programs and publications offered by the Institute.

www.wynja.com/personality/theorists.html
This site presents a number of theorists in the field of personality, including Sigmund Freud, Alfred Adler, and Abraham Maslow.

http://plaza.interport.net/nypsan/freudarc.html
A collection of web links that point to Internet resources related to Sigmund Freud and his works.

http://www.cmhc.com/psyhelp/chap4/
The text of an article on observational learning and Canadian researcher Albert Bandura's role in developing social learning theory.

http://seamonkey.ed.asu.edu/~gail/occse1.htm
A discussion of Bandura's self-efficacy theory, as it relates to an occupational self-efficacy scale.

Chapter 3

Classification and Diagnosis

Philip Firestone

Bill was a 42-year-old man who had been obese most of his life. He suffered from diabetes and high blood pressure, at least partially as a result of his weight. He also had a lifelong history of anxiety. Bill had never worked and, after graduating from high school, had lived with his parents all his life. He cared for both his parents as they became infirm in their old age and was described by all as a very loving and supportive son. Bill was an avowed bisexual, favouring males. He had never had any serious relationships with males or females. However, he was very sexually active. As a young teenager he had been sexually molested for over four years by a wealthy uncle who was well liked by the whole family. From his teenage years on he had preferred sexual activities with teenage boys. He had numerous one-night stands while he was a teenager and continued this pattern as an adult. His days would be taken up by cruising the parks for teenage male street children and teenage prostitutes. He would befriend these children and give them money and drugs in return for sex. He was convicted of sexual offences against these teenagers and was given a probationary term that required he attend treatment, with no time in prison. After his sentence was completed he returned to his sexual offending pattern. The second group of charges resulted in a four-year sentence, with 18 months being spent in prison. Once again he participated in many treatment programs in prison.

After his release from prison, money was in short supply and he felt he should be eligible for a disability pension which would provide approximately $1000 monthly, plus medication and other benefits. After being turned down, he got a lawyer to appeal his case. The lawyer argued that he should be considered for a medical disability, particularly because his pedophilia was a constant source of anxiety for him because of his prison history and the fear that others might find out. Using a previous psychological report, she argued that stress might not only exacerbate his diabetes and blood pressure but increase his risk of further offend-

ing; that Bill's health was seriously compromised by the stress related to his pedophilia; and that full-time work would be overwhelming, resulting in an increased risk of reoffending.

Bill was sent for a psychological assessment, and received the following diagnoses:

- *Axis I.* Pedophilia, sexually attracted to males, exclusive type; generalized anxiety disorder, mild
- *Axis II.* Dependent personality disorder
- *Axis III.* Obesity, diabetes
- *Axis IV.* Criminal record
- *Axis V.* Level of current functioning: 62

The assessing psychologist was not prepared to support the application for a disability pension, because:

- the medical reports did not suggest that Bill's medical condition precluded most types of occupations;
- the generalized anxiety disorder was mild and most people with this problem function adequately in the workplace;
- pedophilia is not considered to preclude most occupations;
- there were medications available to decrease pedophilic urges and alleviate anxiety that Bill could use to allow him to work;
- Bill had many attributes that would make him a good candidate for many jobs

One of the most interesting aspects of this request for a psychological report is the lawyer's insistence that pedophilia be considered sufficiently disabling to allow for social assistance. (If this argument had succeeded in Bill's case, how many men would have become newly eligible for assistance?)

In the realm of medicine and abnormal psychology, a **diagnosis** consists of a determination or identification of the nature of a person's disease or condition, or a statement of that finding. A diagnosis is made on the basis of a **diagnostic system**: a system of rules for recognizing and grouping various types of abnormalities (Glanze, Anderson, & Anderson, 1985).

In order to gather all the information required for a proper diagnosis, a thorough assessment is required. Students often confuse assessment and diagnosis. An **assessment** is a procedure in which information is gathered systematically in the evaluation of a condition; it serves as the basis for a diagnosis. A psychiatric assessment may include interviews with the patient or the patient's family, medical testing, psychophysiological or psychological testing, and the completion of self-report scales or other report rating scales. A diagnostic system provides a number of criteria for a disorder; if a certain number of these criteria or indications

are present, the person is diagnosed as having that particular disorder. Therefore, information from each of the assessment procedures contributes to the formulation of a diagnosis. The term **sign** is often used to designate a certain feature of a category of abnormal behaviour that a clinician can recognize, although the patient is often unaware of it. In contrast, the term **symptom** is used to describe a feature of a diagnostic category that a patient recognizes and may find disturbing. For example, people with agoraphobia are fearful of what may happen when they are away from home. Consequently, they start spending more and more time at home. In the early stages they are often unaware of their decreased excursions from home, so this behaviour could be classified as a sign of the disorder. On the other hand, people with mood disorders often report difficulty with sleep. Because they themselves are aware of the difficulty, it would be classified as a symptom.

THE PERFECT DIAGNOSTIC SYSTEM

The perfect diagnostic system would classify disorders on the basis of a study of presenting symptoms (pattern of behaviours), etiology (history of the development of this behaviour pattern), prognosis (future development of this pattern of behaviours), and response to treatment. In the development of this diagnostic system, a large number of people would have been thoroughly assessed psychologically and physically, in terms of feelings, thoughts, behaviours, and various other important features. A thorough history would have been taken in order to understand how various features developed. These people would then have been observed over a long period of time to assess the natural progression of their problems. In addition, various treatments would have been tried on small groups of these patients, in a controlled fashion, to assess their effectiveness. Diagnostic categories would then be established by figuring out exactly which patterns of presenting problems, with what kind of history, developed in which particular manner and responded differentially to various treatments. Presumably, different symptom clusters, with dissimilar histories and differing normal progression, would signal different syndromes. In the resulting perfect system, each sign or symptom would be found in only one diagnostic category. There would be no overlap in the picture presented by patients. Furthermore, treatment modalities would be so thoroughly developed that we would have in our bag a perfect cure for each diagnostic category, which, with pinpoint accuracy, would alleviate suffering for people who fit that category.

Unfortunately, scientific research is not so neat; nor are human beings. We have not often been able to systematically observe and measure many aspects of functioning in people over long periods of time, even if we knew which features were important to note. Furthermore, it has proven terribly difficult to follow large groups of patients in a controlled fashion. The history of therapeutic interventions has also revealed how difficult it is to implement procedures following strict scientific principles.

However, despite the resulting shortcomings of diagnostic systems to date, most researchers and clinicians are of the opinion that a good diagnostic system is very useful, if not essential (see Table 3.1).

THE HISTORY OF CLASSIFICATION

As we learned in Chapter 1, an interest in classification dates back at least to the Middle Ages. Kraepelin, in the nineteenth century, led the way in developing a systematic classification; however, his categories and descriptors bear little relation to modern systems.

A milestone in the modern development of a comprehensive diagnostic scheme was the World Health Organization's decision to add mental health disorders to the International List of the Causes of Death. In 1948 the list was expanded to become the International Statistical Classification of Diseases, Injuries, and

Table 3.1	Functions of a Good Classification System	
1. Organization of clinical information	It provides the essentials of a patient's condition coherently and concisely.
2. Communication shorthand	It enhances the effective interchange of information, by clearly transmitting important features of a disorder and ignoring unimportant features.
3. Prediction of natural development	It allows accurate short-term and long-term prediction of an individual's development.
4. Treatment recommendations	It allows accurate predictions of the most effective interventions.
5. Heuristic value	It allows the investigation and clarification of issues related to a problem area. It also enhances theory-building.
6. Guidelines for financial support	It provides guidelines to services needed, including payment of caregivers.

Causes of Death (ICD), a comprehensive listing of all diseases, including abnormal behaviour. The American Psychiatric Association published its own classification system, the *Diagnostic and Statistical Manual* (DSM), in 1952. However, DSM, and its second edition DSM-II (APA, 1968), proved highly unsatisfactory. These two volumes were very brief and contained only vague descriptions of the diagnostic categories. They were greatly influenced by psychoanalytic theory, focussed on internal nonobservable processes, were not empirically based, and contained few objective criteria, as shown in this excerpt from the preamble to the specific diagnostic categories in DSM-II (APA, 1968, p. 39), describing "Neuroses" (emphasis added):

Anxiety is the chief characteristic of the neuroses. It may be felt and expressed directly, or it may be controlled unconsciously *and automatically by* conversion, displacement *and various other psychological mechanisms. Generally, these mechanisms produce symptoms experienced as subjective distress from which the patient desires relief.*

As a result the system proved quite unreliable; using this system, it was not unusual for clinicians to come up with widely differing diagnoses for the same person.

In 1980 the American Psychiatric Association published a greatly changed diagnostic manual, DSM-III, which was followed with a more modest revision in 1987, DSM-III-R. DSM-III introduced several significant differences. First of all, in an attempt to improve reliability, field trials were used to substantiate their content. Some 12,500 patients and 550 clinicians were involved in trials (Widiger & Trull, 1991).

DSM-IV Multiaxial Classification System, First Four Axes

Axis I Clinical Syndromes	Axis II Personality Disorders	Axis III General Medical Conditions
Disorders usually first diagnosed in infancy, adolescence	Paranoid	Infectious and parasitic diseases
Delirium, dementia, amnesia, and other cognitive disorders	Schizoid Schizotypal	Neoplasms Endocrine, nutritional, and meta-bolic diseases
Substance-related disorders disorders	Antisocial Borderline	Diseases of the blood and blood-forming organs
Schizophrenia and other psychotic disorders	Histrionic Narcissistic	Diseases of the nervous system and sense organs
Mood disorders	Avoidant	Diseases of the circulatory system
Anxiety disorders	Dependent	Diseases of the respiratory system
Somatoform disorders	Obsessive-compulsive	Diseases of the digestive system
Factitious disorder		Diseases of the genitourinary system
Dissociative disorders		
Sexual and gender identity disorders		
Eating disorders		
Sleep disorders		
Impulse control disorders not elsewhere classified		
Adjustment disorders		

Axis IV

Psychosocial and Environmental Problems

Check:

_____ Problems with primary support group (Childhood, Adult, Parent-Child). Specify: _____

_____ Problems related to the social environment. Specify: _____

_____ Educational problem. Specify: _____

_____ Occupational problem. Specify: _____

_____ Housing problem. Specify: _____

_____ Economic problem. Specify: _____

_____ Problems with access to health care services. Specify: _____

_____ Problems related to interaction with the legal system/crime. Specify: _____

_____ Other psychosocial problem. Specify: _____

Furthermore, these versions became atheoretic—that is, they moved away from endorsing any one theory of abnormal psychology, becoming more pragmatic as they moved to more precise behavioural descriptions; to increase precision, they included the required number of symptoms from a list, as well as time elements required to meet the criterion. Perhaps the greatest innovation was the development of a multiaxial requirement. For the first time, in addition to a primary diagnosis, diagnosticians were required to provide substantial patient information, evaluating and rating them on five different *axes* or areas of functioning.

Against this background, the APA charged a task force to begin work on DSM-IV to improve on its previous work. Thirteen work groups were established to cover each major diagnostic category. Professionals from all fields related to mental health were consulted. In addition to comprehensive literature reviews, old data sets were reanalyzed and an additional 12 multisite field trials were conducted to collect new data. These field trials were constituted to ensure that subjects represented diverse socioeconomic, cultural, and ethnic backgrounds. The field trials included 70 sites, and evaluated some 6000 patients. In addition to reliability of the diagnoses these field trials assessed the validity of the diagnoses and set out to establish improved criteria. Clinicians used several draft versions of proposed diagnostic categories in their work and reported back to the work groups on their findings. Representatives from all over the world, including 27 Canadian psychiatrists and psychologists, sat on the committees or consulted with them. The result of this mammoth undertaking was DSM-IV (APA, 1994).

DSM-IV is now used very widely in Canada and the United States. Nations in the European Community more commonly use the WHO's ICD. However, the use of the DSM is becoming widespread throughout the world.

DSM-IV: A MULTIAXIAL APPROACH

One of the major innovations from DSM-III on was the use of multiaxial classifications. Previously, clinicians typically rated patients on the most conspicuous aspect of their abnormal behaviour. Now, for the first time, the system acknowledged that a person's life circumstances as a whole need to be considered; diagnosticians were required to evaluate an individual on a broad array of information that might be of concern. With DSM-IV, clinicians assess patients under five different axes, or aspects, of the person's condition. Each of the five axes addresses a different type of information. See the table "DSM-IV Multiaxial Classification System, First Four Axes." Look again at the opening case for an example of what kinds of information the five axes record for a particular person.

Axis I is most similar to previous diagnostic systems in that it diagnoses the most obvious disorders. Included in Axis I are the psychological disorders that have been recognized for centuries because of their bizarre nature (such as schizophrenia), or the difficulty they pose in the everyday life of individuals (such as mood disorders).

Axis II focusses on the presence of generally less severe long-term disturbances, which may nevertheless interfere with a person's life. Usually individuals with these problems can function in jobs and relationships, albeit with significant difficulty. In our opening case, Bill was found to have a dependent personality disorder; not his most obvious problem but still significant. These less dramatic behaviour patterns were often missed in the presence of overriding Axis I symptoms. As an example, suppose a psychologist is assessing someone with an alcohol use disorder. The psychological and medical problems associated with alcohol abuse may be so severe that the psychologist overlooks a subtler lifelong behaviour pattern of pervasive social inhibition and feelings of inadequacy. This pattern may indicate an Axis II disorder called *avoidant personality disorder*, sometimes present since childhood. Did the personality disorder lead to the alcohol use disorder? Will it affect the required treatment? Maybe and maybe not, but without being directed by Axis II the psychologist might not have seen the whole range of the person's problems.

Axis III covers any medical disorder that might be relevant to the understanding or management of the case. This axis recognizes that medical disorders may cause psychological disorders, or they may affect future development or treatment. Suppose a previously well functioning individual is left partially paralyzed by a car accident and then develops a major depressive disorder. The paralysis has to be considered not only in terms of how it contributed to the depression but also in terms of what treatments are possible and what outcomes can be expected.

Axis IV and Axis V are significant additions to the DSM classification system. Axis IV collects information on the patient's life circumstances, recognizing that individuals live within a social milieu. Suppose that two women have anxiety disorder; one is single, the other has an abusive husband and three children. Although their primary diagnosis is the same, the treatment and expected development of the two women might be quite different. In our opening case, Bill's life and his psychological state would be affected by his criminal record.

Axis V (see table "DSM-IV Multiaxial Classification System, Fifth Axis") measures how well a person is able to cope with the circumstances related to his or her problems. This information can be indicative of the need for treatment and of the person's coping mechanisms and can assist in planning intervention. Suppose that two people both saw children die in a terrible school bus accident, and both are suffering acute stress disorder. One finds himself unable to work and is having suicidal thoughts (Axis V: Level of current functioning: 50). The other is somewhat depressed and experiencing mild insomnia, but generally functioning satisfactorily (Axis V: Level of current functioning: 70). The first person may be given a fast-acting psychotropic medication to make sure he doesn't deteriorate or attempt suicide. The second may need only psychological counselling.

DSM-IV recognizes that not everyone who experiences psychological discomfort is necessarily suffering from a clinically significant condition. Nevertheless, most patients who seek clinical services will satisfy criteria for some condition in Axis I, Axis II, or both.

CATEGORIES OF DISORDER IN DSM-IV

DSM-IV groups all the disorders listed on either Axis I or Axis II into 15 categories, on the basis of broad similarities in how they affect people or how the people suffering from them may appear to the clinician.

Disorders Usually First Diagnosed in Infancy, Childhood, and Adolescence

Included in this broad-ranging category of disorders are the intellectual, emotional, and physical disorders that typically begin before maturity. (We discuss these disorders in Chapter 5.) Under the general classification of "Attention Deficit and Disruptive Behaviour Disorders" are *attention deficit/hyperactivity disorder,* in which the individual displays maladaptive levels of inattention, hyperactivity, or impulsivity, or a combination of these; *oppositional defiant disorder,* in which there is a recurrent pattern of negativistic, defiant, disobedient, and hostile behaviour toward authority figures, and *conduct disorder,* in which children persistently violate societal norms,

DSM-IV   Multiaxial Classification System, Fifth Axis

Axis V

Global Assessment of Functioning Scale (GAF Scale)

Consider psychological, social, and occupational functioning on a hypothetical continuum of mental health/illness. Do not include impairment in functioning due to physical (or environmental) limitations.

Code	Description
100–91	Superior functioning in a wide range of activities, life's problems never seem to get out of hand, is sought out by others because of his many positive qualities. No symptoms.
90–81	Absent or minimal symptoms (for example, mild anxiety before an exam), good functioning in all areas, interested and involved in a wide range of activities, socially effective generally. Satisfied with life, no more than everyday problems or concerns (for example, an occasional argument with family members).
80–71	If symptoms are present, they are transient and expectable reactions to psychosocial stressors (for example, difficulty concentrating after family argument); no more than slight impairment in social, occupational, or school functioning (for example, temporarily falling behind in school work).
70–61	Some mild symptoms (for example, depressed mood and mild insomnia) OR some difficulty in social, occupational, or school functioning (for example, occasional truancy, or theft within the household), but generally functioning pretty well, with some meaningful interpersonal relationships.
60–51	Moderate symptoms (for example, flat affect and circumstantial speech, occasional panic attacks) OR moderate difficulty in social, occupational, or school functioning (for example, no friends, unable to keep a job).
50–41	Serious symptoms (for example, suicidal ideation, severe obsessional rituals, frequent shoplifting) OR any serious impairment in social, occupational, or school functioning (for example, no friends, unable to keep a job).
40–31	Some impairment in reality testing or communication (for example, speech is at times illogical, obscure, or irrelevant) OR major impairment in several areas, such as work or school, family relations, judgment, thinking, or mood (for example, depressed man avoids friends, neglects family, and is unable to work; child frequently beats up younger children, is defiant at home, and is failing at school).
30–21	Behavior is considerably influenced by delusions or hallucinations OR serious impairment in communication or judgment (for example, sometimes incoherent, acts grossly inappropriately, suicidal preoccupation) OR inability to function in almost all areas (for example, stays in bed all day; no job, home, or friends).
20–11	Some danger of hurting self or others (for example, suicide attempts without clear expectation of death, frequently violent, manic excitement) OR occasionally fails to maintain minimal personal hygiene (for example, smears feces) OR gross impairment in communication (for example, largely incoherent or mute).
10–1	Persistent danger of severely hurting self or others (for example, recurrent violence) OR persistent inability to maintain minimal personal hygiene OR serious suicidal act with clear expectation of death.
0	Inadequate information.

Source: Reprinted with permission from the *Diagnostic and Statistical Manual of Mental Disorders*, Fourth Edition. Copyright 1994 American Psychiatric Association.

rules, or the basic rights of others. Other diagnostic categories include *separation anxiety disorder*, in which the child becomes excessively anxious over the possibility of separation from parents or significant others; *mental retardation*, subaverage intelligence with impairments in social adjustment, identified at an early age; *autistic disorder*, in which the child shows severe impediments in several areas of development, including social interactions and communication; and *learning disorders*, in which the person's functioning in particular academic skill areas is significantly below average. Frequently, children may develop disorders that are most commonly seen in adults, such as depression or schizophrenia and these are diagnosed according to the same criteria as those used for adults.

Substance-Related Disorders

These disorders are brought about by the excessive use of substances, such as alcohol, amphetamines, marijuana, cocaine, and nicotine, that affect the central nervous system. When the use of these substances results in social, occupational, psy-

chological, or physical problems, it is considered a mental disorder. Individuals with such diagnoses may be unable to control or stop their use of substances and may be physically addicted to them. On occasion, anxiety and mood disorders can be a result of substance abuse. Such substance-induced mental disorders are categorized in the DSM along with the other disorders whose symptoms they share. For example, excessive intake of caffeine may cause extreme anxiety and panic. Included in the group of substance abuse disorders are: *alcohol use disorder, opioid use disorder, amphetamine use disorders, cocaine use disorders, and hallucinogen use disorders.* These disorders are covered in Chapter 10.

Schizophrenia and Other Psychotic Disorders

These disorders (discussed in Chapter 14) constitute some of the earliest recognized by mental health workers and by those developing diagnostic systems. The disorders known as *schizophrenia* are marked by severe debilitation in thinking and perception. People with schizophrenia suffer from a active and in less need of sleep, and displays flights of somewhat disconnected ideas, grandiosity (an illusion of personal importance that can lead to inappropriate behaviour), and impairment in functioning. Severity of mood disorders can vary. In **bipolar conditions**, both depression and mania are exhibited.

Anxiety Disorders

Anxiety is the predominant disturbance in this group of disorders (discussed in Chapter 7). Individuals who suffer from an anxiety disorder may experience excessive fear, worry, or apprehension. A person can have a fear of a specific object or situation, called a *phobia*, which usually leads to avoidance of the feared stimulus. In other anxiety disorders, people may not be aware of the reasons for their extreme feelings of anxiety or they may exhibit *obsessions* (recurrent, intense thoughts) or *compulsions* (strongly repetitive behaviours), which, when not performed, cause overwhelming distress. Individuals may also experience a lingering anxiety reaction to extraordinarily traumatic events (*acute stress disorder* and *posttraumatic stress disorder*).

Somatoform Disorders

The physical symptoms of somatoform disorders have no known physiological cause but seem to serve a psychological purpose. Individuals with *somatization disorder* have a long history of bodily problems or dysfunctions, for which they have consulted doctors or taken some form of medication. However, the symptoms may be inconsistent with anatomical structures, and the discrepancy suggests a psychological basis for the symptoms. In *conversion disorder* the person reports

Children may develop disorders most commonly seen in adults, such as depression or schizophrenia. These are diagnosed according to the same criteria as those used for adults.

state of *psychosis,* or a loss of contact with reality. They often lose the ability to care for themselves, relate to others, and function at work. Speech may be incoherent, and the person often suffers from *delusions*, such as believing that someone has placed thoughts in his or her head, *hallucinations*, such as hearing voices, *loose associations* (unconnected pieces of thought), and *inappropriate affect,* such as giggling when discussing sad events like someone's illness or death. Essentially people in a psychotic state have lost contact with the world and with others.

Mood Disorders

This category of the DSM-IV involves disturbances in mood that do not seem to be a reasonable response to circumstances. These disorders, which we discuss in Chapter 13, include **major depressive disorder**, in which the person is extremely sad and discouraged and displays a marked loss of pleasure from usual activities. Clinically depressed people often have severe problems sleeping, and experience weight loss and lack of energy. Also included in these disorders is **mania**, a condition in which a person seems extremely elated, more

Compulsive hand washing is one possible manifestation of an anxiety disorder.

the loss of motor or sensory function, for example a paralysis or blindness. Individuals with *pain disorder* experience severe, prolonged, and unexplained pain believed to stem in part from psychological factors. *Hypochondriasis* is the misinterpretation of minor physical sensations as abnormal; individuals become preoccupied with the fear that they have a serious illness. Finally, people with *body dysmorphic* disorder are overly preoccupied with an imagined defect in their appearance. These disorders are covered in Chapter 8.

Dissociative Disorders

Psychological dissociation involves a sudden and profound alteration in consciousness that affects an individual's memory and identity. People with *amnesia dissociation* may forget their entire past or, more selectively, lose their memory for a particular time period. With *dissociative fugue,* individuals suddenly and unexpectedly leave their home and travel to a new locale, start a new life, and forget their previous identity. Individuals with *dissociative identity disorder* (previously known as "multiple personality disorder") possess two or more distinct personalities, each with unique memories, behaviour patterns, preferences, and social relationships.

Depersonalization disorder involves a severe and disruptive feeling of self-estrangement or unreality. (See Chapter 8.)

Sexual and Gender Identity Disorders

The sexual disorders section of the DSM-IV includes three main categories. Individuals who suffer from a *sexual dysfunction* are characterized by disturbance in sexual desire and in the psychophysiological changes that accompany the sexual response cycle. Inability to maintain an erection, premature ejaculation, and inhibitions of orgasm are some examples of their problems. Individuals in the *paraphilias* are characterized by sexual urges, fantasies, or behaviours that involve unusual objects or activities, such as exhibitionism, voyeurism, sadism, and masochism. People with *gender identity disorders* feel extreme and overwhelming discomfort with their anatomical sex and identify themselves as members of the opposite sex. (See Chapter 12.)

Sleep Disorders

Individuals with these disorders display two major categories of sleep disturbances. In the *dyssomnias*, sleep is disturbed

---

Focus *Comorbidity*

As we shall see in following chapters, **comorbidity** is common. That is, no matter what diagnostic system is used, it is common for an individual to meet the criteria for more than one diagnostic condition. In fact, research has demonstrated that comorbidity may be present more than half the time. Is this finding a function of poor diagnostic systems, which have failed to include all the relevant criteria in each condition? Or does it simply reflect the reality of individuals experiencing psychological problems and the complexity of the human mind?

Research has demonstrated, for example, that as many as 50 percent of people suffering from anxiety disorders also have mood disorders. Clearly there is a relationship of some kind between anxiety and mood disorders, but what is that relationship? Do anxiety disorders and mood disorders have the same cause (or set of predisposing factors), whether genetic or environment? Or does one

An Example of Comorbidity

disorder predispose an individual to the other? It seems to make sense that a person suffering serious anxiety, with the attendant feelings of helplessness and hopelessness, may develop depression. In fact, in the majority of cases of comorbidity the anxiety does precede the depression.

When comorbidity exists a frequent question is which disorder to

treat first. Do you treat the problem that came first? Do you treat the problem that is most serious? Do you treat the problem that is most easily treated? What do you do if the most serious problem is one that often takes a long time to resolve, while the less serious problem can be eliminated much more easily? ▲

in terms of amount (for example, not being able to maintain sleep or sleeping too much), quality (the person does not feel adequately rested after sleep), or timing (the person is unable to sleep during conventional sleep times). The *parasomnias* are marked by abnormal events during sleep (for example, *sleep terror disorder* or *sleepwalking disorder*).

Eating Disorders

This category (discussed in Chapter 9) includes extreme eating patterns that significantly impair functioning. In *anorexia nervosa,* the individual refuses to maintain a minimally normal weight for her or his age and height (the majority of sufferers are female). These people avoid eating and become emaciated, often due to an intense fear of becoming fat. In *bulimia nervosa,* there are frequent episodes of binge eating coupled with compensatory activities such as self-induced vomiting or the use of laxatives.

Factitious Disorder

This diagnosis is given to individuals who intentionally produce or complain of either physical or psychological symptoms, apparently because of a psychological need to assume the role of a sick person.

Adjustment Disorders

This diagnosis refers to the development of emotional or behavioural symptoms within three months after a major stressful event, such as divorce or business difficulties. The reaction usually involves distress and impairment in social or occupational functioning, or other symptoms that exceed the reaction one would normally expect to such a stressor. However, the symptoms are not severe enough to meet the criteria for any Axis I diagnosis.

Impulse Control Disorders

This category includes a number of conditions in which people are chronically unable to resist impulses, drives, or temptations to perform acts harmful to themselves or to others. For example, in *intermittent explosive disorder* the person has episodes of violent behaviour which result in the destruction of property or injury to others. In *pathological gambling* the individual is preoccupied with gambling, is unable to stop, and gambles as a way to escape from problems. Those suffering from *trichotillomania* are impelled to pull out their own hair, often to the extent that they have to wear a wig to avoid attracting attention.

Personality Disorders

Individuals with these disorders (discussed in Chapter 11) display an enduring, pervasive, inflexible, and maladaptive pattern of behaviour that markedly impairs functioning or causes subjective stress. The patterns of these behaviours are usually evident by adolescence. The ten distinct personality disorders that make up the category are listed on Axis II. One common example of personality disorder is *antisocial personality disorder*, which usually surfaces before the age of 15, in which the person displays a history of continuous and chronic disregard for and violation of the rights of others. Individuals with this diagnosis are often called psychopaths; they do not appear to feel guilt or shame for transgressing social mores. In *dependent personality disorder,* a person manifests a pattern of submissive and clinging behaviour and fears of separation, which are related to a need to be taken care of.

Delirium, Dementia, Amnesia, and Other Cognitive Disorders

Delirium is a clouding of consciousness, wandering attention, and an incoherent stream of thought. It may be caused by several medical conditions as well as by poor diet and substance abuse. *Dementia*, a deterioration of mental capacities, is typically irreversible, and is usually associated with Alzheimer's disease, stroke, several other medical conditions, and substance abuse. *Amnestic syndrome* involves an impairment in memory when there is no delirium or dementia, and is frequently linked to alcohol abuse.

Other Conditions That May Be a Focus of Clinical Attention

This broad category is used for conditions that are not considered to be mental disorders but still may be a focus of attention or treatment. If a person's medical illness appears to be in part psychological, or exacerbated by a psychological condition, the diagnosis is *psychological factors affecting physical condition* (referred to previously as psychophysiological or psychosomatic disorders). Among the other conditions in this category are academic problems, marital problems, occupational problems, and physical or sexual abuse.

ISSUES IN THE DIAGNOSIS AND CLASSIFICATION OF ABNORMAL BEHAVIOUR

Despite the long history and widespread use of the DSM, and other diagnostic systems for mental health, considerable controversy still exists concerning their use. There are two main arenas of controversy. One body of opinion objects to classification per se, and suggests any classification system for mental disorders is irrelevant at best and inappropriate at worst. The second category of opposition targets the DSM in particular.

Against Classification

Those who object to classification at all make several points.

Medical Model

A substantial number of professionals argue that the whole diagnostic endeavour is flawed because of its adherence to the medical model. Medical disorders are legitimate, they say, because they have a clear indication, such as a lesion, which is a recognizable deviation in anatomical structure, whereas there are no such anatomical deviations in most mental disorders. Society, according to this viewpoint, merely uses the diagnostic process for its own ends (Szasz, 1961). Wakefield (1992) aptly responds to the fallacies inherent in this position by pointing out that there are many medical disorders for which there are no known lesions or anatomical abnormalities. He points out that some medical disorders, such as trigeminal neuralgia, are so classified on the basis of associated dysfunction alone. Furthermore, it is possible that at some point in the future anatomical anomalies may be found to be associated with some disorders.

Another argument rejects the notion that symptoms indicate underlying problems of which the patient is unaware. This notion, say its opponents, is a holdover from medical practice and outdated psychodynamic theories of personality. In medicine, for example, a high fever is often considered a symptom indicative of an underlying problem, say an infection. But is this an accurate analogy to what happens in psychopathology? A case in point might be conversion disorder (see Chapter 8), in which a person suddenly loses a voluntary motor ability such as walking, or a sensory function such as vision, without any medical reason—because of severe psychological distress, or so psychologists believe. The person with the conversion disorder is unaware of the stressor that caused the loss of ability, or the historical events that caused one limb or sense to be affected and not others. The critics argue that there is little evidence for such speculations, and worse, that such conjectures are of little value and may even get in the way of treatment. Therapists may typically spend years with a patient trying to understand the underlying causes of the symptoms. The critics maintain that the disorder is the problem behaviours themselves, not some underlying and unexplored issues the behaviours are alleged to represent. The most sensible approach would be to treat the behaviours themselves, rather than searching for elusive causes.

Stigmatization

Another argument against diagnosis is that it unfairly stigmatizes an individual. Once Jerry is, for example, diagnosed with schizophrenia, he is seen simply as a "schizophrenic," rather than a complex individual, perhaps a skilled musician with a strong social conscience and a volatile temper. The label might also have a major impact socially and occupationally. Once he is labelled, Jerry will find it difficult to get hired as a music teacher or to be elected to public office. Related to this labelling argument is the risk that the individual labelled mentally ill may come to identify with the label, leading to further deterioration or impeding rehabilitation. Wakefield (1992) addresses the stigmatization criticism by stressing that, even if such undesirable consequences do occur on occasion, the flaw lies not in the classification system but in people's reactions. Professionals must guard against the dangers of discouraging or belittling mentally ill people, and must help to educate the public appropriately.

The problems associated with labelling someone mentally ill are brought into focus in the widely acclaimed movie *Shine*, which depicts the life of David Helfgott. David, a teenage piano prodigy, moved from Australia to London, England to accept a music scholarship. He suffered a major mental collapse in the mid-1970s and spent more than a decade in psychiatric hospitals before emerging in the mid-1980s to perform at a Perth piano bar. Although an official diagnosis has not been made available, the fact that he was on the antipsychotic medication Serenac for many years suggests schizophrenia, or some other type of psychotic disorder. His wife reveals that he is still on medication, and that when he stops taking it he deteriorates. He travels under protective circumstances to prevent him from wandering off and cannot perform on consecutive nights. Nevertheless, he is a loving husband, a charming individual, an engaging entertainer, and a prodigiously skilled pianist. Any diagnosis such as "schizophrenia" would fall far short of describing the many attributes that have helped him overcome the problems often ascribed to people with schizophrenia. One also wonders how he would have fared had his wife, Gillian, not been attracted to his many qualities and made a special effort with him.

David Helfgott, whose extraordinary life was documented in the 1996 film Shine.

Source: Peter Wilmoth, David Helfgott, *The Sunday Age*, posted off *Robert Banks Photography* (home page), last modified January 28, 1997, accessed November 18, 1998 <atlas.onthe.net.au/~robb/davetext.html>.
© Peter Wilmoth 5/09/96.

Loss of Information

A frequent charge against diagnosis is that inherent in any label is a loss of information. How can anyone's uniqueness be summarized in a word or two whether the label is favourable (such as "beautiful" or "smart") or unfavourable (such as "lazy" or "aloof")? Despite the intuitive appeal of such an argument, it is important to note that often the information lost is irrelevant to the diagnostic endeavour. An accomplished musician or athlete can be admired for her skill; but she may not be able to use it if she is experiencing major hallucinations that lead to a diagnosis of schizophrenia. On the contrary, the diagnosis may assist in the selection of intervention procedures since it shifts the focus to more clinically relevant issues. The label may also be of considerable assistance in research, as it provides a commonality for professionals in diverse locations.

Criticisms Specific to DSM

Another set of criticisms is related not to diagnosis per se but to flaws in the conceptualization of DSM-IV in particular.

Discrete vs. Continuum

One of the most frequent criticisms of the DSM is that it takes a **categorical** approach to classification: that is, an individual is deemed to either have a disorder or not have a disorder, with no in-between. One reason for this approach is historical. It is mostly psychiatrists who have developed mental health nosologies (classification systems), and, being physicians, they have used the same approach taken in medicine. For example, if a person goes to a physician reporting pain in the ear and fever, the physician will diagnose the person as having a bacterial infection—otitis media—or not having such an infection. There is no in-between. But is this a reasonable model for assessing mental function? A categorical system does not recognize the continuum between normal and abnormal.

Consider the case of a teenager who shows significant levels of opposition and aggression but falls just short of the required criteria for "Conduct Disorder" and therefore does not receive this diagnosis. Does this mean the individual has no problems? And what of the large body of research with conduct-disordered children—are the findings irrelevant to this youngster? This is not merely an academic question for professionals who must advise parents on how to deal with their children, or for psychologists testifying in court. An expert witness may have considerable difficulty convincing the court that a defendant has significant problems and a poor prognosis if the individual falls just short of meeting the DSM criteria for a particular diagnosis.

Thus, people may be denied needed help because they fall just short of the diagnostic criteria. Furthermore, critics allege, a categorical approach does not give a meaningful description of an individual's psychological problems. For these reasons some have advocated a **dimensional** approach to

diagnosis, based on a continuum for mental disorders from nonexistent or mild to severe. Disorders could be measured on a continuous scale, perhaps a Likert-type scale or a numerical rating from 1 to 10.

Yet this approach also has disadvantages. One is that many more people would receive a psychiatric diagnosis. For example, many people who would not, under the current system, receive a diagnosis of depression might be classified as mildly depressed, thus unduly stigmatizing them and increasing the burden on the mental health system. It has been suggested that some disorders, such as schizophrenia, are more appropriately diagnosed using a categorical approach, while others, such as the personality disorders, are more appropriately diagnosed with a dimensional classification system. A variation is to use several personality or psychiatric dimensions in describing an individual, with perhaps a ten-point scale for each dimension. Thus a person might, for example, receive scores of 4, 3, 9, and 8 on measures of depression, anxiety, antisocial personality, and delusional disorder.

Dimensional diagnostic procedures have, in fact, been attempted in the past, but have had little success. Clinicians have not been able to agree on how many dimensions should subsume a given disorder, nor has there been consensus on scoring procedures. Finally, the dimensional strategy does not eliminate the need for categorical decisions, but merely shifts the decision; the diagnostician still faces the decision whether, for example, to rate someone a 4 or a 5 on a Likert-type scale.

Reliability and Validity

The usefulness of any measurement tool rests on two qualities. First it must be **reliable**: that is, it must give the same measurement for a given thing every time. A ruler made of a malleable material that randomly expanded and shrunk would be of little value to a carpenter. Second, it must be **valid**: that is, it must measure what it purports to measure. A rigid ruler would be reliable; but it would be useless as a measure of temperature. (See Chapter 4 for a fuller discussion of validity.) These requirements of reliability and validity are also necessary for systems that measure psychopathology.

Inter-rater reliability refers to the extent to which two clinicians agree on the diagnosis of a particular patient. For example, if a system does not allow clinicians to agree on the signs and symptoms that constitute a specific disorder, inter-rater reliability will remain low. A classic study on the reliability of the diagnostic process was carried out many years ago (Beck, Ward, Mendelson, Mock, & Erbaugh 1962). In this investigation four highly experienced psychiatrists interviewed 153 new inpatients in a psychiatric hospital. Each patient was interviewed first by one psychiatrist and then a few hours later by a second psychiatrist. The psychiatrists were asked to formulate a DSM-I diagnosis based on the interviews. The overall percentage agreement between pairs of raters was rather low, at 54 percent. That is, just over half the time, the two psychiatrists agreed on a given patient's diagnosis. Inter-rater agreement was about this rate for anxiety reaction, schizophrenic reaction, and sociopathic disturbance.

For personality trait disturbance, the rate was only 38 percent, meaning that the majority of the time, the two psychiatrists did not agree.

One might speculate that this disagreement arose because the patient did not give the same report to both psychiatrists. Perhaps a patient might, for example, mention domestic violence during one interview and not the other. Indeed, such discrepancies did occur, but when the authors of the studies analyzed the data, they found this to be the least important cause of poor reliability. A more significant cause was differences between the interviewers, such as different interview techniques or differences in interpretation and in the importance given to certain symptoms. However, the factor most responsible by far for poor inter-rater reliability was the inadequacy of the diagnostic system itself. DSM-I notoriously failed to provide the clearly defined and observable criteria required for good diagnoses.

What about the second standard for any tool, validity? First, validity depends inexorably on reliability. A tool that is not reliable cannot be valid. However, it is possible for a tool to be reliable without being valid, as in the example of the ruler used to measure temperature. In a diagnostic system, validity is determined by whether a diagnostic category is able to predict behavioural and psychiatric disorders accurately. The two most important types of validity for diagnostic systems are concurrent validity and predictive validity. **Concurrent validity** refers to the ability of a diagnostic category to estimate an individual's present standing on factors related to the disorder but not themselves part of the diagnostic criteria. For example, although significant academic underachievement and a downward drift in socioeconomic status are not diagnostic items for schizophrenia, they are clearly found in most schizophrenics. If an assessment of the non-schizophrenic siblings of diagnosed schizophrenics indicated they had better education and higher income, this would be an indication of concurrent validity. One of the major criticisms of the DSM is that it sheds little light on the non-symptom attributes of people with a given diagnosis. Another essential requirement of a good diagnostic system is **predictive validity**: the ability of a test to predict the future course of an individual's development. A key to a clear understanding of a disorder is its progression. As we will see in Chapter 5, a diagnosis of Conduct Disorder in early adolescence has been found to be highly related to a diagnosis of Antisocial Personality Disorder as an adult. If all children with Conduct Disorder were reassessed at 20 years of age, and achieved a diagnosis of Antisocial Personality Disorder, the predictive validity of CD would be perfect. As we shall see later, this is certainly not the case.

Gender Bias

The late 1960s saw poignant criticisms of gender bias and sexism in the mental health system (Chesler, 1972). DSM-I and DSM-II were very influenced by psychoanalytic theory, which has been extensively charged with sexism (Kaschak, 1992; Segal, 1988). In 1974, a task force was set up by the American Psychological Association to investigate gender bias and sex-role stereotyping in mental health assessment and therapy. The first step was to survey female clinicians to determine what practices indicate gender bias or sexism. Four categories were developed: fostering traditional gender roles, bias in expectations and devaluation of women, sexist use of psychoanalytic concepts, and treating women as sex objects, including the seduction of a female patient (which was not specifically labelled unethical by a professional body until 1978). Nonetheless, DSM-III was far from free of gender bias.

Some writers have claimed the DSM describes many psychiatric disorders in a fashion that makes a diagnosis more probable for women, even when no pathology is involved (Kaplan, 1983a, b; Tavris, 1992). They contend that diagnostic categories in the DSM are based on professional assumptions regarding the nature of psychopathology, which are in turn influenced by societal norms that value stereotypic masculine behaviour, such as assertiveness and goal-directed behaviour, over stereotypic feminine behaviour, such as cooperativeness and nurturing others. These feminine behaviours are considered secondary to mental health and may even be seen as signs of emotional immaturity and psychopathology (Cook, Warnke, & Dupuy, 1993).

Another criticism of the DSM is that it does not sufficiently take life circumstances into account, assuming that psychological problems are largely attributable to the individual. Although recent years have seen increased acknowledgement of the extent to which women may be oppressed in Western society, there is still insufficient recognition of these factors in the diagnostic assessment (Cook et al., 1993; Stephenson & Walker, 1979). The DSM has also been accused of medicalizing normal female behaviour related to reproduction. This criticism is particularly relevant to the new diagnostic category of premenstrual dysphoric disorder (PMDD), a disorder similar to premenstrual syndrome. A great deal of controversy has arisen from the addition of a psychiatric disorder aimed solely at women and relating to a natural biological process (for example, Seligmann & Gelman, March 15, 1993).

The personality disorders of Axis II have also come under fire because some seem to correspond to exaggerated female stereotypes (for example histrionic personality disorder, narcissistic personality disorder, and dependent personality disorder), and may be diagnosed more frequently in women than in men. In a classic study (Broverman, Broverman, Clarkson, Rosenkrantz, & Vogel, 1970) questionnaires were sent to psychologists, psychiatrists, and social workers asking what point on a continuum between dichotomous characteristics (such as not at all aggressive to very aggressive) constitutes good mental health. This sort of experiment is termed an *analogue study*; it does not directly detect the clinicians' professional behaviour, but their attitudes, which are assumed to be analogous.

It is the most frequent means of studying gender bias in clinical assessment (Davison & Abramowitz, 1980). In this study, one-third of the clinicians were asked to rate a healthy adult, one-third a healthy male, and the remaining third a healthy female. Results indicated that although the criteria for mental health did not differ between adults and males, the criteria were significantly different between adults and females. In addition, socially desirable traits tended to be assigned to healthy males, and undesirable traits to healthy females. Dependency and emotionality were not seen as necessary characteristics for mental health. Interestingly, there was no difference between the responses of male and female clinicians. This study has been criticized because it is an analogue investigation and because the questionnaires listed more characteristics associated with masculinity than with femininity. Some now consider it dated. However, other research has produced similar findings. Investigations suggest that gender bias in diagnoses is not merely an artifact of the experimental procedure employed. For example, Adler, Drake, and Teague (1990) presented clinicians with case summaries of patients meeting criteria for several different personality disorders. They found that clinicians tended to diagnose these patients in accordance with gender stereotypes. It has also been demonstrated even when males and females are diagnosed with the same personality disorder (histrionic personality disorder and antisocial personality disorder, in this particular experiment), women are judged to be more pathological (Hamilton, Rothbart, & Dawes, 1986).

Cultural Bias

Just as mental health professionals have learned to recognize cultural bias, they have been led by recent developments to grapple with similar concerns related to culture. Millions of immigrants from all over the world have moved into Canada and the United States over the last 20 years. The North American milieu now includes more people of colour, a greater variety of religions, a variety of languages, and a tremendous increase in the variety of cultural practices. Clinicians must, more than ever, be aware of cultural factors that might influence the diagnostic process.

DSM-IV has striven to be atheoretical and to take cultural differences into account. It stresses that an individual's primary social and cultural reference group, as well as his or her unique personal experience, must be taken into account in an assessment (Mezzich et al., 1993). Despite these improvements to the DSM-IV, the designation of behaviour as normal or abnormal is fraught with cultural and professional assumptions, especially considering that disorders in the DSM are determined largely by consensus of English-speaking scientists trained primarily in the United States and, to a lesser extent, in Canada.

It is important to note that some behaviours considered abnormal in white North American culture may not be considered abnormal in other cultures. For example, hallucinations should not necessarily be considered abnormal during North American aboriginal religious ceremonies (Rogler & Hollingshead, 1985). In addition, since the belief that evil spirits can possess an individual is held by many in Hispanic nations such as Haiti or Puerto Rico, such reports should not always be considered a sign of schizophrenia in individuals from this culture. Similarly, it has been noted that the culture of aboriginal children instills a sense of cooperativeness, valuing the group more than the individual. As a result, they fare worse on IQ tests, which tend to be designed as individualistic and competitive (O'Conner, 1989). The same has been reported with African-Americans (Helms, 1992). Furthermore, North American aboriginals are overrepresented in the lower socioeconomic strata, and several studies have shown that IQ tests underestimate the intelligence of people in these strata (Dauphinais & King, 1992; National Commission on Testing and Public Policy, 1990).

The past ten years have seen a particularly large influx of immigrants from the Pacific Rim to the west coast of Canada. Research has suggested that diagnostic procedures with people of Japanese and Chinese origin need to be sensitive to cultural and attitudinal factors. For example, the widely used Minnesota Multiphasic Personality Inventory (MMPI) contains the F (for frequency) subscale. Many items are worded in such a fashion that endorsing them as "true" is different from the way most people in North America would answer. It is often assumed that people who score high on this scale are unable to understand the questions, answering carelessly, or faking an illness. Yet Cheung and Okazaki (1991) found that people in Hong Kong and the People's Republic of China tend to score higher than North Americans on this scale. Thus a relatively high score for a Chinese subject on this scale may not be indicative of this type of responding or faking, but merely of a different cultural background.

Certain syndromes appear only within a particular culture. *Taifin-kyofu-sho,* a syndrome found only in Japan, is characterized by an excessive fear that one will embarrass or offend others. This syndrome afflicts 7 to 36 percent of people treated by psychiatrists in Japan and primarily affects young Japanese men. Interestingly, *taifin-kyofu-sho* differs from social phobia in that the fear is not for oneself, but for others (Chang, 1984; McNally et al., 1990).

Research in the United States has suggested that emotional difficulties may be diagnosed differently in African-American and Hispanic populations than in white populations. Several studies found that clinicians shown a case summary were more likely to diagnose the patient with schizophrenia if told the patient was black. Hospital-based studies have also shown that blacks were overdiagnosed with schizophrenia and underdiagnosed with mood disorders (Garb, 1997). There is also some evidence that psychopathology has been underestimated in Hispanics due to linguistic bias (Sabin, 1975) and the fact that Hispanics may be more reluctant to disclose information to non-Hispanics than to Hispanics (Levine & Padilla, 1980; Lopez, 1989; Lopez & Hernandez, 1986).

ViewPoint *Overdiagnosis?*

How common are mental disorders? One of the most comprehensive and well-constructed epidemiological studies to date has been the Ontario Health Survey, conducted in the Ontario between 1990 and 1991. More than 8000 people were interviewed with a semistructured interview and, if applicable, were given a DSM-III-R diagnosis. They were all people not living in institutions, and were chosen on the basis of census data to be representative of the population of the province. Although it might be expected that there would be national differences, a smaller study conducted earlier by Dr. Bland and a team of researchers from the Department of Psychiatry at the University of Alberta had very similar results (Bland, Orn, & Newman, 1988). The findings of the Ontario Health Survey (shown in the table within this ViewPoint box) are startling. Approximately 19 percent of the population would receive an Axis I diagnosis over a 12-month period. Even more surprising was that Dr. Bland found that if one considered the lifetime prevalence of a psychological disorder, 33 percent of the population would qualify. These findings do not even consider the Axis II disorders. A similar investigation carried out in the United States found that if Axis II disorders are included, the lifetime prevalence of a major psychological disorder approaches some 50 percent. This is a remarkably large segment of the population. The survey also revealed that fewer than 40 percent of people with a psychological disorder had ever received professional treatment (Kessler et al., 1994).

Lifetime and 12-Month Prevalence of DSM-III-R Disorders

	Males 12 Mo.	Males Lifetime	Females 12 Mo.	Females Lifetime	Total 12 Mo.	Total Lifetime
Affective disorders:						
Major depressive episode	7.7	12.7	12.9	21.3	10.3	17.1
Manic episode	1.4	1.6	1.3	1.7	1.3	1.6
Dysthymia	2.1	4.8	3.0	8.0	2.5	6.4
Any affective disorder	8.5	14.7	14.1	23.9	11.3	19.3
Anxiety disorders:						
Panic disorder	1.3	2.0	3.2	5.0	2.3	3.5
Agoraphobia without panic disorder	1.7	3.5	3.8	7.0	2.8	5.3
Social phobia	6.6	11.1	9.1	15.5	7.9	13.3
Simple phobia	4.4	6.7	13.2	15.7	8.8	11.3
Generalized anxiety disorder	2.0	3.6	4.3	6.6	3.1	5.1
Any anxiety disorder	11.8	19.2	22.6	30.5	17.2	24.9
Substance use disorders:						
Alcohol abuse without dependence	3.4	12.5	1.6	6.4	2.5	9.4
Alcohol dependence	10.7	20.1	3.7	8.2	7.2	14.1
Drug abuse without dependence	1.3	5.4	0.3	3.5	0.8	4.4
Drug dependence	3.8	9.2	1.9	5.9	2.8	7.5
Any substance abuse/dependence	16.1	35.4	6.6	17.9	11.3	26.6
Other disorders:						
Nonaffective psychosis	0.5	0.6	0.6	0.8	0.5	0.7
Any disorder	27.7	48.7	31.2	47.3	29.5	48.0

Source: Archives of General Psychiatry, 51: 8–19. Copyright 1994, American Medical Association.

VIEWPOINT *continued*

One interpretation might be that mental health professionals have been rather self-serving and have created a diagnostic system that greatly over-diagnoses individuals (Szasz, 1961).

Critical Thinking Questions

1. A DSM diagnosis reflects a significant disturbance. Is it possible that such a large portion of the Canadian population suffers from psychological problems? Recall from Chapter 1 that one of the criteria for abnormality is relative infrequency in the population. When some of the conditions affect as many as one of four people at one time or another in their lives, and when half of the population experiences one condition or another at some time, can these conditions truly be considered abnormal?

2. Some individuals (especially grandparents) might suggest that the frequency of psychological disorders in our society has increased over the past 25 years. If in fact they are right, what factors may have contributed to such an increase?

3. What features of American society, compared with Canadian society, might lead to a higher proportion of the American population having mental health problems?

4. What features of Canadian society, compared with American society, might lead to a higher proportion of Canadians seeking help for mental health issues?

PANORAMA

The DSM-IV diagnostic system, as we have seen, is far from perfect. However, as the history of classification in the natural sciences has demonstrated, the development of a diagnostic classification system is an ongoing process requiring continual refinement. Classification is an accepted procedure in all sciences and it is very likely that the field of mental health will continue to use it. It is encouraging to note that DSM-IV has made a serious attempt to apply research findings and that it stresses observable behaviour and provides explicit rules for diagnosis. This scientific attitude should allow the detection of flaws in the present system and facilitate the gathering of information. Gradually the diagnostic categories should be refined as we fill in the present gaps in our knowledge and come to recognize how culture and politics have influenced professional concepts of mental health.

There has been a significant increase in the use of technology in the study of psychopathology. We have already experienced the developments and increased information resulting from the use of computers and the types of statistical analyses they allow. In particular, the rapid growth in the neurological sciences and the availability of tools such as positron emission tomography (PET), magnetic resonance imaging (MRI), and single-photon emission computed tomography (SPECT) will continue to offer new diagnostic possibilities. Other chapters in the book will discuss some of the recent discoveries achieved with these technologies, and how they may lead to changes in the present system. Rather than a total abandonment of the current diagnostic system, we are likely to see an increased refinement of diagnostic categories, or on occasion the melding of different diagnostic categories as research fails to support their uniqueness.

SUMMARY

Every science includes a system for categorizing information. In abnormal psychology the perfect diagnostic system would be based on etiology, presenting symptoms, prognosis, and response to treatment. This diagnostic system would also enhance the organization of clinical factors and provide a shorthand that would help professionals communicate easily. The DSMs have progressed considerably in arriving at DSM-IV. The use of a multiaxial classification system has been adopted in recognition of the importance of psychosocial features in the development and maintenance of psychological problems. Many professionals feel that the DSM-IV is still too aligned with the medical model and that it leads to excessive stigmatization and loss of information about individuals. It is also criticized for using categories that do not do justice to the complexity of human behaviour and for displaying gender and cultural biases. As in any other classification system, issues of reliability and validity are central to the diagnostic process.

KEY TERMS

diagnosis (p. 50)
diagnostic system (p. 50)
assessment (p. 50)
sign (p. 50)

symptom (p. 50)
major depressive disorder (p. 55)
mania (p. 55)
bipolar conditions (p. 55)
comorbidity (p. 56)
categorical (p. 59)

dimensional (p. 59)
reliable (p. 59)
valid (p. 59)
inter-rater reliability (p. 59)
concurrent validity (p. 60)
predictive validity (p. 60)

ADDITIONAL RESOURCES

American Psychiatric Association
1400 K Street, N.W.
Washington, DC 20005
(202) 682-6000
(202) 682-6850 fax
apa@psych.org

www.mentalhealth.com/mag1/p51.html#Per
This collection presents hundreds of articles on personality disorders and their classification, diagnosis, and treatment.

www.mentalhealth.com
Internet Mental Health is an encyclopedia of mental health information. It includes information on mental disorders and medications, online diagnosis, and links to other mental health sites.

www.psych.org
The web page of the American Psychiatric Association provides information on the diagnosis and treatment of mental and emotional illnesses. The site provides clinical and research resources and information about other organizations, journals, and publications.

Chapter 4

Psychological Assessment and Research Methods

Philip Firestone

Noah was a boy, aged five years and ten months, whose parents had requested a psychological assessment because his teachers had reported him to be disruptive in class and to be performing below his potential in Grade 1. The parents had been called in to the school for a meeting with all his teachers. All the teachers who had worked with him described him in much the same way, and matched how his parents saw him. Noah was a talkative, happy-go-lucky child, well liked by the other children. He was sometimes a little aggressive, with no evidence of malice. He had difficulty following individual instructions, and frequently did not comply with classroom rules. His teachers wondered whether Noah's mediocre academic achievement and disruptive behaviour might be caused by family or emotional problems.

The psychologist addressed this assessment on three fronts. First, he interviewed Noah's family, starting with the whole family together: Noah, his parents, and his brother, who was three years older. Then he spoke to the parents alone, to each of the boys alone, and to the two boys together. The psychologist also asked the teachers to fill out a checklist widely used to assess classroom behaviour. Finally, Noah's IQ was assessed (Wechsler Intelligence Scale for Children) and he was given a projective test that is widely used in the personality assessment of children (Children's Apperception Test).

The psychologist rated Noah's home environment as fairly good. There was no evidence of marital problems or family issues, beyond the normal strains of raising two young boys. The behaviour checklist showed a problem only on the scales measuring attention/impulsivity, where Noah scored at approximately the 21st percentile for his age group. He scored within normal limits on scales measuring anxiety, depression, and antisocial behaviour. The projective test revealed that Noah had a rich emotional life. He felt involved and loved in his world. His comments suggested he had difficulty accepting general rules of play and was reluctant to share toys. He regarded himself too highly, and did not want to admit that other children might

be better than he at games, sports, or other activities. Noah's IQ was very high. His overall score placed him in the 98th percentile, with good performance in all areas.

The psychologist's report provided to the parents and school included the following interpretations:

- There was no evidence of family issues leading to Noah's problem behaviour.
- Noah's problem behaviour in class was largely a result of difficulty with concentration and impulsivity.
- Noah's personality assessment suggested he was a bit immature.
- Noah's IQ was in the gifted range. His academic performance was indeed below potential.

The report noted that, because he was born in the fall, just before the school's January cutoff for registration, Noah was the youngest boy, and one of the youngest children, in his class. Some of his impulsive actions and failure to pay attention might simply reflect his youth, and might cease to be a problem in another year or so. His intellectual abilities may have allowed him to function as well as he did despite this immaturity. Emotionally, Noah was all right, but may have had a somewhat overinflated self-image—perhaps because he was excessively praised for the precociousness achieved through high intelligence and an older brother's influence. The report suggested since this was only Grade 1, and Noah's problems were not severe, the school simply monitor his behaviour for another year. The only action recommended was that both parents and school be firm in response to his aggressive behaviour to ensure that no one was hurt and that Noah got a clear message of what is acceptable.

The following school year Noah was placed in an accelerated class containing only 12 children. With the increased structure and supervision of a smaller class, Noah did very well academically and his classroom behaviour improved dramatically. However, during free play or recess he still displayed more disruptive and aggressive behaviour than one would like.

ASSESSMENT

As mentioned in Chapter 3, an accurate diagnosis provides a shorthand description of many important attributes of a patient, and allows some predictions about the individual's development. This diagnosis usually results from a **psychological assessment**: a systematic gathering and evaluation of information pertaining to an individual with suspected abnormal behaviour. This assessment can be carried out with a wide variety of techniques to appraise social, psychological, and/or biological factors.

A diagnosis is only as good as the assessment on which it is based; and the assessment, in turn, is only as good as the tools used to carry it out. Therefore, good diagnosis hinges on the development of accurate assessment tools. Think of your car, for example. If the gas gauge is faulty, you can't easily tell when you come to a sudden grinding halt whether your engine is shot or you're simply out of gas.

Although assessments are usually thought of in relation to diagnosis, they may also have other specific purposes. An IQ test may be used to guide school placement, a neuropsychological test to assess the natural progression of a disorder, or a symptom checklist to gauge the success of treatment.

A good assessment tool depends on two things: an accurate ability to measure some aspect of the person being assessed, and a knowledge of how people in general fare on such a measure, for the purposes of comparison. Because this knowledge is derived from research, we turn our attention in the second half of this chapter to research methods. You will also notice that assessment and research often use similar methods—sometimes even the same tools—and must deal with similar issues of reliability and validity.

Assessment Tools: Striving for the Whole Picture

A diagnostician trying to understand someone is attempting to piece together a puzzle. The patient may be able to present a partial description of issues related to the suspected psychological abnormality, from his or her unique perspective. This report gives one piece of the puzzle; but the clinician needs a more objective perspective. Glimpses of the past, revealing the patient's behaviour and experiences at various ages and in various settings will provide a few more pieces, but the puzzle remains incomplete. Missing at this point from the overall picture are accounts of the patient's emotional, cognitive, and physiological states. Sometimes patients cannot report on their own internal states, even when they can accurately describe their observable behaviour. Fortunately, many psychological methods are available to fill in many of the missing pieces. The most useful understanding of a patient draws on a combination of procedures that shed light on a range of different aspects of an individual's functioning.

Reliability and Validity

Of course, to be useful, any test must be both reliable and valid, as discussed in Chapter 3. Several types of reliability are particularly important for psychological tests.

Test-retest reliability refers to the degree to which a test yields the same results when it is given more than once to the same person. If your score on an IQ test is dramatically different from one day to the next, the test does not give much of a measure of intelligence. Test-retest reliability can be evaluated by correlating a person's score on a given test with the same person's score on the same test taken at a later time. The higher the correlation between the two scores (as expressed in terms of a correlation coefficient) the greater the reliability. One obvious problem is that one may improve on a test the second time around because of practice with the procedures or familiarity with the questions. To circumvent this problem, behavioural scientists often attempt to ascertain a test's **alternate-form reliability**. To do this, the test designers prepare two forms of the same test—that is, they decide what construct they want their test to measure, think up questions (or items) that would test that construct, and then word those questions in a slightly different way in order to create a second test that measures the same construct as the first. A high correlation between scores on the first and second test demonstrates alternate-form reliability.

Internal consistency refers to the degree of reliability *within* a test. That is, to what extent do different parts of the same test yield the same results? One measure of internal consistency is **split-half reliability**, which is often evaluated by comparing responses on odd-numbered test items with responses on even-numbered test items. If the scores for these responses are highly correlated, then the test has high split-half reliability. Another method for evaluating internal consistency, **coefficient alpha**, is calculated by averaging the intercorrelations of all the items on a given test. The higher the coefficient alpha, the higher the internal consistency of the test.

Clearly an unreliable measure is useless. However, as discussed in Chapter 3, a reliable measure may be of little value if it is not *valid*. As we shall see later in the chapter, there are several measures of intelligence that have excellent reliability quotients. However, their usefulness is still hotly debated. What exactly is it they are measuring? How well do they predict future functioning? In addition to concurrent validity and predictive validity, discussed in Chapter 3, there are several other types of validities related to psychological tests.

Face validity means that the items on a test resemble the characteristics associated with the concept being tested for. For example, suppose a test of assertiveness asks questions like "How do you react when you are overcharged in a store? When someone cuts in front of you in a lineup?" Because such behaviours relate to the general concept of assertiveness, the test would have face validity.

Content validity goes one step further and requires that a test's content include a representative sample of behaviours thought to be related to the construct (that is, the concept or entity) that the test is designed to measure. For example, the construct of depression includes features such as lack of energy and participation, sadness, and unfavourable self-perception. To have content validity, an instrument designed to assess depression should address such features. A test that focussed only on sadness without considering other features would not have good content validity. However, experience has shown that content and face validity, while they may be relevant early in the development of a test, are not enough, because the human mind is not simple enough to test in such obvious ways.

The concept of **criterion validity** arises because some qualities are easier to recognize than to define completely. Suppose you wanted to know whether a calculator was working properly; one way to test it would be to work out a problem to which you already know the answer: say "6 times 5." If the calculator gives an answer of 368, you know it is not a valid instrument. Now suppose you wanted to develop a test for artistic ability. You design an instrument that asks many questions about creative behaviour and activities. You then give the test to a large group of well-known and highly regarded artists and to a control group of people not identified as artistic. If the artists' test scores are much higher than the non-artists, your test has good criterion validity. Note that this large survey is not an assessment of the people involved:

you start with the assumption that the artists are artistic. It is the instrument that is being tested.

Construct validity refers to the importance of a test within a specific theoretical framework and can only be understood in the context of that framework. This type of validity is especially useful when the construct to be measured is rather abstract. As an example, self-esteem is considered important for success in many endeavours. In order to evaluate how well a measure assesses self-esteem, we would look to a theory for a prediction and see whether the measure correlates well with that prediction. Developmental psychologists suggest that children who are shown a great deal of emotional support and unconditional positive regard should develop more self-esteem than those who are not supported or who are raised in abusive homes. One might compare the scores on the measure of self-esteem in two groups of teenagers, one from intact and nurturing families and the other from homes where there has been documented neglect or abuse. One would judge the construct validity of the self-esteem measure by how closely it was related to the backgrounds of these teenagers.

Clinical vs. Actuarial Prediction

How can one best take all the information available about a patient and put it together? How does one evaluate and interpret a collection of data—interviews, case histories, responses to tests—to describe the patient, make predictions, and come to decisions? These broad questions have been hotly debated for years within the mental health professions. Two very different approaches have been developed. People who endorse the **clinical approach** argue that there is no substitute for the clinician's experience and personal judgement. They prefer to draw on all the available data in their own manner; they are guided by intuition honed with professional experience rather than by formal rules. Those who endorse the **actuarial approach** argue that a more objective standard is needed—something more unbiased and scientifically validated. They rely exclusively on statistical procedures, empirical methods, and formal rules in evaluating the data.

Which method is superior? It has been suggested that the actuarial approach tends to be much more efficient in terms of making predictions in a variety of situations, especially when many predictions must be made and the base of data is large (Meehl, 1959, 1962). In Canada, Dr. Vernon Quinsey (Queen's University) and Dr. Marnie Rice and Grant Harris (the Mental Health Centre in Penetanguishene, and McMaster University) have put clinical and actuarial prediction to the test with sexual offenders. Their question was: Which approach will give a more accurate prediction of which offenders will repeat their crimes? They found that, with this population at least, judgements based on a personal, clinical interpretation of patient information were rather poor predictors of future violence. They point to several factors: (1) low inter-clinician agreement about the dangerousness of particular individuals; (2) disagreement among clinicians about the dangerousness of populations of offenders, as reflected by their estimates of the base rate or proportion of dangerous persons in a population;

(3) overreliance on certain striking information—a history of institutional violence, a diagnosis of schizophrenia, or severity of injury to victims—that actually has little or no relation to the risk that the person will repeat the offence (Quinsey, 1979; Quinsey & Ambtman, 1979; Quinsey & Cyr, 1986; Quinsey & Maguire, 1986; Quinsey, Maguire, & Varney, 1981; Rice, Harris, Lang, & Bell, 1990). Similar factors presumably influence decision-making with other clinical populations. More recently, these researches have developed actuarial procedures that are useful predictors with violent populations (Webster, Harris, Rice, Cormier, & Quinsey, 1994).

BIOLOGICAL ASSESSMENT

In trying to determine the cause of abnormal behaviour, it is important to be aware of any medical conditions that may be causing, or contributing to such behaviour. For example, it has been well established that one form of psychosis may be caused by syphilis (see Chapter 1), which is readily diagnosed with a simple blood test. We also know that disruptions in the functioning of the thyroid may mimic anxiety and depression in previously psychologically stable individuals. When medication stabilizes the thyroid functions, their psychological symptoms abate. Many other medical conditions can also affect behaviour. Therefore, it is important that a general physical examination be conducted as part of an assessment for psychological disorders.

Brain Imaging Techniques

The central nervous system has been the focus of considerable research in the attempt to understand the causes of psychopathology. One of the oldest and most well established techniques is the electroencephalogram (EEG). The EEG uses electrodes placed on various parts of the scalp to measure the brain's electrical activity. These electrical impulses are carried through to special electronic equipment that is able to amplify and record the activity in many parts of the brain. On occasion patients may be asked to carry out a variety of visual or auditory tasks to see how various brain parts respond. Since we know so much about normal brain patterns, deviations in a particular part of the brain might be considered an indication of a problem for further investigation. It has been established that many seizure disorders, brain lesions, and tumours can be detected through EEG examinations.

Neuroimaging techniques can provide both structural and functional information concerning the physiological health of the central nervous system. Prior to the 1970s, brain imaging was done through radiography; it could identify problems with the cerebral vasculature, but could not identify differences in tissue density.

The CAT Scan

At the beginning of the 1970s, rapid developments in computer technology made possible a revolutionary brain imaging technique known as **computerized axial tomography (CAT)**. In

Several years ago a physician referred a seven-year-old boy to me. Michael's mother, a registered nurse, told me he had experienced eight short, unpredictable seizures over a period of three months. The mother and father were very frightened and upset, but Michael remarked he could not remember having the seizures. The seizures had occurred only when his mother was around. On one occasion Michael had a seizure while in the car with his mother, only ten minutes from a hospital. By the time they reached the hospital Michael was fine and there was no medical evidence of any seizure activity. Michael had been given a full medical and neurological examination and declared perfectly healthy. The referring physician suspected Michael might have been faking or holding his breath until he passed out, in order to get attention or sympathy from his parents. I spent several sessions with the family together and with each of them alone. Once, while the parents were in my office at the hospital, Michael fell and had what appeared to be a very short seizure while in the Neurology waiting area. This was the first time someone other than his mother had been present. Once again there were no medical signs. In my opinion, Michael and his parents were a happy, well-adjusted family with no emotional problems, so, although I had identified no cause for the seizures, I stopped seeing the family. About six months later, in the hospital, I saw Michael in a wheelchair being pushed by his mother. A few weeks after I stopped seeing them, Michael had deteriorated rapidly. He started having many more seizures. It was only at that point that physicians were able to diagnose a very rare and progressive brain disorder that would lead to death within a year. The disorder was not diagnosable in its early stages, with the technology available at that time.

This was not the only case I have seen—though it was certainly the most dramatic—in which what appeared to be a psychological disorder was the first sign of some medical problem.

this procedure a narrow band of X-rays is projected through the head and onto scintillation crystals, which are much more sensitive than X-ray film. The X-ray source and detector then rotate very slightly and project another image; to complete the *scan*, the source will rotate a total of 180 degrees, producing a number of images at predetermined angles. Each separate exposure produces a matrix of dark and light areas, which are later combined by a computer to produce a highly detailed *tomograph*—a two-dimensional image or cross-section of the brain. The resolution of this image can be further improved by injecting an iodinitic radiopaque substance to enhance the contrast between different sorts of tissue. The resolutional capability of a CAT scan is in the range of about 1 millimetre in soft tissue and can resolve structures such as cerebral vasculature, ventricles, grey and white matter, and

some subcortical structures such as the thalamus and basal ganglia. This provides a wealth of information about an individual living brain.

CAT scans have confirmed a number of ideas about how the brain works in abnormal psychology. For example, scientists have long suspected that schizophrenia and degenerative neurological disorders such as Alzheimer's disease involve cortical atrophy—that is, the number of brain cells or the size of individual cells shrinks. CAT scans have shown they were right (Gewirtz, Squires, Sharif, & Honer, 1994). Schizophrenics have smaller frontal lobes than normal controls (Andreasen, 1989; Andreasen, Hoffman, & Grove, 1985). Moreover, autistic children evidence atrophy in the cerebellum, and people suffering from bipolar disorder show some tissue loss throughout the brain (Andreasen & Black, 1991).

Magnetic Resonance Imaging

Nuclear magnetic resonance imaging, or simply **magnetic resonance imaging (MRI)**, is a noninvasive technique, developed in the early 1980s, that reveals both the structure and the functioning of the brain. A strong homogeneous magnetic field is produced around the patient's head. This field causes atoms with odd atomic weights (especially hydrogen) to align their electrons parallel to the direction of the field. Brief pulses of radio waves are subsequently introduced, causing these electrons to move in a characteristic gyroscopic manner. When the radio waves are turned off, the electrons return to their original configuration and in doing so emit radio waves of their own at a characteristic frequency, which can then be detected outside a patient's head. By adding a small magnetic gradient to the field, the frequency of radio wave transmission by atoms within the brain is altered to correlate with the gradient, allowing scientists to determine the location of the radio source. The information gathered is then integrated into a computer-generated image of the brain (see Figure 4.1). MRI techniques are capable of discriminating extremely small differences in water concentration. MRI is also a safe technology: because it uses neither high-energy radiation (X-rays) nor injections, it avoids the risks of overexposure and neurological complications.

Positron Emission Tomography (PET)

Positron emission tomography (PET) is a combination of computerized tomography and radioisotope imaging. As in MRI, radiation is detected outside the head. In the case of PET, the radiation is generated by injected or inhaled *radioisotopes*—that is, common elements or substances with the atom altered to be radioactive. Isotopes with half-lives of minutes to hours are required for a PET scan. As the substance is used in brain activity, radiation is given off and detected by the PET equipment. This process allows the scientist to measure a variety of biological activities as the processes occur in the living brain. Recall from Chapter 2 the importance of neurotransmitters in brain activity. Providing a radioactive version of a *ligand*—a common molecule present in the chemical bonding that characterizes neurotransmission—allows the PET scan to show the distribution of various neurotransmitters

Figure 4.1   An Image of the Brain Produced Through Magnetic Resonance Imaging

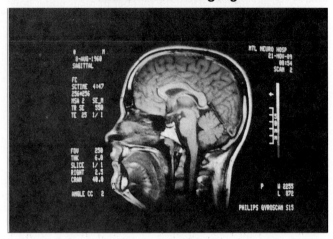

Figure 4.2a   PET Scan Images of a Normal Brain

Figure 4.2b   PET Scan Images of a Schizophrenic Brain

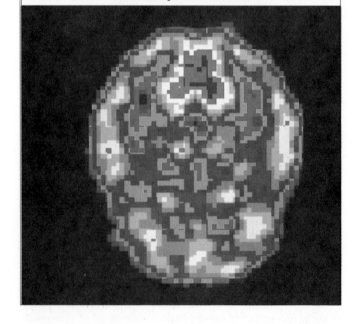

within the brain. Similarly, glucose with a radioactive "label" (so called because it makes the glucose show up for the equipment) allows the rate of metabolic activity to be measured. Thus while CAT scans and MRIs can produce a static image of the brain's anatomy, a PET scan produces a dynamic image of the functioning brain (see Figures 4.2a and b).

Clinicians often use CAT or MRI in addition to PET scans to determine the cause of structural abnormalities, such as reduced blood flow. PET scans have confirmed that there are abnormal patterns of metabolic activity in people with seizures, tumours, stroke, Alzheimer's disease, schizophrenia, bipolar disorder, and obsessive-compulsive disorder; they also show atypical patterns of cortical blood flow as they perform cognitive tasks (Fischbach, 1992).

Neuropsychological Testing

Neuropsychological assessments are used to determine relationships between behaviour and brain function. The **Bender Visual-Motor Gestalt Test** (Bender, 1938) is the oldest and most commonly used of these tests. It is easily administered and is often used to screen children for neuropsychological impairment. The test consists of a series of nine cards containing lines and shapes drawn in black on a piece of white cardboard (see Figure 4.3). Children are asked first to copy the images on another card and then to draw them from memory. Errors in reproducing these lines and shapes may indicate neurological problems, but may also be caused by a tremor in the hand or simple nervousness. But certain *types* of errors are characteristic of neurological impairment: rotation of figures, perseveration (continuing to copy a line past the scale of the original pattern), fragmentation, oversimplification, inability to copy angles, and reversals (Goldstein, 1990; Lezak, 1976).

The main problem with this test is that it produces many false negatives: that is, some people with neurological impairment can complete the test with few errors. Moreover, many normal younger children will make more errors than

older children with brain damage as a result of developmental differences. The Bender is age-normed to help compensate for this shortcoming; that is, results are compared to the results expected for a child of that age. While some clinicians prefer to interpret this test subjectively, others use a

Figure 4.3 The Bender Visual-Motor Gestalt Test

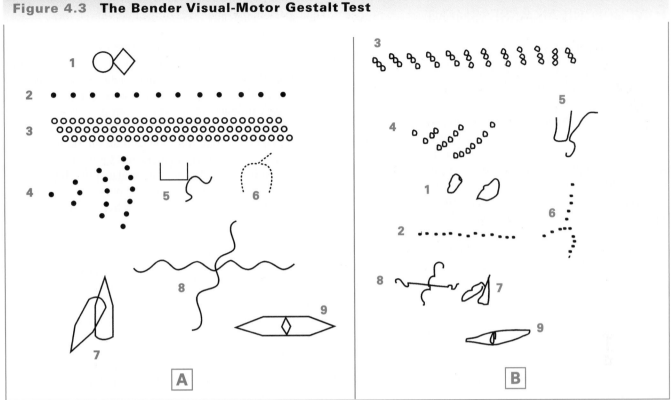

Note: Part A shows the nine images that children are asked to reproduce. Part B shows the drawings of a person known to have brain damage.
Source: Lacks, *The Bender-Gestalt Test*, p. 34. Copyright © 1984 by John Wiley & Sons. Reprinted by permission of John Wiley & Sons, Inc.

standardized scoring system. The test-retest reliability coefficient is 0.7 with the scoring system, and clinicians can discriminate between normal subjects and those with neurological impairment approximately 75 percent of the time (Heaton, Baade, & Johnson, 1978; Pascal & Suttell, 1951).

Newer tests are available. Neuropsychological assessments now usually employ a battery of tests to identify not only the presence of cognitive and motor impairment but also the nature and area of neurological impairment (Goldstein, 1990). By examining the pattern of results and deficits in performance, it is possible to discriminate between various forms of organic damage (Boll, 1985). The most popular neuropsychological battery is the Halstead-Reitan (Reitan & Davison, 1974); the Luria-Nebraska is also widely used. The former was developed by psychologist Ralph Reitan, who adapted tests created by his mentor, Ward Halstead, an experimental psychologist who studies patients with organic brain damage. The Halstead-Reitan consists of the following six subtests, with five more optional tests available:

1. *Category test.* This test measures abstract thinking. The subject is called on to determine the principles that relate images varying in shape, size, location, colour, and other characteristics. Several images are shown on a screen, and the subject is asked to choose, by pressing a button, which ones represent the given category. (A variation of this type of test appears in educational picture books and children's television, as in the familiar jingle "One of these things is not like the others.") Performance on this test is believed to reflect frontal lobe functioning.

2. *Rhythm test.* In this test of concentration and attention, the subject listens to 30 pairs of tape-recorded rhythmic beats, and is asked to identify which pairs are the same and which are different. Performance on this test is associated with right temporal lobe functioning.

3. *Tactual performance test.* The subject is required to fit blocks of various shapes into their corresponding spaces on a board while blindfolded. He or she later draws the board from memory in order to test visual memory.

4. *Tapping test.* The subject taps rapidly on a lever.

5. *Grip strength test.* The subject grasps a dynamometer, which measures grip strength; this test can help identify the location of brain damage.

6. *Auditory test.* The subject is asked to identify aurally transmitted nonsense words.

The tests described above are meant for adults; versions are also available for children aged five and older as well (Nussbaum & Bigler, 1989). The Halstead-Reitan is quite time-consuming, requiring six hours or more to administer, and some time to score as well.

PSYCHOLOGICAL ASSESSMENT

Clinical Interviews

Interviews occur in every realm of life. Chances are you were interviewed before you were admitted to your university program. You've probably done job interviews already, and will do more as you enter your career. Mental health professionals, too, use the interview. The clinical interview is the oldest and the most common assessment tool, used by almost every clinician. It is generally accepted as a useful and comfortable way to gather information from an individual. Practitioners ask about many aspects of the individual's life: medical history, age, marital status, family, education, and lifestyle, as well as the reason the person is seeking consultation.

Not all interviews are the same. Different types of interviews are often used to provide different kinds of information.

The Unstructured Interview

As the name implies, *unstructured interviews* tend to be open-ended affairs that allow interviewers to concentrate on a person's unique style or on certain aspects of the presenting problem. Having no script, the interviewer can pursue a line of questioning to see where it leads. One advantage of the free-flowing interview is that the clinician can follow the patient's lead. Patients are often under considerable stress, and are being asked to reveal very private, personal, and sometimes embarrassing information, which they may find difficult or impossible to discuss with a stranger. In an unstructured interview, it is relatively easy to avoid a sensitive topic until a patient is more at ease.

Although all interviews depend partly on the training, insight, personality, and skills of the interviewer, these factors are essential in the unstructured interview. The major criticism of this type of interview is its poor reliability and validity. The clinician's own theoretical paradigm greatly influences the type of information sought. A psychodynamically oriented interviewer is more likely to ask individuals about their childhood, memories of their parents, sexual history, and dream content. A clinician working from a behavioural perspective may well concentrate on the immediate circumstances surrounding an individual's presenting problem and the contingencies reinforcing maladaptive behaviours. Thus clinicians may tend to uncover only information that fits their paradigm and confirms their hypotheses.

The Semistructured Interview

To avoid the pitfalls of unstructured approaches, *semistructured interviews* have been developed. As in the unstructured interview, the clinician has considerable leeway about what questions to ask, in what order, and with what wording. The questions are guided, however, by an outline that lists certain dimensions of the patient's functioning that need to be covered. The most frequently used semistructured interview in psychiatric settings is the **mental status examination** (see Table 4.1), which screens for patients' emotional, intellectual, and neurological functioning. It is used in formal diagnosis or to plan treatment. The semistructured interview, too, faces problems of reliability and validity.

The Structured Interview

How can an interview get away from the subjectivity of the interviewer and become a reliable procedure? A number of

---

Table 4.1 Dimensions Assessed by the Mental Status Examination

1. *Appearance.* Is the patient clean and well groomed?
2. *Behaviour.* Are there any peculiar aspects to the patient's behaviour, such as atypical speech patterns (speed or cadence), odd mannerisms or tics, strange posture or gait?
3. *Sensorium* (sensory apparatus). Do the five senses appear to be intact?
4. *Affect* (expressed emotional responses). Has the patient expressed anger, anxiety, or any other general state during the interview? Has the patient's affect been inappropriate to the topic (for example, laughing or smiling when sad things were being discussed)?
5. *Orientation.* Is the patient aware of who he or she is, where he or she is, the time, date, and year?
6. *Thought content.* Does the patient describe hearing or seeing things whose existence is questionable? Does the patient seem to have delusions of persecution, grandeur, or the like?
7. *Memory.* How intact is the patient's memory for long-past events and recent events?
8. *Intelligence.* How sophisticated is the patient's vocabulary? How well does the patient express thoughts and ideas, use and understand abstractions and metaphors? Is the patient able to express and understand sophisticated concepts?
9. *Thought processes.* Is thought logical and coherent, or is there evidence of a loosening of associations, apparently unconnected ideas that are joined together?
10. *Insight.* Is the patient aware of his or her situation, and able to appreciate its severity and the necessity for clinical assistance?
11. *Judgement.* Has the patient shown ability to make sound and well-thought-out decisions, in the past and presently?

structured interviews have been developed that are very specific in the order and wording of questions and the rules governing the evaluation of responses. Many of these are designed to look for specific problems, such as behaviour problems of childhood (Edelbrock & Costello, 1984), anxiety disorders (DiNardo, O'Brien, Barlow, Waddell, & Blanchard, 1988), and personality disorders (Widiger & Frances, 1985). Perhaps the most interesting structured interviews are those originally developed for several large epidemiological investigations in the United States in the late 1960s and 1970s. They have been refined over time and now follow the same principle as the decision trees for differential diagnoses found originally in DSM-III and now in DSM-IV. The Structured Clinical Interview for DSM-III-R (SCID) (Spitzer, Williams, Gibbons, & First, 1985) follows the same branching "decision tree" approach (see Figure 4.4). At each point the interviewer is instructed to ask a specific question. Patient responses are rated, and the interviewer is instructed to carry on with another set of questions depending on the patient's response. A "yes" response from the patient leads to a very different set of questions from a "no" response. SCID is the most widely used structured clinical interview. It is available both as a booklet and as DTREE software, a computerized structured interview (First, Williams, & Spitzer, 1996).

Assessment of Intelligence

Intelligence tests were the first assessment tools developed by psychologists to win widespread acceptance; by now, virtually everyone in our society has heard of them. The first scientific study of intellectual functioning was conducted by the biologist Sir Francis Galton (1822–1911) in 1883, to test the hypothesis that intelligence has a hereditary aspect, a concept still being explored. Galton believed that pure intelligence could best be measured by studying physiological cues—for example, the speed of response to a flash of light—an attribute later known as *sensory intelligence*. This was the first attempt to demonstrate the biological correlates of intelligence.

The first widely accepted and successful test of intelligence was designed to predict academic performance. The French psychologist Alfred Binet (1857–1911) was commissioned by the Parisian school board to develop a means of determining which children should receive a public school education and which required special education. He did so by developing separate tests of judgement, comprehension, and reasoning. He was the first to use a large sample of subjects to establish norms for the purpose of describing intelligence. Binet's approach was to take a child's mental age, which was determined by the child's successful performance on age-grouped tests that had been normed, divide it by the child's chronological age, and multiply the quotient by 100. This would result in an **intelligence quotient**, or **IQ**. Theoretically, at least, an individual's IQ was always a reflection of that person's performance compared with the population of others of the same age. Therefore, a person aged 14.8 years who received a mental age score of 15.6 would achieve an IQ of $(15.6/14.8)(100) = 105$. Binet's work developed into the **Stanford-Binet Scales**, which have been revised over the years and are now in their fourth edition. The most recent Stanford-Binet assesses four general kinds of ability: verbal reasoning, quantitative reasoning, abstract/visual reasoning, and short-term memory. It produces separate scores for each of these functions as well as a global IQ score that summarizes the child's ability.

Virtually all contemporary standardized tests of intelligence, as well as other types of psychological tests, share Binet's basic principle of comparison. A person's IQ is a function of how his or her score compares to others of the same age. Convention has dictated that the average be set at 100; those who perform more poorly have lower IQs; those who perform better have higher IQs. (See Chapter 1.)

The most widely used IQ tests were developed by David Wechsler (1896–1981). In 1939 he published the first widely used intelligence tests for adults. The most recent version of the **Wechsler Adult Intelligence Scale**, or WAIS, was published in 1974 and is called the **WAIS-R**. This test was designed to measure diverse aspects of intelligence and consists of 11 subscales: 6 verbal tests (general information, abstract thinking, short-term memory, arithmetic ability, the capacity to recognize and act on well-learned societal rules and expectations, and vocabulary), and 5 performance tests (puzzles, reproduction of designs, manipulation of objects, symbols, and numbers). Figure 4.5 shows two of these performance tests. Average intelligence on this scale is an IQ of 100, with scores below 70 indicating mental retardation, and scores above 130 indicating exceptional intelligence. In 1974 the Wechsler Intelligence Test for Children (WISC) was published. The latest version is the WISC-III, published in 1991. The Wechsler Preschool and Primary Scale of Intelligence (WPPSI) was published in 1967. These Wechsler scales are the epitome of well-designed and -researched assessment tools. They have very good test-retest and split-half reliability and concurrent validity, and readily distinguish between intellectually gifted, learning-disabled, and mentally retarded individuals (Thorndike, Hagen, & Sattler, 1986).

Of all psychological traits, IQ shows the most stability. As demonstrated in Table 4.2, the correlation diminishes with time; but a correlation of 0.78 from 8 to 15 years of age is quite remarkable. It should be noted, however, that more than half of all children show a variation of 10 points or more between early school years and adolescence. Some children have shown as much as a 40-point change within the same time period (Bukatko & Daehler, 1992).

But what does IQ really predict? The typical correlation between IQ scores and academic performance is in the range of 0.50 to 0.70, depending on the IQ tests being studied, the age of the individuals assessed, and how academic performance is measured (Brody, 1992). A strong correlation would be expected, because many of the same skills are required for intelligence tests and for academic success: skills such as verbal ability, rote memory, and reasoning. In fact, one might wonder why the correlation is not even stronger. The

Figure 4.4   Sample Item for SCID

Interview	Rating Scale				Obsessive-Compulsive Disorder Criteria

Obsessions

I would like to ask you if you have ever been bothered by thoughts that kept coming back to you even when you tried not to have them.	?	1	2	3	1. Recurrent, persistent ideas, thoughts, impulses, or images that are experienced as intrusive, unwanted, and senseless or repugnant (at least initially).
If YES: Distinguish from brooding about problems (such as having a panic attack) or anxious about realistic dangers:	?	1	2	3	
What were they?					2. The individual attempts to ignore or suppress them or to neutralize them with some other thought or action.
(What about awful thoughts, or thoughts that didn't make any sense to you—like actually hurting someone even though you didn't want to, or being contaminated by germs or dirt?)	?	1	2	3	3. The individual recognizes that they are the product of his or her own mind and not imposed from without (as in thought insertion).

Go to Compulsions	Describe Obsessions

Compulsions

Was there anything that you had to do over and over again and couldn't resist doing, like washing your hands again and again, or checking something several times to make sure you'd done it right?	?	1	2	3	1. Repetitive, purposeful, and intentional behaviour that is performed according to certain rules or in a stereotyped fashion.
If YES: What did you have to do?	?	1	2	3	2. The behaviour is not an end in itself, but is designed to neutralize or prevent extreme discomfort or some dreaded event or situation. However, either the activity is not connected in a realistic way with what it is designed to neutralize or prevent or it is clearly excessive.
(What were you afraid would happen if you didn't do it?) (How many times did you have to ____? How much time did you spend each day ____?)					

Go to Generalized Anxiety Disorders Section	Describe Compulsions

Key to Rating Scale

? = Inadequate information
1 = Absent or false
2 = Subthreshold
3 = Threshold or true

Source: APA.

explanation seems to be that academic performance is also critically influenced by such factors as family, personality, and community. Some research has demonstrated a weak correlation (correlation coefficients of 0.20 to 0.30) with job trainability and performance. However, there is no evidence that IQ is significantly related to other measures of success in life such as income earned, physical or mental health, or general life satisfaction (Bukatko & Daehler, 1992).

The use of IQ tests has become quite controversial. Do they really measure innate capacities or do they simply

Figure 4.5 **Items Similar to Those on the Performance Subtests of the Wechsler Intelligence Scale**

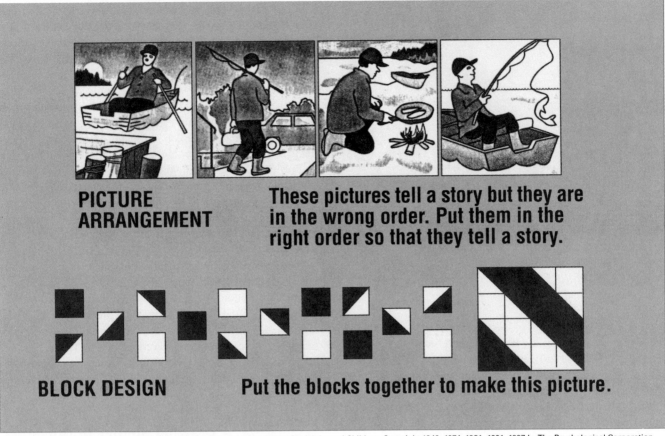

PICTURE ARRANGEMENT

These pictures tell a story but they are in the wrong order. Put them in the right order so that they tell a story.

BLOCK DESIGN

Put the blocks together to make this picture.

measure achievement? The issue of fairness is perhaps the most sensitive. Critics have argued that the IQ differences that have been found in North America between whites, blacks, and people of Asian background are actually a function of poor test construction; others argue that these differences are a function of subjects' socioeconomic environments. See Chapter 3 for a discussion of cultural bias.

Table 4.2 **Correlations of Intelligence from 3 to 15 Years of Age**

Age	3	4	5	6	7	8	9	15
2	.74	.68	.63	.61	.54	.58	.56	.47
3		.76	.72	.73	.68	.67	.65	.58
4			.80	.79	.72	.72	.71	.60
5				.87	.81	.79	.79	.67
6					.86	.84	.84	.69
7						.87	.87	.69
8							.90	.78
9								.80
15								

Source: Adapted from N. Brody, *Intelligence* (New York: Academic Press, 1992), p. 232.

Personality Assessment

The early success of intelligence tests in predicting academic performance stimulated research and study of the measure of personality. While intelligence tests tend to produce total scores, personality assessments usually describe various characteristics that make up an individual's unique personality. A wealth of tests, questionnaires, and rating scales are available that offer shortcuts to understanding an individual and to predicting behaviour. These formal personality tests, and other assessment methods, are widely used for a variety of tasks including research, personnel selection, and diagnosis in clinical settings.

Projective Tests

Projective tests have the longest history in modern personality assessment, and generally have their roots in psychoanalytic principles, although some cognitive-behavioural models use a similar methodology. The theory behind a **projective test** is that a person presented with an ambiguous stimulus will project onto that stimulus his or her unconscious motives, needs, drives, feelings, defences, and personality characteristics. Thus the test reveals information that the person cannot or will not report directly. Projective tests are used to help clinicians form hypotheses about an individual's personality.

Figure 4.6   Inkblots Like Those on the Rorschach Test

Rorschach inkblot test.   The oldest and probably the best known projective test is the **Rorschach inkblot test**. Hermann Rorschach (1884–1922), a Swiss psychologist, was intrigued as a child by the game of dripping ink on paper and folding the paper to make symmetrical figures. He noticed that people saw different things in the same blot, and he believed that their "percepts" reflected their personality. In high school his friends gave him the nickname "Klecks," meaning "inkblot" in German. As a professional, he continued experimenting with hundreds of blots to identify those that could help in the diagnosis of psychological problems. The year following the publication of these blots, at the age of 38, he died of complications from a ruptured appendix. Figure 4.6 shows inkblots like those on the Rorschach test. Each blot is presented on a separate card and is handed to the subject in a particular sequence. Initially, most clinicians used their own very clinical approach in interpreting the results of a Rorschach examination. They would generally use the content of a patient's responses to the inkblots (for example, I see two people fighting), as well as the use of colour, shading, texture, and movement in the interpretation of results. The **Exner system** developed in an attempt to increase reliability and validity by standardizing the scoring of responses (Exner, 1993). Evidence suggests the Exner system may have greater clinical validity for testing schizophrenia than depression or personality disorders (Vincent & Harman, 1991). Although still very controversial, the Rorschach is in wide use and its proponents provide evidence of adequate reliability and validity, as judged by reviews of research conducted between 1971 and 1980 (Exner, 1986; Exner, 1993; Parker, Hanson, & Hinsley, 1988).

Thematic apperception test (TAT).   The **thematic apperception test (TAT)** was developed by psychologists Henry Murray (1893–1988) and Christiana Morgan at Harvard University. *Apperception* is a French word that can be translated as "interpreting (new ideas or impressions) on the basis of existing ideas (cognitive structures and past experience)." The TAT consists of drawings on cards depicting ambiguous social interactions. (See Figure 4.7.) Individuals are asked to construct stories about the cards. It is assumed their tales reflect their experiences and outlook on life and may also shed light on deep-seated needs and conflicts. Respondents are asked what they believe is happening in the scenes, what led up to these actions, what thoughts and feelings the character is experiencing, what happens next, and so on. Psychodynamically oriented clinicians assume that respondents identify with the protagonist or victims in their stories, and project their psychological needs and conflicts into the events they apperceive. On a more superficial level, the stories also suggest how respondents might interpret or behave in similar situations in their own lives. Validity and reliability of scoring techniques are open to the same criticisms as the Rorschach inkblot test.

In general, advocates of projective tests argue that they may yield meaningful material not easily obtained by self-report questionnaires or interviews. Because people want to be judged favourably, many people will give socially desirable responses to questionnaires; that is, consciously or unconsciously, they try to answer according to what they think they ought to be rather than what they are. Projective tests avoid this problem by presenting an ambiguous picture, and by not

Figure 4.7   A Drawing Similar to Those on the Thematic Apperception Test

asking directly about the subject. Because they allow freedom of expression, they may also shed light on areas that a questionnaire might not cover. However, research has not been very supportive of the reliability and validity of many of the projective techniques (Acklin, McDowell, & Orndoff, 1992; Bornstein, Rossner, & Hill, 1994; Burstein, 1989). Rather, it appears that clinicians tend to interpret responses in a way that confirms their own clinical assumptions, without empirical validation of their accuracy. It appears the degree of comfort professionals have with projective methods depends more on their acceptance of the underlying theories than on the reliability and validity of the techniques.

Personality Inventories

More recently there has been a movement to find ways to assess personality that are objective and scientifically valid. A range of instruments have been developed that use scientifically accepted procedures such as standardization, establishment of norms, clinical and control groups, and statistically validated methods of interpretation.

Minnesota Multiphasic Personality Inventory (MMPI). The most widely used objective test of personality is probably the **Minnesota Multiphasic Personality Inventory**, or **MMPI**. It was originally published in 1943 by Hathaway & McKinley. The revised and updated version, the MMPI-2, was published in 1989 by Butcher, Dahlstrom, Graham, Tellegen, and Kraemer. It is "multiphasic" because it assesses many aspects of personality. The MMPI contains 567 questions grouped to form ten content scales plus additional scales to detect sources of invalidity such as carelessness, defensiveness, or evasiveness (see Table 4.3). Each item is a statement; the respondent is asked to check "True," "False," or "Cannot Say." Many items appear to have little face validity, meaning it is difficult to ascertain what the question appears to measure.

To establish the categories and items, the creators of the test compared the responses of a large number of patients with well-diagnosed disorders like depression, anxiety, antisocial disorders, paranoia, schizophrenia, and mania to each other and to the responses of normal, nondiagnosed individuals. The MMPI is based on the *contrasted-groups* method of ascertaining validity: items were chosen only if people known to have the characteristic the scale is intended to measure responded differently to the item than did people who did not have that characteristic. For example, a question would appear on the depression scale only if there is a clear difference between the responses of a group of depressed people and a group of people who are not depressed. This technique establishes concurrent validity, with group membership as the criterion by which the validity of the test is gauged.

As is common with the new breed of actuarially based personality assessments, raw scores are converted into standard scores with a mean of 50 and a standard deviation (a measure of how far from the mean an average score will fall) of 10. An individual's personality profile is depicted as elevation on a graph, which facilitates interpretation. Results of

an MMPI-2 assessment are not a diagnosis, but a profile of personality characteristics compared to normal and pathological groups that may *assist* in forming a diagnosis. As an example, a standard score of 65 or higher on a particular scale places an individual at approximately the 92nd percentile or higher of the revised normative sample, and is considered to be clinically significant. The higher a score, the more likely the presence of a disorder. Although a single scale may be informative, MMPI experts typically interpret the pattern of relative scores from the entire profile. The relative elevations of different scales present a complex picture of a personality. However, in the hands of a trained clinician this profile can provide considerable insight into the functioning of an individual. The Focus box gives an example of how an individual's scores can be analyzed.

Many items on objective tests like the MMPI are obvious testimony of disturbed thoughts and feelings. The transparency of these items makes them fertile ground for faking. MMPI validity scales include the L (lie) scale, the F (infrequency) scale, and the K (defensive) scale, among others. The L scale contains items that refer to minor foibles or flaws in character that nearly all of us possess and admit to readily. People who disavow these foibles may also deny items with more serious clinical implications. The lie scale identifies individuals who are trying to fake good scores. The F scale contains items that were endorsed by fewer than 10 percent of the normal sample. A high F score may suggest random or careless responding, difficulty in reading or comprehending the test items, or an effort to "fake bad" to exaggerate complaints. An irony that clouds interpretation of the MMPI is that abnormal validity scale scores do not necessarily invalidate the test for highly disturbed respondents such as schizophrenics. The K scale measures a more subtle form of distortion, called psychological defensiveness or guardedness—respondents' tendency to conceal genuine feelings about sensitive issues in order to create a favourable impression. The K scale is used as a correction factor; scores on clinical scales that may be biased by defensive tendencies are augmented (corrected) by a fraction of the K scale score.

A concern about the original edition of the test (MMPI) was the narrowness of the group of normal subjects on whom it was standardized. All were white, and most were young married people living in small towns or rural areas near Minneapolis. With the revision (MMPI-II), the test was standardized on a much more representative sample based on census information (Graham, 1990) and modernized in other ways as well. Sexist language was removed, as were test items that seemed aimed at identifying people's religious beliefs.

Millon Clinical Multiaxial Inventory (MCMI). While the MMPI-2 focusses primarily on Axis I disorders (see Chapter 3), the **Millon Clinical Multiaxial Inventory (MCMI)** (Millon, 1981) was developed to help clinicians make diagnostic judgements within the multiaxial DSM system, especially in the personality disorders found on Axis II. Not surprisingly, this actuarially constructed self-report relates particularly well to Millon's theory of personality (Millon,

Table 4.3 The MMPI Scales

Validity Scales

Cannot say scale (?)	Measures the total number of unanswered items
Lie scale (L)	Measures the tendency to claim excessive virtue or to try to present an overall favourable image
Infrequency scale (F)	Measures the tendency to falsely claim or exaggerate psychological problems in the first part of the booklet; alternatively, detects random responding
Infrequency scale (Fb)	Measures the tendency to falsely claim or exaggerate psychological problems on items toward the end of the booklet
Defensive scale (K)	Measures the tendency to see oneself in an unrealistically positive way
Response inconsistency scale (VRIN)	Measures the tendency to endorse items in an inconsistent or random manner
Response inconsistency scale (TRIN)	Measures the tendency to endorse items in an inconsistent or false manner

Clinical Scales

Scale 1	Hypochondriasis (Hs)	Measures excessive somatic concern and physical complaints
Scale 2	Depression (D)	Measures symptomatic depression
Scale 3	Hysteria (Hy)	Measures hysteroid personality features such as "rose-coloured glasses" view of the world and the tendency to develop physical problems under stress
Scale 4	Psychopathic deviate (Pd)	Measures antisocial tendencies
Scale 5	Masculinity-femininity (Mt)	Measures gender-role reversal
Scale 6	Paranoia (Pa)	Measures suspicious, paranoid ideation
Scale 7	Psychasthenia (Pt)	Measures anxiety and obsessive, worrying behaviour
Scale 8	Schizophrenia (Sc)	Measures peculiarities in thinking, feeling, and social behaviour
Scale 9	Hypomania (Ma)	Measures elated mood state and tendencies to yield to impulses
Scale 10	Social introversion (Si)	Measures social anxiety, withdrawal, and overcontrol

Special Scales

Scale A	Anxiety	A factor-analytic scale measuring general maladjustment and anxiety
Scale R	Repression	A factor-analytic scale measuring overcontrol and neurotic defensiveness
Scale Es	Ego strength	An empirical scale measuring potential response to short-term psychotherapy
Scale Mac	MacAndrew Revised Addiction Scale (MAC-R)	An empirical scale measuring proneness to become addicted to various substances

1990). The MCMI consists of 175 self-reported true-false items that yield scores for 20 clinical scales that are associated with DSM categories. The normative sample used to validate the instrument consisted of 1000 people including males and females and representing a wide variety of diagnoses. The clinical groups included patients seen in private practice, clinics, mental health centres, residential settings, and hospitals. The MCMI has been criticized because it consistently underestimates the severity of depressive syndromes (Patrick, 1988) and overdiagnoses personality disorders (Piersma, 1987). Some clinicians suggest the MMPI and MCMI should be used together, on the basis of the assumption that the MMPI is especially useful in diagnosing Axis I disorders and that the MCMI is most useful in identifying Axis II disorders (Smith, Carroll, & Fuller, 1988). Using the MMPI and the MCMI in combination may aid in making more subtle diagnostic distinctions than are possible with either test alone (Antoni et al., 1985, 1986).

A major limiting factor to any self-report test is that many people do not give accurate reports about themselves. Some will lie, and others will fall into what are called *response sets*, or test-taking attitudes that lead them to shade their responses one way or another, on the basis of their own personal traits (for example, some people like to say yes), cognitive traits, or *demand* characteristics (that is, answering as one thinks the tester would wish). A common response set is the *social desirability* set: answering to make oneself look good (Jackson & Messick, 1961). Despite control scales designed to detect such distortions, no professional assumes the problem is eliminated.

Walter Mischel (1968) eloquently argued, with considerable empirical support, that personality tests are flawed by an inherent basic assumption common to all of them: that an individual's personality, or behavioural characteristics, are stable traits, generalizable across situations and over time. Many researchers supported Mischel's view, arguing that predicting a person's behaviour requires knowledge of both the

Focus *The MMPI: A Sample Profile*

MMPI Form

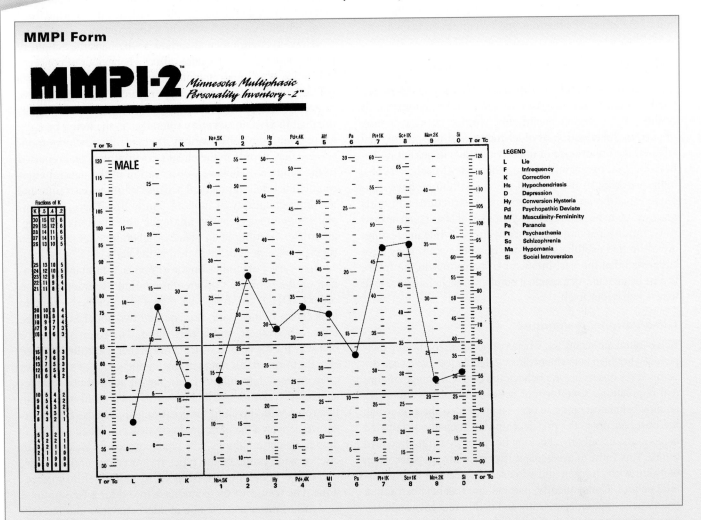

The above is a profile of a patient referred to our clinic by a physician. The physician was concerned about possible schizophrenic ideations, level of depression, and possible suicidal tendencies. It was interpreted by a senior psychologist who specializes in the MMPI, and who knew only the patient's sex, age, level of education, and marital status. This is called a *blind interpretation*.

REPORT

This is a blind analysis of an MMPI profile completed by Mr. Smith on June 18, 1997. This profile is valid. The MMPI profile completed by Mr. Smith suggests that he is currently experiencing a considerable amount of psychological distress in the form of tension, worry, and anxiety. He is a passive, dependent man who is having considerable difficulty coming to grips with his underlying dependency needs. It would not be unusual for such an individual to form very strong passive relationships. He is an angry man, whose anger is modified somewhat by his own self-image as a soft, esthetically inclined individual who has rejected the traditionally masculine role. However, he pays for this role rejection with a high level of anxiety and tension, and also experiences a moderate level of depression.

Although the level of anxiety may produce some interference in his thinking, it is unclear from the profile whether a thought disorder exists. It would be necessary to definitively ascertain this from other data sources.

However, he is a ruminative and obsessive man who tends to externalize sources of anger. He is subtly suspicious of the motives of others but feels uncomfortable in stating this directly. Again, this is reflective of his own difficulty in dealing with anger in a direct, but still very controlled way.

Individuals with profiles such as this often do engage in self-destructive behaviour. However, I would suspect Mr. Smith would give some warning about any such acts. It should be noted that he is highly vulnerable to loss and does have the potential to become seriously disorganized around such issues. Should he sustain the loss of a significant other person, or significant function, he may become acutely suicidal. ▲

person's typical behaviour patterns and the characteristics of the setting, sometimes called the **person by situation interaction** (Endler & Magnusson, 1976). This debate led to a greater awareness of the limitations of general trait theories, and of the effect of situations and incentives on behaviour.

Behavioural and Cognitive Assessment

The development of the DSMs from DSM-I to DSM-IV has been marked by an increased reliance on behaviour that is readily observable and quantifiable. This has been a response, in part, to the rejection of older theories of personality that stressed the importance of underlying traits in predicting behaviour. Led by social learning theorists (Mischel, 1968), many working in the field of psychopathology have concluded that the underlying personality structures and traits assessed by more traditional psychological tests (such as hostility, rigidity, paranoia, or obsessiveness), while interesting, are of limited usefulness in predicting behaviour. They have suggested that the best predictor of behaviour in the future is past behaviour. As a result, a number of techniques arose to assess behaviour itself.

Observational Techniques

Behavioural clinicians try, whenever possible, to observe their patients' troubled behaviours directly. Techniques have been developed for observing the behaviours of a wide range of clinical populations. One form of behavioural observation may employ behaviour rating scales —a preprinted sheet on which the observer notes the presence and/or intensity of targeted behaviours, usually by checking boxes or by filling in coded terms. This form of assessment is particularly popular when working with children and adolescents, because they all attend school. Consequently, parents and teachers can rate a child's behaviour independently and in different environments. One such rating scale, the Child Behaviour Checklist, is considered an excellent tool that can detect a broad array of problems in children, including aggressive behaviour, delinquent behaviour, attention problems, social problems, anxiety, and somatic complaints. It has undergone rigorous and sophisticated research for over a decade, with parents, teachers, and the youths themselves using various versions of the rating scales. The development of these scales has included boys, girls, men, and women from all over the world, resulting in excellent norms based on age and sex. This test also has a computerized version to assist in scoring and interpretation.

However, often behaviour therapists are interested in more focussed rating scales developed for particular populations, in which it is quite clear behaviour problems exist. Raters are required to respond only to a small number of items, most of which are present in all individuals with this problem. These types of rating scales are particularly useful as before-and-after assessments in treatment programs.

Behaviourally oriented therapists often use rating scales before, during, and after treatment. This allows patients or their parents and therapists to assess progress, and perhaps change certain procedures. As an example, the Home

Situations Questionnaire, shown in Figure 4.8, is frequently used by those treating noncompliant and/or aggressive children. This questionnaire would be completed by a parent as part of the initial evaluation, and at various times during treatment, which may last for two or three months.

How do environmental variables—perhaps the actions of parents, siblings, and friends—affect a behaviour of concern? When this is an important question, a clinician may go into a person's everyday environment to record a running narrative of events, using pencil and paper, video, or still camera. This is called **in vivo observation** (literally, "in the living being"). More commonly, observations are made by *participant observers*, key people in the client's environment, and reported to the clinician. However, observation in the natural environment is often impractical because of time constraints and the unpredictability of modern family life. Therefore clinicians sometimes create an **analogue observational setting**: an artificial setting in an office or laboratory set up to elicit specific classes of behaviour in individuals.

In a series of studies on the effects of stimulant medication on the behaviour of attention deficit/hyperactivity disorder (ADHD) children, we set up a room in the hospital to look like a living room. It contained two couches, a coffee table, a bookshelf, and homey items. The room also had a one-way mirror behind which a researcher controlled a video camera to record all interactions. In one series of studies we were interested in children's free play, structured play, and response to frustration. The mother of each child was put in this room with the child for prearranged periods. The mothers were given a list of desired activities and asked their children to do certain things. The whole procedure was meant to elicit a wide range of the types of behaviour children carried out at home and a typical set of mother-child interactions. The results of these studies allowed for a fine-grained analysis of many aspects of a child's behaviour and interactions with his or her mother. A rating scale filled out by a parent at home would not have provided such a wealth of information (Monteiro-Musten, Firestone, Pisterman, Bennet, & Mercer, 1997).

Such observation methods, while useful, are fraught with difficulty. Validity may be undermined by **subject reactivity**, the change in behaviour often seen when people know they are being observed or filmed (Harris & Lahey, 1982). Moreover, because behaviour is often specific to particular situations, observations in one setting cannot always be applied to other settings (Patterson, 1974; Tunnell, 1977). Methodological issues include inconsistency between observers, which may be avoided by training observers properly. Frequent monitoring of observers is also important to avoid *observer drift*, a steady deterioration in accuracy as a result of fatigue or of a gradual, inadvertent change in the criteria over a long period of observation (O'Leary & Kent, 1973). Finally, any assessment requiring observation of individuals, in natural or analogue situations, is so fraught with logistical concerns, and is often so expensive in terms of time, equipment, and scoring procedures, that it becomes very difficult to implement in clinical practice.

Figure 4.8 Home Situations Questionnaire

Child's name _____ Date _____

Name of person completing this form _____

Instructions: Does your child present any problems with compliance to instructions, commands, or rules for you in any of these situations? If so, please circle the word Yes and then circle a number beside that situation that describes how severe the problem is for you. If your child is not a problem in a situation, circle No and go on to the next situation on the form.

Situations	Yes/No (Circle one)		If yes, how severe? (Circle one)								
			Mild								Severe
Playing alone	Yes	No	1	2	3	4	5	6	7	8	9
Playing with other children	Yes	No	1	2	3	4	5	6	7	8	9
Mealtimes	Yes	No	1	2	3	4	5	6	7	8	9
Getting dressed/undressed	Yes	No	1	2	3	4	5	6	7	8	9
Washing and bathing	Yes	No	1	2	3	4	5	6	7	8	9
When you are on the telephone	Yes	No	1	2	3	4	5	6	7	8	9
When visitors are in your home	Yes	No	1	2	3	4	5	6	7	8	9
When you are visiting someone's home	Yes	No	1	2	3	4	5	6	7	8	9
In public places (restaurants, stores, church, etc.)	Yes	No	1	2	3	4	5	6	7	8	9
When father is home	Yes	No	1	2	3	4	5	6	7	8	9
When asked to do chores	Yes	No	1	2	3	4	5	6	7	8	9
When asked to do homework	Yes	No	1	2	3	4	5	6	7	8	9
At bedtime	Yes	No	1	2	3	4	5	6	7	8	9
While in the car	Yes	No	1	2	3	4	5	6	7	8	9
When with a babysitter	Yes	No	1	2	3	4	5	6	7	8	9

—————————————————— For Office Use Only ——————————————————

Total number of problem settings _____ Mean severity score _____

Partly in response to such difficulty, clinicians or researchers may use challenge tests tailored to an individual's problem. This technique is particularly popular when dealing with phobias. We have brought real cats to our office, for example, to gauge the severity of a patient's cat phobia: How close can the patient stand to be to the cat while it walks around? While it is held by someone? Of course, this technique would hardly be possible with a phobia about thunder.

Cognitive-Behavioural Assessment

The thoughts that precede, accompany, and follow maladaptive behaviour are sometimes very important to a clinician's understanding of an individual. But how can they be determined? Cognitive assessment tools are a relatively recent development to address this question through tests and questionnaires carefully constructed to provide reliable, valid information. Kanfer and Phillips (1970) described four sets of variables behavioural and cognitively oriented clinicians are concerned with, sometimes referred to by the acronym **SORC**. The S stands for *stimuli*. In this model a clinician would attempt to establish the particular environmental situations that frequently preceded the problem, or in which the problem often arose. The O stands for *organismic*, referring to physiological or psychological factors within the individual that might increase the probability of a behaviour, such as alcohol, a tendency to low blood sugar, or poor self-esteem. The R refers to the overt *responses*, or the problem behaviour itself; the intensity, frequency, and duration of the behaviour would be important. The C refers to *consequences* of the behaviour, particularly those that might reinforce or punish the behaviour.

Self-Monitoring

As its name implies, self-monitoring converts a patient into an assessor. Subjects are usually asked to note the frequency with which they perform various acts, and sometimes the circumstances surrounding these occurrences and their response to them. Self-monitoring-type tasks have also been used with other, less overt "behaviour" such as thoughts and feelings (Lee & Piersel, 1989). For example, behaviour therapists treating people who are depressed may ask them to monitor their own thoughts and feelings to help them become aware of the sequence of events leading to their self-defeating or self-damaging cognitions. Obviously, this technique depends on a competent, diligent, and motivated self-monitor. It is not appropriate, for example, for children or people with schizophrenia. Self-monitoring has proved to be useful and cost-effective in many different types of behavioural intervention programs (Kratochwill & Sheridan, 1990). Behavioural and cognitive clinicians find it a good way to search for vivid behaviours that will enable them to make a functional analysis of a person's disturbance.

Behaviour rating scales and systems may be categorized as ranging from direct to *indirect*, depending on how closely the observational setting approximates the setting in which the behaviour naturally occurs. Time, resources, and privacy should be considered in choosing an assessment technique. Another distinction is between *broad band* instruments, which seek to measure a wide variety of behaviours, and *narrow band* instruments, which focus on behaviours related to single, specific constructs such as hyperactivity, shyness, or depression (Shapiro & Skinner, 1990). Narrow band tests are appropriate when the psychological problems of a patient are fairly well known.

Behaviourally oriented therapists will often require patients to keep a diary, in which they record factors related to their problems. Dr. Pat McGrath and his colleagues have developed a treatment program for people with migraines. An integral part of the program is the maintenance of a diary, as shown in Figure 4.9, to track the time, place, frequency, possible contributing causes, and coping strategies. Note how the information requested reflects the influence of the SORC model on this self-monitoring tool.

Figure 4.9   A Headache Diary

**Treatment Week 1
Headache Diary**

Fill in this form at breakfast, lunch, dinner, and bedtime each day

Name: _____   Week Beginning: _____

Day	Time	Intensity Rating	Other Symptoms	Medication	Possible Cause	Coping Strategy
	Breakfast					
	Lunch					
	Dinner					
	Bedtime					

Intensity Ratings

0: No headache
1: Headache—I am only aware of it if I pay attention to it.
2: Headache—but I can ignore it at times.
3: Headache—I can't ignore it but I can do my usual activities
4: Headache—It is difficult for me to concentrate; I can only do easy activities.
5: Headache—such that I can't do anything.

Coping Strategy

1. Basic Relaxation

Source: McGrath, Cunningham, Lascelles, & Humphreys (1990).

RESEARCH METHODS

Psychological assessment and diagnosis are inextricably entwined with research. It is research that validates the tools used in assessment. Conversely, psychological assessment and diagnosis provide the descriptive and measurement tools used by researchers in examining the attributes of clinical populations. To the extent that diagnostic criteria are impaired or the tests undependable, the results of research are doomed to be erroneous. Thus, all the issues of reliability and validity discussed at the beginning of this chapter, and in Chapter 3, are also important in research.

One of the primary goals of clinical research is the **description** (defined as the specification and classification of an event) of clinical phenomena. The other is the prediction of behaviour. The two are linked; without some descriptive strategies and subsequent classification scheme it would be difficult to predict the likelihood of future events.

In this section we will review some of the science required in the study of abnormal behaviour. The word **science** comes from the Latin *scientia* ("knowledge") and is defined as "knowledge ascertained by observation and experimentation, critically tested, systematized, and brought under general principles." Behavioural investigators strive to explore human behaviour in the same manner as scientists explore physical phenomena. The assumption is that the scientific method and principles are immutable, whether one is studying the path of the sun, why water turns to ice, or why some people become depressed and others don't. Of course, each field of investigation has its own problems. Those studying human behaviour have obstacles different from those faced by material scientists, while clinical researchers, those who study abnormal psychological behaviour, have their own unique challenges.

All scientific research can be divided into two broad categories: experimental methods of investigation, and nonexperimental methods.

EXPERIMENTAL METHODS

Controlled Experimental Research

One of the distinguishing features of all science is that questions must be posed in a manner that allows clear and precise answers. To allow this clarity, investigators must have as much control as possible over all aspects of the research, but this proves most difficult in clinical studies. The flagship of research into psychopathology is the **experiment**. The well-conducted experiment allows for the greatest confidence in interpreting and generalization of results.

In the experiment, variables are actually manipulated and the effects of these manipulations on other variables are gauged. Large groups of subjects are generally used, and the results are analyzed with proven statistical techniques. In a true experiment subjects are randomly assigned to experi-

mental and control groups. **Random assignment** is a procedure that ensures that each subject has an equal probability of being in either the experimental or control group, guaranteeing the equivalence of these groups. Both groups are then assessed on traits of interest. The **experimental group** is the one that is exposed to a variable that is manipulated, the **independent variable**. Then, the groups are given an assessment on measures the researchers hypothesized would be affected by the manipulation. These behavioural responses constitute the **dependent variables**. The **control group** experiences all aspects of the experiment, including assessments, in a manner identical to the experimental group, except for the manipulation of the independent variable. The responses of the subjects are then analyzed using acceptable statistical methods, and the results are interpreted and discussed. (See Figure 4.10.)

A common question in psychopathology is which treatment is most effective for a certain type of patient. An experiment can address this question. Some of the issues associated with this type of research can be seen in a clinical experiment with children with attention deficit/hyperactivity disorder (ADHD) (Firestone, Kelly, Goodman, & Davey, 1981).

We designed a study to compare the relative effectiveness of two common treatment procedures for ADHD children, stimulant medication and parent training. One of the most important requirements of a good experiment is subject selection. In order that others can replicate the study, subjects should meet well-defined criteria and be well described in terms of any features that may be important. Our experiment would mean little if the children we studied did not actually have ADHD. Therefore we used only children referred to the Hyperactivity Project by physicians who suspected the child had ADHD and required treatment. The next criterion was that subjects meet the DSM-III criteria for the disorder, with symptoms being evidenced at home and school, and starting before three years of age. (Actually, at the time the diagnosis was based on DSM-III and was called ADDH, but for simplicity's sake we will assume that DSM-IV criteria would select the same subjects.) In addition, the children were required to score above cutoffs on well-known behaviour rating scales completed by parents and teachers, and on a test of intellectual ability. As well, children were required to be free of significant medical disorders, brain damage, epilepsy, or psychoses.

Now that we had a suitable sample, subjects had to be divided into treatment groups. Why not let parents choose which intervention they wanted for their child? If parents had been allowed to choose, it might turn out that the parents who chose one treatment over the other might be those with a higher (or lower) education level, a higher (or lower) income, a bias against medication, or some other factor that might influence the outcome. It would then be impossible to say whether any difference in outcome between the groups was caused by the different treatments or by the differences among the parents.

Figure 4.10   Procedure for Experimental Research

Source: D. Steele, "Abnormal Clinical Psychology," Series II, colour transparencies. Upper Saddle River, NJ: Prentice Hall, 1996.

To prevent this bias, parents were randomly assigned to the treatment groups. The parents of the children meeting the study criteria were told that if they agreed to participate they would be randomly assigned to one of the groups. In one group the parents would receive counselling in behaviour modification techniques for ADHD children, and the children would receive methylphenidate (Ritalin) for the four-month duration of the study (PT+M). In addition, they would be encouraged to share what they had learned with their child's teacher. In another group, the parents would be provided with exactly the same counselling but the children would be placed on placebo (PT+P). In a third randomly assigned group, the parents were not given parent training and the children were given methylphenidate (M).

In this experiment the types of treatment being compared (PT+M, PT+P, M) were the independent variable. For descriptive purposes, subjects were assessed on many measures prior to treatment. This is often referred to as a **pretest**. To get a comprehensive picture of the effects of manipulating the independent variable, children were assessed on several dependent variables judged to be important to their functioning (rating scales filled out by parents and teachers, school performance, measures related to attentional abilities). This is often called a **posttest**.

Research experience has revealed that individuals in treatment programs expect to get better, or report improvement to please the experimenter (Shapiro & Morris, 1978). This has been called the **placebo effect**, from the Latin word meaning "I shall please." To avoid having results reflect this effect, all the subjects should have, as nearly as possible, the same expectations. Thus, in the present study, children who were not receiving methylphenidate were given placebo medication. A **placebo** is a substance that looks and feels like the substance being tested, but does not contain the

active ingredient. Although originally used in medication research, the approach has also been adopted to include placebo psychological treatments, such as just spending time talking generally with the subject, or asking the subject to draw and discuss pictures that don't relate closely to the study topic. It is also known that experimenters can unwittingly influence the results. If the experimenter expects that subjects receiving the treatment will show more improvement than the controls, this expectation can be subtly communicated to the subjects. Therefore, to further ensure that expectations would not influence the outcome of the study, a **double-blind** procedure was used: that is, neither the subjects nor the experimenters knew who was getting medication and who was getting a placebo. A senior investigator kept the medication code, which was consulted only in emergencies and after all assessment had been completed. In a perfect experiment, we would have provided a placebo to match the parent training in the M condition. However, resources and ethics precluded this.

As shown in Figure 4.11, the results showed that by the end of the study, children who had received active medication performed significantly better than those who had received the placebo. The addition of parent training did not significantly improve outcomes.

Despite careful construction, this experiment experienced problems common to virtually all research with clinical populations. A key issue in any experiment is validity. The first type of validity to consider is **internal validity**: the degree to which the changes in the dependent variables are a result of the manipulation of the independent variable; this reflects the internal integrity of the study. If no alternative explanations are possible, one has strong internal validity. The other is **external validity**: the generalizability of the findings, or the degree to which the findings in the investigation apply to other

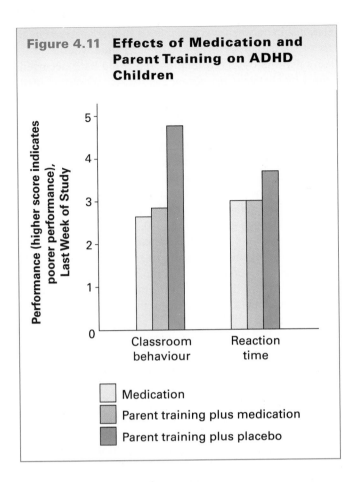

Figure 4.11   Effects of Medication and Parent Training on ADHD Children

Performance (higher score indicates poorer performance), Last Week of Study

Classroom behaviour   Reaction time

☐ Medication
☐ Parent training plus medication
☐ Parent training plus placebo

Pros and cons.   The strength of the controlled experiment is that it allows inference concerning causes and effect, the prime goal in all research. However, the controlled experiment is arguably the most difficult research strategy to implement, because of the need to control for so many factors. If strict control cannot be achieved, the internal validity of any experiment is threatened. Profound ethical dilemmas can arise relating to random assignment. For example, early in the development of a treatment for AIDS, research required that some subjects be provided with active medication, which was withheld from the control group of patients. Is it ethical to withhold treatment, no matter how speculative, from a seriously ill population, and if so, for how long is it reasonable to do so? A similar question came up in our ADHD experiment. Parents had agreed to keep their child in the assigned condition for four months before being informed of their child's medication status. We might have learned more about the effects of the drug by extending the experimental period to two years. But it would have been unacceptable ethically to keep children who were doing poorly on placebo that long; on the other hand, to keep on placebo only those children who showed an improvement would compromise the validity of the experiment. Finally, the rigorous requirements of subject selection and the intervention procedures required in many controlled experiments limit the generalizability of findings.

Quasi-Experimental Methods

Many important questions in abnormal psychology cannot be addressed in a pure experiment, since it is impossible—or, where possible, highly unethical—to create psychological disturbance in individuals in order to carry out investigations. Quasi-experimental studies, which do not face some of the challenges of controlled experiments, have therefore been essential in the development of various nosological (classification) systems, including the DSMs. A **quasi-experimental study** is one in which the subjects in the experimental group are not randomly assigned but are selected on the basis of certain characteristics and in which there is no manipulation of independent variables. Many other scientifically accepted procedures are used.

Some of the issues arising in quasi-experimental investigations can be seen in an investigation of teenagers with migraine headaches led by Dr. Pat McGrath of Dalhousie University, a well-known specialist in the study of pain (Cunningham, McGrath et al. 1987). The study grew out of a notion that people with certain types of personalities—those who were anxious, depressed, and had a poor self-concept—were prone to headaches. A group of adolescents were selected who met accepted medical criteria for significant migraine headaches. In a quasi-experimental design, this group is designated the experimental group. The control group in a quasi-experimental study is selected not through random assignment but through matching: that is, attempting to ensure that the subjects in all conditions are comparable on all variables that might be important to the research except for the key variable: in this case, the presence of migraine headaches.

individuals in other settings. In the present study it appeared the experimental controls were sufficiently stringent to provide good internal validity. However, the external validity might have been problematic. As mentioned previously, the representativeness of the population being studied is extremely important in research. In the present study, 18 of the 91 families meeting the inclusion criteria refused treatment or dropped out right after the pretest. The reasons varied from parents not being prepared to have their children on medication to lack of time and interest. Another 14 families stopped attending after a few sessions, with little or no apparent reason. One might speculate as to the reason for the 35 percent dropout rate, and what effects it had on the outcome of the study. In the present investigation, parent training consisted of approximately 12 individual and group sessions. Would that discourage parents and limit the usefulness of the program? Parents were also expected to read quite a bit. Did this requirement prevent parents with limited education from continuing? We also discovered, despite carrying out pill counts and regularly checking with both parents and schools, that some children were not receiving their medication regularly. Is the external validity of this experiment compromised by the intensive supervision provided to the subjects in the study, and the way supervision was implemented? In Ontario, the nature of the medical care system is such that virtually all health services are free, and so there was no fee for treatment or medication. Would the results of the experiment have differed if families had had to pay for these services?

Selecting the control group in this project presented a particularly intriguing problem. The normal control group was constituted by finding other children attending the same hospital who were the same age and sex as the *migraineurs*, with similar social and medical histories, except that they did not suffer from disorders that involved prolonged pain. However, if the study had proceeded with only these two groups the results would have been *confounded*. A **confound** occurs when two or more variables exert their influence at the same time, making it impossible to accurately establish the causal role of either variable. This is perhaps the most vexing problem facing all clinical research. In the migraine study, if psychological differences emerged between the experimental and control group, two interpretations would be possible: it could be that these psychological differences *led* to the migraines; however, it could also be that the psychological differences *resulted* from the pain endured by the migraineurs. To control for this problem in interpretation, the researchers included a *clinical control group*, as well: a group similar to the control group, but possessing some pathology similar to that of the experimental group. In this study the clinical control group was made up of teenagers who suffered from chronic musculoskeletal pain such as rheumatoid arthritis.

The results revealed that the migraineurs did in fact demonstrate more psychological problems than the normal controls. However, when the three groups were compared it was clear that it was the level of pain, not the source of pain, that was associated with personality and behavioural differences. In the end the results did not support the hypothesis that personality and behavioural styles put one at risk for developing migraines. Rather, it seemed that people who suffer pronounced and prolonged pain respond by becoming anxious and depressed.

Pros and cons.   The quasi-experimental study allows for meaningful analysis of many aspects of psychological disorders that cannot be studied by experiment. In fact, the development of DSM-IV was based largely on such quasi-experimental procedures. Nevertheless, the assignment of subjects on the basis of their personal characteristics limits the cause-and-effect inferences that are possible. In addition, experience has demonstrated that it is difficult to match subjects on all factors but the one in question.

NONEXPERIMENTAL METHODS

Correlational Research

The **correlational method** measures the degree of relationship between two variables and generally requires a large number of participants. It is not invasive; behaviour is not manipulated, just quantitatively measured and then analyzed statistically. Following the measurement of the variables, a statistical procedure called a correlation coefficient is computed. The resulting statistic describing the relationship between two variables is further analyzed by a test of statistical significance to determine whether it is likely that the observed relationship could have occurred simply by chance. *Correlation coefficients* are represented by the symbol r and range in value from -1.00 to 1.00. A *positive correlation,* such as $r = 0.68$, indicates that an increase in one variable is associated with an increase in the other. A *negative correlation,* such as $r = -0.63$, indicates that an increase in one variable is associated with a decrease in the other. When the correlation coefficient is close to zero, there is no significant relationship between the two variables. Generally, psychologists are interested in correlation coefficients greater than $+/-0.30$. Figure 4.12 shows a correlation of 0.47, which is statistically significant, between IQ scores and a measure of reading ability. If you look at the dots, you can see that most children with higher IQ scores (toward the right of the graph) also tend to score higher on reading (toward the top of the graph), but there are many exceptions.

Correlational research is frequently carried out where experimental manipulation is impossible or unethical. For example, in studying the effects of maternal smoking on the developing fetus, it would be unacceptable to randomly assign expectant mothers to groups and force some of them to smoke. Once a reliable correlation is established between two variables, knowledge of one variable allows prediction of the other. However, a common misconception is that if two variables are reliably correlated, a causal relationship must exist. Actually, a significant correlation may have one of three interpretations. First, it is possible that variable A caused variable B. Second, it is possible that variable B caused variable A. Finally, a third variable may be responsible for the occurrence of both A and B.

For example, suppose it is found that children who take violin lessons get higher grades than children who don't. It may be that studying the violin improves academic performance. It may be that only children with high grades are allowed to take violin lessons. Or it may be that a third factor—perhaps parents with an interest in cultural pursuits—leads to both high grades and an interest in the violin. (Can you think of further studies that would clarify the relationship?) Thus, correlational research methods possess no internal validity and cannot establish that a causal relationship exists. Nonetheless, the correlational method has played a major role in the study of abnormal behaviour and still occupies a deserved place as a research method.

Pros and cons.   Correlational research is a relatively inexpensive method of studying the relationship between naturally occurring phenomena. It can indicate whether a meaningful relationship exists between two variables. This knowledge may be of value even if the reasons for the relationship are not evident. Furthermore, it can also be used to illuminate areas that might benefit from more rigorous research strategies. Nevertheless, it is impossible to make cause-and-effect inferences with this design.

Figure 4.12 IQ Scores and Performance on a Reading Test for a Group of Grade 4 Children

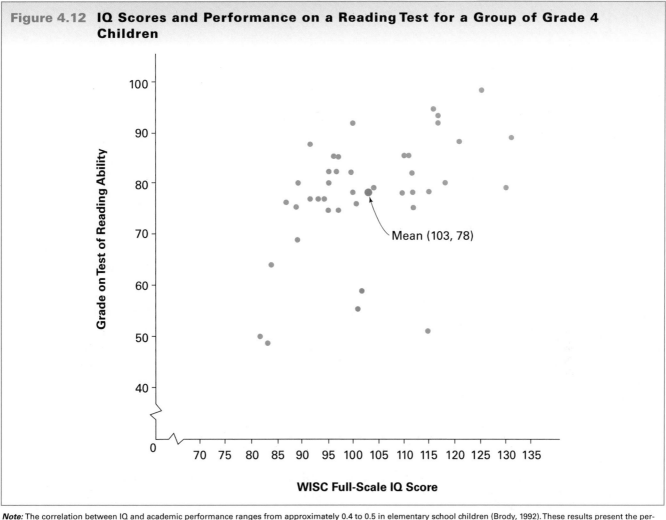

Note: The correlation between IQ and academic performance ranges from approximately 0.4 to 0.5 in elementary school children (Brody, 1992). These results present the performance of a hypothetical group of children in Grade 4. The children were first administered the Wechsler Intelligence Scale for Children (WISC). Several days later, they were administered a group test of reading ability on which the highest possible score is 100. Each dot on the graph represents one child's scores on the two tests. The further the dot is to the right, the higher the IQ score; the higher up on the graph, the higher the reading score. As you can see, the dots follow a rough line; generally the higher the IQ, the higher the reading ability. There are, however, many exceptions. One of the lowest reading scores (55) was earned by a child with an IQ of 101. Yet another child with an IQ of 100 scored 92 on the reading test.

The Case Study

The case study method is undoubtedly the oldest approach to the study of abnormal behaviour and has been extensively used by clinicians to describe patients they have treated. The **case study** is a description of the past and current functioning of a single individual. Since the case study is generally the result of information gathered through intense interactions over long periods, it may be very rich. Variables such as family history, education, employment history, medical history, social relationships, and the patient's level of psychological adjustment are described within the case study. This information is collected primarily by interview, but may be supplemented by test scores, archival records, consultations with family members, and actual observation during the clinical interview (for example, behavioural tics, emotional state, posture). The goal of the case study is a description of an individual's current problem, and its relation to his or her past. Ultimately, it seeks to provide a theory concerning the etiology of a patient's problem or psychological makeup, and/or a course of treatment and outcome.

Pros and cons. As a method of investigating abnormal psychology, the case study possesses definite, albeit limited, advantages. Its approach is classified as *idiographic* in that it offers rich detail and vividness concerning a particular individual that is frequently lost in large studies. In contrast, the *nomothetic* approach, more favoured by scientists, studies large groups of subjects to uncover the basic principles governing behaviour. The case study can be an excellent source for the generation of new hypotheses concerning the etiology and treatment of psychological disorders, which may later be tested under more rigorous statistical controls. In addition, the case study is useful in the description of particularly rare disorders and their treatment. Finally, the case study can be used to supply a counterexample to universally accepted principles, since the existence of only one exception can render a proposition false. As an example, it has often been asserted that all sex offenders have themselves been victimized as children. If one is able to find any sex offender who has not been victimized, this assertion is incorrect. The exception to the rule does not, however, preclude the suggestion there may be a higher incidence of sexual victimization in the history of sex offenders than in that of normal controls.

Several years ago we conducted a study to evaluate a promising new anti-depressant, which appeared to have fewer side-effects than the older families of antidepressants. Fifty consecutive patients diagnosed as suffering from a major depressive episode (DSM-III-R) were offered inclusion in the investigation. They were given full information on the investigation. If they agreed to participate they would be provided with cognitive behaviour therapy over a four-month period. They also had to agree that they would take the medication under investigation, and that one-half the group would receive a placebo for the four-month period. All patients were told that if they did not want to participate, they would be provided with the conventional intervention, which was pretty well the standard of care provided in all hospital outpatient departments. If they agreed to participate, they could withdraw from the study at any time without jeopardizing further treatment at the hospital.

About two months into the study, the research staff brought the plight of a 35-year-old man to my attention. He had a troubled marriage, somewhat related to his mood disorder, when he entered the investigation. His marriage had since deteriorated. The staff were concerned both for him and for his wife, worrying that irreparable damage would be done to the relationship unless he showed more improvement. The staff were "blind" and did not know whether he was on the medication or placebo. Only I knew that he was on placebo and that many, but not all, subjects on the active medication had shown dramatic improvement.

This was the dilemma: On the one hand, the experimental medication *appeared* (but could not yet be proved) to help many of the depressed individuals in this, and other, studies. On the other hand, if every subject showing no improvement while on placebo were taken out of the placebo condition, it would be impossible to determine whether the experimental medication was effective. Then all the work we had done, and the work the subjects had carried out, would be wasted. In addition, future patients might not benefit from a beneficial medication, because we were unable to complete the experiment properly.

Critical Thinking Questions

1. What do you think the responsibility of the researcher should be under these circumstances?
2. What factors should go into the decision-making process?
3. What would you do?

These advantages notwithstanding, the case study has limited use in the study of psychopathology. It does not employ the scientific method or control for rival hypotheses, and so cannot demonstrate cause and effect. Thus, the case study cannot prove a theory. In addition, one cannot be certain of the generalizability (external validity) of the findings. Finally, the clinician's theoretical background has been shown to influence the questions asked and therefore skew the information gleaned. A Freudian, for instance, might focus on childhood conflicts, an Adlerian on power struggles, and a social learning theorist on the antecedents and consequences of behaviour. Thus, although the case study method has an assured position within the field of abnormal psychology, its usefulness will always be limited.

Single-Subject Research

Single-subject designs, like the case study, are based on the intense investigation of an individual subject. However, this approach avoids many of the criticisms of the case study by using experimentally accepted procedures. The variations of this design have several common elements: they use observable behaviours that are quantifiable, they quantify the presence of the behaviour prior to any intervention, they systematically apply readily observable and quantifiable interventions, and they measure the effects of the intervention on the behaviours of the subject. The **ABAB** design, also called the **reversal design**, requires the quantification of behaviour in its naturally occurring environment prior to any intervention. This constitutes the A phase or the baseline of the procedure. Next, in the B phase, the treatment is introduced in a controlled manner for a period of time. The next A phase constitutes the reversal, during which time the treatment is not provided, and the subject is exposed to the original baseline conditions. Finally, the treatment is provided once again and represents the final "B", (Firestone, 1976).

Billy was a four-year-old with ADHD, in a regular preschool program, who was often both physically and verbally aggressive towards other children, using commands, threats, teasing, and verbal conflicts. Children and parents complained regularly about his conduct. He had been told by staff and parents many times not to act in this fashion, to no avail. It was decided to target his physical aggression first. The teachers and researchers first agreed on what constituted physical aggression. For the next five days all adults working in the school, including the researchers, were asked to surreptitiously record every aggressive incident on a prepared chart and to deal with it as they had previously. This generally consisted of separating Billy from the other child, reprimanding him verbally, and sending him to play in another part of the room. At the end of each day all adults gave their charts to the researcher. As expected, and as demonstrated in Figure 4.13, the talk with Billy did little to change his physical or verbal aggression. This constituted the A1 phase of the intervention.

Billy was then told that every time he was aggressive toward another child he would be placed in "timeout": that is, he would have to sit in a chair facing the corner in an unused part of the room until he was quiet for two minutes. As the figure demonstrates, Billy's aggressive behaviour rapidly diminished. This constituted the B1 phase of intervention.

After five days in phase B1, it was decided to stop putting Billy into timeout and return to the approach used before the study started (A2). Within three days, Billy's aggressive behaviour returned to nearly pre-intervention levels. At the request of the parents and teachers it was decided to reinstate the timeout after day 3 of this condition (B2). This time Billy's aggressive behaviour appeared to decrease even more rapidly than it had the first time. Interestingly his activity level did not change.

Pros and cons. The case of Billy demonstrates how a single-subject design differs from a case study. The single-subject design has the advantage of being relatively inexpensive. Moreover, the variables in question are clearly defined, observable, and quite accurately measured, removing the element of personal bias from the observations. An individual's performance can be judged more accurately than in even a well-executed group design, where performance is based on group means.

One problem inherent in this research strategy was demonstrated in Billy's case. While Billy's undesirable behaviour improved dramatically in response to the first intervention, the behaviour did not immediately return to pre-study levels when the intervention was withdrawn. Billy's initial state was not recoverable within the time constraints of the present study. We assume this was a result of some permanence in the change of Billy's behaviour pattern—which is the goal of most treatment. The other, perhaps more important, problem with the ABAB design is an ethical one: can one justify reinstating contingencies that don't work in order to demonstrate that others do? More practically, subjects are often unwilling to give up treatment that works just to preserve the integrity of the research design. This problem appeared in Billy's case, where the adults refused to continue with the second baseline. Finally, results are not generalizable; there is clear support that timeouts are effective with Billy, but we cannot say that they will be effective for all children with similar behaviour. Single-subject design reports are thus usually treated as demonstrations of interventions that warrant further study.

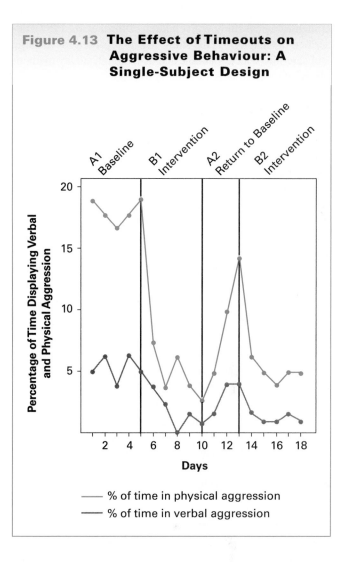

Figure 4.13 The Effect of Timeouts on Aggressive Behaviour: A Single-Subject Design

— % of time in physical aggression
— % of time in verbal aggression

Epidemiological Research

Epidemiology is the study of the incidence and prevalence of disorders in a population. **Incidence** refers to the number of new cases of a disorder in a particular population over a specified time period, usually a year. **Prevalence** is the frequency of a disorder in a population at a given point or period of time. In psychopathology, epidemiological research can help identify the frequency of disorders in various populations and assist in the understanding of their development and maintenance or in the design of intervention strategies.

Perhaps the most famous epidemiological study occurred during a cholera outbreak in nineteenth-century London, England. At that time, John Snow noted that most people coming down with cholera congregated or drank water from one source, the Broad Street Pump. He also noted that rates of cholera were lower upstream from London where the water was less contaminated. He was thus able to demonstrate that the cholera was being spread by contaminated water.

We have no example in psychopathology in which an epidemiological study was able to prevent a disorder. Two Canadian studies, however, are exemplary. Dr. Dan Offord, a psychiatrist at McMaster University, conducted a landmark epidemiological study with children (Offord et al., 1987), described in Chapter 5. This study, highly regarded for its large and carefully selected sample and its thorough survey methodology, gave clinicians valuable information on the common childhood disorders.

Dr. Charles Costello conducted one of the first investigations into the prevalence of fears and phobias in adults, in Calgary, Alberta. In this investigation, 449 women, randomly selected from the Calgary area, were interviewed in their homes by research staff to determine fears related to separation (for example, taking journeys, being in large, open spaces), mutilation fears (injections, hospitals, doctors, blood), nature fears (heights, tunnels, enclosed spaces), social fears, and animal fears. The results revealed that 26 percent of the subjects were completely free of the fears investigated, 19 percent had fears sufficiently intense to cause them to avoid the feared situations or objects, and approximately 5 percent were incapacitated by their phobias (Costello, 1982). (See Figures 4.14 and 4.15.)

Pros and cons.   The advent of epidemiological research strategies allowed for the detailed collection of information concerning the incidence and prevalence of disorders in large populations. Such information is essential for the understanding of factors that contribute to the health of a population and the design of intervention strategies. However, this research strategy does not easily allow inferences concerning cause and effect. The final hindrance to epidemiological research is that it requires very large numbers of subjects in order for relationships between factors to be recognized.

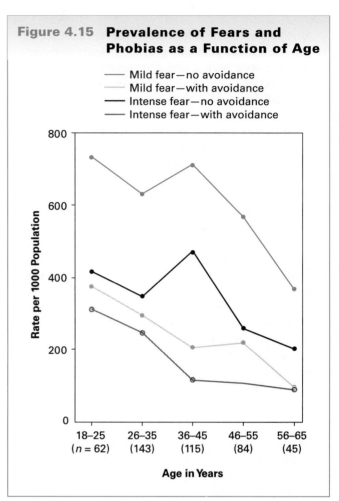

Figure 4.15 Prevalence of Fears and Phobias as a Function of Age

Source: Costello (1982).

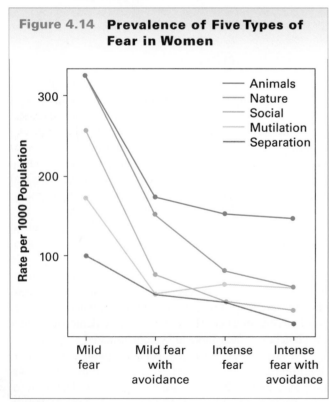

Figure 4.14 Prevalence of Five Types of Fear in Women

Source: Costello (1982).

Studies of Inheritance

Is a person born with a disorder, or a tendency to a disorder, or is it developed through environmental influences? As a general question, this may be termed the nature/nurture debate, and, as we discussed in Chapter 1, the short answer is that there *is* no simple answer: both factors are important. But the question still remains for particular disorders and particular cases: Is the source of a problem genetic or environmental? (In this discussion, *genetic* refers to inherited traits. In fact, some genetic disorders are not inherited but caused by mutation; for example, in Down syndrome, genetic damage occurs to the cells produced by parents whose own cells are normal. Such disorders are not, of course, tracked through family studies.)

Family Studies

Researchers often examine the incidence of a disorder among family members, often including distant as well as close relatives. Genetic similarity between family members is greater than between non–family members. Furthermore, genetic similarity is greater between parents and their children, and between siblings, than it is between cousins, or between aunts/uncles and their nieces/nephews, or between grandparents and their grandchildren. Table 4.4 shows the genetic relationships between family members and non–family members. (Note that the genetic relationship between a parent and child is not exactly the same as between siblings. A child gets half of his or her genes from each parent; therefore, parent and child always have 50 percent of their genes in common. Siblings each get half of their genes from the mother and half from the father, but it is not known which of a parent's genes each child will get. Therefore, two siblings could in theory have anywhere from 0 to 100 percent of genes in common; the *average* genetic similarity between siblings is 50 percent. This distinction will not make any difference in statistical analyses, though in some circumstances it will affect predictions about an individual on the basis of family information.)

In family studies, the patient, or the person who has come to the attention of the clinician or researcher, is called the *index case* or **proband**. If the proband and a comparison person are alike on the characteristic of interest (if, for example, they show the same abnormal behaviour), the two are said to be *concordant* (or to display *concordance*). If the concordance rate for the disorder increases with increasing genetic similarity, this will offer support for, but will not confirm, a genetic basis for the problem. After all, families typically live in, and create, far more similar environments than are found between people from different families. Heredity and environment are thus confounded in family studies. For these reasons, behavioural geneticists have turned to other methods of studying these influences.

Adoption Studies

Adoption studies offer researchers an opportunity to determine the separate effects of genetics and environment on the development of psychological disorders. In the prototypical investigation a group of individuals who were adopted away from their biological parents at an early age and who demonstrate a psychological disorder are studied. The rates of disorder in the biological and adopted parents are then compared. This allows researchers to control for environmental effects, assuming that the children were adopted at birth. Presumably,

if there is greater agreement between adoptees and biological parents than there is between adoptees and adoptive parents, then a genetic link likely exists. Unfortunately, research in this regard has demonstrated how difficult it is to match parent groups. For example, groups of parents who adopt children tend not to be a random representation of the community at large, and this may unduly influence the results. They tend to come from higher socioeconomic strata and tend to have fewer problems such as alcoholism or substance abuse. This is not surprising, since in most jurisdictions parents wanting to adopt children are screened by agencies for suitability.

Cross-fostering is a very great improvement on the traditional adoption study. In this case, one group comprises adopted children, whose biological parents have a disorder and whose adoptive parents demonstrate no psychopathology. The other group comprises adopted children whose biological parents have no disorder but whose adoptive parents develop psychopathology. The comparisons available in this design allow statements concerning the relative impact of genes and environment. The ViewPoint box that follows shows a cross-fostering study of petty criminality among male adoptees.

There are several limitations to adoption studies as a research tool. It is very difficult to obtain full, accurate information concerning the biological parents of adoptees. Frequently, only the mothers are considered in this research, since it is not possible to verify who the fathers are. It is also difficult to control for the contact adoptees have had with their biological parents. Researchers may have difficulty in acquiring large enough samples to allow statistical inferences. Furthermore, adoption studies do not control for the effects of prenatal exposure to toxins, maternal illness, or perinatal trauma; such factors can have significant physiological effects on the fetus, but are not genetically transmitted (Bohman, Sigvardsson, & Cloninger, 1981).

Twin Studies

Examination of the concordance rates among twins has been seen as a more accurate basis from which to infer genetic contributions to disorders, because the genetic similarity between twins is known. For example, identical twins share exactly the same genotype (they have inherited exactly the same genes from their parents), whereas non-identical twins share only half their genotype. Identical twins, also known as **monozygotic (MZ) twins** (from *mono* meaning "one," and *zygote* meaning "fertilized egg"), result from the fertilization by a single sperm of a single ovum. This is followed by an unusual extra division into exactly matched zygotes, which subsequently develop into genetically identical fetuses. Thus, MZ twins have 100 percent of their genes in common. Non-identical (or *fraternal*) twins, also known as **dizygotic (DZ) twins** (from *di* meaning "two") result when two independent sperm separately fertilize two independent ova at approximately the same time. Thus, DZ twins, like non-twin siblings, have, on average, just 50 percent of their genes in common. If there is greater concordance for a disorder among MZ twins than among DZ wins, so the argument goes, we can infer a genetic basis for the disorder.

Table 4.4   Genetic Relationships

Relationship to Proband	Genes Shared
Non–family member	0%
Spouse	0%
Cousin	12.5%
Grandparent	25%
Grandchild	25%
Aunt or uncle	25%
Niece or nephew	25%
Parent	50%
Child	50%
Non-twin sibling (brother or sister)	50%
Non-identical twin (dizygotic twin)	50%
Identical twin (monozygotic twin)	100%

VIEWPOINT *A Cross-Fostering Analysis of Petty Criminality in Male Adoptees*

Results of Cross-Fostering Study

Classification of Predisposition to Petty Criminality		Petty Criminality Observed in Male Adoptees	
Congenital	*Postnatal*	*Total* (n)	*Petty Criminality* (%)
Low	Low	666	2.9
Low	High	120	6.7
High	Low	66	12.1
High	High	10	40

Source: Adapted from M. Bohman, Predisposition to criminality: Swedish adoption studies in retrospect, *Genetics of antisocial behaviour* Gregory Bock and Jamie Goode, eds. [Ciba Foundation Symposium 194] (Chichester, England: John Wiley and Sons Ltd., 1995), pp. 99–114.

These are the results of a cross-fostering analysis of petty criminality (without alcohol abuse) in male adoptees. "Congenital" refers to the characteristics of the biological parents (genetic), whereas "postnatal" refers to the characteristics of the adoptive placement (environmental). The results suggest that if the biological parents have no petty criminal records and their child was adopted by a family that was also free of such activity (Low Low) the probability of the offspring getting involved in this type of criminal behaviour was quite low. If the biological parents had petty criminal records and their child was adopted by a family none of whose members was involved in such activity (High Low), the probability was higher than in the Low Low condition. As might be expected, when the biological parents were petty criminals and their child was adopted away into a family with such behaviour the rates increased to 40 percent. These findings were not replicated for violent criminality. Overall the chart suggests that nature and nurture each play a significant, but far from a definitive, role in the development of petty criminality. As can be seen, even in the highest-risk group (High High), 60 percent of the boys did not grow up to become petty criminals. Nevertheless, the 40 percent criminality rate in this group is far higher than the petty criminality rates in the other groups and should be cause for grave concern.

These results suggest that parents who are involved in petty criminality, and who raise their own children, place them at extremely high risk to become offenders themselves.

Critical Thinking Questions

1. Is society justified in stepping in and monitoring these parents and/or children before the children get involved in criminal activity, even if the parents have not physically abused the children?
2. If these results are accurate, is society justified in treating the children of criminal parents differently from the children of noncriminal parents because of their risk status?
3. Can you think of a number of alternatives to removing children from high-risk families?

It is not easy, however, to amass a large number of subjects for such studies, because only a little more than 1 percent of all children are twins, and only one in three of these are monozygotic. For any particular disorder there will be even fewer to select from, since most disorders occur in only a very small percentage of the population. For example, schizophrenia, a disorder that has been persistently examined for a genetic basis, occurs in only 1 percent of the population. Researchers are going to have to search far and wide to discover enough monozygotic twins where at least one has schizophrenia. Typically, this has forced researchers to examine hospital records back over many years. The difficulty is that, since diagnostic procedures have changed over the years, it is hard to be sure what the sample really includes.

Other important criticisms have been levelled at the basic assumption of twin studies. For example, it is assumed that environmental influences are held constant in these comparisons between monozygotic and dizygotic twins and that therefore only genotypic differences can account for differential concordance rates. Lewontin, Rose, and Kamin (1984) point out that the environment of monozygotic twins is remarkably more similar than that of dizygotic twins. After all, monozygotic twins look alike, they are almost invariably dressed the same by their parents and most everyone, including their parents, have great difficulty telling them apart. Lewontin et al. argue that these facts suggest monozygotic twins will be treated almost identically, that is, the environmental responses to them will be the same. For dizygotic twins, however, who do not look the same (or at least no more alike than non-twin siblings), environmental responses can be expected to differ from one twin to the other. Therefore, according to Lewontin et al. different concordance rates between monozygotic and dizygotic twins could as readily be accounted for in terms of environmental rather than genetic influences. Moreover, identical twins have been found to exert greater influence over each other than do fraternal twins (Carey, 1992).

It is interesting to examine the differences in concordance rates between dizygotic twins and non-twin siblings. Since fraternal twins and non-twin siblings are equally similar genetically, what is one to make of differences in concordance rates between these two groups? Studies of schizophrenia consistently show that dizygotic twins have higher concordance rates than do non-twin siblings. Given that dizygotic twins are born at the same time, go through the same temporal changes, go to the same school, and often share the same friends, it is likely that environmental similarities play a significant role. Even more to the point, same-sex fraternal twins can be assumed to share far more environmental experiences in common than opposite-sex fraternal twins, although these two different sorts of fraternal twins have exactly the same genetic relationships. Six studies (Lewontin et al., 1984) have shown greater concordance among same-sex dizygotic twins than among opposite-sex dizygotic twins, a further indication of environmental influence. Recent research has demonstrated that the mother's health, perinatal trauma, viral infections, and environmental toxins, all interacting with the sex of the fetus, may be implicated in the long-term development of children through nongenetic, physiological processes. These elements may, at least in part, contribute to the higher concordance rates reported in dizygotic, same-sex twins than in dizygotic, opposite-sex twins (Bohman, Sigvardsson, & Cloninger, 1981).

Obviously, it would be ideal to combine twin and adoption strategies by studying large numbers of MZ and DZ twins who suffer from the disorders of interest and were adopted early in life. However, finding sufficient numbers of such individuals who are willing to participate is a demanding task, fraught with myriad logistical difficulties. Nevertheless, there has been a great deal of converging research, using a wide variety of research strategies, with several pathological groups, including schizophrenics, bipolar disorders, and substance abusers. Such studies have generally revealed higher concordance rates for disorders in MZ than in DZ twins, and cannot be simply dismissed. Some scientists have developed statistical procedures to calculate the degree to which genetics, as opposed to environmental factors, is responsible for psychological characteristics using correlational data obtained with the twin study method. In one procedure, the correlation coefficient for DZ twins is subtracted from the correlation coefficient for MZ twins, and the result is then multiplied by 2 (Falconer, 1960). Using this formula, Plomin (1990) has suggested that height is correlated 0.90 among MZ twins and 0.45 among DZ twins. One could therefore conclude that height is 90 percent inherited, and by subtraction determine that 10 percent may be due to environmental factors. However, this simple calculation must be viewed with caution. It is only an estimate of the average contribution of genetics to the development of disorders, and, under extreme circumstances, environment can exert a greater influence than is suggested by this simple computation. For example, factors such as extreme malnutrition or prenatal exposure to toxins may result in the genetic propensity of a trait not manifesting itself.

We have examined a number of different research designs in this chapter, each with particular strengths and weaknesses. Table 4.5 summarizes the pros and cons of all these methods.

STATISTICAL VS. CLINICAL SIGNIFICANCE

In experimental research, the concept of **statistical significance** is crucial, since it is the standard by which most research is judged as valuable or worthy of being published. Basically, experimental results are deemed statistically significant if it is extremely unlikely the obtained results could have occurred purely by chance. The convention in psychological research is to set a significance level of 0.05 (often written as $p = 0.05$, where p stands for "probability"), meaning that if the independent variable exerted no effect whatsoever, the obtained findings would be observed no more than 5 percent of the time, solely by chance. Thus if $p < 0.05$, it seems reasonable to assume that the independent variable is exerting an effect. However, there is a big difference between demonstrating statistical significance and finding a treatment that works in real life.

Suppose a psychologist has developed a treatment for depression and has found, through careful quantitative research, using large groups of subjects, that the intervention significantly decreases symptoms of depression. So she offers this new treatment to a few patients outside the study. Some show no symptom relief. Others score somewhat lower on a scale of depression, or report that some symptoms have decreased, but their lives have not improved in any meaningful way; they still feel depressed. Assuming the clinician correctly administered the treatment, why did a seemingly promising therapy fail to ameliorate the patient's quality of life?

At issue is the concept of **clinical significance**, which refers to a treatment's practical utility, and which does not follow automatically from statistical significance. In a study with a large number of subjects, statistically significant results may demonstrate that small changes are not due to chance. However, it is possible that only a minority of subjects in the group experienced improvement, or that the improvement was measurable but small. Unless change is sufficient to be of value to a patient, the treatment has little merit. In fact, the cost in terms of time and money, and possible side-effects may render the treatment worse than useless. Moreover, some interventions work better in controlled circumstances than in the everyday world. Suppose, for example, that a medication only worked if administered eight times a day at precisely the same time. It might work fine when administered by a nurse in a hospital, but once home, the patient would be unable to stick to the schedule, and the treatment would become ineffective.

To control for the potential irrelevance of statistical significance in research, it has been suggested that it is equally important to evaluate the social validity of a treatment, and attend to the qualitative changes in patients' functioning. This

Table 4.5 Pros and Cons of Different Research Designs

Research Design	Pros	Cons
Controlled experiment	1. Cause and effect can be established	1. Difficult to implement because of control required (internal validity) 2. Ethical problems due to required manipulation of variables 3. External validity problematic
Quasi-experimental	1. Allows research when manipulation of variables is not possible 2. Provides information on pathological groups	1. Cause-and-effect statements compromised by lack of random assignment 2. Difficult to match subjects in different groups
Correlational study	1. Relatively easy and inexpensive to implement 2. Allows study of relationships and between common phenomena variables	1. Cause and effect cannot be established
Case study	1. Very easy to implement 2. Idiographic approach provides rich detail 3. Allows some insight into infrequently occurring disorders 4. Provides for generation of new hypotheses	1. Cause and effect cannot be established 2. Highly biased by clinician's perspective 3. Cannot generalize to other patients or populations
Single-subject design	1. Relatively easy and inexpensive to implement 2. Allows cause-and-effect statements 3. Allows some insight into infrequently occurring disorders	1. Ethically and practically difficult to implement some reversals 2. Impossible to generalize results to other settings or subjects
Twin and adoption studies	1. Allows insight into genetic and environmental contributions to pathology	1. Generally cause and effect cannot be established (some diseases such as Tay-Sachs are the exception)
Epidemiological studies	1. Provides information on the incidence and prevalence of problems	1. Impossible to make cause-and-effect statements 2. Large numbers of subjects required 3. Provides information on factors related to the occurrence of problems

might be accomplished by collecting subjective input on therapy results from patients and significant others in their lives (Wolf, 1978). Another meaningful approach, called **normative comparison**, compares treatment results to non-disturbed samples (Jacobson & Truax, 1991; Kendall & Grove, 1988).

Concern with clinical significance has now grown to the point that many journals will not accept articles (especially those dealing with interventions that have already been well studied) unless the authors can provide data showing meaningful, practical outcomes.

PANORAMA

If there is a unique niche for psychologists in the mental health service spectrum, it is the psychological assessment. Their educational background, which combines the study of the scientific method as well as psychopathology, has prepared them extremely well for the development of tests and other assessment procedures. Consequently, psychologists, more than any other professional group, have been involved in the development and use of psychological tests.

Several trends have been apparent in the development of psychological assessment tools over the past decade. First, recent assessment tools have become much more focussed in the questions they seek to answer. Historically, tests like the Rorschach and the MMPI were used to describe many aspects of personality functioning, defence mechanisms, and even intellectual and cognitive ability. More recently, however, tests have been developed to assess more specific aspects of psychological functioning, such as level of depression, risk of suicide, degree of obsessive-compulsive tendencies, or ability to concentrate.

The development of behavioural assessments also exemplifies this specificity. They strive to assess how individuals actually behave—not how they say they behave—under particular circumstances. Another major thrust has been the attempt to ensure, before new psychological tests are released, that they are constructed on sound psychometric principles and have demonstrated good reliability and validity. Finally, advances in medical technology and in computers have enabled a wealth of sophisticated new assessment techniques, especially as related to specific relationships between brain function and behaviour. Clinicians are therefore now more inclined to use a number of psychological tests, both broad-based and specific.

Research in abnormal psychology has developed in a number of different directions. First, it is evident that small sample investigations have provided, and continue to provide, insight into various psychological disorders and their treatment. However, we have also discovered that humans are more diverse than we once thought. For example, one might assemble a group of people all diagnosed with a mood disorder; yet they may be utterly unlike one another in many ways, complicating analysis of results. To better understand the development and treatment of psychological problems like mood disorders, groups have to be delineated that are more homogeneous by sex, age, speed of onset, etc. However, results with this group will not be generalizable to all people with mood disorders. As a result, large multisite investigations are required to ensure adequate samples of patients and to ensure that findings are not the result of the idiosyncrasies of researchers and their communities. In addition, there has been more interest in epidemiological research. It is hoped that such studies may uncover factors contributing to mental health that will help prevent mental health problems.

SUMMARY

Psychological assessment plays an important role in abnormal psychology, providing a sound system for describing an individual's psychological profile. Good psychological assessment tools need to be both reliable and valid. Two methods for using psychological information in the prediction of behaviour are clinical and actuarial. Biologically based procedures used in the study of psychological problems, include EEG, CAT scan, MRI, and PET. Although the results of most brain imaging assessments cannot be used to help in diagnoses, aside from circumstances in which there is frank neurological impairment, they have contributed greatly to research. A number of neuropsychological tests, are used to study brain-behaviour relationships. Clinical interviews have always been an integral part of any psychological assessment, and recently have developed more structured components. IQ tests were the first psychological tests to gain wide acceptance, and do a fairly good job of predicting school performance. Projective tests, initially based on psychoanalytic theory, were the first personality tests. However, actuarial personality tests like the MMPI, based on more psychometrically sound procedures, have become more favoured among clinicians. With the growing acceptance of social learning theories, behavioural and cognitive-behavioural assessment techniques have become widely accepted. Most of these tests focus on specific behaviour problems, rather than the whole range of personality functioning. A large number of behaviour rating scales are available. Self-monitoring is one example of a cognitive-behavioural assessment.

In the second section of this chapter we reviewed the most common research methods used by psychologists. The controlled experiment is not always possible in human research. However, quasi-experimental and correlational research, if conducted appropriately, can provide a great deal of insight into human behaviour. Although not scientifically rigorous, case studies and single-subject research designs may raise important questions and may point the way to more controlled research. Family, adoption, and twin studies are valuable for the insight they offer into the relative contribution of heredity and the environment. Recently researchers have stressed that it is not enough to simply demonstrate statistically significant results of an intervention. The more important question is whether the treatment offers meaningful relief to the distress or difficulty of people with psychopathology.

KEY TERMS

psychological assessment (p. 66)
test-retest reliability (p. 67)
alternate-form reliability (p. 67)
internal consistency (p. 67)

split-half reliability (p. 67)
coefficient alpha (p. 67)
face validity (p. 67)
content validity (p. 67)
criterion validity (p. 67)
construct validity (p. 68)

clinical approach (p. 68)
actuarial approach (p. 68)
computerized axial tomography (CAT) (p. 68)
magnetic resonance imaging (MRI) (p. 69)

positron emission tomography (PET) (p. 69)
Bender Visual-Motor Gestalt Test (p. 70)
mental status examination (p. 72)
intelligence quotient (IQ) (p. 73)
Stanford-Binet Scales (p. 73)
Wechsler Adult Intelligence Scale (p. 73)
WAIS-R (p. 73)
projective test (p. 75)
Rorschach inkblot test (p. 76)
Exner system (p. 76)
thematic apperception test (TAT) (p. 76)
Minnesota Multiphasic Personality Inventory (MMPI) (p. 77)
Millon Clinical Multiaxial Inventory (MCMI) (p. 77)

person by situation interaction (p. 80)
in vivo observation (p. 80)
analogue observational setting (p. 80)
subject reactivity (p. 80)
SORC (p. 81)
description (p. 83)
science (p. 83)
experiment (p. 83)
random assignment (p. 83)
experimental group (p. 83)
independent variable (p. 83)
dependent variable (p. 83)
control group (p. 83)
pretest (p. 84)
posttest (p. 84)
placebo effect (p. 84)
placebo (p. 84)
double-blind (p. 84)
internal validity (p. 85)

external validity (p. 85)
quasi-experimental study (p. 85)
confound (p. 86)
correlational method (p. 86)
case study (p. 87)
single-subject designs (p. 88)
ABAB (p. 88)
reversal design (p. 88)
epidemiology (p. 89)
incidence (p. 89)
prevalence (p. 89)
proband (p. 91)
cross-fostering (p. 91)
monozygotic (MZ) twins (p. 91)
dizygotic (DZ) twins (p. 91)
statistical significance (p. 93)
clinical significance (p. 93)
normative comparison (p. 94)

ADDITIONAL RESOURCES

American Psychological Association
750 First Street, N.E.
Washington, DC 20002
(202) 336-5500
executiveoffice@apa.org

www.yorku.ca/dept/psych/classics/Binet/binet1.htm
This site contains the text of Binet's New Methods for the Diagnosis of the Intellectual Achievements of Subnormals (1905).

www.cycad.com/cgi-bin/Upstream/Issues/psychology/IQ/apa.html
This site contains a lengthy report of a task force established by the Board of Scientific Affairs of the American Psychological Association. Topics covered include concepts of intelligence, intelligence tests, genes and intelligence, environmental effects on intelligence, and group differences.

www.stf.sk.ca/ps/src/bibliog/multint.htm
An extensive bibliography on the subject of intelligence and brain research is available at this site.

www.phil.gu.se/fu/ro.html
This site discusses the classical presentation of the Rorschach method, including the perceptual and cognitive processes associated with this method. It also addresses the use of the Rorschach method to treat patients with brain damage.

Chapter 5

Behaviour and Emotional Disorders of Childhood and Adolescence

Philip Firestone

On the evening of Sunday, March 27, 1994, Nicholas Battersby was shot while strolling down a quiet Ottawa street. Within a few days, three teenagers were arrested and charged with the killing. Doug, aged 17, was by law a minor, but on his lawyer's advice, he pleaded guilty to manslaughter as an adult. He was sentenced to 4 1/2 years in prison. Doug, who was driving the vehicle, had not shot Nicholas but had shot at other people that evening. The boys reported that they did not know Nicholas and had just been having fun with a shooting spree. Nicholas Battersby was simply in the wrong place at the wrong time.

Doug (not his real name) had an unenviable history. His biological father, a severe alcoholic, left the family when Doug was two years old, and had nothing to do with him after that. Doug's mother was constantly on welfare and he was raised in subsidized housing all his life. His mother has been described as a good and caring mother who provided the best environment she could for her children. But she went from one bad, abusive relationship to another. Doug lived with inconsistency and received poor parenting from the men who passed through his life.

Doug was described as a difficult child from an early age. As far back as kindergarten, his teachers reported he had a poor attitude and a short attention span. Doug was enrolled in special classes and was considered a serious behaviour problem. Psychological testing revealed high-end borderline intellectual abilities. He was also diagnosed as hyperactive and placed on Ritalin, but did not take it for very long. Police files revealed that Doug had been involved with the police well over 50 times, starting from the age of seven, for beating up other children, swarming, general theft, many auto thefts, weapons offences, alcohol- and drug-related offences, and being unlawfully at large. For several years, Doug was virtually always in foster care, detention homes, residential treatment centres, or on probation, but rarely complied with rules. The two other boys involved in the killing had quite similar histories.

Boys like Doug and his pals are very common in the mental health and judicial systems, though few of them actually kill. What diagnosis describes them? How have they come to be as they are? It is evident that many factors contribute to their disturbing behaviour and often a single diagnosis is insufficient. Doug would meet the DSM-IV criteria for attention deficit hyperactivity disorder and conduct disorder. In addition, as a child, he would have been diagnosed with opposition defiant disorder, and likely have qualified for a number of the learning disorders (for example, reading disorder). This comorbidity is more often than not the case in children who display serious behaviour problems early in life, and as in Doug's case, results in a very poor prognosis. Professionals are often stymied by the obstacles to change posed by these children's personal attributes.

HISTORICAL VIEWS OF CHILDHOOD

Virtually all modern theories, whether psychodynamic, behavioural, cognitive, or biological, consider the early years as critical in the development of adult behaviour. Nevertheless, during the latter part of the nineteenth century, children's psychological attributes were simply considered a downward extension of adult psychopathology. Although G. Stanley Hall, in the late nineteenth century, is often credited with developing the study of child psychology as a serious independent discipline, recognizing children were not simply small adults, Lightner Witmer is generally acknowledged to be the first to practise clinical psychology with children (Benjamin, 1996). In 1896 he opened the first North American psychological clinic for children at the University of Pennsylvania. Originally established to work with those who were experiencing academic problems, it quickly encompassed youngsters with emotional problems as well. By the 1930s many clinics treated childhood disorders and by the 1950s it was agreed that children's psychological disorders should be considered independently of adult disorders.

The first *Diagnostic and Statistical Manual* (DSM-I, 1951) made scant reference to the uniqueness of childhood disorders, including them within the adult categories. DSM-II (1968) recognized six independent diagnostic categories for children. Presently, DSM-IV lists some 44 categories of "disorders usually first diagnosed in infancy, childhood or adolescence."

Note, by the way, that different people define when childhood starts and ends slightly differently. Developmental psychologists generally refer to those under two years of age as infants or toddlers; *early childhood* refers to ages two to six, *late childhood* ages six to eleven, *early adolescence* ages eleven to fourteen, *middle adolescence* ages fourteen to eighteen, and *late adolescence* ages eighteen to twenty-one. In the DSM-IV, age eighteen is used as the cutoff point, with those over that age considered to be adults. Eighteen is also the usual legal cutoff, reflected in delinquency statistics. While adolescence is a separate stage from childhood, some of the studies referred to in this chapter have looked at children and adolescents together.

Developmental Psychopathology

In its early years, child psychology had a limited view, studying children by assessing the ages and stages of development. However, by the 1950s it encompassed the study of processes and mechanisms from birth to adulthood. By the late 1960s the term *developmental psychology* emerged as the favoured description of this field. It was also becoming increasingly clear to those working with abnormal behaviour that to effectively diagnose and treat psychological disorders in youth, one must first understand normal child development. How does a normal child at various ages experience and express feeling? How does a problem or a bad experience at one level of development affect the child at a later stage? Such exploration of continuities and discontinuities became a major focus.

In the 1970s **developmental psychopathology** emerged as a field of study in its own right. Its practitioners recognized that the perspectives taken with adults could not encompass the intricacies of normal and abnormal behaviour in an organism undergoing rapid biological, cognitive, and behavioural changes. Developmental psychopathology endorses the following principles:

- Abnormal behaviour (and normal behaviour) is *multide-termined*. It is unusual for any meaningful behaviour pattern to be the result of a single experience or even a single relationship over time. Rather, behavioural and emotional states are the result of a complex interplay between genetics, other biological factors, and repeated interpersonal experiences.

- Influence is reciprocal: a child is influenced by his or her environment and, in turn, influences the environment.

- A child needs certain experiences to develop normally. Failing to get the nurture or the challenge needed at one point places the child at risk for atypical experiences later on.

Risk Factors

How *much* deviation places a child at risk for later pathology? How does abnormal behaviour at one stage in development relate to normal or abnormal development at later stages? These are crucial questions in child development.

One possibility is that, with some problems at least, a childhood disorder persists into adulthood in essentially the same form. Recent longitudinal work suggests that this is the case with serious aggression in childhood. Boys rated as aggressive at eight years of age showed significant continuity in aggression up to 24 years later (Farrington, 1991). Another pathway may be related to **risk factors**. Loeber (1990) describes a risk factor as an event occurring early in a child's life that is predictive of a later outcome. The Ontario Child Health Study (Offord & Bennett, 1994), found that conduct problems in children predict continued psychiatric problems, but that the pattern was different for males and females. Does the difference reflect innate sex differences, or does gender place males and females into different risk paths?

Loeber examines how various risk factors may affect children differently depending on their age or developmental status (Loeber & Keenan, 1994). For example, the death of a parent does not always lead to immediate or later depression. However, depending on the child's age and earlier emotional and social experiences prior to the death, the child may be more sensitive to loss. Years later, a divorce may be more devastating for this person than for others.

Assessing and Treating Children: Special Issues

Right from the beginning, the psychological assessment of a child is different from that of an adult. Most adults seen by mental health professionals have identified themselves as needing help or as having problems, with the exception of court-referred forensic patients or those in serious psychotic states. Children, on the other hand, are more often brought to the attention of professionals because others, generally parents or teachers, feel they need help. Most of the children, especially the aggressive ones, do not feel they have a problem at all and resist the whole assessment or treatment process. (The Focus box discusses this issue in more detail.)

Partly for this reason, parents' and teachers' reports are often considered more important in assessment than the child's own input. The same is true for many aspects of treatment. Professionals often concentrate on instructing parents, teachers, nurses, or residential care workers in how to ameliorate behaviour problems. This is particularly true with psychotropic medication, which few children will readily accept. Professionals focus on getting information on behaviour change from parents and caregivers, and on techniques to ensure children take the medication as prescribed. Children's self-reports are considered of secondary importance and then generally only as they relate to side-effects.

Children often do not have enough cognitive skill to develop insight into their own problems or develop solutions; young children lack even the verbal skills to communicate their problems. Another reason that assessment and treatment must be filtered through the observations of adults is that, nearly always, the involvement of families and schools is necessary to implement treatment.

Prevalence of Childhood Disorders

In DSM-IV the childhood disorders often referred to by professionals as *behaviour problems,* **externalizing problems**, and *problems of undercontrol* are found under Disruptive Behaviour Disorders. The other childhood disorder found in DSM-IV is separation anxiety disorder (SAD), which is commonly classified as a personality problem, emotional problem, or a problem of overcontrol. While children and adolescents can certainly be subject to other anxiety disorders (such as obsessive-compulsive disorder or generalized anxiety disorder) and to depression, the authors of DSM-IV felt that these disorders were fundamentally the same whether the sufferer was a child or an adult, and did not create separate childhood categories. Developmental disorders, also a common concern with children, are discussed in Chapter 6.

The prevalence of childhood psychological disorders has been measured in several different Western countries and found to be remarkably similar. Of course, some differences do occur. Factors such as sources of information (parent, teacher, child), the way information is collected (rating scales, telephone surveys, interviews), and the diagnostic system used will affect prevalence. Differences have also been found between urban and rural environments.

VIEWPOINT *Who Is the Patient?*

Treating children involves special dilemmas for practitioners.

All too often, in any mental health practice, a patient does not participate appropriately or will not accept treatment. Perhaps the patient misses or cancels appointments frequently, or does not follow the therapist's directions. If such noncompliance persists in an adult, the therapists may justifiably stop providing services. But what do you do when an adult's actions affect a child patient? Consider the following, quite common, scenarios.

Critical Thinking Questions

1. A ten-year-old boy with reportedly serious behaviour problems and suspected learning problems is referred for assessment and treatment. His parents are often late for sessions or skip them entirely. They don't want the clinician to contact teachers or other professionals. What should the therapist do?

2. If a clinician is seeing an adult who refuses to take prescribed medication, and the clinician feels that medication is vital, he or she may refuse to continue to treat the patient. But how can this approach be applied to children? What if a child's parents refuse to administer medication that the clinician thinks is essential?

3. What if the parents agree but the child refuses?

One of the landmark epidemiological studies was the internationally acclaimed **Ontario Child Health Study (OCHS)**. The primary objective of the OCHS was to estimate the prevalence of various emotional and behavioural disorders among children four to sixteen years of age (born from January 1, 1966, through January 1, 1979). Four disorders were studied: *conduct disorder (CD)*, hyperactivity (*attention-deficit hyperactivity disorder, ADHD*), emotional disorder, and somatization. These disorders were chosen because of their perceived frequency and adverse affect on quality of life, as well as the cost to society for diagnosis and treatment. The study examined the six-month prevalence rates for disorders overall, and the prevalence of individual disorders for selected geographic and demographic subgroups. Also studied were the use of mental health and social services, ambulatory medical care, and special education for children with or without one or more of the disorders measured in the survey.

The six-month prevalence for any of the disorders surveyed was approximately 18 percent. However, finer analyses showed that rates vary by age and sex (see Table 5.1). Conduct disorder and hyperactivity were more frequent in boys than in girls, regardless of age. Among four-to-eleven-year-old children the rate of hyperactivity was almost twice that of conduct disorder, but the proportion was reversed among children aged twelve to sixteen (Szatmari, Boyle, & Offord, 1989a). Other analyses revealed evidence of more disorders in urban than in rural settings (Offord et al., 1992). Girls had a higher overall rate of emotional disorders than boys, but the difference was almost entirely in the older group; in this group, girls had 2.5 times as many emotional problems as the boys. The same was true for the Somatization category, in which prevalence in younger groups could not be estimated because of low rates.

Table 5.1 Prevalence of Psychological Disorders in Children and Adolescents (per 100)

Age Group (no. of children)	Conduct Disorder	Hyperactivity	Emotional Disorders	Somatization	More Than One Disorder
Boys					
4–11 (721)	6.5	10.1	10.2	—	19.5
12–16 (608)	10.4	7.3	4.9	4.5	18.8
4–16 (1329)	8.1	8.9	7.9	—	19.2
Girls					
4–11 (721)	3.3	3.3	10.7	—	13.5
12–16 (624)	3.4	3.4	13.6	10.7	21.8
4–16 (1345)	3.3	3.3	11.9	—	16.9

Source: Adapted from D. R. Offord et al., Ontario Child Health Study. II. Six-month prevalence of disorder and rates of service utilization, *Archives of General Psychiatry, 44(1987)*, 832–836. Copyright 1987, American Medical Association.

Note: The OCHS used the term *hyperactive* to describe children who met the DSM-III criteria for Attention Deficit Disorder with Hyperactivity. In DSM-IV these children are referred to as Attention Deficit/Hyperactivity Disorder. The term *emotional disorder* describes states reflecting dysphoric mood (excessive crying, thoughts of suicide, deliberate self-harm), compulsive and/or obsessive symptoms, and feelings of tension or anxiety. Somatization refers to the self-perception of a child as being sickly and the presence of recurring physical symptoms (constipation, headaches, nausea) in the absence of any medical disorder.

ATTENTION DEFICIT AND HYPERACTIVITY DISORDER

Six-year-old Zach was referred to the clinic by his pediatrician. During Zach's first six months, his mother was concerned about his poor sleep patterns. By the time he was a year old, she worried that he would hurt himself because he tried to climb out of his crib, and often rocked it so vigorously that it moved across the floor. His mother reported that he had never really walked; he went from crawling to running. Zach generally had several bruises from bumping into, or falling off, furniture and stairs. Although he could watch his favourite television shows, he could not play with toys or other children for more than a few minutes.

His problems increased when he started kindergarten, because he could not follow classroom rules, sit still during circle time, or wait for his turn in games; the latter sometimes led to fights with other children. Zach's Grade 1 teacher described him as overactive, impulsive, and unable to concentrate as his classmates could.

After a full assessment, including interviews and a behaviour rating scale complete by both parents and his teacher, Zach was diagnosed with Attention Deficit/Hyperactivity Disorder, Combined Type.

He was placed on stimulant medication with excellent results. His general behaviour, although far from perfect, was now much more like that of other children his age. His parents were given several counselling sessions on appropriate child-rearing approaches to the hyperactive child, and were also referred to a parents' self-help group sponsored by a local hospital.

The largest number of children seen in mental health clinics are those who behave disruptively, cannot control their activity levels or impulses, or have difficulty concentrating: those diagnosed with **attention deficit hyperactivity disorder (ADHD)**. There are two reasons they are seen so often: because, at approximately 6 percent of the school-age population, ADHD is one of the most prevalent childhood psychiatric disorders (American Psychiatric Association, 1987; Szatmari, 1992); and because these children create such problems in schools and families. As is typical of the externalizing disorders, these behaviours are usually more disturbing to others than to the children themselves.

ADHD is classified within the DSM-IV Disruptive Behaviour Disorders because these children have disturbing effects on parents, teachers, and friends and quickly become misfits (Whalen & Henker, 1985; Whalen, Henker, & Dotemoto, 1980). Having an ADHD child is stressful for the mother, who often feels inadequate as a parent (Johnston &

Mash, 1989; Mash & Johnston, 1983, 1990). In an ingenious set of studies, Dr. Charles Cunningham of McMaster University and several of his associates demonstrated that ADHD children can lead others around them to behave badly. One investigation (Cunningham & Siegel, 1987) paired up a number of boys. Half the pairs included one ADHD child and one normal control; the other half paired two normal controls. In the pairs that included an ADHD child, *both* children were more demanding and disruptive than in the control pairs. It is not surprising that ADHD is one of the most researched disorders of childhood.

ADHD is much more common in boys than in girls, with reported ratios between 3 to 1 (Szatmari, Offord, & Boyle, 1989b) and 5 to 1. Among children referred to clinics, the ratio rises to approximately 8 to 1. Age is another important factor. The OCHS study revealed that the prevalence of ADHD in boys dropped from approximately 10 percent in the 4 to 11 age group to about 7 percent in children aged 12 to 16. By the age of 18, the difference between males and females has disappeared (see Figure 5.1). However, many experts argue that these results are unrealistic, and that the rating scales and the DSM-IV criteria themselves (see DSM table) are more applicable to younger children (Barkley, 1996).

Historical Perspective

For centuries people have recognized a certain pattern of behaviour in children that we now call ADHD. In the mid-1880s German physician Heinrich Hoffman described a

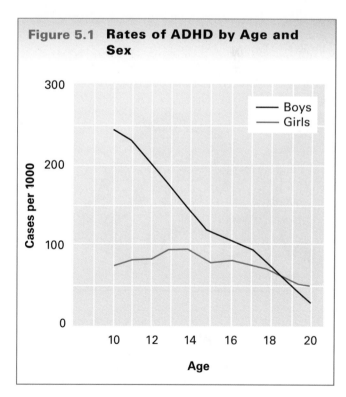

Figure 5.1 Rates of ADHD by Age and Sex

Source: Reprinted from *Journal of Child Psychology and Psychiatry, 34 (1993)*, P. Cohen, J. Cohen, S. Kansen, C. Velez, C. Hartmark, C. Johnson, M. Rojas, J. Book, & E. L. Streuhning, An epidemiological study of disorders in late childhood and adolescence, 851–857, with permission from Cambridge University Press.

DSM-IV Diagnostic Criteria for Attention Deficit/Hyperactivity Disorder

A. Either (1) or (2), 6 or more items, at least 6 months, to a degree that is maladaptive and inconsistent with developmental level:

(1) Inattention

    (a) inattention to details in schoolwork, work, or other activities

    (b) often has difficulty sustaining attention in tasks or play activities

    (c) often does not seem to listen when spoken to directly

    (d) fails to finish schoolwork, chores, or duties in the workplace

    (e) often has difficulty organizing tasks and activities

    (f) often avoids, dislikes, sustained mental effort (such as schoolwork)

    (g) often loses things necessary for tasks or activities (e.g., toys)

    (h) is often easily distracted by extraneous stimuli

    (i) is often forgetful in daily activities

(2) Hyperactivity-impulsivity

    (a) often fidgets with hands or feet or squirms in seat

    (b) often leaves seat in classroom or in other situations

    (c) often runs about or climbs inappropriately (restlessness)

    (d) often has difficulty playing or engaging in leisure activities quietly

    (e) is often "on the go" or often acts as if "driven by a motor"

    (f) often talks excessively

Impulsivity

    (g) often blurts out answers before questions have been completed

    (h) often has difficulty awaiting turn

    (i) often interrupts or intrudes on others (e.g., butts into conversations or games)

B. Some hyperactive-impulsive or inattentive symptoms that caused impairment were present before age 7 years.

C. Some impairment from the symptoms is present in two or more settings (e.g., at school or work, and at home).

D. There must be clear evidence of clinically significant impairment in social, academic, or occupational functioning.

Individuals may be diagnosed as Combined Type, Predominantly Inattentive Type, or Predominantly Hyperactive-Impulsive Type.

Source: Reprinted with permission from the *Diagnostic and Statistical Manual of Mental Disorders,* Fourth Edition. Copyright 1994 American Psychiatric Association.

"The Story of Fidgety Phillipe" appears in Struwwelpeter, *a nineteenth-century book of children's verses by physician Heinrich Hoffman. "I wonder if Phillipe is able / To sit still today at the table?" muses the father in the verse. It turns out that, like many hyperactive children, he is not. Phillipe begins rocking back and forth at the table, loses his balance and clutches frantically at the tablecloth before crashing to the floor, bringing the entire table setting with him.*

hyperactive child in a poem entitled "The Story of Fidgety Phillipe" (Stewart, 1970). The first designation to be accepted by professionals was **minimal brain dysfunction (MBD)**, a term common in the 1940s and early 1950s. The encephalitis epidemic of 1917–1918 had left a number of children with unmistakable organic brain damage. It became clear that a number of brain pathologies, such as encephalitis, birth trauma, lead toxicities, and head injury resulted in children showing difficulty with attention, overactivity, and impulse control. It was reasoned, therefore, that children with this combination of behaviours must have some serious brain dysfunction, as yet undetectable. However, subsequent research failed to uncover neurological signs in MBD, and this theory fell into disrepute.

The lack of hard neurological signs and the influence of psychoanalytic theory resulted in the diagnostic category of Hyperkinetic Reaction of Childhood when DSM-II was published (American Psychiatric Association, 1968). The authors acknowledged overactivity and attention as central to the disorder, but indicated it was a rather benign problem generally diminishing in adolescence. Subsequent research demonstrated that only the most obvious manifestation of this disorder decreased in adolescence, with subtler but perhaps more significant problems often continuing into adolescence and adulthood.

It was primarily the work of psychologist Virginia Douglas (Douglas, 1972) and her associates at McGill University, in the 1960s and 1970s that demonstrated that a higher-than-normal activity level, although bothersome to adults, was not terribly important in the development of ADHD children. Her studies illustrated that the most important deficits of these children—the ones that surfaced repeatedly when compared to normal controls—were an inability to sustain attention and control impulses. Largely as a consequence of this seminal work, attention deficits and impulsivity were recognized as fundamental in this disorder and incorporated in the name used in DSM-III and DSM-IV.

Diagnosis and Assessment

The essential features of ADHD are *age-inappropriate* levels of inattention, impulsivity, and hyperactivity. Anyone who has worked with children realizes that the ability to sit still, to concentrate, and to control impulses is largely age-related. In fact, our whole school system acknowledges this fact in grouping children by age. In making a diagnosis of ADHD one must consider the age of onset, the present age of the child, the behavioural characteristics being displayed, and the pervasiveness of the behaviour. It is important to consider behaviour both at home, as reported by parents and caregivers, and at school, as reported by teachers. As illustrated, children may be diagnosed in DSM-IV as ADHD, *combined type*; ADHD, *predominantly inattentive type*; or ADHD, *predominantly hyperactive-impulsive type*.

Assessment Tools

The assessment of ADHD in children has been advanced by the development of several good behaviour-rating scales.

Table 5.2 shows one of the more popular scales. Typically, both parents and teachers are asked to complete these; respondents are asked to record their perceptions of the child's behaviour over a specific period, compared to other children.

Technology has allowed the development of computerized tests for ADHD children. Dr. Russell Shachar, a psychiatrist at the Toronto Hospital for Sick Children, has carried out considerable research with a computerized continuous performance task, a measure of attention and impulse control. His work has demonstrated that ADHD children who are also diagnosed as Conduct Disorder have very different response patterns from those without such a condition (Schachar & Logan, 1990; Schachar, Tannock, & Logan, 1993).

Comorbidity

Among Ontario school-age children, close to 40 percent of ADHD children also qualify for a diagnosis of conduct disorder (Szatmari et al., 1989b). Barkley (1996) suggests that, in clinic-referred groups, up to 60 percent will be comorbid for oppositional defiant disorder (ODD) by seven years of age, and up to 50 percent will later be diagnosed with conduct disorder (CD). Recently in our own labs we have found that even preschool-aged ADHD children have extremely high rates of comorbidity; 83 percent have a co-diagnosis of ODD and 30 percent of CD (Monteiro-Musten, Firestone, Pisterman, Bennett, & Mercer, 1997). In adolescence, approximately 25 percent will meet the criteria for antisocial personality disorder and alcohol use disorder (Claude & Firestone, 1995; Manuzza & Klein, 1992; Weiss & Hechtman, 1986).

Learning disabilities are also common among ADHD children. Barkley (1996) reports that approximately 25 percent of the school-aged children in his studies have significant learning disabilities. In Ottawa, Dr. Susan Pisterman, who has been studying preschool ADHD children for several years, uncovered even more alarming results. Ninety-one percent of children originally diagnosed as ADHD at four years of

Table 5.2	Conners Teacher Rating Scale			

Child Name: _____ **Age:** _____ **Sex:** _____ **Teacher:** _____

Instructions: Read each item carefully, and decide how much you think the child has been bothered by this problem during the past month.

Not at All	*Just a Little*	*Pretty Much*	*Very Much*	*Classroom Behaviour*
0	1	2	3	Constantly fidgeting
0	1	2	3	Demands must be met immediately—easily frustrated
0	1	2	3	Inattentive—easily distracted
0	1	2	3	Fails to finish things he/she starts
0	1	2	3	Disturbs other children
0	1	2	3	Temper outbursts

Note: These six questions are examples from the rating scale teachers are asked to fill in on their pupils in their class.

Source: © 1989 Multi-Health Systems Inc., 908 Niagara Falls Boulevard, North Tonawanda, NY. 14120-2060, (800) 456-3003. Reprinted by permission.

age demonstrated learning problems at 9 1/2 years of age (Pisterman, Firestone, & Pilon, 1996).

Long-Term Development

Long-term followups of ADHD children show disturbing results. In a U.S. study, eight-year-old ADHD children followed into adolescence were characterized by continuing behaviour problems, inattention, impulsivity, poor school and academic performance, and an indication of emerging alcohol abuse (Barkley, Fischer, Edelbrock, & Smallish, 1990; Fischer et al., 1990). Another followup showed full ADHD syndrome in 40 percent of subjects; almost one in three had conduct disorders or antisocial personality disorder (APD); and one in four showed substance abuse problems (Gittelman & Manuzza, 1985; Manuzza et al., 1991). Among a group of ADHD children in Los Angeles first diagnosed at age nine, half had been arrested by late adolescence, and many had a history of multiple arrests (Satterfield, Hoppe, & Schell, 1982).

Two long-term Canadian studies with clinic-referred children are noteworthy. Drs. Gabrielle Weiss and Lilly Hechtman from the Montreal Children's Hospital have conducted the longest followup ever with ADHD children. At age 25 to 30, ADHD children continued to show problems, albeit not as severe as those in the American studies. Only a third had outgrown all symptoms of ADHD; about 25 percent had developed antisocial personality disorder (APD). They also showed higher-than-average levels of substance abuse and had poorer academic and occupational records (Weiss & Hechtman, 1993).

However, our own study called into question the link between childhood ADHD and a host of other serious problems in young adults. We examined the role of aggression in the long-term development of ADHD children. A group of children diagnosed at age 8 were evaluated at 20 and compared to controls (Claude & Firestone, 1995). Within the ADHD group, we compared those who had shown high levels of aggression when they were first examined at age seven with those who had been inattentive and overactive but not aggressive. The results were quite revealing. As in other studies, our ADHD group showed higher rates of antisocial personality disorder and substance abuse disorders during adolescence than controls. But these rates were attributable primarily to the "aggressive" subgroup. The nonaggressive ADHD group had no more psychiatric diagnoses than the controls, except for the diagnosis of ADHD itself. We also found that the aggressive group had spent an average of 435 days in residential treatment, compared to an average of 75 days for the nonaggressive group.

Etiology

Although no one has been able to explain exactly what causes ADHD, most researchers agree that a biological predisposition to ADHD is highly likely. There may be a variety of neurological etiologies manifested through a common pathway in the central nervous system. However, a precise causal pathway has not been determined. Family studies have revealed increased levels of ADHD and other psychiatric problems in the families of children diagnosed with ADHD compared to controls, and several twin studies have shown greater concordance of hyperactivity in monozygotic than dizygotic twins, supporting a genetic hypothesis (Biederman, Faraone, Keenan, & Tsuang, 1991, 1992). The heritability of ADHD has been estimated at between 30 and 50 percent, a significant component indeed. Nevertheless, if these numbers are correct, at least 50 percent of the variance in ADHD is not accounted for by genetics.

In the late 1970s and early 1980s, Benjamin Feingold (1975) proposed that food additives played a major role in the development of hyperactivity. He pointed to red and yellow food dyes as the major culprits, along with natural salicylates, found in numerous foods. More recently, sugar has been popularized as a major contributor to ADHD. More than a decade of scientific research has been unable to substantiate the role of any of these substances in the etiology of ADHD (Conners, 1980; Krummel, Seligson, & Guthrie, 1996; Prinz, 1985). Some recent correlational evidence suggests that lead from paint in older buildings, industrial pollution, and automobile exhausts can make their way into children, and may be related to attention deficits and other psychological problems (Minder, Das-Smaal, Brand, & Orlebeke, 1994). However, this research has not been well controlled and further work is required. In any case, the majority of children with relatively high levels of body lead do not have ADHD, and most ADHD children do not have elevated body lead readings.

The role of brain functioning in ADHD has received considerable study over the past ten years. Zametkin et al. (1990) used PET scans, which measure the rate of cerebral glucose metabolism of brains, in adults with childhood onset of ADHD and found they had reduced glucose metabolism, indicating less activity, during an auditory attention task. The first comprehensive study using MRI with ADHD and age-matched children was recently completed (Castellanos et al., 1996) and it reports ADHD children had a significantly smaller right frontal region and a smaller right side to the striatum.

Few investigators would endorse a theory suggesting ADHD arises purely from child-rearing or other social factors. There is significant support for the notion that, for the most part, ADHD individuals have a significant biological predisposition that involves brain function. The disorder may be exacerbated by biological forces such as complications of pregnancy and birth, and possibly by environmental toxins such as lead. Family influences may maximize or minimize the expression of the features that lead to a diagnosis of ADHD. Certainly it seems probable that an ADHD child raised in a supportive and nurturing environment will do better than one who receives poor parenting or whose family is dysfunctional or characterized by psychopathology (Hechtman, 1991). However, even in these circumstances, a child would probably not develop ADHD without a biological predisposition to the disorder.

Treatment

Stimulant Medication

More research has been conducted on the effects of stimulant medications on the functioning of school-aged children with ADHD than any other treatment modality for any childhood disorder (DuPaul & Barkley, 1990). Few, if any, interventions have led to the consistent, often dramatic, therapeutic gains evidenced by ADHD children who have taken stimulants (see Figure 5.2). The most frequently prescribed stimulant medication is **methylphenidate (Ritalin)**, with **dextroamphetamine (Dexedrine)** and **pemoline (Cylert)** used much less frequently. There are over 30 years of strong scientific support for the benefits of stimulant medication for hyperactive children. Most likely to improve are hyperactive, restless, impulsive, disruptive, aggressive, and socially inappropriate behaviours. In fact, there is considerable evidence that with appropriate administration of stimulant medication as many as 75 percent of ADHD children show improved attention and classroom behaviour that makes them indistinguishable from normal controls. Academic achievement, however, does not always improve, and children may need special education classes, tutoring, or other remedial help (DuPaul & Barkley, 1990; Rapoport & Castellanos, 1996a).

Interestingly, it has been established that children without problems in regular classrooms also show improved attention and decreased irrelevant activity levels when receiving this medication (Rapoport et al., 1978). More recently we have shown that preschoolers with ADHD taking methylphenidate show the same kind of improvement as school-aged children (Musten et al., 1996).

Behavioural and Psychological Treatments

Numerous experiments have been conducted to establish that operant procedures can control some problem behaviours found in ADHD children. Although interesting laboratory analogues, they are often far removed from the real environment of ADHD children and are limited in clinical usefulness (Backman & Firestone, 1979). Similarly, several studies have used cognitive training to improve attention and control impulsivity and other problems central to ADHD, but these procedures have demonstrated little clinical effectiveness (Abikoff, 1987; Hinshaw & Erhardt, 1993). Several large-scale investigations have shown that intensive behavioural programs in the classroom can sometimes improve the behaviour of some ADHD children. However, practical issues in regular classes make their implementation difficult and there is little evidence of generalization and maintenance of these gains.

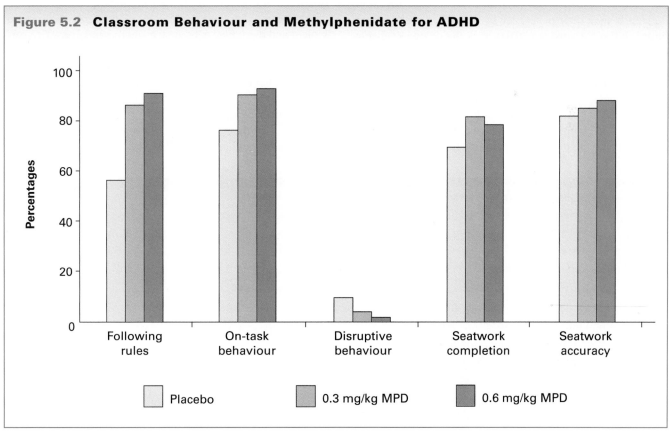

Figure 5.2 Classroom Behaviour and Methylphenidate for ADHD

Placebo   0.3 mg/kg MPD   0.6 mg/kg MPD

Note: The graph shows the differences in various aspects of classroom behaviour for ADHD with placebo and two dosages of methylphenidate (Ritalin) taken just before school and at noon. As shown, medication resulted in improvement in all categories depicted.

Source: W. Pelham, C. Carlson, S. Sams, G. Vallano, M. Dixon, & B. Hoza, Separate and combined effects of methylphenidate and behavior modification on boys with attention-deficit hyperactivity disorder in the classroom, *Journal of Consulting and Clinical Psychology, 61(1993)*, 506–515. Copyright © 1993 by the American Psychological Association. Reprinted with permission.

All this is not to say that psychological intervention should not be used for ADHD children. There is evidence that classroom intervention for academic and behaviour problems can help (Pfiffner & Barkley, 1990) and that it may be beneficial to train parents and teachers in social learning principles, in addition to giving stimulant medication (Gittelman et al., 1980). Furthermore, many children develop significant psychological problems, such as poor social skills and poor self-esteem, as a result of their experiences related to being ADHD. Psychological treatment geared toward these features, rather than the core symptoms of ADHD, should prove valuable. Finally, parent training programs are very helpful in improving the parenting skills, attitudes, and self-esteem of the parents, and reducing their stress, which is undoubtedly beneficial in the long run (Johnston & Mash, 1989; Mash & Johnston, 1983, 1990; Pisterman et al., 1992).

Oppositional Defiant Disorder and Conduct Disorder

Oppositional Defiant Disorder: Description

Refusing to follow instructions, arguing apparently just for the sake of arguing, hostility toward parents and teachers—as parents know, these are common behaviours for most children and adolescents. But children who act this way more frequently than their peers may be diagnosed with **oppositional defiant disorder (ODD)**. It is the degree of disturbance that makes them a concern to parents, schools, and society at large. ODD is usually first seen in the home. Some children then begin to act the same way in other settings, but many are defiant only with family members or people they know well. That sullen, vindictive, foul-mouthed child may turn quiet and compliant at the office of the family doctor or psychologist, who therefore fails to recognize the problem.

Symptoms of ODD (see DSM table) typically emerge before the age of eight and usually not later than early adolescence (American Psychiatric Association, 1994), and affect the child's interactions with parents, teachers, and peers. In some cases children with ODD may go on to develop a more serious category of aggressive behaviour known as conduct disorder (CD).

The diagnostic categories of ODD and CD are frequently discussed together, because many consider there to be little difference between the disorders other than the age at which they are manifested. However, it is important to note only about one in four boys diagnosed with ODD has developed CD three years later (Hinshaw & Anderson, 1996; Loeber, Keenan, Lahey, Green, & Thomas, 1993). Because the two are so closely linked, however, we will discuss etiology and treatment of the two disorders together.

Conduct Disorder: Description

Children with **conduct disorder (CD)** show a "repetitive and persistent pattern of conduct in which the basic rights of others and major age-appropriate societal norms or rules are violated. The behaviour pattern is typically present in a variety of settings such as home, school, or the community" (American Psychiatric Association, 1994). (See DSM table.) Aggression is the greatest concern; the terms *CD* and *aggressive children* are often used interchangeably. As these children get older, their aggression often progresses to more violent and disruptive acts, such as theft, vandalism, fire-setting, truancy, mugging, running away, destroying property, and cruelty to people and animals. The persistence of these disturbing behaviour patterns over time, from early childhood through adulthood, highlights their importance.

Children with CD are often uninterested in school. Regardless of their socioeconomic status, they tend to have lower grades, and are more likely to fail and to drop out of

---

DSM IV   Diagnostic Criteria for Oppositional Defiant Disorder

A. A pattern of negativistic, hostile, and defiant behavior lasting at least 6 months, during which four (or more) of the following are present:

(1) often loses temper

(2) often argues with adults

(3) often actively defies or refuses to comply with adults' requests or rules

(4) often deliberately annoys people

(5) often blames others for his or her mistakes or misbehavior

(6) is often touchy or easily annoyed by others

(7) is often angry and resentful

(8) is often spiteful or vindictive

Note: Consider a criterion met only if the behavior occurs more frequently than is typically observed in individuals of comparable age and developmental level.

B. The disturbance in behavior causes clinically significant impairment in social, academic, or occupational functioning.

Source: Reprinted with permission from the *Diagnostic and Statistical Manual of Mental Disorders*, Fourth Edition. Copyright 1994 American Psychiatric Association.

DSM IV   Diagnostic Criteria for Conduct Disorder

A. A repetitive and persistent pattern of behavior in which the basic rights of others or major age-appropriate societal norms or rules are violated, as manifested by the presence of three (or more) of the following criteria in the past 12 months, with at least one criterion present in the past 6 months:

Aggression to people and animals

(1) often bullies, threatens, or intimidates others

(2) often initiates physical fights

(3) has used a weapon that can cause serious physical harm to others (e.g., a bat, brick, broken bottle, knife, gun)

(4) has been physically cruel to people

(5) has been physically cruel to animals

(6) has stolen while confronting a victim (e.g., mugging, purse snatching, extortion, armed robbery)

(7) has forced someone into sexual activity

Destruction of property

(8) has deliberately engaged in fire setting with the intention of causing serious damage

(9) has deliberately destroyed others' property (other than by fire setting)

Deceitfulness or theft

(10) has broken into someone else's house, building, or car

(11) often lies to obtain goods or favors or to avoid obligations (i.e., "cons" others)

(12) has stolen items of nontrivial value without confronting a victim (e.g., shoplifting without breaking and entering, forgery)

Serious violations of rules

(13) often stays out at night despite parental prohibitions, beginning before age 13 years

(14) has run away from home overnight at least twice while living in parental or parental surrogate home (or once without returning for a lengthy period)

(15) is often truant from school, beginning before age 13 years

B. The disturbance in behavior causes clinically significant impairment in social, academic, or occupational functioning.

Source: Reprinted with permission from the *Diagnostic and Statistical Manual of Mental Disorders*, Fourth Edition. Copyright 1994 American Psychiatric Association.

school (Wolff, Waber, Bauermeister, Cohen, & Ferber, 1982). The more violent CD children tend to have significantly lower verbal and nonverbal intelligence (Farrington, Loeber, & van Kammen, 1990).

CD children are also likely to have poor interpersonal skills, are often rejected by their peers, and tend to be socially ineffective in their interactions with parents, teachers, and other significant adults. One possible explanation is that they appear to be deficient in the cognitive problem-solving skills that underlie most social interactions. When asked to list all the possible responses they can think of for a particular social situation (for example, "another child takes a tool just when you were about to use it") they do not generate as many alternatives as normal children, and are more likely to mention physical force and aggression. They also lack the ability to see someone else's perspective, a fundamental component of good relationships. There is considerable evidence that they are more likely to interpret another child's ambiguous gesture as hostile, which may partly explain their aggressive behaviour (Dodge, 1985). For example, they may take friendly roughhousing and backslapping as an assault; if they are bumped into in a schoolyard or accidentally injured in a game, they may believe the action was purposeful.

Diagnostic Issues

About 5 to 10 percent of children are estimated to have ODD and about 3 to 6 percent are estimated to have conduct disorder, with boys outnumbering girls by approximately 2 to 1 (Offord, Adler, & Boyle, 1986; Rutter, Cox, Tupling, Berger, & Yule, 1975). It is, however, difficult to establish the prevalence of CD. Many children show one or more symptoms but are not considered to have CD. In one study of children attending a primary care pediatric clinic, fewer than half of those identified as having clinical problems proved on interview with parents and teachers to reach criterion for any DSM disorder (Costello et al., 1988). Estimates often group ODD and CD together; yet many youngsters diagnosed with ODD never progress to the more serious CD, and only a minority of youth with CD will develop antisocial personality disorder as adults.

Individuals diagnosed with CD are prone to exhibit ADHD and/or substance abuse. Those with more conduct problems seem more likely to develop substance abuse and antisocial personality disorder later in life (Robins & Price, 1991). Children with both CD and ADHD are at particularly high risk for antisocial behaviour later (Moffitt, 1990). In some communities in the United States, substance abuse and delinquent behaviour has emerged as early as the second grade, perhaps indicating the increased availability of drugs (Loeber, Green, Keenan, & Lahey, 1995).

Although less frequent, there are also reports of above-chance rates of anxiety disorders and depression in CD individuals (Offord, Alder, & Boyle, 1986; Zoccolillo, 1992). Recent investigations have suggested that preadolescent boys with both CD and anxiety disorders are less aggressive than boys with CD alone.

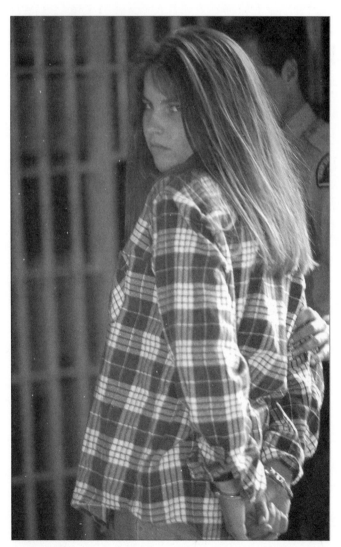

In Canada, many adolescents diagnosed with conduct disorder end up in a variety of institutions, from therapeutic foster homes, to residential treatment centres, to secure care facilities, which are really a form of prison for adolescents.

Etiology

In considering the etiology of conduct disorders, keep in mind the earlier discussion of risk factors (Garmezy, 1985). Factors that contribute to conduct disorder are multifaceted and may include biological or genetic attributes of the child, as well as family and community factors.

Neurological

There are reports that the incidence of subclinical neurological signs (such as poor coordination and poor fine motor skills) is three to four times as high among children with CD than others (Wolff, Waber, Bauermeister, Cohen, & Ferber, 1982), and their IQ is significantly below that of their peers (Moffitt & Lynam, 1994). However, many theorists dispute the claim that these scores demonstrate a biological cause, contending that IQ scores are not reflective of neuropsychological performance.

Temperament

Temperament, which may be considered an inborn style of interacting with the environment, is also identified as important in the backgrounds of conduct-disordered youths. Differences in temperament are usually based on observations such as the child's actions, emotional responsiveness, moods, and social adaptability. Easy-to-manage children tend to be contented, adapt well to environmental change, and show low-intensity responses to change in stimulus. Difficult children, in contrast, are easily distressed, adapt poorly to change, and react intensely to stimuli. Children with a difficult temperament are more likely to be referred for treatment for aggressive behaviour and temper tantrums than are easy children (Thomas & Chess, 1977). Thus, it has been speculated that a difficult temperament may characterize the history of youths eventually diagnosed as conduct-disordered.

Family Links: Genetic or Environmental?

For decades researchers have sought to establish whether certain antisocial behaviour patterns are heritable. Intergenerational patterns of criminal behaviour have been emerging for some time (Frick, 1993). For example, having a parent (especially a father) with antisocial personality means that a child will be much more likely to have CD (Faraone, Biederman, Keenan, & Tsuang, 1991; Frick et al., 1992; Lahey et al., 1988). Criminal and/or alcoholic parents, particularly the father, have also been consistently demonstrated as a characteristic of antisocial youths (Farrington, 1991; Kazdin, 1985). In the OCHS, having a parent arrested was one of the best predictors of conduct disorder.

It is also often found that the parents of aggressive children were themselves aggressive at the same age (Huessmann, Eron, Lefkowitz, Walder, & Leopold, 1984) and that parents of children with conduct disorder are more likely to suffer from various psychiatric disorders than parents of children in the general population. In a six-year longitudinal study of early predictors of conduct disorder, Offord and Keenan (1994) found that 69 percent of the CD children's fathers and 43 percent of their mothers had a substance abuse problem, and that 70 percent of the CD families came from the lowest economic class. This was twice the rate of the non-CD children (Loeber & Keenan, 1994).

All in all, the evidence is overwhelming that there is a link between CD and family. But is the connection genetic or environmental? Consider life in the home of, say, a substance-abusing mother and a father with psychiatric disorders and a criminal record. There is evidence that the mothers of CD children, as a group, may live in poorer psychosocial circumstances. The children may have received poor prenatal nutrition and may have been exposed to pre- and postnatal toxic agents, because of maternal drug abuse and other environmental factors (Needleman, Schell, Bellinger, Leviton, & Allred, 1990). In addition to these medical risks, it is reasonable to suppose that parents with antisocial personality disorder, substance abuse problems, or criminal behaviour will provide poor child-rearing. CD children, it has been suggested, may be part of a deviant family system.

For example, violent offenders often come from families in which there is poor supervision, spousal aggression, and alcoholism, and their parents demonstrate lax, erratic, and inconsistent discipline practices (Glueck & Glueck, 1950; McCord, 1977, 1988; McCord, McCord, & Howard, 1963). Peer groups and socialization practices play a significant role in the development of CD.

Dysfunctional families. Although several variables associated with dysfunctional families (marital conflict, divorce, child abuse) have been implicated in the onset and maintenance of antisocial behaviour in youth (Dodge, Price, Bachorowski, & Newman, 1990; Emery, 1982), the relationship between these variables and the behaviour can be complex. For example, marital conflict between the parents is associated with aggressive behaviour in children; but it seems that it is not so much the conflict itself that has this outcome as the fact that it makes the parents less available to the child or harsher in attitude to the child (Olweus, 1980). Although divorce has been implicated in the onset of conduct problems in boys, increasing evidence suggests that it is not so much the divorce itself that leads to problems as preexisting and ongoing marital conflict (Amato & Keith, 1991). Early physical abuse was a clear risk factor for later aggressive behaviour reported in school and community settings, even with statistical control of familial variables and temperament (Dodge et al., 1990).

Attachment. Researchers have identified several attachment patterns in young children that may predict problem behaviour (see discussion of attachment theory in Chapter 2). For example, an anxious attachment pattern (characterized by excessive clinging) or an avoidant pattern (being uncomfortable with closeness) appears to be associated with ODD in the preschool years (Erickson, Sroufe, & Egeland, 1985). Insecure attachment has also been linked with aggression in elementary school boys (Renken, Egeland, Marvinney, Mangelsdorf, & Sroufe, 1989) but not in girls (Greenberg, Speltz, & DeKlyen, 1993). However, no direct effect of in-

secure attachment to child antisocial behaviour has been established. Instead, researchers suggest that attachment relationships may interact with other factors (Greenberg, Speltz, & DeKlyen, 1993).

Parenting style. A strong predictor of later conduct problems is specific child-rearing patterns, such as poor parental supervision and lack of parental involvement in the child's activities. It has been found that mothers of children with conduct disorder are significantly more likely than mothers of control children to be poor at supervising their child's behaviour and inconsistent in applying discipline. There is also indirect evidence that parental involvement and parental discipline may be related to behaviours associated with ODD. Parents of antisocial youths, compared with parents of normal youths, show less acceptance, warmth, affection, and emotional support to their children, and report less attachment to them (Loeber & Dishion, 1983; Loeber & Stouthamer-Loeber 1986; McCord et al., 1959). There is also considerable evidence that parents of children with CD reinforce antisocial behaviour and ignore and punish appropriate behaviour. (See the Focus box later in the chapter.) This "coercive process," occurring over hundreds, if not thousands, of interactions, may well explain many of the unacceptable behaviours associated with CD (Patterson, 1982).

But before concluding that bad parenting causes CD, consider that much of the research is correlational and merely reflects group differences. Recall from Chapter 4 that correlation does not prove cause and effect. Research on family socialization related to aggression has increasingly recognized that influence can go both ways: yes, parents influence children, but children also influence parents (Lytton, 1990). Anderson, Lytton, & Romney (1986) watched mothers interacting with their own sons and with other boys. They found that all the mothers—whether their own children had conduct problems or were normal—had poorer-quality interactions with the conduct problem children than with normal children. They suggest that the main problem is not the mother but the child's behaviour. It may be that parents of conduct-disordered children show parenting difficulties not because they lack specific parenting skills but because of the stress of living with a very difficult child (McLoyd, 1990; Wahler & Dumas, 1989).

In the end, the attempt to establish a single ultimate cause for the disturbing behaviour patterns of CD is probably futile. *Reciprocal determinism*—that is, the understanding that people and their environments affect each other—is likely to offer a more accurate explanation.

Long-Term Development

One of the most disturbing aspects of conduct problems is their persistence as the child grows. Measures of aggression and antisocial behaviour have shown considerable stability across the life span, with correlations across lengthy intervals similar to those found for IQ (Farrington, 1991; Loeber, 1982; Olweus, 1979). However, the form of the behaviour often changes. For some, argumentative and defiant behaviours that first emerge in preschool and early childhood predate physical aggression and stealing in middle and late childhood, which are followed by sexual assault, substance abuse, and concentrated property destruction in adolescence (Hinshaw & Anderson, 1996). Dr. Richard Tremblay, a psychologist at the University of Montreal, and his colleagues have been carrying out an internationally acclaimed longitudinal study examining early disruptive behaviour and poor school achievement as possible predictors of later delinquent behaviour. As an example of this work, 1034 boys from 53 Montreal schools with low socioeconomic indexes were chosen for participation in a longitudinal study. Findings at 13 years of age confirmed predictions that children who are high in impulsivity, low in anxiety, and low in reward dependence were at greatest risk for antisocial behaviour (Tremblay, Pihl, Vitaro, & Dobkin, 1994). Others have reported that 40 percent of boys and 35 percent of girls who were diagnosed with CD later met the criteria for antisocial personality disorder in adulthood (Zoccolillo, Pickles, Quinton, & Rutter, 1992). Girls, however, show a different pattern than boys. CD in girls is a strong predictor of later problems related to anxiety and depression, in addition to persisting antisocial tendencies (Robins, 1986). Not surprisingly, the more conduct problems a child displays, the more likely the child is to develop a disorder in adulthood, as shown in Figure 5.3 (Robins & Price, 1991). (Note that, by DSM-IV criteria, a diagnosis of conduct disorder is based on 3 of the 15 identified conduct problems.)

Robins (1986) documented that patterns may persist over generations: antisocial behaviour in childhood predicts similar behaviour not only in children but in grandchildren.

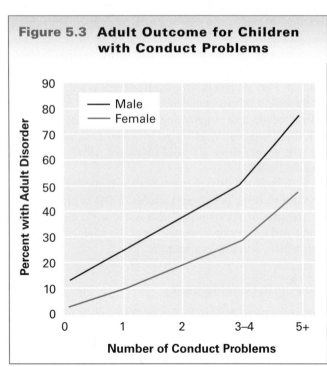

Figure 5.3 Adult Outcome for Children with Conduct Problems

Source: L. N. Robins & R. K. Price, Adult disorders predicted by childhood conduct problems: Results from the NIMH Epidemiologic Catchment Area Project, *Psychiatry, 54(1991)*, 116–132.

People with conduct and antisocial disorders are not only impaired in their own lives but also a heavy burden on society. They often cause suffering to others, and have repeated contact with both medical and correctional institutions, where a great deal of money and professional time is spent treating them (Offord & Waters, 1983). These disorders are thus one of the most costly of the mental health disorders, making effective prevention and treatment techniques essential.

Treatment

Four diverse treatment methods for ODD and CD have been examined in controlled trials: problem-solving skills training, parent management training, family therapy, and school- and community-based treatments (Kazdin, 1993; Pepler & Rubin, 1991). Although well-publicized claims have been made for each of these treatments, results must be viewed with caution. Research has consistently noted that CD in adolescents is extremely difficult to treat, and remains far more impervious to treatment than the externalizing problems among younger children (Kazdin, Mazurick, & Siegel, 1994). Furthermore, conclusions about the effectiveness of treatment are difficult to draw due to the lack of methodological rigour and a shortage of consistent findings (Kazdin, 1987a; Rutter & Giller, 1984). Nevertheless, several of the following treatment approaches are viewed as promising.

Problem-Solving Skills Training

Research has consistently found deficits in problem-solving skills, social perception, and social attributions in CD (Dodge, 1986a, b). These children are more inclined to interpret others' intentions and actions as hostile and to have poor social relations with peers, teachers, and parents. They have a limited repertoire of behavioural responses and fall back on aggression.

Problem-solving skills training usually combines several different procedures including modelling and practice, role-playing, and reinforcement contingencies. In one controlled study, children who received this training showed significant improvement, measured by teacher and parent checklists, which continued up to a year later (Kazdin, Esveldt-Dawson, French, & Unis, 1987b). However, they still were not functioning at a normal level (Kazdin, 1992a); and others have not found that improvements are consistently maintained (Kendall, Reber, McLeer, Epps, & Ronan, 1990).

Parent Training

Parent training (PT) programs are based on a *social learning* causal model. Interactions between the parent and child, or within the family, are considered to inadvertently develop and sustain aggressive and antisocial behaviour. This reciprocal rewarding, between parent and child, of undesirable or inappropriate behaviour has been described as the "coercive process" (Patterson, 1982, 1986). (See the Focus box for an example.) In PT the immediate goals are to develop specific skills in the parents to promote desirable, prosocial behaviours in the child while at the same time applying discipline

Focus   *The Coercive Process*

1. Parent tells Jimmy to go to bed.

2. Jimmy starts to fuss: "I want to play just one more video game."

3. Parent says "No! It is late and you have school tomorrow."

4. Jimmy gets very upset, starts hitting table and screaming hysterically, "Just one more game, just one more game! You're mean, you never let me have any fun!"

5. Parent feels a bit guilty at having spent so little time with Jimmy, and too tired, after a hard day's work, to argue and force the issue. Parent says "Okay, okay, just one more game."

6. Jimmy stops screaming and loses himself in the video game.

7. Parent, relieved the fight is over, goes into kitchen to make some coffee. Is not monitoring the child.

The reward pattern is as follows:

1. Child is rewarded for screaming; probability of screaming is increased.

2. Parent is rewarded for giving in; probability of giving in is increased.

The process is called "coercive" because the child got his reward by using inappropriate and undesirable behaviour.

Every parent has gone through something like the scenario above, yet most children do not develop serious antisocial behaviour. However, if this pattern is typical, and if the family has other risks for the development of conduct disorder (marital conflict, substance abuse, financial problems), and/or the child has a difficult temperament, the parent may be unwittingly reinforcing antisocial behaviour (Patterson, 1982). The most worrisome aspect of coercion is that it can so easily escalate: each time the child is rebuked, makes a fuss, and then the parents give in, he learns to display even more aversive or destructive behaviour.

Treatment pinpoints the coercive process and provides the parent with more tools with which to short-circuit it: both specific parenting skills and general interpersonal skills. The goal becomes to reward only good behaviour. ▲

techniques to minimize undesirable, maladaptive behaviours. Many studies of parent training programs have shown improvements in child behaviour at home, at school, and in the community (Kazdin, 1987a; Miller & Prinz, 1990). However, many parents drop out of the program. Dropouts tend to be single mothers, young mothers, parents from minority groups, and those with lower socioeconomic status—often the families that most need the treatment.

In a recent study, Kazdin, Siegel, and Bass (1992b) evaluated the effects of problem-solving skills training (PSST) and PT combined on children referred for severe antisocial behaviour. As expected, the combined treatment program led to marked changes, as measured by parental reports. The children's antisocial behaviour decreased and prosocial behaviour increased. Parental stress and overall symptoms of dysfunction were reduced. However, no differences were reflected in posttreatment teacher reports. Overall, the evidence on PT is promising, but its effectiveness may be overestimated because most studies have been conducted under ideal conditions in clinical settings.

Family Therapy

Family therapy, in which treatment revolves around changing the family as a system, has claimed success in treating conduct-disordered children. In family therapy, maladaptive behaviour is considered to serve a particular function within the family, reflecting the dysfunction among the family as a whole. Treatment seeks to integrate behavioural social learning, cognitive-behavioural, and family systems perspectives, although there are many variations in approach and technique.

One example, *functional family therapy* (Alexander & Parsons, 1982), has shown some promise with delinquent youth. The main goals of treatment include increased reciprocity and positive reinforcement among family members and establishing clear communications and identifying solutions to interpersonal problems. Outcome studies have shown reduced rates of arrest and self-reported delinquent behaviour. There is also evidence of improved school functioning, peer relations, and family interactions. The limitation is that the most disturbed youths and families may not be willing or able to engage in the process.

School- and Community-Based Treatment

The problem with the clinic-based methods described above is that they are only available to the minority of children who receive professional assistance (Offord et al., 1987). The Ontario Child Health Study (OCHS) revealed that only one in six children who suffered from a psychiatric disorder received mental health services during the preceding six months (Boyle, 1990). Furthermore, when PT is made available, economically disadvantaged, socially isolated, single, or depressed parents—those whose children are at the highest risk—are least likely to join and least likely to benefit from programs (Firestone & Witt, 1982; Kazdin, 1993; Kazdin, Siegel, & Bass, 1990; Prinz & Miller, 1994).

Another approach is to work through schools and the community. Dr. Charles Cunningham and a group of his colleagues at Chedoke Hospital of McMaster University have developed the innovative **Community Parent Education Program (COPE)**, a large-group, community-based version of PT programs (Cunningham, Davis, Bremner, & Dunn, 1993). To make access as easy as possible, COPE sessions have been scheduled at nearby neighbourhood schools and community centres, in the morning, afternoon, and evening (Cunningham, Bremner, & Boyle, 1995). Indeed, the program has succeeded in getting increased attendance by the high-risk families who are often least likely to enroll in clinic-based programs. Economic analyses have indicated that COPE is six times as cost-effective as individual parent training programs.

Community-based prevention programs offer important advantages and should be given priority. Because these programs use community settings, they are available to all children. This not only increases the likelihood of reaching all those who need treatment, but minimizes the stigmatization or labelling that may occur when only those identified as high-risk are treated (Offord & Bennett, 1994). Moreover, an inclusive program gives problem children a unique opportunity to interact with normal children in mixed-gender settings. Studies have indicated that children with aggressive behaviour show improvements when mixed with normal peers, and the presence of females tends to suppress antisocial behaviour in males.

SEPARATION ANXIETY DISORDER (SAD)

Susan was a bright, energetic six-year-old who had recently begun Grade 1. She had loved kindergarten, but now she was growing increasingly reluctant to go to school, and would report various pains and aches at school time. He parents decided to ignore her complaints and wait for her to grow accustomed to her new teacher and environment. However, Susan's anxiety about school was escalating, and she began to be fearful in other situations, especially when she faced separation from her parents. The mere suggestion that she go to a friend's house while they shopped threw her into a panic. She would burst into uncontrollable tears, expressing fears that one of her parents would "get lost and never find their way home" or that she would never see her mom or dad again. Despite constant reassurance that nothing bad would happen to any of them, she became increasingly preoccupied with fears of being alone, either in the house or in unfamiliar places, or with fears that her parents would leave her behind somewhere. Nightmares became common. She would crawl into bed with her parents at night, complaining of scary noises and shadows in her room. Susan's parents were disturbed to see her so upset. Worried about the developing nature of her fears, they sought professional help. At the first interview they told the therapist that Susan's fearfulness had begun shortly after the family moved into a new house to accommodate the new baby on the way.

Fears and worries are part of the normal course of childhood development, and most children will feel anxious at some times. Fears are especially common at certain developmental stages. In one survey, 43 percent of eleven-to-twelve-year-old children expressed some fears, while another 33 percent expressed numerous fears (Abe & Masui, 1981). These findings have been replicated in more recent studies with boys and girls of differing ages, in different countries (Ollendick, King, & Frary, 1989; Ollendick, Matson, & Helsel, 1985). Children are, moreover, not immune to the anxieties, relating to social change and uncertainty, that affect society as a whole. However, since many adults anticipate a certain degree of shyness and fearfulness in children at certain developmental periods, severe problems in functioning may go unnoticed.

Moreover, because anxious children may not be acting out in obvious ways, their problems may be easier to overlook. Anxiety disorders are not seen in mental health clinics as often as the disruptive disorders, probably because these children are not usually tearing the room apart or hitting their classmates; thus, parents and teachers are not driven so quickly to seek help from professionals. The same reason may account for the limited research in this area.

DSM-III-R listed a number of anxiety disorders for children and adolescents. However, on the basis of considerable study, DSM-IV revised the diagnostic categories of childhood and adolescence. Only **separation anxiety disorder (SAD)** remained as a *childhood* anxiety disorder, since it was the only one considered unique to childhood. Children and adolescents can indeed suffer from other anxiety disorders, but they will now be diagnosed for these with the same criteria as adults (Bernstein, Borchardt, & Perwein, 1996). (See DSM table.)

The most obvious sign of SAD is distress, sometimes amounting to panic, upon separation from the attachment figure. Children may also harbour grim, but unfounded, fears that they will be separated from their parents or that harm will befall their parents or other family members. They may cling so close to parents that they are reluctant to sleep alone and may try to avoid going to school so as to remain with the parents. Upon separation, the child may become overwhelmed with feelings of homesickness and loneliness, and may fantasize about being reunited with the attachment figure. Finally, social withdrawal, depression, or difficulties in concentrating may result when these children are not with the attachment figure.

Children diagnosed with SAD often report a host of fears, including animals, monsters, and concerns about death. The parents also report a litany of nighttime problems, including reports of frightening monsters, numerous trips to the bathroom, and general refusal to go to bed.

Although the onset of SAD may occur as early as the preschool years, the average age of children presenting at clinics is about nine years (Last, Francis, Hersen, Kazdin, & Strauss, 1987). In the OCHS, 3.6 percent of girls aged 12 to 16 and 2.4 percent of boys in that age group showed anxiety disorder, and a great deal of comorbid depression was evident (Bowen, Offord, & Boyle, 1990).

DSM IV Diagnostic Criteria for Separation Anxiety Disorder

A. Developmentally inappropriate and excessive anxiety concerning separation from home or from those to whom the individual is attached, as evidenced by three or more of the following:

   (1) recurrent excessive distress when separation from home or major attachment figures occurs or is anticipated

   (2) persistent and excessive worry about losing or about possible harm befalling major attachment figures

   (3) persistent and excessive worry that an untoward event will lead to separation from a major attachment figure (e.g., getting lost or being kidnapped)

   (4) persistent reluctance or refusal to go to school or elsewhere because of fear of separation

   (5) persistently and excessively fearful or reluctant to be alone or without major attachment figures at home or without significant adults in other settings

   (6) persistent reluctance or refusal to go to sleep without being near a major attachment figure or to sleep away from home

   (7) repeated nightmares involving the theme of separation

   (8) repeated complaints of physical symptoms (such as headaches, stomachaches, nausea, or vomiting) when separation from major attachment figures occurs or is anticipated

B. The duration of the disturbance is at least 4 weeks.

C. The onset age is before 18 years.

D. The disturbance causes clinically significant distress or impairment in social, academic (occupational), or other important areas of functioning.

Source: Reprinted with permission from the *Diagnostic and Statistical Manual of Mental Disorders*, Fourth Edition. Copyright 1994 American Psychiatric Association.

Fears differ at different ages. When asked about their anxieties, children aged five to eight most often mentioned worry about harm befalling a parent. Nine-to-twelve-year-olds most often reported excessive distress upon separation; thirteen-to-sixteen-year-olds most often reported physical complaints on school days. Reaction to anxieties are different, as well. Young children often refuse to go to school. Sadness and withdrawal are common among middle children. Adolescents exhibit both physical complaints and school refusal.

SAD may appear suddenly in a previously well-functioning child, often after a major stressor, such as the death or illness of a relative, or moving to a new school or neighbourhood. Onset has also been reported following prolonged vacations or absences from school, and at developmental transitions, such as entry into elementary or junior high school.

So-called school phobia is often a reflection of separation anxiety. For some children, a hug is enough to relieve the distress; others have more persistent problems.

Although there is some evidence that anxiety disorders in general are more frequent in girls (Offord et al., 1987), research has generally not revealed sex differences with SAD. When gender differences in anxiety appear, it is not clear whether girls really do experience more anxiety or if the difference is a result of an artifact, such as girls' greater willingness to admit to having such fears.

Diagnosis and Assessment

Typically, from about six months up to two or three years of age, most children will display some distress when separated from parents. However, children diagnosed with SAD experience severe and excessive anxiety when faced with separation from parents or others to whom they are emotionally attached. Such extreme anxiety, which frequently reaches panic proportions, becomes evident even when the child merely thinks about separation. For a clinical diagnosis of separation anxiety disorder to be made, the anxiety reaction must be well beyond that normally seen in other children of the child's developmental level and at least three of eight possible symptoms of anxiety must be demonstrated for a period of four weeks.

SAD may sometimes be misdiagnosed because the parents describe the child as being quite oppositional, displaying temper tantrums, disobedience, or aggressiveness. However, upon closer examination it becomes apparent that the oppositional behaviour is restricted to anxiety-provoking situations that involve separation from their parents. Thus, before deciding that a child has an oppositional disorder, it is important to examine the situations that elicit the behaviour. Separation anxiety may be the cause even if only certain types of separations evoke the behaviour.

Assessment Methods

It is generally recommended that a multidimensional method of assessment be used when evaluating a child's anxiety problem. Assessment procedures include structured or semi-structured clinical interviews with children and parents, self-report questionnaires, parent and teacher ratings, behavioural observations, and psychological measurements. A complete assessment involves three separate realms: verbal/cognitive, motoric/behavioural, and physiologic.

There are currently several reliable structured and semi-structured interviews available. These include the Schedule for Affective Disorders and Schizophrenia for school-aged children (K-SADS), the Diagnostic Interview for Children and Adolescents (DICA), and the Revised Children's Manifest Anxiety Scale (RCMAS). Each instrument involves detailed, separate interviews with both the parents and the child to evaluate the existence and subsequent severity of the symptoms (see Rapoport & Ismond, 1996, for a comprehensive listing).

Comorbidity

Children with anxiety disorders often have mood disorders as well (Anderson, Williams, McGee, & Silva, 1987; Bowen, Offord, & Boyle, 1990; McGee, Feehan, Williams, & Anderson, 1992). In clinical populations, up to 70 percent of children with anxiety disorders are depressed; approximately 80 percent are reluctant or refuse to go to school (Gittelman et al., 1980); 70 percent show somatic complaints and many also have test anxiety (Biedel, 1988).

Long-Term Development

Children diagnosed with anxiety disorders have also been described by parents, teachers, and peers as socially withdrawn, maladjusted, and having poor school performance (Ialongo et al., 1993; Strauss, Forehand, & Frame, 1986). Anxiety, especially when associated with depression and low self-esteem, may interfere with social behaviour and make it difficult for children to form friendships.

Overall, researchers know very little about the course of SAD if left untreated. It has been suggested that children can simply outgrow the disorder and develop into well-functioning adolescents and adults. However, this possibility seems unlikely, based on long-term followup studies of children treated for school phobia or school refusal (at least some of whom might be diagnosed with SAD). Without intervention, SAD appears to vary, often getting better for a time and then worse if the child undergoes stress or developmental transitions. Approximately 40 percent of children diagnosed with an anxiety disorder continue to exhibit significant symptoms up to four years later (McGee, Feehan, Williams, & Anderson, 1992; Offord et al., 1992). In one study, 75 percent of children with separation anxiety at baseline met diagnostic criteria for agoraphobia at followup (Biederman et al., 1993).

There is also speculation that children with SAD may be at risk for agoraphobia and panic disorder in adulthood (Berg, Butler, & Hall, 1976).

Etiology

Family Links

Separation anxiety, like other anxiety disorders, does run in families. In one study, mothers of children with SAD had a much higher lifetime rate of anxiety disorders (83 percent) than the control group mothers (40 percent) (Last, Strauss, & Francis, 1987). A series of studies showed that mothers who suffer depression together with panic disorder had a 38 percent probability of having a child with separation anxiety

ViewPoint *Gender Differences*

Visit virtually any special classroom for children with intellectual, academic, or behavioural problems, and you will see many more boys than girls. Boys outnumber girls in all psychological disorders of childhood and adolescence except the anxiety and eating disorders. Is this difference caused by the different ways parents rear boys and girls? That does not seem to be a complete explanation, since gender difference in vulnerability is evident as early as conception. Although approximately 1.4 times as many males as females are conceived, by age three there are fewer male children still alive. More males than females die due to miscarriages, birth and pregnancy complications, and diseases of childhood (Klug & Cummings, 1986). This is undoubtedly a function of a biological weakness compared to females.

Critical Thinking Questions

1. Since boys show so many more behavioural and psychological problems in childhood, should they be treated differently, because that is their "normal" or "natural" way of behaving?
2. Should parents and schools be more forgiving of boys' aggressive and disruptive behaviour because they can't help it?
3. On the other hand, should parents and schools be less forceful in making girls get involved in many activities because they often show more anxieties and fears than boys?

disorder (Weissman, Leckman, Merikangas, Gammon, & Prusoff, 1984). There is no concrete evidence, however, linking SAD with specific types of psychopathology in parents.

The possibility that anxiety disorders in general have a genetic component has received increasing attention, since a tendency to anxiety is, to some extent, under genetic control (Marks, 1973; Torgersen, 1976). Most studies have shown a higher incidence of anxiety disorders than expected by chance in relatives. However, the usual question remains: Is the family link one of heredity or of shared environment?

In a twin study, the concordance for anxiety disorder was three times as high in MZ pairs as in DZ pairs, suggesting a significant genetic transmission; but the high number of discordant MZ pairs shows that environment, too, is important (Torgersen, 1983).

Temperament

An increasing body of data from laboratory monkeys supports the hypothesis that high stress reactivity is heritable. Genetically related rhesus monkey infants reared under identical circumstances were more likely to react similarly to stress even if they were not reared by their natural mother and did not interact with each other while growing up. Kagan (1982) reported that human toddlers and preschool children display developmentally stable individual differences in a personality or behavioural characteristic he calls *timidity* or *vigilance*. Some of these children consistently display fearfulness, anxiety, and cautious withdrawal in the face of novelty or challenge, but not in the absence of stress.

Such a temperament in early childhood may be related to anxiety disorders later in life. Kagan and his colleagues have explored the role of **behavioural inhibition** (Kagan, Reznick, & Snidman, 1988). Behaviourally inhibited children show profound avoidance of others in preschool, and demonstrate atypical autonomic nervous system responses when challenged by novelty. In a three-year followup, those with behavioural inhibition had significantly higher rates of multiple anxiety disorders, avoidant disorders, separation anxiety disorder, and agoraphobia than other children (Biederman et al., 1993). Socially withdrawn school-aged children appear to exhibit more internalizing problems than do sociable children. Do low self-esteem, depression, and anxiety problems interfere with social behaviour and lead children to withdraw from their peers? Or does rejection and isolation from their peers cause children to become sad and anxious? The latter seems an inadequate explanation, since only about 30 percent of children who are socially inhibited develop an anxiety disorder (Biederman et al., 1990). Inhibition may be one of several factors that contribute to the development of an anxiety disorder.

Parental Attachment

An insecure bond between parent and child is considered to be an important factor in the development of various anxiety symptoms. Sometimes an insecure bond results from overprotection. When parents have not allowed the child to experience the natural challenges and pains of development, the child may feel ill equipped to deal with change and separation.

Treatment

Treatment of childhood anxiety disorders generally aims to improve interactions between the parent and child. A multimodal approach is typically employed, and should include educating both parent and child about the specific disorder, consulting with primary care physicians and school staff, cognitive-behavioural interventions, and family therapy. More recently, pharmacology has demonstrated some usefulness.

Cognitive-Behaviour Therapy

Cognitive-behaviour therapy integrates behavioural approaches, such as exposure, with cognitive techniques, such as coping self-statements, and has shown considerable success in the treatment of SAD.

Behavioural therapy attempts to enhance self-efficacy, the belief that one can be successful (see Chapter 2). Exposure involves practising the behaviour one is trying to develop, beginning with easy steps. For example, a child who panicked at the idea of a sleepover might start by staying at a neighbour's house, knowing the mother was waiting at home, and gradually work up to longer and further visits.

Cognitive techniques help the individual reframe anxious thoughts in a more hopeful or confident way, resulting in more assertive and adaptive behaviours (Leonard & Rapoport, 1991). Using coping statements, a child is taught to think, "I can walk to school by myself. The school is a safe place to be with friends." When panicked thoughts start coursing through the mind, the child is taught to recognize them, consciously stop, and replace them with coping statements. Typically, children ten years and older can benefit from cognitive techniques.

In one study, Kendall (1994) compared children aged nine to thirteen who had taken 16 weeks of cognitive-behaviour therapy to a control group of similar children on a waiting list. The therapy program consisted of coping self-statements, modelling, exposure, role-playing, relaxation training, and contingent reinforcement. The treated children reported clinically significant decreases in anxiety and depression. In fact, a year later many did not meet diagnostic criteria for an anxiety disorder. Parents are often involved in this type of treatment to ensure that children can use their new skills at home and at school.

Play Therapy

As might be expected, many young children with anxiety disorders are shy or fearful when visiting a clinician. Even if they are comfortable, they may not have the cognitive or verbal abilities to express themselves. In either case, play therapy may be useful for both diagnosis and treatment. In play therapy a child is exposed to a wide variety of toys, artistic materials, and dolls, usually chosen by a therapist based on suspected problems. For example, if the therapist suspects a child's behaviour relates to parental conflict, dolls or puppets might be chosen that could represent a father, mother, and child. The therapist would then engage the child in various activities with these toys and see if the child's play with the dolls seemed to be expressing feelings or thoughts the child could not express in other ways.

Pharmacological Treatment

Surprisingly few studies have evaluated pharmacological treatments for childhood anxiety. Psychotropic medication has not demonstrated consistent evidence of usefulness with this population. Tricyclic antidepressants and benzodiazepines have been widely used to treat SAD, although there is only limited support for their efficacy, and they commonly have undesirable side-effects (Bernstein, Garfinkel, & Borchardt,

1990; Klein, Koplewicz, & Kanner, 1992; Simeon & Ferguson, 1992).

Serotonin reuptake inhibitors, which have fewer and more tolerable side-effects than the older antidepressants, show some promise, but are still in the early stages of investigation. In an initial study of fluoxetane, 80 percent of a group of 20 children with a range of anxiety disorders showed moderate to marked improvement (Birmaher et al., 1995). Double-blind placebo studies will be needed to confirm these results.

In general, SAD is underresearched, perhaps because anxious children are not as disturbing to parents and teachers as disruptive children. In view of the high prevalence and poor prognosis of anxiety disorders in childhood and adolescence, there is a dire need for more research into treatment techniques, and combinations of therapies, that might help these children.

PANORAMA

The past 25 years have seen developmental psychology study children from conception into adulthood. The results have demonstrated that the polarized nature/nurture debate is dead. It is clear that human development, both normal and abnormal, is a dynamic interplay of genetics (for example, random combinations, mutations), biology (for example, maternal nutrition, prenatal exposure to toxins), and the psychosocial environment into which a child is born. The goal of this research has always been to chart human development and determine how various factors affect it. Borrowing heavily from this work, those in the field of childhood psychopathology have developed primary, secondary, and tertiary interventions. The Better Beginnings, Better Futures Project, which originated with the Ontario Ministry of Community and Social Services, is a fine example of a primary intervention program, in which whole communities are targeted with the goal of preventing problems from arising in the first place. Intervention starts with prenatal care and lasts until at least eight years of age. The COPE program in Hamilton is a secondary inter-

vention program. Here many children are helped who show some signs of a problem although they may not yet have a full-blown diagnosable disorder. Both programs treat entire families in their own communities. Tertiary treatment refers to treatment of individuals who demonstrate all the signs of a psychological disorder like ADHD or CD. Traditionally, debates about which treatment works best have pitted dynamically oriented treatment against behavioural treatments, or psychological interventions against psychological interventions. Such polarized approaches are also outdated. Research has demonstrated that most interventions have some merit. A more fruitful question would be "Which treatment works best, for what kind of person, with which disorder, under what circumstances?" Two children with the same diagnosis may do best with very different treatments or combinations of treatment, depending on their developmental stage, personality, or the abilities of their parents. This type of question allows us to address the needs of the child or adolescent, not the theoretical preference of the health care provider.

SUMMARY

The Ontario Child Health Study revealed the six-month prevalence of psychological disorders in children and adolescents was approximately 18 percent, with differences based on age, sex, and location. ADHD is probably the best studied of the childhood disorders, because it is found in at least 5 percent of the general population. In consequence, there are a number of well-validated assessment instruments available. ADHD is often comorbid with CD, and the combination predicts continuing problems into adolescence and young adulthood so-

cially, emotionally, academically, and legally. There is general agreement that ADHD is a biologically based problem, which may be exacerbated or alleviated by the environment. Stimulant medication is the most effective means of improving the behaviour of ADHD children, while they are on it. There is also some evidence that teaching parents and teachers social learning techniques can be beneficial. Other psychological interventions may be helpful in dealing with secondary problems such as low self-esteem or poorly developed social skills.

Many professionals consider ODD a younger version of CD. CD is particularly disturbing, because of the degree of aggression and vandalism associated with it. Children with CD often have other problems, the most serious of which appears to be substance abuse. The number of conduct problems is predictive of the difficulty these children will have as adults. They do poorly in school, drop out early, and are prone to antisocial personality disorder as adults. The major risk factors associated with CD are related to the family. Criminality, family violence, substance abuse, and other psychiatric problems are often present in the families of CD children. These family features may put children at biological risk as well as exposing them to inappropriate parenting. Of all psychological attributes, only IQ has a greater stability over time. Interventions based on social learning theory appear to be the treatment of choice for these children. Recent years have seen the development of community-based treatment programs designed to reach those most in need.

Although children and adolescents have all the anxiety disorders experienced by adults, SAD is the only one considered unique to this age group. Anxiety disorders have not had the research attention of ADHD or CD, presumably because they do not cause the same kinds of problems for schools and communities. The sex differences seen in some other anxiety disorders are not apparent in SAD, but there are age-related differences. There is some evidence of genetic and biochemical contributions to SAD, but the mechanisms are not well understood, and it is clear there is a considerable environmental component as well. Once again, behavioural interventions appear to be the treatment of choice, but more research would be helpful. Traditional medication for anxiety disorders have not been found effective with youngsters, but there is some promise with the new family of serotonin reuptake inhibitors.

KEY TERMS

developmental psychopathology (p. 99)
risk factors (p. 99)
externalizing problems (p. 99)
Ontario Child Health Study (OCHS) (p. 100)
attention deficit hyperactivity disorder (ADHD) (p. 101)

minimal brain dysfunction (MBD) (p. 102)
methylphenidate (Ritalin) (p. 105)
dextroamphetamine (Dexedrine) (p. 105)
pemoline (Cylert) (p. 105)
oppositional defiant disorder (ODD) (p. 106)
conduct disorder (CD) (p. 106)
temperament (p. 108)

problem-solving skills training (p. 110)
parent training (PT) (p. 110)
family therapy (p. 111)
Community Parent Education Program (COPE) (p. 111)
separation anxiety disorder (SAD) (p. 112)
behavioural inhibition (p. 115)

ADDITIONAL RESOURCES

Canadian Institute of Child Health
885 Prom. Meadowlands Drive
Suite 512
Ottawa, ON
K2C 3N2
(613) 224-4144
(613) 224-4145 fax
cich@igs.net

Canadian Paediatric Society
2204 Walkley Road
Suite 100
Ottawa, ON
K1G 4G8
(613) 526-9397
(613) 526-3332 fax
info@cps.ca

Children and Adults with Attention Deficit/Hyperactivity Disorder
8181 Professional Place
Suite 201
Landover, MD 20785
(800) 233-4050
(301) 306-7070
(301) 306-7090 fax
national@chadd.org

www.interlog.com/~hincks/welcome.htm
This site highlights resources provided by The Hincks Centre, a children's mental health centre located in Toronto, that offers outpatient, and residential and day treatment services/assessments to infants, children, and youth.

www.clarke-inst.on.ca
The web site of the Clarke Institute of Psychiatry provides information about mental health issues related specifically to children and youth, including attention deficit hyperactivity disorder, anger and aggression management, and children's mental illnesses.

www.chadd.org
This site for Children and Adults with Attention Deficit/Hyperactivity Disorders contains valuable information on attention deficit disorder as well as details about policy regarding disability issues.

www.cich.ca/html
The Canadian Institute of Child Health web site addresses issues related to children's health and development, including public information, policy development, and outreach to national, provincial, and community groups.

www.cps.ca
The Canadian Paediatric Society promotes quality health care for children and youth. Their web page provides information about national guidelines and standards for pediatric practice, including psychosocial pediatric issues.

Chapter 6

Developmental Disorders

Patricia M. Minnes

Joe proudly points to his baseball cap bearing a picture of Niagara Falls. He eagerly announces that he had a boat ride to the bottom of the Falls, went to the top of a tower in an elevator with windows, and had his own motel room next to Jim and Mary's room. Joe's delight is contagious; one can't help but smile as he talks about the trip organized to celebrate his 50th birthday.

At the age of 12, Joe was institutionalized when his parents could no longer manage his behaviour. His parents were older and lived in the country, a three-hour drive from the institution. Joe saw little of his family and after a few years, lost contact altogether. Joe attended the institutional school and later worked in the workshop. A psychological assessment at the age of 37 found Joe to have a mild developmental handicap. He was able to read, spell, add, and subtract at the primary school level. Joe had fairly well developed verbal skills and good comprehension and could manage personal care with limited supervision. Joe's major problem was his temper. Whenever his routine was changed, Joe would start shouting, swearing, and threatening. When Joe became particularly upset, he would bang his head and scratch himself. After taking psychotropic and neuroleptic medication for many years to control these outbursts, Joe developed coordination and visual problems that were thought to be drug-related.

Joe's institution was scheduled to close in a few years and his assessment indicated that he would be a good candidate for community living. So after 25 years in the institution, he was moved to a new group home. He still worked in the institution's workshop. But Joe would hang around the institution and hide from group home staff when it was time to go home. He had outbursts of temper and his shouting and screaming disturbed the neighbours. He would "borrow" other residents' things and become upset if they did not want to watch his television programs or listen to his favourite music. Joe would also bully a younger resident and would bother one of the female residents by standing close to her, stroking her arm, and staring at her.

Joe was enrolled in a program called Living with Others where he learned the importance of personal space and strategies to manage anger. He practised relaxation exercises and met regularly with a psychologist to talk about his fears and concerns. The psychologist found that change and unexpected events triggered feelings of loss of control related to Joe's long history of abandonment. Joe's outbursts improved to the point where he no longer required medication.

Since he was unhappy at the group home, Joe was considered for a new program called Homeshare, in which adults with developmental disabilities live with families in the community. On Joe's first weekend visit with Jim and Mary, he was anxious and became agitated on three occasions, but he was able to cool off in their large garden. After three more visits over the next two months, Joe asked if he could move in with Jim and Mary. Finding the house too quiet since their youngest son had left for university, Jim and Mary agreed. They were pleased with Joe's progress over the next few months and came to consider him a member of the family.

HISTORICAL PERSPECTIVE

Throughout history and particularly since the mid–nineteenth century, changing attitudes toward people with developmental disabilities have been reflected in policies and models of service delivery (Wolfensberger, 1975).

For centuries, such people were regarded as subhuman, a menace, or an object of dread. In ancient Greece, handicapped infants were left on mountaintops to die or were thrown from the cliffs. While this practice is abhorrent to modern sensibilities, it can be argued that a similar view of disability is reflected in the common current practice of aborting a fetus shown at prenatal screening to have Down syndrome or spina bifida. Moreover, people with developmental disabilities are often given lower priority than others for medical and surgical intervention. There are even those who support euthanasia in cases of severe disability.

Between 1870 and 1890, there was a shift in attitudes toward viewing people with disabilities as objects of pity, burdens of charity, and "holy innocents" (Wolfensberger, 1975). Asylums were built to protect them. However, in the later nineteenth and early twentieth century, genealogical studies by Goddard (1912) and others emphasized that mental retardation was inherited. People with disabilities came to be viewed as a threat to the moral and intellectual fibre of society; the growing *eugenics movement* called for sterilization, the restriction of marriages, and institutionalization to protect society from this threat.

The *medical model* dominated the first half of the twentieth century. Increasing numbers of individuals were viewed as needing medical care and were thus institutionalized. Psychologists played an important role in the diagnosis and classification process through intelligence testing. However, few institutions were able to provide more than custodial care for the growing numbers of residents. As institutions became more crowded, maladaptive behaviours became increasingly difficult for staff, and medication became the treatment of choice.

The late 1950s and early 1960s represented a time of major change in the field of developmental disabilities. It was the time of the civil rights movement in the United States, when freedom from oppression was a major theme. The publication of *Christmas in Purgatory* (Blatt & Kaplan, 1966), a photographic essay about the appalling living conditions of persons with developmental disabilities in institutions, led to litigation and public outcry. In 1968, the International League of Societies for the Mentally Handicapped adopted the *developmental model* to guide educational programming.

At the same time, interest in environmental influences on behaviour and the rise of behaviourism led to the application of operant conditioning techniques in educational programs. For the first time, people with mental retardation were viewed as having potential, and as capable of some learning and development regardless of the degree of disability.

New initiatives were stimulated by the interest shown by U.S. President John F. Kennedy, who had a sister with a developmental disability. Gradually, the medical model was replaced by the philosophy of *normalization* and changing attitudes were reflected in policies promoting the use of least restrictive practices and environments.

From the 1960s to the present, deinstitutionalization, educational mainstreaming, and community-based service delivery have been major goals. People with disabilities have gained increasing visibility through media coverage of the Special Olympics and through television and films that increase public awareness. In the 1990s, advocacy has become an important theme, including self-advocacy through organizations such as People First and the National Association of Retarded Citizens in the United States.

MENTAL RETARDATION

Developmental disorders may be manifested in a number of different ways. There may be unusual physical features, deficits in language, motor ability, and other skills, and patterns of behaviour such as hyperactivity, aggressiveness, or **stereotypy** (the repetition of meaningless gestures or movements).

The terminology associated with developmental disorders varies and can be confusing. For example, in Canada, the terms **developmental handicap** and **developmental disability** are often used interchangeably. The term *mental retardation* is widely used in the United States; however, the terminology was changed in Canada in an attempt to reduce the associated stigma. In Australia, the term *intellectual disability* has replaced *mental retardation*, and in Britain the term *learning disability* has replaced the term *mental handicap*. To add to the confusion, the term *learning disability* as used in North America refers to normal intelligence with specific learning problems (for example, reading, writing, arithmetic) whereas in Britain it refers to significantly subaverage intellectual dysfunction. Moreover, the term *developmental disability* is sometimes used in North America to include autism. In this chapter the term *mental retardation* is used in some instances, because it is more common in the body of professional literature. For the purposes of this section, assume that the terms *developmental disability* and *mental retardation* are synonymous.

Prevalence

The prevalence of mental retardation or developmental handicap is difficult to determine. Information is inconsistent: statistics vary depending upon the classification system, the samples, and the measures used. In addition, the majority of statistics are based on U.S. samples. The data of the Canadian working group on the Epidemiology of Mental Retardation (Health and Welfare Canada, 1988) suggests a prevalence of at least 8 per 1000 altogether, with approximately half (4 per 1000) falling within the mild range (IQ 50–70) and the other half falling within the severe range of mental retardation (IQ < 50). A cross-sectional survey in the Maritime provinces (McQueen, Spence, Garner, Pereira, & Winsor, 1987) determined the prevalence of major mental retardation in children aged seven to ten years to be 3.65/1000. Estimates of older mentally handicapped and developmentally disabled people range from 13,000 to 30,000 people in Canada and from 200,000 and 500,000 in the United States (Janicki, 1989).

DIAGNOSTIC ISSUES

While IQ as measured by standardized intelligence tests is the most basic criterion for mental retardation, there have been important changes in the definition over the years. These include the level of IQ required and the inclusion of deficits in adaptive behaviour. In North America, the American Association on Mental Retardation (AAMR), founded in 1876, has strongly influenced the definition and classification of mental retardation through the publication of classification manuals since 1921. More recently, the AAMR definition (Grossman, 1983) has been incorporated into the DSM criteria (see the DSM table "Diagnostic Criteria for Mental Retardation").

According to the 1983 classification manual (Grossman, 1983), **mental retardation** refers to significantly subaverage intellectual functioning with onset before the age of 18. However, it must also be accompanied by limitations in two or more areas of adaptive behaviour, such as communication, self-care, academic, domestic, social or community skills, leisure, and work. Traditionally, intellectual functioning has been determined on the basis of IQ scores (see Chapter 4). As shown in Figure 6.1, IQ scores are normally distributed, with a mean of 100 and a standard deviation of 15.

The choice of cutoff point, however, has been somewhat arbitrary and has changed several times over the years (Zigler & Hodapp, 1991). For example, for many years, IQ scores falling two standard deviations below the mean were considered to be within the mentally retarded range. Scores within this range were divided into four subcategories: mild

DSM-IV Diagnostic Criteria for Mental Retardation

A. Significantly subaverage intellectual functioning: an IQ of approximately 70 or below on an individually administered IQ test (for infants, a clinical judgment of significantly subaverage intellectual functioning).

B. Concurrent deficits or impairments in present adaptive functioning (i.e., the person's effectiveness in meeting the standards expected for his or her age by his or her cultural group) in at least two of the following areas: communication, self-care, home living, social/interpersonal skills, use of community resources, self-direction, functional academic skills, work, leisure, health and safety.

C. The onset is before age 18 years.

Mild Mental Retardation:	IQ level 50–55 to approximately 70
Moderate Mental Retardation:	IQ level 35–40 to 50–55
Severe Mental Retardation:	IQ level 20–25 to 35–40
Profound Mental Retardation:	IQ level below 20 or 25
Mental Retardation, Severity Unspecified:	When there is a strong presumption of mental retardation but the person is untestable by standard intelligence tests.

Source: Reprinted with permission from the *Diagnostic and Statistical Manual of Mental Disorders*, Fourth Edition. Copyright 1994 American Psychiatric Association.

Figure 6.1 Distribution of IQ Scores

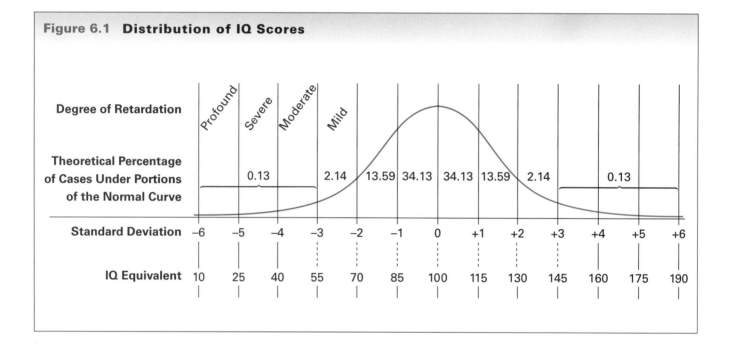

(IQ 50–55 to 70), moderate (IQ 35–40 to 50), severe (IQ 20–25 to 35), and profound (IQ < 20). In 1959, the fifth edition of the AAMR classification manual (Heber, 1959) raised the cutoff to one standard deviation below the mean (IQ < 85), and created a fifth level called "borderline." These changes raised the prevalence of mental retardation from approximately 3 percent to 16 percent of the population, leading to increased demands upon services for persons with disabilities. In 1973 the cutoff was returned to 70; in 1992 it was raised slightly to 75 to accommodate errors in measurement.

A number of other changes were introduced in the ninth edition (AAMR, 1992). While the age of onset, significantly subaverage intelligence, and limitations in adaptive functioning remain the same, the new classification approach is more positive, in that it addresses the person's strengths and capabilities. Furthermore, the criteria represent a broader, more ecological perspective; level of functioning is seen to represent not only the abilities of the individual but also the environmental support or services available to that person (Schalock et al., 1994). Thus, rather than diagnosing someone as having "moderate mental retardation," which gives the impression of a fixed state, the diagnosis might read, in part, "able to complete activities of daily living with limited support." (See Table 6.1.) The DSM has not as yet incorporated the updated approach used in the new AAMR manual, but the new system is being used increasingly by Canadian clinicians.

Table 6.1 Levels of Adaptive Functioning

Degree of Retardation	Preschool 0–5 years	School Age 6–21 years	Adulthood 21+ years
Mild—Intermittent Support	Development of motor, social, and communication skills relatively normal or mildly delayed.	Able to attend school and learn basic reading, spelling, arithmetic but may be several years behind age peers. Will need support and adapted work in high school.	With appropriate education and vocational training, these individuals are able to live relatively independently and often have the skills needed for basic employment. They often require supervision and support with financial matters and in relationships.
Moderate—Limited Support	Delayed motor development and social awareness. Can benefit from training in self-help skills, for example, toileting, feeding, dressing. Can learn to talk and communicate.	Can learn functional academic skills typically found in children in the primary grade levels. Need considerable support in school settings.	Can live semi-independently in the community and may be able to obtain unskilled employment. Require supervision with many aspects of daily life.
Severe—Extensive Support	Poor motor development and limited if any communication and self-help skills.	Training in basic communication and self-help skills is possible through systematic programming. Receptive language or comprehension is usually more advanced than expressive language or speech.	Can develop simple skills and carry out simple tasks with assistance and supervision. Can learn basic self-protection skills with intensive training and practice. Require supervision in most if not all activities of daily living.
Profound—Pervasive Support	Sensorimotor development minimal. Often require nursing care. Limited responses to interpersonal contact and stimulation from the environment.	May be some limited motor development but do not benefit from training in activities of daily living (for example, toileting, feeding, dressing).	May have some motor functioning and speech sounds. Need full assistance and supervision.

Source: Kendall, Philip and Constance Hammen. *Abnormal Psychology.* Copyright © 1995 by Houghton Mifflin Company. Used with permission.

The Challenges of Assessing Intelligence

Although classification systems such as those adopted by DSM and AAMR place heavy emphasis upon IQ, the use of IQ tests has been the subject of considerable controversy in recent years. First, such tests were not devised to take into account sensory, motor, and language deficits, which may contribute to poor performance. Second, when people have had limited experiences because of their disability or when they have lived in institutions, their performance may be limited because the test situation is unfamiliar and overwhelming. They may not understand what is expected of them or may not take the initiative to solve problems (Zigler, Hodapp, & Edison, 1990). For these reasons, IQ scores may not accurately reflect people's cognitive abilities.

Moreover, it is questionable whether scores in the lower end of the scale are meaningful, because the major intelli-

gence tests such as the Wechsler Scales and early editions of the Stanford-Binet were not standardized on people with developmental disabilities with IQ scores lower than 70. Nevertheless, a number of changes in the fourth edition of the Stanford-Binet Intelligence Test (Delaney & Hopkins, 1987) have made it a more useful instrument with persons with developmental disorders. The needs of individuals with disabilities, including mental retardation, deafness, blindness, and visual or motor impairment, are addressed in the Stanford-Binet *Examiner's Handbook* (Delaney & Hopkins, 1987).

Measuring Adaptive Behaviour

The assessment of adaptive behaviour has added greatly to the utility of psychological assessments. The Vineland Adaptive Behavior Scales, which are completed during interviews with parents, teachers, or caregivers, are frequently used for this purpose. The Vineland provides a profile of adaptive skills under the following headings:

1. *Communication.*
   a. receptive language (for example, understanding);
   b. expressive language (for example, speech); and
   c. written language
2. *Daily living.*
   a. personal (for example, eating, dressing, personal hygiene);
   b. domestic; and
   c. community (for example, time, money, telephone, public transport)
3. *Socialization.*
   a. interpersonal relationships;
   b. play and leisure time; and
   c. coping
4. *Motor skills.*
   a. gross motor (for example, movement and coordination of arms and legs); and
   b. fine motor (for example, ability to manipulate objects using fingers and hands)

The Vineland Scales are also particularly useful in that they provide supplementary norms for special populations, including: ambulatory and nonambulatory adults with mental retardation living in residential facilities, adults with mental retardation living in the community, children between the ages of six and twelve years with visual handicaps or hearing impairments, and emotionally disturbed children between the ages of nine and sixteen years. Given the problems of assessing intelligence, the assessment of adaptive skills is particularly important. As indicated in Table 6.1, such skills can be expected to vary according to chronological age and level of intelligence.

Interviewing Strategies

Gathering information from people with developmental disorders is an important aspect of any assessment. However, the reliability of the information gathered is critical. Unfortunately, it is often assumed that people with disabilities cannot give reliable information. On the other hand, some may err by assuming the opposite (Wyngaarden, 1981). When the person himself or herself is the best, or the only, source of information it is up to the interviewer to adapt the questions to the person's level of functioning.

· ·

ETIOLOGY

Developmental disorders have many causes. Some have clear organic causes; some relate to environmental factors; some reflect an interaction between genetics and environment. For example, damage due to an environmental toxin will have different effects on a child depending on inherited factors such as temperament or birth weight. Conversely, genetically based disorders can have different outcomes depending on the availability of medical and educational services. It is not possible in this chapter to provide comprehensive coverage of all causes of developmental disorders. Therefore, a number of disorders have been selected to represent different types of damage occurring at different stages of development.

A more detailed list of examples is outlined in Table 6.2.

Genetic Causes

An Overview of Genetics

In recent years, the field of genetics has become very active, with increasing understanding of the processes of genetic transmission and the identification of genes associated with particular disorders. Basically, the traits we inherit from our parents are carried by thousands of genes found in each of our cells. Genes are found in specific positions on chromosomes. Each human cell contains 23 pairs of chromosomes, each pair including one chromosome from each parent. Forty-four of these are matching and called autosomes. The additional two are called the sex chromosomes. Females have two X chromosomes; males have an X and a Y chromosome. An X chromosome is contributed during conception by the mother and either an X or a Y may be contributed by the father (Patton, Payne, & Beirne-Smith, 1986).

There are three types of inheritance: dominant, recessive, and sex-linked or X-linked. In dominant inheritance, an "individual gene can assume 'control' over or mask its partner and therefore will operate whether an individual gene pair is similar or dissimilar" (Patton et al., p. 164). In recessive inheritance, genes, "in a sense 'recede' when paired with a dissimilar mate and therefore only are influential when matched with another recessive gene" carrying the same trait (Patton et al., p. 164). Dominant inheritance of mental retardation is very rare. Two such disorders are tuberous sclerosis and neurofibromatosis. Disorders associated with recessive inheritance include phenylketonuria, Tay-Sachs disease, and galactosemia. Such disorders may be identified through genetic screening.

In sex-linked inheritance, the abnormal gene is carried on the X chromosome. In females, the gene is generally recessive and will operate only when it appears on both X chromosomes. Disorders transmitted in this way therefore tend to primarily affect males, who have only one X chromosome; the Y chromosome is not able to dominate or override the trait. X-linked disorders associated with mental retardation include Fragile X syndrome (described later in this chapter) and Lesch-Nyhan syndrome.

Inherited disorders can be identified through a blood test. Genetic screening can also determine whether both parents (in the case of recessive disorders) or the mother (in the case of X-linked disorders) carry an abnormal gene and run the risk of bearing a child with the disorder. For example, since Tay-Sachs is found largely among European Jews, some Jewish couples will undergo testing before trying to conceive.

Table 6.2 Disorders Associated with Mental Retardation

Prenatal Causes	Perinatal Causes	Postnatal Causes
Chromosomal Abnormalities	**A. Intrauterine Disorders**	**A. Head or Brain Injuries**
1. Autosomes 　Trisomy 21 (Down syndrome) 　Translocation 21 (Down syndrome) 　Tuberous sclerosis	1. Placental Insufficiency 　a. Placenta previa/hemorrhage 　b. Toxemia/eclampsia	1. Cerebral Concussion 2. Cerebral Contusion or Laceration 3. Intracranial Hemorrhage
2. X-Linked 　Fragile X syndrome	2. Abnormal Labour/Delivery 　a. Prematurity 　b. Premature rupture of membranes 　c. Abnormal presentation, for example, breech	**B. Infections** 1. Encephalitis 　a. Herpes simplex 　b. Measles 　c. HIV
3. Other X Chromosome Disorders 　XO syndrome (Turner) 　XYY syndrome 　XXY syndrome (Klinefelter)	3. Obstetrical Trauma 4. Multiple Birth	2. Meningitis 　a. Streptococcus pneumonia 　b. Influenza type B
Metabolic Disorders	**B. Neonatal Disorders**	**C. Seizure Disorders**
1. Amino Acid Disorders 　Phenylketonuria (PKU)	1. Hypoxia 2. Intracranial Hemorrhage	**D. Toxic-Metabolic Poisons**
2. Carbohydrate Disorders 　Galactosemia	3. Neonatal Seizures 4. Respiratory Disorders	1. Lead 2. Mercury
3. Nucleic Acid Disorders 　Lesch-Nyhan disease	5. Infections 　a. Meningitis 　b. Encephalitis 　c. Septicemia	**E. Malnutrition**
Neural Tube Defects	6. Head Trauma at Birth	**F. Environmental Deprivation**
1. Anencephaly 2. Spina Bifida		1. Abuse 2. Neglect
Environmental Factors		
1. Intrauterine Malnutrition 　a. Maternal malnutrition 　b. Placental insufficiency		
2. Drugs, Toxins, Teratogens 　a. Thalidomide 　b. Alcohol 　c. Cocaine 　d. Methylmercury 　e. Radiation		
3. Maternal Diseases 　a. Diabetes mellitus 　b. Rubella 　c. Syphilis 　d. Toxoplasmosis 　e. Cytomegalovirus 　f. Hypothyroidism		

Source: Adapted from American Association on Mental Retardation, *Mental retardation: Definition, classification and systems of support*, 9th ed. (Washington, DC: AAMR, 1992).

Chromosomal Abnormalities

Whereas inherited disorders occur in the children of parents who carry abnormal genes, other chromosomal abnormalities are not inherited but occur at conception. The best known chromosomal abnormality associated with mental retardation is **Down syndrome**, first described by Langdon Down in 1866. In 1959, the genetic link was discovered by Jerome Lejeune and his colleagues. There are three types of Down syndrome. The most common is **trisomy 21**, which occurs in 95 percent of Down syndrome. Whereas the normal human cell has 23 pairs of chromosomes, one chromosome in each pair provided by each parent, in Down syndrome there is an extra chromosome on pair 21. Thus, persons with Down syndrome have 47 rather than 46 chromosomes. Trisomy 21 occurs in approximately 1 in 700 live births, with a larger proportion of births occurring in older mothers. The incidence increases dramatically from approximately 1 in 350 for women between the ages of 35 and 39 to 1 in 100 after age 40 (Baroff, 1986). More recently, research has indicated that there may also be an increased risk of Down syndrome when the father is over 40, regardless of the mother's age (Hook, Cross, & Regal, 1990) (see Figure 6.2). Down syndrome is discussed in more detail later in this chapter.

Two other causes of Down syndrome are **translocation** and **mosaicism**. In the former, part of the 21st chromosome breaks off and attaches to another. This occurs in approximately 4 percent of cases. This type of anomaly is not associated with maternal age. In mosaicism, cell division occurs unevenly, so that some cells have 45 chromosomes and some have 47. This type occurs in only 1 percent of cases. Whereas individuals with Down syndrome due to translocation have all of the features found in trisomy 21, people with mosaic Down syndrome may have fewer physical characteristics, better speech, and higher intellectual functioning, depending upon the numbers of cells affected.

Prenatal Screening

Prenatal screening for chromosomal abnormalities is possible through **amniocentesis**. This procedure is conducted between the 11th and 18th weeks of pregnancy. With the assistance of ultrasound, a needle is inserted into the amniotic sac via the pregnant woman's abdomen. A small amount of amniotic fluid is withdrawn and cells contained in the fluid are then cultured in the lab. Studies of amniocentesis indicate diagnostic accuracy up to 99.4 percent, with the estimated risk

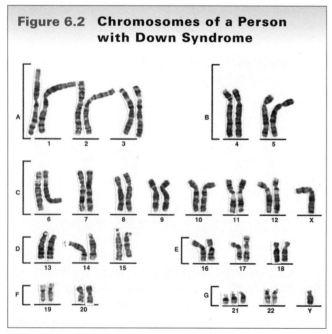

Figure 6.2   Chromosomes of a Person with Down Syndrome

Karyotype (a type of diagram developed from photomicrographs of chromosomes) of a person with the most common type of Down syndrome, showing the third chromosome at pair 21.

of complications such as infection or miscarriage being approximately 0.5 percent greater than in pregnancies without amniocentesis (Baroff, 1986). A more recently developed test known as **chorionic villus sampling (CVS)** involves obtaining cells from the vagina and cervix. This test can be carried out earlier, between the 8th and 12th weeks of pregnancy, but may be less accurate than amniocentesis. If a chromosomal abnormality is found, the parents may choose to terminate the pregnancy. These techniques can also identify inherited genetic abnormalities. Prenatal screening techniques are advocated by those in favour of preventing developmental disabilities, but opposed by many others who advocate for the basic rights of people with disabilities.

Metabolic Disorders

Phenylketonuria (PKU) is the best known of several rare metabolic disorders that can cause mental retardation. PKU has been described as an "inborn error of metabolism." It is caused by an autosomal recessive gene occurring in approximately 1 in 17,000 births. As a result of a recessive gene passed on from each parent, a liver enzyme is inactive, causing an inability to process or metabolize the amino acid phenylalanine. This substance builds up in the brain to toxic levels, leading to mental retardation.

PKU is now detected through a blood test shortly after birth. Affected infants are given a low-phenylalanine diet, which includes primarily fruits and vegetables and eliminates most protein-rich foods such as fish, meat, and eggs. Protein required for development is provided through a special dietary supplement. Followup studies indicate that children started on the diet before three months of age will function intellectually within the normal range, with IQs in the 90s, whereas untreated children often have moderate to severe retardation (Dobson, Kushida, Williamson, & Friedman, 1976). As many foods contain phenylalanine, it is difficult for school-aged children and adolescents to adhere to the diet; however, if the diet has been followed during the preschool years the most damaging effects of the disorder will have already been prevented.

Other disorders include congenital hypothyroidism, hyperammonemia, Gaucher's disease, and Hurler's syndrome. Congenital hypothyroidism occurs in 1 in 6000 children and may be detected through a screening test at birth. If not treated through replacement of the hormone thyroxine, children are small, and have poor muscle tone and severe mental retardation. Hyperammonemia, which occurs in 1 in 30,000 children, involves a deficiency in the enzyme that normally transforms the neurotoxic ammonia (produced when protein is broken down into component amino acids) into urea, which is excreted in the urine. If this process does not take place, ammonia builds up and brain damage or death may occur. Treatment through dietary regulation is less effective than in PKU. Gaucher's disease and Hurler's syndrome also involve deficient enzymes. Both are progressive, neurological disorders associated with mental retardation and early death. Treatment through enzyme replacement frequently has only limited success.

Environmental Causes

The Prenatal Environment

Mental retardation can result if the fetus is exposed to toxins or infections or if the blood supply lacks nutrients or oxygen. Maternal health, therefore, is very important. Inadequate nutrition, the use of alcohol, tobacco, or drugs, infections such as **rubella** or AIDS, and exposure to radiation can all affect infant development.

Maternal infections. Rubella (also known as German measles) during the first three months of pregnancy can lead to mental retardation, visual defects, deafness, heart disease, and other problems. Fortunately, rubella-related problems have declined with routine vaccination.

Fetal alcohol syndrome and fetal alcohol effects. Alcohol consumption during pregnancy can lead to a number of defects of varying degrees. Prenatal and postnatal growth retardation and central nervous system dysfunction are common. Figure 6.3 shows the typical facial features of **fetal alcohol syndrome (FAS)**, including short eye openings, an elongated, flattened area between the mouth and nose, thin upper lip, and flattened cheeks and nasal bridge. Head circumference is frequently below the third percentile. Cleft palate, heart and kidney damage, and vision defects are also found (Streissguth & LaDue, 1987).

FAS is one of the most common known causes of mental retardation, found in 1 to 3 per 1000 live births (Niccols, 1994). **Fetal alcohol effects (FAE)**—a term used to describe children who display some of the symptoms of FAS without meeting all diagnostic criteria—is estimated to occur approximately three times as often as FAS (3–5 per 1000). The incidence of FAS among alcoholics is estimated to be 25 per 1000 (Abel, 1984). The fact that infants born to alcoholic mothers do not always exhibit FAE or FAS reflects the complex interplay of genetic and environmental factors contributing to these disorders.

Figure 6.3 The Facial Features of Fetal Alcohol Syndrome

Source: Streissguth, A. P. & Little, R. E. (1994). "Unit 5: Alcohol, Pregnancy, and the Fetal Alcohol Syndrome: Second Edition" of the Project Cork Institute Medical School Curriculum ("slide lecture series") on *Biomedical Education: Alcohol Use and Its Medical Consequences*, produced by Dartmouth Medical School.

A longitudinal study (Streissguth, Barr, & Sampson, 1990) indicates that binge drinking is particularly risky. The children of women who drank five or more drinks on one occasion were more likely to have developmental delays up to three months in reading and arithmetic and to require special educational support. This study suggests that heavy drinking on even a few occasions may be more damaging than moderate drinking over a longer time. The link between paternal drinking patterns and FAS is not clear and further research is required to determine the impact on fetal development (Jenkins & Culbertson, 1996).

Children with FAS exhibit a range of problems at varying stages of development. Cognitive functioning varies from relatively minor learning problems to severe mental retardation. Learning may also be affected by attention deficits, hyperactivity, and other behaviour problems such as temper tantrums, enuresis (bed-wetting), and eating and sleeping difficulties. It is difficult, however, to distinguish such inherited tendencies from the effects of environmental deprivation resulting from ongoing alcoholism in the family.

Other drugs. Early development of the fetus can also be severely affected by the effects of certain drugs. The anticonvulsant Dilantin, chemotherapy, and hormone therapy have all been found to have teratogenic effects, including facial anomalies, malformed limbs, and a risk of later cancer (Batshaw & Perret, 1986). Congenital limb deficiency, although rare, is one of the best-known examples of teratogenic effects. It received a great deal of attention in the 1950s and 60s when **thalidomide**, a drug prescribed by European physicians for nausea (Tausig, 1962) was found to cause limb deficiencies or malformations in infants (McBride, 1961).

Birth-Related Causes

Advances in obstetric and neonatal intensive care in recent years have reduced the risk of brain damage and mental retardation as a result of birth-related trauma. Nevertheless, extreme prematurity or a lack of oxygen during prolonged or complicated labour and delivery can result in developmental problems including visual deficits, cerebral palsy, and speech and learning difficulties.

Cultural-Familial Retardation

Childhood environment can have an important effect on cognitive as well as physical and emotional development. Psychological and social deprivation due to lack of stimulation and care can impair intellectual development. Poverty, poor nutrition, large family size, lack of structure in the home, and low expectations for academic success may all be contributing factors. Children learn by experience and by modelling adult behaviour; if they are given little opportunity to practise cognitive skills or to watch adults practising them, it seems reasonable that they would not develop as rapidly as children given ample opportunity and encouragement to practise reasoning and communication skills.

In approximately 75 percent of people diagnosed as having a developmental handicap, no organic cause or brain dysfunction has been identified (Zigler, 1967). Most people within this group function intellectually within the mild range. (Figure 6.4 shows the estimated distribution of intelligence for organically based and cultural familial retardation.) They are found more frequently within lower socioeconomic groups, and commonly have at least one parent and possibly one or more siblings with developmental delays or handicaps. As with other disorders (see, for example, the discussion of conduct disorder in Chapter 5), the latter finding can be read two ways: Do children inherit low intelligence from their parents, or do parents with low intelligence create a deprived environment? The uncertain etiology of developmental handicaps in this group is reflected in the term **cultural-familial retardation**. More recently the term *retardation due to psychosocial disadvantage* has been introduced. Debate continues, however, as to the relative contributions of genetic and environmental factors.

Developmental-Difference Controversy

When looking at people near the low end of the normal range of intelligence, a question arises: Is this kind of low cognitive performance a disorder—an instance of pathology—or merely one extreme of normal human variability? Contradictory answers to this question constitute the **developmental-difference controversy** (Zigler & Balla, 1982).

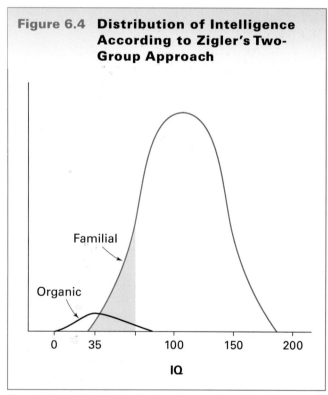

Figure 6.4   Distribution of Intelligence According to Zigler's Two-Group Approach

Source: E. Zigler & R. M. Hodapp, *Understanding mental retardation* (Cambridge: Cambridge University Press, 1991).

The developmental perspective describes cultural-familial retardation as being merely the low end of the normal range of intelligence, the result of the complex interactions of genetic and environmental factors that determine anyone's intellectual functioning. Zigler and colleagues argue, moreover, that motivational and personality factors, such as wariness or *outer-directedness* (reliance on others) may influence intellectual performance. Furthermore, a person with a long history of failure may have low self-esteem; to avoid failure, the person may stop trying, thus further reducing performance.

The difference perspective, in contrast, describes mental retardation as intrinsically different from normal intellectual functioning. One test is to assess how people with low intelligence perform on a cognitive task: Do they do it as a normal younger person of an equivalent *mental age* would, or does their performance show some intrinsic *difference* beyond the level of functioning? There are as yet no clear answers, but, as with other areas of psychology, it seems likely that various factors play a role.

Research with Twins and Adopted Children

Twin studies, as described in Chapter 4, can be used to study the effects of non-pathological inheritance on intelligence. Results of many studies in various countries support genetic effects in that the IQ scores of monozygotic (identical) twins are significantly more concordant than those of dizygotic (fraternal) twins. Studies of identical twins reared apart have found correlations of 0.67 to 0.78 between intelligence tests scores. However, these results may be an overestimate due to similar environments (Achenbach, 1982).

The results of adoption studies also provide some support for the genetic hypothesis. Generally, the IQ scores of adopted children are found to be more similar to those of their biological parents than to those of their adoptive parents (Scarr, 1981). These findings suggest that intelligence test scores are affected more by the genetic makeup of the biological parents and possibly prenatal environmental factors than by environmental input provided by adoptive parents (Achenbach, 1982).

Environmental and Social Deprivation

Early studies of infants reared in institutional settings (Spitz, 1945) demonstrated the critical importance of nurturance and appropriate stimulation for healthy psychological growth and development. Spitz studied infants in a foundling home who were described as wasting away and dying. Although the institutional conditions were hygienic and the infants were given adequate nutrition, their contact with caregivers was limited. Toileting and feeding were carried out in an impersonal manner, toys were not available, and there were few opportunities for physical activity and play. Children remained in their cribs, with the view of the room often blocked by sheets hanging over crib railings.

More recently, Canadian research conducted with infants and children adopted from Romanian orphanages (Ames, 1992) has confirmed many findings from previous studies. Ames and colleagues explored the effects of environmental and social deprivation experienced by children institutionalized in Romanian orphanages. Two groups of children were studied: (1) Romanian orphans who had spent between 8 and 53 months in an orphanage; (2) a group of Canadian-born children who had never been institutionalized and who were living with their natural parents. The children were matched for sex, age, and the adoptive mother's education. A second comparison group included an early adoption group of infants adopted from Romania before four months of age.

This longitudinal study documented the devastating effects of poor nutrition and limited physical and social stimulation (Ames et al., 1997). All of the 46 children at the time of adoption were found to be delayed in developmental milestones and intelligence; 78 percent were also delayed in gross and fine motor skills, personal-social skills, and language. Fewer areas of delay were found among children who had spent less time in institutions, who had access to toys, who were favourites among the caregivers, and who had been kept clean (Morison, 1997).

The orphans who entered an infant development program after adoption were found to progress rapidly. However, approximately three years after adoption, 17 percent of the Romanian children at 4 1/2 years of age (those who had been adopted young) and 56 percent of the older children were not ready for the school grade appropriate to their age. The children who had been in the orphanage longest had the lowest IQs, with a mean score in the low average range. The mean score for children in the early adopted group was within the average range. The Canadian-born comparison group children had the highest IQ scores with a mean score in the high average range.

Physical growth, too, showed long-term effects of early deprivation. According to both Canadian and Romanian norms, 85 percent of the Romanian children at adoption were below the 10th percentile for weight. Three years after adoption, the Romanian children weighed 2.5 kilograms less on average than the Canadian-born children and were approximately 5 centimetres shorter than Canadian-born children and 2.5 centimetres shorter than the early adoption group.

Behavioural and social problems were reported to be more common in the older adoptees than in the Canadian-born and early-adoption groups. These problems included eating difficulties (either refusing solids or not knowing when to stop eating), stereotyped movements (for example, rocking), social withdrawal, being slow to attach, not making needs known, and being indiscriminately friendly.

At followup, the older Romanian children continued to display significantly more behaviour problems than the Canadian-born children and the early-adoption group. Three years after adoption, 36 percent of the Romanian children had behaviour problems requiring professional assistance, including crying, problems with peers, hyperactivity and dis-

tractibility, and disobedience or defiance. Children who had spent less time in the orphanage and who were adopted by families with more time and energy to spend working with the child tended to do better.

Prevention and Early Intervention Programs

Research with children living with their natural families has also confirmed the effect of environmental factors on development. One of the best-known longitudinal studies was conducted by Bradley et al. (1989). This collaborative study examined family environment and cognitive development in the first three years of life. Parental responsiveness and the presence of stimulating play materials were found to be more important than socioeconomic status. The level of parent education, intelligence, and language abilities also played a role.

Several prevention and early intervention programs have been developed to try to fill in gaps in children's environments. Such programs began during the late 1940s and 1950s with early support for mothers and children, including prenatal care, immunization, and nutritional advice. In the 1960s, such programs expanded to include day care and community mental health centres and stimulating early childhood education programs (the U.S. Head Start program being the best known of the latter) (Crocker, 1992).

Evaluative reviews of early intervention and prevention programs (Marfo & Kysela, 1985; Ramey & Ramey, 1992) indicate that they can significantly improve intellectual performance and levels of academic achievement. Several major studies have investigated whether mental retardation related to inadequate environmental conditions could be prevented. Intensive preschool programming, including medical care and nutritional support, was provided to children from infancy until age five.

Martin, Ramey, & Ramey (1990) set out to determine those most at risk for cognitive delay or mental retardation and those who gain the most through participation in intensive early educational intervention. The mother's level of intelligence was found to be the strongest predictor of developmental progress. (Many children in this study came from single-parent households.) Two groups were set up: a control group, in which the children did not receive early educational intervention but did receive medical, nutritional, and social service support; and an intervention group, in which the children received a full-day program.

By the age of three, all of the children in the intervention group with mothers whose IQs were below 70 were tested as functioning within the normal range. All but one of the children in the control group with mothers whose IQs were low had IQ scores within the mild (IQ 55–70) to borderline (IQ 71–85) range of mental retardation. On average, the children in the early intervention group were found to have IQs 20 points higher than the children in the control group. While only 49 percent of the children in the control group had IQs within the normal range, 95 percent of the children in the intervention group were functioning within the normal range with an IQ > 85 (Ramey & Ramey, 1992).

In a later study, Project CARE (Wasik, Ramey, Bryant, & Sparling, 1990), participants received home visits during the first three years as well as the centre-based intervention program. Children who received both home visits and the intensive intervention program were found to be functioning intellectually at a higher level than a control group receiving only health and social service support.

In a longitudinal analysis, children up to the age of twelve years in a similar early intervention program (the Abecedarian Project) were functioning between one- and two-thirds of a standard deviation higher than the children in the control group. At age twelve, only 13 percent of the intervention group had an IQ below 85, compared to 44 percent of the control group (Ramey & Ramey, 1992). Moreover, half as many children in the intervention group had failed a grade (28 vs. 55 percent).

In a summary of the results of these early intervention studies, Ramey and Ramey outline a number of "essential daily ingredients" for the development of young children. These include:

a. encouragement of exploration;

b. assistance in basic skills such as labelling, sorting, sequencing, comparing, and noting means-end relations;

c. reinforcement of developmental achievements;

d. guided rehearsal and extension of new skills;

e. protection from inappropriate disapproval, teasing, or punishment;

f. a rich and responsive language environment; and

g. a supportive and predictable environment in terms of opportunities for learning and patterns of interaction

TWO SPECIFIC DISORDERS

Down Syndrome

Jessica is 14 years old and has Down syndrome. She lives with her parents and a younger brother. Since her birth, Jessica's parents have been determined to give her the best possible opportunities for learning and to integrate her into the community. They were actively involved in an early intervention program focussing on language and motor development. When she was two, they enrolled her in an integrated day care. Jessica attended regular primary school classes but received some help from an educational assistant and a resource consultant. However, her only real friend was Jan, another girl with Down syndrome. The other children tended to avoid Jessica and Jan unless specifically asked by the teacher to do something with them.

Jessica attended Brownies and sang in the church choir but her favourite activity was swimming with the Special Olympics team. At the age of 12, a psycholog-

ical assessment found that Jessica was functioning intellectually in the upper half of the moderate range, but had significantly higher adaptive skills. She could complete most activities of daily living independently or with minimal supervision. She liked to help her mother with the cooking and laundry and liked to watch television or play computer games with her younger brother. Jessica was able to use money and enjoyed shopping for clothes. She could read at a Grade 4 level and do Grade 6 arithmetic.

At age 14, Jessica was preparing to enter high school, but the special education consultant was unsure whether she should be fully integrated. It was decided that she would attend a special class for her weaker subjects (English, history, and geography) but would be integrated for math, music, and physical education. Social isolation continues to be a challenge for Jessica; however, her activities with Special Olympics have provided her with a close circle of friends who also have disabilities.

The physical features of Down syndrome are widely recognized. These include short stature, slanted eyes with an epicanthic fold of skin over the inner corner, a wide and flat bridge of the nose, short, thick neck, stubby hands and fingers, large, protruding tongue, and poor muscle tone. Other associated problems include congenital heart disease, gastrointestinal abnormalities, and congenital cataracts (Pueschel, 1987). The degree of intellectual impairment can range from mild to severe, with the largest proportion functioning within the mild to moderate range; particular difficulties in expressive language are common.

Although life expectancy is higher for people with Down syndrome than it used to be, adults with Down syndrome are at high risk for Alzheimer-type dementia (Dalton & McLachlan, 1986). Research has shown that individuals with Down syndrome over the age of 40 generally show the neuropathological indicators of that dementia (Zigman, Schupf, Lubin, & Silverman, 1987). However, its associated behavioural deterioration (for example, cognitive and visual memory deficits; declines in daily living skills and adaptive behaviour) appears in only 15 to 40 percent of cases (Zigman et al., 1987). The *Dementia Scale for Down Syndrome* (DSDS) developed by Angela Gedye (1995) in British Columbia is designed to detect and rate the severity of dementia among people who are not verbal and cannot follow test instructions. Information is gathered through informant-based interviews. Early results suggest that the instrument has considerable utility, especially when individuals are reassessed every six months.

Early intervention and education have been shown to contribute to the development and adaptive functioning of people with Down syndrome. Indeed, while the range of intellectual ability is broad, many individuals with Down syndrome are

Members of the Kingston Turtles swim team proudly display the trophy they won at a Special Olympics swim meet.

able to attain basic reading, number, and writing skills, and considerable independence in activities of daily living in the community (Cicchetti & Beegly, 1990). Some individuals with Down syndrome are able to function at a much higher level. One example is Christopher Burke, an actor with Down syndrome who has become well known for his role in the television program *Life Goes On*.

Fragile X Syndrome

Ryan is a ten-year-old boy with Fragile X syndrome. He lives at home with his parents and older brother Kurt, who also has Fragile X. Ryan's mother also has a brother with Fragile X and her sister has a daughter who is affected. Ryan attends a class for children with disabilities at the local school. He reads at a Grade 3 level and can do simple addition and subtraction. Ryan has a well-developed vocabulary but he tends to repeat particular phrases from commercials and songs he has heard and his speech becomes especially repetitive when he is agitated. Ryan enjoys being active. He and his brother like to ride their bikes and like to go bowling. They are both on a basketball team organized through the Special Olympics. At home, computer games are a favourite activity.

Both Ryan and Kurt are able to take care of their personal hygiene with relatively little supervision. They make their own beds and help with chores such as washing the dishes, cutting the lawn, and shovelling snow. They are able to use the microwave to make simple meals and enjoy helping their mother with baking.

Ryan's new teacher was concerned about his limited attention span and frequent outbursts, especially during transitions from one task or setting to another. Ryan's parents were also concerned that he was increasingly irritable; if his routine changed unexpectedly, he would have tantrums, swearing repeatedly and sometimes becoming physically aggressive.

After consulting with his parents, the school referred Ryan to the school board's psychologist, who observed Ryan at home and at school. She noted that he was distracted in class by other children's activities and by the many pictures and notices on the walls, arts and crafts materials, and books on the shelves, and that he had the most difficulty staying seated and attentive during class discussions or unstructured time. The teacher rearranged the desks and created some quiet areas set apart by low room dividers. Ryan's desk was placed against the wall and he was given frequent opportunities to sit in one of the quiet areas. A token program was also devised where Ryan could collect stickers for paying attention and staying in his seat during structured class activities. These could be "cashed in" for computer time during unstructured periods.

The psychologist also suggested that Ryan's parents and his teacher develop a pictorial schedule of daily activities, with a copy kept at Ryan's desk and another posted on the refrigerator at home. Reviewing the schedule for the next day helped to prepare Ryan for changes in routine and reminded his parents and teachers to anticipate changes that might trigger extreme responses by Ryan.

Fragile X syndrome, first described by Martin and Bell (1943), was identified as an X-linked chromosomal abnormality in the late 1960s (Lubs, 1969), and the mutation for the gene causing the disorder (FMR-1 gene) was discovered in 1991 (Oberle et al., 1991; Yu et al., 1991). It is characterized by a weakened or "fragile" site on the X chromosome, as shown in Figure 6.5. A person who inherits a Fragile X gene may not be directly affected, but may be a genetic carrier, transmitting the disorder to his or her offspring. Females, because they also have a second X chromosome, are more likely to be unaffected carriers.

Fragile X syndrome is the second most frequently occurring chromosomal abnormality causing mental retardation after Down syndrome, and the most common *hereditary* cause of mental retardation (Dykens, Hodapp, & Leckman, 1994). As this is a relatively recently discovered disorder, prevalence rates vary. Among females, approximately 1 in 400 is estimated to be an unaffected carrier and approximately 1 in 2000 is directly affected. Rates for males with the full mutation range from 1 in 700 to 1 in 1000; approximately 1 in 2000 males is an unaffected carrier.

Physical features include a high forehead, elongated face, large jaw, large underdeveloped ears, and in males enlarged testes. Individuals with Fragile X syndrome display a number of cognitive, behavioural, and physical symptoms, but the degree to which they are affected in any of these varies (Dykens, Leckman, Paul, & Watson, 1988). Moreover, these

Figure 6.5   Schematic Drawing of the Fragile X Syndrome

Source: Hagerman and Boggs, 1983.

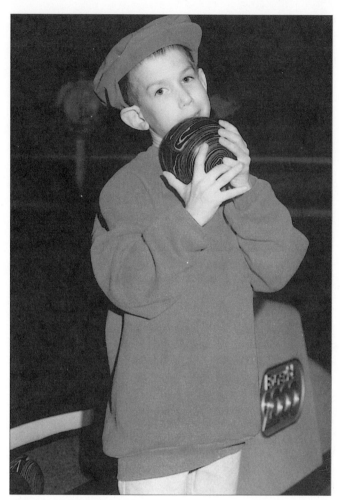

A boy with Fragile X syndrome.

characteristics are often less pronounced in carrier females. For example, intellectual levels in males vary from moderate mental retardation to within the normal range, with declines in IQ appearing around puberty.

Males show a particular pattern of cognitive functioning with weaknesses in sequential processing of information in a particular order (for example, words in a sentence, a sequence of tasks) but strengths in simultaneous processing of information in a more holistic fashion (for example, visuospatial tasks, recognizing a picture despite missing parts) (Dykens, Hodapp, & Leckman, 1987). In contrast, only approximately one-third of females are mildly mentally retarded and most display only learning difficulties involving attention, short-term memory, planning, problem-solving, and understanding mathematical concepts (Dykens et al., 1994).

Receptive language may be relatively well developed in relation to expressive language in males with Fragile X syndrome. Their speech has been described as "jocular, staccato, perseverative and sing-songy" (Dykens et al., 1994). Vocabulary may be well developed and individuals may be able to express themselves relatively well in certain familiar contexts. Males with Fragile X often have particular problems with communication and socialization, but may show

greater strengths in adaptive behaviour, particularly in activities of daily living. Fragile X syndrome is associated with attention deficits, hyperactivity, anxiety, and aggression. Autistic-type behaviours such as hand-flapping, hand-biting, poor eye contact, and an aversion to being touched or oversensitivity to certain textures may also occur (Hagerman, 1987).

Because of a resemblance of symptoms, people with Fragile X may be diagnosed with autism. The diagnosis is easily made by blood test. If the person seems to show any of the facial features suggestive of Fragile X, it is worthwhile testing, both for the guidance of relatives considering childbearing, and because the diagnosis may allow access to specialized intervention programs.

Educational programs that include a good deal of visual information have been found to be particularly effective with students with Fragile X. For example, the Logo reading program (Braden, 1989) involves matching words with symbols or familiar logos from the community (for example, restaurant or road signs). As the child learns the word, the logo is faded out.

THE EFFECT OF DEVELOPMENTAL DISORDERS ON THE FAMILY

Over the past three decades, the experiences and needs of families of children with disabilities have been the focus of numerous publications and research studies (for example, *American Journal of Mental Retardation*, 1989). While there is little doubt that parents of children with disabilities do experience more stress than other parents (Beckman, 1991; Dyson, 1991), factors such as the type and degree of disability and the child's age can affect the degree of stress (Minnes, 1988a).

Furthermore, Canadian and U.S. research has demonstrated that such stress can be buffered by informal social support from friends, family members, neighbours, etc. (Flynt, Wood, & Scott, 1992; Minnes, 1988b; Minnes et al., 1989). In contrast, more formal support from professionals and social service agencies has not been consistently shown to mediate stress. Indeed, parents frequently report interactions with professionals to be stressful (Baxter, 1989; Turnbull, Summers, & Brotherson, 1986).

Family cohesion, open communication patterns, and patterns of organization and control can also help a family cope (Mink, Blacher, & Nihira, 1988; Minnes, 1988b). Studies of siblings of children with disabilities have yielded conflicting results; some report adverse effects (Cuskelly & Dadds, 1992) and others do not (Dyson, Edgar, & Crnic, 1989). Further research is needed on the relationships and interactions between disabled and non-disabled siblings within the family system at different stages of the family life cycle (Skrtic, Summers, Brotherson, & Turnbull, 1984).

Parental reactions to the birth of a child with a disability have been likened to those found in bereavement (Solnit & Stark, 1961). Olshansky (1966), however, suggested that, rather than progressing through the usual mourning process within a given time frame, parents of a retarded child often experience a state of chronic sorrow, a long-term internalization of a depressive mood. In contrast to the view that incomplete resolution of grief is evidence of pathology, he described chronic sorrow as a "natural and understandable response to a tragic fact." The work of Wikler, Wasow, & Hatfield (1981) changed this view. Today the sorrow experience is seen as a periodic rather than a continuous phenomenon; adjustment is interrupted by emotional stress and upheaval at significant transition points when progress in the child's development might be expected to occur. ("At this age, his brother was in high school and borrowing the car"; "If only she were normal, she would be preparing for her confirmation now.")

In a recent Canadian study (Nachshen & Minnes, in press), parents of children with developmental disabilities were asked to discuss the major challenges they had faced. Almost all respondents (93 percent) said their child's diagnosis had been a major issue in their family. Most also identified a number of other stressful experiences, such as explaining to others about their child's disability (74 percent), dealing with doctors and other professionals (74 percent), creating and/or finding opportunities for their child to make friends and participate in activities (74 percent), meeting personal needs (67 percent), choosing the best level of integration for their child (67 percent), dealing with teachers and the educational system (63 percent), and feelings about the cause of their child's disability (63 percent).

Many highlighted the importance of everyday interaction with friends, family, and neighbours (59 percent), meeting the needs of their other children (52 percent), long-term planning for their child (48 percent), meeting the needs of their spouse or partner (44 percent), and maintaining satisfying friendships (41 percent). Many parents expressed concern about the general ignorance and lack of available information on developmental disabilities. They also reported a great deal of difficulty in dealing with inflexibility among professionals, schools, and community organizations. Finally, parents noted that overemphasis on the needs of the disabled child contributed to family disharmony.

Currently, a similar Canadian study is being conducted with senior parents of persons with developmental disabilities (Woodford & Minnes, 1997). Many parents who are now in their late seventies and eighties have kept their children at home for the past 30 to 50 years. During that time they have fought to obtain better services in their communities and have been strong advocates for the rights of persons with disabilities. Ironically, while their efforts have made a great difference to the next generation of people with disabilities, many of these parents have been unsuccessful in making satisfactory life plans for the care and accommodation of their own children when the parents die.

EDUCATION AND INTERVENTION

Mainstreaming and Attitudes Toward People with Disabilities

Legislation introduced in both Canada (for example, Ontario Bill 82, 1980) and the United States requires that children be educated in the least restrictive environment possible, regardless of the severity of their disability. But what is best: education in a separate space, or being integrated into the mainstream? The **contact hypothesis** put forward by Amir (1969) stated that people would grow more comfortable with people of different ethnic groups as they were exposed to them. This hypothesis, applied to disability, suggests that integration should improve general attitudes toward people with disabilities.

Although a number of studies conducted in Canada, Australia, and the United States provide some support for the contact hypothesis, the results are not uniformly positive

(Gething, 1991; King, Rosenbaum, Armstrong, & Miller, 1989). Context is important and we need to consider the quality as well as the quantity of contact (Roper, 1990).

The *normalization movement* has advocated that children with disabilities be treated "as normal" and thus the use of labels has fallen into disfavour. A number of studies have investigated the effect of labels on attitudes (Budoff & Siperstein, 1978; Graffi & Minnes, 1988). Labels can have a protective effect for children who are seen as incompetent. Such findings have interesting, if controversial, implications for educators, suggesting that children might be more accepting of classmates with disabilities if they were given the information to help them understand. If they see unusual behaviour within the context of disability, they can then label the behaviour rather than the person. Some programs in integrated schools emphasize that all of us have greater abilities in some areas and relative disabilities in others.

Training in Community Living Skills

As more people with disabilities live in the community, it becomes especially important for them to learn to look after their own needs as much as possible. Awareness of the importance of adaptive behaviour has also been heightened with its inclusion in the AAMR classification system. In recent years, therefore, many educational programs for people with developmental disabilities have focussed on developing social skills and independent living skills and on reducing or managing maladaptive behaviours. These programs often use *operant conditioning* approaches, which include systematic observation, task analysis, and the use of various shaping and prompting procedures and reinforcement contingencies. Operant conditioning has been found to be very successful in teaching not only basic self-help skills such as feeding and dressing (Hughes, Schuster, & Nelson, 1993; Minnes, 1980; Reid, 1983) but also more complex skills such as social interaction, meal planning, vocational skills, personal hygiene, use of public transport, and use of money (Reid, Wilson, & Faw, 1983).

The Issue of Sex Education

Since the 1970s, there has been much debate about whether people with developmental disabilities should have the right to enjoy sexual activity, marriage, and children. (See the Viewpoint box for a discussion of issues of sterilization, childbirth, and child-rearing.) Given the taboos associated with sexuality even for people without disabilities, it has been difficult for many to accept the concept of people with developmental disabilities engaging in sexual activity.

VIEWPOINT *Who Should Be Parents?*

The eugenic control or prevention of developmental disabilities became an issue of great concern in the late nineteenth and early twentieth centuries. The eugenics movement argued that people with developmental disabilities should not be permitted to have children, as the gene pool would be endangered through the introduction of "inferior" individuals. Procreation by people with developmental disabilities was originally prevented by institutionalization in segregated wards; but later, sterilization became common.

The first American statute in favour of sterilization of people with mental retardation was passed in 1907 in the state of Indiana. More than 30 states eventually passed similar laws (Woodill, 1992). Similar Canadian laws were passed in Alberta in 1928 and British Columbia in 1933 (Dickens, 1982); despite increasing concern about issues of informed consent, they

were not repealed until the 1970s. Between 1907 and 1958, 31,038 sterilizations were performed in the United States on mentally handicapped women (20,048) and men (10,990) and more than 4000 people were sterilized in Alberta and British Columbia (Woodill, 1992). With the risk of unwanted pregnancies removed, many individuals who had been institutionalized for their own protection were moved into the community.

Informed consent for sterilization procedures has been a contentious issue in Canadian and American courts over the years. The question is whether the court may give or withhold consent on behalf of an individual whose competence to understand the nature and consequences of sexual intercourse, pregnancy, and childbearing is questionable (Institute of Law Research & Reform, 1988). However, the well-known case of "Eve" in the Supreme Court of

Canada in the 1980s provided legal support for the equal rights of people with developmental disabilities, including the right to marry, bear, and raise children. This landmark decision stated that involuntary sterilization of a woman with mental retardation because it is deemed to be in the "best interests of the individual" is in violation of the *Canadian Charter of Rights and Freedoms* (Robertson, 1991; Vogel, 1987).

Now that such rights have been established, an increasing number of children are being born to people with disabilities. Concern for the welfare of these children has prompted research to evaluate the competence of such parents. Specialized training programs for parents with mental retardation have been developed in Canada and the United States (Feldman, Case, Towns, & Betel, 1985; Tymchuk, Andron, & Tymchuk, 1990). These programs teach child care skills, such as

VIEWPOINT *continued*

bathing, diapering, and feeding; appropriate parent-child interactions; and safety skills, such as recognizing and preventing household dangers, dealing with common emergencies, and understanding and following instructions on labels for medications and high-risk household products.

An intensive program conducted at Surrey Place Centre in Toronto used concrete training strategies, including verbal instruction, picture books, modelling, and tangible reinforcement (Feldman et al., 1986). The results indicated improvements in child care skills and decision-making strategies.

Using task analysis, reinforced practice, and clear feedback, mothers with mental retardation were also taught to increase their expressions of affection for their child, to provide contingent praise, and to stimulate the child's language through imitation and reflective statements. Mothers were also taught behaviour management skills and strategies to promote generalization, which are critical to success. For such programs to be effective, care must be taken to include training in a number of settings involving different situations to promote generalization of skills. Moreover, followup and "booster sessions" are recommended as maintenance of skills frequently is problematic due to environmental and personal stresses such as abusive relationships, depression, and illness (Tymchuk & Feldman, 1991).

Critical Thinking Questions

1. What are the potential risks and benefits to children of parents with disabilities? Do these differ from risks and benefits to children of parents without disabilities?
2. Should parent training be required of persons with disabilities who wish to have children or should it be available to everyone, possibly through courses in high school?
3. What criteria would you use to determine parenting competence?

Studies in the late 1970s and early 1980s indicated that staff in residences for people with developmental disabilities generally frowned on sexual behaviour, although views ranged from tolerance of behaviours such as kissing and holding hands to lack of acceptance of any sexual activity (Haavik & Menninger, 1981). More recent studies in Canada and Scotland, however, indicate a range of attitudes among residential staff and other professionals working in the field (Murray & Minnes, 1994a; 1994b). Younger and more highly educated individuals were generally more accepting, and professional staff were more accepting than direct care staff. Such findings emphasize the importance of assessing the attitudes of staff before implementing sex education programs.

With increasing numbers of people with developmental disabilities living in the community, recent research indicates that both children and adults with developmental disabilities are at considerable risk for sexual assault and sexual abuse (Sobsey, Grey, Wells, Pyper, & Reimer-Heck, 1991). Although past surveys of reported abuse indicated that incidents of sexual abuse occur four times as frequently in institutions as in community residences (Blatt & Brown, 1986), a more recent survey of women with mental retardation living in community residences reported that 75 to 80 percent had been sexually assaulted (Davis, 1989). There is an urgent need for specialized sex education programs for people with developmental disabilities, especially as people with developmental disabilities who are living more independently in the community are at increasing risk of contracting HIV infections and AIDS (Murray & Minnes, 1994b). Although counselling and psychotherapy have often been seen as inappropriate for people with developmental disabilities, recent initiatives have demonstrated that adaptations can be made to accommodate limited expressive and receptive language skills. Furthermore, programs to help mentally retarded survivors of sexual abuse (for example, Mansell, Sobsey, & Calder, 1992) are now being introduced through interactive-behavioural group therapy, which involves intensive support and the use of role-playing exercises (Tomasulo, 1994; Tomasulo, Keller, & Pfadt, 1995).

MALADAPTIVE BEHAVIOURS AND DUAL DIAGNOSIS

Kevin was a 27-year-old man who had lived in the community since completing a school-to-community program at the local high school six years ago. He lived with his parents until he was 24 and then moved into his own apartment. He continued to have regular, frequent contact with his parents but was able to manage cooking, cleaning, and other activities of daily living without much supervision. Kevin had two volunteer jobs. Three days a week, he helped the cleaners at the local school and on Fridays he did grocery shopping for an elderly neighbour.

Kevin had been assessed as functioning at the top of the mild range of developmental handicap. He could read at the Grade 4 level and understood money fairly well. One of his favourite activities was to take the bus to the mall and hang out. Kevin had been involved in social activities organized by the Association for Community Living but had to stop going because of poor frustration tolerance and angry outbursts. These outbursts tended to occur in unstructured situations; when Kevin did not have a clear idea of what to expect, he could become agitated and would shout and sometimes strike passersby.

Kevin longed to have friends but his behaviour often alienated them. A recent outburst at the grocery store raised concerns about his ability to keep his volunteer jobs. Without such activities during the day, Kevin would be even more socially isolated.

He had recently become involved with a group of teens, some of whom had been charged with shoplifting. Kevin's parents were concerned that his new friends may have been encouraging Kevin to join them on shoplifting sprees and that Kevin might be easily led because he was so eager for acceptance. Whenever they tried to discuss his friends and activities, Kevin became very angry and clammed up.

A recent Canadian survey of aberrant behaviour among more than 900 children, adolescents, and adults with developmental disabilities in Ontario found clinically significant aberrant behaviour in 52.9 percent of children between the ages of four and eleven years, and in 46.8 percent of adolescents and adults (Atkinson & Feldman, 1994). The most frequently reported behaviours found in the children included inadequate self-control or control of anger, attention deficit, withdrawal, enuresis/encopresis, and *pica* (eating inedible substances). The type and intensity of behaviour varied according to the degree of disability and the age and sex of the child. Aggression and depression were the most common psychological problems reported in the older group. The frequency of these behaviours diminished with age and varied according to sex.

Until the 1980s, it was rare for a person with mental retardation to be diagnosed with a psychiatric disorder. Emotional and behavioural difficulties were often attributed to lower intelligence and psychosocial problems (Borthwick-Duffy & Eyman, 1990). It is true, on the one hand, that what looks like disordered behaviour may sometimes be simply an expression of distress. Because people with mental retardation have limited communication skills, they usually express distress, whether physical or psychological, through their behaviour (Sovner & Hurley, 1989). On the other hand, **diagnostic overshadowing**—perceiving deviant behaviours to be a function of the developmental disorder—may cause real psychiatric disorders to be missed (Reiss, Levitan, & Szyszko, 1982). People with developmental disabilities are now generally thought to be at increased risk of developing emotional and behavioural problems similar to psychiatric disorders. Indeed, epidemiological studies indicate that they can develop all types of psychiatric disorders, including less common ones (Sovner & Hurley, 1989).

The co-occurrence of serious behavioural or psychiatric disorders in people with developmental disabilities has been labelled **dual diagnosis**. Prevalence rates of dual diagnosis, obtained primarily in the United States, vary widely. Estimates suggest that approximately 10 to 15 percent of people with developmental disorders have been given a psychiatric diagnosis (Borthwick-Duffy & Eyman, 1990; Campbell & Malone, 1991) and a larger percentage (up to 40 percent), although they have not been given a formal psychiatric diagnosis, are receiving medication, counselling, or therapy from a mental health professional (Davidson et al., 1994; Reiss, 1990).

Behavioural approaches are generally the intervention of choice for maladaptive behaviours such as aggression, destructiveness, and self injury. Recent research has begun to address the relative merits of psychopharmacological interventions either in conjunction with behavioural programs or as an effective alternative (Ellis, Singh, & Landrum, 1993; Williams, Ellis, Ickowicz, Singh, & Singh, 1993). Such studies suggest that this is an important area for further research.

Community-based crisis intervention services are needed for individuals with dual diagnoses (Davidson et al., 1995). Their special needs can be met only if service providers in the fields of mental health and developmental disability combine their resources and expertise. Although the majority of services would be community-based, short stays in inpatient facilities may be required for assessment and treatment of serious crises.

DEINSTITUTIONALIZATION AND COMMUNITY INTEGRATION: HOW EFFECTIVE ARE THEY?

Since the 1970s, services for people with developmental disabilities have been guided by the **normalization principle**, a concept introduced in Scandinavia by Bengt Nirje (1969), which suggested that the lives of individuals with disabilities should be as normal as possible. This principle was applied to services for persons with disabilities in North America by Wolfensberger (1972). Normalization, as defined by Wolfensberger, recommended "utilization of means which are as culturally normative as possible, in order to establish and/or maintain personal behaviours and characteristics which are as culturally normative as possible (Wolfensberger, 1972, p. 28). In other words, people with disabilities should be given the opportunity to have as normal a lifestyle as possible through participation in activities common to members of society of similar age (Zigler, Hodapp, & Edison, 1990).

The influence of this principle has been widespread since the 1970s, contributing to the **deinstitutionalization** of thousands of people with disabilities and the provision of community-based accommodation and services. The evolution of Canadian policies regarding integration can be traced through a review of documents regarding services for people with developmental disabilities. For example, as early as 1973, the importance of being involved in one's community was recognized by the Ontario Ministry of Health in a report called *Community Living for the Mentally Retarded in Ontario: A*

New Policy Focus. In 1974, the mandate of the Developmental Services Act was to help people with disabilities to live in their own homes. Since then the policy focus has been on moving people from institutions into the community and supporting people to remain in the community. In Ontario alone, nine institutions were closed between 1974 and 1996, with the numbers of people with developmental disabilities served in the community increasing from approximately 4600 in 1974 to over 50,000 in 1996. Before the year 2000, approximately 430 people with developmental disabilities in Ontario will move into the community with the closure of three additional institutions. Furthermore, the numbers of residents in the three remaining institutions will be reduced from approximately 2200 to 1750. Similar trends are occurring across Canada. Currently, the social and cultural contexts beyond the immediate home, such as family, friends, work, and leisure, are becoming the focus of research and service delivery. However, the need to evaluate objectives and outcomes has only recently been recognized.

An Acculturation Perspective

The normalization perspective has been criticized by some as failing to recognize the unique needs and characteristics of people with disabilities. Katherine Buell (1995) at Queen's University in Kingston has proposed an approach to evaluating the effects of deinstitutionalization and of the new community-based services. Buell has adapted a framework used in cross-cultural psychology to the field of developmental disabilities (Buell & Minnes, 1994). The **acculturation framework** (Berry, Kim, Power, Young, & Bujaki, 1989) considers the relationship of ethnocultural groups (or minority groups) within a larger society. Four modes of acculturation are defined: segregation, in which the group lives its own separate life, interacting little with the dominant society but maintaining its own identity; marginalization, in which the group has little sense of group identity but has not been accepted by the dominant group; assimilation, in which the group blends into the dominant group; and integration, in which the group participates in the economic, social, and cultural life of the dominant society while maintaining its own identity as a unique cultural entity. Members of ethnocultural groups categorized as integrated according to Berry's framework report less identity confusion and fewer feelings of marginality, depression, and anxiety than those categorized as assimilated, segregated, or marginalized. Buell's adapted framework (shown in Table 6.3) views people with developmental disabilities as a small subculture within a larger dominant group or culture.

From this point of view, a useful way to evaluate integration would be to assess the nature of their relationships with the larger society. This approach led to the development of the AIMS (Assimilation, Integration, Marginalization, Segregation) (Buell, 1995), an outcome measure designed to measure different levels of integration. Traditional institutional care could be considered segregation. The normalization approach, in which people are treated "as normal"—in other words, like everyone else—might be viewed as assimilation. If people with developmental disabilities do in some sense form a subculture, because they are set apart by differences in behaviour, cognition, and communication, would they benefit more from integration, and how could it be achieved? We really don't have a model yet for an integration approach. To date, people with developmental disabilities have generally had few choices about whom to associate with and when; these choices have been made by service providers. Currently, Buell and I are refining the AIMS and conducting a large study comparing levels of community integration and quality of life of people with developmental disabilities and people with acquired brain injuries.

Evaluating Quality of Life

While deinstitutionalization, normalization, and mainstreaming were major issues in the field of developmental disabilities during the 1970s and 1980s, the focus of attention has shifted in the 1990s to evaluating the **quality of life** of individuals with disabilities and their caregivers. But what constitutes quality of life and how can it be measured? There is no consensus, and a number of different approaches have been taken to the measurement of this important construct.

In Canada alone, several authors have developed different conceptual frameworks. For example, the Quality of Life Interview Schedule (QUOLIS) developed at Queen's

---

Table 6.3 **The Adapted Acculturation Framework**

		Issue One: Is it considered valuable to recognize and support the unique characteristics of people with developmental disabilities?	
		Yes	**No**
Issue Two: Is it considered valuable for people with developmental disabilities to maintain relationships with other groups?	**Yes**	Integration	Assimilation
	No	Segregation	Marginalization

Source: M. K. Buell, *Deinstitutionalization of persons with developmental disabilities: Normalization and service delivery evaluation* [Unpublished doctoral dissertation]. (Kingston, ON: Department of Psychology, Queen's University at Kingston, 1995).

University in Kingston (Ouellette-Kuntz, McCreary, Minnes, & Stanton, 1994) is designed specifically to address the needs of adults with severe and profound disabilities. During interviews with two informants who know an individual well in different contexts, quality of life is measured under 12 domains, such as health services and housing and safety. (See Table 6.4.)

QUOLIS contains 78 statements or indicators addressing supports in 12 life domains. Informants are asked to consider each statement, and the interviewer then rates responses on four 7-point scales with regard to four dimensions: availability, accessibility, current level of involvement, and apparent level of satisfaction.

A second approach to quality of life is reflected in the Quality of Life Project led by Renwick, Brown, and Raphael (1994) at the Centre for Health Promotion in Toronto. Their conceptual framework includes three major components of quality of life, each divided into subcomponents. The first component, entitled "Being," deals with the self (answering the question "Who is …?"), under the headings physical, psychological, and spiritual being. The second component, entitled "Belonging," focusses on how people fit into their physical, social, and community environments. The third component addresses strategies people use to achieve hopes and goals related to practical issues, leisure, and aspects of personal growth.

Table 6.4 Approaches to the Measurement of Quality of Life: QUOLIS

QUOLIS Domains	Samples of Basic Indicators
Health services	Primary medical care by physician or health care centre
Family/guardianship	Relative assumes informal guardianship role
Income maintenance	Regular review to ensure suitable public support
Education, training, employment	Coaching in life/vocational skills to promote integration
Housing and safety	Residence permits privacy and use of personal possessions
Transportation	Readily available transport to permit community activities
Social and recreational services	Regular activities provided
Religious/cultural supports	Opportunities for regular involvement
Case management	Individual assigned to ensure the needs of person are met
Esthetics	Ensure opportunities for variety and personal style in clothing
Advocacy	Avoidance of discrimination on basis of disability
Counselling	Relationship with a trained worker to discuss concerns

Source: Adapted from H. Ouellette-Kuntz, B. D. McCreary, P. M. Minnes, & B. Stanton, Evaluating quality of life: The development of the Quality of Life Interview Schedule (QUOLIS), *Journal of Developmental Disabilities, 3(1994),* 17–31.

PERVASIVE DEVELOPMENTAL DISORDERS: AUTISM

Stevie was a five-year-old boy who had been diagnosed with autism. He had been referred to a community behaviour management team because of frequent tantrums, in which he screamed and hit his head and jaw. His parents were concerned that Stevie would seriously injure himself, and were finding it difficult to manage him at home after the school had limited his attendance to three days per week because of his disruptive behaviour.

From the beginning, Stevie's parents knew that there was something different about their son. Stevie was described as a "good" baby. He resisted cuddling and seemed to be quite happy to be left alone. As a toddler, Stevie rarely interacted with his older sister and did not play with toys like other children. He liked to spin the wheels on his toy cars, tricycle, and wagon. He rarely used these toys in the conventional way and would scream if pushed to do so. Stevie's parents also noted his lack of language. Stevie would make repetitive sounds and imitate what was said to him but he did not make spontaneous comments or ask questions.

When Stevie was enrolled in nursery school at the age of four, the teachers recommended psychological assessment. The psychologist observed Stevie at home and at school, recording the frequency and duration of Stevie's outbursts, and their antecedents and consequences. A pattern emerged: when Stevie became frustrated for some reason—perhaps a wheel on a toy had fallen off or another child had taken one of his toys—he would scream and hit his jaw; restraint or comforting by his parents did not help.

Stevie's parents took a course on behaviour management in which they learned to praise and reinforce Stevie when he was behaving appropriately and to not respond or to respond neutrally to inappropriate behaviours. Feeling that Stevie was frustrated by his inability to communicate his needs, the psychologist also referred him to a speech pathologist, who taught him and his parents sign language. As Stevie learned to express his wishes and was reinforced for doing so appropriately, his tantrums and hitting gradually decreased.

Autism (from the Greek *autos*, "self") is the best known of the **pervasive developmental disorders**. Others include Asperger Disorder, Rett Disorder, and Child Disintegrative Disorder. Autism was first identified as a childhood disorder in 1943 by Leo Kanner. He described a sample of 11 children who exhibited a number of distinct characteristics, including a lack of social responsiveness or extreme autistic aloneness, and significantly limited or unusual communication patterns. In addition, Kanner noted unusual patterns of behaviour such as a lack of eye contact, self-stimulation including rocking, spinning, or flapping; self-injury including head-banging or hand-biting; an obsessive interest in particular objects, and an obsessive need for sameness. (See the DSM table "Diagnostic Criteria for Autistic Disorder.") Early terms for this disorder include Kanner's syndrome and childhood psychosis, the latter reflecting the notion of an association with schizophrenia. However, clinical research has shown that autism and childhood schizophrenia are very different in clinical features. Childhood schizophrenia, unlike autism, typically involves hallucinations and delusions, normal language skills, normal IQ, normal development until after the age of six, and frequent remissions and relapses. In addition, schizophrenia, unlike autism, shows a pattern of heritability, and is equally distributed between males and females (Volkmar, Carter, Grossman, & Klin, 1997).

Prevalence

Canadian studies estimate the prevalence of autism at from 4 to 10 per 10,000 births (Bryson, Clark, & Smith, 1988; Szatmari & Mahoney, 1993). Higher estimates—from 10 to 22

DSM-IV Diagnostic Criteria for Autistic Disorder

A. A total of six (or more) items from (1), (2), and (3), with at least two from (1), and one each from (2) and (3):

(1) qualitative impairment in social interaction, as manifested by at least two of the following:

(a) marked impairment in the use of multiple nonverbal behaviors such as eye-to-eye gaze, facial expression, body postures, and gestures to regulate social interaction

(b) failure to develop peer relationships appropriate to developmental level

(c) a lack of spontaneous seeking to share enjoyment, interests, or achievements with other people, i.e., by a lack of showing, bringing or pointing out objects of interest

(d) lack of social or emotional reciprocity

(2) qualitative impairments in communication as manifested by at least one of the following:

(a) delay in, or total lack of, the development of spoken language (not accompanied by an attempt to compensate through alternative modes of communication such as gesture or mime)

(b) in individuals with adequate speech, marked impairment in the ability to initiate or sustain a conversation with others

(c) stereotyped and repetitive use of language or idiosyncratic language

(d) lack of varied, spontaneous make-believe play or social imitative play appropriate to developmental level

(3) restricted repetitive and stereotyped patterns of behavior, interests, and activities, as manifested by at least one of the following:

(a) encompassing preoccupation with one or more stereotyped and restricted patterns of interest that is abnormal either in intensity or focus

(b) apparently inflexible adherence to specific, nonfunctional routines or rituals

(c) stereotyped and repetitive motor mannerisms (e.g., hand or finger flapping or twisting, or complex whole-body movements)

(d) persistent preoccupation with parts of objects

B. Delays or abnormal functioning in at least one of the following areas, with onset prior to age 3 years: (1) social interaction, (2) language as used in social communication, or (3) symbolic or imaginative play.

C. The disturbance is not better accounted for by Rett's Disorder or Childhood Disintegrative Disorder.

Source: Reprinted with permission from the *Diagnostic and Statistical Manual of Mental Disorders*, Fourth Edition. Copyright 1994 American Psychiatric Association.

per 10,000—have recently been suggested, reflecting changes in diagnostic criteria, to include a broader range of disorders in the autism spectrum (Bryson, 1996; Costello, 1996). Autism occurs three to four times as often in males as in females. The difference appears to be among people with higher IQs; no such difference is found among individuals functioning at a lower level (Lord & Schopler, 1987). Approximately one-third of individuals with autism do not speak, and up to half exhibit significant psychiatric and/or behavioural problems, including depression, anxiety, and aggression toward self or others. Epilepsy and sensory impairments are also common (Bryson, 1996). The strongest single predictor of functional outcome among people with autism has consistently been found to be the development of functional speech by the age of five years.

DESCRIPTION

Social Development

Two critical features of autism are social dysfunction and unusual responses to the environment. Such deficits, while frequently described, are less well understood than other aspects of autism (Lord, 1993). From infancy, parents often note the lack of attachment and comfort-seeking behaviours. The child does not anticipate being picked up and does not seek physical contact. Indeed autistic children will often stiffen their bodies or scream in response to being picked up or may seem indifferent. Social interactions are characterized by a lack of reciprocity.

The nature of the social interactions of autistic individuals differs according to developmental level; however, they continue to be deficient or unusual. For example, young children with autism frequently display relatively little interest in social interaction and prefer solitary activities. They may respond with relative indifference to strangers and even to their parents (Volkmar et al., 1997). Abnormal or absent social behaviours are noted in the first two years of life of most children with autism.

Whereas the social environment is of particular interest to normally developing infants and young children, as well as to some children with mental retardation, children with autism are often much more responsive to the non-social environment. Minor changes in the environment (for example, routines, arrangement of furniture or objects) can lead to emotional outbursts. Over time, older individuals with autism may display some attachments to family members and show differential awareness of strangers but they will rarely initiate social interaction (Landry & Loveland, 1988; Sigman & Mundy, 1989). Autistic individuals without expressive language often do not use the non-verbal signals (for example, eye contact) that usually guide social interaction.

Studies of social orientation indicate that children with autism show little interest in the human face and often avoid eye contact. In addition, subsequent preverbal social communication skills such as smiling, pointing, and joint attention are frequently absent or significantly delayed. The lack of these skills hampers subsequent symbolic development, including imitation and symbolic play. Whereas normally developing children, and some older children with mental retardation, readily imitate actions involved in interactive games such as "peek-a-boo" and "pat-a-cake," children with autism rarely initiate social interaction, preferring solitary activities involving repetitive or stereotyped actions with objects (Stone, Lemanek, Fishel, Fernandez, & Altemeier, 1990).

Language Acquisition

The first three years of life see rapid development of expressive language. In normally developing children, verbal skills begin with babbling and progress to single words, short but meaningful phrases, and then sentences. However, approximately 50 percent of children with autism are mute. Those who do develop speech often do not communicate meaningfully. Moreover, those who do develop language often have speech that is abnormal in tone and content. There is some evidence to suggest that children with fluent speech (that is, three-word phrases produced spontaneously and regularly in an effort to communicate) by the age of five are more likely to have higher academic achievement and better developed adaptive skills by adolescence than children without such speech by the age of five (Venter, Lord, & Schopler, 1992). This measure was found to be as effective in predicting outcome as early IQ or language tests (Lord & Paul, 1997). Nonverbal joint attention and play skills prior to the age of five have also been found to predict the acquisition of language (Mundy, Sigman, & Kasari, 1990).

Echolalia is one of the common characteristics of speech in children with autism. In this condition the child will repeat another person's words or phrases, using the same or similar intonation. **Pronoun reversal** is also common; autistic individuals often refer to themselves as "he" or "she" rather than "I," perhaps because they have trouble shifting reference between speaker and listener or a third party. This aspect of language is thought to be related to deficits in joint attention and to difficulties in understanding the perspectives of others and the distinction between self and other (Lord & Paul, 1997).

Although articulation is often clear and there may be quite a good vocabulary, meaningful, spontaneous speech is rare among individuals with autism. Receptive language can also be affected. People with autism may understand relatively short requests but fail to understand more complex information.

Attention, Perception, and Cognition

Children with autism characteristically show abnormal responses to environmental stimulation. As a result, it was hypothesized that high levels of arousal are related to filtering difficulties. For example, autistic individuals may seem underresponsive to certain stimuli (especially to sound) but overresponsive to other stimuli, such as pain or touch (Ornitz, 1989). More recent research, however, has focussed more upon attentional processes. Results to date indicate particular patterns of attention deficits associated with autism. For example, people with autism have difficulty orienting, focussing, controlling, and maintaining attention. On the other hand, they can display selective attention and overfocus in abnormal ways on particular aspects of the environment (Burack, Enns, Stauder, Mottron, & Randolph, 1997). Auditory perception and discrimination are often poorer than visual perception. Such problems are likely to contribute to delayed language acquisition.

Approximately 25 percent of individuals with autism function within the normal range of intelligence. These individuals often have some meaningful speech and are ultimately able to function more independently, although social difficulties limit the degree of community integration possible. Among the remaining 75 percent, a small proportion, often called **savants**, display islets of exceptional ability in areas such as mathematics, music, or art, or unusual feats of memory. A study of more than 5000 autistic children (Rimland, 1978) found extraordinary abilities in 9.8 percent of the sample. This combination of extraordinary skills and significant social deficits was well portrayed by Dustin Hoffman in the widely acclaimed film *Rain Man*. Hoffman's character, Raymond, could memorize all the numbers in the telephone book and remember all the cards played in a poker game.

Overall, about 10 percent of individuals with autism will be fully integrated into the community in adulthood, able to hold a job and live fairly independently. Approximately 60 percent are dependent in many aspects of their life. Poor prognostic signs include the absence of communicative speech by five years (Achenbach, 1982) and an IQ below 60 (Gillberg, 1991).

· ·

DIAGNOSTIC ISSUES

The classification of autism has evolved since it was first included as a diagnostic category in DSM-III in 1980. The wide range of intellectual, social, and language deficits has made diagnostic reliability problematic. To clarify diagnostic categories, several changes were made to the DSM-IV criteria. Subgroups have been classified according to a number of criteria, including level of intelligence, social functioning, and the presence of organic features (Volkmar & Schwab-Stone, 1996). Subgroups include the "core syndrome" of autism, Rett syndrome, and Asperger syndrome. Debate continues as to whether core autism and Asperger's represent points on a continuum of severity, or whether they are different but related disorders (Waterhouse, Morris, Allen, Dunn, Fein, Feinstein, Rapin, & Wing, 1996).

The core syndrome of autism is currently diagnosed by counting the number of autistic symptoms (see the DSM table for autism). Higher symptom counts tend to be associated with lower IQ. Higher-functioning individuals with higher IQ and fewer symptoms are often categorized as having **Asperger disorder**.

Asperger Disorder

Matthew was an 18-year-old man with Asperger syndrome. He was relatively high-functioning, with fairly well-developed expressive language, and was able to read and write. He was not echolalic in the traditional sense but did exhibit other features of autism such as hand-flapping and obsessive behaviour. He was able to interact socially to some extent but in a rather rigid, stilted fashion. In addition, his way of approaching individuals, especially young women, was often intrusive and inappropriate.

Matthew had always lived at home with his parents. He took the bus to school, where he was integrated for computer and physical education and spent the rest of the day in a special class for students who were relatively high-functioning but needed learning support for a variety of reasons. Matthew enjoyed sports, especially swimming and playing basketball with his classmates. He also liked to go to the mall where he could spend his allowance on CDs and computer games. In the past year, he had become very involved with the Internet and spent hours surfing.

Through the school-to-community transition program, Matthew was assigned to a job coach who helped him develop his computer skills to prepare for a work placement at the local library gathering research information from the World Wide Web.

Unlike those with autism, individuals with Asperger disorder do not have significantly delayed cognitive development. Except for social skills, their adaptive behaviour and interest in the environment are age-appropriate, and they may indicate particular interest in social interaction. However, their interactions are frequently odd or eccentric (Volkmar et al., 1997). The most commonly cited social deficits include:

- failure to establish a joint frame of reference for interaction (that is, they may begin to speak seemingly in mid-thought);

- failure to observe social norms or to show awareness of the listener's feelings (for example, making inappropriate personal remarks to strangers);

- repeated reference to preoccupations in conversation (for example, the Internet) and use of stereotyped phrases, often related to these limited areas of interest (for example, "Do you have a Web page?")

The symptoms of Asperger syndrome were noted in the literature long before the syndrome was recognized. In 1944, a year after Kanner first described autistic children, Hans Asperger described a group of children with similar characteristics. There has been ongoing controversy as to whether the syndromes described by Kanner and by Asperger are separate conditions diagnostically or represent different parts of a continuum of "autistic spectrum disorders." Generally, Asperger syndrome has been viewed as a mild version of autism associated with higher intellectual functioning (Gillberg & Gillberg, 1989; Waterhouse et al., 1996).

Child Disintegrative Disorder

Child disintegrative disorder (CDD), although described in the literature in the early 1900s, continues to be less frequently reported and less well understood than autism. The major distinguishing feature of CDD is later onset; after a period of several years of normal development, marked deterioration occurs. The ability to speak in sentences is present before onset of the disorder. Individuals with CDD exhibit behaviours and deficits in social skill and communication similar to those found in autism. The etiology of CDD has not been determined, although it is thought that a neurobiological cause is likely (Volkmar, Klin, Marans, & Cohen, 1997).

Rett Syndrome

Rett syndrome was first described in the 1960s by Andreas Rett in a German report of 22 cases. However, the syndrome did not receive much recognition until several papers were published in the 1980s by Hagberg in Sweden (Hagberg, Aicardi, Dias, & Ramos, 1983). Rett syndrome is a distinct disorder primarily affecting females. Incidence is approximately 1 in 15,000. Rett syndrome is often confused with autism due to similarities in speech problems, lack of social responsiveness, stereotyped behaviours, and, in some cases, screaming and self-injurious behaviour. However, in Rett syndrome there is a unique pattern of cognitive and functional deterioration, which has been divided into four stages (Rett Syndrome Diagnostic Criteria Working Group, 1988). In the first stage, *stagnation* (6 to 18 months from onset), motor development slows and *hypotonia* (poor muscle tone) is noted, as well as loss of interest in play and in the environment. In the second stage, *rapid destructive* (one to three years from onset), developmental milestones are lost and, perhaps most notably, hand use is reduced to stereotyped movements such as wringing, clapping, and mouthing. Expressive language is lost and autistic behaviours as well as irritability occur. Seizures, insomnia, and self-injury are also common in this stage. In the third stage (two to ten years from onset), the child functions within the severe range of mental retardation and may appear demented. *Ataxia* (lack of coordination), *apraxia* (poor movement control), and progressive rigidity occur, along with early *scoliosis* (curvature of the spine), and *bruxism* (teeth-grinding). In the fourth stage (ten years or more from onset), mobility is significantly reduced, and there is progressive muscle wasting and rigidity and growth retardation; expressive and receptive language are absent.

Although the etiology of Rett syndrome is not known, it is thought to be related to a metabolic problem. Brain imaging studies indicate the presence of mild diffuse cerebral atrophy.

Assessment

Due to the multifaceted nature of autism, assessments are usually carried out by a multidisciplinary team, including a psychologist, psychiatrist, speech and language specialist, occupational and physical therapist, and teacher. Audiological and neurological assessments may also be conducted. A comprehensive developmental approach to assessment is strongly recommended to permit accurate documentation of strengths and deficits in various areas of functioning related to adaptation in day-to-day life.

ETIOLOGY

Since Kanner (1943) first presented his 11 cases in the 1940s, the etiology of autism has been a topic of considerable debate. Overall, there have been two major hypotheses.

Psychogenic

The psychogenic hypothesis focussed on family characteristics and the child's environment. Both Kanner and the psychoanalyst Bettelheim (1967) were strong proponents of this view. They described parents of children with autism as highly intelligent, obsessive or rigid, and lacking in warmth. This view led to the term "refrigerator parent," which over the years has been very damaging to parents' self-esteem. Research since the 1950s, however, has not supported this view. There is no empirical evidence that the personality characteristics described by Kanner occur more frequently in parents of children with autism than in other parents (Cantwell, Baker, & Rutter, 1978). Furthermore, the facts that siblings do not all develop autism and that symptoms appear in all cultures point to a biological or organic basis.

Biological

In the past 30 years, the focus of research has shifted from psychogenic to biological factors. Several findings support the biogenic hypothesis. About 30 percent of adolescents with autism have epileptic seizures. Abnormal levels of the neurotransmitter serotonin are found in 30 to 50 percent of children with autism. In addition, a history of prenatal infections such as rubella and problems during pregnancy and delivery are fairly common among mothers of children with autism (Goodman, 1990; Nelson, 1991).

Researchers generally agree that neurobiological factors play an important role in the etiology of autism. New brain imaging technology has led to a good deal of support for this position. For example, the brains of people with autism have been found to be slightly larger and heavier and abnormalities have been found in a number of brain structures (for example, the amygdala, hippocampus, septum, mamillary bodies, and cerebellum) (Denckla, 1996). Neuropsychological studies over the years have produced conflicting results because of inconsistent methodologies, samples, and measures. Nevertheless, findings in general indicate that impairment is not limited to a single area of the brain and there is considerable variability within different functional domains (for example, attention, memory, language). The amygdala, hippocampus, cerebellum, frontal lobes, and basal ganglia have all been associated with symptoms of autism, including problems orienting to social stimuli, motor imitation, joint attention, and empathy. Difficulties are commonly found with executive functions such as inhibition, flexibility, planning, and organization, which are controlled by the frontal lobes (Ozonoff, Pennington, & Rogers, 1991), whereas the degree of language and memory dysfunction varies more widely (Dawson, 1996).

Genetic factors are now considered to play a considerable role in the development of autism; however, the complexities of genetic transmission are not as yet understood (Rutter, Bailey, Simonoff, & Pickles, 1997; Szatmari & Mahoney, 1993). The relatively high frequency of autism among siblings of a person with autism (3 to 5 percent) suggests a strong genetic component, although other factors may also contribute (Smalley & Collins, 1996). The frequent occurrence of autistic features in individuals with Fragile X syndrome and tuberous sclerosis, and evidence that the *phenotype* (the pattern of social, cognitive, and behavioural abnormalities) extends beyond autism, suggest that a number of interacting genes are likely to be involved (Rutter et al., 1997). This complexity makes genetic research difficult; nevertheless, more family studies of affected pairs of relatives are needed, as well as mapping studies to identify the genes contributing to the disorder (Spence, 1996).

TREATMENT AND INTERVENTION

Medications and Nutritional Supplements

Although biological factors in the etiology of autism have received most attention in recent years, biologically based treatments have not been found to be generally effective. Data from the Autism Research Institute on a large sample of more than 6000 children indicate that prescription drugs are frequently the treatment of choice for physicians (Rimland & Baker, 1996).

Drugs generally are used to regulate levels of neurotransmitters (for example, serotonin, dopamine, norepinephrine) thought to contribute to abnormal behaviours frequently associated with autism. Preliminary research evidence summarized by McDougle, Price, & Volkman (1994) suggests that drugs that increase 5-HT neurotransmission (for example, clomipramine) may facilitate reduction of repetitive behaviours and aggression and help improve social skills. Dopamine receptor antagonists such as haloperidol are effective in

reduction of maladaptive behaviours but extrapyramidal side-effects and tardive dyskinesia are less with resperidone. Stimulants such as methylphenidate (Ritalin) may help to reduce distractibility and hyperactivity but more controlled studies are needed to determine particular effects with children with autism. Recent studies of naltrexone (Neo-Synalar, Nupercainal) have shown some benefit in reducing hyperactivity but little effect on social skills and self-injurious behaviour and aggression. While there was considerable interest in fenfluramine in the treatment of social and sensory functioning, more recent controlled studies have not demonstrated significant effects on the core symptoms of autism. However, research data on the six most frequently prescribed medications methylphenidate (Ritalin) thioridazine (Mellaril), diphenhydramine (Benadryl), phenytoin (Dilantin), haloperidol (Haldol), and carbamazepine (Tegretol) indicate benefits in less than one-third of cases and adverse reactions in almost half of cases (Rimland & Baker, 1996).

Alternative approaches including nutritional supplements such as megadoses of vitamin B6 and magnesium, vitamin C, and folic acid have become popular because they do not have the side-effects of prescription drugs. Well-controlled research of their effectiveness is, however, extremely limited (Rimland & Baker, 1996).

Psychodynamic

Psychodynamic intervention was common in the 1940s and 1950s, when psychogenic explanations predominated. Withdrawal of the child from the home was recommended, to a non-threatening environment where he or she could learn to express feelings and take action (Bettelheim, 1967). However, empirical studies have found no evidence that such approaches are effective (Matson, Benavidez, Compton, Paclawskyj, & Baglio, 1996).

Behavioural Interventions

In the 1970s, Ivor Lovaas and colleagues began the Young Autism Project, which offered behavioural programs designed to alleviate symptoms of autism. Such programs, which have also been used with individuals with disorders, focussed on developing self-help skills, language, appropriate social interactions, and academic skills and on reducing maladaptive behaviours including self-stimulation, stereotyped actions, self-injury, and aggression (Lovaas, Koegel, Simmons, & Long, 1973; Lovaas & Smith, 1988).

A recent review of behavioural treatment studies since 1980 (Matson et al., 1996) found that the most frequently addressed aberrant behaviours among people with developmental disabilities and autism were stereotypy, aggression, and self-injurious behaviour. Following functional analysis of the antecedents and consequences of the target behaviour, programs are developed to alter the reinforcement contingencies maintaining the behaviour. The most common behavioural interventions are positive reinforcement of appropriate behaviour (53 percent), aversive stimuli (20 percent), extinction (1 percent), and a combination (26 percent).

With growing concern about aversive procedures such as contingent electric shock, a number of nonaversive procedures have been put forward as alternative interventions with maladaptive behaviour (LaVigna & Donnellan, 1986). For example, functional communication training techniques were developed as a nonaversive approach to reducing aberrant behaviours. Essentially, clients are taught appropriate responses to their environment that they can use instead of inappropriate or maladaptive behaviour (Carr & Durand, 1985). Thus, children would be taught to ask for something beyond their reach rather than having a severe temper outburst.

Studies have indicated that functional communication training produced more appropriate behaviour than timeout even when the client was with adults unfamiliar with the program (Durand & Carr, 1992). However, in cases where self-injury or aggression is particularly severe, it might be considered unethical to use interventions less intrusive than electric shock, which has been shown to quickly reduce the frequency of such behaviours. Nevertheless, the potential for abuse highlights the need for careful regulation and monitoring of such techniques. The questions of client consent, peer reviews, and the qualifications of professionals involved must be considered. Shock is now used only in extreme cases as a last resort, and is not used at all in most facilities (Matson et al., 1996).

Social skills training is another important area of intervention for people with autism, as it is for people with developmental disorders in general. The most frequently addressed behaviours include initiating contact (32 percent), responding appropriately (23 percent), and reciprocal interactions (15 percent). In the vast majority of studies, the intervention of choice is positive reinforcement (using praise, tokens, stickers, etc.) of appropriate behaviour (Matson et al., 1996). Through the use of task analysis, target behaviours were broken down into steps, including prerequisite skills. For example, eye contact and attending would be taught as precursors to asking and responding to questions (Goldstein & Wickstrom, 1986). Skills taught in this way need to be generalized to other individuals and other environments. One approach, particularly with adolescents, has been to train student volunteers from different settings to be peer tutors, so that the autistic person gets used to responding to several different people.

A good deal of attention has been given to language intervention programs, with the majority (87 percent) focussing on expressive language (Matson et al., 1996). Using operant conditioning principles, shaping, and modelling, researchers have successfully taught verbal imitation, labelling, asking questions, and appropriate verbal responding (Lovaas, 1977). A number of other augmentative communication systems have been developed to assist people with autism who do not have functional expressive language. Manual sign language has been found to be effective, alone or as part of a "total communication" approach including oral language; communication boards and talking computers may also be helpful (Barrera, Lobato-Barrera, & Sulzer-Azaroff, 1980; Carr, Binkoff, Kologinski, & Eddy, 1978; Carr & Kologinsky, 1983; Mirenda & Schuler, 1988). (See the Focus box on facilitated communication for an example of an approach that did not fulfill its promise.) Research indicates that such approaches can be effective in helping people with autism communicate independently and spontaneously at a basic level (for example, making requests and appropriate comments). Furthermore, evidence suggests that improved communication skills are often associated with reduced maladaptive behaviours such as tantrums, aggression, and self-injury (Donnellan, Mirenda, Mesaros, & Fassbender, 1984).

Improvements in behavioural approaches over the years have led to increasingly good results. Indeed, recent followup studies have reported significant gains, to the point that some clients are able to function at a normal level (Lovaas, 1987).

Focus *The Dangers of Hope: Lessons from Facilitated Communication and Other Miracle Cures*

For decades, alternative approaches to overcoming various forms of disability have passed in and out of fashion. The success of such movements is a function of "the unhappiness of clients and the vividness of their dreams" (Toch, 1971, p. 44). Parents and caregivers who become strong proponents of alternative approaches frequently ignore concerns raised by professionals and "nonbelievers."

In the 1960s and 1970s, for example, the Doman Delacato technique (Delacato, 1966; Doman, Spitz, Sucman, Delacato, & Doman, 1960) received a good deal of attention. This approach, based on a theory of neurological organization, argued that appropriate physical activity is essential for correct sequential development of the neurological system at each stage of development. Their treatment, applied to children with a wide variety of disabilities, required intensive active and passive involvement in physical activities found in earlier stages of development (Hudson & Clunies-Ross, 1978). Research has generally failed to provide support for the validity of the technique and systematic investigation of the theoretical underpinnings of the approach has led to their rejection (Cummins, 1988;

Focus *continued*

Hallahan & Cruikshank, 1973). Concerns have been raised by organizations and by professionals that the pressure upon parents to follow extremely demanding procedures can lead to neglect of other family members' needs and increased family distress. Nevertheless, parents and caregivers continue to invest enormous amounts of time, money, and energy using "patterning" techniques with their children.

One of the more recent techniques to attract attention is **facilitated communication (FC)**. Claims of dramatic and rapid improvements in behaviour and functioning have given parents great hope. However, research findings have not supported continued use of this type of communication training.

Facilitated communication training (FC), developed in Australia in the 1970s, was introduced to Canada and the United States in 1990 by Douglas Biklen from Syracuse University. The technique was described as a "teaching strategy used with people with severe communication impairment requiring aided communication who are not yet able to access a communication aid independently but for whom direct access with their hands is a realistic and desirable goal" (Crossley, 1992). Individuals with communication difficulties were taught to point to pictures, letters, or objects by a facilitator who provides various types of support to the hand or forearm. Physical support, it was suggested, can overcome neuromotor problems that limit the individual's ability to initiate movements, thus in-terfering with communication. Letterboards, typewriters, or talking computers are often used as part of this process.

The technique aroused great excitement and controversy in Canada, Australia, and the United States (Minnes, 1992; Prior & Cummins, 1992). Remarkable success stories emerged of apparently low-functioning children with autism who suddenly demonstrated the ability to read and produce sentences expressing sophisticated ideas and feelings. However, concerns were soon raised about the "ouija board" effect: Were these really the child's own thoughts, or were facilitators unintentionally influencing the child's choice of symbol through subtle body movements (Rimland, 1991)?

Despite the absence of empirical evidence to confirm independent communication, countless parents, caregivers, and educators became strong proponents of the technique. It became even more important to determine the reliability and validity of this technique when numerous reports were published of people around the world using their new-found communication channel to describe physical and sexual abuse.

Over the next few years, dozens of qualitative and quantitative studies on FC (see Green, 1994) were conducted. Three paradigms were used, particularly in quantitative studies. In the first, questions were asked about information made available to the person being facilitated but not to the facilitator—through headphones, for example (Hudson, Melita, & Arnold, 1993), or as stimulus material blocked by screens from the facilitator's view. In a second approach, called "message passing," questions were asked about events or activities that occurred when the facilitator was not present. A third approach, called a training model or set work design, assessed gains in communication skills over time.

The results of dozens of well-controlled studies indicated that in the majority of cases, messages were not being communicated independently; rather, facilitators were unwittingly influencing the messages being communicated (Rimland, 1993; Wheeler, Jacobson, Paglieri, & Schwartz, 1993). The results of an intensive, multi-method validation study conducted in Toronto by Adrienne Perry, Susan Bryson, and James Bebko did not provide support for the emergence of hidden literacy skills. Moreover, they noted an "abdication effect," whereby students who could perform basic communication tasks independently became passive when a facilitator became involved. Indeed, accuracy levels of one-quarter of participants dropped significantly from 75–80 percent correct in a "no facilitated communication" condition (Bebko, Perry, & Bryson, 1996; Perry, Bryson, & Bebko, 1993).

These and other results point to a number of risks associated with FC. A recent review of the *Canadian Code of Ethics for Psychologists* (Dayan & Minnes, 1995) raised serious ethical questions about choosing this approach over augmentative communication systems with well-documented effectiveness. ▲

The intensive interventions developed by Lovaas and colleagues included one-to-one behavioural treatment, 40 hours per week, for at least two years. The participants were 19 children with autism under the age of four, who were integrated into regular preschool classes. In addition parents were given training sessions. IQ scores increased by 20 points on average, and by the age of seven, nine of the children were able to keep up with a Grade 1 class in all areas. Outcomes for children in the two control groups were poorer, except for one child whose intellectual and educational accomplishments were within the normal range (McEachin, Smith, & Lovaas, 1993). These results led to considerable debate and a number of critical commentaries have been published. The major concerns included the nonrandom assignment of children to experimental and control groups, small sample size, nonrepresentative samples (children were higher-functioning in the experimental group), insufficient measures of the severity of autism, and inconsistent assessment measures.

LEARNING DISORDERS

Mark was a 19-year-old university student, in first-year Applied Science, with a nonverbal learning disorder. Mark had problems understanding and applying concepts in courses such as mathematics. He had particular difficulty understanding graphs and preferred to have information presented in words. Mark liked to participate in study groups because he remembered information more readily after hearing it discussed. Mark was assessed at the University Student Counselling Centre and was found to have above-average intelligence, good auditory memory, but poor visual memory. Mark had a good vocabulary and good rote memory—that is, he could memorize facts easily but couldn't always synthesize or use the information.

Mark had sloppy handwriting and did not express ideas clearly in writing. He was a slow reader because of problems with visual tracking, often losing his place or misreading words. Multiple-choice tests were particularly difficult for Mark because of his slow reading and problems discriminating between words that look alike. If there was a separate answer sheet, Mark's visual tracking problems made transferring from one page to another difficult.

Mark was socially isolated and anxious. He had trouble reading facial expressions and did not catch nonverbal cues. He avoided sports because of his clumsiness.

After Mark's assessment, a learning disabilities specialist was able to arrange some special accommodations. He was given extra time on math exams and others involving graphs and was allowed to write his exams on a computer. In addition, he enrolled in a program to teach him to use verbal strategies in problem-solving.

Learning disorders, frequently referred to as *learning disabilities*, include reading disorders, mathematics disorders, and disorders of written expression. Communication disorders and problems related to poor motor skills may also be included.

Such disorders are usually addressed within an educational rather than a mental health context so they will be addressed only briefly in this chapter.

Learning disabilities in children have been noted in the literature since the late 1800s. A lack of consensus regarding the definition of such problems, however, is reflected in the varied terminology used over the years (for example, *congenital word blindness*, *developmental alexia*, *minimal brain dysfunction*, *perceptual handicaps*, *developmental aphasia*, *dysgraphia*, *dyslexia*, and *dyscalculia*) (Culbertson & Edmonds, 1996). Indeed, Cruikshank (1972) lists 40 different terms used in the literature.

Three major components are commonly found in definitions of learning disabilities (Harrison, 1992):

1. A disparity between estimated potential and measures of current academic achievement (thus, children functioning intellectually within the developmentally handicapped range [IQ below 70] are excluded)

2. An absence of sociocultural factors or physical problems, such as visual impairment or brain injury, that would explain the learning difficulty

3. The assumption that underlying learning processes are dysfunctional

The Ontario Ministry of Education (Ministry of Education, 1978) has adopted the following definition of learning disabilities:

Disorders in one or more of the processes involved in understanding or using symbols or spoken language. The disorder results in a significant discrepancy between academic achievement and assessed intellectual ability, with deficits in at least one of the following areas: receptive language (i.e., listening, reading); language processing (i.e., thinking, conceptualizing, integrating); expressive language (i.e., talking, spelling, writing); and mathematical computations. Such deficits become evident in both academic and social situations. This definition does not include children who have learning problems which are primarily the result of impairments of vision or hearing; motor handicaps; mental retardation; primary emotional disturbance; or environmental, cultural or economic disadvantage. (p. 2)

Although this definition provides useful guidelines, there is a need for further clarification. For example, how large must the discrepancy be between potential and current achievement? How should such discrepancies be measured (Harrison, 1992)?

Prevalence

Without a precise definition, it is very difficult to establish prevalence. Estimates vary from 2 to 15 percent of school-age children (Gaddes, 1976). In recent years, the prevalence of learning disorders among adults has become a topic of concern. Learning disorders in children do not necessarily improve with age. In a recent Canadian followup study, Harrison (1992) found that both the pattern of cognitive skills and the types of academic problems experienced by children with reading disorders and arithmetic disorders continue into adulthood despite intensive remedial assistance, and that these adults experience a number of difficulties whether or not they are still in school. Many students with learning disabilities progress to postsecondary education. Since the 1980s, the number of students entering university or college with known learning disabilities has increased markedly (Gajar, 1992), both because changes in education and social attitude have allowed more of them to progress to university and because current knowledge permits more learning disabilities to be diagnosed. It is estimated that this increase will continue (Shaw & Shaw, 1989).

Learning disorders occur more frequently in males than females, with ratios ranging from 2 to 1 to 5 to 1 (Taylor, 1989). Most people with learning disorders function within the normal range of intelligence but their performance on standardized intelligence tests usually shows significant discrepancies between scores on verbal items and visuomotor and visuospatial items.

DSM-IV criteria for learning disorders (see the DSM table "Diagnostic Criteria for Reading Disorder") include discrepancy between achievement and IQ score and age, as well as significant interference with academic achievement or activities of daily living.

Reading Disorder

Reading disorder, commonly known as **dyslexia**, involves difficulties not only in the recognition but also in the comprehension of words. Reading is often very slow and characterized by omitted, substituted, or distorted words. Such difficulties often extend to spelling as well. (See the DSM table "Diagnostic Criteria for Reading Disorder.") Estimates range from 2 to 8 percent of children in the elementary grades have dyslexia.

Mathematical Disorder

Mathematical disorder, also known as **dyscalculia**, involves problems with recognizing and understanding numerical symbols, sequencing problems, and attention deficits. DSM-IV diagnostic criteria are the same as for reading disorder. Prevalence is not known, but estimates suggest that approximately 6 percent of school-aged children have mathematical disorder (Semrud-Clikeman & Hynd, 1992).

Disorders of Written Expression

Disorders of written expression, or **dysgraphia**, are characterized by limited handwriting skills, spelling, grammatical, and punctuation errors. The DSM-IV diagnostic criteria are similar to those for reading disorder. Information concerning this disorder is limited and prevalence estimates are unreliable, as dysgraphia often co-occurs with dyslexia. Estimates in the 1970s suggest rates between 3 and 4 percent (Culbertson & Edmonds, 1996).

DSM-IV **Diagnostic Criteria for Reading Disorder**
A. Reading achievement, as measured by individually administered standardized tests of reading accuracy or comprehension, is substantially below that expected given the person's chronological age, measured intelligence and age-appropriate education.
B. The disturbance in Criterion A significantly interferes with academic achievement or activities of daily living that require reading skills.
If a sensory deficit is present, the reading difficulties are in excess of those usually associated with it.

Source: Reprinted with permission from the *Diagnostic and Statistical Manual of Mental Disorders*, Fourth Edition. Copyright 1994 American Psychiatric Association.

DIAGNOSTIC ISSUES

Traditionally, psychometric assessment of intelligence has been the primary approach in defining learning disabilities. However, research by Rourke and others indicates that the level of performance does not give a clear picture and that detailed assessment of the patterns of performance is critical (Rourke, 1991). Two of the most commonly cited profiles are those of verbal learning disorders and nonverbal learning disorders. These subtypes have been identified across cultures in the Western world (Korthonen, 1988) and in adults with learning disorders. Moreover, research suggests that particular emotional-behavioural responses may be associated with learning disorders (Rourke, 1991). For example, withdrawal from frustrating situations, regression, somatic complaints, fear reactions to particular situations, depression, clowning, impulsive behaviour, dependency, or passive-aggressive behaviour (Silver, 1979).

Psychometric studies indicate that adults and children with learning disorders show similar patterns (Harrison, 1992). For example, while they frequently demonstrate particular strengths in visuospatial tasks (for example, picture completion, picture arrangement, block design), they have difficulty with tasks requiring concentration, sequencing abilities, auditory processing, and auditory memory (Leonard, 1991). People with reading disorder generally perform better on tasks requiring visuospatial abilities rather than verbal abilities; people with mathematical disorders generally exhibit the opposite pattern (Harrison, 1992).

ETIOLOGY

Research findings to date have been inconclusive. It is generally believed that both biological and psychological causes may be implicated. Exclusionary criteria indicate that the primary cause is *not* mental retardation, emotional disorders, sensory impairments, physical disabilities, cultural-familial disadvantage, or such environmental factors as limited access to education or poor teaching (Johnson & Blalock, 1987).

Until recently, the different phenotypical expressions of learning disabilities or disorders have been viewed as having the same underlying cause (Harrison, 1992). The presence of learning disorders among children with neurological problems (for example, brain injury, epilepsy) has led some to suggest brain dysfunction as a causal factor. However, as not all children with such problems develop learning disabilities, other factors including motivation, information processing problems, and perceptual deficits must be considered.

Brain imaging studies of dyslexia show altered patterns of asymmetry in the language areas of the brain and minor malformations of the cortex (Hynd, Semrund-Clikeman, Lorys, Novey, & Eliopulos, 1990). In addition, single photon emission computed tomography (SPECT) scans report reduced blood flow to the left temporal-frontal region of the brain in children with language disabilities (Lou, Henriksen, & Bruhn, 1990).

The cause of such differences in brain structure is still unclear. Hypotheses about dyslexia include abnormal fetal growth patterns in the brain (Hynd et al. 1990). It has been suggested that high levels of testosterone may stimulate more rapid growth of the right hemisphere or may interfere with left hemisphere development (De Lacoste, Horvath, & Woodward, 1991).

There is some evidence that dyslexia may be inherited; however, the mode of transmission remains unclear due to methodological problems in genetic research (Culbertson & Edmonds, 1996; Pennington & Smith, 1988). Moreover, it is important not to overlook environmental influences.

TREATMENT

A recent review of research on intervention strategies (Bos & Van Reusen, 1991) highlighted motivation, cognitive processing styles, and cognitive-behavioural approaches. The authors emphasize the importance of:

a. bolstering students' self-esteem and stimulating their intrinsic motivation to learn;

b. developing organizational frameworks to help students learn new material and retrieve material already learned;

c. introducing verbal self-instructional techniques, cognitive modelling, and self-regulatory techniques; and

d. promoting generalization and maintenance of skills learned

PANORAMA

Several important trends have emerged in the area of mental retardation over the past four decades. The most obvious is the normalization or deinstitutionalization movement. Families have assumed increasing responsibility for the care and training of people with disabilities and many people with disabilities have been integrated into the community, into the educational mainstream, and into supported employment. Treatment and intervention approaches have moved from the medical model and custodial care to an educational or developmental model in which family members, teachers, and paid caregivers act as mediators in the training process. Furthermore, parent/professional relationships have become more collegial, with the parent and the professional working more as partners.

It is difficult to predict what will happen in the next 10 to 15 years. History has shown that the sociopolitical context affects attitudes and models of service delivery and that historically the pendulum has swung back and forth. While most people would probably like integration to continue, community living poses challenges to staff and clients alike.

Community-based educational and vocational programs, medical and dental care, and leisure activities must be provided. However, given the economic constraints of recent years, adequate funds may not be available for such support. Without it, behaviour problems arise, staff burn out, and community attitudes change. Systematic behavioural interventions and structured programming require staff training and commitment. If funding is not available, agencies may be forced to resort to drugs to manage behaviour and there is a risk that the medical model and custodial care may return. The irony is that effective educational and behavioural technology is available but often not used.

At the same time, although the remarkable advances in genetics in recent years have been very exciting, some have expressed concern that attitudes may become less positive toward persons with developmental disabilities with increasing availability of genetic/prenatal screening and that abortion and euthanasia may gain favour as interventions.

Excellent data from educational and intervention programs are now available that demonstrate that people with

developmental disabilities can live meaningful lives in the community if the appropriate supports are in place. The challenge of the next decade will be to maintain the significant advances made to date in times of economic uncertainty.

An enormous amount of information on autism has been published in the past decade. As Cohen and Volkmar (1997) suggest, numerous advances have been made through research conducted by several different disciplines. For example, our understanding of the genetic aspects of autism has increased and the development of more reliable assessment methods has contributed to research and clinical interventions. Research on cognitive processing in people with autism has helped us to understand some of the social and interpersonal deficits common to autism. Furthermore, the development and refinement of empirically based approaches to language and social skills training have contributed to increased community opportunities and quality of life for individuals with autism and pervasive developmental disorders and their families. In addition, difficult behaviours are now being managed more successfully due to the development of new medications designed to affect transmission of neurochemical substances.

Despite these developments, the lives of family members and caregivers of persons with autism continue to be challenging. In times of stress, caregivers may become frustrated with many unanswered questions and the seemingly slow progress associated with traditional intervention approaches. The lure of new treatments acclaimed by the media and advertised on the Internet can be difficult to resist. While such approaches may provide some hope in the short term, there is a critical need for ongoing well-controlled research to ensure that interventions and treatments are empirically valid and safe.

As regards learning disabilities, over the past 30 years research has broadened our understanding of this problem, and increasing knowledge is reflected in changing educational and psychological practices. In the 1970s, assessments for learning disabilities tended to focus on specific areas of difficulty (for example, auditory, visual, or psycholinguistic deficits) and programs were developed to address these specific difficulties. However, since the 1980s, the focus has shifted from the content of learning to cognitive processes and learning strategies. Students are taught how to learn and helped to develop self-control and self-awareness. For example, they learn planning and organization strategies that can help them become more independent in the classroom. Whether instruction is provided in regular classrooms, in resource rooms, or on a consultation basis, changing community needs and resources need to be recognized. Services must take into account, for example, the ethnic diversity within classrooms and the increasing numbers of children surviving with developmental problems caused by premature birth, fetal drug and alcohol effects, and AIDS. As demands for services for individuals with learning disabilities increase, greater communication is urgently needed between teachers and service providers such as psychologists and researchers.

SUMMARY

Developmental disorders are associated with varying degrees of damage to the brain occurring at different stages of development before, during, or after birth. Damage is manifested in a number of different ways depending upon the condition. There may be unusual physical features, particular types of cognitive, language, motor, or other deficits, and patterns of behaviour (for example, hyperactivity, stereotypy, aggressiveness) associated with different types of disorders. While IQ as measured by standardized intelligence tests is the most basic criterion for mental retardation, there have been important changes over the years in the level of IQ required and deficits in adaptive behaviour.

Mental retardation refers to significantly subaverage intellectual functioning beginning before the age of 18, and accompanied by limitations in two or more areas of adaptive skill such as communication, self-care, academic, domestic, social, or community skills, leisure, and work. A new, more positive approach introduced in 1992 by the American Association for Mental Retardation addresses not only the person's deficits but also his or her strengths and capabilities, and highlights the supports needed to function well in a given environment.

The etiology of developmental disorders in general and mental retardation in particular is complex. In some disorders, the cause is clearly understood. For example, Down syndrome and Fragile X syndrome are chromosomal abnormalities and phenylketonuria is a metabolic disorder caused by the accumulation of phenylalanine in the brain. Screening for chromosomal abnormalities can be conducted before birth through amniocentesis or chorionic villus sampling, or after birth through a blood test.

Mental retardation can also be caused by environmental factors at different stages of development. The fetus can be affected prenatally by maternal malnutrition, toxins such as alcohol or drugs, or maternal infections such as rubella or HIV. Oxygen deprivation during delivery, extreme prematurity, or birth-related trauma can lead to developmental problems such as visual defects, cerebral palsy, and speech and learning problems. The postnatal environment can also significantly affect development. Research with children adopted from deprived environments such as orphanages highlights the importance of nurturance and stimulation in the prevention of mental retardation.

Intervention strategies for people with mental retardation tend to focus on developing social and community living skills and reducing or managing maladaptive behaviours. Task analysis and systematic observation of antecedents and consequences, and training programs using operant conditioning techniques, have helped people with mental retardation to increase their independence. As a result, increasing numbers of people with developmental disabilities are living in the community. Pharmaceutical interventions for some severe behaviour problems associated with dual diagnosis are recommended. Sex education, while controversial, can reduce the risk of abuse while promoting more successful integration into the community. In addition, genetic and supportive counselling for family members and parent training can reduce family stress and improve quality of life for individuals with developmental disorders and their families.

The deinstitutionalization and mainstreaming movements have emphasized the importance of community integration. Evaluation of community-based care and quality of life has become an important area of work for psychologists.

Autism is the best known of the pervasive developmental disorders. It is characterized by a lack of social responsiveness, unusual responses to the environment, and absent or unusual expressive language. There has been much debate about whether the core syndrome of autism is separate from disorders characterized by autistic behaviours, such as Rett syndrome and Asperger syndrome, or whether all these disorders fall on the same continuum. Higher-functioning individuals with higher IQ, more expressive language, and fewer other symptoms are often categorized as having Asperger syndrome.

The focus of research concerning the etiology of autism has shifted from psychogenic to biological factors. Neurobiological and genetic factors are currently considered to play important roles in the development of autism, although the causal processes are still not clearly understood.

As in mental retardation, systematic intervention programs applying operant conditioning principles have been found effective in developing language and social skills and in managing maladaptive behaviour. Intensive early intervention programs using parents and others as mediators have yielded particularly good results.

Learning disorders include problems with reading, mathematics, and writing. Although there has been considerable confusion regarding the definition of learning disorders, common components of definitions include disparity between estimated potential and current academic achievement, IQ greater than 70, problems due to dysfunctional learning processes rather than sociocultural or physical factors, and deficits apparent in both academic and social situations.

Prevalence estimates range from 2 to 15 percent of school-age children; problems continue into adulthood despite remedial assistance. The etiology of learning disorders is not known. Assessment profiles indicate two subtypes: verbal and nonverbal. Particular emotional-behavioural responses such as depression, impulsivity, dependency, or withdrawal may be associated with learning disorders. Intervention strategies focus on self-esteem, motivation, cognitive processing styles, organizational patterns, self-instruction, and self-regulation.

KEY TERMS

stereotypy (p. 121)
developmental handicap (p. 121)
developmental disability (p. 121)
mental retardation (p. 121)
Down syndrome (p. 125)
trisomy 21 (p. 125)
translocation (p. 126)
mosaicism (p. 126)
amniocentesis (p. 126)
chorionic villus sampling (CVS) (p. 126)
phenylketonuria (PKU) (p. 126)

rubella (p. 127)
fetal alcohol syndrome (FAS) (p. 127)
fetal alcohol effects (FAE) (p. 127)
thalidomide (p. 127)
cultural-familial retardation (p. 128)
developmental-difference controversy (p. 128)
contact hypothesis (p. 133)
diagnostic overshadowing (p. 136)
dual diagnosis (p. 136)
normalization principle (p. 136)
deinstitutionalization (p. 136)
acculturation framework (p. 137)
quality of life (p. 137)

autism (p. 139)
pervasive developmental disorders (p. 139)
echolalia (p. 140)
pronoun reversal (p. 140)
savants (p. 141)
Asperger disorder (p. 141)
child disintegrative disorder (CDD) (p. 142)
facilitated communication (FC) (p. 145)
learning disorders (p. 146)
dyslexia (p. 147)
dyscalculia (p. 147)
dysgraphia (p. 147)

ADDITIONAL RESOURCES

Canadian Association for Community Living
Kinsmen Building, York University
4700 Keele Street
North York, ON
M3J 1P3
(416) 661-9611
(416) 661-5701 fax
alem@cacl.ccca.com

Neurologically Disabled of Canada
970 Lawrence Avenue West
Suite 205
Toronto, ON
M6A 3B6
(416) 789-7957
(416) 789-9079 fax
cmha.toronto@sympatico.ca

The Autism Research Foundation
Moss-Rosene Lab
Suite W701
715 Albany Street
Boston, MA 02118
(617) 414-5286
tarf@ladders.org

ladders.org/tarf/
The web site of the Autism Research Foundation, which is dedicated to research on autism and developmental brain disorders. Provides information about research into the underlying neurological basis of autism and related developmental disorders.

web.syr.edu/~jmwobus/autism/
Autism Resources, an extensive collection of sites related to autism.

www.cacl.ca
The web page of the Canadian Association for Community Living. Provides information about people with intellectual disabilities and how to provide supports and services for them to live in communities rather than institutions.

www.roehler.ca
The web page of Roehler Institute, Canada's leading organization to promote the equality, participation, and self-determination of people with intellectual and other disabilities. Provides information about the Institute's research into the causes of marginalization of such individuals and provides information on the Institute's research and findings.

www.and.ca
Site of the Neurologically Disabled of Canada, whose rehabilitation approach involves stimulating the brain's ability to develop despite injury or inadequate development. Provides information about functional rehabilitation programs to individuals with non-progressive neurological disabilities.

www3.sympatico.ca/cmha.toronto/b5cmha.htm
The Canadian Mental Health Association (CMHA) promotes the mental health of all people and ensures the provision of the best possible services for people with mental health problems. This site provides information about CMHA programs, publications, and links.

Chapter 7

Anxiety Disorders

Stéphane Bouchard

Steven Taylor

Brian J. Cox

Janel G. Gauthier

Henry, a 31-year old schoolmaster, came to the hospital seeking treatment. He was agitated and seemed quite nervous; he jumped at any sudden noises. However, he was clear in describing his problems, and his remarks were well organized. Henry said that when he graduated, he found a position teaching primary school. Although he initially enjoyed the work, he gradually developed strange feelings and began to fear that he had a serious disease and was going to die of a heart attack. Despite assurances and examinations by several doctors, he remained convinced that he had a heart problem. Henry told the clinician that he frequently felt anxious and apprehensive, and at those times, his heart pounded like it would explode. When this happened, Henry said, he was sure he was going to die. When the attacks came over him, he had to stop teaching, and, although he went back to work on several occasions once he felt better, the attacks would recur and he finally had to quit his job.

Henry also told the clinician that he was distressed when he had to enter crowded places or cross large, open squares. He avoided public transport because he was afraid he would have an attack and would not be able to get help. Gradually, Henry's fear of having an attack caused him to begin to limit the things he could do and the places he could go. At first, Henry avoided crowds, then he stopped going to shopping malls and no longer visited friends. Finally, Henry gave up his apartment and returned to his parents' home where he all but isolated himself for the three years prior to coming for treatment.

* * *

Joyce was a 38-year-old businesswoman who sought treatment for a debilitating fear of snakes. She described herself as an otherwise well-functioning person. Joyce was very successful in her job as the managing director of a reasonably large company, and she enjoyed tennis and reading. She was happily married and it was her husband's desire to live in the country that brought her to seek treatment for her fear of snakes. When her husband first mentioned the possibility of moving to the country, Joyce did not think it would lead to anything, so she spoke encouragingly about the idea. However, as time went on and her husband became more and more enthusiastic about the idea, Joyce began to realize that he was serious. Joyce also realized, unfortunately, that she had said too many positive things about buying a country place to back out of the plans. Fervently hoping he would renege at the last moment, Joyce remained to all appearances supportive. Finally, they looked at a house that was the fulfillment of their dreams—except that, for her, the fact that it was in the country was a serious defect she was afraid to mention.

When Joyce came to the clinic she was distraught. She said she would either have to be cured of this overwhelming fear quite quickly, or she would have to tell her husband she could not live in the house they were about to buy. Joyce thought this news would devastate her husband and might threaten their wonderful marriage. The dread she felt about walking around the lot they were going to buy and even about living in a house which she thought would inevitably be surrounded by snakes was too much for her, and she had to take a leave from her job. Her worries were, in any case, interfering with the proper execution of her job.

Both Henry and Joyce suffered from anxiety disorders, but their problems were obviously quite different. Henry had a panic disorder that markedly restricted his life, and that seemed—to him, at least—more likely to happen when he was away from the safety of his parents' home. Joyce's problem was much more specific in the features of the world that triggered her fear—a phobia of snakes. However, just because only snakes caused Joyce's distress, and she otherwise was able to function at a high level, it should not be assumed that this was a trivial problem. Joyce very clearly described problems in many aspects of her life that were a direct result of this limited phobia.

In addition to these, there are other anxiety-based disorders. DSM-IV lists twelve. As a group, they form the third most prevalent set of mental disorders, and are associated with considerable personal suffering and socioeconomic costs in lost wages, medical care, and impairment in occupational and social functioning. These disorders are usually chronic if untreated, and may lead to additional psychological problems such as depression and substance abuse. Comorbidity between anxiety and depression is, in fact, common. As discussed in Chapter 13, it is not always possible to determine whether it was the restricted life experiences caused by the anxiety that led to the depression, or whether the fear of recurring depression made the person more vulnerable to anxiety. In either case, the person experiences considerable suffering.

Given the importance of anxiety disorders, it is not surprising that they are the subject of a substantial body of research and one of the most common topics in psychiatric journals. This research has helped refine and demonstrate the effectiveness of a number of forms of treatment Yet only a small proportion of people with anxiety disorders receive empirically validated treatments. According to a survey by the Clarke Institute of Psychiatry, only 15 percent of Canadian hospitals (most located in major metropolitan areas) had specialized anxiety disorders clinics (Swinson, Cox, Kerr, Kuch, & Fergus, 1992). State-of-the-art treatments, such as those described in this chapter, are available only in a few specialized clinics in Canada, although efforts are being made to make these treatments more widely available.

Panic and Anxiety

The term *panic* was coined in reference to the Greek god Pan, a satyr with a penchant for jumping out of the bushes and terrifying travellers by uttering a blood-curdling scream. According to DSM-IV, a **panic attack** is defined as a discrete period of intense fear or discomfort accompanied by at least four of the thirteen somatic, behavioural, and cognitive symptoms. Panic symptoms include palpitations, shaking, chest pain, and fear of dying, going crazy, or losing control.

Anxiety is a blend of emotions (Izard, 1977). It is an affective state "composed primarily of high negative affect, associated with a sense of uncontrollability, and a shift in attention to a focus primarily on the self or a state of self-preoccupation. The sense of uncontrollability is focussed on future threat, danger, or other negative events" (Barlow, 1991, p. 3).

Panic and anxiety share many characteristics; both, for example, are associated with palpitations, nausea, and muscle tension. However, they also differ in many ways. Panic, unlike anxiety, comes on suddenly and is more likely to be accompanied by shortness of breath and fear of dying, going crazy, or losing control. Most importantly, panic attacks can occur unexpectedly, "out of the blue." Panic and anxiety can be normal experiences. For example, a cowboy in the Calgary Stampede probably feels some anxiety, as do many students before or during an exam. A hunter might experience a panic attack when startled by a bear. When there is real danger, anxiety and panic are adaptive reactions; they can motivate a person to escape or avoid threatening situations. However, anxiety excessive for the situation, chronic anxiety when there is no threat, or panic in the absence of danger can be regarded as maladaptive reactions. Everyone at times feels a degree of anxiety or fear that is not entirely justified by the circumstances, and this, too, is normal. But when excessive anxiety or panic occurs more frequently than it does for most people, and when it is intense enough to cause distress and interfere with the person's ability to function, they may represent a type of pathology called, collectively, *anxiety disorders*.

Various medical conditions and toxic substances may also lead to excessive anxiety or anxiety-like symptoms, as may other mental disorders. Diagnostic criteria for all anxiety disorders exclude anxiety that can be better explained by another medical or mental condition.

Prevalence

Although estimates of the lifetime prevalence of anxiety disorders vary, it is clear that they are quite common. As shown in Table 7.1, approximately one-quarter of the population may be expected to develop an anxiety disorder at some point in their lives, although not all of them will seek the help of a mental health professional. Table 7.1 compares data from two large-scale community surveys. Bland, Orn, & Newman (1988) based their findings on structured interviews conducted in 1981 with 3258 Edmonton adults, using DSM-III criteria (APA, 1980). U.S. data, from the more recent and even larger National Comorbidity Study (Kessler et al., 1994), used DSM-III-R criteria (APA, 1987). Differences in prevalence between Canadian and U.S. data are probably due to a combination of population differences, differences in criteria, and different methods of assessment. Yet there are many similarities. Both studies, for example, show that anxiety disorders are quite common, and both show a higher prevalence in women than in men.

HISTORICAL PERSPECTIVE

Mythical and historical accounts of anxiety reactions date as far back as the existence of writing. For example, there is a graphic description in the Epic of Gilgamesh, circa 2000 B.C. During the nineteenth century, anxiety disorders and

---

Table 7.1 Lifetime Prevalence of Anxiety Disorders in Adults (percent)

Diagnosis	Canadian Data			U.S. Data		
	Female	Male	Total	Female	Male	Total
Panic disorder	1.7	0.8	1.2	—	—	—
With agoraphobia	—	—	—	5	2	3.5
Without agoraphobia	—	—	—	—	—	2
Agoraphobia without panic	4.3	1.5	2.9	4	2.1	3.2
Social phobia	2	1.4	1.7	15	11	13.3
Specific phobia	9.8	4.6	7.2	15.7	6.7	11.3
Obsessive-compulsive disorder	3.1	2.8	2.9	2.8	1.7	2.3
Generalized anxiety disorder	—	—	—	6.6	3.6	5.1
Posttraumatic stress disorder	—	—	—	10.4	5	7.8
At least one anxiety disorder	—	—	—	30.5	19.2	24.9

Note: — = no data available.

Source: Canadian data were collected in Edmonton (see Bland et al., 1988). U.S. data are based on the National Comorbidity Survey (see Eaton, 1994; Kessler et al., 1994; Kessler, Sonnega, Bromet, Hughes, & Nelson, 1995; Magee, Eaton, Wittchen, McGonagle, & Kessler, 1996). Data for obsessive-compulsive disorder are from Myers et al. (1984), because this disorder was not assessed in the National Comorbidity Survey.

several other psychological problems (for example, what was then called *hysteria* and is now termed *somatization disorder*) were described as **neuroses**. The term *neurosis* meant a disease of the nervous system and was originally used in the late eighteenth century by William Cullen, a Scottish physician. Early in the 20th century, Freud's views replaced Cullen's idea of a biological basis for the neuroses, although the term was retained. Indeed, Freud's theories were largely derived from his work with anxiety-disordered or hysterical patients. In 1924, Mary Cover Jones published a case study suggesting that clinical methods based on learning principles could be effective in reducing fear in children (Jones, 1924). In those days, however, anxiety disorders were mostly treated by various medical means, including lobotomy (Marks, Birley, & Gelders, 1966). However, fears and phobias did provide the early behaviourists with problems that seemed readily analyzable in terms of the conditioning models that were, at that time, beginning to find a foothold in North American psychology departments.

The first behavioural model of fears and phobias was proposed in the 1920s by Watson (Watson, 1924; Watson & Rayner, 1920). Watson proposed that fears were acquired via classical conditioning, as explained in Chapter 2. Support for this model was found in the case of "Little Albert," an 11-month-old boy who developed a fear of white rats after an experiment in which he learned to associate a rat with a loud noise made by a hammer hitting an iron bar. Watson had earlier shown that sudden loud noises elicit an unconditioned response of fear in infants. Following many repetitions of pairing the rat with the noise, the child began to show a strong fear reaction to the presence of the white rat, even when the animal was presented in the absence of any aversive noise. The little boy's fearful reaction generalized to other similar stimuli, such as a white rabbit and a white dog.

According to Watson's theory, the unconditioned stimulus (UCS, loud noise) naturally elicited an unconditioned response (UCR, fear) in the little boy. Prior to the experiment the conditioned stimulus (CS, white rat) did not lead to fear. With a sufficient number of trials pairing the UCS with the CS, "Little Albert" developed a conditioned response (CR, fear of the rat). While this theory applies primarily to phobias—marked and persistent fears and avoidance of a specific stimulus or situation that is excessive and that interferes with the person's functioning—it also has implications for the development of other forms of anxiety. Watson's theory has been modified over the years but still retains some popularity.

....

ETIOLOGY

The 12 anxiety disorders covered in DSM-IV share many common elements; each also has its own distinct features. We will first discuss general theories that have been advanced to explain anxiety disorders as a whole. Specific explanations of the individual disorders will be discussed in the sections dealing with each disorder.

One of the earliest attempts to explain the origin of anxiety disorders was Freud's (1917) psychodynamic theory. Freud thought there were three types of anxiety that people expressed. **Realistic anxiety** occurs when people are faced with a genuinely dangerous situation. **Neurotic anxiety** results from being persistently prevented (usually by parents) from expressing the impulses of the id. Finally, **moral anxiety** develops when people become so afraid of their id impulses that they see them as threatening.

Freud thought that particular anxiety disorders develop when neurotic or moral anxiety become so strong that they overwhelm the person's defence mechanisms. This may happen, so Freud thought, when the person believes his or her impulses are very dangerous and so threaten his or her capacity to keep them at bay. This might result from repeated punishment as a child for expressing the needs of the id. It may also happen when the defence mechanisms are too weak as a result of parental overprotection, limiting the chances to develop adequate defences.

Psychoanalytic theories, then, whether Freudian or Neo-Freudian, propose that anxiety disorders originate in problematic relations between children and their parents. Overly punitive or overly protective parents can either instill feelings of lack of control over the impulses of the id, or produce weak defence mechanisms. Both allow the person to be readily overwhelmed by anxiety.

Researchers and clinicians in many disciplines have debated vigorously over the years the causes of anxiety disorders. Much of this debate has been about whether nature or nurture is responsible for these disorders. Today, the debate has been largely set aside as irrelevant. Few now believe that the origins of anxiety disorders are exclusively biological or exclusively psychological. Rather, it is widely recognized that many factors are involved in the etiology and maintenance of these disorders, including cognitive, behavioural, emotional, environmental, and biological factors. The notion that these influences all operate interactively is also widely accepted. This is known as the biopsychosocial model (see Chapter 2) and is shown in Figure 7.1. The key point is the reciprocal *determinism* among the five causal factors. Behaviour, for example, is shaped by biological, emotional, environmental, and cognitive influences, but also, in turn, shapes them, in a complex set of interactions.

For the clinician working with anxiety, the biopsychosocial model implies that all five classes of determinants need to be assessed and considered in establishing a treatment plan. To illustrate the interaction between determinants, consider the fear of public speaking. Apprehension about performing in public may lead to physiological arousal (for example, blushing and trembling). The person may then observe that he or she is trembling, and worry that others will notice. This, in turn, can make the person feel even more anxious, which may add to physiological arousal. Reactions from the audience (environmental factors) can also play a role. An enthusiastic audience response may alleviate anxiety, whereas signs of hostility or indifference may increase it. Finally, changes in physiological responses can produce changes in behaviour

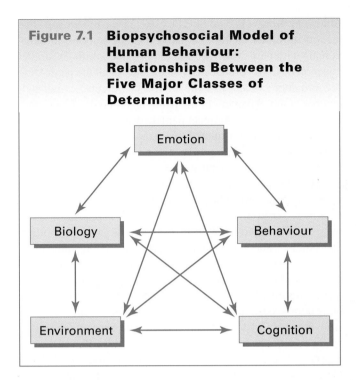

Figure 7.1 Biopsychosocial Model of Human Behaviour: Relationships Between the Five Major Classes of Determinants

that can also affect the environment. For example, if excessive trembling and blushing (biology) are successfully treated, the person may be less anxious about the presentation (emotion), enabling him or her to deliver a better speech (behaviour) that would be better received by the audience (environment), leading the person to believe that he or she is a successful speaker (cognition).

We need, nevertheless, to examine determinants separately in order to understand the full range of possible influences.

Biological Factors

Biological theories emphasize the role of three factors: genetics, neurotransmitters, and neuroanatomy.

Genetics

Inherited factors are important in the development of anxiety disorders. Family studies indicate that up to 25 percent of those suffering from an anxiety disorder have an immediate family member who also suffers from an anxiety disorder. However, as discussed in Chapter 4, this observation does not establish genetic causation: families share not only genes but also environments and learning experiences. Twin studies (see Chapter 4) suggested a genetic role by showing higher concordance for monozygotic than for dizygotic twins, even when environmental factors are controlled. However, studies using powerful statistical methods (for example, Kendler, Neale, Kessler, Heath, & Eaves, 1993) suggest that anxiety disorders arise from a combination of genetic and environmental factors. Little is known about what specific sorts of genetic and environmental factors are involved. In all likelihood, many genes are involved and many different types of learning experiences. Further studies are needed to identify the locations of these genes and the

proteins that they code for. Once these are identified, then we may be able to identify the relationship between genes and neurochemical factors in anxiety disorders.

One possible route for genetic influence is behavioural inhibition. Recent studies (for example, Biederman et al., 1993) suggest that behavioural inhibition to unfamiliar events or people, manifested in young children by behaviours such as withdrawal, seeking a parent, and inhibition of play, is a risk factor for the development of anxiety disorders. Research has also suggested that behavioural inhibition may be genetically determined.

In many cases, the role of genetics in determining behavioural traits is not straightforward. The influence of a gene may be not so much to determine a trait as to create a potential for it, given certain environmental factors. (See also the discussion of penetrance in Chapter 14.) That is, gene-environment interactions can influence the *expression* of a gene. Little is known as yet about the way environmental factors influence genetic expression.

Neurotransmitters and Neuroanatomy

As explained in Chapter 2, one neuron communicates with another by releasing chemicals called neurotransmitters from the terminal button of its axon into the synaptic cleft, the space between the button and the dendrite of an adjacent neuron. Neurotransmitters travel across the cleft to receptors located on the other neuron.

Several different neurotransmitters have been implicated in anxiety disorders. A set of studies by Redmond (1985, 1987) revealed that electrical or drug stimulation of a region of the brain called the **locus ceruleus** induces fear-like behaviours in monkeys. Conversely, removal or drug-induced inhibition of the locus ceruleus reduces anxiety. Moreover, exposure to dangerous or threatening situations results in increased activity in the locus ceruleus. Many of these findings have been replicated successfully with human participants. The locus ceruleus influences arousal and the orienting response toward novel stimuli; according to Redmond (1987), it is the centre of fear and anxiety. Since the locus ceruleus contains close to half of the concentration of norepinephrine in the brain and produces almost 70 percent of all norepinephrine in the body, this neurotransmitter is believed to play an important role in the anxiety disorders. This role is further supported by the antianxiety effects of certain drugs.

Dysregulations of another neurotransmitter, serotonin, may also play an important role. Animal studies have found that destruction of regions of the brain containing serotonin reduces anxiety, while increasing availability of serotonin in the brain induces anxiety (Kahn, Westenberg, & Moore, 1995). The role of serotonin in anxiety disorders is further suggested by the efficacy of a class of drugs known as selective serotonin reuptake inhibitors (SSRIs). These drugs block the reuptake of serotonin in the synaptic cleft, thereby increasing the availability of serotonin to post-synaptic receptors and progressively leading to their regulation (Pecknold, 1990).

It is interesting that the same drugs can be used to treat anxiety, which appears to be associated with high levels of serotonin, and depression, which appears to be associated with low levels of serotonin. (See Chapter 13.) However, the dosages used are different. This observation points up the fact that the relationships between neurotransmission and mental and emotional processes are complex and still imperfectly understood.

GABA is another important substance in the brain related to anxiety. The role of GABA in anxiety was discovered after it was found that a class of drugs known as benzodiazepines reduce anxiety through their action on GABA (Costa & Greengard, 1975). According to one hypothesis, benzodiazepines increase the release of GABA into the synaptic cleft, thereby depleting presynaptic neurons of GABA, which makes the neurons harder to stimulate (Cloninger, 1987; Dorow & Duka, 1986).

Finally, some studies suggest that the dopaminergic system is involved in the etiology of social phobia and obsessive-compulsive behaviour.

Neurotransmitters probably play a complex role in the anxiety disorders, and much remains to be learned. The role of only a handful of neurotransmitters has been studied and neuroscientists are continually discovering new roles and subtypes of neurotransmitters. Different neurotransmitters appear to interact with one another. For example, serotonin affects the activity of the norepinephrine-producing locus ceruleus, and may also influence GABA (Kahn et al., 1995). The amygdala, a structure in the temporal lobe, may play a key role in the coordination of the different neurotransmitters involved in anxiety and panic (Goddard & Charney, 1997; Marks, 1987). In addition to the anatomical links between the amygdala and other regions of the brain potentially involved in fear reactions (most importantly, the locus ceruleus, the hippocampus, and the thalamus), the electrical stimulation of this region induces anxiety in humans, as well as behaviours and symptoms associated with anxiety in animals.

A new and exciting area of research in the neurobiology of anxiety disorders has emerged in the 1990s with the work of Jacques Bradwejn, a Canadian psychiatrist now working in Ottawa, and his collaborations with Claude de Montigny, working in Montreal (Bradwejn & de Montigny, 1984; Bradwejn, Koszycki, & Meterissian, 1990). They initially observed that **cholecystokinin (CCK)**, a peptide found in high concentration in the brain stem, the hippocampus, the amygdala, and the cerebral cortex, induces anxiety in rats. They also found that the effect could be blocked with benzodiazepines. CCK appears to modulate neurons in the brain, with changes in CCK producing changes in anxiety (Harro, Vasar, & Bradwejn, 1993; Palmour, Bradwejn, & Ervin, 1992). Other neuropeptides may also be involved in the etiology or expression of anxiety and panic, as suggested by recent work by Boulenger and colleagues at the University of Sherbrooke (Boulenger, Jerabbek, Jolicoeur, & Lavallée, 1996).

One of the most fascinating findings on CCK comes from studies on the induction of panic in humans. Bradwejn and collaborators demonstrated that one form of CCK, the tetrapeptide fragment CCK_4, induces panic attacks. In one study,

Bradwejn, Koszycki, and Shriqui (1991) gave intravenous injections of either CCK_4 or a placebo saline solution to individuals with panic disorder and to normal controls. A single injection of CCK_4 produced a panic attack in all the panic-disordered subjects and in almost half (46 percent) of normal controls. Only 9 percent of the panic-disordered subjects and none of the control subjects panicked with the placebo injection. Bradwejn postulated that panic and anxiety may involve CCK and that panic disorder may be due to a hypersensitivity to this substance.

The mechanism of this reaction to CCK is still unclear. CCK interacts with other neurotransmitters such as norepinephrine, serotonin, and GABA. Thus, it is possible that a hypersensitivity to CCK may influence the action of other neurotransmitters known to be involved in anxiety and panic. Another possibility is that the panic is a reaction to the very powerful physical sensations caused by CCK_4, such as cardiorespiratory distress. Individuals with panic disorder are known to be particularly fearful of these sensations. It is possible that they experienced a full-blown panic attack in response to these physical sensations, while the controls experienced the same physical sensations, but did not all show the same emotional reaction. To test the latter possibility, future investigations should compare response to CCK_4 with response to a *psychologically valid placebo*: that is, some other substance that produces similarly threatening body sensations through different means. It will also be enlightening to see whether the findings with CCK_4 are specific to panic disorder or generalizable to other anxiety disorders. Ultimately, the development of an effective "anti-CCK" medication would both further research and offer possibilities for treatment.

Psychological Factors

Two-Factor Theory

Variants of conditioning theory have been used primarily to explain phobia, but also may have implications for the development of pathological anxiety as well.

Watson's classical conditioning theory, described earlier, is consistent with anecdotal reports of people who developed phobias after unpleasant experiences naturally occurring with stimuli such as insects or dogs. However, it does not explain the persistence of the phobia. As explained in Chapter 2, Pavlov found that the conditioned response would diminish when the conditioned stimulus is presented repeatedly without the unconditioned stimulus. Yet phobias often persist for years.

During the 1960s and 1970s, the most influential theory of fear and phobias was Mowrer's (1960) **two-factor model** (see also Chapter 2), which has its origins in the work of Pavlov (1928) and Watson and Rayner (1920). The model proposed that fears are acquired by classical conditioning, as proposed by Watson, but maintained by operant conditioning. To illustrate, dog phobia can arise from a traumatic incident where the person is painfully bitten by a dog. Here, stimulation of the pain receptors represents the UCS, which evokes pain and fear (UCR). Through the process of conditioning, pain and fear become paired to the CS (the dog).

The link between the CS and UCS tends to decay over successive trials in which the CS (dog) is presented without the UCS (pain). As this occurs, the CS (dog) tends to elicit an increasingly weak or less frequent CR (fear). Given a sufficient number of trials of CS (dog) without UCS (pain), the CS (dog) should eventually cease to elicit the CR (fear). In the case of many fears, however, this process is blocked from occurring because the person learns that fear can be minimized (at least in the short term) by avoiding or escaping from the CS. In other words, avoidance or escape is a negative reinforcer that prevents classically conditioned fears from being unlearned.

A considerable body of evidence to support this theory has emerged, not only from studies of the experimental induction of fear in animals, but also from clinical observations of people with anxiety disorders and from observations of soldiers. Incidental findings from studies of aversion therapy show a similar effect (Menzies & Clarke, 1995; Rachman, 1990).

Yet many findings are inconsistent with the theory. First, it cannot explain the development of all phobias. Fears are sometimes acquired in the absence of conditioning. For example, many people who are afraid of snakes have never actually encountered one; thus, there has been no opportunity for the CS to be associated with the UCS. Likewise, there are many people who fear flying yet have never been in an aircraft.

Second, researchers often fail to create conditioned fears in the laboratory. Similarly, in real life people sometimes fail to acquire fears in situations that would appear to be fear-evoking: air raids, for example. Moreover, some details about Watson's study, such as the observation that Little Albert was not frightened as long as he was allowed to suck his thumb (Samelson, 1980) are unexplained by either Watson's or Mowrer's theory.

Third, neither conditioning nor two-factor theory can explain why some stimuli are more likely to become feared than others; particularly why some mostly harmless things, like garter snakes and spiders, are common subjects of phobias, yet few people have phobias about such things as guns, matches, and electrical outlets, despite their potential for real harm. Rather than rejecting the two-factor theory, researchers have attempted to modify it to account for these findings.

To account for fear acquisition in the absence of conditioning, Stanley Rachman of the University of British Columbia (1990) proposed a revised model, which postulated there are three ways in which fears can be learned: (1) classical conditioning, (2) modelling (that is, observing others react fearfully), and (3) informational and instructional transmission (for example, receiving fear-evoking information or misinformation from others). According to a recent review of the literature on phobia acquisition by Cox and Taylor (1997), approximately half of clinical phobias are associated with classical conditioning, with a smaller proportion of phobias associated with modelling (vicarious learning) and fear-relevant instruction or information. Some people with phobias are unable to recall the origin of their fears.

Cox and Taylor (1997) noted that so-called conditioning events are also found in about a third of non-fearful people. It may be that aversive conditioning experiences are less likely to produce phobias when the person has a history of fearless contact with the stimulus in question. For example, a person who is bitten by a dog may not develop a phobia if he or she has a history of pleasant encounters with dogs. This has been called *fearless familiarity* (Rachman, 1990).

Biological Preparedness

Seligman (1971) claimed that clinical phobias have a number of characteristics that are inconsistent with the two-factor theory of learning. Phobias, unlike fears conditioned in the laboratory, were said to be (1) rapidly acquired (for example, single-trial learning), (2) resistant to extinction, (3) noncognitive (that is, phobias persist even when the person knows intellectually that the stimulus is harmless), and (4) differentially associable with stimuli of evolutionary significance. The two-factor theory assumed that all neutral stimuli can become fear stimuli. However, some stimuli (for example, small animals) are more likely to be fear-evoking than others (for example, guns, matches, electrical outlets); "only rarely, if ever, do we have pyjama phobias, grass phobias, electric-outlet phobias, hammer phobias, even though these things are likely to be associated with trauma in our world" (Seligman, 1971, p. 312).

Seligman (1971) proposed the **biological preparedness theory**, stating that people and other organisms are biologically prepared to acquire fears of certain stimuli. That is, evolution has predisposed organisms to easily learn those associations that facilitate species survival. As a result of a sufficiently long period of natural selection, organisms are

There is substantial evidence to support specialized biological preprogramming in nonhuman species, but there is less experimental support for the notion that "prepared" fears are more easily acquired than "unprepared" fears in humans.

prepared ("hard-wired") to fear some stimuli, unprepared for others, and contraprepared for still others. That is, they are unlikely to acquire fears of some stimuli like flowers, despite many trials of learning. In evolutionary terms, stimuli such as guns, matches, and electrical outlets have not been around long enough for such preparedness to occur.

There is substantial evidence to support specialized biological preprogramming in nonhuman species. For example, Cook and Mineka (1989) had rhesus monkeys watch videotapes of other monkeys behaving fearfully in response to a toy snake or a crocodile. As a result, the observer monkeys were frightened of these toys when they came in contact with them. In comparison, monkeys who watched spliced videotapes of monkeys showing the identical fear behaviours to artificial flowers or toy rabbits did not become afraid of flowers or toy rabbits.

Evidence from human studies, however, has not been so compelling. McNally (1987) conducted an extensive review of the literature on the subject and concluded that there is very little experimental support for the notion that "prepared" fears are more easily acquired than "unprepared" fears in humans. Likewise, there is no clear support for the hypothesis that prepared associations reflect a primitive, noncognitive form of conditioning.

According to Bandura (1986), it is not ancestral experience that makes people more likely to fear some stimuli than others, but the properties of the stimuli themselves, such as agential hurtfulness (the ability to directly cause harm), intensity, unpredictability, and uncontrollability. These stimulus properties, he argued, do not reflexively lead to fear. Rather, research shows that events lead to fear reactions largely through cognitive processing, which defines the threatening quality of particular objects or situations under different circumstances. Studies examining the role of thought patterns in phobic reactions reveal that, far from being reflexive conditioned reactions, they are usually triggered by frightening irrational thoughts centring on perceived coping inefficacies (which we will explain a bit later).

Cognitive Theories

For years, anxiety disorders have been explained in terms of behavioural theories heavily rooted in experimental psychology with classical and operant conditioning. The primary assumption of these theories is that anxiety symptoms are not the product of physical disease or of deep-seated psychological trauma, but learned maladaptive responses.

Where the various learning theories differ is in the depiction of the exact learning mechanisms and of what is actually learned. In the classical conditioning model, for example, the contiguous pairing of neutral cues (for example, driving a car) with anxiety-provoking experiences (for example, having a car accident) converts the neutral cues to threats that are themselves capable of producing the autonomic arousal of heightened anxiety (for example, fear of driving). The purely operant paradigm conceives anxiety symptoms in terms of behaviours (for example, avoidance or escape) that produce environmental consequences (for example, relief of distress, sympathy), which, in turn, reinforce

behaviours (for example, lead to higher probability of avoidance or escape).

Although many criticisms have been voiced against the traditional conditioning models (Rachman, 1976, 1977), they have nevertheless inspired much clinical research and led to breakthroughs in the treatment of anxiety disorders. More recent behavioural theories of anxiety disorders take into account the cognitive elements implicit in the principal modes of learning. Working from a social-cognitive perspective, Bandura (1986, 1997) viewed anxiety within the context of a comprehensive theory of behaviour change. He proposed that people become fearful mainly because they perceive themselves as unable to cope effectively with potentially aversive events. To the extent that they believe they can prevent, terminate, or lessen the severity of the threat, their apprehension will be reduced. Bandura also suggested that the primary determinant of avoidance behaviour is not anxiety per se but low **perceived self-efficacy**. For example, electricians know they run the risk of electrocution if they fail to flip a circuit breaker before repairing an electrical outlet, yet they do not become anxious; they perform this self-protective response without needing to be prompted by autonomic arousal.

Cognitive theories of anxiety assume that cognitions are the primary determinants of anxiety. According to the cognitive model proposed by Aaron Beck (Beck, 1976; Beck & Emery, 1985), emotions are influenced by the way people think about (appraise) themselves and the world. This appraisal is, in turn, influenced by beliefs, which are the products of prior experiences. People prone to anxiety disorders are thought to hold dysfunctional beliefs about threat or danger. For example, someone suffering from social phobia may hold the unrealistic belief that people tend to be very critical or rejecting of one another. Entering a social situation, this person may think, "People won't like me." This thought can cause the person to selectively search for information that supports the maladaptive beliefs (for example, selective abstraction or overfocussing on unpleasant social experiences), and to interpret ambiguous information in a way that supports the maladaptive beliefs (for example, jumping to conclusions).

Drawing on Beck's theory, Salkovskis (1996, p. 51) has proposed an equation that summarizes the relationship between thoughts (appraisals) and anxiety:

$$\text{Anxiety} = \frac{\begin{array}{c}\text{Perceived probability of threat} \times \\ \text{Perceived cost or awfulness of danger}\end{array}}{\begin{array}{c}\text{Perceived ability to cope with danger} + \\ \text{Perceived rescue factors}\end{array}}$$

As shown in the equation, threat is defined as the product of the appraised "cost" or awfulness of an event and its perceived probability. For example, speaking in public will be appraised as highly threatening if the person thinks it is very likely that he or she will be ridiculed by others, and believe that this will have serious consequences. People may become anxious about a possible event appraised as serious but unlikely events (for example, a tornado) or as less threatening but likely (for example, criticism from others). These two factors are not simply additive; they interact multiplicatively.

Yet, even when people appraise a threat as both probable and awful, they are not always anxious; according to the equation above, this is because they perceive themselves as being able to cope with the demands of the situation (high self-efficacy) (Bandura, 1986, 1988, 1997) or they perceive rescue factors: that is, possible help from other people, change in the environment, or chance. For example, a camper in Glacier National Park may perceive attack by a bear as both probable and potentially awful; yet she may not worry much, reasoning "I can shout and throw food at it; besides, they have park rangers around to deal with trouble." A violinist auditioning for the Montreal Philharmonic Orchestra may think that failure is both likely and costly, yet feel fairly confident. "It's a tough orchestra to get into," he may think, "and if I don't make it, I'll have to scramble to pay the rent. But, after all, I am a pretty good player; and if worst comes to worst and they don't take me, I have lots of friends who can get me other gigs." Self-efficacy, in particular, is a good predictor of whether a person will approach or avoid a threatening stimulus (Zane & Williams, 1993).

Cognitive, as well as behavioural, models of anxiety propose that anxiety is maintained by **avoidance**, or escape behaviour. Avoidance may involve real or imagined danger, and may be physical or cognitive. Avoidance can be subtle. For example, a person frightened of eating in public might avoid dishes that require utensils, such as steak or soup, and choose sandwiches instead. Cognitive avoidance—using mental distraction to avoid thinking about the source of anxiety—is not directly observable.

The short-term effect of avoidance is to reduce or prevent anxiety and it is therefore tempting for people suffering from anxiety or panic attacks. However, avoidance maintains the person's tendency to overestimate danger and underestimate coping and rescue factors. When people avoid a feared situation, it is very difficult for them to correct their faulty appraisal. When they fail to learn the true consequences and probabilities of a feared event, they also fail to increase their perceived self-efficacy to cope effectively. Thus avoidance leads to the maintenance of anxiety disorders.

Cognitive approaches to anxiety are appealing because they seem plausible, have received empirical support in many studies, and have led to effective treatments. However, cognitive models are probably oversimplifications. Cognitive processing in humans is extremely complex, and much remains to be learned. One of the most important limitations of cognitive models of anxiety is that they are not firmly grounded in cognitive science. However, the situation is changing rapidly; cognitive models of anxiety are becoming more complex, and tied more closely to cognitive research. Current models do not suggest that the equation above is wrong. Rather, the models are based on a more comprehensive, multifactorial framework. Beck himself recognized recently the need to develop more complex, nonlinear models of *information processing* to refine our understanding of panic and anxiety (Beck, 1996, pp. 1–3).

It is important to understand how thoughts and beliefs are processed and represented. Theories explaining how information is processed and stored in memory are referred to as **information processing** models. They are often based on a computer analogy. The cognitive "hardware" consists of **cognitive structures** to store information (that is, memory structures), which contain information processing "software" that produce or alter the cognitive contents in memory, and produce thoughts or images in consciousness. In these models, **learning** is conceived as the development of internal representations of stimuli, actions, outcome, and their interrelationships (Barnard & Teasdale, 1991; Davey, 1992; Foa & Kozak, 1986; Lieberman, 1993; Rescorla, 1988; Tryon, 1993).

Such information is stored in long-term memory according to some organization or cognitive structures (Barnard & Teasdale, 1991; Nelson, 1995; Segger, 1994; Squire & Zola-Morgan, 1988). According to Lang (1985) and Foa and Kozak (1986), the *fear structures* form a network containing three types of information: stimulus, response, and meaning. To illustrate, a fear structure of a spider-phobic person contains stimulus information ("Spiders crawl; spiders are hairy; spiders can bite"), response information ("Ugh! I've got to move away from it"), and meaning information ("Spiders are dangerous").

Recent studies suggest that particular types of memory structures are involved in anxiety. For example, when comparing nonanxious individuals to individuals suffering from either high anxiety or an actual anxiety disorder, studies have shown biases in memory. That is, anxious individuals tend to learn and remember more easily information related to threatening stimuli. This finding applies to implicit memory (memories acquired without verbalizable knowledge or awareness) and, sometimes, but not inconsistently, also to explicit memory (conscious recollection) (for example, MacLeod & McLaughlin, 1995).

Cognitive contents are the information acquired and stored in cognitive structures. They include images and beliefs about stimuli. This information is used to assign meaning to events. Cognitive contents include information regarding the probability and costs of stimuli, perceived ability to cope, and potential rescue factors. Cognitive therapists often call cognitive contents cognitive *propositions*, *schemata*, or *core beliefs*.

Indirect support for the causative role of maladaptive cognitive contents in anxiety disorders is provided by the effectiveness of cognitive therapy. For example, a team of researchers in Hull and Quebec City demonstrated that cognitive therapy aiming solely at the modification of beliefs was effective in treating individuals suffering from panic disorder with agoraphobia (Bouchard et al., 1996; Bouchard, Gauthier, Nouwen, & Ivers, 1997). Moreover, using an approach called *multivariate time series analysis*, they showed that reducing the strength of maladaptive beliefs led to improvement in symptoms. Similarly, researchers in Vancouver have shown that treatment aimed at changing maladaptive thoughts is effective in reducing social phobia (Taylor et al., 1997).

Complex **cognitive operations** are performed in order to store, transform, and retrieve information in memory and to process information in general (Barnard & Teasdale, 1991;

Lieberman, 1993; Tryon, 1993). These processes can be biased and can thus lead to distortions in the appraisal of events, in the estimation of probability, and in the availability of coping strategies.

A growing body of research has investigated the role of attentional biases and selective processing of information in anxiety disorders. Numerous studies have confirmed that attentional biases selectively facilitate the processing of information relevant to the disorder. For example, a person with a phobia about blood will be particularly quick to process information about needles. (See Logan & Goetsch, 1993, for a review.) People with an anxiety disorder detect threatening stimuli better and faster than people without an anxiety disorder. Conversely, when presented with information not relevant to their anxiety, they perform at a lower level than controls on a variety of mental tasks, suggesting that their attention is directed to anxiety-relevant information. To illustrate, Mathews, Mogg, Kentish, and Eysenck (1995) asked 24 individuals suffering from generalized anxiety disorder to state the colour of a number of printed words. They were able to do this with words of neutral meaning, but showed impaired performance when presented with words with threatening meanings. This finding suggests that the threat-related content of the words distracted their attention from the task. The subjects' impaired performance disappeared once their generalized anxiety disorder was successfully treated.

Cognitive products are the conscious products of processing cognitive contents from cognitive structures. They consist of thoughts or images and are often produced automatically (without efforts or attention). In anxiety, cognitive products often reflect the presence of threat, danger, low coping capability, and high probability of occurrence of threatening events. They also take the form of questions about uncertainty and are oriented toward future threat (for example, "What if I get sick?" "What if I fail the test?"). In order to explain anxiety, panic, and other emotional disorders, information processing models encompass all these features of cognition. For a more detailed discussion of these models, see Foa and Kozak (1986) and Barnard and Teasdale (1991; Teasdale, 1996).

••

THE ANXIETY DISORDERS

Specific Phobia

Description

A **specific phobia** is a marked and persistent fear and avoidance of a specific stimulus or situation (APA, 1994). The DSM-IV recognizes four subtypes of specific phobia: (1) animal phobia; (2) environmental phobia (for example, heights, storms); (3) blood-injection-injury phobia; and (4) specific situation phobias (for example, elevators, flying). Encountering the phobic stimulus almost invariably provokes anxiety. Most of the time the phobic stimulus is avoided, but it may be endured with significant distress. (See the DSM table "Diagnostic Criteria for Specific Phobia.")

DSM-IV   Diagnostic Criteria for Specific Phobia

A. Marked and persistent fear that is excessive or unreasonable. The fear is cued by the presence or anticipation of a specific object or a situation.

B. Exposure to the phobic stimulus almost invariably provokes an immediate anxiety response. The response may take the form of a situationally bound panic attack (occurring almost invariably immediately upon exposure) or a situationally predisposed panic attack (not always associated with the cue and not necessarily occurring immediately after exposure).

C. The person recognizes that the fear is excessive or unreasonable.

D. The phobic reaction(s) is avoided or else endured with intense anxiety or distress.

E. The avoidance, anxious anticipation, or distress in the feared situation(s):

interferes significantly with the person's normal routine, occupational (or academic) functioning, or social activities or relationships;

or there is marked distress about having the phobia.

Source: Reprinted with permission from the *Diagnostic and Statistical Manual of Mental Disorders*, Fourth Edition. Copyright 1994 American Psychiatric Association.

Fears about one thing or another are very common in the general population. How, then, can we distinguish between normal fear and clinical phobia? For a diagnosis of phobia, the fear, avoidance, and worries related to the phobic stimulus must interfere significantly with the person's life, and the phobic reaction must be considered excessive or unreasonable. Finally, specific phobia is ruled out as a diagnosis if the focus of apprehension is more typical of other anxiety disorders such as agoraphobia, social phobia, or obsessive-compulsive disorder.

Most phobic reactions are associated with autonomic arousal, but there is one notable exception. Blood-injection-injury phobias are usually associated with an initial rise in heart rate and blood pressure followed by a reduction in arousal, which sometimes leads to fainting.

Agoraphobia is not a specific phobia, but rather a cluster of phobias where many situations are avoided; we will discuss this disorder in the section on panic disorder. Claustrophobia (fear of enclosed spaces) and acrophobia (fear of heights) are often associated with agoraphobia but may also exist as independent and specific phobias.

Specific phobias are quite common. As shown in Table 7.1, Bland's survey in Edmonton found a prevalence of 7.2 percent, and the U.S. National Comorbidity Survey found a somewhat higher rate of 11.3 percent. Both showed higher rates in women than in men. A survey of 449 women in Calgary (Costello, 1982) found higher rates yet. Costello's sample showed a lifetime prevalence of 24.4 percent for mild fears and of 19 percent for phobias. (See Chapter 4, and Figures 4.14 and 4.15.) The most prevalent were animal fears, followed by fears of environmental events, social situations, mutilation, and separation from significant others.

The development of subclinical fears is a common but typically transient occurrence in children. There is a predictable pattern of the rise and fall of many fears. This has been called the "ontogenetic parade," and has been extensively reviewed elsewhere (for example, Marks, 1987). Fear of separation from the caregiver is common at 6 to 22 months, and typically wanes after 30 months. Fear of unfamiliar adults also is common at 6 to 9 months. It typically subsides by 20 to 24 months but may persist as shyness. Fears of animals, darkness, and imaginary creatures typically emerge between two and six years, and decline thereafter for many (but not all) children. Fear of school appears when the child begins attending school, at three to six years. It may gradually decline then reemerge when the child moves from elementary school to high school. Social-evaluative fears often emerge or intensify during adolescence.

The fluctuating course of fears over the life span may be due to maturational factors such as the development of endocrine and other biological systems necessary for fear responses to occur. Developmental milestones such as learning to walk and developmentally linked life experiences, such as starting school, may also play a role in influencing the course of fears. To illustrate, fear of heights appears to arise as the child becomes increasingly mobile (Scarr & Salapatek, 1970). The development of fears also may be influenced by the child's cognitive capacities for recognizing potential dangers, combined with his or her self-perceived ability to control these events (Ollendick, Yule, & Ollier, 1991).

Specific phobias are similar to subclinical fears in that they often emerge in childhood or adolescence, and often before age 25. However, there is a considerable variability in age of onset of specific phobias, and it appears that they can occur at any point in the life span. Compared to subclinical fears, phobias are more likely to be chronic, especially if untreated.

Assessment and Diagnostic Issues

Many self-report instruments have been developed to assess phobia, fear and avoidance. The most popular self-reports are the Fear Survey Schedule, Version II (Geer, 1965) and Version III (Wolpe & Lang, 1964) and the Fear Questionnaire (Marks & Mathews, 1979). Of particular interest in the assessment of phobias is the behavioural avoidance/approach test (BAT). The BAT is an assessment strategy that can be adapted for the assessment of any avoidance behaviour and is the most direct measure of avoidance. Individuals are asked to carry out a feared or avoided task and their actual performance is measured, as well as self-reported anxiety level and measures of arousal, such as heart rate. The task is divided into a hierarchy of steps of progressively feared situations and the individual is instructed to go as far as possible in the accomplishment of the task. For example, a person with a snake phobia would be asked to move as close as he or she could to a snake. The instructions are standardized because changes in the procedure influence the results. Examples of BAT are walking a predetermined distance in a shopping centre, climbing a ladder, or staying alone in a closed and dark closet for a set length of time.

Etiology

Neo-conditioning theories (for example, Davey, 1992) regard classical and operant conditioning as processes that draw on cognitive mechanisms such as expectations and memory representations of the CS and UCS. Here, UCS-CS links are acquired when the conditioned stimulus is perceived as a *predictor* of the occurrence of the unconditioned stimulus. To illustrate, a person with a fear of driving might learn that poorly lit, wet roads are predictive of life-threatening motor vehicle accidents. The strength of the conditioned fear is a function of two factors: (1) the strength of the UCS-CS link (which is influenced by the perceived probability that a given event will lead to a given outcome) and (2) the perceived aversiveness of the UCS (for example, the perceived dangerousness of motor vehicle accidents). Expectations about one's coping abilities also may influence conditioned fears.

The neo-conditioning approach also entails a revised view of operant conditioning of avoidance behaviour. Avoidance is determined not by the experience of fear itself, but by the individual's *expectation* of whether a given behaviour (for example, driving in the rain) will lead to an aversive outcome (for example, a fatal motor vehicle accident). According to this perspective, avoidance behaviour is not reinforced by reduction of fear; it is reinforced by full or partial confirmation of one's expectations (for example, by a "close call" while driving). The neo-conditioning model is shown in Figure 7.2.

According to the neo-conditioning perspective, UCS evaluation (and reevaluation) can influence the acquisition, extinction, and inflation of fears. Thus, mild conditioned fears can escalate into phobias when the UCS is reevaluated as more threatening. For example, a person might acquire a mild fear of spiders after sustaining a painful but harmless spider bite. The fear may escalate into a phobia if the person later learns that spider bites may be lethal. Thus, the perceived dangerousness of the UCS is inflated from a harmless painful bite to a painful and potentially life-threatening bite. As a consequence, the nature of the CS changes (that is, spiders now become predictive of life-endangering events) and the conditioned fear increases accordingly. The neo-conditioning model proposes that the CS and UCS are represented as cognitive contents in long-term memory.

Panic Disorder and Agoraphobia

Description

There are four defining elements of panic disorder, the most important of which is the presence of unexpected panic attacks. Panic attacks are discrete periods of intense fear or discomfort accompanied by at least 4 of 13 symptoms (see the DSM table "Diagnostic Criteria for Panic Disorder Without Agoraphobia," which lists diagnostic criteria for the disorder when unaccompanied by avoidance behaviours, as discussed later). The onset of the attack is sudden and often accompanied by a sense of imminent danger and urge to flee. Panic attacks can occur in a variety of other disorders; but in panic

Figure 7.2 The Neo-conditioning Model of Phobias

Source: Reprinted from *Behaviour Research and Therapy*, 14. G. C. L. Davey, Classical conditioning and the acquisition of human fears and phobias: A review and synthesis of the literature, 29–66. © 1992. With permission from Elsevier Science Ltd., The Boulevard, Langford Lane, Kidlington, 0X5 1GB, U.K.

disorder they occur spontaneously and without apparent triggers. Also part of the criteria is that at least one of the attacks is followed by persistent concerns about having additional attacks, worry about the implication or consequences of the attacks (for example, worry about "going crazy"), or a significant change in behaviour as a result of the attacks.

In panic disorder, the attacks sometimes occur out of the blue, without apparent triggers. They can also occur when the person is relaxed, even during sleep (*nocturnal panic*).

Panic attacks may also be triggered by exposure to specific stimulus (for example, enclosed spaces). Panic attacks are labelled "situationally bound" if the stimulus always triggers an attack, and "situationally predisposed" if exposure often but not always triggers a panic attack.

Panic disorder is often accompanied by avoidance behaviours. Avoidance may be subtle or severe and manifest. Such behaviours are labelled *agoraphobia* when avoidance is extensive and associated with apprehension about having a panic attack or panic symptoms in places or situations from which escape is difficult or in which help is not available.

Agoraphobia involves avoidance of a cluster of situations, such as enclosed spaces, travelling far for home, being alone in or outside the home, driving on a bridge or in a tunnel, using the subway, or going into crowded places. Contrary to common belief, agoraphobia is not restricted to fear of open spaces. Even the name, derived from the Greek word *agora* ("marketplace"), refers not to open spaces per se but to public spaces.

The diagnosis of agoraphobia without history of panic disorder is also possible. The essential features of this disorder is the fear of the occurrence of panic-like symptoms or limited-symptom panic attacks (panic attacks with fewer than four symptoms). The current theory is that the dichotomy between panic disorder and agoraphobia is artificial. Some studies found very few cases where the onset of agoraphobia was totally unrelated to panic symptoms. Thus, agoraphobia would represent a learned avoidance response to either full-blown panic attacks or a smaller set of panic symptoms. However, this theory is not without controversy and the central role of panic has been questioned. Some authors, such as Isaac Marks (1987), suggested that panic is one feared event in

Focus *Did Darwin Suffer from Panic Disorder with Agoraphobia?*

We all know that Charles Darwin travelled the world and, on the basis of his observations, proposed a theory of evolution that radically changed our view of the world. But what is less known is that Darwin suffered from a variety of disabling symptoms that may well have been manifestations of panic disorder with agoraphobia. Recently, Barloon and Noyes (1997) studied in detail Darwin's biography, his own personal writings, and comments from his physicians. They concluded that he was afflicted with panic attacks and severe agoraphobic avoidance.

Before and during his voyage on the *Beagle*, he travelled widely and gave no indication of such disorders. He was then in his mid-twenties. But about two years after his return in England, his lifestyle changed significantly. At age 28 he writes: "I have awakened in the night being slightly unwell and felt so much afraid though my reason was laughing and told me there was nothing and tried to seize hold of objects to be frightened of" (Barloon & Noyes, 1997, p. 138). Later he wrote: "constant attacks ... makes life an intolerable bother and stops all work" (p. 138), "My nervous system began to be affected so that my hands trembled and my head was often swimming" (p. 138), "I dreaded going anywhere, on account of my stomach so easily failing under any excitement" (p. 139), and "Of late, anything which flurries me completely knocks me up afterwards and brings on violent palpitations of the heart" (p. 139). In his letters he frequently referred to discrete and sudden attacks that left him drained. He reported nine of the thirteen symptoms of panic attacks, including worrying excessively about his health, and being very sensitive to stress. He was very afraid to leave his house without his wife or to stay at home alone. His symptoms were chronic and punctuated with brief periods of remission.

Alternative explanations would be the presence of medical conditions, but he did not suffer from any known medical illness. Others have suggested organic diseases (for example, chronic brucellosis or a virus cough during his voyage). But these explanations do not fit the clinical picture as well as panic disorder with agoraphobia.

Post mortem biographical analyses are obviously subject to biases and flaws. But, since Darwin noted that "ill-health ... has saved me from the distraction of society and its amusements" (p. 140), perhaps panic disorder and agoraphobia contributed to the development of his theory of evolution. ▲

DSM-IV Diagnostic Criteria for Panic Disorder Without Agoraphobia

A. Both (1) and (2):
  (1) recurrent unexpected panic attacks:
    Panic attacks are discrete periods of intense fear or discomfort in which at least four of the following symptoms developed abruptly and reached a peak within 10 minutes:
    (1) palpitations, pounding heart, or accelerated heart rate
    (2) sweating
    (3) trembling or shaking
    (4) sensations of shortness of breath or smothering
    (5) feeling of choking
    (6) chest pain or discomfort
    (7) nausea or abdominal distress
    (8) feeling dizzy, unsteady, lightheaded, or faint
    (9) derealization (feeling of unreality) or depersonalization (being detached from oneself)
    (10) fear of losing control or going crazy
    (11) fear of dying
    (12) paresthesias (numbness or tingling sensations)
    (13) chills or hot flashes

  (2) at least one of the attacks has been followed by at least 1 month of one or more of the following:
    (a) persistent concern about having additional attacks
    (b) worry about the implications of the attack or its consequences
    (c) a significant change in behavior related to the attacks

B. Absence of agoraphobia.
  Agoraphobia is defined as:

A. Anxiety about being in places or situations from which escape might be difficult (or embarrassing) or in which help may not be available in the event of having an unexpected or a situationally predisposed panic attack or panic-like symptoms.

B. The situations are avoided; or endured with marked distress or with anxiety about having a panic attack or panic-like symptoms; or require the presence of a companion.

C. The anxiety or phobic avoidance is not better accounted for by another mental disorder.

Note: All DSM criteria for anxiety disorders require that the problem not be caused by a medical condition or better explained by another disorder.

agoraphobia, but not necessarily the only one. For example, there are reports of patients who developed avoidance of a cluster of situations typical of agoraphobia because they were afraid of having diarrhea away from home or were elderly and afraid of falling. Another example is a recent study conducted with children by Biederman et al. (1997). In their sample, agoraphobia without a history of panic disorder was more prevalent (15 percent) and had an earlier age of onset than panic disorder with agoraphobia (4 percent) and panic disorder without agoraphobia (2 percent).

The onset of panic disorder is typically around late adolescence or young adulthood; the Edmonton epidemiological study, for example, found an average age of onset of 19 for males and 21 for females (Bland et al., 1988). Panic disorder afflicts more females than males and is often underdiagnosed by health care professionals. Panic disorder typically develops after a stressful life event. Because of the severe and spontaneous nature of the initial panic attacks, it is not unusual for people with panic disorder to present at general hospital emergency rooms believing they are having a heart attack. The disorder is often chronic, and is characterized by severe impairment, punctuated by episodes of remission. Agoraphobia is sometimes so severe that the afflicted person is unable to leave his or her home.

Claims that panic disorder is related to separation anxiety in childhood have been made but they remain unsubstantiated (Bouchard, Bolduc, Gauthier, & Boisvert, 1995; Thyer, 1993). More than 50 percent of individuals with panic disorder have another mental disorder such as depression, substance abuse, generalized anxiety disorder, or personality disorders. Panic disorder with agoraphobia is often accompanied by social fears and a perception of incompetence in social situations (Marchand, Goupil, Trudel, & Bélanger, 1995). Individuals with panic disorder are among the most frequent users of health services among people with mental disorders, and have a poor quality of life. Yet it often takes seven or eight years before a person can receive appropriate treatment for panic disorder. Delays result both from the failure of health care workers to diagnosis panic disorder and from the limited treatment resources.

Assessment

Two phenomena need to be assessed in this disorder: panic attacks and avoidance behaviour. Avoidance is traditionally assessed with BAT, the Mobility Inventory (Chambless, Caputo, Jasin, Gracely, & Williams, 1985) or the agoraphobia subscale of the Fear Questionnaire (Marks & Mathews, 1979). A recent review of validated self-reports for panic disorder (Bouchard, Pelletier, Gauthier, Côté, & Laberge, 1997) has revealed the existence of ten instruments assessing physiological sensations and cognitive aspects of panic. The most popular measures of fear of anxiety sensations are the Body Sensation Questionnaire (Chambless, Caputo, Bright, & Gallagher, 1984), the Agoraphobic Cognitions Questionnaire (Chambless et al., 1984), and the Anxiety Sensitivity Index (Peterson & Reiss, 1992). It is worth mentioning that several studies have now shown that the Anxiety Sensitivity Index predicts whether a person is at risk for experiencing panic attacks, and possibly panic disorder (Maller & Reiss, 1992; Taylor, 1999). Studies conducted by Sherry Stewart at Dalhousie University in Halifax also reveal that women with high scores on the Anxiety Sensitivity Index tend to drink more alcohol in order to cope with anxiety and panic (for example, Stewart & Zeitlin, 1995; see also Taylor, 1999).

Etiology

The cognitive model of panic proposed by David M. Clark (1986) is one of the most widely cited models of panic, and it has led to innovations in the treatment of panic disorder. Although panic attacks often occur unexpectedly, this does not mean that panic is without cause. According to Clark's theory (1986), panic attacks arise from the catastrophic misinterpretation of arousal-related bodily sensations. That is, when a person experiences arousal-related bodily sensations, he or she misinterprets the sensations as a sign of impending death, insanity, or loss of control. This interpretation naturally leads to intense anxiety, which increases arousal and the intensity of the feared sensations. The more intense sensations further alarm the person, who by now may be convinced that the catastrophe is imminent—and so on, in a vicious circle that culminates in a panic attack (see Figure 7.3).

People prone to panic attacks are said to have elevated **anxiety sensitivity**. That is, they tend to catastrophically misinterpret arousal-related bodily sensations because they believe the sensations to have harmful consequences, such as death, insanity, or loss of control. For example, they are likely to misinterpret caffeine-induced palpitations as a sign that they are about to go into cardiac arrest or shortness of breath due to humidity as a sign of impending suffocation. Similarly, most of us have had the sensation when very fatigued that the things around us are flat, unconnected, or not quite real ("derealization"). Instead of taking this hollow feeling as in-

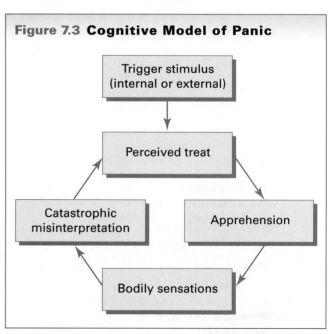

Figure 7.3 Cognitive Model of Panic

Trigger stimulus
(internal or external)

Perceived treat

Apprehension

Bodily sensations

Catastrophic
misinterpretation

Source: Reprinted from *Behaviour Research and Therapy*, 24. D. M. Clark, A cognitive approach to panic, 461–470. © 1992. With permission from Elsevier Science, The Boulevard, Langford Lane, Kidlington, U.K. OX5 1GB.

dicating a need for sleep, a person with anxiety disorder takes it as a sign that he or she is about to go crazy. Fear of arousal-related bodily sensations also leads the person to be more attentive to his or her body. Thus, the person is more likely to notice, and thereby become alarmed by harmless, but unusual, bodily sensations.

In this model, agoraphobia is regarded as avoidance of situations that induce feared bodily sensations. Thus, individuals with panic disorder often fear and avoid activities such as jogging, drinking coffee, watching suspenseful movies, and even having sex (a potent source of bodily sensations). People can learn to fear arousal-related bodily sensations through a variety of life experiences. Beliefs that these sensations are dangerous appear to be a predisposing factor for panic attacks and panic disorder.

The cognitive model of panic has been supported by the findings from several studies (see McNally, 1994, for an extensive review and Schmitdt, Lerew, & Trakowski, 1997, and Clark et al., 1997, for more recent studies). One of the strongest pieces of evidence is that artificially induced panic attacks can be blocked by providing different interpretations of body sensations. For example, when asked to hyperventilate, anyone will experience sensations such as dizziness and increased heart rate; subjects with panic disorder will generally become anxious in response to the sensations aroused. This anxiety is decreased if the person is told that the sensations are signs of good psychological adjustment and increased if the person is told that the sensations are signs of passing out (Salkovskis & Clark, 1990). Manipulations of expectancies have similar effects when people receive infusion of sodium lactate (van der Molen, van den Hout, Vroemen, Lousberg, & Griez, 1986), a substance that induces arousal-related bodily sensations. Similar findings have been found with people who are vulnerable to panic disorder but not currently suffering from it. Similarly, clients who have had cognitive treatment for panic disorder are less likely to become anxious in response to physically induced sensation than they were before treatment. Little research has yet been conducted with CCK_4.

Self-efficacy and perceived control are important, and have been shown to influence the induction of panic by procedures such as CO_2 inhalation.

Social Phobia

Bart was a 32-year-old computer system analyst. He described a history of having difficulty in social situations since his mid-teenage years. He was single, and, because of his restricted social life, had developed few personal relationships. His major fears were eating in public and any kind of public speaking. When his work forced him to do either, he felt intense anxiety and distress. He was afraid of being scrutinized, embarrassed, and humiliated, and experienced palpitations, trembling, shortness of breath, and sweating. His anxiety had compromised his ability to

work. He managed to work at home but avoided assignments that would require appearing in public. He had turned down promotions to avoid having to make presentations to staff. He avoided social events and gatherings where he might be invited to speak and relied on alcohol to face up to social situations he could not avoid. His physician had given him a beta blocker which helped a little by controlling his tremor in public but did not ease his anxiety. He gave no description of unexpected panic attacks. He had had one episode of depression at the age of 26 when an affair ended. A review of his family history showed that his mother was very protective.

Description

Most people know what it is like to feel anxious in social situations. However, social phobia is more than shyness. People with social phobia are intensely afraid of social or performance situations in which they may be subject to scrutiny or evaluation by others. This is often accompanied by worry about what other people are thinking about them. Although social phobia and agoraphobia are both characterized by fear of public places, the foci of the fears are different. When standing in the middle of a lineup at the grocery store, a person with agoraphobia would be afraid that the people in front

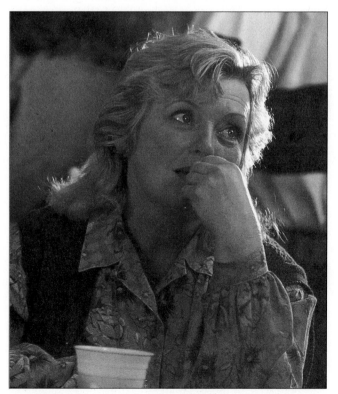

Gathering with friends in a restaurant sounds like fun to most people, but can be terrifying to someone with a social phobia.

of him or her in the lineup were blocking the exit; in contrast, the person with social phobia would be afraid of those behind him, thinking that they were judging him or her.

Many people are apprehensive about speaking in public or interacting with others. However, to be diagnosed as having social phobia, the fear must be considered excessive or unreasonable by the person. (See the DSM table "Diagnostic Criteria for Social Phobia.") The feared situations are often but not always avoided; they can be endured with intense discomfort. Typically avoided situations are being the centre of attention, public speaking, signing one's name in public, eating in public, and using public washrooms. Individuals with social phobia are particularly prone to anticipatory anxiety and often engage in detailed and critical ruminations about past social events or interactions. A subtype of generalized social phobia is diagnosed when the person is afraid of most social situations.

The most recent estimates of prevalence of social phobia are much higher than those obtained at the end of the 1980s. For example, as shown in Table 7.1, U.S. estimates from the 1994 National Comorbidity Study are almost eight times as high as those from the 1988 Edmonton study. This discrepancy can be attributed to changes in diagnostic instruments and criteria, most notably the elimination from the DSM of the stipulation that social phobia could not be diagnosed in the presence of other disorders such as avoidant personality disorder. A telephone survey conducted in Winnipeg (Stein, Walker, & Ford, 1994) confirmed the effect of changing diagnostic criteria. When they used more liberal criteria, 31 percent of their 526 participants acknowledged "being much more nervous than other people" when speaking in front of a large audience. When they applied DSM-III-R criteria the prevalence of social phobia dropped to 7.1 percent—lower than U.S. figures, but still high enough to suggest that social phobia is one of the most prevalent anxiety disorders.

DSM-IV Diagnostic Criteria for Social Phobia

A. A marked and persistent fear of one or more social or performance situations in which the person is exposed to unfamiliar people or to possible scrutiny by others. The individual fears that he or she will act in a way that will be humiliating or embarrassing.

B. Exposure to the feared social situation almost invariably provokes anxiety, which may take the form of a situationally bound or situationally predisposed panic attack.

C. The person recognizes that the fear is excessive or unreasonable.

D. The feared social or performance situations are avoided or else endured with intense anxiety or distress.

E. The avoidance, anxious anticipation, or distress in the feared social or performance situations interferes significantly with the person's normal routine, occupational functioning, or social activities or relationships, or there is marked distress about having the phobia.

Source: Reprinted with permission from the *Diagnostic and Statistical Manual of Mental Disorders,* Fourth Edition. Copyright 1994 American Psychiatric Association.

The onset of social phobia is usually during late childhood or adolescence and the onset of puberty may play an important role. The course of the disorder is often chronic and typically fluctuates in severity according to social and environmental stressors. More females are afflicted with social phobia but it appears that more males seek treatment for the disorder. The latter observation contrasts with patterns found in other anxiety disorders. Individuals with social phobia, especially with generalized subtype, also tend to be unmarried and to have a poor quality of life. A study by van Ameringen, Mancini, Styan, and Donison (1991) from McMaster University in Hamilton showed that, as for most anxiety disorders, comorbidity is very high with other anxiety disorders (70 percent), major depression (70 percent), and alcohol abuse (28 percent). Alcohol is often used as a way of alleviating social anxiety. However, alcohol use does not help the person overcome his or her social phobia and can create problems of its own. Contrary to popular belief, most individuals with social phobia have adequate social skills. However, they use them ineffectively when they are anxious or they view their own performance very critically.

Assessment and Diagnostic Issues

It is sometimes difficult to distinguish between social phobia and panic disorder with agoraphobia. Structured diagnostic interviews are often useful in making this distinction. This kind of interview should be used whenever possible with all anxiety disorders, especially by practitioners beginning their clinical training.

The two most widely used diagnostic interviews are the Anxiety Disorders Interview Schedule (ADIS; DiNardo, Brown, & Barlow, 1994) and the Structured Clinical Interview for DSM-IV (SCID; First, Spitzer, Gibbon, & Williams, 1995). The ADIS was specially developed to assess anxiety disorders. It also assesses depression and contains screening questions on other disorders, such as substance use disorders, psychotic, and organic disorders. It provides clinical data on features typical to anxiety disorders, such as panic symptoms, avoidance behaviour, and factors influencing anxiety. The SCID is used to diagnose numerous mental disorders including, but not limited to, anxiety disorders. The SCID has greater breadth than the ADIS, but does not assess each anxiety disorder in as much depth. Both instruments, as for any other diagnostic tool, require clinical judgement and adequate training.

Among the self-report measures, the most popular are the Social Avoidance and Distress Scale and the Fear of Negative Evaluation (Watson & Friend, 1969), the Fear Questionnaire (Marks & Mathews, 1979), the Social Phobia and Anxiety Inventory (Turner, Beidel, Dancu, & Stanley, 1989), and the Social Interaction Anxiety Scale and Social Phobia Scale (Mattick & Clarke, 1988). Cox and Swinson (1995) have provided a review of self-report and other assessment strategies for social phobia.

Etiology

The cognitive model presented in Figure 7.4 was developed by David M. Clark and Adrian Wells (1996). A similar model

Figure 7.4 Cognitive Model of Social Phobia

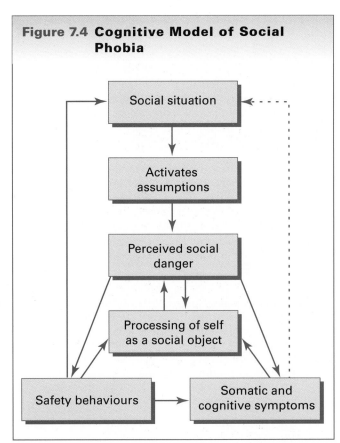

Source: From D. M. Clark, Panic disorder and social phobia, in D. M. Clark and C. G. Fairburn, eds., *Science and practice of cognitive-behaviour therapy* (New York: Oxford University Press, 1996), pp. 119–154. Reprinted with permission of Oxford University Press.

was published by Rapee and Heimberg (1997). For individuals with social phobia, the perceived threat from social stimuli comes from maladaptive beliefs about themselves (for example, "I'm stupid" "I'm vulnerable") and about social interactions (for example, "Unless everybody loves me I'm worthless" "Unless I'm perfect people will reject me"). These beliefs are often held more intensely during social encounters than in nonsocial situations. People with social phobia also appear to have very high standards for their own social performance. The activation of such beliefs increases arousal, somatic symptoms (for example, blushing, shaking), and cognitive symptoms (for example, concentration difficulties). It also leads to subtle avoidance and safety behaviours to try to reduce anxiety.

An important aspect of this model is its emphasis on selective attention. People with social phobia focus on themselves while in social situations. When they become anxious, they closely monitor their thoughts and the way they are behaving toward other people. This shift in attention prevents them from adequately processing the information around them (for example, from listening and responding warmly and spontaneously). Thus, individuals with social phobia may appear stiff, preoccupied, and aloof to others. This increases the likelihood that others will, in fact, reject or avoid them.

According to Clark and Wells, this shift in attention explains the difference between shyness and social phobia. Although shy people may be anxious in a new social situation, they will effectively process the surrounding information and are therefore more likely to eventually become actively engaged in and enjoy social interactions.

The findings from several studies are consistent with Clark and Wells' model. Studies have shown that individuals with social phobia selectively attend to socially threatening stimuli. For example, research by Lynn Alden and colleagues at the University of British Columbia has shown that in social interactions, people with high social anxiety tend to believe that their social behaviour (for example, conversation skills) will fall short of what others expect of them. In other words, socially anxious individuals believe that others hold them to standards that they cannot attain (Wallace & Alden, 1991). Other studies have not only confirmed the importance of self-focussed attention but shown that it diminishes with successful treatment (for example, Woody, Chambless, & Glass, 1997).

Obsessive-Compulsive Disorder

Edna was a 33-year-old single woman who described having obsessions and compulsions for as long as she could remember. Her primary symptoms were contamination obsessions and related compulsions. She complained of unwanted, intrusive thoughts of being contaminated with germs. As a result of her contamination fears, she tried to avoid touching doorknobs, rubbish bins, and all other objects that might be covered in dirt or germs. If she had to touch these objects, she then felt compelled to wash and rewash her hands until they felt clean. At times she washed up to three hours a day, using strong disinfectants and sometimes medicinal alcohol. She would also frequently check whether she had come into contact with germ-bearing objects. In her calmer moments, Edna acknowledged that her contamination fears were excessive. However, when she came in contact with a "contaminant" she was flooded with thoughts that she is in danger of contracting some terrible disease. Her obsessions and compulsions worsened whenever she read media stories about diseases such as flesh-eating disease; she therefore tried to avoid reading newspapers and watching news programs on TV. Looking back on her childhood, Edna recalled that both parents were excessively controlling. Her mother was a perfectionist and emphasized cleanliness. Edna was criticized whenever her room was messy or whenever she got dirty while playing. She also recalled her mother frequently warning her of the dangers of touching "dirty" objects, such as garbage bins.

Description

Obsessive-compulsive disorder (OCD) is a common anxiety disorder that typically begins in adolescence or early adulthood. OCD tends to be chronic, with symptoms waxing and waning over time, often in response to life stressors. OCD is characterized by recurrent obsessions, compulsions, or both. **Obsessions** are thoughts, images, or impulses that are persistent, markedly distressing, and egodystonic: that is, they are experienced as intrusive or unacceptable; the person regards them as alien, uncontrollable, and not the kind of thought that he or she would want to have. Common obsessions include repetitive thoughts of violence, sex, contamination, urges to arrange things in a particular order, or repeated doubts about the adequacy of one's actions.

Note that it is not only people with OCD who have intrusive thoughts. Most people have such thoughts from time to time (Rachman & de Silva, 1978). Unwanted intrusive thoughts occurring in the general population have similar themes to clinical obsessions (for example, violence, contamination, sex) but are less distressing, do not last as long, and are easier to dismiss.

Compulsions are repetitive behaviours (overt actions or cognitive acts) performed in response to an obsession, or according to certain rules or in a stereotyped manner. Typically, the person feels compelled to perform the compulsion to prevent or alleviate distress or to prevent some feared event. However, either the compulsive activity is clearly excessive, or it is not a realistic response to the perceived threat. The person often recognizes the compulsions to be excessive or unreasonable and may want to resist them. He or she derives no pleasure from the activity, although it may relieve tension. Common compulsive behaviours include repeated washing and cleaning, checking, seeking reassurance, repeating actions, and ordering or arranging objects. Examples of cognitive compulsions include repeated counting, rehearsing particular phrases, or thinking "good" thoughts to replace or undo "bad" (obsessional) thoughts. It is interesting to note that 50 percent of the participants in a nonclinical sample acknowledged sometimes performing ritualistic acts such as checking or ordering things "in a correct manner" (Muris, Merckelbach, & Clavan, 1997). The fact that both intrusive thoughts (with content similar to those in clinical samples) and ritualistic behaviours are so common suggests a continuity between normal and obsessive behaviour. (See the DSM table "Diagnostic Criteria for Obsessive-Compulsive Disorder.")

Assessment and Diagnostic Issues

Behavioural methods, self-report inventories, and observer-rated scales have been developed to assess obsessions, compulsions, and related symptoms such as fear and avoidance of stimuli that trigger obsessions and compulsions (for example, "contaminated" objects such as doorknobs or trash cans). Among the more useful self-report questionnaires is the Maudsley's Obsessional Compulsive Inventory (Hodgson & Rachman, 1977), which contains four subscales: (1) compulsive washing, (2) compulsive checking, (3) obsessional slowness and repetition, and (4) obsessional doubting and

---

DSM-IV Diagnostic Criteria for Obsessive-Compulsive Disorder

A. The presence of either obsessions or compulsions:
Obsessions as defined by (1), (2), (3), and (4):

   (1) recurrent and persistent thoughts, impulses, or images that are experienced, at some time during the disturbance, as intrusive and inappropriate and that cause marked anxiety or distress

   (2) the thoughts, impulses, or images are not simply excessive worries about real life problems

   (3) the person attempts to ignore or suppress such thoughts, impulses, or images, or to neutralize them with some other thought or action

   (4) the person recognizes that the obsessional thoughts, impulses or images are a product of his own mind

Compulsions as defined by (1) and (2):

   (1) repetitive behaviours or mental acts that the person feels driven to perform in response to an obsession, or according to rules that must be applied rigidly

   (2) the behaviours or mental acts are aimed at preventing or reducing distress or preventing some dreaded event or situation; however, these behaviours or mental acts either are not connected in a realistic way with what they are designed to neutralize or prevent, or are clearly excessive

B. At some point during the course of the disorder, the person has recognized that the obsessions or compulsions are excessive or unreasonable.

C. The obsessions or compulsions cause marked distress, are time consuming, or significantly interfere with the person's normal routine, occupational functioning, or usual social activities or relationships.

Source: Reprinted with permission from the *Diagnostic and Statistical Manual of Mental Disorders*, Fourth Edition. Copyright 1994 American Psychiatric Association.

---

conscientiousness. Among the most useful clinician-rated measures is the Yale-Brown Obsessive-Compulsive Scale (Goodman, Rasmussen, Price, Mazure, Heninger, & Charney, 1989). These and other measures are reviewed in detail in Taylor (1995). A group consisting of most of the leading international scientists working on the cognitive aspects of OCD, the Obsessive Compulsion Cognitions Working Group (1997), reached consensus on six domains of beliefs that should be measured when assessing OCD: responsibility, perceived importance of thoughts, concerns over the controllability of thoughts, perceived threat, intolerance of uncertainty, and perfectionism. These beliefs appear to play an important role in the maintenance and possibly the origin of OCD.

Etiology

There are many psychological and biological theories of OCD, but no one theory predominates. Few theories have been subject to extensive empirical investigation. Many theories offer only sketches of putative mechanisms. Some account for only a subset of obsessive-compulsive phenomena, while others fail to account for the widespread occurrence of similar phenomena in the general population.

One of the most comprehensive theories is Salkovskis' (1985, 1989) cognitive-behavioural model of OCD, drawing from learning theory and cognitive theory (Beck, 1976; Beck & Emery, 1985), which has led to some promising new developments in treatment. Key elements of this model are illustrated in Figure 7.5.

Salkovskis' theory begins with the observation that more than 90 percent of the general population experience cognitive intrusions (that is, intrusive thoughts, images, or impulses). Why do these become clinical obsessions for only a minority of people?

Salkovskis (1985, 1989) argued that cognitive intrusions reflect the person's current concerns. Intrusions are automatically triggered by internal or external stimuli. Harm-related thoughts, for example, may be triggered by seeing sharp objects. These trigger stimuli can be regarded as reminders or retrieval cues for the current concerns.

Salkovskis proposed that cognitive intrusions develop into obsessions only when intrusions are appraised as posing a threat for which the person is personally responsible. Intrusive thoughts are not intrinsically upsetting, but become the source of discomfort when they elicit disturbing thoughts in people with an inflated sense of responsibility. The Obsessive Compulsion Cognitions Working Group (1997) defined responsibility as "the belief that one has the power which is pivotal to bring about or prevent subjectively crucial negative outcomes. This may be actual, that is, having consequences in the real world, and/or at a moral level."

To illustrate, suppose a woman, Beth, sees her set of sharp kitchen knives and the thought or image of stabbing her child flashes through her mind. Salkovskis argues that most people would regard such a thought as meaningless and harmless—"mental garbage." But Beth may appraise the thought as having serious consequences for which she is personally responsible. "Having thoughts about stabbing my child means that I really want to hurt her"; she thinks. "I am a bad mother for having such thoughts; God might punish me." She is now distressed and tries to **neutralize** the threat by suppressing the thought or by acting to prevent it from coming true.

Several studies show, however, that attempts to suppress unwanted thoughts are worse than useless (see Wegner, 1989, for a review). For example, in a series of studies, Wegner and colleagues instructed subjects to try not to think of white bears. Paradoxically, they thought of white bears more frequently than controls given no instructions. Such findings, although not always replicated, are consistent with the view that obsessions are partly due to attempted thought suppression. This paradoxical effect holds true for most people. People with OCD, however, seem to make especially strong efforts to suppress their thoughts, which may result in a great rebound of these thoughts. The same effect is produced by other common neutralization strategies, such as trying to replace the "bad" thought with a "good" thought, or the use of distracting thoughts. Such strategies merely become reminders of the obsessional thoughts (Freeston, Ladouceur, Rhéaume, & Blais, 1995).

Appraisals of intrusions may also lead to compulsions. A person who believes that he or she is responsible for the intrusive thought and its consequences may try to prevent anticipated harm. For example, Beth may remove all the knives from her house to stop herself from acting on the thoughts of stabbing her child.

Salkovskis (1985, 1989) advanced two main reasons why compulsions tend to persist and to be excessive. First, they are negatively reinforced by immediate distress reduction. Second, they prevent the person from learning that the dire appraisals are unrealistic; that thoughts of harm need not lead to harmful acts. In turn, by acting as reminders, compulsions maintain obsessions. For example, every time Edna washes her hands she is reminded of contamination.

Mood-dependent recall is also thought to influence intrusions, whether or not the mood is produced by appraisals of intrusions. Anxious mood may trigger intrusions; depressed or dysphoric mood may make increase the likelihood of experiencing negative thoughts.

Why do some people, but not others, experience negative thoughts in response to cognitive intrusions? Life experiences shape the basic assumptions we hold about ourselves and the world (Beck, 1976). Of particular importance here are assumptions about personal responsibility, perfectionism, and the consequences of negative thoughts (Frost & Steketee, 1997; Rhéaume, Ladouceur, Freeston, & Letarte, 1995). Salkovskis (1985) proposed that assumptions about blame, responsibility, and control play an important role in OCD, as

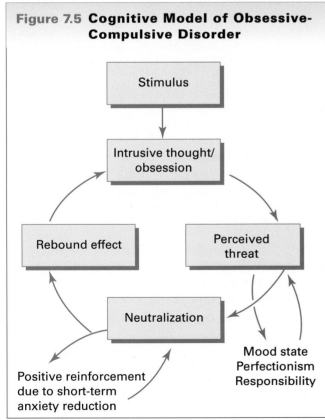

Figure 7.5 Cognitive Model of Obsessive-Compulsive Disorder

Stimulus

Intrusive thought/obsession

Rebound effect

Perceived threat

Neutralization

Positive reinforcement due to short-term anxiety reduction

Mood state
Perfectionism
Responsibility

Source: Adapted from P. M. Salkovskis, Cognitive-behavioural factors and the persistence of intrusive thoughts in obsessional problems, *Behaviour Research and Therapy, 27(1989),* 677–682; and R. Ladouceur, M. H. Freeston, & J. Rhéaume, Traitement cognitif et comportemental du trouble obsessionnel-compulsif. Partie 1. Modèle explicatif, *Revue Québécoise de Psychologie, 17(1996),* 91–107.

illustrated by beliefs such as "Having a bad thought about an action is the same as performing the action" ("thought-action fusion") and "failing to prevent harm is the same as having caused the harm in the first place." These assumptions can be acquired from very strict moral or religious training, or from other experiences that teach the person to adhere to excessively high codes of conduct and responsibility. Some people seem to fall into a sort of magical thinking common in children. ("If I wish you were dead, or imagine you dead, you may die, and it will be my fault.")

Salkovskis' model has the advantage of containing several readily testable hypotheses, which have generally been supported in studies. It has been found that not all intrusive thoughts are aversive (for example, Edwards & Dickerson, 1987). Moreover, studies support the view that unwanted intrusive thoughts can be distinguished from negative thoughts (Clark, 1992; Freeston, Ladouceur, Thibodeau, & Gagnon, 1992).

Studies by Rachman and colleagues support the view that personal responsibility influences the frequency and duration of compulsive rituals. Lopatka and Rachman (1995) experimentally manipulated the perceived responsibility of 30 compulsive checkers. Participants were asked to perform a variety of actions (for example, lock the door, turn the stove on and off). After performing each action the participants rated his or her level of discomfort and strength of urge to check. These actions were performed under three conditions: (1) low responsibility (where the experimenter explicitly assumed all responsibility for any aversive consequences), (2) high responsibility (where the experimenter explicitly emphasized that the participant was responsible for any aversive outcome), and (3) a control condition without any manipulation of perceived responsibility. As predicted, decreases in responsibility were followed by significant decreases in discomfort and in the urge to check, and there was a trend for increases in responsibility to be followed by increases in discomfort and in the urge to check.

Posttraumatic Stress Disorder

Description

Posttraumatic stress disorder (PTSD) is characterized by three clusters of symptoms, which arise after the person is exposed to a traumatic stressor: (1) recurrent reexperiencing of the traumatic event (for example, flashbacks, nightmares, intrusive thoughts), (2) avoidance of trauma-related stimuli and numbing of general responsiveness, and (3) persistent symptoms of increased arousal (for example, hypervigilance, exaggerated startle response). (See the DSM table "Diagnostic Criteria for Posttraumatic Stress Disorder.")

PTSD is often chronic, and persists for at least one year after the trauma in approximately 50 percent of cases. The most common precipitating events are combat trauma, physical and sexual assault, natural disasters, and motor vehicle accidents. Community-based studies indicate that PTSD has a lifetime prevalence of 1 to 14 percent, depending on diagnostic methods and type of population (see Table 7.1). Not surprisingly, it occurs at a much higher rate (3 to 58 percent)

DSM-IV Diagnostic Criteria for Posttraumatic Stress Disorder

A. The person has been exposed to a traumatic event in which both of the following were present:

(1) the person experienced, witnessed, or was confronted with an event or events that involved actual or threatened death or serious injury, or a threat to the physical integrity of self or others

(2) the person's response involved intense fear, helplessness, or horror

B. The traumatic event is persistently reexperienced in one (or more) of the following ways:
(1) recurrent and intrusive distressing recollections of the event, including images, thoughts, or perceptions
(2) recurrent distressing dreams of the event
(3) acting or feeling as if the traumatic event were recurring
(4) intense psychological distress at exposure to internal or external cues that symbolize or resemble an aspect of the traumatic event
(5) physiological reactivity on exposure to internal or external cues that symbolize or resemble an aspect of the traumatic event

C. Persistent avoidance of stimuli associated with the trauma and numbing of general responsiveness, as indicated by three of the following:

(1) efforts to avoid thoughts, feeling, or conversations associated with the trauma
(2) efforts to avoid activities, places, or people that arouse recollections of the trauma
(3) inability to recall an important aspect of the trauma
(4) marked diminished interest or participation in significant activities
(5) feeling of detachment or estrangement from others
(6) restricted range of affect
(7) sense of foreshortened future

D. Persistent symptoms of increased arousal, as indicated by one of the following:

(1) difficulty falling or staying asleep
(2) irritability or outburst of anger
(3) difficulty concentrating
(4) hypervigilance
(5) exaggerated startle response

E. Duration of the disturbance is more than 1 month.

F. The disturbance causes clinically significant distress or impairment in social, occupational or other important areas of functioning.

Source: Reprinted with permission from the *Diagnostic and Statistical Manual of Mental Disorders,* Fourth Edition. Copyright 1994 American Psychiatric Association.

in groups exposed to traumatic events (for example, combat veterans, victims of natural disasters or criminal violence). For example, Kuch and Cox (1992) assessed 124 Jewish Holocaust survivors who had emigrated to Canada after World

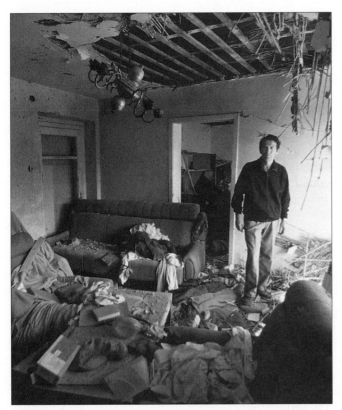

PTSD occurs at a much higher rate in groups exposed to combat, natural disasters, or criminal violence.

War II. Survivors of the Auschwitz extermination camp were three times as likely to meet diagnostic criteria for PTSD than the survivors who had not been in concentration camps. Comorbid psychiatric disorders have been estimated to occur in 62 to 98 percent of cases of PTSD, with the most common being other anxiety disorders, major depression, and substance-abuse disorders.

Two subtypes of PTSD are defined in DSM-IV: acute (duration of less than three months) and chronic (more than 3 months). PTSD that begins more than six months after the trauma is specified as "delayed onset." In any case, the symptoms must be present for at least one month to give the diagnosis of PTSD. If the onset and the remission of symptoms occur within one month of the trauma, the condition may be diagnosed as acute stress disorder (APA, 1994).

It is important to note that not all survivors of traumatic events will develop PTSD. The cause of PTSD is not the traumatic event itself, nor a weak personality, but the interaction between a traumatic event, personality factors, and how the individual deals with the event.

Many trauma victims react with PTSD symptoms soon after exposure to a traumatic event. For example, as many as 90 percent of rape victims report intrusive thoughts, numbing, and hyperarousal symptoms shortly after the assault. However, in most cases the symptoms remit spontaneously within three to six months after the trauma.

The age of onset and the course of PTSD vary considerably depending, in part, on the nature of the traumatic stressor. PTSD tends to become chronic if it lasts for more than three months and is not treated. The duration and intensity of the emotional reaction to the traumatic event as well as the uncontrollability of the event are significantly related to the development of PTSD. Poor social support is also a risk factor for the development of PTSD. Significant distress is caused not only by the direct reaction to the traumatic event, but also by the aftermath of the event, including shame, guilt, anger, or irritability.

Assessment

As is the case for other anxiety disorders, the assessment of PTSD includes a variety of measures targeting features not specific to the disorder (for example, MMPI). The most widely used self-report measures of PTSD symptoms include the Revised Impact of Event Scale (Horowitz, Wilner, & Alvarez, 1979) and the Mississippi Scale for combat-related PTSD (Keane, Caddell, & Taylor, 1988). Many scales developed to assess PTSD are specific to the traumatic event, such as the Accident Fear Questionnaire (Kuch, Cox, & Direnfeld, 1995) and the Veronen-Kilpatrick Modified Fear Survey (Resick, Veronen, Kilpatrick, Calhoun, & Atkinson, 1986). Among the most widely used clinical interviews is the Clinician Administered PTSD Scale (Blake et al., 1995).

Psychophysiological methods are also used to assess PTSD. They usually take the form of measuring heart rate, blood pressure, skin conductance, or muscular tension while presenting to the person visual and auditory stimuli related to his or her traumatic experience. Psychophysiological methods are useful because they provide an objective measure of reactions to trauma-related stimuli.

Etiology

Current cognitive theories of PTSD are consistent with neo-conditioning models, and emphasize cognitive factors such as expectations and appraisals about the meaning of aversive experiences. Such models include the emotional processing model of Foa and colleagues (Foa & Kozak, 1986; Foa, Steketee, & Rothbaum, 1989) and similar models (for example, Chemtob, Roitblat, Hamada, Carlson, & Twentyman, 1988).

These models propose that PTSD symptoms arise from a fear structure stored in long-term memory during and after the trauma. The traumatic experience is thought to be so intense that it causes fear-conditioning to a wide range of stimuli (for example, sights, sounds, odours, and bodily sensations associated with the trauma). Such stimuli can serve as reminders of the trauma, thus activating the fear structure and thereby producing hyperarousal and intrusive recollections of the trauma. Avoidance and numbing symptoms are thought to arise from mechanisms for deactivating the structure (Foa, Zinbarg, & Rothbaum, 1992).

Horowitz (1986) and others have suggested that traumatic events are processed ("worked through") according to a mechanism in which intrusion symptoms alternate with avoidance and numbing symptoms. In this way, avoidance and numbing regulate the amount of exposure to trauma-related stimuli.

Focus · *Cultural Differences in Dealing with Anxiety*

The solution to nightmares according to Ojibwa legend:

The dream catcher is fashioned from a hoop of red willow with a webbing of animal sinew which takes the form of a web. ... Attached at the bottom of the loop are a bead ... and a feather. It is hung above a sleeping area in a place where the morning light can hit. The nature of the dream catcher will attract all sorts of dreams to its web. When bad dreams come, they do not know the way through the web and get caught in the webbing, where the first light of day causes them to melt away and perish. The good dreams, knowing the way, go through the centre of the web and slide down the feather to the sleeper below. ...

There was a time in Ojibwa history when the people were being tormented by nightmares. The elders and "medicine people" all tried to solve this problem on their own, but no one made progress against the dreams; so a council of all the people was called. During this council one elder had a vision of a spider's web in a hoop with a feather and bead attached that would catch the bad dreams while letting good dreams pass through. The elders went to work fashioning dream catchers in the manner prescribed by the vision and when the people started using them, the bad dreams went away.

Although the dream catcher was not meant specifically for the treatment of nightmares associated with PTSD, it is a nice illustration of how other cultures might deal differently from Western culture with anxiety and its symptoms. Students may have the false impression that the principles taught in many classrooms in Canada—and in Western culture in general—apply to everybody. It is important to remember that culture is a part of the biopsychosocial model outlined so often in this book.

For example, the prevalence of anxiety symptoms such as nervousness and shortness of breath is different in India (48 percent and 8 percent respectively) than in Nigeria (9 percent and 32 percent respectively) (Inkeles, 1983). The Western pharmacopoeia is much less effective in China, possibly because of the differing attributions of the causes of anxiety (Good & Kleinman, 1985).

It is crucial to understand cultural diversities in order to tailor interventions adequately. Language may be important in therapies that use words. This point is illustrated by the case of a woman suffering from OCD, who did not improve with exposure to English-language audiotape recordings of her ruminations; when the recordings were made in Cantonese, her native language, the treatment became very effective (Martin & Tarrier, 1992). Other cultural factors come into play as well. The strategies to engage people in treatment and to conduct cognitive-behavioural interventions are different with people from Latin America (Organista & Muñoz, 1996), with more emphasis on self-disclosure and adaptations to the cognitive-restructuring techniques. Similar flexibility is necessary with Orthodox Jews (Paradis, Friedman, Hatch, & Ackerman, 1996), where the view of mental illness as a disease to be concealed, the fear that the therapist will not respect religious beliefs, values and laws, or the potential contribution of family members and the community may interfere with treatment. In a culture where religious beliefs have an important role, it might be useful to discuss with the client collaboration with a spiritual leader. ▲

Source: Dreamcatcher: *Anishnabe as Remembered by WayaGola.* Original text by Jim Shupe on **www.lib.uconn.edu/Native/dreamcat/dreamfaq.html.** Accessed June 1997.

Foa et al. (1992) proposed that avoidance and numbing involve two separate mechanisms. Avoidance is said to be regulated by strategic effortful processes, whereas numbing may be mediated by more automatic mechanisms.

The strongest argument in favour of the information processing model is the suggestion by Foa and Kozak (1986) that treatment of PTSD would not be effective in reducing symptoms unless the information stored in memory were sufficiently activated for emotional processing to occur. This hypothesis was supported by a study by Foa, Riggs, Massie, and Yarczower (1995). They found that people who experienced more fear when reexperiencing the trauma during exposure treatment benefitted more from treatment.

Janoff-Bulman (1992) advanced our understanding of why particular events are traumatic by proposing that traumatic events shatter one or more of three fundamental beliefs:

- the world is fundamentally good;
- events occur according to logical and fair rules; and
- I am a worthwhile person

Following a traumatic event, such as rape, the radical change in these beliefs would lead to a sense of vulnerability. However, more research is needed to demonstrate that these three beliefs are fundamentals and were strongly held before the trauma in people suffering from PTSD.

Generalized Anxiety Disorder

Description

Generalized anxiety disorder (GAD) is a specific group of symptoms with, at the core, the tendency to worry excessively about a number of events and activities. The worrisome thoughts are unrealistic, difficult to control, and excessive and include major issues as well as everyday concerns (for example, well-being of family members, finances, work, health, school). The worry is not transient; the DSM-IV requires that the anxiety must be present more days than not for a period of at least six months.

Because research began later on GAD than on other anxiety disorders, much less empirical information is available. Studies conducted in the United States, England, and Australia suggest that onset of GAD is gradual, and often occurs in childhood or adolescence. In fact, more than 60 percent of individuals with GAD state "I've always been a worrier." However, clients tend to wait more than 25 years before consulting for treatment. Twice as many women as men suffer from GAD.

People with GAD typically have a strong sense of loss of control over external and internal events. They tend to have a poor quality of life and very often suffer from other disorders such as depression, social phobia, panic disorder, or specific phobia.

Assessment and Diagnostic Issues

Important changes in the classification of GAD have been made since it was first described in the DSM-III (APA, 1980). It was originally conceived as a residual disorder, diagnosed only if no other anxiety or mood disorder was present. The DSM-III-R recognized that GAD could exist concurrently with other disorders, provided that the sphere of worry was not limited to the other disorder. Also, the duration requirement was increased from one to six months to ensure that the anxiety was truly chronic. Because it is often chronic, begins at an early age, and is considered by some as being a vulnerability factor for other mental disorders, it has even been suggested that GAD is a personality disorder (for example, Sanderson & Wetzel, 1991). However, GAD remains in the anxiety disorders section of the DSM-IV.

The DSM-IV criteria also reduced the overlap between panic disorder and GAD, and reinforced the importance of pervasive, chronic, and uncontrollable worry as a hallmark of GAD. In contrast to panic attacks, worries are accompanied by symptoms less associated with autonomic arousal and more with chronic anxiety (see the DSM table "Diagnostic Criteria for Generalized Anxiety Disorder"). Finally, GAD is not diagnosed if the worry and anxiety result from another psychological disorder, such as anticipatory anxiety in panic disorder.

Associated symptoms reflecting **autonomic hyperactivity** are now listed for panic disorder, and symptoms reflecting motor tension as well as **vigilance** and **scanning behaviours** are now listed for GAD. Individuals with GAD differ from individuals with other anxiety disorders largely on these symptom clusters (Brown, Marten, & Barlow, 1995). GAD is characterized by three key features: uncontrollability of worry, intolerance of uncertainty, and ineffective problem-solving skills.

Worries are different from obsessions. Both include negative thoughts. However, obsessions can also take the form of images and impulses while worries are more often verbal

DSM-IV Diagnostic Criteria for Generalized Anxiety Disorder

A. Excessive anxiety and worry, occurring more days than not for at least 6 months, about a number of events or activities.

B. The person find it difficult to control the worry.

C. The anxiety and worry are associated with at least three of the following six symptoms (with at least some symptoms present more days than not for the past 6 months).
   (1) restlessness or feeling keyed up or on edge
   (2) being easily fatigued
   (3) difficulty concentrating or mind going blank
   (4) irritability
   (5) muscle tension
   (6) sleep disturbance

E. The anxiety, worry, or physical symptoms cause clinically significant distress or impairment in social, occupational, or other important areas of functioning.

Source: Reprinted with permission from the *Diagnostic and Statistical Manual of Mental Disorders,* Fourth Edition. Copyright 1994 American Psychiatric Association.

thoughts rather than images. Second, obsessions are more intrusive than worries. The latter are generally more voluntary and ruminative. Third, the content of the worries is perceived by people as more realistic, more egosyntonic, and more variable than the content of obsessions.

Although it does not specifically assess GAD, Spielberger's (1983) State-Trait Anxiety Inventory is often used to measure both normal anxiety in nonclinical samples as well as anxiety levels in people with anxiety disorders. **State anxiety** refers to a transient emotional experience comprising tension and apprehension (that is, how a person feels right now). **Trait anxiety** refers to a proneness or tendency to experience state anxiety under stressful or threatening conditions (that is, how an individual generally feels). Other measures of anxiety can be used with individuals with GAD, including the Beck Anxiety Inventory (Beck, Epstein, Brown, & Steer, 1988). A measure that is more consistent with the recent diagnostic emphasis on worry in GAD is the Penn State Worry Questionnaire (Meyer, Miller, Metzger, & Borkovec, 1990). This measure focusses on the frequency and uncontrollability of worry rather than the content of the worry.

Although not designed specifically for GAD, the Hamilton Anxiety Rating Scale (Hamilton, 1959) is often used by clinicians and in clinical research to assess clinical anxiety. The Hamilton scale assesses several cognitive and somatic symptoms of anxiety. It is not an ideal instrument for assessing any particular anxiety disorder, because it incorporates symptoms characteristic of a number of anxiety disorders. Because it has been used in so many treatment studies over the years, however, it continues to be employed so that study outcomes can be directly compared to previous findings.

Etiology

Several of the theoretical approaches used to explain anxiety in general appear to apply to GAD, but especially the perception of threat and information processing (Rapee, 1991; Tallis & Eysenck, 1994).

Dugas, Gagnon, Ladouceur, & Freeston (1998) proposed a model of this disorder (see Figure 7.6). According to these authors, one of the key elements underlying the perception of threat in GAD is an intolerance of uncertainty (Dugas et al., 1998; Freeston, Rhéaume, Letarte, Dugas, & Ladouceur, 1994; Tallis & Eysenck, 1994). People with GAD react with strong anxiety to uncertain or ambiguous situations, feeling that something terrible is about to happen or that things are out of control.

David Barlow also highlighted three variables that interact to perpetuate emotional arousal and worry: ineffective problem-solving, cognitive avoidance, and the belief that worrying can predict negative outcomes (Barlow, 1988; Craske, Barlow, & O'Leary, 1992). Individuals with GAD do not lack problem-solving skills; rather they show poor problem orientation (Davey, 1994). Problem orientation means the appraisal of everyday problems, including reaching a belief that the problem can be solved and that the person has the ability to solve it by following certain steps (Maydeu-Olivares & D'Zurilla, 1996). For example, a recent study showed that individuals with GAD tend to repeat the first step of problem-solving (identifying the problem and potential threat) without proceeding to further steps (Dugas, Letarte, Rhéaume, Freeston, & Ladouceur, 1995). Borkovec (1985) also suggests that worry may be an attempt to engage in problem-solving. ("There's a tough test tomorrow. I'd better go home and worry.")

Emotional arousal may interfere with attentional processes in chronic worriers, including those with GAD. That is, they may be distracted by their distress from focussing on problem-solving. They may also have difficulty generating possible solutions or selecting the most appropriate ones.

Borkovec and colleagues (for example, Borkovec & Inz, 1990) speculate that worry is a strategy for avoiding somatic arousal and threatening images. Because worrying is a conceptual process, it leads to the suppression of images and is accompanied by inhibition of the activity of the sympathetic nervous system (Borkovec, Shadick, & Hopkins, 1991). But research has also shown that worry is self-perpetuating. Attempts to resist worrying or to distract from the worries just make it worse in the long run, in a similar fashion to the unsuccessful neutralization strategies discussed in relation to OCD.

Ironically, many individuals with GAD believe that worry serves another useful function: preventing adverse outcomes. It is true that thinking about an event in order to find (and implement) a solution can help to prevent adverse consequences—when the event is the kind the person can have some control over. For example, it might be useful to prepare for negotiations by anticipating the other person's arguments and planning responses. But for some individuals with GAD it is as if "planning the event in advance" creates a perception of control over outcomes and even *potential* threats. They may preview a car trip, for example, by imagining all the bad weather and accidents that could befall them, feeling that this will somehow protect them. By the time the trip begins, they may be too fearful to go, or too upset to drive safely.

With intolerance to uncertainty as a background, all these elements interact and are influenced by mood state and life events. As the vicious circle builds, the person's thoughts may be occupied almost exclusively by worries about the focus of concern and his or her inability to cope with it.

Other Anxiety Disorders

Three more anxiety disorders are listed in DSM-IV. *Anxiety disorder due to a general medical condition* is self-explanatory. Similar diagnostic criteria applies to a *substance-induced anxiety disorder*, but with a drug, toxin, etc. as the causal agent. The clinical presentations of these disorders vary according to the causative agent, and treatment may involve treating the underlying medical condition or withdrawing the person from the substance inducing the anxiety disorder.

The remaining category of anxiety disorder is labelled *anxiety disorder not otherwise specified* ("anxiety disorder NOS") and includes symptoms that do not meet diagnostic criteria of any other anxiety disorder, such as a combination of anxiety and depressive disorder, or phobic symptoms secondary to the social impact of stuttering.

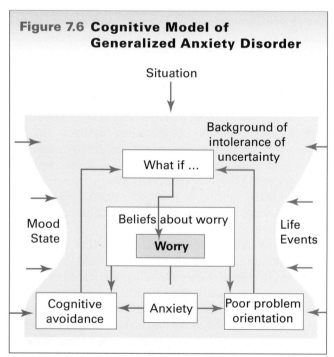

Figure 7.6 Cognitive Model of Generalized Anxiety Disorder

Source: Reprinted from *Behaviour Research and Therapy*, 36 (2), M. J. Dugas, F. Gagnon, R. Ladouceur, & M. H. Freeston (1988), Generalized anxiety disorder: A preliminary test of a conceptual model , 215–226, Copyright 1998, with permission from Elsevier Science Ltd., The Boulevard, Langford Lane, Kidlington 0X5 1GB, UK.

TREATMENT

Anxiety disorders may be treated by means of pharmacotherapy or psychotherapy. The effectiveness of the two modes is comparable. However, relapse more often occurs after drugs are discontinued. Furthermore, some people have difficulty tolerating the side-effects and many people prefer nonpharmacological treatments. Cognitive-behavioural treatments tend to have a lower relapse rate, possibly because these therapies involve teaching skills to manage anxiety, which allow people to continue to use their skills after the formal course of treatment has been completed. Interestingly, there is evidence that psychological variables can predict relapses after drug treatment. For example, relapse from drug treatment of panic disorder is predicted by whether the person believes that anxiety sensations are harmful (anxiety sensitivity). Such findings support the biopsychosocial hypothesis that biological and psychological treatments are effective through mechanisms interacting with one another and operating at different levels.

More than 400 forms of psychotherapy have been described, but very few have been put to the test. Forms of therapy that have not been empirically validated are considered experimental. Ethically, it is essential to offer therapies shown to be effective. Although no treatment is able to eliminate all symptoms for all clients, controlled outcome studies have confirmed the effectiveness of some interventions. For some disorders, treatments are still in development; for others, well-established treatments are available and researchers are concentrating on refining our understanding of the mechanism of change.

An ideal treatment should not only alleviate symptoms, but be relatively cost-effective and accessible to those who could benefit from it. The traditional therapeutic qualities of empathy, warmth, support, and positive therapeutic alliance are a prerequisite for effective treatment, but are not enough in themselves; effective strategies must be used. We will describe each strategy separately, but keep in mind that they are often combined in practice.

Pharmacotherapy

Only three drugs have to date been approved for the treatment of panic by the Health Protection Branch (HPB) of Health Canada, although many others have been shown to be effective. The reason for this is the stringent requirements for the marketing of drugs. Before a new drug can be marketed for general use, the pharmaceutical company must conduct preclinical trials (for example, animal studies) and treatment-outcome studies using human subjects, including safety studies, and then apply for HPB approval. The drug may be marketed only for the application for which it has received approval. Because seeking HPB approval is an expensive process, a company may not seek to market a drug approved for one condition as use in another condition, even if it has been empirically established in other countries as effective. This limitation does not, however, prevent physicians from using their clinical judgement to prescribe the drug. For example, the drugs approved in Canada as anti-panic agents are alprazolam (Xanax), paroxetine (Paxil), and sertraline (Zoloft). However, many other drugs in the same classes have been shown to be effective (for example, tricyclic antidepressants, SSRIs) and are used to treat anxiety disorder in Canada. Drugs are prescribed by physicians on the basis of the diagnosis, the individual's characteristics, potential side-effects, and interactions with other drugs.

The most important classes of drugs used to treat anxiety disorders include selective serotonin reuptake inhibitors (SSRIs), benzodiazepines, tricyclic antidepressants, monoamine oxidase inhibitors (MAOIs), and reversible inhibitors of monoamine oxidase (RIMAs). None of these drugs are effective for all anxiety disorders. For example, benzodiazepines are of limited value in the treatment of posttraumatic stress disorder. The mechanisms of the various drugs are not yet fully understood but involve variables discussed in the section on the biological models.

At various doses many of these drugs are effective in reducing or, in some cases, eliminating symptoms of anxiety and panic (for a review see Lydiard, Brawman-Mintzer, & Ballenger, 1996).

Exposure Techniques

Exposure therapy was the first psychological treatment to be thoroughly validated for anxiety disorders. It is defined as "any procedure that confronts the person with a stimulus which typically elicits an undesirable behaviour or an unwanted emotional response" (Marshall, 1985, p. 121). Fear-inducing stimuli may be internal (for example, body sensations, thoughts, images, worries) or external (for example, situations, objects, animals, individuals, places). External stimuli may be presented as *imaginal*, *representational* (through audio or video), *virtual* (through computer technology), or *in vivo* (in real life). Exposure may begin at low intensity and be progressively increased, or the initial stimuli may be designed to elicit the strongest emotional response the person can tolerate (*flooding*). The treatment can also take the form of **response prevention**: that is, blocking avoidance behaviours (Marshall, Gauthier, & Gordon, 1979). Finally, the rate of exposure may be massed or spaced over time and the duration of each exposure may be brief or prolonged.

Overall, exposure therapy has been found to be most effective when it is prolonged, massed, and carried out in vivo. Distractions will impede progress, so it is important to encourage the person to focus strongly on the stimulus during exposure. To ensure maximal effectiveness, each exposure should continue until the anxiety has subsided or is reduced. This may take anywhere from a few minutes to a few hours, depending on the severity of the disorder. Ideally, exposure should be repeated until an increase in perceived self-efficacy and a reduction in undesirable behaviours and beliefs are observed. The effects of exposure can also be enhanced by modelling (demonstrating) the appropriate behaviour for clients before exposure (for example, touching a spider in the case of spider phobia).

When it comes to homework assignments, progressive in vivo exposure is preferred (that is, starting with small steps and working up), because it is easier for clients to complete. Moreover, progressive exposure teaches them a method that they can use in their daily life to overcome their fear. It is important to remember that even graded exposure can be very demanding on clients. Therefore, any exposure assignments are always negotiated.

Exposure for individuals with panic disorder involves provoking the feared sensations (interoceptive exposure) by methods such as hyperventilation, exercising, or spinning in a chair. A client who suffers from agoraphobia would be asked to enter feared situations such as grocery stores, churches, or driving alone in the car. Individuals with social phobia would be asked to engage in social activities or behave "foolishly." Individuals with PTSD would be asked to recall and describe the traumatic event according to a predetermined hierarchy (imaginal exposure). Individuals with obsessive-compulsive disorder would be asked to refrain from engaging in the ritualistic behaviours while exposed to feared stimuli (response prevention), or listening to audio recordings of their obsessions. For exposure purposes, individuals with generalized anxiety disorder would imagine the realization of their worst fears and focus on these scenarios until anxiety has abated.

All of these exercises evoke some degree of distress. However, the aim is not to endure panic and anxiety, but to develop more adaptive internal representations of stimuli and their non-threatening consequences as well as a more accurate evaluation of the probability of various outcomes and the effectiveness of coping strategies.

Cognitive Restructuring

Cognitive therapy encompasses a wide array of techniques intended to eliminate maladaptive thoughts and images. Founders of cognitive therapy include Albert Ellis, Aaron Beck, and Donald Meichenbaum of the University of Waterloo (see also Chapter 13 and Chapter 16). **Cognitive restructuring** involves three steps: (1) identifying maladaptive cognitive contents (automatic thoughts, beliefs), processes, and products; (2) challenging the maladaptive cognitive contents by helping the client to examine the evidence for or against a belief; and (3) developing more adaptive cognitive contents and processes.

In doing so, it is essential not to engage in arguments or confrontation. The therapist must encourage the client's collaboration as a scientist to assess every aspect of a situation in order to find the most plausible interpretation. This process is called "collaborative empiricism." Cognitive restructuring is very different from "positive thinking," in which a false illusion of safety may be created. The plausible interpretations may not be entirely "positive," but will be more realistic. Faulty appraisals are corrected during the therapy session with the therapist, and between sessions via homework exercises. Clients are trained to use a homework sheet called

"dysfunctional thoughts record" (see Table 7.2). At the beginning, three columns are used to help the client to identify his or her maladaptive thoughts, but later in therapy more columns are added to find alternative explanations and reduce the intensity of the initial emotion. Reappraisal of probabilities, consequences, and coping capacities is a difficult task that requires expertise on the part of the therapist and practice on the part of the client.

Behavioural experiments are often used to test the validity of beliefs. Although they may involve some form of exposure to feared stimuli, the exposure is less intensive than in exposure therapies and not repeated. Other strategies are often combined with cognitive restructuring, such as rehearsing coping self-statements, identifying errors in logical thinking, or providing information found to be useful and helpful to clients.

Relaxation Training

The aim of **relaxation training** is to decrease physiological arousal. Relaxation exercises are widely available through books, audiotapes, and brief courses offered in hospitals, health services, and community centres. For many people, relaxation is synonymous with Jacobson's progressive relaxation. The first step of this technique is to tense and release the tension in a predetermined sequence of muscular groups. Once the client has mastered the technique, the second phase involves only releasing the tension.

This strategy, developed in 1960s, has been included in many stress reduction packages. It was also used in systematic desensitization, an early exposure-based treatment (Wolpe, 1958), in which the client was trained in a relaxation exercise and then asked to imagine fear-evoking stimuli. Before and after imagining each stimulus, the person was asked to relax. Thus, relaxation was thought to inhibit the anxiety response.

Variant techniques have been used with different muscle groups or without the tensing phase. Other techniques such as positive imagery, meditation, or breathing exercises are also effective. No single technique is best for everyone, and one should be sought that meets the client's needs, interests, and capacities. Practice is also essential in learning to relax effectively and rapidly.

Problem-Solving

For individuals with generalized anxiety disorder, training in **problem-solving** (D'Zurilla & Goldfried, 1971) can significantly reduce anxiety and worry. Many people tend to think of problems in broad, vague, and catastrophic ways that allow of no possible solution. Problem-solving training helps them to divide problems into manageable units that can be systematically analyzed and solved.

Problem-solving involves the following steps:

1. Identify the specific, objective details of the problem, rather than thoughts or feelings about it.

Table 7.2 Homework Sheet Used for Cognitive Restructuring by a Patient Suffering from Panic Disorder

Client/file no. **1701-D**   Group and week: **B-5**

Situation	Emotion (intensity in %)	Thoughts (believability in %)	Alternative Interpretation (believability in %)	Re-rate Emotion (intensity in %)
At the restaurant	Anxiety (80%)	It will be full of people, it will be hot and I will faint (90%)	It doesn't matter how many people are there (30%) This is emotional thinking (100%) Hot does not equal fainting (80%) I've never fainted in all my panic attacks before (> 500) (100%) Faint=decrease in blood pressure and I can't faint because my panic will increase my blood pressure (85%)	Anxiety now at 20%
My heart was racing in my chest without any warning	Panic (100%)	I will have a heart attack and die (80%)	Don't know—must ask therapist and find an exercise to convince me of the contrary	Panic still at 100%
People were laughing at the store	Anxiety (75%) Depressed (60%)	These people were laughing at me (90%) I'm screwed up and I'll stay like that forever (50%)	I can't read minds (100%) They were laughing at the baby (40%) I'm not silly—see notes from last therapy session (90%) I'm getting better; my panic attacks are less frequent (90%)	Anxiety now at 50% Depression now at 0%

2. Let the mind go and think of all the possible solutions, no matter how foolish, silly, or ridiculous they may sound.

3. Rank-order these solutions from most to least practical and reasonable.

4. Decide on a specific plan to carrying out the best solution.

5. Put the plan for the best solution into action.

6. If this action is not successful, move down the list to the next-best solution; try again until the problem is resolved or alleviated.

A more detailed presentation of each step can be found in D'Zurilla (1988) and D'Zurilla and Goldfried (1971).

Other Techniques

Many treatment packages combine exposure, cognitive restructuring, and techniques for specific disorders. Breathing retraining is often used in panic disorder. The client is trained to detect inappropriate breathing patterns and substitute controlled diaphragmatic breathing.

For individuals with social phobia, outward focus implies shifting attention to process external stimuli by monitoring and analyzing aspects of the environment such as people's behaviours or expressions. However, attention must be paid to ensure that outward focus does not become an avoidance strategy. In Montreal, Stravynsky and his colleagues (Stravynsky & Greenberg, 1989) have also shown that social skills training is useful for people with social phobia, even if they have good social skills; by requiring them to practise feared behaviours, it serves as a form of exposure therapy.

A new and controversial method of treating anxiety disorders is Eye-Movement Desensitization and Reprocessing (EMDR; Shapiro, 1995). EMDR consists of imaginal exposure to fear-evoking images while systematic saccadic eye movements are produced. Saccades (rapid shifts of focus) are typically induced by asking the person to track a therapist's finger as it moves rapidly from side to side. Coping statements are also introduced while the scene is being imagined. Treatment typically takes one to four sessions. Recently, it has been suggested that eye movements in EMDR can be replaced with other lateral, stereotypic motor movements. The theory behind EMDR (Shapiro, 1995) is that exposure to trauma produces neuronal changes that disrupt the physiological balance between excitatory and inhibitory systems in the brain, which prevents appropriate processing of traumatic memories. EMDR purportedly restores this balance and reverses the neural pathology, thus allowing appropriate reprocessing and integration of the traumatic memories. This theory has been widely criticized. However, some evidence suggests that the treatment is effective for some anxiety disorders, such as posttraumatic stress disorder (Van Etten, & Taylor, 1997).

Treatment Effectiveness

Anthony and Swinson (1996) conducted for Health Canada an excellent review of all the methodologically reliable studies and concluded that there is impressive support for the effectiveness of cognitive-behavioural therapy for anxiety disorders.

According to many reviews (for example, Antony & Swinson, 1996) and consensus reports (for example, Association/Troubles Anxieux du Québec [ATAQ], 1996), cognitive-behaviour therapy is the most effective psychological treatment for panic disorder. Outcomes are comparable to those of pharmacotherapy in the short term, and appear to be more enduring.

Two studies conducted by Richard Swinson and Brian Cox demonstrated that some adaptations of traditional cognitive-behaviour therapy are effective: telephone-administered behavioural interventions (Swinson, Fergus, Cox, & Wiskwire, 1995), and providing clients with reassurance and exposure instructions delivered in the general hospital emergency room (Swinson, Soulios, Cox, & Kuch, 1992). Guylaine Côté, now at the University of Sherbrooke, and Janel Gauthier also demonstrated that minimal therapist contact and the use of a self-help book was as effective as 17 weeks of in-person cognitive-behaviour therapy (Côté, Gauthier, Laberge, Plamondon, & Fournier, 1994). The rate of panic-free participants was above 80 percent and remained constant at a five-year followup. Marked improvement in agoraphobic avoidance was also reported. For example, at the five-year followup, a participant had been to the top of the CN Tower without panicking and another had taken a ferry from North Sidney (Nova Scotia) to Port-aux-Basques (Newfoundland), a five-hour trip, without experiencing any anxiety.

A review of 42 outcome studies has revealed that exposure, cognitive restructuring and social skills training are all effective interventions in social phobia (Taylor, 1996). However, cognitive restructuring combined with exposure tended to be most effective. A similar study has confirmed the effectiveness of exposure-based treatments for PTSD (Van Etten & Taylor, 1997).

Obsessive-compulsive disorder was long considered one of the most difficult psychological disorder to treat, but at least 16 studies have reported good outcomes with behavioural and cognitive-behavioural therapy. A meta-analysis has also found both pharmacotherapy and behavioural therapy to be effective (Cox, Swinson, Morrison, & Lee, 1993). Cognitive-behavioural therapy has recently been confirmed effective for obsessions without compulsions (Freeston et al., 1997).

Complex clinical studies have examined the relative contribution of various treatment strategies, their mechanism, and their interactions with pharmacotherapy. For example, in a sample of 60 individuals with generalized social phobia, Taylor et al. (1997) found that those receiving cognitive restructuring did better than those receiving a placebo. However, receiving cognitive restructuring did not facilitate subsequent exposure therapy.

Although cognitive-behaviour therapy is generally effective, it does not help everyone with anxiety disorder. Marshall and Gauthier addressed this issue in a comprehensive review of outcome studies published in 1983 but still relevant today (Marshall & Gauthier, 1983). They determined that cognitive-behavioural therapy is more likely to succeed if it is:

1. conducted by well-trained therapists;
2. based on a good understanding of the theoretical model relevant to each disorder;
3. based on a correct diagnosis;
4. planned only after a case formulation or functional analysis;
5. attentive to the needs of the client; and
6. monitored closely

Finally, it is important to point out that no treatment is a panacea: empirically validated treatments generally lead to improvements but not to total cure. More studies are needed to reliably establish long-term effectiveness (Milrod & Bush, 1996), to help patients achieve completely normal levels of functioning, and to assess the effect of comorbid disorders.

PANORAMA

The first psychological theories of anxiety were proposed almost a century ago, yet only recently have sufficient empirical data been gathered to form reliable scientific theories leading to effective treatments. Further research is needed to refine existing theories and improve treatment effectiveness. For example, outcome studies often show significant improvement in the specific symptoms of panic frequency or agoraphobic avoidance; but more comprehensive assessments have revealed that many clients do not reach the level of functioning usually found in nonanxious individuals.

Availability of effective, empirically validated treatment also appears to be a problem. In the United States, Barlow (1994) estimated that fewer than 40 percent of those presenting with anxiety disorder were receiving adequate psychological treatment. Swinson's data showed a similar trend in Canada (Swinson et al., 1992). Dissemination of effective treatment is a crucial issue in Canada at a time when pressure is mounting from government and third-party payers to deliver briefer and more effective treatments. Clinicians need continuing education to keep up to date with current treatments. More research should also focus on making established treatments more cost-effective and accessible, perhaps through self-help books, videoconferencing, or even the Internet.

More research is also needed on combining psychological and pharmacological treatments. Many believe that two effective interventions should be more effective than either one alone. It is often argued that pharmacotherapy acts more rapidly and help clients to benefit more from psychological treatments. So far, however, this claim has found little empirical support (for example, Marks et al., 1993).

SUMMARY

Anxiety disorders are prevalent and chronic conditions. They cause considerable suffering and can seriously impair functioning and quality of life. Anxiety disorders appear to have biological and psychological causes that interact with one another in complex ways. Genetics is clearly a predisposing factor, but explains at most 40 to 50 percent of anxiety disorders.

Neuroanatomical and neurochemical factors are involved in panic, anxiety, and their disorders. Serotonin, GABA, norepinephrine, and in some cases dopamine and neuropeptides are linked to anxiety reactions. Although many areas of the brain may be involved, the locus ceruleus and the amygdala appear to be most important.

It was initially thought that anxiety could be explained by classical and operant conditioning principles. They cannot, however, account for the full clinical picture of anxiety disorders. Current thinking is based on a biopsychosocial model with perceived threat, low self-efficacy, and avoidance as core features.

Specific phobias are characterized by a panic reaction triggered by specific cues and reinforced by avoidance behaviour. Neo-conditioning models are used to explain the disorder and exposure to the anxiety-provoking cues is still the best psychosocial treatment available.

Panic disorder is defined by the presence of panic attacks that often occur unexpectedly. Agoraphobia is said to be the avoidance of places where panic attacks could occur, and often accompanies panic disorder. The conceptual models of panic disorder all focus on how internal bodily sensations are perceived or associated with threat (anxiety sensitivity). Treatments aiming to change this perception of threat often take the form of cognitive restructuring and exposure to internal sensations or agoraphobic cues.

The essential feature of social phobia is a fear of acting in a way that will be humiliating. Thus, social situations or performances are avoided, or endured with significant distress. It is believed that underlying mechanisms behind social phobia include devaluating beliefs toward oneself, very high standards of performance, self-focussed attention, and avoidance. The effectiveness of cognitive restructuring, exposure, and social skills training have been confirmed by empirical studies.

The defining elements of obsessive-compulsive disorder are the presence of unwanted intrusive thoughts and repetitive stereotyped behaviours. An inflated sense of responsibility, perfectionism, and cognitive avoidance are thought to be the core of this debilitating disorder. Although drugs such as SSRIs, benzodiazepines, and tricyclic antidepressants are very popular (as for other anxiety disorders), exposure and cognitive restructuring are effective treatment strategies.

Posttraumatic stress disorder develops after exposure to a traumatic event. The individual is afflicted by reexperiencing of the event, avoidance of stimuli related to the trauma, and increased arousal. Comprehensive and validated psychosocial models have yet to be proposed, but difficulty in emotional processing is a key variable. Empirically validated treatments include exposure and other cognitive-behavioural techniques.

The central feature of generalized anxiety disorder is chronic worry. Intolerance of uncertainty, beliefs about worry, cognitive avoidance, and difficulties in problem orientation are all involved. Cognitive-behavioural therapies addressing these variables are effective.

KEY TERMS

panic attack (p. 153)
neuroses (p. 154)
realistic anxiety (p. 154)
neurotic anxiety (p. 154)
moral anxiety (p. 154)
locus ceruleus (p. 155)
cholecystokinin (CCK) (p. 156)
two-factor model (p. 156)
biological preparedness theory
    (p. 157)

perceived self-efficacy (p. 158)
avoidance (p. 159)
information processing (p. 159)
cognitive structures (p. 159)
learning (p. 159)
cognitive contents (p. 159)
cognitive operations (p. 159)
cognitive products (p. 160)
specific phobia (p. 160)
neo-conditioning theories (p. 161)
anxiety sensitivity (p. 164)
obsessions (p. 168)

compulsions (p. 168)
neutralize (p.169)
autonomic hyperactivity (p. 173)
vigilance (p. 173)
scanning behaviours (p. 173)
state anxiety (p. 173)
trait anxiety (p. 173)
response prevention (p. 175)
cognitive restructuring (p. 176)
relaxation training (p. 176)
problem-solving (p. 176)

ADDITIONAL RESOURCES

Anxiety Disorders Association of
    America
11900 Parklawn Drive
Suite 100
Rockville, MD 20852
(301) 231-9350
anxdis@aol.com

Obsessive-Compulsive Foundation
P.O. Box 70
Milford, CT 06460-0070
(203) 878-5669
(203) 874-2826 fax
info@ocfoundation.org

www.behavior.net/column/meichenbaum/index.html
www.aaets.org/arts/art39.htm
These sites contain transcripts of interviews with Canadian psychologist Donald Meichenbaum about treating patients who have posttraumatic stress disorder.

www.adaa.org
Web site of the Anxiety Disorders Association of America. Provides information on a range of anxiety disorders, including phobias, obsessive-compulsive disorder, and posttraumatic stress disorder.

www.ocfoundation.org/indright.htm
Site of the Obsessive-Compulsive Foundation. Provides information about the latest techniques to treat OCD, as well as a listing of publications and research endeavours.

www.UQAH.UQUEBEC.CA/BOUCHARD/ATAQ.HTM
This French-language site provides information on anxiety disorders and treatment.

www.nimh.nih.gov/PUBLIST/SPECIFIC.HTM
Information on anxiety disorders and their treatment, from the U.S. National Institute of Mental Health.

Chapter 8

Dissociative and Somatoform Disorders

Philip Firestone

Dorothy Joudrie, a Calgary socialite, and Earl Joudrie, one of Canada's top business executives (Chairman of the Board of Algoma Steel, Gulf Canada Resources, Unitel Communications, and Canadian Tire Corporation), had met at Dorothy's very posh home to discuss some aspects of their impending divorce, after more than 25 years of an often very stormy marriage. Earl had also returned to pick up some personal papers and some items of sentimental value, including family photos. As he left through the garage, Dorothy calmly approached him and deliberately shot six bullets into Earl, at point-blank range. Her husband reported that, as he lay bleeding on he floor of the garage, she asked, in a calm voice, "How long is it going to take you to die?" After a few minutes she snapped out of her tranquillity and began crying hysterically. At this point she immediately rushed to call emergency services to help her husband.

Dorothy was charged with attempted murder. During her sensational trial it was revealed that she had been an alcoholic for many years, and often had little or no insight into her behaviour. For example, after being charged with the shooting of her husband she requested to get out on bail quickly in order to play her weekly bridge game. She testified their relationship had been marked with consid-erable domestic violence and Earl had beaten her for years. The beatings had stopped 18 years prior to the shooting. She reported absolutely no memory of the shooting. The defence emphasized the beatings that Earl had inflicted on his wife. They also stressed the calm, deliberate manner in which Dorothy shot Earl. Even Earl underscored that his wife's serene demeanor surrounding the shooting was very unlike her. All psychiatrists, even the prosecution's, agreed with the opinion that Dorothy appeared to be in a dissociative state during the shooting.

After two days of deliberations, Dorothy was found not guilty by a jury of 11 women and 1 man who decided she was suffering from a mental disorder at the time of the shooting. She was found not criminally responsible since the jury believed the psychiatric testimony that she was unable to form the necessary intent to commit a crime. As a result, Dorothy was able to trade the rough privation of a prison for the treatment, relative comfort, and freedom of a mental hospital. She was released from hospital after a short stint there. Earl commented after the verdict, "I'm not looking for vengeance at all, but some son of a bitch shot me six times and that seems to have been forgotten in this whole mess."

Dissociative and somatoform disorders have been known throughout recorded time and have usually been seen as variants on the same problem. They have generally been considered as one of the neuroses, because anxiety is regarded as the predominant underlying feature in the etiology of these disorders. In DSM-II, these psychological problems were classified as Hysterical Neuroses. However, with DSM-III, the emphasis in classification of psychological disorders shifted from etiology to observable behaviour, a trend even more evident in DSM-IV. So even though most professionals still believe anxiety is central to these two diagnostic categories, the fact that their behavioural patterns are so different from each other has resulted in two independent groupings.

Current thought suggests somatoform and dissociative disorders are different, but are both characterized by physical symptoms and/or behaviour that are thought to be caused by or exacerbated by the way people think or their ideas (Merskey, 1995). There has been more confusion and debate about these types of problems than almost any other psychological disorders. Nevertheless, they have played an important role in psychological thought from ancient times to the present.

Patients with somatoform and dissociative disorders are extremely common in medical practice. For example, Devine and Merskey (1986) estimated that 38 percent of patients coming to a primary care physician with pain of any kind as a symptom have pain that cannot be attributed to any known physical cause. One study has indicated that 10 percent of adults living in Winnipeg may be suffering from a dissociative disorder (Ross, 1991). Unfortunately, most health professionals view people suffering from somatoform and dissociative disorders with disfavour, as fakers or malingerers. The idea that people without identifiable organic cause for their complaints are somehow psychologically weak or craven leads to blame and feelings of unworthiness.

HISTORICAL PERSPECTIVE

The Hippocratic writings make some reference to dissociative and somatoform symptoms but it is not until Plato that there was much consideration of causation. The Platonic view was that a wandering womb (*hysteros*) caused these symptoms (Merskey, 1995). Such a reference to a gender difference in the frequency of dissociation is interesting since it has been supported by recent epidemiological research, which suggests a female-to-male ratio of approximately 5 to 1 (Peterson, 1991). It is not clear whether this is a function of biological vulnerability or differential help-seeking attitudes, or whether females are more likely to suffer the trauma that seems to be related to dissociation (Ross, 1989).

Although there are references to dissociation throughout Greek and Roman mythology, it was emphasized in early Christianity, where it was seen as the result of demonic possession, and exorcism was the favoured treatment (Ross, 1989). Only after the decline in the acceptance of possession as an explanation for abnormal behaviour did more psychologically based theories develop (Putnam, 1989). Many of the pioneers of modern psychological theories, such as Binet, Charcot, and Jung, wrote about dissociation, especially as it related to the development of multiple personalities, as well as the role of hypnosis in its treatment. However, it was Breuer and Freud, in their classic 1895 publication *Studies in Hysteria*, who identified severe psychological trauma as important in the etiology of dissociation and established a relationship between dissociation and hypnotic-like states. They described in some detail the usefulness of hypnosis in the treatment of such patients. The book consisted primarily of case studies of female patients suffering from dissociation, most of whom had been sexually abused. Several of these patients also suffered from somatoform disorders. For example, the first case described "Anna O." (treated by Breuer), a 21-year-old woman who developed visual and hearing problems, total paralysis of both legs and her right arm, with partial paralysis of her left arm, nervous cough, and periods of disturbed consciousness in which she seemed to be quite a different person. The classic Freudian view of somatoform and dissociative disorders began with such cases and was developed over several years.

The most dramatic of the dissociative disorders, previously called *multiple personality disorder* and now called *dissociative identity disorder*, received considerable attention up to the end of the first decade of the 1900s despite its rarity. However, two factors led to a decline in its acceptance thereafter. First, Freud repudiated his patients' reports of being sexually abused by their fathers, suggesting that in reality they simply had fantasies of such seductions. This view tended to discredit both patients' reports and hypnosis as a meaningful intervention. The later ascendancy of biological theories in the etiology of psychological disorders also directed attention away from earlier explorations of dissociation.

Edward Shorter, a historian at University of Toronto, has written a fascinating history of somatization (Shorter, 1992), and Harold Merskey, a psychiatrist from London, Ontario, has just published the second edition of his delightful history of dissociative disorders (Merskey, 1995). Each tracks changing views of these baffling disorders.

"Anna O." (Bertha Pappenheim) (1859–1936) developed a bizarre range of physical and psychological symptoms. Her case was influential in the development of Freud's ideas.

DISSOCIATIVE DISORDERS

Dissociative disorders are characterized by severe disturbances or alterations of identity, memory, and consciousness. The defining symptom of the dissociative disorders is **dissociation**, the disruption of mental processes involved in memory or consciousness that are normally integrated (Spiegel & Cardena, 1991). Normally there is a unity in our consciousness that gives rise to our sense of self. We know who we are. We know our names, where we live, and what we do for a living. But with the dissociative disorders, these simple aspects of daily living are bizarrely disturbed. People may lose knowledge of their family or of what they have been doing for the last few days, weeks, and even years.

There is general agreement that dissociation occurs in a minor way to most of us. Someone sitting in an office, in a trance-like state, daydreaming of a tropical holiday, is undoubtedly, for a short period, undergoing an experience that is not *associated*, or integrated, with his or her surroundings. If normal functioning is not impaired by these occasional lapses and if the person can "snap out of it," there is no concern about pathological dissociation. However, there is a problem when one is unable to control these drifts of consciousness or behaviour. Putnam (1989) suggests that the

hallmarks of a pathological dissociative reaction are an alteration in sense of identity, varying from amnesia to alternating identities, and a disturbance of memory for events occurring during a period of dissociation, ranging from dreamlike recall of events to complete amnesia. Psychological trauma and emotional distress are commonly viewed as causal factors, even though people suffering from dissociative disorders may not be aware of any underlying emotional or psychological conflicts.

In earlier editions of the DSM, dissociative disorders were categorized as neuroses. This may seem a strange categorization, since the criteria for dissociative disorders do not include overt anxiety, which is the defining characteristic of the neuroses. The theory was, however, that loss of memory or changes in identity serve the purpose of hiding the underlying sources of anxiety from conscious awareness. Four types of dissociative disorders will be discussed in this chapter: dissociative amnesia, dissociative fugue, depersonalization, and dissociative identity disorder, which, prior to the publication of DSM-IV, was commonly referred to as multiple personality disorder. Table 8.1 outlines the characteristics of these four disorders.

Table 8.1 Types of Dissociative Disorders

Disorder	Description	Comment
Dissociative amnesia	Inability to recall important personal information	Can be used as a legal defence. Suppressed memories of sexual abuse would fit into this category.
Dissociative fugue	Sudden, unexpected flight from home; inability to remember past and who one is	Typically, someone turns up in another province or country wandering about unaware of his or her identity.
Dissociative identity disorder	Presence of two or more personalities	Formerly known as multiple personality disorder. The classic case is "The Three Faces of Eve" (Thigpen & Cleckley, 1957).
Depersonalization disorder	Feeling of being detached from oneself	Depersonalization experienced for a short period of time is very common and not pathological.

There is little good-quality research available on the prevalence rates of dissociative disorders, and generally these conditions have been viewed as quite rare. However, a Canadian study conducted in Winnipeg by Dr. Colin Ross, a psychiatrist at the University of Manitoba, suggested higher rates. In this investigation, individuals responded to questions on the Dissociative Experience Scale (Bernstein & Putnam, 1986). The results indicated that approximately 10 percent of adults reported symptoms often found in those suffering from a dissociative disorder: 7 percent with dissociative amnesia, 3 percent with dissociative identity disorder, 2 percent with depersonalization disorder, and 0.2 percent with dissociative fugue (Ross, 1991). However, the Dissociative Experience Scale is not intended as a diagnostic instrument but as a screening tool to be used in conjunction with a diagnostic workup, so these findings of symptoms are somewhat difficult to interpret. More recent research using standardized measures like the Dissociative Experience Scale and face-to-face interviews suggests that as many as 6 percent of the general population may experience occasional dissociative symptoms (Mulder, Beautrais, Joyce, & Ferguson, 1998), and a much smaller number actually suffer from a full-blown disorder.

DISSOCIATIVE AMNESIA

Everyone, at one time or another, forgets certain things. We forget what we went shopping for or where we put our keys, we forget a name or a loved one's birthday. Such forgetting is normal. In **dissociative amnesia**, however, a person does not forget just certain items. In this state there is a real and complete memory loss for extensive and important actions and/or personal information. Dissociative amnesia is characterized by a sudden onset, typically in response to a traumatic event or extremely stressful experience, and by an equally sudden re-

turn of memory. (see DSM table.) Memory loss stemming from substance abuse, head trauma, or other brain pathology is not considered dissociative amnesia.

In one form of dissociative amnesia, the memory loss is **localized**: the person cannot remember what happened during a specific period of time, quite often the first few hours after a traumatic experience. The person forgets some, but not all, of what happened during a given period, as in the Dorothy Joudrie case at the beginning of this chapter. Quite often in this condition the memory loss is for a disturbing event. A war veteran, for example, may remember a specific battle in great detail, but have no memory of the death of a close friend during the same battle. It has been estimated that between 5 and 14 percent of all mental disorders that emerge during warfare are cases of dissociative amnesia, making it the most common of the dissociative disorders (Loewenstein, 1991).

Generalized amnesia, in which an individual forgets his or her entire life history, and **continuous amnesia**, in which a person can remember nothing following a certain point in time, are two other subtypes of dissociative amnesia but both are extremely rare. Curiously enough, habits, tastes, and skills are retained in these dissociative states even though personal information may not be remembered. For example, an amnesic patient may continue to smoke even though he has no idea when he started smoking or even where he bought his last pack of cigarettes. Continuous amnesia is rare as a dissociative form of amnesia, but quite common in cases of amnesia having an organic basis. The forgotten or partially forgotten period is called the *amnesic episode*. During an amnesic episode a person experiencing difficulties with memory may not be aware of such difficulties. This individual may wander around aimlessly, or act puzzled or confused. Later, in an attempt to recall the events of the amnesic episode the individual may become aware of and quite distressed by this memory deficit.

Focus *Repressed Memory or False Memory?*

At the age of 23, Alana sought help from a therapist because of feelings of anxiety and depression and a general feeling that her life was not working out well. She had had several relationships with boyfriends that ended unpleasantly and she was concerned about her ability to make meaningful relationships. After several sessions of therapy, following efforts to recall her early relationship with her father by the use of hypnosis, she remembered, in a vague way at first, but subsequently in increasing detail, that her father had sexually abused her during her childhood. She was shocked but learned from her therapist that these traumatic memories had been **repressed** in order for her to survive in the family all these years. Although she had been somewhat distant from her father, she had not remembered this abuse for 17 years. She confronted her parents and both her father and mother denied any sexual abuse. With support from her therapist, she took her accusation to the police who, after some investigation, charged her father with sexual abuse. Her father claimed total innocence. After he was charged, he consulted a lawyer and learned about **false memory syndrome** (Loftus, 1993) in which people are induced by therapists to remember events that have never occurred. Loftus believes that therapists implant the memories by using leading questions and repeated suggestion and having patients use visualization and hypnosis to recover memories. For a riveting account of how Alana's father's lawyer could at-

tack the credibility of the story, read Loftus and Ketcham's book *Witness for the Defense: The Accused, the Eyewitness, and the Expert Who Puts Memory on Trial* (Loftus & Ketcham, 1991).

The concept of repressed memory derives from Freudian theory, which suggests that severely traumatic events can be entirely forgotten in order to protect the child from the severe anxiety from the event. This theory became clinically prominent with the publication of two influential books by Dr. Judith Lewis Herman, a psychiatrist at Harvard University (Herman, 1981, 1992). The suggestion in the first book was that incest could be remembered with little difficulty. The later book suggested that childhood trauma usually leads to repression or dissociation. The trauma and dissociation are pivotal to all dissociative disorders.

Dr. Joel Paris, a professor of psychiatry at McGill University, has pointed out the implicit assumptions associated with the trauma-repression hypothesis: (a) that the mind records memories of childhood accurately; (b) that sexual and physical abuse in childhood are frequently repressed or dissociated; and (c) that otherwise inaccessible traumatic memories can be accessed through psychotherapy and/or hypnosis. He goes on to cite considerable memory research that indicates most experiences are not recorded as with a video camera, but are distorted by various life events. Furthermore, they are often far from factually correct. In fact, as Loftus (1993) has pointed out, experimentally im-

planted false memories, once accepted as true by subjects, are reported as fact with enormous conviction, and are often embellished over time.

Furthermore, the theory that trauma causes repression has had little empirical support. There is little experimental evidence that memories can be repressed (Singer, 1990). To the contrary, studies with adults reveal that very traumatic events tend to cause the intrusive memories commonly associated with posttraumatic stress disorder (Horowitz, 1993). Nevertheless, it should be noted that, because this repression is believed to occur only with significant trauma, controlled research is not possible.

Finally, because there is no objective way to determine whether a memory elicited in psychotherapy is true or false (aside from corroborating evidence) it is generally impossible to establish the veracity of the recovered memory. There is considerable evidence that hypnosis can implant highly detailed but untrue memories. It is for this reason that in most jurisdictions, courts do not admit evidence that have emerged in hypnotic states (Paris, 1996).

In summary, most memory researchers do not accept that significant events such as repeated sexual abuse are likely to be completely forgotten for extended periods of time. It is generally accepted that because of guilt, shame, or fear of reprisal, children may not reveal their abuse, but they do not usually forget it. This, of course, does not prove that all such recovered or repressed memories are false. ▲

DISSOCIATIVE FUGUE

Dissociative fugue is the loss of memory with the added dimension of physical flight. Fugue derives from the Latin *fugere* ("to flee"), from which the word *fugitive* is also de-

rived. Two important features must be present for diagnosis: (1) sudden and unexpected travel away from home or work; (2) the inability to recall one's past and confusion about personal identity. (See DSM table.) A person suffering from dissociative fugue leaves the comfort of home and familiar surroundings, and assumes a completely new identity. These new

DSM-IV Diagnostic Criteria for Dissociative Amnesia

A. The predominant disturbance is one or more episodes of inability to recall important personal information, usually of a traumatic or stressful nature, that is too extensive to be explained by ordinary forgetfulness.

Note: DSM-IV criteria for dissociative and somatoform disorders require that the symptoms not be due to the effects of a substance, to a physical cause, or to other psychological disorders that would better explain the symptoms. Most sets of criteria include that the symptoms cause clinically significant distress or impairment in social, occupational, or other important areas of functioning.

Source: Reprinted with permission from the *Diagnostic and Statistical Manual of Mental Disorders*, Fourth Edition. Copyright 1994 American Psychiatric Association.

identities can be quite elaborate, lasting for years, and individuals may display behaviour that is very different from their previous habits. People suffering from dissociative fugue have even been known to remarry, oblivious to their existing spouses and families! More commonly, however, the fugue is less dramatic and much briefer. When these individuals emerge from their fugue state they may find themselves in unknown places surrounded by strangers. To confuse matters, a complete amnesia for their fugue period may then occur. Recurrences of dissociative amnesia are extremely rare, as is the disorder itself, affecting only 0.2 percent of the population. As with dissociative amnesia, dissociative fugue usually follows a severely stressful event. Stressors such as marital discord, personal failures, natural disasters, and service during war may precipitate a state of fugue. There is some evidence avoidance plays an important role in the development of both disorders; some adolescent runaways are suspected of being in a state of fugue (Loewenstein, 1991).

It is important to distinguish a fugue state from malingering. Making a false claim of amnesia in order to escape responsibility would constitute malingering. As an example, a person very dissatisfied with his or her life might run away and establish a new identify; when finally found, such a person might claim to be amnesic to avoid blame.

DEPERSONALIZATION DISORDER

Have you ever experienced *déjà vu*, the brief but very odd feeling that an event has happened before? Have you ever suddenly felt like a stranger or like a robot during social interactions? Such experiences are called **depersonalization**, and are quite normal, as long as they are occasional and transitory. In fact, they are reported to occur in up to 70 percent of young adults (Ross, 1991). It is only when such experiences are persistent, recurring, and personally distressing that they are considered pathological. (See DSM table.)

Depersonalization disorder has a sudden onset and is usually confined to adolescence or early adulthood. Individuals suffering from depersonalization feel unreal and disconnected from the self. Their experiences include feeling as though they are in a dream and are outside observers of their own thoughts, actions, and bodies. All depersonalization experiences are "as if" feelings involving only limited splitting between conscious and unconscious mental processes. For example, a person may say "I feel as if I'm outside my body, as if I'm an alien." But the person does not believe this to be literally so. In this way, depersonalization is unlike schizophrenia, in which the illusory experiences are interpreted as real and may constitute part of a delusional belief.

Although depersonalization is listed with the dissociative disorders, it does not share with the other disorders the common feature of memory loss or identity confusion. This has sparked some controversy among diagnosticians over the appropriateness of its categorization. Some suggest it should not even be considered a disorder because of its frequent occurrence in the general population.

DSM-IV Diagnostic Criteria for Depersonalization Disorder

A. Persistent or recurrent experiences of feeling detached from, and as if one is an outside observer of, one's mental processes or body (e.g., feeling like one is in a dream).

B. During the depersonalization experience, reality testing remains intact.

Source: Reprinted with permission from the *Diagnostic and Statistical Manual of Mental Disorders*, Fourth Edition. Copyright 1994 American Psychiatric Association.

Jane is 32 years old, is unmarried, and has been employed as a clerk in the women's shoe section of a department store for eight years. She is lonely and depressed and has been on Prozac (fluoxetine) for a year. She manages reasonably well and has not missed work more than two days a month, and although she has thought of suicide she has not made any attempts. Two months ago, because she was not getting better, her family doctor referred her to a psychologist. He interviewed Jane extensively and "discovered" that she had multiple personality (DSM-IV diagnosis of Dissociative Identity Disorder). Four of Jane's "personalities" have been uncovered so far. Tanya is a more outgoing personality than Jane normally manifests; she likes flamboyant clothing, talks loudly, and is also more creative, enjoying drawing. Carrie is shy, childlike, and eager to please; she seems to know very little about Jane's life. Joanne is a dogged and determined personality, who takes over when Jane feels too overwhelmed or tired to cope with life. Devon is a "male" personality who sometimes takes over when Jane is overwrought and goes for long, rapid walks in neighbourhoods Jane would find frightening. Jane has been seeing the psychologist twice a week and is very pleased with his work.

DSM-IV Diagnostic Criteria for Dissociative Fugue

A. The predominant disturbance is sudden, unexpected travel away from home or one's customary place of work, with inability to recall one's past.

B. Confusion about personal identity or assumption of a new identity (partial or complete).

Source: Reprinted with permission from the *Diagnostic and Statistical Manual of Mental Disorders*, Fourth Edition. Copyright 1994 American Psychiatric Association.

When her case is reviewed by the insurance company that covers the extended health coverage at her workplace, they decide to stop covering the cost of her treatment because, according to their medical advisers, the diagnosis of dissociative identity disorder (multiple personality) is scientifically dubious. Jane attempts suicide by consuming 30 Prozac tablets and 30 aspirin. She calls her mother, who takes her to the emergency department of the local hospital. She is discharged the next morning to be followed up by the mental health team in three days.

DISSOCIATIVE IDENTITY DISORDER

Imagine finding yourself in a place you don't recognize and having no idea how you got there, dressed in clothes you don't remember putting on, and having strangers tell you about things you have done but don't remember: things that are totally out of character for you. These are just a few examples of the bizarre experiences of people with Dissociative Identity Disorder. Dissociative Identity Disorder is the new DSM-IV label for what was formerly called Multiple Personality Disorder (MPD). The new name is based on a defining feature of this disorder, that certain aspects of a person's identity become detached or dissociated. The name was also intended to end the misconception that multiple people are somehow living inside one body.

Dissociative identity disorder (DID) is the most severe and chronic of the dissociative disorders and is characterized by the existence of two or more unique personalities in a single individual. (See DSM table.) Each personality, or **alter**, may be a very distinct entity, having its own constellation of behaviour, tone of voice, and physical gestures. Sometimes the personalities may be almost polar opposites. Various personalities may require different eyeglass prescriptions and have different allergies (Miller et al., 1991). The alters may also differ in the age and gender they claim to be, as well as race and family history (Coons, Bowman, & Milstein, 1988). A formal diagnosis requires that the existence of alters be chronic and severe (causing personal distress) and not result from the ingestion of some drug.

Alters may or may not be aware of one another. There are generally three kinds of relationships: *mutually amnesic* (no awareness of one another), *mutually cognizant* (well aware of one another), and *one-way amnesic* (some are aware of others but this awareness is not reciprocated). For DID to be diagnosed there must be at least two alters which exert control over the person's behaviour, causing the person to suffer lapses in memory for the period of time the other alter was in charge.

The transition from one alter to another is called a **switch**. A switch occurs suddenly and is often precipitated by stress or some other identifiable cue in the surrounding environment. Artificial precipitants like hypnotic suggestion can also elicit such change (Brende & Rinsley, 1981; Smith, 1993).

New postures, facial expressions, and patterns of facial wrinkling can emerge during a switch. Researchers have also found physiological differences between alters in autonomic nervous system activity, blood pressure levels, and even menstrual cycles (Putnam, Zahn, & Post, 1990).

It is commonly believed the age of onset for dissociative identity disorder is during childhood, even though it is not usually diagnosed until adulthood. Many researchers believe a single episode, or recurring episodes, of abuse may be considered as the major determinant in the development of this disorder (Beitcham et al., 1992; Bliss, 1984; Briere & Runtz, 1988; Kluft, 1987; Sanders & Giolas, 1991). Furthermore, there are reports that as many as 97 percent of DID patients have been physically and/or sexually abused during their childhood (Ross et al., 1990). DID occurs three to nine times as often in women as in men (APA, 1994); it has been suggested that this prevalence reflects the greater risk of sexual abuse in women.

Until the late 1980s MPD was generally considered to be rare. The first case of MPD to be formally reported was in 1817 (Boor, 1982), and by the early 1960s a literature review was able to identify only 77 cases, most of which were reported between 1890 and 1920 (Sutcliffe & Jones, 1962). By 1970, 100 cases had been reported in professional journals, by the mid-1970s, 200 cases had been reported, rising to 300 cases by the late 1970s and then doubling by the early 1980s! This rapid increase in reported cases led to much debate over the true prevalence of MPD. It was suggested that this increase was a result of the increasing prevalence of child sexual abuse, which is hypothesized to play a major role in the etiology of dissociative disorders (Kluft, 1987). However, it is not clear that child sexual abuse is increasing (Feldman et al., 1991); some argue that only the recognition of abuse is growing.

As the incidence of DID rose, considerable skepticism was expressed concerning its very existence (Dell, 1988). In fact, there is considerable evidence that the dramatic increase in the diagnosis of DID is largely a North American phenomenon. This diagnosis is rarely made in France despite the fact that French theorists played an important role in the early work on multiple personality disorder and the French are still very influential in psychodynamic theory and practice. Furthermore, DID is rarely diagnosed in Great Britain, Russia and India, Japan, and Switzerland (Spanos, 1996). To add to the confusion, however, research with psychiatric patients in the Netherlands and Turkey reports dissociative identity disorder rates similar to those found in the United States (Tutkun et al., 1998). It is unclear whether these differences are due to cultural influences or to different characteristics of those seeking psychiatric help.

Part of the notoriety of this diagnosis arose from its use as a legal defence in several sensational U.S. court cases in the 1970s and 1980s. Billy Milligan was the first person in U.S. history to be found not guilty of major crimes by reason of insanity, because he suffered from multiple personality disorder. He was found not guilty of a series of rape/abductions by reason of insanity and sentenced to a mental institution, only to be released six years later. Another widely publicized case was that of Kenneth Bianchi, better known as the Hillside Strangler. Unlike Milligan, Bianchi was found guilty of his crimes and his defence based on multiple personality disorder was rejected. The trial raised the question of whether MPD was a true disorder or just an act to avoid punishment or to achieve otherwise unattainable goals (Dell, 1988).

Merskey (1992) has argued the phenomenon of DID or MPD is created by the power of suggestion, similar to that of hypnotic suggestion. For example, in laboratory studies, hypnotized subjects have been shown to have an increased tolerance to pain when given various suggestions, such as that a particular body part is numb and insensate (Kihlstrom, 1984). Could multiple personalities likewise be the result of suggestions? If a person who had had a blackout were told that another part of his or her being would like to come forward and talk, would that be enough to develop an alter? To counteract such skepticism, some researchers have looked to physiological measures, since they are regarded as less subject to conscious control, and have demonstrated greater differences in autonomic nervous system activity of MPD patients than for controls (Putnam, Zahn, & Post, 1990). Yet even this evidence is not conclusive; research into biofeedback has shown that some individuals can develop remarkable control over a great number of autonomic functions.

DSM-IV Diagnostic Criteria for Dissociative Identity Disorder

A. The presence of two or more distinct identities or personality states (each with its own relatively enduring pattern of perceiving, relating to, and thinking about the environment and self).

B. At least two of these identities or personality states recurrently take control of the person's behavior.

C. Inability to recall important personal information that is too extensive to be explained by ordinary forgetfulness.

Note: In children, the symptoms are not attributable to imaginary playmates or other fantasy play.

Source: Reprinted with permission from the *Diagnostic and Statistical Manual of Mental Disorders,* Fourth Edition. Copyright 1994 American Psychiatric Association.

However, there is an increase in support for a move away from the disease model toward a sociocognitive perspective in understanding DID. According to Dr. Nick Spanos, multiple identity enactments are seen in many cultures, and just like the phenomenon of DID in North America, they are socially constructed; "It is context bounded, goal-directed, social behaviour geared to the expectations of significant others, and its characteristics have changed over time to meet changing expectations" (Spanos, 1994, p. 143).

VIEWPOINT *Multiple Identities: Disorder or Role-Playing?*

Dr. Nick Spanos, a distinguished Canadian psychologist from Carleton University in Ottawa, who died in an airplane crash in 1994, was one of the most articulate opponents of DID. He proposed that multiple personalities are produced by role-playing. According to Spanos, cases of DID are not legitimate diagnoses but are iatrogenic conditions unintentionally caused by practitioners (Spanos, 1994). During the same time as the Bianchi trial, Spanos and his colleagues were working on an ingenious experiment to support the possibility that a person may adopt another personality in order to avoid punishment (Spanos, Weekes, & Bertrand, 1985). The experimental manipulations used in the study were derived from an actual interview with Bianchi himself.

In the Spanos study, undergraduate students were told they would play the role of an accused murderer, who has pled not guilty despite a wealth of evidence. They were also told that they would take part in a simulated psychiatric interview, which might involve hypnosis. The subjects were then assigned to one of three experimental conditions: the Bianchi condition (consisting of a rudimentary hypnotic induction and instruction to let a second personality come forward), the Hidden Part condition (hypnosis with a suggestion that they may have hidden parts of themselves), and a "control" condition (subjects were not hypnotized and were given even less explicit information about the possible existence of any hidden part). Subjects were then interviewed by a "psychiatrist'" (experimental assistant) who probed for a second personality and who asked questions about the facts of the murder. Eighty-one percent of the subjects in the Bianchi condition

adopted a new name, and many admitted guilt for their murders.

In an additional exploration, those who had acknowledged another personality were given a personality test in each of their two personalities. The results indicated considerable differences between the two personality conditions. The Spanos study demonstrated that under certain demand conditions some individuals seem able to assume additional personalities. It is clear from research results that some individuals are particularly susceptible to suggestion and may develop additional states that are "personality-like." However, these laboratory analogues have not approached the breadth and intensity of behaviour found in many real patients seeking help for DID. Nor does the fact that role-playing is possible prove that all cases of DID are enactments.

VIEWPOINT *continued*

Critical Thinking Questions

1. Our legal system has recognized diminished responsibility for those inebriated while committing certain acts that cause grave harm to others (for example, killing someone while driving drunk, or assaulting someone while drunk). Some professionals have suggested that individuals suffering from Dissociative Identity Disorder should be treated the same way. They argue that if an individual's alter that is not under the control of someone's stronger and predominant personality commits a serious offense, the individual should not be seen as fully responsible. Do you think this is reasonable? What options would you suggest?

2. There is considerable evidence that some psychotherapists are particularly likely to have patients who demonstrate DID after they enter therapy. There is also considerable evidence that some individuals are particularly susceptible to revealing or developing DID only after they have entered psychotherapy.

Do you think there should be guidelines concerning procedures to be followed in the event that a therapist suspects DID in a patient?

3. Proponents of the existence of DID present evidence that in certain DID patients there is some indication of different physiological (for example, autonomic) states portrayed by different alters. Do you think this is strong evidence in support of the diagnosis of DID? Are there alternative explanations for this type of phenomenon?

ETIOLOGY

Dissociative disorders have always fascinated professionals and have resulted in a considerable body of literature. Nevertheless, compared to most other disorders, there has been relatively little systematic research into these disorders.

The majority of cultures that have been studied acknowledge conditions in which another entity takes over the body and mind of an afflicted individual. In some societies these dissociative experiences or trances are not viewed as pathological but are valued as part of religious experiences.

Putnam (1989) proposes that the vast majority of dissociative disorders are a result of intense psychological trauma. Dissociation can be a normal process initially used by an individual to handle traumatic experiences. However, in some individuals under some circumstances it can develop into a maladaptive or pathological process leading to a dissociative disorder.

Despite the skepticism of some professionals concerning DID, the reference to trauma in the history of those demonstrating dissociation and DID has considerable support. There have been many reports of physical and/or sexual abuse rates of more than 50 percent in patients diagnosed with DID (Ross, 1991; Tutkun, Sar, Yargic, Ozpulat, Yanik, & Kiziltan, 1998). In a very interesting New Zealand investigation, a randomly selected group of more than 1000 individuals were given a face-to-face semistructured interview. More than 6 percent reported some dissociative experiences. There was a significant positive correlation between childhood physical and/or sexual abuse and the measures of dissociation. However, the correlation was moderated by whether individuals had a psychiatric problem: if childhood abuse resulted in a psychological problem, then the problem had a significant dissociative component (Mulder, Beautrais, Joyce, & Ferguson, 1998).

Psychodynamic theories, many of which predated sophisticated epidemiological studies, have eloquently proposed that dissociative disorders are a function of the fundamental defence mechanism of massive repression. Generally, the repression wards off the anxiety precipitated by a severe psychological trauma. Consistently with psychodynamic theories, most of these traumatic events occur during childhood. More recent theorizing has accepted that in vulnerable individuals, dissociative amnesia and fugue may also arise years after experiencing stress as an adult. For example, it is common for individuals to experience amnesia or fugues years after dangerous military conflict, natural disasters such as floods or fires, or extreme marital conflict. In the psychodynamic view, these overwhelming traumatic events, which often have no apparent solution, cause such psychic pain that the only defence is to avoid thinking of or remembering these experiences. Repression then acts to spare the person this intolerable pain. Amnesia or fugue, which are the ultimate in avoidance of psychic pain, are possible results of these repressed traumas.

In dissociative identity disorder, the psychodynamic theorists suggest that repeated trauma, such as that associated with sexual or physical abuse, may lead a child to fantasize about being another person who is safely watching or protected from the abuse. This fantasy can become extremely pathological and develop into other personalities (Schreiber, 1973).

The behavioural view, although expressed differently, has many similarities to the psychodynamic perspective. Both hold that the dissociative disorders are a result of traumatic events and that individuals develop methods of reducing the associated anxiety. Furthermore, both acknowledge that individuals are unaware of the origin of their disorder. Behavioural theorists refer to learning theories: thoughts and actions that relieve anxiety or enhance pleasurable states are repeated. In the initial stages of a dissociative disorder, these thoughts or behaviours may be fortuitous, but as their immediate consequences are relief or pleasure, they are elaborated and strengthened. This sequence presents a blueprint for the development of alters in dissociative identity disorder.

TREATMENT

Whereas dissociative amnesia and fugue often self-correct within a short period time with few lingering problems, the prognosis for multiple personality disorder is not so optimistic. There is little evidence these individuals get better without professional help. However, even though there have been many decades of treatment for individuals with dissociative disorders, the treatment programs are not well developed. Furthermore, there have been very few attempts to evaluate the success of treatment for these individuals.

Psychodynamic interventions are probably the most widely used form of treatment for individuals suffering from dissociative disorders. The traditional approaches of free association, examining the unconscious, and identifying defence mechanisms (such as repression), seem to fit the hypothesized development of these problems. These explorations are well suited to the recovery of memories, whether repressed or forgotten. Therefore, many non-psychodynamic clinicians are quite supportive of this approach for the dissociative disorders (Loewenstein, 1991).

As mentioned earlier, there is some support for the belief that hypnotic states are implicated in the development and maintenance of the dissociative disorders (Merskey, 1992).

There is also growing evidence that people with dissociative disorders score higher on measures of hypnotizability (Frischolz, Lipman, Braun, & Sachs, 1992). In fact, psychoanalysis has its roots in the work of Mesmer and Charcot, who believed that hypnosis was key to the treatment of patients with dissociative symptoms. So it is not surprising that hypnosis has long been used for the treatment of the dissociative disorders. Clinicians use hypnosis to assist patients in recovering otherwise inaccessible memories. They may also use hypnosis to find other personalities or identities in such individuals.

There is no evidence of medication having any significant role in the treatment of dissociative disorders. However, antidepressant and antianxiety medications are often used to treat the depression and anxiety often evident in these patients. One other medication, sodium amobarbital (Amytal), often called "truth serum," has found a role in the treatment of individuals with dissociative identity disorders. This medication sedates people and lowers their inhibitions, which often leads to the recall of previously unreported events (Spiegel, 1994). As is true of most medications, Amytal does not work for everyone and sometimes people forget what they recalled under the influence of the medication. Because of the limited effectiveness of medication on the dissociative disorders, it is generally used only in conjunction with other forms of treatment.

SOMATOFORM DISORDERS

Somatoform disorders describe a set of disorders that have as their basis the occurrence of physical symptoms for which there is no known physical cause, excessive preoccupation with minor physical symptoms, or excessive concern about normal bodily functioning. The Somatoform Disorders category of the DSM-IV includes Conversion Disorder, Hypochondriasis, Somatization Disorder, Pain Disorder, and Body Dysmorphic Disorder (see Table 8.2). Somatoform disorders often appear to be physical disorders, but when investigated, no evidence of physical disorder can be found. The lack of evidence, however, does not necessarily indicate that there *is* no physical cause but merely that there is no *known* physical cause sufficient to account for the symptoms. It is not uncommon that individuals in the early stages of medical diseases are misdiagnosed as having somatoform disorders (Slater & Glithero, 1965).

Somatoform disorders must be distinguished from malingering and factitious disorders. **Malingering** is deliberately pretending to be ill in order to achieve some specific objective (for example, receiving insurance money, evading military service, avoiding an exam). Similarly, people with **factitious disorders** deliberately fake or bring on symptoms of illness (for example, they might take excessive amounts of laxatives or other medication) to gain their doctor's attention and thus satisfy a need to play the role of a patient. People with somatoform disorders, on the other hand, truly believe that they have a serious physical problem. It has been estimated that between 30 and 80 percent of patients who visit primary care physicians have symptoms for which no physical cause can be found (Barsky & Klerman, 1983). For obvious reasons, these patients are not likely to seek psychological help, so only a very small number are ever treated by mental health professionals.

CONVERSION DISORDER

Conversion disorder occurs when a person experiences motor symptoms (for example, paralysis) or disturbances in sensory functioning (for example, loss of vision) that appear to be a result of a neurological problem, but for which no physical cause can be found. (See DSM table.) This disorder was previously known as "hysteria," from the Greek word *hystera* ("uterus"). Hippocrates thought that this disease was restricted to women and that it was caused by the wandering of the uterus throughout the body in search of a child. (See Chapter 1.) At the time, marriage was considered the best cure for hysteria.

Freud was the first to use the term "conversion" in describing this disorder. He hypothesized that these symptoms developed as a result of repressed anxiety, which was rechannelled and converted into a physical symptom. For example, unconscious psychosexual conflict (and its resulting anxiety) concerning masturbation might result in a paralysis of the hand. Conversion disorder usually develops in response to severe stress in adolescence or early adulthood (Folks, Ford, & Regan,

Table 8.2 **Somatoform Disorders**

Somatization Disorder	Multiple symptoms including pain, gastrointestinal problems, sexual problems, pseudo-neurological symptoms.	Best described as having multiple symptoms without known cause.
Conversion Disorder	Symptoms are involuntary motor or sensory functions, for example hysterical blindness, paralysis, or lack of feeling (anesthesia).	Conversion disorders are now quite unusual and are seen primarily in very poorly educated individuals or in primitive societies.
Pain Disorder	Pain without sufficient known physical cause.	Pain disorder is very common and a leading cause of lost days of work.
Hypochondriasis	Excessive concern about serious illness when there is no underlying illness.	The most common diseases people worry about are cancer and heart disease. Often leads to "doctor shopping."
Body Dysmorphic Disorder	Severe preoccupation with defect in appearance in any part of the body.	Also known as dysmorphophobia. There may be ideas of reference ("Everyone is looking at my ugly nose").

1984). DSM-IV diagnostic criteria stipulate that the disorder must not be feigned (as in malingering or factitious disorder) and that psychological factors are judged to be the primary cause of the symptom. These symptoms must also cause significant distress or social or occupational impairment.

There are three categories of conversion symptoms: *sensory*, *motor*, and *visceral*. Sensory symptoms include **anesthesia** (loss of sensitivity), **hyperesthesia** (excessive sensitivity), **analgesia** (loss of sensitivity to pain), and **paresthesia** (bizarre sensations such as tingling). Motor symptoms include paralysis (usually restricted to one limb or side of the body), tremors, and tics. Patients may also experience **aphonia**, which is an inability to talk above a whisper. Visceral symptoms include a persistent "lump in the throat," choking, coughing, belching, and nausea.

Although conversion disorders can be extremely difficult to diagnose, there are certain factors that differentiate them from true neurological problems. People with conversion disorder frequently (but not always) show signs of *la belle indifference* or surprising unconcern about the severity of their symptoms. Those with the disorder also often do not experience secondary symptoms consistent with their primary complaint. For example, someone with limb paralysis might not exhibit the signs of atrophy usually seen with such a problem. Or the dysfunction experienced by conversion disorder patients may be selective. A person may be unable to write, but able to use the same muscles to perform other activities. People suffering from conversion-disordered blindness may nonetheless avoid bumping into furniture. Finally, unlike true neurological disorders, symptoms of conversion disorder can sometimes disappear under hypnosis or with drugs.

One of the criteria traditionally used to diagnose conversion disorder is that the symptoms do not make anatomical sense. **Glove anesthesia** is an example. The patient experiences loss of sensation only on the part of the hand that would be covered by a glove (see Figure 8.1), although the nerve fibres in the hand run all the way up the arm. Nevertheless, a disease commonly diagnosed today—carpal tunnel syndrome—can cause symptoms that are very similar to glove anesthesia. Indeed, more frequently than we would like, a physical complaint originally diagnosed as a conversion disorder later turns out to be a true medical illness (Bridges, Goldberg, Evans, & Sharpe, 1991). Misdiagnosis can occur because medical technology cannot always pick up diseases in their early states.

DSM-IV Diagnostic Criteria for Conversion Disorder

A. One or more symptoms or deficits affecting voluntary motor or sensory function that suggest a neurological or other general medical condition.

B. Psychological factors are judged to be associated with the symptom or deficit because the initiation or exacerbation of the symptom or deficit is preceded by conflicts or other stressors.

C. The symptom or deficit is not intentionally produced or feigned (as in Factitious Disorder or Malingering).

D. The symptom or deficit cannot, after appropriate investigation, be fully explained by a general medical condition, or by the direct effects of a substance, or as a culturally sanctioned behavior or experience.

E. The symptom or deficit causes clinically significant distress or impairment in social, occupational, or other important areas of functioning or warrants medical evaluation.

F. The symptom or deficit is not limited to pain or sexual dysfunction, does not occur exclusively during the course of Somatization Disorder, and is not better accounted for by another mental disorder.

Source: Reprinted with permission from the *Diagnostic and Statistical Manual of Mental Disorders*, Fourth Edition. Copyright 1994 American Psychiatric Association.

Figure 8.1 Glove Anesthesia

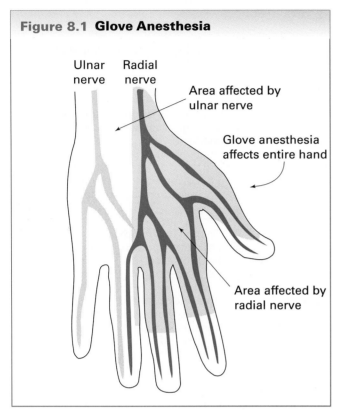

Source: Comer (1995).

The non-coloured area represents the area affected by the ulnar nerve and the coloured area represents the area affected by the radial nerve. It would be expected that a person with nerve damage would have loss of sensation in one of these areas. However, people with glove anesthesia lose sensation in the entire hand and part of the arm.

The most famous case of conversion disorder is that of "Anna O.," referred to earlier. She developed conversion symptoms while caring for her dying father. While sitting by his bedside one day, she imagined that she saw a black snake trying to attack him. When she tried to reach for the snake, she found she could not move her arm. She then imagined that the fingers of her right hand turned into small black snakes. After this episode, she experienced paralysis in her right hand and side. In addition, she had periods of deafness and also became unable to speak her native tongue (German), although she remained fluent in English.

Conversion disorder appears to have declined in prevalence. During the late nineteenth century, Freud, Breuer, and the French physician Jean Martin Charcot (1825–1893) reported treating many cases of hysteria. Today, prevalence estimates range from about 1 to 3 percent (Carson, Butcher, & Mineka, 1998). The decline may reflect, at least in part, a decline in misdiagnosis due to our increasing understanding of neurological symptoms, as was discussed with glove anesthesia. Although women are more often diagnosed with conversion disorder, 20 to 40 percent of cases occur in men (Folks et al., 1984). During World War I, conversion disorder was diag-nosed frequently in soldiers who had experienced extremely difficult conditions and intense combat (Merskey, 1995).

HYPOCHONDRIASIS

Do you have friends or relatives who are always complaining of some disease or disorder even though they are quite healthy? We usually say they are "hypochondriacs." **Hypochondriasis** is defined as excessive preoccupation with fears of having a serious illness, despite physicians' assurances that these fears are groundless. (See DSM table.) The ancient Greeks called the region below the ribs *hypochondria*, and thought that it was linked to changes in mood and mental functioning. Ulcers, for example, were once classified as part of the "hypochondriacal syndrome." As we learn more about the causes of disease, fewer illnesses are included in this category (Barsky, Wyshak, & Klerman, 1986).

Hypochondriasis is diagnosed when an individual misinterprets minor bodily symptoms (for example, occasional heart palpitations) as evidence of a serious disease, and the preoccupation persists for at least six months despite appropriate medical evaluation and reassurance. In order to be diagnosed with this illness, the patient must also experience significant distress or disruptions in occupational or social functioning.

Hypochondriacs may complain of a variety of symptoms, but are often unable to adequately describe them. They are likely to read a popular magazines on medical topics and then become convinced that they have the latest illnesses. They tend to seek medical advice frequently, but are often disappointed when no sign of illness is found. "Doctor shopping" is common, and interactions with doctors are often dissatisfying and fraught with tension. For their part, physicians often become frustrated with hypochondriacs because of the apparent waste of medical time. Hypochondriacs also tend to use large amounts of over-the-counter medication and herbal remedies designed to relieve vague symptoms such as "tired blood."

DSM-IV Diagnostic Criteria for Hypochondriasis

A. Preoccupation with fears of having, or the idea that one has, a serious disease based on the person's misinterpretation of bodily symptoms.

B. The preoccupation persists despite appropriate medical evaluation and reassurance.

C. The belief in Criterion A is not of delusional intensity (as in Delusional Disorder, Somatic Type) and is not restricted to a circumscribed concern about appearance (as in Body Dysmorphic Disorder).

D. The preoccupation causes clinically significant distress or impairment in social, occupational, or other important areas of functioning.

E. The duration of the disturbance is at least 6 months.

Source: Reprinted with permission from the *Diagnostic and Statistical Manual of Mental Disorders*, Fourth Edition. Copyright 1994 American Psychiatric Association.

It is estimated that between 4 and 9 percent of patients seen in general medical practice suffer from hypochondriasis (Barsky, Wyshak, Klerman, & Latham, 1990). Although like other somatoform disorders it was once considered to affect primarily women, it actually affects men and women equally often (Kellner, 1986; Kirmayer, Robbins, & Paris, 1994). It can occur at any age, but peak periods for onset occur in adolescence, middle age, and after the age of 60 (Kellner, 1986).

The key symptom of hypochondriasis is excessive fear of developing a serious illness, making it somewhat difficult to distinguish from anxiety disorders such as panic disorder. Hypochondriasis is often comorbid with mood and anxiety disorders (Barsky, Wyshak, & Klerman, 1992; Noyes, Kathol, Fisher, Phillips, & Suezer, 1994). Like sufferers of panic disorder, hypochondriacs often overreact to and misinterpret somatic symptoms. However, the focus of the preoccupation differs somewhat. Patients with panic disorder are concerned with immediate effects of an illness (for example, I will have a heart attack and die here), whereas hypochondriacs are more concerned about the long-term implications of their symptoms to their health. This is a rather fine distinction, however, and Barlow and Durand (1995) have concluded that hypochondriasis is essentially an anxiety disorder.

SOMATIZATION DISORDER

Terri, 34, has had sporadic back pain for several years; each bout of pain would clear up after a few days' rest and lots of aspirin or ibuprofen. But three years ago everything seemed to go wrong. One day at her secretarial job, she twisted to catch a piece of paper that slipped from her desk and her back "went out." She went home and just never got better. Neither her family doctor nor an orthopedic surgeon could find anything wrong, so she was denied Workers' Compensation.

Terri's pain is constant but is made worse by activity. Her pain is worst in her lower back but she has pains all over. She walks bent over. Her right arm is often numb or tingling. She has had migraine headaches since she was 14; now she has dull headaches almost every day, which sometimes peak into a migraine. She also has premenstrual distress and cramping menstrual pain. She feels bloated and has a lot of gas. She spends most of her time watching TV or resting. She takes 16 aspirin with codeine a day, which she buys over the counter. She sleeps terribly and is depressed. She ruminates about killing herself.

Her husband Gary was supportive for a long time but now mostly avoids her. They have not had sex for 18 months. He worries about Terri but feels she has not helped herself. Both are furious with the doctors who have not helped at all. Gary wonders if he should get out of the marriage now while he is still young enough to find someone else. He feels guilty for having these thoughts.

Somatization disorder was formerly called *Briquet's syndrome* after Paul Briquet, a French physician who first described the condition in 1859. It is characterized by multiple complaints of physical ailments that do not appear to have any organic basis. A wide range of symptoms are reported. Table 8.3 shows the range and frequency of reported symptoms in a 1962 sample. These symptoms typically begin in early adulthood (before the age of 30) and last for years (Cloninger, Martin, Guze, & Clayton, 1986). To meet DSM-IV diagnostic criteria, the individual must complain of four pain symptoms at four different sites (for example, head, neck, joints, back), two gastrointestinal symptoms (food intolerances, diarrhea, vomiting), one sexual symptom other than pain, and one pseudoneurological symptom (for example, limb paralysis for which there is no apparent physical cause). These symptoms must cause significant impairment in social and occupational functioning.

Patients suffering from somatization disorder often appear overdramatic and discuss their symptoms in excruciating detail. They typically present their current symptoms as part of a long medical history, and may even keep daily records of bowel movements and other bodily functions. Many believe that they have been sick for their entire lives. They are likely to visit numerous physicians and consume massive amounts of over-the-counter medication.

People with somatization disorder, hypochondriasis, or pain disorder often become frustrated with physicians and embark on an intense search for the drug or device that will solve their problems.

Table 8.3 Reported Symptoms in a Sample of Patients with Somatization Disorder

Symptom	Percent Reporting	Symptom	Percent Reporting	Symptom	Percent Reporting
Dysapnea (laboured breathing)	72	Sudden fluctuations in weight	16	Back pain	88
Palpitation	60	Anorexia	60	Joint pain	84
Chest pain	72	Nausea	80	Extremity pain	84
Dizziness	84	Vomiting	32	Burning pains in rectum, vagina, mouth	28
Headache	80	Abdominal pain	80	Other bodily pain	36
Anxiety attacks	64	Abdominal bloating	68	Depressed feelings	64
Fatigue	84	Food intolerances	48	Phobias	48
Blindness	20	Diarrhea	20	Vomiting all nine months of pregnancy	20
Paralysis	12	Constipation	64	Nervous	92
Anesthesia	32	Dysuria (painful urination)	44	Had to quit working because felt bad	44
Aphonia (loss of voice above a whisper)	44	Urinary retention	8	Trouble doing anything because felt bad	72
Lump in throat	28	Dysmenorrhea (painful menstruation, premarital only)	4	Cried a lot	70
Fits or convulsions	20	Dysmenorrhea (prepregnancy only)	8	Felt life was hopeless	28
Faints	56	Dysmenorrhea (other)	48	Always sickly (most of life)	40
Unconsciousness	16	Menstrual irregularity	48	Thought of dying	48
Amnesia	8	Excessive menstrual bleeding	48	Wanted to die	36
Visual blurring	64	Sexual indifference	44	Thought of suicide	28
Visual hallucination	12	Frigidity (absence of orgasm)	24	Attempted suicide	12
Deafness	4	Dyspareunia (painful sexual intercourse)	52		
Olfactory hallucination	16				
Weakness	84				
Weight loss	28				

Source: After M. Perley & S. B. Guze, Hysteria: The stability and usefulness of clinical criteria, *New England Journal of Medicine, 266(1962)*, 421–426.

....

PAIN DISORDER

Christina is a bright and personable 14-year-old, well liked by her teachers and peers. A straight-A student, she was active in team sports until she developed a constant, burning pain in her right flank and upper leg three years ago. The pain was exacerbated by walking. After two years, it spread until she hurt all over.

She had her appendix removed but the pathology report found no evidence of inflammation. She was referred to the children's hospital, where she got a "million-dollar workup," including investigation for potential sexual abuse, gynecological problems, rheumatological problems, cancer, orthopedic disorder, kidney disease, gastrointestinal disease, and neurological problems. She has had CAT scans, X-rays, MRI studies, nerve conduction studies, and dozens of blood and urine tests. All have tested normal.

Her pain makes walking difficult. She has often been awakened from sleep by her pain. Yet, when asked "How are you?" she says she is doing fine. She has stopped all sports and other extracurricular activities. She has not missed much school and is still at the top of her class. She plans to go to medical school and become a pediatrician. Her mother has frequent migraine headaches. Her father has been on disability for two years because of heart disease. He had had significant pain from angina but, after an angioplasty, is about to return to work. Christina's younger brother has knee pain.

Christina was helped by encouragement and support from a psychologist, who taught her progressive relaxation and cognitive techniques, and also received some relief of pain from anesthetic blocks. When her leg pain was in remission, the other pains gradually subsided. The pain clinic thought her pain was due to undetectable nerve damage and sensitization that produced the rest of her pain.

Chronic pain is a major health care problem that affects approximately 50 million Americans (and by rough extrapolation about 5 million Canadians) and costs billions of dollars in health care and lost productivity (Turk & Okifuji, 1998). As a result, **pain disorder** is the best studied of the somatoform disorders. (See DSM table.) Pain has historically been divided into two separate categories: either it is due to organic pathology or it is due to psychological problems. Although this model has been thoroughly discredited and most health professionals would deny a unifactorial approach to chronic pain, the simplistic notion that pain must be one thing or the other, either organic or psychogenic, continues to dominate most thinking. For example, there are three subgroups of Pain Disorder in the DSM-IV: Pain Disorder with a Medical Cause, Pain Disorder with a Psychological Cause, and Pain Disorder with Both Medical and Psychological Causes. The criteria for diagnosis of pain disorder in the DSM-IV are not very helpful, because they are so vague (characteristics of the pain or body location are not described) and because no guidance is given on how to decide whether pain is due to psychological factors. In some cases, such as in arthritis, it is easy to see where the pain is coming from. However, in many situations, such as most low-back pain and most headaches, it is very difficult to determine the cause. Complicating diagnosis is the fact that there is no way to directly measure pain, and that pain thresholds vary widely among individuals. For example, the same electrical shock may be quite painful to one person and barely noticeable to another.

Very often, when no medical cause can be found, psychological causes are inferred by exclusion. This might work well if medical investigations could discern all organic causes of pain, but they cannot. Indeed, there is growing evidence of organic impairment as the cause of several chronic pain disorders once thought to be purely psychological, including whiplash, fibromyalgia, and regional pain (Teasell & Merskey, 1997). There is a constant interplay between psychological and physiological factors in pain. For example, even the most obviously physiologically caused pain (such as extraction of wisdom teeth) is highly influenced by psychological factors (Gidron, McGrath, & Goodday, 1995).

DSM-IV Diagnostic Criteria for Pain Disorder

A. Pain in one or more anatomical sites is the predominant focus of the clinical presentation and is of sufficient severity to warrant clinical attention.

B. The pain causes clinically significant distress or impairment in social, occupational, or other important areas of functioning.

C. Psychological factors are judged to have an important role in the onset, severity, exacerbation, or maintenance of the pain.

D. The symptom or deficit is not intentionally produced or feigned (as in Factitious Disorder or Malingering).

Note: The disorder may be categorized as Pain Disorder Associated with Psychological Factors, Pain Disorder Associated with both Psychological Factors and a General Medical Condition, or Pain Disorder Associated with a General Medical Condition.

Source: Reprinted with permission from the *Diagnostic and Statistical Manual of Mental Disorders*, Fourth Edition. Copyright 1994 American Psychiatric Association.

BODY DYSMORPHIC DISORDER

Scott is 20 years old and a second-year psychology student. He is a bit shy and has had few girlfriends. Scott is an only child from a fairly ordinary family. His father, an auto mechanic, used to drink too much but has been sober since joining Alcoholics Anonymous five years ago. His mother, a secretary, is nervous in social situations but does very well with close friends and family.

Scott has a terrible secret tormenting him. He is convinced his penis is too small. Because he was so worried about it, six months ago he stopped going to the gym to play basketball and lift weights with his chums. He had noticed someone looking at him once in the shower and later heard people laughing in the locker room; he was sure that they were laughing about his penis size. About two months ago, he stopped going to the pub with buddies on the weekend because he didn't want to go into the lavatory to urinate lest others see his minuscule penis. He went to his doctor and said he wasn't feeling well but was afraid to ask him about penis size. He looked in *Playgirl* and saw that the centrefold was much better endowed than he was. All he can think about is the size of his penis. He got good grades in first term but is now avoiding classes because he is very preoccupied and he is sure that the rest of the class can tell about his problem.

Body dysmorphic disorder occurs when an individual is unusually and excessively preoccupied with some aspect of his or her personal appearance. This can be an imagined defect or can be an exaggeration of an existing trait. Individuals with this disorder commonly complain about excessive facial hair, or the shape of the nose, mouth, or jaw (see Table 8.4). Some people spend many hours each day examining their "defect" in the mirror, whereas others attempt to avoid looking at it entirely. Plastic surgery does little to alter their perceptions of their deformity. People with this disorder also frequently feel that everyone is looking at them or that everything that happens to them is somehow related to their defect—a way of thinking called "ideas of reference." Suicidal ideation and attempts occur frequently in people diagnosed with body dysmorphic disorder (Phillips, 1991).

Body dysmorphic disorder is diagnosed when an individual's preoccupation with his or her imagined defect impairs social or occupational functioning or causes clinically significant distress (APA, 1994). It must not be better accounted for by another disorder; dissatisfaction with size and body weight, for example, is better explained by anorexia nervosa or bulimia nervosa. However, these somewhat vague criteria and significant overlap with other disorders have led some to question whether its status as a separate diagnosis is

Table 8.4 Location of Imagined Defects in 30 Patients with Body Dysmorphic Disorder*

Location	n	%
Hair[1]	19	63
Nose	15	50
Skin[2]	15	50
Eyes	8	27
Head/face[3]	6	20
Overall body build/bone structure	6	20
Lips	5	17
Chin	5	17
Stomach/waist	5	17
Teeth	4	13
Legs/knees	4	13
Breasts/pectoral muscles	3	10
Ugly face (general)	3	10
Ears	2	7
Cheeks	2	7
Buttocks	2	7
Penis	2	7
Arms/wrists	2	7
Neck	1	3
Forehead	1	3
Facial muscles	1	3
Shoulders	1	3
Hips	1	3

1. Involved head hair in fifteen cases, beard growth in two cases, and other body hair in three cases.
2. Involved acne in seven cases, facial lines in three cases, and other skin concerns in seven cases.
3. Involved concerns with shape in five cases and size in one case.

* Total is greater than 100% because most patients had "defects" in more than one location.

Source: K. A. Phillips, S. L. McElroy, P. E. Keck, H. G. Pope, & J. L. Hudson, Body dysmorphic disorder: 30 cases of imagined ugliness, *American Journal of Psychiatry, 150(1993)*, 302–308. Copyright 1993, the American Psychiatric Association. Reprinted by permission.

warranted (Hollander, Cohen, & Simeon, 1993; McElroy, Phillips, Keck, Hudson, & Pope, 1993). For example, excessive preoccupation and frequent checking are consistent with a diagnosis of Obsessive Compulsive Disorder (OCD). In addition, although many patients with body dysmorphic disorder are aware that they are overly concerned with their appearance, many are convinced that their defect is a legitimate source of concern. Such individuals could also be diagnosed with a delusional disorder (Phillips, McElroy, Keck, Pope, & Hudson, 1993).

Because people with body dysmorphic disorder tend to be very secretive about their concerns, prevalence figures for this disorder are difficult to obtain. One survey of college students found that 70 percent reported dissatisfaction with their bodies, and 23 percent met the criteria for the disorder (Fitts, Gibson, Redding, & Deiter, 1989). But it is likely that these results reflected a large percentage of students who were concerned primarily about their weight. It has been estimated, however, that approximately 2 percent of patients

requesting plastic surgery have body dysmorphic disorder (Andreasen & Bardach, 1977).

Social and cultural factors can also play a role in determining whether people think they are ugly or attractive. What is considered a deformity in one culture may well be a sign of beauty in another. It was once common practice in China, for example, to bind girls' feet, since tiny feet were considered beautiful. In Burma, women wear brass rings in order to elongate their necks. In our culture, ideal body size and shape have changed throughout the centuries. As discussed in the chapter on eating disorders, pressure to conform to an often unrealistic cultural ideal can be quite strong. Should a person responding to this pressure—perhaps a woman concerned that she has small breasts or a bit of facial hair, or a man distressed by a receding chin—be considered as having a disorder?

DIAGNOSTIC ISSUES

Differential Diagnosis

It is often difficult to differentiate between the various somatoform disorders, and their diagnostic criteria in the DSM-IV are based primarily upon theory and clinical wisdom rather than research (APA, 1994). Somatization disorder shares many characteristics with conversion disorder and both are often diagnosed in the same patient (Folks et al., 1984). Somatization disorder is differentiated from hypochondriasis in that patients with somatization disorder are more likely to be preoccupied with their *symptoms*, and are not as concerned with what those symptoms might mean. Hypochondriacs, on the other hand, are convinced that they have a serious disease. Also, whereas conversion disorder typically develops in adolescence or early adulthood, the onset of hypochondriasis can occur after the age of 30 (Noyes et al., 1994).

Somatization disorder is estimated to affect less than 1 percent of the North American population (Robins et al., 1984). This may be due, in part, to the number and specificity of DSM criteria. One Montreal study observed a prevalence rate of 17 percent when less rigorous criteria were applied. However, when DSM-III criteria were used in a primary care setting the prevalence dropped to less than 1 percent (Kirmayer & Robbins, 1991). In North America, somatization disorder is diagnosed more commonly among unmarried women from lower socioeconomic classes (Swartz, Blazer, George, & Landerman, 1986). In some countries, however, the disorder is more commonly diagnosed among men, whereas in others no sex differences in prevalence rates are observed (Swartz, George, Blazer, & Escobar, 1991). It is generally believed that somatization disorders are more common in cultures where overt expression of emotion is discouraged.

Somatization disorder is likely to occur with other disorders. Patients often experience anxiety and depression (Brown, Golding, & Smith, 1990). In addition, marital difficulties, suicide attempts and antisocial behaviour are also common in these individuals (Kirmayer, Robbins, & Paris, 1994). Katon et al. (1991) suggest that the high comorbidity of somatization disorder with anxiety and depression could be due to several factors. It is possible that anxiety and depression cause a person to be more attuned to physical symptoms. On the other hand, chronic, unexplained physical symptoms may result in anxiety and depression. Finally, it is also possible that both somatization disorder and anxiety and depression are caused by a third, yet unexplained, disorder.

Problems with DSM-IV

There are serious problems with the DSM-IV classification of Somatoform disorders. The first major problem is that Somatization Disorder, Conversion Disorder, and Pain Disorder are diagnoses of exclusion. In other words, there are generally no positive signs of the disorder, just the absence of evidence that symptoms are caused by a known medical problem. In other words, these are diagnoses based on our inability to find out what causes a disorder.

In the case of Pain Disorder, it would not be unusual for a patient to go to four different physicians with the same symptoms and receive four different diagnoses. For example, Terri, described in the case, would likely be diagnosed as having a somatoform disorder if she went to a psychiatrist, fibromyalgia if she went to a rheumatologist, migraine if she saw a neurologist, and irritable bowel syndrome if she were seen by a gastroenterologist. These are not just different names that different subspecialties have devised for the same disorder but are thought to be quite different disorders with different treatments indicated.

The second problem with the DSM-IV is that for a disorder to be present there must be significant interference with the normal life of the person. The difficulty is that individuals may have the same severity of symptoms and yet experience different levels of interference with everyday activities. Moreover, the cause of the interference with daily activities may not be the same as the cause of the pain symptoms. In chronic conditions especially, the effects of the changes, or believed changes, in bodily state (pain, nausea, swelling, etc.) have wide-ranging effects on all aspects of a person's daily life and the lives of those around him or her. For example, a person who has back pain may have soft-tissue damage (which typically cannot be objectively detected), have an unrewarding or punishing job, be fearful of increased activity leading to more pain, and be subject to the advice of professionals and peers alike. In fact the disability associated with chronic conditions is often better predicted by the stress caused by a disorder than by the disorder itself. It is ironic that the diagnosis of "pain without disease" makes the physician look at social and psychological factors for a cause; yet, at the same time, being told there is no medical reason for a pain makes the patient more socially disabled and psychologically more likely to be anxious and depressed.

The arbitrariness of the DSM-IV has also been criticized. There are, as in all classification systems of behaviour, some artificial aspects of the somatoform disorders classification. For example, a person with four pain symptoms, two gastrointestinal symptoms, one sexual symptom, and one pseudoneurological symptom would be classified as having Somatization Disorder, but someone with three pain symptoms, three gastrointestinal symptoms, one sexual symptom, and one pseudoneurological symptom would not. It is not clear how this problem can be solved other than by using such labels judiciously. Experienced physicians tend to use these systems as guidelines rather than hard-and-fast rules.

ETIOLOGY AND TREATMENT

Psychodynamic Models

Psychoanalytic theory provides the most well-developed explanation of the development of somatoform disorders. As mentioned, Freud first used the term "conversion" to describe the way in which anxiety resulting from unconscious psychosexual conflicts was channelled into pseudoneurological symptoms. In the course of treating hysterical patients, Freud developed many of the main ideas of psychoanalytic theory. However, this theory has not been completely supported by research. For example, the theory predicts that the development of symptoms of conversion disorder should reduce anxiety in the patient (because it has been converted). This is why we expect to see *la belle indifference* in conversion disorder patients. Although some patients do indeed exhibit *la belle indifference*, it has also been shown that many of them actually experience *higher* levels of anxiety than other patients (Lader & Sartorius, 1968; Simon & von Korff, 1991).

Even though several other psychodynamic models have been applied to somatoform disorders, all emphasize the role of a psychic trauma—often an unconscious mental conflict—in the development of symptoms. If the symptoms affect the body—such as paralysis or pain— they are referred to as conversion symptoms and the disorder is called *hysteria*, or, in modern terms, one of the somatoform disorders. In other cases, where the symptoms are related to memory and consciousness, the result is dissociative disorders. The symptoms may be symbolically related to the conflict, as in the case of a 16-year-old girl, Miss Katharina, who developed hysterical shortness of breath, difficulty swallowing, dizziness, vomiting, and excessive fear of death after seeing her uncle having sex with her cousin (Breuer & Freud, 1974). Her uncle had attempted to molest her several times before and it was only when she saw the two having intercourse that she realized what the uncle had been trying to do to her. She informed her aunt and her uncle and aunt divorced. Katharina felt responsible for the divorce and guilty. Her mental conflict was too threatening to be resolved in the conscious world. She repressed all memory of the connection between the events with her uncle and the symptoms. When Freud uncovered the relationship between her emotional state, the memories, and her symptoms and interpreted the vomiting as disgust, her symptoms immediately resolved. This treatment was carried out, not with years of psychoanalysis, but during a conversation when she approached Freud on a trail in the Alps one afternoon during his holidays (Breuer & Freud, 1974/1893–1895).

Two concepts, primary gain and secondary gain, are also central to the psychodynamic model. **Primary gain** is the avoidance of the unresolved conflict. **Secondary gain** is the attention and avoidance of responsibility that the symptom brings. Treatment involves unearthing the relationship between the symptom and the repressed conflict. While Freud focussed on psychosexual conflict, later psychodynamic theorists addressed other types of conflict. Thousands of soldiers in World War I, who had previously functioned well, developed symptoms after horrific battle experiences, leading those working with them to explore conflicts over self-preservation. The idea of secondary gain through illness as a prime motivation for sickness behaviour remains a very popular one and is often used with somatoform disorders.

More recent psychodynamic approaches to somatization disorders have emphasized other aspects. For example, Ford and Folks (1985) emphasized the importance of early chaotic family relationships, lack of mature adult relationships, and a difficulty in expressing or verbalizing emotional feelings. The lack of ability to express feelings has been termed *alexithymia* and the Toronto Alexithymia Scale, developed by a team of Canadian psychologists and psychiatrists (Taylor, Parker, Bagby, & Acklin, 1992), is recognized as the best instrument in the area.

Treatment of somatoform and dissociative disorders using a psychodynamic model has focussed on individual therapy designed to understand the underlying unresolved conflict, much as Freud did with Ms. Katharina, or to examine the problem of expression of feelings. Unfortunately, there has been little careful research on the efficacy of psychodynamic therapy. In addition, the length of traditional dynamic therapy has extended, in some cases, from the single session used by Freud on the footpath in the Alps to many months and often years.

During World War I, thousands of soldiers faced with unendurable anxiety and conflicts over self-preservation developed conversion disorder.

Behavioural Models

Proponents of a behavioural etiology of somatoform disorders believe that people adopt symptoms in order to achieve a particular end. Like people who are malingering, they take on the role of a sick person in order to reduce stress or gain some other positive reward (Ullman & Krasner, 1975). It is thought that individuals with such disorders have previous experience with the symptoms they later develop and that they have been rewarded for having these symptoms in the past. Within this theory there is no mention of whether the processes are conscious or unconscious; therefore, it is somewhat inconsistent with the current diagnostic categorization of somatoform disorders as separate from malingering and factitious disorder. This model is concerned with what happens before a behaviour occurs (its *antecedents*), the behaviour itself, and what happens after the behaviour occurs (its *consequences*). The persistence of a behaviour can best be explained by the strength of the bond that is developed by its antecedents and consequences.

Since the behaviourists have studied pain more extensively than other somatoform disorders, the model of pain can be used as an example. Fordyce (1976) described this model in detail in the understanding of chronic pain. In particular he draws our attention not simply to the range of pain behaviours and the way others respond in a solicitous or punishing manner, but also to the fact that the person suffering pain often stops engaging in the full range of usual social, family, and other behaviours. The person may stop going to parties, practising hobbies, etc.

Behavioural treatment programs are based on the identification of pain-related behaviours that were exacerbating suffering: for example, stimulus conditions such as working at a stressful job or taking excessively difficult courses. Responses of others that maintain disability are then identified. This was a radical move away from the treatment of chronic pain as something resulting from organic illness to an understanding of it as psychologically mediated and maintained.

Modelling, although not emphasized by Fordyce, is also an important construct in behavioural understanding of somatization and dissociative disorders. Sam Mikail and Carl von Baeyer, two Canadian psychologists, have examined the link between parental somatizing and child somatizing. Similarly, McGrath and Goodman (1998) have found a very significant aggregation of pain complaints within families. Several researchers have found that children with recurrent abdominal pain have an increased rate of relatives with somatizing symptoms (Routh & Ernst, 1984; Walker, Garber, & Greene, 1991).

Cognitive-Behavioural Model

The cognitive-behavioural model of pain has been developed by a large number of researchers and clinicians and has been among the most vigorous areas of clinical and research activity. Don Meichenbaum, a psychologist at the University of Waterloo, was among the foremost developers of cognitive behaviour therapy (Meichenbaum, 1977). Meichenbaum's major contribution has been to take seriously the critics of the behavioural model and recognize the central role of thoughts or inner speech in our emotions and reactions to the external world.

In this model, thoughts and behaviours that both cause and maintain suffering would be noted and identified. For example, the therapist would help Terri identify the activities she avoided (walking, social encounters, etc.) and the environment in which the avoidance occurred, as well as her patterns of thinking at the time. The therapist would then work to change the environmental contingencies and encourage Terri to recognize when she had unhelpful punishing thoughts and replace them with more realistic patterns of thinking. (See Chapter 7 for a model of this process, and Chapter 2 for an in-depth description of cognitive-behavioural therapy.) This model has been hugely influential and popular, as it seems to account for people's inner or private worlds as well as the immediate world around them.

This model promotes treatments that are often adopted by teams of professionals and delivered to groups of patients. A common strategy is a four-to-five-week inpatient treatment program for severely disabled chronic pain patients such as that run by Eccleston in Bath, England. Another example is a less intensive program such as an eight-week cognitive-behavioural outpatient program for those with migraine headache (McGrath, Cunningham, Lascelles, & Humphreys, 1990). Such a program has been shown to be effective in randomized controlled trials (McGrath et al., 1992; Richardson & McGrath, 1989).

The cognitive-behavioural model has produced the most effective treatments tested in a large number of randomized controlled trials. Results have been strongest in the area of pain because it is much easier to assemble a large enough sample of sufferers to conduct a trial.

Treatment of Pain

A growing body of literature on the treatment of pain suggests that most chronic pain with significant handicap can be effectively treated with cognitive-behavioural methods offered as part of an inpatient or day hospital multi-disciplinary pain clinic program. The most significant change is often not the amount of pain that individuals suffer but the amount of disability, the number of hospitalizations and surgeries, and the return to productive work (Turk & Okifuji, 1998). Turk and Okifuji (1998) have estimated that for each patient treated by a multidisciplinary pain clinic, the savings in medical costs and disability alone (not including lost productivity) would amount to more than one hundred thousand dollars. Unfortunately, such clinics are not available for most patients with chronic pain.

Headache (both tension headache and migraine headache) can also be effectively treated with cognitive-behavioural methods. As an example, a cognitive-behavioural program developed at the Children's Hospital of Eastern Ontario in Ottawa demonstrated that weekly therapy over a 12-week period was effective in reducing the suffering of patients with such headaches. Interestingly, similar results were achieved

with three sessions with a therapist and the addition of audiotapes, manuals, and telephone contact (McGrath et al., 1992; Richardson & McGrath, 1989).

Of course, a careful and thorough history and medical examination and appropriate medical treatment should always be undertaken in individuals with pain. However, continuing, unnecessary medical investigations and medical interventions may do more harm than good. Not only do investigations cost time and money; an excessive search for what might be wrong medically may make it difficult for an individual to adapt to pain and get on with life. There is no need, however, to tell a person "Your pain has no physical cause." The person may respond to such a statement by becoming anxious and angry and insisting on a physical cause. It is more useful to simply state that no physical cause has been found, but that techniques are available that may be helpful whatever the cause.

Cognitive-Perceptual Model

Talking about thoughts and feelings as well as behaviour makes a lot of sense when we consider our own experience of illness, or the worry about illness. In normal, everyday life we may think we are ill or have caught something. Indeed, recently increased knowledge about ranges of symptoms tends to lead to worry, a problem encountered so often in medical training that it has acquired the name "medical student's disease." That is, medical students often finish a lecture or course of reading on an illness and feel that they themselves have the symptoms described, and must have that illness. This phenomenon is thought by some to be similar to the pattern of thinking and feeling experienced by people with somatoform disorders.

This model takes as its starting-point a change in environment and plots the many factors that may affect how we perceive these changes. For example, suppose the room temperature drops by 1 degree C. Will you notice this change? If your body registers the temperature drop, it will send a message to your brain. You may, however, be too involved in something else (such as reading a fascinating chapter) and therefore not notice. If the chapter is not so interesting, more of your attention is available, and you will notice.

Delia Cioffi (Cioffi, 1991), who developed this idea, emphasizes that the way we interpret or understand events is as important as what happens in the physical world. Suppose you think you may be getting a head cold; you are probably more aware than usual of changes in your body. This overattentiveness is magnified for someone like Terri, who experiences pain and suffering from an unknown cause and hence is often worried and afraid that there may be something dreadful going on in her body. She is very aware of all of the changes in her body, as she has learned to pay attention to them. After all, they may be important—they may tell her something about her condition and what to do about it.

The same process may be going on with Scott, who is more aware of his own image. He is more likely to pay attention to his reflection in windows of shops he passes. He also checks his body more often than other people, trying to confirm or allay his worries.

Cioffi goes further with this idea, saying that it is not only what people observe that counts but what they think about when they do pay attention to their bodies. If you notice the slight drop in temperature, you may decide that it is meaningless or that there is a draft in the room. On the other hand, if you have recently heard that sudden drops in temperature are the first sign of the bubonic plague, you may start to think about all of the dreadful things that are likely to beset you and your loved ones. Before you know it, you will have decided who will get all of your possessions when you die and how many people will pack the cathedral at your funeral.

This process of thinking about illness and worrying about illness is often called "hypochondriacal thinking," although in truth many people have such thoughts about bodily changes being due to illness or disease. Such thoughts become a problem only when they exacerbate or create suffering. Worrying thoughts about what may be causing the pain can often drive a relentless and unproductive search for a cure from health professionals. Similarly, many men who have smaller-than-average or even average-size penises may be aware that they don't look like the *Playgirl* centrefold, and perhaps regard it wistfully. The difference with Scott is that he has strong, frequent thoughts about the inadequacy of his penis.

The psychological models outlined above have a lot in common. The strength of the cognitive-perceptual model is that it encourages us to look at the ways in which we make sense of the changes in our body and how we try out our theories on other people.

No specific treatments have been developed from the cognitive-perceptual model. However, cognitive-behavioural treatments have learned from the cognitive-perceptual model and incorporated efforts to change the interpretation of sensations in somatoform disorders.

Biological Models

Right and Left Brain

Some limited evidence suggests that certain somatoform disorders may have a biological component. Ford and Folks (1985) found that symptoms of conversion disorder are more likely to appear on the left side of the body in areas that are controlled by the right side of the brain. The right side of the brain has been linked to emotional arousal, and especially negative arousal. The left hemisphere, on the other hand, is responsible for verbal capacity. This research suggests that the emotional right side of the brain depends upon the verbal left side to describe and interpret emotional experiences. It is possible, then, that with somatoform disorders, the left side of the brain is prevented from interpreting the emotional experiences of the right side. Thus sufferers are not able to connect their physical symptoms with stressful emotional experiences. This theory must be further tested.

Biopsychosocial

Other researchers have found evidence of a biopsychosocial component to the development of somatization disorder. This finding comes from numerous studies that have observed a link between somatization disorder and antisocial personality disorder (APD). Somatization disorder is more common among women with parents who have APD (Sigvardsson, von Korring, Bohman, & Cloninger, 1984). Lilienfeld (1992) found high rates of APD in first-degree relatives of somatization disorder patients. In addition, both APD and somatization disorder tend to begin early in life, run a chronic course, are more common among those of lower socioeconomic classes, are difficult to treat, and are associated with substance abuse, marital discord, and suicide attempts (Goodwin & Guze, 1984; Lilienfeld, 1992). Because APD tends to be diagnosed more often in males and somatization disorder is more common in females, it has been hypothesized that these two disorders are gender-specific expressions of the same underlying biological processes (Guze, Cloninger, Martin, & Clayton, 1986).

Gate Control Theory of Pain

Ron Melzack, a psychologist at McGill University in Montreal, developed the internationally recognized gate control theory of pain together with Patrick Wall, a physiologist from the United Kingdom (Melzack & Wall, 1965). This theory liberated us from thinking of pain as a simple physical stimulus such as tissue damage yielding a specific response, pain. The gate control theory provides the possibility that a given injury or amount of tissue damage will have different effects on different people at the same time or on the same person at different times.

The **gate control theory** hypothesized the existence of a regulating mechanism in the laminae of the dorsal horn of the spinal column. This "gate" regulates input from the a-delta and C fibres. So, for example, peripheral stimulation by vibration or a small electrical current will often block pain. Similarly, changes in mood or emotion will influence the perception of pain. The gate control theory did not detail the role of psychological factors but, unlike other biological theories, it did make explicit allowance for psychological factors.

Although the gate control theory has been challenged and subsequently overtaken by a cascade of different findings, it is one of the most influential models in medicine and the original paper is one of the most widely cited papers ever. This work has influenced a generation of pain researchers.

PANORAMA

Dissociative disorders continue to be some of the most puzzling psychological problems faced by clinicians. Even though their clinical presentations have been recognized since the late 1980s, there is a paucity of systematic research in this area. It appears they occur more frequently now than in the past, but the increase may be one of reporting rather than of true prevalence. Dissociative amnesia and dissociative identity disorder (previously called "multiple personality disorder") have achieved an exceptional level of notoriety, sometimes resulting in the whole concept of dissociation being discredited. Proponents of the Repressed Memory Syndrome and the False Memory Syndrome more frequently argue the merits of their respective positions in the public media than in scientific forums. The increased reporting of dissociative identity disorder and its relationship to childhood sexual abuse seems to have mirrored its popularization in books and movies. The fact that multiple personality disorder has been used as a defence in several highly publicized trials of serial killers has not helped the image of this disorder. However, although one might dispute the frequency of occurrence of these disorders, and argue about the processes involved and their etiology, it is probably inappropriate to deny their existence altogether. Significant numbers of individuals suffer from dissociative symptomatology, and they have been in the care of respected and talented mental health professionals who support the existence of the dissociative disorders. Hopefully, the near future will see increased research that will help clarify the whole area.

Individuals with somatoform disorders constitute a large proportion of patients seeking medical care. This represents a great deal of human suffering and a sizeable cost to our health care system. Recently, there has been an increase in research with these problems. More sophisticated medical and psychological techniques have determined that some problems previously thought to be based entirely on psychological processes do in fact have an organic basis. Chronic pain is probably the most thoroughly studied of the somatoform disorders and in some ways may be used as a model for the other disorders in this category. The current approach is to interpret an individual's pain, even when organically based, as having a significant psychological component. Psychologically based interventions are being developed to help individuals minimize their pain and develop coping mechanisms to enhance their daily lives. Recent work in the area is focussing on greater specificity, evaluating the necessary and sufficient components of the treatment packages in relation to more specific types of pain as well as the other somatoform disorders.

SUMMARY

Dissociative disorders are characterized by severe disturbances of identity, memory, and consciousness. In dissociative amnesia there is a real and complete memory loss of extensive and important personal information. This is usually of sudden onset in response to stressful events. With dissociative fugue the memory loss is accompanied by physical flight to new locations. A person may move to a new town and assume a completely new identity, while remembering nothing of his or her previous life. Individuals suffering from depersonalization disorder feel they are in a dream and are outside observers of their own thoughts, actions, and bodies. In dissociative identity disorder, a person's identity is split into two or more unique personalities. Each personality or "alter" may have his or her own constellation of behaviour, mannerisms, and tone of voice. Most theories agree that dissociative identity disorders are a result of massive repression, often involving painful childhood events. This repression acts to protect individuals against the pain and anxiety associated with these events. Psychodynamically oriented treatment is often used to try to uncover these repressed memories, and hypnosis has proven to be a valuable tool as well.

Somatoform disorders encompass a set of disorders in which individuals have physical symptoms for which there is no biological basis. Conversion disorder occurs when a person experiences motor symptoms such as paralysis, or disturbances in sensory function, for which there is no physical cause. A psychogenic cause is suspected when the area affected does not correspond to anatomical divisions. Hypochondriasis is diagnosed when an individual continuously misinterprets minor bodily symptoms as evidence of a serious disease, despite medical evaluations to the contrary. In somatization disorders individuals also report multiple symptoms which have no organic basis. However, unlike people with hypochondriasis, they are concerned only with the symptoms, not with what the symptoms may mean. Most theories suggest that these disorders are related to anxiety that is not expressed overtly, but is transformed into physical complaints. Behavioural theories also focus on the reinforcement conditions that sustain these ailments.

Chronic pain is a major health care problem, and the best studied of the somatoform disorders. Research has demonstrated that there is a constant interplay between psychological and physiological factors even in physiologically caused pain such as the extraction of wisdom teeth. A growing body of literature supports the finding that most chronic pain can be effectively treated with cognitive-behavioural methods.

KEY TERMS

dissociative disorders (p. 183)
dissociation (p. 183)
dissociative amnesia (p. 184)
localized (p. 184)
generalized amnesia (p. 184)
continuous amnesia (p. 184)
repressed (p. 185)
false memory syndrome (p. 185)
dissociative fugue (p. 185)

depersonalization (p. 186)
dissociative identity disorder (DID)
  (p. 187)
alter (p. 187)
switch (p. 187)
somatoform disorders (p. 190)
malingering (p. 190)
factitious disorders (p. 190)
conversion disorder (p. 190)
anesthesia (p. 191)
hyperesthesia (p. 191)
analgesia (p. 191)

paresthesia (p. 191)
aphonia (p. 191)
la belle indifférence (p. 191)
glove anesthesia (p. 191)
hypochondriasis (p. 192)
somatization disorder (p. 193)
pain disorder (p. 195)
body dysmorphic disorder (p. 195)
primary gain (p. 198)
secondary gain (p. 198)
gate control theory (p. 200)

ADDITIONAL RESOURCES

International Society for the Study of
  Dissociation
60 Revere Drive
Suite 500
Northbrook, IL 60062
(847) 480-0899
(847) 480-9282 fax
info@issd.org

Sidran Foundation
2328 W. Joppa Road
Suite 15
Lutherville, MD 21093
(410) 825-8888
sidran@sidran.org

www.issd.org
The International Society for the Study of Dissociation (ISSD) brings together professionals dedicated to the search for answers to improve the quality of life for all patients with dissociative disorders. This site provides information about ISSD, guidelines for treatment, and web links.

www.sidran.org
The web site of the Sidran Foundation, an organization that studies trauma and dissociation.

noah.cuny.edu/illness/mentalhealth/cornell/conditions/dissocid.html
A fact sheet outlining the cause, treatment, and self-management of dissociative identity disorder.

Eating Disorders

Fred J. Boland

Julie was 19 years old and in her first year at university. She weighed 46 kilograms (102 pounds), which, on her 167 centimetre frame, gave her an emaciated appearance. Her **body mass index** (weight in kilograms over height in metres squared) was 16.5. The body mass index is an indicator of how much fat you have on your body, and Canadian guidelines suggest a range between 20 and 27 as healthy for women.

Julie did not socialize much with other students and tended to isolate herself from her three female housemates. She studied very hard, but had difficulty concentrating. Any grade lower than an A was unacceptable. She disciplined herself to exercise for at least an hour each day and rigidly controlled what she ate. Her skin had taken on a yellowish colour and her housemates irritated her by asking if she was sick and commenting on how little she ate. In response she would often lie about her food intake. To further avoid the issue, she started eating alone in her room. One day, after an exercise session, she fainted. Concerned, her housemates called her parents, who insisted, despite her protestations, that she seek help.

A medical exam indicated that severe dehydration, a serious electrolyte imbalance, and an irregular heartbeat threatened Julie's life. She was hospitalized to correct these conditions and a refeeding program was initiated to bring her weight up to a safer level. She was intensely anxious about eating and weight gain, but did begin therapy with the hospital's eating disorder team, which continued after discharge. A thorough assessment resulted in a DSM-IV Axis I diagnosis of anorexia nervosa: restricting type.

During therapy it became clear that Julie's eating disorder had started in early adolescence. The changes to her body made her feel fat, ugly, embarrassed, and afraid. She felt she stood out from her thinner peers.

She told her mother she wanted to lose weight. Her mother, who was also dieting at the time, helped her prepare nutritious low-calorie meals, bought her an exercise video, and complimented her on her increasingly slim figure, as did her peers.

Although Julie lost 5 kilograms, she still felt and saw herself as fat. She took over all food preparation, carefully documenting the caloric and fat content of each food before selection. Her dieting became increasingly rigid and repetitious. She exercised strenuously every day and weighed herself morning and evening. Julie seemed to take pride in her weight loss. However, if she ever gained even half a kilogram she became anxious that she was becoming fat. Any attempts by her parents to insist on healthier eating were met with resistance.

By the time she was 17, her weight had dropped to 44 kilograms. Whenever possible, she would avoid social eating occasions. When she couldn't, she picked at her food, saying she wasn't hungry. She had not menstruated in over a year, but it did not bother her, nor did the dangers of her very low weight. Her pursuit of thinness was paramount.

In her last semester of high school her weight dropped to 43 kilograms. She fainted in class twice during one week. Her heartbeat was slow and irregular. Her parents and family doctor arranged hospitalization and just before going to university her weight climbed to 49 kilograms. She later told her therapist : "They forced me to gain weight in the hospital, but I made up my mind I would lose it again when I went away to university."

In the past few years eating disorders have been a frequent topic of popular books, magazine articles, and talk shows. Everyone seems to know of some famous athlete (for example, Nadia Comaneci) or entertainer (for example, Karen Carpenter) who has suffered from anorexia or bulimia nervosa. The most famous of all was the late Princess Diana, who courageously went public in her battle with bulimia nervosa. **Anorexia nervosa** is characterized by the pursuit of thinness to dangerously low weight levels, while **bulimia nervosa** is characterized by a binge-purge syndrome in people who are generally in the normal weight range.

Many of the core symptoms of these disorders are extreme manifestations of characteristics displayed by normal people. Anorexia nervosa patients have an intense desire to be thin and a terror of becoming fat. But many girls, young women, and even older women feel the same way, only less intensely. People with bulimia nervosa are often extremely dissatisfied with their bodies. But body dissatisfaction, in lesser degrees, is very widespread and experienced by the majority of females and a sizeable proportion of males. David Garner, a psychologist who did a great deal of his research on eating disorders at the Toronto General Hospital, surveyed 4000 readers (3452 women and 548 men) of *Psychology Today* (January 1997). Among women, 24 percent reported that they would sacrifice more than three years of their life to achieve their weight goals, and 15 percent would sacrifice more than five years. Fully 86 percent said they would like to lose weight. Among men, 11 percent said they would sacrifice three years to attain their weight goals. However, many men who are dissatisfied actually want to gain weight, a goal rare among women.

The stigma of fatness goes well beyond the legitimate medical consequences of obesity (Garner & Wooley, 1991). The media and fashion industry continue to bombard us with incredibly thin female models and, for that matter, incredibly well-sculpted men. Dieting for appearance reasons is widespread in Canada, the United States, and other industrial countries. Diet books and magazine articles are extremely popular and the diet industry is a multibillion-dollar business. There is no doubt that thin is in and fat is out. What part these sociocultural forces play in eating disorders is not fully known. But corresponding with the rise of the current emphasis on thinness and the stigma associated with fatness has been an increase in the prevalence of eating disorders.

Psychologists and other health professionals have observed over the past two decades a large increase in the number of individuals seeking help for eating disorders. Over the same period there has been a burgeoning of research interest as scientists and clinicians try to understand these disorders, develop better treatments for them, and attempt to prevent their development.

In this chapter we will describe the main eating disorders, their possible causes, and their treatment.

HISTORICAL PERSPECTIVE

According to historians (Silverman, 1995), the first clear case of anorexia nervosa was described by Richard Morton in 1689. He referred to the problem as "nervous consumption." It was not until 1873 that William Gull coined the term *anorexia nervosa* to describe cases of self-starvation.

The word *bulimia* goes back to the ancient Greek words *bous* ("ox") and *limos* ("hunger"), literally "ox-hunger" (Parry-Jones & Parry-Jones, 1995). Throughout the ages there have been many references to uncontrollable eating and purging, but it was not until the 1970s, when increasing numbers of young women started to seek help for binge-purge problems, that the terminology became clarified. Boskind-Lodahl (1976) used the term *bulimarexia*, while Palmer (1979) used *dietary chaos syndrome*. DSM-III used the term *bulimia* (American Psychiatric Association, 1980), but *bulimia nervosa*, a term introduced by Russell (1979), came into widespread use and is the one accepted term used today.

DIAGNOSTIC ISSUES

Anorexia Nervosa

A central feature of anorexia nervosa is the pursuit and maintenance of an extremely low body weight. DSM-IV (American Psychiatric Association, 1994) uses the criterion of refusal to maintain even a minimal expected weight for the person's age and height. The guideline given is 85 percent of expected weight, but many individuals with the disorder go much lower. Note that many people with anorexia are in their early teens and still growing. A young person would meet these criteria if weight *gain* during a period of growth is less than 85 percent of expected weight gain. (See the DSM table.)

A second criterion is an unrealistic, phobic-like fear of gaining weight or becoming fat. Eating obviously makes people with anorexia nervosa anxious, especially in social situations.

A third is disturbances in the experience of body weight and shape, a sense of self-worth strongly tied to weight and shape concern, or denial of the serious consequences of such a low body weight. Far from recognizing their dangerously low weight as a problem, people with anorexia often appear to take pleasure in the weight loss.

In females past puberty, the absence of at least three consecutive menstrual cycles (associated with low levels of

> ## DSM-IV Diagnostic Criteria for Anorexia Nervosa
>
> A. Refusal to maintain body weight at or above a minimally normal weight for age and height (e.g., weight loss leading to maintenance of body weight less than 85% of that expected; or failure to make expected weight gain during period of growth, leading to body weight less than 85% of that expected).
> B. Intense fear of gaining weight or becoming fat, even though underweight.
> C. Disturbance in the way in which one's body weight or shape is experienced, undue influence of body weight or shape on self-evaluation, or denial of the seriousness of the current low body weight.
> D. In postmenarcheal females, amenorrhea, i.e., the absence of at least three consecutive menstrual cycles. (A woman is considered to have amenorrhea if her periods occur only following hormone, e.g., estrogen, administration.)
>
> **Restricting Type:** during the current episode of Anorexia Nervosa, the person has not regularly engaged in binge-eating or purging behavior (i.e., self-induced vomiting or the misuse of laxatives, diuretics, or enemas)
>
> **Binge-Eating/Purging Type:** during the current episode of Anorexia Nervosa, the person has regularly engaged in binge-eating or purging behavior (i.e., self-induced vomiting or the misuse of laxatives, diuretics, or enemas)

Source: Reprinted with permission from the *Diagnostic and Statistical Manual of Mental Disorders*, Fourth Edition. Copyright 1994 American Psychiatric Association.

estrogen) is the final diagnostic indicator. This criterion poses an interpretation problem in young girls who have never menstruated and in those who only menstruate while taking birth control pills. Generally, such cases are still seen as meeting the criteria for anorexia nervosa.

In males who develop anorexia nervosa, there is often a loss of potency and of interest in sex associated with the low levels of testosterone that accompany the disorder. This was originally suggested by Russell (1970) as a criterion that would parallel the loss of menstruation; however, DSM-IV does not require this in male cases. (Note that we will sometimes use the pronouns "she" and "her" in this chapter, since the large majority of people with eating disorders are female. However, in most cases comments may be understood as generally referring to all sufferers.)

At 162 centimetres and 45 kilograms, Karen clearly met the DSM-IV weight criterion for anorexia nervosa. At 22, she had been eating-disordered for seven years. Initially, she had lost weight by avoiding certain foods such as meat and sweets, and by exercising religiously. Within months, her dieting became increasingly rigid and she found herself constantly obsessed about food and battling her chronic hunger. Rapidly a pattern emerged: after a week or so of semistarvation or liquid fasts, her attempt at eating a small meal would fail and turn into a binge, during which she would consume a great deal of the forbidden foods she so strenuously sought to avoid. These episodes terrified her and she would attempt to rid herself of the unwanted calories by vomiting and using laxatives. Although there were subsequent periods of maintaining a rigid dieting pattern without binge eating, her predominant pattern of maintaining her very low weight was to alternate rigid dieting with binge-purging. In the year prior to treatment she also reported vomiting and taking laxatives even after non-binge meals.

For research purposes as well as for clinical considerations, DSM-IV subtypes anorexia nervosa into **restricting type** and **binge eating/purging type**. About half of anorexia nervosa patients are of the restricting type and half of the binge eating/purging type. In the restricting type, the person relies on a rigidly controlled, very low intake of food to maintain her low weight. Julie, described in the case study that opened this chapter, illustrates this group. In the binge eating/purging type, illustrated by Karen, dietary restraint breaks down fairly regularly and the person binges. To maintain a very low weight and rid the body of the unwanted calories, the person then engages in self-induced vomiting and/or abuse of laxatives, diuretics, or enemas. In its criteria for anorexia nervosa, DSM-IV does not precisely define what constitutes a binge or specify a frequency of binge eating and purging, allowing for subjective interpretations on the part of the clinician and patient. Sometimes an anorexic will mainly purge, but not go on eating binges. Such a patient would be classified under the binge eating/purging type. In both subtypes, people often exercise excessively to burn off calories.

The fact that these two subtypes are in the same diagnostic category indicates that they have a great deal in com-

mon. Nevertheless, the distinction between subtypes is important. The binge-purge behaviour has to be specifically addressed in treatment. In addition, purging leads to a variety of medical problems. There is also evidence that the binge eating/purging subtype is associated with more impulsive behaviours, such as substance abuse, stealing, self-mutilation, and suicidal ideation and behaviour (DaCosta & Halmi, 1992). Moreover, a review of treatment outcome studies shows that the binge-purge subtype has a poorer long-term prognosis (Steinhausen, Rauss-Mason, & Seidel, 1991).

Bulimia Nervosa

Vicki was 24 when she first sought treatment for her eating disorder. At 163 centimetres and 61 kilograms, her weight was in the normal range. As a teenager, she had gained weight, reaching 71 kilograms when she was 17. At that time her self-esteem was low, and she felt ugly and repelled by her own body. She made up her mind to go on a diet by cutting out all sweets and junk food and skipping lunch. She found it very difficult but managed to lose 5 kilograms, which delighted her. However, during the Christmas holidays she gained most of it back. At New Year's she started a very extreme diet, sometimes fasting for two or three days at a time, and at other times getting by with a liquid diet preparation that amounted to 600 calories per day. In three weeks her weight dropped to 58 kilograms but she was feeling very stressed and obsessed with food.

That Friday night, when she was home alone, she had her first severe binge. She had just wanted to treat herself and at first the cookies and ice cream were a relief. But her pleasure soon turned to anxiety as she couldn't seem to stop. She had blown her diet and felt out of control. She ended up eating a huge amount of food and was sure she would become fat again. She went to bed feeling bloated, nauseated, depressed, and drained. Tomorrow she would fast. She promised herself it wouldn't happen again.

Shortly after, Vicki took a job as a waitress at a bar-restaurant and moved to her own apartment. Her pattern of strict dieting and fasting followed by binge eating recurred with increasing frequency. Within a month she started to vomit after her binges. The vomiting relieved the bloating and got rid of the dreaded calories. She felt guilty about the vomiting but anything was better than becoming fat. Although she was able to follow rather stringent diets for a while, they seldom lasted long before she would revert to her binge-purge pattern. When she felt especially stressed from work or relationship problems, she binged and purged four, even six times a day.

Far from recognizing their dangerously low weight as a problem, people with anorexia often appear to take pleasure in their weight loss, an attitude to pathology referred to as egosyntonic.

Vicki had problems establishing intimacy and her relationships tended to be short-term and volatile. At least once a week she would get drunk. She felt she lived a double life, having to hide her binge eating and purging. Her teeth were badly eroded by the vomit. Occasionally her throat would bleed and there was a puffiness under her chin that would not go away. Her stomach was chronically upset and she felt tired and unmotivated. Nevertheless, her major concern was that the treatment might make her fat again.

A thorough assessment at the eating disorder clinic led to the DSM-IV Axis I diagnosis of Bulimia Nervosa/Purging Type. Substance Abuse and Depression were also added as Axis I diagnoses, as well as an Axis II diagnosis of Borderline Personality Disorder (see Chapter 11 for a description). The psychologist thought the depression was secondary to the eating disorder and substance abuse and that it should lift with successful intervention in the latter two disorders. He also noted that symptoms of eating disorder and substance abuse overlapped with those of the personality disorder and suggested reassessing for the latter after treatment of the Axis I disorders.

DSM-IV Diagnostic Criteria for Bulimia Nervosa

A. Recurrent episodes of binge eating. An episode of binge eating is characterized by both of the following:

(1) eating, in a discrete period of time (e.g., within any 2-hour period), an amount of food that is definitely larger than most people would eat during a similar period of time and under similar circumstances

(2) a sense of lack of control over eating during the episode (e.g., a feeling that one cannot stop eating or control what or how much one is eating)

B. Recurrent inappropriate compensatory behavior in order to prevent weight gain, such as self-induced vomiting; misuse of laxatives, diuretics, enemas, or other medications; fasting; or excessive exercise.

C. The binge eating and inappropriate compensatory behaviors both occur, on average, at least twice a week for 3 months.

D. Self-evaluation is unduly influenced by body shape and weight.

E. The disturbance does not occur exclusively during episodes of Anorexia Nervosa.

Purging Type: during the current episode of Bulimia Nervosa, the person has regularly engaged in self-induced vomiting or the misuse of laxatives, diuretics, or enemas

Nonpurging Type: during the current episode of Bulimia Nervosa, the person has used other inappropriate compensatory behaviors, such as fasting or excessive exercise, but has not regularly engaged in self-induced vomiting or the misuse of laxatives, diuretics, or enemas

Source: Reprinted with permission from the *Diagnostic and Statistical Manual of Mental Disorders*, Fourth Edition. Copyright 1994 American Psychiatric Association.

Bulimia nervosa is an eating disorder characterized by recurrent episodes of binge eating followed by some form of compensatory behaviour aimed at ridding the body of the excessive calories consumed. (See the DSM table.) Unlike anorexia nervosa, people with bulimia nervosa are generally in the normal weight range. One important question arises: What exactly is a binge? Almost everyone has overeaten at certain times, for example, at an all-you-can-eat buffet of tempting food. Does that constitute a binge? There is also a subjective component to judging a binge. For example, a patient might say she binged because she had an unplanned doughnut, even though her total consumption for the day was under 600 calories.

To deal with these difficulties, DSM-IV offers two criteria to define a **binge**. First, the amount of food eaten in a set period of time (for example, a one- or two-hour period) must be definitely more than most people would consume in a similar period and circumstances. Thus, the doughnut would not qualify as a binge. Second, the person must feel out of control over what she eats, how much, or whether she can stop. This feeling is very unpleasant and frightening; quite different from what most people feel overindulging at the free buffet.

Self-reports from patients with bulimia nervosa contribute to an understanding of what constitutes a binge. In one study of 25 outpatients, an average of 3415 calories were reported to be consumed during a binge, with a range of 1200 to 11,500 calories (Mitchell, Pyle, & Eckert, 1981). In another study, where patients kept a food diary for one week, the average consumption during a self-defined binge was 1173 calories with a range of 45 to 5138 calories (Rossiter & Agras, 1990).

Binge eating has also been studied in the laboratory. In one study six patients with bulimia nervosa were given large amounts of their preferred food and were asked to binge in their typical fashion. The average binge contained 4394 calories with a range of 1436 to 7178 calories. In another laboratory study (Walsh, Hadigon, Kissileff, & LaChaussée, 1992), patients with bulimia nervosa were shown to consume almost three times as much during a binge (3583 vs. 1271 calories) as non-eating-disordered controls, who were also instructed to have a "typical binge."

Together, these studies show that a person with bulimia nervosa consumes more food during a typical binge than a non-eating-disordered person would consume during the same period of time and in similar circumstances. Clinical reports also show that binge eating in bulimia nervosa patients is accompanied by feelings of loss of control, the second criterion defining this eating disturbance.

A second diagnostic criterion for bulimia nervosa is that the person must engage in recurrent compensatory behaviour aimed at preventing weight gain. A person who compensates mainly by self-induced vomiting (which is most typical) or the use of laxatives, diuretics, or enemas is classified as **purging type**. One who mainly fasts or exercises to excess is classified as **nonpurging type**. The purging type is encountered far more frequently than the nonpurging type.

For a DSM-IV diagnosis of bulimia nervosa, the binge eating and purging must occur at least twice a week over a period of at least three months.

The final diagnostic criterion is that the person's self-evaluations must be seriously influenced by concerns about body weight and shape. A characteristic feature of bulimia nervosa and anorexia nervosa is a disturbance in the way the person views or feels about her body shape and weight. Body image disturbance has two main components. The first is a perceptual component; **body image distortion**. Generally, eating disorder patients see themselves as larger than they really are. The second component has to do with affect and attitude; **body image dissatisfaction**. The person feels fat and unhappy about her body weight and shape.

Initially, researchers thought body image distortion was most important. However, research showed that there are only mild to moderate differences between eating-disordered patients and women who are not eating-disordered on this dimension. The real difference is in feelings and attitudes: people with eating disorders feel much worse about their bodies than controls (Cash & Brown, 1987). A recent *meta-analysis* of 66 studies (a statistical evaluation of the significance and strength of variables of interest across different studies) confirmed body dissatisfaction to be more important than body distortion (Cash & Deagle, 1997). Bulimics and anorexics showed similar levels of body image distortion, but bulimics showed stronger body dissatisfaction. It is possible that the lower weight of the anorexic, although dangerously maladaptive, serves to make her feel less dissatisfied with her body. However, relative to controls both groups show a strong overvaluation of weight and shape concerns. That is, not only were they unhappy with their bodies, but this dissatisfaction undermined their feelings of self-worth and self-esteem.

Atypical Eating Disorders

When we think of eating disorders, what typically comes to mind are anorexia nervosa and bulimia nervosa. However, there are a variety of other atypical eating disturbances (Herzog, Hopkins, & Burns, 1993) that DSM-IV classifies as "eating disorders not otherwise specified" (EDNOS). In most cases this is because the person fails to meet one of the criteria for anorexia nervosa or bulimia nervosa. For example, a woman is still having regular menstruation even though she meets all the criteria for anorexia nervosa, or she has all the symptoms of bulimia nervosa but only binges and purges once a week. Cases where the person persistently induces vomiting without binge eating or where the person chews a large amount of food but spits it out without swallowing it would also fall into the EDNOS category. (See DSM table.)

Binge Eating Disorder

Joe, a 40-year-old bus driver who lived alone, was recently diagnosed with Type II (adult onset) diabetes. His family doctor had referred him to a hospital-based obesity treatment program. At 172 centimetres and 108 kilograms, Joe's BMI was 35 (obesity is commonly defined as a BMI of 30 or more) indicating a large amount of body fat. During the assessment it became clear that Joe had developed a particular eating pattern that contributed to his obesity and that he described as "addictive." Two to four evenings a week, which almost always included weekends, he would watch TV in his kitchen while consuming 3500 to 5000 calories of food, usually in the form of meats, breads, sweets, and various snack foods. On mornings after he binged he would skip breakfast but usually eat lunch. He had tried to diet several times on his own but seldom lasted for more than a week. He had also tried without success to break his binge eating pattern. He maintained that he binged more frequently in the winter than in the summer. He also acknowledged binge eating more when he was stressed or depressed. Joe did not exercise, nor did he ever try to avoid the caloric consequences of binge eating by vomiting, laxative use, or other methods.

Although it is not an official eating disorder, DSM-IV lists "Binge Eating Disorder" as a special case of EDNOS. It describes people who have clinically significant eating binges, as defined in the criteria for bulimia nervosa, but who do not engage in extreme means (fasting, strict dieting, purging) to compensate for the calories consumed during the binge (Marcus, 1993). (See DSM table.) It is estimated that up to 30 percent of individuals in treatment for obesity have a binge eating disorder (Spitzer et al., 1992).

DSM-IV Diagnostic Criteria for Eating Disorders Not Otherwise Specified

The Eating Disorder Not Otherwise Specified category is for disorders of eating that do not meet the criteria for any specific eating disorder. Examples include:

1. For females, all of the criteria for Anorexia Nervosa are met except that the individual has regular menses.
2. All of the criteria for Anorexia Nervosa are met except that, despite significant weight loss, the individual's current weight is in the normal range.
3. All of the criteria for Bulimia Nervosa are met except that the binge eating and inappropriate compensatory mechanisms occur at a frequency of less than twice a week or for a duration of less than 3 months.
4. The regular use of inappropriate compensatory behavior by an individual of normal body weight after eating small amounts of food (e.g., self-induced vomiting after the consumption of 2 cookies).
5. Repeatedly chewing and spitting out, but not swallowing, large amounts of food.
6. Binge eating disorder, recurrent episodes of binge eating in the absence of the regular use of inappropriate compensatory behaviors characteristic of Bulimia Nervosa.

DSM-IV Research Criteria for Binge Eating Disorder

A. Recurrent episodes of binge eating. An episode of binge eating is characterized by both of the following:

  (1) eating in a discrete period of time (e.g., within any 2-hour period), an amount of food that is definitely larger than most people would eat in a similar period of time under similar circumstances

  (2) a sense of lack of control over eating during the episode (e.g., a feeling that one cannot stop eating or control what or how much one is eating)

B. The binge eating episodes are associated with three (or more) of the following:

  (1) eating much more rapidly than normal

  (2) eating until feeling uncomfortably full

  (3) eating large amounts of food when not feeling physically hungry

  (4) eating alone because of being embarrassed by how much one is eating

  (5) feeling disgusted with oneself, depressed, or very guilty after overeating

C. Marked distress regarding binge eating is present.

D. The binge eating occurs, on average, at least 2 days a week for 6 months.

  Note: The method of determining frequency differs from that used for Bulimia Nervosa; future research should address whether the preferred method of setting a frequency threshold is counting the number of days on which binges occur or counting the number of episodes of binge eating.

E. The binge eating is not associated with the regular use of inappropriate compensatory behaviors (e.g., purging, fasting, excessive exercise) and does not occur exclusively during the course of Anorexia Nervosa or Bulimia Nervosa.

Source: Reprinted with permission from the *Diagnostic and Statistical Manual of Mental Disorders,* Fourth Edition. Copyright 1994 American Psychiatric Association.

Assessment

Assessment for diagnostic purposes is usually made by clinical interview exploring DSM-IV criteria for eating disorders. A history of body weight will determine whether the patient has ever met the weight criteria for anorexia nervosa and provide an estimate of what might be an appropriate weight range for that person. It is important to assess for attitudes and beliefs about body weight and shape, a central aspect of the psychopathology of eating disorders. A dietary history explores for the presence, frequency, and severity of binge eating and the past and present use of aberrant weight loss methods (for example, strict dieting, fasting, purging behaviours, exercise patterns, etc.). Menstrual history is explored for the presence of amenorrhea, and sexual history is commonly explored, especially for the presence of any sexual abuse.

It is important to determine the extent to which the patient is experiencing symptoms of starvation. As will be seen later, many of the symptoms associated with eating disorders are the result of maintaining weight and food intake at a semistarvation level.

The interview is generally broadened to also explore for other disorders which may be present (for example, substance abuse, depression, personality disorders) and to assess the person's past and current social and family situation.

A medical examination that looks for the physical consequences and medical complications associated with eating disorders complements a psychological assessment. Information from both assessments can be used in educating and motivating the patient.

To avoid missing salient features of the eating disorder, many clinics use a structured interview that systematically covers relevant areas. One of the best is the Eating Disorder Examination (EDE; Fairburn & Cooper, 1993). The EDE has good reliability and validity; allows for a DSM-IV diagnosis; provides numerical rating for many symptoms; and provides normative data on dietary restraint, bulimic behaviour, and eating, weight, and shape concerns. The EDE is also useful for research purposes and for evaluating progress in treatment.

Many clinics also use a variety of self-report inventories to supplement the structured or unstructured interview. The Eating Disorder Inventory (Garner, 1991), which yields a variety of scale scores relevant to eating disorder pathology, is popular. Finally, psychometric instruments such as the Beck Depression Inventory (Beck & Beck, 1972) and the Symptom Checklist 90 (Derogatis, Lipman, & Covi, 1973) are commonly used to screen for, or verify, associated psychopathology.

Prevalence

There is little doubt that over the past few decades there has been an increase in the prevalence of eating disorders, primarily bulimia nervosa.

Fairburn and Beglin (1990) reviewed more than 50 studies of the prevalence of bulimia nervosa and noted how difficult it is to get accurate prevalence rates. Some studies are based only on university students, who may not be representative of women in general. Findings also differ according to the method of assessment. For example, self-report questionnaires tend to produce much higher rates than studies using clinical interviews. They make the point that even interview studies may be biased, since many who have eating disorders may choose not to participate. Also, the particular age group surveyed makes a large difference to rates reported. Finally, over the periods surveyed the diagnostic criteria have changed, becoming more tightly defined.

One of the best prevalence studies to date was carried out by Paul Garfinkel and colleagues (1995) on a broad urban and rural community sample of females ($n = 4285$) and males ($n = 3831$), between the ages of 15 and 65 living in Ontario. The authors randomly selected one person from each household and conducted a structured interview to determine whether he or she suffered from bulimia nervosa. They found that the lifetime prevalence of bulimia nervosa was 1.1 percent for females and 0.1 percent for males. An additional 22 females and 6 males met all but one of the criteria (Garfinkel et al., 1995). Because of some of the difficulties and biases noted earlier by Fairburn and Beglin (1990), these estimates may be on the low side. The authors did not report the prevalence of anorexia nervosa, but average rates from a number of studies suggest a prevalence of 0.3 percent in females (Hoek, 1995). Bear in mind that the rates would be higher in a sample consisting of young women. It is generally agreed that only about 5 to 10 percent of eating disorders occur in males.

One thing is certain: since the 1970s, hospitals and clinics have experienced an upsurge in patients seeking help for eating disorders, mainly bulimia nervosa. David Garner and Christopher Fairburn (1988) plotted the rates of referral to the Toronto General Hospital and Clarke Institute of Psychiatry from 1975 to 1986 (see Figure 9.1). In 1975 there were few cases of bulimia nervosa. From 1979 to 1981 the number of cases of bulimia nervosa were roughly equivalent to numbers for anorexia nervosa, restricting type, and anorexia nervosa, bulimic type. By 1986 the number of cases of bulimia nervosa outnumbered the other eating disorders by a margin of 5 to 1.

CLINICAL DESCRIPTION
Anorexia Nervosa

To see an adolescent girl with severe weight loss and a sickly, jaundiced complexion is a moving experience for most of us.

How, you ask yourself, could anyone voluntarily seek such a state? By what path did she arrive at such an emaciated condition, seemingly pleased with her skin-and-bones appearance, denying the seriousness of her condition, and determined not to gain weight to a normal level?

Two related motivations are apparent: a desire to be thin so strong she will sacrifice her health, maybe even die for it; and an intense fear of being fat. These motivations are translated into avoidance of many foods and the adoption of a very low food intake, often consisting of calorie-reduced and high-fibre foods. Irrational cognitions and attitudes toward food abound. While eating, many anorexics cut their food into tiny pieces, eat very slowly, and adopt other rituals such as eating their foods in a particular sequence. Eating makes them anxious, and conflicts with parents and others who encourage them to eat sensibly are common. To give the impression that they are eating more they will sometimes secretly dispose of food. This is often facilitated by their preference for eating alone. Their semistarved state leaves them preoccupied and obsessed with thoughts of food (see the Slim Chance Awards Focus box). Indeed, many love to cook and prepare food for others while eating little themselves.

The majority of anorexics exercise excessively as a way of burning calories. Many count calories for both food and

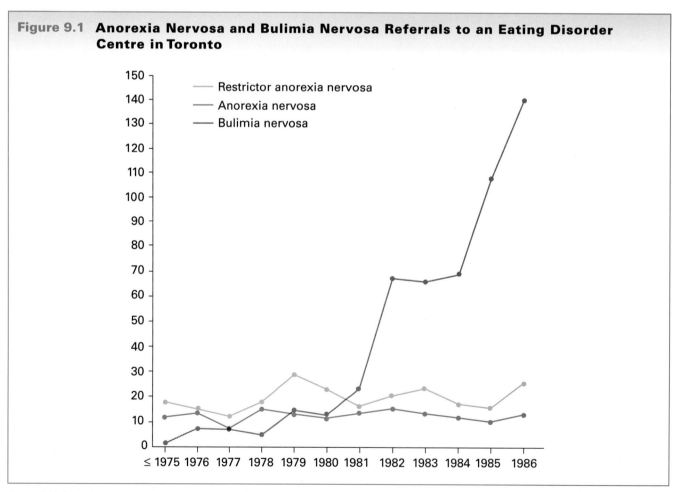

Figure 9.1   Anorexia Nervosa and Bulimia Nervosa Referrals to an Eating Disorder Centre in Toronto

Source: D. M. Garner & C. G. Fairburn, Relationship between anorexia nervosa and bulimia nervosa: diagnostic implications, in D. M. Garner & P. E. Garfinkel, eds., *Diagnostic Issues in Anorexia Nervosa and Bulimia Nervosa* (New York: Brunner/Mazel, 1988). © 1988 by Brunner/Mazel. Reprinted by permission.

exercise ("If I run five miles I will be allowed a muffin"). Even when they are not deliberately exercising, many show a general restlessness that is linked to their state of starvation.

The anorexic is in a constant all-encompassing battle with her hunger and body weight. Some clinical scientists believe that this battle reflects control conflicts in other aspects of her life (Bruch, 1973; Crisp, 1970). In restrictive anorexia, the rigid dieting and overactivity are sufficient to maintain a very low body weight. In the binge eating/purging subtype (about 50 percent of cases), the restraint breaks down and the anorexic binges, or at least eats more than intended. In these cases the lower weight is maintained by purging (vomiting, laxative, and diuretic abuse). Some people who don't binge use purging to achieve the desired low weight. The irony about laxative abuse is that it is not very effective; while quite damaging to health, it only eliminates about 15 percent of calories consumed (Bo-Linn, Santa Ana, Morawski, & Fordtran, 1983). Nevertheless, laxatives, along with diuretics, produce weight loss due to dehydration, and any weight loss is welcomed by the anorexic.

Patients with the binge eating/purging subtype of anorexia nervosa tend to have more comorbidity (for example, substance abuse) than the restricting subtype and to be more like bulimia nervosa patients in terms of family characteristics (high conflict, low cohesion). Finally, the binge eating/purging anorexics have a poorer long-term treatment outcome than restricting patients.

As noted earlier, anorexics are more likely than normal controls to see themselves as larger than they are, though not all do. They feel considerable dissatisfaction with their bodies, though not as strongly as do bulimics. This dissatisfaction may be directed at the whole body or focussed on one or two body parts, such as the stomach or thighs. In both anorexia and bulimia nervosa, self-worth hinges largely on shape and weight.

Relationships with family and peers are often disturbed. Most sufferers exhibit social withdrawal, depression, and anxiety, symptoms that are often related to their semistarved state.

In the great majority of anorexia nervosa patients the onset of the disorder is preceded by a period of dieting. However, dieting alone cannot account for the disorder. In the section on etiology we will consider other predisposing factors.

Bulimia Nervosa

The onset of bulimia nervosa is usually at around 18 years of age. Like anorexia, it is typically preceded by a period of increasingly strict dieting and the strong linking of weight and shape concerns to self-worth. Since people with bulimia nervosa maintain their weight in the normal range, or close to it, and since they are usually secretive about their behaviour, family and friends often suspect nothing.

Bulimics are not able to tolerate the hunger associated with strict dieting as well as the restricting anorexic and may show other signs of poor impulse control. As dietary restraint breaks down, binge eating emerges. Most binge eating takes place in the late afternoon and evening, and it is more likely on weekends. The foods consumed during a binge are usually those the bulimic forbids herself when dieting, such as cakes, ice cream, cookies, chips, and other snack foods (Knight & Boland, 1989). These foods are best characterized as sweet fats, since the proportion of calories derived from fat is about the same as that derived from carbohydrates (Kaye et al., 1992). Binge eaters may not consume a higher proportion of carbohydrates overall than non-eating-disordered individuals, but they consume a great deal more during binges.

Because bulimics share with anorexics a phobic-like fear of gaining weight, the binge eating is very threatening to them. Usually, for a period of six to nine months, there is a pattern of alternation between binge eating and attempts to compensate by periods of restrictive eating. However, this pattern generally breaks down and the person starts to purge within half an hour of the end of the binge—in the great majority of cases by self-induced vomiting. Initially the bulimic may use her fingers, a spoon, or even an emetic to help her vomit, but with time she often learns to vomit at will. She may abuse laxatives and diuretics along with vomiting or instead of vomiting (Freeman et al., 1998). Once purging begins, an increase in binge eating is often observed.

Although the exact prevalence is unknown, a small subset of individuals satisfy all the other criteria for bulimia nervosa but purge calories following binge eating by fasting and excessive exercise. While these behaviours serve the same function as purging by vomiting, laxative, and diuretic abuse, they are more acceptable to society and are not associated with such physically damaging effects. This pattern is referred to in the DSM-IV as bulimia nervosa/nonpurging type. Few studies have compared the two subgroups of bulimia nervosa, but indications are that the purging type is more seriously disturbed.

There is a great deal of overlap between the symptoms of anorexia nervosa and bulimia nervosa. Common to the two are a fear of weight gain and of losing control; a strong desire to be thin; restrictive eating practices; excessive exercise; undue emphasis on weight and shape in self-evaluations; low self-esteem; and a tendency to depression and other psychopathology.

Therefore it is not surprising that sometimes a person may move from one diagnosis to another. For example, a person may initially meet the criteria for anorexia nervosa but, through treatment or through natural recovery, regain her weight back to acceptable levels and experience regular menses. However, she may still be unhappy with her body and very anxious about becoming fat. Thus, she may start to diet again but this time develop a pattern of binge eating and purging that satisfies the criteria for bulimia nervosa. Even more common is switching between subtypes. About 50 percent of individuals with anorexia nervosa binge and/or purge (Garfinkel, Moldofsky, & Garner, 1980). According to Hsu (1988), restricting types switch to binge eating/purging types about twice as often as in the other direction.

Medical Consequences

Although their exact frequency is difficult to determine, serious medical consequences are associated with anorexia and bulimia nervosa, especially if purging is involved (Goldbloom & Kennedy, 1995; Kaplan & Woodside, 1987; Mitchell, 1995).

Because of their starvation condition, the skin of anorexia nervosa patients takes on a yellowish colour, and they grow very fine body hair called *lanugo*. In both anorexia nervosa and bulimia nervosa those who purge by vomiting do considerable damage to their teeth because of acidic content from the stomach.

Dehydration occurs in a large proportion of patients, especially in those who purge by using vomiting, laxatives, and diuretics. Very dry skin and hair are common. More seriously, the purging can deplete the body of potassium and chloride, resulting in an imbalance of electrolytes, compounds in the body that conduct electrical impulses. **Electrolyte imbalance** can seriously compromise renal, bowel, and brain functioning. It also affects heart functioning and a number of deaths due to cardiac arrest have been reported (Mitchell, 1986). For these reasons, eating-disordered individuals have increased mortality rates (Hsu, 1980; Theander, 1985).

Problems with the gastrointestinal tract are common. Vomiting can cause the salivary glands to swell, giving the appearance of puffy cheeks. Perforations of the esophageal area and delayed gastric emptying have been reported. Constipation is common, especially in those who have abused laxatives. One of the most serious complications of severe binge eating and purging is gastric dilation, which can result in rupture and the spilling of stomach content into the body cavity. This is often fatal.

Amenorrhea (failure to menstruate) occurs in anorexia nervosa patients and in a considerable proportion of bulimia nervosa patients. Many others have irregular menstruation. In males with anorexia nervosa a loss of sexual interest and potency is observed.

Finally, eating disorders, especially anorexia nervosa, are associated with osteoporosis (bone loss) due to low calcium intake and absorption.

The Binge-Purge Cycle

Because binge eating is present in a number of different eating disorders, it is receiving increasing research attention (Fairburn & Wilson, 1993). A significant minority of individuals also engage in *subclinical* binge eating—that is, binges, which may or may not be associated with purging, that do not meet the criteria for an eating disorder but are nonetheless disturbing to them (Vanderheyden & Boland, 1987). What triggers binge eating? How does the binge-purge cycle develop and how is it maintained?

Triggers

The factors that trigger a binge episode cannot always be neatly separated from the longer-term factors that contribute to the development or maintenance of an eating disorder. For example, dieting is likely involved in the development of bulimia nervosa; it serves as a trigger of binge eating; and it and also contributes to maintaining the pattern. Here we are concerned with the immediate triggers of binge eating—what happens just prior to a binge.

Stress and emotional distress. One important trigger is *stress and emotional distress*, associated with such mood states as anxiety, depression, frustration, and rejection (for example, Abraham & Beumont, 1982; Davis, Freeman, & Garner, 1988). While there is general agreement that aspects of the binge offer at least temporary relief from distressed states such as anxiety (Schlundt & Johnson, 1990), there is no agreement yet on how this happens. Is the binge a general coping mechanism for dealing with distress (Johnson & Connors, 1987)? Does it simply distract the person from other problems in her life (Hawkins, Fremouw, & Clement, 1984)? Does the binge reduce painful self-awareness of perceived faults by allowing the individual to focus her cognitions on the immediate stimulus in front of her—the binge food (Heatherton & Baumeister, 1991)? Further research is needed to clarify these questions.

Dieting. Although not all binge eating is triggered by dieting, there is a strong relationship between the severity of dieting and the severity of binge eating (Polivy & Herman, 1985; Vanderheyden & Boland, 1987). People with bulimia nervosa diet chronically, often skipping meals, or eating very lightly early in the day only to binge in the evening. Prior to the binge, they are often quite hungry and obsessed by thoughts of food. Moreover, there is some evidence that dieting increases self-reported stress (Rosen, Tacy, & Howell, 1990); thus, acute hunger may interact with the more general stress/distress factor.

Forbidden food. People with bulimia nervosa have built up a pattern of binge eating on rich, tasty foods that they normally exclude as forbidden during their strict dieting. The simple availability of these foods can take on the power to trigger binge eating. One possible explanation is a *deprivation effect*: denied during dieting, the foods increase in salience and are the focus of craving. A second possibility is that the repeated pairing of these foods with binge eating produces a conditioned association such that the food cues elicit a response of binge eating (Booth, Lewis, & Blair, 1990). (See the discussion of conditioning in Chapter 2.) This trigger is likely to interact with other triggers. One can imagine that if a person is suffering some type of distress and is hungry and obsessed with thoughts of food, the presence of rich foods that have offered relief in the past may tempt her into a binge.

When people with bulimia try to eat foods that they have labelled forbidden, the situation gets worse. A long series of clever experiments by Peter Herman and Janet Polivy of the University of Toronto show that eating forbidden food can disinhibit eating in restrained eaters (Herman & Mack, 1975; Herman & Polivy, 1988; Polivy & Herman 1985, 1991). That is, the cognitive restraint that usually controls their food intake breaks down. For most purposes, the term **restrained eaters** is synonymous with dieters, and we will usually use the more common term. Technically, a *restrained eater* is defined as one who receives a high score on a scale (for example, the Restraint Scale, Herman & Polivy, 1980) that measures diet and weight history and concerns with food and dieting. As you probably know if you have ever dieted, when dieters are induced to eat food that they would normally avoid, it has the effect of breaking their diets (Polivy & Herman, 1985). Indeed, even a small amount of forbidden food, such as 100 calories of ice cream, tends to disinhibit subsequent eating much more than a larger portion of "virtuous" food, such as 500 calories of cottage cheese and fruit (Knight & Boland, 1989). Both dieters (Polivy & Herman, 1985) and bulimia nervosa patients (for example, Garner & Bemis, 1985) are very prone to dichotomous thinking. These black-and-white, all-or-nothing thinking patterns are thought to play a part in binge eating. If a person with bulimia nervosa eats even a small amount of forbidden food, she is prone to think "I broke my diet. There is no point now in watching what or how much I eat." The result is a binge.

Alcohol.   Bulimia nervosa patients report that ingesting alcohol can precipitate a binge (Abraham & Beumont, 1982). Laboratory studies (Polivy & Herman, 1976a, 1976b) have also shown that alcohol has a disinhibiting effect on dieters. Alcohol, of course, is a well-known disinhibitor of many behaviours (see Chapter 10).

Solitude.   Finally, the simple circumstance of being alone can serve as a trigger. Bulimia nervosa patients do most of their binge eating in private (Abraham & Beumont, 1982; Davis et al., 1988). Apart from the general tendency shown by eating-disordered individuals to withdraw socially, gorging oneself and vomiting are embarrassing and people try to hide it. Normally, most people eat more in company than when alone (De Castro, 1990). But for the bulimic, social situations tend to inhibit binge eating and privacy disinhibits social constraints on acceptable eating behaviour. In fact, being interrupted by another person can stop a binge. Being alone is also likely to interact with other triggers. For example, loneliness may exacerbate feelings of anxiety and depression.

Some individuals also, no doubt, have less obvious triggers that are unique to them.

Consequences of Binge Eating

People seek help for bulimia nervosa because of the adverse consequences of binge eating. They report feeling embarrassed, depressed, out of control, dissatisfied with their bodies and their relationships. They may also be suffering a number of physical symptoms associated with their disorder. Yet the patient is unable to stop binge eating and purging. A look at the immediate and delayed consequences of bingeing and purging will help us understand why it is so hard to break the cycle.

The *immediate consequences* of a binge—those that happen in the first 30 minutes—are mainly rewarding. First, there is the pleasure of eating rich, tasty food. Second, there is at least temporary relief from hunger. Third, there is temporary relief from negative mood states and stress (Abraham & Beumont, 1982; Hawkins & Clement, 1984). These are powerful positive and negative reinforcers and, because they are immediate, can tend to control behaviour more than long-term, but delayed, adverse consequences.

From about 30 minutes onward, depending in part on how fast the person is eating, *delayed adverse consequences* come into play (Lingswiler, Crowther, & Stephens, 1989).

The person experiences feelings of being out of control, and of shame, disgust, and depression. She probably felt unhappy before the binge, but is even worse after. Yet, rather than stopping her from repeating the pattern, this very misery may help reset the stress/distress trigger for the next binge.

As the binge progresses, anxiety over weight gain grows (Abraham & Beumont, 1982); to relieve this anxiety, the binger is likely to purge.

Finally, there is bloating, abdominal pain, headache, and fatigue, which often play a part in stopping the binge (Lingswiler et al., 1989). Bloating and abdominal pain provide another motive for purging.

Most people with bulimia nervosa *purge* by vomiting, generally within 30 minutes of the end of a binge. Vomiting offers two powerful, negative reinforcers that help lock in the binge-purge pattern: it relieves the painful bloating and reduces anxiety over weight gain. Eventually, the purging can come to play a large part in controlling binge eating; the person will often not binge unless there is an opportunity to purge shortly thereafter (Rosen & Leitenberg, 1982). However, the purging also resets one of the triggers of binge eating by placing the person back into a state of hunger. Overall, while the individual may feel she has undone many of the consequences of the binge, she is left with a sense of fatigue, depression, and self-loathing, and has done much to set herself up for the next binge.

The same cycle, in less obvious form, is also evident in those who use other forms of purging. For example, after a binge, the person may promise herself that she will go on a very strict diet for the next few days in order to rid herself of the calories consumed during the binge. This would put her in a state of hunger and exacerbate any stress/distress she may experience, leaving her open to another binge.

ETIOLOGY

At this point we do not know the etiology of eating disorders, but it is highly unlikely that any single factor will turn out to be the cause. Rather, multiple factors appear to interact, probably at different times during development. In the absence of sure knowledge, many theories arise, often stressing different risk factors.

Sociocultural Pressure and Body Dissatisfaction

Hilda Bruch (1978) was one of the first to suggest that the media and fashion industry contribute to the development of eating disorders by propagating the notion that a women cannot be loved or respected unless she is thin. Since that time, Canadian researchers (Garner, Garfinkel, Schwartz, & Thompson, 1980) and others (for example, Wiseman, Gray, Mosimann, & Ahrens, 1992) have consistently documented that our culture creates enormous pressures for women to be thin. This pressure tends to be present in all industrial societies (DiNicola, 1990). One can see this for oneself by looking at the models in women's magazines, at the mannequins in shop windows, and at female singers, actors, and other admired and rewarded entertainers.

In a clever use of available data, Garner et al. (1980) showed that while examples of "ideal" women (*Playboy* centrefolds, Miss America contestants) became thinner from 1960 to 1978 (see Figure 9.2), the average North American woman's weight increased. A more recent review (Wiseman et al., 1992) shows that this stress on thinness is still very much with us, although the average woman's weight has further increased (Kuczmarski, 1992). Witness the top modelling prospect chosen by the Ford Modelling Foundation in 1997, a 14-year-old Canadian girl who, at 180 centimetres tall and 56 kilograms (*Globe and Mail*, 1997), meets the weight criteria for anorexia nervosa (less than 85 percent of expected for her height and age). Thus, a large gap has been created between the ideal body offered up to women and the actual bodies of the vast majority of women. The result is body dissatisfaction. Not only do women who are overweight by objective standards feel dissatisfied, but so do a large proportion of average-weight and even underweight women (Garner, 1997).

Thinness has also become associated in our culture with many other valued attributes, including self-control, competence, success, acceptance, beauty, femininity, and attractiveness. Conversely, fatness and obesity (the anti-ideal) have developed unappealing associations, such as stupidity, laziness, ugliness, and a lack of femininity (Garner, Rockert, Olmstead, Johnson, & Coscina, 1985; Wilfley & Rodin, 1995). Given this message, it is not surprising that women will pursue the former and avoid the latter, even at risk to their health. Feminist writers and researchers in particular have made us more aware of the damaging effects of our culturally prescribed standards for women (for example, Fallon, Katzman, & Wooley, 1994; Striegel-Moore, 1995).

Differential Socialization

Ruth Striegel-Moore offers an enlightening developmental perspective on this situation. Noting that the massive majority of eating disorders develop in young women, she points out differences in the socialization process for girls and boys as a

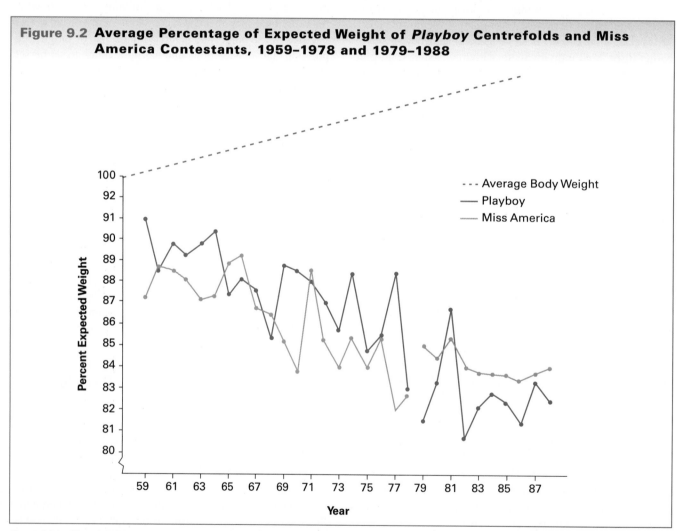

Figure 9.2 Average Percentage of Expected Weight of *Playboy* Centrefolds and Miss America Contestants, 1959–1978 and 1979–1988

Source: Adapted from C. V. Wiseman, J. J. Gray, J. E. Mosimann, & A. H. Ahrens, *International Journal of Eating Disorders 11(1992)* (1), 87; and D. M. Garner, The 1997 body image survey *results, Psychology Today, 30* (1), 30–44.

Thinness is associated in our culture with self-control, competence, and beauty, among other attributes.

contributing cause (Striegel-Moore, 1993; Striegel-Moore, Silberstein, & Rodin, 1986). She argues that girls are socialized from early life to pay more attention to appearance and attractiveness than boys. Beauty remains a central concept to women's identity throughout their lives. In a culture where attractiveness is nearly synonymous with thinness, is it any wonder that women internalize the thin ideal and avoid the anti-ideal of fat? She also argues that females define themselves more in terms of their relationships than males, and pay more attention to cues of approval and disapproval from others, especially as regards their looks.

Studies on a sample of Canadian girls suggest that weight and shape dissatisfaction rise throughout adolescence (Leichner, Arnett, Rallo, Srikomenswaran, & Vulcano, 1986). Striegel-Moore notes that when boys go through adolescence they put on a layer of muscle, thus moving them closer to the male ideal, whereas girls put on a layer of fat, moving them away from the ideal female body. In addition, adolescence is a time when public self-consciousness is high and young girls may feel that any perceived flaw in their body is on display. For girls, more than for boys, body image also emerges as an issue in sexuality and dating, achieving autonomy, and forming an identity. Adolescent girls are thus particularly prone to body image dissatisfaction (Striegel-Moore, 1993; Striegel-Moore et al., 1986).

Dieting

With the increase in body dissatisfaction occurring during adolescence there is a corresponding increase in dieting and the use of aberrant weight loss methods, such as vomiting, laxative abuse, and diet pills (Leichner et al., 1986). Table 9.1 shows how common such methods were in repeated surveys of New York State teenage girls carried out at the same schools over a seven-year period.

Dieting can take the form of fasting for one or more days at a time, avoiding many different foods, consuming commercial low-calorie liquid diet preparations, or generally cutting back on the amount eaten. It can also involve the use of appetite-suppressant drugs such as amphetamines. Books and magazine articles tout dozens of different variations on the diet theme, all claiming that their particular diet will bring about effortless and lasting weight loss, usually rapidly. (The Focus box on the Slim Chance Awards highlights a few of the many products available to those searching for an easy way to lose weight.) In some cases, these diets come close to recommending behaviours seen in eating-disordered individuals (Wooley & Wooley, 1982). Regardless of the particular pattern adopted, dieting is so widespread among females that it is considered normative (Polivy & Herman, 1987). The great majority of this dieting is in the service of appearance rather than of health, and many investigators see it as a major risk factor for eating disorders.

The great majority of cases of anorexia and bulimia nervosa are preceded by periods of restrictive dieting (Abraham & Beumont, 1982). In one prospective study, 15-year-old schoolgirls were identified as either dieters or non-dieters. One year later they were reassessed for eating disorders. Dieters were eight times more likely to develop an eating dis-

Table 9.1	Adolescent Girls' Use of Drugs and Vomiting to Lose Weight		
	1984	**1989**	**1992**
High School*	*n* = 311	275	253
Middle School**	*n* = 131	120	114
Have you ever used drugs/medications such as Dexatrim or Acutrim to help you lose weight?			
High school	28.0% (87)	14.2% (39)	11.9% (30)
Middle school	0.8% (1)	1.7% (2)	6.1% (7)
Have you ever used laxatives such as Ex-Lax or Correctol to help you lose weight?			
High school	5.5% (17)	4.4% (12)	3.2% (8)
Middle school	1.5% (2)	0% (0)	1.8% (2)
Have you deliberately vomited in an effort to lose weight?			
High school	16.1% (50)	13.5% (37)	15.4% (39)
Middle school	3.8% (5)	3.3% (4)	11.4% (13)

* Grades 9–12.
** Grades 7–8.
Source: Adapted from L. Phelps, R. Andrea, F. G. Rizzo, L. Johnston, & C. M. Main, Prevalence of self-induced vomiting and laxative/medication abuse among female adolescents: a longitudinal study, *International Journal of Eating Disorders 14(1993)* (3), 377.

Focus *The Year's "Worst" Weight Loss Products:*

1997 Slim Chance Awards

On "Rid the World of Fad Diets and Gimmicks Day," the *Healthy Weight Journal* and the Task Force on Weight Loss Abuse, National Council Against Health Fraud, present annual "Slim Chance Awards" for the worst products around. These awards "affirm the sad fact that there's no end in sight to weight loss quackery, get-rich-quick schemes, and con artists who profit by defrauding vulnerable consumers." The 1997 awards, which follow, "represent a large number of similar products being heavily advertised today."

WORST PRODUCT: EQUINOX WEIGHT MANAGEMENT SYSTEM

The Equinox Weight Management System is an herbal program based on the quack theory that our bodies must be detoxified for proper balance and function of digestive and enzyme systems. It includes Equi-Lizer Fast Start capsules (claimed to suppress appetite, stimulate calorie consumption, and burn fat), Equi-Lizer Steady Burn capsules (claimed to increase thermogenesis and stabilize appetite), Equi-Lizer NightTime Formula (claimed to promote weight loss while you sleep, reduce sugar's ability to produce fat, reduce toxins, and help detoxify your body), Protein Plus

ChromeMate capsules ("essential to keep calorie-burning capacity at its peak"), Equi-vites Multi-vitamin tablets, and Equi-Lizer Almond Bars. Combination costs about $164 a month. Multi-level company.

MOST OUTRAGEOUS: ABSORBIT-ALL PLUS

Full-page newspaper ads across the country in July 1996 touted Absorbit-ALL PLUS in blaring headlines, all the more ridiculous in this day of cautious claims, "Guaranteed to blast up to 49 pounds off you in only 29 days! Blocks up to 15 times its weight in fat, blasts up to 50% of your body fat in record time, obliterates up to 5 inches from your waistline, and zaps 3 inches from your thighs before you know it!" Just more chromium picolinate mixed with mysterious ingredients like "Asian root fat blockers" in a pill that "stimulates your metabolic rate and prevents lean muscle loss while the fat just melts away!" $49.95 + $5.95 shipping and handling, for 30-day supply.

WORST CLAIM: SVELT PATCH

The Svelt PATCH—a stick-on patch to be attached anywhere on the body—purportedly absorbs fat, triggers fat burning, speeds up metabolism,

stimulates thyroid, fights water retention, prevents muscle loss, controls appetite, and maintains weight loss, all illegal drug claims. "Fucus—a natural algae" is the active ingredient here, supposedly absorbed from the patch into the body. Each patch lasts 24 hours, and a four-week supply costs $42.95.

WORST GADGET: SLIMMING INSOLES

Insoles that slip into your shoes, are covered with small knobs, and cause "weight loss with every step you take" are one of the most highly advertised weight loss gadgets on the market today. The knobs are claimed to stimulate foot reflex centres that control kidneys, bladder, and stomach through acupressure—"a 5,000-year-old Chinese therapy." The theory is that weight problems are often linked to "under-performance of the dietary system." Therefore, when these organs are primed to function efficiently through acupressure, your metabolism "works normally and does not store fat!" Testimonials claim no dieting or exercise needed. "I lost 74 pounds!" Cost $19.95. ▲

Source: Adapted from *Healthy Weight Journal*, January/February 1997. © 1997, Healthy Weight Journal. See the website for *Healthy Weight Journal* at www.healthyweightnetwork.com/hwj.htm.

order than non-dieters (Patton, Johnson-Sabine, Wood, Mann, & Wakeling, 1990). Even in the much rarer cases in which binge eating occurs first in the progressive development of an eating disorder, it is often followed by dieting and the development of a cycle of dieting, binge eating, and purging. For these and other reasons some investigators have argued that in some susceptible individuals dieting, especially strict dieting, may precipitate or even cause an eating disorder (Garner & Garfinkel, 1980; Polivy & Herman, 1985; Rodin, Silberstein, & Striegel-Moore, 1985).

Normal males in the Keys, Brozeck, Henschel, Mickelsen, and Taylor, (1950) semistarvation study (see the Focus box) suffered psychologically during food deprivation and developed many of the symptoms we see in anorexia and bulimia

nervosa. Bear in mind that the majority of adolescents and young adult females who diet are not overweight by recommended standards. Yet studies and reviews show that this type of dieting is also associated with a variety of ill effects, including low self-esteem, depressed mood, feelings of failure, and increased stress levels (Berg, 1995; Rosen, Tacy, & Howell, 1990). Even with the obese, however, there is a major current debate over whether dietary treatments do more good than harm (see Garner & Wooley, 1991, for a critique of obesity treatments and Brownell & Rodin, 1994, for a rebuttal). All agree that the great majority of individuals who lose weight by dieting or dietary treatments eventually gain it back.

Why is it so easy to regain lost weight? Why is dieting so hard on both the body and the emotions? Many researchers

Focus   *Starvation and the Symptoms of Eating Disorders*

David Garner and colleagues did much to bring to the attention of therapists and researchers the remarkable similarities between people placed on a semistarvation diet and those with eating disorders (Garner et al. 1985). They summarized the results of an early experiment by Keys, Brozek, Henschel, Mickelsen, & Taylor (1950).

Keys had studied 36 young men who had volunteered for a semistarvation experiment as an alternative to military service. The men were housed together during the first three months and were allowed to eat normally. Tests showed they were psychologically and physically healthy. During the next six months they were given a daily allotment of food that amounted to half their normal daily intake (about 1200 calories) and they lost about 25 percent of their original body weight. During the next three months they were refed and permitted to gain back their weight.

During the weight-loss period the men became obsessed with thoughts of food and eating. They read cookbooks, collected recipes, talked about food and daydreamed about it. Three changed their career plans and later became chefs. The men experienced intense hunger and cravings for food. Some could not tolerate it and binged, sometimes vomiting afterward. During the refeeding period, binge eating was commonplace, with some saying they felt hungry even after a large meal. Even months after the refeeding periods, some of the men still had abnormal eating patterns.

The semistarvation period was associated with an increase in depression, irritability, anger, apathy, hypochondriasis, and personality changes. Many of these symptoms persisted during the refeeding period.

The dieting affected the men socially. They withdrew from each other and complained of feeling socially inadequate. Their sexual interest declined sharply and in some cases their relationships with women suffered.

The men reported impaired concentration, alertness, and judgement, and their productivity declined considerably.

For ethical reasons, the Keys et al. study would not be carried out today. Nevertheless, we can learn from it. These men were psychologically and physically healthy at the start of the experiment. They did not start with the same motivations, attitudes, and beliefs as the girls and women who develop eating disorders. Nevertheless, during the period of the semistarvation diet, and for months afterwards, many of them showed the cognitive, emotional, and behavioural patterns that characterize anorexia and bulimia nervosa. Their struggle to regain control of their eating, even after the period of deprivation had ended, suggests that the experience of starvation helps induce and perpetuate the symptoms of eating disorders. ▲

favour the notion that we have a comfortable biological weight range that our bodies seek to maintain. One version of this that has gained increasing attention is the concept of a **set point** (Keesey, 1986, 1995). We each arrive at our individual weight through a complex interaction between nature and nurture. However, according to Keesey, in the long run, this weight is fairly stable and difficult to change. When humans or animals are underfed or overfed, a biological mechanism seeks to maintain weight by either slowing or speeding up metabolism, much as a thermostat maintains a stable room temperature by causing the furnace to cut in or cut out in response to changes in temperature.

The implications of a set point mechanism for the strict dieting seen in eating disorders has been thoroughly explored by Garner et al. (1985) and Garner and Wooley (1991). If anorexic and bulimic individuals attempt to maintain a weight that is significantly below their set point, this will generate forces pulling them back toward their normal set point. In anorexia nervosa, for example, decreases of more than 30 percent have been observed in **basal metabolic rate** (the amount of energy used by a resting person to maintain vital functioning). Many of the symptoms seen in eating-

disordered individuals, and also in the men in the Keys et al. (1950) experiment may be due to the consequences of being significantly below normal set point.

So far, in discussing the possible causes of eating disorders, we have attempted to link sociocultural pressures to body dissatisfaction and dieting, noting that the socialization process for women interacts with their development to put them particularly at risk for eating disorders. However, while dieting and body dissatisfaction may be necessary to the development of eating disorders, they can hardly be considered a sufficient cause. After all, the majority of women in Canada feel some body dissatisfaction and diet at some point in their lives, but only about 2 or 3 percent of them go on to develop a clinical eating disorder. Clearly, other predisposing factors are involved.

Low Self-Esteem

It is well recognized that eating-disordered patients have low self-esteem (for example, Garfinkel & Garner, 1982)—that is, a poor evaluation of their own perceived central attributes. Body-esteem is an important component of general self-esteem (Mendelson & White, 1985) and body dissatisfaction is likely to decrease self-esteem (Heatherton & Polivy, 1992). Low self-esteem is associated with a higher score on a measure of eating disorder pathology (Attie & Brooks-Gunn, 1989). Moreover, chronic dieters with low self-esteem are more likely to disinhibit their eating after consuming forbidden food than those with high self-esteem (Polivy, Heatherton, & Herman, 1988). However, data linking self-esteem to eating disorders are correlational and other interpretations can be made. Does poor self-esteem make people fail at dieting, or does failure at dieting, or developing a binge-purge pattern, lower self-esteem? Or could the effect go both ways, so that initially low self-esteem is lowered even further by abnormal eating patterns (Herman & Polivy, 1993)?

Conceivably, low self-esteem could lead to dieting even if it were not initially associated with body dissatisfaction. Suppose a girl has low self-esteem because of academic failure. She may seek to compensate by being admired for being more than usually slim, with all the connotations that image carries of beauty, self-discipline, and success.

Obesity and Early Menarche

The above analysis applies to all girls growing up in our culture. However, certain factors would accentuate this pressure in individual girls. People who develop anorexia or bulimia nervosa have a higher incidence of childhood obesity and an earlier onset of puberty than normal controls (Crisp, 1970; Fairburn, Welch, Doll, Davies, & O'Connor, 1997). Such factors may increase body dissatisfaction, lower self-esteem, and encourage early dieting (Fairburn et al., 1997; Striegel-Moore et al., 1986). They may also increase the incidence of teasing about weight and shape, which is also reported by eating-disordered individuals (for example, Fairburn et al., 1997).

Psychodynamic Factors

Crisp (1970) has hypothesized that the central feature of anorexia nervosa is an **avoidance of psychosexual maturity**. The anorexic's fears of maturity are transferred to her body, which can be controlled by deprivation and brought back to a prepubescent state. One might guess that such motivation might be particularly strong in a girl who experiences early menarche.

Bruch (1973) held that a **pervasive sense of ineffectiveness** at dealing with life was an underlying vulnerability in eating disorders. The anorexic combats these feelings by exercising narrow control of one area of her life—her weight and what she eats. Garfinkel and Garner (1982) have incorporated these concepts as well as others into a multidimensional theory of anorexia nervosa. The concepts are somewhat difficult to operationalize, but eating disorder patients do show higher-than-normal levels on scales measuring fears of maturity and a sense of ineffectiveness (Garner, Olmstead, & Polivy, 1983). However, at least in the case of ineffective-

ness, eating-disordered patients cannot always be differentiated from people with other psychiatric problems (Steiger, Goldstein, Mongrain, & Van der Feen, 1990). More research is needed to clarify whether these concepts are associated with eating disorders in particular or with psychiatric disturbances in general. Moreover, do these patterns *predate* the development of eating disorders, or have they developed as a *consequence* of the eating disorder? Finally, many of these concepts arose through the study of anorexia nervosa and it will be important to determine how well they apply to bulimia nervosa.

Irrational Cognitions

According to cognitive and cognitive-behavioural theories, the development of rigid thinking and overvalued ideals plays an important role in causing and maintaining eating disorders. Eating disorder patients, especially anorexia nervosa patients, do exhibit many irrational cognitions, even when compared to other psychiatric groups (Steiger, Goldstein, Mongrain, & Van der Feen, 1990).

The central belief is that weight and shape are of extreme importance and must be controlled at all costs (Fairburn, 1981, 1985; Garner & Bemis, 1982, 1985). From this starting-point, the eating-disordered individual follows a certain logic (albeit a maladaptive one) to conclude :

- "Fat is terrible and I must avoid it completely."
- "My worth can be judged by my weight."
- "I can't be happy, attractive, and successful unless I am thin."
- "If I eat any unplanned food I am a weak person."

Eating disorder patients are prone to **cognitive errors** in their reasoning. For example, when it comes to dieting, they exhibit a *dichotomous* thinking style: it's A or B, all or nothing. ("If I eat any forbidden food I have totally broken my diet.")

Earlier we saw how this thinking style can contribute to binge eating. Such cognitive errors can extend to other areas as well ("If I don't get A's on my courses I am a failure"). People with eating disorders tend to magnify any perceived defect ("If I gain two pounds it will be terrible and everyone will notice"). They jump to conclusions ("If I gain any weight I will become fat").These thought patterns engender fear and anxiety, lower self-esteem and coping ability, contribute to binge eating, and encourage strict dieting and purging behaviour.

But how do these irrational beliefs and cognitive errors develop in the first place? That's not clear. Various factors may be involved and may differ from one person to another. However, once these thought patterns become entrenched they play a powerful role in maintaining eating-disordered behaviour.

Personality and Personality Disorders

Another hypothesis is that one or more personality traits, or outright personality disorders, may predispose some people to an eating disorder. In an insightful review of this literature, Vitousek and Manke (1994) note that many early studies described eating-disordered patients as shy and inhibited, conforming and compliant, perfectionist and obsessive. Later studies that divided eating disorders into subgroups tended to find bulimics to be more outgoing, impulsive, and unstable in mood than restrictors. Many recent studies have reported increased incidence of a variety of personality disorders in eating-disordered patients. The most common pattern is for anorexia nervosa to be associated with obsessive-compulsive personality disorder and bulimia nervosa with borderline personality disorder (see Chapter 11).

It is difficult to draw firm conclusions about the relationship between personality and eating disorders. As Vitousek and Manke (1994) observe, all the studies of premorbid personality are retrospective and open to many sources of bias. We come back to the chicken-and-egg dilemma: Is the personality trait the cause of the eating disorder or its effect? Recall that the males in the Keys et al. (1950) semistarvation study showed dramatic personality deterioration after they started the semistarvation diet. Moreover, the personality disorders observed in eating disorder patients often disappear spontaneously once the eating disorder is successfully treated.

Genetic Predisposition

Could there be an inborn predisposition to eating disorders? The relatives of anorexia nervosa patients do show a higher prevalence of eating disorders than the relatives of psychiatric patients with other diagnoses (Strober, Morrell, Burroughs, Salkin, & Jacobs, 1985).

One twin study supported the notion of a genetic basis. This study looked at 16 monozygotic (identical) twin pairs in which one twin had anorexia nervosa; in nine of the pairs (55 percent) the other twin also had the disorder. In fraternal (dizygotic) twin pairs, the corresponding figure was 7 percent (Holland, Hall, Murray, Russell, & Crisp, 1984). A study of bulimia nervosa in identical and fraternal twins suggested a similar genetic component, accounting for as much as 50 percent of the variance (Kendler et al., 1991).

Since twins are normally raised together, it is difficult to estimate the role of shared environment. There is also the possibility that identical twins may be treated more alike than fraternal twins, thus exaggerating the genetic component. Nevertheless, these studies strongly suggest a genetic predisposition to develop an eating disorder in some individuals.

Genetics do appear to be an important influence—though by no means the only one—on personality traits (Carey & DiLalla, 1994). Strober (1995) has hypothesized that what is inherited, in the case of anorexia nervosa, restricting type, are personality traits, such as a tendency to become anxious and worried, to like order and routine, and to avoid novelty. These traits in no way guarantee the development of an eating disorder, but they do bring the individual into conflict with the changes and pressures of adolescent development. She may adapt by developing rigidly controlled eating patterns and an obsession with weight and shape.

For bulimia nervosa, Strober (1995) suggests that the inherited disposition includes excitability, impulsiveness, a tendency to seek sensation, and difficulty in accepting disappointment or rejection. People with these traits might have trouble sticking to rigid diets and suffer periodic binge episodes as a result. He notes that bulimia nervosa is associated with increased risk of substance abuse and mood disorders.

These are general hypotheses and much research is needed to properly test them. The increase in eating disorders seen over the past 25 years has corresponded to the increase in sociocultural pressure stressing thinness and stigmatizing fatness. On the surface, it is difficult to see genetics playing a large part in this increase. However, sociocultural pressures might affect girls with certain inherited temperamental traits more than their peers; if these girls also suffer low self-esteem, or experience childhood obesity and/or early menarche, the challenges of adolescence may push them into an eating disorder.

Personality traits may also interact with other inherited features. Childhood obesity, a known risk factor for eating disorders, has been shown to have a fairly strong genetic component (for example, Stunkard, Foch, & Hrubec, 1986). Obesity and inherited personality traits together may leave a girl especially vulnerable to eating disorders.

The Family

Family systems theory views eating disorders as a symptom of **dysfunctional family** communication and relationship patterns (Root, Fallon, & Friedrich, 1986). Family studies show that both bulimia nervosa patients and anorexics who binge and purge perceive their families as less expressive, communicative, disclosing, cohesive, and nurturing and more conflicted than the families of normal controls (for example, Humphrey, 1988, 1989; Kog & Vandereycken, 1989). Families of restricting anorexics exhibit low expressiveness and poor communication, but are not characterized as lacking cohesion or in conflict (Humphrey, 1988).

However, while these patterns consistently emerge, it is not clear that they are specifically associated with eating disorders. One key variable seems to be the presence of depression. In a study carried out in Ottawa, Blouin, Zuro, and Blouin (1990) compared depressed bulimia nervosa patients, bulimia patients who were not depressed, and normal controls. Only the depressed bulimics described their families as high in conflict and low in cohesion and expressiveness. Bulimics who were not depressed were indistinguishable from normal controls. Two other studies that included both psychiatric controls and normal controls, found no differences in family perceptions between the eating-disordered group and the psychiatric control group; both groups showed more perceived family dysfunction than the normal controls (Stuart, Laraia, Ballenger, & Lydiard, 1990). These two studies suggest that family dysfunction may be associated not so much with bulimia in particular as with the development of psychopathology in general. Another possibility is that the dysfunction in the family is the result of having to live with a seriously disordered family member. It is also possible that perceptions of the family are distorted by the respondents; it seems reasonable that being depressed or disturbed may cloud one's perception of one's family.

However, a recent study does suggest some more specific associations (Fairburn, Welch, Doll, Davies, & O'Connor, 1997). This study interviewed women with bulimia nervosa, and matched samples of both healthy controls and psychiatric controls. The bulimics reported more parental alcoholism and obesity, low parental contact, high parental expectations, and a family history of teasing about shape, weight, or eating. The greater the exposure to these factors the greater was the risk of developing bulimia nervosa.

We still have much to learn about the role of the family in eating disorders. Some research suggests that fathers of bulimics are distant and nonsupportive (Steiger, Van der Feen, Goldstein, & Leichner, 1989). If this is true it may accentuate the role of the mother. Mothers pass on many values about weight, shape, and dieting—values that may be helpful or harmful (Pike & Rodin, 1991).

It is also possible that family characteristics such as conflict and limited cohesion or expressiveness, even if they do not in themselves cause eating disorders, may aggravate existing tendencies. In any case, if family dysfunction is present, it often has to be addressed during treatment, especially if the person is still living at home.

Socioeconomic Status

After over one hundred years of observation, to quote Gard and Freeman:

the prevailing wisdom concerning the relationship between eating disorders and socioeconomic status in both the professional and lay person's mind, is that there is an increased prevalence of eating disorders in high socioeconomic status groups. (Gard & Freeman, 1996, p. 1)

These authors then proceed to demolish this "myth" with a cogent analysis of the literature since 1970. Between 1973 and 1985 they found eight studies reporting a link between anorexia nervosa and higher socioeconomic status. However, these studies were strongly biased because they were based on small uncontrolled patient samples, or surveys of students from predominantly private schools. They note that these patient samples may not be representative of eating disorders in the general population and that individuals with eating

disorders from upper socioeconomic groups are more likely to be seen by health professionals. Furthermore, students from private schools are not representative of students in general or of women in general. Since that time, eight studies using better sampling procedures and methodology have failed to find a relationship between higher socioeconomic status and anorexia nervosa and nine studies have failed to find this relationship with bulimia nervosa. Indeed, four of the anorexia nervosa studies and four of the bulimia studies showed an opposite trend (Gard & Freeman, 1996). At this point, the safest conclusion is that there is no proven relationship between socioeconomic status and eating disorders.

Mood Disorders

There is a strong association between eating disorders, especially bulimia nervosa, and depression (for example, Cooper & Fairburn, 1986; Hudson, Pope, & Jonas, 1984; Laessle et al., 1987). In the study by Hudson and colleagues, almost 90 percent of the bulimia nervosa patients also suffered depression. Could bulimia nervosa itself be a variant of mood disorder?

Research suggests that, on the contrary, the depression is secondary to the eating disorder. Sequential analysis shows that in the great majority of cases the depression does not precede the eating disorder (Laessle, Kittle, Fichter, Wittchen, & Pirke, 1987). Also, the depression associated with bulimia appears to be different from that seen in pure depression—with more anxiety and obsessional ruminations and less sadness and suicidal ideation (Cooper & Fairburn, 1986). In addition, if depression and eating disorders had the same etiology, one would expect an increased rate of eating disorders in young women who have primary depression. However, Strober and Katz (1987) found that the rate is no different than the base rate in the general population. Finally, successful treatment of bulimia nervosa usually relieves depressive symptoms, even though depression is not directly targeted in treatment.

Substance Abuse

Reviews of the literature suggest that the rate of alcohol and/or drug abuse in eating-disordered patients is about 17 percent, while the rate of eating disorders in women with substance abuse is about 20 percent (Holderness, Brooks-Gunn, & Warren, 1994): many times the expected rate in the general population of women (see Chapter 10). The association is highest in individuals with bulimia nervosa and higher in the binge-purge type of anorexia nervosa than in the restricting type.

Why do eating disorders and substance abuse sometimes go together? Krahn (1991) and Wilson (1995) have reviewed a number of possible explanations. One possibility is that they have a common genetic and biological basis. Some have, indeed, suggested that eating disorders can best be viewed as a type of addiction, though there are major problems with this model. (See ViewPoint box.)

ViewPoint *Are Eating Disorders Addictions?*

There are many similarities between alcohol and drug abusers and individuals with eating disorders (Wilson, 1995). Both groups report cravings, experience feelings of losing control, and hide the behaviour. Both groups appear to use their substances to deal with stress and bad emotional states. For both, their substance (food, alcohol, or drugs) becomes a central focus in their lives and they will persist in the behaviour despite adverse psychological, physical, and social consequences.

You might be thinking, with all these similarities and the high co-morbidity between the two disorders, why don't we just consider eating-disordered individuals "food addicts" (a popular lay term that implies an **addiction model** of eating disorders).

However, an insightful analysis by Wilson (1993, 1995) discounts such a model. First, alcohol and drug abusers do not have a drive to avoid consuming their substance; they seek it out. Eating-disordered individuals, on the other hand, try their best to avoid food because of threatened weight gain. Second, eating-disordered patients are dominated by weight and shape concerns and eating makes them anxious. These concerns are not central to substance abusers and there is no strong anxiety associated with indulging.

Wilson raises the question of how addiction models could ever handle anorexia nervosa, restricting type. It is difficult to argue that this group is addicted to starvation while those with the binge-purge type are addicted to food. He notes, as well, that there are no parallels in eating disorders to the phenomena of tolerance and physical dependence, concepts central to alcohol and drug addiction.

Finally, Wilson and others have argued that the addiction model is unhelpful in treatment. To stress abstinence or avoidance of foods such as sweets would be a backward step, since a major focus of treatment is to normalize eating patterns. In addition, unless patients learn to handle these tempting "forbidden" foods, they will be in danger of relapse.

Critical Thinking Questions

1. Are substance abuse disorders and eating disorders just different manifestations of an underlying predisposition (for example, genetic, biochemical, or personality)?

2. Substance abuse disorders are more common in males, whereas eating disorders are more common in females. To what extent do differential cultural pressures on males and females determine the psychopathology each is prone to develop?

3. There is evidence that substance abusers use their substances to cope with life problems and that individuals with bulimia nervosa also use binge eating to cope with stress. Does using one substance (for example, cocaine) to cope predispose a person to use a very different substance (for example, food) as a coping device? How would you test this hypothesis?

Another possibility is that deprivation of food, especially rich food, may enhance the reward value of other substances like alcohol and drugs. A third possibility is that both disorders may reflect a third, more basic disorder of impulse control. At this point we do not know, but it is worth recalling that alcohol is known to disinhibit eating in dieters and to trigger bulimic binges.

Sexual Abuse

Most eating disorders emerge by the time the individual is 18. Sadly, surveys have also reported that before that age about half of young females and about a third of males have been sexually abused in some fashion (see Chapter 12). Since sexual abuse is so damaging to the child's self-esteem, feelings about her body, sense of control, and other aspects of functioning, some investigators thought sexual abuse might be a necessary and sufficient cause of eating disorders (for example, Waller, 1991).

While there is still much we do not know, the evidence from well-controlled studies does not support this specific hypothesis. Eating-disordered patients do show a higher incidence of sexual abuse than normal controls. However, a better control would be women with other types of psychiatric problems (Connors & Morse, 1992). Studies have shown rates of sexual abuse among those with eating disorders are either lower than, or no different from, those among psychiatric controls (Folsom et al., 1993; Palmer & Oppenheimer, 1992). Thus, any association appears not to be specific to eating disorders. Nonetheless, it is possible that in certain individual cases, sexual abuse may contribute to an eating disorder. It may also interact with other risk factors to contribute to the development of an eating disorder. In any case, the association of sexual abuse with so many different psychiatric problems should concern all of us.

Careers Stressing Thinness

Women who choose careers in dancing, modelling, or sports such as gymnastics that stress very lean physiques appear to be at increased risk for eating disorders (Druss & Silverman 1979; Garner & Garfinkel, 1978; Garner & Rosen, 1991).

In recent years athletes in particular have been in the spotlight. When we first surveyed a sample of university athletes from different sports we found no indication that either male or female athletes were any more at risk for eating disorders than other students. In fact, the athletes tended to have better body-esteem and self-esteem (Wilkins, Boland, & Albinson, 1990). A wider review of the evidence suggests that the increased risk is limited to athletes in sports that stress appearance or an extremely lean body (Garner & Rosen, 1991).

One problem with questionnaire surveys is that athletes may underreport symptoms. Probably the best study of athletes to date was carried out in Norway by Sundgot-Borgen (1993). He first surveyed more than 500 elite female athletes and more than 400 controls and found no real difference between the groups in the percentage at risk for eating disorders. However, he then selected all those scoring in the "at risk" range on the questionnaires and gave them a clinical interview and medical examination. It turned out that 18 percent of the athletes vs. 5 percent of controls suffered from some type of eating disorder. It is not known whether this high rate would hold up in less-elite athletes. Among dancers, for example, those at the most competitive school showed the highest incidence of eating disorder symptoms (Garner & Garfinkel, 1980).

Elite athletes are under enormous performance pressures and stress. As well, there are great financial and other rewards for reaching the top. Just as some athletes resort to steroid use to give them a competitive edge, others may use aberrant weight control methods. At least one group of athletes appears to do both. An Ottawa study showed that competitive male bodybuilders engage in considerable steroid use and also exhibit a great deal of eating-disordered pathology (Blouin & Goldfield, 1995) (see Table 9.2). Again, is it the bodybuilding that causes the eating problems, or are men with excessive concerns about their shape drawn to bodybuilding?

In any case, mental health professionals are recognizing the need to target athletes, parents, and coaches with

To achieve those rippling muscles, some bodybuilders may work out, train, take drugs, and engage in eating-disordered behaviour.

education and other prevention and intervention efforts (Garner & Rosen, 1991).

Eating Disorders in Males

Much of this chapter is devoted to research carried out with females. However, it is estimated that from 5 to 10 percent of cases of anorexia nervosa (Andersen & Mickalide, 1983) and bulimia nervosa (Pope & Hudson, 1986) occur in males. Because eating disorders occur so frequently in females, there may be a bias against recognizing or diagnosing eating disorders in males. Also, males may be more secretive about disturbed eating and less willing to seek help for what they might consider a women's problem. Nevertheless, this subgroup is receiving increasing research attention (for example, Andersen, 1990).

Are eating disorders different in males than in females? This is the question addressed by most studies on males. The answer appears to be no. A review (1989) by Howard Steiger, Director of the Eating Disorder Program at the Douglas Hospital in Montreal, found little or no difference between males and females with either anorexia nervosa or bulimia nervosa in age of onset, socioeconomic status, symptomatology, or etiological factors related to personality or family. Such findings are reflected in other reviews as well (Andersen, 1995).

Steiger argues, therefore, that the same factors operate to produce eating disorders in males and females, except that in females they are more active and powerful. For example,

Table 9.2	**Psychological Characteristics of Bodybuilders and Comparison Groups**		
Measure	**Body-building**	**Running**	**Martial Arts**
Body image and eating measures:			
	Mean (SD)	*Mean (SD)*	*Mean (SD)*
Drive for thinness[a,b]	75.2 (1.8)	67.8 (1.6)	66.6 (1.9)
Bulimia[a,b]	78.0 (1.8)	69.6 (0.7)	69.2 (0.8)
Body dissatisfaction[a]	58.6 (3.0)	47.5 (2.9)	41.7 (2.6)
Drive for bulk[a,b]	17.5 (0.9)	7.7 (0.7)	9.2 (0.9)

[a]Bodybuilders vs. martial artists $p < 0.05$.
[b]Bodybuilders vs. runners $p < 0.05$.

Note: Scores are of standardized measures of these characteristics and are derived from questionnaires administered to a volunteer sample of 43 bodybuilders, 48 runners, and 48 martial artists.

Source: Adapted from A. G. Blouin & G. S. Goldfield, Body image and steroid use in male bodybuilders, *International Journal of Eating Disorders (18)1995* (2), 162. © 1995 by John Wiley & Sons. Reprinted by permission of John Wiley & Sons, Inc.

girls hit puberty earlier than boys, and their bodies change more radically; women experience stronger sociocultural pressure to achieve thinness than men.

Among males, however, homosexuals and bisexuals may be at greater risk (Herzog, Norman, Gordon & Pepose, 1984; Schneider & Agras, 1987). Andersen (1995) estimates that approximately 20 percent of males with eating disorders are homosexual—a higher rate than the general population, but still a minority. The pattern does not apply to females: lesbians are not at higher risk than heterosexual women. The general explanation for gay men's increased risk is that, since they tend to place more emphasis on attractiveness than heterosexual men (Silberstein, Mishkind, Streigel-Moore, Timko, & Rodin, 1989), they experience more cultural pressure to achieve thinness. Steiger has raised the possibility that males who develop eating disorders, regardless of their sexual orientation, show more identification with the feminine. This would also be consistent with the general hypothesis, but we have to be cautious in our interpretations. It is difficult to accumulate samples of males with eating disorders and even more difficult to accumulate samples of homosexual men with eating disorders. More research is obviously needed.

Biological Mechanisms

Many hormones and neurotransmitter substances have been hypothesized to be involved in the development or maintenance of eating disorders. Insulin and serotonin are the most interesting.

When we eat a meal, the hormone insulin is released in order to metabolize carbohydrates, transport glucose into the cells, and store fats. This is referred to as the *postprandial response*. However, insulin can also be released in anticipation of eating in order to prepare the body for expected food. This is referred to as the *cephalic response*. Since high levels of insulin have an appetite-stimulating effect, one hypothesis suggests that bulimics may have an exaggerated cephalic response to thoughts of food or the mere presence of food and that this may serve to trigger binge eating (Powley, 1977). It is known, for example, that obese individuals have an exaggerated cephalic response to seeing food (Rodin, 1985). However, in laboratory comparisons of bulimia nervosa patients and normal controls, no differences were found in cephalic insulin response (Johnson, Jarrell, Chupurdia, & Williamson, 1994). Thus, this hypothesis is not supported.

Another hypothesis linking insulin to binge eating concerns the postprandial response. Earlier we noted that refined carbohydrates (sugars) are a major component of binge food. Could the insulin response to carbohydrates lead to increased hunger that might trigger a binge? In an interesting study with normal subjects Spitzer and Rodin (1987) were able to show that when fasting subjects consumed glucose they later increased the amount of food they consumed. The following sequence of events has been proposed to explain this response:

1. Since glucose (refined carbohydrates) is easily absorbed from the gut, glucose levels rise rapidly in the blood.

2. The body releases a corresponding amount of insulin to deal with this rise.

3. Blood sugar levels fall rapidly, rendering the person somewhat hypoglycemic (low blood sugar). No longer needed, insulin also declines.

4. The low blood sugar level makes the person feel hungrier.

Could this sequence apply to binge eating in bulimia nervosa patients? Again, laboratory research comparing bulimia nervosa patients to normal controls (Johnson et al., 1994) suggests that acute hypoglycemia may indeed be involved in the binge-purge cycle, but that the key feature associated with the hypoglycemic response is purging. In this study, bulimics showed the same insulin response after a high-carbohydrate meal as normal controls when they did not purge. However, when the bulimics purged after the high-carbohydrate meal, blood glucose levels and insulin levels showed a dramatic decline relative to nonpurging controls, thus leaving them in a state of acute hypoglycemia. Since this state is associated with increased hunger, it is speculated that this may set the stage for the next binge. Johnson and colleagues note that it is not uncommon for bulimia nervosa patients to engage in binge eating and purging several times a day. This would fit the carbohydrate-insulin reaction pattern described above.

The case appears even stronger for the involvement of serotonin, a neurotransmitter involved in mood disorders and the control of appetite. Wurtman and Wurtman (1984) and others have suggested that it may also be involved in eating disorders, especially bulimia nervosa. The main hypothesis is that bulimics have low levels of brain serotonin, which increases craving for carbohydrates, the consumption of which results in an increase in serotonin. Again insulin is critically involved.

The level of serotonin in the brain is controlled by how much of its precursor, tryptophan, crosses the blood-brain barrier. Tryptophan comes from a variety of foods in our diet (for example, bananas). But having tryptophan circulating in the blood does not guarantee that it enters the brain to be converted to serotonin. This appears to depend on what type of food we consume during a particular meal. When we eat a protein-rich meal, very little tryptophan enters the brain, not only because animal protein contains little tryptophan but also because it is high in five other large amino acids that have priority over tryptophan in crossing the blood-brain barrier. However, when we eat a carbohydrate-rich meal, the strong insulin release that accompanies it (much stronger than that seen after a protein meal) has the effect of lowering the level of these other large amino acids, thus facilitating an influx of tryptophan into the brain, where it is available to be turned into serotonin. High levels of serotonin are associated with satiety, which may contribute to the temporary relief from hunger experienced by the bulimic during a binge with a high carbohydrate content. It has been shown, for example, that administration of a drug like fenfluramine that increases the level of serotonin in the brain has a direct effect of suppressing food intake (Silverstone & Goodall, 1986). Since both dieters and bulimics tend to avoid carbohydrates between binges the net effect would be lowered insulin and serotonin levels, which might cause craving for carbohydrates, a common component (along with fats) of binge food.

In addition, bulimics have a very high frequency of associated depression. Since depression is associated with lower levels of serotonin (see Chapter 13), the consumption of a large amount of carbohydrates might, at least temporarily, improve their mood due to the increase in serotonin levels. In effect they would learn that bingeing makes them feel better. As you will see in the section on treatment, antidepressant medications, which almost all increase the level of serotonin, have been found useful in the short term treatment of bulimia nervosa. This lends some weight to the argument that serotonin is involved in eating disorders.

There is another interesting connection between bulimic symptoms, mood, and central serotonin activity. Arthur and Jane Blouin and colleagues (1992) asked 31 bulimia nervosa patients at the Ottawa Civic Hospital and 31 normal comparison subjects to report their binge eating, purging, and mood over a twelve-month period. Figure 9.3 shows that symptoms vary according to a seasonal pattern, becoming more frequent in the winter when daylight diminishes and decreasing as the days get longer. They also noted that the numbers of people seeking help for bulimia nervosa at their clinic follow the same pattern.

The authors note that this pattern is also seen in seasonal affective disorder (SAD), a state of dysphoria that, by definition, varies with available light (see Chapter 13). Central serotonin levels also show seasonal variation, being lowest in December and January (Carlsson, Svennerholm, & Winblad, 1980). Fenfluramine, a drug that increases serotonin levels, has proven effective in the treatment of both SAD (O'Rourke, Wurtman, Wurtman, Chebli, & Gleason, 1989), and bulimic bingeing (Robinson, Checkley, & Russell, 1985), lending credence to the hypothesis that serotonin deficits underlie both disorders. Further research is needed to determine the degree to which serotonin irregularities play either a causal or a maintaining role in eating disorders. It is possible, for example, that serotonin deficits are a result of dieting, which often involves avoidance of carbohydrates.

In summary, it is apparent that a variety of risk factors may be involved in the etiology of eating disorders, with various theories accentuating different factors. People with eating disorders are a heterogeneous group, with different histories and personality characteristics. Some were overweight at one time, others were not; some were sexually abused, others were not; some are depressed or have a substance abuse problem, others do not; and so on. Cause and effect can also be very tricky to determine: even if an association exists, one must question whether the variable precedes the eating disorder, merely coexists with it, or is a consequence of the disorder. To determine which factors are critical and how they interact in a given individual, we need prospective longitudinal studies—studies that would follow samples of young girls from before the age at which eating disorders start. By noting their physiological, personal, and environmental characteristics and then finding out which ones eventually develop eating disorders, we will gain insight that will no doubt lead to more effective treatments.

Figure 9.3 **Seasonal Variation in Binge Eating, Purging, and Feeling Worst Among Bulimics**

Note: These data are taken from a modified Seasonal Pattern Assessment Questionnaire, administered to 31 bulimics and 31 normal comparison subjects.

Source: A. Blouin, J. Blouin, P. Aubin, J. Carter, C. Goldstein, H. Boyer, & E. Perez, Seasonal patterns of bulimia nervosa, *American Journal of Psychiatry 149(1992)* (1), 76. Copyright 1992, the American Psychiatric Association. Reprinted by permission.

TREATMENT

Because anorexia nervosa and bulimia nervosa have a great deal in common, similar treatment strategies have evolved. There are, however, important differences. People with bulimia nervosa are generally more willing to seek treatment than those with anorexia nervosa. Hospital care is more often needed for anorexics because of dangerously low body weight, although a person with either disorder may need to be hospitalized for other medical complications or to prevent suicide. Sometimes a lack of programs means that hospital care is the only way to get effective treatment. Even when hospitalization is required, a major part of therapy takes place on an outpatient basis.

Treatment of Anorexia Nervosa

Many types of treatment have been used with anorexia nervosa patients, singly or in combination. These include various forms of psychodynamic psychotherapy (Herzog, 1995), cognitive therapy (Garner, 1986), cognitive-behavioural and behavioural therapy (Channon, de Silva, Hemsley, & Perkins, 1989), family therapy (Russell, Szmukler, Dare, & Eiler, 1987), educational therapy (Garner et al., 1985), and various types of antipsychotic and antidepressant medication (Walsh & Devlin, 1992). Treatments may be individual or group; may be inpatient, day-patient or outpatient; and may be directed primarily at younger adolescents or at adults. Regardless of treatment used, it is difficult to engage the anorexic in the therapeutic process because of the egosyntonic nature of the symptoms. Relapse is common and treatment generally requires considerable therapeutic resources.

Nutritional management is important, especially early in treatment (Beumont & Touyz, 1995). The first priority must be to make sure the person gains enough weight for safety, on purely medical grounds. Moreover, very low weight is associated with cognitive deficits, so patients will probably not benefit much from psychotherapy until they regain some of the weight. Also, as noted earlier, many of the psychological symptoms of anorexia nervosa are actually effects of starvation. Eliminating or reducing these effects through a more normal diet is often considered a prerequisite to later therapy.

Forced feeding, through a tube or other means, is used only as a last resort. More often, hospital privileges are made contingent on eating prescribed meals and gaining weight. Regardless of the type of long-term therapy used, an educational component is often included, targeting nutrition and body weight (Beumont & Touyz, 1995).

There are very few comparative treatment studies of anorexia nervosa, in part because it is difficult to accumulate patient samples. According to reviews, pharmacological agents in the treatment of anorexia nervosa have failed to demonstrate a clinically significant impact (Walsh, 1995; Walsh & Devlin, 1992). Similarly, the results of a controlled trial of cognitive-behavioural and behavioural treatment were disappointing, with few differences from a control treatment condition (Channon et al., 1989).

One of the few therapies to receive support in a controlled trial is **family therapy** (Russell et al., 1987). Twenty-one adolescents with anorexia nervosa were first given ten weeks of inpatient treatment to restore their weight to 90 percent of normal. They were then discharged and randomly assigned to either family therapy or cognitive-behaviour therapy. Twelve months later, nine of ten patients in family therapy but only two of eleven patients in cognitive-behaviour therapy were doing well. A second study (Le Grange et al., 1992) also supported family therapy. Although the numbers of patients in these studies are small, the results are promising and should encourage larger, multisite trials.

A review of four decades of outcome research in anorexia nervosa shows that almost all studies are uncontrolled, with many possible sources of bias (Steinhausen, Rauss-Mason, & Seidel (1991). In a recent summary of 68 of these outcome studies totalling 3104 patients, Steinhausen (1995) estimates that, on average, about 40 percent of anorexia nervosa patients recover while another one-third improve.

Treatment of Bulimia Nervosa

As with anorexia nervosa, many different approaches have been tried with bulimia nervosa. There are many well-controlled trials of bulimia nervosa treatments. The two treatment approaches that have received the most research attention are antidepressant medication and cognitive-behavioural therapy.

Antidepressant Medication

Double-blind studies of antidepressant medication as the primary treatment of bulimia nervosa show that both the older tricyclics, such as amitriptyline (Elavil), imipramine (Tofranil), and desipramine (Norpramin), and the newer serotonin reuptake inhibitors, such as fluoxetine (Prozac) and sertraline (Zoloft), relieve symptoms significantly more effectively than placebo (Mitchell & de Zwaan, 1993; Walsh, 1995; Walsh & Devlin, 1992). Reviews note, however, that outcome studies tend to be short-term, with little followup to see whether improvement is lasting. Indications are that there is a high relapse rate, especially when medication is discontinued. The mechanism by which antidepressants reduce bulimic symptoms is at present unknown. However, it may not be through alleviating depression, as the effective dosage with bulimia nervosa patients can be lower than therapeutic dosages used in the treatment of depression. Further, even bulimics who are not depressed tend to benefit.

Cognitive-Behavioural Therapy

Cognitive-behavioural therapy has more empirical support than any other treatment. This approach was first used for bulimia by Christopher Fairburn (1981) and is outlined in both a treatment manual (Fairburn, Marcus, & Wilson, 1993) and a self-help book (Fairburn, 1995b).

Cognitive-behavioural therapy emphasizes the role of irrational cognitions: beliefs and attitudes that base self-worth on shape and weight; the tendency to set perfectionistic standards, and the use of dichotomous thinking patterns and other cognitive errors. As we said earlier, self-esteem is often low to begin with, and is further undermined by the binge-purge behaviour.

The first phase of treatment emphasizes educating patients about their disorder and using behavioural techniques (for example, not eating alone, delaying purging, using social support) to interrupt the binge-purge cycle. Patients are encouraged to reduce dieting, to weigh themselves less often, and to eat three meals and one or two snacks per day. Normalizing eating is considered very important because it eliminates hunger, a trigger of binge eating, and gets rid of any effects of starvation. It also helps to recondition the patient to cues of hunger and satiety.

During the second phase, a concerted effort is made to deal with distorted cognitions associated with weight, shape, and eating. The patient is helped to identify her overvalued ideals of beauty or thinness, her irrational thoughts, and her cognitive errors, to challenge them, and to restructure them in a more rational and healthy way. Effort continues at eliminating dieting and improving body image and self-esteem. The patient is offered techniques to handle "forbidden foods" and other triggers of binge eating, and is helped to improve her problem-solving skills and coping skills in general.

The final phase is aimed at maintaining progress and planning strategies to prevent relapse. The therapist helps the patient analyze "dangerous" situations and plan carefully how she will cope with them to avoid lapsing into bingeing, thus increasing her confidence in her own strength. She also works out with her therapist how she will deal with any lapse that does occur to prevent it from turning into a full-scale relapse.

Cognitive-behavioural treatment is usually offered on an individual basis and generally involves 16 to 20 sessions over a period of three to four months.

Reviews of many studies (Craighead & Agras, 1991; Fairburn, Agras, & Wilson, 1992; Wilson, 1995) all point to the success of this form of therapy. Binge eating and purging is reduced by about 80 percent on average; about half of patients are able to stop bingeing and purging completely. Attitudes towards weight and shape improve as well as self-esteem, personality functioning, and depression (Garner et al., 1993). Followup of patients for as long as six years shows that beneficial changes are maintained and relapse rates are low (Fairburn, 1995b).

Comparative reviews show cognitive-behavioural treatment to be more effective than antidepressant medication, behavioural treatment alone, supportive psychotherapy, supportive-expressive psychotherapy, and stress-management therapy (Fairburn, 1995b; Wilson, 1993, 1995).

Interpersonal Therapy

Only one other treatment so far tested compares favourably to cognitive-behavioural therapy in terms of long-term outcome. This is *interpersonal therapy*, in which the focus is on resolving problems the bulimic has with various relationships

in her life. The two therapies showed similar outcomes one and six years after treatment (Fairburn, Norman, Welch, O'Connor, Doll, & Peveler, 1997). So far, this is the only study that has carefully evaluated interpersonal therapy.

No treatment helps *all* individuals with bulimia nervosa. Wilson (1996) has addressed the question of what to do when our best treatment—cognitive-behavioural therapy—fails. Among the strategies suggested are broadening the focus of cognitive-behavioural therapy to include a greater stress on interpersonal conflicts and relationships. Wilson also suggests various forms of exposure treatment (for example, Rosen & Leitenberg, 1985) that aim to reduce the anxiety aroused by cues that trigger bingeing such as forbidden foods, weighing, or tight clothes. (Note the similarity to exposure treatments for obsessive compulsive disorder, discussed in Chapter 7.) When borderline personality disorder is also present, it may be helpful to specifically address this disorder in treatment. Similarly, when both substance abuse and eating disorders are present, treatments for both can be integrated in various ways (Boland, 1997).

A Graduated System of Care

Health care systems in Canada are under considerable financial pressure. Cutbacks, closings, and reorganizations are the order of the day. We must continue somehow to offer good treatment for eating disorders but do it in as economical a way as possible. Some centres across Canada have evolved a *graduated system of intervention*, an idea supported by Fairburn (1995) and others. The idea is that only a minority of individuals with eating disorders need expensive inpatient treatment or even day treatment programs. Most can benefit substantially from outpatient treatment, and not all need the same intensity of treatment or the same amount of a therapist's time. Over the past few years many hospitals in Canada have initiated brief, psychoeducational groups, which appear to help many patients with eating disorders (Olmstead et al., 1991). Those who do not benefit may then be offered more intensive treatments such as cognitive-behavioural or body-image therapy.

Self-help groups, such as the Anorexia Nervosa and Bulimia Association, are available in many communities and can be very useful. These support groups may offer help directly and may help people who have received professional treatment to maintain progress afterward. Also available are a variety of self-help manuals, including one that follows the principles of cognitive-behavioural therapy (Fairburn, 1995a).

Prevention

In Canada, the National Eating Disorders Information Centre (see Additional Resources at the end of this chapter) has done a great deal to disseminate information on eating disorders. Recently they have made available resource kits for teachers to use in prevention efforts. However, so far prevention efforts have been disappointing. They do indeed increase information about the disorders but they do not change critical behaviours such as dieting (for example, Paxton, 1993).

A recent prevention program aimed at 13- and 14-year-old girls in a British school suggest that we must be cautious (Carter, Stewart, Dunn, & Fairburn, 1997). The program, largely based on cognitive-behavioural principles, targeted dieting, body image, and other aspects of eating disorders. As in other prevention studies, the girls increased their knowledge about eating disorders. It was less typical but even more encouraging that dieting and similar behaviours actually decreased in the period immediately following the intervention. Disappointingly, however, these effects had disappeared at a six-month followup; in fact, the girls were actually dieting more than they had before the program (see Figure 9.4). We cannot necessarily conclude that the program made the girls diet more. The authors did not include a control group that did not receive the intervention, so it is possible that the increase observed might have simply come with growing older, and perhaps might have been even larger without the program. Nevertheless, we have to be careful that our prevention efforts do not backfire by sensitizing children to weight and shape concerns, only to produce increases in behaviours like dieting. This study also points up the importance of followup; had the study ended after the initial posttest, the authors would have missed this reversal.

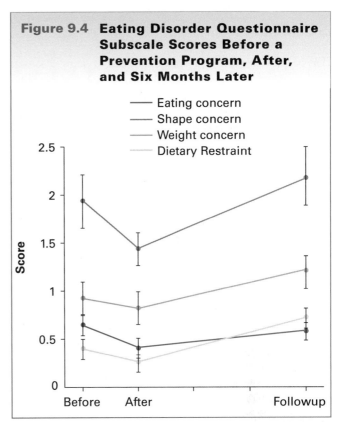

Figure 9.4   Eating Disorder Questionnaire Subscale Scores Before a Prevention Program, After, and Six Months Later

Note: These scores measure the eating disorder-related attitudes and behaviours of 13- and 14-year-old girls in a British intervention study.
Source: J. C. Carter, D. A. Stewart, V. J. Dunn, & C. G. Fairburn, Primary prevention of eating disorders: Might it do more harm than good?, *Eating Disorders, 22(1997),* 167–172.

PANORAMA

The differentiation of anorexia nervosa and bulimia nervosa into purging and nonpurging subgroups, and the isolation of binge eating disorder as a separate entity, have allowed for a finer analysis of symptoms, etiology, and predictors of treatment outcome. Recent genetic studies show a considerable hereditary disposition to developing eating disorders. Future research will concentrate on what constitutes this disposition. Heritable personality tendencies and neurochemical irregularities are potential candidates. Whatever the mechanism, it is generally agreed that it would have to interact with one or more other risk factors (for example, sociocultural factors, dieting, bodily changes, developmental challenges of adolescence, family factors) in order for an eating disorder to emerge. This nature/nurture interaction is likely to be present in a sizeable proportion of eating disorder cases, even though others will likely show no genetic loading. Future comparisons of those with and without a genetic loading will further enlighten us.

Studies comparing eating disorder patients with both psychiatric and normal control groups are helping to tease apart specific factors from those associated with psychopathology in general. Many believe that both a specific and a general factor must be present for a clinical eating disorder to emerge. Longitudinal studies are needed to disentangle factors that may predispose a person to develop an eating disorder from those that may precipitate the disorder, help maintain it, or simply represent a consequence of it.

Family therapy appears to be the most promising treatment for adolescent anorexia nervosa patients, while cognitive-behavioural therapy appears to be the treatment of choice for bulimia nervosa. In the future we are likely to see more integration of treatment approaches (for example, cognitive-behavioural and interpersonal therapy), especially in difficult cases. Advances in pharmacological agents are also likely to prove valuable. Finally, there is a need for a successful recipe for prevention.

SUMMARY

The past few decades have seen an increase in eating disorders such as anorexia nervosa and bulimia nervosa, and the number of people who seek help for them. Anorexia nervosa is characterized by a refusal to maintain normal body weight. The pursuit of thinness and a strong fear of gaining weight and becoming fat are central to the disorder. About half of anorexics maintain their very low weight by restricting their food intake and avoiding many foods. For the other half, dietary restraint breaks down and they binge or at least eat more than intended. In order to maintain their dangerously low weight they engage in purging. In both subgroups body image disturbance is apparent, and weight and shape concerns are unduly tied to self-worth.

Bulimia nervosa is characterized by a repetitive binge-purge cycle. Unlike anorexics, bulimics maintain their weight at or near the normal range for their height. They share with anorexics a strong desire to be thin and a fear of becoming fat. If they purge by vomiting (the great majority), or abuse laxatives, diuretics, or enemas, they are considered *purging type*. If they compensate for their binges by excessive exercise or fasting, they are classified as *nonpurging type*. Severe body dissatisfaction is characteristic of bulimics and, as in the case of the anorexic, the bulimic's self-worth is largely determined by weight and shape concerns.

DSM-IV also recognizes a variety of atypical eating disorders that are classified as "eating disorders not otherwise specified"; generally, these do not quite fit the criteria for anorexia or bulimia nervosa. The most notable in this category is binge eating disorder, in which the person binges as in bulimia nervosa but does not regularly purge or otherwise compensate.

Although many etiological theories accentuate one or two risk factors, it is likely that eating disorders are multi-determined, with different factors more important for different individuals. The stage is set by sociocultural values favouring thinness and stigmatizing fatness, and a differential socialization pattern that stresses appearance for females. This has led to widespread body dissatisfaction and dieting among females, and in a small proportion of individuals has precipitated a clinical eating disorder. What makes this group susceptible? Potential contributors are childhood obesity and/or early menarche, possibly because they accentuate the general factors noted above and expose this subgroup to teasing about weight and shape. Low self-esteem, a pervasive sense of ineffectiveness, a history of sexual abuse, and family dysfunction may also play a part, but their contribution may be to a wide variety of psychopathology rather than specifically to eating disorders. Biological factors, such as low levels of serotonin, may contribute to binge eating, but whether this association is a cause, consequence, or maintaining factor is unclear. More recent studies suggest a hereditary predisposition to develop eating disorders, perhaps through inherited personality traits such as obsessiveness and anxiety tendencies in anorexics, and sensation-seeking and impulsive tendencies in bulimics.

Depression and personality disorders co-occur frequently with eating disorders, but it seems likely that these disorders are less a cause than an effect, often remitting with successful treatment of the eating disorder. Substance abuse also frequently co-occurs with bulimia nervosa; possibly both disorders represent an underlying impulsivity. Further research is needed to clarify these issues.

Treatments for anorexia nervosa have included psychodynamic, cognitive, cognitive-behavioural, educational, and family therapy, as well as various antipsychotic and antidepressant medications. Nutritional and behavioural management to bring the anorexic's weight up to a safer level is always the first priority. In addition, antidepressant medication has proven beneficial for bulimia nervosa in the short term, but side-effects and relapses are a problem in the longer term. The most empirically validated treatment appears to be cognitive-behavioural therapy, which generally reduces binge eating and purging by about 80 percent on average. For adolescents, family therapy appears to have the best outcome. To date, prevention efforts with school children have increased knowledge of eating disorders, but have done little to actually change critical behaviors such as dieting.

KEY TERMS

body mass index (p. 204)
anorexia nervosa (p. 204)
bulimia nervosa (p. 204)
restricting type (p. 206)
binge eating/purging type (p. 206)
binge (p. 207)

purging type (p. 207)
nonpurging type (p. 207)
body image distortion (p. 208)
body image dissatisfaction (p. 208)
electrolyte imbalance (p. 212)
amenorrhea (p. 212)
restrained eaters (p. 212)
set point (p. 217)
basal metabolic rate (p. 217)

avoidance of psychosexual maturity (p. 218)
pervasive sense of ineffectiveness (p. 218)
cognitive errors (p. 218)
dysfunctional family (p. 219)
addiction model (p. 221)
nutritional management (p. 225)
family therapy (p. 225)

ADDITIONAL RESOURCES

National Eating Disorders Information
    Centre
CW 1-211 200 Elizabeth Street
Toronto, ON
M5G 2C4
(416) 340-4156
(416) 340-4736 fax
mbeck@torhosp.toronto.on.ca

Anorexia Nervosa and Bulimia
    Association
767 Bayridge Drive
P.O. Box 20058
Kingston, ON
K7P 1C0
(613) 547-3684
anab@www.ams.queensu.ca

www.ams.queensu.ca/anab
The web site of the Anorexia Nervosa and Bulimia
Association. Provides information about eating disorders.

www.concernedcounseling.com/ccijournal/conference/
eating_disorders_diagnosis_treatment.html
An interview with Dr. David Garner, a psychologist who
conducted much of his research on eating disorders at the
Toronto General Hospital, in which he discusses the diagnosis and treatment of eating disorders.

www.nedic.on.ca
The site of the Toronto-based National Eating
Disorders Information Centre. Provides information
and resources about diagnosing and treating eating disorders.

www.sfwed.org
A comprehensive collection of resources about eating disorders.

Chapter 10

Substance-Related Disorders

Philip Firestone

Marilyn Keyes

Yolanda Korneluk

At the age of 45, Gareth found himself in group therapy describing how he had lost his job and almost lost his life. When he thought back to how it had all begun, he found it difficult to pinpoint when using drugs and alcohol ceased to be fun and social activity, and began to be necessary to maintain day-to-day functioning. Somehow, he had gone from having the world by the tail as an executive at a software company to living in a treatment facility, wondering if he would ever be able to stay off drugs and rebuild his life.

At first, Gareth drank to keep up with his co-workers and business clients, many of whom regularly had "liquid lunches." Although he didn't really like the way alcohol made him feel in the afternoon, he soon found that a little of "the hair of the dog" at the bar after work helped him to feel better for the drive home. He also found alcohol more pleasing at parties and was able to drink more without getting drunk.

At a party held by a business associate, Gareth was introduced to cocaine, which gave him the energy for extended parties and alleviated the hangovers he often experienced after a night of drinking. He was also amazed by the way that cocaine improved his concentration, energy, and creativity. When high on cocaine he could work longer hours without taking a break, and he began to feel as if he could accomplish anything he set his mind to. The only drawback was the cost of the cocaine, but even that he could handle because he was doing so well in his job.

As he began to use cocaine more frequently, Gareth found that he often needed alcohol or "downers" to help him relax and fall asleep in the evenings. His physician was willing to prescribe barbiturates when Gareth explained that he was in a high-pressure job and had trouble sleeping because he worked work odd hours and travelled to different time zones. Of course the barbiturate and alcohol use at night meant he was often groggy in the morning and needed cocaine to help him function. His co-workers began to notice changes in Gareth's personality and decreased productivity. Gareth was in danger of losing his job.

One night, this cycle of abuse caught up with Gareth. He had been drinking with some customers right after work and came home at about 7:00 pm. Tired, he decided to skip dinner and have a nap but couldn't sleep, so he took a couple of sleeping pills and had another stiff drink. The combination of barbiturates and a considerable amount of alcohol on an empty stomach resulted in a loss of consciousness. When his wife got home around 8:00 pm, she found him asleep on the sofa, and could not awaken him. She immediately phoned 911; help arrived in time. The interview in the emergency room later that evening revealed the drug roller coaster Gareth was on. His physician and wife insisted that he go directly to a treatment facility and he agreed.

Historically, virtually every culture has employed some legally or socially sanctioned drugs to alter moods or states of consciousness. In our culture, the most widely used substances are alcohol, tobacco, and caffeine, all of which are legal and (at least to some extent) socially acceptable. Many people begin their day with a cup of coffee and a cigarette. Parties and other social events for adults almost always include alcohol. And although the immediate effects of these substances are usually pleasant, history is full of accounts of the devastating long-term impact of addictive substances.

. . . .

HISTORICAL PERSPECTIVE

Alcohol and drug use has been around longer than recorded history. Mead, an alcoholic beverage naturally formed by the fermentation of honey, was probably the first alcohol that humans consumed. The ancient Egyptians were known for their drinking, and wine was extensively used by the Hebrews.

Opium derivatives were once widely used in Asian cultures, as well as in ancient Greece and Rome. Therapeutically they were taken to relieve pain or induce sleep. However, the euphoria these drugs produced resulted in their wide use to enhance pleasure. In the Andes, for thousands of years, native populations occasionally chewed the leaf of the coca plant to relieve fatigue and increase endurance. The flower of the peyote cactus has long been used by tribes in South and Central America as part of religious ceremonies. The chemical contained in this flower was valued for its ability to alter consciousness and results in hallucinations similar to those caused by LSD.

The effects of substance abuse were particularly grim as the Europeans colonized North and South America. When Canadian aboriginal people were introduced to European brandy they discovered a means of being transported into a strange new world of experience. In an inebriated state, people committed crimes and acts of self-destruction previously unheard of (Douville & Casanova, 1967). A hunter might trade his entire winter's catch of furs for a jug or two of whiskey, leading to misery and starvation. As a final insult, liquor reduced resistance to many imported diseases (Eccles, 1959).

South American cultures suffered similar effects. Prior to the arrival of the Spanish, alcohol was consumed only collectively, as part of religious ceremonies. A few years after the conquest, aboriginal people commonly used alcohol to escape from the confusion of their disrupted world (Bethell, 1984). There was also a striking increase in the use of coca leaf in the Andes. Formerly only used with the permission of the Inca (king) or his governor, coca became indispensable for Quechua mine workers because it enabled them to work almost without eating (Bethell, 1984).

Diagnostic Issues

Defining Substance-Related Concepts

There are several concepts associated with substance-related disorders that require explanation. In DSM-IV the term **substance intoxication** is used to describe a reversible and temporary condition due to the recent ingestion of (or exposure to) a substance. To qualify for this diagnosis a person must demonstrate clinically significant maladaptive behavioural or cognitive changes, such as belligerence, disturbed perception, altered mood, and impaired thought processes or motor behaviour, as a direct result of the substance.

Substance abuse refers to recurrent substance use that results in significant adverse consequences in social or occupational functioning. (See DSM table.) For example, a person intoxicated by a substance or recuperating from its use may fail to fulfill major obligations, such as a university examination. Interpersonal relationships may deteriorate or come to an end as a result. Substance abuse may also include using the substance in hazardous situations, such as drinking and driving, with catastrophic consequences. The term *addiction* has commonly been used to describe lack of control over substance use, to the point that a person may feel enslaved. DSM-IV uses the term **substance dependence** to describe this condition. (See DSM table.) There are two forms of dependence: **physiological** and psychological. The first is defined largely in terms of **tolerance** and **withdrawal** symptoms. Tolerance means that the person needs increased amounts of the substance to achieve the same effect. Individuals suffering from withdrawal experience unpleasant and sometimes dangerous symptoms such as nausea, headache, or tremors when the addictive substance is removed from the body. These physiological events are a result of the changes the body has undergone in order to adapt to the continued presence of the drug. Additional ingestion of the specific drug, or one that is closely related, will alleviate these symptoms. Of course this is part of the vicious circle that maintains dependence.

Psychological dependence, a more recent concept, is also known as **habituation** and refers to being psychologically accustomed to a substance or activity as a consequence of regular usage. When the substance or activity is unavailable, feelings of restlessness, irritability, and uneasiness may be experienced. An indication of psychological dependence is spending increasing amounts of time obtaining or using the substance, and restricting work and social activities that preclude substance use. For example, a person might stay away from an otherwise desirable party if smoking is not allowed.

DSM-IV Diagnostic Criteria for Substance Abuse

A maladaptive pattern of substance use leading to clinically significant impairment or distress, as manifested by one (or more) of the following, occurring within a 12-month period:

(1) recurrent substance use resulting in a failure to fulfil major role obligations at work, school, or home (for example, repeated absences or poor work performance related to substance use; substance-related absences, suspensions, or expulsions from school; neglect of children or household)

(2) recurrent substance use in situations in which it is physically hazardous (for example, driving an automobile or operating a machine when impaired by substance use)

(3) recurrent substance-related legal problems (for example, arrests for substance-related disorderly conduct)

(4) continued substance use despite having persistent or recurrent social or interpersonal problems caused or exacerbated by the effects of the substance (for example, arguments with spouse about consequences of intoxication, physical fights)

DSM-IV Diagnostic Criteria for Substance Dependence

A maladaptive pattern of substance use, leading to clinically significant impairment or distress, as manifested by three (or more) of the following, occurring at any time in the same 12-month period:

(1) tolerance, as defined by either of the following:

   (a) a need for markedly increased amounts of the substance to achieve intoxication or desired effect

   (b) markedly diminished effect with continued use of the same amount of the substance

(2) withdrawal, as manifested by either of the following:

   (a) the characteristic withdrawal syndrome for the substance

   (b) more of the same (or a closely related) substance is taken to relieve or avoid withdrawal symptoms

(3) the substance is often taken in larger amounts or over a longer period than was intended

(4) there is a persistent desire or unsuccessful efforts to cut down or control substance use

(5) a great deal of time is spent in activities necessary to obtain the substance (for example, visiting multiple doctors or driving long distances), use the substance (for example, chain-smoking), or recover from its effects

(6) important social, occupational, or recreational activities are given up or reduced because of substance use

(7) the substance use is continued despite knowledge of having a persistent or recurrent physical or psychological problem that is likely to have been caused or exacerbated by the substance (for example, current cocaine use despite recognition of cocaine-induced depression, or continued drinking despite recognition that an ulcer was made worse by alcohol consumption)

Specify if: **With Physiological Dependence:** evidence of tolerance or withdrawal (that is, either Item 1 or 2 is present)

Without Physiological Dependence: no evidence of tolerance or withdrawal (that is, neither Item 1 nor 2 is present)

Polysubstance Abuse

Research into the short- and long-term effects of substance use and abuse is plagued by the issue of **polysubstance abuse**, the simultaneous misuse or dependence upon two or more substances. In fact, concurrent dependence appears to be the rule rather than the exception. For example, 95 percent of problem drinkers also smoke cigarettes and are likely addicted to both (Istvan & Matarrazo, 1984). Research has shown that more than half of cocaine users are dependent on alcohol (Higgins, Budney, Bickel, Foerg, & Badger, 1994), and more than half of all amphetamine users also abuse benzodiazepines (Darke, Ross, & Cohen, 1994). Opioid addicts often abuse alcohol, barbiturates, synthetic hypnotics, cocaine, and other compounds as well (Anglin, Almog, Fisher, & Peters, 1989). Sometimes the pattern is that of concurrent, alternating use. To prevent the excessive excitement, irritability, and insomnia associated with chronic amphetamine use, addicts will often consume barbiturates when they want to "come down" or sleep. Later, amphetamines will be used to reduce the sedative effects or morning drowsiness caused by the barbiturates. Polysubstance abuse appears to be on the rise and is more common in young people (Newcomb, 1994). In Canada, aboriginal youth are at particular risk for polysubstance abuse (Yukon Bureau of Statistics, 1990).

There are a number of health and treatment concerns related to polysubstance abuse. Combining drugs is physically dangerous because they are often **synergistic**. That is, the combined effects of the drugs exceed or are significantly different from the sum of their individual effects. For example, mixing alcohol and barbiturates or opioids may depress central nervous system functioning to a much greater degree than any of these substances alone. Amphetamines and other stimulants, when combined with alcohol, cause physical damage greater than the damage that would be caused by the drugs taken separately (Comer, 1997). To complicate matters, individuals with a history of polysubstance abuse are likely to have more diagnosable mental problems than individuals who abuse only one substance (Darke et al., 1994). When treatment is considered, the drug that presents the more immediate threat to health (for example, opioids, cocaine, alcohol) tends to overshadow others (for example, smoking, marijuana). However, it is not clear which dependence should be treated first, or whether all should be treated at the same time.

In a study of Ontario high school students, Gordon Walsh and Edward Adlaf (1995) of the Addiction Research Foundation developed a useful classification based on the degree and pattern of drug use. They found that about 60 percent of 15-to-17-year-olds drink on occasion, and that about 20 percent of 17-year-olds used drugs other than alcohol and tobacco. Of the latter group, they identified the vast majority (85 percent) as *recreational drug users*, characterized by occasional cannabis use in addition to alcohol and tobacco use. Individuals in this group were less likely to use "hard" drugs. *Mood modifiers* (4 percent) described students who frequently used mood-altering substances (barbiturates and stimulants) in addition to cannabis. *Tranquillizer users* (3 percent) used drugs infrequently, but tended to prefer those with tranquillizing effects and rarely used cannabis, hallucinogens, or stimulants. *Excessive users* (6 percent) reported using a large amount of many kinds of licit and illicit drugs in the previous year. Finally, *frequent illicit users* (2 percent) almost exclusively used illicit drugs, including heroin, speed, LSD, and cocaine.

Solvent use, although by no means limited to Native youth, has become a serious problem in some aboriginal communities. The First Nations and Inuit Community and Youth Solvent Abuse Survey (Kaweionnehta Human Resource Group, October 1993) indicated that one in five aboriginal youth have tried solvents. Of these, 68 percent are males between 12 and 19 years of age. In British Columbia, however, a full 40 percent of solvent abusers are between the ages of 4 and 11.

Focus *Aboriginal Canadians*

Issues related to substance abuse in Canada's aboriginal populations are of growing social concern. In a recent survey by Statistics Canada (1993), Native Canadians identified unemployment (67 percent), alcohol abuse (61 percent), drug abuse (48 percent), suicide (25 percent), family violence (39 percent), and sexual abuse (25 percent) as significant problems in their communities. Evaluating the impact of each of these concerns, however, is made extremely complex by the unique current and historical economic, social, and political factors experienced by Canada's First Nations and Inuit people.

Alcohol use on reserves does not appear to be more prevalent than elsewhere in Canada, with the majority reporting two drinks or fewer per month (60 percent) and only 2 percent reported that they drank alcohol daily. However, the rate varied widely by region, with those in Ontario and British Columbia reporting daily drinking rates of 19 percent and 21 percent respectively (Statistics Canada, 1993). Although the rate of alcohol use by aboriginal Canadians does not appear to be greater than that of other Canadians, there is some evidence that the impact of alcohol may be greater in these communities. Rates of health problems associated with alcohol use, including dependency, alcoholic psychosis, and liver disease are significantly higher in aboriginal populations (Scott, 1994). This may in part be due to significantly higher rates of use for most other drugs, such as nicotine, marijuana, solvents, heroin, and stimulants, which can compound the deleterious health effects of alcohol.

Focus *continued*

Gfellner and Hundelby (1995) compared drug use among Native and white adolescents over a four-year period. Alcohol, cigarettes, and marijuana were the most frequently used substances by both groups of adolescents. Although both groups had similar rates of alcohol use, Native youths reported smoking twice as much and using marijuana three times as much as white adolescents. Native youths also reported higher rates of use of most other drugs, including medicinal and non-medicinal tranquillizers, hallucinogens, stimulants, and solvents (see Table 10.1).

Similar results were obtained by other researchers examining the prevalence of substance abuse among native students in Quebec (Hindmarsh, Porter-Serviss, & Opheim, 1994; Lalinec-Michaud, Subak, Ghadirian, & Kovess, 1991). ▲

Table 10.1 Percentage of Native and White Students Who Had Used Drugs in the Previous Year, 1993

Substance	Group	1993
Cigarettes	White	29.1
	Native	63.3*
Alcohol	White	70.3
	Native	73.7
Marijuana	White	10.4
	Native	36.9*
Glue	White	3.5
	Native	4.3
Solvents	White	3.5
	Native	6.4*
Barbiturates NM	White	2.6
	Native	7.2*
Barbiturates M	White	5.1
	Native	12.2*
Heroin	White	2.1
	Native	5.5*
Speed	White	3.3
	Native	9.8*
Stimulants NM	White	5.5
	Native	8.5
Stimulants M	White	4.3
	Native	7.2*
Tranquillizers NM	White	1.9
	Native	4.2*
Tranquillizers M	White	2.3
	Native	3.8
LSD	White	4.7
	Native	14.4*
PCP	White	2.0
	Native	5.1*
Other hallucinogens	White	4.5
	Native	9.4*
Cocaine	White	2.6
	Native	4.7
Crack	White	3.4
	Native	8.1*

M=medical use; NM=non-medical use

*Significant between-group (white/native) difference in percentage of adolescents who used the drug.

Source: Adapted from B. M. Gfellner and J. D. Hundelby, Patterns of drug use among Native and white adolescents, 1990–1993, *Canadian Journal of Public Health, 86(1995)* (2), 95–97. Reprinted with permission.

Solvent use is accompanied by serious medical problems, including respiratory difficulties, liver and kidney problems, blood abnormalities, and CNS damage.

Treatment of aboriginal people for substance abuse problems is complicated by several factors. First, many substance abusers (particularly solvent abusers) are very young and come from distressed home environments. In addition, there is a higher than expected rate of suicide among aboriginal people, which may, in turn, be an indicator of the presence of other psychiatric disorders in addition to substance abuse. Finally, many aboriginal people end up in treatment because the situation at home ends up in violence. Although these are also risk factors for other Canadians entering treatment, they may be particularly relevant for intervention programs implemented with aboriginal populations because of the high rates of such problems in these communities.

"When did things start to fall apart?" thought Marianne. Certainly, the car accident had a lot to do with it. She could still vividly remember that evening five years ago. She was to have gone to Florida with Luc that week, but he told her he wanted to end their relationship. Instead she had driven the five hours to Toronto to take a computer graphics course. Driving home after three gruelling days, she fell asleep at the wheel and crashed into a wall of rock. She awoke in the hospital with a fractured spine.

Fortunately, she was able to walk again. Three weeks later she went back to an empty home and a long recuperation. The medications provided by the hospital helped control the pain and let her sleep. Combined with alcohol, she discovered, they worked even better. The alcohol also dulled her nagging worries about the future.

Eventually her injuries healed and she again found employment. She managed to stop taking the pain medication, but kept on drinking. Alcohol dulled the back pain, and it made her feel good. She fell into the habit of having a few drinks alone at home each night, often falling asleep in front of the television. She often resolved not to drink that night, but the loneliness and the back pain were too much to bear without alcohol. Yet she convinced herself she was not really an alcoholic because she never drank during the day and was never really drunk. Nevertheless, her concentration was off, her work began to suffer, and her social life dwindled. She finally realized she had a problem and made inquiries about professional services but, as yet, was too ashamed and frightened to admit that she needed help.

The devastation wrought by alcohol addiction is not a new thing. This woodcut captures the misery suffered by the addicted in 18th century London.

ALCOHOL

History of Use

Alcohol has been called the "world's number one psychoactive substance" (Ray & Ksir, 1990). By 6400 B.C. people had discovered how to make alcohol in the form of beer and berry wine. The distillation process in which the fermented solution containing alcohol is heated and the vapours are collected and condensed in liquid form again to create what were first called "spirits" is believed to have been discovered in Arabia. In addition to the Egyptians and the Hebrews, there is ample evidence that the Greeks enjoyed wine, and later Roman emperors were notorious for their insobriety. It is reported the people who met Columbus in the Caribbean had their own form of beer, and the distillation of whiskey was commonplace in Ireland by A.D. 1500, and occurred on a large scale in America by the eighteenth century.

Concern for overuse of alcohol and attempts to regulate its consumption date back to earliest recordings of its use. All attempts to suppress alcohol in Europe and America from the fourteenth to the twentieth century have failed. In the United States, the Prohibition came into effect in 1920, and did effectively reduce overall alcohol intake. However, there was widespread disrespect for the law, leading to the growth of organized crime and bootlegging, some of which originated in Canada. Concern about this lawlessness, as well as an appreciation of the revenues to be gained by taxing liquor sales, led to the repeal of Prohibition soon after the Depression began. As might be expected, there was a gradual increase in alcohol consumption; per capita consumption equaled pre-Prohibition levels by the end of World War II, and continued to rise until it peaked in 1980/81.

Canadian Consumption Patterns

Canadian consumption followed a comparable pattern. From 1971 to 1987, consumption of beverage alcohol in Ontario increased steadily from 732 million to 999 million litres. However, since 1987, alcohol sales have dropped considerably, with beer and wine consumption down 13 percent and 16 percent respectively, while the use of spirits has declined 27 percent. In 1993 more than 10,000 Canadians were interviewed, as part of a larger survey, about their alcohol habits. Approximately three of every four Canadians reported drinking alcohol in the previous 12 months, while 18 percent were former drinkers, and 8 percent had never imbibed alcohol. This was a significant reduction from the 84 percent reporting consuming alcohol in a 1978 survey. Although this reduction may in part reflect an increased awareness of the health risks of drinking, demographics is also a factor. The proportion of Canadians over 60 years of age—a group that drinks less than younger Canadians—is increasing. Young adults are more likely to drink, and to drink heavily; consumption peaks in the mid-twenties, then decreases. Men are more likely than women to be current drinkers and report higher levels of consumption. Single people are more likely to be both casual and heavy drinkers; high-income earners and those with a postsecondary education are also more likely to be current drinkers. However, those with the least education and those out of work reported the heaviest drinking.

Alcohol researchers suggest there is a direct relationship between the overall level of consumption within a population and the number of alcohol-dependent people. Moreover, there is a relationship between an individual's consumption and that person's risk. On the basis of consumption statistics, Adlaf, Ivis, and Smart (1994) categorize 18 percent of the Ontario population as at no risk for alcohol dependence (abstainers), 62 percent as low-risk (1–14 drinks per week),

14 percent as moderate-risk (15–35 drinks per week), and 6 percent as high-risk (35 or more drinks per week) for alcohol dependence (Adlaf, Ivis, & Smart, 1994).

Effects

Ethyl alcohol is the effective chemical compound in alcoholic beverages. It reduces anxiety, produces euphoria, and creates a sense of well-being. It also reduces inhibitions, which adds to the perception that alcohol enhances social and physical pleasure, sexual performance, power, and social assertiveness.

Yet it appears that some of the short-term effects of ingesting small amounts of alcohol are as strongly related to these expectations as they are to its chemical action on the body. In an interesting body of research, subjects were told falsely that their drink contained alcohol. These subjects were found to behave more aggressively (Lang, Goeckner, Adessor, & Marlatt, 1975), and to report greater sexual arousal (Wilson & Lawson, 1976) than subjects who were not led to believe they were consuming alcohol. In another study, women who actually were given alcohol reported feeling more sexually aroused by an erotic film as alcohol intake increased. However, a physiological measure of arousal (vaginal vasocongestion) contradicted self-report measures (Wilson & Lawson, 1976). It would appear that in some individuals expectations regarding alcohol's effects are more potent than the actual physical responses.

Unlike most orally ingested psychoactive substances, alcohol does not require digestion to enter the bloodstream. Since ethanol is water-soluble, it can pass directly into the blood from the stomach, although most of it is absorbed from the small intestine. The bloodstream quickly carries it to the central nervous system. The rate and peak level of absorption depend on how quickly the alcohol gets through the stomach and into the intestine. If alcohol is consumed on a full stomach, such as with a meal, passage to the intestine is more gradual than when consumed on an empty stomach.

Once the alcohol reaches the blood supply, it travels throughout the body and enters most tissues. Alcohol level is usually expressed as a percentage of blood. For example, if there are 80 millilitres of alcohol in 100,000 millilitres of blood, **blood alcohol level (BAL)** is 0.08 percent. Alcohol is removed by the liver at essentially a constant rate of 7 to 8 millilitres of ethanol per hour. Thirty millilitres of liquor, 150 millilitres of wine, and one beer have equivalent absolute alcohol content of 15 millilitres. If rate of intake equals rate of metabolism, then BAL will remain stable. If more than one drink is consumed every two hours, then BAL will climb. Because alcohol does not distribute much into fatty tissues, an 80-kilogram lean person will have a lower blood alcohol level than an 80-kilogram fat person who drinks the same amount of alcohol. The lean person has more fluid volume in which to distribute the alcohol. Alcohol is further broken down in the stomach by the enzyme **alcohol dehydrogenase**, and recent research has shown that women have significantly less of this enzyme. The lower levels of alcohol dehydrogenase in women and the fact that men tend to have a lower proportion of body fat mean that a woman will usually have a higher BAL (and therefore be more intoxicated) than a man of the same body weight consuming the same quantity of alcohol (Frezza et al., 1990; National Institute on Drug Abuse, 1992a).

Short-Term Effects

The effects of alcohol vary with the level of concentration of the drug (yes, it is a drug) in the bloodstream. In addition, alcohol has what is termed a biphasic effect. The initial effect of alcohol is stimulating, resulting in pleasant feelings as blood alcohol level rises. After the blood alcohol level peaks and begins to decline, alcohol acts as a depressant, and many may experience increases in negative emotions.

Alcohol causes deficits in eye-hand coordination, which can be seen at BALs as low as 0.01 (alcohol only makes one *think* one is the best pool player), and drowsiness shows up on vigilance tasks at levels of 0.06. A 40 percent decrease in steadiness, as measured by the amount of swaying, is evident at a BAL of 0.06. Decreased visual acuity and decreased sensitivity to taste, smell, and pain are evident at BALs as low as 0.08. Furthermore, at BALs of 0.08 to 0.1, reaction time slows by about 10 percent, performance on standard intelligence tests falls, memory is poorer, and perception of time is altered. (Five minutes seems like eight—an interesting challenge to the adage "Time flies when you're having fun.") Alcohol begins to affect driving performance at about 0.05 and the curve starts to rise sharply at about 0.08, the legal limit of impairment in many jurisdictions. At the same time that objective measures show poorer performance, the loss of inhibition often gives a person increased confidence (Wallgren & Barry, 1971).

The adverse symptoms of "the morning after the night before" are familiar to many, but not well understood. The symptoms of hangovers range from upset stomach, fatigue, headache, thirst, depression, anxiety, to general malaise. Some believe that these symptoms are a result of withdrawal from the short- or long-term addiction to alcohol. This notion is supported by the popularly recommended cure of "the hair of the dog that bit you." This remedy may appear to minimize the symptoms, but it really only spreads them out. An analgesic for the headache, rest, and time are probably the wisest "cures."

Another theory of the cause of hangovers is that they are a reaction to the congeners in alcohol. Congeners are natural products of the fermentation and preparation process and vary between alcoholic beverages. Beer has an approximately 0.01 percent congener level and wine has about 0.04 percent. The congener levels of distilled liquor varies. Vodka, which is a mixture of pure alcohol and water, has the lowest congener level, at about the same level as beer; while some spirits have up to 0.2 percent congeners. In a study entitled "Experimental induction of hangover" (Chapman, 1970), results showed that bourbon drinkers were twice as likely to have a hangover as vodka drinkers with the same BAL, and the higher the BAL level, the more likely the drinker was to have a hangover.

The extreme thirst that accompanies a hangover is related to alcohol's ability to cause the fluid inside the body's cells to move outside the cells, causing cellular dehydration. In addition, the diuretic effect that causes the body to excrete more fluid than is taken in, an effect that can be quite inconvenient in certain circumstances, contributes to the increase in thirst. Finally, the nausea and stomach upset result because alcohol is a gastric irritant. In addition, the accumulation of acetaldehyde, a byproduct of the metabolism of alcohol, is quite toxic, which contributes to the nausea and headache. The fatigue experienced the next day can often be attributed to alcohol's interference with normal sleep patterns and the increased level of activity during the revelry of the evening before.

Long-Term Effects

Because alcohol is ubiquitous in our society it is rarely seen as a dangerous drug. In fact, it is a favourite part of many social activities. However, chronic alcohol consumption is related to many diseases. Because alcohol travels though the body in the bloodstream it comes in contact with every organ, directly or indirectly affecting every part of the body. Factors related to the severity of damage include an individual's genetic vulnerability, frequency and duration of drinking, and the severity and spacing of binges (Gordis, 1991). Because alcohol is high in calories, heavy drinkers often reduce their food intake. However, not only are these calories of little nutritional value, but alcohol interferes with the absorption of nutrients in food that is eaten. Consequently, severe malnutrition and related tissue damage can result. Prolonged alcohol use, with concomitant reduced protein intake, is damaging to the endocrine glands, pancreas, and, especially, to the liver. Alcohol has also been associated with cancers of the mouth, tongue, pharynx, larynx, esophagus, stomach, liver, lung, pancreas, colon, and rectum. Finally, the effects of alcohol and nicotine are compounded to increase cancers of the oral region (Gapstur, Potter, Sellers, & Folson, 1992; Longnecker, 1994).

Heavy alcohol use has been associated with damage to the heart muscle (cardiomyopathy), high blood pressure, and strokes. On the other hand, there is recent evidence that moderate alcohol consumption is related to a lower incidence of heart attacks. This finding has prompted discussions of a possible protective factor. The suggestion is that consuming 2 to 3 ounces of alcohol per day may raise HDL cholesterol ("good cholesterol"), which in turn increases blood flow through the coronary vessels (Bofetta & Garfinkel, 1990; Razay, Heaton, Bolton, & Hughes, 1992).

It has been a popular belief that consumption of alcohol permanently kills brain cells and research has demonstrated that the brains of alcoholics demonstrate tissue reduction, particularly in the hypothalamus and thalamus. Cell loss in these areas is associated with Korsakoff's psychosis, a disease characterized by impaired memory and a loss of contact with reality. However, research is conflicting and there is some evidence of brain axon regrowth in the cortex following an extended period of abstinence (Jensen & Palkenberg, 1993; Segal & Sisson, 1985).

Fetal Alcohol Syndrome

As far back as the eighteenth century there was some suspicion that alcohol interfered with fetal development. However, it was not until 1973 that researchers described *fetal alcohol syndrome (FAS)* as a unique set of features caused by chronic maternal alcohol consumption. Alcohol enters the fetus from the mother's bloodstream. The results of most studies indicate that fetal levels of alcohol are comparable to maternal levels, or even higher (Berk, 1993). Investigators suspect alcohol in the fetus can interfere with cell duplication and migration in the primitive neural tube and hence affect the development of the brain. In addition, heavy drinking draws oxygen away from the fetus that is vital for cell growth in the brain and other parts of the body (Berk, 1993). The effects of alcohol can be increased by smoking and other drugs. Since a great number of women who drink also smoke, their children are at even greater risk.

Diagnostic criteria for FAS include growth retardation, a pattern of abnormal features of the face and head, and evidence of central nervous system abnormalities including abnormal neonatal behaviour, mental retardation, or other evidence of abnormal neurobehavioural development. The presence of some of these symptoms in a child who does not meet diagnostic criteria for the syndrome is called *fetal alcohol effects (FAE)*. (See Chapter 6 for further description and a facial diagram.)

Not all children of drinking mothers show these abnormalities and some show others such as eye and ear defects, heart murmurs, malformation of organs, undescended testicles, birthmarks, and abnormal fingerprints.

Is there a safe level of alcohol consumption for an expectant mother? It is impossible to answer that question. Moderate drinking—defined as the equivalent of two martinis a day—has been associated with lower birth weight in newborns. Four to six drinks a day led to noticeable mild physical effects and dysfunction. Scientific data do not demonstrate that occasional consumption of one or two drinks definitely causes alcohol-related birth defects but neither do they indicate any safe level of use.

In a general survey conducted by Statistics Canada in 1993, respondents were asked whether their drinking had adversely affected their social life, physical health, happiness, home life or marriage, work, or finances in the previous 12 months. At least one problem was endorsed by over 9 percent of all current drinkers, with the most common problems related to health and finance. Men were more likely to report problems than women and were three times as likely to drive after drinking two or more drinks in the previous hour. Problems for youth were somewhat different. They related to legal violations such as driving while impaired, injuries, drinking large amounts at a single sitting, decreased school performance, and arguments.

According to a Canadian Centre for Substance Abuse study (Single, Robson, Xie, & Rehm, 1997) alcohol use costs Canadians a staggering $7.5 billion a year in increased health care and law enforcement and reduced productivity. (See

Table 10.2 for a breakdown of the ways in which alcohol, tobacco, and illicit drugs impose costs on the Canadian economy.) In particular, drinking and driving has been recognized as a major social problem. It is estimated that in 1992, 6700 Canadians lost their lives as a result of alcohol consumption. The largest alcohol-related cause of death was motor vehicle accidents (estimated at 1470), followed by liver cirrhosis and suicide. In addition, there were an estimated 86,000 hospital admissions related to alcohol, the largest number being caused by accidental falls, followed by alcohol dependence and motor vehicle accidents.

Etiology

More than 93 percent of Canadians have used alcohol for considerable periods of time. Alcohol is advertised on television, radio, and magazines. It is available in every community and we are encouraged to imbibe at most social gatherings. There is no stigma attached to drinking alcohol; in fact, people are often pressed to explain why they are abstaining. With such extensive social influence, why do only some people become dependent on alcohol, while others do not? There is extensive research into the etiology and

Table 10.2   The Costs of Alcohol, Tobacco, and Illicit Drugs in Canada, 1992

	Millions of Dollars			
	Alcohol	Tobacco	Illicit Drugs	Total
1. Direct health care costs: total	**$1,300.6**	**$2,675.5**	**$88.0**	**$4,064.1**
1.1 Morbidity:				
General hospitals	666.0	1,752.9	34.0	2,452.9
Psychiatric hospitals	29.0	—	4.3	33.3
1.2 Comorbidity	72.0	—	4.7	76.7
1.3 Ambulance services	21.8	57.2	1.1	80.1
1.4 Residential care	180.9	—	20.9	201.8
1.5 Nonresidential treatment	82.1	—	7.9	90.0
1.6 Ambulatory care: physician fees	127.4	339.6	8.0	475.0
1.7 Prescription drugs	95.5	457.3	5.8	558.5
1.8 Other health care costs	26.0	68.4	1.3	95.8
2. Direct losses associated with the workplace	**14.2**	**0.4**	**5.5**	**20.1**
2.1 EAP and health promotion programs	14.2	0.4	3.5	18.1
2.2 Drug testing in the workplace	NA	—	2.0	2.0
3. Direct administrative costs for transfer payments	**52.3**	**—**	**1.5**	**53.8**
3.1 Social welfare and other programs	3.6	—	NA	3.6
3.2 Workers' compensation	48.7	—	1.5	50.2
3.3 Other administrative costs	NA	NA	NA	NA
4. Direct costs for prevention and research	**141.4**	**48.0**	**41.9**	**231.1**
4.1 Research	21.6	34.6	5.0	61.1
4.2 Prevention programs	118.9	13.4	36.7	168.9
4.3 Training costs for physicians and nurses	0.9	NA	0.2	1.1
4.4 Averting behaviour costs	NA	NA	NA	NA
5. Direct law enforcement costs	**1,359.1**	**—**	**400.3**	**1,759.4**
5.1 Police	665.4	NA	208.3	873.7
5.2 Courts	304.4	NA	59.2	363.6
5.3 Corrections (including probation)	389.3	NA	123.8	513.1
5.4 Customs and excise	NA	NA	9.0	9.0
6. Other direct costs	**518.0**	**17.1**	**10.7**	**545.8**
6.1 Fire damage	35.2	17.1	NA	52.3
6.2 Traffic accident damage	482.8	—	10.7	493.5
7. Indirect costs: productivity losses	**4,136.5**	**6,818.8**	**823.1**	**11,778.4**
7.1 Productivity losses due to morbidity	1,397.7	84.5	275.7	1,757.9
7.2 Productivity losses due to mortality	2,738.8	6,734.3	547.4	10,020.5
7.3 Productivity losses due to crime	—	—	NA	NA
Total	**7,522.1**	**9,559.8**	**1,371.0**	**18,452.9**
Total as % of GDP	1.09%	1.39%	0.20%	2.67%
Total per capita	$265	$336	$48	$649
Total as % of all substance-related costs	40.8%	51.8%	7.4%	100.0%

Source: E. Single, L. Robson, X. Xie, & J. Rehm, *The costs of substance abuse in Canada* (Ottawa: Canadian Centre on Substance Abuse, 1997), p. 15.

maintenance of alcohol abuse and many of these theories have been adopted for other types of substance abuse, so some generalization is possible.

Genetic Factors

It is an accepted fact that alcohol abuse and dependence runs in families but, as we have seen in other chapters (see Chapter 4), this does not disentangle the genetic and environmental influences. Twin studies have confirmed that monozygotic twins are more similar than dizygotic twins in their tendencies to develop problems with alcohol abuse and dependence. The concordance rate for monozygotic twins has been found to be approximately 56 percent, compared to approximately 29 percent for dizygotic twins (Kaiji, 1960; Kendler, Heath, Neale, Kessler, & Eaves, 1992). However, these studies fall prey to the criticisms mentioned in Chapter 4. Adoption studies (also explained in Chapter 4) shed further light. An influential series of studies by Goodwin (1976, 1979, 1985) compared offspring of alcoholics raised by their biological parents with offspring of alcoholic parents raised by non-alcoholic foster parents, as well as offspring of non-alcoholic parents. (Adopted offspring had been separated from their biological parents within the first few weeks of life.) Sons of alcoholics were about four times as likely as sons of non-alcoholics to become alcoholics, whether raised in their family of origin or in a foster family. Although the influence of genetics was not found to be as strong for females in this study, a subsequent report did reveal a significant genetic influence on daughters of alcoholics (Bohman, Cloninger, von Korring, & Sigvardsson, 1984).

On the basis of drinking history, two types of alcoholics have been identified. **Type I Alcoholics** begin drinking in their mid-twenties to thirties and do not typically develop problems with their drinking until middle age. These drinkers tend to have relatively few social and occupational problems but are at risk for developing liver disease. This type appears to have a lower heritability component than **Type II Alcoholics**. The latter develop drinking problems earlier in life, and show antisocial behaviour that can take the form of fights and arrests, but they experience few medical difficulties. This type of alcoholism appears to be highly heritable by sons, but not by daughters (McGue, Pickens, & Svikis, 1992; Pickens et al., 1991).

Twin and adoption studies provide evidence for a genetic contribution to the development of alcohol disorders, but what exactly is inherited? Genetic research provides some evidence that there is an association between a gene on chromosome 11 that is involved in the sensitivity of certain receptor sites for the neurotransmitter dopamine, which forms part of the reward system of the brain. The brains of alcoholics have been found to have one form of this gene (DRD2) significantly more frequently than brains of non-alcoholics (Blum et al., 1990; McBride, Murphy, Lumeng, & Li, 1990).

Another genetic factor that may be involved in alcoholism is the ability to metabolize alcohol. Alcohol is broken down in the liver into a byproduct called acetaldehyde, which is further broken down by the enzyme aldehyde dehydrogenase.

If acetaldehyde is allowed to build it causes serious illness. In certain individuals, particularly those of Asian descent, aldehyde dehydrogenase seems to be absent, resulting in unpleasant physiological responses and therefore a reduced risk for development of alcohol abuse (Goedde & Agarwal, 1987; Yoshida, Huang, & Ikawa, 1984).

It is important to note that being a son or daughter of an alcoholic does not predetermine alcoholism. Although vulnerable, many offspring of alcoholics do not become alcoholics, and many alcoholics are born to non-alcoholic parents. Undoubtedly, environmental factors and personal choice play significant roles in the development or avoidance of problems with alcohol.

Neurobiological Influences

Biological marker studies attempt to show that alcoholism is inherited by establishing an association between alcoholism and other inherited characteristics. (See also discussions of linkage analysis in Chapters 13 and 14.) Biological processes of alcoholics, of non–problem drinkers, and of children of both are compared to determine markers of vulnerability to alcohol. One such marker is brainwave activity that can be measured by electroencephalographic (EEG) techniques. Sons of alcoholic fathers have higher than normal rates of the fast beta wave (Gabrielli et al., 1982), and show less EEG change after alcohol consumption than sons of non-alcoholic fathers (Ehlers & Schuckit, 1990). Evoked potentials have also been implicated. These are brief changes in EEG responses to external stimuli, such as flashes of light or loud sounds. The P300 response occurs about 300 milliseconds after the presentation of a stimulus and is believed to indicate an individual's attentional abilities. Sons and daughters of alcoholics show smaller P300 amplitudes than offspring of non-alcoholic fathers (Hill & Steinhauer, 1993; Steinhauer & Hill, 1993). A similar pattern was found in chronic alcoholics who were no longer drinking (Porjesz & Begleiter, 1983).

Heart rate increases following the consumption of alcohol have also been studied. Men with alcoholic relatives show larger increases in heart rate (Finn, Zeitouni, & Pihl, 1990). In addition, those with the greatest increases in heart rate were more inclined to drink alcohol regularly (Pihl & Peterson, 1991). It has been suggested that heart rate increase is a measure of sensitivity to the stimulating properties of alcohol, and may be viewed as an index of reward (Wise & Bozarth, 1987).

Another potential marker for alcohol disorders may lie in the functioning of the enzyme monoamine oxidase (MAO), which is involved in the metabolism of the neurotransmitters dopamine and norepinephrine. (See Chapter 13.) Low MAO activity has been found in alcoholics, particularly those classified as Type II. The suggestion is that this reduced activity is involved in alcohol's effect on the reward systems of the brain, and may be a risk factor for alcoholism. MAO levels are also involved in a variety of other psychiatric conditions which are not related to substance abuse (Altman et al., 1996; see also Chapters 7 and 13).

The neurotransmitter serotonin has also been implicated in the development of alcoholism. Low levels of serotonin have been associated with impulsivity, aggression, and anti-social behaviour—characteristics linked to Type II alcoholism—and to alcohol craving in both animals and humans. However, serotonin is difficult to measure, making it an impractical marker for alcoholism (Tabakoff & Hoffmann, 1991).

Although each of the aforementioned biological markers have shown interesting relationships to alcoholism, none has so far been found clinically useful in diagnosing substance abuse or in predicting of which individuals will grow up to be alcoholics. Like the genetic factors discussed earlier, at the present time, these biological markers might be considered indications of a vulnerability to alcoholism and merit further investigation.

Psychological Factors

While one clear profile of an addictive personality has not been established, certain personality characteristics seem to be associated with alcoholism. A number of studies using the Minnesota Multiphasic Personality Inventory (MMPI) have found such an association to unconventionality, disregard for established social customs, as well as impulsivity and inability to tolerate frustration and profit from experience (Cox, 1987). The MacAndrew Scale of the MMPI, which was developed as a means of identifying alcoholic personality characteristics, has identified two personality types. Some studies have shown that up to 85 percent of male alcoholics can be distinguished by this scale, and are termed *primary alcoholics*; these men are characterized as bold, aggressive, and hedonistic. The second type, termed *secondary alcoholics*, can be identified by a separate set of 18 MMPI items and are referred to as *punishment avoiders*. They use alcohol to cope with their tension and depression (Cox, 1987). Since these studies were conducted with individuals who already have drinking problems, it is unclear whether these personality factors are the cause or the consequence of the disorder.

The tension-reduction, or anxiety-relief, hypothesis suggests that drinking is reinforced by its ability to reduce tension, anxiety, anger, depression, and other unpleasant emotions. However, support for this hypothesis is inconsistent, probably because alcohol has variable effects on tension, depending on how much is consumed, and only certain individuals experience stress reduction after ingesting alcohol. It appears that the subjective effects of alcohol depend largely on the expectancies of the drinker. These expectancies are developed early in childhood by observing adult drinking behaviours and media messages about the feelings and good times that can be had with alcohol. The **alcohol expectancy theory** proposes that drinking behaviour is largely determined by the reinforcement that an individual expects to receive from it. Among the expectancies identified by a group of social drinkers were that alcohol positively transforms experiences, enhances social and physical pleasure and sexual performance and experience, increases power and aggression, alters personal characteristics and improves social skill, and reduces tension (Goldman, Brown, & Christiansen, 1987).

Nevertheless, most of these subjective experiences are a function of expectation and attitude and not a drug effect. In fact, alcohol's pharmacological effects can have the opposite effect of expectation in regard to tension reduction, mood, sexual performance, and social skills.

In support of the expectancy theory, alcoholics and non–problem drinkers have both been found to drink more when told their drinks contain alcohol, regardless of the beverage's alcohol content (Marlatt, Demming, & Reid, 1973). Alcoholics and heavy social drinkers can be distinguished by a measure of their alcohol-related beliefs. Alcoholics and heavy social drinkers are more likely than non–problem drinkers to believe that alcohol use will result in positive outcomes (Thombs, 1993). Longitudinal research with adolescents supports the impact of alcohol expectancy on future drinking behaviour. Positive expectancies of alcohol effects predicted higher levels of subsequent alcohol use (Smith, Goldman, Greenbaum, & Christiansen, 1995).

Sociocultural Factors

Alcohol use is influenced by such social and cultural factors as family values, attitudes, and expectations that have been passed on from generation to generation. It seems people who are introduced to drinking as a rite of passage in an environment where excessive drinking is socially accepted (and indeed encouraged by peer pressure) face increased risk of developing alcoholism. In some subcultures, an individuals' use of chemicals is seen as a sign of maturity, and this adolescent peer subculture may encourage repeated episodes of substance abuse. Social learning also influences expectancies and, as we have seen, individuals with positive expectancies are most likely to be the heaviest drinkers. Cultural and familial traditions and attitudes toward alcohol use combine to influence the individuals expectations of the effects of alcohol and their drinking patterns.

Evidence for cultural influence on drinking patterns can be found in comparisons of alcoholism in different countries. While the consumption of alcohol is worldwide, the patterns of alcohol abuse differ from country to country. In France, where daily drinking is common, alcoholics are usually steady drinkers who rarely show a loss of control and are prone to physical disorders rather than social disruptions. Although daily drinking is also acceptable in Italy, drinking is usually restricted to mealtime and consumption limited, and there is a much lower rate of alcoholism than in France. In England, Ireland, and North America alcoholism is often manifested by bouts of extremely heavy drinking and often associated with loss of control and disastrous social consequences. In Muslim countries, where consumption of alcohol is discouraged on religious grounds, alcoholism rates are very low (Rivers, 1994).

Drinking patterns in the home also influence an individual's use of alcohol. Adolescents' drinking tends to mirror that of their parents. If parents use alcohol to cope with stressful situations or associate heavy drinking with celebration, children will likely adopt the same attitudes. In general, the more parents drink, the earlier their children begin to drink. However, there is less linkage between parent and child drinking patterns when parents are either nondrinkers or very heavy drinkers (Barnes, Farrell, & Cairns, 1986; Harburg, Davis, & Caplan, 1982). Children of alcoholics may mimic parents' behaviour or react by being totally abstinent. Children of parents who drink no alcohol also tend to the extremes of drinking behaviour, either drinking heavily or not at all (Lawson, Peterson, & Lawson, 1983).

The exact etiology of alcohol abuse and dependence has yet to be resolved, but many researchers agree that it is a multidetermined disorder influenced by biological, psychological, and sociological factors. Evidence for a genetic contribution to the development of alcohol abuse and dependence is strong, but it cannot explain why some people with family histories of alcoholism do not develop drinking problems. Nor does it account for the fact that most of the people who develop these disorders do not have family histories of these problems. Individuals develop expectations about alcohol, must chose to use alcohol, and decide on the manner in which it will be used. The individual with biological and/or psychological vulnerabilities may respond to social influences and personal stressors in a manner that promotes the development of drinking problems. Different combinations of risk factors and environmental liabilities create multiple paths to the development of alcohol use disorders.

Treatment

Alcohol and drug abuse have probably been around as long as the drugs themselves. Early admonitions against the overuse of alcohol were of a moral nature, and those who lacked the fortitude to resist temptation were punished. A more liberal view of alcohol and other drug use arose during World War II, when many soldiers engaged in substance abuse. A number of treatment programs have been developed for alcoholics, each with its own proponents and some evidence of effectiveness. The differing patterns of alcohol abuse suggest that there are various contributors to alcohol dependence, and it may be that some treatments, or combination of treatments, are better suited for some alcoholics under some conditions.

The Minnesota Model

Most professionals agree with most components of the Minnesota model, which has been the most common treatment for alcohol use and dependence. This model views alcoholism as a disease. For people who show signs of withdrawal, treatment begins in a hospital or detoxification clinic under medical supervision, and often includes prescription drugs. Following detoxification treatment for the physical dependence, treatment of the psychological dependence begins. This component includes education about the consequences of alcohol use and abuse, individual counselling for psychological issues, and group therapy to improve interpersonal skills. Abstinence is the goal, since it is assumed that people with the alcoholism "disease" will never be able to drink in a controlled way. Participants are usually required to attend Alcoholics Anonymous meetings, and encouraged to keep going after treatment to address the danger of relapse.

Pharmacotherapy

Medication has been used in the treatment of alcoholics to assist in detoxification, to reduce the pleasurable effects associated with drinking, and to produce nausea when alcohol is consumed. To make detoxification more bearable, benzodiazepines (tranquillizers) have been administered to alcoholics as a first step in treatment. Since these medications mimic the effects of alcohol, they minimize the effects of withdrawal. Doses are gradually decreased as withdrawal proceeds. The use of benzodiazepines is controversial because of the danger of substituting one addiction for another, and because most alcoholics do not experience withdrawal symptoms severe enough to warrant this intervention (Wartenberg et al., 1990).

Medication can also be prescribed as a method of reducing the immediate gratification that accompanies drinking. Naltrexone, an **antagonist drug**, targets the neurotransmitters that mediate alcohol's effects on the brain and "blocks" the pleasurable effects of alcohol. In addition, it helps reduce the sensation of craving. Preliminary studies have shown that naltrexone does help some alcohol abusers abstain from alcohol use (O'Malley et al., 1992; Volpicelli, Alterman, Hayashida, & O'Brien, 1992). However, its success depends on the compliance of the individual. Naltrexone may serve as a useful addition to psychological therapy that includes helping the individual reexamine expectations of alcohol.

Another drug approach is to make the experience of drinking extremely aversive. **Antabuse** (disulfiram) and CCC (citrated calcium carbamate) block the action of the metabolizing enzyme acetaldehyde dehydrogenase, resulting in a buildup of acetaldehyde in the body. Like people who naturally lack this enzyme, people who drink alcohol after taking Antabuse experience increased heart rate, nausea, vomiting, and other unpleasant effects. Patients are instructed to take the medication each morning, before the desire to drink becomes overwhelming. This treatment offers some protection from unplanned drinking, but once again compliance is a major hurdle.

Psychological Therapy

Alcoholics Anonymous. Alcoholics Anonymous (AA) works with more alcoholics than any other treatment organization, and is the most successful known approach to treatment. AA does not use professionally trained staff; it is a self-help group, "a fellowship of men and women who share their experience, strength, and hope with each other that they may solve their common problem and help others to recover from alcoholism" (AA Grapevine, Inc., New York, NY, cited in Rivers, 1994, p. 268). AA got its start in 1935 in a popular Protestant religious following, the Oxford Movement. The movement, dedicated to redeeming mankind through striving for absolute good, consisted of small groups that met weekly for prayer, worship, and discussion. Two members, physician Dr. Bob and stockbroker Bill W., had been trying unsuccessfully to quit drinking, and found the fellowship of the group helpful. They invited more and more alcoholics into the group, and when the meetings became too large, they broke away and founded Alcoholics Anonymous.

The AA treatment is based on a disease model and the goal is complete abstinence. AA members believe there is no cure for alcoholism; there are only alcoholics who drink and alcoholics who do not drink (in recovery). They believe they are powerless to control drinking and must rely on a "Higher Power" to help them (see Table 10.3). Members are encouraged to attend meetings often and regularly, as social support is central to the program. Members who have stayed sober for a period of time serve as sponsors for newcomers.

There are over 20,000 AA groups holding 25,000 meetings each week all over the world. A large survey of a stratified random sample of North American members showed that 59 percent drop out in the first year of membership; but 83 percent of members who have stayed sober more than one year will remain in the Fellowship another year; after five years, the proportion rises to 91 percent (Chappel, 1993). AA is an effective treatment for some, and many people credit it with saving their lives. Others find it difficult to embrace because of its reliance on spirituality and its adoption of the disease model.

Behavioural treatment. The behavioural approach treats alcoholism as a learned behaviour. Alcohol, an unconditioned stimulus, elicits unconditioned responses in the form of pleasant physical reactions. Alcohol becomes associated with these pleasant responses. (See Chapter 2 for an explanation of conditioning theory.) Therefore, some behavioural interventions

attempt to condition an aversive response to alcohol by pairing alcohol with an unpleasant stimulus. For example, the sight, smell, and taste of alcohol may be presented while the alcoholic is nauseated and vomiting as a result of taking an emetic drug. Theoretically, over time the sensation of nausea should be elicited by presence of alcohol without the emetic drug (a conditioned response), and the previous positive associations with drinking become negative. Even though a number of theoretically sound procedures have been used, aversion therapy alone has had limited success, but it can be combined with other treatments (Costello, 1975; Nietzel, Winett, Macdonald, & Davidson, 1977).

Other behavioural treatments are based on operant conditioning principles (see Chapter 2). *Contingency management* has been used to manipulate reinforcement contingencies for alcohol use. Contracts between patients and treatment programs may be established, that specify rewards (or punishments) contingent on small steps toward sobriety. A more comprehensive operant program is the Community Reinforcement Approach (CRA; Azrin, 1976). A spouse, friend, or relative who is not a substance user is recruited to participate in the program; both participants learn behavioural coping skills, and how to develop contingency contracts. They learn to identify antecedents to drinking, the circumstances in which drinking is most likely, social reinforcers, and the consequences of drinking. They are also taught how to arrange reinforcement contingencies to reward sobriety rather than reinforce drinking. Finally, this comprehensive intervention program also helps alcoholics develop new recreational options that don't involve alcohol and reduce stress through improvements in practical areas of life, such as employment, finances, and education.

Relapse Prevention

Whether the goal of treatment for alcoholics is complete abstinence or controlled drinking, the long-term results of most programs are disappointing. Most treated alcoholics eventually relapse and develop problems with alcohol again. Relapse prevention treatment aims to avoid relapses if possible, and to manage a relapse if and when it occurs (Marlatt & Gordon, 1985). **Relapse** is seen as a failure of a person's cognitive and behavioural coping skills to cope with the problems of alcoholism. Maladaptive behaviour is seen as a result of self-defeating thoughts and self-deception that can bring about "inadvertent" slips. Apparently innocent decisions based on distorted beliefs can chain together to create circumstances that increase the risk of drinking. The relapse prevention techniques attempt to help individuals identify these distorted beliefs and replace them with adaptive ones. High-risk situations are identified for each individual and strategies developed to deal with them. For example, if a person has a history of drinking in response to interpersonal conflict, he can be taught to recognize the early stages of an argument and talk issues over more calmly, or to leave and go for a walk before tensions mount too high. People are taught to view lapses not as overwhelming failures that will inevitably lead to more drinking but as temporary occurrences brought on by a specific

---

Table 10.3 The Twelve Steps of Alcoholics Anonymous

1. We admitted we were powerless over alcohol—that our lives had become unmanageable.
2. Came to believe that a Power greater than ourselves could restore us to sanity.
3. Made a decision to turn our will and our lives over to the care of God as we understood Him.
4. Made a searching and fearless moral inventory of ourselves.
5. Admitted to God, to ourselves, and to another human being the exact nature of our wrongs.
6. Were entirely ready to have God remove all these defects of character.
7. Humbly asked Him to remove our shortcomings.
8. Made a list of all persons we had harmed, and became willing to make amends to them all.
9. Made direct amends to such people wherever possible, except when to do so would injure them or others.
10. Continued to take personal inventory and when we were wrong promptly admitted it.
11. Sought through prayer and meditation to improve our conscious contact with God as we understood Him, praying only for knowledge of His will for us and the power to carry that out.
12. Having had a spiritual awakening as the result of these steps, we tried to carry this message to alcoholics, and to practise these principles in all our affairs.

Source: Alcoholics Anonymous.

situation, from which a person can recover. Initial evaluations have shown relapse prevention to be useful in treating alcohol dependence (Baer et al., 1992).

Marital and Family Therapy

An individual's pattern of substance abuse is unavoidably linked to close social relationships, though not necessarily caused by these relationships. In family and marital therapy, the relationship, rather than the alcoholic, is seen as the patient. Family therapy focusses on issues of interaction and the notion that a family unit attempts to maintain equilibrium. Established patterns of interaction and resistance to change can inadvertently support alcohol abuse by one member of the family. Family members may have established roles for themselves that are defined by the substance abuse and have become so enmeshed in the drinking problem that they actually prevent changes in the abuse pattern. Such people are described as *codependents*. Even if there is no codependency, marital conflict, such as spousal nagging about drinking, can stimulate bouts of heavy drinking.

In an alcoholic's family other existing or potential problems are often overshadowed by the alcohol abuse. In a sense, the abuser becomes a scapegoat. When the individual stops drinking, other troubling issues may develop or become evident. For example, a potentially depressed spouse may manage the depression by dealing with the problem of an alcoholic spouse. When this diversion is no longer available, the depression may unfold. Children of alcoholics often try to be "extra good" and supportive during the drinking phase, and may react to a parent's quitting by acting out. Family members may have reduced their communication because of fear of causing the alcoholic to become violent or drink more, and the communication may remain subdued after cessation of drinking. Each of these areas provide potential targets of therapeutic interventions in the families of alcoholics.

Involving the spouse and other family members in alcohol-related treatment has been found to enhance the effectiveness of alcoholism programs (Bowers & Al-Redha, 1990). The addition of marital therapy to familial involvement in alcohol-focussed counselling sessions has further enhanced treatment. Alcohol abusers who received marital therapy were found to drink less, report greater marital satisfaction, and experience fewer marital separations 18 months later compared with abusers whose spouses were only included in the alcohol-related treatment (McCrady, Stout, Noel, Abrams, & Nelson, 1991).

Controlled Drinking

Originally, controlled drinking research was used to test the critical hypotheses of the popular disease concept of alcoholism (Pattison, Sobell, & Sobell, 1977). Marc and Linda Sobell (researchers who worked for many years at the Addiction Research Foundation) studied a program for teaching alcoholics to drink in moderation in comparison with an abstinence-oriented program similar to AA (Sobell & Sobell, 1973, 1976). Subjects in the study were 40 male alcoholics in a treatment program and thought to have a good prognosis.

Overall results over more than two years of followup indicated that the controlled drinking group were functioning well for 85 percent of the days, as compared to 42 percent of the days for the abstinence group.

These results were challenged in a subsequent paper. Pendery, Maltzman, and West (1982) reported that they had contacted the men in the Sobell study ten years later and found that only one of the men in the controlled drinking group continued to maintain a pattern of controlled drinking; four had died from alcohol-induced problems. This reevaluation made headlines. The Sobells were charged with scientific misconduct and ethical violations. However, these charges were later refuted by an independent investigative committee. Pendery et al. (1982) had not provided followup data on the abstinence group—who, it turned out, had fared no better than the controlled-drinking group. This controversy has created lasting mistrust between proponents and opponents of controlled drinking programs.

Recent research suggests that controlled drinking is a viable alternative to abstinence-based treatment for individuals who are not physically dependent on alcohol (Miller, 1983; Nathan, 1987b). Problem drinkers who are not physically dependent on alcohol and have not suffered severe consequences may recognize that they can benefit from modifying their drinking practices. Yet they may not wish to be labelled as alcoholics, nor willing to accept the drastic treatment goal of abstinence.

The Addiction Research Foundation advises that abstinence is clearly the appropriate treatment goal for drinkers who have had a long career of heavy drinking, where drinking has come to be a pervasive and integral part of their lifestyle, or for those who have suffered serious consequences. However, if they are unwilling to accept abstinence as a treatment goal, they may benefit from treatment aimed at harm reduction (ARF, 1992).

BARBITURATES

There are a number of drugs considered **depressants** because they inhibit neurotransmitter activity in the central nervous system. We have seen that alcohol is one of these substances, although it was not developed for this purpose. Barbituric acid, produced in 1903, was one of the first drugs developed as a treatment for anxiety and tension. Since then there have been many derivatives of this sedative-hypnotic drug, including those with the brand names Seconal, Tuinal, and Nembutal. Barbiturates were widely prescribed until the 1940s, when their addictive potential became known. Barbiturates are commonly known as "downers," or according to the colour of their brand-name versions (for example, "blues," "yellow jackets," and "red birds"). Now, another group of drugs belonging to the sedative-hypnotic class called benzodiazepines (for example, Valium and Librium) are more frequently prescribed. Although these are generally thought of as safer alternatives to barbiturates, they too can be addicting if misused.

Derivatives of barbituric acid are odourless, white, crystalline compounds, usually taken as tablets or capsules.

Long-acting forms are now also available for prolonged sedation. Shorter-acting versions, used to treat sleeplessness, are thought to be more addicting.

Prevalence

The 1993 General Survey on Drugs carried out by ARF (Single, MacLennan, & MacNeil, 1994) indicated that the use of tranquillizers (including barbiturates and antianxiety agents) is fairly low in Canada. In this survey, 3.8 percent of respondents indicated that they had used prescribed tranquillizers during the previous month. Their use is most common among lower income groups (7.8 percent), and among the elderly (10.6 percent). In a survey of Ontario high school students (ARF; Adlaf, Ivis, Smart, & Walsh, 1995) use of prescription barbiturates fell from 8 percent in 1989 to 5 percent in 1995. About 3 percent used non-medicinal barbiturates.

Effects

In small doses (50 milligrams or less), barbiturates cause mild euphoria. With larger doses (100–200 milligrams), slurred speech, poor motor coordination, and impairment of judgement and concentration occur. Initially, users may be combative and argumentative, but the larger dosages eventually induce sleep. The behaviour observed at this dosage is similar to that seen in alcohol intoxication. In fact, DSM-IV criteria for sedative, hypnotic, or anxiolytic intoxication are very similar to those of alcohol intoxication. Very large doses of barbiturates lower respiration, blood pressure, and heart rate to dangerous levels. The diaphragm muscles may relax excessively, causing suffocation. Coma is also a common outcome. Many people taking barbiturates are unaware that their effects are amplified when mixed with other drugs. As an example, the combination of barbiturates with alcohol greatly increases the sedative qualities of the barbiturate—the effect that nearly killed Gareth in the chapter-opening case. This combination has led to many deaths, both accidental and suicidal.

Chronic use of barbiturates can cause what appears to be a constant state of alcohol intoxication. Long-term use causes depression, chronic fatigue, mood swings, and paranoia. It may also result in dramatic personality changes and serious impairments of memory and judgement.

Dependency

Tolerance to barbiturates develops rapidly. With regular use, increasingly higher doses are needed to achieve sedative effects. A user attempting to abstain abruptly may experience extreme withdrawal reactions including delirium, convulsions, sleep disruptions, and other symptoms similar to those experienced with alcohol withdrawal. Withdrawal from barbiturates takes much longer and is significantly more dangerous than alcohol withdrawal (Cambor & Millman, 1991).

Treatment

Treatment for barbiturate abuse is very complicated and can require prolonged hospitalization. Treatment usually involves administering progressively smaller doses of the abused drug to minimize withdrawal symptoms. Initially, an individual is given the barbiturate in a dose about 40 percent of its usual size. After this, the dose is reduced by about 10 percent per day until the user is no longer dependent. At this stage, many individuals experience **abstinence syndrome**, which is characterized by insomnia, headaches, aching all over the body, anxiety, and depression, and which can last for months (Cambor & Millman, 1991). In addition to the pharmacological interventions, psychological and educational programs are usually advised to treat barbiturate dependency. Peer support groups on the same model as AA, but focussing primarily on narcotic users, have been set up in most large Canadian cities (Halikas, 1993).

STIMULANTS

Stimulants refer to a class of drugs that have a stimulating or arousing effect on the central nervous system and create their effects by influencing the rate of uptake of the neurotransmitters dopamine, norepinephrine, and serotonin at receptor sites in the brain. The increased availability of these neurotransmitters affects the nucleus accumbens, which is the primary reward centre for the brain. As a group, stimulants are the most commonly used and abused drugs. They include nicotine, amphetamines, cocaine, and caffeine.

Tobacco

Tobacco use (in the form of cigarettes, snuff, chewing tobacco, cigars, and pipes) constitutes one of the leading public health concerns in Canada. A recent survey estimated that the number of Canadian deaths directly attributable to tobacco use is approximately 41,000 per year (Illing & Kaiserman, 1995). This number includes adult smoking-related diseases (for example, lung cancer and emphysema), childhood illness linked to maternal smoking (for example, respiratory illness), and deaths due to smoking-related fires. Smoking prevention and cessation programs have become a priority for national health campaigns. Moreover, society bears major costs related to tobacco use. As shown in Table 10.2, and graphically in Figure 10.1, the costs to society related to tobacco are higher than the costs related to alcohol, and much higher than all costs related to illicit drugs.

Nicotine comes from the tobacco plant *Nicotiniana tabacum*, which is a member of the nightshade family. Indigenous to South America, it is now grown in many places throughout the world. In Canada, it was originally grown by the Petun, Neutral, and Huron tribes of southwestern Ontario, who introduced it to French settlers. These colonists began

Figure 10.1 Total Social Costs per Capita of Tobacco, Alcohol, and Illicit Drugs

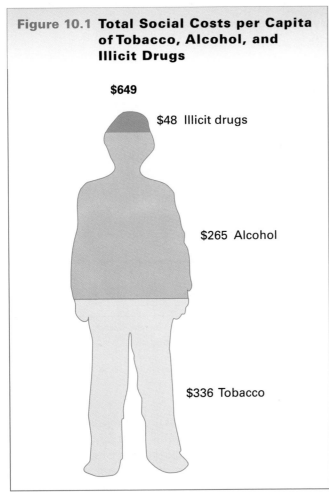

$649

$48 Illicit drugs

$265 Alcohol

$336 Tobacco

Source: E. Single, L. Robson, X. Xie, & J. Rehm, *The costs of substance abuse in Canada* (Ottawa: Canadian Centre on Substance Abuse, 1997).

cultivating and trading tobacco as early as 1652. Commercial cultivation began in the 1800s, and Canada now ranks among the top ten tobacco-producing countries, producing over 100 million kilograms annually. The tobacco industry in Canada employs approximately 6000 people, plus another 51,000 seasonal workers.

Prevalence

It is estimated that 27 percent of Canadians over the age of 15 smoke cigarettes. This represents a decline from 1965, when approximately 50 percent of Canadians smoked regularly. Increased awareness about the adverse health effects of tobacco probably have a lot to do with this decline, as well as increasing tobacco prices (Mummery & Hagen, 1996). Nevertheless, tobacco use may be rising once again. In 1994, tobacco sales increased by 10 percent from the previous year.

The rates of smoking vary according to age groups with the highest usage among those aged 20 to 24. Thirty-seven percent of Canadians in this age range smoke, whereas only 14 percent of those over the age of 65 do so. Of particular concern to public health officials are the increasing rates of smoking

among people under the age of 20. About 30 percent of 18- and 19-year-olds are smokers, and most smoke daily. One reason for the increase may be the availability of low-nicotine cigarettes, which are easier to get used to, and might more easily lead to addiction (Silverstein, Feld, & Kozlowski, 1980). Another possible reason is the increasing sale of individual cigarettes. In addition, although there are strict laws governing the advertisement of tobacco, many critics have claimed that cigarette ads specifically target young people.

Effects

Nicotine is a CNS stimulant related to the amphetamines. It is an extremely potent chemical and the ingestion of only a few drops, in its pure form, can cause respiratory failure. Lower dosages can interfere with thinking and problem-solving, and can cause extreme agitation and irritability along with mood changes. However, the very small amount of nicotine present in a cigarette is not lethal and can increase alertness and improve mood. When inhaled, nicotine enters the lungs and reaches the brain in seconds. The pleasure centres of the brain seem to have receptors specific to this chemical (Benowitz, 1990).

Although the short-term consequences of smoking are minimal, the long-term health risks associated with smoking are significant. Smoking has been implicated in the development of lung, esophagus and larynx cancer, other cancers, emphysema, respiratory illness, heart disease, and other chronic conditions. Most of these illnesses are not caused by the nicotine in cigarettes but by the carbon monoxide and other chemicals found in tobacco. Although many of the health risks associated with smoking can be minimized five to ten years after a person quits smoking, lung damage is often irreversible (Jaffe, 1985). The health hazards of second-hand (or passive) smoke can be even more dangerous. Because there is no filter for these substances, second-hand smoke contains greater concentrations of ammonia, carbon monoxide, nicotine, and tar than the smoke inhaled by the smoker. As a result, passive smoking is associated with significant health risks in nonsmokers including heart disease, lung cancer, and childhood asthma.

Smoking during pregnancy is associated with problems including low birth weight, spontaneous abortion, stillbirth, and infant illness and disability. Women who smoke during pregnancy have double to triple the risk of having an underweight baby and 12 times the risk of delivering prematurely. There has been a decline in rates of smoking during pregnancy from 28 percent in 1983 to 18.7 percent in 1992. This was due in part to a general decline in the overall population smoking rates as well as to increased numbers of women who quit during the first trimester (Stewart et al., 1995).

Dependency

Dependence produced by nicotine is thought to be even greater than that produced by other addictive substances, including alcohol, cocaine, heroin, and caffeine (see Figure 10.2; Franklin, 1990) Nicotine dependence develops quickly, and although

Figure 10.2 Relative Addictiveness of Commonly Used Substances

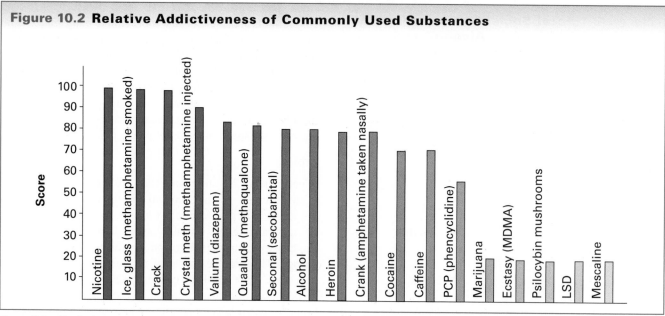

Source: D. Franklin, Hooked–not hooked: Why isn't everyone an addict? *Health, 1990,* November/December, 39–52 (Chap. 12). Research by John Hastings.

This figure represents experts' assessment of how easy it is to get hooked on various commonly used substances (both legal and illegal) and how difficult it is to stop using them. The numbers given are relative rankings based on the experts' scores for each substance.

extremely large doses are required to produce intoxication, its behavioural effects are severe enough to classify many tobacco users as having a substance abuse disorder according to DSM-IV criteria. Smokers become addicted not only because of nicotine's mood-enhancing abilities but to prevent the effects of withdrawal, which can be quite severe.

So in smoking we have a situation that is extremely conducive to dependence: heavy nicotine use does not cause intoxication or behavioural impairment, it is legally and socially acceptable, and it is relatively inexpensive. One can smoke all day and avoid the severe withdrawal symptoms—a perfect recipe for addiction. People addicted to nicotine display behaviours much like those of other substance abusers: they often need a cigarette to start their day, they frequently smoke more than they anticipate, and they often spend a great deal of time looking for more cigarettes. Some smokers change their social plans in order to have continuous access to cigarettes. Furthermore, almost all smokers continue to do so despite the knowledge they are seriously damaging their health. There has been some suggestion that some people are more sensitive to the effects of nicotine, and thus become dependent more quickly (Pomerleau, Colins, Shiffman, & Sanderson, 1993).

Treatment

Many Canadian municipalities have instituted tough smoking bylaws, including reductions or bans in public places such as restaurants, shopping malls, and buses. In addition, it is no longer acceptable to smoke in most workplaces. (Less than 20 years ago, smoking was even allowed in many Canadian university lecture halls!) Recently, leaders in some municipalities have fought for total smoking bans in bars and restaurants.

This has been met with a great deal of resistance from business owners who argue that profits, especially on alcohol, will decline if smoking is not allowed on the premises. Nevertheless, the trend is toward smoke-free public environments.

Despite greater restrictions on smoking in public places and ever-increasing knowledge about the health risks associated with smoking, it can be a difficult habit to break. Most smokers attempt to quit at least once, and the vast majority do so without professional help. Others seek help in the form of psychological and/or biological treatment programs.

Psychological treatments. The psychological interventions designed to help people stop smoking are usually behavioural or cognitive in nature. As such, they typically help individuals develop skills such as self-monitoring, goal-setting, and reinforcement. Some interventions attempt to reduce the pleasure experienced by the smoker by forcing them to smoke far more cigarettes than they would normally, although the adverse nature of these programs has probably contributed to their lack of success (Sobell, Toneatto, & Sobell, 1990). Other smoking cessation programs involve abrupt abstinence ("cold turkey") or include a period of reduction before the client quits for good.

Overall, psychological smoking cessation programs have produced mixed results. While some programs report significant reductions in levels of smoking by the end of the treatment period, most people begin smoking again within a year (Etringer, Gregory, & Lando, 1984). It seems that programs that include frequent, ongoing contact with participants are the most helpful, although abstinence rates reported by such interventions rarely exceed 33 percent after one year (Shiffman, 1993).

Biological treatments. Biological treatments work on the principle of nicotine replacement. They help to reduce cravings and other physiological withdrawal symptoms, by maintaining a steady level of nicotine in the system. The idea is to break the behavioural habits associated with smoking while simultaneously reducing craving. Although these treatments seem to be helpful in reducing the severity of withdrawal symptoms in the short term, many have questioned their long-term efficacy. Increasingly, these interventions are being used in conjunction with psychological therapies (Doherty, Dinnunen, Militello, & Garvey, 1995).

Nicotine gum is chewed for about 20 minutes per piece whenever the smoker craves a cigarette. Although it appears this method of nicotine replacement is helpful in alleviating the physiological symptoms of withdrawal, there is evidence that some people can become dependent upon the gum. In addition, chewing large quantities of the gum can allow high levels of nicotine to enter the blood, which can have adverse effects on a fetus and people with cardiovascular problems. The most effective use of nicotine gum may well be in conjunction with a psychological treatment program (Hall, Tunstal, & Rugg, 1985; Killen, Fortmann, & Newman, 1990).

The nicotine patch replaces nicotine transdermally through a band-aid-like patch worn on the arm. The advantage of this method over nicotine gum is that it delivers a constant supply of nicotine to the system. Therefore, the smoker does not have to worry about consuming too much. However, continuing to smoke while using the patch is dangerous. Nicotine patch programs usually involve gradually reducing the amount of nicotine supplied to the wearer. Like nicotine gum, the patch seems to be helpful in reducing withdrawal symptoms but probably works best when combined with other forms of intervention.

A new approach to nicotine replacement is nasal spray. The spray is inhaled much like an antihistamine and delivers nicotine to the system much faster than the gum and patch methods. The advantage to this delivery method is that it more closely approximates the effects of smoking a cigarette. However, for the same reason, the spray is potentially more addictive than other nicotine replacement systems. More research is necessary in order to examine the efficacy of this treatment (Perkins et al., 1996).

Amphetamines

Amphetamines and related drugs have effects on the body similar to those of the naturally-occurring hormone adrenaline. The two most commonly abused forms of amphetamine are methamphetamine (with street names such as "speed" when injected, and "ice" or "crystal" when smoked in a purified form) and dextroamphetamine (a legally prescribed medication sold under the name Dexedrine). Other street names for these drugs are "bennies," "uppers," "glass," "crank," and "pep pills." Another drug in this class has recently become popular: methylene-dioxymethamphetamine (MDMA), known as "Ecstasy" (or simply "E") is chemically an amphetamine, but is known primarily for its hallucinogenic effects.

Amphetamines were originally developed as a nasal decongestant and asthma treatment in the 1930s. In addition to shrinking mucous membranes and constricting blood vessels, it was discovered they also increased alertness and concentration. Consequently, they were used to treat narcolepsy (a sleeping disorder) and later attention deficit and hyperactivity disorder (ADHD). Later, the appetite-suppressant qualities of amphetamines also led to their use as a treatment for obesity. Currently, only dextroamphetamine (or Dexedrine, used in the treatment of ADHD) is legally manufactured in Canada. Other amphetamines and related drugs are manufactured illegally in home laboratories.

Prevalence

The rate of amphetamine and other illicit drug use in Canada is difficult to determine for a number of reasons. First, unlike alcohol and tobacco (which can be measured by the shot or the cigarette) most drugs have no accepted units of measurement. Moreover, because the majority of sales of such drugs are illegal, there are no consumer records or indexes of availability. Thus it is difficult to define and monitor addiction, or to gauge the social impact of illicit drug use.

Between 1950 and 1970, stimulants were widely consumed by truckers, athletes, students, and others wishing to increase alertness and enhance performance. Since then, amphetamine use in Canada has declined markedly, although there have been reports of recent increases in the use of amphetamine-like drug combinations called "lookalike" stimulants, such as "wake-up pills" (ARF, 1997).

In an ARF survey, approximately 3 percent of Canadian adults reported having used amphetamines at least once in their life (Giesbrecht, Glicksman, Douglas, & Loranger, 1992). Use is somewhat higher among youth; 6.5 percent of Ontario students in Grades 7 to 13 reported using stimulants other than cocaine at least once during the preceding year (Adlaf, Smart, & Walsh, 1993).

Effects

At low doses, amphetamines increase alertness and allow the user to effectively focus attention, offering improved performance on cognitive tasks. At higher doses, they induce feelings of exhilaration, extraversion, and confidence, although usually not to the same degree as is experienced with cocaine. At very high doses, restlessness and anxiety can occur.

Chronic amphetamine use is associated with feelings of fatigue and sadness, as well as periods of social withdrawal and intense anger. Repeated high doses can cause hallucinations, delirium, and paranoia, a condition known as **toxic psychosis**. In order to combat undesirable effects such as sleeplessness, many amphetamine users also become dependent upon depressant drugs such as tranquillizers, barbiturates, and alcohol to induce sleep. This can lead to a roller-coaster-like vicious circle of drug use (Stein & Ellinwood, 1993).

The physical effects of amphetamines include increased or irregular heartbeat, fluctuations in blood pressure, hot or cold flashes, nausea, weakness, and dilation of pupils. Prolonged use usually leads to weight loss. At very high doses, amphetamines can induce seizures, confusion, and coma. The periods of intense anger associated with prolonged amphetamine use may also contribute to the prevalence of violent death in Canada. Regular amphetamine users were four times as likely to die from violent causes as nonusers (ARF, 1997).

Dependency

Amphetamine tolerance and dependence develops very quickly. The effects of amphetamines do not last long, and users often experience a post-high "crash" marked by feelings of fatigue, irritability, sadness, and craving. Withdrawal from amphetamines also often causes periods of apathy and prolonged sleeping.

Cocaine

Cocaine comes from the *Erythroxylon coca* bush, indigenous to various areas in South America. Its stimulating effects have long been known to the people of these regions, who chew on the leaves to reduce fatigue and induce euphoria. Throughout the 1800s, cocaine was viewed as harmless; it was sold in cocaine-laced cigarettes, cigars, inhalants, and crystals, and was the principal ingredient in a variety of commercial products, including Coca-Cola (Musto, 1992). In 1911, cocaine use was restricted in Canada and is now only occasionally used legally as a local anesthetic for minor surgeries.

In the 1960s and 70s, cocaine became a popular recreational drug. Due to the high cost, its use was generally limited to those in middle- and upper-income groups. Recently, however, cocaine has fallen in price as cheaper forms such as crack have been introduced.

Cocaine is usually sold on the street in powder form. This powder is often snorted, but can also be rubbed into the skin or mixed with water and injected. Another method of cocaine ingestion is called "freebasing" and involves purifying cocaine by heating it and smoking the residue. (See Table 10.4 for a comparison of methods of taking substances.) Crack is made by dissolving powdered cocaine in a solvent, combining with baking soda, and heating it until it forms a crystallized substance (a "rock"), which is then smoked. The process itself is potentially dangerous, because the solvents are highly flammable. It is popular, however, because of its cheapness, since the cocaine used need not be as refined as cocaine for snorting. This method of ingestion also increases the rate of metabolizing the drug, and makes it more addictive.

The short-term effects of cocaine appear soon after its ingestion and wear off very quickly. Crack is especially fast-acting, and may wear off in a few minutes. In small amounts, cocaine use in any form brings produces feelings of euphoria, well-being, and confidence. Users become more alert and talkative, and experience reduced appetite, increased excitement, and energy, due to the stimulation of the higher centres of the central nervous system. It appears these effects are primarily achieved by increasing the availability of dopamine at important neuronal sites in the brain. With high doses, the central nervous system is overstimulated, leading to poor muscle control, confusion, anxiety, anger, and aggression.

Continuous use may result in mood swings, loss of interest in sex, weight loss, and insomnia. As with amphetamines, chronic use of cocaine can also lead to toxic psychosis experienced as delusions and hallucinations.

Physical symptoms of cocaine use include increased blood pressure and body temperature, as well as irregular heartbeat. Users may also experience chest pain, nausea, blurred vision, fever, muscle spasms, convulsions, and coma. Death can occur as a result of cocaine's impact upon the brain centres that control respiration.

Table 10.4 **Methods of Taking Substances**

Method	Route	Time to Reach Brain
Inhaling	Drug in vapour form is inhaled through mouth and lungs into circulatory system.	7 seconds
Snorting	Drug in powdered form is snorted into the nose. Some of the drug lands on the nasal mucous membranes, is absorbed by blood vessels, and enters the bloodstream.	4 minutes
Injection	Drug in liquid form directly enters the body through a needle. Injection may be intravenous or intramuscular (subcutaneous).	20 seconds (intravenous) 4 minutes (intramuscular)
Oral ingestion	Drug in solid or liquid form passes through esophagus and stomach and finally to the small intestines. It is absorbed by blood vessels in the intestines.	30 minutes
Other routes	Drugs can be absorbed through areas that contain mucous membranes. Drugs can be placed under the tongue, inserted anally and vaginally, and administered as eyedrops.	Variable

Source: M. J. Landry, Understanding drugs of abuse: The process of addiction, treatment and recovery (Washington, DC: American Psychiatric Press, 1994), p. 24.

Crack, a fast-acting and highly addictive form of cocaine, is smoked with a special pipe.

Prevalence

The restriction on cocaine use by the Canadian government in the early 1900s led to a decline in its use throughout the first half of the century. This decline coincided with an increase in amphetamine use. When amphetamine use waned in the 1950s and 1960s, cocaine's popularity again increased (ARF, 1997).

About 4 percent of males and 2 percent of females in Ontario report having used cocaine or crack at least once. Most, however, use it only occasionally. Although it is more likely to be used by people in their 20s and 30s, surveys by ARF indicated that 3 percent of Canadian students in Grades 7 to 13 had tried cocaine during the previous year (Adlaf, Smart, & Walsh, 1993; Hindmarsh, Porter-Serviss, & Opheim, 1994).

Dependency

Until fairly recently, cocaine was not thought to be addicting. However, more recent research has revealed that cocaine produces intense psychological dependence and results in severe withdrawal symptoms. Cocaine users often feel a crash as the drug begins to wear off, which results in intense craving, depression, and paranoia, followed by fatigue. The craving for cocaine experienced during withdrawal gradually reduces in intensity, but can take more than a month to disappear completely (Gawin & Kleber, 1986; Weddington et al., 1990).

Treatment for Amphetamine and Cocaine Abuse

Treatment for stimulant abuse is complicated by several factors. Stimulant users are also likely to use other drugs in order to counteract some of the effects of the stimulants. As a result, many are dependent upon alcohol or other depressants, making it difficult to decide which dependency to treat first. In addition, people who abuse more than one drug often have comorbid mental disorders, and it is difficult to determine whether one of these conditions predates the other.

Psychological treatments. Psychological treatments for stimulant abuse developed in the 1980s were often modelled after the 12-step programs for alcohol. Intervention programs, which normally have abstinence as a goal, have also focussed on group therapy, individual counselling, and developing relapse prevention skills (McClellan et al., 1993). Cognitive-behavioural interventions examine the thoughts and behaviours that precede and maintain stimulant abuse (Joe, Dansereau, & Simpson, 1994). Recently, community outpatient programs have become popular in which individuals are rewarded with money and social outings if they remain drug-free. There is some evidence that these programs are superior to 12-step programs, but this is far from conclusive (Higgins et al., 1993).

Biological treatments. Biological treatments are usually used as adjuncts to psychological interventions for stimulant abuse. Antidepressants may be prescribed to combat the depression that frequently occurs during withdrawal. In addition, dopamine-enhancing drugs (for example, bromocriptine) may be given in order to reduce cravings. Studies have so far failed to find that these medications alone improve outcomes (Campbell, Thomas, Gabriellu, Liskow, & Powell, 1994; Eiler, Schafer, Salstrom, & Lowery, 1995). Again, they are probably most beneficial when used in conjunction with a good psychological treatment program.

Caffeine

Caffeine, the world's most popular stimulant, was first isolated from coffee beans in 1820. It had, however, been used for centuries before that. Tea was drunk in China at least as early as the ninth century, but tradition places its discovery much earlier. Coffee was recorded in Ethiopia in the fifteenth century, and was then stated to have been drunk from time immemorial. Soon after that time, the substance became controversial among Moslems in North Africa and Arabia; some used it to keep awake during long religious ceremonies, although others claimed that it was an intoxicating beverage and thus forbidden by the Koran. Nevertheless, coffee became the national beverage of the region. Both coffee and tea were introduced to Europe in the seventeenth century. Coffee houses played an important social role in seventeenth- and eighteenth-century England, and tea became a staple of British life by the end of the eighteenth century.

Prevalence

Canadians consume approximately 2200 tonnes of caffeine per year. This is the equivalent of about 2 1/2 cups of coffee per day per person, although caffeine is found in a variety of other foods and beverages (see Figure 10.3). It is also a common ingredient in many over-the-counter pain medications, cough and cold remedies, and diet pills. Like other stimulants, it produces a release of the neurotransmitters dopamine, serotonin, and norepinephrine.

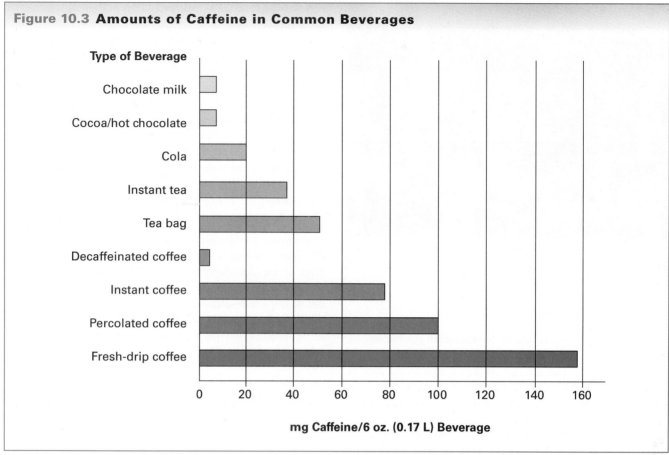

Figure 10.3 Amounts of Caffeine in Common Beverages

Source: From M.T. Nietzel, M. L. Speltz, E. A. McCauley, & D. A. Bernstein, *Abnormal Psychology* (Boston: Allyn and Bacon, 1998). Copyright © 1998 by Allyn & Bacon. Reprinted by permission.

Effects

In general, caffeine is less harmful than other stimulants. At low doses (100–150 milligrams, approximately one cup of brewed coffee), caffeine can increase attention, improve problem-solving skills, and improve mood. Higher doses cause increased jitteriness, nervousness, gastrointestinal discomfort, and insomnia. At doses exceeding 1000 milligrams per day, caffeine can cause muscle tremors, agitation, excessive talkativeness, disorganized thinking, and rapid or irregular heartbeat. Prolonged use of 350 milligrams per day or more can result in physical dependence. Long-term consumption of more than 650 milligrams per day may cause chronic insomnia, persistent anxiety and depression, and irregular heartbeat. Approximately 20 percent of Canadians are described as physically dependent upon caffeine (that is, they consume 350 milligrams per day or more), and roughly 4 percent consume more than 650 milligrams per day. Cessation of caffeine use can cause withdrawal symptoms that include headaches (which can only be relieved by caffeine consumption), drowsiness, and irritability (Silverman, Evans, Strain, & Griffiths, 1992). The DSM-IV has several classes of caffeine-related disorders, including caffeine intoxication, caffeine-induced anxiety disorder, and caffeine-induced sleep disorder.

OPIOIDS

Opioids (also known as narcotics) are a class of CNS depressants—drugs whose main effects are the reduction of pain and sleep inducement. Opium, the alkaloid from which opioids are derived, comes from the seeds of the opium poppy, which is indigenous to Asia and the Middle East. Natural opiates (for example, morphine and codeine) are refined directly from opium, whereas semisynthetic opiates (for example, heroin) are derived from natural opiates. Synthetic opiates (for example, methadone, Darvon, Demerol) are drugs manufactured to have effects similar to those of the other opiates.

Opioids can be taken as tablets, capsules, suppositories, or syrups, or in the form of an injection. In pure form, heroin appears as a white, odourless, bitter-tasting powder which can also be snorted. Most heroin users, however, prefer to mix heroin with water and inject it to produce a more intense high. This is known as "mainlining."

Heroin, the most commonly abused opioid, was originally introduced in 1898 as a replacement for morphine and was viewed as relatively harmless. It was not until the early 1900s that it was discovered that heroin is even more addictive than morphine. Morphine and codeine are the only naturally derived opioids in common clinical use in North America.

Morphine remains a mainstay of analgesia for severe pain, such as that experienced by terminally ill cancer patients, and codeine is present in many common medications such as cough syrups and painkillers. Although synthetic opiates are used frequently today as analgesics, they can also produce dependence.

Prevalence

In 1992, only 0.4 percent of Canadians report ever having tried heroin (Geisbrecht, Glicksman, Douglas, & Loranger, 1992); it was more common among lower-income people. Although police seizures of heroin declined dramatically between 1991 and 1992 (Royal Canadian Mounted Police [RCMP], 1994), a 1994 survey by ARF reported that heroin use among undergraduate university students may be on the rise. While in 1988 only 0.3 percent of university students reported using heroin over the previous 12 months, that number rose to 1.1 percent in 1993 (Glicksman, Newton-Taylor, Adlaf, Dewit, & Geisbrecht, 1995). However, even if the street use of heroin is not a major Canadian problem, the use of prescription forms of opioids by Canadians is of considerable concern. Surveys have found that 8 percent report using prescription forms of codeine, morphine, or Demerol in the previous month (Adlaf, Ivis, & Smart, 1994). Opioids were most likely to be used in British Columbia (12 percent) and least likely to be used in Quebec (3 percent), those between the ages of 25 and 34 years were most likely to use prescription opioids (11 percent), and women report greater use than men (9.0 percent versus 7.4 percent; Single, MacLennan, & MacNeil, 1994).

Effects

Opioids mimic the effects of **endogenous opiates**, or the body's natural painkillers. Known as **exogenous opiates**, narcotics affect receptor sites located throughout the body, including the brain, spinal cord, and bloodstream. The narcotics bind to receptor sites at these locations and in turn reduce the body's production of endogenous opiates. Thus, someone who stops using exogenous opiates may experience increased pain sensitivity (Cambor & Millman, 1991).

Heroin is perhaps the most addicting of all opiates, in part due to the sensations associated with using the drug. About one minute after injecting heroin, the user experiences an intense pleasurable rush. After this subsides, a euphoria characterized by dulled sensations and dreamlike sedation is produced, and the user may appear drunk. Heroin also acts as an appetite suppressant and even small doses cause restlessness, nausea, and vomiting (ARF, 1997).

At higher doses, heroin has extremely dangerous effects. Pupils constrict, the skin may turn blue and feel cold and clammy, breathing slows, and coma and respiratory depression causing death can occur. A major problem is that the impact of any dose can be difficult to determine. In fact, heroin addicts sometimes die from a dosage level that they had

previously tolerated. It appears that this is more likely to occur when the drug is taken in an environment that is different than the one in which the drug is usually taken although it is not clear why this is so (Szab'o, Tabakoff, & Hoffman, 1984). In addition, because heroin is produced in an uncontrolled manner and sold on the street, it is often cut with other drugs and its purity is difficult to determine. Many deaths have resulted when for some unknown reason the heroin that is sold at a street level is purer than usual, so that the user unwittingly injects a higher dose.

Chronic users may develop a number of physical conditions. Chronic respiratory and pulmonary problems may develop as a result of the effects of heroin on the respiratory system. Endocarditis, an infection of the lining of the lungs, occurs as a result of the use of unsterilized needles. The use of unsterilized injection equipment can also cause abscesses, cellulitis, liver disease, and brain damage. The risk of HIV infection among intravenous drug users is significant, although the introduction of needle exchange programs seems to have been successful at reducing the spread of HIV through needles (Caplehorn & Ross, 1995).

Dependency

The withdrawal symptoms associated with heroin are extremely severe and begin about eight hours after the last dose. Along with increased pain sensitivity, the user may experience dysphoria, a dulling of the senses, anxiety, increased bodily secretions (runny eyes and nose), pupil dilation, fever, sweating, and muscle pain. Thirty-six hours after a dose, muscle-twitching, cramps, hot flashes, and changes in heart rate and blood pressure can occur in addition to sleeplessness, vomiting, and diarrhea. These symptoms gradually diminish over a five-to-ten-day period. Partly because of the intensity of these symptoms, relapse of opioid abuse is extremely common (ARF, 1997).

Treatment

The treatment for opioid abuse typically involves the use of medications. Drugs such as naltrexone act as opioid antagonists and help to alleviate initial symptoms of withdrawal, while **methadone**, a heroin replacement, is often used to reduce the craving after initial withdrawal symptoms have abated. Higher doses are given in the early stages of treatment and are then gradually decreased. This approach is not without problems. Many heroin addicts become dependent on methadone, and may require maintenance therapy for up to 20 years. Furthermore, the reduction in narcotic use is often accompanied by an increase in the use of other drugs. However, people receiving methadone maintenance therapy are less likely to commit crimes to support their habit (Bertschy, 1995) and are at less risk of HIV infection than people using heroin (Rosenbach & Hunot, 1995). Most experts agree that methadone therapy works best in conjunction with good individual and group psychological programs, as well as ongoing peer support (Bertschy, 1995).

When Derek was 16 and in Grade 11, his older brother turned him on to grass, and he liked it. Derek began to occasionally smoke with his brother during the week. He could get marijuana for other kids from his brother, which made him very popular.

Although Derek's parents and brother had dropped out of school early, Derek seemed academically gifted. But as his smoking became more frequent, his work habits deteriorated and his attendance dropped. Within a few months he met suppliers who could provide him with cheaper marijuana and other drugs as well. Derek was now spending more time dealing than doing schoolwork, and he failed his year. But he was earning as much in a day or two as his father did in a week of casual labour.

By the end of the next school year word of his services reached the ears of the principal. Derek's apartment was raided and a sizeable cache of drugs was seized. Derek was sentenced to 18 months in prison.

Upon release 6 months later, Derek was adamant about going straight. He returned to school and got a job waiting tables. But grades didn't come as easily as before, the other students were all much younger, and the double workload was tiring. He slowly slipped into seeing some of his old acquaintances and smoking the odd joint. When other students asked for drugs, he found it hard to refuse. Derek soon gave up his job and started selling, and using, a variety of drugs.

Derek was referred to one of the authors for a pre-sentencing report, after being found guilty of possession of a variety of drugs for the purpose of trafficking. This time he was also charged with possession of a large number of stolen goods, including a very expensive stereo system. Derek claimed he had received the goods as payment for drugs and did not know they had been stolen.

CANNABIS

Marijuana and hashish come from the hemp plant *Cannabis sativa*, indigenous to Asia but now grown in many parts of the world. The hemp plant was originally (and still is) cultivated for its strong fibres, which can be processed into cloth and rope. However, its medicinal and psychotropic properties soon became known, and it was used to treat rheumatism, gout, depression, and cholera, as well as for pleasure. Marijuana consists of the leaves and flowers of this plant, which are dried and crushed. Hashish, made from the resin produced by the plant, is a much stronger form of **cannabis**. Although both forms are most often smoked in cigarette form (called a "joint") or in a pipe, they can also be chewed, added to baked goods, or prepared in a tea. Other names for

marijuana and hashish are "pot," "weed," "grass," "dope," "reefer," and "bud."

Prevalence

Marijuana is the most commonly used and most widely available illicit drug in Canada (RCMP, 1994). In general, however, marijuana use appears to be declining among Canadian adults since it peaked in the late 1970s and early 1980s. In 1989, 7 percent of Canadian adults reported having used marijuana in the previous year, whereas in 1993 this dropped to 4 percent. (Single, MacLennan, & MacNeil, 1994). Twenty-seven percent of men and 17 percent of women reported ever having tried cannabis products; current users were most likely to be between the ages of 20 and 40 years (Geisbrecht et al., 1992).

Although rates of marijuana use among adults appear to be stabilizing or declining, use among high-school students is on the rise. As with adult populations, student use peaked in the late 1970s, when 32 percent of adolescents reported using cannabis in the previous 12 months. This reached a low point in 1989, when only 12 percent reported using these drugs. Since then, however, rates have again begun to rise, and by 1995, 23 percent of Ontario high school students reported marijuana or hashish use in the past 12 months. Approximately 5 percent of Canadian Grade 12 students reported weekly use of cannabis (Adlaf, Ivis, Smart, & Walsh, 1995).

Effects

The psychoactive effects of cannabis are caused primarily by the chemical delta-9-tetrahydrocannabinol (**THC**). Although the exact mechanisms by which THC exerts its influences is not fully understood, it appears as if it acts upon specific cannabinoid receptors in the body and mimics the effects of naturally occurring substances including the endogenous opiates (Bouaboula et al., 1993). The concentration of THC in marijuana and hashish has increased about fivefold since the 1960s and 1970s, making it difficult to accurately measure the effect of specific doses.

Cannabis involves mild changes in perception along with enhancement of physical experiences. With relatively small doses, most users report feeling mildly euphoric and sociable. A sense of well-being and relaxation usually begins within minutes of ingesting the drug and lasts for two to three hours. Some people find the drug stimulating, however, and occasionally panic or anxiety is also experienced. At high doses, cannabis has been known to cause hallucinations, although it seems that this most often occurs when the user has a preexisting mental disorder. Individuals under the influence of marijuana show deficits in complex motor skills, short-term memory, reaction time, and attention (Wilson, Ellinwood, Mathew, & Johnson, 1994). Physical effects include itchy, red eyes, and increased blood pressure and appetite.

Long-term users often suffer greater lung problems than tobacco smokers, including deterioration in the linings of the trachea and bronchial tubes, which may be a result of holding unfiltered smoke in their lungs for long periods of time. In addition, marijuana and hashish contain much greater concentrations of some known carcinogens (for example, benzopyrene) than tobacco, and there is also some evidence that chronic marijuana use can result in fertility problems for both men and women.

Some long-term users develop **amotivational syndrome**: a continuing pattern of apathy, profound self-absorption, detachment from friends and family, and abandonment of career and educational goals. Although the amotivational syndrome is thought to be related to the alteration of brain function caused by chronic cannabis use (Musty & Kabak, 1995), it may also be related to depression in long-term users. There is evidence that about 30 percent of regular cannabis users also have symptoms of depression (APA, 1994; Cambor & Millman, 1991). It is unclear whether depression leads to increased cannabis consumption or whether it is a result of prolonged use.

Therapeutic Effects of Marijuana

Marijuana has been used in the treatment of several diseases, including cancer, AIDS, and glaucoma. It has been shown that THC can help to alleviate nausea and encourage eating in cancer and AIDS patients. In the treatment of glaucoma, THC has been used to relieve pressure within the eyes. Because it is both illicit and thought to be "bad for one's health," most jurisdictions do not currently allow marijuana consumption for therapeutic use, even in extreme cases.

Dependency

It has long been believed that marijuana is not addictive, but there is recent recognition that regular marijuana use results in both tolerance and withdrawal symptoms, although withdrawal is milder than with other addictive substances. Symptoms include mild irritability, nausea, diarrhea, loss of appetite, restlessness, sleep disturbances, and drug craving (ARF, 1997; Jones, 1983). There are few documented treatment programs designed specifically for cannabis use.

HALLUCINOGENS

Hallucinogens are drugs that change a person's mental state by inducing perceptual and sensory distortions or hallucinations. They are also called *psychedelics*, which comes from the Greek words for "soul" and "to make manifest." There are many different kinds of hallucinogens, but the most well known are lysergic acid diethylamide (LSD or "acid"), mescaline, and psilocybin. Many of these drugs are derived from plants, but others are produced in the laboratory.

LSD was first discovered in 1938 by Swiss chemist Albert Hoffman, who was investigating ergot, a fungus that affects cereal plants such as wheat and rye. In 1943, he accidentally ingested some of the compound he had isolated from this fungus, and subsequently had the first recorded "acid trip." Later, he also extracted psilocybin from a mushroom called *Psilocybe mexicana*.

Hallucinogens can be ingested in capsule or tablet form, or as a liquid applied to small pieces of paper (for example, stamps or stickers) and then placed on the tongue. Mescaline is found in the head of the peyote cactus and is chewed or mixed with food or water. Psilocybin is also chewed or swallowed with water. The effects of hallucinogens usually begin within an hour of ingestion and last between six and twelve hours.

Prevalence

In Canada the use of hallucinogens peaked in the 1960s. In 1992, about 5 percent of adult Ontario residents reported having tried LSD at least once. People between the ages of 20 and 40, and those in upper-income groups (above $40,000 per year) were more likely than those in lower-income groups to have tried the drug. As with other drugs, men reported higher rates of current hallucinogen use (4 percent) than women (3 percent). Hallucinogen use appears to be on the rise among student populations. A recent survey of over 8000 students in western Canada and the Northwest Territories found that hallucinogen use among students in Grades 6 to 12 nearly doubled from 1987 to 1992, when 6 percent of students reported that they had used hallucinogens in the previous year. Use of hallucinogens in university student populations is also higher than in other adult groups (Glicksman, Newton-Taylor, Adlaf, Dewit, & Geisbrecht, 1995).

Effects

The subjective effects of hallucinogens depend upon a number of variables, including the personality of the user and the amount of drug ingested. A person's expectations regarding the

Timothy Leary was one of the leaders of a movement that extolled hallucinogens as part of a quasi-spiritual quest to expand consciousness and live life on a higher plane.

effects of hallucinogens appear to play a large role in determining their reaction. In addition, the setting in which the hallucinogens are taken appears to be very important. Users who feel uncomfortable or unsafe in their environment may experience anxiety and fear, which can sometimes escalate into panic or psychotic-like episodes. A very small number of individuals are left with a prolonged psychotic disorder, long after the drug has worn off.

People taking hallucinogens report a number of sensory experiences, including vivid visual hallucinations. Objects may waver, shimmer, or become distorted (for example, limbs may appear very long). People commonly see colourful "halos" around objects; moving objects leave visible trails. Users may also experience *synesthesia*, a transference of stimuli from one sense to another, such "hearing" colours or "feeling" sounds.

Hallucinogens have an excitatory effect on the CNS and mimic the effects of serotonin by acting upon serotonin receptors in the brain stem and cerebral cortex. LSD, for example, affects the sympathetic nervous system and causes dilated pupils, increased heart rate, elevated blood pressure, and increased alertness. Most hallucinogens are not physiologically dangerous even in high doses. However, hallucinations may lead to a risk of injury if there are extreme distortions in sense of distance, depth, or speed.

One of the most frightening and inexplicable consequences of hallucinogen use can be the occurrence of "flashbacks"—unpredictable recurrences of some of the physical or perceptual distortions experienced during a previous trip. DSM-IV includes a diagnosis called Hallucinogen Persisting Perception Disorder, which is applied if flashbacks cause significant distress or interfere with social or occupational functioning.

Dependency

It is widely thought that hallucinogens have little addictive potential, although they may induce psychological dependence. Even heavy users of hallucinogens rarely consume the drug more than once every few weeks, partly due to the fact that tolerance develops within a few days of continuous use. When this occurs, a user no longer experiences the hallucinogenic effects of the drug, although the physiological effects are still manifested. Abstinence from the drug for a few days to a week lowers tolerance to normal levels. Hallucinogens do not appear to cause noticeable withdrawal effects, even after long-term use.

Because hallucinogens do not appear to be addictive, few programs have been developed specifically to treat hallucinogen dependence. Those that have been developed generally focus on addressing the user's psychological dependence on the drug.

VIEWPOINT *Gambling: An Addiction?*

Many Canadian provinces have recently legalized gambling in casinos and through "video lottery terminals," which allow you to gamble in bars and restaurants in the comfort of your own neighbourhood. Social gambling has been part of many societies and can be recreational and provide exciting and exhilarating entertainment. In fact, most people have been social gamblers at one time or another. They limit the frequency of gambling, and the time and money spent, and suffer no repercussions. However, there is another group of gamblers who will "risk their reputation, their family's security, their life's savings, their work, their freedom, or their safety on the turn of a card, a roll of the dice, or the legs of a horse" (Custer, 1982). They are preoccupied with gambling and unable to resist despite staggeringly negative consequences. Such people are commonly called "compulsive gamblers"; mental health professionals refer to them as *pathological gamblers*.

Approximately 8 percent of Ontario residents aged 18 to 74 are *problem gamblers*, and 0.9 percent are *probable pathological gamblers* (Stirpe, 1994). The internationally acclaimed Donwood Institute's Problem Gambling Program, in Toronto, describes the typical patient as a male who has experienced problems with gambling for eight years, and has lost some $95,000.

There is a common pattern of development and progression of pathological gambling. Generally an adolescent begins by betting small amounts of money. There is often a winning phase where initial "luck" is quickly replaced by skillful gambling. The person begins to feel exceptional. This phase may continue for some time. The pathological gambler invariably has a history of a big win, followed by unreasonable optimism and larger bets. Gambling is now an obsession, and gambling activities that were once social events become more solitary.

Inevitably there comes a losing streak, which is intolerable to the pathological gambler, and since the bets are much larger now, the winning pool is quickly depleted. The gambler must get the money back, and begins to "chase" losses. He or she bets more frequently, more heavily, and often with a sense of urgency that diminishes his or her betting skills. The gambler's search for money with which to gamble intensifies, borrowing increases, and more time is spent in gambling activities than in fulfilling home or work obligations. In some cases, after exhaustion of all legal sources of loans, the gambler resorts to lies or loan sharks.

At this point the gambler may confess to family and friends and plead for money to bail him- or herself out, in return for a promise to quit. This money is then also gambled and lost. Desperation sets in and, to continue gambling to recoup the loss or to repay the debt, a previously law-

VIEWPOINT *continued*

abiding individual may resort to criminal activity. Eventually, gamblers are in danger of injury, divorce, loss of job, imprisonment, or death.

Many parallels between pathological gambling and alcohol/drug dependencies have been noted. Some pathological gamblers have such great difficulty quitting they even experience withdrawal-like symptoms when attempting to stop. In fact, the diagnostic criteria for pathological gambling were intentionally patterned after those for substance dependence. In addition, the frequent co-occurrence of chemical dependence and pathological gambling in the same individuals has been used as further evidence of a relationship between the two. It has been suggested that gambling and other addictive disorders are functionally equivalent forms of behaviour that satisfy similar needs and that these behaviours may be regarded as cross-addictions. As a result, an addiction model of pathological gambling has gained increasing acceptance among clinicians. The methods of Gamblers Anonymous, established in Los Angeles in 1957, were fashioned after the 12-step model of Alcoholic Anonymous (AA).

Gambling shares many characteristics with substance use. Both generate short-lived pleasurable feelings and provide relief from negative feelings, and both ultimately create cravings to repeat the behaviour. Both have the ability to alter mood and level of arousal, and arguably, to induce an altered state of perception. When engaged in excessively, both behaviours lead to harmful consequences for the individual and society. Yet certain individuals are unable to control the frequency or amount of the behaviour.

The issue of whether addiction can occur without the ingestion of a substance is the topic of lively debate. Some researchers argue in favour of a physiological definition of dependence that requires neurophysiological changes in response to the presence of a foreign substance, while others adhere to the psychological aspect of dependence. DSM-IV criteria for diagnosis of substance dependence can be with or without physiological dependence. DSM-IV has categorized pathological gambling as a disorder of impulse control, yet patterned the diagnostic criteria for this disorder after those for substance dependence.

Critical Thinking Questions

1. Should gambling be considered an addiction?

2. What about other activities to which some individuals appear "hooked"? For example, there is ample evidence that there are some people that spend an inordinate number of hours "surfing the Net" or playing video games like Nintendo.

3. If an "activity," as opposed to a substance, is considered addictive by virtue of being included in DSM-IV, should it then be regulated like other substances? For example, we regulate the age at which individuals can purchase cigarettes and alcohol. Should there also be strict regulations about attending bingo and casinos?

4. Should our health care system (and hence our taxes) be required to provide free services to individuals such as this? Should it be considered a health problem, since unlike alcohol there is no evidence of damage to our body from gambling?

PANORAMA

Substance abuse is an ever-growing problem in our communities. The full impact of both illicit drugs and substances previously considered benign, such as tobacco and alcohol, is just now surfacing. Research has demonstrated that the health, social, and economic costs associated with substance abuse is staggering. There are a variety of drug abuse patterns, and individuals who abuse substances or who become dependent do so for a variety of reasons. It is clear that genetic makeup, personality characteristics, family experiences, and community attitudes must all be considered potential contributors to substance use. As a result, recent comprehensive treatment programs attempt to address the unique combination of factors that result in any individual abusing drugs. However, treatment is difficult, and too often unsuccessful, so there has

been an ever-increasing emphasis on prevention aimed at the most vulnerable population: children and adolescents. Governments and schools have provided such programs in schools and through the public media. Their goal is to urge children to consider the serious health and social consequences of smoking, drinking, and using other drugs. The results of these programs vary according to the time frame and the substance under consideration. As we have seen, tobacco consumption has dropped dramatically over the past quarter-century. In addition, alcohol consumption has decreased, and the number of fatal automobile accidents involving youthful drivers has dropped substantially (Hingson, 1993). The frequency of FAS has also been reduced by programs that have educated women to the perils of drinking during pregnancy (National Institute on Drug Abuse, 1992b). However, alcohol, smoking, and drug abuse prevention programs geared to reducing consumption overall have been less successful. Information gained from research may allow future prevention programs to become more effective by tailoring interventions to the populations most at risk for the development of specific drug problems.

SUMMARY

Alcohol and drugs have been around since recorded history. Many drugs were originally used in moderation, or as part of religious ceremonies. However, more recently they have been consumed in a more widespread fashion, and many individuals develop patterns of abuse and dependence on the substances they consume. DSM-IV sets out the criteria for substance intoxication, substance abuse, and substance dependence. One of the major problems with substance abusers is the phenomenon of polysubstance abuse. Research has demonstrated that concurrent dependence may be the rule rather than the exception.

Alcohol is the world's number one psychoactive substance. Alcohol consumption has dropped considerably in Canada but is still abused by a substantial proportion of the population. Research criteria suggest 20 percent of Canadians may be at moderate to high risk of developing alcohol dependence. The short-term effects of alcohol may result in positive feelings, but over time it acts as a depressant. Alcohol causes deficits in coordination, vigilance, and reaction time. These physical and psychological effects can result in accidents. In the long term, alcohol abuse results in negative consequences economically, socially, and medically. It poses a major health risk to individuals and is a significant burden on the health care system.

Barbiturates are considered depressants because they inhibit neurotransmitter activity in the central nervous system. Originally developed as a treatment for anxiety, they proved to be very addictive and presently are rarely used for this purpose; rather they are prescribed, usually on a time-limited basis, for sleep problems. The euphoria produced by small doses turns to poor motor coordination at higher doses, and can prove fatal in too large a dose. This results from the barbiturate's action on the part of the brain that controls breathing. Barbiturates are also dangerous because their effects are greatly amplified when they are mixed with other drugs such as alcohol.

Stimulants are so labelled because they stimulate or arouse the central nervous system, and do so by influencing the neurotransmitters dopamine, norepinephrine-and serotonin. Tobacco, is the most widely used stimulant, and perhaps the most addicting. Approximately 27 percent of Canadians smoke. Although short-term effects appear to enhance mood and alertness, long-term nicotine use contributes cardiovascular disease, cancer, and other chronic conditions. It is also a serious risk to fetal development. It is one of the few drugs that affects others—through second-hand smoke. Most communities enforce smoking bans in the workplace and indoor public places. They have also initiated prevention programs in schools and the media. As a result, the proportion of the population that smokes has dropped considerably from 1965. Unfortunately, smoking in teenagers has not diminished over the past ten years. Treatment programs often include biological interventions that provide diminishing amounts of nicotine through chewing gums, transdermal skin patches, and nasal inhalers.

Amphetamines are another group of drugs that produce effects similar to those of adrenaline. Three percent of Canadians report having used amphetamines once in their life. These drugs can be smoked, snorted, or taken intravenously and are very addictive. The short-term effects of low dosages of amphetamines include increased alertness and ability to focus attention. This may lead to enhanced cognitive performance. Higher dosages, preferred by drug addicts, may produce feelings of exhilaration, but restlessness and anxiety may also be present. Prolonged use may lead to paranoia, toxic psychosis, or periods of chronic fatigue or a "crash" when the drugs wear off.

Cocaine's stimulating effects have long been known to the indigenous people of South America. It became a popular recreational drug, for the wealthy, in the 1960s and 1970s. However, with the more recent drop in its street price, cocaine and its derivative "crack" have become more common in all segments of the community. In the 1990s approximately 3 percent reported using cocaine once, but a much lower number reported repeated use. Cocaine can be snorted, smoked, or injected intravenously. No matter what the route, its effects are very short-lived, sometimes lasting only a few minutes. Like other stimulants, it produces euphoria, a sense of well-being, confidence, and increased energy. Continuous use may result in mood swings, weight loss, decreased interest in sex, insomnia, delusions, and hallucinations. Cocaine produces intense psychological dependence and severe withdrawal symptoms.

Opioids (also known as narcotics) are CNS depressants whose main effects are the reduction of pain and sleep inducement. Heroin was developed as a replacement for morphine to control pain. Medically it can be taken orally or injected. Most heroin users inject morphine for the intense, pleasurable "rush" it produces. This is generally followed by a dull euphoria and dreamlike sedation. Only 0.4 percent of Canadians report having tried heroin, although recent statistics report more than 1 percent of university students reported using it over the previous 12 months. At higher dosages heroin can be very dangerous, since it affects the part of the brain that controls respiration. Overdoses result in coma and respiratory depression. As with most drugs taken intravenously, infection, particularly HIV and hepatitis, is a constant problem.

Cannabis sativa, or marijuana, is the most commonly used illicit drug in Canada. Approximately 12 percent of Ontario residents report using marijuana occasionally. Marijuana use results in mild euphoria and changes in perception. Another common effect is increased appetite. Also, a deterioration in attentional abilities, complex motor skills, and short-term memory is associated with marijuana. Prolonged use may lead to the amotivational syndrome and depression in some users. Although it is less addicting than most other drugs, there is some evidence that regular marijuana use results in both tolerance and withdrawal.

Hallucinogens, also called psychedelics, induce perceptual and sensory distortions or hallucinations. They are not addicting. One of the most frightening and inexplicable consequences of hallucinogen use can be the occurrence of "flashbacks"—unpredictable recurrences of some of the physical or perceptual distortions experienced during a previous trip.

It is clear that alcohol, tobacco, and illicit drugs are a major health hazard and cost our country billions of dollars annually, in direct and indirect expenses. There is evidence that educating communities has had some positive effects with alcohol and tobacco use; but there is a disturbing trend for increased use of several illicit drugs, particularly by teenagers and young adults.

KEY TERMS

substance intoxication (p. 232)
substance abuse (p. 232)
substance dependence (p. 232)
physiological (p. 232)
tolerance (p. 232)
withdrawal (p. 232)
psychological dependence (p. 232)
habituation (p. 232)
polysubstance abuse (p. 233)
synergistic (p. 233)

ethyl alcohol (p. 236)
blood alcohol level (BAL) (p. 236)
alcohol dehydrogenase (p. 236)
Type I Alcoholics (p. 239)
Type II Alcoholics (p. 239)
alcohol expectancy theory (p. 240)
antagonist drug (p. 241)
Antabuse (p. 241)
relapse (p. 242)
depressants (p. 243)
abstinence syndrome (p. 244)
stimulants (p. 244)

nicotine (p. 245)
amphetamines (p. 247)
toxic psychosis (p. 247)
opioids (p. 250)
endogenous opiates (p. 251)
exogenous opiates (p. 251)
methadone (p. 251)
cannabis (p. 252)
THC (p. 252)
amotivational syndrome (p. 253)
hallucinogens (p. 253)

ADDITIONAL RESOURCES

Centre for Addiction and Mental Health
33 Russell Street
Toronto, ON
M5S 2S1
(416) 595-6878
(416) 595-6881 fax
noursej@cs.clarke-inst.on.ca

Canadian Centre on Substance Abuse
75 Albert Street, Suite 300
Ottawa, ON
K1P 5E7
(613) 235-4048
(613) 235-8101 fax
rgarlick@ccsa.ca

Alcoholics Anonymous
475 Riverside Drive
New York, NY 10015
(212) 870-3400
(212) 870-3003 fax

www.arf.org
The Addiction Research Foundation, an agency of the Ontario Ministry of Health founded in 1949, is one of the world's preeminent facilities for research into drug use and abuse. It has been a collaborating centre of the World Health Organization, participating in national and international investigations. ARF has a large staff of scientists who carry out basic and applied research, publish a journal, and disseminate comprehensive information to professionals, community agencies, and the public.

www.camh.net
The Centre for Addiction and Mental Health (CAMH) was formed in early 1998 through the amalgamation of the Addiction Research Foundation, the Clarke Institute of Psychiatry, the Donwood Institute, and Queen Street Mental Health Centre. CAMH's goal is to better understand, prevent, and provide care for addiction and mental illness. This site provides information about various types of addictions, mental health, and community health and education.

www.ccsa.ca
The web site of the Canadian Centre on Substance Abuse, an organization working to minimize the harm associated with the use of alcohol, tobacco, and other drugs. Provides useful statistics, databases, publications, and web links to other sources.

www.alcoholics_anonymous.org
The web site of Alcoholics Anonymous. Gives information about the causes, effects, and treatment of alcoholism.

www.marininstitute.org
A database containing citations for over 13,000 articles and news stories about the alcohol beverage industry, alcohol policy, and prevention efforts.

www.ncadd.org
A comprehensive menu of information and advice as well as dozens of links to other organizations that have used computer technology in the fight against alcohol and other drug addictions.

Chapter 11

The Personality Disorders

Ralph C. Serin

William L. Marshall

Brian, a 43-year-old man, is preoccupied with the idea that people are trying to hurt or humiliate him. He responds angrily to casual remarks, which he interprets as critical or denigrating of him. For example, a co-worker once remarked, "That's a nice tie you're wearing, Brian." Brian angrily shot back, "What I wear is none of your business." When his therapist asked why he had responded that way, Brian said his co-worker was obviously criticizing his dress sense. He could give no reasonable support for this assumption, but still bore a grudge against the man who made this apparently innocent comment.

Brian told his therapist he has no friends he could really trust. "My so-called friends are always trying to make me feel foolish or they take advantage of my good nature." It was clear to the therapist that Brian had trouble trusting her.

However, in most other ways, Brian seems normal. He does not have the systematic delusions or hallucinations typical of schizophrenics, and his thoughts are not disordered. He has held the same job for more than 20 years, attends church regularly, although his family, fellow church members, and co-workers all consider him to be overly sensitive and unpredictable.

*   *   *

Margaret, 36, is a very successful accountant. Her fastidious nature, extreme orderliness, and conscientiousness care for even the smallest details of her job have earned her the respect of her clients and colleagues. She frequently criticizes other people's sloppiness, and often reorganizes her co-workers' desks when they are out.

Margaret does not have many friends and none of her co-workers wants to spend free time with her because she is as obsessively meticulous about other aspects of her life. For instance, when one colleague accepted an invitation to dinner at Margaret's house,

Margaret escorted her to the living room, complaining that she was five minutes early, and told her to sit in a specific chair. When the guest asked for a drink, Margaret told her she could only drink at the dining table, because she might spill on the sofa or carpet. At the supper table, Margaret was as formal and precise as she was at work. Every aspect of the meal was neatly arranged, and the plates were removed after each course as soon as Margaret finished eating. Conversation was stilted and focussed on work. The guest was ill at ease, and never saw Margaret socially again.

*   *   *

People meeting Andrew, who is in his late twenties, at first usually find him charming. He is talkative, enthusiastic, and very happy to share aspects of his life with others. He does dress rather flamboyantly, but he seems nice and friendly. Unfortunately, once people get to know Andrew, they notice that he only wants to talk about himself and constantly tries to be the focus of attention. Once when Andrew was having lunch with his friends Ted and Mike, Ted described his mother's distressing illness, and Mike tried to allay his fears. Andrew interrupted to describe in detail his appendectomy at the age of 15. Both his friends were annoyed at Andrew's insensitivity and tried to direct the con-

versation back to Ted's mother, but Andrew appeared not to notice and continued with his self-focussed story.

Brian, Margaret, and Andrew are in many aspects fairly normal people, but their personal style (or personality) is upsetting to others and may also lead to some degree of personal distress for them. None of them has any Axis I clinical disorder, but clearly each has a problem in social functioning, and shows behaviour and thinking characterized by a single feature: suspiciousness in Brain's case, fastidiousness in Margaret's, and attention-seeking in Andrew's. These three people would very likely meet the diagnostic criteria for an Axis II personality disorder.

What Is Personality Disorder?

Personality disorders are essentially maladaptive personality traits. What *is* personality? And where do you draw the line between a normal personality trait (even though it may not be especially attractive) and a disorder?

All people display some consistency in their behaviour and thought. We readily describe our friends (and our enemies) as friendly or hostile, kind or cruel, shy or outgoing, sensitive or thick-skinned, etc. Actually, all of us display a range of responses, being more gentle at one time and

rougher at another, or quite trusting of A but somewhat suspicious of B. However, we consider a quality to be characteristic of someone ("He is generous," "She is creative," etc.) only if it is persistently displayed over time and in various situations. These persistent features are described by personality theorists as **traits**; every person manifests several traits, the combination of which describes his or her personality.

DSM-IV defines personality traits as "enduring patterns of perceiving, relating to, and thinking about the environment and oneself that are exhibited in a wide range of social and personal contexts" (American Psychiatric Association, 1994, p. 630). What is not acknowledged in this definition (or in the similar ones used in most textbooks) is that while most people's behaviour patterns are "enduring," they are also modified by context. Even a loud, garrulous person is usually quiet and restrained at a funeral. People with personality disorders, however, tend to be more rigid and inflexible; typically, they display the same personality characteristics independent of circumstance. In fact, DSM-IV says that it is only when personality traits are inflexible and maladaptive (that is, significantly interfere with the person's functioning) that they constitute a personality disorder.

Although it is not clearly stated in the DSM, people with personality disorders also show a far more restricted *range* of traits than most people. For example, if asked to describe a friend, you might think of a number of adjectives: generous, friendly, calm, ambitious, forgetful, and so on. All these characteristics together make up the complex whole that is an individual personality. In contrast, people with personality disorders can be characterized by a single dominant—and in their case, dysfunctional—trait. Think of Margaret in the opening case. Many women are organized and punctilious, even excessively so, yet are quite normal. Margaret fits the description of personality disorder because her neatness is:

1. *rigid:* she is equally fastidious about everything in her life, apparently unable to determine which details justify such care and which do not;

2. *maladaptive:* she is unable to have a social life because of this one trait; and

3. *dominant:* she may be thought of at work as Margaret the Fussbudget or Margaret the Neatnik; people may be unable to define other aspects of her personality; even she herself may have little self-concept beyond this all-consuming trait

Clusters of Disorders

DSM-IV lists ten specific personality disorders, organized into three broad **clusters**: (A) odd and eccentric disorders (paranoid, schizoid, and schizotypal); (B) dramatic, emotional, or erratic disorders (antisocial, borderline, histrionic, and narcissistic); and (C) anxious and fearful disorders (avoidant, dependent, and obsessive-compulsive). Table 11.1 presents the clusters with characteristic features. The principles on which these disorders have been grouped have been challenged (Frances, 1985). Clusters A and C do seem to have enough features in common to make reasonable groups, but Cluster B is a rather confusing and heterogeneous group. The clinical usefulness of the clusters is questionable.

Prevalence

The best estimates suggest that approximately 6 to 9 percent of the population will have one or more personality disorders during their life (Merikangas & Weissman, 1986). However, prevalence is hard to determine because the criteria

Table 11.1 Personality Disorders Listed in DSM-IV

Personality Disorders	Characteristic Features
Cluster A	
Odd and Eccentric Disorders	
Paranoid	Pervasive suspiciousness of others
Schizoid	Emotional detachment
Schizotypal	Eccentric behaviour and social isolation
Cluster B	
Dramatic, Emotional, or Erratic Disorders	
Antisocial	Disregard for others, rule-breaking, impulsive
Borderline	Labile mood, unstable relationships
Histrionic	Attention-seeking, dramatic emotional displays
Narcissistic	Grandiosity, egocentricity
Cluster C	
Anxious and Fearful Disorders	
Avoidant	Sensitivity to criticism, avoidance of intimacy
Dependent	Cannot function independently, forfeits own needs
Obsessive-Compulsive	Inflexibility, need for perfection

Source: APA, 1994.

are open to interpretation. Prevalence rates vary from one study to another as a function of the method used for specific diagnoses. For example, self-report measures will likely yield lower estimates of antisocial personality disorder than structured interviews, because people are reluctant to admit to antisocial traits and behaviours. Other disorders, such as those in Cluster C, may be overrepresented by self-report questionnaires, since people who are somewhat anxious may endorse particular items even though the associated symptoms are not severe enough to merit a clinical diagnosis.

Table 11.2 describes lifetime prevalence data from a community study conducted in the United States. Unfortunately, there are no similar data for Canada. Most studies in Europe have revealed somewhat lower rates for most of the disorders (Maier, Lichtermann, Klingler, Heun, & Hallmayer, 1992). Prevalence rates among psychiatric patients are generally higher than in the community at large, and higher again among inpatients than outpatients. For example, borderline personality disorder, the most commonly diagnosed personality disorder among patients in treatment, was reported in 11 percent of outpatients and 19 percent of inpatients (Widiger & Frances, 1989). Between 10 and 15 percent of outpatients display schizotypal personality disorder (Bornstein, Klein, Malon, & Slater, 1988), compared to 20 to 30 percent of inpatients (Widiger & Rogers, 1989). Antisocial personality disorder is common among psychiatric patients but much more common among prisoners. In psychiatric outpatients the prevalence is near 5 percent, but jumps to 12 to 37 percent for psychiatric inpatients. In prison populations the rates range from 30 to 70 percent (Widiger & Rogers, 1989). These highly variable rates for prisoners presumably reflect differences in the diagnostic criteria used and the particular populations sampled.

Assessing prevalence is complicated by the fact that many people with personality disorders never come to the attention of mental health professionals. The reason these disorders appear on Axis II of DSM-IV is that they do not have the pronounced symptoms of those on Axis I ("clinical" disorders), and do not impair functioning as severely. Although objective evaluation of personality-disordered patients does show that their lives are adversely affected, their actual abilities appear relatively intact (Millon, 1996). They are thus less likely to be referred to a mental health professional. Research shows that 80 percent or more of people with personality disorders never seek treatment for their problems (Drake & Valliant, 1985). Many of them, in fact, are *egosyntonic*: that is, they do not believe they have a problem at all— or, at least, the problem is not in themselves. One can easily imagine how Brian, in the opening case, sees the problem as the nastiness and disloyalty of others, and Margaret sees the problem as others' carelessness. Intervention for this group must initially address the question of motivation: Is the person ready for treatment?

HISTORICAL PERSPECTIVE

The first clear statements of personality disorder were made in 1801 by Pinel, whose work we discussed in the first chapter of this book. Pinel described what he called *manie sans délire* ("insanity without delirium"). People with this disorder,

Table 11.2 Lifetime Prevalence in a Community Survey

Disorder	Percentage
Cluster A	
Paranoid	0.4
Schizoid	0.7
Schizotypal	3.0
Cluster B	
Antisocial	3.0
Borderline	1.7
Histrionic	3.0
Narcissistic	(None found)
Cluster C	
Avoidant	1.3
Dependent	1.7
Obsessive-Compulsive	1.7

Source: Adapted from Zimmerman & Coryell, 1990.

Pinel said, displayed irrational anger, uncontrollable stealing, and persistent lying, but were otherwise intellectually intact. This description was the predecessor of what was to become known as *psychopathy* or antisocial personality disorder. (We will discuss the development of this concept more fully in the section on that disorder.)

The early psychoanalysts, including Sigmund Freud, described a range of character disorders that went well beyond the earlier reports of psychopathic features. The psychoanalysts claimed that many of their patients had fixed personalities that were either hysterical, narcissistic, masochistic, melancholic, or obsessive-compulsive. In fact, the personality disorders were, until recent years, identified with the psychoanalytic movement, and the early versions of the diagnostic manual defined these disorders in psychoanalytic terms. When it became apparent that such descriptions generated unreliable diagnoses, the authors of the diagnostic manual quite sensibly turned to more behavioural criteria. This change to more observable criteria occurred with the publication of DSM-III, which also, for the first time, placed these disorders on a separate axis (Axis II) from the clinical disorders.

Karl Abraham, in the 1920s, was probably the first writer to explicitly elaborate a set of personality disorders, and he was followed by Wilhelm Reich, who in 1925 described four types of character pathology (Blashfield & Davis, 1993). The first edition of the DSM had 16 different specific categories of personality disorders, most of which were dropped or renamed in subsequent revisions.

The concepts of hysteria and paranoia both have a long history dating back to the Greeks, but in this century they have evolved into personality disorders. Kraepelin's (1913) classification system included paranoid-like personality as a disorder, which he believed was a precursor of paranoid psychosis. In fact, quite a number of the present personality disorders were originally seen as either the first signs of a developing psychosis or characteristics that predisposed the person to psychosis. For example, Rado (1956) introduced the term *schizotypal* to refer to the genotype for the later development of schizophrenia, and Hoch (1909) described a "shut-in" personality (now known as schizoid personality disorder) that he said preceded schizophrenia. An avoidant personal style was initially mentioned by Horney (1945) and was later given its current name, *avoidant personality disorder*, by Millon (1969), who has played a very important role in the identification of personality disorders.

As noted, the present set of personality disorders first appeared in DSM-III and subsequent revisions have essentially refined the criteria. Personality disorders are now well-established disorders, although not without controversy.

DIAGNOSTIC ISSUES

The personality disorders present more diagnostic problems than most of the Axis I disorders: the diagnostic criteria have relatively low reliability (Rogers, Duncan, Lynett, & Sewell,

1994); the etiology of these disorders is poorly understood (Marshall & Barbaree, 1984); and there are few effective treatments (Kelly et al., 1992).

Beyond that, however, there have been challenges to the DSM-IV definitions of personality disorder. Canadian researcher W. J. Livesley and his colleagues (Livesley, 1986; Livesley, Schroeder, Jackson, & Jang, 1994) have criticized the categorical approach of the DSM, according to which a person either has or does not have a personality disorder, arguing that personality is better viewed as a constellation of traits, each of which lies along a continuum. (We'll discuss this concept in more detail a bit later.)

There are, in fact, many unresolved problems with the notion of personality disorder. To rephrase the question we asked at the opening of the chapter, is there really such a thing as personality disorder, as distinct from normal variation in personality traits? The vast majority of clinicians would agree that the answer is yes; some people consistently show maladaptive, inflexible, and restricted ways of behaving and thinking that are best described as personality disorders. The problem is not so much whether these disorders exist but how they can be defined in a way that is not prejudicial, is reliable, and leads to effective treatment. Further research is needed before a clearly defined set of criteria is developed.

The clearer set of definitions in DSM-IV has led to far greater research attention in recent years. Over time, we can hope that this research will result in more reliable criteria that will allow more accurate diagnosis and better treatment.

Gender and Cultural Issues

In addition to the general criticisms, many writers have suggested that the diagnostic criteria, and their interpretation, reflect gender and cultural biases, which contribute to the broader problem of unsatisfactory reliability.

DSM-IV does require that diagnosticians ensure that the client's functioning does not simply reflect a normative response in the client's society of origin. As our population becomes increasingly culturally diverse, clinicians may misdiagnose if they do not take adequate precautions to determine whether certain attitudes and behaviours are appropriate for distinct cultures or societal subgroups. For example, a child growing up in an inner-city slum may learn that he or she has to "look out for number one" to survive. To a more privileged clinician who sees him as an adult, such self-interested strategies may look like psychopathology. In North America, an adult who would not take a job without her father's permission might be suspected of dependent personality disorder; but in some traditional Asian societies she would just be a dutiful daughter.

Similarly, a number of authors have suggested that the diagnostic criteria for some personality disorders are gender-biased (Kaplan, 1983). For example, the emphasis on aggression in the criteria for antisocial personality disorder may lead to underdiagnosis in females because of gender differences in the prevalence and expression of aggression. Others are concerned that the clinician's own gender bias or acceptance of sex-role stereotypes may influence the diagnosis (Ford & Widiger, 1989; Pantony & Caplan, 1991). For instance, clinicians have been shown to be reluctant to diagnose males as having histrionic personality disorder or females as having antisocial personality disorder (Widiger & Spitzer, 1991). Henry and Cohen (1983) have suggested that clinicians typically overdiagnose borderline personality disorder in women. On average, 80 percent of the subjects identified as borderline by structured interviews are women (Widiger & Trull, 1993). How can we tell whether these results reflect a true difference in prevalence, gender-biased criteria, or gender-biased application of the criteria?

To test this question, Warner (1978) had 175 mental health professionals make a diagnosis after reading a case history. The patient was described as a woman in half the cases and as a male in the other half, but the case description remained otherwise identical. Of those clinicians who were given the "female" case, 76 percent diagnosed the patient as suffering from a hysterical personality disorder (the earlier name for histrionic personality disorder), while only 49 percent applied that diagnosis when the patient was described as a man.

Ford and Widiger (1989) took another approach: they analyzed a number of real cases of patients, and found that while the specific diagnostic criteria for histrionic personality disorder were found with equal frequency among men and women, women were significantly more likely to be diagnosed with histrionic personality disorder.

A third comparison also supports the idea of gender bias: diagnoses among patients reveal a significantly higher prevalence of histrionic personality disorder for women than for men; yet an epidemiological community survey of over 3000 adults revealed the same prevalence (2.2 percent) in males and females (Nestadt et al., 1990). This suggests a gender bias either in the likelihood that a person with histrionic features will be referred to a psychiatric clinic or in the application of the diagnosis among those referred.

Attempts have been made to diminish these biases. For example, histrionic personality disorder used to be called *hysterical personality*. The name itself was biased: you may recall from Chapter 1 that the term *hysteria* is derived from the Greek word for uterus, considered to be the source of disorders in women, and the word *hysterical* has since traditionally been applied to women. It was thought that changing the name to reflect the actual behaviour (*histrionic* means "excessively theatrical") might reduce gender biases. However, the change of terminology does not appear to have changed attitudes substantially. Histrionic personality disorder is still diagnosed much more commonly in females than in males (Reich, 1987) and studies that ask subjects to rate the diagnostic criteria indicate that most people view the features of the disorder as decidedly feminine (Sprock, Blashfield, & Smith, 1990).

Reliability of Diagnosis

Concerns about cultural and gender insensitivity underscore longstanding larger concerns about the reliability and validity of personality disorder diagnoses. Such concerns have governed revisions to the DSM since 1980. For instance, the early field trials with DSM-III (American Psychiatric Association, 1980) revealed rather poor inter-rater reliability for the personality disorders (see Chapter 4). Subsequent examinations have failed to produce any better results (Dahl, 1986). Rogers, Dion, and Lynett (1992) found only three of thirteen studies provided evidence for satisfactory reliability for the diagnosis of antisocial personality disorder. Strategies such as using structured interviews and expanding the breadth of information collected appear to increase reliability. However, these procedures take longer and few clinicians appear willing to spend the extra time. Since cost-efficiency in mental health services is being increasingly emphasized, it may prove all but impossible to spend the time necessary to use these suggested diagnostic procedures.

Comorbidity and Diagnostic Overlap

One further problem with the diagnosis of personality disorders concerns their independence from each other and from Axis I disorders. The terms *comorbidity* and *overlap* are often used synonymously in the literature but in fact refer to two conceptually distinct features of diagnosis. *Comorbidity* should be used to describe the co-occurrence in the same person of two or more different disorders. **Overlap**, on the other hand, refers to the similarity of symptoms in two or more different disorders (that is, some of the same criteria apply to different diagnoses).

Ideally, diagnostic criteria for different disorders should be distinct, but for personality disorders, the criteria remain sufficiently vague or require such inference by the clinician that overlap seems certain. For example, the principal criterion for paranoid personality disorder is pervasive distrust of others. But how is the clinician supposed to identify this? A distrustful person may not show this quality in the clinician's office. On the other hand, if a client does show distrust at a first appointment, it may well be no more than the reasonable caution of a person dealing with a stranger on important personal matters. From interviews with the client and discussions with family members, the clinician must infer the presence or absence of pervasive distrust. It is, of course, all too easy to make an error of inference. From quite similar behaviours a clinician might infer distrust (which is a feature of paranoid personality disorder) or hypersensitivity to criticism (which is a feature of avoidant personality disorder). In fact, some degree of suspiciousness about the motivation of others characterizes both these otherwise quite different disorders.

Whereas early versions of the DSM required clinicians to choose one primary diagnosis and exclude all others, DSM-IV encourages multiple diagnoses if appropriate. This approach makes diagnosis easier, but it complicates the task for researchers, who generally require a single, clear diagnosis to identify study samples. Multiple diagnoses confront them with difficult decisions that may lead to a confound in interpretations of their findings. Multiple diagnoses also compli-

cate the task of choosing a course of treatment, and make prognosis difficult.

This similarity of symptoms across disorders also results in blurred boundaries between diagnoses, perhaps confusing clinicians. Morey (1988) found that eight of the personality disorders diagnosed according to DSM-III-R (American Psychiatric Association, 1987) overlapped in their diagnostic criteria with other diagnoses by as much as 50 percent. This represented a marked increase in overlap from DSM-III. Yet even by DSM-III categories, as many as two-thirds of patients who receive one diagnosis of a personality disorder also meet the criteria for at least one other personality disorder (Clarkin, Widiger, Frances, Hurt, & Gilmore, 1983).

In particular, comorbidity in borderlines has been the focus of considerable debate. Patients diagnosed as borderline have been found to commonly have schizotypal features, and comorbidity has been observed between borderline diagnoses and other personality disorders (Pfohl, Coryell, Zimmerman, & Stangl, 1986). For example, 47 percent of borderlines met the criteria for antisocial personality disorder and 57 percent met the criteria for histrionic disorder in one study (Widiger, Frances, & Trull, 1987). Figure 11.1 illustrates comorbidity of borderline diagnosis with other personality disorders as determined by Widiger, Freiman, and Bailey (1990). These findings were replicated by Morey (1988), who also reported high diagnostic comorbidity in borderlines with paranoid, histrionic, narcissistic, avoidant, and dependent personality disorder diagnoses. Furthermore, comorbidity between borderline personality disorder and mood disorders has led to suggestions that borderline disorder might be best classified as a subtype of affective disorder (Nakdimen, 1986).

Millon (1996) presented an overview of the likelihood of specific overlap in DSM-IV diagnoses for the personality disorders. For instance, he rank-ordered diagnoses in order of their likelihood of overlapping criteria with antisocial personality disorder. In ascending order, Millon found that sadistic personality, narcissistic personality, and substance abuse all shared features that might be considered to overlap with antisocial disorder. Furthermore, he provided a concise clinical description of the unique features for each potentially overlapping disorder that was meant to assist clinicians to more accurately distinguish among a rather heterogeneous group of patients. For instance, in distinguishing other disorders from antisocial personality, he noted that narcissistic individuals are similarly egocentric, but tend not to be impulsive. Also, relative to antisocial patients, the borderline's manipulative behaviour tends not to be aggrandizing nor aimed at gaining power. Millon's descriptions highlight pervasiveness, severity, and motivation, as well as personality style, and indicate that a diagnosis should be much more than a simple compilation of behaviours or symptoms.

Additional examples of diagnostic imprecision include avoidant disorder patients manifesting symptoms (for example, social inadequacy and hypersensitivity to criticism) that are remarkably similar to those in social phobics (an Axis I disorder).

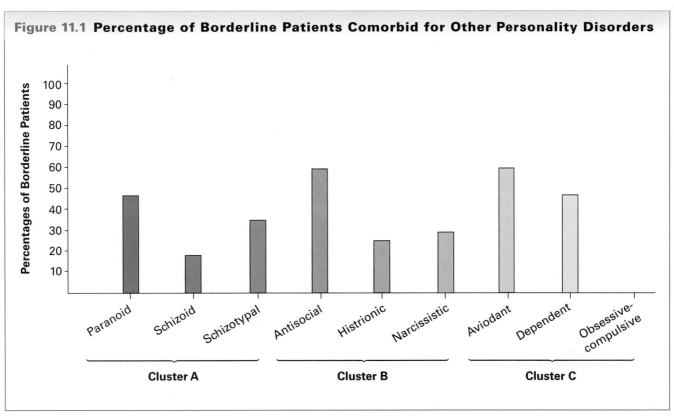

Figure 11.1 Percentage of Borderline Patients Comorbid for Other Personality Disorders

Source: Adapted from Widiger, Freiman, & Bailey, 1990.

Dimensional vs. Categorical Classification

One suggestion to address this problem of overlap is the adoption of a dimensional rather than a categorical system of classification (Widiger & Costa, 1994). As discussed in Chapter 3, *categorical* systems provide criteria for inclusion (that is, behaviours, traits, and symptoms); a person who has enough of these criteria to meet some agreed-upon threshold receives the diagnosis in question. *Dimensional* systems present prototypical descriptions, whereby extreme scores represent membership in a group or diagnosis. For example, extraversion is considered to be a dimensional trait by most personality theorists. People who are assessed as sociable, active, talkative, fun-loving, and person-oriented are described as being extraverted. In fact, everybody is understood by personality theorists (for example, Eysenck, 1977) to lie at some point along the dimension of extraversion from very extraverted through somewhat extraverted to not very extraverted. A categorical model, by contrast, would specify the presence or absence of several features to defining a person as either extraverted or not.

Dimensional systems, however, raise other concerns. How many dimensions are needed to classify patients as having one or another personality disorder? Arguments have been made for three to five dimensions (Widiger & Trull, 1992), but as many as ten have also been suggested (Millon, 1983). What score, or scores, would serve as cutoff points? These questions have practical implications for the development of a relatively simple and effective dimensional classification model.

The most popular dimensional approach in personality research is the five-factor model of Costa and McCrea (1992). Table 11.3 describes the features of this model. The basic traits in this model include neuroticism, extraversion, openness to experience, agreeableness, and conscientiousness. *Neuroticism* refers to emotional instability and the expression of negative emotions such as anxiety, depression, and anger. *Extraversion* refers to activity level, particularly interactions with others and ease of expression of positive emotions. *Openness to experience* refers to curiosity and willingness to consider new ideas. *Agreeableness* refers to concern for others and cooperativeness. *Conscientiousness* refers to self-discipline and reliability. A person may be scored separately on each dimension. Note that the dimensions are not parallel to each other. On the dimension of neuroticism, a high score represents difficulty, while a high score on openness to experience or agreeableness is desirable; on the dimension of extraversion, an extremely high or extremely low score may represent a problem.

Together, a reasonably comprehensive description of an individual's behaviour and interactions is provided by scores on these five dimensions. Although such a dimensional system was considered for both DSM-III-R and DSM-IV, failure to reach consensus led to the retention of the categorical approach (Widiger, Frances, Spitzer, & Williams, 1988).

Table 11.3 Five-Factor Model of Personality

Global Traits	Characteristics of the High Scorer	Characteristics of the Low Scorer
Neuroticism Identifies individuals prone to psychological distress, unrealistic ideas, excessive cravings or urges, and maladaptive coping responses	Worrying, nervous, emotional, insecure, inadequate, hypochondriacal	Calm, relaxed, unemotional, hardy, secure, self-satisfied
Extraversion Assesses quantity and intensity of interpersonal interaction, activity level, need for stimulation, and capacity for joy	Sociable, active, talkative, person-oriented, optimistic, fun-loving, affectionate	Reserved, sober, unexuberant, aloof, task-oriented, retiring, quiet
Openness to Experience Assesses proactive seeking and appreciation of experience for its own sake, toleration for and exploration of the unfamiliar	Curious, broad interests, creative, original, imaginative, nontraditional	Conventional, down-to-earth, narrow interests, not artistic, not analytical
Agreeableness Assesses the quality of one's interpersonal orientation along a continuum from compassion to antagonism in thoughts, feelings, and actions	Soft-hearted, good-natured, trusting, helpful, forgiving, gullible, straightforward	Cynical, rude, suspicious, uncooperative, vengeful, ruthless, irritable, manipulative
Conscientiousness Assesses the individual's degree of organization; contrasts dependable, fastidious people with those who are lackadaisical and sloppy	Organized, reliable, hard-working, self-disciplined, punctual, scrupulous, neat, ambitious, persevering	Aimless, unreliable, lazy, careless, lax, negligent, weak-willed, hedonistic

Source: Oltmans & Emery. Abnormal Psychology, Prentice Hall.

Etiology

Unfortunately, very little is known about the causes of personality disorders. However, there has been much speculation. In this section we will briefly cover the main areas of theorizing. Where there are more detailed accounts and evidence, it will be covered in the next section, under the specific disorders.

Psychodynamic Views

Psychoanalysts see personality disorder as resulting from disturbances in the parent-child relationship, particularly in problems related to separation-individuation (Mahler, Pine, & Bergman, 1975). This is the process by which the child learns that he or she is a separate individual from the mother and other people and acquires, as a result, a sense of himself or herself as an independent person (see Chapter 2). Thus, difficulties in this process, according to psychodynamic theorists, result in either an inadequate sense of self (for example, borderline, narcissistic, or histrionic personality disorders) or problems in dealing with other people (for example, avoidant or antisocial personality disorders).

Kernberg (1954), for example, says borderline people have learned through experiences with their frustrating parents to see themselves and others in contradictory and extreme terms. They see their parents as dangerous, depriving, and hurtful, yet at the same time consider them good, loving, and

nurturing. These views of their parents are later transferred to all other people. Thus, borderline people see new friends as perfect, but soon change their minds and see them as completely nasty.

There is clear evidence that personality-disordered adults are far more likely than other people to have had disrupted childhoods, including the loss of a parent through death, divorce, or abandonment (Robins, 1966) or parental rejection (McCord & McCord, 1964). However, this evidence has also served to bolster other environmental theories of personality disorders, particularly attachment theory (Ainsworth & Bowlby, 1991) and learning-based theories (Turkat & Levin, 1984).

Attachment Theory

Attachment theory says that children learn how to relate to others, particularly in affectionate ways, by the way in which their parents relate to them. When the attachment bond between parent and child is good (that is, the parents are loving, encouraging, and supportive), the child will develop the skills and confidence necessary to relate effectively to others. The parent-child bond serves as a template for all later relationships (Bowlby, 1977). When this bond is poor, the child will lack confidence in relations with others, fearing rejection, and will lack the skills necessary for intimate relationships.

This analysis has been applied to various personality disorders (Links, 1992; Patrick, Hobson, Castle, & Howard, 1994), and the evidence appears to support the hypothesis

(Coons, 1994; Torgersen & Alnaes, 1992; West, Keller, Kinks, & Patrick, 1993). Researchers in Vancouver (Bartholomew, 1990; Dutton, Saunders, Starzomski, & Bartholomew, 1994) have shown that if parent-child attachments are poor, the child will typically develop adult relationship styles characterized by ambivalence, fear, or avoidance. Poor attachments typically lead to deficits in developing intimacy (Marshall, Hudson, & Hodkinson, 1993), and various maladaptive ways of dealing with interpersonal relationships (Marshall & Barbaree, 1984). This explains why personality disorders usually emerge during late adolescence, when the demands for social interaction become preeminent. Consistently with these claims, Goldberg, Mann, Wise, and Segall (1985) found that personality-disordered patients typically described their parents as uncaring, overprotective, or both.

Cognitive-Behavioural Perspectives

Cognitive strategies or schemata (for example, beliefs, assumptions, and attitudes) are said to develop early in life. Cognitive-behavioural theorists argue that in the case of personality-disordered individuals, these schemata become rigid and inflexible (Shapiro, 1981). Linehan (1987) claims that these people come from families who consistently invalidate the child's emotional experiences and oversimplify the ease with which life's problems can be solved. Accordingly, they learn that the way to get their parent's attention (and, as a consequence, the attention of others) is by a display of major emotional outbursts. Linehan's theory has been applied primarily to borderline patients but it could readily apply to other types of personality disorder, particularly to the dramatic, emotional, or erratic disorders of Cluster B.

Parents may also model inappropriate personal styles themselves, and there is considerable evidence that modelling is a powerful influence on children's behaviour (Bandura, 1977). In addition, parents may inappropriately reward or punish behaviour and the expression of attitudes. Parents of children who engage in antisocial behaviour, for example, have been shown to reward or punish their children noncontingently (Snyder, 1977): that is, their responses are not related to the child's behaviour (see Chapter 5). Marshall and Barbaree (1984) classified the diagnostic criteria for all the personality disorders along nine cognitive-behavioural dimensions, as shown in Table 11.4. They outlined a social learning theory, proposing that the responses characterizing personality disorders were learned from early experience, especially with parents. A large body of literature indicates the disruptive, abusive, and inappropriate parenting received by these people. To avoid aversive experiences, or in imitation of their parents, the children adopted personal styles that were

Table 11.4 Cognitive-Behavioural Classification of the Features of Personality Disorders

Cognitive-Behavioural Dimension	Personality Disorder	Diagnostic Criteria
1. Inappropriate assertiveness	Histrionic Borderline Dependent	Easily influenced by others Inappropriate intense anger Unable to express disagreement
2. Interpersonal aversiveness	Borderline Antisocial	Unstable interpersonal relationships Deceitful and irresponsible
3. Dominance/submission	Dependent Obsessive-compulsive	Needs others to assume responsibility for his or her life Insists that others do things exactly his or her way
4. Dysfunctional social cognitions	Schizotypal Paranoid Narcissistic	Magical beliefs and suspiciousness Suspects others are exploiting him or her Grandiose sense of self-importance
5. Social anxiety	Avoidant Histrionic	Afraid of being criticized or rejected Uncomfortable when not the centre of attention
6. Dysfunctional affiliation	Borderline Schizoid Dependent	Frantically avoids abandonment Neither desires nor enjoys relationships Goes to excessive lengths to obtain nurturance from others
7. Inappropriate emotions	Borderline Antisocial Schizoid	Emotional instability Lack of remorse Emotional coldness
8. Compulsions	Obsessive-compulsive	Perfectionism and inflexibility
9. Antisocial behaviour	Antisocial Borderline	Failure to conform to social norms; aggression Impulsivity that may hurt others

Source: Adapted from W. L. Marshall & H. E. Barbaree, Disorders of personality, impulse and adjustment, in S. M. Turner & M. Hersen, eds., *Adult psychopathology: A behavioral perspective* (New York: Wiley, 1984), pp. 406–449.

immediately rewarding, although dysfunctional in the long term. As a result of both negative (reduction in aversiveness) and positive (immediate satisfaction) reinforcing consequences, these personal styles become entrenched and, over time, more inflexible. Although this theory has some intuitive appeal, and there is supporting evidence of difficult childhoods, it remains, like most etiological accounts, largely speculative.

Biological Factors

Biological accounts of personality disorders have been most thoroughly explored with antisocial personality disorder and we will discuss them more thoroughly when we describe that disorder. Various biological theorists have claimed that personality disorders either have a genetic basis or are the result of disturbed neurotransmitters or brain dysfunction. Research has revealed a genetic influence in the following personality disorders: antisocial (Carey & Gottesman, 1996), paranoid (Kendler & Gruenberg, 1982), schizotypal (Nigg & Goldsmith, 1994), and borderline (Widiger & Trull, 1993). However, Rutter et al.'s (1990) review found no support for the claim that juvenile delinquency (that is, antisocial behaviour) is inherited. Cadoret et al. (1995) concluded that, although there was evidence of a heritable factor in antisocial personality, environmental experience also plays a significant role. Cloninger, Svrakic, and Przybeck (1993) have proposed that specific disturbances in neurotransmitter systems characterize particular types of personality disorders. Both Schalling (1993) and Virkkunen and Linnoila (1993) concluded from their reviews that antisocial personality-disordered patients have reduced levels of the neurotransmitters serotonin and norepinephrine, and Raine's (1993) meta-analysis of 29 recent studies confirmed these conclusions.

Finally, Andrulonis and colleagues (1981) reported high rates of neurological dysfunctions, encephalitis, epilepsy, and minimal brain damage in borderline patients, all of which they suggested caused dysfunctions in the limbic system (part of the temporal lobe of the brain). Cowdry and Gardner (1988) found that anticonvulsants, which work on the limbic system, helped borderline patients. Also, impairment in eye-tracking responses, which is taken to be indicative of brain dysfunction, has been found (Zemishlany, Siever, & Coccaro, 1988) in all Cluster A disorders (that is, paranoid, schizoid, and schizotypal).

Research to date is limited, but what there is supports these biological accounts (Depue, Luciana, Arbisi, Collins, & Leon, 1994). The strongest support, as we will see, comes from research with antisocial personality disorder.

Most Likely Etiologies

As with most psychological problems, personality disorders are probably caused by many factors. There is clear evidence of biological, family, and learning processes, and there is some support for psychodynamic accounts. However, so far there has been little attempt to develop a synthesis of the various explanations. Research in this field is still largely in the early stage of single-factor theories, as discussed in Chapter 2.

Biological explanations seem to dominate for Cluster A disorders. Biological and attachment theories for Cluster B disorders (antisocial, borderline, histrionic, and narcissistic) both have support. There has been very little investigation of Cluster C disorders (avoidant, dependent, and obsessive-compulsive) despite their prevalence (Morey, 1988).

....

THE SPECIFIC DISORDERS

The bulk of recent research has focussed on antisocial personality disorder and borderline personality disorder. Accordingly, we will emphasize these two, giving briefer descriptions of the remaining disorders.

CLUSTER A: ODD AND ECCENTRIC DISORDERS

Paranoid Personality Disorder

Pervasive suspiciousness of other people's motives and a tendency to see everything everyone does as a personal attack are the primary features of patients diagnosed as having a **paranoid** personality. These are the people who, for example, walk past a clutch of giggling teenagers and assume they are the butt of the joke; who take a clerk's comment "It's not my department" as a personal rebuff. They consistently misread the actions of others as threatening or critical, and they expect other people to exploit them. They are overly vigilant and take extreme precautions against potential threats. They believe that other people intend to hurt them, and they are reluctant to share anything personal for fear it might be used against them. In addition, they are typically humourless and eccentric, and are seen by others as hostile, jealous, and preoccupied with power and control. Not surprisingly, they have difficulty with relationships, as most people cannot tolerate their need to control and particularly their destructive jealousy. Paranoid people often become socially isolated, which only exacerbates their feelings of persecution.

DSM-IV	**Diagnostic Criteria for Paranoid Personality Disorder**

Pervasive distrust and suspiciousness without justification, as indicated by 4 or more of the following:

1. Suspects others are trying to exploit or harm him/her
2. Doubts the loyalty of friends
3. Afraid to confide in others
4. Sees hidden meaning in benign remarks
5. Persistently bears grudges
6. Consistently believes others are attacking his/her character
7. Believes that sexual partner is unfaithful

Source: Reprinted with permission from the *Diagnostic and Statistical Manual of Mental Disorders,* Fourth Edition. Copyright 1994 American Psychiatric Association.

These features, identified in both the diagnostic criteria (see DSM table) and clinical reports, have been confirmed in research. For example, Turkat and his colleagues have found that, compared with normal subjects, paranoid adults report far more thoughts of others wishing them ill and also recall more such thoughts from their school days (Turkat & Banks, 1987); they have greater difficulty dealing with ambiguity and are more suspicious (Thompson-Pope & Turkat, 1988), and they are more likely to misread social cues as evidence of hostility by others (Turkat, Keane, & Thompson-Pope, 1990).

Since paranoid personality occurs quite commonly in the relatives of schizophrenics, a genetic link with schizophrenia has been proposed and it has been suggested that paranoid personality disorder may in fact be a subtype of schizophrenia (Kendler, Masterson, & Davis, 1985). However, paranoid schizophrenics, as defined by DSM, experience complex delusions and auditory hallucinations (see Chapter 14 for a description), whereas these symptoms are absent in paranoid personality disorder. There is also a significant diagnostic overlap between paranoid personality and both avoidant and borderline personality disorders (Morey, 1988). Furthermore, in a large-scale study among adolescents in upstate New York, paranoid disorder was found to be one of the four most persistent types of personality disorder (Bernstein et al., 1993).

Schizoid Personality Disorder

Individuals with this condition seem determined to avoid intimate involvement with others and they display little emotional responsiveness. These clients often indicate that they rarely experience intense emotions and may be puzzled by the enthusiasms of others. **Schizoid** clients are typically loners who are cold and indifferent toward others. In fact, they seem not to enjoy relationships of any type, apparently preferring to be alone. They like solitary activities and do not seek or seem to desire sexual relations. Most lack the skills for effective social interaction; but, more than that, they appear uninterested in acquiring such skills.

Little methodologically sound research has been done on this disorder. As a consequence, knowledge has not advanced over the past several years, and clinical speculations remain unfettered by data. To further complicate analysis, changes in definition make it difficult to compare recent study results with data from the 1980s and earlier. After DSM-III-R refined the criteria for schizotypal personality disorder, the frequency of diagnosed schizoid disorder rose from 1.4 percent to 11 percent, apparently due to reassignment of people who would previously have been diagnosed as schizotypal (Morey, 1988). Many studies confound schizoid and schizotypal features and do not, therefore, permit any reasonable conclusions.

Schizotypal Personality Disorder

Jennifer was 24 years old when her parents brought her to a hospital outpatient clinic, worried because her unusual behaviour seemed to be getting worse. Despite the warmth of the day, Jennifer was wearing a shirt, a sweater, a rather ragged sleeveless jacket, a loose skirt with a pair of sweat pants underneath, boots, and long socks pulled up over the pants.

Her parents said Jennifer had been a nice child but had always had trouble forming friendships because she did not trust others. In her teens, Jennifer developed a fascination with astrology, keeping a scrapbook of her daily horoscope. As an adult, she also began collecting occult paraphernalia. She was sure that one of her ancestors had been a witch, and that her own thoughts could sometimes cause people to do things.

As her parents related her history, Jennifer sat quietly to one side staring at the psychologist. She seemed surprised when he spoke to her, and asked why he wanted her to speak and when she could leave. The psychologist persuaded her to be interviewed alone.

Jennifer said there was nothing wrong with her, although she was concerned that she had no close friends. She also complained that her co-workers were trying to get her fired, although the remarks she reported sounded quite innocent. In the middle of this discussion, Jennifer suddenly asked, "Do you hear those ethereal sounds emanating from the upper reaches of the building?" After a puzzled moment, the psychologist discovered that she was referring to sounds from the hospital kitchen down the hall. Jennifer seemed reassured, but still somewhat dubious.

Over the course of several sessions, Jennifer never became comfortable with the therapeutic relationship and never discussed her problems openly. After a few sessions she seemed to lose interest and stopped coming for treatment.

The major presenting feature of patients such as Jennifer is eccentricity of thought and behaviour. Many **schizotypal** people are extremely superstitious. Their ideation and behaviour are peculiar, and these features tend to turn other people away so that they often become socially isolated. No doubt this isolation from others increases the likelihood that they will have unusual thoughts and perceptions, since they have little opportunity to check the accuracy of their cognitions. Their thinking tends to be magical and full of odd beliefs. For instance, they may believe that aliens frequently abduct earthlings or that horoscopes actually predict the future. They typically believe in paranormal phenomena such as telepathy and clairvoyance. While such beliefs in themselves are no sign of mental disorder, schizotypal people will create odd, idiosyncratic combinations of beliefs or interpret commonplace occurrences in bizarre ways.

Although their beliefs, perceptual experiences, speech, and behaviours are quite odd and tend to isolate them from others, they are not usually considered to be so eccentric as to meet the criteria for delusional or hallucinatory experiences. There is, however, considerable disagreement on this issue. For example, McGlashan (1994) claimed that transient psychoses characterize these patients, and Kendler (1985) concluded that schizotypal disorder is simply a subtle form of schizophrenia. Research examining biological features has found strong similarities between schizotypal patients and schizophrenics (Siever, 1985), and many family members of schizophrenics exhibit schizotypal symptoms (Kendler, 1985). Indeed, Widiger and Shea (1991) suggest that schizotypal disorder may be a prodromal (early or premonitory) or residual stage of schizophrenia.

There is also considerable diagnostic overlap between schizotypal disorder and other Cluster A disorders, as well as avoidant personality disorder, and, to a lesser degree, borderline personality disorder (Morey, 1988). In fact, some have questioned whether the distinctions between Cluster A disorders have any meaning or value (Livesley & West, 1986).

Perhaps because of the schizophrenic-like features of this disorder, antipsychotic drugs have been a common treatment. Low doses of such drugs somewhat relieve cognitive problems and social anxiety (Goldberg et al., 1986); antidepressants have also been somewhat beneficial (Markovitz, Calabrese, Schulz, & Meltzer, 1991). Overall, medication has been of modest benefit (Gitlin, 1993). Controlled studies of psychological treatments have not been reported. Generally the long-term prognosis for schizotypal patients is poor.

CLUSTER B: DRAMATIC, EMOTIONAL, OR ERRATIC DISORDERS

This grouping in DSM-IV seems odd. Histrionic and borderline disorders may both be perceived as dramatic; but what does that have to do with antisocial personality? Indeed, none of the descriptors of Cluster B seem to fit antisocial personality disorder except for the limited range of emotional expression. In fact, it has been suggested that antisocial patients belong to a separate category of personality disorders (Lykken, 1995).

Antisocial Personality Disorder

John was an enigma to many. He was a bright and personable man, whom many said had great potential. Yet, by age 21, he had amassed a remarkable criminal history. His first recorded conflict with the police occurred at the age of 8 when he was caught stealing. Already, however, teachers had noticed his bullying behaviour in the playground. John's family life was characterized as chaotic, with little structure. Soon he was involved in various petty crimes, finally being sent to a juvenile youth centre at 14 after several unsuccessful foster home placements. His criminal behaviour continued unabated, escalating to robbery, assaults, and finally armed robbery. As a youth, he frequently absconded from training school.

Although drugs and alcohol were a major part of John's lifestyle, he was impulsive and took risks even when sober. He liked to drive fast cars and dared his pals to dangerous races or games of chicken. Surprisingly, in others areas of his life, John was a careful planner. He would carefully plan out certain crimes or methodically mete out revenge.

John knew how to be engaging, especially with women. However, he usually only bothered to turn on the charm when he wanted something. He considered sex to be a conquest and bragged about his prowess. Once he had slept with a woman, he would quickly drop her. Surprisingly, many women forgave John, perhaps hoping to convince him to settle down.

To the careful eye, however, John's behaviour had a grandiose quality. He also had difficulty shifting mental gears. Once John was pursuing a goal, he seemed unable to consider other options. At times he followed the same course of action even when it was clearly not in his best interests. For example, once when John was planning to break into a particular house, he learned that the police were staking out a drug dealer's apartment next door. Nevertheless, he went ahead with the break-in and, not surprisingly, was caught red-handed.

John made outrageous claims; for example, he claimed to be a professional athlete in several different sports, all at the same time. When asked what occupation he might wish to pursue, he would propose lawyer or businessman, although he had never held a job for more than four months. He recounted such goals with a panache that was at odds with his situation.

John could give the impression of being very attentive, leading people to disclose a great deal about themselves. When asked later, they would report a very close relationship, yet they knew almost nothing about John, who carefully avoided revealing details about himself. From the outside, his interactions with others appeared shallow and egocentric, but those he chose to permit into his inner circle were beguiled. John could not trust others. He moved a great deal, saying he had wanderlust. Part of his reason for moving may have been a need to meet new people who would accept him at his word.

It was as if there were two Johns. The outward John was often outgoing and devil-may-care. The inner John was a loner, appearing not to require the company of others. His contact with others could be mercurial and unpredictable. If guile didn't get him what he wanted, he might easily become aggressive and violent. It was as if it was all an act, with his performance delivered as part of a script. John always seemed to know the right words to say. For instance, he could express apparent remorse during therapy sessions, but then commit crimes on his way home. It was as if his words and deeds were disconnected. Despite his protestations that he could change, he seemed to be confirmed in a life of crime.

John's personal style is quite typical of men diagnosed as having antisocial personality disorder (APD). On the surface, he is charming and persuasive, but this covers up a self-centred and, in his case, criminal lifestyle. Not all people with antisocial personality commit crimes, although most of them who are so diagnosed by clinicians do have a criminal record. This may simply reflect the fact that it is their criminal behaviour that brings them to the attention of psychiatrists or psychologists. However, certainly the characteristics of APD do predispose people to crime, and unlawfulness is one of the examples that DSM-IV provides for the disregard that antisocial personalities display toward others (see DSM table on Antisocial Personality Disorder).

The essential distinguishing feature of APD is a "pervasive pattern of disregard for, and violation of, the rights of others that begins in childhood or early adolescence and continues into adulthood" (American Psychological Association, 1994, p. 645). Many people with antisocial personality disorder would, as children, have met the criteria for conduct disorder although, as noted in Chapter 5, by no means all youths with conduct disorder go on to develop APD. Moffitt (1993) has shown that conduct disorder that begins before adolescence is far more likely to persist into adulthood, when

DSM-IV	**Diagnostic Criteria for Antisocial Personality Disorder**

Pervasive disregard for and violation of the rights of others as indicated by 3 or more of the following:

1. Repeated illegal acts
2. Deceitful/lying
3. Impulsiveness
4. Irritable and aggressive
5. Recklessness
6. Consistently irresponsible
7. Lack of remorse

Source: Reprinted with permission from the *Diagnostic and Statistical Manual of Mental Disorders*, Fourth Edition. Copyright 1994 American Psychiatric Association.

it would be called APD, than conduct disorder that first appears in the early teens.

The DSM-IV criteria for the diagnosis of APD presents seven exemplars reflecting the violation of the rights of others: nonconformity, callousness, deceitfulness, irresponsibility, impulsivity, aggressiveness, and recklessness. Three or more of these must be met for the diagnosis to be applied.

Perhaps no other disorder so sharply calls into question the concept of responsibility and the line between the moral and

Focus *Murder and Madness*

Few events in recent Canadian history have received more media coverage than the trials of Paul Bernardo and Karla Homolka. Bernardo and Homolka, at that time husband and wife, abducted two teenage girls and held them captive for several days, while they repeatedly and brutally sexually assaulted them. On the videotapes they made of their own acts, these cold-blooded offenders displayed a clear contempt for the suffering of their victims. After several days of torture and brutality, the girls were murdered and their bodies disposed of. When these callous crimes were revealed in the mass media, the public was outraged—all the more so because a woman was involved. A further public outcry greeted the deal worked out by Crown prosecutors (who did not then have access to the videotapes) that allowed Homolka to be charged with manslaughter rather than murder, and to serve only 12 years in jail, in exchange for testifying against Bernardo.

The public mind faced a serious dilemma—the same mixed reaction raised by every particularly shocking murder. On the one hand, the public understandably wants people like Bernardo and Homolka to be held responsible for their crimes and suitably punished. On the other hand, many cannot imagine that any sane person could commit such awful acts. Part of this response is a desire to distance ourselves from violence and cruelty. We want to believe that we could not possibly do such things, so we find some relief in the idea that the Bernardos of the world are insane. But are they?

Neither Bernardo for Homolka attempted to enter a plea of not guilty by reason of insanity, so the court did not have to try to resolve the issue. In fact, fewer criminals plead insanity than one might think. An insanity plea is entered in fewer than 1 percent of crimes; when such a plea is made in a murder case, it is successful only 18 percent of the time (McGreevy,

Steadman, & Callahan, 1991). Among unsuccessful pleas were that of Jeffrey Dahmer (who murdered, dismembered, and cannibalized as many as 15 men in Milwaukee) and David Berkowitz ("Son of Sam," who killed 6 and wounded 7 in New York City in 1976/77). Furthermore, it should be noted that those found not guilty by reason of insanity typically spend more time incarcerated (in psychiatric institutions) than do those who are found guilty (who spend their time in prisons).

In fact, more than 90 percent of mentally ill people have no history of, or propensity for, violence (Monahan, 1992), although the rate of violent behaviour is somewhat higher among psychotic patients (that is, those diagnosed as having schizophrenia, bipolar disorder, or major depression) than among normal people (Swanson, Holzer, Ganju, & Jono, 1990). Young, poor males with a history of general criminal behaviour are, in fact, at far greater risk of being violent than any

Focus   *continued*

group of mentally ill patients (Monahan, 1992).

The majority of violent people who are assigned a DSM diagnosis are abusers of alcohol and other drugs; the rate of violence in this group is 12 to 16 times as high as in the normal population. Yet most people do not consider them to be insane, nor do the courts.

If most murderers and violent offenders are not insane (that is, psychotic), then should they be considered to have a personality disorder? After all, surely their behaviour is abnormal enough to justify some diagnosis. Psychiatrists and psychologists are not necessarily free of the same feelings toward these crimes that the general

public hold. They, too, may want, on the one hand, to punish serial killers and, on the other hand, to distance themselves from such people. It is difficult for diagnosticians to set aside their horror and make an impartial diagnosis. Consequently, many violent offenders are identified as personality-disordered, with most being diagnosed as having APD.

Since past violent behaviour is one of the diagnostic criteria for APD, this is not surprising, but does it help us deal with these offenders? Probably not, since a diagnosis of APD is often taken to mean that the person is intractable to treatment; efforts at rehabilitation may, therefore, be abandoned. Such a diagnosis also typically

enters into judgement about future risk of violence; since predictions of dangerousness typically overestimate future risk (Webster, Ben-Aron, & Hucker, 1985), the person may be detained longer than public safety really requires. The public may feel safer with these offenders behind bars, but it's an expensive approach for the taxpayer, since it costs about $70,000 per year to keep a person in jail in Canada.

In any case, these dilemmas are not likely to disappear. Our courts and prisons will continue to have to deal with the complex issues of sanity and behaviour. Deciding that violent offenders must have a personality disorder does not resolve these issues, and may cause more problems than it solves.

---

the psychological. As discussed in the Focus box on murder and madness, people have a tendency to consider all violent crime to reflect disorder. Two grounds of distinction are persistence and pervasiveness. Recall that personality is generally understood to be stable, and that people with personality disorders are more fixed in their traits than normal people. If a woman with no history of violence murders her husband, we will probably focus on the act itself rather than the personality of the killer. If a man who drives safely, did well in school, and has a good relationship with his family is caught robbing banks, we will probably see the robberies as a career choice—choice to act immorally—rather than a sign of disorder. Contrast these examples with the case of John, for whom dishonesty, aggression, recklessness, and a lack of intimacy characterize every aspect of his life from childhood on.

Historical Perspective

The description of a persistent pattern of antisocial behaviour has a long clinical tradition (Pinel, 1809). Pritchard (1835) described some male criminals as suffering from "moral insanity" and he said that a man of this type was "incapable, not of talking and reasoning upon any subject proposed to him, for this he will do with great shrewdness and volubility, but of conducting himself with decency and propriety in the business of life" (p. 15). Pritchard thought it was the "moral principles of the mind" that were "perverted or depraved" in these men. Later in the nineteenth century, the term **psychopath** was introduced to describe these people, and it was assumed that their behaviour was the result of a hereditary defect (Preu, 1944). Sociologists began to take an interest in this problem in the early part of the twentieth century, and not surprisingly they saw social conditions as the

critical factors. Accordingly, they replaced the term *psychopath* with **sociopath** (Birnbaum, 1914).

Originally the terms *psychopath* and *sociopath* were used to describe most, if not all, males who committed criminal or other antisocial acts. Over time, however, the concept began to be more narrowly applied such that now both antisocial personality disorder and psychopathy are used only for those antisocial individuals who have a clear personality disorder.

The most influential book ever published on antisocial personality disorder was Hervey Cleckley's (1964, 1976) *The Mask of Sanity*. Cleckley spent most of his career studying what were then called psychopaths. From his clinical experience he derived 16 features (see Table 11.5) that he claimed clearly distinguished these people (by this time it was accepted that women, too, could be psychopathic although it remained almost an exclusively male diagnosis). Cleckley's work markedly influenced all subsequent writers and remains influential.

Diagnostic Issues

The term *psychopathy* has, to some degree, been replaced by **antisocial personality disorder (APD)**, perhaps because *psychopath* was considered to have pejorative connotations (Harding, 1992)—which is not surprising, considering the behaviour of the people who bore the label. *Psychopathy*, however, is a resilient term and has enjoyed a resurgence in use in correctional and legal settings (Hare, 1996). The two terms are often used interchangeably, which leads to confusion, since they do not now hold exactly the same meaning.

Let us examine this subtle but important difference. As discussed in Chapter 3, early versions of the DSM focussed on internal processes, and the diagnostic categories were quite

Table 11.5 Features of Psychopaths According to Cleckley

1. Superficial charm and good intelligence
2. Absence of delusions
3. Absence of nervousness
4. Unreliable
5. Untruthful and insincere
6. No remorse or shame
7. Poorly motivated antisocial behaviour
8. Failure to learn from experience
9. Egocentric and unable to love
10. Shallow emotions
11. Poor insight
12. Poor interpersonal relations
13. Impersonal sex life
14. No long-term plans
15. Rarely suicidal
16. Reckless

Source: Adapted from H. Cleckley, *The mask of sanity*, 5th ed. (St. Louis: Mosby, 1976).

Dr. Robert Hare.

unreliable, since different clinicians would make different inferences about something that, after all, they could not actually observe. Later versions, therefore, have moved more and more toward measurement of behaviour rather than feeling or thought, and have become more reliable.

The APD criteria in DSM-IV (see the DSM table on Antisocial Personality Disorder) represent a reduced and simplified version of the DSM-III-R criterion set. Three DSM-III-R items were dropped (parental irresponsibility, failure to sustain a monogamous relationship, and inconsistent work) because they failed to meet acceptable levels of (1) association with antisocial personality disorder, (2) evidence concerning prevalence, and (3) inter-rater reliability (Rogers et al., 1994; Widiger & Corbitt, 1993). Nevertheless, Widiger and Corbitt concluded that the DSM-IV diagnostic criteria were 98 percent concordant with the DSM-III-R diagnosis.

The question remains, however: Granted the current criteria show improved inter-rater reliability, are they measuring what they are supposed to measure? Or does the reliance on behavioural indexes run the risk of measuring not so much personality as simply destructive or criminal activity (Hare, Hart, & Harpur, 1991)? Employing essentially behavioural criteria may yield a group of antisocial individuals who are markedly variable in terms of personality traits (Blackburn, 1992). This concern is underscored by the results of recent studies (Rogers, Duncan, Lynett, & Sewell, 1994) comparing DSM-IV and other measures of APD (including the ICD-10 of the World Health Organization, 1990, and the PCL-R, which we will discuss in a moment).

One reason for this concern is that a DSM diagnosis of APD may change over time (Rogers et al., 1994). Personality disorders are understood to be more or less unchangeable features, much like the personality traits we all hold. Antisocial personality disorder is generally believed to have an early onset and a long course; yet, using DSM-III criteria, diagnosis was inconsistent over time (Helzer, Spitznagel, & McEnvoy, 1987). It remains to be seen whether DSM-IV criteria are

more stable. Could it be, then, that our assumptions about the stability of personality disorder are flawed? Could APD be more likely than other personality disorders to change over time? Could it even be possible that psychopathy is not truly a personality disorder but something else? Well, maybe; but before considering such possibilities, most theorists would suspect the criteria themselves.

In fact, diagnostic tools other than DSM-IV are gaining prominence in the forensic literature. The Psychopathy Checklist—Revised (PCL-R), which was devised by the University of British Columbia's Robert Hare (Hare, 1991), enjoys widespread popularity as both a research instrument and a clinical tool. The advantage of the PCL-R is that it scores both behavioural *and* personality features. However, it can be reliably scored only by someone (usually a psychologist) trained in its administration. Independent information must also be available on the subject's history, because psychopaths typically lie about their past. Studies of the PCL-R have revealed that a combination of two factors, personality traits and lifestyle instability, is *necessary* and *sufficient* for a diagnosis of psychopathy—and probably for a realistic diagnosis of the condition APD is meant to describe (Hare, Hart, & Harpur, 1991). Such an approach appears more likely to eventually yield a dimensional model of APD (Rogers et al., 1994) which, as we have seen, many feel to be more appropriate for personality disorders than a categorical model.

Psychopathy, as measured by the PCL-R, has been demonstrated to be a more reliable and more specific construct than APD (Hare, 1983) and has greater predictive validity (Hare, 1991). Recent studies, for example, confirm the value of PCL-R scores in predicting future violent behaviour (Salekin, Rogers, & Sewell, 1996). Also, psychopaths, as defined by the PCL-R, have records of a greater number and variety of criminal offences than nonpsychopaths (Kosson, Smith, & Newman, 1990) and they are more likely to display current violence (Serin, 1991). Many researchers and clinicians continue to use the concept of psychopathy rather than following DSM-IV criteria.

Prevalence

Lack of a common yardstick, while the debate continues on the relative usefulness of the concepts of APD and psychopathy, leads to some confusion in attempting to determine prevalence.

DSM-IV reports prevalence rates for APD of approximately 3 percent in males and 1 percent in females for community samples. The United States National Comorbidity Survey (Kessler et al., 1994) reports a somewhat higher prevalence of 5.8 percent in males and 1.2 percent in females.

The prevalence in forensic settings (prisons and hospitals for psychiatrically disturbed criminals) can be expected to be higher, since, as we have seen, criminal behaviour is a preeminent feature of antisocial personality. Yet DSM-IV does not estimate prevalence in institutions. Estimates in Great Britain (Chiswick, 1992) indicate that approximately 25 to 33 percent of patients in Special Hospitals (hospitals for the criminally disordered) are psychopathic; this number may be expected to be higher than comparable rates in prison, because these hospitals take those criminals considered to have a psychiatric disorder while those who do not are simply imprisoned.

Hare (1983, 1985) reported higher estimates in Canadian prisons; using DSM-III-R criteria, approximately 40 percent were diagnosed as having APD. Another correctional sample (Hart & Hare, 1989) shows the relative overdiagnosis using DSM-III criteria (50 percent prevalence of APD) compared with an early version of the Psychopathy Checklist (12.5 percent prevalence of psychopathy). Quebec researchers Côté and Hodgins (1990) found still higher rates, using yet another assessment strategy, the Diagnostic Interview Schedule (Robins, Helzer, Croughan, & Ratcliff, 1981). In a random sample of 495 male inmates, Côté and Hodgins diagnosed 61.5 percent as APD using the Diagnostic Interview criteria. Rates of psychopathy among Canadian prisoners also appear to vary according to security level, with a higher percentage of psychopaths in maximum security prisons (Wong, 1984).

Etiology of APD

How does a person come to be antisocial—to have a callous disregard for others, impulsivity and poor self-regulation, rule-breaking and criminality, and exploitation of others?

Family environment.   As noted earlier, particular problems in childhood are strongly predictive of adult antisocial behaviour, and the family context is significant. Disruptive family life and inconsistent or harsh discipline by parents seem to set the stage for children (particularly boys) to show aggressive and otherwise antisocial behaviour (Robins, 1966). In addition, Loeber (1990) and Robins (1986) have shown the following to be risk factors for an adult diagnosis of APD: fighting, truancy, school failure, lying, stealing, discipline problems, poor social skills, antisocial friends, and low socioeconomic status.

These observations have led to a variety of family intervention strategies aimed at preventing these children from continuing their antisocial ways into adulthood (see Chapter 16 for more details of these approaches). Briefly, these interventions attempt to modify the family dynamics so that discipline and mutual respect are enhanced, as well as targeting the risk factors mentioned above (Henggeler & Schoenwald, 1993; Patterson, 1982). These approaches have produced consistently good results (Borduin et al., 1995), although it appears necessary to repeat treatment over time (Kazdin, 1987).

Patterson's work (Patterson, 1982; Patterson & Bank, 1986; Patterson, Reid, & Dishion, 1992) also implicates the family in the processes that lead to conduct disorder in children (see also Chapter 5). Patterson and his colleagues have developed a model showing how problems escalate as both parent and child react badly to each other's responses. Since early-onset conduct disorder often leads to APD (Moffitt, 1993), we may conclude that inept parental discipline and other disruptive aspects of family life are significant in the etiology of APD.

Genetic links.   What is clear is that antisocial tendencies often run in families. Recall the studies cited in Chapter 5 that showed that the children of parents with antisocial personality disorder were more likely to have conduct disorder. These findings can also be interpreted to support a genetic explanation. Swedish adoption studies (see Chapter 4) showed that adopted children whose biological parents were criminals had an increased likelihood of criminal behaviour, even when raised in families with no such tendencies. Can similar assumptions be made about antisocial personality disorder? Raine's (1993) meta-analysis of 29 genetic studies indicated that 51.5 percent of monozygotic twins were concordant for criminal behaviour, compared to 20.6 percent of dizygotic twins. These figures clearly suggest a genetic component, but the high concordance for dizygotic twins points to environmental influence as well. There appear to be genetic factors that, in combination with early experiences such as exposure to criminal activities in the family, poor parenting, neglect, and physical abuse, interact to make children vulnerable to developing a psychopathic lifestyle and personality (Mealey, 1995).

Self-regulation.   Various psychological explanations have also been proposed that focus on psychopaths' inadequate self-regulation. Lykken (1957), for example, suggested that psychopaths are essentially fearless. This **fearlessness hypothesis** claims that psychopaths have a higher threshold for feeling fear than do other people. Events that make most people anxious (such as the expectation of being punished) are thought to have little or no effect on psychopaths.

In order to examine his theory, Lykken (1957) conducted a series of studies, one of which involved the use of electric shocks as punishers. He constructed a task that he called a "mental maze," in which subjects had to learn a complex sequence of 20 lever presses (see Figure 11.2). There were four levers, from which subjects had to choose 1 on each of the 20 series. If the subject pressed the correct lever, a green light came on. If he chose one of the other levers, a red light came on. This was explained to subjects before they started. They were also told that from time to time they would be given a shock at random, to keep them alert. In fact, the shocks were not random. On each trial, pressing a particular one of the three incorrect levers not only turned on the red light, but also gave the subject an electric shock. Learning the sequence of correct lever presses was called the **manifest task** and was meant to determine whether the subjects had a generalized learning problem. The disguised task, called the **latent task**, was the association between particular lever presses and shocks. It was this latter task that Lykken was particularly interested in, because his fearlessness theory predicted that

Figure 11.2 Lykken's Lever Apparatus to Test Avoidance Learning

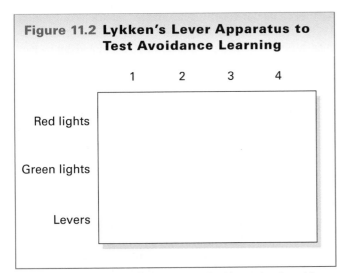

Lykken (1957) devised this apparatus for his study of avoidance learning in psychopaths. The participants had to learn a sequence of 20 correct level presses.

Source: D.T. Lykken, A study of anxiety in the sociopathic personality, *Journal of Abnormal and Social Psychology, 55(1957),* 6–10.

Figure 11.3 Effects of Different Types of Punishment on Psychopaths

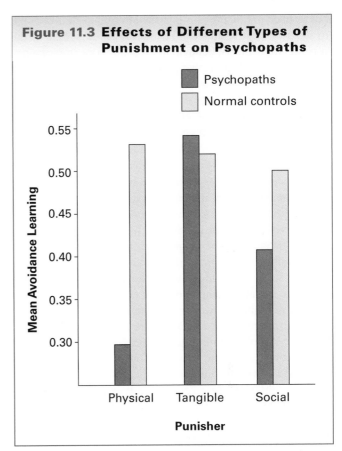

Source: Adapted from F. J. Schmauk, Punishment, arousal, and avoidance learning in sociopaths, *Journal of Abnormal Psychology, 76(1970),* 325–335.

psychopaths would fail to learn this while nonpsychopaths would quickly learn to avoid pressing the levers that produced shocks. This is precisely what Lykken found.

From these and similar observations from studies that also used electric shock as punishers, Lykken and other theorists concluded that psychopaths were unresponsive to punishment as a result of their fearlessness, and this was why they failed to learn society's rules. It was assumed by these theorists that children acquire prosocial behaviours and beliefs largely by being rewarded for good behaviour and punished for bad behaviour. If psychopaths are unresponsive to punishment, then they will be unaffected by their parents' feedback and, as a result, will not acquire the constraints that prevent most people from behaving in an antisocial way.

Subsequently, however, some social learning theorists questioned the validity of Lykken's conclusions. Schmauk (1970), for example, suggested that Lykken's findings might be relevant only to shocks and other types of physical punishment. Schmauk pointed out that, as children, psychopaths appear to have been exposed to severe physical punishment from their parents or guardians that was frequently not contingent upon their behaviour. As a result, Schmauk suggested, psychopaths may have learned to be either indifferent to physical punishment or oppositional to such attempts at controlling them.

To test this idea, Schmauk repeated Lykken's study but employed three different kinds of punishers: physical (electric shocks), tangible (subjects lost money for errors), and social (reprimands by the experimenter). With electric shocks as punishers, Schmauk replicated Lykken's findings, and he obtained similar results with the social punishers. That is, in response to both types of punishers, the psychopaths performed very poorly relative to nonpsychopaths. However, when psychopaths lost money for pressing the wrong lever, they quickly learned to avoid the shocked levers; in fact, they learned faster

than did nonpsychopaths under any of the punishment conditions (see Figure 11.3). Schmauk concluded that psychopaths were not completely fearless or unresponsive to punishment, but were differentially responsive to different kinds of punishment as a result of early learning experiences.

Stewart (1972), one of Schmauk's students, pursued the issue of response on the part of psychopaths. Schmauk had suggested that psychopaths were not unresponsive to physical punishment, but rather did the opposite of the punisher's intention, presumably as a way of exercising some degree of control in the face of aversive experiences. **Oppositional behaviour** has been thoroughly examined in children (Campbell, 1990). It is commonly displayed by boys who are severely and noncontingently punished by their parents—as studies show many psychopaths were during their childhood (Loeber & Stouthamer-Loeber, 1987; Patterson, 1982). Stewart had psychopaths and nonpsychopaths engage in a sentence completion task; each sentence could be completed so that its meaning was either aggressive or passive. Half of each group of subjects was given an electric shock every time they produced an aggressive meaning, and the other half were shocked for passive meanings. The nonpsychopaths did what you would expect: they stopped completing sentences in a way that led to a punished meaning and began completing sentences only in a way that avoided punishment. The psychopaths did exactly the opposite: they increased the frequency with which they completed punished meanings and all but stopped producing non-punished meanings. It is difficult to see how these results can be interpreted other than as deliberate oppositional behaviour. Stewart's data strengthened Schmauk's conclusions that psychopaths do, in fact, respond to physical punishers but in quite the opposite way from most people. What implications does this finding have for the prison system, in which people are first punished by being jailed and then, while in jail, punished for infractions of rules?

Course and Prognosis of APD

Robins and Regier (1991) reported the average duration of APD, from the onset of the first symptom to the end of the last, to be 19 years. (Note that, since the diagnosis of APD is not given to children, some people may have been displaying antisocial behaviours for longer than this reported duration.) This remittance over time of symptoms has been called the *burnout* factor, meaning that as they age, offenders get fed up with constantly being in trouble; eventually the perceived costs of offending outweigh the benefits. Many theorists expect symptoms to disappear by the fourth decade of life. However, Arboleda-Florez and Holley (1991) have presented data refuting the burnout view; they found, on the contrary, that many APD patients continue to display an antisocial style as they get older, despite repeated adverse consequences. Furthermore, Harpur and Hare (1994) described data suggesting that personality style, as reflected by Factor 1 of the PCL-R, does not appreciably change with age.

These conflicting data are confusing and it is hard to make sense of them. It may be that psychopathy and APD are more distinct than some researchers appear to think. A partial explanation may lie in the finding of Correctional Services of Canada researchers Porporino and Motiuk (1995) that released prisoners with both APD and substance use are more likely to reoffend than ex-offenders who have only one or the other disorder.

One confounding factor may be simply that a number of people with APD have, by their middle years, earned long-term jail sentences. Stuck in jail, they have no opportunity to commit new criminal offences, the "symptom" measured in some studies. It is also possible that some people continue as antisocial and uncaring of others as ever in their feelings, but act out in a less severe or obvious way, perhaps because they are tired of going to jail, or perhaps because by middle age they have less restless energy for criminal exploits. Such ideas remain speculation.

Since the notion of psychopathy depends less on behaviour and more on personality style than DSM-IV's APD, it may be that psychopathy will prove to be less age-dependent than the DSM-IV diagnosis. On the other hand, APD is one of the disorders that affects others as much or more than the disordered person. From society's point of view, it doesn't matter so much how these people feel as how they act; if the violent, illegal, and hurtful acts stop, the most socially important measure of APD has, in fact, changed.

Treatment for APD

Reviews by Canadian researchers of the literature on treatment efficacy for APD patients, and for psychopaths in particular,

have been unequivocally pessimistic (Suedfeld & Landon, 1978; Wong & Elek, 1990). Many of the early studies, however, suffered from poor methodology. As pointed out by Paul Gendreau of the University of New Brunswick, programs delivered in previous decades did not reflect contemporary knowledge of effective treatment programs for resistant clients, so it may be premature to discount the potential for modifying the destructive behaviours of these clients. Unfortunately, recent treatment studies have been no more encouraging. Yet therapists have not given up hope. Approximately two-thirds of psychiatrists think that psychopaths are sometimes treatable (Tennent, Tennent, Prins, & Bedford, 1993).

Treatment of other groups of resistant clients suggests a **responsivity factor**. That is, treatment must be responsive (or matched) to a particular client's needs and interpersonal style. Interventions may be ineffective if they are of insufficient intensity (Gendreau, 1996), viewed by patients as irrelevant (Miller & Rollnick, 1991), or seen as involuntary (Gabbard & Coyne, 1987). Several of these issues have been considered as they apply to prisoners with APD, yet they remain untested hypotheses. Researchers at the Oak Ridge Mental Health Centre in Ontario (Rice, Harris, & Quinsey, 1996) have pointed out that, far from being matched to inmates' specific problems, treatment programs tend to be determined more by the orientation of the therapist or director, with some targeting personality features and others criminality.

There is an ethical issue in dealing with people who lack freedom of movement. Inmates in Canadian prisons are not forced to take psychological treatment. Many are eager to participate, though the sincerity of their desire to change may be suspect, as discussed in the ViewPoint box on the topic of motivation.

Treatment is more effective if clients can form an effective therapeutic alliance (Gerstley et al., 1989). There are two barriers to such an alliance, however; first, psychopaths are characteristically unable to form relationships; and second, some therapists themselves dislike the clients. Treatment, according to current views, should be aimed at symptom reduction and management, rather than cure (Quinsey & Walker, 1992). Changing the basic personality style may be an unrealistic goal. Yet, if a client avoids destructive behaviour, society's need to be protected has been well served, as well as the client's own need to avoid the consequences of such behaviour.

Psychopaths tend to exploit unstructured programs, masking their resistance with verbal skills, and inappropriate intervention may do more harm than good (Rice, Harris, & Cormier, 1992). Attrition from treatment programs is also high and this has proved to be predictive of subsequent reoffending. Lastly, in substance abuse treatment, APD patients fare more poorly than other patients (Alterman & Cacciola, 1991). Hospitalization is not generally effective. Prognosis is, however, better for clients who have a treatable anxiety or depressive feature to their behaviour (Gabbard & Coyne, 1987).

Many of the recent developments in treatment programs for criminal populations have come from Canadian researchers in forensic hospitals (for example, Rice et al., 1996) and in prisons (for example, Serin & Kuriychuk, 1994).

VIEWPOINT *Motivation for Treatment: The Client's or the Therapist's Responsibility?*

Personality-disordered clients are notoriously resistant to treatment, and are often judged to be unmotivated to change. Of course, most people resist change to some extent. It means giving up what is familiar, however unpleasant or dysfunctional it may be, and entering unknown territory. In fact, few of us willingly change our beliefs, attitudes, or behaviours unless we are convinced that we are wrong and that the change will benefit us in some way: by bringing us more in line with others' thinking, perhaps, or by making us feel better.

Many people with personality disorders are reluctant to enter treatment because they do not think there is anything wrong with them. Individuals with APD characteristically think they have the right idea of how to behave to maximize benefits to themselves; they don't care if that behaviour causes problems for others. In treatment they may simply repeat what they think the therapist wants to hear without really accepting any challenges to their current way of thinking. People with paranoid personality disorder are likely to distrust a therapist and may, therefore, be unable to enter the sort of relationship necessary to produce change. The focus of narcissistic patients is so self-centred and self-assured that they may interpret challenges to their behaviour as simply the jealous therapist's attempt to demean them. Dependent personality clients are, by definition, afraid to function independently, so although they may willingly enter treatment at the urging of a friend, they are likely to resist attempts to make them more assertive and decisive.

Some therapists insist that it is clients' responsibility to decide whether they want to change. Since most personality-disordered people are either reluctant or afraid to change, these therapists may refuse to treat them, concluding that nothing can be done for them. In fact, despite the overall prevalence of personality disorders (which is substantially higher than that for schizophrenia, mood disorders, and eating disorders) very few therapists have attempted to treat these clients.

Let us consider an example. Canadian federal penitentiaries now offer a variety of therapeutic programs in areas related to the risk of reoffending (for example, training in controlling anger, solving problems, and maintaining relationships, or treatment of substance abuse or sexual offending). Most inmates who enter these programs do so to help them get early parole or transfers to a more comfortable (less secure) prison. Their motivation is not change but a way to get out of prison. Some therapists consider it inappropriate to admit offenders with these motivations into treatment. But if access were refused on these grounds, most of the treatment programs would be shut down for lack of clients, and many dangerous offenders would go untreated.

Typically, all inmates willing to enter the program are accepted, whatever their reasons. Treatment providers consider it their job to convince inmates that it is in their own best interests to participate fully. To do this, they must show them that treatment will reduce their chances of returning to prison and will equip them to function more effectively in society and thereby increase their enjoyment of life. Of course, such attempts are not always successful, although far more inmates do come to participate fully than most people would expect. The important point here is that the therapist takes responsibility for motivating clients rather than seeing self-motivation as a necessary characteristic.

The same approach appears to be essential in other personality disorders as well. Instilling motivation is a critical component in all successful treatment programs for personality disorders.

Critical Thinking Questions

1. If a male prisoner enters treatment simply to get released from custody, and indicates that he sees nothing wrong with his behaviour, would the effort required to motivate him to participate effectively be so great as to waste the therapist's valuable time that could be better spent on self-motivated clients?
2. Should motivation to change be based on self-interest or a concern for the harm one's behaviour does to others?
3. Is the self-centredness of narcissistic patients a complete block to effective treatment or is there some way we could engage them effectively in treatment?

While treatment targets for these samples have sometimes obscured the distinction between criminality and antisocial personality, they typically include some combination of targeting aggressive and antisocial attitudes and beliefs, impulsivity or poor self-regulation, anger, and substance abuse, while striving to enhance assertiveness, social skills, empathy, problem-solving, and moral reasoning. Structured program materials are available for many of these targets; however, techniques for measuring treatment gains remain relatively unsophisticated. In particular, self-reports are of little use in people with a reason to deceive the assessor and plenty of practice in lying.

Pharmacotherapy has also been used to manage antisocial or threatening behaviour or acting-out, particularly in prisons and hospitals. Long-term drug use may bring side-effects, and noncompliance is always an issue (Harris, 1989). While short-term use of antipsychotic, antianxiety, and sedative medications is not uncommon, improvements are rarely sustained and patients do not gain the skills to deal with future situations. For some patients, medication may reduce arousal level sufficiently for them to more fully participate in cognitive-behavioural treatment (Rice & Harris, 1993).

Borderline Personality Disorder

Mary was raised in an abusive alcoholic family, which resulted in several placements in foster homes. Contact with her family was "all or nothing." They were either in daily contact or would not speak for months. She readily attributed any personal difficulties to her chaotic family background. In early adolescence she developed an interest in poetry and became preoccupied with fantasies of becoming a world-renowned poet, at the same time as she was struggling to get through high school.

After she threatened suicide, her family doctor referred her to a therapist. Mary showed up an hour late for her first appointment, yet demanded indignantly to be seen immediately. Her speech seemed affected. She was short, quite overweight, and so heavily made up as to camouflage her natural features, and she looked older than her stated age. She immediately tried to gain control of her first interview, declaring that she had no desire to waste her time with a "shrink" and demanding that a report be submitted to her doctor indicating that she did not have any psychological problems.

Throughout Mary's life she had had problems with her female friends. She complained they had no understanding of friendship, were not trustworthy, and could not fulfill her needs. Late one evening when she felt deeply lonely, Mary called many friends to come and stay with her. When none could come immediately, she severed all ties with them. Yet she often expressed envy of her friends, and ruminated about how they perceived her.

Mary's opinion of her psychologist vacillated from session to session; she would gush about how lucky she was to have "the best" therapist and then, in a sudden burst of hostility, accuse him of utter incompetence. This characteristic feature of vacillating between idealizing and devaluing other people is called "splitting." Mary was emotionally labile within and between sessions, with severe and rapid mood swings. Temper outbursts were a frequent occurrence over trivial matters.

Mary had attempted suicide several times, always after breaking up with a boyfriend. After her most recent and severe attempt, Mary expressed confusion regarding her sexual orientation. She had great difficulty interacting with others. At times she felt completely overwhelmed and asked to go back to hospital, while at other times she said she would rather kill herself than go to hospital.

Fluctuations in mood, an unstable sense of their own identity, and instability in their relationships characterize **borderline personality disorder (BPD)** patients. This overriding instability in all aspects of their functioning makes borderlines unpredictable and impulsive and, along with their irritability and argumentative style, these features tend to seriously interfere with their relationships. However, they seem unable to tolerate being alone and accordingly become desperate about relationships, typically alternating between idealizing and devaluing their partners.

Historical Perspective

The term "borderline" comes from early identification of people as *borderline psychotics* (a term no longer commonly used) or as people whose functioning was borderline. Millon (1992) has described the origins of the present conceptualization of borderline personality disorder. In an examination of four influential reports on what was variously called *borderline personality organization* (Kernberg, 1967), *the borderline syndrome* (Grinker, Werble, & Drye, 1968), *borderline states* (Knight, 1953), and simply *borderline patients* (Gunderson & Singer, 1975), Perry and Klerman (1978) found that criteria varied. Only one of the criteria (the patient's maladaptive and inappropriate behaviour at interview) appeared in all four reports.

Spitzer, Endicott, and Gibbon (1979) concluded that the label "borderline" had been used up to that time to identify two different constellations of symptoms: (1) instability and vulnerability and (2) a set of features that had been described as "borderline schizophrenia." The former constellation provided the basis for identifying BPD in DSM-III while the latter became *schizotypal personality disorder*.

Diagnostic Issues

Considerable overlap and even confusion between borderline and schizotypal disorders remain (Rosenberger & Miller, 1989; Serban, Conte, & Plutchik, 1987). Oddly enough, the DSM-III characteristic (intolerance of being alone) that most accurately distinguished borderlines from schizotypals (McGlashan, 1983) was dropped from the diagnostic criteria in DSM-III-R and DSM-IV. (See DSM table.)

Debate continues concerning the nature of borderline disorders (Millon, 1986). Widiger, Miele, and Tilly (1992) found considerable inconsistencies in research aimed at evaluating the diagnostic formulations, which they attribute to differences in research samples, settings, and interpretations of the diagnostic criteria. Diagnosis using DSM criteria has low reliability (Hurt, Clarkin, Koenigsberg, Frances, & Nurmberg,

DSM-IV Diagnostic Criteria for Borderline Personality Disorder

Pervasive instability and impulsivity as indicated by 5 or more of the following:

1. Frantically avoids real or imagined abandonment
2. Unstable and intense relationships
3. Unstable self-image
4. Impulsivity in at least 2 areas (e.g., sex, substance abuse, binge eating)
5. Recurrent suicidal behaviour or gestures
6. Emotional instability
7. Chronic feelings of emptiness
8. Difficulty controlling anger
9. Transient paranoia or dissociative symptoms

Source: Reprinted with permission from the *Diagnostic and Statistical Manual of Mental Disorders*, Fourth Edition. Copyright 1994 American Psychiatric Association.

1986). Dimensional ratings (using rating scales and structured interviews) have been shown to improve reliability (Widiger, Miele, & Tilly, 1992). This disagreement makes it very difficult to compare or synthesize research findings.

Prevalence

Borderline personality disorder has a lifetime prevalence of approximately 2 percent of the population and is thought to be more common in women than in men. BPD, which typically begins in adolescence, has been shown to display reasonable stability over time (Barasch, Frances, Hurt, Clarkin, & Cohen, 1985). However, Stone (1993) reported that of patients diagnosed during early adulthood as borderline, only 25 percent still met the diagnostic criteria in middle age.

Etiology of BPD

The etiology of BPD has been debated for many years with different views emphasizing childhood experiences, biological factors, psychodynamic processes, or social learning. Certainly the evidence strongly implicates disruptions in the family of origin and childhood abuse and neglect (Links, 1992; Marziali, 1992). Borderline patients typically recall their parents as either neglectful (Paris & Frank, 1989) or abusive (Bryer, Nelson, Miller, & Krol, 1987). Briere and Zaidi (1989), in the examination of 100 women seen at an emergency service, found that a woman who was sexually abused in childhood was five times as likely to be diagnosed with borderline personality disorder.

Any consideration of childhood experience, of course, faces the problem of dealing with retrospective data: the question of the accuracy of recall. Nevertheless, findings to date suggest attachment problems as a significant etiological factor in borderline disorder. BPD patients have major problems with adult relationships, and this may be understood to result from a fear of, or ambivalence about, intimacy.

People who have problems with adult intimacy are considered to have developed these difficulties as a result of poor parent-child attachments (Berman & Sperling, 1994), which fail to instill the self-confidence and skills necessary for

effective intimacy (Bartholomew, 1989) and fail to provide an adequate template for adult intimate relationships (Bowlby, 1988). For example, many adults who as children had poor relationships with their parents have an interpersonal style described as **anxious ambivalent**. These adults strongly desire intimacy with others and consequently, persistently seek out romantic partners. However, once they begin to get close to their partner, they become anxious and begin to back away from the relationship. While they desire closeness, they appear to be afraid of it. This is precisely the relationship style that characterizes borderline patients. The features of borderline disorder may then be seen as attempts to adjust to their desire for but distrust of intimacy.

Murray (1979) has suggested an association between minimal brain dysfunction and the development of borderline disorder. He proposed that the distorting effects of minimal brain dysfunction on perceptual processes may interfere with effective parent-child relationships and that these effects may continue to disrupt relationships throughout the life span. The confused perceptions, emotional instability, and poor impulse control typical of minimal brain dysfunction are said by Murray to lead to the development of borderline behaviour. Research has generally supported the idea that a subset of borderlines have soft neurological signs (Marziali, 1992), but the evidence is certainly far from convincing.

Available evidence suggests a relatively high incidence of borderline features in the first-degree relatives of BPD patients (Links, 1992), and this has been taken by some to suggest familial transmission of the disorder (Baron, Risch, Levitt, & Gruen, 1985). Of course, familial transmission of a disorder may be the result of environmental rather than genetic factors. In a Norwegian twin study, Torgersen (1984) found no support for a genetic contribution to the development of either BPD or schizotypal disorder, but the sample was small.

Histrionic Personality Disorder

Attention-seeking behaviours distinguish people with **histrionic personality disorder**. They are flamboyant, overly dramatic in their emotional displays, and overresponsive to events others would consider trivial. They constantly seek the spotlight and cannot stand being ignored. However, because they are self-centred and come across as insincere and shallow, they cannot hold other people's attention for long and typically have few friends. (Recall Andrew, in the opening cases to this chapter.) Their need for attention makes them demanding and inconsiderate; not surprisingly, their relationships are often short-lived and emotionally tumultuous. They are often flirtatious, and seem unable to develop intimacy in relationships. Their behaviour causes considerable distress to themselves and to others with whom they become involved.

Histrionic people are frequently depressed and often suffer from poor health (Nestadt et al., 1990). There is considerable overlap with borderline personality disorder. Widiger et al. (1992) found that 57 percent of borderline patients also meet the criteria for histrionic personality disorder.

Narcissistic Personality Disorder

Narcissistic people grandiosely consider themselves to have unique and outstanding abilities. They have an exaggerated sense of self-importance; indeed, egocentricity is the hallmark of these patients. They are so preoccupied with their own interests and desires that they typically have difficulty feeling any concern for others, although they themselves are easily hurt. Their self-esteem is readily shattered by criticism from others, presumably because they desire only admiration and approval. Their self-absorption frequently leads to an obsession with overblown fantasies of success. They expect, and demand, to be treated as special, and this, along with their lack of empathy, leads them to exploit others. Like histrionic patients, the typical behaviour of narcissists alienates others, and they are frequently lonely and unhappy. When frustrated or slighted, narcissists can become vengeful and verbally or physically aggressive.

Ronningstan and Gunderson (1990) claim that research has validated these features as characteristic of narcissistic personality disorder. However, while Morey (1988) has reported a remarkable increase (from 6.2 percent of patients to 22 percent) in the application of the diagnosis from DSM-III to DSM-III-R, Zimmerman and Coryell (1989) could find no cases of narcissistic personality disorder in a sample of 800 community subjects. When narcissism is diagnosed, there is considerable overlap with borderline personality disorder (Morey, 1988).

According to Greek myth, the beautiful youth Narkissos fell in love with his own reflection in a spring; to punish him for his excessive self-love, the gods transformed him into the flower called the narcissus.

CLUSTER C: ANXIOUS AND FEARFUL DISORDERS

Cluster C includes avoidant, dependent, and obsessive-compulsive disorders. Again, the cluster does not seem to be particularly meaningful: while the first two share anxieties and fears as primary features, the obsessive-compulsive person is more characterized by a preoccupation with orderliness and rules. Information is sparse regarding etiology and effective intervention specific to these disorders.

Avoidant Personality Disorder

Burt was a bright government clerk in his thirties, who was distressed because he had won no promotions over the past eight years. He had been offered promotions three times, but had turned them all down because they would have meant dealing with the public, and he was afraid of making mistakes. His bosses had offered him no further chances.

At the clinic, it took several interviews before Burt was comfortable enough to explain his problem. Once he was able to speak more freely, Burt described himself in negative terms. He said he was not good with people and that people who did not know him well would think he was stupid. Although Burt seemed pleasant and quite likeable, he said he had few friends; those he did have were people he had known for years. He was very cautious about forming new relationships because he feared rejection; most people, he felt, would not like him once they got to know him.

A pervasive pattern of avoiding interpersonal contacts and an extreme sensitivity to criticism and disapproval characterize **avoidant** people. They actively avoid intimacy with others, although (unlike people with schizoid disorder) they clearly desire affection and suffer from loneliness. Social discomfort and a fear of criticism are common features. Avoidant clients restrict social interactions to those they trust not to denigrate them; but even with these people, they refrain from getting too close. These fears cause problems for them not only in interpersonal relationships but also in their choice of jobs, academic pursuits, and leisure activities. Their avoidance of intimacy also distresses other people who may wish to form a close relationship with them.

People with avoidant styles were identified in the literature for many years prior to the inclusion of this personality disorder in the diagnostic manual. For instance, Horney (1945) noted that there were people who found interpersonal relationships of any kind to be such an intolerable strain that "solitude becomes primarily a means of avoiding it" (p. 73). Millon (1969) was the first to use the term *avoidant personality* to describe people who actively avoided social interactions. He suggested (Millon, 1981) that a child rejected by his or her parents would lack self-confidence and later avoid others for fear of further rejection. This notion fits with the extensive literature on parent-child attachments and the consequences for adult relationships of parental rejection. While some children who have poor parental bonds develop an anxious/avoidant relationship style (typical of BPD), others grow up to be so afraid of intimate relationships that they become avoidant of any depth in whatever relationships they form.

Trull, Widiger, and Frances (1987) found considerable overlap between avoidant personality disorder and dependent disorder, and Morey (1988) reports overlap with borderline disorder. There is also considerable overlap with social phobia (Turner, Beidel, Dancu, & Keys, 1991); the distinction appears to be one of severity (Holt, Heimberg, & Hope, 1992).

Dependent Personality Disorder

Dependent people appear to be afraid to rely on themselves to make decisions. They seek advice and direction from others, need constant reassurance, and seek out relationships where they can adopt a submissive role. Dependent patients not only allow, but seem to desperately need, others to assume responsibility for important aspects of their lives. They seem unable to function independently and typically ask their spouse or partner to decide what job they should seek or what clothes they should buy. They subordinate their needs to those of other people in their lives, even people they hardly know. This style often gets them involved in abusive relationships or destroys relationships with partners who could be beneficial to their lives. (See DSM table.)

Reich (1990) observed that the relatives of male dependent patients were likely to experience depression, whereas the relatives of female dependents were more likely to have panic disorder. Panic-disordered patients have also been found to have comorbidity with various personality disorders, including dependent disorder (Johnson, Weissman, & Klerman, 1990).

Obsessive-Compulsive Personality Disorder

Inflexibility and a desire for perfection characterize this disorder. It is the centrality of these two features, and the absence of obsessional thoughts and compulsive behaviours, that distinguish this personality disorder from the Axis 1 obsessive-compulsive disorder. (See Chapter 7 for a description of this disorder.) Recall Margaret in the opening cases. Preoccupation with rules and order make these people rigid and inefficient as a result of focussing too much on the details of a problem. Obsessive-compulsive personality patients also attempt to ignore feelings, since they consider emotions to be unpredictable. They tend to be moralistic and judgemental, which leads to problems in dealing with others.

Turkat and Levin (1984) could find no reports in the literature that they considered at all helpful in understanding obsessive-compulsive personality disorder. Most of the research they reviewed was concerned with the psychoanalytic notion of the anal-retentive character, which has lost much of its credibility in recent years. This anal-retentive characteristic of patients with obsessive-compulsive personality disorder refers to their orderliness, miserliness, and obstinacy, and was said by Freud to originate in the anal stage of psychosexual development.

Very little research on this disorder has emerged over the years since DSM-III-R was published, except that which concerns distinguishing this personality disorder from obsessive-compulsive disorder. While studies using projective techniques or clinical interviews find co-occurrence of the two disorders (Cawley, 1974; Slade, 1974), studies using objective measures have found a clear independence. In fact, Joffe, Swinson, and Regan (1988) found that avoidant, dependent, and schizotypal personality disorders were all more likely to co-occur with Axis I obsessive-compulsive disorder.

TREATMENT

It is difficult to evaluate treatment for personality disorders for two main reasons: first, many of these people see nothing wrong with their own characteristic personality style and so do not seek treatment; second, dropout rates are extremely high. As clients, these people pose a serious challenge for the therapist. All of them have considerable difficulty with relationships and this affects the therapeutic alliance. Also, most have problems maintaining focus on the therapeutic process between sessions. Patients being treated primarily for an Axis I disorder tend to do more poorly if they also have a personality disorder (Reich & Green, 1991). Some doubt exists about the potential for effective treatment, since personality, and thus personality disorder, is considered to be stable. Although efforts have intensified in recent years to developing treatment programs specifically for personality disorders, outcome data is limited.

Essentially three approaches have been developed: (1) object-relations therapy, (2) cognitive-behavioural approaches, and (3) medication.

Object-Relations Therapy

Leading proponents of an object-relations approach have been Otto Kernberg (1975) and Heinz Kohut (1977). In their view, treatment should be aimed at correcting the flaws in the self that have resulted from unfortunate formative experiences. The relationship with the therapist serves as a vehicle for confronting,

---

DSM-IV Diagnostic Criteria for Dependent Personality Disorder

Pervasive and excessive need to be taken care of as indicated by 5 or more of the following:

1. Unable to make decisions without advice
2. Needs others to take responsibility for major areas of functioning
3. Unable to express disagreement
4. Lacks capacity to do things independently
5. Goes to excessive lengths to get support
6. Feels helpless when alone
7. Desperate need for relationships
8. Unrealistic fears of being alone

Source: Reprinted with permission from the *Diagnostic and Statistical Manual of Mental Disorders*, Fourth Edition. Copyright 1994 American Psychiatric Association.

in a supportive way, the patient's defences and distortions. This process is slow and, if successful, produces gradual changes. Thus, treatment is seen as necessarily long-term.

In a controlled evaluation of this approach, Stevenson and Meares (1992) treated 30 borderline patients. At one-year followup, 30 percent no longer met DSM criteria for borderline personality disorder. Clarkin and his colleagues (Clarkin et al., 1992) demonstrated that Kernberg's psychodynamic treatment approach (Kernberg, Selzer, Koenigsberg, Carr, & Appelbaum, 1989), combined with antidepressant medication, was effective in reducing a range of specific symptoms of BPD patients (see Figure 11.4). Single case reports of similar treatment programs with narcissistic patients have also been encouraging (Kinston, 1980). Although Walsh (1990) has suggested that a psychotherapeutic approach emphasizing a supportive relationship and aimed at enhancing social skills may be useful with schizotypal patients, there have not, as yet, been any controlled studies. Generally, more extensive and rigorous evaluations are required to determine the true value of this approach.

Cognitive-Behavioural Approaches

Beck (Beck et al., 1990) has extended his cognitive analyses to the personality disorders and suggested that treatment must correct the cognitive distortions of these patients in order to be successful. His treatment is directed at challenging the core beliefs thought to underlie the problems of personality-disordered patients. **Cognitive restructuring**, as this challenging of core beliefs is called, provides the basis for change, along with skills training and behavioural practices. To date, however, adherents of this promising approach have not produced controlled evaluations. This is understandable, since the approach has been applied only recently and Beck et al. (1990) claim that cognitive therapy will take far longer with personality disorders than with other disorders.

The **dialectical behaviour therapy** developed by Linehan (Linehan & Heard, 1992) has specifically targeted borderlines. One of the main features of this approach is the acceptance by the therapist of the patient's demanding and manipulative behaviours. In addition, several standard behavioural procedures are used, such as exposure treatment for the external and internal cues that evoke distress, skills training, contingency management, and cognitive restructuring. The dialectical process describes "both the coexisting multiple tensions and the thought processes and styles used and targeted in the treatment strategies" (Linehan and Heard, 1992, p. 249).

Linehan, Armstrong, Suarez, Allmon, and Heard (1991) compared the treatment outcome of 22 female borderline patients assigned to dialectical behaviour therapy with 22 patients given "treatment as usual." After one year of treatment, those assigned to dialectical behaviour therapy had made fewer suicidal attempts and had spent less time in hospital than those allocated to the other treatment program. Moreover,

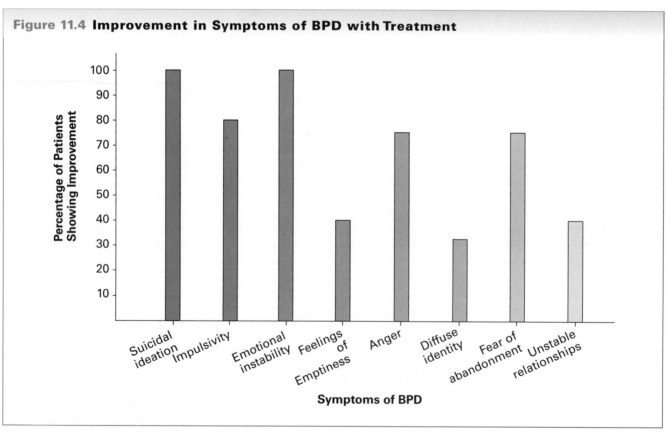

Figure 11.4 Improvement in Symptoms of BPD with Treatment

Source: Adapted from Clarkin et al., 1992.

only 17 percent of the dialectically treated patients dropped out, compared to 60 percent of the other group. Depression and hopelessness diminished for both groups, in similar degree. To date there is no published work on the application of dialectical therapy to other personality disorders.

Canadian therapist Ariel Stravynski and his colleagues (Stravynski, Lesage, Marcouiller, & Elie, 1989) have applied behavioural approaches employing social skills training and desensitization to the problems of avoidant-personality-disordered patients. However, the long-term benefits of these programs have not been evaluated, and Alden (1989) observed that most of the treated patients remained socially uncomfortable.

Pharmacological Interventions

Borderline patients have been successfully treated with a variety of pharmacologic agents including amitriptyline (an antidepressant), thiothixene (an antipsychotic), and carbamazepine (an anticonvulsant). It has been suggested that different subtypes of borderline patients may be differentially responsive to either antipsychotic or antidepressant medications. Goldberg et al. (1986), for example, found antipsychotics to be most effective with borderlines displaying psychotic-like features, while Cole, Saloman, Gunderson, Sunderland, and Simmonds (1984) found maximal improvements for antidepressants with those borderline patients who also met the criteria for major depression. In addition, Waldinger and Frank (1989) indicate that medications may facilitate psychotherapy with borderline patients.

Goldberg et al. (1986) also found low doses of thiothixene to be beneficial with schizotypal-disordered patients; they also seem to respond to antidepressants (Markowitz et al., 1991); however, the benefits of any medications with schizotypal disorder are modest at best (Gitlin, 1993). Medication has been used with antisocial patients for short-term management of threatening behaviour. However, the limited improvement, noncompliance, and long-term side-effects suggest at best a modest role, perhaps in combination with other interventions.

PANORAMA

Other than the rather extensive research on antisocial and borderline personality disorders, and to a lesser extent on schizotypal patients, the personality disorders remain largely a neglected domain in the field of psychopathology.

The criteria for personality disorders remain somewhat subjective despite attempts by the authors of DSM-IV to specify all criteria in observable terms. In addition, there is the continued problem of diagnostic overlap, which is more troublesome with the personality disorders than elsewhere. Whether switching from a categorical classification to a dimensional system is the best solution to this problem is not clear, although research focussing on dimensional analyses seems more likely to enhance our understanding of these disorders.

As we saw throughout this chapter, personality-disordered patients all seem to have poor relationships with their parents. Perhaps this common childhood feature is the origin of their difficulties with being appropriately intimate with others. This suggests that attachment theory may be the best way to understand the origins and current features of these patients, and that dealing with relationship issues may provide an effective treatment approach. What evidence there is on attachment analyses, and the corresponding treatment of these disorders, encourages some degree of optimism with this approach.

Perhaps the most serious deficiency in our knowledge concerns treatment of these disorders. Presently there are few treatment alternatives available, and for most of the personality disorders, very little has been tried in a systematic way, except perhaps for borderline disorder. As we have seen, some clinicians think antisocial personality disorder is treatable, despite mounting evidence to the contrary. Greater and more systematic efforts are needed to develop ways of more effectively helping these people.

Controlled, long-term outcome studies of large numbers of patients are required to determine the effectiveness of treatment, particularly in the light of the existing pessimistic view. For the low-incidence personality disorders such studies may not be feasible, but some settings may have sufficient numbers for such investigations. Nevertheless, sample size alone should not deter researchers from attempting to make progress in the assessment and treatment of personality disorders.

SUMMARY

Personality disorders are essentially maladaptive personality traits. All people have more or less consistent characteristics that make up their personality. Personality disorders are distinguished from normal personality traits by being rigid, maladaptive, and monolithic. People with personality disorders typically have many intact abilities but have impaired functioning (especially socially) because of their disorder.

Personality disorders were first clearly described in the early nineteenth century. The present set of personality disorders first appeared in DSM-III as Axis II, separate from the Axis I "clinical" disorders.

The DSM-IV lists ten disorders, grouped into three clusters: Odd and Eccentric Disorders (paranoid, schizoid, schizotypal), Dramatic, Emotional, or Erratic Disorders (antisocial, borderline, histrionic, narcissistic), and Anxious and Fearful Disorders (avoidant, dependent, obsessive-compulsive). Axis II diagnoses tend to have lower reliability than Axis I, and there is considerable comorbidity as well as overlap among these disorders. Some researchers suggest that a dimensional model would be more useful for personality disorders than DSM's categorical classification. Many have argued that the diagnostic criteria reflect cultural and gender bias.

Etiological explanations have focussed on psychodynamics, attachment theory, cognitive-behavioural perspectives, and biological factors such as genetic, neurotransmitters, or brain dysfunction. There is little clear data.

Of the ten DSM-IV disorders, two have received the bulk of research attention. Antisocial personality disorder is a major problem for society, because affected individuals are prone to commit crimes and otherwise act in harmful ways. The essential feature of APD is a pervasive, ongoing disregard for the rights of others. Special diagnostic issues and confusion over prevalence and research outcomes arise because APD is similar to, but not identical with, the older construct of psychopathy. The latter, as measured by the PCL-R, fo-

cusses on emotional and interpersonal processes as well as behaviour, whereas the DSM-IV's criteria for APD are largely behavioural. Social and family factors have been cited as etiological factors for APD; there is some support for genetic factors as well. Studies have shown that psychopaths respond to physical punishment by opposing the intent of the punisher. There is conflicting data on whether people with APD "burn out" in middle age. Treatment outcomes are generally poor; more studies are needed on programs that target the client's specific problems.

Borderline personality disorder is characterized by fluctuations in mood, an unstable sense of identity, and instability in relationships. Diagnostic criteria are still debated. Disruptions in the family of origin are the most common etiological explanation.

Treatment for personality disorders in general is difficult to evaluate, because many patients never seek treatment. Three main approaches have been tried: object-relations therapy, cognitive-behavioural approaches, and medications. There are few well-controlled studies of any treatments for most of the disorders.

KEY TERMS

traits (p. 260)
clusters (p. 261)
overlap (p. 264)
paranoid (p. 268)
schizoid (p. 269)
schizotypal (p. 269)
psychopath (p. 272)
sociopath (p. 272)

antisocial personality disorder (APD) (p. 272)
fearlessness hypothesis (p. 274)
manifest task (p. 274)
latent task (p. 274)
oppositional behaviour (p. 275)
responsivity factor (p. 276)
borderline personality disorder (BPD) (p. 278)

anxious ambivalent (p. 279)
histrionic personality disorder (p. 279)
narcissistic (p. 280)
avoidant (p. 280)
dependent (p. 281)
cognitive restructuring (p. 282)
dialectical behaviour therapy (p. 282)

ADDITIONAL RESOURCES

Canadian Psychiatric Association
260-441 MacLaren Street
Ottawa, ON
K2P 2H3
(613) 234-2815
(613) 234-9857 fax
cpa@medical.org

American Psychological Association
750 First Street NE
Washington, DC 20002-4242
(202) 336-5500
executiveoffice@apa.org

www.mentalhealth.com/dis/p20-pe05.html
This web site includes a description of borderline personality disorder, online diagnosis, and research papers and magazine articles.

www.ohsu.edu/cliniweb/F3/F3.709.597.html
Links to sites on personality disorders.

www.mentalhealth.com/mag1/p51.html#Per
This collection includes hundreds of articles on personality disorders and their treatment.

Chapter 1 2

Sexual and Gender Identity Disorders

Myles Genest

William L. Marshall

When David phoned for an appointment, he asked whether he could arrange to arrive at the office unseen by other clients to avoid recognition. He said that his problem was "impotence," so the therapist encouraged him to bring his wife to the initial interview.

David had always doubted the adequacy of his sexual responsiveness. He had first tried to have intercourse at the age of 20 while on a road tour with his university football team. After a night of drunken revelry, some of the guys hired a prostitute for the night. Rather than admit to being a virgin, David went along, despite his anxiety. He tried to take his turn with the woman, but couldn't. He was so ashamed that he begged the prostitute not to tell anyone, but later he boasted about his prowess.

Although he could masturbate to orgasm and develop an erection when he did so, David believed that he wasn't as "highly sexed" as most guys, because he didn't share his classmates' fascination with pornography and ribald jokes. He became upset by his continued masturbation, believing that it was an abnormal sexual outlet, and worried about whether he could have intercourse. The episode with the prostitute confirmed David's worst fears. To avoid facing such embarrassment again, he broke off relations with women as soon as they made any sexual overtures. Eventually, he stopped dating entirely.

David had graduated and was an engineer when he began to develop a strong friendship with Alicia, a colleague in his office. He admired her for bucking the establishment in a male-dominated field, and they often talked over coffee or lunch. Eventually she made it clear that she was interested in more than friendship. Before he knew it, David had agreed to marriage. He felt that he had led her on by allowing such a close bond to develop and hoped that in the security of a caring relationship, his capacity for a sexual relationship with a woman would grow.

David was nevertheless panicked by the thought of meeting his wife's sexual demands. Alicia did not seem to expect sex before marriage and, to his relief, when he finally admitted his problem to her the week before their marriage, she was understanding and calm and said they would work it out together. On their honeymoon, David found he was able to have intercourse on several occasions. Many more times, however, Alicia was interested but David couldn't get an erection and quickly backed out of the encounter.

As the years passed, Alicia remained the sexual initiator, and David grew more and more anxious. He began to stay up late, working until Alicia was asleep. Gradually, conflict between them increased. Alicia, who was thinking of children by now, began to press David "to do something about your impotence." David became more anxious about failure with each unsuccessful attempt, and he would sometimes try to satisfy Alicia with oral sex. This always left him feeling inadequate and he emotionally withdrew, leaving her upset.

By the time they sought therapy, David and Alicia felt quite hopeless. They saw therapy as a last-ditch effort to save their marriage, but they were also motivated by the joint desire to have children.

* * *

Graham was a pleasant, attractive undergraduate when he first appeared at a clinic seeking treatment for a fetish. During his first two years he had been an attentive student and had very good marks but his third-year grades had fallen so far that Graham decided to repeat the year. He was again doing poorly. He told the therapist he had become so preoccupied with his fetish that he couldn't pay attention to lectures or study.

Graham grew up as a rather lonely boy. His parents, in their mid-forties when he was born, considered displays of affection and emotion inappropriate. Determined that he succeed at school, they rewarded him when he got top marks and set strict study rules that all but precluded friendships.

When Graham was nine years old he discovered the pleasures of masturbation. Since it was one of his few sources of satisfaction, he began to masturbate more and more often. Then his pretty teenage cousin came to visit for a few days. One day Graham was on his way to the bathroom to masturbate when he saw a pair of her blue jeans lying on the floor with other laundry. He had already thought about his cousin several times during masturbation since she had arrived, and the sight of a piece of her clothing increased his excitement. He quickly picked up the jeans, took them into the bathroom, and fondled them while he masturbated. This became a frequent ritual for the next several days. After the cousin left, Graham used any pair of blue jeans he could get hold of, pretending they belonged to his cousin.

Since this exciting ritual was one of Graham's few pleasures, it quickly became entrenched and was especially frequent when he was under stress. Blue jeans are a common sight on a university campus. Away from his parents' watchful eyes, Graham allowed his studies to slip as he turned more and more to his fetish for pleasure. Finally he began to steal blue jeans from dormitories and laundromats and the fear of being caught, plus his failing grades, led Graham to seek treatment.

Graham was quite good at casual chat and could form superficial relationships, but lack of skill and fear of rejection held him back from real intimacy. He had had three girlfriends but after a few months all of them wanted more than he could give and broke up with him.

Here then was a lonely, emotionally starved young man who turned to a fetish for pleasure and comfort, but as he retreated further and further into the fetish, the costs became greater than the benefits.

These two cases illustrate some of the range of the disorders covered in this chapter. Both problems are sexual in nature, but David's is a type of sexual dysfunction—a persistent failure to achieve satisfaction in sexual relations—while Graham's is a *paraphilia*—a redirection of sexual desires toward what is generally considered to be an inappropriate object, or person, or behaviour. This chapter will also describe what are called *gender identity disorders*: the condition of people who feel ill at ease with their biological sex and are comfortable only when they present themselves as belonging to the opposite gender.

HISTORICAL PERSPECTIVE

Conceptions of the appropriateness or deviance of human sexual behaviours has varied considerably throughout history (Bullough, 1976). Sex is one of the most discussed human behaviours, although these discussions are often superficial and skirt substantive issues. For example, sex education often takes the form of a recitation of knowledge about physiological functioning and anatomical facts rather than about the actual behaviours and the associated thoughts and feelings. Most people define *abnormal sex* as any sexual behaviour they do not themselves engage in, or wish to engage in.

Brown (1985) suggests that the Judeo-Christian tradition has had a significant influence on notions about appropriate and inappropriate sexual behaviours within our society. He contends that the prevailing attitudes at the time the Bible and the Talmud were written condoned "sex between men and very young girls in marriage, concubinage, and slavery" (p. 23). Not surprisingly, some of the remarks in these historic documents are in conflict with today's values. Christian notions of acceptable sexual behaviour evolved in the West primarily through the teachings of St. Augustine. St. Augustine declared that sexual intercourse was permissible only for purposes of procreation, only when the male was on top, and only when the penis and vagina were involved. Thus, oral-genital sex, masturbation, anal sex, and presumably all forms of precoital activities were considered sinful, as were sexual activities with someone who could not conceive, such as a child or a same-sex partner.

Science in the sixteenth and seventeenth centuries offered support for these Christian teachings by attributing all manner of dire consequences to so-called excessive sexual activity. These views were popularized in 1766 by Tissot in his treatise on the ills of onanism (solitary masturbation). Tissot attributed a whole variety of ills to masturbation and recommended that the state establish controls on sexuality, although just how they were to enact these controls was not made clear. Popular writers on sex in the eighteenth century took up Tissot's claims with gusto. The Reverend Sylvester Graham and Dr. John Harvey Kellogg in the eighteenth century published treatises declaring that masturbation caused numerous problems including lassitude, dullness, defective development, untrustworthiness, and even ill health and round shoulders. Parents were warned to watch for these signs and at all costs prevent the destructive behaviour. Excessive sexuality could be counteracted by healthy activities and a diet of bland foods. Graham developed Graham crackers and Kellogg developed corn flakes to meet the need for such foods.

Krafft-Ebing (1901) published the first strictly medical textbook on sexual aberrations, called *Psychopathia sexualia*. Again, masturbation was blamed for numerous illnesses. The range of sexual behaviours considered to be deviant was initially extremely broad, including whatever was thought to differ from prevailing beliefs about acceptable practices. Accordingly, up to the early part of the twentieth century, deviance included a variety of sexual practices that are no longer officially listed as deviant.

Research on sexuality has not progressed at the same rate as has research on other human problems, apparently as a result of notions concerning the privacy of sex. Such notions have encouraged the general public to view with suspicion researchers who examine sexuality. The publication of Alfred Kinsey's research (Kinsey, Pomeroy, & Martin, 1948; Kinsey, Pomeroy, Martin, & Gebhard, 1953) investigating human sexual practices was greeted with animosity by the general public, the media, and many of his scientific colleagues, apparently because his findings upset established beliefs about sexuality. His data revealed that masturbation, oral-genital sex, and homosexuality, for example, were engaged in by far more people and with far greater frequency than was previously believed. Masters and Johnson's (1966) study was greeted with much the same animosity. Recently, two surveys of sexual practices in the United States were stopped as a result of political pressure, despite the fact that they had already been carefully screened and approved by scientific communities (Udry, 1993). Perhaps even more illustrative are the funding levels provided by the National Institute of Mental Health (NIMH), the primary source of research funding in the United States. Despite the well-established damage that sexual offenders cause to society, NIMH devoted $1.2 million in 1993 to research on this topic, while spending $125.3 million on studies of depression (Goode, 1994).

DIAGNOSTIC ISSUES

As in all other areas of human functioning, it is necessary to have at least an approximate idea of what is normal (including some indication of the frequency of behaviours) in order to define abnormal functioning. Simple frequency, however, will not always do. For example, most, if not all, men occasionally ejaculate too rapidly during sexual intercourse; and for an unknown, but apparently significant number, this is a persistent problem (Gebhard & Johnson, 1979). Even if most men ejaculated rapidly upon being sexually aroused, would this be considered normal? It certainly would be from a statistical point of view, but if the man and his partner were dissatisfied and sought help, the diagnosis of a problem would nevertheless be likely.

In sex, then, satisfaction with present functioning is an important diagnostic criterion, reflected in DSM-IV's definition of sexual dysfunctions. A problem for reliable diagnoses is that DSM-IV's criteria require diagnosticians to make somewhat subjective judgements: to decide, for example, whether a client's experiences are "persistent," "recurrently deficient," "minimal," or "delayed," or cause "marked distress or interpersonal difficulty." There are no perfectly objective standards for these qualities, which will in any case vary within the same individual from one time and setting to another.

For the paraphilias, on the other hand, the question of the satisfaction, or distress, of the person suffering from the disorder is not quite so straightforward. Graham, the young man with the fetish described at the beginning of this chapter, was sufficiently distressed by his problem that he sought help. Presumably a person could have a fetish (or some other odd sexual interest that did not hurt anyone) and not be upset by it. In that case, would the person have a diagnosable problem? Not according to DSM-IV, which requires that distress be experienced. Clinicians, however, characteristically apply a diagnosis of fetishism whether or not the person is distressed by the behaviour. In fact, it appears that the majority of fetishists are only occasionally distressed by their sexual interests—when a friend or family member finds out, for example.

For the other paraphilias, such as exhibitionism and pedophilia (an attraction to sex with children), DSM-IV is not clear about *who* must experience distress for the diagnosis to be made. Need the person with the paraphilia feel distress? Or does the distress of victims count? In practice, most clinicians ignore this criterion of distress. Few clinicians, for example, would hesitate to diagnose and treat a man who had repeatedly exposed his genitals to a woman simply because the exhibitionist reported enjoying the behaviours.

Surprisingly, perhaps, many men who sexually molest children do not meet DSM-IV criteria for pedophilia because they do not *persistently* molest (or persistently imagine molesting) children. Similarly, most men who rape women do not engage in or fantasize sadistic acts with their victims, which is a necessary DSM-IV criterion for sexual sadism, the only relevant diagnosis in these cases. The diagnostic criteria for paraphilias, then, seem to reflect an insensitivity to public concerns about sexual abuse and to ignore the fact that most people consider sexual offenders to be distinctly aberrant.

Of course, as we saw in Chapter 11, just because the public thinks an act—murder, for example—is aberrant does not mean the person committing the act is mentally disordered. A distinction here between the requirements for legal insanity and DSM-IV disorders may be helpful. The only DSM-IV disorders that are relevant to the legal notion of insanity are those that involve a loss of contact with reality or impairment in the person's ability to recognize an act as wrong. Paraphilia does not fit this description; sexual offenders know what they are doing and know it is wrong. They must, therefore, be held responsible for their crimes.

At the same time, research has revealed that sexual offenders differ from normal people on many aspects of their functioning, and they clearly upset others by their behaviour. It seems sensible, therefore, to consider all sexual offenders to be in need of corrective interventions, whether or not they have a diagnosable disorder. However, these corrective interventions are best seen as attempts to rehabilitate criminals rather than treatment for a diagnosable disorder.

NORMAL SEXUAL RESPONSE

To identify abnormal functioning, we need some idea of what constitutes normal sexual behaviour. Unfortunately, because of the secrecy surrounding sex, it is hard to determine how frequently various sexual behaviours occur, even quite normal activities. Very few people, for example, will acknowledge openly that they masturbate, and yet anonymous surveys reveal that very high proportions of the population (81 percent of males and 45 percent of females) engage in this activity (Kinsey et al., 1948, 1953).

Research has revealed considerable cultural differences in what is considered normal. One of the few studies that have directly compared sexual behaviour in Canada to that in other countries, examined 2230 students from the United States, Canada, England, Germany, and Norway (Luckey & Nass, 1969). The European students were more likely to have had premarital intercourse, with the differences especially notable among women; Canadian and U.S. samples differed little.

Some norms for sexual behaviour also change with time. Beginning in the mid-1960s, liberalization of attitudes toward sexuality appeared to be accompanied by greater sexual experience. (There are few earlier statistics available, since mores did not allow the questions to be widely asked.) A study of Canadian university students reported that, from 1968 to 1978, the percentage of female students who had had intercourse increased from 32 to 58 percent, and of male students from 40 to 62 percent (Barrett, 1980).

A more recent survey of 1655 teenaged girls in Nova Scotia suggests the trend is continuing: 71 percent of the 18-year-olds, 59 percent of the 16-to-17-year-olds, and 31 percent of the 14-to-15-year-olds reported being sexually active (Day, 1990).

William Masters and Virginia Johnson (1966) were the first investigators to study and document the physiological stages that take place in the normal human sexual response. They noted the changes that occur in the body with increased sexual arousal, orgasm, and the return to the unaroused state, and referred to this sequence as the **sexual response cycle**. Masters and Johnson divided the sexual response cycle into four stages: excitement, plateau, orgasm, and resolution.

During the *excitement* phase, the genital tissues of both males and females swell as they fill with blood (vasocongestion). This causes erection of the penis in men and engorgement and lubrication of the vaginal area in women.

Sex therapists William Masters and Virginia Johnson.

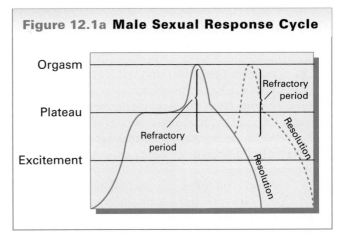

Figure 12.1a shows a typical pattern of physiological changes in male sexual response, characterized by a period of mounting excitement, a plateau phase, and a brief, intense orgasm followed by a return to baseline. In some cases, after a refractory period, a second rise in excitement and orgasm may occur. While male responses vary in some aspects, both within and across individuals, the overall pattern remains the same.

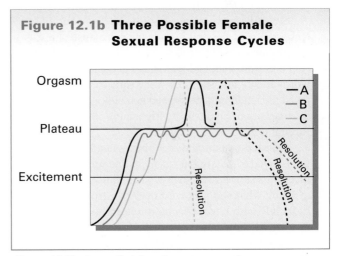

Figure 12.1b shows that female response patterns are more variable. Line A shows a pattern similar to the typical male cycle. Lines B and C represent other common response cycles, but by no means exhaust the possibilities. Note that, although line B does not show an orgasmic response in physiological terms, women experiencing such a response will report orgasm.

Source: Adapted from W. H. Masters & V. E. Johnson, *Human sexual response* (Boston: Little Brown, 1966), p. 5.

Other areas, such as the testes and nipples, also become engorged and there is an increase in muscular tension. Heart rate increases and breathing becomes more rapid and shallow. The *plateau* phase consolidates this arousal, with additional swelling of penis and vaginal tissues. In men, the testes become elevated and may reach 1 1/2 times their unaroused size. In women, the clitoris retracts underneath the clitoral hood and the inner part of the vagina expands. During *orgasm*, both sexes experience rhythmic, muscular contractions at about eight-second intervals. In men, orgasm comprises two stages, which quickly follow one another. First, seminal fluid collects in the urethral bulb, at the base of the penis. As this happens, there is a sense of orgasmic inevitability and nothing can prevent ejaculation from following. Within two or three seconds, contractions lead to expulsion of the ejaculate from the penis. Women experience contractions of the uterus and of the pelvic muscles surrounding the vagina during orgasm. Blood pressure and heart rate reach a peak during orgasm and there are involuntary muscular contractions. Following orgasm, the body gradually returns to its prearoused state, in the stage that Masters and Johnson called *resolution*. Shortly after ejaculation, men experience what is called a refractory period, during which they are unresponsive to sexual stimulation. Women, however, may be able to experience multiple orgasms without any refractory period. Figure 12.1 describes the sexual response cycles of men and women derived from Masters and Johnson's research.

Helen Singer Kaplan (1979) proposed an alternative model of sexual stages, consisting of desire, excitement, and orgasm. An important contribution of her work was the distinction of desire as primarily a psychological component to the sexual response. She also treated the stages as independent components, and noted that normal sexual experiences do not necessarily follow the full sequence described by Masters and Johnson. Thus, a couple's sexual encounter may sometimes involve excitement followed by diminished arousal without orgasm. To suggest that this sequence is not part of normal sexual experience is not only an inaccurate description of people's experiences but encourages an unhealthy expectation that people should always proceed through a predetermined pattern of sexual behaviour.

Sexual Dysfunctions

Joan came for help at the insistence of her best friend, in whom she had confided. Recently, Joan had become interested in a man. Ron, she believed, was gentle and caring, and she wanted to return his affection. Joan had never had an orgasm; she thought that this had contributed to the breakdown of her only previous relationship and was afraid it would mar things with Ron.

Joan had been reared in a strict religious family in which the word "sex" had never been spoken. Anything to do with the body was held to be shameful and disgusting. Her parents never showed open affection, and, although her mother hugged her, her father merely shook her hand when she left home for university.

Shy and obedient, Joan had always avoided embarrassing conversations at school and was totally unprepared for her first menstruation. Thinking she was dreadfully sick, she raced home, and was chided by her mother for making such a fuss. Joan had never touched her own body except while washing, and felt uncomfortable even seeing herself undressed in a mirror.

Sexually inexperienced when she was courted by Robert, Joan tolerated his advances because she was too embarrassed to protest. She believed she should stop him from making love to her, but could not find the words to say no. She grew very fond of him and enjoyed the tenderness he showed her, although she found the intensity of his sexuality frightening and completely foreign to her own experience.

Joan felt constricted by Robert's needs, which she felt obliged to satisfy but resented. She was completely unable to express her own wishes, but expected him to know what she wanted. Finally, in frustration, she broke off with him, refusing to return his phone calls or open his letters.

Joan had read some popular materials about sexuality in the last several years, and begun to think there was something wrong with her. The books suggested that she shouldn't be afraid or ashamed of her own sexuality but she couldn't shake these feelings.

As this case illustrates, multiple factors (for example, shame and ignorance about sex, anxiety about sex, lack of experience with physical affection, and low self-confidence) may contribute to the development of sexual dysfunctions. Joan's problem clearly developed over time, becoming worse the more she worried about it. By the time someone like Joan consults a therapist, the problem has typically become complex and involves secondary difficulties such as relationship problems and low self-esteem.

DSM-IV (American Psychiatric Association, 1994) uses an amalgamation of Masters and Johnson's (1966) and Kaplan's (1979) components of the sexual response in classifying sexual dysfunctions. It categorizes them according to which of the three phases is affected: desire, arousal, or orgasm. A separate category deals with instances in which pain is the primary complaint. (See DSM table.)

Each of the sexual dysfunctions can be further classified into several subtypes. For example, if the person has always experienced the problem, then the disorder is called **lifelong sexual dysfunction**; if it is of fairly recent onset, then it is said to be an **acquired sexual dysfunction**. In addition, sexual dysfunctions may be apparent with all partners and even during solitary sexual activity, in which case they would be termed **generalized sexual dysfunctions**; when the problem is apparent only with one partner (for example, the client's spouse) then they are known as **situational sexual dysfunctions**.

We know very little about the prevalence of sexual dysfunctions and even less about their incidence (Spector & Carey, 1990). Existing epidemiological studies are few and suffer from methodological shortcomings. Table 12.1 shows estimates of the prevalence of sexual problems, although these problems were not defined in DSM-IV terms.

In reviewing reports from a wide variety of studies, Bancroft (1989) found that a lack of sexual interest was the most common complaint of women attending sex clinics, whereas Kaplan (1974) reported orgasmic dysfunction to be the most common problem among women.

Altogether, the evidence suggests that some degree of sexual dysfunction is very common. Stephen Levine, past president of the Society for Sex Therapy and Research, recently observed: "The lifetime prevalence of sexual dysfunctions may be so high that almost every man or woman who lives a long life can be expected to qualify for a diagnosis at some time" (Levine, 1989, pp. 215–216). However, data from one of the most frequently cited surveys (Frank, Anderson, & Rubinstein, 1978) suggests caution in interpreting survey findings. Frank et al. evaluated 100 couples who were not seeking treatment for any sexual or other disorder. These researchers noted that individuals may experience sexual difficulties without necessarily being dissatisfied with their marriages or even with their sexual relations. Forty percent of the men and 63 percent of the women reported at least occasional sexual dysfunctions, but these did not detract from their overall enjoyment of their sexual relationship. Among a Swedish sample of 58 randomly selected men, there was a similar absence of a relation between sexual dysfunction and satisfaction (Nettelbladt & Uddenberg, 1979).

Sexual Desire Disorders

In Woody Allen's *Annie Hall*, Annie and her partner, Alvy, are shown in separate conversations with their therapists. While the two agree on the number of times a week they engage in sex, Alvy says to his therapist "We never have sex," while Annie says "We have sex all the time." Obviously, the same data were regarded differently by these two people. Both Kinsey and Masters and Johnson found that the frequency of masturbation among men varied from less than once per month to

DSM-IV Diagnostic Criteria for Sexual Dysfunction

Characterized by disturbances in sexual desire and disruptions in the psychophysiological changes that normally occur in the sexual response cycle, with these causing distress and interpersonal difficulties.

Sexual Desire Disorders	
Hypoactive sexual desire disorder	Persistently deficient or absent sexual fantasies and desires
Sexual aversion disorder	Persistently extreme aversion to, and avoidance of, sexual contact with another person
Sexual Arousal Disorders	
Female sexual arousal disorder	Persistent inability to generate and maintain adequate lubrication/swelling response of sexual excitement
Male erectile disorder	Persistent inability to generate or maintain adequate erection
Orgasmic Disorders	
Female orgasmic disorder	Persistent delay in, or absence of, orgasm following normal sexual excitement phase
Male orgasmic disorder	Persistent delay in, or absence of, orgasm following normal sexual excitement phase
Premature ejaculation	Persistent ejaculation with minimal sexual stimulation, either before or shortly after penetration
Sexual Pain Disorders	
Dyspareunia	Persistent genital pain during intercourse
Vaginismus	Persistent involuntary spasm of the musculature of the outer third of the vagina

Source: Reprinted with permission from the *Diagnostic and Statistical Manual of Mental Disorders*, Fourth Edition. Copyright 1994 American Psychiatric Association.

Table 12.1 Prevalence of Sexual Dysfunctions

Females		Males	
Lack of interest	59%	Lack of interest	33%
Being turned off	36%	Being turned off	26%
Difficulty becoming excited	48%	Difficulty achieving erection	7%
Difficulty maintaining excitement	33%	Difficulty maintaining erection	9%
Problems achieving orgasm	46%	Inability to have an orgasm	15%
Reaching orgasm too fast	11%	Premature ejaculation	36%
Any problems	77%	Any problems	50%

Source: Adapted from E. Frank, C. Anderson, & D. Rubinstein, Frequency of sexual dysfunction in "normal" couples, *The New England Journal of Medicine, 299(1978),* 111–115.

several times per day. However, all of these men regarded their own frequency as "normal"; they thought that a man with higher frequencies was "abnormal," and they considered lower frequencies to be indicative of "low sex drive." These two examples illustrate both the differences among individuals in sexual interest or desire and the subjective nature of people's definition of the "normal" frequency of sexual desires.

In DSM-IV, sexual desire disorders are subdivided into two categories: **hypoactive sexual desire disorder** and **sexual aversion disorder**. For a diagnosis of hypoactive sexual desire disorder, DSM-IV requires a persistent or recurrent deficiency of sexual fantasies and desire for sex, causing marked distress or interpersonal difficulty. Note that desire is not the same as arousal; we are talking here not about the

presence or absence of a physiological response, but about the person who "just doesn't feel like it." Sexual aversion disorder is diagnosed if there is persistent or recurrent, extreme aversion to, and avoidance of, almost all genital sex with a partner, causing marked distress or interpersonal difficulty. Sexual aversion disorder may also include panic attacks, extreme anxiety, and avoidance of partners.

Hypoactive desire is among the most difficult dysfunctions to define, because of the importance of context. Desire may occur in some situations but not in others, and sexual activity may occur without desire, in both males and females. Social pressures for high levels of sexual interest may play a role in elevating performance pressure and creating unrealistic expectations. Partners differ in their desire and a partner with intense desire may label the other as having a problem (Rosen & Leiblum, 1989). As Alvy and Annie illustrate, what is considered deficient or normal varies a great deal among individuals.

In fact, some have criticized the existence of such a diagnosis as a reflection of culturally imposed standards that are typically male-centred and hypersexual. The very term *hypoactive* implies an established standard—but whose? A population average? A clinical consensus? However it is defined, a standard of desire is value-laden and many question its appropriateness.

Sexual Arousal Disorders

Sexual arousal disorders involve difficulty becoming physically aroused when the person desires such arousal. In the case of males, sexual arousal or lack of arousal is usually gauged by penile erection, not the only physiological response but certainly the most obvious. Female sexual arousal, however, is less directly evident, and women can have intercourse without arousal. Perhaps for this reason, female sexual arousal disorder may be the least understood sexual dysfunction (Spector & Carey, 1990). Note, again, the difference between desire and arousal. We are talking here not about the person who is "not in the mood" but about someone who is emotionally and mentally interested in sex but who does not become physiologically aroused. This disorder is probably underdiagnosed in women. A woman who is not aroused will, naturally, not experience an orgasm, and such women may be misdiagnosed as having orgasmic dysfunction (Wakefield, 1987). This does not happen with men. The failure to achieve an erection is diagnosed quite separately from a failure to ejaculate (a male orgasmic disorder).

The DSM-IV diagnostic criteria for **female sexual arousal disorder** include a persistent or recurrent inability to attain or maintain arousal "until completion of the sexual activity," and the presence of marked distress or difficulty. DSM-IV defines the presence and maintenance of arousal in terms of genital vasocongestion. A woman may, however, be physiologically aroused (that is, she may experience the lubrication and swelling that accompany vasocongestion) but be unaware of it (Heiman, 1975). Since this criterion of arousal is rarely measured directly, and typically rests on the woman's reported arousal, misdiagnosis may occur. It might, then, have been better for DSM-IV to have retained from the earlier version of the manual the criterion of subjective arousal.

Because this diagnosis has largely been neglected, it is difficult to estimate its prevalence. Forty-eight percent of a community sample of women reported "difficulty getting excited," and 33 percent endorsed having "difficulty maintaining excitement" (Frank, Anderson, & Rubinstein, 1978).

Male erectile disorder is present, according to DSM-IV, when there is a persistent or recurrent inability to reach or sustain an erection "until completion of the sexual activity" and resultant distress. The previous term for this problem, *impotence*, acquired such negative connotations that it has been abandoned in the official nomenclature, although it is still widely used by the general public and by many practitioners.

Erectile problems, while certainly not new, have gained increased public attention, partly because of current expectations for lifelong sexuality, women's increased expectations of sexual satisfaction, and media attention (Tiefer & Melman, 1989). Erectile dysfunction is the most common complaint of men who seek assistance for sexual problems (Bancroft, 1989; Spector & Carey, 1990). About 2 percent of Kinsey's total male sample (Kinsey et al., 1948) reported permanent erectile difficulty and 42 percent reported at least occasional erectile problems (Gebhard & Johnson, 1979). At sex therapy clinics, men complaining of erectile dysfunction make up from 36 percent to 53 percent of the patients (Spector & Carey, 1990).

Erectile problems can be devastating for men. Difficulty attaining or maintaining an erection often leads to embarrassment, depression, even suicidal inclinations. Because the problem carries such connotations about masculinity, men with erectile difficulty are likely to delay seeking help and to avoid confronting the problem, and may try home remedies, such as alcohol, before approaching a professional. The relationship with a sexual partner is likely to be affected, not just by the erectile problem, but by the avoidance, depression, and other secondary problems that follow. As a result, by the time a man and his partner seek help, the problem is likely to seem overwhelming and to be much more complex and intractable than it might have been earlier.

Orgasmic Disorders

Orgasmic disorders are some of the most commonly reported sexual dysfunctions. Both males and females may experience difficulty in reaching orgasm.

The DSM-IV diagnostic criteria for **female orgasmic disorder**, also known as **anorgasmia**, require a persistent or recurrent delay in, or absence of, orgasm following normal excitement, causing marked distress or interpersonal difficulty. As with other sexual dysfunctions, it is evident that this diagnosis calls for subjective judgements in determining, for example, what constitutes "persistent" or "recurrent," what amounts to a "delay," and what is "normal excitement."

Kinsey was the first researcher to pay attention to female orgasms, counting them for women as he did for men (Kinsey et al., 1953). In his work, Kinsey noted that women were more likely to experience orgasm through masturbation than with a partner, a finding that has since been replicated (Spector & Carey, 1990). These observations led to marked changes in the way women's sexual functioning was viewed, and today female orgasmic disorder is typically cited as the most common sexual problem presented at sex clinics. The rates among clinical samples range from 18 percent to 76 percent (Spector & Carey, 1990).

Male orgasmic disorder is defined in the same way as female orgasmic disorder, but is much less common. DSM-IV criteria require a persistent or recurrent delay in, or absence of, orgasm following normal excitement, causing marked distress or interpersonal difficulty. In these men, orgasm may be possible only with oral or manual stimulation or only during erotic dreams, but not during intercourse.

Between 1 percent to 8 percent of men attending clinics report orgasmic disorder, as do 1 percent to 10 percent of community samples (Spector & Carey, 1990). The dysfunction appears, however, to be more frequent (up to 17 percent) among males seeking marital therapy, and is reported as the second most frequent dysfunction among gays seeking sex therapy (Spector & Carey, 1990).

Premature Ejaculation

Premature ejaculation occurs when the man persistently ejaculates with minimal stimulation and often before or immediately following intromission (entry of the penis into the vagina). As with all sexual dysfunctions, if early ejaculation does not cause marked distress or interpersonal difficulty, the diagnosis is not made.

Determining what constitutes "premature" has presented problems in assessment and research. One approach has been to use a time limit, such as within one or two minutes of intromission. The Kinsey data would suggest that this criterion would lead to a high rate of diagnosis, for 26 percent of his male sample reported ejaculating within two minutes of intromission (Gebhard & Johnson, 1979). LoPiccolo (1978) had argued that a minimum of four minutes of sexual stimulation before ejaculation occurs is a reasonable criterion for effective functioning. This standard was widely adopted prior to DSM-IV, which defines as dysfunctional ejaculation occurring with minimal stimulation. The DSM-IV definition allows the diagnostician to take into account both the client's notion of what is satisfactory and what the clinician sees as a reasonable duration of sexual stimulation prior to ejaculation.

An alternative criterion has been movement-oriented, such as before 20 seconds of rapid thrusting. Masters and Johnson (1970) suggested a couple-oriented criterion, diagnosing premature ejaculation when it occurred at least 50 percent of the time before the partner's orgasm. In a survey of more than 700 women, Darling, Davidson, and Cox (1991) reported an average preferred length of intercourse of over eleven minutes, which is longer than most males typically take to ejaculate (Spector & Carey, 1990). Voluntariness of control, that is, the male's sense of having control over ejaculation, has also been used as a criterion.

However it is defined, premature ejaculation appears to be the most common sexual complaint of males in the community (Grenier & Byers, 1995), and yet it is a less frequent complaint at sex therapy clinics than erectile disorder (Spector & Carey, 1990). It seems that, for most men and their partners, premature ejaculation is not a sufficiently serious problem to lead them to seek treatment.

Sexual Pain Disorders

Dyspareunia refers to genital pain associated with intercourse. Painful intercourse is rare among men, and usually associated with infections, inflammation, or physical anomalies. For DSM-IV diagnosis, dyspareunia must cause marked distress or interpersonal difficulty and must not be caused exclusively by lack of lubrication or by vaginismus, which is a separate disorder. Yitzchak Binik, at McGill University's Department of Psychology, and his Ph.D. student, Marta Meana, surveyed 26 years of published work on dyspareunia (Meana & Binik, 1994). They noted that some experts claim lack of lubrication is the most common cause of the problem, yet DSM, as noted, excludes all of these cases.

The true incidence and prevalence of dyspareunia are unknown. There are prevalence reports varying from 2.6 percent to 33 percent, but all studies have serious limitations (Glatt, Zinner, & McCormack, 1990; Meana & Binik, 1994) including varying definitions of the disorder. It has been claimed that dyspareunia is the second most common female dysfunction and that it is increasingly reported in clinics.

One study in New York (Glatt et al., 1990) surveyed 324 women in their early thirties. Thirty-three percent of these women had persistent dyspareunia at the time of the study; in addition, almost 30 percent had previously experienced dyspareunia. In 34 percent of the cases of dyspareunia, the women reported an important adverse effect on their relationships and 48 percent reported a decrease in frequency of intercourse as a result. Fewer than half of those still experiencing dyspareunia had ever consulted a health care professional about the problem.

Vaginismus is the persistent involuntary contraction of the muscles in the outer third of the vagina upon attempts at penetration. The muscle contractions prevent penetration by the penis, and usually by a tampon or a speculum during a gynecological examination. If penetration is attempted, it may be extremely painful or impossible. Vaginismus may become so severe that even the anticipation of vaginal entry may trigger it. Some instances clearly relate to painful trauma (rape or traumatic gynecological exam) but most cases are lifelong (Bancroft, 1989). Some cases may spontaneously remit, but DSM-IV suggests a chronic course unless treatment is received. No reliable data are available on the general incidence of vaginismus. John Lamont (1978) reported that at the Human Sexuality Clinic at McMaster University in Hamilton, 47 percent of all patients seen between 1972 and 1976 received a diagnosis of vaginismus; other clinic reports have varied from 12 percent to 55 percent (Spector & Carey, 1990).

Etiology of Sexual Dysfunctions

Most of the research on the causes of sexual dysfunctions has focussed on specific disorders, although all these disorders possess common factors to some degree. Clearly, both physical and psychological factors are involved in the development of most if not all sexual dysfunctions, although one factor or another may be more important in a given case. The ViewPoint box discusses procedures to identify organic and psychogenic features of specific disorders, but the results are not to be understood as a determination of which set of influences apply, but rather of their relative importance.

VIEWPOINT *Male Erectile Disorder: Organic or Psychological?*

One of the major treatment and research issues concerning male erectile disorder is whether the problem is of organic origin or psychologically induced. The question is important, because one would not expect psychological treatments to be effective if the problem has a physical cause. It was at one time believed that as many as 95 percent of all cases of erectile disorder were psychologically caused (Masters & Johnson, 1970). Recently, however, it has been estimated that between one-third and two-thirds of men with erectile failure have some degree of organic impairment (LoPiccolo, 1992).

One test for physical or psychological origin is whether a man has erections during sleep (Fisher, Gross, & Zuch, 1965). Nighttime erections are measured using what is called **nocturnal penile tumescence** (NPT). NPT measures require the client to sleep in a laboratory over several nights with a device attached to his penis. This device records changes in the circumference of the penis as a result of the blood inflow that produces an erection. The figure here shows the most commonly used device. Originally this procedure, called **phallometry**, was developed to assess, during waking hours, a man's preferences for various sexual acts or particular sexual partners (see the Focus box).

The rationale for NPT is the assumption that the interpersonal, attitudinal, and emotional factors that prevent effective functioning when the man is awake will not be influential during sleep (Rosen & Beck, 1988). However, some studies indicate that NPT may be more affected by psychological phenomena than its advocates claim (Schiavi, 1992). For example, simply the stress of being assessed seems to affect the frequency of erectile responses during sleep, particularly on the first night of testing (Jovanovic, 1969). Also, depression, which is a common feature of men with erectile disorder, influences the frequency and duration of nocturnal erections (Roose, Glassman, Walsh, &

This phallometry device records changes in the circumference of the penis.

Cullen, 1982). More to the point, recent evidence indicates that NPT responses can be impaired in psychogenic cases (Buvat, Buvat-Herbaut, Lemaire, Marcolin, & Quittelier, 1990). Nevertheless, advocates of NPT claim that nighttime erections will either be absent or markedly diminished in men with organic erectile dysfunction (Karacan, 1970). Indeed, several studies have shown lower NPT in men with erectile dysfunction than in normal men (Rosen & Beck, 1988).

Clinicians also examine the man's history of sexual functioning, the presence of any known similar problems in family members, his current and past medical history, his use of medications and nonprescription drugs, his age, and his serum testosterone. Circulating testosterone is considered to stimulate sexual behaviour (Rosen & Beck, 1988) and low levels of serum testosterone are associated with erectile difficulty (Spark, 1991). Various drugs (for example, antihypertensive and antidepressant medication and alcohol) have been shown to lower sexual interest. Increasing age in men is related to an increased likelihood of erectile problems (Segraves & Segraves, 1992), as are diseases such as diabetes, peripheral neuropathy, and vascular disorders (Malatesta & Adams, 1984).

If a man has had erectile difficulties all his life, the possibility of an organic basis is increased. If his problem is of recent onset, and is not associated with changes in medication or physical disease, it is more likely that his erectile dysfunction is psychogenic. Obviously if the erectile difficulty is situational (for example, it occurs with one partner but not with others), psychological factors must be at the basis of the problem. When there are clear indications of erectile dysfunction in other male members of the client's family, organic causes are suggested.

Queen's University researchers Marshall, Surridge, and Delva (1981), using information gathered on these various factors, found that each of their clients could be categorized as belonging to one of three groups. The first group was classified as having organic signs because they had physical diseases or were suffering from the consequences of surgery. The second group, which they identified as having psychogenic origins to their disorder, reported chronic marital discord and depression, and were clearly anxious about their performance. The final group in Marshall et al.'s classification had mixed organic and psychological signs, so the researchers concluded that the basis for their problem was uncertain. To test the accu-

VIEWPOINT *continued*

racy of NPT measures, Marshall and his colleagues focussed on the first and the second group, where the cause was believed to be known. (It is the third group, of course, for whom the tests could be most useful clinically.) Marshall et al. were, on the basis of NPT responses, able to correctly classify 9 of the 10 organic group and 7 of the 10 psychogenic clients. When a criterion of fewer than two NPT episodes per night was used to identify organic causes, while three or more erections identified a psychogenic basis, all but one of the 20 subjects were correctly classified.

While this study was taken to support the value of NPT assessments, recent critics (LoPiccolo, 1992) have suggested that the idea of attempting to distinguish organic and psychogenic causes of erectile dysfunction is misplaced because many, if not most, cases involve both. Support for this claim comes from studies demonstrating that psychological treatment can be effective even when there are clear signs of physical impairment (Carey, Wincze, & Meisler, 1993). Nevertheless, this issue, and the associated investigative strategies, including NPT assessments, remain central

in the work of clinicians dealing with clients who have erectile dysfunction.

Critical Thinking Questions

1. Why do clinicians think it is necessary to distinguish organic from psychogenic origins for male erectile disorder?
2. If a man who has daytime erectile difficulties fails to show any erections during sleep, does that mean his problems must be organic in origin?
3. What are the present limits to evaluations aimed at distinguishing psychogenic from organic causes of male erectile disorder?

Almost everyone experiences some sort of sexual performance difficulty at one time or another. Excessive alcohol, for example, may cause a temporary lessening of desire or interfere with erection or orgasm. After a long period without sex, or the first time with a new partner, a man may ejaculate prematurely. Usually the problem disappears with the situation that caused it. But a person who is very upset by such an experience may so carefully monitor his or her responses during the next sexual encounter that dysfunctioning may occur. This second perceived failure, of course, only leads to greater anxiety, and a chronic dysfunction may emerge.

Sexual Desire Disorders

People with sexual desire disorders are generally not interested in anything sexual (Nutter & Condron, 1985), a pattern also apparent in depressed patients. This similarity has led to speculation that hypoactive sexual desire may result from depression. Consistently with this idea, Schreiner-Engel and Schiavi (1986) found that 73 percent of men and 71 percent of women with low desire had a history of mood disorders, while only 32 percent of matched normal males and 27 percent of matched normal females had a similar history. Furthermore, in 88 percent of the men and 100 percent of the women with a history of depression, their sexual desire disorder began shortly after the onset of their mood disorder. Kaplan (1979) emphasizes other psychological factors in sexual desire disorders. She notes the prevalence among these clients of dysfunctional attitudes about sex, relationship problems, and a strict upbringing that has associated sexual pleasure with guilt. Indeed, these appear to be factors in all sexual dysfunctions.

In addition to psychological difficulties that may precipitate sexual dysfunctions, abnormal hormonal functioning may cause problems. Certainly hormones such as **prolactin**, **testosterone** (the so-called male sex hormone), and **estrogen** (the so-called female sex hormone) are involved in sexual activity and desire, and variations in the levels of these

hormones can lower or increase sex drive (Rosen & Leiblum, 1995). However, the evidence suggests that abnormal hormonal levels play a part in only a few cases of sexual desire disorder (Kresin, 1993).

Sexual Arousal Disorders

There is clear evidence that sexual abuse often leads to impairment of sexual arousal in women (Morokoff, 1993). Troubled relationships and general stress appear to lessen arousal, as do hormonal factors.

Male erectile disorder may be caused by vascular disease, neurological deficits, priapism (permanent erection, which can damage erectile structures), diabetes, and various medications, including drugs to treat blood pressure and mood-altering drugs (Bancroft, 1989). Masters and Johnson (1970) estimated that psychological factors were primary in 95 percent of the cases of erectile dysfunction. Recent estimates suggest something closer to a 50/50 split between biogenic and psychogenic origins (Everaerd, 1993). However, problems with the studies make these estimates unreliable. In many cases, both psychological and organic causes may be important.

Perhaps the most commonly reported factor associated with arousal disorders, and to some extent all sexual dysfunctions, is what Masters and Johnson (1970) originally called performance anxiety. **Performance anxiety** is the response of dysfunctional people who feel they are expected to perform sexually. Worried that their performance will not be up to the expectations of their partner, they become *spectators* of their own behaviour, monitoring their own sexual performance and the perceived responses of their partner. When this happens the person's focus is on the performance rather than on enjoyment of the sexual experience. Like the watched pot that never boils, the spontaneous sensory response of sexual arousal is blocked. However, anxiety can affect sexual functioning simply as a result of increased activity in the sympathetic branch of the autonomic nervous system. When sympathetic activity occurs, as happens when someone is anxious, its activity inhibits the parasympathetic branch. Since sexual arousal is associated with activation of the parasympathetic branch, inhibition of this branch by sympathetic activity will interfere with sexual arousal and may, as a result, cause sexual dysfunction.

Abrahamson and his colleagues (Abrahamson, Barlow, & Abrahamson, 1989) examined this idea in a controlled laboratory study. They had men with and without erectile difficulties watch an erotic film under three conditions: (1) demand distraction, in which they also monitored their erectile responses by watching feedback of their arousal revealed by penile plethysmography (see the Focus box on measuring sexual arousal for a description of this procedure); (2) neutral distraction, in which they were required to estimate the length of a line displayed on a separate TV monitor; and (3) a no-distraction condition where they simply watched the erotic film. The dysfunctional men showed a significantly lower erectile response under the demand condition than they did under either of the other two conditions. For the normally functioning men, on the other hand, the demand condition increased erectile response, presumably because for them feedback about their arousal enhanced their sexual feelings. These results clearly support the idea that when dysfunctional men monitor their sexual arousal it interferes with their erectile responses.

Orgasmic Disorders

Orgasmic disorders are generally thought to involve primarily psychological factors, but certain medical conditions (for example, heart or circulatory problems) and some medications can cause anorgasmia in women. Again, relationship difficulties are common, although it is often hard to know whether these difficulties preceded or were caused by the sexual dysfunction. Limited sexual techniques, a lack of understanding of their own response, and a partner who does not understand their needs may all play a role, as does an inability to let go and allow the natural response to sexual stimulation to occur. As shown in the case of Joan, these barriers are more difficult to overcome if a woman feels constrained in discussing sex with her partner or in exploring techniques.

Premature Ejaculation

Premature ejaculation is also thought to be primarily psychologically caused. Bancroft (1989) has noted that boys' first sexual experiences usually involve masturbation, where rapid ejaculation is no disadvantage, and may even be an advantage. This may produce a conditioned response of rapid ejaculation, which may subsequently prove too fast for his partner; if the man worries about it, his performance anxiety may exacerbate the problem.

Vaginismus/Dyspareunia

Most researchers have concluded that vaginismus is primarily psychogenic in origin. It is thought that conditioned fear of intercourse produces the involuntary contractions. This conditioned fear is assumed to result from unpleasant or traumatic sexual experiences such as rape or child sexual abuse.

However, there is no systematic research available to support these popularly held clinical opinions. Beck (1993) points out that most of the published literature on vaginismus is no more than clinical reports which, while to some extent informative, do not provide a sound basis for inferring the causes of the problem. The same is true for dyspareunia.

Treatment of Sexual Dysfunctions

Psychological Interventions

Until the publication of Masters and Johnson's (1970) book describing their treatment approach, there was very little literature on therapy for sexual dysfunctions. Masters and Johnson described a comprehensive and intensive approach that required couples to live in their clinic for two weeks. Many aspects of Masters and Johnson's approach have been retained or modified at other clinics, so that most programs now share a number of common elements. Most programs see sexual dysfunctions as involving two people and, as a consequence, they typically insist that both partners attend treatment.

Communication and exploration. The majority of programs begin with an extensive assessment of the couple, including a detailed sexual history. This is typically followed by sex education, where information is provided and maladaptive ideas about sex are challenged. Procedures are provided for enhancing communication between the partners, not only about sexual matters, but about all issues that may cause disharmony. Effective sexual communication first requires each partner to develop an understanding of his or her own sensations and bodily responses. Acceptance of their own bodies may be limited because of embarrassment or guilt. Accordingly, sex therapists often suggest exercises in which clients privately explore their own bodies and use masturbation to become aware of their own arousal response. Clients also learn to communicate their specific sexual preferences to one another so that they can give each other sexual pleasure.

Sensate focus. The final component in sex therapy programs is what Masters and Johnson (1970) called **sensate focus**: essentially a form of desensitization applied to sexual fears (see the description of desensitization for phobias in Chapter 7). It is assumed that once the sexual dysfunction has developed, the person develops performance anxiety or fear, which serves to worsen and entrench the problem. This fear, then, must be overcome and sensate focus is the most frequently employed technique.

We cannot illustrate sensate focus with all the disorders, but one example should be sufficient. No matter what the disorder, the couple is initially instructed not to attempt intercourse until sufficient progress has been made. In the first step, they undress together with the light on to desensitize any embarrassment they may have about being naked together. They next take turns at massaging or touching one another all over except the genital or breast areas. They are learning to enjoy touching and being touched without any fear of imminent demands for sex. After several sessions of this, each person begins to tell the partner during the touching exercises what he or she enjoys. All of these sessions are interspersed with discussions with the therapists, meant to enhance communication skills and to identify and deal with any problems that arise during the touching sessions. As the couple becomes comfortable and they each begin to expand their enjoyment of the associated physical pleasures, they progress to the next stage, genital and breast touching. There is still, however, a moratorium on sexual intercourse to allow the couple to enjoy sexual sensations and arousal without the fear of having to perform. The aim is to eliminate spectatoring, allowing each partner to relax and focus on his or her own pleasure. Once the couple can maintain their pleasure without fear, they are advised to enter the last stage of sensate focus, which is designed specifically for the problem that brought them to the clinic.

In this final stage, the ban on sexual intercourse is lifted. However, the couple is instructed to progress slowly and to follow a particular gradual program aimed at overcoming the specific dysfunction. For premature ejaculation, for example, this part of sensate focus involves several steps. First, to avoid adding the muscular tension of supporting himself to the tension that builds with sexual excitement (which would encourage rapid ejaculation) the man lies on his back. His partner straddles his legs and stimulates his penis; when he feels the earliest sign of an orgasmic response, he tells her to stop. Sometimes just stopping is not enough to prevent the man from ejaculating. In those cases, the woman is instructed to apply the "squeeze technique," pressing hard with her thumb on the ventral side of the penis just below the head. Although it is not painful, the squeeze technique diminishes arousal and prevents ejaculation. The couple repeats this process until the man can withhold his ejaculatory response for extended periods. At this point the woman inserts the man's penis into her vagina and essentially repeats the same cycle until the man can tolerate sexual intercourse without orgasm long enough to maximize his partner's pleasure.

Evaluation of psychological treatment. Masters and Johnson (1970) claimed that over 80 percent of their clients were successfully treated for their various dysfunctions. However, they used a rather loose criterion of success and did not follow up their clients long enough to properly evaluate the maintenance of their gains.

More recent and careful evaluations have shown that premature ejaculation and vaginismus are most successfully treated with the type of therapy outlined above (Beck, 1993). Success rates as high as 80 percent for vaginismus and 90 percent for premature ejaculation have been reported. Erectile dysfunction has not fared so well, although as many as 70 percent of men with this disorder have been found to recover sufficient erectile capacity to have intercourse (Hawton, Catalan, & Fagg, 1992). For problems such as low desire or orgasmic dysfunction in women, directions to engage in self-masturbation appear to enhance the effects of comprehensive therapy (LoPiccolo, 1990).

Overall, psychological sex therapy has been quite successful in treating sexual dysfunctions. Some cases in which it is not successful may be attributable to undetected physical problems.

Physical Treatments

Physical treatments are best used in conjunction with psychological approaches, even in cases where there is a clear organic cause. In erectile disorder that has a physical basis, for example, there are nevertheless psychological features once the disorder is established. Such a man will very likely become afraid of failing and develop performance anxiety, which may remain a problem even after the physical cause has been corrected.

Medications of one kind or another have been shown to be helpful in some cases of sexual dysfunction. Antidepressants, for example, can delay the ejaculatory response and have led to improved sexual satisfaction in some men (Althof & Seftel, 1995). Of course, history is full of stories attributing the power of sexual stimulation to an almost endless list of supposed aphrodisiacs (Tannahill, 1980). Almost all presumed aphrodisiacs that have been evaluated failed to produce reliable effects.

However, one substance has received particular attention in recent years. Yohimbine hydrochloride was systematically evaluated by urologist Al Morales and his colleagues at the Impotence Clinic in Kingston, Ontario. Yohimbine rapidly increases heart rate and blood pressure and, thereby, increases blood flow to the penis. This ought to increase the probability of a man treated with yohimbine being able to achieve an erection. In an early study Morales and his colleagues (Morales, Surridge, Marshall, & Fenemore, 1982) demonstrated that 43 percent of patients diagnosed as having an organic basis to their erectile disorder recovered sufficient erectile capacity to have satisfactory intercourse with their partners. Several other studies have also shown benefits for yohimbine in treating erectile disorder in men (Segraves & Segraves, 1992). A later study by Morales et al. (1987) did not find significantly higher success rates for yohimbine over placebo with men whose problems were organically based. However, it is possible that recording data as either successful or not successful, rather than reflecting a spectrum of change, may have obscured improvements. Surprisingly, the drug was dramatically effective with erectile disorder judged to be psychogenically caused. Of these men treated with yohimbine, 62 percent subsequently had satisfactory erections, compared to only 16 percent of the placebo-treated patients (Reid et al., 1987).

Recently, considerable publicity has accompanied the announcement of a new medication for male erectile disorder. Sildenafil (marketed under the trade name "Viagra") was described by Goldstein et al. (1998) in the *New England Journal of Medicine* as having specific pharmacological effects on the corpus cavernosa in the penis in a way that ought to increase penile response to sexual stimulation. Accordingly, Goldstein and his colleagues evaluated its effects on men who could not generate and maintain an erection of sufficient quality to have intercourse. Their careful examination of these men revealed that some had an organic basis to their problem, others had psychogenic causes, and some had both organic and psychogenic problems. This is a particularly difficult group, given that many had organic causes to their erectile difficulties.

Goldstein et al. conducted two double-blind studies. The first study targeted 532 men with erectile difficulties, while the second included 329 men with this disorder. In both studies, Viagra was compared to a placebo pill, and in both cases, it proved remarkably effective. Sixty-nine percent of all attempts at intercourse were successful for the men taking Viagra, while only 22 percent of the attempts were successful on the placebo. Furthermore, increased doses were associated with improved erectile functioning. Only 6 to 18 percent of the men reported uncomfortable side-effects, such as headaches, flushing, and dyspepsia.

While Goldstein et al. found little in the way of troublesome side-effects, it is too early in the clinical use of Viagra to rule out the possibility of more problematic effects with long-term use. However, in view of sildenafil's promise of an easy treatment (Viagra is taken orally and only when the man wants to have sex) for this very difficult problem, the fact that Goldstein et al.'s results hold up is very encouraging. Future studies of its long-term effects should establish its usefulness more clearly.

Surgical interventions for women with sexual pain disorders were at one time quite common. These treatments were based on the mistaken assumption that increasing the vaginal opening would decrease the pain. Unfortunately, these procedures all too often simply eliminated all sensation. Surgery can be helpful with males with erectile dysfunction when the cause has been identified as a vascular blockage preventing adequate blood flow to the penis (Mohr & Beutler, 1990).

The most common physical treatment for sexual dysfunctions has been physical implants for men with erectile disorder. While a number of different implants were used in the past, currently the most popular approach is to implant in the penis inflatable silicone cylinders. (See Figure 12.2.) These cylinders are joined to a reservoir of fluid that has been inserted into the man's abdomen along with a tiny pump in the scrotum. To produce an erection, the man presses the pump, which pushes fluid from the reservoir into the cylinders. As the cylinders fill, they cause the penis to become erect. These implants have been very popular and the early evidence indicated that the patients and their partners were quite satisfied (Anderson & Wold, 1986). However, followup studies have shown that 40 percent of men with implants and their partners are not satisfied, in the long term, with the results. Fears associated with silicone implants and concerns about the invasiveness and irreversibility of the procedure appear to have reduced the popularity of this approach in recent years (Thomas & LoPiccolo, 1994).

Direct self-injection of the muscle relaxant papaverine is a recent technique that seems to enhance erectile capacity (Mohr & Beutler, 1990). However, many men find the procedure painful, or at least unpleasant, and the repeated injections can produce scar tissue. High refusal rates and numerous dropouts have limited the use of this procedure (Althof & Turner, 1992).

Figure 12.2 Penile Implant

Source: R. C. Rosen and S. R. Leiblum, eds., *Erectile disorders: Assessment and treatment* (New York: Guilford Press, 1992).

GENDER IDENTITY

Boys are expected to act like boys, and they are allowed little latitude before they are labelled "sissies." Girls who play hockey and prefer trucks to dolls are tolerated much better. Even so, when she was growing up, Leslie Feinberg was such a tomboy that she was rejected on all sides (Gilbert, 1996). As she matured, the female role chafed so much that eventually Leslie moved to New York and began to pass as a man. She dressed like a man, acted like a man, and expected others to treat her like a man.

In making this transition, Feinberg identified herself as "transgendered," or simply "trans." She rejected her categorization as female and insisted on having the right to live as she pleased without harassment. Her transformation dealt with more than gender: Feinberg became a spokesperson for a new movement of those in society who have been marginalized. These are the women and men who feel that they are the victims of cruel accidents of biology—that they were born the wrong sex.

Most people are gonadally, genetically, hormonally, genitally, reproductively, and socially the same sex as they "feel" they are. If they have ovaries, they also have a clitoris, vagina, uterus, and breasts, XX chromosomes, and heightened estrogen levels at puberty. They are treated as female by parents and others, and have a private, internal sense of femaleness. If they have testicles, they have a penis, beard, male pattern of body hair, XY pair of chromosomes, heightened testosterone levels at puberty, and a sense of maleness. It is the sense of being female or male that constitutes an individual's gender identity.

Three aspects of the development of gender identity are separable: sexual orientation, gender role, and gender identity. **Sexual orientation** refers to the preferred age and sex of the person's partner. Gays and lesbians have a same-sex orientation, whereas heterosexuals have an opposite-sex orientation. **Gender role** is the collection of those characteristics that a society defines as masculine or feminine. Because roles relate to social standards, ideas about gender role change over time and from culture to culture. **Gender identity** refers to a person's basic sense of self as male or female, the first signs of which appear between 18 and 36 months of age.

In some instances these "variables of gender" (Money, 1987) do not all coincide. In rare cases where the actual biological variables are discordant, **hermaphroditism** occurs, with the reproductive structures being partly female and partly male. When the biological variables are consistent, but are discordant with the person's sense of self, gender identity disorder occurs.

Gender Identity Disorders

A "trans" activist, such as Leslie Feinberg, might appear to fulfill the DSM-IV criteria for **gender identity disorder** (GID, previously known as transsexualism—see the DSM table "Gender Identity Disorder"). She has experienced a "strong and persistent cross-gender identification" and reported "persistent discomfort with ... her sex or sense of inappropriateness in the gender role of that sex" (American Psychiatric Association, 1994, p. 537). This latter feature (that is, discomfort with biologically endowed sex) is referred to as **gender dysphoria**. Thus, if a biological male says he does not feel like a male but rather feels like a female trapped in a man's body, then he would be experiencing gender dysphoria. The diagnosis of gender identity disorder also requires, however, that there be "clinically significant distress or impairment in social, occupational, or other important areas of function-

---

DSM-IV Diagnostic Criteria for Gender Identity Disorder

A strong and persistent cross-gender identification.

(a) In children, GID is shown by four or more of the following:

1. Repeated desire to be the other sex
2. Preference for, or insistance on, wearing clothes that are stereotypically of the other sex
3. Preference for cross-sex roles in play
4. Desire to play stereotypical games of the other sex
5. Preference for playmates of the other sex

(b) In adults, GID is shown by:

1. Desire to be other sex
2. Frequent attempts to pass as other sex
3. Desire to live as other sex
4. Conviction that he/she has the feelings and reactions of other sex

Source: Reprinted with permission from the *Diagnostic and Statistical Manual of Mental Disorders*, Fourth Edition. Copyright 1994 American Psychiatric Association.

---

ing" (p. 538). Feinberg argues that she is perfectly well-adjusted to her transgendered life, although society may have difficulty with it. Such individuals may fulfill some of the cross-gender requirements for the diagnosis, but they do not completely fit the criteria because their gender identity appears not to result in severe distress.

Because they feel that they are physically the *wrong* sex, people with gender identity disorders may cross-dress (known as transvestism) or attempt in other ways to rid themselves of secondary sex characteristics. They may request hormonal treatment, or other physical alterations, such as electrolysis to remove facial hair, in attempts to assume the role of the other sex. In some instances, they undertake surgery to change their anatomy, and are then known as transsexuals.

Green and Blanchard (1995) report that gender identity disorder occurs more commonly in children than in adults, with 3 percent of boys and 1 percent of girls identified as having the disorder. In fact, the gender dysphoria associated with gender identity disorder most commonly begins in childhood; most adults having this disorder report gender-role conflicts and transsexual feelings occurring at a very early age (Tsoi, 1990). However, in adults the prevalence of gender identity disorder is quite low: approximately one in 30,000 men, and one in 100,000 to 150,000 women (American Psychiatric Association, 1994).

Some individuals with GID are attracted to those of the biologically opposite sex, some are attracted to the same sex, some are attracted to both, and some are attracted to neither. There seem to be significant differences between these groups of "gender dysphorics," especially between the homosexual group and the rest.

Homosexual gender dysphoria occurs among people with GID who are attracted to individuals of the same biological sex—for example, men who feel they are women and are attracted to men. They do not find cross-dressing sexually arousing (as do transvestites), but are drawn to it as part of their cross-gender identification because they see themselves as really females. Although Blanchard (1989) has provided some information about female homosexual gender dysphorics, most of the information about this group comes from studies of males. These men report having been attracted only to other men from their earliest sexual awareness (Zucker, 1990a). Many were effeminate as children and were ostracized and labelled "sissies" by their peers. Although most male homosexual gender dysphorics report this sort of childhood, not all effeminate and cross-gender-identified boys become homosexual gender dysphorics. Many of these children begin to show more masculine behaviour beginning at puberty (Green, 1987). Some of them, however, remain effeminate, discontent with their male sex, and continue to engage in cross-gender behaviour, while a small minority eventually become transsexuals, having surgery to change their physical sexual characteristics.

One of the world's foremost centres for the investigation and treatment of gender problems is at the Clarke Institute of Psychiatry in Toronto. Ray Blanchard, head of its Clinical Sexology Program, has noted that homosexual male gender

Ray Blanchard, head of the Clinical Sexology Program at the Clarke Institute of Psychiatry in Toronto.

dysphorics claim that their attraction to other men is actually heterosexual, because they are really women. Because many gender-dysphoric people dislike their own genitals and do not want them touched, their sexual contact tends to be as receptive partner in oral or anal sex, or they avoid sexual contact altogether.

Heterosexual gender dysphoria occurs among those who are attracted to the opposite sex but who are nevertheless drawn toward presenting themselves like the opposite sex. Thus, this group consists of men who like to dress as women but who are attracted to women; and women who like to appear as men but are attracted to men. Unlike homosexual gender dysphorics, the heterosexual males with this disorder typically were not effeminate as children. They do, however, develop an interest in cross-dressing, which in adolescence leads to sexual excitement and masturbation, and is known as transvestic fetishism, which we will discuss later in this chapter. As researchers at the Clarke Institute have found, not all transvestic fetishists experience gender dysphoria (Freund, Watson, & Dickey, 1991a), but heterosexual gender dysphoria is generally preceded by transvestic fetishism. This specific subgroup of male transvestites fantasize being female, in both sexual and nonsexual interactions. Often in adulthood and middle age their sexual response to cross-dressing is lessened, but the desire to cross-dress remains and cross-gender wishes escalate. They describe their experience as one of comfort or well-being when they cross-dress. Some even come to describe sexual arousal as a nuisance that interferes with their activities (Blanchard, 1990).

Interestingly, Blanchard (1989) contends that heterosexual gender dysphoria is uncommon among women because its precursor, fetishistic cross-dressing, is virtually absent.

Etiology of Gender Identity Disorders

Very little is known about the origins of gender identity disorder. Unfortunately, what data are available present a rather confusing picture, although most authorities in the field consider the problem to result from some as yet unspecified combination of biological and psychological factors.

A tragic "test case" that offers some insight into the nature/nurture debate emerged accidentally when one of a pair of male monozygotic twins had his penis cut off during a botched circumcision (Green, 1987). Instead of undertaking the repeated, difficult, and unsatisfactory surgeries to reconstruct a penis, the physician and parents elected to "reassign" the boy as a girl. Thus, nature (that is, the hereditary component) was held constant between the twins because of their identical genetic makeup. Only the nurture component varied for the two: one twin was subsequently reared as a girl, the other as a boy. The reports indicate that the reassigned twin became feminine in behaviour and interests. At puberty, she was given hormonal replacement therapy in order to develop breasts and other female secondary sex characteristics. This case is still cited by many writers as evidence that "gender identity is something one *learns* at a very young age" (Barlow & Durand, 1995, p. 419). Such conclusions overlook followup information on the reassigned twin (Green, 1987). The professionals who studied this case maintained that, as a young adolescent, the child "had a very masculine gait, ... looks quite masculine and is ... being teased ... they ... call her cave-woman" (Diamond, 1982, p. 183). These psychiatrists claimed that she had not adjusted at all well to being a female. Thus, the outcome for this single case is far from clear and, contrary to the initial reports, it is difficult to take it as evidence for the importance of either genetics or environment in the development of gender identity.

Some theorists have suggested that disturbances in gender identity may be caused by either genetically influenced hormonal disturbances or exposure during fetal development to inappropriate hormones. Yalom, Green, and Fisk (1973), for example, found that young boys whose mothers took female hormones during pregnancy showed fewer so-called masculine behaviours than did boys whose mothers were not exposed to these hormones. A problem with this type of research, however, concerns the issue of what constitutes masculine or feminine behaviour. Certainly, it is common for children to show some supposedly gender-atypical behaviours and interests, and in today's more tolerant climate more parents are comfortable with boys playing with dolls or girls engaging in rough-and-tumble play. In any event, careful reviews of the literature have not offered much support for the hormonal hypothesis (Bancroft, 1989).

Psychodynamic and behavioural theories of human behaviour emphasize the importance of early childhood experiences and the family environment. For psychoanalytic theory, the basic conflict resulting from a boy's failure to separate from the mother and develop an independent identity creates a gender identity problem (Meyers & Keith, 1991). Behavioural theory (Bernstein, Steiner, Glaiser, & Muir, 1981) suggests that the basis of gender identity disorder lies in encouragement by parents of gender-inappropriate behaviours, combined with the lack of a same-sex adult model and overprotection by the opposite-gendered parent. Somewhat contrary to expectations about the influence of early family life, Green (1978), in a study of boys raised by transsexual parents, found them all to develop into appropriately adjusted adults with no evidence of gender identity problems. More importantly, perhaps, Green (1976) found no differences in the behaviours and attitudes of the parents of gender-identity-disordered boys and the parents of normal boys. The parents of gender-identity-disordered boys did nothing to encourage cross-sex behaviours, and, in fact, most actively discouraged such behaviour. In addition, many children diagnosed as having gender identity disorder grow up to be free of such problems (Zucker, Finegan, Deering, & Bradley, 1984).

To date, there is little support for any theory of the origin of gender identity disorder, but, as noted earlier, most theorists now consider both biology and experience to play a part.

Treatment of Gender Identity Disorders

Kenneth Zucker has worked extensively with gender-identity-disordered children at the Clarke Institute. When parents present cross-gender-identified children for treatment, the clinician faces a difficult issue. Some feel it is inappropriate to try to change gender identity, but Zucker (1990b) notes that there are several reasons for treating these children: elimination of peer ostracism, treatment of any underlying psychopathology in the children and their families, and prevention of transsexualism in adulthood. Attempts have been made to encourage gender-appropriate and discourage cross-gender behaviour among these children through behavioural, psychodynamic, and family therapies. In the short term, these interventions

may affect cross-gender behaviour, but little is known about their long-term impact on gender disorders of children.

Some heterosexual and more homosexual gender dysphorics eventually request hormonal treatment or surgery to "reassign" them to the opposite sex (Kockott & Farhner, 1987). Jeremy Baumbach, a psychologist at the Yukon Family Services Association in Whitehorse, and Louisa Turner, at Case Western Reserve University School of Medicine (Baumbach & Turner, 1992), noted that not all gender dysphorics request hormonal or surgical reassignment. Those with the highest desire for surgical sexual reassignment appear to be those who are the most sexually aroused by imagining themselves as having the sexual organs of the opposite sex (Blanchard, 1993). Typically, clinics require candidates for hormonal or surgical treatment to live in the role of the opposite sex for one to five years before they are accepted for treatment (Clemmensen, 1990). This "real-life test" helps ensure that patients are able to function fully in the desired gender role before potentially irreversible measures are undertaken.

Clarke Institute researchers have found that hormonal therapy assists in developing the desired secondary sex characteristics (Dickey & Steiner, 1990). Males treated with feminizing hormones show breast enlargement, increased fat deposits, and decreased muscle mass, body, and facial hair. Their capacity to have erections and to ejaculate diminishes. Treatment of women with testosterone leads to an increase in muscle bulk and facial hair, deepening of the voice, enlargement of the clitoris, and suppression of ovarian function.

Sexual reassignment does not consistently produce the desired results. As Dickey and Steiner (1990) note with female-to-male surgery, "Although many patients appear happy with the results of phalloplasty, the shortcomings and complications are myriad. These include scarring of the abdominal wall, strictures, fistulas, urinary incontinence, infections, and often extrusion of testicular prostheses. The created organ lacks sensation and is nonerectile. The aesthetic appearance ranges from marginal to grotesque" (p. 150). For men, the surgery involved in reassignment is generally more

Left-hand photo shows Dr. Richard Raskin before surgery; right-hand photo, taken after sex-reassignment surgery, shows the same person in the new identity of Dr. Renée Richards. Richards competed professionally on the women's tennis circuit.

successful. Similar postsurgical problems may occur as with phalloplasty, although they are less common and may be reduced by, for example, having the client wear a vaginal mould during healing.

However, in the majority of cases, transsexuals are pleased with the results of surgery. A series of patients at the Clarke Institute were followed for one year (Blanchard, Steiner, Clemmensen, & Dickey, 1989). None of the reassigned 61 homosexual females or 36 homosexual males regretted the surgery. Four of the 14 reassigned heterosexual males did have regrets. Not surprisingly, postoperative adjustment was also related to the success and completeness of the surgery. In many cases, when surgically changed transsexuals express unhappiness or psychological problems, these are attributed to their sex-change surgery, but such difficulties may have existed before the surgery. Most clinics now offer psychotherapy and counselling both before and after surgery for their transsexual clients and clients receiving such counselling appear to do better (Green & Fleming, 1990).

SEXUAL PREFERENCE DISORDERS

Shortly after his 50th birthday, Joseph Fredericks was sent to prison for life for the murder of an 11-year-old boy. Fredericks had kidnapped the boy from a shopping mall in Brampton, Ontario, and then repeatedly raped him before stabbing him to death.

In his second year at school, Fredericks had been assessed by a school psychologist who concluded that his intelligence was extremely low. Fredericks was taken from his poverty-stricken parents and placed in an institution for the retarded (as they were then called), where he knew no one and lost all contact with the parents he loved. Many years later it was discovered that Fredericks' intelligence was quite normal.

Fredericks was introduced to sexual activities by older residents of the institution. Frightened at first, he soon sought out other boys for sex. There was little else to do in the institution and sex became his only pleasure.

At 17, Fredericks was considered too old for the institution and sent out into the world with a little money in his pocket, but no idea what to do with it. He didn't know how to find a room or a job. Because he was assumed to be incapable of learning, he had been taught no job skills. He went on welfare until he found casual work. Since he had no friends or relatives that he knew of, Fredericks soon began to seek out the company of young boys, the only people he had ever learned to relate to. He was arrested for sexual molestation soon after leaving the institutional and repeated this behaviour over the next 30 years. In 1985, he was sent to Kingston Penitentiary for five years, but released after serving two-thirds of his sentence because he was considered to pose no great risk to the community.

Evidently, this conclusion was disastrously mistaken, for within a few weeks he had murdered the little boy.

Joseph Fredericks and Graham, the young man whose case was described at the beginning of this chapter, illustrate the opposite ends of a continuum of harm to others that the *paraphilias* represent, and we might wonder why these two very different individuals are placed in the same general category by the diagnostic manual. Clearly, Graham's eccentric sexual behaviour hurt no one but himself (except for the inconvenience occasioned to those from whom he stole the jeans). Joseph Fredericks, on the other hand, was an extremely dangerous man. The two, however, have similarities: both were lonely, alienated from others, unable to establish effective adult relationships, and both had childhood experiences that established patterns of non-normative sexual responding that endured into adulthood. Both were attracted to these early sexual experiences because of the emotional emptiness of their lives. Sexually deviant activities became their only source of pleasure.

Sexual preference disorders, for the purposes of this chapter, will refer to those disorders listed in DSM-IV as paraphilias, plus additional sexual anomalies, such as child molestation, incest, and rape, that are not included in DSM-IV's list of paraphilias. Indeed, it seems peculiar that the most abhorrent and dangerous sexual offenders are all but excluded from the official diagnostic manual. Although DSM-IV offers a cautionary statement indicating that the diagnostic manual does not encompass "all the conditions for which people may be treated" (American Psychiatric Association, 1994, p. xxxvii), to omit such high-frequency and damaging behaviours does rather diminish the value of the manual for those who do clinical or research work with sexual offenders.

DSM-IV describes unusual sexual interests as **paraphilias**, which means "beyond the usual" (*para*) form of love (*philia*). According to the diagnostic manual, paraphilias are characterized by "recurrent, intense, sexually arousing fantasies, sexual urges, or behaviours" (American Psychiatric Association, 1994, p. 522) concerning the particular focus of the paraphiliac's desire. (See DSM table.) In practice, however, people have usually been diagnosed as having a paraphilia only if they are considered to actually prefer the eccentric sexual behaviour over more normative, sexual behaviours. This is because prior versions of the diagnostic manual appeared to demand this or, at least, were interpreted that way by diagnosticians. The changes in DSM-IV to include actual sexual behaviours are an improvement and may lead to changes in diagnostic practices more consistent with the range of behaviours dealt with by clinicians. To date, however, clinicians have treated numerous sexual aberrations despite the fact that many of these clients (for example, most rapists and many child molesters) did not meet DSM diagnostic criteria. Clinicians are concerned to deal with harmful behaviours whether or not these are driven by abnormal preferences.

Homosexuality (that is, sexual relations between persons of the same gender) is no longer identified in the diagnostic

DSM-IV Diagnostic Criteria for Paraphilias

Recurrent, intense, sexually arousing fantasies, urges, or behaviors involving: (1) nonhuman objects; (2) the suffering or humiliation of oneself or one's partner; or (3) children or other nonconsenting persons.

Exhibitionism
Recurrent, intense fantasies, urges, or behaviors involving exposure of one's genitals to an unsuspecting stranger.

Frotteurism
Recurrent, intense fantasies, urges, or behaviors involving touching or rubbing against a nonconsenting person.

Pedophilia
Recurrent, intense fantasies, urges, or behaviors involving sexual activity with a prepubescent child (generally under 13 years).

Sexual Masochism
Recurrent, intense fantasies, urges, or behaviors involving being humiliated, beaten, bound, or otherwise made to suffer.

Sexual Sadism
Recurrent, intense fantasies, urges, or behaviors involving acts that cause physical or psychological suffering to another person.

Transvestic Fetishism
Recurrent, intense fantasies, urges, or behaviors involving cross-dressing (i.e., dressing in the clothes of the opposite sex).

Voyeurism
Recurrent, intense fantasies, urges, or behaviors involving watching an unsuspecting person who is either naked, disrobing, or engaged in sexual activity.

Source: Reprinted with permission from the *Diagnostic and Statistical Manual of Mental Disorders*, Fourth Edition. Copyright 1994 American Psychiatric Association.

manual as a disorder. Up to and including DSM-II, homosexuality was listed as a disorder and people (mostly males) with this sexual orientation were subjected to treatment aimed at changing their attraction from same-sex to opposite-sex partners. Homosexuality was also illegal, and all too often homosexuals were imprisoned. In 1973, the American Psychiatric Association's Nomenclature Committee recommended that homosexuality be eliminated from the list of disorders. However, they also suggested the addition of "sexual orientation disturbance" to refer to those homosexuals who experienced conflict with their sexual orientation or who wished to change their orientation. Accordingly, DSM-III included **egodystonic homosexuality** to refer to conflicted homosexuals and, although this category has been dropped from DSM-III-R and DSM-IV, both include, as one possible form of a Sexual Disorder Not Otherwise Specified, "persistent and marked distress about sexual orientation" (American Psychiatric Association, 1994, p. 538).

In this chapter we will not discuss homosexuality as a topic, as we consider it to be a personal preference that is essentially no one else's business. Evidence indicates that homosexuals have no more psychological problems than heterosexuals, despite the continuing prejudices of many other

people (Gagnon & Simon, 1973; Siegelman, 1979). Interestingly, a recent study (Adams, Lohr, & Wright, 1995) found that those men who expressed strong distaste or hostility to homosexuals showed far greater sexual arousal to males than did those males who were tolerant of homosexuality. Perhaps this marked aversion to homosexuality (often called *homophobia*) may be driven by a desire to cover up the man's own unacknowledged sexual feelings.

Sexual Variants

Fetishism

DSM-IV describes **fetishisms** as sexual behaviours in which the presence of "nonliving objects" (the fetish object) is "usually required or strongly preferred for sexual excitement." Most researchers and clinicians, however, also include an excessive attraction to particular body parts, with the feet being a common fetish. These latter types of fetishisms have been called "partialisms," by which is meant a sexual fixation on specific parts of a person's body.

Since it is mostly men who appear at clinics for treatment of fetishisms, it is often presumed that these fixations are primarily found in males, although there is no clear evidence that this is so. Of the fetishistic objects that have been reported in the literature, women's underwear or women's shoes appear to be among the most common, but there are reports of fetishisms for leather, rubber, plastic, babies' diapers, furs, and purses. Indeed, almost any object, or even behaviour, can become a fetish. King (1990), for example, described a man who became sexually aroused whenever other people sneezed.

The fetishist typically likes to smell or rub the object against his or her body or, in some cases, wear the article or have his partner wear it. When the articles worn by the fetishist are clothes of the opposite sex, it should be called *transvestic fetishism*, which we will describe in more detail in a moment. As we saw in Graham's case, some fetishists are driven to steal their desired objects. It is often this theft that gets them into trouble with the law, rather than their actual sexual behaviour.

Very little is known about the psychological adjustment of fetishists, but many of those who appear for treatment seem in all other aspects to be quite normal. For example, Paul, described in the cases that opened Chapter 1, was unhappy as a teenager because he feared ridicule, but grew up to be a happily married, well-adjusted man. Most people assume that such an odd behaviour must imply a deeply disordered mind, but that does not seem typically to be the case (Gosselin & Wilson, 1980). A fetishist who accepts his own feelings, odd though they may seem to others, and who has found ways of meeting his desires that do not harm others and do not interfere with his social functioning does not seem to pose a problem. And indeed, since he would not meet the criterion of distress, he would not be diagnosed by DSM-IV standards as having a disorder.

We know very little about the origin of fetishes, although many fetishists report that their unusual sexual attraction began in childhood. As we saw in Graham's case, a coincidence of sexual excitement in a young boy and accidental exposure to a particular item (in that case, blue jeans) can entrench a fetish. Conditioning has often been invoked to explain the etiology of fetishisms and Stanley Rachman, now at the University of British Columbia, demonstrated in a laboratory study that males could acquire sexual arousal to women's boots as a result of conditioning experiences (Rachman, 1966). What Rachman did was pair sexual arousal (stimulated by pictures of nude females) with exposure to women's boots, and he found that subsequently the men who experienced these pairings displayed sexual arousal to the boots. In this study, the UCS was the pictures of nude females, the UCR was sexual arousal, and the CS was the women's boots. The subsequent responses of these subjects to the women's boots was the conditioned response (CR). However, as Baron and Byrne (1977) point out, if it was simply fortuitous associations between sexual arousal and some object, then there should be many fetishists who are attracted to pillows or ceilings since sexual arousal occurs very frequently at bedtime or upon waking. There are, however, no reports in the literature of such fetishisms.

Transvestic Fetishism

A person who *cross-dresses*—wears the clothing associated with the opposite sex—in order to produce or enhance sexual excitement is said to be a **transvestite** (or to have a transvestic fetish). Most transvestites who appear at clinics are males, so it is assumed that this is primarily a male behaviour, but again, there is no evidence that this is so in the population at large.

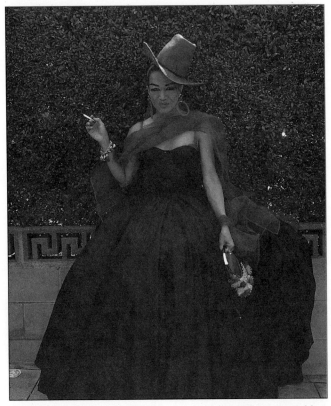

Transvestic fetishists like this man are sexually aroused by cross-dressing.

People cross-dress for various reasons. Performers who earn their living impersonating people of the opposite sex are not transvestites unless they are sexually excited by their work, which few seem to be. Men who wear women's clothing to attract other men are better understood as homosexuals who adopt a particular style to make themselves appealing (called "drag queens" in the argot of the street). Most transvestites, on the other hand, are clearly heterosexual. Indeed, many male transvestites report that they most enjoy heterosexual intercourse when dressed in their favourite women's garments although they sometimes have difficulty finding a willing partner. Prince and Bentler (1972) found that 89 percent of the over 500 transvestites they surveyed were heterosexual and most of them were married and had children. Fifty percent of the wives in that study accepted their husbands' practices.

Although the literature on transvestites is not extensive, some evidence suggests that most appear to be reasonably well-adjusted, if a bit shy (Gosselin & Wilson, 1980), although Wise et al. (1991) found a high incidence of anxiety, depression, interpersonal sensitivity, and social alienation among transvestites. If these findings turn out to be generalizable, such difficulties may result not from the transvestism directly but from being social outcasts. The majority of transvestites experienced sexual arousal to female clothes during adolescence and, for most, these feelings persisted into adulthood (Buhrich & McConaghy, 1977). However, 91 percent claimed that the frequency and intensity of sexual arousal associated with cross-dressing had diminished with age.

Sadomasochism

People who derive sexual pleasure from inflicting pain or humiliating others (**sadists**) have a paraphilia that may be considered either a sexual variant (if it involves cooperative, willing partners) or a sexual offence (if it involves unwilling partners). **Masochists**, on the other hand, who enjoy experiencing pain or humiliation, cannot usually force their desires on others.

These two disorders were previously considered to be a single paraphilia, presumably because some of these people alternate between the roles of the giver and receiver of pain. It is now clear, however, that most sadists and masochists exclusively adopt one or the other role. The majority (85 percent) of both types are heterosexual (Moser & Levitt, 1987), have a childhood onset, and do not wish to change their sexual practices (Spengler, 1977). The limited research available suggests that sadists and masochists are otherwise conventional in their lifestyles and have above-average educational attainment.

Elaborate rituals and the use of a variety of equipment (for example, handcuffs, masks) typically accompany sadistic and masochistic behaviours and there is a successful commercial industry offering the necessary paraphernalia. In addition, dominatrix prostitutes make a living by punishing or belittling their (mostly male) masochistic clients. In some cases the prime aim of the sadist seems to be to humiliate and degrade the partner, who is required to behave submissively or engage in humiliating acts. Physical restraints may be used and rape may be simulated with a willing partner. Some masochists also prefer these sorts of behaviours. Other sadists desire to physically hurt their partners by spanking, whipping, etc. For most, the sadistic elements are ritualized and symbolic rather than actual painful experiences. However, some sadists find ritualized sadism with a willing partner unsatisfying; they want to *really* hurt or impose their will on an uncooperative partner. These sadists will be considered in more detail in the later section dealing with rape.

It has been suggested that sadistic or masochistic pleasure occurs far more frequently than is evident by clients attending clinics for treatment (Moser & Levitt, 1987)—which would make sense if most sadists and masochists are content with their own practices. Evidence from surveys suggests that approximately 5 to 10 percent of men and women enjoy such activities (Barbach & Levine, 1980); few of them would meet the diagnostic criteria of sexual sadism or masochism.

DSM-IV notes, under the category of sexual masochism, one particularly dangerous form which they call **hypoxyphilia**, and others have called **autoerotic asphyxia** or **asphyxiophilia**. This particular behaviour involves the deliberate induction of unconsciousness by oxygen deprivation, produced by chest compression, strangulation, enclosing the head in a plastic bag, or various other techniques. Oxygen deprivation is usually self-induced and follows a ritualistic pattern, terminating, when successful, in orgasm and automatic release from the oxygen-depriving technique. Unfortunately, these automatic release strategies do not always work and there have been numerous reports of death among asphyxiophiliacs (Hazelwood, Dietz, & Burgess, 1983).

Stephen Hucker, a Canadian psychiatrist, has studied this unusual disorder for several years (Hucker, 1985, 1990). He reports that hanging is the most common method of producing asphyxia, although many place plastic bags over their heads, while others inhale anesthetics or have their chests compressed. In fact, elaborate bondage is typically associated with the ritual leading to asphyxia (Hazelwood et al., 1983) and there is also evidence of masochistic stimulation including self-administered electric shocks or burns (Hucker, 1985).

Unusual Sexual Variants

New-Zealand-born psychologist John Money (1984), claims there are many more paraphilias than are listed in the diagnostic manual. He suggests there are at least 30 or more different types, although DSM-IV has a category that would accommodate these, called "paraphilias not otherwise specified." Sexual satisfaction derived from receiving enemas (klismaphilia) occurs frequently enough that pornographers cater to such interests, as they do to people who are sexually aroused by urination (urophilia) or defecation (coprophilia). Some of these rarer paraphilias, however, involve activities that break the law, such as sex with corpses (necrophilia), or with animals (bestiality), or that take the form of obscene telephone calls (scatologia). All of these unusual sexual variants, although occasionally described in the literature, are far too infrequently seen at clinics to permit adequate descriptive research.

Sexual Offences

DSM-IV lists four specific paraphilias involving sexual desires that, if enacted, constitute a criminal offence. **Pedophilia** describes recurrent fantasies or behaviours involving sexual activity with prepubescent children, **exhibitionism** involves exposure of the genitals to an unsuspecting stranger, **voyeurism** entails secretly looking at naked people, while **frotteurism** is touching or rubbing against a nonconsenting person for the purpose of sexual pleasure. Also, as we have seen, the category of "Paraphilias Not Otherwise Specified" in DSM-IV lists three other disorders that constitute illegal acts.

Exhibitionism

Exhibitionism is the most frequently occurring sexual offence in Western countries. For example, Rooth (1973) reported that over one-third of all sexual offences recorded in Canada, England, Germany, Hong Kong, and the United States involved exhibitionism. In a study of 142 exhibitionists, Abel et al. (1987) found that these men had committed in excess of 70,000 acts of exposure for an average of 514 acts per offender. As many as 30 to 50 percent of adult women say that on at least one occasion they have been the victims of an exhibitionist (DiVasto, Kaufman, Jackson, Christy, Pearson, & Burgett, 1984). Furthermore, exhibitionists have the highest rate of reoffending, with up to 57 percent being reported again within four years of being originally convicted (Marshall, Eccles, & Barbaree, 1991). Exhibitionism is obviously a very persistent and frequent behaviour. Worse, a number of them go on to other offences. Freund (1990), for example, found that many exhibitionists also peep into windows to watch women undressing or having sex (voyeurism), and as many as 12 percent had also committed rape.

Canadian researchers Ron Langevin and Rubin Lang (1987) report that the majority of exhibitionists are married, and that most report quite satisfactory sexual relations with an adult woman. In fact, sexual problems (other than their offensive behaviour) are rare among exhibitionists (Lang, Langevin, Checkley, & Pugh, 1987) and they appear to be as maritally well-adjusted as other men (Langevin, 1983). These offenders do not appear to share any distinctive personality features, and very few suffer from any type of psychopathology (Smukler & Schiebel, 1975). The age of onset of exposing behaviour is typically in the early twenties (Blair & Lanyon, 1981), often during a period of transitory interpersonal problems.

Voyeurism

Voyeurs are commonly called "peeping toms" after the man who supposedly broke the agreed-upon rule not to look at Lady Godiva as she rode naked through the streets of Coventry in protest against the heavy taxes imposed by her husband. However, these offenders are not quite as innocuous as the legendary Tom. Voyeurs seek sexual excitement by observing unsuspecting people who are undressing, are already naked, or are engaged in sexual acts. Like most other types of sexual offenders, voyeurs are typically male.

Although many voyeurs also engage in exhibitionistic behaviours, most do not appear to graduate to more dangerous behaviours. However, the available research on voyeurs is quite limited; we really do not know how many attempt to enter the building after seeing a victim undressing, but some certainly do. Abel (Abel et al., 1987) found that voyeurs quite frequently display other paraphilias, and some had also raped women.

In their study of voyeurs, Langevin, Paitich, and Russon (1985) found that, while these men had a somewhat greater than average number of sexual partners and their adult relationships were approximately normal, the majority reported poor relationships with their parents. They did not identify at all well with either of their parents and their childhood environment was described as frequently emotionally cold and hostile.

Frotteurism

Almost all detected frotteurs are male. *Frotteurism* (or *frottage*—from the French *frotter*, "to rub") refers to touching or rubbing up against a noncompliant person so that the frotteur can become sexually aroused and, in many cases, reach orgasm. These offences typically occur in crowded places such as busy sidewalks, stores, or shopping malls, or on packed public transport. The impersonal nature of this type of sexual contact is considered by some authorities (Money, 1987) as essential to the pleasure of the frotteur. Abel et al. (1987) found that while some frotteurs keep the contact brief and furtive to make it appear accidental, others seem unconcerned about being detected and are more intrusive and aggressive, fondling the victim's genitals, buttocks, or breasts, or rubbing the penis vigorously against the victim until orgasm occurs. Observations like these encouraged Langevin (1983) to view frotteurism as a form of sexual aggression belonging to the same category as rape. He pointed out that both are aggressive forms of direct sexual touching without the consent of the victim.

Child Molestation

Sexual offences against children occur far more commonly than most people suspect, although it is difficult to accurately estimate offence rates. The official police records do not always make clear the age of victims of sexual assault and offenders frequently plea-bargain and accept a lesser conviction. Researchers have attempted to get around these problems by surveying adults and asking if they were the victims of childhood sexual abuse or by asking them if they had ever molested a child.

The Canadian Committee on Sexual Offenses Against Children and Youth (1984), chaired by Chris Badgley, Professor of Social Work at the University of Calgary, conducted sophisticated national surveys in an attempt to determine the rates of child sexual abuse. They found that one-third of Canadian males and over one-half of Canadian females reported being sexually victimized, with over four-fifths of these incidents occurring before the age of 18. Sixty-two percent of the female victims and 70 percent of the male victims were under the age of 12 at the time of the assaults. Surveys in other countries have revealed quite similar results (for example, Russell, 1984; Wyatt, 1985). In addition, Finkelhor and Lewis (1988) found that as many as 17 percent of adult males who had never been convicted of a sexual offence nevertheless indicated that they had sexually molested at least one child.

However, surveys that have asked adults to recall childhood abuse are rarely able to check the veracity of these reports, and, in fact, many people refuse to participate in these studies. Haugaard and Repucci (1988) found that when they were able to ensure complete participation of all who were contacted, the percentage who identified themselves as childhood victims of sexual abuse was significantly less than when the participation rate was lower. Furthermore, the definitions of sexual abuse provided by the researcher have varied across surveys. When clear descriptions of different types of abuse are provided, 68.6 percent of child victims report being fondled, and about half (49.5 percent) indicate that the abuser used no force or threats.

These difficulties notwithstanding, the consistent impression from these surveys is that a considerable number of children are sexually abused. This is obviously an important social problem, because the effects of victimization may be considerable and long-lasting. Children who are sexually abused commonly exhibit emotional disturbances, alcoholism or drug dependence, eating and sleeping disorders, inappropriate sexual behaviours, behavioural and social problems, failing school grades, and various other short-term effects. They may also suffer problems later in life such as depression, anxiety, low self-esteem, difficulties fulfilling the role of a parent, inability to trust others, poor intimate relationships, and sexual dysfunctions. Briere (1988) reports that more intrusive forms of sexual abuse generally lead to more severe and long-lasting consequences. These effects are the same as those described for posttraumatic stress disorder in the chapter on anxiety disorders. While the severity of the effects varies, they can be devastating to victims and their families, and they also represent an inestimable financial burden on society. While Canada is at the forefront in developing effective ways to cope with this problem, there is still a long way to go.

In defining child molesters, the questions arise of the age of the abuser and the victim. When the offender is an adult and the victim is prepubescent, the issue seems clear enough; but what about an offender who is a child or an early adolescent? When two children engage in sexual interactions it may be difficult to distinguish exploratory play from assault. These issues have received increasing attention in recent years with the increase in awareness of the number of juvenile sexual offenders and their frequent aggressiveness (Barbaree, Marshall, & Hudson, 1993). To date, however, there is no firm agreement on where the boundary lies between sexual abuse and exploration among children. Researchers typically suggest that an act be considered molestation only if there is a five-year age difference between the two young people, but most clinicians would not hesitate to call a 12-year-old boy who sexually assaults a 9-year-old girl a child molester.

Many researchers have found that men who molest their own children (incest offenders) are far more similar to nonoffenders than men who molest other people's children (Frenzel & Lang, 1989; Freund, Watson, & Dickey, 1991b; Marshall, Barbaree, & Christophe, 1986; Quinsey, Chaplin, & Carrigan,

1979). It has been suggested that incest offenders, rather than being driven by deviant desires to have sex with children, simply take the opportunity arising from their power over their children to satisfy their sexual needs.

The great majority of adults who sexually abuse children are men. However, recent research and clinical reports have suggested that there may be a greater proportion of females who sexually abuse children than was previously thought (Elliot, 1993). Finkelhor and Russell (1984) estimated from their survey research that between 87 percent and 94 percent of female child victims, and between 76 percent and 85 percent of male child victims, were abused by men. Among sexual offenders who report being abused as children, as many as 22 percent of Canadian sexual offenders give accounts of childhood molestation by women (Dhawan & Marshall, 1995).

Unfortunately for parents seeking to protect their children from sexual abuse, the majority of child molesters appear to be so trustworthy that few people attempt to restrict their access to children. As a greater proportion of cases of child molestation get reported, it is apparent that offenders may come from any socioeconomic level. Offenders from the wealthier end of the social spectrum seem less likely to be reported, apparently for fear of embarrassment to the family, or for fear of the loss of the income of the offenders. They seem to benefit from their reputable image throughout the judicial process: even if these offenders are reported they are less likely to be prosecuted; if prosecuted, they are less likely to be convicted; and if convicted, they are less likely to receive an extended prison sentence (Marshall & Barrett, 1990).

What distinguishes child molesters from other males? Researchers have examined a diverse array of features. While some differences between groups have been found, in most cases the distinction between child molesters and others is incomplete; that is, many child molesters appear quite normal on most of the measures. For example, it is often claimed (Kalichman, 1991) that child molesters show patterns of disturbed personality on measures such as the Minnesota Multiphasic Personality Inventory (MMPI). However, when Marshall and Hall (1995) examined these findings in more detail, they found that in almost all the studies the average scores of the child molester groups were within normal limits. This means that even when child molesters scored on average higher than comparison subjects, they nevertheless showed normal personality functioning.

One promising area of research is intimacy skills. It is assumed that all people seek intimacy (Perlman & Duck, 1987) but, depending upon their self-confidence and skills, not all achieve it. The capacity for and the skills necessary to achieve intimacy in adult relations are thought to be primarily instilled within the parent-child bond. Marshall (1989) proposed that because child molesters characteristically had poor relationships with their parents, they grew up lacking in confidence and bereft of intimacy skills. This deficit turned them away from effective relationships with adults and toward children, whom they would see as nonthreatening.

This theory integrates a range of currently known facts about child molesters. For instance, it has been found that child molesters were typically either emotionally rejected by their parents, neglected by them, or physically and sexually abused by them (Awad, Saunders, & Levene, 1984; Finkelhor, 1984). In addition, child molesters perceive children to be less threatening and more attractive than adults (Howells, 1978). Most importantly, research has shown that child molesters are significantly deficient in intimacy and are extremely lonely. This finding has been confirmed by studies in Canada and New Zealand (Seidman, Marshall, Hudson, & Robertson, 1994), the United States (Bumby & Hansen, in press), Australia (Smallbone & Dadds, 1997), and England (Garlick, Marshall, & Thornton, 1996). Fortunately, they can be trained to overcome these difficulties and to develop effective relationships with adults (Marshall, Bryce, Hudson, Ward, & Moth, 1996).

Rape

The term *rape*, in its traditional sense, refers to forced vaginal penetration of an unwilling female's vagina by a male assailant's penis. Not only did this definition exclude the rape of males, it placed quite unnecessary emphasis on penile-vaginal intercourse. In terms of legal processes, this requirement of demonstrated forced vaginal intercourse in order to obtain a conviction of rape caused so many problems that Canadian legislators decided to change the law. Rape, as a criminal offence, and various lesser sexual crimes, were replaced in 1983 in Canadian law by three crimes of sexual assault. These three different types of sexual assault are defined by varying levels of forcefulness by the offender and incur, upon conviction, increasing lengths of possible sentences. These improvements in the law served to make clear the assaultiveness of these crimes, and to diminish the legal relevance of whether penetration had occurred. This is quite reasonable, since the severity of psychological damage caused by an incident of sexual assault does not depend only on whether the vagina was penetrated, but on many other factors as well. Over and above the sexual objectification many offenders also make a point of degrading and humiliating their victims and may physically hurt them. The current Canadian laws better reflect the reality of sexual assault than did the earlier rape laws.

Since sexual assault laws have not been similarly modified in most jurisdictions of the United States, nor in other countries, most researchers continue to use the terms *rape* and *rapist*. For convenience, we will use these terms, but this should not be taken to imply support for the old laws. The recent Canadian laws, we believe, are superior to any in the world in terms of encouraging victims to report and in having the courts focus on the appropriate issues.

Because of these changes, and because there are now restrictions on questioning the victim in court about her previous sexual experience, more victims do appear to be coming forward. Nevertheless, sexual assault remains a markedly underreported crime. Koss (1985) found that, although 13 percent of the women she studied acknowledged that a male had forced them to have sex, only half considered it to be rape. Furthermore, of those who did identify themselves as rape victims, only 8 percent had reported the offence to the police. The victim was less likely to report the assault to the police, or even construe it as rape, if she had been romantically involved with the offender. This finding does much to explain low reporting rates; as Figure 12.3 reveals, strangers actually constitute a very small percentage of rapists. Of the 91 rape victims in one study (Kilpatrick, Best, Saunders, & Veronen, 1988), 24 percent had been raped by their husbands and another 17 percent by their dating partner. Until quite recently, forcible sex by a spouse was not covered by the sexual assault laws of most countries and it is still excluded from these laws in many places. (Husbands are no longer immune to charges of rape in Canada.)

Koss (1992), from a thorough analysis of survey data, concluded that the real rate of rape was six to ten times as high as the officially recorded statistics. Relying on estimates such as these, Marshall and Barrett (1990) took the official Canadian figures for 1988 and multiplied them by four (a conservative strategy) to estimate the true frequency of rape in Canada. This calculation suggested that more than 75,000

women are raped in Canada every year, at the frightening rate of one every seven minutes.

Most people expect rapists to have personality defects. How could someone do such a thing, they reason, if he were not disturbed? In fact, very few rapists appear to have been suffering from any disorder at the time they offended (Scully & Marolla, 1983). As noted earlier, unless rapists meet the criteria either for sadism or for a personality disorder, they would not be given a DSM-IV diagnosis, and the incidence of sadism among rapists appears to be no more than 10 percent (McConaghy, 1993).

In an interesting analysis of a 27-year-old man serving a seven-year sentence for rape in a Canadian penitentiary, Barbaree (1990) found that the man showed greater sexual arousal to both rape and nonsexual assault on a woman than he did to consenting sex. (See the Focus on measurement of sexual arousal.) This pattern is just what we would expect

Focus   *Measurement of Sexual Arousal*

When clinicians ask sexual offenders, or men who have one or another of the sexual variants, about their preferred sexual behaviours or sexual fantasies, these men typically report quite normal sexual interests. Yet their actual behaviours suggest otherwise. Consequently, it has been assumed that these men do not usually tell the truth. It seems understandable that they would lie, since they are all too aware that other people (including perhaps the clinician asking them the questions) consider their sexual behaviours to be either repugnant or reprehensible. Also, in the case of sexual offenders, they may be reluctant to tell the truth for fear of getting into further serious trouble.

Because most clinicians believe aberrant behaviour is driven by deviant desires, a technology has been developed to assess sexual preferences independently of what the offender says. This technology, called *phallometry*, measures the man's erectile responses (that is, the degree to which he gets an erection) while he watches or listens to sexual depictions that include both appropriate sexual stimuli (for example, an image of a naked female or a scene of two consenting adults having sex) and

inappropriate stimuli (for example, images of children or a scene of a man forcing a resisting woman to have sex). The relative degree of arousal to these two classes of stimuli is thought to reflect the man's true sexual preferences.

Kurt Freund was the first to develop this technology in the early 1950s. Since then this assessment procedure has been modified and improved in several ways, and is in common use in treatment programs throughout the world.

Gene Abel (Abel, Barlow, Blanchard, & Guild, 1977) reported the first assessment of rapists using this approach. He found that these offenders showed greater arousal to forced sex than did nonrapist males, and these findings were confirmed by Canadian researchers (Barbaree, Marshall, & Lanthier, 1979; Quinsey & Chaplin, 1982). However, all these early studies examined rather small samples of subjects. In later, larger sample studies (for example, Baxter, Barbaree, & Marshall, 1986; Hall, 1989; Wormith, Bradford, Pawlak, Borzecki, & Zohar, 1988) the differences between rapists and normal men disappeared; both groups showed a stronger preference for consenting sex.

Canadian studies examining the preferences of exhibitionists (Langevin et al., 1979; Marshall, Payne, Barbaree, & Eccles, 1991) and men who sexually abused their daughters (Frenzel & Lang, 1989; Marshall, Barbaree, & Christophe, 1986; Quinsey, Chaplin, & Carrigan, 1979) have similarly found no differences between these offenders and normal males. In fact, it is only with nonfamilial child molesters (men who sexually abuse other people's children) that the results with phallometric assessments are at all clear. As a group, these child molesters show greater sexual arousal to children than they do to adults (Frenzel & Lang, 1989; Freund, Watson, & Dickey, 1991b; Marshall et al., 1986; Quinsey et al., 1979). However, even in these cases only approximately half of the nonfamilial child molesters appear deviant, with very few of the single-victim offenders displaying deviant arousal (Freund & Watson, 1991).

Despite the continued popularity of phallometric measures, the scientific evidence in support of its use is quite limited and in most cases should cause serious doubts about its value (Marshall, 1997).

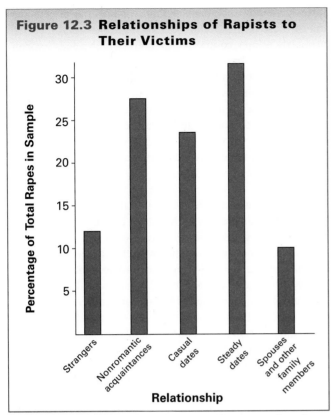

Figure 12.3 Relationships of Rapists to Their Victims

Note: These data are drawn from a large-scale survey of women attending colleges in the United States.

Source: Adapted from Koss, 1988.

of a sadistic rapist, and the details of this man's offence revealed that it was particularly vicious. Furthermore, he described himself as having enjoyed hurting his victim. Sadists, in fact, are the only rapists who are consistently identified as deviant by phallometric assessments. Not surprisingly, serial sexual murderers are far more frequently found to be sadistic. In one study, 86 percent of serial sexual murderers reported violent fantasies and, compared with other murderers, had higher rates of other paraphilias, particularly transvestic fetishism (Prentky et al., 1989). Fortunately, serial sexual murderers are rare.

Etiology of Sexual Offending

Over the years, many theorists have speculated about the origins of sexual offending. Behaviourists have tended to view such offending as being sexually motivated and consequently they have offered explanations that focus on the misdirection of sexual desires. As we saw with fetishes, the most frequently cited of these explanations is the claim that accidental sexual experiences result in classical conditioning processes making deviant sexual practices attractive.

Conditioning theories. McGuire, Carlisle, and Young (1965) were the first to propose that conditioning was the basis of acquired preferences motivating men to engage in unusual or offensive sexual behaviours. A young male, for example, might be caught in the act of masturbating by an

attractive woman, and this association between high sexual arousal and a woman seeing his exposed penis might, according to this conditioning account, serve to entrench an attraction to (or preference for) exposing his penis to women. Similar accidental associations between sexual arousal and seeing younger children were said to be the conditioning bases of future child molestation, while masturbating to pornographic images of, or to thoughts of, sexually assaulting a woman were said to instill a preference for rape.

A similar theory, that assumes sexual offenders are aroused by their deviant acts, was advanced by Kurt Freund, who began his outstanding career in his native Czechoslovakia but lived and worked in Toronto from the 1960s until he died in 1996. Freund outlined what he called a **courtship disorder theory** of sexual offending. Freund (1990) suggests, by analogy with animal courtship behaviour, that there are four phases in human sexual interactions: (1) looking for and appraising a potential partner; (2) posturing and displaying oneself to the partner; (3) tactile interaction with the partner; and (4) sexual intercourse. Freund's notion of courtship disorder suggests that fixation at any one of these stages produces sexual offending. Fixation at stage 1 would result in voyeurism; at stage 2 in exhibitionism; at stage 3 in frotteurism; and at stage 4 in rape.

These theories have some intuitive appeal so long as we accept that these offensive behaviours are sexually motivated. However, not everybody accepts that sexual crimes are driven exclusively, if at all, by sexual desires. Also, as is evident in the Focus box, phallometric assessments have not consistently shown that sexual offenders have the types of sexual preferences that conditioning or courtship disorder theories would predict. Furthermore, Marshall and Eccles (1993), in their review of the relevant literature on animal and human sexual behaviour, found little supporting evidence for conditioning theories.

Feminist theories. Feminist theories of sexual offending are quite diverse, but there are common threads. Most feminists vigorously hold men to be personally, as well as collectively, responsible for sexual assault. Feminist theorists typically see sexual abuse as arising naturally out of the sociocultural environment of our societies, which they see as essentially patriarchal (Brownmiller, 1975; Clark & Lewis, 1977). In this context, these theorists point to the differential ways parents and other influential people (for example, peers and teachers) respond to boys and girls. Girls, according to this analysis, are encouraged to be submissive, cooperative, nurturing, and emotional, and to defer to males in most, if not all, matters. Boys, on the other hand, are encouraged to be dominant and competitive and are discouraged from displaying any emotions (other than perhaps anger), particularly those that might serve a nurturing and supportive role toward others. This approach to bringing up boys and girls finds support in the entrenched, essentially patriarchal structures of society, which serve to limit the power and influence of women and children. Feminists see this as setting up women and children to be dominated by, and to be subservient to, adult males. This power differential, so these views suggest, provides few constraints on men's behaviour toward women and children and facilitates sexual abuse.

Feminist theorists typically see rape as a nonsexual, or pseudosexual, offence. They emphasize instead offenders' apparent anger toward women, as seen in their efforts to humiliate the victim and to exercise power and control. Canadian psychologist Juliet Darke (1990) examined both what rapists said about their own motives and victims' perceptions. Both sources revealed that over 60 percent of rapes involved some form of intentional humiliation of the victims. Consistently with feminist analyses, Seidman et al. (1994) found that rapists attending community clinics were more angry toward women than were matched, nonoffending males. In addition, Garlick et al. (1996) found that rapists blamed women for their loneliness, and their loneliness and lack of intimacy was found to be strongly related to feelings of hostility toward women (Marshall & Hambley, 1996). Rapists have also been found to consider aggression an appropriate response to an excessive demand, whereas most other males think that a firm but polite refusal is the acceptable response (Marshall, Barbaree, & Fernandez, 1995). Marshall et al. (1995) also found that rapists scored high on a measure of overassertiveness and tended to respond to difficult social interactions with verbal, and sometimes physical, aggression.

Consistently with the idea that patriarchal structures encourage rape, Sanday (1981), in her examination of data from 156 tribal societies, found higher rates of rape in societies characterized by patriarchal systems. In these rape-prone societies, women were seen as the property of men and were excluded from all positions of power and influence. These societies, where violence was endemic, had far higher rates of sexual assault than societies where both sexes were treated more equally. Rape was less common in societies in which women were respected and had an equal say in religious, political, and economic matters.

There is a fairly extensive body of literature concerning how likely men say they would be to rape a woman. Feminists typically take these data to support their theories. Malamuth, for example (1986; Malamuth, Heavey, & Linz, 1993), has found that in studies of men who had never been charged with rape, as many as 30 percent (and even higher in some studies) said that they would rape a woman if they knew they could get away with it. These figures, taken at face value, are quite startling and appear to strongly support feminist claims. However, questions of interpretation arise. Malamuth's measure asks men to rate on a 5-point scale the likelihood that they would rape, and he counts all those who indicate *some* likelihood of raping. It is hard to know how these respondents understand the notion of likelihood, but it is possible (perhaps even likely) that those who mark less than 5 on this scale mean that it is *unlikely* they would rape, except possibly in very unusual circumstances. Moreover, it is hard to know how to rate a response that amounts to a guess about what the respondent might do in a purely hypothetical situation.

Despite some problems with the evidence taken to support feminist views of sexual assault, the analyses offered by feminists have radically changed and expanded our understanding of these crimes. They have made it clear that these are primarily crimes committed by men (which needs explaining in any theory of sexual assault) and that there are clear sociocultural bases to sexual offending. Most importantly, lobbying by feminists has changed the way we deal with sexual abuse as a society. The investigation and prosecution processes have been made far easier on victims than they were just a few years ago, and the offenders who are identified are more likely to be convicted and jailed than excused and let go, as so many were in the past.

Comprehensive theories. Marshall and his colleagues (Marshall & Barbaree, 1990; Marshall, Hudson, & Hodkinson, 1993) have integrated a broad range of evidence to suggest that the childhoods of sexual offenders create a vulnerability and a social inadequacy in these growing males that makes them readily attracted to deviant sexual behaviours. These deviant acts, unlike prosocial sexual behaviours, require little social skill, have no built-in obligations to others, and do not require the offender to be concerned about the other person's needs or rights. Deviant sexual acts, then, might appeal to males who are lacking in social skills and who are self-centred. Also, sexual offences provide the opportunity to exercise power and control over others, and this is particularly satisfying to powerless males who lack self-confidence.

As we have seen, sexual offenders do typically have disrupted childhoods and there is clear evidence that such experiences leave the child feeling unlovable, lacking in self-confidence, with poor social skills, and with a propensity for antisocial behaviour (Loeber, 1990). In this theory, however, it is not just poor parenting that produces sexual offending.

Sociocultural factors, accidental opportunities, and transitory states all contribute to the complex of influences that set the stage for sexual offending. Sanday's (1981) research revealed that those societies with high rates of sexual assaults were characterized by an acceptance of violence and by male dominance over women and children. Violence is all too frequently presented by the media in our society as an acceptable and, indeed, even rewarded way to deal with problems (Geen, 1983), and men are still portrayed in many popular sitcoms as the dominant figures. A vulnerable young male would be expected to find these images of males (as dominant and violent) attractive, and he might subsequently look for ways to act as powerfully as the men in the stories. There is in fact evidence that these media portrayals do increase violent and controlling behaviours in the viewers (Geen, 1983). Sexually assaulting a woman or a child certainly puts the offender in a position of power over the victim and allows the offender to control what happens—and, of course, it produces the added satisfaction of sexual gratification.

Transitory states such as anger, depression, intoxication, and boredom have been found to immediately precede sexual offending (Pithers, Beal, Armstrong, & Petty, 1989), but Marshall's theory suggests that it is only vulnerable males who will respond in abusive ways to such circumstances. Even under these conditions, a vulnerable male cannot offend unless he has an opportunity, or creates one.

The implications of Marshall's account that have been examined have generally been confirmed. In addition, the general theory has led to more precise subtheories including the role in sexual offending of self-esteem, empathy (Marshall, Hudson, Jones, & Fernandez, 1995), and relationships (Ward, Hudson, Marshall, & Siegert, 1995). These more specific theories have, in turn, generated research that has, for the most part, supported these accounts.

There are other comprehensive accounts of sexual offending (for example, Finkelhor, 1984; Hall & Hirschman, 1991) that have the same advantages as Marshall's theory. That is, they integrate a breadth of currently available knowledge and they have generated clearly testable implications. A final clear advantage of all the theories considered here is that the results of studies examining their implications have increased our understanding of these puzzling and destructive offenders. The more we know about sexual offenders, the better we will be able to deal with them in a way that effectively reduces the future harm they might otherwise cause.

Treatment of Sexual Offenders

Prior to the 1970s, most treatment programs for sexual offenders were derived from some form of psychoanalytic theory. However, the programs were not very effective (Furby, Weinrott, & Blackshaw, 1989), so clinicians turned to other models for direction.

Behaviour therapy. Behaviour therapists were just beginning in the late 1960s to extend their treatment theories to sexual deviates. Bond and Evans (1967), for example, developed a simple approach to treatment based on the assumption that these offensive behaviours were driven by deviant sexual preferences. They thought that all that was necessary in treatment was to eliminate these deviant preferences (for example, a sexual attraction to children, or to forced sex, or to exposing) and the offending would disappear. Typically, sexual preferences in these early studies were modified by associating the deviant thoughts with a strongly aversive event, such as an electric shock to the calf muscles. This turned out to be a rather naive notion; but good science progresses from simple conceptualizations to more complex ones only when the simple approach fails to produce results. Recently, Rice, Quinsey, and Harris (1991) examined their own similar, quite limited treatment program, which they had offered at the Oak Ridge Mental Health Centre in Ontario during the 1970s and early 1980s. They found that this program was ineffective.

Comprehensive programs. As a result of the lack of benefits from these early behavioural interventions, more comprehensive approaches began to emerge. American psychiatrist Gene Abel and his colleagues (Abel, Blanchard, & Becker, 1978) were among the first to develop such programs. Similar programs were developed in Canada (Lang, Pugh, &

Langevin, 1988; Marshall, Earls, Segal, & Darke, 1983). Therapists have also adapted relapse prevention strategies from the field of addictions (Pithers, Marques, Gibat, & Marlatt, 1983).

These comprehensive programs typically attempt to overcome sexual offenders' tendency to deny or minimize their offending. They work to improve self-esteem and social and relationship skills, to enhance empathy, and to alter offence-supportive attitudes and deviant sexual preferences. Various other offence-related problems are also addressed, such as substance abuse, anger, and an inability to handle stress. Sexual offenders are trained to identify factors that might increase their risk of reoffending, and they are taught ways to deal with these problems should they arise.

Benefits of treatment. Recent attempts to evaluate the effectiveness of treatment for offenders have been hampered by the difficulty of doing methodologically sound outcome research. For example, a satisfactory evaluation would require that sexual offenders be randomly allocated to groups receiving either treatment or no treatment, yet many clinicians are understandably reluctant to deliberately withhold treatment from these dangerous offenders. However, enough appraisals show apparently successful outcomes to encourage optimism about the value of treatment with these difficult clients (Marshall, Jones, Ward, Johnston, & Barbaree, 1991).

In an evaluation of the Kingston Sexual Behaviour Clinic's community-based programs for child molesters and exhibitionists, Marshall and his colleagues (Marshall & Barbaree,

Table 12.2 Reoffence Rates of Treated Sexual Offenders

	Treated Offenders	Untreated Offenders
Community Program		
Kingston Sexual Behaviour Clinic:		
Child molesters	8.0	18.0
Exhibitionists	12.0	24.0
Prison Programs		
Kingston Penitentiary: Mixed group of sexual offenders	11.0	35.0
Minnesota Prison:		
Child molesters	8.6	20.8
Rapists	14.5	27.3
Saskatchewan Penitentiary:		
Child molesters	9.5	14.6*
Rapists	5.0	
New Zealand's prison:		
Child molesters	3.2	20.0**

*Mixed group.
**An estimate of recidivism based on previously released offenders.

Source: Adapted from Marshall & Anderson, 1996.

1988; Marshall, Eccles, & Barbaree, 1991) found that treated offenders had much lower reoffence rates than did matched, untreated sexual offenders. Prison-based programs also seem to be successful. Davidson (1984) reported a positive evaluation of Kingston Penitentiary's early program for the period 1973–1978, and Minnesota's quite comprehensive prison program also showed less reoffending among treated offenders (Steele, 1993). In addition, two recent evaluations have also supported the effectiveness of treating sexual offenders in prison. Both Saskatchewan's penitentiary program and New Zealand's prison program have produced reductions in the reoffence rates of their treated sexual offenders (Marshall & Anderson, 1996). Table 12.2 shows the results of several programs.

By apparently reducing reoffence rates, treatment saves the women and children whom these men might have assaulted from considerable suffering. In addition, given the very high costs of police investigation and jails, treating sexual offenders actually saves taxpayers a great deal of money (Marshall, 1992). Table 12.3 presents a calculation of estimated financial benefits.

Table 12.3 Cost-Benefit Analysis of Treating Sexual Offenders

	Rate of Reoffence		
	Untreated	*Treated*	*Reduction in Reoffenders*
Community	43%	16%	27%
Prison	35%	11%	24%
Reduction in number of victims	=	50+	
Cost per reoffender	=	$200,000	
Cost to treat 100 offenders	=	$500,000	
Dollars saved by treatment (per 100 offenders):			
Savings (25* × 200,000)	=	$5,000,000	
Less costs	=	$500,000	
TOTAL SAVINGS	**=**	**$4,500,000**	

*This is an approximate average of the reduction in reoffenders as a result of treatment.

Source: Adapted from W. L. Marshall, The social value of treatment for sexual offenders, *Canadian Journal of Human Sexuality, 1(1992)*, 109–114.

PANORAMA

Over the past 30 years in particular, we have learned a lot about human sexual behaviour, although there is still much to learn. Our understanding of some, but not all, of the sexual dysfunctions is now sufficiently extensive to permit reasonably reliable diagnoses and to produce reasonably effective treatment methods. There are still difficulties, however, with distinguishing organic from psychogenic causes of erectile disorder. Since this distinction is critical to treatment decisions, further research must focus on identifying the features characteristic of organic and psychogenic etiology.

Gender identity disorder presents problematic issues. Is it appropriate, for example, to assist those who wish to surgically alter the physical attributes of their biological sex? Should we rather counsel them and try to help them to accept their biological endowment? Both alternatives have problems and perhaps the best approach is to allow sex change surgery only after a long period of counselling. This is, in fact, what most gender clinics presently do.

Sexual variants are not really a problem to anyone except the afflicted person. These people could, and perhaps many do, find an outlet, whether solitary or with a cooperative partner, that does not upset others. There does not seem to be any reason why they cannot live out their lives with their eccentric sexual behaviour kept private. Not so for sexual offenders. These people, mostly males, cause considerable distress to others and society has a responsibility to protect its citizens, particularly those who are most vulnerable, such as children. Canadians have been at the forefront in developing effective means of assessing and treating these offenders and in developing methods for predicting their future risk. While progress has been made, we still have a long way to go. However, now that this is a clear public issue, we are hopeful that even more progress will be made over the next several years.

SUMMARY

Definitions of healthy or normal sexual behaviour are dependent upon social values, ethics, information, and history. Our understanding of sexual normalcy has changed as the primary sources of information have shifted from speculative theories to science. However, the progress of scientific understanding has been severely hampered in this area by biases against the open investigation and discussion of sexuality.

The sexual response cycle identified by Masters and Johnson consists of parallel stages in men and women: excitement, plateau, orgasm, and resolution. Problems in these stages occur commonly, but do not always become serious enough to warrant a diagnosis of dysfunction. Many couples deal with difficulties by adapting their sexual practices to accommodate them.

Hypoactive sexual desire appears to be increasingly present at sex therapy clinics, particularly among men. There is little information on the origins of this problem, although sometimes it is a result of earlier sexual trauma. Female sexual arousal disorder is little understood although it may occur relatively frequently. Male erectile disorder, the most common complaint among men seeking sex therapy, appears to involve a cycle of negative expectations and responses to sexual stimuli, including critical self-observation, called spectatoring. Female orgasmic disorder is the most common sexual problem presented at clinics. There are no consistent psychological differences between women who have orgasms and those who do not. Male orgasmic disorder is uncommon. Premature ejaculation is the most common male sexual complaint, although it does not always lead men and their partners to seek treatment. Anxiety and learning an overly rapid sexual response have been suggested as causes of premature ejaculation, but there is little evidence supporting this. Dyspareunia and vaginismus are sexual pain disorders that have received little attention, although they appear to be common.

The origins of sexual dysfunctions have received much less research attention than most types of disorders, although they are among the most common human problems. Treatment for these problems, however, has proliferated since the early 1970s, and appears to be quite successful. There is evidence that psychological treatments produce benefits for many clients. Physical interventions are most commonly used for male erectile disorder, and are effective for many clients; surgical intervention, because it is typically irreversible, is seen as a last resort.

Gender identity disorder is defined as a strong identification with the opposite sex. People who experience gender identity disorder may be homosexual or heterosexual. Some cross-dress and some seek to change their physical appearance to that of the desired sex through hormone treatment or surgery. Sexual reassignment surgery is chosen by a minority of people with GID; those who have the surgery generally say they are satisfied with results.

Paraphilias, as defined by the diagnostic manual, are disorders characterized by deviant sexual interests. In this chapter we have included other sexual behaviours for which there may or may not be associated deviant interests. Some of these behaviours involve activities that do not require a partner, and therefore are not inherently hurtful to or abusive of another person. These disorders we have called "sexual variants," while those that involve the abuse of another person we have called "sexual offences." Sexual offending is far more frequent than most people believe; surveys show a considerable number of women and children are victimized by these offenders.

The primary sexual variants are fetishisms, transvestic fetishisms, and sadomasochisms; the primary sexual offences are exhibitionism, voyeurism, frotteurism, child molestation, and rape. Most of those who display these disorders are men. Many appear quite similar to normal males, although group studies have found differences between sexual offenders and normal men on a number of factors. For example, most sexual offenders appear to have experienced disturbed childhoods and have difficulties in establishing satisfactory adult relationships.

Various theories have attempted to identify the etiology of aberrant sexual behaviour. Those that take a narrow view of the factors that cause sexual offending, however, do not seem able to account for the full scope of the problem. More comprehensive accounts not only integrate current knowledge, they also appear to have facilitated the development of more specific theories.

Treatment of sexual offenders, while still in the early stages of development, appears to reduce the propensity to offend. When treatment is effective, it not only prevents considerable suffering but also saves money.

KEY TERMS

sexual response cycle (p. 288)
lifelong sexual dysfunction (p. 290)
acquired sexual dysfunction (p. 290)
generalized sexual dysfunctions (p. 290)
situational sexual dysfunctions (p. 290)
hypoactive sexual desire disorder (p. 291)
sexual aversion disorder (p. 291)
female sexual arousal disorder (p. 292)
male erectile disorder (p. 292)
female orgasmic disorder (p. 292)
anorgasmia (p. 292)
male orgasmic disorder (p. 292)

premature ejaculation (p. 293)
dyspareunia (p. 293)
vaginismus (p. 293)
nocturnal penile tumescence (p. 294)
phallometry (p. 294)
prolactin (p. 295)
testosterone (p. 295)
estrogen (p. 295)
performance anxiety (p. 295)
sensate focus (p. 296)
sexual orientation (p. 299)
gender role (p. 299)
gender identity (p. 299)
hermaphroditism (p. 299)
gender identity disorder (p. 299)
gender dysphoria (p. 299)
homosexual gender dysphoria (p. 299)

heterosexual gender dysphoria (p. 300)
paraphilia (p. 302)
egodystonic homosexuality (p. 303)
fetishisms (p. 303)
transvestite (p. 304)
sadists (p. 304)
masochists (p. 304)
hypoxyphilia (p. 305)
autoerotic asphyxia (p. 305)
asphyxiophilia (p. 305)
pedophilia (p. 305)
exhibitionism (p. 305)
voyeurism (p. 305)
frotteurism (p. 305)
courtship disorder theory (p. 309)

ADDITIONAL RESOURCES

SIECCAN, The Sex Information and
    Education Council of Canada
850 Coxwell Avenue
East York, ON M4C 5R1
(416) 466-5304
(416) 778-0785 fax
sieccan@web.net

Canadian Psychological Association
151 Slater Street
Suite 205
Ottawa, ON K1P 5H3
(613) 237-2144
(613) 237-1674 fax
iparisien@cpa.ca

Lesbian and Gay Community Services
    Center
One Little West 12th Street
New York, NY 10014
(212) 620-7310
(212) 924-2657 fax
webmaster@gaycenter.org

www.cmhc.com/disorders/sx40.htm
Description of gender identity disorder and links to other
resources.

www.public.asu.edu/~ide4bubu/sexlinks/dysfunct.html
A collection of links to information on sexual problems.

www.leaderu.com/offices/rekers/docs/cross.html
This article discusses cross-sex behaviour and addresses diagnostic considerations and issues.

www.gaycenter.org/gip/html
Information on gender identity provided by the
Gender Identity Project of the Lesbian and Gay
Community Services Center.

Chapter 13

Mood Disorders and Suicide

Zindel V. Segal

H. Bruce Ferguson

Linda was a young lawyer who had just moved to Vancouver to take on an important post with the litigation group of a respected law firm. She and her husband were looking forward to getting to know the city in their spare time. As Linda's work demands started to mount, she found herself feeling insecure about her abilities and staying later at the office to make sure that things were done properly. As it became increasingly clear that long hours and work on weekends were expected of Linda, she and her husband began to argue more frequently and their relationship grew more distant. Linda noticed that her weight had started to drop, but she attributed the weight loss to a schedule so hectic that it left her little time for lunch. When Linda started waking up two or three hours earlier than usual and couldn't get back to sleep, she merely took advantage of her wakefulness and went into work early. Linda noticed other changes as well, such as her lack of interest in socializing with her colleagues and a nagging fear that people at the office were talking about her behind her back. Linda also started to dress in a casual and unkempt manner, feeling that it was too difficult to get dressed day in and day out. This caused problems at the office where the dress code was more formal.

At one point, Linda stayed at home and did not leave her bedroom for seven days. When the office called she instructed her nanny to say she had the flu, but would not take calls. If her husband asked her what was going on she would grow sullen or become irritable with him for second-guessing her. At this point, it dawned on Linda's husband that the changes in her behaviour and feeling states were not temporary and would not right themselves without some type of intervention. He convinced her to speak with a psychologist, who diagnosed a major depressive disorder, unipolar type, and recommended a 20-session course of cognitive behaviour therapy.

* * *

As human beings, our lives are continually enriched by the sheer variety of emotions we can experience. These can range from powerful surges of feeling to subtle, nuanced sensitivities, each of which may, in themselves, be pleasant, neutral, or aversive. This capacity allows us to respond to the demands of our surroundings and to feel that our lives are deep and vibrant. Yet, when mood is disordered, the very things that once made life seem full can make existence so difficult to bear that taking steps to end it seems like a plausible solution. In this chapter we will examine the different types of mood disorders, the theories that attempt to explain their causes, and how they are treated. The first important question to consider is what a mood disorder is apart from the normal ups and downs we all experience in the course of our everyday lives.

* * *

It had been five months since Brent and Jodie had broken up and he was ready to start dating again. More and more of his friends were married and Brent wondered whether he would remain single forever. He hit it off immediately with Paula, a friendly woman with an open grin. Brent and Paula spent hours chatting on the phone. They would even jest about how they would furnish a house if they got married.

Brent began to think of the two of them as a couple and was hurt when Paula was not available. When he asked her why she was limiting her involvement, she said that she wasn't ready for a relationship because she was still getting over her divorce. Eventually Brent realized that he had no future with Paula and decided to break up.

Over the next few weeks, Brent found that his need for sleep increased, he was often irritated by little things his co-workers did, it was hard to get up for work, and he was not eating as much as he used to. It wasn't that his appetite was gone so much as that food and other things were less interesting to him. He felt sad a good deal of the time and worried about ever being able to maintain a long-term relationship. With time, and the steady support of friends (some of whom suggested that Paula was a jerk for leading him on when she had no intention of getting seriously involved), he began to feel better. "Who knows," he concluded. "I guess the timing just wasn't right."

In the second case above, Brent became sad and started to experience a number of other physical changes that may be associated with depression when his romance ended. Some would call such a condition a mild or *situational* depression, meaning that the sad mood appeared to be triggered by a stressful life event. This is a normal reaction to feelings of disappointment and regret, not considered a disorder. But how does this state differ from the more serious range of responses called clinical depression or mood disorder?

There is general agreement that an altered mood state should be diagnosed as **mood disorder** (also called **affective disorder**) only when it is severe enough to interfere with a person's social and occupational functioning (for example, ability to work or go to school) and when the range of symptoms is not limited to the person's feelings, but affects other bodily and behavioural systems as well. With these guidelines in mind, we can see why the drop in Brent's mood falls within the range of normal mood swings, while Linda's difficulties represent a clinical depression.

HISTORICAL PERSPECTIVE

Changes in mood, whether mild or extreme, have been recognized as an important marker of a person's emotional stability since the advent of modern medicine (McCann & Endler, 1990). The Roman physician Galen (A.D. 129–198) was among the first to extend ideas on the relationship between bodily fluids (humours) and emotional temperament, including depression, first proposed by Hippocrates (460–377 B.C.). In Galen's time, depression was thought to result from an excess of black bile from the spleen (also called *melancholer*). Dryness was one of the physical properties thought to be associated with black bile, and so treatment involved finding ways of restoring the balance among the humours in the body, which was often done by regulating the environment in which the patient lived, for example by increasing moisture.

By the time the British physician Robert Burton wrote about depression (1621/1977) in the seventeenth century, the term *melancholia* was used to describe the condition. The treatment of depression continued to stress physical interventions: either removing a carefully measured amount of blood from the patient, or inducing the patient to vomit, both of which were intended to restore balance to the humours initially described by Hippocrates.

DIAGNOSTIC ISSUES

More recently, the diagnosis of mood disorders has been approached by a listing of core features thought to make up the syndrome, along with a timeline for the persistence of symptoms. There are two important criteria for a diagnosis of clinical disorder. The first is *duration*: we would not want to label someone as having a clinical problem if the difficulty is temporary or fleeting. The second is *severity*. For example, someone who finds it difficult to fall asleep only on occasion or only for 20 minutes would not be considered to be displaying a clinical symptom. It is only when multiple symptoms of depression co-occur and meet these two criteria that the likelihood of an affective disorder being present increases.

Mood disorders are usually classified into two broad categories according to the types of changes observed in the patient's feeling states. If the change in mood is only in the direction of depression or lowered mood, followed by a return to normal mood with recovery, then the diagnosis is likely to be one of the **unipolar disorders**. If the change in mood occurs in both directions, that is, the patient at one time or another experiences both depression (mood lowering) and mania (mood elevation), then the diagnosis is likely to be one of the **bipolar disorders**.

UNIPOLAR AFFECTIVE DISORDERS

Major Depressive Disorder

Symptoms of **major depressive disorder** include persistent feelings of sadness, loss of interest or ability to feel pleasure, unexplained weight loss, difficulty sleeping, fatigue, difficulty concentrating, feelings of worthlessness or guilt, suicidal thoughts, and either agitation or slowing down. (See the DSM table "Diagnostic Criteria for Major Depressive Episode.") To arrive at this diagnosis it must also be established that the patient is not suffering from other disorders that may present as depression, such as schizoaffective disorder (see Chapter 14) or a delusional disorder (see Chapter 17). In addition, it is important to determine whether there has been a manic, hypomanic, or mixed episode of mania and depression in the past. If there is evidence of the latter, the diagnosis is more likely to be bipolar disorder.

Diagnostic criteria require that a major depressive episode last at least two weeks, but episodes usually last much longer; a duration of six to nine months is typical.

DSM-IV   Diagnostic Criteria for Major Depressive Episode

Has the patient experienced five or more of the following symptoms **continuously at least over a two week** period and in a way that departs from the patient's normal functioning?

1. The patient reports that he/she feels depressed or sad most of the day.
2. There is a loss of interest or ability to derive pleasure from all or nearly all activities that were previously enjoyed.
3. Significant weight loss when not dieting or weight gain or a decrease or increase in appetite nearly every day.
4. There is difficulty sleeping through the night or the need for more sleep during the day.
5. The patient is noticeably slowed down or agitated throughout the day.
6. The patient reports feeling fatigued or a loss of energy nearly every day.
7. Feelings of worthlessness or extreme or inappropriate guilt.
8. The patient reports difficulties with concentration or the ability to think; this can also be seen by others as indecisiveness.
9. Recurrent thoughts of death or ideas about suicide without a specific plan for doing so or a suicide attempt.

Source: Reprinted with permission from the *Diagnostic and Statistical Manual of Mental Disorders*, Fourth Edition. Copyright 1994 American Psychiatric Association.

Prevalence and Course

Major depression has been called the common cold of mental illness, because so many people are affected by it. It is estimated that about 5 percent of Canadians suffer from depression. The Ontario Health Survey, for example, found a rate of 4.5 percent in Ontario (Offord et al., 1994). Prevalence is roughly twice as high for women as for men. These figures, however, capture only those people who would qualify for a clinical diagnosis of major depressive disorder. They do not reflect the larger number who might admit to being depressed from time to time at levels of severity which may not meet strict diagnostic criteria for major depressive disorder. If these looser criteria are used, the figures for depression jump to as high as 27 percent (Canadian Task Force on the Periodic Health Examination, 1990).

Depression used to be seen as a self-limiting and discrete disorder (Keller, 1994). It was believed that a person who had recovered from an episode of depression was unlikely to become depressed again. Understandably, this view led to an emphasis on treatments to alleviate the symptoms associated with the episode.

As further evidence has accumulated, however, the picture of the course taken by this disorder has changed dramatically. It is now estimated that at least 50 percent of patients who recover from an initial episode of depression will have at least one subsequent depressive episode (Paykel et al., 1995), and that patients with a history of two or more past episodes will have a 70 to 80 percent likelihood of recurrence in their lifetimes (Consensus Development Panel, 1985). Some researchers believe that the pattern is even more entrenched: according to Angst et al. (1973), "single episodes are extremely rare and if only time of observation can be extended beyond 15 years they are practically never observed" (p. 500).

The period of remission between episodes may be a few months or several years. Moreover, it is not unusual for people to have low mood and other symptoms of depression at subclinical levels between episodes.

It is hardly surprising, then, that depression entails significant costs for both its sufferers and society as a whole. A 1989 estimate of the total costs for major depression in Canada was $27 billion (Canadian Mental Health Association, 1995), which would include not only medical and drug costs but lost productivity due to absenteeism at work, unemployment, or permanent disability. In fact, recent data show that in terms of the numbers of days spent entirely in bed due to any type of medical illness, depression ranked second, just behind heart disease and ahead of such physically incapacitating diseases as arthritis (see Figure 13.1).

Underdiagnosis

There is, however, a large discrepancy between the number of people suffering from depression, as reported by epidemiological studies (for example, Myers et al., 1984) and the number who actually get help for the condition. As with mental disorders in general, depression may be underdiagnosed because there is no obvious marker for the condition. If you have chest pains or a suspiciously coloured spot on your skin, you may decide that you need to consult a doctor. Many of the symptoms of depression, however, do not point clearly to an emotional problem. You might feel that constant fatigue or problems with sleep are due to being overworked or not having a vacation in a while. (See the Focus box on rationalizing depression.) Symptoms such as fatigue and weight loss may also suggest various medical illnesses (Wells, 1996). So even if you went to see a doctor, you might be investigated for a medical problem and the

Figure 13.1 Days Spent Entirely in Bed: Depression and Other Medical Conditions

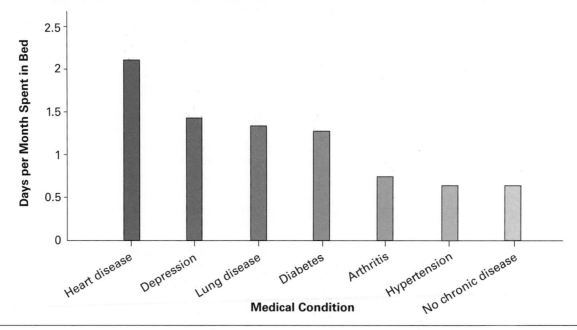

Source: Reprinted by permission of the publisher from *Caring for Depression* by Wells, Sturm, Sherbourne and Meredith, Cambridge, Mass.: Harvard University Press, Copyright © 1996 by the Rand.

Focus   *Rationalizing Depression*

When people think of depression, they tend to think only of altered mood. Yet depression can also have powerful effects on how people think, and these changes are likely to be different at various points in the course of the disorder. Early on, there may be a form of denial, in which sufferers minimize their symptoms.

Paradoxically, depression can make it difficult for us to acknowledge that we are depressed. Instead, we often consider a number of alternative explanations for the changes in thought and feeling we experience, until things reach the point where we feel too overwhelmed to do anything about the condition. Why should this be so? Remember that depression often carries with it a strong tendency to become self-critical and to blame oneself for anything that goes wrong. Taking care of oneself by being attentive to changes in one's mental health flies in the face of this austere, critical attitude. In *In the Jaws of the Black Dogs*, noted

Canadian design critic John Bentley Mays describes his struggles with depression. This excerpt shows how depression can lead to denial:

If I woke up with the familiar lethargy, and could not pull myself out of bed and get dressed until noon, or spent an afternoon crying the scant, drizzling tears peculiar to depression—here's the lie—it was just the doleful sound of winter rain blowing against the window panes, or the bitter, unremitting cold that sometimes comes in February. When the weather was glorious, some other cause would come to mind. ... Fickle weathers, of course, had nothing to do with the drawing near of such thoughts. Bad weather makes many sane people feel low ... when not stirring the simmering pot of lies within, I find much to love in the coldest days of winter. ... Apart from heavy thunderstorms, I love the cold

rains of autumn and spring. ... But on mornings of the nearing of my silent, ancient enemy, I forget all that, and blame what is close at hand; even weather I would otherwise find delightful. Thoughts of worthlessness whirl around in my head, casting out all happier thoughts; and one thing after another slips out of my control. The bills are not paid, the garbage not taken out, the book lies unread beside my chair, the article unwritten. And there come upon me those afflictions I blame everything but depression for; the rasping dryness of spirit, crippled awareness of whatever is lovely and kindly, exhaustion lingering and irremediable. And, worst of all, the after-image burned into my eyes by the nearness of the dogs, the vision of myself as waste and ruin. ▲

Source: John Bentley Mays, *In the jaws of the black dogs* (New York: Viking Press, 1995), pp. xiii–xiv. Reprinted by permission.

---

diagnosis of depression might be missed. With older people, there is the particular risk that depression will be misdiagnosed as dementia; difficulty in concentrating and loss of interest in activities may be taken for the memory deficits and flattened affect of Alzheimer's-type dementia (see Chapter 17).

Finally, one of the strongest deterrents to accurate diagnosis of depression is the stigma still associated with this condition. It is not uncommon for people to think that if they are depressed they should just "pull up their socks and get on with it," or "soldier on through the difficult times" without getting help. By preventing sufferers from seeking a diagnosis and appropriate help, such attitudes actually make it harder to recover. In fact, one form of psychotherapy for depression starts by educating patients about the fact that depression is an illness. This recognition relieves guilt by entitling patients to reduce their own expectations about how much they should do for themselves and others—as they would if they had, for example, a broken leg (Klerman, Weissman, Rounsaville, & Chevron, 1984).

Comorbidity

The most frequent comorbid condition with depression is anxiety. There is considerable symptom overlap between these two conditions: poor concentration, irritability, hypervigilance, fatigue, guilt, memory loss, sleep difficulties, and worry may suggest a diagnosis of either disorder. When a person has both clinical depression and anxiety disorder, it may be difficult to ascertain which set of problems developed first, but usually mental disorder is long-standing; comorbidity is rarely found among people who have recently fallen ill.

While it is likely that both anxiety and depression are related neurobiologically, the physiological basis for comorbid conditions is still unknown. At a psychological level, it seems reasonable that the second disorder can result from demoralization with the lack of recovery from the first. For example, an agoraphobic patient who spends much of her time in the house because she is afraid to go out on her own will experience social withdrawal, which may predispose her to depression. Conversely, a person who has become unable to work because of depression may become very worried, and predisposed to anxiety disorder.

As common as comorbidity seems to be, the treatments for depression and anxiety, by and large, continue to focus on treating one disorder at a time. The lack of an integrated treatment means that a patient treated only for depression may still suffer from anxiety.

Diagnostic Specifiers

While formal diagnostic categories are important in conveying information about the core features of a syndrome, we can also learn about the disorder by studying patients who present with variations of these features. For example, epidemiological surveys suggest that many people who would not meet the strict criteria for a diagnosis of major depressive disorder nevertheless experience significant levels of distress. If someone has only three out of the five required symptoms, for example, is he or she considered free of depression? What if one of these symptoms is particularly severe? Even within the group that meet the criteria, there can be considerable differences in presentation. To capture this natural variation in the expression of affective disturbances, a number of diagnostic categories are used. **Specifiers**—so called because they increase the specificity of diagnoses—convey important information about salient features of a patient's depression that might be otherwise overlooked. Specifiers thus lead to the creation of homogeneous subgroups, aid in treatment selection, and can improve the prediction of the course of illness (DSM-IV, 1994).

An important specifier used in conjunction with a diagnosis of major depression is "**with melancholic features**." Prominent in this type of depression is **anhedonia**, a loss of pleasure or interest in almost all activities or a lack of reactivity to usually pleasurable events. In addition, depressed mood is worst in the morning. Sleep disturbance featuring early morning awakening is also common, as is significant weight loss and psychomotor retardation or agitation (DSM-IV, 1994).

Other diagnostic categories define conditions that do not meet the full criteria for major depressive disorder.

Dysthymic Disorder

Dysthymic disorder or **dysthymia**, sometimes thought of as chronic sadness, manifests many of the same symptoms as major depression, except that they are less severe. Its distinguishing feature is the fact that it persists for at least two years with only brief times when mood returns to normal. A patient who reports having felt down more days than up over the past two years should be evaluated for this disorder. (See the DSM table "Diagnostic Criteria for Dysthymic Disorder.")

One of the problems with dysthymia is that its protracted nature can undermine many areas of the sufferer's life. People with episodic disorders may mobilize their adaptive capacities and try to cope with the problem in the short term, perhaps by containing it, tolerating it, or distracting themselves from it. As dysthymia drags on in its chronic course, however, the sufferer's coping responses may gradually wear down, and subtle changes in personality may occur. Barely able to remember what a good mood feels like, a long-term sufferer may judge the habitual mild sadness to be normal and therefore not seek help (Wells, Sturm, Sherbourne, & Meredith, 1996).

Seasonal Affective Disorder

The observation of elevated rates of depression and mania during the fall and spring has suggested that seasonal changes in the amount of sunlight available may trigger faulty regulation of circadian rhythms, leading to affective disturbance

DSM-IV   Diagnostic Criteria for Dysthymic Disorder

A. Depressed mood for most of the day, for more days than not, as shown either by self-report or observation by others, for at least 2 years.

B. Two or more of the following symptoms are present when the person is depressed:

 1. Poor appetite
 2. Insomnia or hypersomnia
 3. Low energy or fatigue
 4. Low self-esteem
 5. Poor concentration or difficulty making decisions
 6. Feelings of hopelessness

C. Over the 2-year period, the person has never been without the symptoms in Criteria A and B for more than 2 months at a time.

D. No Major Depressive Disorder has been present during the first 2 years of the disorder.

E. No evidence of a past Manic Episode, a Mixed Episode or Hypomanic Episode, and patient does not meet criteria for Cyclothymic Disorder.

F. Symptoms cause clinically significant distress or impairment in social or occupational areas of functioning.

Source: Reprinted with permission from the *Diagnostic and Statistical Manual of Mental Disorders*, Fourth Edition. Copyright 1994 American Psychiatric Association.

(Wehr & Rosenthal, 1989). People with **seasonal affective disorder (SAD)** seem to be vulnerable to environmental changes in sunlight and show a pattern of mood problems that are cyclic and time-limited. SAD may be unipolar or bipolar. People with unipolar depression may become depressed in late fall, or in late spring. Some have one episode a year, lasting typically three or four months (for example, from December to March or June to September); some may have two episodes a year. People with bipolar disorder may become depressed in the winter and manic in the summer.

The prevalence of SAD is greater at latitudes farther from the equator (such as Canada's) since there is more seasonal variation in hours of sunlight. Epidemiological data indicate that the prevalence of SAD is in the range of 4 to 6 percent and that the typical patient is female with an onset in early adulthood.

A seasonal relationship to mood swings is likely if the patient has experienced at least two depressive episodes during a particular time of the year and such seasonal episodes outnumber nonseasonal episodes. Interestingly, many of the symptoms for SAD are the reverse of those typically found in major depression. Patients will often report an increase in appetite, weight gain, and a greater need for sleep. Although these symptoms may strike some as a form of "hibernation" similar to that found in other species, it is important to remember that SAD is not limited to fall/winter periods but has a spring/summer cycle as well.

Although the mechanism by which it works it still not clearly understood, phototherapy is effective for most people with seasonal affective disorder.

The hormone melatonin, which is secreted by the pineal gland in response to changes in dark/light intensity, has been implicated in SAD. Since this hormone can be inhibited by prolonged exposure to bright light, patients with SAD have been treated with phototherapy. Patients receiving phototherapy are asked to sit in front of a light box for between two and six hours per day, preferably in the morning. It is estimated that about 80 percent of patients will respond to this regimen, with noticeable improvement occurring in a majority of patients. What is still unknown is the mechanism of this effect. While there is some evidence that exposure to bright lights slows melatonin production in individuals with SAD, it is unclear whether this is the pathway by which phototherapy achieves its effects.

BIPOLAR AFFECTIVE DISORDERS

Norman Endler, a noted Canadian psychologist, has described his experiences with bipolar depression (Endler, 1982, pp. 84–86). Here he describes the experience of mania:

"It was great to be alive again. It was inconceivable that I had recovered so rapidly and so well. One day, I was down in the dumps, destined to be an emotional cripple for the rest of my life; the next I was back to my normal self as if nothing had happened. ... I resumed my regular tennis program and my regular social life. My sex life was better than ever before. I ate and slept regularly. I felt neither tense nor anxious. In fact, I felt good. But most of all I talked. Gee whiz, did I

ever talk. I talked from morning until night. I talked incessantly. I talked nonstop and then more so. I told everyone about my illness, my treatment, and my recovery. I referred to the ECT by telling everyone how I had my brain "zapped." I was not really fully aware of my behavior nor of the effect that it had on others. ... I didn't stop to analyze my thoughts, feelings or behavior. I was critical of others and occasionally told some people off publicly. I was not so concerned about others as I had been nor of the effect my behavior had on them. I was aggressive, talked incessantly, and interrupted others while they were speaking. Whenever I had a thought I felt compelled to utter it, and I didn't always censor my thoughts and feelings. At times I seemed to have lost my sense of judgment. Except for my wife, ... no one else told me that my behavior was qualitatively different from what it had been. I was having a good time. I was ... preoccupied with myself, but ... I was making my wife miserable."

Source: Reprinted from Norman S. Endler, *Holiday in Darkness*. Reprinted with the permission of the publisher, Wall & Emerson, Inc., Toronto, Canada.

Mania

The word **mania** has its origins in the Greek term *mainomai* meaning "to be mad." Whereas the symptoms of depression may be all too easy to overlook, the hallmarks of manic episodes are flamboyance and expansiveness. In fact, extreme or prolonged cases of mania are considered bona fide psychotic states, implying that the person is experiencing a break with reality. Less severe or briefer episodes are called **hypomanic**, meaning that the individual's state of mind would not be considered psychotic, but nevertheless represents significant impairment.

As with depression, the diagnosis of mania is made on the basis of criteria related both to how long the episode lasts and the number of symptoms experienced (see the DSM table "Diagnostic Criteria for Manic Episode"). A manic episode must be at least one week long. Such episodes typically do not last much longer than a week.

A person experiencing a manic episode may go on shopping sprees, engage in sexually promiscuous behaviour, take on numerous, unrealistic work commitments, brag, and dominate others socially. In general, the person shows intolerance when the world does not cooperate with his or her momentary needs. For example, one patient remembered being in such a hurry to get things done that he skipped out on paying a hotel bill because the person standing in line in front of him was taking too long to check out.

Although the symptoms associated with most mental disorders are unpleasant and unwanted, patients report that some aspects of the manic state are enjoyable and intoxicating. The patient's mind often seems clear, sharply focussed, and able to

DSM-IV Diagnostic Criteria for Manic Episode

I. The patient's **mood is abnormally and consistently elevated**, expansive or irritable for at least one week.

II. During the time that the patient's mood was elevated, were three or more of the following present to a significant degree?

- Excessive self-esteem or grandiosity.
- Less need for sleep.
- More talkative than usual or feels a pressure to keep talking.
- The patient reports that he/she feels that his/her thoughts are racing.
- The patient is easily distracted.
- The patient is agitated and there is an increase in behavior aimed at achieving a specific goal of his/hers.
- Impulsive acts aimed at increasing the sensation of pleasure (e.g., shopping sprees, promiscuity, etc.).

Source: Adapted from American Psychiatric Association, *Diagnostic and statistical manual of mental disorders,* 4th ed. (Washington, DC: APA, 1994).

Source: Reprinted with permission from the *Diagnostic and Statistical Manual of Mental Disorders,* Fourth Edition. Copyright 1994 American Psychiatric Association.

make connections between things that had previously seemed unrelated. (More often than not, these dazzling insights don't seem so profound once the patient is not feeling so high.) Some cognitive functions may, in fact, be enhanced, although impulsiveness may interfere with other cognitive tasks. People often report being able to use their abundant energy to complete a great deal of work. It is this wonderful ability to make sense of things and to solve difficult problems and the tremendous sense of power over one's environment that manic patients are reluctant to give up (Jamison, 1995). Caught up in a wave of enthusiasm and expansiveness, these people often deny they are having difficulties and are thus unlikely to take appropriate remedial action. Indeed, a desire to hang on to the pleasurable feelings may be one reason for poor compliance with effective treatments such as lithium, which reduces the grandiosity and expansiveness. Similarly, when patients feel discouraged or stressed they may stop taking their medication in order to bring back the high experienced during the manic state.

Bipolar I and Bipolar II

When episodes of depression alternate with episodes of mania or hypomania, this is called bipolar disorder. This disorder has been classified into two types: **Bipolar 1**, in which there are one or more manic episodes and usually one or more depressive episodes; and **Bipolar 2**, in which there is at least one hypomanic episode and one or more episodes of major depression. As these categories suggest, it is very rare for an individual to experience an episode of mania without an accompanying depression at some point in his or her life. The depressions last much longer than the manic episodes, typically six to nine months as in unipolar disorders. Between episodes, people may have normal mood, or may have periods of dysthymic-type symptoms.

Bipolar disorder is less common than major depression, with estimates running between 0.8 to 1.6 percent of the population (Kessler et al., 1994). As Table 13.1 indicates, bipolar disorder differs from unipolar disorder not only in the presence of manic episodes; the features of depressive episodes also differ. Unlike major depression, bipolar depression is evenly distributed between men and women.

Bipolar depression has a mean age of onset in the early twenties, with the highest risk period being between the ages of 20 and 29. Rates of suicide are very high, running from anywhere between 10 to 15 percent if left untreated. In addition, the chronic nature of this condition and the unpredictability of the sufferer often take a heavy toll on those closest to him or her. As a result, there is an increased rate of joblessness, divorce, and financial difficulties in this population (U.S. Department of Health and Human Services, 1993).

Recently there has been interest in the fact that creative individuals appear to be overrepresented among sufferers of bipolar disorder (see Table 13.2). One view holds that mood swings and creativity are related because familiarity with extreme aspects of human experience provide the artist with the raw materials for creative expression; another possibility is that the cyclic rhythms of mood swings correspond to the nature of creative output (Andreasen, 1987). Although this

Table 13.1 Differences in Symptom Patterns Between Unipolar and Bipolar Depression

Symptom	Unipolar	Bipolar
Activity level	Agitated	Marked slowing
Sleep	Insomnia	Hypersomnia
Age of onset	Late teens–early 20s	Thirties
Family history	Strong familial risk for unipolar depression	Strong familial risk for unipolar and bipolar depression
Gender	More common in women	Fairly evenly distributed
Pharmacotherapy	Lithium mostly used as augmentation to first-line antidepressant medication	Lithium is treatment of choice

Table 13.2 Poets and Bipolar Disorder (partial listing of major American poets with documented histories of bipolar disorder)

	Pulitzer Prize in Poetry	Treated for Major Depressive Illness	Treated for Mania	Committed Suicide
Hart Crane (1899–1932)		•	•	•
Theodore Roethke (1908–1963)	•	•	•	
Delmore Schwartz (1913–1966)		•	•	
John Berryman (1914–1972)	•	•	•	•
Randall Jarrell (1914–1965)		•	•	•
Robert Lowell (1917–1977)	•	•	•	
Ann Sexton (1928–1974)	•	•	•	•
Sylvia Plath* (1932–1963)	•	•		•

*Plath, although not treated for mania, was probably Bipolar II.

Source: From MANIC-DEPRESSIVE ILLNESS by F. K. Goodwin & K. R. Jamison. Copyright © 1990 by Oxford University Press, Inc. Used by permission of Oxford University Press, Inc.

association has been noted over many years, it is not clear whether it captures a true causal element, or whether it merely reflects the way certain lives may be romanticized. Artists' celebrity status may attract biographers who cast about for details that speak to the sensational and pathological in their lives; thus, it may be not so much that poets and movie stars are more likely to suffer such symptoms than plumbers and accountants as that we are more likely to know about them.

As with unipolar disorders, there are a number of diagnostic categories that describe people who do not meet the full criteria for bipolar disorder but have related symptom profiles.

Rapid Cycling Depression/Mania

A person who moves very quickly in and out of depressive and manic episodes—four or more episodes of mania and/or depression in one year—may have a particularly severe type of bipolar disorder called **rapid cycling depression/mania**. These patients often do not respond as strongly to pharmacotherapy, which may relieve only some of the symptoms. In fact, there is a risk in some patients that standard pharmacotherapy can induce rapid cycling. One estimate suggests that as many as 15 to 20 percent of patients with bipolar disorder may demonstrate this rapid cycling. Because the usual progression of the disorder is toward more frequent episodes of depression and mania, some (for example, Post, 1992) have suggested that a seizure model emphasizing the autonomous kindling of new episodes may be one of the mechanisms responsible. While there is no hard data to confirm or contradict this view, it is interesting to note that anticonvulsant medication is sometimes used with success in treating this condition.

Cyclothymia

As with unipolar disorder, bipolar disorder exists in a less severe form. It is possible for a person to experience a long-standing pattern of alternating mood episodes that do not meet the criteria for major depressive or manic episode. Criteria for a diagnosis of **cyclothymic disorder**, or

cyclothymia, include a duration of at least two years with recurrent periods of mild depression alternating with hypomania. These periods may alternate with other times when the person's mood is normal for up to two months. During periods of mild depression, sufferers often feel worthless, but when they are hypomanic their view of themselves is inflated. This type of shifting between personality traits, combined with mood volatility, often leads to imbalances in interpersonal relationships. Others may be drawn to the traits exhibited by a person in the hypomanic phase, but find the person less appealing when his or her mood starts to drop. Thus social support may erode just when it is most needed.

Figure 13.2 shows the spectrum of mood variability, from mood swings only slightly wider than normal (cyclothymic personality) through the ups and downs of cyclothymic disorder to the sharp swings of bipolar disorder.

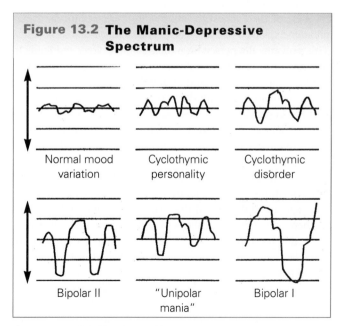

Figure 13.2 The Manic-Depressive Spectrum

Normal mood variation

Cyclothymic personality

Cyclothymic disorder

Bipolar II

"Unipolar mania"

Bipolar I

Source: Adapted from MANIC-DEPRESSIVE ILLNESS by F. K. Goodwin & K. R. Jamison. Copyright © 1990 by Oxford University Press, Inc. Used by permission of Oxford University Press, Inc.

ETIOLOGY

Although the definitive causes of mood disorders are still unknown, most researchers agree that depression is multifactorial, involving a complex and dynamic interaction of social, biological, and psychological (for example, cognitive, behavioural, affective, motivational, personality) variables. This is reflected in the different models that have been proposed to explain how depression develops. Most of the following section refers primarily to major depression. However, since many studies have not distinguished between unipolar and bipolar disorder, it is difficult to discuss the etiology of these disorders separately.

Psychological Models

Among the psychological theories, we consider those models that view depression as resulting from early deprivations in the parent-child relationship, negatively biased information processing, or high levels of life stress.

Psychodynamic Models

The psychodynamic perspective on mood disorders is based on Freud's (1917) early writings on the meaning of loss and his understanding of how different individuals respond to this event. He suggested traumatic events as early as the oral stage of psychosexual development may lead an individual to be vulnerable to loss later in life. The general psychodynamic model views depressive symptoms as the products of conflicts that are likely unconscious. These symptoms, although they may reflect disturbances in somatic functioning (for example, insomnia, loss of appetite), have important symbolic meanings. It is this unresolved conflict that results in depression and the goal of treatment is to address it directly, rather than through providing relief from the symptoms themselves.

One of the earliest psychodynamic formulations of depression explained its occurrence as due to unconscious hostility. This prevents the person from being able to love and leads to feelings of guilt and worthlessness. Freud held that powerful feelings, such as anger and disappointment, are stirred up in response to loss through death or abandonment, but that instead of expressing these feelings against the person who has left, the depressed individual turns them toward himself or herself. This mechanism has been called "anger turned inward." Freud drew an important distinction between the natural process of mourning or grief following a loss and the more incapacitating response of melancholia. In both cases, the mourner feels sad about the loss of the loved person, but in melancholia there are additional feelings of guilt, shame, and self-blame.

Later work focussed on the effects that an ambivalent attitude toward the lost love object can have for the survivor. By expressing anger at the love object for leaving, the person becomes vulnerable to internal criticism by the superego, the mind's protector of standards and codes of moral behaviour. (See Chapter 2.) This criticism contributes to feelings of inadequacy, anhedonia, and possibly suicide, the ultimate act of self-punishment.

A depressive personality? More recently, a number of revisions of the psychodynamic framework have been presented that build on Freud's observations but emphasize the role of early childhood events, especially loss of self-esteem and a continual turning to others for approval and acceptance. Premorbid personality—that is, the personality displayed before the individual became depressed—has been an important factor in psychodynamic models of depression. The suggestion here is that certain traits may make individuals especially vulnerable to depression. People with a depressive personality style tend to rely excessively on others for validation and approval. When they don't receive such reinforcement, their self-esteem drops sharply. They may also become adept at eliciting and insisting on a steady flow of approval from those they are intimately involved with.

While much of the evidence for this concept has come from anecdotal reports of clinical cases, there have been some efforts to document the effects of certain personality styles on the development of depression. One of the most comprehensive was conducted by Hirschfeld et al. (1989), who found little predictive power for premorbid traits predicting the onset of depression. There was some indication in this study that dependency features may be related to depression, but it was unclear whether this was a cause of the disorder or a factor that prolonged the disorder once it developed.

Attachment and depression. Bowlby (1980) studied how **disruptions in attachment**, especially to the early parent-child relationship, affect later personality development and how certain personality types were vulnerable to depression. He noted that one of the first tasks of the infant was to form a reliable bond with the parent and that the nature of this bond could determine the child's personality. Attachments could be secure, avoidant (being uncomfortable with intimacy), or anxious/ambivalent (excessively clinging, feeling that others were not as close as one would wish). Weak affectional bonds in early childhood and poor social relations later in life have been shown to contribute to depression (Burbach & Borduin, 1986). In fact, there is evidence that intimacy and social support can protect against depression when the person must face difficult circumstances (Brown, Andrews, Harris, Adler, & Bridge, 1986). According to this theory, the route by which some of the more common risk factors for depression operate (for example, presence of a depressed or alcoholic parent, neglect or abuse in childhood) is to weaken social bonds, thereby leaving the person susceptible to depression.

Blatt (1974) was one of the first to investigate more specific descriptions of the different types of depressive states that arise from patterns of interaction between children and their parents. When parents act in ways that leave their child feeling deprived, rejected, confused, or overindulged, the child's sense of self may embody conflicts relating to affection, care, and love. When depressed, a person with this background may be demanding of others, exhibit clinging behaviours, seek constant reassurance, and fear the loss of intimate relationships. Blatt has labelled this **anaclitic depression**. If parents are overly critical, controlling, intrusive, and punishing, the child's sense of self may embody conflicts relating to identity, competition, and aggression. A person with such a background may develop **introjective depression**, carrying feelings of inferiority, inadequacy, self-criticism, and guilt.

When some of the major premises of this approach to depression are examined empirically, the evidence for them is limited. For example, how can we assess whether people hold unconscious hostile feelings for those they love? Assessments of the thoughts and dreams of depressed persons show that themes of loss and failure predominate, not anger and hostility, as the theory would predict (Beck & Ward, 1961). Yet Blatt's approach has been supported by studies looking at differences on a questionnaire he developed to assess the two different types of depression. Depressed patients who scored in the elevated range on the anaclitic subscale of the Depressive Experiences Questionnaire showed a different symptom profile than patients who had high scores on the introjective subscale (Robins, Block, & Peselow, 1989).

Cognitive Models of Depression

There are a number of cognitive views of depression each of which builds on the basic observation that how people think can have a profound influence on how they feel. The approach developed by A. T. Beck (1967) initially grew out of clinical observations of depressed patients and was later supported by experimental work conducted by Martin Seligman and his colleagues (Seligman, 1975).

As was typical for his time, Beck adopted a traditional psychoanalytic perspective to understand the repetitive, negative, and self-defeating nature of his depressed patients' thinking. However, Beck found little support for the commonly held view that these thoughts reflected important symbolic processes related to unconscious anger. In his sessions, he began to spend less time interpreting the thoughts that patients were reporting for their hidden meaning and more time working directly with these thoughts.

A depressed accountant describes being informed by the president of his firm that the contract position for which he was initially hired will expire in two months. The president goes on to tell him that the firm is very pleased with his work and will consider him for future consulting opportunities. In retelling this incident to his therapist, the patient remembers thinking "I am being fired; once again, this means I have failed. If I were more competent she would have found a way to keep me on. The only reason she's saying those things about my performance is because she pities me." Even though the patient knew at the time of hiring that the position was time-limited, and that "rationally, I know that they haven't misled me," he continues to feel as if this outcome confirms a deeper sense of his own inadequacy.

This case illustrates one of Beck's observations: that depressed patients often report a **negative cognitive triad** of thoughts about the future, the world around them, and themselves. Like this accountant, they tend to see themselves as worthless, helpless to change the events in their lives, and hopeless about the future.

Notice also that in trying to understand why he was let go, the patient was drawn to interpretations that were likely to reinforce his own beliefs about his shortcomings. Beck proposed that depressed patients often perceive the cup as half empty rather than half full because their views are biased by **negative schemata**. A *schema* is a set of interconnected beliefs, information, and examples used to organize and simplify subsequent information on a topic. All of us use schemata of some kind to deal with the wealth of information around us, but some people apply schemata overly rigidly, and some people begin with extreme or unrealistic schemata. A person with a negative schema of the world or a negative self-schema will expect things not to work out, and therefore tend to look for evidence that they have not worked out, and miss information that paints a different picture. Although negative schemata are not directly detectable, they lead to certain types of thinking errors or cognitive distortions that are easily observed. (See the discussion in Chapter 9 on how cognitive error can also contribute to the maintenance of eating disorders.)

Among the more common types of thinking errors or cognitive distortions are

- *overgeneralization:* drawing a broad conclusion on the basis of a single incident (for example, "I failed the last exam; therefore I have no chance of passing the next one");
- *all or nothing thinking:* seeing a situation only in extreme terms (for example, "If I get above 80 percent on this exam I am a success; otherwise I am a failure"); and
- *arbitrary inference:* drawing a conclusion on the basis of skimpy evidence (for example, "He did not smile at me; therefore he dislikes me")

It is important to recognize that cognitive distortions in and of themselves do not cause depression; in fact, these ways of thinking are normally distributed in the population. The same types of cognitive error, applied to different schemata or to schemata about other areas, can lead to different conclusions. For example, a person with a schema about the shortcomings of certain ethnic groups may apply a cognitive error to reinforce her prejudices, but will not become depressed. Rather, the combination of negative expectations about oneself and one's future and the rigid thinking that lies behind cognitive errors cause depressed people to misinterpret events in their lives, and these interpretations make it more likely that a sad mood will follow. With time, the mood changes may last for longer and lead to behavioural withdrawal, so that the person starts on a vicious *downward spiral*, which often ends in clinical depression.

There is a good deal of evidence supporting this type of model as well as the more general association between thinking and feeling in depression. Singer and Salovey (1988) have shown that mood and memory influence each other, so that it is easier to recall unhappy memories when one's mood is low and vice versa.

In a specific application of this theory, Williams and Broadbent (1986) demonstrated that the autobiographical memories of depressed patients who had attempted suicide were more general and lacking in detail than in nondepressed psychiatric control patients. They suggest that the difficulty in remembering specific examples of mastery or good experiences interferes with problem-solving ability and, as a result, may be one reason why these patients view suicide as an option.

A second prominent cognitive approach to depression is that of **learned helplessness/hopelessness** (Abramson, Metalsky, & Alloy, 1989). The earliest formulations of this model were based on experimental work using a paradigm in which dogs were exposed to inescapable shock. Seligman (1975) noted that the dogs' reactions to this experience mirrored many of the symptoms exhibited by depressed individuals: mood change, passivity, loss of appetite, and sleep disturbance.

Translating this finding to humans, the learned helplessness model of depression postulated that a basic cause of depression is the expectation that bad events will occur and there is nothing to be done to prevent them. Depression was seen as arising from people's lack of control over bad events in their lives and the types of explanations they used to understand this lack of control. A depressive reaction was most likely to be associated with explanations of bad events in terms of causes that were internal to the individual, stable, and global. The critical factor is not the presence of the event itself, nor even the lack of control, but the person's interpretation of the situation.

For example, suppose two people—Marie and Louise—had both lost most of their possessions in a fire caused by an overloaded electric circuit. Neither had smoke alarms in her apartment. Marie explains the fire as caused by a freak accident and the landlord's carelessness; she sees herself as a heroine recovering from disaster with the help of friends. "I'll sue the landlord!" she says. "And my next apartment, I'll get a properly run place." Louise explains the fire as caused by her own stupidity in overloading the circuit and her weakness in not demanding a smoke alarm. "Things like this happen to me. I'm not the kind of person who can get a decent place to live or look after a place." Although both are upset by their loss, only Louise is at risk for depression.

In their extension of this work, Abramson et al. (1989) propose that hopelessness is an immediately preceding and sufficient cause of depression and that there is a chain of events that builds toward the development of hopelessness in individuals and, subsequently, results in depression. Although no single link in the chain leads to hopelessness in and of itself, each contributes significantly. Hopelessness develops when a distressing event in an important area of the individual's life is coupled with attributions about the event that are stable and global and have implications for the person's view of himself or herself. The specific cognitive risk factor in this model is a general tendency to explain events in terms of stable and global

causes, to view adverse events as having extremely adverse consequences, and to see bad events as lowering self-esteem.

This model of depression has been studied widely and there is good support for the notion that depressed and nondepressed persons exhibit differences in their thinking. For example, Seligman, Abramson, Semmel, and Von Beyer (1979) have shown that depressed patients differed from nondepressed controls in the explanations they gave for bad outcomes. Depressed patients tended to see failure or rejection as being their fault and due to personal characteristics that are stable parts of their personalities, whereas nondepressed controls took less responsibility for the same events. This shows that the way in which people explain failure or defeat can have important effects on their subsequent moods.

In fact, the most recent work on the role of attributions has suggested that there may be a specific subtype of depression that is defined by high levels of negative thinking, as opposed to other types of symptoms (Abramson, Metalsky, & Alloy, 1989). One of the most intriguing features of this approach is the possibility of finding ways to prevent depression by studying the effects of various strategies used with dogs to prevent them from succumbing to learned helplessness. If an animal learns that it has control over important events such as shock and food, it may be less susceptible to learned helplessness.

Perhaps humans can prevent depressive reactions by learning new responses. For example, in the *structured mastery approach*, people are encouraged to take constructive action first, rather than getting blocked at the stage of considering whether it will work—get up, take exercise, go out for dinner with a friend. (As a well-known commercial put it, "Just do it.") In a related technique of *immunization*, people are encouraged to acknowledge and monitor moderately low moods before they can become self-reinforcing, and to recognize that low mood need not prevent them from doing things to look after themselves. Interestingly, one study using this framework with 10-to-13-year-old children showed a reduction in depressive symptoms, as well as fewer conduct problems compared to a control group (Jaycox, Reivich, Gillham, & Seligman, 1994).

Life Stress Perspectives

Cognitive and psychodynamic models of depression have been criticized by some for not paying enough attention to the role of environmental triggers of depression and for focussing instead on concepts that exist largely in the minds of the depressed people themselves (Coyne & Gotlib, 1983). In the diathesis-stress framework (see Chapter 2), which recognizes the relationship between life stress and development of affective disorder, depression is seen as developing from the interaction between a constitutional vulnerability (diathesis) and marked levels of stress. Even low levels of stress can trigger the disorder in a person who is extremely vulnerable constitutionally. Conversely, even people who are not predisposed to depressive disorder can develop depression if exposed to severe enough stress, such as the experience of war, disaster, or prolonged deprivation.

Sometimes, such a response is self-limiting and resolves when the stressful event has resolved; this is called **adjustment disorder**. However, where the stress is particularly severe, major depressive disorder may develop that will not resolve spontaneously.

The work of Brown and Harris (1978) established the link between distressing life events and long-term effects. Specifically, they found that early childhood loss, such as the loss of a parent before the age of 12, was a powerful predictor of depression in adulthood. There was also a strong association between the onset of depression and recent losses, such as being fired from work, marital separation, or doing poorly at school (Monroe & Simons, 1991). For example, Roy and Kennedy (1984) compared a sample of 72 Canadian depressed patients with never-depressed orthopedic patients and found significantly greater levels of early loss and current marital difficulties in the depressed subjects. A Canadian research team was also among the first to show that this relationship held not only for unipolar depression, but for bipolar depression as well (Kennedy, Thompson, Stancer, Roy, & Persad, 1983; see also Hammen, Ellicott, Gitlin, & Jamison, 1989).

Yet stress does not always lead to depression. In fact, only about 10 percent of people experiencing severe losses go on to develop depression. Why do these people become depressed when the other 90 percent do not? One answer is that certain environmental factors are protective, even in the presence of significant life stress. In the sample of women studied by Brown and Harris (1978), women who had an intimate partner, held a job outside the home, had fewer than three children still at home, and subscribed to a system of religious beliefs were less likely to become depressed after recent loss events. Perhaps these factors help to protect them against the development of a pervasive sense of hopelessness and lack of options and, in this way, help to keep depressive reactions at bay (Rutter, 1985).

A second hypothesis is that distressing life events are more likely to lead to depression when the type of difficulties are in areas of the person's life that he or she feels insecure about. This view is more integrative than the models presented above, because it draws a number of different factors together in its explanation of how depression is triggered. Neither high levels of stress nor specific personality/constitutional characteristics alone are sufficient causes of depression. Rather, it is when these two factors interact that the risk for depression is greatest. This has been called the **congruency hypothesis**. *Congruent* stressful events are those that match the person's specific vulnerability, whereas noncongruent events do not.

Evidence in support of this view comes from a Canadian study examining the development of depression in people with two different personality types: dependent personality and self-critical personality. Dependent traits include being clingy in relationships or looking to others for self-esteem, whereas self-critical traits involve being very self-punitive about making mistakes or feeling that one has to live up to unreasonably high standards at all times. All participants in the study were in remission from a previous episode of major depression suffered up to one year earlier. The study posed the question of whether relapse would be more likely to be triggered by congruent or noncongruent stressful life events. Subjects who were interpersonally dependent were found to become depressed more often when they suffered a breakup of a relationship than when they failed a course or were given a poor evaluation at work (Segal, Shaw, Vella, & Katz, 1992). These subjects were generally able to handle stress related to their jobs or schoolwork without getting depressed, but if the stress was related to an important interpersonal relationship they ended up getting depressed.

Interpersonal Effects of Mood Disorders: A Vicious Circle

As we pointed out earlier, living with a chronic affective disorder can lead to changes not only in how sufferers view themselves but also in how they are viewed by those around them. Interpersonal relationships may be damaged; and there is a good deal of evidence that these changes in relationships in turn contribute to maintaining and exacerbating symptoms (Coyne, 1976; Gotlib & Hammen, 1995).

In general, these relationships are described as conflict-ridden and lacking in mutuality. Significant others commonly go through two stages of response. At first they are sympathetic and do what they can to help. But after a while, they begin to resent the ceaseless quality of requests from the depressed person and express this feeling indirectly through mixed messages of support and rejection. Couples where one spouse is depressed, for example, typically show greater negative expressiveness and emotional outbursts than nondepressed couples. There may also be a greater imbalance between the things that they say to one another and their nonverbal communication about the same topic.

People with depression are often unable to maintain intimate relationships, perhaps because their feelings of worthlessness lead them to expect rejection, or perhaps because others find their depressed mood hard to take. Unfortunately, the added burden of loneliness only worsens their state of mind.

One explanation could be that the types of personality characteristics that become pronounced in depression upset the balance of power in the relationship. If a depressed person is emotionally dependent and socially inactive, his or her deep needs may place an inordinate strain upon an important few relationships. Over time, this burden leads to resentment and hostility.

What effect does this conflict have on the disorder itself? The best evidence we have comes from the work on **expressed emotion (EE)**. (See Chapter 14.) This concept describes the amount of criticism, hostility, or overinvolvement the depressed person is exposed to in his or her interpersonal environment. A home in which interactions are characterized by repeated very critical remarks by a spouse, partner, or other family member would be considered to be a high-EE environment. Using this framework, Hooley and Teasdale (1989) reported that unipolar depressed patients who were discharged from hospital into high-EE home environments were more likely to suffer a relapse within nine months than patients who returned to low-EE environments. Thus, living with a critical spouse or other family member may be one of the avenues through which interpersonal difficulties influence relapse.

Another possibility is that personal relationships erode in depression not only because others react with hostility but, more importantly, because depressed people themselves limit their relationships. Using an innovative focus group strategy, Coyne and Calarco (1995) interviewed people who had a history of depression, but were not currently depressed. Those who had had multiple experiences of depression interacted differently; usually they had lowered their expectations of what they could get from relationships with others and had also scaled back their ambitions. It seems understandable that a depressed person would try to protect herself or himself from hoping for too much, given past experiences. However, this approach to relationships may itself contribute to the maintenance of symptoms as others react by drawing back. It might also prevent individuals from learning alternative interpersonal skills that could help them obtain supportive social relationships.

Biological Models

Biological theories propose that depression is the result of an organic dysfunction and that the nature of the dysfunction can be detected through studies of the genetics, biochemistry, or neurophysiology of depression. Studies of somatic processes in depression have been ongoing over the past century, but it was only through the discovery of antidepressant medications in the 1950s that more precise hypotheses about the relationship between biological processes and affective disorder could be formulated. Investigations of the pathways through which somatic treatments for depression achieved their effects, for example, provided clues to physical systems that might be responsible for mood regulation. Advances in the reliable diagnosis of depressive syndromes and the use of computer-aided visual imaging have also helped in the search to uncover mechanisms of brain functions in depression.

Genetic Evidence

Can affective disorders—or a vulnerability to such disorders—be inherited? Perhaps a better way to put the question is this: How much influence does heredity assert over the way in which depression develops, and how much influence does environment assert?

It has long been observed that depression runs in families; that is, the close relatives of people suffering from depression are more likely to have depression themselves than the general population. Yet it is hard to know how much of this effect arises from genetic influence and how much from nurture; siblings and parents, after all, share the same family environment. If we noted that attending medical school or law school followed a strong familial pattern, we would not want to conclude that there is a "medical practitioner" or "legal practitioner" gene. Rather, the effects of the family's culture and attitudes toward education would more likely be responsible.

One method that has been used to tease apart familial from genetic contributions to developing depression is the family study (see Chapter 4). In this design probands are identified who clearly meet the criteria for a diagnosis of affective disorder. The next step involves systematically locating and interviewing family members to find out if they have ever suffered from the disorder. The concordance for varying degrees of genetic relationship are calculated.

It has been found that first-degree relatives of people with unipolar disorder have a prevalence of 25 to 30 percent for depression and second-degree relatives have a prevalence of between 12 percent to 15 percent—still significantly higher than the rate for the general population (Palmour, 1989; Torgersen, 1986). The link is even stronger for bipolar disorder: first-degree relatives of patients with bipolar depression are at significantly higher risk of developing mood disorders of any type than are first-degree relatives of unipolar depressed patients. (Because early studies in this area did not distinguish between these two types of disorders, they often yielded an underestimate of the true level of heritability.)

Adoption studies have also supported the notion of heritability. In an early study using this method, Mendlewicz and Rainer (1977) found rates of 32 percent in the biological parents of affectively ill adoptees as compared to 12 percent in their adoptive parents. In interpreting these findings, however, we must remember that adoption is an unusual event to begin with, and so the families who give up their children for adoption may themselves be predisposed to heightened life stress and adversity. Nevertheless, the finding is suggestive.

Further recent evidence for a heritable component in unipolar depression comes from a twin study conducted by McGuffin, Katz, and Rutherford (1991). They found higher rates of concordance for depression among monozygotic twins (53 percent) than dizygotic twins (28 percent).

The genetic findings in depression have led to two broad conclusions. First, there is evidence of genetic transmission for a range of disorders that includes the more formal diagnostic categories of unipolar and bipolar affective disorders, along with eating disorders, suicide, and schizoaffective disorder. The evidence for a genetic contribution is stronger for bipolar disorder than for unipolar depression (Hammen, 1991).

Given that a disorder appears to have a genetic component, questions remain about the exact type and mechanism of transmission. A more specific method used to isolate the genetic contribution to mental disorder is called **linkage analysis**. This method capitalizes on what is already known about the chromosome pattern for a particular, more easily observable trait (such as red-green colour deficiency) that appears to be linked with affective disorder. (See Chapter 14 for a discussion of similar linkage studies relating to schizophrenia.) If it can be established that the traits are indeed linked genetically, the observable trait can be considered a genetic marker for affective disorder, and it will be assumed that the same chromosome that carries that trait also carries a gene that increases a person's risk for mood disorder.

To examine the proposed relationship, family pedigrees are collected and studied for cases in which both depression and the linked trait are present. The important question then becomes whether the linkage pattern can be replicated across a new series of pedigrees (Sevy, Mendlewicz, & Mendelbaum, 1995). A good deal of research on the genetics of affective disorder has focussed on the X chromosome and on chromosome 11.

Early findings using this method were reported by Winokur, Clayton, and Reich (1969), who examined whether manic depressive illness was transmitted on the X chromosome. The argument in favour of X-linked heritance came from observations that data from family studies showed a greater risk of transmission to females than to males, and two family pedigrees in which bipolar disorder was prominent also showed a strong association with red-green colour deficiency (commonly called colour-blindness), an X-linked trait. These findings, however, have not been replicated. Perhaps there is a subtype of bipolar disorder with X-linked heritance, but at present the evidence does not support this view.

One of the problems of studying family pedigrees is that marriage often introduces genetic diversity, which makes drawing conclusions about the familial transmission of disorder harder to verify. More recent work has tried to address this problem by studying communities in which in-group marriage is the norm. In this way, the genetic contribution to disorder might be seen more clearly. Sephardic Jewish families and the Old Order Amish have been two such groups. Egeland et al. (1987), for example, reported success in conducting linkage analysis (Egeland et al., 1987) in a community of the Old Order Amish in Pennsylvania, with a tendency for bipolar disorder being associated with a gene on chromosome 11. However, other studies of different Amish pedigrees and three studies of Icelandic pedigrees have failed to replicate this finding. Furthermore, in cases where other linkage studies have reported some success, it is not always at the same site. What this suggests is that while a tendency to mood disorder can be inherited, there is likely not one single "depression gene." This heterogeneity precludes a straightforward charting of genetic pathways.

Neurotransmitter Deficiency Theories

In studying the biochemistry of the brain, depression researchers have postulated a number of neurochemical disturbances that are correlated with changes in mood. Much of this work has examined various neurotransmitters, including norepinephrine, dopamine, serotonin, and acetylcholine. *Neurotransmitters* are chemical substances manufactured at the neuron and released at the *synapse*, or gap between one neuron and another (see Chapter 2 and Chapter 14). The synapse is the central point of neural communication, and when a neurotransmitter is released it can have the effect of exciting other neurons around it, which would increase the chance of those neurons firing, or it can have the opposite effect and inhibit neighbouring neurons, thereby reducing the chances of their firing. At a very simple level, many neurotransmitter-based theories of depression suggest that it is characterized by low rates of neural firing in selected brain areas. This underperformance is due to an absence or shortage of the neurotransmitters needed to activate neighbouring neurons.

Neurotransmitters such as serotonin and norepinephrine are part of a larger group of molecules called the **catecholamines**; these chemicals have been implicated most directly in models of depression. According to the monoamine hypothesis (Schildkraut, 1965), differing levels of these neurotransmitters can disrupt mood regulation and bring on other symptoms of depression. For example, a shortage of norepinephrine, dopamine, or serotonin is thought to cause depression through decreasing the amount of neuronal activity in specific brain regions, while an excess of these neurotransmitters is thought to cause mania due to increased neuronal activity. The hypothesis is intuitively appealing, in that the biochemical activity postulated mimics the behavioural signs of the disorder itself. That is, it is easy to understand that an excess of neuronal activity could lead to excitement and restlessness and slowed activity to depression and lethargy. Moreover, the theory is appealing because the remedy seems straightforward: it seems reasonable that increasing the levels of available monoamines should alleviate depression, and that decreasing them in manic patients should alleviate mania (McNeal & Cimbolic, 1986).

This framework has, understandably, generated considerable research. However, findings have been contradictory (Thase & Howland, 1995). The evidence for lower overall levels of monoamine synthesis or increased breakup of monoamines in depression is inconsistent. On one hand, the supportive evidence comes from the finding that when vulnerable patients are given drugs that lead to a reduction in amines, they become depressed. On the other hand, giving patients drugs that lead to more monoamine creation does not always produce an antidepressant effect. Moreover, when antidepressant drugs that increase monoamines are effective, mood changes occur roughly one week after these neurotransmitters have been made available at the neuronal level. This time lag would not be predicted by the model; rather, one would expect that reversing the chemical imbalance would lead to rapid change in mood.

Another group of theories have looked beyond the relative availability of neurotransmitters at the synapse to suggest that depression is due to an altered or diminished function at the receptor neuron (postsynaptic neuron). In this case, normal levels of neurotransmitter would have little effect in terms of excitatory influence and the neuron would be less likely to fire. Changes in the postsynaptic receptor may explain why it usually takes 10 to 14 days for antidepressant medication to have its effect.

Electrophysiological Findings and Sleep Disturbances

Some researchers have investigated the neural basis of emotion in an effort to understand how disturbances of that system may be implicated in affective disorders. One approach has been to study the electrical currents on the scalp that are caused by cortical activity, using electroencephalography (EEG). The most notable findings have come from readings of alpha band activity, a type of brain wave seen when the brain is at rest. A number of studies have shown an association between depression and a resting pattern of asymmetry, with higher alpha readings in the left frontal region of the brain than in the right frontal region (suggesting lower levels of cortical activity in the left frontal cortex). This finding meshes well with other neurobiological evidence of lower activation levels in the frontal lobes of depressed patients. **Frontal cortex EEG asymmetry** has therefore been suggested as a marker of risk for major depression. Data from a number of studies have shown that this asymmetry reliably distinguishes depressed from nondepressed individuals and remitted-depressed patients from never-depressed controls, and is stable across phases of depression (Henriques & Davidson, 1990). Thus it appears that what the EEG shows is not a reflection merely of mood, but also of the underlying disorder.

A study by Harmon-Jones and Allen (1997) examined the relationship between resting frontal EEG asymmetry and a number of temperamental variables. They found a significant correlation between asymmetry and a self-report measure of emotional dysregulation, specifically related to **approach motivation**, or the ability to seek reward. Depressed people often have a marked deficit in approach motivation, which is related to symptoms such as anhedonia (the inability to derive pleasure from activities) and social withdrawal. The noted association with a particular EEG pattern suggests a fundamental biobehavioural system for approach-related motivation. An index created from a measure of frontal cortex asymmetry may hold clinical promise as a way to identify individuals at risk for psychiatric disturbance, particularly depression, in which deficits in approach motivation are central.

Sleep research also supports a role for biological processes in depression. It is well documented that depressed patients often complain of problems sleeping. They may find it hard to get to sleep, or may wake during the night or too early in the morning (Ford & Kamerow, 1990). Recordings of brain-related electrical activity taken from the scalp have verified this clinically based observation by showing that depressed patients have different sleep patterns than nondepressed controls. EEG studies indicate that depressed patients show a decrease in slow-wave sleep and an earlier onset of *rapid eye movement (REM)* sleep, which is often associated with dreaming and more restful sleep. (See the discussion of sleeping patterns in Chapter 17.) For example, the first period of REM sleep in nondepressed adults starts about 70 to 90 minutes after the person has fallen asleep. Depressed patients, however, tend to start having REM sleep at 60 minutes or less (Reynolds & Kupfer, 1987).

Such findings support the biological model of depression: it seems unlikely that such variations in neurophysiological patterns would be caused by psychological factors. In addition, the decrease in slow-wave sleep is consistent with reduced activity of the neurotransmitter serotonin, and falls in line with predictions from the monoamine hypothesis (Thase & Kupfer, 1987).

The monitoring of sleep responses is also useful in explaining the mechanisms through which antidepressant drugs have their effects. For example, patients who responded to antidepressant medication show a marked suppression of REM sleep (Wu & Bunney, 1990). A group of Canadian researchers was among the first to show that REM suppression can also be achieved by waking a sleeper about to enter the REM phase of the sleep cycle and that this can also delay depressed mood (Knowles et al., 1979).

···

TREATMENT

Most episodes of depression will improve within a few months even if untreated. For treatment to make a difference, it needs to achieve its effects sooner and perhaps in a more enduring way. That is, the most effective treatment will not only alleviate depressed mood during the current episode but help to prevent the next episode, or at least to reduce its severity.

If depression is self-limiting, does it need to be treated at all? The answer is clearly yes. First, not all mood episodes clear up on their own. Even if they did, the social cost in terms of family strain and reduced productivity, the increased risk for suicide during a depressive episode, and the sheer unhappiness of sufferers make a compelling case for timely intervention.

Over the past 20 years, a number of new treatments, both psychological and somatic, have been developed that enable clinicians to treat depressed patients more quickly and comprehensively. While relapse or the return of symptoms following recovery remains a problem, the acute features of a depressive episode can now be managed with greater confidence. Furthermore, as the stigma associated with having a clinical depression has decreased and public education has increased awareness of the signs and costs of this disorder, more people have been able to get effective help. However, many depressed people still endure their disorder without seeking treatment and greater public awareness of availability of effective intervention is needed (Shuchter, Downs, & Zisook, 1997).

Psychological Treatments

Cognitive Therapy

A person's emotional reactions are determined, in part, by what he or she thinks. Cognitive therapy (CT) takes this as the starting-point for a series of treatment interventions that strive to teach patients to become aware of the meanings they place on various events in their lives and to observe how these views may contribute to the emotional reactions that follow (Beck, 1967). CT is a structured form of treatment with a focus on what can be done in the present to address depression-producing ways of thinking and behaving. Patients are asked to learn to recognize negative thought patterns that accompany depression and to record these on thought-monitoring sheets. Once this occurs, patients can evaluate the degree of fit between objective reality and their particular understanding of things.

The therapist's role is to work collaboratively with the patient to identify negative beliefs and to devise behavioural tests of these beliefs so that the patient can begin to collect evidence that either supports or fails to confirm them (Beck, Rush, Shaw, & Emery, 1979). In this way, the patient learns how to respond to negative thought patterns by bringing to mind evidence that

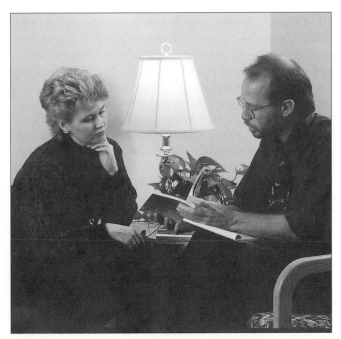

Cognitive therapists often set their patients homework; exercises that allow them to start practising more constructive ways of thinking and interacting, one small step at a time.

does not support these interpretations and allows interpretations that are less likely to lead to a depressive reaction.

Patients also learn to recognize silent assumptions or themes that underlie many of their negative beliefs. For example, suppose a patient reports that he expects to fail at work, feels inept when he plays sports, and feels rejected by friends. He may be operating with a general view or schema or himself as *inferior* or *flawed*. By practising various cognitive and behavioural responses to this schema, the person can learn to generate new views of himself and apply them to anticipated or actual situations.

Of all the psychological treatments for depression, CT is among the most thoroughly evaluated. In more than 15 comparative studies, CT and antidepressant medication were found to be equally effective in reducing depression (Segal & Shaw, 1996). New research is now looking at whether it is possible to enhance response to treatment by combining pharmacotherapy and cognitive therapy. The following list describes some of the more common interventions used in cognitive therapy.

Behavioural strategies. Behavioural interventions are especially helpful for dealing with patients' lack of energy or motivation to do things. For example, the withdrawal typical of severely depressed patients, particularly in early phases of treatment, may be due to response inhibition supported by negative expectations. In this approach, therapist and patient identify smaller behaviours patients can still perform—possibly something as simple as deciding to get out of bed, or keeping track of daily activities. Having done *something*, the patient may note some change in negative thoughts, or may find evidence that can be used against self-defeating thoughts such as "I can't do anything" (Beck et al., 1979).

Activity scheduling. This exercise starts with getting patients to record a baseline measure of their activities and corresponding moods. In the next phase, patients list the tasks, responsibilities, and especially the pleasant activities that they want to integrate into their schedules. Following this, a daily schedule can be worked out in which patients designate specific time slots for engaging in selected activities. These activities should include both pleasure- and mastery-related events. Patients are then asked to predict how much pleasure and/or mastery they expect to get from each of the scheduled activities. Finally, patients are asked to monitor their behaviour, noting the actual degree of pleasure and/or mastery they derived from the scheduled activities. These actual pleasure and mastery ratings can be compared to patients' earlier ratings in order to obtain an index of the accuracy of their predictions (Lewinsohn & Graf, 1973).

Graded task assignments. In selecting and scheduling pleasant events and mastery tasks, cognitive therapists try to maximize the likelihood of their successful completion. One way to do this is to anticipate potential obstacles and to come up with a contingency plan. Another approach involves grading tasks so that patients start with the easiest, and then move on to greater challenges. Tasks may be simplified by breaking them down into smaller units (Williams, 1992). For example, whereas cleaning the house may represent an overwhelming prospect for a seriously depressed patient, smaller components of the task, like making the bed, may be more manageable. After the patient has made the bed successfully, other components of the larger task may be undertaken.

Testing beliefs through behavioural experiments. Fundamental to most cognitive interventions is training in self-monitoring. Patients are encouraged to bring ongoing records of thoughts, images, and feelings surrounding problematic situations to the therapy session. These records are preferable to retrospective accounts of events, since they are a more direct data source and are less likely influenced by memory biases.

Once a negative belief is identified, therapists encourage patients to regard these thoughts as scientific hypotheses that then can be subjected to empirical (rather than strictly logical) examination. Automatic thoughts reported in the form of propositions (for example, "Everyone I know dislikes me") can usually be tested quite readily. However, automatic thoughts are frequently expressed in the form of questions (for example, "What do people think of me?"). Such queries can be translated into propositions via appropriate probes (for example, "Do you have any thoughts about what the people you know think of you?", "What runs through your mind as you consider that question?", etc.).

Designing effective experiments can require a good deal of creativity and ingenuity on the part of both therapist and patient. One means of generating ideas for experiments involves considering, *a priori*, the kind of evidence that could either support or refute the hypothesis in question. For example, to test the thought "Everyone I know dislikes me," the therapist and patient might first consider how people generally signal their dislike for another person (for example, they might fail to return a greeting). Next, an experiment could be designed in which, say, the patient would greet a random sample of acquaintances, and take note of whether the greetings were reciprocated. A series of such experiments could help weaken the subjective plausibility of patients' negative automatic thoughts, and may provide evidence for more reasonable alternatives (for example, "Many, if not most, of the people I know seem to respond to me in a favourable manner"). (See the discussion and chart on cognitive restructuring in Chapter 7.)

Operationalizing negative beliefs.   Automatic thoughts often have an absolute, black-and-white quality. Examples of such thoughts are "I'm a weakling," "I'm a bad parent," and "I'm a stupid person." These constructs (weak, bad parent, stupid person) allow little sense of gradation, and can generate intensely negative affect. One means of introducing some sense of gradation involves working with patients to operationalize these constructs. As a first step, patients are asked for specific definitional criteria for the construct in question (for example, "A weakling is someone who is not strong enough to stand up to others"). Therapists may suggest a Likert-type scale (for example, a

"weakling scale") that patients can use to rate the extent to which they, and other people they know, meet the definition. Most typically, these ratings will fall into the intermediate range. As a result, patients may find that they do not meet their own criteria for the label. More reasonable thoughts can then be considered (for example, "I have been able to stand up for myself on some things, and have given in on others"; "I am not totally without resources, but a human being who, like everyone else, has strengths as well as weaknesses"). Patients are trained to practise this approach whenever they notice themselves thinking in terms of these absolutist negative beliefs.

Interpersonal Therapy

Interpersonal therapy (IPT; Klerman et al., 1984) emphasizes that depression often arises as a result of disruptions in an individual's social adjustment. This model places greater emphasis on understanding the roles played by family and friends and the patient's reactions to significant life stressors. Troubled or unresolved relationships are seen as contributing to depressed moods and locking the person into a cycle of ineffective coping.

One common cause of depression, according to this model, is an abnormal grief reaction, in which mourning has been prolonged or avoided. Until the process is worked through, the person will not be able to establish new relationships. Interpersonal role disputes, such as marital arguments or friction with workmates or friends, are also commonly experienced in depression. Role transitions—such as leaving home for university, becoming a parent, changing careers, or retiring—may also trigger depression if the person does not adapt well. Finally, people may be prone to depression if a deficit in interpersonal skills prevents them from building and maintaining relationships.

There are three distinct phases to treatment. In the early phase the goal is to enable the patient to deal with depression. Symptoms are reviewed, the diagnosis is confirmed, the need for medication is evaluated, and the patient is offered education about depression. Patients are reassured that they have a genuine illness, which they need not hide or feel stigmatized by, and are entitled to the lowered expectations of the "sick role," as they would be for a broken leg.

The second phase of treatment involves examining interpersonal problems. Unlike CT, IPT does not try to change patients' negative schemata directly, focussing on relationships instead. Nor does it assign homework or other structured exercises for patients to complete between treatment sessions.

When reaction to a death is involved, IPT therapists work with patients to help them reconstruct the relationship with the departed, paying special attention to the expression of guilt, self-blame, or unfulfilled expectations (Klerman et al., 1984). When a dispute is involved, therapists urge patients to acknowledge it and seek clarification of the issues. Once the patient makes the link between the depression and the continuation of the dispute, he or she may gain motivation to address this issue. One way to do this is by outlining alternative courses of action and evaluating the costs and benefits associated with each one.

When a role transition preceded depression, the therapist will help the patient explore the benefits and opportunities of the new role, and the social skills and relationships that accompany it. Feelings of restriction and loss are addressed by having the patient review areas of mastery not related to the new role.

If the patient lacks relationships, the therapist will review past relationships and behaviours that may serve as model for initiating new social contacts. Social skills training may also be used to give the patient practice with social behaviours.

Termination, the final phase of IPT, prepares patients to effect change on their own, without relying on the therapist.

In a number of comparative studies, IPT has been shown to be as effective as antidepressant medication (Elkin et al., 1989).

Somatic Treatments

Antidepressant Pharmacotherapy

The discovery of drugs with antidepressant properties occurred partly by accident. It started with the observation that certain forms of medication used to combat high blood pressure induced depression-like symptoms in patients. Drugs such as reserpine were known to decrease the levels of the neurotransmitters serotonin and norepinephrine; from there it was just one more step to the idea that depression might be relieved by drugs that increase the levels of these neurotransmitters.

At present there are three major classes of antidepressants: **monoamine oxidase inhibitors** or **MAOIs, tricyclics**, and **selective serotonin reuptake inhibitors (SSRIs)**. Common MAOIs include isocarboxazid (Marplan), phenelzine sulfate (Nardil), and tranylcypromine sulfate (Parnate). Tricyclics include amoxapine (Asendin), amitriptyline (Elavil), imipramine (Tofranil), and doxepin (Sinequan). SSRIs include fluoxetine (Prozac), sertraline (Zoloft), and paraxetine (Paxil). Each type of drug takes a different route to increase the available levels of neurotransmitters. MAOIs inhibit the release of substances that break down neurotransmitters, allowing them to remain in the synaptic space for longer periods and stimulate greater rates of neuronal firing. Tricyclics enable more neurotransmitters to be released into the synaptic cleft. SSRIs, as their name suggests, delay the process of reuptake of neurotransmitters so that they remain available longer to maintain optimal neuronal firing rates.

A typical course of treatment would be six months of acute treatment, followed by one year of continuation, often at a lower dosage. The research evidence suggests that antidepressant medication is superior to placebo in removing the symptoms of major depression and that anywhere from 50 to 70 percent of patients will respond to the drugs. Many of these compounds, however, carry significant side-effects. MAOIs require close monitoring of patients' diets and restrictions of foods containing tyramine, such as certain cheeses, chocolate, and red wine; in combination, such foods and MAOIs may increase risk of hypotension, stroke, or circulatory problems. Tricyclics can produce blurred vision, constipation, dry mouth, and dizziness.

The SSRIs produce the fewest side-effects and are the least toxic. They are thus often preferred, because patients will stay on them for longer periods of time and have a lower risk of overdosing. The popularity of the SSRIs was recently enhanced by claims that these drugs will do more than just treat depression, but can also enhance personality. Kramer (1994), in his bestselling book *Listening to Prozac*, has described cases in which shy and socially awkward patients became socially confident and popular by taking Prozac. Unfortunately, these anecdotal descriptions were never supported by any empirical proof of changes on objective measures of personality and in time the manufacturer of Prozac posted advertisements in scientific journals that reminded practitioners that the drug was intended only for legitimate medical disorders.

Mood Stabilizers

The history of medication-based treatments for bipolar disorder extends back to the late 1930s, when opium-related drugs and barbiturates were used unsatisfactorily for the treatment of depression and mania. The introduction in the 1950s of lithium salts and antipsychotic drugs for the treatment of mania and depression was considered an important advance. Patients taking **lithium carbonate** usually describe it as flattening out the peaks and valleys of the illness, allowing them to regain a measure of stability in their lives along with less disruption for family members. Evidence has accumulated that lithium has preventive effects for both unipolar depression and bipolar disorder and today lithium prophylaxis is considered the treatment of choice for bipolar disorder (Schou, 1997).

Yet availability of effective treatment by no means guarantees that people with a history of the disorder will make full use of it. Compliance with lithium treatment was only 35 percent in one study (Kupfer et al., 1997). Relapse often occurs when patients decide on their own to stop taking the medication. They may have several reasons for this decision.

Some patients are sometimes unwilling to give up the exhilaration of hypomanic states. Others report that lithium dulls their senses, and don't see why they should take it when they feel well (Goodwin & Jamison, 1990).

Another reason for rejecting lithium is concern about long-term toxic effects. A number of side-effects have been documented, such as *polyuria* (excessive urination) and reduced kidney function, which are not always reversible. Because people are expected to stay on lithium for years, and because the difference between a therapeutic and a toxic dosage is quite small, people worry about the long-term effects on their bodies. Regular monitoring of blood lithium levels and kidney function is important both to prevent kidney damage and to reassure patients.

Concerns about toxicity also need to be seen in context. Several studies have shown lower mortality rates for bipolar disorder patients receiving long-term lithium than for patients not receiving such treatment. In one study, drawing on data from a number of centres, mortality was not significantly higher than the rate for the general population, a noteworthy finding given the high rates of suicide in bipolar disorder. Whether lithium lowers mortality through preventing suicide is still open to speculation, since the analysis did not examine other variables that might account for this finding (Schou, 1997).

Lithium is not, however, effective for all patients. As many as 40 percent of bipolar patients do not show a strong response to treatment; lithium's effectiveness declines over time, from 83 percent at one year to 37 percent at five years (Kupfer et al., 1997). It is also less effective in treating the depressive phase of the disorder than the manic phase. In fact, it is widely accepted that treatments for the depressive phase lag behind more effective treatments for mania or unipolar depression.

A novel integrative focus may be provided by recent research into a question that has not yet been studied widely: *How* does relapse occur in bipolar disorder? Specifically, do life events trigger relapse? Johnson and Miller (1997) completed monthly assessments over a one-year period on a sample of 67 individuals who had been hospitalized for bipolar disorder. Individuals reporting severe life events took up to three times as long to achieve recovery as patients without such events. These findings were not due to differences in medication compliance, and are among the first to suggest that the psychosocial environment may play an important role in the course of bipolar disorder.

A more complex psychopathological model of this disorder may emerge that could provide the basis for multimodal interventions serving specific bipolar populations, such as those with dual diagnoses or those sensitive to environmental stress. A recent cognitive-behavioural treatment manual, for example, proposes psychological interventions in conjunction with medication and family support (Basco & Rush, 1996).

Electroconvulsive Therapy

Almost everyone knows about electroconvulsive therapy, or shock treatments. Unfortunately, much of the public's knowledge of this therapy has been obtained from popular depictions such as the one in the movie *One Flew over the Cuckoo's Nest*. In this movie, the Jack Nicholson character is given many unwanted and inappropriate shocks, rendering him a grotesque figure suffering memory loss and brain damage. As a result of such images, the public view bears little relationship to the practice of electroshock therapy today.

Convulsions elicited by electrical stimulation were first used to treat severe psychosis. In 1938, Cerletti and Bini pioneered this technique following earlier work indicating that pharmacologically induced seizures produced improvement in schizophrenics (see Chapter 1 for more historical background). They used the term *electroshock* for their method, but argued that the electrical current was used only to induce convulsions and that the current had no direct effect on the illness. Electroshock, or *electroconvulsive therapy (ECT)* as it has become known, is the only convulsive therapy in use today.

ECT was first used in the United States in 1940. Over the following decade its use spread throughout the continent, and by the 1950s the technique had been accepted into the mainstream of psychiatric practice (Weiner & Coffey, 1991). Soon after its general use began, it was recognized that ECT

produced better results with patients with major mood disorders than with schizophrenia (Enns & Reiss, 1992). The early use of ECT was very different from current practice. Many more shocks were given and at higher intensities than are now applied. Also, ECT was given to many patients with diagnoses for which the technique is no longer used. ECT treatment declined during the 1960s and 1970s, partly in response to the introduction of effective pharmacotherapeutic treatments and to a very vocal anti-ECT lobby.

Since the end of the 1970s, however, there has been a marked turnaround. Comprehensive reviews of past research have led to more standardized practice, and recent research has improved our knowledge of the conditions under which ECT works and the types of disorder for which it is most effective (American Psychiatric Association, 1978, 1990; Enns & Reiss, 1992; Pankratz, 1980; Weiner & Coffey, 1991). ECT is now used mainly for major depression and bipolar disorder; it is also used, less commonly, in acute schizophrenia with prominent affective or catatonic symptoms. It is important to note ECT is most commonly used as a last resort rather than a first line of treatment. It is generally used in the most severe cases in which individuals have not responded to other forms of therapy.

How does ECT work? Despite the long history of this technique, its mechanism is still not understood. It has been established that a generalized cerebral seizure is a necessary though not a sufficient condition. It appears that it may not be the seizure itself that produces improvement so much as some aspect of the process or aftermath of seizure generalization (Weiner & Coffey, 1991). This is an area that requires and deserves more research attention.

ECT is generally administered under well-defined protocols with a psychiatrist, an anesthetist, and a nurse present. The physician must obtain the patient's signed, formal, informed consent, or, in the case of a clearly incompetent patient, consent from the responsible person according to local law. Informed consent means that the physician must first explain in detail the treatment technique and the expected benefits and risks, as compared to the expected benefits and risks of alternative treatments, or no treatment.

ECT is typically administered two to three times per week to a total course of between six and twelve treatments. The treatments are modified by the use of brief anesthesia, muscle relaxants, and oxygen. Electrode placement can be unilateral or bilateral. Electrical stimulus intensity is often adjusted so that it only moderately exceeds the seizure threshold, and brief pulse stimuli are used, since they result in fewer adverse effects. During the procedure, it is routine to monitor cardiac functioning and the electroencephalogram. In general, it is accepted that to be effective, cerebral seizures must be at least 25 seconds in duration.

With the development of the current treatment guidelines, the rate of complications and adverse effects has been markedly reduced. The mortality rate is comparable to that reported for brief general anesthesia. Nausea, headache, and muscle soreness are commonly reported but these respond to symptomatic treatment.

The main adverse effect of concern is memory impairment. Immediately after the seizure, there is usually a period of confusion. After the confusion clears, there is usually both retrograde amnesia (forgetting events prior to the seizure) and anterograde amnesia (forgetting of events after the seizure). These usually subside in the weeks following the therapy but can be distressing to patients during therapy. A small proportion of patients complain of continuing memory impairment following ECT; however, this complaint is controversial and it has yet to be clearly documented with empirical tests that memory impairment actually occurs (Enns & Reiss, 1992).

Reviews of research indicate that bilateral electrode placement, higher stimulus intensity, sine waveform stimulus, more frequent treatments, concomitant psychotropic drugs, and higher anesthetic dose are associated with greater memory interference than unilateral nondominant electrode placement, moderately suprathreshold stimulus intensity, brief pulse waveform, less frequent treatments, and more moderate doses of anesthetic (Enns & Reiss, 1992). The choice of electrode placement (unilateral versus bilateral) and stimulus intensity involves a tradeoff between efficacy and the unwanted side-effects of memory impairment. Resolution of these opposing interests depends on the individual case and must be made by skilled psychiatrists in consultation with their patients.

It is clear that ECT is a safe and effective treatment and should continue to be widely available as a therapeutic option. As in so many other areas, future practice and development must be guided by sound empirical research.

....

SUICIDE

Suicide—the intentional taking of one's own life—has been with us as long as recorded history. The Greeks and Romans regarded suicide as a rational and acceptable, even noble, course of action in certain circumstances. However, attitudes in North America have tended to be shaped by the Judeo-Christian tradition, which regards life as a gift from God and the taking of life as sin. These religious injunctions against suicide resulted in the persecution of those who attempted to take their own lives and in the bodies of suicides being buried in cemetery areas reserved for criminals, drunks, and unbaptized children. In fact, in many Western countries, attempted suicide has been removed from the criminal codes only recently.

Attitudes have changed. While suicide remains somewhat taboo as a subject of general discussion, social and clinical scientists have established a solid knowledge base regarding suicide. Vigorous public debate is ongoing regarding the ethics and legality of assisted suicide for individuals suffering from terminal disease and intractable pain. While this debate is not within the scope of this book, we should note that increased openness in discussion has allowed progress in understanding this complex human behaviour. This discussion of suicide and attempted suicide appears in this chapter because the majority of suicides occur among people who manifest mental illness, most frequently mood disorders.

Who Commits Suicide?

Philosophers and authors from Seneca to Shakespeare have often written of suicide as part of their endless quest to understand the meaning of the human condition. We have a much more pragmatic interest in this discussion: prevention. Knowledge of the demographics and epidemiology of suicide is fundamental to understanding the causes of suicidal behaviour and may help clinicians assess the risk of suicide in an individual in crisis.

Throughout the Western world, suicide has for many years been among the top five to ten causes of death. Every year of the past two decades, approximately 3500 Canadians and 30,000 Americans have killed themselves. These facts make suicide an important public health and social issue in our two countries. Furthermore, more than 90 percent of the individuals who complete suicide (that is, who are successful in a suicide attempt) suffer from a diagnosable mental disorder, most frequently mood disorders. Despite these statistics, suicide and mental illness in general have been relatively neglected in terms of research and public attention.

Overall, Canadian suicide rates increased from the mid-1950s to the mid-1980s and appear to have started to decline, as shown in Figure 13.3. Throughout these changes, suicide rates have been much higher among men than among women. The most recent figure for Canada is 12.69 suicides per 100,000 population; broken down by sex, the rates are 5.34 per 100,000 females and 20.16 per 100,000 males. Interestingly, females are more likely to attempt suicide but males are more likely to die because they use more lethal suicide methods. Rates in the United States are slightly lower but have followed similar patterns.

The changes in suicide rates have not been the same for all age groups. For older Canadians (aged 60 to 79), rates have stayed relatively stable; however, for young Canadians, rates have risen dramatically. Figure 13.4 shows the remarkable change for 15-to-19-year-olds. People in their twenties, an age group with higher suicide rates to begin with (see Figure 13.5), showed a similar increase. In both age groups the large changes were mainly for males. Thus, the overall rise in suicide rates over the past forty years has been largely due to increases in the rates for teenage and young adult males. Adolescent boys have reached rates equal to those previously found for adult males and the rates of men in their twenties are now roughly equal to those of the elderly, long a high-risk group. (See Chapter 17 for a discussion of suicide risk among the elderly.)

It is also noteworthy that while suicide is the sixth most frequent cause of death in the general population of Canadians, it is second to motor vehicle accidents as the most frequent cause of death among teenaged boys aged 15 to 19. This marked increase in rates for young males has a large impact on the potential years of life lost to suicide and serves to underline the importance of suicide as a social and health issue.

The fact that suicide is affected by psychosocial factors is borne out by the existence of cultural, ethnic, and regional variations. Cross-national comparisons are difficult because

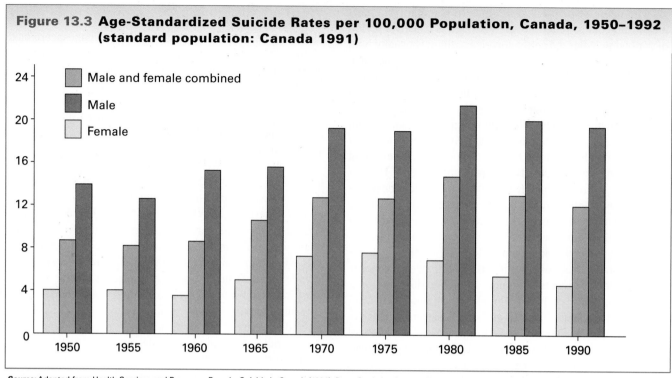

Figure 13.3 Age-Standardized Suicide Rates per 100,000 Population, Canada, 1950–1992 (standard population: Canada 1991)

Source: Adapted from Health Services and Programs Branch, *Suicide in Canada* (1994). Data: Statistics Canada. Reprinted by permission of University of Toronto Press.

of differences in methods of death certification and reporting across countries. However, with this caveat, Canada and the United States have suicide rates that fall in the midrange. The highest rates are found in Germany, Scandinavia, Eastern Europe, and Japan, while the lowest are in the traditionally Catholic countries such as Italy, Spain, and Ireland (Blumenthal, 1990; Sainsbury, 1986). Generally, the increases in rates in North America over the past two decades have been parallelled throughout the Western world.

There are also regional variations evident within countries. In Canada, Quebec and Alberta have higher than average suicide rates for both males and females; Newfoundland and Ontario have lower rates (*Suicide in Canada*, 1994). In the United States, rates are much higher in the Western mountain states than in the mid-Atlantic states.

Race and ethnic group also have important effects on suicide rates. In the United States, Caucasians kill themselves at much higher rates than African-Americans or Hispanics

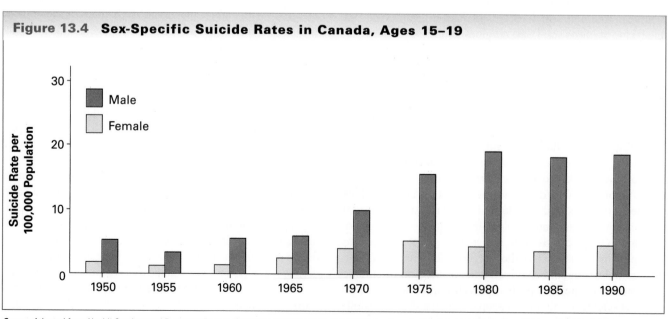

Figure 13.4   Sex-Specific Suicide Rates in Canada, Ages 15–19

Source: Adapted from Health Services and Programs Branch, *Suicide in Canada* (1994). Data: Statistics Canada. Reprinted by permission of University of Toronto Press.

Figure 13.5 Canada Suicide Rates by Age Group (average annual rate for 1989–1992)

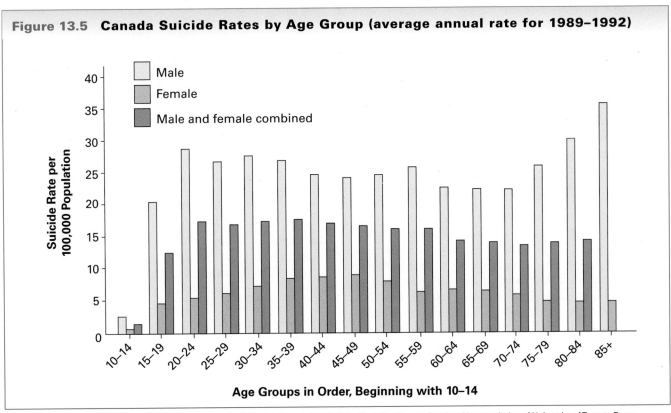

Source: Adapted from Health Services and Programs Branch, *Suicide in Canada* (1994). Data: Statistics Canada. Reprinted by permission of University of Toronto Press.

(Buda & Msuang, 1990). In contrast, the suicide rates for Native Americans are very high, although there is some variation across tribes (Berlin, 1987).

In Canada, suicide rates vary both across aboriginal groups and from community to community. In general, suicide rates for aboriginal groups may be up to twice as high as those for the general population (*Suicide in Canada*, 1994) and suicide is regarded as one of the most serious health and social problems faced by their communities in the 1990s. Most startling are the extremely high rates of suicide among aboriginal youth, including Inuit. As shown in Figure 13.6, the rates for aboriginal youth are approximately five times as high as those of non-native youth—even given the increases in overall youth suicides.

Over the past few years, media, politicians, and native leaders have attempted to explore the reasons for this disturbing trend, and to find ways to counteract what some have called an epidemic. Extreme social changes over the past few generations, wide gaps in experience that make it difficult for adults to provide role models or continuity for youth, poverty, joblessness, hopelessness, and high rates of substance abuse have all been suggested as contributing factors.

The Role of Mental Illness in Suicide

Retrospective analyses ("psychological autopsies"), conducted in a variety of settings, have revealed that approximately 90 percent of those who complete suicide are mentally ill at the time of their death (Black & Winokur, 1990). Studies have found that up to 70 percent of suicides were clinically

Figure 13.6 Suicide Rates Among Aboriginal and Nonaboriginal Youth

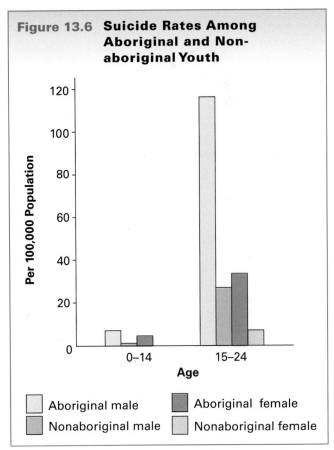

Source: *The Globe and Mail*, November 16, 1996. Reprinted with permission. Data: *Vital Statistics & Indian Health Data*, March 16, 1994 (Health Canada); Statistics Canada.

depressed (Barraclough, Bunch, Nelson, & Sainsbury, 1974) and that as many as 75 percent of adolescent suicides had an existing mood disorder (Brent & Kolko, 1990). Although there is clearly an association between mood disorders and suicide, it is important to remember that the majority of people with mood disorders do not kill themselves or even attempt suicide. Lifetime risk of suicide among the mood-disordered is estimated to be approximately 20 percent (Goodwin & Jamison, 1990).

What causes some depressed people to attempt suicide while others do not? The question is clearly an important one for clinicians. A ten-year followup study of a large number of patients with major depressive illness found that six factors were predictive of suicide within the first year: panic attacks, severe anxiety, reduced ability to concentrate, insomnia, moderate alcohol abuse, and reduced capacity for enjoyment. Suicide after one year was associated with severe hopelessness or suicidal thinking at the time of the original illness and a history of suicide attempts (Fawcett et al., 1990). Despite these significant associations, a study using stepwise multiple regression, a sophisticated statistical technique, to predict suicide in almost 2000 patients with mood disorders was unable to identify any of the 46 patients who completed suicide (Goldstein, Black, Nasrallah, & Winokur, 1991). Thus, given our current understanding, it seems that we cannot predict suicide even among a group at high risk.

After mood disorders, alcohol and substance abuse represents the most frequent diagnosis among victims of suicide. About 25 percent of people who commit suicide in the United States have been reported to have alcoholism. Substance abuse may be more important in the suicides of young people. Mixed substance abuse was identified in 67 percent of youth and young adult suicides and in 46 percent of suicides in adults aged 30 and over (Rich, Young, & Fowler, 1986). Approximately 10 percent of persons with schizophrenia complete suicide (Miles, 1977). Suicide risk appears to be greatest during the first three months of an inpatient hospitalization in young males who unemployed, unmarried, and depressed (Roy, 1986). Finally, studies reviewed by Tanney (1992) showed increased rates of suicide for anxiety disorders, as well as antisocial and borderline personality disorders.

Other Risk Factors

Suicide attempts occur much more frequently than completed suicides. Data from a large epidemiological study (18,571 adults) in the United States showed that the rate of attempted suicide was 300 per 100,000, or approximately 23 times the rate of suicide (Moscicki, 1989). The characteristics of attempters are quite different from those of suicide completers (see Table 13.3); this has led to some debate about whether suicide and attempted suicide (also called *parasuicide*) are distinct phenomena or different aspects of the same phenomenon. However, the importance of parasuicide as a risk factor is evident from the report that 10 to 13 percent of suicide attempters go on to take their lives.

Not surprisingly, people with terminal illness are more likely to commit suicide. Studies from large urban groups in the United States have reported suicide rates for AIDS patients

Table 13.3 Contrasting Suicide Attempters and Suicide Completers

	Attempters	Completers
Sex	More often female	More often male
Age	Younger	Older
Means	Low lethality (for example, pills, wrist laceration)	High lethality (for example, firearms, hanging)
Setting	High chance of rescue	Low chance of rescue
Frequent diagnoses	Dysthymia, borderline personality disorder	Mood disorder, schizophrenia, substance abuse

that are 36 to 50 times the population rate (Marzuk et al., 1988; Zeck et al., 1988). People in custody also appear to represent a group at increased risk. A Correctional Services Canada publication (1992) reported that although the rate of suicides among inmates had decreased through the 1980s, it remained at least six times that of the general Canadian population.

Psychological Factors

Researchers have attempted to isolate psychological factors that might help us understand or predict suicide. While prediction is as yet beyond us, we have accumulated some knowledge that is helpful in working with suicidal individuals. A number of studies have reported a significant association between hopelessness and suicide (Beck et al., 1990). It appears that the belief that things will not get better in the future is more instrumental than depression in the decision to take one's life. Another approach has concentrated on the cognitive characteristics of suicide attempters. Research results indicate that suicidal individuals are more rigid and constricted in their thinking, and therefore less likely to find solutions which would be acceptable alternatives to suicide (Linehan, Camper, Chiles, Strosahl, & Sherin, 1987). Finally, it is now clear that, in vulnerable individuals, stressful life events play an important role in risk for suicide. Up to 39 percent of persons completing suicide experienced a stressful life event in the preceding six weeks (Rich, Fowler, Fogarty, & Young, 1988). The majority of these events related to interpersonal conflict, rejection, loss, or failure (Blumenthal, 1990).

Biological Factors

The potential importance of biological factors in suicide was suggested by studies of children adopted at birth. Comparisons of biological and adoptive relatives for persons committing suicide provided evidence for a weak genetic factor in suicide (Schulsinger et al., 1979). An inherent difficulty in such research is that one cannot determine whether what is inherited is a tendency to suicide or disorders (for example, depression) or behaviours (for example, impulsivity) that might put individuals at increased risk for suicide.

As our capacity to study the neurobiology of the brain and nervous system has developed, these techniques have been used to investigate possible neurochemical mechanisms underlying suicide. Studies have examined, post mortem, the brains of suicide victims (Beskow et al., 1976; Mann et al., 1986; Paul et al., 1984). Other studies have looked at suicide attempters, examining their cerebrospinal fluid (Äsberg et al., 1976), platelets (Pandey et al., 1990), and hormone release following a pharmacological challenge (Mann & Arango, 1992). Such studies provide consistent evidence for a hypoactive serotonin system. Low levels of serotonin have been associated with high levels of aggression (Brown et al., 1982) and high levels of impulsivity (Spoont, 1992). Thus, it is possible that low levels of serotonin may lead to a predisposition to act impulsively and aggressively, which in turn may make a person vulnerable to suicide.

How Can We Best Understand Suicide?

Early attempts to understand suicide produced two general approaches. The first, termed a *statistical-social model*, places a major emphasis on social and environmental influences as determinants of mental and physical health. The alternative approach focusses on psychological factors and mental disorders and could be called a *clinical model*.

Nineteenth-century pioneering sociologist Émile Durkheim (1897/1951) proposed that the broad social context is central to the genesis of suicide. He studied the association between social factors and suicide and proposed two general hypotheses. The first is that suicide is inversely related to the degree of integration of a society—that is, the degree to which people are tied to their society. The second is that the motivation for suicide changes with changing values of a society. He associated lack of integration with what he called **anomie**: a quality of feeling rootless and normless, lacking a sense of intimate belonging. He believed that the division of labour in modern societies undermined the social ties experienced by people in traditional societies, who worked alongside friends and neighbours. This factor, according to Durkheim, explained why suicide rates were higher among Protestants, males, the wealthy, and the unmarried than among Catholics or Jews, females, the poor, and married people.

From his study, Durkheim identified three types of suicide. Egoistic suicide results from personal economic hardship or social adversity and explains the increase in suicide rates during economic slumps. Anomic suicide "results from man's activity lacking regulation and his consequent sufferings" (1951, p. 258). Altruistic suicide was identified as being motivated by the desire of the individual to fulfill some higher purpose; modern examples include terrorist suicide bombings.

Our review of factors affecting suicide rates makes it clear that sociocultural factors do play an important role. Suicide rates vary across and within countries, perhaps reflecting differences in religious approaches or attitudes toward suicide. The disturbingly high rates of suicide among young people, and particularly young aboriginal people, would be explained by Durkheim as reflecting their sense of loss of identity and confusion, and the disintegration of social and cultural supports within families and native groups. Although there is much that is reasonable in Durkheim's hypotheses, his theory does not acknowledge a role for mental disorders and alcohol/substance abuse in suicide. Since we now know that these factors are important to the majority of suicides in our society, it is clear that Durkheim's theoretical position can provide only partial explanations of suicide.

Freud (1957) proposed that suicide resulted from unconscious hostility directed inward. The notion was that rejection by or loss of someone ambivalently loved and hated can lead to introjection of that person; aggression is then directed inward to "punish" that person. A second hypothesis suggested that the death instinct, thanatos, can turn inward and become so strong as to make persons kill themselves. While Freud's hypotheses sparked interest in psychological aspects of suicide risk, they have not proved generally useful in explaining suicide or in intervening with suicidal individuals.

Current approaches to understanding and dealing with suicide owe much to the work of Shneidman (1987). He proposed that suicide was most commonly a solution to remove the person from a situation that was causing unbearable pain. Shneidman portrayed the suicidal act as a "cry for help" and highlighted the ambivalence that individuals feel about ending their lives; they do so because their constricted cognition does not allow them to see alternative courses of action that offer hope.

A model of suicide has emerged as a complex, multidetermined behaviour resulting from the interplay of a number of factors. *Risk factors* include genetic/family history, biological factors, psychological factors, history of exposure to suicide, and mental illness; *precipitating factors* may include stressful life events, availability of means, and opportunity. Set against these are *protective factors*, such as a strong social support network, intact personal relationships, hopefulness, and treatment for disorders. Depending on the result of the interaction of these factors in a given individual at a particular time, that person's threshold for a suicide attempt may be exceeded.

Combining Shneidman's view with this threshold approach (Blumenthal & Kupfer, 1988) facilitates our understanding of suicide, allows professionals to intervene effectively with suicidal individuals, and provides a theoretical basis to guide broader efforts in suicide prevention.

Can Suicide Be Prevented?

Given that suicide is complex and determined by multiple factors, it seems reasonable that a number of parallel initiatives, on several levels, would be required to prevent suicide, or to reduce suicide rates in populations (Boldt, 1985; Shaffer, Garland, Gould, Fisher, & Trautman, 1988). The broadest prevention approach involves *primary preventions*, which aim to change situations, attitudes, or conditions that predispose individuals toward suicide. More focussed approaches, called *secondary* or *tertiary interventions*, target individuals who have already made suicidal threats or attempts.

An example of a primary preventive initiative is universal public education programs to increase life skills and positive coping strategies, perhaps taught in high school. An integral part of such programs would be teaching the signs of mental/emotional distress and reducing the stigma of seeking help for such problems. Educational programs often contain information about suicide, identifying risk factors and providing guidelines for obtaining help. Such high school programs have not been shown to be successful. In fact, although the duration and depth of such programs has been quite limited, concern has been expressed that they may be dangerous. Might they sensitize students, planting the idea of suicide in vulnerable teens, thus increasing rather than decreasing their risk (Shaffer et al., 1988)?

Other attempts at reducing suicide rates have focussed on the means, by restricting access to more lethal methods of attempting suicide. There are two successful interventions of this type. In Britain in the 1950s, 40 percent of all suicides were by means of self-asphyxiation with domestic cooking gas. In the 1960s, domestic gas made from coal was replaced by natural gas, which has a carbon monoxide content of only 2 percent and by 1971, suicides by self-asphyxiation had fallen to less than 10 percent (Kreitman, 1976). Similarly, in the United States, the decrease in the carbon monoxide content of automobile emissions has coincided with a decrease in the rate of suicide by asphyxiation. Although these statistics do not prove a preventive effect (because it is impossible to know whether people sought other means to commit suicide), we do know that suicide is often an impulsive act. Intuitively it seems reasonable that removing the easiest means of suicide will give prevention a better chance.

Currently the most frequent means of suicide are firearms and hanging for males, and poisoning and hanging for fe-

VIEWPOINT *Can Suicide Be Contagious?*

Media reports of suicides, especially of famous personalities, may become a model or stimulus for other suicides (Phillips & Carstensen, 1986). The notion is that such contagion would be most likely to affect those already at risk. Phillips (1979) reported that the suicide rate increased by 12 percent in the month after Marilyn Monroe's death. Also, Gould (1990) documented an increase in suicides in a particular community following a suicide widely publicized in local media. While these findings have not been replicated, it appears that adolescents may be particularly vulnerable to cluster suicides and that highly publicized suicides (or a local suicide receiving a lot of public attention) may place young people at heightened risk (Gould, 1990).

What can explain this phenomenon? One possibility is that there is a copycat element at work here. The fans of the celebrity, trying to emulate the qualities of the admired figure, may see his or her act as a meaningful choice, a bold, romantic statement made in the face of an uncaring world. They see themselves as, like their hero, taking a stand against the world and having the same sort of dramatic effect on those around them as did the original event. On the contrary, Williams (1997) suggests that media-inspired suicide is not an attempt at mimicry so much as an emotional effect. Learning that an idealized person has taken his or her life could engender feelings of hopelessness. Life without the admired figure would seem dreary. The fan may wonder how life can be meaningful if someone who had everything the celebrity had nevertheless chose suicide? Hopelessness is one of the few psychological variables that distinguishes between those who attempt and those who successfully commit suicide. Maybe one way of measuring the harmful effects of excessive media coverage of the self-inflicted deaths of celebrities is to examine the degree of hopelessness it leaves in the minds of the viewers.

Under such conditions it is essential that professionals, teachers, parents, and peers be alert for teens already at risk: those who are depressed, who have drug or alcohol problems, who have previously attempted suicide, or who have recently experienced rejection or failure.

It is important to be attentive to threats of, or allusions to, suicide and not to be coerced into keeping such confidences secret. They should be reported to someone who can act immediately to arrange help for the young person. Remember Shneidman's (1987) view that most suicides are ambivalent about death: their act is a mal-adaptive solution to a problem that produces unbearable pain, but that may be temporary.

We still do not understand exactly how media coverage of suicide may produce increases in suicide rates and which individuals are most vulnerable to such influence. Nevertheless, there is agreement among experts that media reports should not glorify or give undue attention to suicide. It is important that the event be reported factually, and that the perspective be presented that the suicide was not a normal response to the individual's problems.

Critical Thinking Questions

1. Why do teens seem to be the most vulnerable to following reports of celebrity suicide with attempts of their own?

2. What message do you think a celebrity who takes his or her own life is trying to send to others? Is this the same message that is conveyed in the media report of the event?

3. What types of information could media reports of suicide contain that might make them less likely to portray these acts in romantic or desirable ways to people that might be at risk?

males; thus, these are the methods that have to be made less available. Certainly the high rate of suicide by firearms by young males makes a strong argument in favour of legislation limiting access to firearms. In the case of poisoning, a similar argument can be made for restricting access to lethal doses of prescription drugs.

In the sphere of secondary/tertiary interventions, the greatest attention has been given to suicide prevention centres and crisis or suicide hotlines. Telephone hotlines are usually anonymous and offer immediate support, while avoiding potential embarrassment or issues of control for callers. Many are staffed by volunteers supervised by mental health professionals. Most give information on how to access appropriate clinical services; some play a more active role in arranging appointments and followup. Most hotlines do not offer therapy but will break confidentiality if the operator feels the caller is at immediate risk.

At this time, the effectiveness of hotlines in reducing suicide has not been clearly established. It has been suggested that they do not reach the people at highest risk, and therefore have a limited effect (Shaffer et al., 1988). It is clear that such services could improve overall functioning through standardized training for telephone operators and intervention protocols (*Suicide in Canada*, 1994). In addition, it has been recommended that all *gatekeepers* (individuals who refer to the mental health system) and mental health professionals receive specific training in identifying and intervening with persons at risk for suicide (*Suicide in Canada*, 1994).

Treating Suicidal Individuals

Identifying and treating individuals who are at risk for suicide requires skilled mental health professionals. In general, the strategy is first to ensure adequate supervision of the attempter, next to deal with life crises as effectively and quickly as possible, and then to concentrate on decreasing risk factors and increasing protective factors. For most individuals, this will involve appropriate psychological and somatic treatment of any existing disorder.

Therapists avoid assigning blame or fault, and encourage patients to talk about suicide openly and straightforwardly. A problem-solving theory of suicidal behaviour is usually advanced and a key goal of the therapist is to convince the person that suicide is a maladaptive and ineffective solution. In most cases, the suicide attempter's family, partner, or friends will be encouraged to become involved in the therapeutic process. Anti-suicide contracts between therapist and attempter are often used to help manage the initial crisis period. (For a sample contract, see Chapter 17.) Once some degree of stability and confidence has been established, a longer-term intervention plan is needed.

Past approaches to therapy with suicide attempters have not been very effective (Liberman & Eckman, 1981; Trautman 1989). We can hope that interventions based on current models of suicidal behaviour combined with therapies proven effective for disorders such as depression (for example, cognitive behaviour therapy) will be more successful.

PANORAMA

With increasing awareness of the prevalence of affective disorders, it is likely that the stigma associated with these problems will be reduced. More accepting attitudes in society may lead to an increasing number of people who recognize their disorder and seek treatment.

The good news is that it is clear that several effective treatments for depression exist, including pharmacotherapy and psychotherapy. With the advances of the past 25 years, people have a much greater chance of receiving adequate care for an acute episode of unipolar or bipolar illness. And if the first treatment tried does not work, there are alternatives.

Where problems persist is in the recognition that affective disorders are not single-episode events, but rather, tend to recur in peoples' lives even after successful recovery. The challenge now is to reduce the rate of relapses or recurrences. One problem is that compliance with medication often falls off with time, sometimes triggering a relapse. New treatments are needed, aimed at preventing the return of depressive episodes in both unipolar and bipolar disorders. We have seen that psychological factors such as stress or distressing life events can have powerful effects on the speed of recovery and the length of remission. How can we protect recovered depressed patients from falling ill again? Pharmacological strategies ask patients to continue taking their antidepressant medication for two to three years. The challenge for psychological treatments will be to draw on an understanding of the connection between the brain systems, cognition, and the body to offer ongoing prevention.

SUMMARY

Epidemiological data indicate that mood disorders are among the most common mental disorders, yet these difficulties largely go unrecognized and untreated, even though effective interventions are available.

Diagnosis of a mood disorder implies interference with social and occupational function, and bodily and behavioural symptoms as well as mood change. Duration and severity are both considered. Unipolar disorders involve depression followed by a return to normal mood. Bipolar disorders involve alternating periods of depression (lowered mood) and mania (elevated mood).

Symptoms of major depressive disorder include feeling sad or depressed most of the day, loss of interest or ability to derive pleasure from activities, weight loss, insomnia, fatigue, feelings of worthlessness or guilt, difficulty concentrating, and suicidal thoughts. Dysthymic disorder manifests many of the same symptoms as major depressive disorder in a less severe form. Seasonal affective disorder (SAD) involves mood disturbance that is cyclical and time-limited. SAD may be unipolar or bipolar and often responds to treatment with intense light.

Bipolar disorder involves periods of depression as well as periods of mania or hypomania. Because some people enjoy the mood elevation of mania, compliance with treatment can be a problem. People with four or more episodes of mania and/or depression in one year meet the criteria for rapid cycling depression/mania. Cyclothymic disorder is a milder version of bipolar disorder.

Most researchers agree that mood disorder is multifactorial, involving the interaction of social, biological, and psychological variables. Freud viewed depression as stemming from anger turned inward. More recent psychodynamic models have focussed on ambiguous feelings toward a lost love object and on disruptions of early attachment.

Cognitive models stress the mood-lowering effects of specific beliefs and expectations held by depressed individuals. These models hold that problems in affective regulation stem from the way in which rigid and self-punitive beliefs avoid being disconfirmed by the individual's experiences so that dysphoric moods are increasingly supported by the interpretation of events in the person's life.

The life stress perspective proposes that depression arises when a vulnerable person undergoes distressing life events. A severe enough psychological trauma can lead to depression even in a person who is not particularly vulnerable. It has also been suggested that people with dependent or self-critical personalities are prone to depression. Being depressed can undermine relationships; in turn, lack of social support and exposure to high levels of negative expressed emotion can lead to a relapse.

Biological models of depressive disorders have marshalled an enormous amount of research into the mechanisms of brain functions in depression. Much of this work has shown a connection between depression and a breakdown of neurotransmitter synthesis or changes at the level of neuroreceptor sensitivity. EEG abnormalities also suggest a neurological basis for the disorder. Genetic research suggests that mood disorder, particularly bipolar disorder, has a marked heritability, although no specific chromosome location has been established.

Treatments for depression have improved greatly over the past two decades. Psychological treatments, such as cognitive therapy, emphasize integrative strategies of behavioural and cognitive techniques at different points in treatment. Early interventions may stress the need for activating and motivating depressed patients to reengage with their environment, while later in treatment more focussed work on depressogenic beliefs would take place. Other psychological treatments emphasize the patient's need to come to terms with recent losses or role changes. Somatic treatments for depression involve medications (monoamine oxidase inhibitors, tricyclics, and serotonin reuptake inhibitors) that increase the availability of neurotransmitters. Newer developments involve reducing side-effects. Electroconvulsive therapy (ECT), despite its bad public image, is another effective and safe technique. Lithium remains the treatment of choice for bipolar disorder.

Suicide is a major social and health issue. Rates of suicide have risen sharply among young people in the last half of the twentieth century, and are far more common among aboriginal people. Suicide involves social factors, as seen in the variation across cultures and nations. Psychological factors are also important: the vast majority of suicides have a mental disorder at the time of death, most often depression. Hopelessness, rigid thought patterns, and severe life stressors appear to increase risk. Yet researchers remain unable to predict individual risk of suicide. So far, most attempts to prevent suicide, on either a population or an individual basis, have demonstrated little effectiveness. We can hope that interventions based on current models of understanding suicide will prove more effective.

KEY TERMS

mood disorder (p. 317)
affective disorder (p. 317)
unipolar disorders (p. 317)
bipolar disorders (p. 317)
major depressive disorder (p. 317)
specifiers (p. 320)
with melancholic features (p. 320)

anhedonia (p. 320)
dysthymic disorder (p. 320)
dysthymia (p. 320)
seasonal affective disorder (SAD) (p. 320)
mania (p. 321)
hypomanic (p. 321)
Bipolar 1 (p. 322)
Bipolar 2 (p. 322)

rapid cycling depression/mania (p. 323)
cyclothymic disorder (p. 323)
cyclothymia (p. 323)
disruptions in attachment (p. 324)
anaclitic depression (p. 324)
introjective depression (p. 325)
negative cognitive triad (p. 325)
negative schemata (p. 325)

learned helplessness/hopelessness
(p. 326)
adjustment disorder (p. 327)
congruency hypothesis (p. 327)
expressed emotion (EE) (p. 328)
linkage analysis (p. 329)

catecholamines (p. 329)
frontal cortex EEG asymmetry
(p. 330)
approach motivation (p. 330)
role transitions (p. 332)
monoamine oxidase inhibitors
(MAOIs) (p. 333)

tricyclics (p. 333)
selective serotonin reuptake inhibitors
(SSRIs) (p. 333)
lithium carbonate (p. 333)
anomie (p. 339)

ADDITIONAL RESOURCES

Mood Disorders Association of British
Columbia
2730 Commercial Drive
Suite 201
Vancouver, BC V5N 5P4
(604) 873-0103
(604) 873-3095 fax
mda@lynx.bc.ca

Canadian Association for Suicide
Prevention
1615 10th Avenue SW
Suite 201
Calgary, AB T3C 0J7
(403) 245-3900
(403) 240-0299 fax
masecard@sympatico.ca

National Depressive and Manic-
Depressive Association
730 N. Franklin Street
Suite 501
Chicago, IL 60610-3526
(800) 826-3632
(312) 642-7243 fax
myrtis@aol.com

www.psychiatry.ubc.ca/mood/md_home.html
This site provides general information about mood disorders.

www-fhs.mcmaster.ca/direct
The Depression Information Resource and Education Centre at McMaster University's Faculty of Health Sciences offers a range of resources about depression.

www.psycom.net/depression.central.html
Depression Central is a major collection of mood disorder and depression resources.

www.execpc.com/~corbeau/
This award-winning site is a collection of resources about many psychological disorders, including mood disorders and suicide.

www.siec.ca
The site of the Suicide Information and Education Centre provides statistics, research data, program information, and curriculum details from over 22,000 documents.

Chapter 14

Schizophrenia

Richard W. J. Neufeld
Jeffrey R. Carter
Ian R. Nicholson
David N. Vollick

Chris, who published his account of his schizophrenia (Fleshner, 1995), was a systems programmer analyst at a major insurance company who also freelanced on the side. Chris had become increasingly introspective. Concerned that his life was coming to an end, he fasted and studied the New Testament Book of Revelation. Tormented by his preoccupation with death, Chris also experienced moments of "mystical emotional gratification."

Chris was gripped by the belief that thoughts and ideas could be transferred from person to person. "I thought people could transfer themselves, their thoughts and minds, from one body to the next, but it was more complex than that. In fact, when this transfer occurred, you could actually 'see' the person from whom the transfer had been taken."

Chris remained competent and efficient at fairly high-level work assignments. But as Chris's delusions occupied more of his thoughts, and as their frightening nature increased his stress, job demands for accurate assimilation of information under time constraints became increasingly oppressive.

To return to Chris's own account: "I was responsible for loading copies of programs for the online system programmers. This authority was given to one person to consolidate the process and avoid costly errors. It was usually quite stressful on Fridays because the online transfer would happen Thursday night. This meant the freshly changed program might develop problems the following morning, thus requiring a 'dynamic load' to change the erroneous copy to a working copy. So one Friday, I imagined that the end of the world was coming and those programmers who wanted their names in the 'book of life' (Rev. 20:12) would have to go through me to save their lives, or was it the end of their lives? I didn't know. It was so real. I felt as though I was a demon and a saviour, holding the key to all these people's lives, and the computer was actually determining their fate via every key I punched. I imagined the file cabinets (full of microfiche) were in fact transcripts of every thought and every statement anybody had ever made—the necessary 'good' by which to judge each individual's salvation. Instead of a merciful judgement, it was a financial enterprise in which corruption pervaded every corner. The 'higher-ups' would have the power to manipulate records that would incriminate or discredit them.

"I dealt with the concept of killing people (via the dynamic load process) by denying it was actually happening and being totally unaware of the killing. I was imagining myself a pawn in a giant game of deception against humanity. I lived all this as if it were reality. It was terrifying. However, now I know this was all due to my then undiagnosed mental disorder.

"Back then my delusions caused tearfulness at times and consequently my boss suggested I see a psychiatrist. I did go and see one, but I was too sick by then to be able to realize all this was in my imagination. I was certain the therapist did not have my best interests in mind and in fact considered him a part of the corrupt system of knowledge/judgment that I referred to earlier. Trusting your therapist is essential in getting on the road to mental health."

* * *

Robert was 23 when he appeared for his second admission to a psychiatric hospital at the urging of his parents because of, in his own words, "the social pressure to perform." His tone of voice was expressionless and he grimaced as he spoke. Robert answered questions in a peculiar and illogical way. He said that concentrating on the questions was like "looking into a bright sun." When asked how he was feeling, Robert answered, "I'm as sure as you can help me as I have ice cubes in my ears." When asked to telephone his family, Robert refused because "insects come out of the little holes."

The results of physical and neurological examinations were within normal limits. Robert's IQ on the Wechsler Adult Intelligence Scale was 98, but he had considerable difficulty on comprehension questions because of his illogical speech. On the ward he was withdrawn and slept 15 hours a day, but never felt that he had enough rest. Robert heard voices, but seemed less interested in them than in the numbness of his eyebrows, which he attributed to a bee sting received some months earlier.

During his hospitalization, Robert became preoccupied with his misdeeds as an adolescent. He repeatedly asked to be sent to jail, saying little work would be expected of him there. Robert felt pressure from his parents to work, but he had little motivation to work and had no career plans.

Robert was dedicated to his diet, fasting for long periods and drinking no liquids of certain colours. He described himself as a "urine reservoir" and received "messages," from soap commercials for example, warning him against using excessive amounts of coloured soap.

Source: Adapted from R. L. Spitzer, A. E. Skodol, M. Gibbon, & J.B.W. Williams, *Psychopathology: A case book* (New York: McGraw Hill, 1993).

These two cases illustrate a disorder we have come to call *schizophrenia*. The disorder undoubtedly is among the most serious, as well as the most puzzling, within the domain of psychopathology. Its effects on the individual's daily functioning and productivity can be devastating. For example, some 20 percent of schizophrenic patients attempt suicide; half of them succeed (Shuwall & Siris, 1994).

Schizophrenic symptoms are often first manifested in the late teens to the mid-thirties, frequently preceded by signs of maladjustment during earlier years. Vocational and social development is usually impaired. In some cases, symptoms may emerge in the forties or fifties, disrupting what may have been satisfactory, or even exemplary, marital adjustment and occupational achievement.

The clinical term **schizophrenia** (*schizein* in Greek means "to split," and *phrenos* means "mind") was coined by an early investigator, Eugen Bleuler. It conveyed the idea that a "schism" had occurred among the functions of the personality, whereby some functions, such as emotional responses, had split away from others, such as thought processes. In addition, thought processes were considered to be dislodged from the environment. Schizophrenia is not, however, to be confused with *dissociative identity disorder* (previously known as "multiple personality disorder"), in which an individual displays separate and distinct personalities.

Behaviour in some instances appears to be autistic, in the sense of being governed by internal stimuli or private events. (*Note:* "Autistic" is used here only in a general sense; *autism* as a pervasive developmental disorder—see Chapter 6—is a quite different disorder from schizophrenia.) The individual may be unresponsive to environmental stimuli that would normally prompt reactions, or may respond in a way that suggests a distorted interpretation of the stimuli. Ordinary objects or events seem to take on a marked personal significance.

Overall, adverse changes in thought, perception, emotion, and motor behaviour are associated with the disorder of schizophrenia. Many affected individuals report feeling that they are observers, rather than initiators, of their own behaviour, an experience labelled **depersonalization** (Foulds, 1965).

One of the most pronounced aspects of schizophrenia is the disruption of cognitive transactions. Thought and language appear to become loosened from the normal constraints that make for coherent sequences of ideas and distinguish fantasy from reality. Often, some notion or theme involving malevolent forces or inordinate personal power increasingly commands the individual's attention. When the preoccupation becomes a main priority of daily activities, it may be so disruptive as to require the attention of caregivers, or sometimes the police. A period of hospitalization is likely to follow.

Other instances of schizophrenia show a progressive erosion of the integrity of psychological functions. Occupational or educational performance may decline, and the frequency and richness of social interactions fall off. Family and marital relations almost inevitably are strained. Often daily activities become so irregular that hygiene and diet suffer.

The two case studies above illustrate the disabling behavioural tendencies commonly associated with schizophrenia. They exhibit two somewhat differing sets of symptoms, which can be viewed as alternative expressions of this disorder. In the first case, Chris displays a fairly high level of intellectual functioning, apart from disturbing beliefs that intrude into his occupational activities and social transactions. Even his aberrant belief system, or delusional network of thoughts, although not grounded in fact, is fairly well integrated in its own right. This internal consistency often incorporates hallucinations, such as Chris's visions of thought transference. The auditory hallucinations that are most common also tend to agree with the substance of the delusions. Voices may provide a running commentary on the persecutory or grandiose topic with which the individual is preoccupied. In the next case, Wagner (1996) provides an example of his own delusional preoccupation, which largely revolved around malicious forces.

> "I was, and despite medication at times still am, sensitive to casual remarks. Sometimes even a 'Hello' or 'How are you?' can feel threatening or of cosmic significance. I hear the voices of abusively cruel people talking to me constantly, even when no one is present, and often such talk is a running commentary on every one of my daily activities. Listening to the radio is impossible because of the personal messages I am sent, either by the DJ or by the sequence of music and advertisements." (p. 400).

Note that distinguishing delusions or hallucinations from mere eccentricities or cultural expectations can at times be difficult. However, in most cases the thoughts of schizophrenics are so clearly aberrant that observers have no trouble identifying them as delusional or hallucinatory. Delusions and hallucinations generally reflect responses to private, internal stimuli. When they are triggered by external events, these events are grossly distorted. Difficulties in living, and referral to mental health personnel, often result when delusions or hallucinations lead to conspicuous actions, dominate behaviour for long periods of each day, or persist despite contradictory evidence.

The second case at the beginning of this chapter demonstrates a different pattern of schizophrenia, characterized by much less effective functioning. Chris was able to keep doing his work effectively despite interference from the disorder; in Robert's case, not only was he unable to work, but his self-maintenance had deteriorated to the point of imperilling his physical well-being. His thinking is also more disrupted; his delusions and hallucinations, apart from being bizarre, are not well integrated but are scattered and of superficial content.

Positive and Negative Symptoms

The foregoing comments have emphasized the **positive symptomatology** of schizophrenia. Positive is used here, of course, not in the sense of *good*, but in the sense of something noted for its presence. Briefly, *positive symptoms* are those that have apparently replaced normal behaviours, or express extravagant versions of normal behaviours. People with schizophrenia may also display an erosion of normal patterns of experience and conduct described as **negative symptomatology**. They appear to lose their intensity. Language may become impoverished, with little apparent effort or success at communication. The person may become withdrawn socially and exhibit little interest in the pursuits he or she used to enjoy. Attention span may be markedly reduced.

The decline in intellectual efficiency is generally accompanied by a decline in academic or occupational achievement. Whereas Chris's symptoms were positive, Robert displays both positive and negative symptoms. His good grades and popularity in elementary school gave way to a sharp decline in scholastic achievement and a tendency to become withdrawn and quiet.

People who experience schizophrenic disorders often report that their symptoms and subjective experiences are aggravated by environmental stressors (see the ViewPoint box). This relationship can be seen in Chris's report. Another patient reports: "College brought even greater stresses, and with them a certain paranoia" (Wagner, 1996, p. 399). Owing, in part, to such subjective experiences, some researchers have examined normal mechanisms of coping with stress, hoping this would illustrate the difficulties of schizophrenic patients. These studies have been complemented by an examination of the way in which schizophrenic patients deal with stress (Nicholson & Neufeld, 1989).

Incidence/Prevalence

Lifetime prevalence for schizophrenia has been found to be approximately the same in Canada and the United States. According to DSM-IV (American Psychiatric Association, 1994), lifetime prevalence estimates range from 0.5 percent to 1 percent, while the incidence rate is considered to be 1 per 10,000 per year. Of all those diagnosed with schizophrenia, 42 to 50 percent have a subdiagnosis of **paranoid schizophrenia**, in which delusions are a predominant symptom, often accompanied by hallucinations related to the delusional theme.

There were 30,118 individuals treated for schizophrenic disorders in Canadian psychiatric and general hospitals during 1992/1993 (Statistics Canada, 1995): 17,700 males and 12,418 females. Of this total, 8681 entered psychiatric hospitals and 21,432 were admitted to general hospitals. Most of those who were treated (61 percent) were between 25 and 44 years of age; the most common subdiagnosis (37 percent) was paranoid schizophrenia. Following paranoid schizophrenia in prevalence is the **undifferentiated** category of subdiag-

nosis, which involves a mixture of paranoid and other symptoms and occurs in 21 percent of patients. The third most frequent diagnostic categorization is that of **residual schizophrenia** (20 percent) which is said to be a feature of chronic schizophrenia, and may be "continuously present for many years with or without acute exacerbations" (American Psychiatric Association, 1994, p. 289). For a patient to be diagnosed with residual schizophrenia, any previous prominent delusions and hallucinations must have subsided.

....

HISTORICAL PERSPECTIVE

The schizophrenic syndrome has been known for thousands of years. Sanskrit writings from the fourteenth century B.C. have references to the disorder. Because schizophrenic symptoms are so bizarre, in ancient and medieval times they were often thought to indicate possession by demons. As we saw in Chapter 1, demonology proposes that some evil being, such as the devil, dwells inside a person and controls his or her mind. The writings of some ancient Babylonians, Chinese, Egyptians, and Greeks seem to reflect this idea. However, Canadian psychiatrist and theologian John White (1983) suggests that the Hebrews differentiated between demonic possession and mental illness as early as the time of David (circa 1000 B.C.). This distinction was apparently lost by the fifteenth century, when the Roman Pope issued the *Malleus maleficarum* ("The Witches' Hammer"), an explicit guide to the Inquisition. This guide attributed loss of reason to witchcraft and prescribed an exorcism ritual to be conducted "at least three times a week, so that through many intercessions the grace of healing may be obtained" (Kramer & Sprenger, 1928/1970, p. 184). Florid psychotic symptoms were often misconstrued as confessions of heresy (Zilboorg & Henry, 1941), and both relapsed and impenitent heretics were often burned at the stake.

German and French psychiatric texts in the nineteenth century include several references to variants of schizophrenia. Lasèque used the term *délire de persecution* to describe a patient in 1852, and in that same year, Morel described a *démence précoce* which was marked by severe intellectual deterioration, withdrawal, and bizarre mannerisms that started in adolescence. In 1871, an illness which resulted in a "silly" deterioration was described by Hecker, who noted that it tended to appear at puberty.

The first modern description of schizophrenia, however, appeared in 1893, when Emil Kraepelin used the term *dementia praecox* to describe a narrow group of psychotic disorders. By 1898, Kraepelin elaborated his descriptions by dividing the single major category into three forms: catatonic, hebephrenic, and paranoid. Common to these forms were several symptoms that marked them as part of the same overall disorder, including progressive mental deterioration (*dementia*) and onset during puberty or adolescence (*praecox*). This description was expanded in the 1899 edition of

Kraepelin's *Textbook of Psychiatry*. Kraepelin emphasized the importance of knowing the course of the disorder: diagnostic judgement might be suspended pending observations on how behaviour and symptomatology were unfolding. Many practitioners resisted this idea; others disagreed with Kraepelin's observation that more than 80 percent of patients with dementia praecox had severe intellectual deterioration. In fact, his views were considered so radical that they were not initially adopted.

Kraepelin revised his categories several times in the years before his death in 1927, the last complete version appearing in 1913. In this version, he described dementia praecox as "a series of states, the common characteristic of which is a peculiar destruction of the internal connections of the psychic personality. The effects of this injury predominate in the emotional and volitional spheres of mental life" (Kraepelin, 1913, p. 3).

During the time in which Kraepelin was revising his texts, Eugen Bleuler's (1911/1950) text on schizophrenia appeared. It has been influential for several reasons. First, Bleuler introduced the term *schizophrenia* to overcome what he saw as the difficulties in the label *dementia praecox*. The new term reflected Bleuler's view that the central characteristic of the syndrome was the disintegration of personality due to a loosening of associations. Second, Bleuler retained Kraepelin's three categories and added a fourth, simple schizophrenia. Third, he declared that the group of schizophrenias should be viewed as a single clinical entity, as they had four primary characteristics in common: disorders of association, autism,

Emil Kraepelin (1856–1926) provided the first modern description of schizophrenia.

ambivalence, and affect. Bleuler's view has dominated the majority of theory and research on schizophrenia from the publication of the English translation of his text in 1950 to the development of DSM-IV in 1994.

DESCRIPTION

It is important to preface a review of the specific symptoms of schizophrenia with two observations. First, there are no symptoms unique to the disorder, or that define it. For example, a number of mental and physical disorders cause hallucinations. Second, while the symptoms of schizophrenia seem unusual, most modern theorists (for example, Costello, 1994) believe that such features are present in less intense, less persistent, and less debilitating forms in normal people. It is, therefore, not any single symptom but a unique *combination* of certain symptoms at certain levels that are important in the diagnosis of schizophrenia.

Perhaps the best way to approach this issue is to review the list of symptoms described in DSM-IV (see the DSM table "Diagnostic Criteria for Schizophrenia"): delusions, hallucinations, disorganized speech, grossly disorganized or catatonic behaviour, and negative symptoms.

Delusions

Delusions are false beliefs that are strongly held, even in the face of solid contradictory evidence. It is important to recognize that delusions differ from false beliefs related to a person's cultural or religious background. For example, although most people believe that a bite from a highly poisonous snake could be fatal, certain religious groups believe faith will offer protection from the bites of serpents. These people would not be considered delusional. A delusion can be highly integrated into every aspect of a person's life, or it may be simply a false belief about one small aspect of a person's life (for example, that a pet can read the person's mind).

There are several forms of delusions. One of the more common forms in schizophrenia is *persecutory* delusions (sometimes called "paranoid" delusions), in which people believe they are being attacked, cheated, persecuted, or conspired against in some way. These people often believe they are the target of an organized group (for example, the RCMP, the Mafia), who they believe intrude into various aspects of their lives through such activities as opening mail, videotaping from secret cameras in the home, or following them in public places.

Religious delusions are also common in schizophrenia; people often believe that their unique interpretations of religious texts give them the means to save or destroy the world.

Grandiose delusions involve beliefs that a person has special powers (for example, the ability to read thoughts), has special knowledge (for example, the only true understanding of the Dead Sea Scrolls), or has the persona of a famous historical figure (for example, Napoleon, Jesus Christ).

DSM-IV Diagnostic Criteria for Schizophrenia

A. *Characteristic symptoms:* Two or more of the following, each present for a significant period of time during a 1-month period (or less if successfully treated):
   (1) delusions
   (2) hallucinations
   (3) disorganized speech (e.g., frequent derailment or incoherence)
   (4) grossly disorganized or catatonic behavior
   (5) negative symptoms (i.e., affective flattening, alogia, or avolition)

Note: Only one Criterion A symptom is required if delusions are bizarre or if hallucinations consist of a voice keeping a running commentary on the person's behavior or thoughts, or 2 or more voices are conversing with each other.

B. *Social/occupational dysfunction:* For a significant portion of the time from the onset of the disturbance, the patient is functioning well below their usual level in one or more of the following areas: work, interpersonal relations, and/or self-care.

C. *Duration:* Continuous signs of the disturbance must persist for at least 6 months. This 6-month period must include at least 1 month of symptoms (or less if successfully treated) that meet Criterion A. This 6-month period may also include prodromal or residual periods. During these prodromal or residual periods, only negative symptoms or less severe symptoms in Criterion A may be present.

D. *Schizoaffective and Mood Disorder exclusion:* No Mood Disorders have occurred at the same time as active phase symptoms. If there have been mood episodes, their duration has been briefer than the duration of the active or residual periods.

E. *Substance/medical exclusion:* The disturbance is not due to the direct effects of a drug, medication, or general medical condition.

F. *Relationship to Pervasive Developmental Disorder:* If there is a history of Autistic Disorder or another Pervasive Developmental Disorder, the additional diagnosis of Schizophrenia is made only if prominent delusions or hallucinations are also present for at least a month (or less if successfully treated).

Source: Reprinted with permission from the *Diagnostic and Statistical Manual of Mental Disorders*, Fourth Edition. Copyright 1994 American Psychiatric Association.

Delusions of reference are convictions involving common, everyday occurrences, objects, or people having special personal significance. One example is the belief that the jacket colour worn by the morning television news broadcaster is a special signal about what clothes should be worn that day.

Schizophrenic people also occasionally have *somatic* delusions, involving beliefs about the body. An example is an 80-year-old woman who believed she was pregnant with Pierre Trudeau's child, although she had never met Trudeau. Another example is a man's belief that his stomach was being eaten from within by ants.

If a delusion is considered bizarre, its mere presence is enough to meet the criteria for a diagnosis of schizophrenia. If the delusion is not bizarre, then it must be combined with another symptom, such as hallucinations, for a diagnosis of schizophrenia. This distinction thus becomes an important diagnostic point. What do we mean by *bizarre*? Recall the distinction made in both Chapter 11 and Chapter 17. A delusion is bizarre if it is clearly impossible, not understandable, and not directly related to an individual's life experience or cultural background. A non-bizarre delusion, while equally false, is conceivably possible. Delusions such as the notion that co-workers are trying to get one fired or that a neighbour is scheming to get possession of one's house would not be considered bizarre.

Hallucinations

Hallucinations, the second DSM-IV defining symptom, are false perceptions occurring in the absence of any relevant stimulus. These perceptual abnormalities may occur within any sensory modality, with auditory hallucinations being the most common form. Schizophrenic patients may report voices, noises, or other sounds that have no external origin. These sounds are most commonly experienced as conversations or as voices commenting on the person's thoughts or behaviours. The voices may or may not be recognizable to the person. For example, a man may hear his deceased mother commenting on his history of masturbation, or the devil speaking through a heating vent, urging him to kill himself. If certain auditory hallucinations are present, no other symptoms are necessary for the diagnosis. If these are not present, but other types of hallucinations are, the diagnosis requires at least one other symptom to be present.

Other, less common forms of schizophrenic hallucination occur in the tactile, olfactory, and visual systems. Visual hallucinations of schizophrenia tend to be less well-formed than those generated by such things as psychedelic drugs (for example, LSD). An example of a schizophrenic visual hallucination is a light flashing in one's peripheral vision, which disappears when one turns to look at it directly. Olfactory hallucinations are false perceptions of smells, such as the smell of burning flesh coming from outside a person's window. An example of a tactile hallucination (also known as a *haptic* hallucination) is a false perception of ants crawling under the skin.

Patients sometimes say that they know it is their illness causing the hallucination, though this insight often does not occur until progress has been made in treatment. The earmark of hallucinations, however, is a lack of control over the experience.

Disorganized Speech

Disturbed belief patterns, as evidenced by systematized delusions and thematic hallucinations, fall into the category of **thought-content symptomatology**. Although the beliefs and perceptual experiences expressed are irrational, the ability to express them coherently may be more or less intact. **Thought-form symptomatology**, in contrast, refers, as the name suggests, to disorganized and incoherent expression of trains of ideas that are loosely connected and subject to irrelevant intrusions.

These symptoms, which form the third characteristic of schizophrenia, are most commonly apparent in **disorganized speech**. Speech may be disorganized in different ways. For example, *derailment* occurs when discourse appears to "go off the rails"; the person allows one topic in a conversation to slide into another, loosely related but irrelevant, topic. To illustrate, one patient stated: "I can hear the rules from the … the tapes, the ones in my teeth, that my dentist put in … I went to the dentist as a child … I had a lot of friends as a child … my friends and I used to play a lot of games … the people on TV play a lot of games with my mind." Often, each phrase may make sense and be related to the next, but the person is soon far from the original topic and seldom returns to it.

Sometimes people will use words that make no sense. They may deliberately create their own **neologisms**: reasonable-sounding but nonexistent words. For example, one patient created the term *doctoramazine* to describe the drug she thought her doctor had injected into her brain whenever she saw him on the ward. Nonsense sounds may also result inadvertently when the person's thought patterns are so disorganized that ordinary words become jumbled. This pattern of speech is sometimes referred to as "**word salad**" or **schizo-aphasia**.

Another common aspect of schizophrenic language is excessive concreteness, a deficient ability to use abstract language, such as metaphors or similes. The phrase "a rolling stone gathers no moss," for example, may signify to a schizophrenic person simply a lack of vegetation on moving rocks.

Any combination of these language disturbances can be found in schizophrenia. It is generally believed that disorganized speech reflects severe disturbances of thought. Such disturbances are often found at lesser, nonclinical levels in the close relatives of schizophrenic patients (Romney, 1990).

Grossly Disorganized Behaviour

Next on DSM-IV's list of characteristic symptoms of schizophrenia is grossly disorganized or catatonic behaviour. **Grossly disorganized behaviour** is exemplified by the patient who lined his hat with tin foil to keep government agents from stealing his thoughts via special laser beams, or the man who urinated in corners because, he said, toilets contained holy water.

Inappropriate emotional reactions constitute another form of disorganized behaviour. The individual may begin to giggle when discussing the death of a parent. Some people react in a "silly" manner to all situations. Often these behaviours are combined with such severe agitation and poor impulse control that the person has difficulty carrying out daily self-maintenance functions, such as eating or washing.

Catatonia

Catatonia describes a wide range of behaviours. In *stuporous catatonia*, there is a marked decrease in a person's reaction to his or her environment, sometimes reaching a level of complete unawareness. *Catatonic rigidity* describes the behaviour of a schizophrenic who maintains rigid, sometimes bizarre postures and who resists efforts to be moved. *Catatonic negativism* refers to a state of active resistance to all instructions or attempts to be moved. *Catatonic posturing* occurs when a person takes on inappropriate or bizarre positions for extended periods. Many catatonic people also display *waxy flexibility*, in which their catatonic posturing can be altered by others (for example, an arm held in a fixed position can be moved by someone else) with the person's passive acceptance. *Echopraxia*, in which the person imitates someone else's movements, or *echolalia*, the persistent echoing of another's words or phrases, can both be present in catatonic schizophrenia. Seemingly purposeless, unstimulated, and excessive motor activity or general agitation of speech and behaviour, often following a period of catatonic rigidity or stupor, is called *catatonic excitement*.

The latter should not be confused with tardive dyskinesia: involuntary movements of the face, tongue, and neck, and sometimes the arms and legs. The latter is one of the most common side effects of antipsychotic medications often used to treat schizophrenia. Nonprofessionals often interpret such side-effects (called *extrapyramidal*) as part of schizophrenic symptomatology, whereas they are actually a response to these drugs that anyone might show. These effects are common following the long-term use of antipsychotic medications, and are usually irreversible.

Persons with schizophrenia may display catatonic rigidity, maintaining bizarre postures and resisting efforts to move them.

Negative Symptoms

All of the preceding symptoms can be described as *positive symptoms*: as we explained earlier, these are changes in behaviour that are additions to, or replacements of, normal behavioural functioning. DSM-IV's fifth set of schizophrenic criteria are *negative symptoms*, reflecting a decline in functioning from normal levels. Such types of symptoms include, for example, impoverishment in emotional expression, in reactivity, and in subjective experience. The terms *affective flattening* or *emotional blunting* are often used to describe these responses. Negative symptoms also include slowed thinking or *thought blocking*, where the person's train of thought is interrupted or lost before completion. Another common negative symptom, labelled **avolition**, comprises a loss of energy, motivation, or interest in activities, including grooming, education, or physical exertion. Also included in this symptom grouping is **anhedonia**, defined as the inability to experience pleasure. *Asociality* describes social withdrawal, with a resulting decrease in friendships, and a lack of intimate relationships. Finally, **attentional deficits** have been widely described in the literature on negative symptomatology. These deficits include distractibility, poor concentration for an extended period, and a tendency to drift away from ongoing activities, including conversations.

Although people with schizophrenia may also display symptoms of anxiety and depression, these are distinct from negative symptoms (Norman & Malla, 1991). However, the distinction is difficult to make by focussing on an individual symptom. Instead, the diagnostician should look at the entire constellation of symptoms to see whether other symptoms of these disorders are present.

In general, negative symptoms tend to become more prominent after schizophrenia has continued for several years. Prominent negative symptoms when someone is first diagnosed suggest a poor prognosis (Hustad, Beiser, & Iacono, 1992).

The Three-Factor Model

Although there has been considerable research on the positive/negative symptom dichotomy, there has been increasing dissatisfaction with this simple division. For example, a recent review by Nicholson, Chapman, and Neufeld (1995) found little consistency across studies in the definition of positive and negative symptoms. Peter Liddle (1987) of the University of British Columbia, examined the symptomatology of patients with schizophrenia using the statistical technique of factor analysis, a technique that can determine symptoms whose severities tend to rise and fall together. Liddle's results indicated that the symptoms could be divided into three separate syndromes. The first syndrome, *psychomotor poverty*, included poverty of speech, lack of spontaneous movement, and various aspects of emotional impoverishment. The second group of symptoms was labelled *disorganization*, and included inappropriate emotional displays and disorganized thought processes. The third group, entitled *reality distortion*, involved delusions and hallucinations. Several studies

have replicated Liddle's findings (for example, Malla et al., 1993), suggesting that these are more useful distinctions than the simple positive/negative categorization.

Similar groupings have also been found in studies of the close relatives of schizophrenic patients (Bassett, Bury, & Honer, 1994), and it has been suggested in DSM-IV that these factors might be used as alternate dimensional descriptors of schizophrenia. As a result, DSM-IV placed these factors into a group of indicators recommended for further investigation and for possible inclusion in later editions of the diagnostic manual.

Research at the University of Western Ontario has focussed on the relationships of Liddle's three symptom factors to measures of neurological functioning. Ross Norman, Ashok Malla, and their colleagues have found that different patterns of neurological functions correlate with the different symptom dimensions. The relations have been found for various areas of functioning, such as movement planning, cognitive performance, neurological "soft signs" (relating to the integration of complex motor activity), and EEG coherence (the systematic associations among signals from different parts of the brain). For example, Norman et al. (in press) found that the level of disorganization symptoms was inversely related to visual memory performance, and the level of reality distortion symptoms was inversely related to verbal memory performance. The psychomotor poverty symptoms were related to some aspects of verbal functioning.

....

DIAGNOSTIC ISSUES

Related Disorders

A number of disorders share certain features with schizophrenia, but they are viewed as being distinct in other ways.

For example, people with **delusional disorder** (see Chapter 17) have one or more non-bizarre delusions, but do not have other characteristic schizophrenic symptoms. Their functioning is usually not markedly impaired and their behaviour is not obviously unusual, apart from their delusions, which may have disruptive effects. The primary determinant of whether the diagnosis is delusional disorder or schizophrenia is the bizarreness of the delusional content.

To illustrate the nature of non-bizarre delusions, we will describe two typical types. In the erotomanic type, the individual believes himself or herself to be the object of another person's amorous interests. In some instances, the belief can lead to stalking a celebrity who the delusional patient claims has been directing remarks to him or her through the media. The object of the delusion may become the central focus of the person's life.

Another so-called non-bizarre delusion is the jealous type, in which the deluded person suspects his or her lover of being unfaithful, usually on the basis of vague and overinterpreted evidence (for example, a telephone call home not being answered quickly enough, foreign hairs on clothes). Sometimes called the "Othello syndrome," this common delusion is more prevalent in men than in women, and often leads to physical assaults or even to homicide.

Delusional disorders, unlike schizophrenia, tend to develop in middle or later adult life. It is possible, however, for them to develop at the younger ages more typical for the onset of schizophrenia.

There is strong evidence that the paranoid subtype of schizophrenia and delusional disorder may be etiologically linked, with some researchers suggesting that they express essentially the same disorder in differing levels of severity (Munro, 1988; Romney, 1987). However, in delusional disorders the internal logic and highly specific content of false beliefs tend to be more organized, elaborate, and less bizarre than is the case with paranoid schizophrenia.

The symptomatology of several other disorders overlaps with that of schizophrenia. A person who displays sufficient symptoms for both an affective episode (depression, mania, or mixed) and schizophrenia is diagnosed as having **schizoaffective disorder**. There is no firm rule as to which set of symptoms predominate in the clinical presentation. During the course of a person's symptomatology, the proportion of mood symptoms to psychotic symptoms can change quite dramatically. It is still unclear how this disorder relates to other disorders. Is it a type of schizophrenia, a type of affective disorder, or some third, unique disorder? We really do not know.

Delusions and hallucinations may be secondary to some other disorder or external cause. Psychotic symptoms can result from a number of different medical conditions, including epilepsy, brain tumours, Huntington's disease, migraine headaches, metabolic disorders, renal disease, and some autoimmune system disorders. In **substance-induced psychotic disorder**, the individual displays prominent hallucinations and delusions that result from the ingestion of a chemical substance (for example, cocaine, marijuana, or an environmental toxin such as carbon monoxide or paint fumes).

Brief psychotic disorder is diagnosed when an individual has a sudden onset of at least one prominent psychotic symptom that lasts for at least one day but less than one month, followed by a full return to premorbid levels of functioning.

Schizophreniform disorder involves the presence of symptomatology similar to that of schizophrenia, but whose duration is between one and six months, the lower limit for a diagnosis of schizophrenia. This is a somewhat problematic disorder, since the feature that distinguishes it from schizophrenia is simply its duration. What purpose is served by applying different diagnoses to essentially the same symptoms, simply because one has a longer duration?

The final disorder related to schizophrenia that we will discuss is not included in DSM-IV, but is present in other diagnostic systems. In the former USSR, the diagnostic category of **sluggish schizophrenia** or *slowly progressive schizophrenia* was widely used. In reviewing Soviet research on this disorder, Merskey and Shafran (1986) found its symptom picture to resemble Western psychiatry's simple schizophrenia. However, sluggish schizophrenia also included social maladaptation, defined as illegal acts committed against social institutions, and the so-called delusions of this disorder—which on their own were considered sufficient grounds for a diagnosis—could include ideas about reforming political systems. This category of supposed psychosis appears to have been used in the former Soviet Union to incarcerate political dissidents in psychiatric hospitals. Such use underscores the potential abuse of diagnostic systems for political ends. It highlights, furthermore, the safeguard inherent in empirically validating proposed classification practices.

Subtypes of Schizophrenia

Is schizophrenia a single disorder or a collection of disparate but related disorders? Although DSM-IV has settled on the idea that there is a unifying characteristic to these disorders, the argument that there are important differences among these patients has not gone away. There is, in fact, considerable evidence for the unity of schizophrenia, with similarities among subtypes exceeding the differences (Heinrichs, 1993; Nicholson & Neufeld, 1993). However, the subdivision of schizophrenia into subtypes is a time-honoured clinical practice.

The Five Classic Subtypes

The subtypes and the model for their assessment that was originally proposed a century ago by Emil Kraepelin and Eugen Bleuler continues to form much of the basis for the current system. DSM-IV recognizes five subtypes of schizophrenia (summarized in Figure 14.1), defined primarily by predominant symptomatology at the time of assessment.

The presence of the **paranoid subtype** of schizophrenia is determined by the patient's preoccupation with one or more delusions or by frequent auditory hallucinations. It is thought to be the least severe of the five official subtypes. Many researchers traditionally divide schizophrenia into paranoid and nonparanoid forms (Neufeld, 1991). Indeed, the second of the two DSM-IV diagnostic criteria for assignment to the paranoid subtype is that there be an absence of prominent disorganized speech, disorganized behaviour, catatonic behaviour, and flat or inappropriate emotions.

The **disorganized subtype**, in contrast, is characterized by disorganized speech, clearly disorganized behaviour, and markedly flat or inappropriate affect. This subtype is generally viewed as being the most severe.

The **catatonic subtype** is defined by the presence of stupor, rigidity, negativism, odd posturing, excitement, and echopraxia or echolalia.

The **undifferentiated subtype** of schizophrenia is a more general "wastebasket" category for patients who display prominent symptoms but who do not fall easily into one of the previous three categories.

The **residual subtype** of schizophrenia is diagnosed when a person who previously met the criteria for one of the other four types has no current delusions, hallucinations, disorganized speech, grossly disorganized behaviour, or catatonic behaviour. Individuals with residual schizophrenia nevertheless continue to show evidence of disturbance by the continuation of either negative symptoms or very mild levels of earlier positive symptoms, which have lessened either with the passage of time or through treatment.

Figure 14.1 The Classic Subtypes of Schizophrenia

Schizophrenia

DSM-IV includes five subtypes of schizophrenia, as shown below:

Catatonic

At least two of the following psychomotor disturbances:

- immobility (including waxy flexibility or stupor)
- excessive motor activity (seemingly purposeless)
- extreme negativism (resistance, rigidity of posture) or mutism
- posturing (peculiar voluntary movements, bizarre positions), repetition

Paranoid

Preoccupation with one or more delusions or frequent auditory hallucinations

Absence of prominent schizophrenic symptoms such as disorganized speech or behavior, or flat or inappropriate affect

Disorganized

Presence of:

- disorganized speech
- disorganized behavior
- flat or inappropriate affect

Does not meet criteria for catatonic type

Residual

No longer active symptoms of schizophrenia, and does not meet criteria for any subtype

Continuing evidence of disturbance indicated by negative symptoms or two or more symptoms of schizophrenia in mild forms.

Undifferentiated

Meets criteria for schizophrenia but does not meet criteria for catatonic, paranoid, or disorganized subtype

Source: Kendall, Philip and Constance Hammen, *Abnormal Psychology.* Copyright ©1995 by Houghton Mifflin Company. Used with permission.

Harold was a single black man who attended a day hospital in a community mental health centre. Harold's illness first emerged at the age of 19. He was studying voice and working in a music store, when suddenly he left his church and spent all his free time with a fundamentalist Christian group. He entered into "consecrations" involving fasting and abstaining from sex and alcohol, and claimed to be an "ambassador of Christ"; he quit his job, feeling that his employer treated him like a slave; he began making bizarre gestures; and he was picked up by the police after shoplifting in an obvious manner, explaining that "everything belongs to God."

Admitted to hospital, he was agitated and unable to sleep. He heard the voice of God and saw the face of the devil. He was in hospital for three months and was treated with antipsychotic medications. He functioned relatively well for nine months after discharge but then his symptoms recurred. Over the next eight years, Harold was hospitalized seven times. Most of these episodes began with increasing preoccupation with religion, followed by agitation, delusions, hallucinations, and incoherent speech. He also began to drink heavily and use marijuana. He made suicidal gestures on two occasions, and was treated with antidepressants as well as antipsychotics.

After his therapist left for vacation, he appeared in the emergency room of a local hospital complaining of hearing voices, seeing colours, and being confused, depressed, and fearful. He was hospitalized and put on prolixin, a long-acting, injectable antipsychotic, and within two weeks the delusions, hallucinations, and anxiety had disappeared. Over the next five years he stayed out of hospital but was unable to return to work. He spent his days at the day hospital, where he organized a patients' chorus. He claimed to be content with his life.

Source: Adapted from R. L. Spitzer, A. E. Skodol, M. Gibbon, & J.B.W. Williams, *Psychopathology: A case book* (New York: McGraw Hill, 1993).

Alternative Systems of Subtyping

Although the classic subtypes continue as separate diagnostic categories in DSM-IV, support for them has lessened over the past 20 years. For example, the percentage of patients diagnosed as suffering from catatonic schizophrenia has decreased dramatically in developed countries. This decrease in frequency of patients being diagnosed as catatonic may be the result of effective drug treatment, or it may be due to inaccurate diagnoses in the past. For example, Boyle (1991) suggests that earlier in the twentieth century, many cases of *encephalitis lethargica* (sleeping sickness) were misidentified as catatonic schizophrenia. There is also a greater recognition that people with schizophrenia do not readily fall into one or another distinct subtype, increasing the proportion of patients diagnosed as "undifferentiated." Because of these and other problems, alternative forms of subtyping have been proposed.

Some theorists believe that, instead of focussing on behavioural symptoms for subdividing schizophrenia, research efforts should be directed at identifying biological subtypes. These theorists believe that biological research to date has been inconclusive because schizophrenia is a biologically heterogeneous disorder. It was hoped that by investigating patient samples with and without certain biological abnormalities (for example, enlarged brain ventricles or abnormalities in neurotransmitter systems), new specific subgroups would emerge. Toronto-based researchers Heinrichs and Awad (1993) had 104 schizophrenic patients complete four neuropsychological tests aimed at assessing the functioning of different parts of their brains. They found five subtypes of patients who could be grouped according to scores on these tests. These groups also differed on other measures, including age, duration of illness, and cumulative hospitalization. It remains to be seen whether these groups will be replicated by other researchers, but this does seem to be a promising start. However, the utility of Heinrichs and Awad's subtypes in terms of its value for prognosis and treatment has yet to be established.

A Two-Factor Model for Classification

Because of the problems encountered in the numerous attempts over the years to subdivide patients, there has been a growing tendency to view schizophrenia in terms of a single disorder with numerous, yet related, manifestations. Early in the century, Bleuler (1911/1915) wrote "at the present time, we cannot solve the problem of dissecting schizophrenia into its natural subdivisions" (p. 227). In an attempt to overcome some of the difficulties present in subdividing symptom patterns, Nicholson and Neufeld (1993) developed a two-factor model of schizophrenia (see Figure 14.2).

The model incorporates two independent continuous factors: severity of disorder and severity of symptoms. The first factor has paranoid schizophrenia as the less severe form of the disorder and nonparanoid subtypes as the more severe form. The more severe form of the disorder is related to longer duration, poorer social competence, and some evidence of more pervasive impairment on tests of cognitive and neuropsychological functioning. An individual located at an intermediate position on this factor (such as point F on Figure 14.2) would display a mixture of paranoid and nonparanoid symptoms. Because paranoid and nonparanoid types are presented not as exclusive, but as points on a continuum, this model can be used to describe patients who exhibit more than one form of symptom or whose symptoms change as the disorder progresses. The model is consistent with the findings that different symptoms are related to clinically relevant variables (for example, paranoid symptoms are associated with better

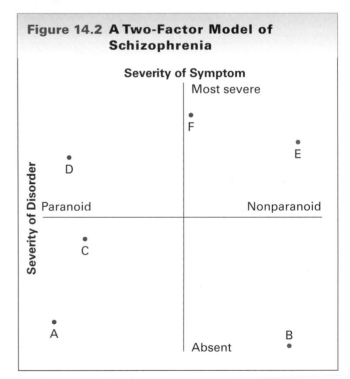

Figure 14.2 A Two-Factor Model of Schizophrenia

Note: Points A to F represent hypothetical patients.

Source: to come

functioning prior to formal diagnosis), and that nonparanoid symptoms are associated with a worse prognosis.

The second factor, severity of symptoms, relates to the frequency and prominence of the symptoms displayed, irrespective of their form. It is possible for a symptom to be severe but to be indicative of a milder form of the disorder. Point D, for example, might represent a person with intense paranoid delusions but no catatonic behaviour or disorganized speech, whereas point B might represent a person with mild thought-form symptomatology. As Bleuler (1911/1950) wrote, "it is extremely important to recognize that [the symptoms] exist in varying degrees and shadings on the entire scale from pathological to normal." For example, delusions, hallucinations, and disorganized speech are seen not only in severe forms of the disorder, but also at low, subclinical levels in nonpsychotic individuals.

A number of well-documented clinical phenomena can be accommodated within this two-factor model. For example, the effects of antipsychotic medication appears to bear primarily on the severity of symptom factor rather than on the severity of the disorder. Although medications control the expression of the symptoms, there is no evidence that they affect the severity of the underlying disorder.

Initial research on Nicholson and Neufeld's (1993) model has been supportive. In a recent study (Nicholson & Neufeld, 1995), 100 patients with schizophrenia were assessed using a wide range of measures of various symptoms. For each symptom, the results were supportive of a continuous factor. In other words, patients did not fall into separate groups on any of the set of symptoms. Thus, the results are compatible with the idea, basic to the model, that all schizophrenics are from a single group, rather than from different groups differentiated by their symptomatology. However useful some may consider subtypes to be for research or clinical practice, subdividing patients into distinctive categories appears to be artificial.

ETIOLOGY

Schizophrenia has a complex etiology. It may be a family of disorders, yet distinct etiologies associated with proposed subtypes have yet to be specified. Exceptions can be found for every hypothesized etiological factor suggested here. In a 1989 address to the Canadian Psychiatric Association, Zbigniew Lipowski warned against the trend in psychiatry to oscillate between overemphasizing psychodynamics and social issues and overemphasizing biological issues. Lipowski pointed out that human behaviour cannot be fully explained from any one theoretical perspective. With this caveat in mind, the question "Which theory best explains schizophrenia?" is less appropriate than "How do the respective theories fit together to explain schizophrenia?"

Our current understanding of schizophrenia has developed from the **vulnerability-stress perspective** (Zubin & Spring, 1977). That is, for whatever reason, certain individuals are vulnerable to schizophrenia, and these people develop

symptoms when they are exposed to certain stressors. (Recall the more general stress-diathesis theory, described in Chapter 2, that applies to psychological disorder as a whole.)

Although valuable in generating research, the vulnerability-stress perspective has certain shortcomings. In particular, vulnerability does not appear to be stable. A more recent theory, known as the *dynamic vulnerability perspective* (Neufeld & Nicholson, 1991; Nicholson & Neufeld, 1992), has addressed this problem by recognizing that the interactions among components are complex and mutually reinforcing (see Figure 14.3 and the ViewPoint box).

In this model, genetic endowment influences vulnerability, the ability to cope, and cognitive appraisal of stressful events and environmental demands. Vulnerability affects symptoms. Symptoms, stress, and subjective appraisal of environmental demands and threats, in turn, all influence coping. The circuit is complete because coping influences subsequent vulnerability.

Further, in this model, stress, coping, and appraisal are all interrelated. Cognitive dysfunctions (such as impaired in-

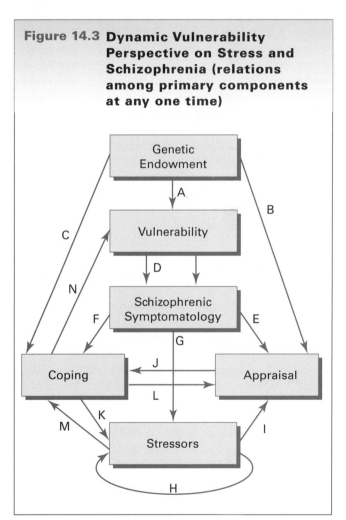

Figure 14.3 Dynamic Vulnerability Perspective on Stress and Schizophrenia (relations among primary components at any one time)

Source: I. R. Nicholson & R.W.J. Neufeld, A dynamic vulnerability perspective on stress and schizophrenia, *American Journal of Orthopsychiatry, 62(1992),* p. 122. Reprinted with permission from the *American Journal of Orthopsychiatry.*

formation processing and memory and language disturbances) can be viewed not only as a consequence of vulnerability and stress, but also as immediate causes of some symptoms.

VULNERABILITY

What factors, then, play a role in vulnerability to schizophrenia?

Developmental Influences

Efforts to draw firm conclusions about the etiology of schizophrenia are often frustrated because causes and effects of the disorder are confounded. While examining the development of schizophrenia over time would make the risk factors clear, the low incidence of the disorder makes such longitudinal studies prohibitively expensive. One alternative research strategy is to conduct **high-risk studies**, such as the Danish (Mednick & McNeil, 1968) and McMaster-Waterloo (Steffy, Asarnow, Asarnow, MacCrimmon, & Cleghorn, 1984) projects. The subjects in these studies were the children of schizophrenic mothers, who were therefore considered especially likely to develop the disorder themselves. The high-risk method yields several advantages. First, the order of events is disentangled so that researchers can identify signs for schizophrenia that predate the onset of symptoms and the educational, occupational, and social difficulties. Second, because no one knows which of the subjects will develop schizophrenia, the data, in principle, are free from researcher bias. Finally, the data collected are uniform across all subjects. Disadvantages of this method include its cost and problems arising from changes over time in research methodology and diagnostic criteria.

Jane Ledingham (1990) at the University of Ottawa reviewed the findings of high-risk studies. She found few differences between high-risk and low-risk children that specifically predicted schizophrenia. One difference was that high-risk children tended to have difficulty with attention tasks (such as repeating a series of digits back to the experimenter). High-risk children who later developed schizophrenia tended to have poor neuromotor test scores. Further, she noted that among people with schizophrenia, those with a family history of the disorder are more likely to be chronically ill and to exhibit fewer paranoid symptoms.

Ledingham suggested that alternative criteria for designating high risk might include behavioural markers. For example, Ledingham and Alex Schwartzman at Concordia University in Montreal (Ledingham, 1981; Ledingham & Schwartzman, 1984) argue that the presence of both aggression and withdrawal in childhood tends to predict schizophrenia in later life. Ledingham also advocated examining biological markers, such as a hyperresponsive pattern of skin conductance (that is, the sweat response), where the amplitude of response is larger than normal, but returns to a resting state faster than is normal (Mednick, 1962).

Three other research methodologies have been helpful in determining the developmental course of schizophrenia. First, *retrospective* studies ask people who are now diagnosed with schizophrenia and their relatives to recall the patients' childhood experiences and behaviours. Second, *followup* studies examine past records and the current status of adults who received treatment for childhood disorders. Third, in *followback* studies, data that had been collected prospectively from large numbers of children are retrieved, with the focus on people who now have schizophrenia.

The results of these three approaches are similar (Hanson, Gottesman, & Heston, 1990). Some, but not all, people who develop schizophrenia show early personality abnormalities. For example, some show abnormalities in childhood that are described as schizoid (that is, having difficulty expressing emotion and functioning in social relationships) or schizotypal (that is, having cognitive or perceptual distortions and discomfort with close relationships). The childhood scores of people who later develop schizophrenia on standard intelligence tests are sometimes lower than the scores of their siblings and correlate poorly with the siblings' scores. Finally, males who later develop schizophrenia appear more likely than females to display abnormalities in childhood.

Genetic Factors

Current evidence indicates that genetic factors play an important role in at least some forms of schizophrenia. Research on this topic is difficult, however, because the gene(s) that are associated with schizophrenia have reduced penetrance (that is, certain environmental factors are necessary for the person to develop symptoms even when genetic factors are clearly implicated). One strategy for determining whether a disorder has a genetic component is to examine the concordance rates within families. Figure 14.4 summarizes the results of many studies that employed this strategy. Clearly, people who are genetically more closely related to people with schizophrenia are at increased risk. At the same time, the genetic component alone is not sufficient to explain the incidence of schizophrenia. Consider that only about 10 percent of people who have a parent with schizophrenia develop the disorder, and that 90 percent of people who have schizophrenia have no first-degree relative with the disorder. Also, if schizophrenia were purely genetic, the concordance rate for monozygotic twins should be 100 percent and they should show the same symptoms. As shown in Figure 14.4, the concordance rate for monozygotic twins is less than 50 percent. The remarkable case of the Genain sisters illustrates both the importance of genetic influence and its limitation (Carson & Butcher, 1992). The monozygotic quadruplets all developed schizophrenia before the age of 25; however, their symptoms differed greatly and only two developed the more serious symptoms of the disorganized subtype.

One limitation of concordance studies is that they do not adequately separate genetic influences from environmental effects. In a classic study, Heston (1966) examined 97 people who had been raised by adoptive parents and whose mothers either had or had not suffered from schizophrenia. In this study, all of those diagnosed as suffering from schizophrenia were in the group whose mothers had schizophrenia.

Figure 14.4 Prevalence of Schizophrenia Among Relatives of Schizophrenics

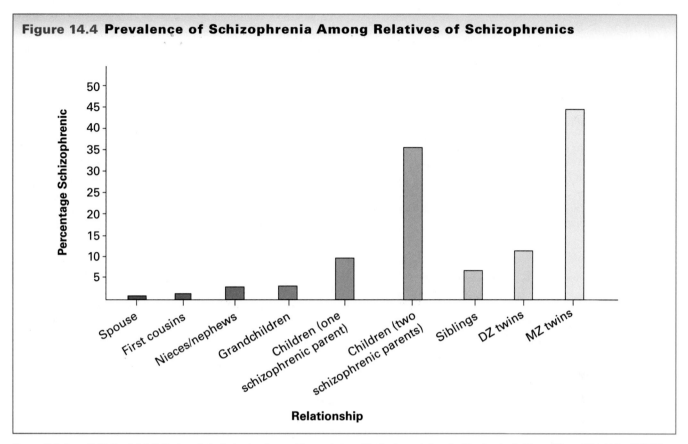

Source: Data from: M. McGue & I. I. Gottesman, A single dominant gene still cannot account for the transmission of schizophrenia, *Archives of General Psychiatry, 46(1989),* 479; and I. I. Gottesman, P. McGuffin, & A. E. Farmer, Clinical genetics as clues to the "real" genetics of schizophrenia: A decade of modest gains while playing for time, *Schizophrenia Bulletin, 13(1987),* 29.

Further, the children of mothers with schizophrenia were more likely to suffer from less severe but similar disorders than the control group. The findings from this and similar studies suggest a genetic predisposition toward schizophrenia symptoms that is independent of child-rearing environment.

A technique called *linkage analysis* is a powerful new tool in genetic research. This approach assumes that when two genes are close together on a chromosome they tend to be inherited together. To conduct a linkage analysis, the researcher must first find a marker gene (that is, a gene associated with an easily identifiable trait). If the marker gene and the disease of interest tend to be found together within a specific family, the researcher can conclude that the gene associated with the disease is related (or linked) to the marker gene.

While at the University of British Columbia, Anne Bassett (1989; Bassett, Jones, McGillivray, & Pantzar, 1988) investigated the family of a schizophrenic patient of Asian descent who had subtle facial features (such as a slightly misshapen skull, protuberant forehead and ears, and widely spaced eyes) and other physical abnormalities similar to those of his maternal uncle, who also suffered from schizophrenia. The linkage analysis suggested that schizophrenia may be associated with an additional copy of part of chromosome 5q. This case was initially received enthusiastically, but subsequent studies have found an association with chromosome 5q in some families (Sherrington et al., 1988) but not in others (Kennedy

et al., 1988), leaving many researchers skeptical about this particular suggested genetic basis of schizophrenia (for example, McGuffin & O'Donovan, 1993).

Another potential marker for schizophrenia is eye-tracking dysfunction (Iacono, Bassett, & Jones, 1988). Eye-tracking consists of two major components, *smooth pursuit* (keeping slowly moving targets focussed) and *saccades* (enabling rapid shift of focus). In general, the eye movements of people with schizophrenia are less efficient and more erratic than those of people without the disorder. Figure 14.5 shows the actual movement of a target and the eye-tracking of two members of the same family. The connection between eye-tracking and schizophrenia, which has been studied since the beginning of the twentieth century (Clementz & Sweeney, 1990), has been described as "one of the most robust findings in schizophrenia research" (Sweeney et al., 1994, p. 222), and has generated intense recent interest (Levy, Holzman, Matthysse, & Mendell, 1993). However, much of this interest has centred on the relationship between eye-tracking and the attentional problems of schizophrenic patients rather than on a linkage analysis.

Research on eye-tracking dysfunction has highlighted an important question in genetic research on schizophrenia: Can the disorder be transmitted by a single gene with reduced penetrance (Meehl, 1962; 1989) or must multiple genes be involved? Various mathematical models of the probability of

Figure 14.5 Samples of Eye-Tracking

A.

Actual movement of target

B.

Tracking by woman with no symptoms
of schizophrenia

C.

Tracking by her brother, who has a
history of schizophrenia

Source: Based on W. G. Iacono, A. S. Bassett, & B. D. Jones, Eye tracking dysfunction is associated with parital trisomy of chromosome 5 and schizophrenia, *Archives of General Psychiatry, 45(1988),* 1140.

transmission have been constructed. Models involving multiple genes seem to be the most promising (McGuffin & O'Donovan, 1993), but some researchers such as Philip Holzman and his colleagues (Holzman et al., 1988) suggest that a single gene might be sufficient, at least in some cases.

Biochemical Influence

Genes influence biological processes through hormones and neurotransmitters; it is the neurotransmitters that have received the greatest attention in schizophrenia research. As was described in Chapter 2, neurotransmitters are chemicals released by one neuron and subsequently absorbed by a second neuron, which they may either activate or inhibit.

For many years, researchers have suggested an association between the neurotransmitter **dopamine** and schizophrenia. In this view, the dopamine receptors (particularly the D_2 receptors) are either too numerous or too sensitive. The idea that such anomalies generate schizophrenia symptoms is based on three lines of evidence. First, neuroleptic medications reduce hallucinations and delusions, and Philip Seeman at the University of Toronto has demonstrated that these drugs inhibit the release of dopamine (Seeman & Lee, 1975). In particular, the clinical effectiveness of different neuroleptic medications is directly related to the extent to which they block the transmission of dopamine (Creese, Burt, & Snyder, 1976; Seeman, Lee, Chau-Wong, & Wong, 1976). Second, the density of D_2 receptors is greater in certain areas of the brain among people with schizophrenia (Wong et al., 1986). Third, overdoses of amphetamine—the effects of which are

known to be mediated by dopamine (for example, Robbins, 1990)—produce symptoms similar to those of paranoid schizophrenia. Also, amphetamine use produces latent inhibition (the process by which a stimulus becomes less effective after repeated presentation), hyperactivity, and stereotyped motor behaviour, each of which is found in some people with schizophrenia.

However, Carleton University researchers Larry Kokkinidis and Hymie Anisman (1980) found that amphetamine also affects several other neurotransmitters, especially norepinephrine. They hypothesize that a combination of increased dopamine and decreased norepinephrine may be the cause of chaotic behaviour among some people with schizophrenia. Kokkinidis and Anisman also suggest that normal dopamine activity, combined with reduced norepinephrine activity, may result in attention deficits, such as difficulty in disregarding irrelevant stimuli. Finally, they indicate that increased dopamine activity and normal norepinephrine activity may result in heightened arousal.

Evidence is now accumulating (Deutsch, Mastropaolo, Schwartz, Rosse, & Morihisa, 1989) that another neurotransmitter, glutamate, is also involved. Glutamate receptors can be found in many of the brain areas implicated in schizophrenia. Further, there is good reason to believe that there is a strong interaction between glutamate and dopamine transmission. In addition to dopamine, norepinephrine, and glutamate, other neurotransmitters (for example, serotonin and aminobutyric acid) may be involved in schizophrenia (Carlsson & Carlsson, 1990). Obviously, the neurotransmitter basis of schizophrenia is complex.

Prenatal and Perinatal Influences

Several sources suggest that prenatal and perinatal factors may contribute to schizophrenia. This could be one explanation for the fact that dizygotic twins have higher concordance rates than non-twin siblings. Complications of pregnancy and delivery are predictive both of schizophrenia and of neuroanatomical anomalies related to schizophrenia.

The possibility that a viral infection during pregnancy may contribute to schizophrenia was suggested as early as 1845 (Tsuang & Faraone, 1994). Fetuses exposed to influenza epidemics during the second trimester are more likely to develop schizophrenia as adults than either those who are not exposed or those who are exposed during the first or third trimesters (Sham et al., 1992). The timing of the exposure appears more clinically relevant than the type of infection.

Neuroanatomical Factors

Even before the development of modern brain imaging techniques, researchers were aware of the association between schizophrenia and many neurological anomalies, such as cortical atrophy (reduced volume of the outermost layer of the brain) and enlarged ventricles (the fluid-filled cushions that support the brain). Investigating neuroanatomical factors might lead to important information about schizophrenia, but researchers must be careful when trying to attribute causality. Genetics can influence biochemistry, which can influence neuroanatomy, but other factors, such as stress, can also change biochemical variables. Environmental factors can also directly affect the structure of the brain. In short, we cannot be sure whether certain neurological anomalies cause schizophrenic symptoms or whether they are a consequence of the symptoms.

Three specific brain areas have been implicated in schizophrenia: basal ganglia, frontal lobes, and temporal lobes.

The basal ganglia (a group of subcortical structures on either side of the thalamus that contribute to movement and cognitive functions) appear to be involved, because they contain many dopamine receptors. In addition, people suffering from lesions in the basal ganglia have symptoms more like schizophrenia than people with lesions to any other structures (Pentalis, Barnes, & Nelson, 1992).

Neufeld and Williamson's (1996) review shows that people suffering from paranoid schizophrenia experienced greater deficits on some frontal lobe tasks than people suffering from other forms of schizophrenia. Two such tasks are the Continuous Performance Task (CPT; Rosvold, Mirsky, Sarason, Bransome, & Beck, 1956) and the Wisconsin Card Sorting Task (WCST; Grant & Berg, 1948). The CPT involves pressing a response key when a symbol that is presented for about a second meets a certain criterion. The version of the CPT that people who suffer from schizophrenia find especially difficult requires the person to respond if the current symbol is the same as the previous symbol (Cornblatt, Lenzenweger, & Erlenmeyer-Kimling, 1989). The WCST requires subjects to sort a set of cards showing various symbols. They are required to detect the sorting rule strictly on the basis of the tester's feedback as to whether a response is correct. Sullivan et al. (1993) found that people who suffer either from schizophrenia or from frontal lobe damage tend to make *perseverative* errors on the WCST: that is, they continue to sort according to rules applicable to a previous train of responses.

However, the most challenging, and most promising, theories about neuroanatomical factors are those that emphasize the interrelations among brain structures. For example, many researchers believe that there is an association between enlarged ventricles and negative symptoms of schizophrenia; recently Robert Zipursky and his colleagues at the Clarke Institute of Psychiatry in Toronto found decreases in the size of both frontal and temporal lobe brain structures corresponding to increased ventricle size (Zipursky et al., 1994).

Peter Liddle and his colleagues (for example, Liddle, Barnes, Morris, & Haque, 1989; Liddle & Morris, 1991) have identified deficits in two different but overlapping systems incorporating the prefrontal cortex that relate to many of the symptoms of schizophrenia. The first is the dorsal system (the top of the prefrontal cortex), which connects to the basal ganglia and the hippocampus (a structure nested deep between the temporal lobes involved with learning and memory). This system is associated with initiating activity. Deficits in

this system may account for psychomotor poverty symptoms, such as flattened affect and a slow response on some cognitive tasks. Second is the ventral system (the bottom of the prefrontal cortex), which connects to the temporal lobes, the basal ganglia, the amygdala (an almond-shaped structure associated with emotional regulation), and the hippocampus. This system is involved in inhibiting irrelevant activities. Deficits in this system may account for disorganization symptoms, including unusual speech patterns, erratic behaviour, and flat or inappropriate affect.

The temporal lobes are associated with language functions. Liddle's work identifies this area with reality distortion symptoms, such as hallucinations and delusions, that are central to the paranoid subtype of schizophrenia. Structures at the centre of the temporal lobe (for example, the amygdala) may be decreased in size among some people suffering from schizophrenia (Barta, Pearlson, Powers, Richards, & Tune, 1990; Suddath et al., 1989). In addition, mounting evidence suggests that abnormal functioning in the pathways connecting the temporal and frontal lobes may be implicated in schizophrenic dysfunction (for example, Frith et al., 1995).

Neurodevelopmental Factors

Are the brain abnormalities presumed to underlie schizophrenia congenital or do they develop later? Weinberger (1987) argues that an anomaly may not become clinically important at the time of its onset. He suggests that early anomalies may interact with the normal development of the brain to produce schizophrenic symptoms much later. Weinberger predicts that anomalies may show themselves among preschizophrenic children in subtle ways, such as neuromotor deficits, attention deficits, and personality and social deficits.

Essential to such theories is the claim that specific brain abnormalities develop early and symptoms are triggered later by nonspecific events. In contrast, Michael Pogue-Geile (1991) suggests that the brain anomalies specific to schizophrenia precede the onset of overt clinical symptoms by only a few years. This approach assumes that the genetic defects involve genes whose behavioural consequences are precipitated at adolescence. The late-onset approach also assumes that the penetrance of these genes can be increased by nonspecific events (such as delivery complications and viral infections).

One process that potentially relates brain development to schizophrenic symptoms concerns synaptic density (the number of synapses in a given area of the brain) (Feinberg, 1982/1983). Synaptic density varies over the life span and across brain regions. Apparently synaptic density normally declines during late childhood and then levels out during adolescence (Goldman-Rakic, 1987; Huttenlocher, 1979, 1984). The incidence of schizophrenia is related to the variability in maturation rates related to sex and social class: people who mature late are more likely to have low synaptic density and a higher incidence of schizophrenia (Saugstad, 1989). Specific investigations are under way regarding the hypothesis that a decline in synaptic density may mediate some schizophrenic symptoms (for example, Hoffman et al., 1995). If this line of research proves fruitful, additional work will be necessary to determine the specific causes of reduced synaptic density.

Personality Factors

The relationship between personality variables and vulnerability to schizophrenia is complex. Research in this area is less well developed than research regarding biological signs of the disorder. Clinical observations suggest that people with schizophrenia harbour intense rage, but are unable to express it. They appear incapable of asserting themselves appropriately, especially toward their parents. In some cases, a family dynamic emerges in which parents are overinvolved and the child who later develops schizophrenia is overdependent. In this situation, the person with schizophrenia experiences inner conflict between a desire for the parents to continue to meet his or her needs and a desire for autonomy. Other emotionally charged inner conflicts, such as sexuality issues, seem to elicit the same coping difficulties.

The personality traits that increase vulnerability to schizophrenia are not clear, but some broad trends emerge. The behavioural pattern of both aggression and withdrawal among high-risk children is consistent with the idea of intense inner rage. In addition, clinical observations suggest that difficulties in social relationships during adolescence are associated with the most chronic cases of nonparanoid schizophrenia. Carson and Butcher (1992) suggest that people with schizophrenia feel inadequate and devalued, and this inhibits appropriately assertive behaviour. These feelings may also lead to exaggerated attempts to defend the self emotionally with excessive fantasy or regression to a less demanding stage of development. Psychoanalytic theory considers schizophrenia a retreat from reality when life is too difficult for the person to accept. In this model, people with weak egos are said to be especially vulnerable to the disorder.

STRESS

According to the stress-vulnerability framework, even in a person vulnerable to schizophrenia, a stressor is usually in-

VIEWPOINT *Stress and Schizophrenia: A Puzzling Set of Relations in Need of "Chaos Theory"?*

Unsettling events, such as moving, changing jobs, or loss of income, can precede the initial occurrence of schizophrenic symptoms (Norman & Malla, 1993a). The more striking relations between stress and symptoms, however, occur after the onset of the disorder. Everyday sorts of troubles—things like losing possessions, the disruption of home repairs, or squabbles with a roommate—can be significantly related to the subsequent level of symptoms. Positive symptoms, specifically delusions and hallucinations, are most closely associated with the levels of subjective stress during the preceding months. The empirical association between stress and symptom level has been fairly well demonstrated. But how should we interpret this association?

Stress may predict symptoms but does it cause them? This question is challenging, because symptomatology itself may be a catalyst for stressful incidents. For example, suppose that before a delusion is fully developed, a person becomes suspicious and jealous and acts in a grandiose manner.

This behaviour may make her friends draw away from her and her supervisor become more critical. Looking back, an observer would notice that a period of social isolation and difficulty at work preceded her delusion, but these effects would be byproducts of the delusional process rather than active agents of its development.

Researchers of stress-schizophrenia relations have tried to avoid incorrect causal inferences in several ways. One approach has been to isolate stressors that are clearly independent of symptoms (Spring, 1981; Spring & Coons, 1982)—economic recessions or natural disasters, for example. Restricting analyses to such upheavals permits methodological neatness; unfortunately, it does not allow researchers to consider the common, day-to-day stresses believed to be most psychologically meaningful.

An alternative method has been to try to allow for the effects of symptoms on stress by estimating their effects statistically and adjusting measures accordingly (Norman &

Malla, 1994). This approach carries its own risks of error: one may adjust the stress measure too much or too little; or the statistical adjustment may reduce the validity or reliability of the measures (Lees & Neufeld, 1994). Often, however, this research tactic is the only way to deal with stress-symptom relations and preserve any amount of their richness.

Relations between environmental stressors and symptomatology are probably complex and reciprocal: it seems reasonable that stress will affect symptoms, which, in turn, will affect stress levels. In addition, these intricate interactions unfold over time. Such features suggest a third method of investigation: constructing and testing quantitative models of the dynamic interactions among the variables of interest (Neufeld, 1989; Nicholson & Neufeld, 1992).

This research approach represents a systems perspective on the problem, whereby the variation in one factor is intrinsically bound up with that of the other factor. Construction of the theovolved in development of the active disorder. Moreover, after the onset of schizophrenia, there is often a relationship between stress and symptom severity (see the ViewPoint box).

Family Dynamics

Family dynamics and schizophrenia is a complicated area that requires more rigorous investigation. The major challenge is to disentangle the factors that contribute to the disorder from the effects of the disorder. Early research in this area misled many professionals into believing that poor parenting caused schizophrenia.

The psychoanalyst Fired Fromm-Reichmann (1948) claimed that psychotic states made sense if they were viewed as responses to a schizophrenogenic mother. These mothers were described as cold, conflict-inducing, rigid, rejecting, overprotective, and insensitive. Similarly, Bateson and colleagues (Bateson, Jackson, Haley, & Weakland, 1956) argued that schizophrenia resulted from repeated exposure to a double-bind situation. A double-bind occurs when a person is involved in an intense relationship wherein the other person (often a parent) expresses conflicting messages. For example, a parent may complain that the child never gives hugs, but stiffen and pull away whenever the child does try to give a hug. Neither Fromm-Reichmann's theory nor Bateson's is supported by current evidence (McGuffin & Morrison, 1994; Tsuang & Faraone, 1994); nevertheless, they contain a grain of truth. Negative affect and communication deviance are not, by themselves, sufficient to produce schizophrenia but they are associated with increased risk of schizophrenia among people who already possess a genetic predisposition to the disorder (Cannon, Barr, & Mednick, 1991).

One of the important issues in current research on family influences is the role of expressed emotion in the course of schizophrenia. As developed by sociologist George Brown and his colleagues (Brown, Carstairs, & Topping, 1958), the concept of **expressed emotion** refers to the display of specific attitudes and behaviours, such as hostility, criticism, and overinvolvement, by the relatives of people who suffer from schizophrenia. High levels of expressed emotion by family members, especially critical comments and emotional overinvolvement, are related to the patient's likelihood of relapse (Cole & Kazarian, 1993; Kazarian, 1992). (See Figure 14.6.) The Level of Expressed Emotion (LEE) scale developed by Canadian psychologists Cole and Kazarian (1988) has

ViewPoint *continued*

retical model requires that the rate of change of any one variable at a given point in time be specified in terms of its own value at that point, as well as the values of other variables in the "system." Thus, in regard to a variable's own values, stressor levels hypothetically may increase at a certain pace if their existing level is only moderate, or they may decrease to some degree if they have reached some unsustainable ceiling. A second influence, in this case, is that of symptom level, which, if relatively high, may tend to send stressor level rapidly upward, or, if relatively low, may have little effect. Construction of theoretical systems models requires the implementation of differential equations, one to express the rate of change of each variable in the system.

Such quantitative methods have become less cumbersome, and the math less daunting, with the advent of user-friendly computer software (see, for example, Koçak, 1989). The methodology remains challenging, but it does deliver a payoff. First, it provides a way to succinctly express interactions that would otherwise be too complex to describe. Moreover, it avoids the risks of the methods described earlier: undermining the reliability and validity of measures through statistical adjustments, on the one hand, or, on the other hand, inferring a causal relationship between two measures that are actually both effects of the same process, if the modelled change in each one is distinct from that of the others, and is nonlinear in structure. (The formal mathematics are too long and technical to elaborate here.)

This method of investigation is within the realm of the quantitative methods popularly identified with *chaos theory* (Gleik, 1992), an interesting recent approach to various natural phenomena observed in fields ranging from ecology to meteorology.

Critical Thinking Questions

1. Viewing stress and schizophrenia symptomatology in terms of nonlinear dynamic systems (chaos theory) specifies that the variables are in continual flux, each being affected by its own momentary state as well as that of the other variable(s), in specific ways. Empirical evaluation therefore requires ongoing monitoring of the system variables (stress and symptomatology). How might these variables be practically measured? If the changes in each variable over time were found to be predictable using a systems analysis, how might the results be applied to the benefit of the patient?

2. Another way to examine effects of stress on symptomatology is to employ experimental manipulations. Doing so, of course, raises ethical concerns. What ethical concerns come to the fore, and how might an experimental approach be implemented ethically?

3. Assume that stress and symptomatology indeed affect one another reciprocally. What is it about the nature of stress, on the one hand, and symptomatology, on the other, that should result in their mutual influence?

Figure 14.6 Expressed Emotion and Relapse Rates

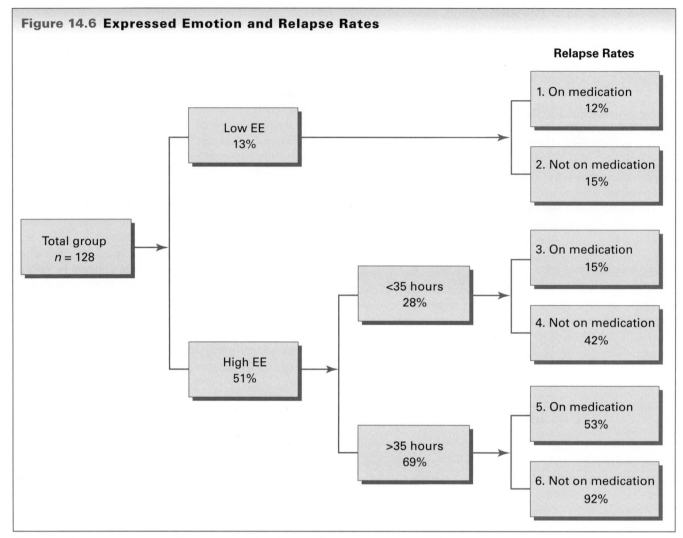

Rates of relapse from recovery back to schizophrenic episodes in a sample of 128 British patients followed for nine months after hospital discharge, as a function of maintaining antipsychotic medication or not, exposure to negative expressed emotion (EE), and weekly duration of exposure to high levels of EE.

Source: Adapted from Vaughn & Leff, 1976.

demonstrated both concurrent validity (Kazarian, Malla, Cole, & Baker, 1990; Kazarian, Mazmanian, McDermott, & Olinger, 1991) and predictive validity (Cole & Kazarian, 1993).

Of course, it may be that increased expressed emotion is simply the result of the stress experienced by a family when one member begins to show schizophrenic symptoms. This explanation, however, is countered by the observation that interventions designed to reduce expressed emotion, such as family education and social skills training, reduce the risk of relapse (Hogarty et al., 1986).

Cultural Influences

Culture seems to influence the specific symptoms that a person suffering from schizophrenia will exhibit. Canadian researcher Ihsan Al-Issa (1968), noted for his work on cultural factors in psychopathology, concluded that the symptoms of schizophrenia tend to form different patterns across cultures. For example, he found that auditory hallucinations are most common in Western culture, and that Africans tend to display less violence, more blunting of affect, and a higher rate of visual hallucinations than Europeans and North Americans. Also, religious delusions are especially common among Christians and Muslims. Similarly, the delusion that thoughts are inserted into the patient's mind from an outside source is most common among people from developed countries, and passivity is most common among people from the Middle East (Coffey, MacKinnon, & Minas, 1993). Hispanic schizophrenic patients often suffer from nervousness and physiological problems rather than changes in emotional expression (Escobar, Randolf, & Hill, 1986; Ruiz, 1985.)

Al-Issa also found changes in symptoms over time within cultures. For example, delusions of grandeur have been decreasing in Western countries over the past 100 years. Overall, Al-Issa concluded that schizophrenia seems to affect the area of functioning most stressed by the patient's culture. Recent research appears to support this hypothesis (Carter & Neufeld, in press).

Curiously, people who experience schizophrenia in developing countries appear to have better outcomes than people in developed countries (Jablensky et al., 1992). Several explanations for this surprising finding have received empirical support (Lin & Kleinman, 1988). First, people in developing countries tend to focus more on the community than on individuals, and this may increase social support for people with schizophrenia. Second, the extended-family characteristic of developing countries provides more support for the family members than the nuclear family of Western culture. Third, people with schizophrenia can return to work more easily in traditional societies. Finally, the stigma of mental illness tends to be lower in developing countries.

Social Status

Hollingshead and Redlich (1958) examined people with schizophrenia in New Haven, Connecticut, and found that they were three times as likely to come from the lowest socioeconomic class as from any other class. (See Figure 14.7.) These observations were repeated in New York City (Srole, Langner, Michael, Opler, & Rennie, 1962) and in European countries (Kohn, 1968).

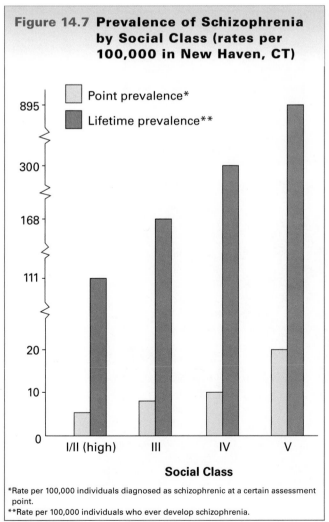

Figure 14.7 Prevalence of Schizophrenia by Social Class (rates per 100,000 in New Haven, CT)

*Rate per 100,000 individuals diagnosed as schizophrenic at a certain assessment point.
**Rate per 100,000 individuals who ever develop schizophrenia.

Source: Data from A. B. Hollingshead & F. C. Redlich, *Social class and mental illness* (New York: John Wiley, 1958).

Two explanations have been offered for these findings. First, it may be that people who have the disorder drift to a lower social status as a result of their symptoms. This is called the **social selection theory**. Certainly, one of the requirements for a diagnosis of schizophrenia is an ongoing reduction in functioning. Second, lower social status could be a factor in the development of the disorder. As noted in the ViewPoint, the stress of daily life is related to the severity of symptoms. Being a member of the lowest social class may result in poorer education, increased stigmatization, and fewer opportunities for economic success. To the extent that these factors increase daily stress, social class could influence symptomatology. This is called the **sociogenic theory**. Clinical data and demographic studies support both hypotheses.

Labelling Theory

Is the stigma of schizophrenia the cause of the disorder? Scheff (1984) proposed that what we typically call "mental illness" is actually a social role (see Chapter 2). According to labelling theory, many people engage in deviant behaviour, but only a few are assigned diagnostic labels; powerful social forces induce people to behave in ways congruent to the label assigned to them.

Labelling theory alone is clearly inadequate to explain the markedly distinct behaviour and thought patterns of schizophrenia. Moreover, the actual behaviour of people with schizophrenia does not match popular misconceptions; therefore, they could hardly be simply acting out the label. Yet it may be possible that the stigma leads to social isolation, which becomes a stressor influencing symptoms. Schizophrenia may be a particularly burdensome stigma to carry because of inaccurate popular notions of the disorder as being characterized by random acts of violence and "multiple personalities."

COGNITIVE FACTORS

The history of experimental research in schizophrenia is fairly rich in studies of cognitive functioning. Documentation of deviations in information processing has historically been one of psychology's main contributions, if not *the* main contribution, to the understanding of schizophrenia. Research on memory and information processing has been motivated in good part by the prominence of thought disorder in the overall symptom picture (Chapman & Chapman, 1973; Maher, 1966). Abnormalities in basic cognitive functions have been viewed as possible sources of disturbed thought, and potentially other symptoms, such as distorted affect and motor abnormalities (George & Neufeld, 1985). After all, to interpret accurately and respond appropriately to events in the environment, including the behaviour of others, one must first be able to process information about these events appropriately.

Moreover, cognitive efficiency influences the ability to cope and thus the level of stress. Impaired cognitive faculties compromise the person's ability to reduce stress; increased stress, in turn, may further compromise cognitive function.

Studies of cognitive process can now be more directly linked to studies of neuroanatomical abnormalities through new technologies like **functional magnetic resonance imaging (fMRI)** (see Figures 14.8a and 14.8b). This technique allows observation of neurophysiological activity accompanying specific cognitive tasks. The more we know about the perceptual and memory processes involved in such tasks, the more we will be able to understand the relevance of these observations.

Information Processing

Information processing in people with schizophrenia has been studied at every level from the simple detection of a visual stimulus to more complex transactions involving short-term and long-term memory functions. Most studies have dealt with the processing of visual rather than auditory information.

Basic processing of visual stimuli begins with a short-term store, lasting approximately 100 milliseconds. Registration of stimuli during this phase involves little active analysis, and is not unlike a visual aftereffect or "iconic image." The second phase of early visual processing involves very-short-term visual memory, thought to occupy from 100 to 600 milliseconds following stimulus presentation. At this point, a more active analysis of stimulus features occurs, in that properties of meaning and coherence of the feature contribute to identification of the presented item (Knight, 1993). Failure to adequately process stimulus elements at this level are thought to adversely affect subsequent information processing that depends on output from these initial phases of analysis. For example, a person may have difficulty deciding whether a face is familiar or not if the physical properties of the face have not already been effectively perceived.

Reviews of findings on early visual processing indicate that to develop the initial store of visual information schizophrenic people need a longer exposure to the visual stimu-

Figure 14.8 fMRI Images Showing Brain Region Activation of Never-Treated Schizophrenic (14.8a) and Normal Subject (14.8b) During Word-Fluency Task

a.

b.

Note: In this study, subjects were asked to think of words beginning with a given consonant. In Figure 14.8a, the patient displays activation in Broca's Area, right caudate area extending into the motor cortex, and left medial temporal regions. Decreased activation occurs in the right medial-temporal regions. Unlike the normal subject, the patient displays no activation in anterior cingulate (shown in Figure 14.8b, area A) and thalamic regions (shown in Figure 14.8b, area B).

Source: Courtesy of the Tesla-4 Imaging Group, Robarts Research Institute, London, Ontario.

lus than other people. This is particularly true of **process schizophrenic** patients: those with a poor history of adjustment prior to being diagnosed with the disorder. In addition, this iconic image may be sustained for a shorter period of time, at least in the case of paranoid schizophrenic subtypes (Broga & Neufeld, 1981a; Neufeld, 1991).

When it comes to the very-short-term visual memory, process schizophrenic subjects appear to have difficulty in quickly identifying stimulus items and finding and using meaningful segments of the items (Knight, 1993). Meaningful segments are those whose features coincide with information held in long-term memory (for example, the typical juxtaposition of facial features).

Turning to that aspect of short-term memory which has been called "working memory," paranoid schizophrenic patients in particular have been found to be susceptible to interference and prone to forget experimental stimuli. Schizophrenic patients have shown increased interference from distracting stimulation when recall has emphasized the meaning of stimuli (Pogue-Geile & Oltmanns, 1980). Distraction may take its toll in part because of diminished active rehearsal of task-relevant stimulus material (Broga & Neufeld, 1981b; Koh & Kayton, 1974).

However, once stimulus items have been encoded, schizophrenic patients display normal facility in extracting and manipulating the items or their properties in order to draw the inferences necessary for task completion. To illustrate, in a memory scanning task, subjects are required to indicate whether a presented item (for example, a word) is among those in a set of recently memorized items. Schizophrenic patients have repeatedly been shown to carry out the item comparison in working memory with normal speed and accuracy. More elaborate versions of such functions, as required for problem-solving, verification of verbal statements, and comparison of items with respect to phonemic (sound) and spatial (nonverbal) properties, are also unimpaired in schizophrenia (Neufeld, 1991).

The contribution of long-term memory to information processing among schizophrenic patients again presents a picture of strengths and weaknesses. The network of semantic (that is, meaning) relations among verbal stimuli appears to be unaffected in this disorder, as is that of spatial or nonverbal properties (Highgate & Neufeld, 1986; Neufeld, 1991). On the other hand, the use of dimensions of meaning (for example, connotations of pleasantness, potency, and excitability) in organizing initially disconnected stimuli seems to suffer. They would generally have no difficulty when asked to rate an item on a specific dimension, but have trouble spontaneously using a range of dimensions to decide which items (for example, words or faces) are more similar or dissimilar overall. While they have no difficulty recognizing previously presented items, they show inferior memory of items whose recall benefits from initial organization in terms of shared meaning, and they are impaired in language and communication (for example, Koh, 1978; Neufeld, 1991).

Encoding. Between the initial phases of stimulus registration and the more elaborate steps required for task completion comes a component of information processing called **stimulus encoding**. Encoding involves translating the stimulation from its raw physical form into a format amenable to higher-order cognitive operations, such as information extraction, taking place in short-term or working memory. For example, identifying whether a presented shape is included in a recently memorized set may be helped by deciphering curves, straight lines, and intersections. Likewise, interpreting a sentence may require recognizing it as a statement or a question.

Schizophrenic patients have been reliably found to take longer to complete encoding processes on a variety of tasks. Analyses indicate that the cause of this slowness is not a reduced rate of completing the stages of encoding, but an increase in the number of stages taken. Elements already encoded may be repeated, or more elements may be encoded than are needed for the other processes involved in task performance. This combination is analogous to travelling in an automobile that runs efficiently, but taking an unnecessarily circuitous route to a destination.

This reduction in encoding efficiency is seen as fundamental to diminished performance of other cognitive functions (for example, Neufeld & Williamson, 1996). Poor encoding efficiency has also been tied to the symptomatology of delusions and hallucinations. The content of the delusions and associated hallucinations that characterize paranoid schizophrenia is often internally coherent and well integrated. At the same time, it is at considerable variance with known facts. This combination of properties is compatible with the profile of cognitive strengths and weaknesses described here (Neufeld, Vollick, & Highgate, 1993).

Encoded material submitted to other processes, such as those involving short-term and long-term memory, may be dealt with efficiently, ultimately making for internal consistency of ideas and inferences. The encoded material that is submitted, however, may be wanting. Encoding operations often take place with respect to normally rapid speech, or quickly changing scenes. If the encoding takes longer than normal, the listener (or viewer) may miss important information. The unimpaired processes of short- and long-term memory are then applied to only the fractions of information available, resulting in inferences that are internally consistent but false: a description of typical thought-content symptomatology. Potentially exacerbating this problem is a tendency for paranoid patients to draw inferences about the presence of stimuli or their properties more readily than others (Broga & Neufeld, 1981b): in other words, to jump to conclusions on the basis of scraps of imperfectly assimilated information.

Reaction time crossover. Reaction time is the most elementary processing task in which performance abnormalities in schizophrenia have been identified. Richard Steffy and his colleagues at the University of Waterloo (Bellissimo & Steffy, 1972, 1975; Steffy & Galbraith, 1980) have been among the most productive researchers of reaction time in schizophrenic subjects.

In most studies of early visual processing, choice-reaction-time paradigms are used. Here, the individual is required to indicate which of two or more briefly displayed stimuli has been presented. In simple-reaction-time paradigms, the individual is required merely to indicate as quickly as possible that a given stimulus has appeared.

During simple-reaction-time trials, the interval between the beginning of the trial and the onset of the stimulus to which a response is required can vary from trial to trial, in an irregular fashion. Conversely, the interval can remain constant or regular over a series of trials. In addition, both irregular and regular intervals can be relatively long (for example, 5 seconds) or short (for example, 1 second). A succession of trials with stimuli at regular intervals obviously offers more predictability than a succession of irregular-interval trials. Not surprisingly, all subjects, both schizophrenic and normal controls, react to stimuli more quickly in regular-interval than in irregular-interval trials when the trials are short (for example, 1 second). For normal controls, patients with other disorders, and reactive schizophrenics (those who were fairly well adjusted before developing schizophrenia), the difference in reaction time between regular and irregular intervals diminishes as the intervals increase in length (for example, to 5 seconds). The pattern differs with process schizophrenics (those with poor premorbid adjustment); for this group, with a long interval, reaction speed is actually faster for irregular intervals. This phenomenon is known as reaction-time crossover, and a representative set of such results is presented in Figure 14.9.

Reaction-time crossover has served as a behavioural marker in studies of heritability of schizophrenia (for example, Cromwell, Elkins, McCarthy, & O'Neil, 1994) and it has been examined as a potentially useful index for prognosis (Steffy & Waldman, 1993). There is no accepted explanation of why this reliable finding occurs, but mathematical models seem promising, as they do in attempts by theorists to explain encoding differences.

Language

Turning our attention to language, disorder of both thought content and thought form have been identified from speech samples since the observations of Bleuler and Kraepelin. Studies of the composition of language samples have indicated that speech abnormalities can be understood at least in part in terms of the types of information processing deficits discussed above (for example, Schwartz, 1982).

Other observations have focussed on the structure of units of speech as compared to that of control subjects. For example, Maher (1972) has observed that the speech of schizophrenic patients reveals reduced ability to prevent remote associations from intruding. For example, the following quote shows loose and idiosyncratic associations with words, not governed by the context of the first part of the sentence:

I wish you a happy, joyful, healthy, blessed and fruitful year, and many good wine-years to come as well as a healthy and good apple-year, and sauerkraut and cabbage and squash and seed year. (Gray, 1991, p. 635)

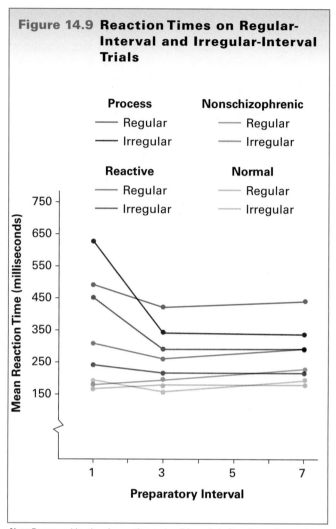

Figure 14.9 Reaction Times on Regular-Interval and Irregular-Interval Trials

Note: Process schizophrenics are those who did poorly before diagnosis; reactive schizophrenics are those who were relatively well adjusted before the emergence of schizophrenia. The third group are psychiatric controls: patients with disorders other than schizophrenia. The fourth group are normal controls.

Source: Steffy, R. A., & Waldman, I. (1993).

This inability to stick to a topic is a type of inhibitory deficit, a problem receiving considerable theoretical attention as it applies to all areas of psychological functioning in schizophrenia (Beech et al., 1991; Maher et al., 1995). The concept of inhibitory deficit was described simply by one young person, who explained, "My stopper's broken. People have a thing that starts and stops them. Mine's broken."

Added to inhibitory difficulties may be problems of associating basic units of speech (morphemes) with their meanings in the context of discussion (Neufeld, 1984; Schwartz, 1982, 1984). For example, the word "blue" has a number of possible meanings. But a normal person has no doubt about the meaning of the statement, "I felt blue about so-and-so's death." A schizophrenic may interpret the word here as referring to a colour, or a type of music, or aristocratic blood.

Still others have noted a failure to take account of cues indicating speech idiosyncrasies with respect to the needs of the listeners (Harrow & Miller, 1980). Most people tailor their speech somewhat to the other person in a dialogue, using more formal or casual speech, a higher or lower vocabulary, to match the listener's needs. Without much conscious thought, we monitor the other person's response. Schizophrenics have difficulty doing this, and are less aware of consensual interpretations. Harrow and Miller, for example, offered subjects interpretations of proverbs. The proverb "People who live in glass houses shouldn't throw stones" may be interpreted to mean "People in the public eye can be constantly monitored; therefore, they should not make false accusations, because everyone will know where the accusations originated." Most

people recognize this interpretation as an atypical slant on the proverb; schizophrenics are less likely to do so.

Other researchers have noted difficulties in encoding the meaning of words into a format facilitating various verbal tasks (George & Neufeld, 1985) and an overreliance on relations among specific words ("lexical cohesion") at the expense of relations among groups of words or phrases (Rochester & Martin, 1979). The latter pattern is shown by the sentence quoted earlier, in which the phrase "a fruitful year" started a train leading to apples and squash rather than remaining in context. Such observations indicate the presence of a complex communication failure, involving both cognitive deficiencies and a diminished sense of audience.

Focus *Schizophrenia: Creativity and Behavioural Survival Value*

Schizophrenia can be devastating to an individual's productivity and quality of life (Romney, 1995). How are we to understand the continued existence of this disorder, given its apparent disadvantage with respect to competition for survival resources? Is there some favourable aspect to this seemingly destructive affliction?

At the level of subjective impression and clinical lore, there appears to be a surprising frequency of individuals with outstanding life achievements whose close relatives have suffered from this syndrome, or, in some instances, who themselves have suffered. Such individuals range from Nobel laureate scientists to prizewinning writers. For example, Michael Smith, a molecular geneticist from the University of British Columbia, has a close relative who has suffered from the disorder, and has himself contributed generously from his Nobel Prize winnings to Canadian research on schizophrenia. Quantum physicist Richard Feynman has an indication of schizophrenia in his family history (Gleik, 1992); and Albert Einstein's second son was diagnosed with paranoid schizophrenia. The son of Kurt Vonnegut (the popular 1960s and 1970s author of such works as *Slaughterhouse Five* and *Cat's Cradle*) was diagnosed with this disorder in

1971 while living in a commune in British Columbia. Mark Vonnegut's story, including detailed descriptions of several psychotic episodes, was presented in his own book, *The Eden Express* (1975).

Perhaps schizophrenia represents some extreme location on distributions of traits whose endurance has positive value (Crow, 1995). Heston (1966) studied foster children whose biological mothers had schizophrenia. He found that these offspring had greater occupational success at more creative jobs, and had more innovative recreational activities, than did controls. Dykes and McGhie (1976) of Queen's University compared creative individuals and schizophrenic patients with respect to their performance on a set of cognitive measures. They observed that performance patterns of these two groups deviated in similar ways from those of noncreative controls. Hasenfus and Magaro (1976) also found certain overlap in information processing types between schizophrenic and creative individuals, as identified by standardized psychometric tests (Wallach & Kogan, 1965). According to Dykes and McGhie, these two groups share a tendency to sample a wider range of environmental stimuli than do others. What the schizophrenic subjects appeared not to

share was the creative individuals' ability to inhibit this tendency when called for by task constraints for correct performance.

Several writers have examined cognitive-behavioural aspects of schizophrenia within the context of survival value. Crow (1995) has written:

Territoriality is ... relevant to the family unit surviving on its own. Less social interaction but more inventiveness, a tolerance of low levels of stimulation, and an ability to remain alert and attentive for long periods of time are at a premium, proneness to schizophrenia might have its origin in relation to social abilities of this type. (p. 16)

Interestingly, Cromwell and his students (personal communication) have observed that relatives of schizophrenic patients score higher than others on avocational creative activities, marked by solitary, as opposed to group-shared undertakings.

Allen and Sarich (1988), in their Darwinian analysis, have speculated:

... what has been selected for—in the non-pathological possessors of the schizophrenia genotype—is simply to take back a bit of the individuality surrendered to the group during tens of millions of years of evolution of interactive sociality in our lineage. (p. 17) ▲

Summary of Etiological Factors

As we have seen, the causes of schizophrenia are varied and complex. Although contributing factors are interrelated, they can be divided into three groups: (1) vulnerability, (2) stress, and (3) cognitive dysfunction.

Vulnerability can stem from a variety of sources. There appears to be a strong genetic component, as shown by high concordance rates within families. Prenatal and perinatal events, such as viral infection and delivery complications, also seem to have an influence. Developmental issues, such as the combination of tendencies toward aggression and withdrawal, have some power to predict future schizophrenic episodes. Some neurotransmitters and neuroanatomical anomalies have also been related to schizophrenic symptoms.

In terms of stress, day-to-day events seem to have the most influence, but family dynamics (especially high expressed emotion), culture, and social class also have roles to play.

Cognitive functioning can be impaired in a variety of ways, potentially fostering other clinical symptoms, including those of thought and affect. Difficulties in encoding, memory, and language appear to dominate.

TREATMENT

Pharmacotherapy

Currently, medications such as the neuroleptics (antipsychotic agents) are considered the primary intervention for schizophrenia (Oyewumi, 1992; Seeman & Seeman, 1992). The neuroleptics are understood to decrease dopamine levels in the brain, and have been in widespread use since their introduction in 1955. Although evidently capable of controlling many of the bizarre thoughts and behaviours that typify acute episodes of schizophrenia, treatment with neuroleptics has its problems.

In the first place, they do not cure schizophrenia. In addition, while pharmacotherapy has been shown to reduce relapse rates in the first year after hospital discharge from approximately 68 percent to approximately 40 percent (Hogarty, 1984, 1993), by the second year as many as 50 percent of those still on the medication have relapsed. Thus, as Hogarty (1984) stresses, pharmacotherapy clearly is not a panacea for schizophrenia. He argues that it needs to be combined with interventions that address other apparent agents of relapse, such as high expressed emotion in families, or poor social and interpersonal skills. With such accompanying interventions, Hogarty notes, relapse rates have been reduced to as low as 15 percent. This reduction in relapse rate makes sense when considered in light of the clinical finding that neuroleptics, although able to attenuate so-called positive symptoms (for example, delusions, hallucinations, thought disorder), have little or no effect on negative symptoms (for example, flat affect, poverty of motivation, paucity of speech). It is precisely the negative symptoms that respond to the additional interventions advocated by Hogarty.

Neuroleptics also produce several troublesome side-effects, which often lead to noncompliance with prescribed drug regimens. One prominent side-effect is tardive dyskinesia, a form of central nervous system damage that affects one in four people taking long-term neuroleptic treatment. Tardive dyskinesia causes uncontrollable involuntary movements, which are irreversible in approximately 50 percent of the cases. The newer antipsychotic medications (for example, clozaril [Clozapine]) and risperidal [Risperidone]) appear to have substantially reduced side-effects (Sigmundson, 1994) compared to traditional compounds (for example, chlorpromazine, trifluoperazine, Haldol, or thioridazine), but another review of the literature (Cohen, 1994) suggests that this claim may be premature. Cohen reviewed a number of reports on pharmacotherapy and found that Clozapine appears to produce more side-effects than previously claimed.

Two other problems have been encountered with the use of neuroleptics. First, they control symptoms for some but by no means all schizophrenic patients (Cohen, 1994; Seeman & Seeman, 1992). Second, according to Cohen (1994), clinicians often do not adhere to prescribing guidelines. Indeed, on balance, Cohen found neuroleptic therapy to be so problematic that he was prompted to say "the field is in crisis and that major paradigmatic change is absolutely necessary" (Cohen, 1994, p. 152).

Hospital Treatment

Manfred Bleuler (1974), the son of pioneer Eugen Bleuler, observed that the prognosis associated with schizophrenia had improved considerably during his lifetime. Schizophrenia no longer meant an illness invariably worsening over time, resulting in continuing deterioration and hospitalization. He believed that this improvement stemmed primarily from advancements in nursing and hospital care. Research has supported Bleuler's contention in that ward atmosphere has been demonstrated to exert a significant short-term influence on outcome (Beck, 1978). This effect, however, may be either beneficial or detrimental, depending on such factors as the clarity of patient-staff roles and limits set on patient behaviour.

We will describe two hospital milieu programs. Wilmer's (1976) "therapeutic community" avoided the use of seclusion, restraints, and electroshock treatments. Medication was administered in limited amounts to avoid supposedly adverse effects on learning, concentration, perceptual, and creative abilities. Therapy involved a Jungian analytic approach, music and art therapy, psychodrama, and family counselling.

Jackson and Cawley's (1992) hospital milieu program was developed from the idea that schizophrenia represents a regression of a vulnerable individual to what Freud termed a "primary process" level of functioning. Winnicott (1965) claimed that this type of functioning results when normal psychological development is arrested by overwhelming traumatic experiences. Regression, he believed, was an attempt to solicit a safe and reassuring environment. Thus, the main aim of therapy was the psychodynamic exploration and resolution of the traumatic experiences and their attendant painful emotions. The interventions were tailored to the specific needs of each individual patient and the treatment program was long-term (average stay for a patient was nine months); early release was not the principal goal. This program is reported (Jackson & Cawley, 1992) to have generated excellent outcomes for a number of schizophrenic patients who had responded poorly, or not at all, to pharmacotherapy, electroconvulsive therapy, and leucotomy.

In 1964, a Canadian Royal Commission on Health Services advocated that mental disorders no longer be distinguished from physical illnesses (Goering, Wasylenki, & Grisonich, 1992). Goering et al. pointed out that this report may have spawned a move in the focus of treatment away from provincial psychiatric hospitals to psychiatric wards within general hospitals. Between 1960 and 1976, the number of beds in psychiatric hospitals decreased markedly (from 47,633 to 15,011) and the number of beds in psychiatric wards in general hospitals increased (from 844 to 5836) in Canada. Goering et al. suggested that this change seems to have created two streams of mental health care. In one stream, the new general hospital psychiatric wards treat less ill, short-term patients who had previously never been admitted to a psychiatric treatment centre. In the second stream, the psychiatric hospitals treat mostly long-term inpatients, as well as some short-term inpatients and outpatients who have proven to be management problems in general hospital settings.

Note, however, that the total number of beds for psychiatric patients has decreased. With widespread use of neuroleptics, a number of schizophrenic patients have been released from psychiatric hospitals to live in the community (Seeman & Seeman, 1992). However, deinstitutionalization has had its problems: too often, shortfalls in government funding have meant the "community" has had no services to offer these patients; nor, in many cases, have hospitals and community mental health programs worked together (Goering et al., 1992). These problems were reflected in a comparative review of outcome studies. Test and Stein (1978) found the community programs superior only in that they reduced length of stay in hospital. They uncovered no differences in symptom reduction, which was linked primarily to antipsychotic medication, or in psychosocial functioning.

To resolve these difficulties, Goering et al. (1992) advanced the following intervention model. First, resources from the psychiatric institutions should be reallocated to community mental health programs. Second, patients and their families should be involved in all phases of treatment planning and implementation. Finally, hospital and community mental health programs should be synthesized into a comprehensive system. Three provinces (British Columbia, New Brunswick, and Ontario) recently adopted strategies based on Goering et al.'s model. To mention one example, the British Columbia Society Partnership Program involves patients and their families in all phases of treatment planning and implementation (Small & Sudar, 1995).

Family Therapy

As the vulnerability-stress model becomes more widely accepted, theorists have increasingly recognized that schizophrenic individuals do not live in a vacuum but are part of a behavioural system, the family (Kazarian & Malla, 1992). Interest in the influence of interpersonal relations has further been renewed by the recent trend to deinstitutionalization. As former inpatients are discharged to their families, the observation has been confirmed that schizophrenic people appear to be especially vulnerable to the expressed-emotion component of a family's interactions.

Family interventions concentrating on reducing the adverse climate in high-expressed-emotion families have produced reduced relapse rates for schizophrenic patients (Kazarian & Malla, 1992). Several interventions have been developed to foster social proficiency and decrease stressors.

The program offered at Victoria Hospital in London, Ontario, exemplifies these approaches. During the first phase, family members are invited to discuss all aspects of their experiences with the patient. The strengths and weaknesses of each family member are evaluated. Members make a commitment to assist treatment efforts and work out a mutually agreeable treatment contract. They then attend a one-day workshop to learn about current theories of the causes of schizophrenia, available treatments, and the strategies families can use to cope with problems. The final phase involves exploring with each family the need for additional therapy sessions to work toward rehabilitation. Whether the family cooperates or not, rehabilitation goals are pursued for at least a year.

The family intervention studies reviewed by Kazarian and Malla (1992) demonstrated effectiveness. One study randomly assigned to one of four groups 103 patients who met the diagnostic research criteria for schizophrenia or schizoaffective disorder, and who resided with families who met the criteria for a high-expressed-emotion designation. Patients in all groups received medication. Additionally, one group received family treatment, one group received social skills training, one group received both family treatment and social skills training, and the final group received no treatment. During the one-year followup, no patients in the group receiving both treatments relapsed, compared to relapse rates of 19 percent in the family treatment group, 20 percent in the social training group, and 41 percent in the no-treatment group.

Psychodynamic Therapy

Individual psychoanalytic or psychodynamic therapy for schizophrenia declined sharply in the 1960s after negative findings of two of four outcome studies, and the demonstrated efficacy of pharmacotherapy in the 1950s. Freud himself thought that people with schizophrenia made poor candidates for treatment. Many contemporary critics have argued that psychodynamic therapy is at best ineffective with schizophrenia (Mosher & Keith, 1980).

However, some reviews of the literature (Beck, 1978; McGlashan, 1994; Mosher & Keith, 1980; Wasylenki, 1990) suggest that the efficacy of psychodynamic treatment is still in question. Past outcome studies have suffered from various methodological flaws, including a lack of precision about therapists' training, experience, and orientation and the treatment process (Beck, 1978; Mosher & Keith, 1980). In addition, treatment-outcome measurements have often been restricted to reduction in positive symptoms—the area in which pharmacotherapy is most effective—ignoring other measures such as reduction in negative symptoms, return to premorbid level of functioning, enjoyment of life, and personal insight (Mosher & Keith, 1980).

Therapy Based on Learning Models

Although major features of schizophrenia may not be learned, learning-based interventions have proven useful in molding socially acceptable behaviour. These interventions include selectively reinforcing appropriate behaviour, token economies, and training in the social skills necessary to live in the community. One Canadian study found that social skills training was effective in reducing negative symptoms, which are typically not affected by neuroleptics (Dobson, McDougall, Busheikin, & Aldous, 1995).

Cognitive therapy has also been found to be useful in ameliorating the consequences of hallucinations, delusions, and thought disturbances. This intervention helps patients to understand their symptoms in a less stigmatizing manner (Kingdon & Turkington, 1991) or to analyze their delusional beliefs (Alford & Correia, 1994).

A cognitive-behavioural program, Integrated Psychological Therapy, has been effective in reducing psychopathology scores and hospital readmission rates (Brenner, Hodel, Roder, & Corrigan, 1992). This program helps patients to discern environmental stimuli relevant to tasks at hand, develop task-facilitative concepts, correctly respond to social cues, and communicate effectively.

Group Therapy

Group therapy is based on the premise that, under the guidance of a therapist, patients with similar psychopathology can help each other. Group therapy with schizophrenic individuals concentrates on supporting each other and developing basic social and interpersonal skills. These goals contrast with those of traditional group therapy, which include the development of insight into, and resolution of, interpersonal issues.

Beck (1978) and Mosher and Keith (1980) evaluated the group therapy literature. They concluded that group psychotherapy was more effective than individual psychotherapy when the level of functioning within the community was examined. Mosher and Keith found that group therapy did not reduce relapse rates or levels of psychopathology but appeared to improve social and interpersonal skills among outpatients.

PANORAMA

A complex set of biological and psychological factors is evidently involved in the etiology of schizophrenia. Studies of family concordance rates, genetic linkage analyses, investigations of biological mechanisms, and examination of birth defect occurrences, and possibly viral infections, together suggest a strong component of biological susceptibility to schizophrenia. Nevertheless, the constellation of factors precipitating clinical symptomatology comprises a mixture of constitutional vulnerability and psychological stress. It can be argued that extreme vulnerability can cause schizophrenia even without significant environmental stress; similarly, extreme stress may precipitate the disorder with minimal vulnerability.

Treatment strategies also incorporate a mixture of biological and psychological modalities. Pharmacotherapy is the primary intervention, but appears to control symptoms rather than cure the disorder. Pharmaceutical research will likely be directed to developing antipsychotics with more specific action and fewer side-effects.

Adjunct treatments involving social skills training and family-oriented therapy appear to have promising effects, although the mechanisms of such effects are not clearly understood. The efficacy of cognitive-behavioural treatments may improve with the incorporation of available knowledge on information processing, perception, and sensation in schizophrenia. Rehabilitation efforts are shifting away from hospitalization and a goal of making patients manageable toward community-based models involving more patient autonomy and a goal of adjustment to living in the community.

Increasingly, it is recognized that more sophisticated methodologies capitalizing on technological developments and formal theoretical models will improve the outlook for understanding and treating schizophrenia. In particular, methods involving computer simulation, electrical and magnetic measurement of biological mechanisms, and quantification of psychological and biological processes will increasingly dominate research endeavours and care programs.

SUMMARY

Although there are indications that schizophrenia has been a disturbance of behaviour and experience since ancient times, it was not until the late nineteenth and early twentieth centuries that the disorder was systematically studied. The symptomatology of schizophrenia takes multiple forms, including delusions, hallucinations, disorganized speech and behaviour, and negative symptoms. Current subtypes include Paranoid, Catatonic, Disorganized, Undifferentiated, and Residual Schizophrenia. More often than not, however, the symptoms considered to distinguish the separate subtypes tend to coexist rather than being clearly differentiated.

For a substantial number of patients, there is a predominance of delusions, frequently accompanied by hallucinations, over other symptoms. The prominence of such a pattern denotes paranoid schizophrenia, the most frequently diagnosed subtype. Empirical analysis of symptom configurations have suggested the possible importance of the separation of delusions and hallucinations from the remaining symptomatology, which has given rise to the suggestion that the paranoid-nonparanoid distinction is the one most relevant for research and possibly for clinical purposes. A synthesis of empirical findings indicates that paranoid schizophrenic symptomatology is indicative of a less severe form of disorder than nonparanoid symptomatology. Furthermore, there appear to be gradations among patients in the relative presence of paranoid and nonparanoid symptomatology, rather than abrupt differences in one or the other.

The etiology of schizophrenia is, to say the least, complex, and its investigation is challenging. The etiology entails what undoubtedly are intricate interactions among genetic and biological factors and environmental influences, including family interactions. Brain systems implicated in the disorder include the dopamine system and possibly other neurotransmitters, such as glutamate and serotonin, with the latter having commanded increasing attention. In addition, several neuroanatomical structures have been the focus of attention in schizophrenia research. In particular, the cognitive-organizational functions of the frontal cortex are considered to be disrupted in schizophrenia.

Several aspects of memory and information processing are unfavourably affected, but others remain intact. The speed of transacting cognitive operations is not impaired; however, it may be applied less efficiently. Each of the stages of converting stimuli into a useful cognitive representation (that is, encoding) proceed at a normal rate, but additional stages are included beyond the normal complement. Cognitive-behavioural markers that have been useful in studies of heritability and prognosis have included eye-tracking dysfunction and reaction-time crossover.

Therapy for schizophrenia has primarily taken the form of pharmacotherapy, with neuroleptics being thought to act on the dopamine system, but possibly also other neurotransmitter systems. Sociopsychological treatments have been shown to be useful in reducing relapse rates. Of special promise are those treatments directed toward patterns of family interaction involving a high degree of expressed emotion.

Clearly, schizophrenia remains an enigmatic and conceptually challenging disorder, despite numerous inroads into understanding the psychological and biological processes involved. Important advances in knowledge can be anticipated with continuing developments in biological measurement technology, rigorous documentation of deviant psychological processes, and the establishment of the relationships between findings from biological and psychological levels of investigation.

KEY TERMS

schizophrenia (p. 346)
depersonalization (p. 346)
positive symptomatology (p. 347)
negative symptomatology (p. 347)
paranoid schizophrenia (p. 347)
undifferentiated (p. 347)
residual schizophrenia (p. 347)
delusions (p. 348)
hallucinations (p. 349)

thought-content symptomatology (p. 349)
thought-form symptomatology (p. 350)
disorganized speech (p. 350)
neologisms (p. 350)
word salad (p. 350)
schizo-aphasia (p. 350)
grossly disorganized behaviour (p. 350)
avolition (p. 351)
anhedonia (p. 351)

attentional deficits (p. 351)
delusional disorder (p. 351)
schizoaffective disorder (p. 352)
substance-induced psychotic disorder (p. 352)
brief psychotic disorder (p. 352)
schizophreniform disorder (p. 352)
sluggish schizophrenia (p. 352)
paranoid subtype (p. 352)
disorganized subtype (p. 352)
catatonic subtype (p. 352)
undifferentiated subtype (p. 352)

residual subtype (p. 352)
vulnerability-stress perspective
    (p. 355)
high-risk studies (p. 356)
dopamine (p. 358)

expressed emotion (p. 361)
social selection theory (p. 363)
sociogenic theory (p. 363)
functional magnetic resonance
    imaging (fMRI) (p. 364)

process schizophrenic (p. 365)
stimulus encoding (p. 365)

A D D I T I O N A L   R E S O U R C E S

The Schizophrenia Society of Canada
75 The Donway West
Suite 814
Don Mills, ON M3C 2E9
(800) 809-HOPE
(416) 445-8204
(416) 445-2270 fax
info@schizophrenia.ca

Association for the Neurologically
    Disabled of Canada
59 Clement Road
Etobicoke, ON M9R 1Y5
(416) 244-1992
(416) 244-4099 fax
info@and.ca

Canadian Psychiatric Association
260-441 MacLaren Street
Ottawa, ON K2P 2H3
(613) 234-2815
(613) 234-9857 fax
cpa@medical.org

www.schizophrenia.ca
The site of the Schizophrenia Society of Canada provides a
range of resources about schizophrenia.

www.pslgroup.com/schizophr.htm
Medical news and information about schizophrenia and
schizophrenia-related disorders.

www.mentalhealth.com/p20-grp.html#Schizo
This collection includes hundreds of articles on
schizophrenia.

Chapter 15

Psychophysiologic Disorders

Kenneth M. Prkachin
Glenda C. Prkachin

George was a 32-year-old high school teacher whose specialty was music. He was referred for psychological evaluation by his family physician. For 16 months George had been consulting his doctor about chest pains, which had caused him great anxiety because he was convinced he was having a heart attack. Within the past year, George had consulted his doctor 37 times about his symptoms, and had undergone extensive medical tests, none of which had provided an explanation of George's symptoms. Although there was no unusual history of heart problems in his family and he was within a normal weight range for his height, George was a smoker and lived a sedentary lifestyle.

Psychological evaluation revealed a man obviously distressed over his physical condition, but whose agitation extended beyond that. He readily expressed grievances with other people in his life: his principal for being demanding and incompetent, his wife for her sexual performance, his father for his coolness, and numerous other individuals or classes of individuals for a litany of reasons. His daily life he described as "going all out." He was up at 5:00 am, at work with early band practice, and usually finished at 6:30 each night. En route home, he would pick up a six-pack of beer and a sandwich to eat on the fly. At home, he would prepare his lessons for the next day, then finish the six-pack and go to sleep.

By reputation he was an extremely effective music teacher. His bands were always competitive in provincial championships and for the preceding two years had been adjudicated the best in the province. Yet he claimed that these achievements gave him no pleasure as he was most often preoccupied with the deficiencies in his students' performances.

George's case is representative of many people who are referred for psychological or psychiatric evaluation, yet it does not readily fit into the diagnostic framework provided by the DSM. The presenting problem (recurrent chest pain) is one that is ordinarily dealt with in clinical medicine, yet there are behavioural (drinking, smoking), psychological (inability to experience pleasure, hard-driven, hostile, and agitated) and social (isolation) characteristics that seem relevant to the symptoms he is experiencing and to his general life. Moreover, a substantial scientific literature suggests that George's symptoms may be explained, at least in part, by psychological and behavioural variables that were identified in his psychological evaluation. Perhaps even more important, there is also reason to believe that psychological therapies that target the psychological and behavioural characteristics George displayed may be effective in alleviating his distress.

This chapter focusses on applications of psychological theories and findings to the explanation of physical illness and disease. This is an area that has traditionally been part of the field of psychopathology—hence its inclusion in this book—but it is emerging as a specialty of its own, called "health psychology" or "behavioural medicine."

HISTORICAL PERSPECTIVE

The idea that psychological processes can have an impact on bodily states, even to the extent of producing physical disease, has a long history in the Western intellectual tradition and may be even more deeply embedded in other cultures. Cannon (1942) discussed the phenomenon of voodoo death. A member of a culture in which voodoo is practised may, over the course of hours or days, die as a consequence of learning that he or she has been cursed. Cannon took this phenomenon quite seriously, and attributed it to physiological processes elicited by threat and fear. As Western medicine evolved during the first half of the twentieth century, most practitioners and scientists have paid little attention to psychological-physiological relationships.

There has, however, been a continuing body of work that has recognized the importance of psychological processes in physical health. In the early years of the science of psychopathology, the area that emphasized them came to be referred to as *psychosomatic medicine* and the health problems as *psychosomatic disorders*. In common usage, this term often implies imaginary illness—the experience of symptoms (headaches, for example) with no underlying pathophysiologic cause. Yet practitioners and scientists are quick to point out that the disorders in question usually involve identifiable disturbances (lesions) in bodily structures and functions and are in no way imaginary or feigned. The term also implies a **dualistic** view of mind and body as separate entities, subject to different laws. To avoid such implications, the DSM-II changed the terminology to "psychophysiological disorders."

For many years, clinicians and investigators interested in this field devoted their attention to a set of disorders that were thought to be primarily determined by psychological and physiological forces and that came to be known as the "classic psychosomatic disorders." Included in this set were gastrointestinal ulcers, ulcerative colitis, hypertension (high blood pressure), asthma, and arthritis. These disorders were probably considered together for a number of reasons. First, because evidence available at the time could not identify a specific pathophysiologic cause for the disorders, dualistic thinking led people to assume that the roots of the disorder must be psychological. Second, there was evidence suggesting distinct psychological features in patients suffering from these disorders. Such thinking both supported and contributed to the early work of psychodynamically oriented theorists, who posited specific psychological etiologies for each of the classic psychosomatic disorders. Helen Flanders Dunbar (1935), one of the earliest theorists in this area, suggested, on the basis of her clinical work, that specific disorders were the natural consequence of specific emotions and personality traits. The psychoanalyst Franz Alexander (1950) argued that the roots of classic psychosomatic disorders lay in characteristic intrapersonal conflicts. According to this theory, people who were prone to get high blood pressure had a chronic sense of rage, generated by intrapsychic forces, but inhibited expression, appearing unassertive and overly compliant. This conflict was thought to have physiological consequences that led to clinical disease. The specific symptomatology was often seen as symbolic of the underlying conflict. Such formulations have been largely supplanted by other views based in empirical research. Nevertheless, they are of more than historical interest, since elements of them persist. For example, there is considerable evidence that something related to the experience or expression of anger may play a role in risk of premature death from cardiovascular disease.

Interest in this field was revitalized in the late 1970s with a new perspective that emerged out of the realization that many, perhaps all, disease states are influenced directly or indirectly by social and psychological factors. In an influential review of contemporary developments in medicine, psychiatry, and the social sciences, the psychiatrist George Engel (1977) argued that the biomedical model of disease should be expanded to what he called a "biopsychosocial" model (see Chapter 2). Engel's argument was based on a vast range of observations supporting the view that a range of factors, including psychological characteristics and societal forces, must be taken into account in order to explain both the origins of many diseases and the nature of health.

At about the same time, many psychologists became interested in the apparently broader role that psychological factors and behaviour play in states of health and illness. For example, health care around the world began to reflect the idea that pain, both chronic and acute, could be influenced by psychological factors (Melzack & Wall, 1982) and treated using psychological techniques (Fordyce, 1976). A number of behaviours, such as smoking and the use of other drugs, had already been identified as increasing risk of morbidity and mortality from disease. Interest intensified as people realized how much such risk factors contributed to the leading causes of death in Western societies, and as behavioural therapy techniques offered apparently successful methods for controlling such behaviours. Increasing evidence justified the belief that other psychological variables, such as stress and characteristic styles of behaviour, were also associated with increased risk of disease.

All of these activities and interests converged in a new branch of psychology—whose concepts will be the focus of this chapter—variously called psychosomatic medicine, behavioural medicine, or health psychology. **Behavioural medicine** usually refers to application of the methods of behaviour modification to the treatment or prevention of disease: for example, the use of psychological techniques to control pain in patients undergoing medical procedures, or interventions to improve the diabetics' ability to control their blood glucose. The broader term, **health psychology**, refers to any application of psychological methods and theories to understand the origins of disease, individual responses to disease, and the dimensions and determinants of good health. In addition to interventions to treat disease, prevent illness, or promote health, health psychologists attempt to explain such things as how

people develop risk of disease, how beliefs and attitudes may affect health-related behaviours, how communication in health care settings may be improved, and how the health of entire populations or communities may be enhanced. In this chapter we shall highlight a number of key concepts, findings and issues that health psychology has contributed to the study of psychopathology, focussing on those disorders that reflect the impact of psychophysiological variables.

DIAGNOSTIC ISSUES

Recall from Chapter 3 the multiaxial system of classification In DSM-IV. When a major element of the disorder is a diagnosable medical condition, that condition will be noted on Axis III; the particular medical condition can be coded according to the International Classification of Disease 9-Clinical Modification system (ICD). On Axis I, under the category "Other Conditions That May Be a Focus of Clinical Attention," a specific code means "Psychological Factor Affecting Medical Condition" (see DSM table). The particular psychological factor involved should then be specified: it may be an identifiable Axis I (for example, Major Depressive Disorder) or Axis II disorder (for example, Borderline Personality Disorder) or may be psychological symptoms that do not meet the threshold for diagnosis of a disorder, such as anger or anxiety, personality traits or coping styles (for example, excessive job involvement or hostility), maladaptive health behaviours (for example, smoking, alcohol use), or stress-related physiological response.

PSYCHOSOCIAL MECHANISMS OF DISEASE

The idea that psychological processes may affect disease is widely held in our culture. People are said to have "died of a broken heart" or "worked themselves to death." Such notions may be vast oversimplifications; yet, as we will see in this chapter, they do have some basis in reality.

If there is indeed a relationship between psychological factors and disease states, how does this connection work? A scientifically oriented person will not be convinced without finding some biologically plausible mechanism through

DSM-IV Psychological Factors Affecting Medical Condition

The designated psychological factor must
(i) be correlated with the development, exacerbation, or delayed recovery from the medical condition,
(ii) interfere with treatment,
(iii) place the individual at additional risk to his or her health or
(iv) precipitate the symptoms of the condition.

Source: Reprinted with permission from the *Diagnostic and Statistical Manual of Mental Disorders,* Fourth Edition. Copyright 1994 American Psychiatric Association.

which those factors may influence disease. A **mechanism** is a process, an activity of a living system, that mediates the influence of an antecedent factor on disease. For example, a person with AIDS may actually die of pneumonia or sarcoma. The ultimate cause of those diseases is infection by the *human immunodeficiency virus* (HIV), but (to greatly simplify our example) the mechanism of disease is the effect of that virus in decreasing the competence of the immune system.

What, then, are the mechanisms through which psychological factors may be responsible for illness and disease? To answer this question we must first specify what we mean by "illness and disease." In this chapter we have used this seemingly redundant phrase intentionally. Although the terms "illness" and "disease" are often thought of as synonyms, there is a subtle distinction. Illness is marked by *symptoms*, which (as described in Chapter 3) are subjective reports of internal states. When you have the flu, you may complain of feeling hot and tired and of having aches and pains in various parts of your body. An interested observer, such as a physician or a concerned family member, cannot see, hear, or feel the heat, fatigue, and pain that you feel.

By contrast, disease is marked by *signs*: objective indications of an underlying disease process, observable either directly by a person with appropriate training or indirectly through the administration of a specific test. Although the feeling of feverishness that you report when you have the flu is a symptom, the high temperature that your mother measures with a thermometer is a sign. When a sign involves the specific disruption of bodily tissue—as in a gastric ulcer—or of the normal function of a bodily system—as in high blood pressure—those disruptions are called **lesions**.

This distinction between illness and disease, symptom and sign, is important because it alerts us to the various ways, or mechanisms, by which psychological factors may, in principle, contribute to ill health. Certainly, one of the principal determinants of illness is disease. We often report pain and distress when we are experiencing a disease state. Ordinarily, the throbbing pain of a migraine headache or the ache of arthritis would not be there, and would not be reported to the doctor, without some underlying dysfunction. On the other hand, because symptoms are reports of subjective experiences, they may also be influenced by other factors that influence perception, independently of disease processes (Mechanic, 1978). Examples of this are abundant in most people's experiences. For example, have you ever endured a headache in silence because to do so was the expected behaviour in the situation? Have you ever missed a day of school or work because you were feeling "sick," even though you may not have had aches, pains, or a temperature? If so, your subjective report of your symptoms of distress were being affected by more than the underlying disease state. What these examples illustrate is that psychological factors may influence illness by affecting our perception of, attention to, or tolerance of bodily signals (Mechanic, 1978).

But what of lesions, pathological changes in the structure or functioning of body systems? What are the mechanisms by which psychological factors might influence body systems? To answer this, we must consider what is known about the ways in which body tissues may be affected by behaviours and psychological processes. A *behaviour*, for the purposes of this discussion, is a discrete and at least potentially observable act, such as eating, exercising, smoking cigarettes, and so on. A *psychological process* is not observable directly, but may be inferred on the basis of other phenomena that are. For example, we cannot see another's depression, but we can see evidence, in the facial expression, in the way the individual speaks, in changes in sleeping and sexual habits, even in the individual's responses to a questionnaire that allow us to infer with some confidence that depression is present.

Psychological influences on body tissues can take place as a consequence of the effects of behaviours, particularly if those behaviours are repeated frequently over weeks, months, or years. For example, there is no longer any reasonable doubt that the effects of repeated smoking of tobacco are toxic. This is not because the act of smoking is inherently pathogenic but because it repeatedly exposes body tissues to tar and nicotine, which are themselves the proximal causes of disease. There are many other examples of behaviours that promote disease by exposing body tissue to pathogenic substances. By contrast, there are behaviours that have beneficial effects. Exercise, for example, contributes to the improvement of cardiovascular fitness.

Psychological influences on body tissues can also take place as a consequence of psychological processes. A host of such influences have been postulated, ranging from perceptual schemata (the ways in which people characteristically interpret experience) through personality and social characteristics to emotions and emotion-like states. (Hereafter, we will use the term "psychosocial variables" to refer to this broad class of psychological and social characteristics and variables.) How could such influences affect body tissue?

There are three general body systems that are responsive to psychosocial variables: the endocrine system, the autonomic nervous system, and the immune system. Although we will discuss these systems separately, current evidence indicates that the three systems affect each other.

The Endocrine System

The endocrine system consists of a number of organs within the body that manufacture biologically active substances called hormones and, when the occasion is right, secrete these substances into the bloodstream. Figure 15.1 displays a number of the most common endocrine organs in the human body. The hormones will circulate with the blood until they reach a "target" such as the heart, the liver, or the bones, where they will cause certain characteristic changes.

Several endocrine hormone systems are known to be highly responsive to psychosocial variables. Perhaps the best known is the system of interacting organs commonly called the *hypothalamic-pituitary-adrenal-cortical (HPA) axis*. An axis is a subsystem consisting of different organs that act in concert in a cascade of effects. The HPA axis, depicted in Figure 15.2, begins with the hypothalamus, a brain structure that

Figure 15.1 **The Endocrine System**

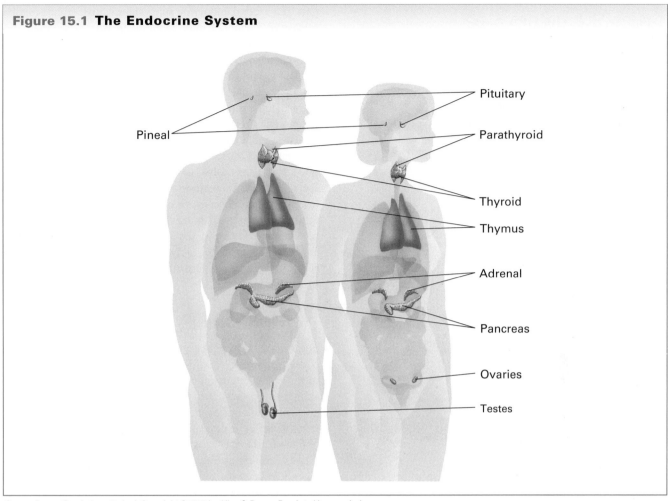

Pineal
Pituitary
Parathyroid
Thyroid
Thymus
Adrenal
Pancreas
Ovaries
Testes

plays a vital role in controlling a large number of body functions. When activated, the hypothalamus causes the pituitary gland, with which it is connected by nerve fibres and blood supply, to secrete a substance called adrenocorticotrophic hormone (ACTH) into the circulation. The targets for ACTH are the cells in the adrenal cortex, the outer layer of the adrenal glands, which is located above the kidneys. When these tissues are stimulated, they in turn secrete a substance called cortisol (sometimes referred to as a glucocorticoid) into the circulation. Cortisol is a highly active hormone that produces a variety of effects in the body, including suppression of inflammation, mobilization of glucose from the liver, increasing of cardiovascular tone, production of immune system changes, and inhibition of the activity of other endocrine structures (Herman, Prewitt, & Cullinan, 1996). These features of glucocorticoid response are a defence mechanism, promoting immediate survival and inhibiting unnecessary activity, but are maladaptive when prolonged or exaggerated. In particular, there is evidence that glucocorticoids suppress immune system function, enhance the development of atherosclerosis (see below), and contribute to neuronal damage in the brain (McEwen & Stellar, 1993; Sapolsky, 1996). The hypothalamus is responsive to psychosocial influences; in particular, the pituitary-ACTH-cortisol cascade seems to be a marker of psychological distress (Lundberg & Frankenhaeuser, 1980).

The Autonomic Nervous System

The second major body system that is responsive to psychosocial influences is the autonomic nervous system (see Chapter 2). Most people have found themselves perspiring before some important event such as an examination or a date, or blushing after doing something embarrassing. Most people are aware, as well, of changes that take place in their bodies during other emotional states: the heart pounding, butterflies in the stomach, dryness in the mouth, and so on. Many of these body changes reflect the activity of the autonomic nervous system (ANS). The term *autonomic*, which comes from the same root as "autonomous," derives from the belief that this system operates unconsciously and out of the control of the individual. Although this assumption is not totally correct, under ordinary circumstances we have little awareness or direct control of the operation of the ANS. Refer to Figure 2.2 for a diagram of the main structures in this system. As described in Chapter 2, the ANS consists of two anatomically

Figure 15.2 The HPA Axis

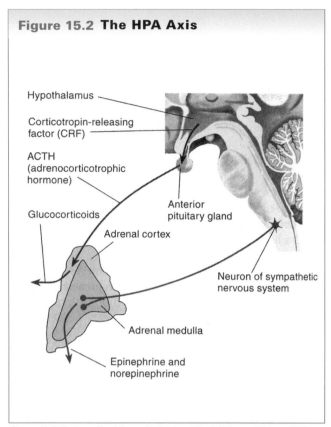

Hypothalamus

Corticotropin-releasing factor (CRF)

ACTH (adrenocorticotrophic hormone)

Glucocorticoids

Anterior pituitary gland

Adrenal cortex

Neuron of sympathetic nervous system

Adrenal medulla

Epinephrine and norepinephrine

Source: N. R. Carlson, *Physiology of behaviour,* 6th ed. (Allyn and Bacon, 1998). Copyright © 1998 by Allyn and Bacon. Reprinted by permission.

distinct parts. The sympathetic branch consists of nerve fibres that emanate from the thoracic and lumbar (or middle) regions of the spinal cord and make contact with a large number of body organs: the heart, the stomach, blood vessels, etc. Notice, however, that most (but not all) organs that are innervated by the sympathetic system are also innervated by the parasympathetic branch, consisting of fibres that emanate from the cranial and sacral (or end) regions of the spinal cord.

The sympathetic and parasympathetic systems act like the accelerator and brakes, respectively, of the organs to which they connect. When the sympathetic system is aroused, it tends to produce changes that prepare the body for vigorous action, such as increased blood pressure, heart rate, and perspiration and decreased digestive activity. Many of the effects of the sympathetic system would be dangerous for the individual if they went on too long. For example, prolonged increases in blood pressure could damage brain or vascular tissues. The parasympathetic branch "applies the brakes" to such changes to return the body to a more quiescent state that is within the body's tolerance. It is rare, however, for only one system or the other to be activated; rather, the level of activity of the body systems that are innervated by the ANS is usually determined by the relative balance of input from the sympathetic and parasympathetic systems.

In comparison to endocrine effects, which rely on the bloodstream to convey hormones to target organs, ANS effects are rapid because they take advantage of the speed of nervous conduction. The sympathetic system itself, however, is

part of a second endocrine subsystem whose effects involve release of hormones into the bloodstream: the sympathetic-adrenal medullary (SAM) axis. Nerve fibres from the sympathetic system stimulate the cells of the inner region of the adrenal gland, the adrenal medulla, to secrete the hormones epinephrine and norepinephrine. These belong to a broader class of hormones known as catecholamines and are also known as adrenaline and noradrenaline. When they are released into the bloodstream, epinephrine and norepinephrine circulate to a variety of target organs where they can have powerful effects. Most of us are aware of some of these effects: we refer to exciting events as producing an "adrenaline rush" and describe risk-takers as "adrenaline junkies." Although such descriptions may not be quite accurate technically, they do convey the idea that catecholamines increase energy and activate the body. Notice how the effects are complementary to, or synergistic with, the direct effects of the sympathetic system.

The Immune System

Yet a third body system responsive to psychosocial factors is the immune system. Our understanding of this potential mechanism is in its infancy because solid evidence of the responsiveness of the immune system to psychosocial influences is much more recent. The immune system comprises a network of cells and organs that defends the body against external, disease-causing forces (for example, bacteria, viruses, fungi) or internal pathogens (for example, cancerous cells) known as *antigens*. The immune system performs this function through the complex actions of a variety of white blood cells (Guyton, 1991). These cells are produced and stored in locations throughout the body, including the thymus gland, the lymph nodes, the bone marrow, and the small intestines, and they exert their effects as they circulate in the bloodstream. As shown in Figure 15.3, there are three general categories of immune response—nonspecific, cellular, and humoral—each of which depends on different cell types or courses of action. In **nonspecific immune responses**, circulating white cells called granulocytes and monocytes identify invading antigens and destroy them by *phagocytosis*: engulfing and digesting them. **Cellular immunity** is based on the action of a class of blood cells called T-lymphocytes. The "T" designation refers to the locus of their production, the thymus gland. Cellular immunity results from a cascade of actions of various types of T-lymphocytes. Initially, an antigen is presented to T-lymphocytes by other cells called *macrophages*. This will cause the T-cells to proliferate (reproduce) and then circulate in the body. Several other types of T-cells participate in an immune episode. *Helper T-cells* secrete substances called *lymphokines* (among these are the interleukins and interferon) that control the responses of other types of T-cell. One group of these, the so-called *natural killer (NK)* cells attack foreign or mutated cells directly. Suppressor T-cells play a role in inhibiting the actions of both the helper and the NK cells, thereby providing a negative feedback mechanism to control the immune episode. In the

Figure 15.3 The Immune System

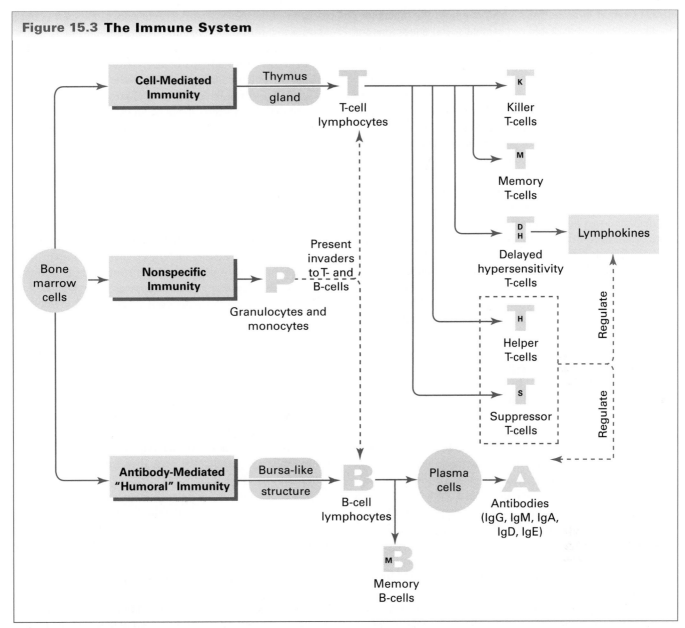

course of an immune episode, certain T-cells become permanently altered and are thereby rendered into *memory T-cells*, which will be stored in the body in anticipation of the next time it needs to counter the threat of invasion. It is this process that is responsible for our building up immunity to certain kinds of microorganisms, so that we may come down only once with certain diseases such as chicken-pox.

In **humoral immunity**, invading antigens are also presented by macrophages to B-lymphocytes. ("B" stands for bursa, an organ in which such cells are produced in birds. They derive from the liver and bone marrow in humans [Guyton, 1991].) This causes the B-cells to reproduce—a process reinforced by the lymphokine secretion from the helper T-cells. Some of the activated B-cells remain as memory B-cells. Others go on to be plasma cells, secreting anti-

bodies called immunoglobulins that neutralize antigens in a number of different ways, such as clumping, presenting the antigen to phagocytic cells, or rupturing the antigen.

Only recently have scientists become aware of the responsiveness of the immune system to psychosocial influences. Studies in the new field of **psychoneuroimmunology** have left little doubt, however, that the immune system can be affected by learning experiences, emotional states, and personal characteristics. For example, exposure of subjects to acute stressors in a laboratory setting, such as making them perform an extemporaneous speech, consistently produces changes in immune system function, such as increased numbers of natural killer and suppressor T-cells and reduced T-cell proliferation (Cohen & Herbert, 1996). Cohen and colleagues (Cohen, Kaplan, Cunnick, Manuck, & Rabin,

1992) studied immune function in cynomolgus (macaque) monkeys exposed to stable or unstable social conditions for 26 months. Unstable conditions, which were produced by changing the monkeys in the experimental colony every month, produce a variety of indications of stress in the affected animals. Blood samples taken from animals exposed to social disruption showed impairment of the ability of T-cells to proliferate, indicating a suppression of immune system functioning. Interestingly, impaired immune system functioning was also observed in animals who showed less affiliative behaviour, such as contacting or grooming other animals, an observation about the stress-modifying effects of social variables.

Cohen and Herbert (1996) have provided a simplified model that posits three pathways through which psychosocial variables might influence immune activity: (1) by the direct action of the central nervous system on organs and structures of the immune system; (2) as a secondary consequence of the hormonal changes discussed above; and (3) by changes in behaviour (for example, poor dietary habits) that reflect personal characteristics or adaptations to changing life conditions.

The Psychology of Stress

The mechanisms identified thus far help us to understand some of the physiological processes that can mediate disease. But how might they be activated by psychological influences?

It is next to impossible to be a sentient human being these days without reading or hearing something about "stress." Stress has become one of the most pervasive ideas in psychology. Ideas with such popular appeal should be viewed with caution; sometimes a notion that appears to explain much may explain nothing. Yet the concept also has considerable appeal in the scientific literature and is central to much theory, research, and intervention in health psychology. What, then, do we mean by stress and how can the concept help us understand health and disease?

Most of us have an implicit understanding of the term. As you are reading this text, you may be cramming for two or three or five final exams, the outcome of which may determine whether you will ever achieve your career goals. If so, you know something about stress. As discussed in Chapter 7, post-traumatic stress disorders can result from extreme stress; depression may also sometimes be caused or exacerbated by events that most of us would call stressful (see Chapters 13 and 17). In the case that opens this chapter, one of the salient features of George's life was that he was constantly on edge, albeit largely because of his own attitudes.

These are but a few of many uses of the term. But how can we view stress so as to understand its impact on health? As it turns out, the term is used in a number of different ways by researchers and the concept has evolved considerably as it has gained popularity. Although this variation can be frustrating and confusing for the student, it is not at all unusual for a useful scientific concept. In the scientific literature, the term has been used in three ways: (1) to refer to a *stimulus*, or a property of the external world, (2) to refer to a *response*, or (3) to refer to a *transaction* that mediates stimulus and response.

The earliest influential views of stress emphasized its properties as a response, particularly as a set of physiological changes. The eminent McGill University physiologist Hans Selye (1956) articulated a theory of stress that began with his early studies of the effects of an ovarian extract in rats. He noticed, at first, that animals treated with regular injections of this extract showed characteristic changes, including enlarged adrenal glands, degenerated immune system organs, and ulcers in their stomach linings. To his surprise, however, a control group of rats injected with a simple saline solution showed the same changes! Rumour has it that Selye was a bit of a klutz at injecting rats and his clumsiness caused the observed reactions. To his credit, he realized this and came gradually to the understanding that the critical determinant of the effects he observed must have been something common to both conditions, namely change, unpleasantness, and a need to adapt. Later experiments confirmed that physiological changes could be produced by a wide variety of conditions involving both physical and psychological challenges. Integrating the results of many experiments and observations, Selye proposed that they all reflected the same underlying process, a process he defined as stress.

Selye proposed that this process was a consequence of adaptation to demands placed on the body and argued that it followed a precise natural history. In the first phase, **alarm**, the body faced with an adaptive challenge mobilizes its defences. If the challenge persists, the body then enters the **resistance** phase, during which it actively fights or copes with the challenge through immune and the neuroendocrine changes such as those described above. In the short term, these adaptive responses enhance the body's ability to ward off threats. However, if the challenge persists further, the body reaches the **exhaustion** phase: it has depleted its energy stores and can no longer maintain resistance, and characteristic tissue changes occur. At this point, the organism may succumb to a disease of adaptation, such as an ulcer. This **general adaptation syndrome (GAS)** served as the first formal description and definition of stress. Note that, according to this model, stress is inferred from a set of bodily changes; that is, stress is defined by a response. Note, as well, that by this definition any event that can bring about the characteristic set of changes is a *stressor*. This implication of the "stress as response" perspective has been the source of considerable controversy.

Others have taken the position that stress may be viewed as a kind of stimulus. Even in the GAS model it is implicit that some event must take place to set off adaptation effects. Perhaps it would be helpful to characterize those events, or their psychological consequences, as stress. In another well-known line of research, investigators have attempted to characterize the stimuli that elicit stress through identifying more or less universally difficult events. The earliest and most famous of these attempts was the Social Readjustment Rating Scale by Holmes and Rahe (1967). These investigators developed a list of events in life that required change. These events, such as divorce, marriage, trouble with the law, and taking out a mortgage, were scaled according to the relative degree of change that they entailed and assigned points through a process of psychophysical scaling (marriage served as the standard against which all other changes were assessed and was assigned an arbitrary change value of 50). Note that it is implicit in this approach that stress is a property of the environment—that is, a stimulus.

Scores of studies that shown that events in the Social Readjustment Rating Scale increase the likelihood of a variety of psychological and physical diseases (Holmes & Masuda, 1974). Nevertheless, the approach has been the subject of a number of serious criticisms; one of the most important is that such major events are not representative of the common sources of stress in our lives. Kanner, Coyne, Schaefer, and Lazarus (1981) suggested that people's day-to-day lives are more affected by smaller events, or "hassles," such as troubling thoughts about the future, too many responsibilities, fear of rejection, problems with a lover, feeling conflicted about what to do, or not having enough money for entertainment. They developed a scale to assess the frequency of such events and how upsetting people found them. There is some evidence that a measure of the intensity of hassles predicts symptoms of physical illness (Weinberger, Hiner, & Tierney, 1987).

Neither the stress-as-response nor the stress-as-stimulus approach has been totally satisfactory to most contemporary students of the issue. Defining stress by its physiological dimension forces us to consider very different processes as identical. For example, your heart rate will increase if you are frightened or if you walk up a flight of stairs—if you are punched or if you are kissed. If we view stress only as a set of physiological responses, we are at risk of glossing over fundamental distinctions and of paying insufficient attention to antecedent factors that may play a substantial role in determining physiological responses. Defining stress as stimulus is equally inadequate, because people vary so dramatically in what stimuli or events provoke physiological arousal or subjective distress. Divorce would constitute a highly undesirable, disturbing event for many people; yet for some it may be a liberating experience. For you, taking your next psychology exam may be a welcome opportunity to consolidate and demonstrate your learning. For your classmate it may be an occasion of great trauma. It is essential to take into account the individual's perspective when accounting for stress and its effects.

This view, which has been articulated most forcefully by Richard Lazarus and his colleagues (for example, Lazarus & Folkman, 1984) has been designated the **transactional model** of stress. It conceives of stress as a property neither of stimulus nor of response, but rather as an ongoing series of transactions between an individual and his or her environment. Central to this formulation is the idea that people constantly evaluate what is happening to them and its implications for themselves. The eminent stress researcher Robert Sapolsky provides the following example:

It's two o'clock in the morning and you're lying in bed. You have something immensely important and challenging to do *the next day. ... You have to get a decent night's rest, but you're still wide awake. ... [S]omewhere around two-thirty, when you're lying there clammy and hyperventilating, an entirely new, disruptive chain of thoughts will no doubt intrude. Suddenly, ... you begin to contemplate that nonspecific pain you've been having in your side, that sense of exhaustion lately, that frequent headache. The realization hits you—I'm sick, fatally sick! ... When it's two-thirty on those mornings, I always have a brain tumor. They're very useful for that sort of terror, because you can attribute every conceivable nonspecific symptom to a brain tumor and convince yourself it's time to panic. (Sapolsky, 1994, pp. 1–2)*

In the transactional model such evaluations are called **appraisals**. Appraisals can take different forms, but one of the most critical is the appraisal of threat (see Chapter 7 for a discussion of appraisal as an element in the development of anxiety). When faced with an event that may have adaptational significance, such as the experience of symptoms of illness or a final examination worth half of one's grade, it is *as if* the individual poses the following question: Is this a threat to me? (Note italics. Lazarus' view is that such appraisals may occur quite unconsciously so that they can only be described metaphorically.) This evaluative process is called **primary appraisal** and it sets the stage for further events that may or may not lead to stress. If the individual concludes that the event poses no threat, the process comes to an end and the person continues evaluating subsequent events. If the individual concludes that there is an element of threat, a further set of **secondary appraisals** takes place, involving the metaphoric question "Is there anything I can do about this?" The individual may have a number of available options, such as seeking the advice of a physician or trying to find out more about what will be on the final examination. Such approaches have been termed *problem-focussed coping* because they attempt to identify and rectify the source of the threat. Alternatively, the individual may focus on mollifying the bad feelings associated with the perception of threat. Such *emotion-focussed coping* might involve engaging in diverting thoughts or activities or taking drugs to induce a different feeling state. The individual will then evaluate the effectiveness of such coping activities. If the individual concludes that his or her coping is effective, stress will be minimized. If not, the appraisal of threat will be reconfirmed. Thus, the transactional model views stress as emanating from the balance between primary and secondary appraisals of threat and coping, respectively, and thus as the product of a repeating cycle.

Although the transactional model is very popular and has a certain intuitive appeal, we must ask how it helps us account for the relation between psychosocial factors and bodily processes contributing to disease states. The first answer to this question is an empirical one: the transactional model grew out of evidence that the way a person perceives a potentially threatening event plays an important role in the extent to which he or she will respond physiologically to that event. In a series of classic studies, Lazarus and colleagues were able to demonstrate this by measuring autonomically mediated reactions to films that many people would find gruesome or uncomfortable to watch. In one study, for example, subjects watched an anthropological film depicting a coming-of-age rite among Australian aboriginal people (Speisman, Lazarus, Mordkoff, & Davidson, 1964). In this film, young males are subjected to a procedure called subincision in which the underside of the penis is cut open—in public and without pain relief. Needless to say, subjects viewing this film often show substantial indications of autonomic arousal. However, subjects shown this film after instructions based on an "intellectualization" strategy (emphasizing the importance and the meaning of the ritual in its cultural context and minimizing the discomfort of the ceremony) or a "denial" strategy (downplaying the pain), showed less arousal than subjects whose instructions accentuated the discomfort and risks of the ritual. Thus, the way one thinks about (or appraises) events can modify the physiological response to those events, presumably through altering the stress-transaction process. Such findings have a direct implication for intervention: if one can manipulate the way people make stress-related appraisals, perhaps by cognitive or behavioural therapy techniques, presumably one can thereby alter physiological responses to stress to treat or prevent stress-related disease.

A second answer to the practical utility of the transactional model is that it can help us organize the way we think about psychosocial influences on disease. Shortly, we will review evidence that certain social conditions, personality characteristics, emotions, and perceptions are associated with disease states. Many of these variables are thought to exert their effects, at least in part, through the processes proposed within the transactional model. The model, then, encourages us to ask such questions as "How would the availability of a supportive social network affect appraisal or coping processes?" or "What are the likely consequences of a particular coping process to a depressed person?" An organizing model that guides thinking about the processes engaged under potentially threatening conditions can be very valuable (at least as long as it does not blind us to alternative explanations).

Psychosocial Factors That Influence Disease

Beginning with the work of Selye, hundreds of studies have taken place of the effects of stress on bodily responses and health outcomes. Those effects can be quite complex and other variables can play an important role. Social status, controllability, and social support are three of the most important.

Social Status

Social status refers to an individual's relative position within a social hierarchy. Many human environments are organized hierarchically, with some people occupying high positions that accord them status and power, others low positions, and most people falling somewhere in between. Social status may

be represented by economic status, in which the wealthy may enjoy substantial privileges and influence, while the poor have little. Differences in social status are also observed in other species, where they may be studied with respect to their implications for human differences. Sapolsky (1990), for example, has conducted numerous studies on stress responses among baboons in Kenya, who can be reliably stratified according to a dominance hierarchy.

The influence of social status on health should come as no surprise. It has been summarized by the eminent University of British Columbia health economist Robert Evans (1994) as follows: "Top people live longer." Marmot and colleagues (Marmot, 1986; Marmot, Kogevinas, & Elston, 1987; Marmot & Theorell, 1988) have reported on one of the most extensive studies to address this issue. The Whitehall Study collected large amounts of information on the health habits and health status of 10,000 British civil servants over approximately 20 years. One of the major features of the Whitehall study was that participants could be ordered along a gradient of occupational and income status from clerical workers at the low end to administrators at the top. The Whitehall study produced a number of important observations, which not only establish the importance of social status as a variable influencing health status, but also suggest that its effects are more subtle than one might imagine. For one thing, 40-to-64-year-old men in the lowest-status positions were between three and four times more likely to die in a ten-year period than men in the highest positions. Moreover, it was not just a matter of a difference between the highest- and the lowest-status individuals; there was a *gradient* to this effect that applied across the range of social status (see Figure 15.4). As Evans (1994) has pointed out, none of these people would be considered to be impoverished, suggesting that something other

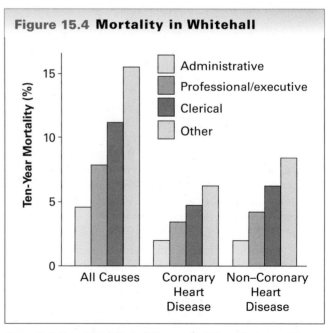

Figure 15.4 Mortality in Whitehall

Source: M. G. Marmot & J. F. Mustard, Coronary heart disease from a population perspective, in R. G. Evans, M. L. Barer, & T. R. Marmor, eds., *Why are some people healthy and others not?* (New York: Aldine de Gruyter, 1994), p. 206.

than deprivation is responsible for the differences. One suggestion as to what might be responsible comes from Sapolsky's (1995) studies of baboons.

In baboons, social status can be assessed by observing such things as which animals will defer to others when competing for food, avoid eye contact, or make submissive gestures. The physiological correlates of social status can be studied by analyzing blood samples. Dominant and submissive baboons differ in a wide variety of measures (Sapolsky, 1995). Dominant males show reduced concentrations of cortisol, higher levels of high-density lipoprotein cholesterol (the so-called "good cholesterol" associated with reduced risk of heart disease in humans), lower blood pressure, and higher levels of circulating lymphocytes than submissive baboons under resting conditions. In other words, dominance is associated with changed neuroendocrine, autonomic, and immune profiles. When stressed, perhaps in a fight, dominant baboons show a larger response on many of these parameters, but a faster return to resting conditions, suggesting that they are better able to recover from provocation. There is a parallel between these findings and further observations that have been made on the Whitehall civil servants. Marmot and Theorell (1988) found that although all grades of civil servants showed elevated blood pressure during the workday, the blood pressures of administrators dropped significantly more than that of lower-grade workers when they went home.

Thus, social status may have an effect on longevity through some of the stress-related physiological effects with which it correlates. Some of these effects may, in turn, depend on other psychosocial factors.

Controllability

A person's ability to control potentially stressful events often reduces their harmful effects (Seligman, 1975). Interestingly, there is evidence that people do not even need to truly *have*

Here the baboon in the centre is showing dominant status. Baboons make good subjects of the effects of status, because their hierarchies are clearly marked and consistent. In this way these animals resemble members of highly structured human hierarchies, such as feudal systems and the civil service.

control over events to experience these benefits, they need only *believe* they have control. In one study (Geer, Davison, & Gatchel, 1970), subjects were shocked while performing a reaction time task. After the first part of the study, half the subjects were led to believe that they could reduce the shocks by reacting more quickly, while the other half were told that all shocks would be reduced. Subjects who were led to believe that their behaviour could influence the shocks showed lower skin conductance arousal (a response mediated by the sympathetic system) than those who were not led to believe they had control—even though all experienced the same shocks.

There is also a sizeable literature indicating that people differ with respect to how much control they believe they exert in their daily lives. People who have an **internal locus of control** see themselves as the masters of their own destiny, whereas those with an **external locus of control** see themselves as being buffeted by the random events of the world. There is evidence that people with an internal locus of control are protected against the harmful effects of stress on their health. For example, Krause and Stryker (1984) found that men with an internal locus of control experienced fewer health problems in the face of economic and job problems.

Ideas about psychological control have influenced explanations of the effects of job stress on disease. Karasek, Theorell, Schwartz, Pieper, and Alfredsson (1982) proposed a model that characterizes occupations on two dimensions: psychological demand and decision control. Psychological demand refers to factors such as the workload, time constraints, and pace of activities involved in the job; decision latitude refers to whether the job provides the opportunity to exercise skills or discretion to control activities. Jobs have been categorized on these dimensions in surveys of workers or by having people rate their own jobs on characteristics that reflect the concepts of demand and decision latitude. Figure 15.5 presents the results of one such exercise. Some jobs are rated as involving both high demands and low control (for example, being a waiter or postal worker), a combination that has been described as high-strain. Other jobs (for example, being a forester or night watchman) which are rated as low in psychological demand or high in decisional control are described as low-strain. Note that such designations are based on the averaged responses of a variety of workers and may not accurately describe the experience of all individuals in those occupations.

High strain has been shown to be associated with increased risk of morbidity and mortality due to cardiovascular disease (Karasek, Baker, Marxer, Ahlborn, & Theorell, 1981) in prospective studies. LaCroix and Haynes (1987) found that men and women in high-strain positions were anywhere from one-and-a-half to five times as likely to develop coronary heart disease over a ten-year period as those in low-strain positions.

Social Support

One of the most pervasive and consistent psychosocial variables that has been related to health status is social support: the extent to which an individual feels connected to other

Figure 15.5 **Karasek Job Strain Model**

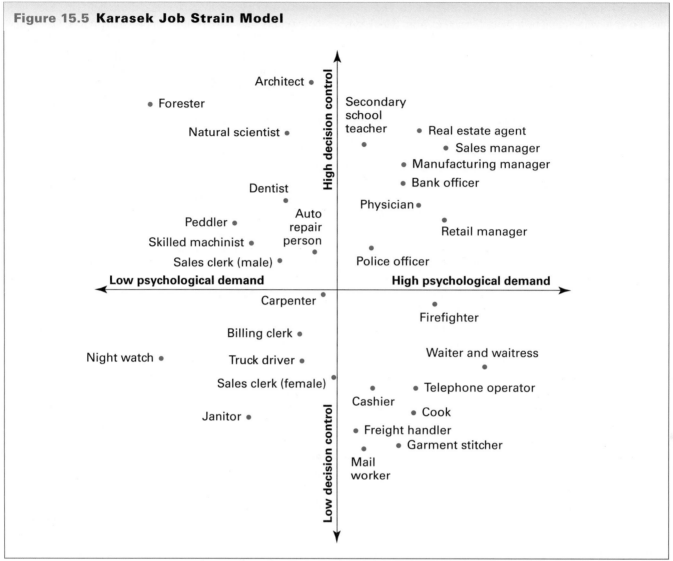

people in meaningful ways. It is usually assessed by asking people about the number of others with whom they have frequent contact, whether there is anyone they feel comfortable confiding in, whether they are involved with social groups, etc. Social support appears to be associated with effects on a remarkably wide range of health indicators. House, Landis, and Umberson (1988) reviewed a series of studies showing that the presence of social support is associated with reduced mortality, especially in men. The beneficial effect of social support was comparable in magnitude to the well-known harmful effect of smoking.

The absence of social support also appears to exacerbate existing disease. Williams et al. (1992) and Case et al. (1992) both found that among patients with diagnosed coronary heart disease or a history of heart attack, those with minimal social support were less likely to survive than those with adequate social support.

Social support may even play a role in the impact of stressful events in nonhuman primates. Sapolsky observed that socially unskillful baboons (for example, those who had difficulty determining whether a rival was threatening or not), and baboons that did not play or groom with others had elevated basal blood cortisol concentrations.

Although the effects of social support have been well documented, the reasons for these effects are a matter of some controversy. Certainly one possibility is that social support may be associated with material support in times of stress. Social support may also provide a means of discovering or testing coping strategies or a way of altering stress appraisals, as suggested by the transactional model. Yet another possibility, implied by the findings of Sapolsky and others, is that there is some direct connection between social interaction and physiological states—that, in some as-yet-unexplained manner, social interaction and/or a sociable attitude stimulates or inhibits hormone release.

We will return to some of these issues elsewhere in this chapter. For now, however, let us turn to some specific disease states.

DISEASE STATES AND PSYCHOSOCIAL FACTORS

Psychosocial factors have been considered possible contributors to many diseases; indeed, it has been argued that all diseases have a psychosocial component. After a brief look at infectious disease, we will focus on two specific diseases for which psychosocial factors have been particularly implicated. These can serve as examples or models for the examination of such factors on other medical conditions as well.

Infectious Disease

Sarah is a student in her first year of medical school. It is her fifth at university. She is in very good health, a competitive athlete, and careful to watch her diet. She had just finished a gruelling set of exams and was on an airplane, flying home for Christmas break, when she noticed the first symptoms of what she recognized as a flu. By the start of the next day, she was experiencing full-blown symptoms: high temperature, aches and pains, a deep cough, and a runny nose. Sarah, who is not used to being sick, was amazed by the intensity of her bout with the flu. She was totally without energy and barely able to make it out of bed on Christmas morning. Eventually, her symptoms improved, but there were still residual effects when she returned to the university for studies after the break.

Many people attribute the onset or the intensity of infectious diseases such as colds or the flu to the stresses and strains of daily life. Furthermore, the symptoms of some infectious diseases, such as genital herpes, often seem to be exacerbated (made worse or made to flare up) during periods of emotional turmoil. What is the evidence that such casual observations may be valid?

Several studies have addressed the issue of whether stressful life conditions predict or increase the likelihood of infectious diseases (Cohen & Herbert, 1996). In one of the most intriguing, Cohen, Tyrrell, and Smith (1993) exposed healthy individuals to nasal drops containing various respiratory viruses or uninfected saline. Subjects were quarantined for seven days after experimental exposure and during this time a number of indications of progression of infection were measured, including severity of cold symptoms, immune system indications of infection taken from nasal fluids, and measurements of mucus in nasal tissue. Prior to the study, subjects were assessed with respect to the number of stressful life events that had occurred to them in the previous 12 months, the perceived stressfulness of their lives, and their current level of negative emotions. Subjects with higher perceived stress and negative affect were indeed more likely both to

have clinical evidence of a cold and to show "hard" immune system changes indicative of infection than subjects with lower stress. The underlying mechanism by which psychological stress might increase susceptibility to infection is unknown, but may reflect the functioning of the HPA axis.

There have been several studies of psychological influences on diseases mediated by the herpes viruses; for example, genital herpes, cold sores, and mononucleosis. One of the features of herpes infections is that, once a person is exposed, they remain in his or her body in a latent state and may only manifest in clinical disease occasionally. Hoon and colleagues (Hoon et al., 1991) studied herpes symptoms in college students and reported that the general effect of stress on vulnerability to disease was associated with their recurrence.

It is perhaps natural to suspect that such stress effects on infectious diseases must be mediated by influences of stress on the immune system. For example, Glaser and colleagues (Glaser, Pearl, Kiecolt-Glaser, & Malarkey 1994) measured the presence of antibodies to Epstein-Barr virus in medical students known to be infected with the virus, during a baseline period and during their fall and spring examinations. Both examination periods were associated with increases in levels of antibodies to the virus, indicative of reactivation of the virus. However, we still have no clear understanding of the precise nature of the immune mechanisms responsible.

One Sunday morning, Marty awakened with a peculiar burning sensation in his stomach. He attributed it to having overdone things the night before. He skipped breakfast, as he was inclined to do, and spent a typical Sunday morning watching football. The aching increased until the normally stoic Marty began complaining. After a late lunch it got better. Throughout the next two weeks the burning pain returned periodically, but not every day, so he didn't really think much was amiss. Anyway, he was getting married that month and had no time to think about it. During Marty's honeymoon, the pains increased. An hour into the drive home, Marty had to pull the car over because he was experiencing extreme pain and vomiting blood. He was taken to the nearest hospital where he was diagnosed with a perforated ulcer. He was told he was lucky to be alive.

Although he recovered well following hospitalization and changes to his diet, Marty's marriage did not thrive and after a few years he and his wife divorced. He would later confide to friends that the weeks and months leading up to his marriage were full of psychological conflict for him due, among other things, to his ambivalent feelings about getting married. He felt that he had limited options. He attributed his ulcer to his psychological condition at the time.

Ulcer Disease

If you were asked to name a disease determined by stress and emotion, there is a good chance ulcers would come to mind. The association has been long established in the media and public consciousness, perhaps because we are very conscious of the influence of emotional states on the gut. Most of us have experienced discomfort in the stomach during emotionally charged times and so it is not difficult to believe that emotional distress may lead to disease of the gut. Indeed, the ulcer was one of the limited set of disorders that Alexander and others viewed as psychosomatically caused and it has been the focus of substantial theoretical analysis. As we shall see, there is some truth to these preconceptions. However, ulcer disease also illustrates the complexity of disease processes, since recent research has suggested a bacteriological cause of ulcers.

First of all, what is an ulcer? A gastric ulcer is an erosion in the lining of the stomach or duodenum. Ulcers can be life-threatening when they perforate but even when they don't they can produce excruciating pain. The events leading to an ulcer are thought to involve an interaction between the stomach's own digestive juices and its natural defence. The digestive juices, one of which is hydrochloric acid, are produced and secreted in the stomach in order to digest food. They are highly corrosive to living tissue, including the stomach itself, which is normally protected by a mucosal lining. Ulcers occur when the digestive fluids penetrate the mucosal lining, thus leaving the stomach or duodenal wall defenceless against their corrosive action.

But what role might psychosocial factors play in the development of such lesions? Here we are left to piece together lines of information from clinical observations and experimental studies in animals and humans. Clinicians have long observed that stressful life circumstances are often associated with the development of ulcers in patients. Alexander (1950) argued that a very specific but unconscious psychological conflict involving an unsatisfied desire for love, symbolized by food, produced a state of chronic readiness to eat and digest which, by stimulating physiological accompaniments of digestion, produced breakdown of the stomach lining and consequent disease. The treatment would then involve psychoanalysis geared toward uncovering the underlying conflict.

Little research has supported either the etiologic or the therapeutic components of Alexander's theory and its influence is mostly of historic interest. There have, however, been significant advances in our understanding of other psychological dimensions of the disease. Many of these follow from the understanding that the brain is an important regulator of the stomach and gut, through several of the autonomic and neuroendocrine mechanisms described earlier. We know, for example, that during stress-induced sympathetic arousal, blood flow is diverted away from the stomach lining to the skeletal muscles. It has been suggested that this may decrease the effectiveness of the mucosal lining of the stomach in protecting it against digestive juices, since blood vessels within that lining are thought to play a role in the deactivation of gastric fluids (Pinel, 1997).

Hydrochloric acid appears to be a necessary but not a sufficient factor in the development of ulcers. Another factor is slow, rhythmic contractions of the stomach (slower than two per minute) that are different from the more frequent rhythmic contractions associated with the feeding cycle (Weiner, 1996). When such contractions occur in rats, gastric erosions develop shortly thereafter (Garrick et al., 1989). Although this association has not been observed in humans, the animal observations make the argument for stress as a factor in ulcer disease more plausible. (See the Focus box for a discussion of causal inference.)

But what is the evidence that stress can cause ulcers in animals? Since Selye's original observation first inspired the general adaptation syndrome, several different methods have been used to demonstrate that manipulations of stress can produce ulcers. One common method is to restrain experimental animals by wrapping them tightly in a tube or some other device; restrained animals reliably show the development of more gastric ulceration than controls (Brodie, 1971). Although this is a coarse procedure that does not provide a very realistic model of human stressors, it has the advantage of reliability and gives experimenters the opportunity to investigate further some of the mechanisms responsible for ulcers.

Such research has indicated that various brain regions involved in the regulation of emotional states are crucial for the development of restraint-induced ulcers. Peter Henke of St. Francis Xavier University, for example, has done extensive research showing that direct manipulation of the central nucleus of the amygdala by electrical stimulation increases gastric ulceration (Henke, 1988, 1992), whereas other manipulations, such as electrical stimulation of areas of the hippocampus that, in turn, affect the amygdala, are associated with reductions in ulceration due to restraint stress (Henke, 1990). Such findings not only help to establish the importance of brain regions in determining whether or not ulceration will occur during stress, but given the importance of these regions in current theories of emotion, they emphasize the relevance of emotional changes to the etiology of ulcers (LeDoux 1993).

Perhaps the most elegant studies implicating psychological factors in the development of ulcers were reported in the late 1960s and early 1970s by Jay Weiss of Rockefeller University. Weiss was interested in separating the physical and the psychological aspects of stress. The stressor he employed was electric shock delivered to the rat's tail by an electrode. In one study (Weiss, 1970), rats were exposed to shock predicted by a warning signal (a beeping tone). Another group of rats was exposed to both shocks and tones, but the events occurred at random so that the tones did not reliably predict the aversive shocks. Another group was exposed to identical environmental conditions, but no tones or shocks. Examinations of the stomachs of these animals indicated that

Focus — *Inferring Causality in Health Psychology*

Is there a will to live? Does stress cause cancer? Does a particular kind of personality make one likely to become arthritic? Today, while there is increasing acceptance of the contribution of psychological factors to illness and disease, many people, including health psychologists, continue to be extremely skeptical. How do we begin to sort out reasonable answers to such questions?

As explained in Chapter 4, the gold standard for establishing causality is the experimental study, in which an investigator manipulates one possible causal variable, while holding all other variables constant, and observes the effects of this manipulation on an outcome variable. In the health sciences, however, it is often difficult, for practical or ethical reasons, to meet the strictures of the experimental method. The development of a disease such as rheumatoid arthritis, for example, may occur over many years, and is difficult to study in a laboratory. Similarly, it would obviously be unethical to conduct a study in which people were exposed to severe stress to establish the role of stress in disease. Epidemiological and correlational research (discussed in Chapter 4) can fill in some of the gaps. Hill (1965; see also Timmreck, 1994) has outlined a number of criteria that may be applied in order to evaluate whether a psychological variable plays a causal role. A basic criterion is *association*. The case that there is some significant relationship is further supported by *consistency* across numerous studies and *strength* of association—that is, the

variability in a psychological variable accounts for a great deal of the variability in an outcome. Yet none of these criteria show that the relationship is one of cause and effect. The fourth criterion, *precedence*, requires evidence that the alleged cause existed *before* the outcome developed. A common but expensive means of establishing precedence is the **longitudinal study**, in which a large group of people are evaluated with respect to the existence of psychological or behavioural features and are then followed up, often years or decades later, to determine whether they have developed a disease. There have been several influential longitudinal studies that have helped establish precedence for psychological variables. The final criterion relates to the logic of explanation. There must be both a biologically and a psychologically plausible mechanism linking a characteristic to the disease or illness outcome.

Animal models or analogue studies are often used to investigate possible mechanisms (American Psychosomatic Society, 1996). For example, Anisman and his colleagues (Sklar & Anisman, 1979) at Carleton University have conducted studies investigating the influence of stressful experiences on growth of malignant tumours in mice to clarify the processes by which stress might affect cancer. Of course, the things done to experimental mice are not much like the stresses humans experience, and mice are not humans; we must be very careful when generalizing from one species to another. However, it

may be possible to illuminate the forces that affect human disease.

In an analogue study (also discussed in Chapter 4), real-life circumstances may be mimicked in a laboratory and their influences evaluated experimentally. For example, Ewart, Taylor, Kraemer, and Agras (1991) were interested in physiological reactions to marital disputes in hostile and non-hostile people. They staged arguments in a laboratory and measured the effects on men and women of both hostility and disputes. Of course there is no guarantee that the artificial laboratory setup mimicked conditions in the natural environment realistically. However, to the extent that such a study reveals theoretically coherent outcomes, it can help build up a plausible explanation of the relationship between, say, hostility or marital disputes and a health outcome.

A final test of causality is the intervention trial. If a particular psychological or behavioural variable plays a causal role in a disease, it should be possible to either prevent or treat the disease by changing that variable. Such trials follow all the logic of experimentation discussed earlier; again, the gold standard is considered to be the randomized controlled trial in which people are randomly assigned either to receive a treatment or not. (See Chapter 16 for a fuller discussion of the experimental evaluation of therapies.) There have been several influential controlled intervention trials in this field. ▲

the unshocked rats had very little stomach ulceration; rats that were exposed to shocks without warning showed extensive stomach ulceration. The interesting finding was that rats

that were shocked after a warning tone showed degrees of ulceration only slightly higher than the unshocked rats. Note that rats in the two "shock" conditions received the *identical* number and intensity of shocks; the only factor that could have explained why one group had more lesions than the other was the *predictability* of the stressor.

In a later study, Weiss (1971) investigated the effects of controllability: the ability to escape from or avoid a stressor. In these studies rats were placed in cages with a wheel (see Figure 15.6). For two of the groups of rats, shock was administered through an electrode attached to the tail, while the third group received no shocks. In one of the shocked groups, turning the wheel would delay the shock, or stop it if it had started. In the other group, turning the wheel had no influence on the administration of the shock. However, because they were wired up in series, these two rats received *exactly* the same number and intensity of shocks. The difference was that one group of rats was able to control the stress, while the other was not. The results parallelled those found in the predictability study: the unshocked rats showed little ulceration; the animals that received shocks they could not control showed substantial degrees of ulceration. The rats that could control shock stress showed only about one-third as much ulceration as the rats that could not control shock. Although we must be cautious when making comparisons with humans, these studies provide very strong evidence that manipulation of psychological variables can affect gastric ulceration. Moreover, they are consistent with evidence already reviewed that suggests that lack of control mediates the effects of potentially stressful events.

While studies of restraint and other forms of stress have helped to map the neural pathways that may be implicated in stress effects, there has been relatively little research in recent years extending these concepts to ulcer disease in humans. So far, our knowledge of stress and its psychosocial determinants has had little effect on the treatment or prevention of ulcers.

In recent years, considerable excitement has been aroused in the medical community by the discovery of a bacterium, *Helicobacter pylori*, that is believed to play a primary causal role in the genesis of ulcers (Rathbone & Healey, 1989). The bacterium is present in the stomachs of large proportions of individuals with ulcer disease and antibodies to it are present in their serum. Moreover, treatment with drugs to eliminate *H. pylori* produces improvement in affected patients (Graham et al., 1992). Does this discovery mean that stress is no longer

---

Figure 15.6 **Weiss's Apparatus for Investigating the Effects of Controllability**

To shock control   To shock source   No connection to shock source

Rats in shock-stress experiment. The rat on the left receives a shock through its tail, but can control the shocks by turning the wheel; the rat in the middle receives the same shocks, but wheel activity in the middle cage has no effect on shocks; the rat on the right receives no shocks.

Source: From Weiss, J. (1972). Psychological factors in stress and disease. Copyright © 1972 by Scientific American, Inc. All rights reserved.

relevant to ulcer disease? Not at all. Although it is highly likely that *H. pylori* plays an important role in the genesis of ulcer disease, it cannot be said that that role is an exclusive one. As Weiner (1996) has pointed out, antibodies to the bacterium have also been found in the serum of healthy controls. The bacterium also appears in association with a number of other diseases, calling into question its specificity of action. Finally, patients have been shown to improve even though the infection has not been eradicated. In any case, the discovery of a bacterial agent is in no way inconsistent with the findings that implicate psychological conditions. It seems reasonable that psychological factors, such as stress, would lead to vulnerability to a physical agent. As discussed in this chapter, and in earlier chapters in this book, interactions between mind and body are complex, and there is rarely a single factor that accounts for any condition.

Cardiovascular Disease

Diseases of the cardiovascular system—the heart and the blood vessels—are the leading cause of death and disability in Western societies. The two disease states that account for most of these deaths are **ischemic heart disease**, in which blood supply to the heart becomes compromised, leading to a **myocardial infarction** (heart attack), and stroke, in which the blood supply to the brain is interrupted, leading to death of neural tissue. The disease processes underlying both endpoints are sufficiently similar that they are considered two sides of the same coin. In Canada, heart disease and stroke account for approximately 41 percent of deaths per year (Heart and Stroke Foundation of Canada, 1992). Raw mortality statistics, however, do not tell the whole story. Cardiovascular diseases are responsible for more **potential years of life lost (PYLL)**—a measure calculated by subtracting age of death from an individual's life expectancy—than any other cause of death except cancer and injuries. For example, it has been estimated that in 1995, premature death from cardiovascular disease resulted in approximately 90,000 years of life lost for Canadian women and approximately 204,000 for Canadian men (Heart and Stroke Foundation of Canada, 1998). Cardiovascular disease also causes significant suffering and disability among survivors. Techniques for early identification and treatment have increased the chances of survival, and advances in rehabilitation have also improved the prospects for recovery. Nevertheless, many people face a life of diminished abilities, anxiety, and suffering, and their family members must also adjust to the consequences of the disease.

Because of its preeminence as a health problem in contemporary society, cardiovascular disease has been the focus of intensive research, and a great deal has been learned about the disease. This knowledge has paid off in a dramatic decline in death rates, which have dropped by almost 50 percent since the 1950s. As part of this research, the behavioural and psychological processes related to developing, triggering, and recovering from cardiovascular disease have been well studied. In this section, we will summarize the major concepts and findings in this area.

Cardiovascular Disease Processes

To understand how psychosocial processes may contribute to cardiovascular disease, you need a basic understanding of the disease processes themselves. The cardiovascular system provides nutrients and oxygen, the basic requirements for life, to all tissues of the body, and serves as a highway for the elimination of waste products as well. To do this, the heart acts as a pump, delivering blood, with its various constituents—platelets, plasma, etc.—through an extensive branching network of arteries, arterioles, capillaries, venules, and veins. The blood vessels consist of an opening, or lumen, and layers of cells that serve as the "tubing." The control of blood supply within this closed system is an intricate matter affected by a number of factors. It is sometimes helpful to think of an analogy with a water pumping system where the heart is the pump and the vasculature is a hose. As the heart pumps, the blood constituents will be transmitted through the tube in cycles that correspond to the pumping action. The peak of the wave of blood flow corresponds to the contraction of the left ventricle of the heart, the main chamber that pumps blood into the major arteries of the body at a point during the cardiac cycle called the *systole*. But when the pump is at rest, at a point in the cardiac cycle termed the *diastole*, blood will still be flowing, albeit at a much reduced pressure. The pressure of the blood flowing through the vasculature is commonly measured in your doctor's office with the use of a sphygmomanometer (blood pressure cuff) and expressed in two numbers: **systolic blood pressure/diastolic blood pressure**, in terms of the number of millimetres of mercury displaced by the measurement device (for example, "130/70").

Persisting with our analogy of the pump and hose, we can see that the pressure within the hose can be influenced by two factors. The first is the simple amount of blood being pushed into the hose with each beat of the pump; the more blood, the greater the pressure, everything else being equal. The second is the diameter of the tubing. Think of a garden hose. What happens if you squeeze it? (See Figure 15.7.) The pressure of the fluid within increases and the spray will be longer. Much the same thing happens when the diameter of the blood vessels

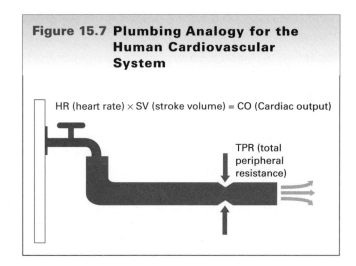

Figure 15.7 Plumbing Analogy for the Human Cardiovascular System

HR (heart rate) × SV (stroke volume) = CO (Cardiac output)

TPR (total peripheral resistance)

is narrowed. Thus, blood pressure is a consequence of two major variables: **cardiac output** (the amount of blood pumped by the heart) and **total peripheral resistance** (the diameter of the blood vessels). Cardiac output is itself determined by two other variables: the rate at which the heart beats (commonly measured in beats per minute) and the amount of blood ejected from the heart (stroke volume).

This excursion into the physiology of the cardiovascular system is important, because it allows us to begin to explain the mechanisms through which psychological factors can affect disease processes. Recall from our discussion of the autonomic nervous system that one of its targets is the cardiovascular system. Sympathetic and parasympathetic fibres can affect both cardiac output and peripheral resistance. Activation of components of the sympathetic system affecting beta-adrenergic receptors on the heart will speed up the rate at which it beats, producing an increase in cardiac output and blood pressure. Activation of other components of the sympathetic system affecting alpha-adrenergic receptors can cause constriction of the blood vessels, again yielding an increase in blood pressure. Activity of the parasympathetic system opposes these effects. Complex feedback mechanisms, involving blood pressure receptors located in the carotid artery, allow the hypothalamus to regulate blood pressure. In this way, the brain is always adjusting output and resistance to maintain blood pressure within certain limits.

Recall, as well, that the neuroendocrine system also influences the cardiovascular system. In particular, release of the catecholamines epinephrine and norepinephrine from the adrenal medulla reinforces the changes produced by sympathetic nervous system arousal, producing increased heart rate, peripheral resistance, and blood pressure. In addition to these effects, however, note that the catecholamines are distributed to the heart and vasculature by circulating *through* the bloodstream. Catecholamines can thereby not only affect the ongoing activity of the heart and vasculature, but also interact with blood constituents, such as the blood cells, themselves. Thus these two basic physiological systems, both of which are regulated by the brain and consequently responsive to psychological influences, are ideally located to exert an ongoing influence on the system in which cardiovascular disease takes place.

Cardiovascular Risk Factors

Deaths due to myocardial infarction can result from disturbances in the normal pumping rhythm of the heart (**arrhythmias**) or from compromised supply of blood to the heart itself. These proximal causes of death, as well as stroke, are influenced primarily by an underlying disease state called **atherosclerosis**: a buildup of deposits, known as *plaques*, on the walls of the blood vessels. The growth of atherosclerotic plaques can ultimately narrow the openings of arteries enough to compromise the blood supply to the heart or the brain, leading to myocardial infarction or stroke (see Figure 15.8).

Atherosclerotic plaques are quite complex structures built up from matter deposited on arterial linings over the course of a lifetime: primarily lipids (blood fats, especially cholesterol),

but also blood platelets and cell fibres. Autopsy studies have shown the development of atherosclerosis (**atherogenesis**) as early as two years of age. Most people show signs of atherosclerosis by their thirties. These observations emphasize the long time frame over which the disease process develops. Over decades, subtle influences on the disease process can play an important role. On the other hand, the slow development of the disease process gives plenty of scope for preventive interventions.

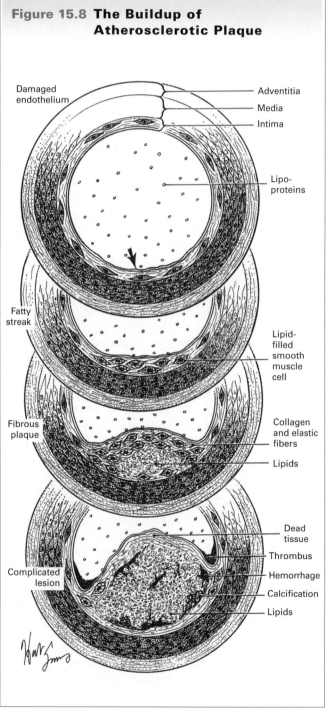

Figure 15.8 The Buildup of Atherosclerotic Plaque

Damaged endothelium — Adventitia — Media — Intima — Lipo-proteins

Fatty streak — Lipid-filled smooth muscle cell

Fibrous plaque — Collagen and elastic fibers — Lipids

Complicated lesion — Dead tissue — Thrombus — Hemorrhage — Calcification — Lipids

Source: M. DeBakey & A. Gotto, *The living heart* (New York: Grosset & Dunlap, 1977), p. 111.

But what do atherosclerotic plaques have to do with behavioural or psychosocial variables? For one thing, individual health-related behaviours may contribute directly to atherogenesis. Dietary factors, such as frequent consumption of fat and cholesterol, may make lipids available for plaque formation. Smoking, too, is thought to play a role in atherogenesis. High blood cholesterol and cigarette smoking are considered major **controllable risk factors** for cardiovascular disease. Exercise is a **protective factor** that is thought to reduce risk of cardiovascular disease, at least in part through the prevention of atherosclerotic buildup. Another potential source of atherogenesis lies in the consequences of the ANS and endocrinal regulatory mechanisms discussed above.

Blood pressure can vary quite substantially over the course of a day. Large variations can cause turbulence in the blood vessels, particularly at branch points, which applies shear stress powerful enough to damage the cells of the vessel walls. According to one theory of plaque formation, lipids, blood platelets, and other constituents recruited to fix the walls become gathering spots for other atherogenic material. Additionally, circulating neuroendocrine factors such as the catecholamines may contribute to plaque formation by affecting the tendency of blood platelets to adhere to one another.

Yet another factor that contributes to risk of cardiovascular disease is **hypertension**, a characteristically high level of resting blood pressure (defined as a reading of more than 140/80 under precisely defined conditions in the doctor's office) Hypertension can result from a variety of background causes, but in approximately 90% of cases it is "essential," meaning that a simple cause cannot be identified.

Psychosocial Factors in Cardiovascular Disease

The activity of the cardiovascular system is clearly and sometimes profoundly altered by psychosocial stimuli. In one study, healthy young men were exposed to four standardized situations, each lasting three minutes, after resting comfortably for 30 minutes (Prkachin, Carew, Mills, & McCarthy, unpublished manuscript). In one situation, they worked on a difficult concept-formation test. In a second, they performed mental arithmetic. In a third situation, they performed another common laboratory stress task, the Stroop colour-word conflict test, in which subjects identify the colour of ink in which a colour-word is written (for example, the word "red" written in blue ink) as rapidly as possible. In the fourth situation, a female research assistant entered the room and sat staring silently at the subject, who was told he had three minutes to make a favourable impression. Systolic and diastolic blood pressure increased for all four tasks, most dramatically the uncomfortable "favourable impressions test" (Borkovec, Stone, O'Brien, & Kaloupek, 1974). Hundreds of similar studies using the **stress reactivity paradigm** have shown that a host of cardiovascular functions are responsive to changes in psychological conditions.

In 1984, Krantz and Manuck formally hypothesized that the risk of cardiovascular disease increases with **cardiovascular reactivity**: how much an individual's cardiovascular function changes in response to a psychologically significant stimulus.

The study of cardiovascular reactivity has provided some important insights. Commonly measured cardiovascular functions such as heart rate, blood pressure, and peripheral resistance can be influenced readily by psychological stressors (Turner, 1994), but so too can hormones such as epinephrine, norepinephrine, and cortisol (Dimsdale & Ziegler, 1991; Kuhn, 1989). More subtle changes in the cardiovascular system, such as the percentage of blood pumped by the left ventricle during each beat (Ironson et al., 1992; Legault, Langer, Armstrong, & Freeman, 1995) and even abnormalities in the motion of the heart's chamber walls can also be produced by psychological stress (Rozanski et al., 1988). Mills and Prkachin (1993), at the University of Waterloo, even found that exposure to psychological stressors could reverse the reduction in "stickiness" of blood platelets produced by "healthy" dietary supplements.

Manuck and colleagues (Manuck, Kaplan, Adams, & Clarkson, 1989; Manuck, Kaplan, & Clarkson, 1983) have also provided experimental evidence that cardiovascular reactivity contributes to the development of atherosclerosis in cynomolgus monkeys raised in an experimental colony. The monkeys in these studies were fed a high-cholesterol diet. Heart rate was measured at rest and while the monkeys were threatened by a "monkey glove" that had been associated with previous episodes of capture. At the end of each study, the researchers measured atherosclerotic deposits on the arteries serving the animals' hearts. Monkeys that showed a higher increase in heart rate in reaction to threat also showed significantly greater atherosclerotic deposits. In other work, Kaplan et al. have shown that social disruption in colonies of cynomolgus monkeys can promote the development of atherosclerosis, even if the animals are not fed an atherogenic diet (Kaplan et al., 1983).

Recent evidence suggests that these findings generalize to humans. David Spence and colleagues at the University of Western Ontario have been studying a large sample of middle-aged men and women for several years. A number of measurements were taken, including an ultrasound assessment of plaque buildup on the carotid arteries. The best predictor of worsening atherosclerosis over a two-year period was the magnitude of systolic blood pressure increase during a difficult version of the Stroop colour-word conflict test (Barnett, Spence, Manuck, & Jennings 1997).

Psychological Factors in Cardiovascular Disease

The great Canadian physician William Osler was one of the earliest students of the modern era to draw attention to the association between styles of behaviour and heart disease. He described the typical patient with atherosclerosis as a "keen and ambitious man, the indicator of whose engine is always at 'full speed ahead'" (Osler, 1910, p. 839).

American cardiologists Friedman and Rosenman (1959) hypothesized the existence of a pattern of behaviour that increases risk of myocardial infarction and death, demonstrated by "any person who is aggressively involved in a chronic, incessant struggle to achieve more and more in less and less time, and if required to do so, against the opposing efforts of other things or other persons" (Friedman & Rosenman 1974,

p. 67). Friedman and Rosenman developed a structured interview to identify people with this behaviour pattern, which they termed Type A. This was an important advance, because it lent itself to systematic epidemiological investigations. In the landmark Western Collaborative Group Study, Friedman and others did comprehensive assessments of the health and health habits of more than 3000 people, who were followed systematically over the next ten years. Mortality statistics revealed two important findings. First, people diagnosed as Type A were approximately twice as likely as others to die from heart disease. Second, risk associated with Type A behaviour was independent of other risk factors for heart disease, such as smoking. This appeared to be the first clear identification of a psychological characteristic that met conventional criteria for designating something a "risk factor."

Not all studies, however, have confirmed an association between Type A behaviour and heart disease. Part of the reason may be incorrect assessment for Type A in earlier studies, as discussed in the focus on Type A. But subsequent evidence suggests that the risk factor lies in only some of the components of the Type A pattern. Look again at the variety of characteristics or behaviours subsumed under the Type A label: hyperalertness, time-urgency, job involvement, competitiveness, and hostility.

According to recent studies, it is not this man's stressful job and drive to get ahead that put him at risk so much as the hostility he is expressing.

Do these components always go together? It is possible, for example, to imagine someone who is hyperalert but not competitive, or time-urgent but not hostile. (See the focus box.)

Focus   *Are You a Type A?*

Like stress, the concept of Type A behaviour has become part of popular culture. Many people, particularly university students, seem almost to pride themselves on being "Type A," despite the implication of health risk. This self-identification is understandable, given the ways Type A has been described in both the professional and popular literature. The emphasis is often on Type A individuals as busy, achievement-oriented, committed to and perhaps overidentified with their jobs, typically engaged in multiple tasks and pressed for time. What student (or single parent, middle manager, or taxi driver) would not use such terms to describe himself or herself at one time or another?

But people who identify themselves as Type A are very often wrong. This is because the characteristics referred to above are usually *not* the main distinguishing features in epidemiologic studies or clinical settings. The gold standard for assessing Type A behaviour is the *structured interview*

(Chesney, Eagleston, & Rosenman, 1981). This interview is designed as a kind of behavioural trap for people who are Type A. The questions focus on themes such as job involvement, competitiveness, anger, and time pressure. But it is the style of presentation of the questions that is critical for eliciting Type A characteristics, and it is the style with which the interviewee responds that is pivotal in establishing the diagnosis. In other words, it is more a matter of *how* you say things than of *what* you say. Indeed, when people are trained in diagnosing Type A from interviews, they are often admonished not to listen to the words.

The features that contribute to the diagnosis—the Type A *stylistics* as they are called—are generally behavioural markers of the key Type A characteristics of hyperarousal, competitiveness, hostility, and anger-proneness. For example, in assessing hyperarousal, an evaluator will listen for a high rate of speaking, an emphatic speaking style, speech that contains

clipped words or sentences, or quick responses to questions. In assessing competitiveness, the evaluator will listen for behaviours such as interrupting, talking over top of the interviewer, or challenging the interviewer. Hostility or anger-proneness are indicated by a certain tone of voice or certain categorical attitudes about people. Increasingly, nonverbal behaviours such as changes in facial expression are being incorporated into the assessment of Type A behaviour (Chesney, Ekman, Friesen, Black, & Hecker, 1990).

Often these behavioural markers are inconsistent with what people say about themselves. For example, a person may report being extraordinarily busy and pressured, yet speak at a calm, measured pace. Regardless of how objectively busy and pressured that person is, he or she would be unlikely to be diagnosed as Type A by the formal assessment systems used today. ▲

The focus of recent research has shifted to identifying which specific components most directly affect risk of heart disease.

Consistently, measures of hostility have been associated with symptoms of heart disease and death. Hecker, Chesney, Black, and Frautschi (1988) reanalyzed data from the Western Collaborative Group Study, including the results of the structured Type A interviews, and determined that hostility was the main characteristic accounting for increased risk of heart disease. A number of studies using the Cook-Medley hostility scale—a questionnaire derived from the MMPI (Cook & Medley, 1954)—have also documented this association. For example, Barefoot, Dodge, Peterson, Dahlstrom, and Williams (1989) studied the health status of 118 lawyers who had been given the MMPI about 28 years earlier when they were healthy young adults. High hostility scores were associated with a significant increase in the likelihood of death at followup.

Not all studies have confirmed this association. However, a meta-analysis of studies in the field (Booth-Kewley & Friedman, 1987) supports the conclusion that hostility and related characteristics are a factor in cardiovascular morbidity and mortality. (Meta-analysis is a method of examining the findings of many studies as a whole. See Chapter 16 for a fuller discussion.)

But just what is this characteristic called hostility? The words we use to describe psychological characteristics or behaviours are imperfect and often fail to capture all their elements. In the case of hostility, the construct seems to involve several different features. Barefoot (1992) emphasizes three components: affective features involving a tendency to respond with anger and contempt; a cognitive/attitudinal dimension involving a tendency to view other people with cynicism and to impute bad intentions to others; and a behavioural dimension involving both direct and subtle aggressiveness and antagonism. Consistently with this analysis, subscales of the Cook-Medley scale measuring cynicism, hostile affect, and aggressive responding all predicted likelihood of early death in the study by Barefoot et al. (1989).

But how would hostility lead to health risk? What mechanism would apply? In a comprehensive analysis, Timothy Smith (1992) outlined five possible models. The **psychophysiological reactivity model** suggests that hostile people are at higher risk for various diseases because they experience exaggerated autonomic and neuroendocrine responses during stress. The **psychosocial vulnerability model** suggests that hostile people experience a more demanding interpersonal life than others. The **transactional model**, a hybrid of the first two models, posits that the behaviour of hostile individuals constructs, by its natural consequences, a social world that is antagonistic and unsupportive. Both interpersonal stressors and the lack of social support increase vulnerability. The **health behaviour model** suggests that hostile people may be more likely to engage in unhealthy behaviours (for example, smoking, drug use, high-fat diets) and less likely to have healthy practices, such as exercise. A final theory is that the link between hostility and poor health outcomes is the result of a third variable, **constitutional vulnerability**, with which they are both associated.

It is difficult to pick and choose among these alternatives because there is evidence to support each of them. For example, several studies have supported the hypothesis that hostile people show enhanced physiological arousal to psychological stress. Interestingly, however, the responses may occur only when the stressful conditions are relevant to the hostility characteristic. For example, hostile subjects differed from non-hostile subjects in their cardiovascular responses to a word-identification test only when subjects were also exposed to social harassment (Suarez & Williams, 1989). Prkachin, Mills, Kaufman, and Carew (1991) found that, unlike non-hostile people, hostile subjects showed a "slow burn" effect, in which their blood pressure increased gradually during a difficult computer task when they were led erroneously to believe their performance on the task was below par. Both the psychosocial vulnerability and the transactional model derive support from studies showing that hostile people have fewer social supports and more stressful life events (Hardy & Smith, 1988; Smith & Frohm, 1985). Finally, several studies have shown that hostile people smoke more, abuse alcohol more, consume more calories, and engage in less exercise than non-hostile people (Smith, 1992).

One relevant set of observations involves the physiological response to anger. Ironson et al. (1992) asked subjects to recall and describe an event that had made them angry, while measuring the proportion of blood ejected from the left ventricle by an imaging technique called radionuclide ventriculography. Decreased left ventricular ejection fraction (LVEF) is an indicator of compromised cardiovascular function. LVEF decreased during anger recall in coronary artery disease patients, but not in normal controls.

In recent years, evidence has emerged about the importance of another psychological characteristic—depression—in cardiovascular morbidity and mortality. Frasure-Smith, Lesperance, and Talajic (1993), from McGill University, studied over 200 patients who had recently survived a heart attack. When they had recovered sufficiently, patients were interviewed and categorized as depressed or not according to modified DSM-III-R criteria. You might wonder, wouldn't anybody having had such an experience be depressed? Indeed, sadness and worry are extremely common in such circumstances; however, people do vary in their reactions. In this study, only 16 percent of patients met the criteria for a major depressive disorder. The researchers followed these patients up six months later—an important milestone, because most deaths following a heart attack occur within that time. Depression soon after the heart attack was associated with a greater than fivefold increase in the risk of dying within six months—independently of other predictors such as disease severity and history of previous heart attack. Carney, Freedland, Rich, and Jaffe (1995) have reviewed other studies and concluded that there is consistent evidence that depression is associated with cardiovascular disease morbidity and mortality; however, most of these studies relate to people already being treated for heart disease. An interesting prospective study looked at a community sample—people born in the community of Glostrup, Denmark, in 1914 (Barefoot &

Schroll, 1996). They were assessed in 1964 and 1974 for depression, using an MMPI scale, as well a variety of physical characteristics. This study implies that the relation between depression and health risk is generalizable to a broader segment of the population. It is impossible to conclude from this study that depression precedes cardiovascular disease, because the sample was already middle-aged when depression was assessed; thus, it is possible that participants could have already developed subclinical heart disease. Risk varied with degree of depression in a graded fashion, leading the authors to conclude that whatever underlying process is involved, it reflects a continuum rather than a specific psychiatric condition.

Carney et al. (1995) have reviewed potential explanations of the impact of depression on cardiovascular disease. Two possible explanations—that the relationship simply reflects the severity of cardiovascular disease (that is, the worse the heart condition, the more depressed the patient) or that the relationship is a consequence of toxic effects of antidepressant medication—cannot be supported by the available evidence. Three other possibilities each have some support. Like the health behaviour model of hostility, there is some evidence that depression may be associated with other risk factors for heart disease, such as high blood pressure and smoking, and this association may be responsible for increased mortality. However, in both the studies of Frasure-Smith et al. (1993) and Barefoot and Schroll (1996) depression was still associated with mortality even when the effects of associated risk factors were taken into account. Another closely related possibility is that depression may affect the extent to which people follow cardiac treatment plans. If depressed people are less likely to take heart medications, for example, their likelihood of untoward consequences may increase. Yet another possibility currently under active investigation is that the relationship reflects alterations in autonomic and neuroendocrine regulation of the heart associated with depression. Depression has been found to be associated with a number of changes in autonomic function, such as increased heart rate and decreased variability of the heart rate, that are themselves predictors of complications of heart disease (Carney et al., 1995).

As we have seen, research over the past 10 to 15 years has yielded an abundance of new information about the relationship between psychosocial variables and cardiovascular disease. As this research has progressed, our ideas about the manner in which such influences operate have become more complex and more refined. We will doubtless learn much more as we move into the next century.

TREATMENT

If psychosocial factors contribute to physiological disease, it seems sensible that psychological approaches would be useful in treatment. A variety of such approaches have been developed, with varied results. Broadly speaking, two classes of intervention characterize work in this field: (1) generic approaches to the management of stress and related problems and (2) interventions directed toward specific psychosocial variables thought to play a role in the etiology of disease.

Generic stress management programs attempt to address either the physiological arousal response or the behaviours and thought processes that may play a role in eliciting arousal. Relaxation training is often used to prevent or inhibit arousal of stress-induced sympathetic and neuroendocrine responses. Techniques range from teaching the control of specific muscle groups to autogenic training, a multifaceted technique that encourages people to invoke images of warmth and heaviness.

Cognitive-behavioural techniques, which are also commonly used, focus on helping the individual identify thinking styles that promote stress, such as negative self-statements, and devise new ways of thinking and acting to counteract stress. (See Chapter 16, and compare with the examples of cognitive treatments described in Chapters 7 and 13.) Such methods are often informed implicitly or explicitly by Lazarus' transactional model and can be seen as attempts to modify appraisal and coping processes.

One influential series of interventions was performed and evaluated by Dean Ornish and colleagues (Billings, Scherwitz, Sullivan, Sparler, & Ornish 1996). Patients with evidence of coronary heart disease were given aerobic exercise, a low-fat, low-alcohol, low-sodium vegetarian diet, group support meetings, and stress management involving stretching, relaxation, breathing techniques, meditation, and guided imagery. At one and four years, these interventions were associated with a significant reduction in atherosclerotic lesions of the coronary arteries, compared to controls (for example, Gould et al., 1995). Of course, with a multifactorial intervention such as this, it is difficult to be certain about the specific importance of the stress management aspect of the intervention. However, internal analyses of the data indicated that the amount of practice patients devoted to stress management, along with dietary fat and cholesterol intake, predicted the extent of coronary lesions, suggesting that something about the stress intervention was important.

Linden and Chambers (1994), of the University of British Columbia, reported on a meta-analysis of stress management in the treatment of hypertension. Their results indicated that stress management could be as effective as the standard prescription drugs when the interventions were targeted and individualized to the patients' problems.

A variety of treatment techniques have been developed to address specific psychosocial variables. Most of this work has been informed by a cognitive-behavioural, transactional perspective. Probably the best-known example of such techniques is the Recurrent Coronary Primary Prevention Project (Friedman et al., 1986). Patients who had suffered a documented heart attack were assigned to one of two conditions. In the first condition, the patients received a standard cardiac counselling intervention involving education about risks and risk factor control. In the second condition, patients also underwent intensive counselling to change Type A behaviours. The Type A counselling, which took place in group sessions over 4 1/2 years, included education about Type A behaviour, developing self-awareness about triggers to Type A behaviour, reducing time-urgency, anger, and hostility, and increasing patience and empathy. After three years, patients who had received the Type A counselling program showed a reduction in measured Type A behaviour; they also had just over half as many recurrences of cardiac events as the control patients.

Although it is possible that the specific skills targeted in the Recurrent Coronary Prevention Project or in Ornish's intensive lifestyle intervention program may be critically important for therapeutic benefits, it is worth noting that the interventions also address several other relevant psychosocial variables. In particular, the programs emphasize and encourage social support. Indeed, as these types of intervention have evolved, they have begun to place greater emphasis on group interaction and on encouraging emotional communication (Billings et al., 1996). Undoubtedly such experiences can contribute to the development of new ways of appraising and coping. Emotional communication may also enhance ability to "process" emotional experience and promote new ways of interacting with others. There is evidence that all of these changes may play a role in promoting health and preventing disease.

PANORAMA

We have taken a long and winding excursion through the study of psychosocial influences on illness and disease. Even so, there are important areas we have not even looked into. For example, there are substantial literatures on psychosocial determinants of cancer (Spiegel & Kato, 1996), diabetes (Surwit & Williams, 1996), and pain (Turk, 1996). It is difficult to overstate the tremendous expansion of research, knowledge, and treatment that has taken place in this field since Engel's (1977) description of the biopsychosocial model. The study of psychosocial influences on illness and disease has become one of the most active areas of psychology. In addition it has attracted clinicians and scientists from many other disciplines: endocrinology, neuroscience, immunology, cardiology, clinical medicine, nursing, and epidemiology, to name but a few. It has also begun to affect public health policies throughout the Western world. Given the amount of research and attention currently being devoted to the area, our knowledge will no doubt continue to grow.

SUMMARY

There is a long history of attempts to explain the origin of illness and disease by psychological processes. Advances in psychological and physiological methods have lent a new credibility to these ideas. Increasingly, scientists have attempted to explain the occurrence of certain diseases by focussing on the physiological changes known to accompany psychological states. Such changes can be mediated in complex ways by the autonomic, neuroendocrine, and immune systems and their interactions. In addition, researchers have identified psychosocial characteristics that enhance risk and theorized about how these variables exert their effects. There is evidence that a number of disease states, including the common cold, ulcers, and heart disease, can be understood, at least in part, by examining psychological and psychophysiological variables. Findings in this area have already contributed to the development of promising treatments for physical disorders.

KEY TERMS

dualistic (p. 374)
behavioural medicine (p. 375)
health psychology (p. 375)
mechanism (p. 376)
lesions (p. 376)
nonspecific immune responses (p. 378)
cellular immunity (p. 378)
humoral immunity (p. 379)
psychoneuroimmunology (p. 379)
alarm (p. 380)
resistance (p. 380)
exhaustion (p. 380)

general adaptation syndrome (GAS) (p. 380)
transactional model (p. 381)
appraisals (p. 381)
primary appraisal (p. 381)
secondary appraisals (p. 381)
internal locus of control (p. 383)
external locus of control (p. 383)
longitudinal study (p. 387)
ischemic heart disease (p. 389)
myocardial infarction (p. 389)
potential years of life lost (PYLL) (p. 389)
systolic blood pressure/diastolic blood pressure (p. 389)
cardiac output (p. 390)

total peripheral resistance (p. 390)
arrhythmias (p. 390)
atherosclerosis (p. 390)
atherogenesis (p. 390)
controllable risk factors (p. 391)
protective factor (p. 391)
hypertension (p. 391)
stress reactivity paradigm (p. 391)
cardiovascular reactivity (p. 391)
psychophysiological reactivity model (p. 393)
psychosocial vulnerability model (p. 393)
transactional model (p. 393)
health behaviour model (p. 393)
constitutional vulnerability (p. 393)

ADDITIONAL RESOURCES

Institute for Work and Health
250 Bloor St. East
Suite 702
Toronto, ON M4W 1E6
(416) 927-2027
(416) 927-4167 fax
pbirt@iwh.on.ca

Canadian Institute for Health
    Information
377 Dalhousie Street
Suite 200
Ottawa, ON K1N 9N8
(613) 241-7860
(613) 241-8120
lpoirier@cihi.ca

Heart and Stroke Foundation of
    Canada
160 George Street
Suite 200
Ottawa, ON K1N 9M2
(613) 241-4361
(613) 241-3278 fax
itstaff@hsf.ca

www.uwlax.edu/HPER/Courses/HED-354/GAS.html
A general discussion of the components comprising the
general adaptation syndrome.

www.nhrc.navy.mil/Pubs/Abstract/71/15.html
A comparative study of Swedes and Americans based on
the Social Readjustment Rating Scale.

www.children.metrotor.on.ca/taskforce/must.html
The determinants of health are explored from a his-
torical perspective, including a discussion of the
Whitehall Study.

www.hsf.ca
The web site of the Heart and Stroke Foundation of Canada
offers current health news and statistics about cardiovascular disease and stroke among Canadians.

Chapter 16

Therapies

John Hunsley
Catherine M. Lee

Stephanie was 17 years old when her mother called a psychologist because she was concerned that Stephanie was depressed: she had scratch marks on her forearms, always dressed in black, listened to music full of themes of despair and destruction, and had written about death in her personal diary.

Stephanie's parents had divorced when she was 10. She had appeared to adjust very well to the divorce; her school grades had remained excellent, she helped around the house, and her mother considered her to be a perfect child. Both Stephanie's parents remarried, her father when she was 13 and her mother when she was 14.

Stephanie's mother and stepfather reported that since starting high school Stephanie had become moody and easily burst into tears. She accused them of being controlling and unreasonable about chores, and they now felt that they "walked on eggshells." Stephanie's father reported that she no longer seemed interested in visiting him and was disrespectful and sullen toward his new partner.

Stephanie agreed to attend a first therapy session with her mother. When asked about herself she gave only brief answers and seemed uncomfortable. She did, however, agree to meet individually with the psychologist. Stephanie acknowledged that she was dissatisfied with her life, that she felt irritable and moody, and did not get along well with her family. She showed the psychologist scars on her arm from using a nail file to hurt herself. She said that she sometimes had thoughts that life was not worth living, but did not have plans to kill herself.

The therapist first worked with Stephanie to develop a safety plan, including crisis and emergency services she could phone if she had thoughts of hurting or killing herself. Stephanie next began monitoring her mood. Together with the therapist, she began to notice that her mood fluctuated with her activities, school pressures, tiredness, and family interactions.

The therapist helped Stephanie to plan her weeks so that there was a mixture of work and enjoyable activities. She learned to problem-solve to manage the demands of schoolwork. Next the therapist invited Stephanie's parents to attend a session. The family talked about reasonable expectations for a 17-year-old. They discovered that chores were negotiated and monitored much as they had been when Stephanie was much younger and began to experiment with regular household meetings. In a session with her father and stepmother, the family discussed how they could maintain contact in a way that fit Stephanie's developmental needs for greater autonomy and more time with her friends. They began to experiment with developing a more mutually respectful style of interaction.

Over several months, Stephanie's mood improved and family members found her more pleasant to be around. In therapy Stephanie worked to identify stressors that might make her prone to slip back into depression. She developed awareness of the early signs and planned ways to quickly get back on track. Short-term therapy that focussed on Stephanie's feelings, behaviours, and thoughts was successful in lifting her depression and in helping her to fight depression in the future.

Throughout this book, we have discussed treatments in the context of the various disorders. In this chapter, in order to more fully explore issues related to treatment, we re-examine the range of therapies available to treat mental disorders as a whole and the context within which these therapies are offered. We also consider in more detail what treatments are effective, and how effectiveness can be determined.

Biological Treatments

The first treatments for psychological disorders were biological (see Chapter 1). Practices such as bleeding, often by cuts to the body or application of leeches, were designed to correct biological imbalances presumed to underlie psychological symptoms. In the latter part of the nineteenth century there was a proliferation of physical strategies designed to calm disturbed behaviour. For example, disturbed patients were protected from self-harm by physical restraints and were subjected to prolonged warm baths, or were placed under cold packs designed to pacify them.

During this century, medical practitioners have experimented with diverse biological interventions. Here we will focus on the most controversial strategy, electroconvulsive therapy, and the most common, psychopharmacology.

Electroconvulsive Therapy

Clinicians in the 1930s noticed that patients with schizophrenia who spontaneously experienced epileptic seizures subsequently showed a reduction in schizophrenic symptoms. They reasoned that if seizures could be provoked, psychotic symptoms would be reduced. As now practised, electroconvulsive therapy (ECT) involves the application of an electrical current to the patient's temples.

With the advent of effective antipsychotic medication, the procedure was abandoned in the treatment of schizophrenia. It is still used to treat severe depression that has not responded to other treatments. ECT used to be associated with serious side-effects including disorientation and memory loss, broken bones, and in rare cases (1 in 10,000) death due to cardiac failure (Avery, 1993). Recently, however, adverse effects have been minimized through less intense, briefer currents, often on only

Electroconvulsive therapy (ECT) involves the application of an electrical current to the patient's temples.

one side of the brain, and shorter courses of treatment. Anesthesia and muscle relaxants reduce distress and the risk of injury. Patients receive a full medical and neurological evaluation beforehand and are monitored during the procedure.

To date, the mechanism by which ECT reduces depressive symptoms is not understood. Nevertheless, there is considerable evidence of its effectiveness in ameliorating severe depression that has not responded to other treatments. (See Chapter 13; also see Chapter 2 for psychologist Norman Endler's account of his "miraculous" recovery.) Although ECT has been associated with symptomatic recovery, there is no evidence that it reduces the likelihood of relapse. Even with its present state of sophistication, ECT is generally considered a treatment of last resort.

Psychopharmacology

A number of pharmacological agents have been found to affect the individual's psychological functioning; these are known as **psychoactive agents**. Within medicine and pharmacology, it is accepted that the ideal method for developing medications is first to understand the pathological process by which a disorder develops, then to identify an agent that will change that process. In reality, things don't always work out so neatly. Science has not clearly established biochemical mechanisms that account for most psychological disorders, and the discovery of classes of psychoactive drugs has often occurred serendipitously; that is, physicians carefully monitoring a patient's reaction to a drug have observed unanticipated benefits in other areas. For example, a major class of antidepressants, the monoamine oxidase inhibitors (MAOIs) was originally developed for the treatment of tuberculosis; the observation that administration was associated with an elevation of mood lead to experimentation with their use in the treatment of depression.

After case studies show beneficial effects, medication trials are conducted to systematically assess drug efficacy (see Table 16.1; see also Chapter 4 for further discussion and example of blind trials).

Drugs may be classified in many ways. We group them here according to their application in the treatment of different types of disorder: antipsychotic, antidepressant, anxiolytic (antianxiety), mood-altering, and psycho-stimulant. Commonly prescribed examples of these medications are listed in Table 16.2.

Antipsychotic Medication

Antipsychotic medications are often also referred to as neuroleptics or major tranquillizers. Prior to their development in the 1950s, patients diagnosed with schizophrenia typically spent their lives confined in psychiatric institutions. Those receiving chronic care on "back wards" had their physical needs met and were contained in hospitals. The chances of return to the community were slender and by the time their symptoms abated in middle and later life, they were unequipped for life in the community.

The development of phenothiazines and related major tranquillizers offered the possibility of reducing psychotic symptoms such as hallucinations. Freedom from debilitating and alarming symptoms offered relief to many patients. Following stabilization on the drug, formerly institutionalized patients were able to return to the community. This made possible the policy of deinstitutionalization in which hospital stays were reserved only for the acute phase of the disorder and patients were rapidly returned to the community. The economic benefits of this process are clear and the advent of the antipsychotic medication was heralded as a major breakthrough.

Unfortunately, for some patients the major tranquillizers are associated with major side-effects known as **extrapyramidal effects**. One type of extrapyramidal effect is similar to the symptoms of Parkinson's disease. These Parkinsonian effects include stooped posture, muscular rigidity, a distinctive shuffling gait, and occasional drooling. These side-effects, which are evident within a few weeks of taking major

Table 16.2 Psychotropic Medications

Type/Generic Name	Brand Name	Treats:	Side-Effects
Antipsychotics *Phenothiazines* chlorpromazine thioridazine fluphenazine trifluoperazine	Thorazine Mellaril Permitil Stelazine	Psychotic symptoms: agitation, delusions, hallucinations, violent or aggressive behaviour (especially schizophrenia)	Variable effectiveness; uncomfortable side-effects; long-term: tardive dyskinesia
Butyrophenone haloperidol	Haldol		
Dibenzodiazepine clozapine olanzapine risperidone	Clozaril Zyprexal Risperdal		Fewer side-effects
Anxiolytics alprazolam chlordiazepoxide diazepam lorazepam oxazepam busiprone propranolol clomipramine meprobamate	Xanax Librium Valium Ativan Serax BuSpar Inderal Anafranil Equinil, Miltown	Anxiety, tension, panic attacks	Drowsiness, lethargy; variable effectiveness
Antidepressants *MAO Inhibitors* isocarboxazid phenelzine tranylcypromine selegiline	Marplan Nardil Parnate Eldepryl	Depression, panic disorder	Multiple side-effects, may be dangerous; special diet necessary
Tricyclics amitriptyline clomipramine doxepin imipramine nortriptyline	Elavil Anafranil Sinequan Tofranil Pamelor	Severe depressive symptoms; panic disorder, OCD	Effects may take time, may cause discomfort
SSRIs fluoxetine sertraline paroxetine fluvoxamine	Prozac Zoloft Paxil Luvox	Depression, OCD, panic disorder	Few side-effects
Mood Stabilizers lithium carbonate lithium citrate	Eskalith, Lithane Cibalith-S	Bipolar disorder	High toxicity
Stimulants dextroamphetamine methylphenidate pemoline	Dexedrine Ritalin Cylert	Hyperactivity, distractibility, learning disorders	Unpredictable, troublesome side-effects

tranquillizers, may be relieved by anti-Parkinsonian drugs, which in turn may have their own unpleasant side-effects. Another extrapyramidal effect evident after prolonged administration of antipsychotic medication is known as *tardive dyskinesia*. Patients suffering from tardive dyskinesia evidence strange muscular movements such as eye-twitching and tongue-thrusting. Of particular concern is the fact that the symptoms may occur not only during administration of the medication, but also after it has been discontinued (see Chapter 14).

Because schizophrenia is a chronic disorder, patients must adhere to a long-term medication regimen. Physicians must carefully calibrate the dosage to maximize symptomatic control and to minimize side-effects. Drug maintenance has been found to reduce the risk of relapse. However, many patients may be tempted to discontinue their medication when they are feeling symptom-free, increasing the risk of a relapse. During the past ten years a new generation of antipsychotic medications with fewer extrapyramidal effects has been tested (Keith, 1997). The first of these, clozapine, is effective compared to standard antipsychotics, but is associated with serious health risks (Skelton, 1995). Among the new antipsychotics, olanzapine shows the most promise. Olanzapine has been demonstrated to be as effective as standard antipsychotics in the treatment of positive symptoms such as hallucinations, it has minimal to no extrapyramidal effects, and is superior to standard antipsychotics in reducing negative symptoms such as withdrawal (Keck & McElroy, 1997).

Anxiolytics

Anxiolytics are agents that alleviate symptoms of anxiety and muscle tension. They reduce activity in parts of the central nervous system, which lowers activity in the sympathetic nervous system leading to lower respiration and heart rates and decreased muscle tension. Barbiturates were the first class of drugs widely used for the treatment of anxiety. Over the years, practitioners became concerned when they observed that patients develop tolerance for barbiturates, requiring larger doses to achieve the same effects. Large doses of barbiturates are highly toxic, which unfortunately made them a common choice for suicide attempts.

A second class of anxiolytics, the benzodiazepines, offered effective control of anxiety without toxicity at high doses. (See Chapter 7 for a discussion of possible mechanisms.) Unfortunately, benzodiazepines are also addictive. After prolonged use of this class of drugs, sudden withdrawal can provoke convulsions that may be life-threatening. Consequently, patients must be carefully monitored and the dose gradually reduced. Like barbiturates, benzodiazepines are dangerous when taken in combination with alcohol.

Benzodiazepines have been demonstrated to be effective in the treatment of panic disorder, generalized anxiety disorder, and social phobia (Lydiard, Brawman-Mintzer, & Ballenger, 1996). However, anxiety symptoms may reemerge

on withdrawal. It is often recommended therefore, that medication be used in conjunction with cognitive-behavioural interventions that help the individual learn to cope with stressful situations (Lydiard et al., 1996; Michelson & Marchione, 1991). There is evidence that regular use of minor tranquilizers by depressed patients is associated with poorer outcome (Wells & Sturm, 1996).

Antidepressants

Drugs used in the treatment of depression fall into three major categories (see Chapter 13): the monoamine oxidase inhibitors (MAOIs), the tricyclics (TCAs), and the selective serotonin reuptake inhibitors (SSRIs). A major drawback of MAOIs is the severe dietary restrictions they impose. In combination with MAOIs, common foods such as yeast, chocolate, and beer that contain the enzyme tyramine can cause a life-threatening increase in blood pressure.

The second group of antidepressants are the tricyclics. This group of antidepressants is associated with nuisance side-effects such dry mouth, blurry vision, constipation, and lightheadedness.

The most recently developed group of antidepressants are the SSRIs, of which Prozac is the best known. The SSRIs are at least as effective as other classes of antidepressants, with fewer adverse effects. Nevertheless, side-effects such as nausea, diarrhea, headache, tremor, and sleepiness can occur.

With any of the antidepressants, improvement is typically evident after one to two weeks of treatment, with optimal response by the third or fourth week. Thirty to 50 percent of patients do not respond favourably to antidepressants. However, 30 to 50 percent of those who do not respond to one class of antidepressants will respond to another. Unfortunately, it is impossible to predict which class of antidepressants will be most effective for a given patient (Thase & Kupfer, 1996). Many mildly depressed individuals are prescribed a dosage of antidepressants below effective levels (Wells & Sturm, 1996). Antidepressants bring symptomatic relief to many individuals in the acute phase of a depressive disorder, but there is less evidence of their influence on relapse. Furthermore, although TCAs and SSRIs are often prescribed for depressed children and youth, a recent review (Sommers-Flanagan & Sommers-Flanagan, 1996) found no double-blind trials that demonstrated their effectiveness with young people.

Lithium

Lithium salts have long been the medication of choice for bipolar disorder (see Chapter 13). Lithium and related mood stabilizers have been shown to reduce rapid cycling between depressive and manic or hypomanic states. It has been demonstrated to have antidepressant effects in 30 to 50 percent of patients (Thase & Kupfer, 1996).

Side-effects of lithium at therapeutic dosages may include nausea, dizziness, weight gain, and mild diarrhea. Of greater concern, however, is that lithium has a narrow window of effectiveness, with low doses being ineffective and high doses being highly toxic. Physicians must carefully monitor patients' blood lithium levels.

Stimulants

Stimulants are the class of drugs most commonly used in the treatment of children with attention deficit and hyperactivity disorder (see Chapter 5). They are short-acting compounds with an onset of action within 30 to 60 minutes and peak clinical effectiveness one to five hours after administration.

Stimulants such as Ritalin reduce hyperactive and impulsive behaviour, permitting the child to sustain attention. Compared to other classes of drugs, stimulants have received intense study. A review of 153 studies including 5768 participants (Spencer et al., 1996) found a 70 percent response rate in the treatment of uncomplicated attention deficit disorder. Common side-effects are appetite suppression and sleep disturbance. Less frequently, patients report mood disturbance, headaches, abdominal discomfort, and fatigue.

VIEWPOINT *Should Psychologists Prescribe Medication?*

In the past few years, many psychologists and psychological associations in the United States have begun to advocate for prescription privileges for psychologists (DeLeon, Fox, & Graham, 1991). They argue that, with appropriate training, psychologists could competently offer a range of psychosocial and pharmaceutical treatments for mental disorders. They point out that many other health professionals, such as nurse practitioners and dentists, have prescription privileges. There are several arguments for their position, including that (1) many major mental disorders (such as schizophrenia) are best treated with medication, (2) it might be more cost-effective for psychologists to prescribe for their patients rather than referring to psychiatrists or physicians, and (3) underserved groups such as the elderly, the chronically mentally ill, and those living in rural areas would benefit from expanded opportunities to receive pharmaceutical treatment from mental health professionals.

Perhaps not surprisingly, many American physicians are concerned about the possible effects of allowing psychologists to have prescription privileges. Both the American Psychiatric Association and the American Medical Association have expressed concern that the prescription of psychotropic medication by less than fully trained medical practitioners could pose a risk for patients. Not all American psychologists are

comfortable with the push for prescription privileges either. For example, Hayes, Walser, and Follette (1995) argue that the provision of education required to competently prescribe would occur at the expense of training in psychological assessment and interventions. Furthermore, they express concern that the biological and pharmaceutical training required of psychologists might be inadequate. As an illustration, they point to the Hawaii Prescription Privilege Task Force, which first advocated two years of additional training for psychologists but eventually suggested that 100 hours would be sufficient.

Will the drive for prescription privileges begin in earnest in Canada? At this point, the Canadian Psychological Association (CPA) has not taken a stand on the issue of prescription privileges for (appropriately trained) psychologists, although there is ongoing discussion of this issue in the CPA Section on Psychopharmacology. There are, however, important differences in the American and Canadian approaches to reducing health care costs. The tendency in the United States is to have less expensive professionals provide basic health care, whereas in Canada many provinces emphasized reducing "duplication" of services. As Dozois and Dobson (1995a) point out, provincial governments would be likely to perceive psychologists writing prescriptions as duplicating the services provided by

psychiatrists. Furthermore, as emphasized in the *Canadian Code of Ethics for Psychologists*, psychologists are encouraged to promote the public interest by working with other health care disciplines. Rather than competing with medically trained professionals, Canadian psychologists may choose to use their expertise in psychosocial interventions to complement the services offered by physicians and other health care professionals (Dozois & Dobson, 1995b; McCrea, Enman, & Pettifor, 1997).

Critical Thinking Questions

1. What might the right to prescribe medication do to the profession of clinical psychology and to the traditional skills of the clinical psychologist to provide psychotherapy?

2. Is the scientific evidence regarding the effectiveness of psychotropic medications strong enough to justify clinical psychologists' seeking prescription privileges?

3. As described above, graduate-level training in psychopharmacology may require two years of training in addition to the six to seven years of training (after the bachelor's degree) currently required in clinical psychology Ph.D. programs. How might required training in psychopharmocology affect your decision to apply to enroll in such a program?

Limits on Effectiveness

It is clear that several classes of drugs, including antipsychotics, anxiolytics, stimulants, and antidepressants, have demonstrated their effectiveness in controlling diverse psychological symptoms. However, no class of drugs is effective for all people with a particular disorder and it is not possible to predict who will respond to a particular class of drugs. A major problem is that approximately 40 percent of individuals who are prescribed psychotropic medication do not comply with the prescribed regimen (Fast & Preskorn, 1993). Consequently, experts recommend monitoring blood plasma levels when appropriate to adjust the dose to increase efficacy and minimize side-effects.

Psychoactive medication has freed many people from debilitating symptoms. However, medication may not enable the individual to learn new skills or to process information in a different way. The evidence suggests that medication may be helpful in symptom control, but without concomitant psychological interventions the person may be prone to relapse and chronic disorder (Biederman, Spencer, & Wilens, 1997).

PSYCHOTHERAPY: A DEFINITION

Any attempt to define psychotherapy is fraught with difficulty. As an example, we can all recall an experience in which talking about a problem with a parent or a good friend made us feel better. But is this psychotherapy? In current terms psychotherapy may be best defined as a process in which a professionally trained therapist systematically uses techniques derived from psychological principles to relieve another person's psychological distress or facilitate growth. Psychotherapy is practised by professionals from many disciplines, including psychology, psychiatry, social work, medicine, and nursing. In Canada, the title *psychotherapist* is not licensed or restricted in any fashion; anyone can advertise his or her services as a psychotherapist. People would therefore be well advised to enquire into the training and professional background of a therapist.

Persons, Curtis, and Silberschatz (1991) illustrated the similarities and differences between psychodynamic and cognitive-behavioural therapies by discussing the treatment of a 25-year-old man who came to a mental health clinic complaining of depression and difficulties relating to people. John was highly self-critical, felt guilty and fatigued, and had little motivation. At his work at an engineering firm, he wasted time on minor tasks, and then stayed in the evening in a futile attempt to catch up. He had no friends and was not dating. John said his father was rigid and authoritarian and had never been interested in him; when he tried to talk with his parents, his father always criticized him and his mother interrupted with irrelevant comments.

Curtis and Silberschatz, the psychodynamic therapists, suggested that John's unconscious identification with his parents caused his current problems and that treatment should focus on helping him develop insights into how his feelings about his parents had inhibited him throughout his life. From their perspective, a key aspect of therapy involves helping John monitor his reactions to the therapist, particularly unconscious expectations that the therapist sees him as incompetent and attempts to control him.

Persons, the cognitive-behavioural therapist, viewed John's problems as stemming from (1) a belief that he doesn't deserve to have a good life, (2) a belief that if he attempts to make changes in his life, something bad will happen, and (3) social skills deficits. The therapist would point out John's dysfunctional beliefs whenever they occur and help him to challenge their validity, as well as helping him rehearse appropriate social interaction skills and providing accurate feedback on social behaviour.

THEORETICAL ORIENTATIONS OF PSYCHOTHERAPY

Many types of psychotherapy have been developed during this century, but which ones are practised by therapists today? Surveys show the major schools of psychotherapy to be psychodynamic, cognitive-behavioural (including behavioural and cognitive approaches), humanistic-experiential, and integrative or eclectic.

The main approaches define a set of founding assumptions that guide therapy (see Chapter 2). Each approach has distinctive techniques or interventions. There is considerable "cross-pollination" as approaches evolve. Adherents of particular approaches are becoming more tolerant of other schools and more aware of areas of overlap (Orlinsky & Howard, 1995). Approaches to psychotherapy are under constant revision. Therefore, criticisms that may appropriately be levelled at an early form of a therapy may no longer apply to later forms of the therapy.

Psychodynamic Approaches

We can trace the roots of psychodynamic therapy to the work of Freud in the first half of this century. On the basis of clinical work with patients suffering from neurotic disorders, Freud developed a theory that psychological problems have their roots in very early childhood and in unconscious conflicts (see Chapter 2). The main goal of Freudian psychoanalysis is to help patients understand the unconscious factors that drive and control their behaviour. Classic psychoanalysis is an intensive process, generally entailing several visits each week and requiring years of treatment. Treatment requires two types of self-exploration. Patients must obtain insight into the nature of their problems, and they must examine these insights in order to understand how past conflicts continue to affect them. Classic psychoanalysts rely heavily on five basic techniques:

1. *Free association.* In this method, the individual is required to say everything that comes to mind without censoring out seemingly unimportant or embarrassing thoughts. The patient generally lies on a couch or sits comfortably in a chair, while the psychoanalyst sits out of view to minimize his or her influence. It is the analyst's task to help the patient recognize unconscious motives and conflicts expressed in the spontaneous speech.

2. *Dream interpretation.* Dream analysis is another procedure for uncovering unconscious thoughts. Freud described dreams as "the royal road to the unconscious." Freud assumed that during sleep, ego defences are lowered, allowing repressed thoughts to surface in disguised form. The therapist's task is to distinguish between the manifest content of the dream (which is consciously remembered by the client), and the more important latent content (the unconscious ideas and impulses that have been disguised).

3. *Interpretation and denial.* During this stage, the therapist begins to interpret what the client says or does. Slips of the tongue, forgetfulness, and the client's behaviour may indicate unconscious impulses, defence mechanisms, or conflicts. Generally, the therapist will first interpret behaviour that the client is already on the verge of understanding. Later, the therapist will interpret the unconscious conflicts that induce defence mechanisms. It is common for clients to deny the analyst's interpretations at first, and this denial is taken as a sign that the analyst is correct.

4. *Analysis of resistance.* During the process of free association or dream interpretation, clients may become resistant—for example, being unwilling to discuss certain topics, missing or arriving late for appointments, joking during the session, or remaining silent. Resistance prevents painful or difficult thoughts from entering awareness; thus, therapists must determine the source of resistance if the client is to deal effectively with the problem.

5. *Analysis of transference.* The core of psychoanalytic therapy is **transference**, which occurs when the client responds to the therapist as he or she responded to significant figures from his or her childhood (generally the parents). Freud believed that individuals unconsciously reexperience repressed thoughts during transference, making it essential to the resolution of the client's problems. So, for example, a patient who experienced a parent as cold and unresponsive might experience the therapist as similarly cold and unresponsive. The client's reliving of a difficult past relationship recreates the neurosis in real life to a certain degree, and is often referred to as transference neurosis. By recognizing the transference relationship and remaining neutral, the therapist is able to help the client work through the conflict. The therapist must be careful not to allow his or her personal feelings, needs, or fears interfere with his or her relationship with the client (countertransference).

Throughout his life, Freud continued to modify his theories and his therapeutic strategies. In addition, many former disciples of Freud developed their own modifications of his work. This family of therapies is referred to as "psychoanalytic psychotherapy," "psychoanalytically oriented therapy," or "psychodynamic therapy." Naturalistic observations have shown that across these approaches, therapists engage in a blend of interpretive and supportive statements (Henry, Strupp, Schacht, & Gaston, 1994). The following are some examples of psychodynamic therapies.

Brief Psychodynamic Psychotherapy

Primarily developed by Alexander and French (1946), this psychoanalytically oriented therapy uses Freudian techniques in an active, flexible manner. Therapy tends to be short-term: sessions occur twice a week rather than every day. Goals are concrete, conversation replaces free association, therapists are empathic rather than emotionally detached, and interpretations focus on current life events rather than childhood fears and conflicts.

Ego Analysis

Ego analysts, such as Karen Horney, Erik Erikson, Anna Freud, and Heinz Hartmann, argued that Freudian analysis was too focussed on the unconscious sexual and aggressive motivation. They believed that individuals are capable of controlling their own behaviour. **Ego analysts** use Freudian techniques to explore the ego rather than the id. Therapists help clients understand how they have relied on defence mechanisms to cope with conflicts.

Adler's Individual Psychology

Alfred Adler proposed that sexual and aggressive instincts are less important than the individual's striving to overcome personal weakness. Adler's **individual psychology** proposes that mental disorders are the consequence of deeply entrenched mistaken beliefs, which lead individuals to develop a maladaptive style of life that protects them from discovering their own imperfections. Adlerian therapists interpret dreams in terms of current behaviour, offer direct advice, and encourage new behaviours.

Interpersonal Psychodynamic Therapy

Harry Stack Sullivan, the American psychiatrist who developed **interpersonal psychodynamic psychotherapy**, believed that mental disorders resulted from maladaptive early interactions between child and parent. This type of therapy is a variation of brief psychodynamic therapy and emphasizes the interactions between the client and his or her social environment. Interpersonal therapists provide feedback to help the client understand how his or her interpersonal styles (such as hostility or dependence) are perpetuating or provoking conflicts. The therapist also helps the client learn to interact with others in more flexible and positive ways, and must be careful not to reinforce the client's maladaptive behaviours.

Time-Limited Dynamic Psychotherapy

More recent psychodynamic approaches, such as **time-limited dynamic psychotherapy (TLDP)** (Binder, Strupp, & Henry, 1995), tend to be briefer and to involve the client in face-to-face contact with the therapist, but retain Freud's emphasis on analysis of transference as a central mechanism of therapeutic change. The TLDP therapist also helps identify patterns of interaction with others that strengthen unhelpful thoughts about oneself and others. Recent research in psychodynamic therapy has underlined the importance of the **therapeutic alliance**. The quality of the relationship between therapist and client is recognized to be a predictor of therapy outcome. Consequently, approaches such as TLDP place greater emphasis on interpersonal processes than did early psychoanalytic formulations.

Humanistic-Experiential Approaches

Whereas psychodynamic approaches focus on the person's unconscious processes, humanistic and experiential approaches focus on the person's subjective experience, giving particular attention to nonrational and emotional aspects of experience. Humanistic-experiential approaches place emphasis not on the past but on the person's current experience. In contrast to psychoanalytic formulations that view individuals as dominated by primitive urges that must be constrained, humanistic-experiential approaches place considerable emphasis on the individual's free will and encourage the client to take responsibility for personal choices.

Client-Centred Therapy

Carl Rogers developed client-centred therapy in the 1940s as an alternative to psychoanalysis. **Client-centred therapy** emphasizes "the warmth and permissiveness of the therapist, a permissive climate in which the feelings of the client could be freely expressed" (Rogers, 1942). Rogers believed that psychological problems arose when personal growth was stunted by judgements imposed by others. (See Chapter 2 for more on Rogers' theories.) This created conditions of worth in which the client believes that he or she must meet the standards of others in order to be a worthwhile person. Rogers was very explicit in defining the therapist qualities that facilitate the client's growth: genuineness, empathy, and "unconditional positive regard." The therapist strives to provide an environment in which the client feels accepted. Self-acceptance follows, and this in turn leads to self-knowledge and dissipation of bad feelings. In the client-centred approach, clients are not diagnosed, evaluated, or given advice, rather, they are valued as unique individuals.

Existential Therapy

Existential therapists base their work on existential philosophers such as Sartre and Kierkegaard. Existential therapy is concerned with the importance of the human situation as perceived by the individual, with the ultimate goal of making the client more aware of his or her own potential for growth and making choices. Existential therapists do not follow any particular procedures but emphasize the uniqueness of each individual. They challenge and confront the client on past and present choices. The therapist helps the client relate authentically to others through the developing of the therapeutic encounter. Existential therapists share themselves, their feelings, and values with the client. This type of therapy is concerned with human existence and the lack of meaning in a person's life, and works best with those who are having conflicts regarding their existence, or those with anxiety or personality disorders rather than psychoses.

Gestalt Therapy

Gestalt therapy was developed by Frederich (Fritz) Perls and emphasized the idea that distortions exist in an individual's awareness of his or her genuine feelings and that these distortions are responsible for impairments in personal growth and behavioural problems. Gestalt therapists focus on helping clients become aware of feelings and needs that have been ignored or distorted and recognizing that these needs are a part of themselves and should be accepted. The goal is to help the client gain increased awareness. To do this, clients must integrate both their inner feelings and their external environments. Therapists encourage clients to experience what is going on in the here and now by asking questions such as "How do you feel when you think about that?" or "What thoughts are running through your head now?" Clients are instructed to communicate directly by talking to people rather than about them (using "I" statements). One of the most popular Gestalt techniques is the empty chair technique, used to make the client more aware of his or her genuine feelings. For example, if a young woman had an unresolved conflict with her ex-boyfriend, she would be instructed to face an empty chair and imagine that her boyfriend was in it, and speak as though she were talking directly to him. Gestalt therapists will often interpret dreams, looking at the importance the dream has to the client at that moment. They also attend to nonverbal cues and ask clients to focus on their body and what meaning these paralinguistic cues are delivering.

In recent years, there has been substantial growth in the range of humanistic-experiential approaches. Psychologist Les Greenberg and his colleagues at York University in Toronto developed a *process experiential approach*, in which the client enters into an empathic relationship with a therapist who is very responsive to his or her experience (Elliot & Greenberg, 1995). Al Mahrer, at the University of Ottawa, formulated a different type of experiential therapy. Mahrer's experiential approach treats each session with a client as an opportunity to enable the client to become a qualitatively new person by (1) accessing deeper "ways of being" in the session and (2) freeing the person of the sense of "bad feeling" that was most apparent in the session (Mahrer, 1996).

Perhaps the greatest contribution of the humanistic approaches has been the emphasis on the human qualities of the therapist. Research has established that therapists working with different approaches are more effective when their clients feel that they are genuine, that they make efforts to understand their experience, and that they accept them despite their problems. To date, however, there have been few studies assessing the effectiveness of humanistic and experiential approaches (Greenberg, Elliot, & Lietaer, 1994).

Cognitive-Behavioural Approaches

Although the distinctions between behavioural, cognitive, and cognitive-behavioural therapies continue to be debated, the overlap in both techniques and theoretical underpinnings is so great that the leading professional association in the area (the Association for the Advancement of Behavior Therapy) views them as making up a single orientation.

The term *behaviour therapy* was first used in the 1950s to describe an operant conditioning treatment for psychotic patients (Lindsley, Skinner, & Solomon, 1954). Skinner's work in the application of operant conditioning produced dramatic changes in the behaviour of populations that were previously considered untreatable, such as the chronically mentally ill and the mentally retarded. The core features of behavioural approaches are that problem behaviours are considered to be learned behaviours and that faulty learning can be reversed through the application of learning principles. (See Chapter 2.)

Originally, behaviour therapy applied empirical findings associated with classical and operant conditioning. However, over the past 30 years the field has broadened to include research findings and theories from areas such as perception, cognition, and the biological bases of behaviour. Behavioural therapists focus on present thoughts and behaviours as opposed to childhood history. Accordingly, behavioural interventions focus on specific targets, such as dealing with phobias and changing maladaptive behaviours. A discussion follows of some examples of behavioural interventions.

Systematic Use of Reinforcement (Contingency Management)

Systematic programs that use reinforcement to encourage and maintain effective behaviour work well in situations where the therapist has considerable control over the client, such as institutional environments.

Token economies. In the **token economy**, appropriate behaviours are rewarded with tokens, which may be exchanged for desired objects or privileges. This approach has been effective in improving the self-help and social skills of schizophrenic patients and behavioural problems displayed by children. Token economies tend to effectively modify specific behaviours, but may not generalize to new situations beyond the institutional environment.

Response shaping. **Response shaping** is a method used to shape behaviour to gradual approximations of what is expected. This method is used extensively with children's behaviour problems or difficulties. For example, a mentally retarded child who is unable to get dressed independently can be taught the process gradually by being rewarded for putting on one item at a time until he or she is eventually able to handle the entire task.

Behavioural contracts. A *behavioural or contingency contract* is a formal, often written, agreement between two or more parties, generally the therapist and client, that specifies the consequences of client behaviours. Behavioural contracts may be applied to problems such as marital difficulties, family disruptions, substance abuse, and obesity. Behavioural contracts can facilitate therapy by specifying clear goals and outlining clear expectations and rewards.

Aversion Therapy

Aversion therapy involves the use of painful or unpleasant stimuli (such as electric shocks, unpleasant aromas, or nausea-producing drugs) to decrease unwanted behaviours (such as smoking, problem drinking, overeating, and disturbing sexual practices). For example, an alcoholic attempting to stop drinking may be required to drink after being given a drug that causes nausea when mixed with alcohol.

Aversion therapy is controversial and has been debated extensively by clinicians. Many clinicians doubt that aversion therapy produces long-lasting changes that will generalize beyond treatment. Aversion therapy alone does not appear to teach adaptive behaviours to replace the maladaptive acts, and is generally reserved as a last-resort treatment for dangerous behaviours (such as self-abuse), or used briefly, in conjunction with techniques that promote more adaptive behaviour.

Extinction

Extinction is based on the idea that learned behaviours weaken and disappear over time if they are not reinforced. The two main techniques relying on the principle of extinction, also called exposure therapy, are *implosion therapy* and *flooding* (see Chapter 7). In implosion, the client imagines anxiety-arousing scenes, and the therapist attempts to elicit an "implosion" of anxiety. In a safe environment, the client will repeatedly imagine a fearful scene and express anxiety. Eventually, after imagining the worst and realizing that nothing is going to happen, the client's anxiety will be extinguished. Flooding, also called *in vivo* exposure, occurs in situations where the client can be exposed to a real-life anxiety-provoking stimulus. For example, a client with an intense fear of dogs may be brought to a kennel full of dogs in order to demonstrate that the feared consequences will not occur.

Joseph Wolpe's work drew on classical conditioning processes, reasoning that pairing anxiety-provoking stimuli with responses incompatible with anxiety would eliminate the anxiety response. In the process of **systematic desensitization**, fear-inducing stimuli are arranged in a hierarchy. Next, individuals are trained in techniques to achieve deep muscle relaxation. They are then required to imagine the first item on the hierarchy while remaining relaxed. They gradually progress through the hierarchy while maintaining their relaxed state. If they become anxious, they stop visualizing until they have regained their relaxed state (see Chapter 7).

Assertiveness Training

Assertiveness therapy is most effective in interpersonal situations where anxiety can be traced to lack of self-assertiveness. Programs tend to follow stages in which the desired behaviours are first practised in the therapy session and later generalized to real-life situations. The therapist generally encourages and guides the client to practise new, more appropriate assertive behaviours and more effective interpersonal skills. For example, clients may learn "refusal skills," conversational skills, social problem-solving, and responding appropriately to insults. Assertiveness training is offered to couples experiencing relationship problems, aggressive individuals, and shy, socially awkward individuals.

Biofeedback Training

In the biofeedback treatment approach, sensitive instruments are used to give the client prompt, exact information on physiological processes such as muscle activity, brain waves, skin temperature, heart rate, and blood pressure. This approach has been used to treat several clinical disorders, including high blood pressure, seizures, incontinence, migraine headaches, and Reynaud's disease (a circulatory disorder). Through operant conditioning procedures, clients are taught to control and influence the physiological process causing them problems. Although biofeedback has been shown to have successful outcomes, there is little empirical validation that it reliably leads to lasting improvements.

Cognitive-Behavioural Approaches

The idea that the way we think and feel influences our behaviour is not new. From the writings of the ancient Greeks on, writers have suggested that the way we interpret our experience affects how we feel and behave (Meichenbaum, 1995). Albert Bandura drew attention to ways that learning could take place by observation and imitation (see Chapter 2). Bandura's work was first applied to children, but has been found to have important applications for adults as well. Bandura also focussed on internal processes that facilitate skill development. He noted that in helping an individual to develop new behaviours, it is important to reward coping as well as mastery. For example, a person making fumbling attempts to learn to skate should be encouraged for persistence and effort, even in the absence of an accomplished performance. Self-efficacy, which refers to a person's sense of his or her own competence to learn and perform new tasks, is often found to be the best predictor of behaviour, such as approaching a phobic stimulus or attempting a new behaviour. Bandura's work laid the foundation for approaches that emphasize the importance of cognitions in mediating behavioural responses (Craighead, Craighead, & Ilardi, 1995).

With their roots in Bandura's learning theory, cognitive-behavioural approaches draw on knowledge developed in other branches of psychology. For example, using paradigms developed in information processing, D'Zurilla and Goldfried (1971) introduced a problem-solving approach to the field of behaviour therapy. This approach was applied in the treatment of diverse problems such as weight control, clinical depression, and social skills deficits. Using concepts developed in understanding cognitive development, Donald Meichenbaum from the University of Waterloo developed **self-instructional training** to train individuals in effective strategies for talking themselves through difficult challenges (for example, stay calm, focus on the task, don't get carried away by your anger).

An essential feature of behavioural approaches is the application of scientifically derived principles in the treatment of problems. Throughout therapy, progress is assessed to determine whether the strategy should be modified. Behavioural treatment requires clear identification of goals and is oriented toward the future. Behaviour therapists are very active in evaluating the outcome of their interventions, but until recently have devoted less attention to studying the process of therapy or the role of the therapeutic relationship (Emmelkamp, 1994).

Other, more purely cognitive approaches such as Albert Ellis' rational-emotive therapy and Aaron Beck's cognitive therapy (see Chapter 2) are based on the assumption that an individual's perception of events, rather than the events themselves, affect adjustment, and consequently they focus on identifying automatic thoughts, changing maladaptive patterns of thinking that are associated with distress, anxiety, and depression (Hollon & Beck, 1994). Like their behavioural "relatives," cognitive and cognitive-behavioural approaches rely on the application of empirically derived strategies in the treatment of diverse disorders including depression, anxiety disorders, eating disorders, attention deficit disorders, chronic pain, personality disorders, and marital distress (Dobson & Shaw, 1995). Cognitive approaches foster a collaborative relationship in which the therapist and client work together to identify problems, test hypotheses, and reevaluate beliefs. Treatment response is continuously monitored and treatment is tailored to the needs of individual clients. Chapter 7 discusses in more detail cognitive techniques in the treatment of anxiety; Chapter 12 describes cognitive and behavioural treatments for personality disorders; and Chapter 13 discusses a cognitive approach to depression.

Eclectic and Integrative Approaches

So far, we have highlighted the distinctive features of each approach to psychotherapy. This "compare and contrast" strategy illustrates how therapists who were dissatisfied with the dominant theories of the time split off from the mainstream and started new schools of thought. It is ironic that the history of psychotherapy, a discipline devoted to helping people, has been marked by some bitter criticism and rejection of opposing views.

Over the years, a number of therapists have observed the similarities and overlaps between apparently different approaches. These ideas were further developed by Jerome Frank in his 1961 book *Persuasion and Healing*. Frank looked not only at twentieth-century psychotherapy, but also at primitive shamanism, religious conversion experiences, and placebo effects in drug treatment. He defined psychotherapy as a process whereby a person who was demoralized about some part of life sought help from a socially sanctioned healer. This separates psychotherapy from the conversations we may have with a friend, a hairdresser, or someone met on the bus. The first ingredient in healing is hope: either explicitly or implicitly, the therapist conveys an expectation that the client's life will change as a result of the psychotherapeutic process (Roberts, Kewman, Mercier, & Hovell, 1993). The second ingredient is an alternative explanation for the problem. Within schools the types of explanation differ, so, for example, a psychodynamic therapist works on the assumption that distress is related to early childhood experiences, whereas a cognitive therapist emphasizes the way the client thinks about the situation. According to Frank, regardless of their accuracy, these interpretations offer a way to understand the problems the person is facing. The third ingredient is that the client is expected to think, feel, or act in a different way. Changes in thoughts, feelings, or behaviours have been found to have ripple effects, so that a person who engages in more pleasant activities may be less likely to feel depressed, a person who thinks that a poor grade is unfortunate but not disastrous may be less likely to feel hopeless, etc.

Frank's analysis of psychotherapy was influential in promoting the development of new therapeutic practices and frameworks that draw upon selected aspects of various dominant schools of therapy. The appeal of the resulting eclectic (that is, using techniques stemming from diverse orientations) or integrative (that is, developing a conceptual model to guide treatment based on elements of diverse orientations) approaches is evident in surveys of psychotherapists. Across numerous surveys over the past 30 years, at least a third of therapists identify themselves as disciples of a particular school of therapy, but claim to have integrated aspects of diverse approaches (for example, Hunsley & Lefebvre, 1990). In a climate of fiscal restraint when health service providers are required to be accountable and furnish evidence that the service they offer is effective, therapists are increasingly motivated to attend to research findings (Goldfried & Norcross, 1995) and to combine the best elements of different schools of therapy.

PSYCHOTHERAPY: TREATMENT MODALITIES

In addition to different theoretical approaches to therapy, there are also distinctive modalities of delivering therapy—to individuals, couples, families, and groups.

Individual Therapy

Early therapy was conducted exclusively in an individual format, with one person (the client or patient) and one therapist. Contacts with other family members were strictly avoided lest they contaminate the all-important therapeutic relationship. Individual therapy is also practised with children. Some forms of individual child psychotherapy appear very similar to adult "talk" therapy. Other approaches use children's play as the medium of communication.

After six years of marriage Judith and Rick are considering separation. They report that they have drifted apart, no longer enjoy each other's company,

and both dread their frequent arguments and irritations. Rick suffers headaches and Judith feels moody and overwhelmed. Both are committed parents who enjoy playing with their young son and infant daughter.

Before they had children, Rick jogged and Judith took aerobics. They enjoyed restaurant meals together and shared a love of jazz. Since the birth of the children, exercising and evenings out have been replaced by trying to get in a couple of hours of work after the children settle for the night. Judith, who works four days a week at a management position, feels disappointed that she shoulders the major responsibility for child care. Rick, however, assumes that he needs to work overtime at his high-tech job to compensate for Judith's reduced income. He is frustrated that she seems negative and critical of him.

After assessing their situation, the couple therapist explains to Rick and Judith that they are in a very taxing phase of life and have slipped out of the habit of nurturing their relationship. The therapist notes that men and women often react differently to stress, so that each feels the other is being unreasonable. At the therapist's suggestion, they begin to schedule regular pleasant times together. Next they work on clearly expressing needs to one another. They also practise problem-solving to cope with having too little time and too many responsibilities. As the couple gets back in the habit of enjoying being together, they become more relaxed in their interactions with each other and develop more realistic expectations of one another.

Couples Therapy

In the nineteenth century, marriage was considered a lifetime commitment to live together and to raise a family. The personal qualities of each partner and their enjoyment of life together were not relevant to the stability of the marriage. In the twentieth century, marriage is considered to be a partnership based on mutual interests and companionship. With the liberalization of Canadian divorce laws in 1968 and 1985 it became possible for one partner to end an unsatisfying marriage.

At the same time as divorce became easier in Western countries, there was increased interest in developing therapies to help couples resolve their difficulties. In couples therapy, the focus is on the marital relationship. Partners (who may be married, cohabiting or dating, and may be of any sexual orientation) may have conjoint sessions but may also each meet separately with the therapist.

The goal is to enhance each partner's satisfaction with the relationship. Early response to developing problems appears to be make couples therapy more effective. In recent years, couples treatments have also been found to be effective for problems originally thought of as individual, such as depression or alcoholism in adults and conduct disorder in children (Hunsley & Lee, 1995; Rohrbaugh, Shoham, Spungen, & Steinglass, 1995). Couples therapy may be based on different theoretical orientations. The best-known approach is based on behavioural and social learning principles. Therapists seek to enhance communication and conflict resolution skills, as well as helping both partners to be more realistic in their expectations about their relationship. Canadian psychologists Sue Johnson and Les Greenberg developed and evaluated an experiential approach to couples therapy, **emotionally focussed therapy**. Drawing upon elements of experiential therapy and structural family therapy, the goal of the therapy is to modify distressed couples' constricted interaction patterns and emotional responses by fostering the development of a secure emotional bond.

Family Therapy

The origins of family therapy can be found in social work and in the child guidance movement (Clarkin & Carpenter, 1995). Family therapy is practised by therapists of diverse orientations, including cognitive-behavioural and psychodynamic. Although early family approaches viewed the family as the source of a family member's problems, many current family approaches make no such assumption but consider the family to be an important part of the solution to problems. A common goal of family approaches is to identify interactions between family members that may inadvertently contribute to problems. Family approaches often involve **reframing** the problem, or presenting a novel explanation for it, after which family members are required to carry out various tasks designed to change their ways of interacting with one another (Seaburn, Landau-Stanton, & Horwitz, 1995). The goals of family therapy are to enhance communication and negotiation in the family, so that each family member's well-being is promoted.

The goals of family therapy are to enhance communication and negotiation in the family.

Group Therapy

Many critics of psychotherapy note that it is expensive. Working with a number of clients in a group format substantially reduces the cost for each person. After World War II, therapy groups were developed to address the needs of various underprivileged groups. Many current cognitive-behavioural treatments, originally developed for use in individual therapy, have been modified for use in a group format. There are also important theoretical reasons for seeing clients in a group. In addition to the shared therapeutic experience of hope for change, the group contest offers feedback from other people (Rosenbaum & Patterson, 1995) and a place to practise ways of relating to others. *Universality*—the awareness that other people share similar experiences or feelings—can reduce feelings of stigma (Ballinger & Yalom, 1995). Participation in a group offers exposure to solutions that have worked for others and may also lead to feelings of cohesion or belonging.

THE CONTEXT OF PSYCHOTHERAPY

Who Provides Psychotherapy?

Clinical psychologists are among the main providers of psychotherapy. Surveys over the years have found that most clinical psychologists are actively involved in offering some form of therapeutic service, be it individual, couple, family, or group therapy. Although many clinical psychologists identify themselves as having either a psychodynamic or a cognitive-behavioural orientation (with fewer describing themselves as humanistic-experiential), the most commonly endorsed orientation is eclectic. For example, in their survey of Canadian clinical psychologists, Hunsley and Lefebvre (1990) found that 98 percent of their respondents provided psychotherapy; most provided individual therapy (86 percent provided individual therapy for adults, 59 percent provided individual therapy for children/adolescents), many provided couples (60 percent) or family (47 percent) therapy, and only a minority provided group therapy for adults (22 percent) or children/adolescents (10 percent). As regards their theoretical orientation, 47 percent defined themselves as eclectic, 25 percent as cognitive, 22 percent as behavioural, 19 percent as psychodynamic or psychoanalytic, and 15 percent as humanistic-experiential. Many who did not choose "eclectic" did choose more than one orientation, suggesting a degree of eclecticism in their practice. For those who were explicitly eclectic, the most commonly reported orientations contributing to their practice were behavioural (35 percent) and cognitive (35 percent).

The research, to date, does not provide much evidence that therapists' professional training or years of experience are directly related to the outcome of treatment, although professionally trained therapists are more effective than non-professional therapists when therapy is shorter than 12 sessions (Beutler, Machado, & Neufeldt, 1994). Because most clients attend fewer than 12 sessions of psychotherapy, there may be substantial advantages to selecting a trained mental health professional as a therapist. Accordingly, people seeking psychotherapy should adopt a "consumer rights" attitude, and before treatment they should question therapists about their training, experience, and therapeutic methods. Also, though many potential clients do not ask about confidentiality issues, financial arrangements, or treatment alternatives (Braaten, Otto, & Handelsman, 1993), they should raise these matters. Table 16.3 offers suggested questions.

Who Seeks Psychotherapy?

People seek therapy for a multitude of reasons. Many have significant emotional distress that interferes with their daily functioning; previous chapters have described the range of disorders such individuals may be experiencing. Some seek therapy for advice and assistance in coping with the demands of social roles, such as parent, spouse, or employee. Some people may come to therapy for aid in coping with recent trauma (for example, rape) or loss (for example, death of a loved one). Some seek assistance in addressing questions related to personal identity, values, or self-knowledge.

Drawing upon American epidemiological surveys, Vessey and Howard (1993) found that some groups of people are more likely to seek psychotherapy. For example, two-thirds of psychotherapy clients are female, half have university education, half are married, and the majority are young-to-middle-aged adults. Unfortunately, Vessey and Howard's analysis also suggested that many of those most in need of such services (that is, those suffering from a psychological disorder) never seek professional help.

A similar picture is evident in Canada. Responses to the recent National Population Health Survey (NPHS) show similar sociodemographic characteristics among those who reported consulting a psychologist for health or mental health reasons (Hunsley, Lee, & Aubry, in press), as shown in Table 16.4. Users of psychological services experienced more stress and distress than the population at large, and were less satisfied with their life situation. Again, unfortunately consistently with American data, Hunsley and colleagues' analysis found that many who could benefit from therapy had not received it. For example, many Canadians suffering from depression had received neither therapy (from a psychologist, social worker, or other kind of counsellor) nor antidepressant medication.

The Duration of Treatment

For many people, the word "psychotherapy" conjures up notions of a lifestyle of regular and frequent sessions with a therapist. Nothing could be further from the truth. The majority of people who receive psychotherapy attend fewer than 10 sessions! Across a range of therapy clinics, across European and North American settings, across a range of clients presenting problems, and over the past 50 years, the picture of the duration of psychotherapy is remarkably consistent (Garfield, 1994; Phillips, E. L., 1991). A large minority of clients come for only one or two sessions, and the median number of therapy sessions is in the range of 5 to 13 sessions.

Although many of the currently used psychotherapies are designed to be short-term in nature (that is, 20 or fewer sessions), there is obviously some concern that many people who start treatment may terminate prematurely, thereby receiving less than optimal benefit from therapy. A number of researchers have attempted to understand the phenomenon of premature termination, with strikingly little success. Although a host of client characteristics have been hypothesized to contribute to premature termination or to treatment failure, many have failed to be empirically confirmed or have

Table 16.3 Informed Consumers: Questions to Ask a Potential Therapist

1. What are your professional qualifications?
2. Have you worked with this kind of problem?
3. How would you describe the way you work?
4. How many times do you think it will be necessary for me to see you?
5. What are the treatment options for me? Are there clinics or other practitioners who also work with problems like this?
6. What is the research evidence on the best type of treatment for my problem?
7. What can I expect from treatment? How will I be different at the end of treatment?
8. How much do you charge? Do you have a sliding fee scale?

Table 16.4 Characteristics of Canadians Who Receive Psychological Services

1. Women are twice as likely as men to consult a psychologist.
2. Although Canadians with university education make up 13 percent of the population, they make up 22 percent of the clientele of psychologists.
3. Although parents and children in single-parent families make up 8 percent of the Canadian population, they make up 20 percent of the clientele of psychologists.
4. People who experience pain that interferes with their daily lives are twice as likely as other Canadians to seek psychological services.
5. Canadians who receive psychological services also tend to be frequent users of other health care services.
6. Canadians who feel so unhappy that they believe life is not worthwhile are five times as likely as other Canadians to seek psychological services.
7. Whether measured by the number of stressful events in their past or the number of ongoing current stressors, users of psychological services are more likely than other Canadians to report high levels of stress.

been found to contribute very little to the prediction of termination (Baekeland & Lundwall, 1975; DuBrin & Zastowny, 1988; Pekarik, 1985). A major problem in this research area is that many researchers have equated premature termination with treatment failure. Clearly this is unwarranted, as the number of therapy sessions attended is not necessarily related to whether the client's condition has improved.

EVALUATING THE EFFECTS OF PSYCHOTHERAPY

Historical Context

With growing awareness of health care costs and a more sophisticated clientele, service providers face increasing demands to be accountable—to demonstrate that the services they offer are effective in treating the problem for which the person sought therapy. The history of research evaluating the effectiveness of psychotherapy is relatively brief; little empirical evidence was available prior to the 1960s. Since that time, though, there has been a veritable explosion in this line of research, so that there are now literally thousands of studies examining the effect of many different forms of therapy for many different types of problems.

As is often the case in science, research attention to a phenomenon is sparked by a controversy or a challenge to the accepted view. The current abundance of psychotherapy outcome research is due, in large part, to Hans Eysenck's 1952 article in which he argued that the rates of improvement among clients receiving psychodynamic or eclectic therapy were comparable to rates of remission of symptoms among untreated clients. On the basis of his review of the limited data available, he contended that about two-thirds of people with neurotic disorders (for example, anxiety disorders, depression) would improve within two years, regardless of whether they were treated by psychotherapy. In other words, Eysenck argued that there was no evidence psychotherapy had any demonstrable effect!

Not surprisingly, Eysenck's review evoked strong reactions from psychotherapists and psychotherapy researchers. Many critical responses to his review were published in scientific journals by leading proponents of psychotherapy. Perhaps the most important result of the ensuing debate was the emerging emphasis on the need for solid research design in evaluating psychotherapeutic effects. Vocal critics of Eysenck's position, such as Luborsky (1954) and Bergin (1971), claimed that Eysenck erred in comparing improvement rates across studies. For example, they argued that adequate control groups (that is, clients who did not receive treatment) were not available in many studies and that Eysenck's criteria for establishing clinical improvement were arbitrary and biased against finding positive therapeutic effects. These criticisms were, in turn, addressed by Rachman (1971) in his review of the growing empirical evidence. Like Eysenck, he concluded that there was no evidence to substantiate the claims of effectiveness made by psychotherapy proponents.

Throughout the 1970s, the debate about the effectiveness of psychotherapy grew, as did the number of published studies on therapy outcome. By this time behavioural therapies were being used by a growing number of psychologists. As empirical verification of outcome was a key element of the behavioural approach to treatment, there were soon many published studies examining the effect of these therapies. Researchers attempting to understand and integrate the burgeoning number of empirical articles on psychotherapy (including psychodynamic, behavioural, and other approaches) faced a formidable challenge in attempting to draw reasonable conclusions. As a result, the debate about the effectiveness of therapy was muddied by the fact that proponents and critics of psychotherapy often drew upon different studies to support their respective positions.

Meta-analysis

Chapter 4 reviewed the procedures generally used to evaluate the effectiveness of interventions in single studies. In attempting to reach conclusions derived from several studies, researchers have typically employed qualitative (that is, nonnumerical) methods. The reviewer provides a narrative account of the various studies, their strengths, weaknesses, and findings, and then draws conclusions about the state of knowledge. However, these methods were unable to gather information across numerous studies using a number of different patient populations and wide variety of outcome measures. As a response to this challenge "meta-analytic" techniques were developed. **Meta-analysis** is simply a method of quantitatively reviewing previous research. An analogy to a typical research study may be helpful in understanding the nature of meta-analysis. As described in Chapter 4, a typical psychotherapy outcome study involves the collection of data from multiple research participants. These data are then summed and overall trends in the group of participants are examined with the use of statistical procedures such as analysis of variance. The same general process occurs in meta-analysis, except that the "participants" in a meta-analysis are research studies, not individual clients.

In a single research study, similar data are collected from all participants. Obviously this is not possible in a meta-analysis, for the original research studies are likely to have employed a range of measures for collecting their data. Therefore, in meta-analysis, the results of prior research are combined by developing a common metric (basically a z transformation) to be used across the studies. The metric is called an **effect size** and is calculated as the difference between the means of the experimental (that is, the treatment) group and the control group, divided by the standard deviation of either the control group or the pooled sample of both groups. In some instances, where two treatments are compared to one another, the effect size is the difference between the two treated groups, divided by the standard deviation of the control group or the pooled standard deviation of all groups (treated and untreated) in the study. Effect sizes can be calculated from raw data, group means, and standard deviations, or from inferential statistics reported in the original research studies (for example, correlations, F-tests, t-tests).

There are numerous advantages to meta-analysis over traditional research reviews or single empirical studies. For example, statistical analysis, not the reader's impressions, are used to determine the pattern of findings when a literature is reviewed. Moreover, by including data from many studies, the number of research participants on whom conclusions are based is dramatically increased. This greatly enhances the meta-analyst's power to detect an effect in the literature and the generalizability of the conclusions drawn on the basis of the literature. As a result of these methodological and statistical strengths, meta-analysis is increasingly being used to determine the current state of knowledge about the effects of psychotherapy and to assist in the development of health care policies regarding the provision of psychotherapy.

An Overview of Current Evidence

Smith, Glass, and Miller (1980) reviewed 475 controlled studies of psychotherapy, including both studies published in scientific journals and unpublished dissertations. Their overall finding was that, broadly defined, psychotherapy for any disorder or problem was clearly effective. Indeed, their estimate was that psychotherapy had an average effect size of 0.85; that is, the difference in the dependent variables (such as measures of symptomatology) between the treated and untreated groups was 0.85 standard deviation units. This value means that the average person receiving therapy was better off after therapy than 80 percent of people who did not receive therapy.

These researchers also calculated the effectiveness of various types of treatment. For example, psychodynamic therapy had an effect size of 0.69, Gestalt therapy had an effect size of 0.64, and cognitive-behavioural therapy had an impressive effect size of 1.13. A subset of the studies they reviewed included direct comparisons of differing forms of treatment. For example, there were 57 studies in which therapies they termed "verbal" (including psychodynamic, cognitive, and humanistic therapies) were compared with "behavioural" (behavioural and cognitive-behavioural therapies) treatments. An analysis of this subset of studies yielded an effect size of 0.77 for the verbal therapies and 0.96 for the behavioural therapies. Caution is required, however, in interpreting the differences among therapies, because clients treated by each differ in the type and severity of problems.

Smith and colleagues conducted many other analyses of their data. For example, they found that the effect of therapy was unrelated to the duration of therapy. Another provocative finding was that there was no correlation between therapists' years of experience and the size of the therapeutic effect. These findings spurred researchers to address, in more sophisticated ways, the role therapist experience and treatment duration may have in therapy outcome.

Since the initial meta-analysis of the effectiveness of psychotherapy, dozens of meta-analytic studies have been published. Initially these studies focussed on replicating the findings of Smith et al. (1980), and, indeed, other researchers obtained similar findings. Subsequent meta-analyses have had a narrower focus. For many researchers, the question of whether psychotherapy is effective has been answered with a resounding yes. Attention has therefore turned to the different effects of treatments on specific disorders (that is, what works for whom) and the effects of therapist and client characteristics on the process and outcome of treatment.

Comparisons: The "Dodo Bird Verdict"

Are there important clinical differences in the outcome of differing forms of psychotherapy? In an influential review of the literature, Luborsky, Singer, and Luborsky (1975) concluded that all psychotherapies produce equivalent effects. Quoting the dodo bird in *Alice in Wonderland*, they pronounced that "Everybody has won, and all must have prizes." Since the Luborsky et al. review, many psychotherapists and researchers have endorsed this view, citing meta-analytic findings such as Smith et al. (1980).

Not all researchers have accepted this perspective. As Shadish and Sweeney (1991) suggested in their review of the comparative treatment literature, there are good reasons why we shouldn't let dodo birds tell us which therapies have won. The competition in *Alice in Wonderland* involved a caucus race in which competitors started at different points and ran in different directions for half an hour. Lewis Carroll's not-so-subtle jab at political committees is hardly a model for scientific evaluation of psychotherapy. If one examines the comparative treatment literature without imposing some structure on it (analogous, perhaps, to allowing the competitors in the race to start at different points and run in different directions) it is going to be difficult to see if there are important differences between therapies.

Careful examination of comparative effectiveness is crucial, because the acceptance of the equivalence of psychotherapies is tantamount to accepting the null hypothesis. Yet the failure to find a significant difference does not necessarily mean that no difference exists. Methodological limitations, such as small sample sizes, may limit the ability to draw conclusions. In fact, Kazdin and Bass (1989) found that almost half of the studies that found no differences between treatments had too few research participants to detect differences that may have existed. Furthermore, conclusions are highly dependent on the manner in which the researcher chooses to categorize therapies. For example, Smith et al.'s (1980) classification of "verbal therapies" included psychodynamic, cognitive, and humanistic approaches—but what do they really have in common? As good an argument could be made for grouping cognitive with the behavioural therapies, to which they are strongly related. Combining data in this way may lose important differences in the effects of these very dissimilar treatments.

Using meta-analytic approaches, a number of investigators are now finding significant differences between treatment. Weiss and Weisz (1995) recently evaluated the relative effectiveness of behavioural (including cognitive) versus nonbehavioural (psychodynamic and humanistic) treatments for children and adolescents. Their meta-analysis examined 105 studies of treatments for problems including anxiety disorders, depression, and social skills deficits. Past reviews of the literature have found that behavioural treatments tend to be superior to nonbehavioural ones, but some researchers have commented that this perhaps the effect size in behavioural studies is higher not because of the true strength of the treatment but because of superior study design. Weiss and Weisz therefore coded the studies in their analysis for a number of methodological features, including random assignment, attrition, therapist experience, and whether the treatment delivered actually matched the theory. They found that in fact the nonbehavioural treatment studies were of higher methodological quality.

Weiss and Weisz found that the behavioural treatments had an effect size of 0.85 (that is, 0.85 standard deviation units better than the no-treatment control group), whereas the effect size for nonbehavioural treatments was 0.42. When they statistically controlled for methodological quality of the studies, the effect sizes of the behavioural and nonbehavioural treatments were 0.86 and 0.38 respectively. The difference was even stronger in the ten studies in their sample that directly compared behavioural and nonbehavioural treatments.

Can we conclude, then, that cognitive-behavioural therapies are the most effective? Not necessarily. It is accurate to say that, at the present time, there is more evidence to support the effectiveness of this group of treatments than there is for any other approach. However, this is due, in large part, to the fact that cognitive-behaviouralists have a tradition of empirically substantiating treatment effects. There may well be other effective approaches that have not been the object of as much empirical investigation.

Psychodynamic therapies, in particular, despite their widespread use, have received very little empirical attention. This has begun to change, largely through the efforts of prominent psychodynamic researchers/therapists such as Lester Luborsky and Hans Strupp (cf. Henry et al., 1994). A growing number of studies are appearing in which short-term psychodynamic therapy is systematically evaluated.

Three recent meta-analyses have attempted to provide a definitive answer to the question of treatment effectiveness. Their results are striking in their discrepancies. Svartberg and Stiles (1991) reported that short-term psychodynamic therapies had a small effect at the end of therapy, and no discernible effects within a few months of therapy ending. They also found that compared to alternative treatments included in the studies they reviewed (mostly cognitive-behavioural treatments), psychodynamic approaches were significantly less effective. In contrast, Crits-Christoph (1992) reported that psychodynamic approaches were effective, and were comparable to alternative treatments. Most recently, Anderson and Lambert (1995) reviewed the literature and concluded that psychodynamic approaches were effective (although less effective than in Crits-Christoph's analysis) and were comparable to alternative treatments. A lack of consistency in meta-analytic findings is often an indication that there are important considerations (such as the role of therapist skill, the diagnosis of patients receiving treatment) that may moderate the effectiveness of treatment. In light of such contradictory findings, one can, perhaps, only conclude that the overall effectiveness of short-term psychodynamic approaches remains an open question.

Effects of Psychotherapy for Specific Disorders

Let us now turn to the effects of psychotherapy for specific disorders. There is now extensive evidence that there are effective psychotherapeutic treatments for many Axis I disorders. In particular, many treatments for anxiety and affective disorders have been developed over the past 15 years.

Anxiety Disorders

It is now commonly accepted that treatment for specific phobias, for example, must involve an element of exposure. That is, the individual with a phobia must begin to confront the object of the phobia. The person is also encouraged (in various ways, depending on the exact nature of the treatment) to accept that the surge of anxiety is normal, not life-threatening, and will soon diminish (see Chapter 7).

Other anxiety disorders are also being effectively treated by psychotherapy. In their meta-analytic review of treatments for panic disorder, Gould, Otto, and Pollack (1995) found that cognitive-behavioural treatments that combined cognitive restructuring (that is, challenging the beliefs and expectations held by the patient) and interoceptive exposure (that is, exposing the patient to bodily symptoms similar to those experienced in a panic disorder) were highly effective. Indeed, it is common to find that approximately 75 percent of patients treated in this manner are panic-free by the end of treatment—and this improvement is typically long-term. Abramowitz (1997) recently reported large effect sizes for two types of treatment of obsessive-compulsive disorder. The first involved a combination of exposure to the object of the obsession or compulsion and response prevention (for example, the patient is encouraged to abstain from rituals such as washing or checking); the other was cognitive therapy including cognitive restructuring and thought-stopping (that is,

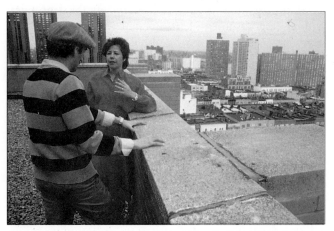

The individual with a phobia must begin to confront the object of the phobia.

using distractions to actively disengage the person from obsessive thoughts). Cognitive-behavioural treatments have also been found to be effective in treating generalized anxiety disorder (GAD; for example, Borkovec & Costello, 1993). Given the high level of comorbidity associated with GAD, it is encouraging to note a "ripple effect"; Borkovec, Abel, and Newman (1995) found that other symptoms decreased when the GAD symptoms were effectively treated (see Chapter 7).

Effective treatments are also available for childhood anxiety disorders. Barrett, Dadds, and Rapee (1996) provided a family-based treatment to children (aged 7 to 14 years) with separation anxiety, overanxious disorder, or social phobia. The treatment combined individual cognitive therapy for the child (including cognitive restructuring, coping strategies, and exposure) and sessions in which parents were (1) encouraged to use reinforcement strategies (such as praise, privileges, and tangible rewards) when the child dealt appropriately with fears, (2) taught to become aware of their own responses to stressful situations, and (3) given information on communication and problem-solving. Twelve months after treatment, 95 percent of children did not meet diagnostic criteria. This same research team also recently reported they have been successful in developing early intervention strategies for children at risk for developing anxiety disorders (Dadds et al., 1997).

Mood Disorders

Researchers have found a number of psychologically based interventions to be effective in the treatment of clinical depression. In general, extensive research suggests that cognitive (and cognitive-behavioural) therapy is effective in treating depression (Dobson, 1989), as is interpersonal psychotherapy, which helps the person learn new ways of interacting with others (Frank & Spanier, 1995). (See Chapter 13.) Indeed, the major National Institute of Mental Health Treatment of Depression Collaborative Research Program found comparable results for these two treatments (Elkin, 1994). Both cognitive therapy and reminiscence therapy (in which clients are encouraged to review their life and the ways in which they have dealt with challenges and stresses) have been found to be effective in treating depression in the elderly (Scogin & McElreath, 1994).

Many Canadian psychologists have been involved in developing cognitive-behavioural treatments for depression and for other disorders. Although initial efforts focussed on establishing the effectiveness of this form of treatment, recent work has attempted to separate the components of cognitive therapy to determine the "essential ingredient." Keith Dobson, of the University of Calgary, collaborated with U.S. colleagues in a study that randomly assigned people with major depression to one of three treatment conditions (Jacobson et al., 1996). A behavioural activation treatment focussed only on increasing patients' physical activity, social interactions, etc. The second treatment added interventions to help patients modify negative automatic thoughts. The full cognitive therapy condition included both of these components as well as work to alter the underlying dysfunctional beliefs that are hypothesized to be make someone

vulnerable to depression. Much to the researchers' surprise, there were no discernible differences between the three treatments, in either the short or the long term, leading them to conclude that the active ingredient of cognitive therapy for depression may be behavioural activation (Gortner, Gollan, Dobson, & Jacobson, 1998). Although replication of such findings is essential, Dobson and colleagues' study certainly requires close attention by proponents of cognitively oriented treatments.

Eating Disorders

Psychotherapy researchers have been actively examining the effects of treatment for other Axis I disorders. For example, cognitive-behavioural therapy and interpersonal psychotherapy are also effective in treating bulimia (for example, Wilfley et al., 1993; see also Chapter 9). Researchers were hopeful that interpersonal psychotherapy would help those for whom cognitive therapy was relatively ineffective; unfortunately, recent empirical evidence indicates that this is not the case (Agras et al., 1995).

Childhood Disorders

A number of treatments have been developed to treat childhood disorders. The symptoms of oppositional defiant disorder and conduct disorder can be substantially reduced through treatments that focus on improving children's social and problem-solving skills or that focus on improving the parents' parenting skills (Webster-Stratton & Hammond, 1997; see Chapter 5). Child therapy researchers have been especially active in developing effective treatments that can be offered in very cost-effective ways, such as the use of well-trained nonprofessionals or videotape-based psychoeducational programs for enhancing skills (for example, Webster-Stratton, 1994). Such researchers have also been able to develop moderately effective child-focussed and parent-focussed treatments for addressing child physical abuse and neglect (Wolfe & Wekerle, 1993).

Sexual Dysfunctions

Since the groundbreaking work of Masters and Johnson (1970), there has been considerable attention to the development of psychological treatments for sexual dysfunctions. Reviewing the research in this area, Rosen and Leiblum (1995) concluded that there are clearly effective treatments for erectile disorder and for female orgasmic disorder. For many other sexual dysfunctions, such as disorders of desire, currently available treatments are less effective. One of the major obstacles to the development of effective treatments is that other psychological disorders (for example, depression) and relationship problems (for example, marital conflict, social skills deficits) may be intertwined with the sexual dysfunction. It is therefore not surprising that there is a tendency for interventions for sexual dysfunction to include multiple components, such as educational material on sexuality and sexual arousal, social skills training, communication training, cognitive restructuring, and guided masturbation training.

Sleep Disorders

Psychotherapy researchers have been actively involved in devising interventions for sleep disorders. To date, much of their attention has been devoted to insomnia. As sedatives can lead to poor-quality sleep, possible addiction, and rebound insomnia on withdrawal, there is a pressing need for effective psychological interventions, especially for older adults (see Chapter 17). In their recent meta-analytic review, Murtagh and Greenwood (1995) concluded that current interventions are effective in reducing the time required to fall asleep, enhancing the quality of sleep, and lengthening the duration of sleep. Treatments include strategies such as relaxation training, sleep restriction (that is, limiting the time spent in bed to the time one is asleep), and *stimulus control* (for example, going to bed only when sleepy, getting out of bed if unable to fall asleep). Canadian psychologist Charles Morin of Laval University has been at the forefront of work in this area, including modifying treatments for use with older adults suffering from insomnia (Morin, Kowatch, Barry, & Walton, 1993).

Axis II Disorders

Despite a number of impressive breakthroughs in the treatment of psychological distress, there remain a large number of disorders for which little effective treatment is available. For example, the majority of Axis II disorders have received little or no attention by psychotherapy researchers. The one major exception is Linehan's multicomponent cognitive-behavioural treatment (including training in emotional awareness and control, problem-solving, and stress management) for borderline personality disorder (for example, Linehan, 1993; see Chapter 11). The development of effective interventions for personality-disordered individuals must remain a priority for psychotherapy researchers.

Family Involvement

There is a growing trend to involve family members in treatment efforts, and current evidence is that such treatments are clinically effective (Shadish et al., 1993). Some theorists earlier in this century saw family members as causing or contributing to disorders (for example, the "schizophrenogenic" mother—see Chapter 14). Indeed, some therapists expected that, to maintain the family's psychological equilibrium, family members would actively undermine the treatment. Alternatively, family members were expected to develop symptoms as the identified patient receiving treatment improved. Fortunately, there is no evidence to support either position; in fact, improvement in the identified patient may lead to enhanced psychological functioning in other family members (Hunsley & Lee, 1995). Current therapeutic approaches typically include family members, who are particularly well-placed to assist the patient in achieving and maintaining treatment goals. For example, some cognitive-behavioural interventions for agoraphobia include the patient's partner as an active participant. Although this approach may not be more effective than individual treatment, dropout rates appear lower (Dewey & Hunsley, 1990), perhaps because of the increased support and acceptance from the partner.

Marital Therapy

The past decade has witnessed a growing literature on the effectiveness of treatments for marital distress. The most widely studied marital therapy is behavioural marital therapy, developed by Jacobson and Margolin (1979). This therapy focusses on improving the communication between partners and encouraging more constructive interactions. Although this treatment has been found to have relatively large effect sizes in meta-analytic studies (0.95; Hahlweg & Markman, 1988), current evidence indicates that fewer than 50 percent of treated couples will be able to maintain happy marriages in the years following treatment (Jacobson & Addis, 1993). Interestingly, behavioural marital therapy, used as a treatment for depressed clients who are maritally distressed, appears to be effective in diminishing depressive symptomatology (Beach & O'Leary, 1992).

Although researchers only began evaluating the effects of emotionally focussed marital therapy (Greenberg & Johnson, 1988) in the mid-1980s, present indications are that it may be more effective than behavioural therapy in reducing marital conflict and helping couples to reestablish happy marriages (effect size of 1.31; Johnson, Hunsley, Greenberg, & Schindler, in press).

Generalizing to Clinical Settings

The evidence we have presented on the effectiveness of psychotherapy in the preceding sections has one major potential limitation—all studies were conducted in a research context. To meet the requirements of increasingly demanding experimental designs, researchers must carefully screen potential research participants to ensure that they fit criteria for their study, randomly assign participants to conditions, provide thorough training to therapists, and monitor the adherence of these therapists to the model of therapy they are supposed to use. All of these factors mean that the results of such experimental studies may not generalize to the "real world" of clinical services, where patients must receive services and are rarely turned away. Furthermore, few therapists are supervised as closely as those involved in randomized clinical trials.

Because of such concerns, psychotherapy researcher Neil Jacobson (1995) has warned mental health professionals that they may be overselling the benefits of psychotherapy. Can psychotherapy, as it is commonly practised, yield the effects obtained in experimental studies?

Two recent analyses of the published literature have attempted to determine the extent to which the effects of research trials on psychotherapy for children, adolescents, and adults generalize to real clinic settings. In their 1992 review of the literature on psychotherapy for children and adolescents, Weisz, Weiss, and Donenberg (1992) concluded that

Focus *Self-Help or Hype?*

A review of strategies for treating psychological disorders is incomplete without a discussion of self-help strategies. Psychologist Jerry Rosen (1993) noted that the self-help "industry" is a multimillion-dollar-a-year business. Every year more self-help books, audiotapes, videotapes, and computer programs are released. When browsing bookstores or surfing cable television channels we are faced with a range of self-help products inviting us to master anxiety, lose weight, parent effectively, or heal our inner child. Some of these materials are derived from effective treatment programs. Others are media products marketed in association with charismatic presentations. Many represent first-hand accounts of an individual's struggle with a particular problem or a therapist's experience in treating a problem. Rosen questions whether this flood of material is "self-help or hype?"

Millions of dollars of sales imply that people find self-help appealing. Recent surveys of practising psychologists (Marx et al., 1992; Starker, 1988) found that the majority of practitioners (1) reported that their clients found self-help materials to be useful and (2) sometimes suggested self-help books to clients, although psychodynamically oriented practitioners were less likely to do so. Few therapists thought the materials were harmful. Most therapists agree that therapy is not the only effective option for people who want to quit smoking, overcome a fear of flying, alter their eating patterns, or address any other issue that could be the focus of therapy. On the other hand, it is a large leap to claim that self-help approaches are as effective as psychotherapy.

Just as the claims of therapists regarding the effectiveness of therapy must be put to an empirical test, so must the claims of the promoters of self-help material. Over the past 20 years, several reviews of the research literature on self-help treatments have concluded that self-help strategies can be effective in altering symptoms and problematic behaviours (Glasgow & Rosen, 1978; Gould & Clum, 1993; Scogin et al., 1990). It appears that social skills deficits, fears, depression, headaches, insomnia, and parenting problems can be treated effectively with self-help material. On the other hand, current self-help treatments for smoking, alcohol consumption, and overeating are relatively ineffective (Gould & Clum, 1993). Overall, these findings are encouraging, for it appears that self-help materials can be effective in dealing with significant psychological concerns and disorders. The potential benefit to public health is obvious, for a self-help program offers a service to those people who may not have access to, or who may not wish to access, a mental health professional.

Yet caution is in order in generalizing from these findings. First, most outcome studies looked at self-help material on the basis of therapist-administered treatments that had already been empirically established as effective. Even a quick scan of commercially available self-help products reveals that the overwhelming majority are based on the author's experience, either as a problem-sufferer or as a practitioner who has treated the problem. Second, research participants in the outcome studies have been screened to determine that the self-help treatment being offered is appropriate. Even an effective self-help program is of little value to consumers who have misdiagnosed their problems and are therefore embarking on the wrong type of self-help program. Although self-help methods can be useful, buyers are encouraged to beware and to carefully consider whether the material is known to be effective in helping people, or whether it merely represents effective marketing. ▲

there are beneficial effects of psychotherapeutic treatment. However, when they examined the scant literature on the effects of treatment as routinely provided in clinical settings (six studies), they were forced to conclude that there is no evidence that psychotherapy, as practised in non-research-oriented settings, had any effect at all.

To determine whether such a conclusion applies also to treatments for adults, a group of psychotherapy researchers who had previously published meta-analytic studies joined forces to review the pertinent literature (Shadish et al., 1997). They were able to identify only 56 studies (out of approximately 1000 included in their own and other meta-analyses) that met criteria for clinical relevance (that is, treatment provided in a non-university setting, with referred patients and ex-perienced, professional therapists). Of those, only 15 met additional criteria for "treatment as usual." They did find a significant positive effect for psychotherapy for adults (effect sizes of 0.68 and 0.58 for the sets of 56 and 15 studies respectively).

These two meta-analytic studies have pointed up a glaring gap in our knowledge of the benefits of psychotherapy. Researchers have steadily improved the internal validity of treatment studies by using randomized clinical trials and homogeneous groups of patients and training and monitoring the therapists. However, maximizing the internal validity of a study always comes with a cost, namely a reduction in external validity. (See Chapter 4 to review these concepts of validity.) Psychotherapy researchers are increasingly aware of the need for research that possesses reasonable external validity without entirely sacrificing the controls necessary for sufficient internal validity. No standard design has yet emerged. Some researchers promote the use of advanced correlational designs, using multiple regression analyses or structural equation modelling. In these designs, variables are not controlled or eliminated as in true experiments. Rather, they are measured and their influence on the outcome of treatment is assessed through sophisticated statistical means. Other researchers propose quasi-experimental designs that do not use random assignment. Instead, the control group is obtained by evaluating the effect of alternative treatments in a separate clinical setting with a comparable patient population.

In an excellent example of this type of research, Howard and colleagues (Howard, Kopta, Krause, & Orlinsky, 1986) studied the "dose" of psychodynamic therapy (measured by the number of sessions) and its "effect" on patients. Using data from a major outpatient clinic in Chicago, they found a positive relationship between dose and effect, with diminishing returns at higher levels. A meta-analysis of data from fifteen other studies found that after eight weekly sessions, 53 percent of patients were improved; after 26 sessions, the number rose to 74 percent; and after 52 sessions it rose to 83 percent. These findings are important both because they indicate a relationship between therapy duration and outcome and because they show that many patients can benefit from even a limited number of sessions.

Howard has gone on to examine how different elements of psychological functioning respond to doses of psychodynamic treatment. Improvements in subjective well-being occurred very quickly, whereas reductions in symptomatic distress and improvements in overall life functioning required more sessions (Howard et al., 1993). In a subsequent study, Howard and colleagues found that patients' acute distress was alleviated first in therapy, followed by reductions in chronic distress and in long-standing characterological difficulties (Kopta et al., 1994).

A recent survey conducted by *Consumer Reports* (Consumer Reports, 1995) provides a different, and very visible, example of nonexperimental methodology. With the assistance of prominent clinical psychologist Martin Seligman, the editors of *Consumer Reports* included questions about psychotherapy in their 1994 annual consumer questionnaire. Of approximately 180,000 readers 2900 completed the section on psychotherapy. More than 80 percent reported substantial improvement in psychological functioning. Moreover, the longer the treatment, the greater the psychological improvement reported. Those whose choice of therapist or duration of treatment was limited by their insurance coverage did not improve as much as those whose coverage was not limited (Seligman, 1995). Critics have argued that the exclusive reliance on retrospective self-report and the absence of a control group renders the survey results meaningless (for example, Jacobson & Christensen, 1996). Despite such criticism, this survey has captured the attention of the public, the media, organized professional psychology, and policy makers in the health care system.

APTITUDE X TREATMENT INTERACTIONS

As we have seen, there are a large number of psychological interventions that are fairly effective in treating a wide range of disorders. However, not everyone benefits from treatment. It seems intuitively obvious that what works for one person may not work for another. If only we could determine who is best suited for each type of therapy! Indeed, there is a line of research that attempts to identify client or therapist characteristics that will pinpoint the best treatment for an individual. **Aptitude X treatment interaction (ATI) research** has been promoted as the crucial next stage of psychotherapy research.

Suppose a researcher wishes to test the hypothesis that depressed people lacking in interpersonal skills would do better in group therapy than individual therapy. To test this, the researcher would need to recruit depressed people, including those who are lacking in social skills and those who are not, and then randomly assign them to one of the two treatments. In analyzing the data, the researcher would first examine with analysis of variance statistics the main effect of treatment (Was one treatment better overall than the other?) and the main effect of client social skill (Overall, do those low or high in social skills show greater improvement in their depression?). Only then can the researcher examine the interaction effect to determine whether group treatment was particularly beneficial to those with low social skills.

Designing ATI research poses a number of methodological challenges (Dance & Neufeld, 1988; Smith & Sechrest, 1991). First, there should be compelling theoretical reasons for examining particular client and/or therapist characteristics. Next, the researcher must be able to compare at least two treatments in one study, which requires substantial research funds. Finally, since analysis of variance requires that main effects be tested before interaction effects, large sample sizes are necessary to ensure sufficient statistical power.

To date, only a minority of ATI studies have yielded significant findings, possibly because of methodological limitations. More recently, though, well-conceptualized and well-designed ATI studies are providing important information on how best to match treatments to client needs. For example, Beutler and colleagues (Beutler et al., 1991) examined the effect of client reactance potential: a tendency to react against authoritative directions. Sixty-three depressed clients were randomly assigned to group cognitive therapy (CT), focussed expressive psychotherapy (FEP, a group experiential treatment), or supportive, self-directed therapy (S/SD, using telephone contacts and self-help materials). Clients who scored high on a self-report measure of reactance potential were found to improve more in the S/SD treatment than in either of the other two treatments. Those scoring low on this measure improved significantly more in CT than in the S/SD treatment. People who dislike being directed may be more suited to a treatment approach that allows them to proceed at their own pace, on their own initiative.

The promise of ATI research is obvious, as optimal matching of clients to treatments should result in improvements in client health, and ultimately reduce health care costs.

EMPIRICALLY SUPPORTED TREATMENTS: GOING PUBLIC WITH OUR RESEARCH

Over the past decade, health care systems in most Western countries have been restructured. Governments, insurance companies, hospital boards, and health care professionals are beginning to recognize the importance of basing health care services on established scientific findings rather than practitioners' assumptions. Psychotherapy is not exempt from this trend, and there is growing pressure to develop standards for **evidence-based practice**.

In 1993, the American Psychological Association's first Task Force on Promotion and Dissemination of Psychological Procedures set out to (1) develop criteria to determine whether a psychosocial intervention has been demonstrated empirically to be effective and (2) suggest methods for educating clinical psychologists, third-party payers, and the public about effective psychotherapies. Current criteria for an **empirically supported therapy** (Chambless et al., 1996) are presented in Table 16.5. The first task force, along with two subsequent task forces, also released a list of treatments that were considered to have met these criteria. In the U.K. a group of psychotherapy researchers working with the National Health Service have developed similar criteria and lists of treatments (Roth & Fonagy, 1996).

The momentum behind this initiative continues to grow. For example, the American Psychological Association now requires that clinical psychology training programs and internships train students in some empirically supported treatments. However, not all psychologists are supportive of such moves. Many researchers feel that the criteria for "empirically supported" are too lax. Conversely, many practitioners object to the development of an "empirically supported" list, fearing that health care agencies and companies will refuse to support any other therapies.

Nevertheless, it is clear that this work will have a lasting impact on psychotherapy. The Section on Clinical Psychology of the Canadian Psychological Association has begun to

---

Table 16.5 Criteria for Designation as an Empirically Supported Therapy

One of two sets of studies are necessary:

I. At least 2 group design studies (that is, randomized clinical trials), demonstrating efficacy by being:
   A. Superior to pill, psychological placebo, or another treatment
   B. Equivalent to an already established treatment, in studies with adequate statistical power (that is, at least 30 participants per group)

II. At least 10 single-case-design studies demonstrating efficacy. These studies must have:
   A. Used good experimental designs
   B. Compared the intervention to another treatment, as in I (A)

Furthermore, for both criterion I and criterion II:
   A. Studies must be conducted with treatment manuals.
   B. The characteristics of the participants must be clearly described.
   C. Treatment effects must have been found by at least two different researchers or research teams.

Source: Adapted from D. L. Chambless, W. C. Sanderson, V. Shoham, S. B. Johnson, K. S. Pope, P. Crits-Christoph, M. Baker, B. Johnson, S. R. Woody, S. Sue, L. Beutler, D. A. Williams, & S. McCurry, An update on empirically validated therapies, *The Clinical Psychologist, 49(1996)* (2), 5–18.

---

consider how clinical psychology in Canada should be influenced by this work (Hunsley, Dobson, Johnston, & Mikail, 1998). Some possibilities include requiring training in empirically supported treatments in Canadian clinical psychology training programs and internships and promoting continuing education opportunities for practising clinical psychologists to learn these treatments.

In the eyes of many clinical psychologists, the field of psychotherapy research has matured sufficiently to warrant such changes. In the relatively short time since Freud, psychotherapy has moved from being an esoteric set of practices based entirely on speculation and supposition to an essential health care service with substantial foundations in solid scientific knowledge.

PANORAMA

Once people suffering from a psychological disorder decide to seek treatment, they often face a difficult decision—whether to take medication or to begin psychotherapy. As we have indicated in this chapter, there is evidence that both options can be helpful. Conversely, it is clear that neither option works for all people.

Researchers have examined treatment outcomes associated with these two alternatives for a number of disorders. In many instances, including the treatment of agoraphobia (Michelson

& Marchione, 1991), panic (Gould, Otto, Pollack, 1995), generalized anxiety disorder (Gould, Otto, Pollack, & Yap, 1997), obsessive-compulsive disorder (Abramowitz, 1997), enuresis (Houts, Berman, & Abramson, 1994), and depression (Antonuccio, Danton, & DeNelsky, 1995), both pharmacotherapy and cognitive-behavioural interventions appear to be effective. In general, cognitive-behavioural treatments for these and many other nonpsychotic disorders tend to be comparable or superior to the most effective medications.

Moreover, although the combination of psychotherapy and pharmacotherapy is frequently endorsed in clinical practice, there is little evidence that such a combination improves on the short-term success of either medication or therapy.

People often assume that medication should be the first line of treatment for psychological disorders. This may indeed be the case for some disorders, such as schizophrenia and bipolar affective disorder; yet there is reason to be cautious in drawing this conclusion about pharmacological treatment in general. Effective medications may be underused by some physicians (Wells & Sturm, 1996) and medications with no demonstrated efficacy may be routinely administered by others (for example, antidepressants for depressed children and adolescents: Sommers-Flanagan & Sommers-Flanagan, 1996). In addition, medication may lead to relief of symptoms without changing the personal or environ-mental characteristics that created the problem (Rickels, Schweizer, Case, & Greenblatt, 1990; Schweizer, Rickels, Case, & Greenblatt, 1990). Also emerging is evidence that the cost of pharmacotherapy for the treatment of psychological disorders may be greater than previously recognized (Antonuccio, Thomas, & Danton, 1997). In the final analysis it may be unwise to ask whether pharmaceutical or psychological treatments are best. Some individuals may not be good candidates for psychological interventions on the basis of their diagnoses, personal characteristics, and social conditions. Likewise some people may not be good candidates for psychotropic medication. People's preferences must also be considered. In the end, the most reasoned approach to patient care should ask what treatment, or combination of treatments, might work best for a given individual at a particular point in time.

SUMMARY

The most commonly employed biological treatments for mental disorders are electroconvulsive therapy (ECT) and psychopharmacology. ECT appears to be a highly effective intervention for psychotic depression. Typically it is used only after the patient has not improved with other treatments. Although the precise mechanism by which ECT affects depression is not understood, current practices have made it a safe medical treatment that has fewer side-effects than in the past. Drugs have proven to be effective in treating a wide range of disorders, including psychotic disorders, anxiety disorders, affective disorders, and attention deficit disorder. Although patient compliance and discontinuation of treatment continue to be a concern, recent classes of medication have far fewer side-effects than earlier drugs.

Psychotherapeutic interventions for mental disorders and other psychological problems come in a variety of orientations (including psychodynamic, humanistic-experiential, and cognitive-behavioural) and are offered in a variety of modalities (individual, couple, family, group). Psychodynamic approaches emphasize the role of unconscious processes in determining psychological disorders and interpersonal problems and assume that much of the client's distress stems from patterns developed early in life. Humanistic-experiential approaches focus on emotional aspects of subjective experience, highlighting the impact of affect in the client's current life situation. Cognitive-behavioural approaches centre on the role of internal (thoughts, images, emotions, bodily sensations) and external (objects, interpersonal interactions) stimuli in shaping the client's adaptive and maladaptive reactions. Numerous attempts have been made to combine these theoretical approaches in practice (eclectic therapy) and in theoretical rationale (integrative therapy).

Unlike biological treatments, which can only be administered by a physician, a wide range of mental health professionals (for example, psychologists, physicians, psychiatrists, social workers) may offer psychotherapeutic services. People seek psychotherapy for a broad range of reasons, including dealing with a mental disorder, adjusting to life transitions and losses, and seeking a fuller understanding of themselves. The majority of psychotherapy clients are women, have relatively high levels of education, and are young-to-middle-aged adults. Research across treatment settings clearly shows that, although some clients receive therapy for many months or years, most clients have five to thirteen sessions.

The history of psychotherapy has been very controversial, with many debates about the merits and effectiveness of the different forms of psychotherapy. From hundreds of randomized controlled trials of psychotherapy and on meta-analytic summaries of these studies, it is clear that psychotherapy, in general, can be effective in treating many disorders and problems. Debate continues, however, about differences in efficacy among the various therapeutic approaches.

Current evidence indicates that there are effective treatments for many Axis I disorders (for example, depression, anxiety disorders, insomnia, conduct disorder). Although many of these of treatments are cognitive-behavioural in orientation, there is growing evidence supporting the use of some psychodynamic and humanistic-experiential treatments. Developing effective treatments has been a focus of many researchers; now one of the major trends in current psychotherapy research is examining whether the results of these empirical studies generalize to the treatments routinely offered in clinical settings. Aptitude X treatment interaction research seeks strategies to optimize the fit between client and treatment approach. Given the growing demands by the public and the health care system for evidence-based health care practices, it is clear that psychotherapy research will have an increasing effect on the nature and type of psychotherapeutic services available.

KEY TERMS

psychoactive agents (p. 399)
extrapyramidal effects (p. 399)
transference (p. 404)
ego analysts (p. 404)
individual psychology (p. 404)
interpersonal psychodynamic
    psychotherapy (p. 404)

time-limited dynamic psychotherapy
    (TLDP) (p. 405)
therapeutic alliance (p. 405)
client-centred therapy (p. 405)
token economy (p. 406)
response shaping (p. 406)
aversion therapy (p. 406)
systematic desensitization (p. 406)
self-instructional training (p. 407)

emotionally focussed therapy (p. 409)
reframing (p. 409)
meta-analysis (p. 411)
effect size (p. 411)
aptitude X treatment interaction (ATI)
    research (p. 417)
evidence-based practice (p. 418)
empirically supported therapy
    (p. 418)

ADDITIONAL RESOURCES

Centre for Addiction and Mental Health
33 Russell Street
Toronto, ON M5S 2S1
(416) 595-6015
(416) 595-6881 fax

Canadian Psychiatric Association
260-441 MacLaren Street
Toronto, ON K2P 2H3
(613) 234-2815
(613) 234-9857 fax
cpa@medical.org

Canadian Psychological Association
151 Slater Street
Suite 205
Ottawa, ON K1P 5H3
(613) 237-2144
(613) 237-1674 fax
iparisien@cpa.org

www.personal.kent.edu/~iacp/
The site of the International Association for Cognitive
Psychotherapy provides a range of resources about cognitive psychotherapy.

www.ect.org
This resource site about electroconvulsive shock treatment
(ECT) includes studies and statistics, news, media articles,
and writings from medical practitioners, activists, and survivors, and identifies truths and misinformation about ECT.

www.aamft.org
The American Association for Marital and Family
Therapy provides various resources about marital and
family therapy.

www.blarg.net/~charlatn/depression/DepMeds.html
A collection of articles from *The Essential Guide to
Prescription Drugs*, including information about various
drugs used to treat depression.

Chapter 17

Mental Disorders and Aging

V. Jane Knox

William L. Gekoski

Just after Laura S. retired at age 65, her only daughter, Stephanie, was killed in a mountain-climbing accident. Laura and her daughter, a single pediatrician, had always been very close and people often remarked that they seemed more like sisters than like mother and daughter. Immediately after hearing the terrible news, Laura began a whirlwind of activity. First, she arranged singlehandedly to have Stephanie's body returned home from Nepal. Next, she planned an elaborate funeral. During these few days, Laura barely slept and never shed a tear. She displayed no sadness, and showed anxiety only about funeral details. Laura wanted everything to be perfect for Stephanie. Her friends praised her strength of character, but her husband, Mark, was silently worried about the frantic pace of activity.

For a few weeks after the funeral, Laura's state of agitation persisted. She could not sleep and usually declined food at mealtime. Migraine headaches, an occasional problem for her before, became almost daily occurrences.

Then, just when Mark had convinced himself that Laura's reactions were normal in the face of such a terrible loss, she began to behave in ways that caused him serious concern. Laura had not cried to this point, but now she began to cry often, sometimes for hours at a time. She still could not sleep well, but now when she was awake she seemed to have little energy for anything that Mark might suggest. She preferred to sit alone in the den doing nothing at all. Laura talked of nothing but Stephanie and of her desire to be reunited with her daughter. Often she said that she, not Stephanie, should have been the one killed. At other times she would say that Stephanie was with them, that she could see Stephanie sitting in a chair next to hers. When Laura began to speak to Stephanie as though she were really in the room, Mark decided it was time to seek professional help.

Mark made an appointment for Laura with a clinical psychologist, who first conducted a thorough diagnostic workup and then met with the couple. The psychologist reassured them that Laura was not mentally ill. Rather, she was suffering from normal bereavement, particularly because her daughter's death was premature and unexpected. Mark was especially relieved to learn that hallucinating the presence of Stephanie was not an unusual reaction within the first months after a death. When the psychologist learned that Stephanie's birthday was two weeks away, she pointed out that such anniversaries are commonly times at which symptoms of bereavement worsen. She recommended that Laura begin bereavement counselling right away.

Changing Demography

In all the developed countries, older adults are the fastest-growing age group. Although different chronological ages are used to define older adults for different purposes, we will use the most conventional dividing line, and say that an older adult is anyone over 65. Table 17.1 shows the growth of the older population in Canada in 20-year intervals between 1951 and 2011 (projected). A number of important observations can be made from the table. Let's consider first what happens to the over-65 group. In 1951, a mere 7.8 percent of the population fell into this category. By 1991, approximately 11 percent of the Canadian population was over 65, and it is projected that by 2011 the percentage will increase to 14.5 percent. By 2031, Statistics Canada (1994) expects that 21.8 percent of the population will be over 65. Among those over age 65, the fastest-growing subgroup is that of people over age 80. From 1991 to 2011, for example, the Canadian population is projected to increase by 30.8 percent, and the over-65 population by 57.8 percent, while the over-80 population is projected to grow by 111.3 percent—more than double.

There are a number of reasons for these trends, including the aging of the large cohort of baby boomers and their low birth rate. A major reason, of course, is improvements in both preventive health care and medical treatments. Advances in public health (for example, immunization, safer drinking water. etc.), workplace safety, and environmental

Table 17.1 Canadian Population, 1951–2001 (projected)

	Population		
Year	**Total**	**65+**	**80+**
1951	14,009,000	1,086,000	149,000
1971	21,680,001	1,744,000	342,000
1991	27,073,000	3,161,000	657,000
2011	35,420,000	4,981,000	1,388,000

	Percentages		
Year	**65+**	**80+**	**Of 65+ Who Are 80+**
1951	7.8	1.1	13.7
1971	8.1	1.6	19.2
1991	11.7	2.4	10.8
2011	14.1	3.9	27.9

Note: The first two percentage columns show the percentage of the *total* Canadian population that was (or will be) over 65 and over 80 respectively. The third column shows the percentage *of the over-65 population* that is actually over 80 years of age.

Sources: Adapted from E. G. Moore & M. W. Rosenberg, *Growing old in Canada* (Statistics Canada Census Monograph Series) (Toronto: ITP Nelson, 1997), Tables 1.1 and 5.1; Statistics Canada, Census Analysis Division, Population projections 1993–2041: Canada, provinces and territories (Ottawa: Minister of Industry, Science, and Technology, 1994); Census of Canada 1951–1991.

protection prevent potentially fatal medical problems, and newly developed and more effective medications and surgical procedures can prolong life. In addition, factors such as greater affluence and higher levels of educational attainment are seen as contributing to increased longevity. More affluent, better-educated people are likely, for example, to have less dangerous jobs, jobs requiring less physical wear and tear on their bodies, better nutrition, and better health care.

What do these changing demographics mean for the mental health field? As the proportion of older adults in the population increases, there will be a disproportionate increase in older as opposed to younger adults with mental disorders. In light of this, we are almost certainly not training enough practitioners who are knowledgeable about, or specialists in dealing with, mental disorders in the older adult population. Nor are we likely to have enough community support services or beds in institutional settings to accommodate the projected numbers of older adults with mental disorders.

Changes in Prevalence in Old Age

Some mental disorders, such as schizophrenia, become less prevalent as we age. Some appear to be equally prevalent regardless of age: for example, obsessive-compulsive disorder. But, one mental disorder, dementia, is much more prevalent in older adults (American Psychiatric Association, 1994). Although dementia, the loss of cognitive ability, does occur in younger people, it is rare and generally secondary to another disorder such as substance abuse or AIDS. Dementia, as a primary mental disorder, is clearly a disorder of old age. According to 1991 Canadian data, dementia affects 2.4 percent of the population aged 65 to 74, 11.1 percent of the population 75 to 84, and 34.5 percent of the population 85 and over (Canadian Study of Health and Aging Working Group, 1994). Dementia will be considered in greater detail in a separate section below.

Increased Vulnerability in Old Age

A person is more likely to develop a mental disorder at times of increased vulnerability (Gatz, Kasl-Godley, & Karel, 1996). When people are vulnerable, they may become unable to cope with previously manageable problems or situations. Have you ever found that something as simple as a cold or headache has reduced your ability to cope with a difficult situation, perhaps an exam? To take a more dramatic example, a person might be able to cope with being laid off from work, or with a spouse being diagnosed with a terminal illness; but if both happened close together, the person might be overwhelmed and might begin to show signs of depression or anxiety. The first blow may be said to have increased the person's emotional vulnerability to the point that he or she is unable to cope with the second. At some point in old age, most people experience increased vulnerability—both physically, as various organ systems begin to be compromised, and psychologically, with losses in areas such as social support (due to death of friends and relatives), and independence (due to loss of driver's licence or relocation from home to institution). Some losses typically occur suddenly, such as the death of a spouse or friend, relocation, hospitalization, or loss of a driver's licence. Other losses, such as vision and hearing, and problems with pain, mobility, incontinence, and finances tend to be more ongoing.

A loss of either type, because it taxes the individual's capacity to cope, may directly or indirectly increase vulnerability to mental disorders. Often a single loss can have widespread effects. For example, loss of hearing not only deprives the individual of the kind of easy interactions with people that most of us take for granted, but may be used as a reason to withdraw from meaningful and rewarding activities and may even lead to suspiciousness or depression. In the extreme case, increased vulnerability may result in death. For example, research clearly shows the loss of spouse increases the risk to an older person's mortality for an extended period (Ferraro, 1989).

Older adults often experience multiple losses, though the nature and degree of loss varies from person to person. There are also wide individual differences in how loss is dealt with. Many older people are prepared for some of the losses they experience and so their vulnerability is only slightly increased. People with highly successful coping strategies can be extremely resilient in the face of new losses (Aldwin, 1994).

Common Myths About Mental Disorders and Aging

One of the most common myths about aging is that the development of pathology must be accepted as a part of normal aging and therefore need not be treated (Birren & Renner, 1980). However, by definition, things that are *pathological* cannot be *normal*. The distinction between normal and pathological is most clearly seen with respect to physical well-being. Normal processes are seen as universal, genetically based, and having developed through evolution to serve the needs of the species. Clearly, puberty and menopause are normal processes of biological development. Pathology, on the other hand, refers to something that deviates from normal, is not universal, is not necessarily genetic in origin, and does not contribute to the individual's well-being.

Gerontologists from many disciplines believe that there is such a thing as a normal aging process: that in the absence of a pathological condition such as heart disease or cancer, a normal process of systems slowing down in old age will ultimately cause some system to stop functioning and the person will die of old age rather than of any particular disease (Hayflick, 1988). Although it is not yet clear exactly what governs the normal aging process, there is a great deal of evidence of various kinds to support the notion that there *is* a **normal aging** process (Fries & Crapo, 1981). Although it is true that older people are more likely than younger people to develop some sort of pathology, this is not because pathology is part of normal aging, but simply because the longer one lives, the greater the likelihood of experiencing those conditions that trigger pathology. Even if the majority of older people have a pathological condition, that does not mean the condition is normal, only that it is typical. Pathologies routinely compromise quality of life. Most gerontologists believe that as we learn how to prevent pathology, and/or intervene to stop or delay pathology, more and more older adults will die of old age, without suffering pathology-related incapacities.

How is all of this relevant to mental disorders in old age? In two ways. First, mental disorders often develop as part of, or secondary to, physical pathologies (Parkinsonian dementia is an example). Second, like physical pathologies, mental disorders in older adults are not part of normal aging. The literature is clear on this point: stable mental health is typical as we age, even into advanced old age (Birren & Renner, 1980). When dramatic behavioural changes do occur in older adults they likely reflect a pathological condition, or some factor, such as medication, which mimics pathology (Butler & Lewis, 1982). Mental disorders should be cause for concern in old people, as they are in younger people, and should be treated.

Another myth concerns treatment. It is widely believed, among health care professionals and among the general population (including older adults themselves) that older adults do not respond well to treatment for mental disorders (Zivian, Larsen, Gekoski, Knox, & Hatchette, 1994; Zivian, Larsen, Knox, Gekoski, & Hatchette, 1992). This belief is simply false. The evidence is clear that, no matter what the treatment modality, older adults are no less responsive than their younger counterparts (Gatz, Popkin, Pino, & Vanden Bos, 1985; Smyer, Zarit, & Qualls, 1990). How did this myth develop? We do not know for certain, but there are a number of likely contributors. First, there is the stereotype of older adults as rigid and set in their ways. It is not a big leap to the conclusion that older people are less able to acquire new ways of thinking and behaving than are younger people. Second, the fact that fewer older adults are treated for mental disorders may lead some to assume that this is because treatment is less successful with them. Finally, a number of studies have found that health care professionals prefer all other age groups over older adults (Zivian et al., 1992). Perhaps this prejudice leads them to assume that treatment will not be successful.

HISTORICAL OVERVIEW

Historically, older adults with mental disorders were typically seen as eccentric rather than ill. Their "eccentricities" were generally tolerated by those around them as long as their aberrant behaviour did not seriously interfere with the family or occupational commitments of others. When they became too disruptive, they were isolated, either in a variety of institutions or at home. Such eccentricities were seen both as part of normal old age and as something about which nothing

could be done. Starting in the 1930s, psychiatric treatment—psychosurgery or sedation—was available, although limited to the most disruptive of older adults suffering from mental disorders. More commonly, however, "treatment" for such people continued to be isolation in some form of institution.

The idea that mental disorders in older adults can and should be treated is a relatively new one. Kermis (1984) has argued that as recently as 1972 the clinical psychology of aging was virtually nonexistent, and that even the most widely used assessment tools were not normed for people over 65. Today there is at least nominal acceptance in clinical psychology of the value of treating older adults with mental disorders.

AGE-SPECIFIC ISSUES OF DIAGNOSIS AND TREATMENT

Recognizing and treating mental disorders in older adults is complicated by a number of factors particularly relevant to this population (Gatz et al., 1985; Smyer, Zarit, & Qualls, 1990). Getting the diagnosis correct may be extremely difficult because similar sets of symptoms may be the result of more than one disorder. The most common example is that an apparent memory impairment may be caused by early dementia or by depression. Differential diagnosis is possible but requires appropriate knowledge and open-mindedness on the part of the practitioner.

Polypharmacy—the concurrent use of multiple medications—can also complicate diagnosis of mental disorders in older adults. Side-effects of medications may mimic, or obscure, symptoms of mental disorder.

Some older adults may not acknowledge symptoms because they perceive a stigma attached to mental disorders. Societal attitudes may compromise diagnosis as well, if practitioners, older adults, and their families believe that certain mental disorders are part of normal aging. Consider the following common remarks:

Mother seems so anxious, but she would never agree to see a psychiatrist. I'm sure she would be too embarrassed. What if someone saw her coming or going?

Uncle Joe is getting more and more forgetful—but what can you expect from someone his age?

Dad seems very depressed, but you know that he won't talk about what is bothering him.

Aunt Sally seems so confused, but the doctor says that at her age we should be thankful she is alive.

In addition, professional training often does not focus on issues important in diagnosing mental disorders in older adults.

The same factors may also impede the treatment of older adults, even if they are accurately diagnosed. (See the Focus box "Older Adults: The Missing Clients" for further discussion of these issues.)

Focus

Older Adults: The Missing Clients

By any yardstick—admissions to psychiatric facilities, attendance at community health clinics, representation in caseloads—older adults are underrepresented as users of mental health services. Why? Probably not because they have fewer mental disorders; the best estimates available suggest that mental disorders occur at at least the same rate as in other age groups. Certainly not because treatment does not work; it does. Then why are older people's mental health needs underserved? According to Gatz et al. (1985), the reasons fall into three categories: client barriers, therapist barriers, and systemic barriers.

There are a host of possible client barriers:

- older adults' belief that they are too old for treatment to be effective;
- shame or embarrassment about admitting to a mental disorder;
- discomfort with a younger therapist;
- a wish to remain self-reliant; and
- a reluctance to consider psychological processes (this is referred to as not being *psychologically-minded*)

Systemic barriers include:

- the paucity of mental health professionals specializing in older adults;
- logistical difficulties with transportation and mobility;
- costs for uninsured services; and

- other people's attitudes and beliefs

Evidence on the last point comes from a Canadian study by Zivian et al. (1994). The authors asked a random selection of visitors to the Ontario Science Centre about their views of mental disorders across the life span. Men and women of all ages thought that psychotherapy would be of less benefit to older patients than to younger ones. Would these people encourage an older friend or relative to seek treatment for a mental disorder? Well, maybe. But perhaps not as enthusiastically as they would a younger sufferer. Another line of evidence comes from a recent study of Canadian family physicians (Mackenzie, 1997). The doctors indicated that they thought treatment for mental disorders was likely to be more effective for younger patients than for older ones. The family physician is often the first person with whom an older patient discusses symptoms of a mental disorder. You might expect that, being less optimistic about the outcome, physicians would be less likely to refer older patients to mental health professionals. And there is plenty of evidence that this is the case (Gatz et al., 1985; Macdonald, 1986; Waxman & Carner, 1984).

As for therapist barriers, it is well documented that psychologists and psychiatrists are reluctant to treat

older adults and prefer to work with younger clients (Zivian et al., 1992). Why? There are a number of reasons.

- unresolved issues with their own parents or with their own aging process;
- fear that the client might die while in treatment;
- concern that they will be considered a low-status therapist;
- the belief that older people cannot benefit from treatment;
- the belief that mental disorders are a normal part of aging; and
- the belief that treating older people is a waste of resources

Unfortunately, older clients are not likely to be better served by the next generation of therapists. DeRyck, Gekoski, Knox, and Zivian (1996) found that graduate students training as clinical psychologists underestimated the benefit of treatment for older adults and rated them as their least preferred client group. There is some room for optimism, though: the more professional experience students had with older clients, the more positive they were about them. Still, we have a long way to go if the mental health needs of the fastest growing segment of our population are to be met. ▲

Comorbidity is more likely to occur, and more likely to create treatment problems, for older than younger adults. The appropriate treatment for one disorder may be incompatible with the otherwise optimal treatment for the second. For example, one of the medications thought to slow the progression of Alzheimer's disease should not be taken by people with kidney disease.

PREVALENCE OF MENTAL DISORDERS IN OLDER ADULTS

An awareness of prevalence should alert practitioners to what mental disorders to look for in older adults and thus should

contribute to accurate diagnosis. Moreover, it will allow us to ask *why* there are changes in prevalence over the life span. The answers to such questions may well offer important insights into prevention and treatment strategies. Unfortunately the information we have is extremely limited (Abraham & Crooks, 1984; Gatz & Smyer, 1992).

Epidemiological information on mental disorders is typically available from psychiatric hospital admissions, community mental health clinic attendance, or from major surveys. In each case, a variety of factors may cause the data to differentially underestimate prevalence for older adults. First, older adults are less likely to seek treatment and less likely to acknowledge that they are in treatment or that they have a mental disorder. Given changes in the popular culture, it is not surprising that younger people are less likely than older adults to see mental disorders as stigmatizing and thus more willing to admit having these disorders. Nor do the attitudes of their families and of society in general encourage the optimism that would lead them to seek treatment. The inaccurate beliefs and negative attitudes of practitioners also discourage them from seeking to diagnose mental disorders in older adults or to offer treatment, again leading to underreporting. Finally, family physicians are more likely to refer younger people with mental disorders to mental health professionals, but to treat older adults with mental disorders themselves rather than to refer them (Goldstrom et al., 1987). The family physician may not want to embarrass the patient or the patient's family by referral to a specialist, or may believe that the specialist will not have an effective treatment available, or may believe that the patient, if referred, would not go to the specialist. Whatever the reason, patients treated by family physicians are less likely to be counted in the statistics.

Before looking at actual prevalence rates, let us review the concepts of prevalence and incidence introduced in Chapter 3. Let us say we are interested in the prevalence of schizophrenia in a young (25–34) and in an old (65–74) age group. The percentage of people in each age group who *currently* have schizophrenia is referred to as the **point prevalence** for that age group. This percentage includes those people who had the disorder prior to entering this age group as well as those who newly developed the disorder while in the age group in question. Incidence refers to the percentage of people in an age group who developed the disorder for the first time while in the age group. Both incidence and point prevalence information are useful in resource planning, because in some cases, a newly developed disorder may call for different treatment than a long-established one. To avoid confusion, we should also mention lifetime prevalence: the percentage of people in a group who have *ever* had the disorder, whether or not they still have it. Unless otherwise specified, prevalence data in this chapter are point prevalence estimates.

The range of prevalence estimates for mental disorders in older adults is very wide—from 2 percent (Kramer, Taube, & Redick, 1973) to 40 percent (Kral, Eastwood, Kedward, McCormak, & Jones, 1983). How can there be such utterly different estimates? Different techniques (for example, census-type surveys, admission rates) have been used in generating the various estimates; some estimates have been corrected for presumed underreporting in older adults; some estimates are based on Canadian and others on U.S. sources. Taking these considerations into account, the best guess would put overall prevalence of mental disorders in older adults at between 10 and 25 percent. These estimates suggest that prevalence rates for older adults are roughly similar to rates for younger people. The prevalence of some particular disorders, however, differs dramatically at different points in the life span.

THEORETICAL FRAMEWORKS OF AGING

Because the way we conceptualize things has a strong influence on our actions, it is useful to look at what theories have been used or could be used to help us better understand the causes of mental disorders in older adults. There are two ways to approach the task of looking at theoretical frameworks for understanding mental disorders in older adults. The first involves considering theories that have been developed in an attempt to understand the causes of mental disorders, and ask what these theories have to say about mental disorders in older adults. The second approach involves considering theories developed specifically to understand aging and older adults, and asking what light they might shed on our understanding of mental disorders in older adults. Chapter 2 outlines several different theoretical frameworks for thinking about mental disorder, including biological, psychodynamic, behavioural, cognitive, and humanistic or existential.

With few exceptions, theorists have not extended, adapted, or refined any of these approaches to fit specifically the clinical experience of older adults. It is not clear whether they have concluded that a particular framework can be applied without adaptation to older adults, or they have simply not asked the question.

Much of psychoanalytic theory, for example, deals with how the early development of personality structures and unconscious processes can lead to mental disorders later in life. However, nothing in this approach differentiates between mental disorders in 25-year-olds and 75-year-olds. Not only did Freudian theory fail to differentiate the adult years, one of Freud's legacies was his explicit position that psychotherapy with older adults was ill-advised. It could be argued that traces of this legacy are evident to this day.

In contrast, Erik Erikson (1950) extended psychoanalytic theory in a number of ways, one of which was to suggest that the critical issues for successful functioning are different at different points in development. Erikson did not, however, focus on the implications of his lifespan approach for understanding mental disorders at different points in the life course.

Let us turn to an examination of theoretical approaches to understanding aging and old age. A number of approaches focus on how older adults adjust to or cope with age-related changes and may inform our thinking about mental disorders in older adults. Three approaches are of particular interest here: social breakdown/social reconstruction, activity/disengagement, and selective optimization with compensation. Let us look at each of these in turn.

Social Breakdown/Social Reconstruction

According to this view, the stage is set for psychological breakdown by a precondition of vulnerability or susceptibility. Causes of increased vulnerability might include increasing forgetfulness, limited mobility, or grief resulting from the death of one's spouse. Each can make it more difficult to cope. Also, vulnerability may lead, as shown in Figure 17.1, to the older person being labelled by others as deficient or incompetent. Others may then start to treat the older person as sick or dependent, thus limiting the person's opportunities to use his or her skills. The result is the loss or weakening of those skills, which in turn leads the older person to identify him- or herself as sick, dependent, or inadequate. This self-perception increases the person's vulnerability, and the cycle may repeat itself until an actual breakdown occurs. It is easy to imagine how a sequence of losses might result in several passes through this cycle until finally a full-blown breakdown occurs. Kuypers and Bengston (1973) suggested that interventions by family and by society can break the **social breakdown** cycle, or even reverse it, starting a cycle of **social reconstruction**. Interventions include counselling, changes in the environment, and education, and can work at any point in the cycle. Which type of intervention will be most effective may depend on where the person is in the cycle.

Activity/Disengagement

Mental disorders in older adults may be better understood against the backdrop of how successful aging is perceived. Activity theory and disengagement theory both arise from the area of social gerontology and are the most frequently invoked theories of successful aging. These two theories have generally been seen as diametrically opposed, so that when all the evidence is in only one will be supported.

Activity theory holds that people who age successfully are the ones who maintain the activity level they had in middle age (Maddox, 1963). More strenuous or demanding activities (such as tennis, employment) can be replaced by less demanding activities (such as golf, hobbies). What is important is that the amount of activity be kept up. If it declines, psychological involvement in life declines with it, and sets the stage for the development of physical and/or mental disorders.

Disengagement theory, on the other hand, holds that as people move into old age, it is normal and natural to slow down as the individual and society begin to separate or *disengage* from each other (Cumming & Henry, 1961). One example of disengagement is when an elderly woman stops holding an annual holiday dinner for her family, but is content to simply be a dinner guest at the home of a child or grandchild. From this perspective, aging successfully involves accepting disengagement, and it is the person who refuses to disengage who is at higher risk for mental disorders.

Which of these two theories has received empirical support? Both have received considerable support. Research has shown that successful aging is a result of at least two factors, only one of which is activity level. The other is personality. If personality and activity levels are considered jointly, a number of different, but equally successful, pat-

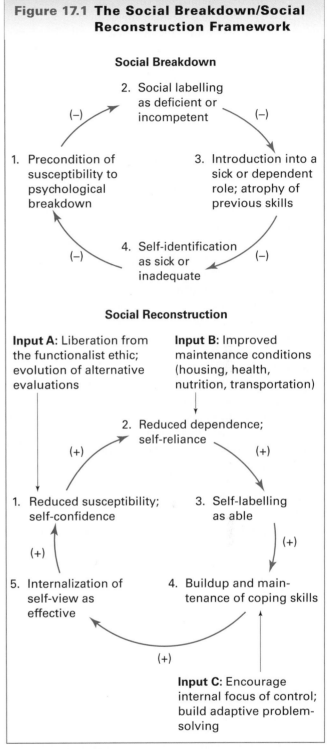

Figure 17.1 The Social Breakdown/Social Reconstruction Framework

Source: J. Kuypers & V. Bengston, Competence and social breakdown: A social-psychological view of aging, *Human Development 16(1973),* 37–49. Reproduced with permission of S. Karger AG, Basel.

terns of aging emerge (Neugarten, Havighurst, & Tobin, 1965). Among these are the *disengaged*, people who are highly satisfied by disengaging from activities and watching the world go by, and the *reorganizers*, people who are highly satisfied by maintaining earlier activity levels. Thus, both activity theory and disengagement theory can be considered useful. Not all people age successfully, of course, and research has also identified some unsuccessful patterns of aging, including *dependent*, *apathetic*, and *disorganized*. It would be expected that people exhibiting less successful patterns of aging would be more prone to mental disorders.

Selective Optimization with Compensation

This is a recently developed theoretical framework (Baltes & Baltes, 1990) which holds that even within the context of normal aging and in the absence of pathology, old age brings losses of abilities and skills. Successful aging entails optimizing remaining skills and compensating where possible for reduced abilities. For example, response speed slows in old age due to changes at the synaptic level. In the normal course of our activities, we emphasize both speed and accuracy of response. When speed slows, then shifting emphasis to accuracy will allow high levels of performance to continue into old age with an accompanying sense of mastery or self-efficacy. Games focussing on accuracy, such as chess, will be favoured over games in which timing is critical, such as charades.

The selective optimization/compensation framework could be used to maximize functioning in people with certain mental disorders by building on strengths and avoiding weaknesses. For example, activities that do not have heavy memory demands, such as bingo, will afford greater gratification to dementia patients. This theoretical framework is especially attractive, as it seems to be equally appropriate for dealing with all older adults, whether or not they suffer from physical or mental pathology.

The remaining sections of this chapter will focus on specific mental disorders as they are manifested in older adults. Emphasis will be on disorders that are more common in old age or manifested differently in old age.

Mood Disorders

Mrs. S., 73, was referred to an outpatient psychological clinic by her family physician with symptoms of sleeplessness, appetite loss, and feelings of hopelessness and despair. Mrs. S. lost her husband of nearly 50 years about eighteen months ago. Shortly thereafter, at her children's urging, she moved from the family home to a senior's apartment complex. Now she thinks the move might have been a mistake. Compared to her house, the apartment feels tiny and holds no fond memories. Mrs. S. reports that she is still depressed over her husband's death. She had spent much of the last several years caring for him and now feels she has too little to occupy her time. Mrs. S. worries that her memory might be failing, though tests show this not to be the case. She is also concerned that her children seem too busy with their own lives to spend enough time with her.

Perhaps because of the belief that older people have a lot to be depressed about—declining health, loss of those close to them, shrinking resources, reduced options—it is commonly assumed that they are most likely to experience mood disorders. Yet the data show quite the opposite is true for the major DSM-IV mood disorders (major depression, bipolar depression, dysthymic disorder). Major depressive disorder is nearly four times as common in younger adults as in older adults, and bipolar disorders are sixteen times as common. The milder form of depression, *dysthymic* disorder, is approximately twice as common at younger as at older ages (Weissman et al., 1988).

It is possible, however, that depressive disorders are underestimated in older adults because the diagnoses are missed, or because the symptoms are mistaken for dementia. We will talk about this issue later in the chapter. Moreover, although the clusters of symptoms that form the diagnostic criteria for the mood disorders may be seen less frequently in older individuals, symptoms of depression are not uncommon. In one recent survey, 15 percent of older adults reported significant depressive symptoms that did not meet the criteria for a specific depressive syndrome (Koenig & Blazer, 1992a). See Chapter 13 for a full discussion of mood disorders and their symptoms.

Suicide

In all age groups, depressive disorders are more common in women than in men. But when it comes to the most serious consequence of depression, suicide, men of all ages are at greater risk (De Leo & Ormskerk, 1991). In one study, older Canadian men were approximately three times as likely to commit suicide as older women (Leenaars & Lester, 1992). Older people are more likely than younger people to commit suicide. Moreover, a greater proportion of suicide attempts are more successful in older people. In the general population, anywhere between one in eight and one in twenty suicide attempts results in death. Among those over 65, an estimated one in four attempts is fatal (Blazer, 1991; McIntosh, 1985), presumably because elderly people use more lethal methods and take more precautions to prevent intervention. Older people who are suspected of being suicidal present a special challenge to mental health professionals. It can be helpful to have an older patient sign an "antisuicide contract" at the beginning of treatment. An example of such a document is shown in Table 17.2.

Among older individuals, a number of factors (in addition to being male) place a person at greater risk of suicide. Being divorced or widowed increases the risk, as does having a low income. And not surprisingly, older people who abuse alcohol or who are mentally disordered or depressed are more likely to kill themselves (De Leo & Ormskerk, 1991; Kastenbaum, 1992). Interestingly, Canadian and U.S. patterns are somewhat different. The Leenaars and Lester (1992) study referred to above compared Canadian and U.S. suicide rates across the life span. Since 1977, suicide rates have been higher in Canada—except among older men; Canadian men over the age of 65 are actually at lower risk of suicide than their U.S. counterparts. Suicide prevention is important in both countries, of course, so if this difference continues to be found it will be important to explore the causes and their implications.

Etiology

What predisposes an elderly person to depression? It seems that both physical health and social supports are involved; the combination of a weak support network and poor physical health places elderly people at particular risk (Phifer & Murrell, 1986).

The etiology of depression is not a simple matter. A variety of contributing factors may play a greater or a lesser role, depending on the particular depressive disorder and the age of the individual. (See the discussion of risk factors in Chapters 2 and 5.) For example, heredity has been shown to be important in the development of both major depressive disorder and bipolar disorder (Egland, Gehard, & Pauls, 1987). However, when either of these disorders occurs for the first time later in life, hereditary factors are less likely to be a primary cause. Stressful life events can also influence older adults differently than younger adults. For instance, an older person who loses a loved one is less likely to become depressed (George, Blazer, & Hughes, 1989). This might seem curious at first, but if you think about it, it makes sense. Older people are more likely to have experienced the death of friends and relatives and to be somewhat emotionally prepared, whereas death can seem like a bolt out of the blue to younger adults.

Let us turn now to a consideration of what we know about the main DSM-IV mood disorders in older individuals.

Depressive Disorders

One of the most common psychiatric ailments in older adults is major *depressive disorder (MDD)*. Prevalence rates for MDD among older adults range from 0.1 percent to 0.8 percent in older men and from 0.6 percent to 1.8 percent in older women (Weissman et al., 1988). Rates jump dramatically, however, when institutionalized older adults are considered. Parmalee, Katz, and Lawton (1989) found that 11.3 percent of nursing home and congregate housing residents suffered from MDD, and according to Zarit (1980) estimates of MDD among those admitted to geriatric hospitals range from 21 percent to a whopping 54 percent.

Dysthymic disorder is a chronic depression that has lasted at least two years but is not severe enough to warrant a diagnosis of MDD (see Chapter 13). As with MDD, dysthymic disorder is more common in younger than older adults, and more common in women than men. Among women over 65, prevalence is 2.3 percent as compared to 1 percent for males in the same age range (Weissman et al., 1988). Again, rates are

---

Table 17.2 A Sample Antisuicide Contract

I, _____ (patient's name), as part of my treatment program, agree to the following terms:

1. One of my major treatment goals is to live life with more pleasure and less unhappiness.

2. I understand that becoming suicidal stands in the way of achieving this goal, and I would like to overcome this tendency. Therefore, I agree to learn better ways to deal with my distress.

3. Because I understand that learning to deal with my distress will take time, I agree, in the meantime, not to kill myself between today and _____ (proposed date).

4. If at any time I feel unable to resist suicidal impulses, I agree to call _____ (name & number) or (phone number). If this person is unavailable, I agree to call _____ (name & number)

or

to go directly to _____ (hospital or agency & address).

5. My therapist, _____ (name), agrees to work with me during therapy sessions to help me learn constructive alternatives to suicide and self-injurious behaviour and to be available as much as is reasonable for crises.

6. I agree to abide by this agreement until it expires or until my therapist and I explicitly renegotiate it. I understand that it is renewable at or near _____ (date).

_____	_____
Signature	Date

_____	_____
Therapist's signature	Date

Source: *Adapted from W. J. Fremouw, M. De Perczel, & T. E. Ellis, Suicide risk: Assessment and response guidelines* (New York: Pergamon Press 1990). Copyright © 1990 by Allyn & Bacon. All rights reserved. Reprinted by permission of Allyn and Bacon.

---

much higher—between 4 and 8 percent—among the institutionalized elderly population (Blazer, 1989).

Diagnostic Issues

What does MDD look like in older individuals? Well, in addition to *dysphoria* (feeling sad) or *anhedonia* (a lack of ability to take pleasure in things), a diagnosis of MDD requires that four other symptoms be present from a list of affective symptoms (for example, feelings of worthlessness or guilt), cognitive symptoms (for example, difficulty concentrating or making decisions) and somatic symptoms (for example, weight gain or loss, primary insomnia, fatigue). (See table in Chapter 13.) MDD often looks different in older adults than in younger adults. Older individuals with MDD are more likely to report weight loss and other somatic symptoms and less likely to report feelings of worthlessness or guilt (Blazer, 1989; Wallace & Pfohl, 1995).

With older adults it is often difficult to determine whether one is seeing a case of depressive disorder or something else. There is the difficult issue of differentiating between dementia and MDD. Depressive symptoms can also be caused by diseases, medical conditions, and drugs that may be more common among older people. As many as half of people with Parkinson's disease develop depressive symptoms (Sano, Stern, & Williams, 1989) and depressive symptoms are associated with a number of other diseases including stroke (Robinson, Lipsey, & Price, 1985) and cerebrovascular disease (Kramer & Reifler, 1992). If it can be demonstrated (through physical examination, laboratory tests, and so forth) that depressive symptoms are the direct physiological consequence of one of these medical conditions or drugs, the person is not considered to have either MDD or dysthymic disorder.

Treatment

Both MDD and dysthymic disorder are typically treated with psychotherapy, drug therapy, electroconvulsive therapy (ECT), or some combination of the three. Earlier in this chapter we made the point that, despite evidence to the contrary, older patients are commonly assumed to be poor candidates for psychotherapy. Well, the treatment of depressive disorders is a good example of "evidence to the contrary." Short-term therapy has been shown to produce significant improvement in older MDD patients (Gallagher & Thompson, 1982; Thompson, Gallagher, & Breckenridge, 1987). These authors compared three therapeutic approaches—cognitive therapy, behavioural therapy, and brief dynamic psychotherapy—and found them to be equally effective with older MDD patients.

As for drug therapy, the weight of the evidence suggests that antidepressants and other chemical treatments are as effective in older patients as they are in younger ones (Koenig & Blazer, 1992b). The problem is that many of these drugs produce side-effects that are tolerated less well, particularly among the frail elderly, than among younger patients. Natural age-related changes such as reduced renal clearance and more sensitive drug receptor sites in the brain can increase side-effects and reduce drug tolerance. Drug interactions can also cause trouble for people on multiple medications (Nakra & Grossberg, 1990).

Partly because of problems with drug treatments, ECT is often used to treat older people with either MDD or dysthymic disorder. There is some evidence that it is more effective with them than with younger people (Koenig & Breitner, 1990), but a high percentage experience complications, some of them serious ones, such as cardiorespiratory problems, confusion, and falls (Burke, Rubin, Zorumski, & Wetzel, 1987). Physicians are usually advised to proceed cautiously with ECT in older patients and to consider other treatments first (Wolfe, Morrow, & Fredrickson, 1996).

Given the potential problems with use of drugs and ECT, you might expect there to be a bias in favour of psychotherapy for this patient group. Not so. Elderly MDD patients are significantly more likely to receive pharmacotherapy and electroconvulsive therapy and significantly less likely to be treated with psychotherapy than patients of younger ages (Brodaty et al., 1993).

The course of MDD is characterized by episodes of relapse and remission. Older patients tend to have longer episodes, but the prognosis may be no worse (Brodaty et al., 1993). In fact, there is some evidence that the long-term prognosis may actually be better. When Blazer, Fowler, and Hughes (1987) compared middle-aged and elderly MDD patients one to two years after treatment, 27 percent of the elderly group but only 9 percent of the middle-aged group were considered recovered, although residual symptoms were somewhat more likely in the older patient group. On the other hand, older depressed patients who are also physically ill or who are institutionalized have a much poorer prognosis (Baldwin & Jolley, 1986).

Bipolar Disorder (BPD)

Bipolar disorder (BPD) most commonly occurs for the first time in late adolescence or early adulthood (early-onset), so that most older individuals with this disorder have had it for a number of years. It has been estimated that only about 10 percent of elderly patients with BPD are diagnosed after the age of 50 (late-onset) (Yassa, Nair, & Iskandar, 1988). The overall prevalence for BPD in older adults has been estimated at 0.1 percent (Weissman et al., 1988), with no difference between men and women.

Diagnostic Issues

Bipolar disorder involves manic episodes: periods of persistently elevated mood that is either expansive or highly irritable. BPD is also associated with at least three of the following: grandiosity, decreased need for sleep, rapid speech or pressure to speak, flight of ideas, distractibility, increased activity, and excessive involvement in pleasurable activities. (See Chapter 13 for a more detailed description and diagnostic criteria.) A manic episode may or may not alternate with depressive episodes. This describes the classic picture of BPD, and it is not uncommon in older patients.

Atypical features of the disorder, however, occur more often in older people than in younger ones, making diagnosis difficult. The most common of these atypicalities is a mixture of manic and dysphoric symptoms (Broadhead & Jacoby, 1990). In older adults, too, irritability and hostility can sometimes mask an elevated mood. To make matters more difficult, manic episodes can occur as a consequence of certain medical conditions or drugs that are more common in the elderly population (multiple sclerosis, for example).

Treatment

Bipolar disorder is typically treated with the drug lithium. This treatment is highly effective in younger adults. It is effective for older adults, too, but can pose some special problems for them. Side-effects, such as delirium, tremors, and renal problems, can have more serious consequences, particularly in frail older people. Moreover, many medical conditions that preclude the use of lithium (such as hypertension and heart disease) are more common in older adults; drug interaction effects are a concern; and older individuals respond more slowly to lithium, so that additional medications often have to be used, at least initially (Foster, 1992).

Some consider ECT the treatment of choice for BPD in older adults at high risk for drug or medical complications (Janicak, Davis, Preskorn, & Ayd, 1993), but as Wolfe, Morrow, & Fredrickson (1996) point out, there is very little good research on the subject so the pros and cons of ECT are less clear than we might like.

SLEEP DISORDERS

All her life Rose slept soundly, got up early, and was energetic. Now, in her seventies, things have changed. She often finds it hard to fall asleep and then often awakens in the middle of the night, worrying about her husband's worsening angina attacks, her daughter's marriage, and her son's difficulty finding a good job. Sometimes her husband wakes her to get her to stop snoring. She feels guilty about her snoring waking him and yet resents being woken once she's finally fallen asleep. At the suggestion of friends, she has experimented with eating and drinking various supposedly sleep-inducing things before bed. So far nothing has helped. Rose tries to sleep in, but finds it hard to sleep once it is light. When she gets up she feels tired and often finds herself dozing off during the day. This has happened in church and in social situations, and has been very embarrassing. Finally, at her husband's urging, she has made an appointment to discuss the problem with her physician.

It is clear from the literature on sleep and sleep disorders that older adults report much greater levels of dissatisfaction with the quality of their sleep than younger adults. As many as 40 percent of older adults complain of sleep problems (Vitiello & Prinz, 1994). The primary complaints reported are light sleep, frequent awakenings during the night, awakening too early in the morning, and sleepiness during the day. The literature also confirms that older adults, especially women, use more sedatives or hypnotic medications than younger adults (Vitiello & Prinz, 1994). But although survey data and anecdotal reports strongly suggest that sleep disturbances are more common in older adults, the vast majority of sleep disorder research has occurred with younger adults (Ford & Kameron, 1989). Unfortunately, it is not clear how much of what we know about sleep disorders can be generalized to older adults.

Diagnostic Issues

Whether reports of sleep disturbance actually warrant the diagnosis of sleep disorder depends on the quantity (intensity and/or persistence) and quality of the sleep disturbance. DSM-IV identifies ten sleep disorder categories and provides diagnostic criteria for them. Several are extremely rare in older adults (for example, narcolepsy, sleepwalking disorder) and so we will not discuss them here. Criteria are given here in the DSM tables for primary insomnia and breathing-related sleep disorder.

DSM-IV Diagnostic Criteria for Breathing-Related Sleep Disorder

A. Sleep disruption, leading to excessive sleepiness or insomnia, that is judged to be due to a sleep-related breathing condition.

B. The disturbance is not better accounted for by another mental disorder and is not due to the direct physiological effects of a substance (e.g., a drug of abuse, a medication) or another general medical condition).

Source: Reprinted with permission from the *Diagnostic and Statistical Manual of Mental Disorders*, Fourth Edition. Copyright 1994 American Psychiatric Association.

DSM-IV Diagnostic Criteria for Primary Insomnia

A. The predominant complaint is difficulty initiating or maintaining sleep, or nonrestorative sleep, for at least 1 month.

B. The sleep disturbance (or associated daytime fatigue) causes clinically significant distress or impairment in social, occupational, or other important areas of functioning.

C. The disturbance does not occur exclusively during the course of another mental disorder.

D. The disturbance is not due to the direct physiological effects of a substance (e.g., a drug of abuse, a medication) or a general medical condition.

Source: Reprinted with permission from the *Diagnostic and Statistical Manual of Mental Disorders*, Fourth Edition. Copyright 1994 American Psychiatric Association.

Diagnosing and treating sleep disorders in older adults is complicated by a number of factors (Vitiello & Prinz, 1994; Woodhouse, 1993), which must be considered before a diagnosis of primary sleep disorder can be made.

- Information about sleep quantity and quality typically comes from self-reports and there is always a question as to whether they are distorted by unrealistic expectations.

- Sleep disturbance can be secondary to a host of physical and mental disorders and medications for such disorders. Treating the disorder or changing the medication may alleviate the sleep disturbance.

- There are age-related changes in sleep that appear to be universal, and thus might be considered normal.

- Sleep characteristics and patterns vary widely between individuals; such differences may be especially great among old people.

- Sleep is affected by what sleep researchers and clinicians call *sleep hygiene*: such habits as the time of going to sleep, sleeping alone or with someone, eating, drinking, and exercising prior to going to sleep. These habits may change with age; for example, retirement may change an individual's time of going to bed and of awakening. On the other hand, established sleep habits may no longer be conducive to quality sleep. For example, because sleep is lighter in older adults, sleeping with someone else in the bed may become a cause of frequent awakening and difficulty falling back to sleep.

Normal Changes in Sleeping Patterns

Sleep comprises five stages (Daly, 1989). In rapid eye movement (REM) sleep, electroencephalographic (EEG) activity is similar to that which occurs during waking activity, rapid conjugate eye movements occur (that is, the eyes move together), and muscle tone is decreased. Non–rapid eye movement (non-REM) sleep, is divided into the remaining four stages. In stage 1, low-amplitude, fast-frequency, irregular EEG activity occurs. In stage 2, the activity is more *synchronous* (regular). Stages 3 and 4 are marked by slow EEG waves; stage 4 is deemed to be the deepest level of sleep, because more intense stimulation is required to rouse someone at this stage. Laboratory studies have shown age-related changes of three types:

- *Changes in EEG activity.* Stage 2 EEG activity is less synchronous than in young adults; the slow waves in stages 3 and 4 are lower in amplitude and there are fewer of them.

- *Changes in the organization of sleep stages.* For example, although the number of REM sleep periods does not change, successive REM periods no longer increase in length.

- *Changes in the circadian rhythms,* or sleep-wake cycles. For example, older people may nap more, and may shift their cycle, going to bed and rising much earlier, or much later, than previously.

There is evidence that changes in endocrine and temperature rhythms also occur, so that it can be said that our basic circadian rhythms shift, as we age, to a less stable, less clear-cut organization (Dement, Laughton, & Carskadon, 1982). It may be that we have not yet really appreciated the effects of changing circadian rhythms on the functioning of older adults. Older adults are likely to spend more time in bed than younger people, but less of it asleep. Vitiello and Prinz (1994) conclude that:

Each of these age-related sleep changes—decreases in total sleep time, stage 4 sleep, and REM sleep; increases in wakefulness during the night, frequency of stage shifts, and sensitivity to environmental stimuli—may contribute to the characterization of the sleep of the elderly as "lighter" or more fragile than that of younger individuals. All of these changes may reflect normal, age-related neuronal alterations in brain areas controlling sleep physiology. ... (p. 640)

It is against these well-documented age-related changes in sleep that we must try to identify sleep disorders—pathologies that go beyond the normal age-related changes.

The three most common sleep disorders in older adults are primary insomnia, nocturnal myoclonus, and sleep apnea. We will consider each of these in turn.

Primary Insomnia

Primary insomnia is typically defined in terms of both nocturnal and daytime symptoms. Nocturnal symptoms include difficulty falling asleep, frequent awakenings, shortened sleep, and non-restorative sleep. Daytime symptoms include fatigue, sleepiness, depression, and anxiety (Ancoli-Israel, 1989; Daly, 1989; Vitiello & Prinz, 1994). DSM-IV diagnostic criteria (see DSM table) require the symptoms to persist for at least one month, to be perceived as stressful, and to not be secondary to any other disorder. Prevalence estimates in older adults range from 12 percent to 50 percent (Woodhouse, 1993). This great variation in estimates results mostly from differences in the criteria used in various studies. Virtually all studies, however, find the highest rates among the oldest old people (Vitiello & Prinz, 1994).

Etiology and Diagnostic Issues

Primary insomnia can result from a wide variety of causes, occurring either singly or in combination. Bootzin and Perlis (1992) group the various possible causes into the categories shown in Table 17.3: physical disorders, substances, circadian rhythm problems, psychological factors, and poor sleep environment or habits.

Given that many of the symptoms of primary insomnia are the same as those characteristics of sleep which normally change as we age, drawing a line between normal and pathological is difficult if not arbitrary.

Treatment

Sedatives or hypnotics are the most common treatments for primary insomnia. These drugs are often successful, particularly when the primary insomnia is transient. Problems can arise, though, when primary insomnia is persistent, because older adults are "at particularly high risk for drug tolerance, dependence, drug interactions, hangover effects, and severe withdrawal reactions" (Daly, 1989, p. 485).

There is an alternative. Behavioural and cognitive therapies have been shown to be highly effective in treating primary insomnia (Reynolds, 1991; Scharf & Jennings, 1990). Generally, these approaches involve educating the patient about the normal age-related changes in sleep and training

Table 17.3 **Causes of Primary Insomnia**

Physical disorders	Periodic movements during sleep, restless legs, gastroesophageal reflux, sleep apnea, fibromyalgia, arthritis, chronic pain, cardiac problems
Substances	Caffeine, nicotine, alcohol, hypnotics, tranquillizers, other prescription medication, substances of abuse
Circadian rhythm problems	Shift work, jet lag, delayed sleep phase syndrome, advanced sleep phase syndrome
Psychological factors	Stress, psychopathology, nightmares, inactivity, reinforcement for insomnia
Poor sleep environment or habits	Extended time in bed, naps, irregular schedule, bed as a cue for arousal

Source: R. R. Bootzin, & M. L. Perlis, Nonpharmacological treatments of insomnia, *Journal of Clinical Psychiatry, 53(1992)* (Suppl. 6), 37–41. Copyright 1992, Physicians Postgraduate Press. Reprinted with permission.

him or her in ways to improve sleep hygiene. A wide range of procedures have been shown to be helpful, including techniques such as biofeedback and progressive relaxation training, and changes to habits—eliminating naps, reducing time in bed, avoiding stimulants before bed, not lying in bed awake, and not exercising before bed.

Most clinicians who specialize in sleep problems argue that pharmacological treatment should be used only as a last resort (Vitiello & Prinz, 1994). And even before behavioural or cognitive treatments are attempted, there should be a careful assessment to rule out the possibility that the symptoms are a consequence of some other disorder or medication. Unfortunately, although primary insomnia is more common among them, older adults are less likely than young adults to be referred to sleep disorder clinics for full assessment and appropriate treatment. Instead, they are commonly treated with sedatives or hypnotics prescribed by their family physician.

Nocturnal Myoclonus

The second most common sleep disorder in older adults is **nocturnal myoclonus**, or periodic leg movement during sleep. In this disorder, the person kicks or jerks or flexes his or her legs and feet every 20 to 40 seconds for a number of periods throughout the night. In some cases, the leg movement wakes the individual and thus creates insomnia.

Prevalence estimates range from 4 percent to 31 percent in older insomniacs and from 25 percent to 60 percent in a general population of older adults (Ancoli-Israel, 1989), with incidence appearing to rise with age (Vitiello & Prinz, 1994). This disorder is not recognized as such in DSM-IV, but it is routinely diagnosed and treated at sleep disorder clinics. Very little is understood about the etiology of nocturnal myoclonus.

Treatment has been almost exclusively pharmacological and not tremendously successful. Although dopaminergic drugs have had some success in reducing the leg movements, the side-effects are substantial. Benzodiazepines do not reduce leg movements but are often successful in reducing the awakenings resulting from the leg movements. Nocturnal myoclonus often occurs in conjunction with the third of the common sleep disorders in older adults: breathing-related disorder or sleep apnea.

Sleep Apnea

In **sleep apnea**, there are episodes of cessation of breathing (apnea) that last at least ten seconds (Ancoli-Israel, 1989; Vitiello & Prinz, 1994). Diagnosis requires that there be at least five such episodes per hour of sleep.

This disorder results in hypoxemia (low blood oxygen saturation) and awakenings from sleep. Because quality and quantity of nighttime sleep is disturbed, during the day the sufferer will typically fall asleep at theatres, concerts, or boring meetings, take short, involuntary naps, have difficulty waking up and getting going in the morning or after a nap, and often have a headache for an hour or two in the morning. Difficulty concentrating and remembering may also occur.

If the disorder is severe or left untreated, weakened cardiac functioning can occur and can be fatal.

Between 25 percent and 33 percent of older adults have this disorder (Hoch et al., 1992) with it being markedly more common in men than in women and with increasing age (Vitiello & Prinz, 1994).

Etiology

Three types of sleep apnea have been identified: (1) obstructive apnea due to blockage of the upper airways, generally indicated by snoring; (2) central apnea due to impairment of activation in the medullary respiratory centre in the central nervous system; and (3) mixed apnea, in which both obstructive and central apnea are present. The etiology of central apnea is unclear.

Diagnosis

Obstructive apnea is the most common form and is easily recognized. The sufferer during sleep will have periods of no breathing followed by a restorative gasp and then a snore and sometimes a sharp muscle movement. Severity is typically related to obesity. This disorder is likely substantially underdiagnosed and undertreated in older adults (Ancoli-Israel, 1989).

Treatment

Treatment involves losing weight, learning to avoid sleeping on one's back, and avoiding of respiratory depressants such as alcohol and hypnotic medication. In addition, respiratory stimulants are often helpful. Treatment may also involve *continuous positive airway pressure* (CPAP) which involves wearing while sleeping a mask attached to an air compressor, which keeps the upper airways open. As a last resort, surgery can modify the upper airway structures. Treatment can be effective, although compliance can be a problem with respect to weight loss and use of CPAP.

ANXIETY DISORDERS

Mr. Wallace, a 68-year-old widower, came to the psychological clinic at the insistence of his sister. Since shortly after his retirement three years previously he has been experiencing what he calls "attacks." During these attacks his heart pounds and sometimes he has pain in his chest and trouble breathing. He trembles all over and feels that he is going to die. According to Mr. Wallace the attacks were infrequent at first—no more than once a month. Two years ago his wife died and since then the attacks have become more frequent, averaging one or two a week. His sister says Mr. Wallace seems totally preoccupied with these attacks and worries continually about when the next one might occur. Their father died of a heart attack and Mr. Wallace is convinced that sooner or later one of his attacks will prove fatal too. A recent medical examination found no evidence of heart disease, blood pressure problems, or other medical conditions that might be producing his symptoms. Nonetheless, Mr. Wallace remains convinced that he has an undiagnosed life-threatening disorder and anticipates the next attack with dread.

Anxiety symptoms are a serious problem for a large number of older adults. In one study of community-residing individuals over the age of 55, 17 percent of the men and nearly 22 percent of the women reported anxiety significant enough to warrant some form of intervention (Himmelfarb & Murrell, 1984). Most of these people, however, would probably not meet DSM-IV criteria for specific anxiety disorders. (See Chapter 7 for criteria and a full description of anxiety disorders.) For example, in a survey of randomly selected residents of Edmonton, 1.5 percent of those over 65 could be diagnosed as having *obsessive-compulsive disorder*. As for *panic disorder*, which is what Mr. Wallace in the case above has, 0.3 percent of older adults in the survey received this classification (Bland, Newman, & Orn, 1988). The prevalence of the other anxiety disorders in the survey fell within the same general range. These percentages may not seem very high, but anxiety disorders in elderly people are among the most frequent psychiatric conditions. Unfortunately, they are also among the least studied in this age group (Sheikh, 1992).

Does the prevalence of anxiety disorders change with age? Studies in both the United States (Kramer, German, & Anthony, 1985; Weissman et al., 1988) and Canada (Bland, Newman, & Orn, 1988) suggest that these, and most other mental disorders, actually become *less* prevalent with age. When these results were first reported they received a lot of attention because they were contrary to a widely held belief that mental disorder rates increase with age.

Should we take these findings at face value? Probably not; for several reasons, underreporting is likely in older age groups. First, as we have said before, mental disorders in

Trying to cope with daily life in the face of major losses and worsening chronic conditions can push the vulnerable older adult beyond worrying into a full-fledged anxiety disorder.

general may be underestimated because the current generation of older adults tend to see mental illness as a stigma (Pasnau & Bystritsky, 1990). There is also reason to believe that older individuals have a higher threshold for reporting anxiety symptoms (Sheikh, 1992).

Diagnostic Issues

Accurately detecting and diagnosing anxiety disorders in adults can be problematic. For example, among the more common diagnostic tools are anxiety scales: paper-and-pencil tests that ask the respondent (usually the patient himself or herself) about various symptoms of anxiety. Most of the available scales have been normed and validated with younger adults and it is not clear that a score obtained by an elderly individual should be interpreted the same way as for a younger person. For example, many of the symptoms on the typical anxiety scale are somatic (feelings of dizziness, heart palpitations, and so forth). Now, these symptoms are not exclusively those of anxiety; they can also be the result of cardiovascular, respiratory, and endocrine disorders or of dementia. Given that these medical problems are more common in older people they may endorse somatic symptoms on anxiety scales for the "wrong" reasons. We need scales developed especially for older people; but they have not yet been created.

Etiology

Anxiety symptoms have been found to be associated with medical illnesses in older adults (Heidrich, 1993; Raj, Corvea, & Dagon, 1993) and may have physical causes. Unfortunately most studies in this area have been *cross-sectional*—measuring the medical illnesses and the anxiety symptoms at the same time—so it is not possible to know whether one caused the other or whether, perhaps, a third factor caused both. (See the discussion of causal relation in Chapter 4.) *Longitudinal* studies are needed, which would follow older adults over time to see whether the development of physical illness is followed by the appearance of anxiety symptoms.

Treatment

How should anxiety disorders be treated in older patients? Even though there is little research on psychological methods of managing anxiety in the elderly population (Sheikh, 1992), these methods are generally favoured over pharmacological treatments (Jenike, 1989; Pasnau & Bystritsky, 1990). There are a couple of reasons for this preference. The first is the risk of side-effects with elderly patients in general, but particularly with those who are physically ill or for whom medical causes of anxiety symptoms cannot be ruled out. Second, although empirical evidence is lacking, there is no reason to expect that treatments such as cognitive-behavioural therapy would be less effective for older anxiety patients than for younger adults (Gurian & Goisman, 1993; Pasnau & Bystritsky, 1990; Sheikh, 1992; Turnbull, 1989). At the present time, cognitive-behavioural therapy appears to be the treatment of choice for anxiety in people of all ages.

In the rest of this section we will focus on three types of anxiety disorder included in the DSM-IV, *social phobia, specific phobia*, and *generalized anxiety disorder*. (See the tables in Chapter 7.) Most surveys indicate that these disorders are somewhat more common than the other anxiety disorders in older segments of the population.

Social Phobias

Social phobia involves an excessive and persistent fear of social situations in which embarrassment may occur, such as public speaking or eating out. A person with a social phobia will typically experience anxiety symptoms on trying to enter the situation in question. Left untreated, social phobias are typically chronic and persist into old age (Blazer, George, & Hughes, 1991). So some older individuals with social phobias have had them for a good part of their lives. On the other hand, it may be that some social phobias begin in late life. Some things that might have been easy at earlier stages can become a source of discomfort in later years. For example, dentures can make eating awkward. Might a phobia about eating in public result? Maybe. Unfortunately, there have not been any systematic studies in the area so we can only speculate.

Specific Phobias

Specific phobias are diagnosed when there is a persistent fear of a particular object or situation (other than a social situation) that is severe enough to result in distress or inability to function. Particularly in urban areas, elderly individuals are often phobic about being victims of crime. In one British study, 66 percent of the elderly people surveyed reported that they did not go out at night for fear of victimization (Clarke & Lewis, 1982). Is this just a realistic concern about being in a dangerous situation? Not according to Clarke and Lewis, who report that of all age groups, older adults are actually the *least* likely to be targets of crime.

Generalized Anxiety Disorder (GAD)

Generalized anxiety disorder is characterized by excessive anxiety on most days for at least six months. At least 6 of a set of 18 particular symptoms must be present (trembling, shortness of breath, dizziness, primary insomnia are examples). In older adults, symptoms of anxiety often coexist with symptoms of depression, which can make differential diagnosis tricky (Gurian & Goisman, 1993). The distinction has important implications, because treatment for these two disorders differs. In most cases, anxiety is secondary to depression and so treatment generally focusses on the latter (Lader, 1982).

PSYCHOTIC DISORDERS

Mrs. J., an 80-year-old widow, was referred for psychiatric consultation by her family physician. Mrs. J. had lived alone in the family home since her husband's death four years ago. She reported that she had been having difficulty sleeping and attributed it to her fear that her next-door neighbours were trying to coerce her into selling them her home. According to Mrs. J, these neighbours telephoned and banged on her door at all hours of the day and night yelling at her that she must discuss the sale. Mrs. J. had contacted the police on more than one occasion to complain about her neighbours' behaviour but said they did not seem to believe there was a problem. Mrs. J. had also tried to enlist the help of her only daughter but reported that the daughter was on the neighbours' side because she wanted money from the house sale. According to Mrs. J., "everyone wants me to crumble under the strain so they can get me out of the house." Mrs. J.'s daughter revealed that although the neighbours had approached her mother about buying her house once several years ago, both she and the police were convinced that no approaches had been made since that time. Aside from her paranoid delusions (false beliefs about people trying to take her house from her) and her hallucinations (hearing the voices of her neighbours yelling at her), Mrs. J. did not seem disturbed.

Psychotic disorders are among the more serious mental disorders at any age, including the later years. We will focus our attention here on *schizophrenia* and the diagnostic category into which Mrs. J. fits, *delusional disorder*.

Schizophrenia

Schizophrenia typically begins to manifest itself in the late teens or twenties The symptoms include two or more of the following: delusions, hallucinations, disorganized speech, disorganized behaviour, and negative symptoms such as lack of will, flattening of affect, or lack of logical thought. (See Chapter 14 for a full description.) Diagnosis also requires that the individual be dysfunctional socially or occupationally and that the disturbance have persisted for at least six months. Naturally, other potential diagnoses must be excluded. This more common schizophrenia is sometimes referred to as *early-onset schizophrenia* to distinguish it from *late-onset schizophrenia*, which first appears after the age of 45. There are important differences between the two, as we will see in a moment.

Early-onset schizophrenia becomes relevant to this chapter when these people grow into old age. Unfortunately, many do not. People with early-onset schizophrenia have a higher death rate than the general population, largely because of increased suicide rates (Allebeck, 1989). It was believed for many years that the disease followed a deteriorating course with age, so that those who do survive would have a poor long-term prognosis. Recent longitudinal studies do not support this view. On the contrary, it appears that schizophrenic symptoms either disappear or decrease substantially over time in a significant number of patients (Harding, Brooks, Ashikaga, Strauss, & Breier, 1987; Jeste, Manley, & Harris,

1991; Ruskin, 1990). The disease is a highly variable one, though, and middle-aged and old people may remain seriously impaired. Some evidence suggests that the nature of their symptoms may change with age, with a decrease in "positive" symptoms, such as delusions and hallucinations, and an increase in "negative" symptoms, such as withdrawal and flattened affect (Ruskin, 1990).

Late-onset schizophrenia is not common; in one recent Canadian study only 2.4 percent of all admissions to a psychogeriatric unit over a four-year period were diagnosed as late-onset schizophrenics (Yassa, Dastoor, Nastase, Camille, & Belzile, 1993).

Diagnostic Issues

The diagnostic criteria for late-onset schizophrenia are the same as those for early-onset schizophrenia, but the particular symptoms are likely to be different. Late-onset cases are less likely to have disorganized speech, lack of logical thought, and flattened affect (Jeste et al., 1991); hallucinations and delusions are likely to be more florid and bizarre (Rabins, 1992). The content of these delusions and hallucinations is commonly persecutory, so people with late-onset schizophrenia are most likely to resemble the *paranoid schizophrenic* subtype. Because delusions of persecution are associated with a number of disorders that occur in older individuals—dementia and delusional disorders, for example—differential diagnosis can be a problem (Jeste et al., 1988; Pearlson et al., 1989, Howard, Castle, Wessely, & Murray, 1993). To complicate matters, psychotic symptoms in this age group can also be caused by a number of medical illnesses, including Addison's disease, Parkinson's disease, brain tumours, and certain vitamin deficiencies.

Etiology

The etiology of late-onset schizophrenia is not well understood. Family studies suggest that genetics plays a lesser role than in early onset schizophrenia (Jeste, Harris, & Paulsen, 1996); the disease is slightly less prevalent among relatives of late-onset schizophrenics than among relatives of early-onset schizophrenics (Jeste, Harris, & Paulsen, 1996). For a time it was thought that hearing loss and impaired vision were part of the etiology of late-onset schizophrenia, particularly in people with paranoid symptoms. Recently, though, Prager and Jeste (1993) have found that late-life schizophrenics appear to have greater deficits when tested with their glasses or hearing aids on, but when the corrective devices are removed are no more impaired than older people in a control group. It still may be that part of the problem for these patients is that they are not hearing or seeing adequately, but better assistive devices may be what is called for.

Treatment

Neuroleptic drugs are the treatment of choice for schizophrenics of all ages. There has not been much research on the effects of neuroleptics in older schizophrenics, but there do appear to be age differences (Jeste, Lacro, Gilbert, Kline, & Kline, 1993). Most seriously, older patients are at greater risk for dangerous side-effects, particularly tardive dyskinesia (an involuntary movement disorder involving abnormal repetitive movements of the lips, mouth, tongue, limbs, and/or trunk).

Delusional Disorder

Delusional disorder typically begins in middle or late life. There are several subtypes of delusional disorder and they are defined in terms of the content of the delusions. The most common is the persecutory type. Others include, for example, grandiose, jealous, and erotomanic types. In a study by Post (1966), approximately one-quarter of patients with late-onset psychosis received a diagnosis of delusional disorder. Overall, though, the disorder is rare—about 0.3 percent of the population is the estimate given in DSM-IV. A number of studies have shown that the majority of people with delusional disorder would not have been considered normal before the onset of their illness. Often these people have successful work histories, but have had social or interpersonal problems, perhaps appearing aggressive, hostile, withdrawn, or suspicious (Christenson & Blazer, 1984; Kay, Cooper, Garside, & Roth, 1976).

Diagnostic Issues

The characteristic feature of delusional disorder is the presence of one or more delusions that persist for at least a month. (See the table for DSM diagnostic criteria.) But—and this is where one can see how differentiating between this and late-onset schizophrenia can get tricky—the delusions must not be bizarre in nature. That is, they must fall within the realm of the plausible. If you take a look back at the case of Mrs. J. at the start of this section, you will probably agree that her account of her neighbour's behaviour *could* be believable. But you can also probably imagine how in some cases it would be difficult to draw the line. Other diagnostic criteria include a lack of marked impairment in functioning, no evidence to suggest that there is a chemical or medical cause of the symptoms, and absence of symptoms of schizophrenia.

Etiology

The etiology of delusional disorder is not fully known but a number of contributing factors have been suggested. There is some evidence that immigrants are more likely be diagnosed as having a delusional disorder (Gurian, Wexler, & Baker, 1992). Why would this be? One possibility is that cul-

---

> **DSM-IV Diagnostic Criteria for Delusional Disorder**
>
> A. Non-bizarre delusions (i.e., involving situations that occur in real life, such as being followed, poisoned, infected, loved at a distance, or deceived by spouse or lover, or having a disease) of at least 1 month's duration.
>
> B. Apart from the impact of the delusion(s) or its ramifications, functioning is not markedly impaired and behavior is not obviously odd or bizarre.
>
> C. The disturbance is not due to the direct physiological effects of a substance (e.g., a drug of abuse, a medication) or a general medical condition.

Source: Reprinted with permission from the *Diagnostic and Statistical Manual of Mental Disorders*, Fourth Edition. Copyright 1994 American Psychiatric Association.

tures have different standards, some being more tolerant or even encouraging of particular beliefs than others. So something considered normal in one's country of origin may be seen as worthy of a diagnostic label in another.

There is evidence that genetics plays a role in the development of delusional disorder, since families of patients with delusional disorder have been shown to have an increased incidence of schizophrenia (Winokur, 1977).

Treatment

As with schizophrenia, neuroleptic drugs are effective treatments. But there are two problems. First, many elderly people with pervasive delusions do not see a need for help (Christenson & Blazer, 1984). ("Why should I go to a doctor just because they're trying to steal my house? A good lawyer is what I need!") Second, when they do get appropriate medical attention, they often do not take prescribed medication.

DEMENTIA

Mrs. L. was 76 when she and her family first noticed that she was beginning to be forgetful. In conversations she would repeat things and be unable to answer questions about recent events. Soon she noticed that she was beginning to make errors at work, and so she retired from a part-time bookkeeping job that had been a great source of satisfaction for her. Her adult children convinced their parents to move from the family home to an apartment in a life care centre. Her family was surprised that Mrs. L. showed little emotion as she disposed of treasured possessions and left her home of many years. In the new apartment, Mrs. L.'s forgetfulness worsened. Once a voracious reader, she stopped reading entirely and spent her days playing game after game of solitaire. Less than two years after the move, Mrs. L.'s husband died. Although they had been married for 59 years and had been very close, Mrs. L. did not appear to grieve. She had trouble remembering that her husband was no longer alive. When her children phoned her, she would ask the same two or three questions over and over. Once fastidious, she no longer bathed or changed her clothes without prompting. In the year following her husband's death, Mrs. L. was able to remain in her apartment with daily assistance from a homemaker and close monitoring by the life care centre staff. This was not expected to be possible for very much longer.

Dementia is the most common mental disorder in older adults and, many argue, the cruellest, gradually robbing sufferers of their memory, judgement, and reason, their personal dignity,

and finally, their very sense of self. In the early stages it may be almost as difficult for loved ones to stand by helpless as it is for the sufferer; in the later stages, it is almost certainly more distressing for family and friends.

Dementia, from the Latin *de* ("from" or "out of") and *mentis* ("mind"), refers to a large category of disorders that have in common the individual's loss of his or her former level of cognitive functioning, that is, loss of ability to remember, think, reason. The causes of this loss and the specific patterns of loss differ for various specific disorders grouped together in the general category of dementia.

For a long time dementia was commonly known as *senility* or *senile dementia* because the mental deterioration was thought to be simply the result of the normal aging process (Blazer, 1990). We now know that this is not the case, that dementia is a pathology which, although relatively common in older adults, is not universally present. Consequently, the terms *senile dementia* and *senility* are, quite appropriately, out of favour.

According to recent studies, of Canadians over the age of 65, 8 percent (about 250,000) meet the criteria for some form of dementia (Canadian Study of Health and Aging Working Group, 1994). Because of the dramatic growth of the older-adult segment of the population, unless prevalence rates change, we can expect about 600,000 cases of dementia in the over-65 population in the year 2021. Prevalence rates accelerate sharply with age, as can be seen in Table 17.4 (p. 441). Women are twice as likely as men to develop dementia.

There are many forms of dementia—DSM-IV lists 13—and so it is not surprising that attempts have been made to categorize or classify the different types. Dementias may be classified by etiology, prognosis, symptoms, treatments, etc. No system is uniformly accepted, and DSM-IV uses no categorization system, but many clinicians and researchers consider the distinction between primary and secondary dementia important (Read, 1996).

In **primary dementia**, whatever its actual etiology, the major manifestation is the progressive, irreversible loss of one's former level of cognitive functioning. Examples are Alzheimer's, Picks, and Creutzfeldt-Jakob diseases. In **secondary dementia**, the symptoms of cognitive loss are secondary to—that is, follow as a result of—other disorders and, although irreversible, are not inherently degenerative. For example, dementia may occur as part of the end stage of a variety of diseases such as Parkinson's, Huntington's, AIDS, and cerebrovascular (multi-infarct) disease.

Pseudodementias also occur: disorders that produce cognitive impairment similar to dementia but can be reversed (Foster & Martin, 1990). Depression, nutritional deficiency, thyroid disorder, and a number of other diseases can cause symptoms that mimic dementia, such as forgetfulness, inability to concentrate, poor judgement, faulty reasoning, and lability or flattening of affect. Such symptoms may also occur as side-effects from many medications, such as hypnotics, but are transient and disappear when their underlying cause is treated.

Primary Dementia

Primary dementia is typically marked by a set of five psychological/behavioural features or symptoms, which typically occur in the following order (Butler & Lewis, 1982):

1. *Impairment of memory.* This is usually the first symptom. The person forgets to carry out simple requests, or repeats in conversation something that was just said a few minutes earlier. Initially, others typically attribute these symptoms to fatigue, stress, or similar causes, and the sufferer him- or herself will initially try to cover up with an excuse. Sometimes sufferers will try to mask their lapse of memory by fabricating, guessing, or trying to change the subject. Many clinicians and caregivers argue that at this stage the greatest distress results not from the memory loss itself but from the embarrassment it causes.

2. *Impairment of intellect.* At some point, the ability to solve problems, to reason, to figure things out begins to be affected. Sufferers may not be able to follow tasks to completion or to develop and execute a plan. They will typically be able to follow instructions singly or to follow a list of things to do. Living alone can become a problem as the sufferer starts having trouble with activities of daily living: cooking, bathing, grooming, etc. For example, a person may undress to take a bath, then not know why she is undressed, and dress again without bathing. Or a person might decide to cook something, then wonder why an ingredient is on the counter and put it back in the cupboard. Difficulty with thinking things through will often leave the sufferer feeling confused and often extremely distressed.

3. *Impairment of judgement.* Not surprisingly, as memory and intellectual impairment progress, making decisions becomes difficult and people may make bad, even dangerous, decisions. At this stage sufferers may be bilked by unscrupulous people, give away expensive items, hand over large amounts of cash, sign away assets, and so on. If left in a car with the motor running while a companion runs into a store, the sufferer—even one who has not driven for years—may move to the driver's seat and drive off, with no destination and no purpose in mind.

4. *Impairment of orientation.* Later in the course of dementia, sufferers begin to lose their sense of orientation with respect to time, place, and person. That is, they will not know what day of the week it is, or what date, or even what year; will have no idea where they are, and will not recognize friends and relatives. Ultimately, a sufferer will not even know his or her own name or personal history.

5. *Lability and shallowness of affect.* Later still, the person may lose most of his or her personality, the unique set of characteristics that define an individual. Extreme changes in affect may occur—from screaming and yelling obscenities to quiet sobbing to staring apathetically into space. These behaviours are often unrelated to the person's premorbid personality. So, a gentle, mannerly person might suddenly begin to swear like a trooper and hit out at people. The sufferer may also go through periods of showing very little affect at all. For example, told of the death of a close friend in a car crash, the person might look up vaguely and simply say "oh" in a flat voice.

These five behavioural features typically occur in the order listed above, each new feature being superimposed upon the previous one. What differs substantially is the interval between the onset of successive features, the rate of decline, and which specific areas of knowledge are most affected. Usually the most practised behaviours remain intact longest, so that, for example, a woman may remember a lifelong habit of sewing but forget how to use the new stove.

The most common of the primary dementias is **Alzheimer's disease**. Alzheimer's is, in fact, the most common of all the dementias, accounting for approximately two-thirds of all cases of dementia in Canada (Canadian Study of Health and Aging Working Group, 1994). Prevalence rates increase steeply with age (see Table 17.4, p. 441).

Generally, Alzheimer's disease is described as progressing through three stages. The Alzheimer's Society of Canada refers to these as *first, middle,* and *late.* Reisberg (1983) uses the terms *forgetfulness phase, confusion phase,* and *dementia phase.*

In the first stage, the victim exhibits memory difficulties, problems with concentration, unclear thinking, difficulty finding words, and errors in judgement. The initial signs are first recognized sometimes by the victim and sometimes by those close to the victim. Depression, isolation, and marital and/or family strain is common during the first stage.

During the middle stage, existing symptoms become more severe and some of a wide range of additional symptoms occur: speech and language difficulties, problems in orientation as to time and place, sleep difficulties, difficulties in employment or social situations, urinary incontinence, feelings of helplessness, flattening of affect, agitation, irritability, and wandering. Although at this point the victim is not yet bedridden, the caregiver's role becomes quite demanding.

In the late stage, the ability to communicate is lost and memory impairment is profound. A variety of physical symptoms develop: stooped posture, increasing immobility, total incontinence, increasing vulnerability to conditions such as pneumonia, congestive heart failure, etc., as the individual approaches a vegetative state. Some Alzheimer victims create problems for those around them by wandering, repetitive actions, agitation, aggression, socially inappropriate remarks or actions, extreme argumentativeness, or following (shadowing) caregivers (Kociol & Schiff, 1989).

Estimates of depression in Alzheimer's patients are as high as 25 percent (Foster & Martin, 1990). Although steadily downhill and always fatal, the course of the disease is variable. Death, typically due to respiratory or cardiac failure, occurs on average eight to ten years after diagnosis.

Diagnostic Criteria

Alzheimer's, like all forms of dementia, is very difficult to diagnose in its earliest stages, and diagnosis is typically made by ruling out other causes of the behavioural symptoms observed. The DSM table shown here lists the criteria used, but in many cases, definitive diagnosis is not possible until histological examination following autopsy. Even then, in some cases definitive diagnosis is impossible, often because the same individual is suffering from multiple forms of dementia.

Primary dementias other than Alzheimer's are relatively rare. Although their symptoms are in many ways similar to those in Alzheimer's, each has some characteristics which are unique. These diseases can be differentiated from Alzheimer's with some difficulty, the benefit resting in differences in how the disease is managed (Davies, 1988; Raskind & Peskind, 1992; Read, 1996). For example, caregiving expectations and plans will differ depending on the rate of progression of different diseases.

In Pick's disease, although many of the symptoms are like those in Alzheimer's, distinctive personality change is common, such as disinhibition of social and sexual behaviours (Raskind & Peskind, 1992). Overeating is also common. Age of onset tends to be younger than in Alzheimer's and activity levels are likely to be lowered rather than heightened as in Alzheimer's, so wandering is not generally something caregivers have to deal with. The course of the disease is variable but, like Alzheimer's, can extend over as much as 15 years after diagnosis.

Creutzfeldt-Jakob disease is even rarer than Pick's. Its symptoms include muscle jerks and it has a very precipitous course; it is usually fatal within two years of diagnosis (Raskind & Peskind, 1992).

Dementia caused by Huntington's disease is also rare. Before cognitive symptoms develop, victims typically experience involuntary muscle movements (chorea) which at first might seem to be fidgeting or restlessness. The fidgeting is controllable at first, but typically becomes uncontrollable. Along with the deterioration of cognitive function, often substantial personality changes and/or mental disorders such as depression, anxiety. or psychosis can develop. Onset is insidious and usually begins in the early forties, but occasionally later. The Huntington's victim ultimately suffers the cognitive impairments characteristic of dementia, and so, even though the disease is usually thought of in terms of the initial involuntary muscle movements, Huntington's is generally categorized as a form of primary dementia.

At the moment, differential diagnosis between the types of primary dementia is more important for researchers than for dementia patients, because relatively little is available in the way of treatment. However, as we learn more about each disorder and begin to develop more effective pharmacological treatments that will at least slow, if not stop, the progression of the disorder, we will need to be able to diagnose earlier in the course of the disease.

Etiology

Alzheimer's disease.   What causes the devastation of Alzheimer's disease? It seems clear that the etiology is physiological. There are two dramatic differences between the brains of Alzheimer's victims and normal old people (Foster & Martin, 1990). The first is the presence of excessive amounts of plaques (collections within a nerve cell of nerve cell and supportive tissue debris suspended in a protein substance called amyloid) and neurofibrillary tangles (clusters of intertwined filaments in nerve cells that in the normal brain are not tangled). (See Figure 17.2, next page) Greater numbers of plaques and tangles are related to poorer functioning and even death of nerve cells. The second difference is substantial shrinkage of the cortex in Alzheimer brains.

The question, of course, is what causes these changes. One hypothesis is genetic. The evidence for genetic involvement is twofold (Raskind & Peskind, 1992). First, individuals with Down syndrome (a genetic disorder) who live beyond age 40 generally show neuropathological indicators of Alzheimer's. Second, Alzheimer's has been shown to run in families. In such families, about 50 percent of those at risk develop Alzheimer's. However, familial Alzheimer's is estimated to make up only 15 percent of all Alzheimer's victims. Recent evidence has suggested the possibility of there being an Alzheimer's gene on chromosome 21, but the evidence is inconsistent. It has been suggested that Alzheimer's may have a number of forms, each associated with different genes or gene combinations.

A second hypothesis involves abnormalities in the amyloid and/or other proteins in nerve cells (Raskind & Peskind, 1992). A third hypothesis focusses on acetylcholine deficiencies, as these are known to disrupt memory (Read, 1996). A fourth hypothesis focusses on aluminum, because excessive aluminum has been shown to increase neurofibrillary tangles and because of some epidemiological evidence that Alzheimer's rates are higher in certain populations with high aluminum content in their water (Read, 1996). Each hypothesis is being

---

DSM-IV   Diagnostic Criteria for Dementia of the Alzheimer's Type

A. The development of multiple cognitive deficits manifested by both:

   (1) memory impairment (impaired ability to learn new information or to recall previously learned information)

   (2) one (or more) of the following cognitive disturbances:

      (a) aphasia (language disturbance)

      (b) apraxia (impaired ability to carry out motor activities despite intact motor function)

      (c) agnosia (failure to recognize or identify objects despite intact sensory function)

      (d) disturbance in executive functioning (i.e., planning, organizing, sequencing, abstracting)

B. The cognitive deficits in criteria A(1) and A(2) each cause significant impairment in social or occupational functioning and represent a significant decline from a previous level of functioning.

C. The course is characterized by gradual onset and continuing cognitive decline.

Source: Reprinted with permission from the *Diagnostic and Statistical Manual of Mental Disorders*, Fourth Edition. Copyright 1994 American Psychiatric Association.

Figure 17.2 **Normal Brain Tissue Contrasted with That of an Alzheimer's Patient**

The slide on the left shows a normal brain; the slide on the right shows a brain from a person with Alzheimer's.

aggressively investigated. Although we do not have the answer yet, substantial advances have been made.

Other primary dementias. The etiology of Pick's disease is unknown. The changes caused by the disease in the cells of the frontal and temporal cortical areas of the brain are relatively distinctive and different from the plaques and tangles in the Alzheimer's brain cells (Conn, 1996).

Creutzfeldt-Jakob disease is known to be caused by a slow virus (Raskind & Peskind, 1992). This disease was brought to public attention a few years ago by the "mad cow" scare in Britain. Some British beef cows were infected with a virus related to Creutzfeldt-Jakob, and some fear that a number of Britons may have contracted the disease before the contaminated beef stocks were destroyed. There is at present no screening test to tell us whether we can expect an increase in Creutzfeldt-Jakob dementia over the next few years.

The cause of Huntington's disease has been established as genetic, and heritability is 50 percent. Genetic screening now makes it possible to establish whether one will develop the disorder.

Treatment

One approach to treating primary dementia has been to seek drugs that will reverse, stop, or at least slow the progression of the disease (Whalley, 1989). Emphasis in seeking effective treatment has focussed on Alzheimer's, because it is the most common of the primary dementias. Progress has been limited, but in recent years several drugs have been developed which may slow the progression of the disease. One, Cognex (Tacrine) has been approved in the United States (but not in Canada) and has begun to be used widely there. Unfortunately, it is only thought to be helpful in the early stages of the disease and has substantial side-effects in some people. A new drug, Aricept, similar to Cognex but with fewer

side-effects, has recently been approved for use in both the United States and Canada. Several other drugs are currently in the clinical trial stage of research.

So far, the more widespread approach to treatment has been to focus on secondary symptoms common in dementia, such as agitation, anxiety, and depression. For the most part, the antidepressants, antipsychotics, and neuroleptics that ameliorate these symptoms in other populations also work with Alzheimer's patients. Some are contraindicated, however, because of side-effects that are especially undesirable in Alzheimer's patients. For example, some drugs cause hyperactivity, which worsens Alzheimer's symptoms such as wandering or verbal or physical abusiveness.

Behavioural treatments have been developed to manage some of the troublesome behaviours of Alzheimer's sufferers (Mace, 1990). Behaviour modification, caregiver counselling, and changes to the physical or psychosocial environment are all used to ensure patient safety, improve quality of life, and control costs. Such programs often allow the patient to be managed with less medication and fewer restraints than might otherwise be needed.

Alzheimer's represents a heavy burden for caregivers, which, as one would expect, increases as the disease progresses. Approaches such as caregiver support, respite, and special adult day care programs appear to ease the burden for caregivers in the middle stage. In the final stage of the disease, the Alzheimer's patient typically requires such intensive care that institutionalization is necessary.

Secondary Dementia

When cognitive impairment is the result of a disease in which the primary manifestations are physical, it is called *secondary dementia*.

Symptoms are generally like those described in primary dementia (Read, 1996), but show more variation. Not all of the five general features of dementia may occur, or they may occur in a different order, or a symptom may be intermittent rather than becoming progressively worse.

Etiology

Secondary dementia can result from a number of diseases such as Parkinson's, amyotrophic lateral sclerosis (ALS; also known as Lou Gehrig's disease), HIV infection (AIDS), or alcoholism. Cognitive impairment occurs when the disease process cause the death of brain cells. Many people with these disorders never develop dementia.

By far the most common cause of secondary dementia, however, is vascular disease. In **vascular disease**, the arteries that supply the brain are partly blocked. When blood flow is reduced beyond a certain point, a *stroke* occurs (Read, 1996), meaning that brain cells have died. The area affected by a stroke can be large or small. An area of nonfunctioning cortex due to a major stroke or a series of small strokes can lead to dementia. Vascular dementia is the second most common form of dementia in Canada, accounting for about 18 percent of cases (Canadian Study of Health and Aging Working Group, 1994). Prevalence increases with age, as shown in Table 17.4.

Diagnostic Issues

Generally, the symptoms of vascular dementia are like those of Alzheimer's, even though the underlying pathology is quite different (Raskind & Peskind, 1992). However, the average onset of vascular dementia is earlier and the disease tends to progress in steps, rather than gradually, as an increasing number of discrete areas are affected and rendered nonfunctional. Sufferers of vascular dementia often show greater day-to-day fluctuation in the degree and nature of impairment. These differences are often subtle and it is often extremely difficult to determine whether an individual's dementia is Alzheimer's or vascular. Even computerized scanning and imaging devices often do not give a definitive answer; histological analysis at autopsy does usually allow clear differentiation (Raskind & Peskind, 1992). To complicate matters further, some—perhaps many—patients suffer from *both* forms of dementia.

Treatment

Blood-thinning medication is often prescribed for vascular disease to lessen the likelihood of further strokes (Foster & Martin, 1990). In other respects, treatment focusses on management, and is similar to that for primary dementia. As more treatments are developed for specific pathologies, accurate diagnosis. will become even more important.

Pseudodementia

The most important diagnostic distinction is between true dementia, of whatever type, and pseudodementia—reversible cognitive impairment caused by conditions such as nutritional deficiency, thyroid problems, or depression. This distinction is essential, because the treatment approaches will be completely different, as discussed in the Focus box. Although differentiating dementia from pseudodementia requires considerable skill on the part of the clinician, it can be done. Yet too often cognitive impairment is assumed to be primary dementia without a full neuropsychological assessment, meaning that patients with pseudodementia do not get the help they need. This diagnostic error leads to a great deal of unnecessary suffering and the loss of years of fulfilling life for many patients. The best example is depression, the most common cause of pseudodementia, and a highly treatable disorder (Storandt & Vanden Bos, 1994).

Table 17.4 Prevalence of Dementias by Age in Canada

Age Group	All Dementias	Alzheimer's Dementia	Vascular Dementia
65–74	2.4	1.0	0.6
75–84	11.1	6.9	2.4
85+	34.5	26.0	4.8
85–89	22.8	16.7	3.4
90–94	40.4	32.3	4.6
95+	58.6	43.3	6.7

Source: First three rows based on report of Canadian Study of Health and Aging Working Group, Canadian Study of Health and Aging, Study methods and prevalence of dementia, *Canadian Medical Association Journal, 150(1994),* 899–912.

Focus *Differential Diagnosis: Dementia vs. Depression*

People who are depressed often display symptoms that are the same as or similar to those exhibited by people suffering from dementia: low affect level, lack of concentration, sadness, confusion, indecisiveness, irritability, dissatisfaction, and personal devaluation.

Forgetfulness, too, can be a symptom of either disorder. In dementia, forgetfulness is usually the first symptom to appear and is due to memory loss. But depressed people also frequently complain about not being able to remember things. Why? Well, depressed people often have trouble concentrating, and so when new information is presented to them they may not attend to it properly. Later on, they cannot retrieve it, because it was not encoded in the first place. If this is taken as evidence of memory loss, family and even health care professionals may jump to the incorrect

Focus *continued*

Characteristics of Depression and Dementia

	Depression	Dementia
Rate of progression	Fast	Slow
Course	Uneven (from week to week)	Even (over months or years)
Memory loss	No true loss	Yes
Memory complaints	Common	Rare (tries to hide losses)
General affect	Depressed	Flat or variable
Feelings of self-worth	Poor	Variable
Unhappy mood	Persistent	Appropriate to situation
Awareness of condition	Exaggerated	Minimal
Distress over condition	Intense	Little or variable
Efforts to cope	Minimal	Maximal
Prior psychopathology	Likely	Unlikely
Worst time of day	Early in morning	Late in day or when fatigued
Substance use	May abuse	Rarely abuses

Source: Adapted from A. LaRue, C. Dessonville, & L. F. Jarvik, Aging and mental disorders, in J. E. Birren & K. W. Schaie, eds., *Handbook of the psychology of aging*, 2nd ed. (New York: Van Nostrand Reinhold, 1985), pp. 664–702.

conclusion that they are seeing a case of dementia. If the depressed person shows other symptoms that occur in both disorders, such as difficulty thinking and concentrating, an incorrect diagnosis is even more likely.

The failure to differentiate depression from dementia can be tragic. Depression is a treatable disorder; at the present time dementia is not. So a depressed person with a misdiagnosis of dementia will not receive treatment from which he or she could almost certainly benefit—treatment that might make the difference between a normal, active life and one of withdrawal and dependency.

The implications are clear. Before concluding that someone has dementia, every effort should be expended to rule out alternative diagnoses, especially the diagnosis of depression. In distinguishing between depression and dementia, the following items can be used as part of the process of *differential diagnosis*—that is, the systematic consideration of specific characteristics whose presence or absence distinguishes one disorder from another.

Differential diagnosis can be particularly complicated when the same individual suffers from both dementia *and* depression—which is not uncommon. Approximately 25 percent of people with dementia also suffer from depression. Accurate diagnosis of both disorders is important, because the progression of dementia is typically slow, so the patient is likely to have considerable time to benefit from treatment for depression. ▲

PANORAMA

In recent years there has been considerable progress in our understanding of mental disorders in older adults. Through research efforts, progress has occurred on a number of fronts. We now know that, although the age profile of prevalence rates does vary by disorder (for example, schizophrenia is more likely in late adolescence or early adulthood, and dementia is more likely to occur in older adults), overall the prevalence rate for mental disorders is similar across the adult life span. We also know that treatments effective with younger adults are equally effective with older adults. Although there is less solid evidence on this point, many gerontologists and mental health professionals believe that successive generations of older adults are becoming more willing than earlier generations to acknowledge and seek treatment for mental disorders.

The evidence now shows that, for many mental disorders in older adults, behavioural or psychotherapeutic techniques alone can be as effective as pharmacological therapy. This finding has important practical implications in that it makes it possible to avoid unpleasant and sometimes risky side-effects of medication to which older adults are particularly vulnerable.

Lastly, knowledge of dementia has increased. We now know that there is a genetic component in at least a substantial percentage of cases. Evidence is also beginning to emerge regarding correlates of dementia. Continued progress on this front should lead to identifying nongenetic causes, giving hope that effective preventive approaches can be developed. New medications have been developed that appear to slow the progress of dementia, thus increasing the quality of life both for dementia patients and their caregivers.

Unfortunately, these hopeful developments have been slow to filter both into public awareness and into the consciousness of health and mental health professionals. It is still the case that more older adults than younger adults with mental disorders are undiagnosed and untreated. Mental disorders, especially depression and dementia, continue to be incorrectly viewed as part of normal aging rather than as pathological conditions that can be successfully treated or managed. The result is unnecessary reduction in the quality of life for many old people and their families.

For the future, education is the key—of professionals and of the public, so that mental disorders are recognized when they exist, and so that older adults, their friends and family, and the health care professionals who work with them seek appropriate treatment. Having prominent older adults with mental disorders go public will also help raise awareness and increase the likelihood of accurate diagnosis and treatment.

SUMMARY

It is a widely held belief that mental disorders are more common in older than in younger adults, but the data suggest that the opposite is the case, with two notable exceptions—sleep disorders and dementia. There are, however, a variety of reasons why prevalence may be underestimated for older adults. True overall prevalence is probably similar for older and younger adults. It is also widely believed (by health professionals, family members, and old people themselves) that it is normal for people to develop certain mental disorders as they age, and that treatments for mental disorders are ineffective in older adults. These false beliefs probably contribute to the fact that older adults are less likely to receive treatment for mental disorders. As a result, the quality of life is unnecessarily reduced for many old people.

Theoretical approaches to mental disorders do not offer specific insights into these disorders in older people. Similarly, theoretical approaches to aging developed by gerontologists are of limited use when it comes to psychopathology, because they focus on successful aging and normal age changes.

Mood disorders are less prevalent in older than in younger adults but they are among the most common mental disorders in older adults. Furthermore, many older people have symptoms of depression without meeting all the criteria necessary for a formal diagnosis. Mood disorders are highly treatable and treatment is just as effective for older as it is for younger adults.

Sleep disorders become more common as people age. Normal age-related changes in sleep—greater difficulty falling asleep, less time spent in deeper sleep—increase the likelihood of sleep disorders. Sleep disorders can be treated but at all ages treatment efficacy varies.

Anxiety disorders are less prevalent in older than in younger adults, but they represent a substantial proportion of the mental disorders experienced by the older segment of the population. There are several treatments for these disorders and client age does not influence their effectiveness.

Psychotic disorders are less common in older than in younger adults. Age can complicate treatment, because side-effects of medication are a greater concern in older people.

The final disorder we discuss, dementia, is truly a mental disorder of aging. Its prevalence increases dramatically with age. Primary dementia results from the gradual degeneration of brain cells that affect cognitive functioning. To date, no treatment is available to prevent, stop, or reverse the disorder, and the challenge is to manage the client's behaviour as it deteriorates. This can be a devastating burden for the caregiver. The symptoms of secondary dementia and pseudodementia are similar to those of primary dementia, but their causes are different. Differential diagnosis can be difficult, but it is essential to ensure no one is denied treatment where it would be effective.

KEY TERMS

normal aging (p. 423)
polypharmacy (p. 424)
point prevalence (p. 426)
social breakdown (p. 427)
social reconstruction (p. 427)

activity theory (p. 427)
disengagement theory (p. 427)
primary insomnia (p. 432)
nocturnal myoclonus (p. 433)
sleep apnea (p. 433)
late-onset schizophrenia (p. 436)
delusional disorder (p. 436)

dementia (p. 437)
primary dementia (p. 437)
secondary dementia (p. 437)
pseudodementias (p. 437)
Alzheimer's disease (p. 438)
vascular disease (p. 441)

ADDITIONAL RESOURCES

Alzheimer Society of Canada
20 Eglinton Avenue West
Suite 1200
Toronto, ON M4R 1K8
(416) 488-8772
(800) 616-8816
(416) 488-3778 fax
expert@alzheimer.ca

Rotman Research Institute
Baycrest Centre for Geriatric Care
3560 Bathurst Street
Toronto, ON M6A 2E1
(416) 785-2500
(416) 785-2378 fax
inquiries@rotman-baycrest.on.ca

National Institute on Aging
Building 31
Room 5C27
31 Center Drive
Bethesda, MD 20892-2292
nihinfo@od.nih.gov

www.ncoa.org
The site of the National Council on Aging provides a range of resources about the effects of aging.

www.uottawa.ca/academic/med/epid/core1.htm
An abstract of the Canadian Study of Health and Aging, which sought to determine the prevalence of dementia among various age groups in Canada.

www.alzheimer.ca/alz/content/html/disease-en/disease-csha-eng.htm
The results of a 1991 study to determine how many Canadians have dementia and the patterns of caring for people with dementia.

www.hookup.net/mall/aging/agesit59.html
The Aging Research Council helps researchers find information related to the study of the aging process. Information about different theories of aging is available here.

www.rotman-baycrest.on.ca
The Rotman Research Institute studies the brain and behaviour in people with conditions such as stroke and Alzheimer's disease.

Chapter 18

Mental Health Law and Ethics

James R. P. Ogloff

Maureen C. Olley

Lindsey A. Jack

In the fall of 1983, Owen Swain was charged with assault and aggravated assault after he attacked his wife and his two children. During the incident he was fighting with the air and talking about spirits. When the police came, they found him in an excited state, rambling in a "dialect" about religious themes. At trial, Mr. Swain testified that at the time he believed his family was being attacked by devils and that he had to protect them by carrying out certain acts.

After he was arrested, he was transferred to a psychiatric hospital, where he remained for almost two months. Mr. Swain was treated with antipsychotic medication and released. For the next six months, while on bail, he continued to see a psychiatrist and take his medication.

At his trial, over the objections of Mr. Swain and his lawyer, the Crown raised the issue of insanity. They argued that Mr. Swain was legally insane at the time of the attacks. He was found not guilty by reason of insanity (NGRI).

At that time in Canada, being found NGRI resulted in the accused being detained in a secure hospital automatically for an indeterminate period. Mr. Swain eventually appealed to the Ontario Court of Appeal and later to the Supreme Court of Canada, arguing that it was a violation of the *Charter of Rights and Freedoms* for the Crown to raise the issue of insanity and for persons found NGRI to be automatically confined to a secure facility. In 1991, the Supreme Court of Canada upheld Mr. Swain's appeal, which led to sweeping reforms of the insanity defence—now called the *not criminally responsible on account of mental disorder (NCRMD) defence.*

As the Swain case makes clear, some people with mental illness come into contact with the law. In fact, the area of mental health law has developed to deal with people who are mentally ill. Mental health law emphasizes that mental illness exists within the social culture of our society. As we will see in this chapter, a number of legal issues arise in the context of mental illness. Most notably, people whose mental illness causes them to be at risk for harming themselves or others may be hospitalized, even against their will, and, as the Swain case shows, people whose mental illness leads them to commit a criminal offence may be dealt with under the unique mental disorders of the *Criminal Code* of Canada.

Just as mental illness must be considered within the broader context of our society, so too must the behaviour of psychologists and other mental health professionals. As professionals, the behaviour of psychologists is governed by ethical guidelines that have been developed by professional associations and licensing boards and by the laws of our society (Ogloff, 1995; Ogloff & Olley, 1998; Reaves & Ogloff, 1996a). In addition to discussing the legal issues that affect people with mental illness, this chapter will provide an introduction to the professional and legal regulation of psychologists. We turn first to a discussion of mental health law, and how our society attempts to deal with and accommodate mentally ill people.

MENTAL HEALTH LAW

Historically, the laws of Canada have evolved from what is known as English common law (Rose, in press). Principles of law were developed gradually over time as judges decided individual cases and began to establish rules from those cases. Although Canada has its own constitution and is no longer dependent on English common law, many of our present laws have their roots in the principles that were developed over many centuries. People in our society have a number of rights and freedoms, enshrined in the *Canadian Charter of Rights and Freedoms* (*Constitution Act*, 1982), which set the limits on how much the state can interfere with us and our freedom.

Canada is one of the few countries in the world that explicitly extends such constitutional rights to people who are mentally ill. Section 15 (1) of the *Charter*, the "Equality Rights" section, provides that

Every individual is equal before and under the law and has the right to the equal protection and equal benefit of the law without discrimination and, in particular, without discrimination based on race, national or ethnic origin, colour, religion, sex, age or mental or physical disability.

In common law, the King (or Queen) of England had two responsibilities that are relevant to our discussion here. First, the King established laws to protect people from the criminal acts of others. His authority, and obligation, to prosecute and imprison—or execute—people who commit crimes is known as the state's "police power." Second, he was obligated to protect and to provide care for those incapable of caring for themselves. In a very real sense, the King was the "father of the country" and, as a father, had the responsibility to care for three groups: mentally ill people, mentally retarded people, and children. His authority to limit the liberty of these people is based on the *parens patriae*, or, literally, the power and obligations the King had as "father of the state." Like criminals, those who could not care for themselves in society were often hospitalized or institutionalized, in this case "for their own good" (although, as Chapter 1 makes clear, the treatment they received was generally custodial at best and brutal at worst).

Today the power of the King has been replaced by the power and obligations of the state. On the basis of the above discussion, there generally are two general circumstances under which mentally ill people in our society can lose their liberty. The first occurs when they are charged with and convicted of an offence, or found to be NCRMD, formerly known as NGRI (both discussed above), and imprisoned or held in custody as Mr. Swain was. The second occurs when it is believed that the person's mental illness has caused him or her to present a danger to others, or when the mental illness may lead to the person's being in danger of harming himself or herself.

On the basis of the distinctions above, mentally ill people may fall under control of the criminal law or under what is known as civil law.

Criminal Law and Psychology

The purpose of criminal law is to protect people from the acts of criminals. On occasion, individuals with mental illness commit crimes, are arrested, and enter the criminal justice system. The prevalence of mental illness among offenders generally has been found to be higher than for people in the general population. A number of studies examining the prevalence of mental disorder in jail populations have been conducted. Specific rates of mental illness reported for jail inmates vary considerably across studies. Prevalence rates of mental illness among random samples of inmates range from 3 percent (Petrich, 1976) to 59 percent (Schuckit, Herrman, & Schuckit, 1977), depending upon the criteria and diagnostic system used. Not surprisingly, higher prevalence rates have been obtained when samples have consisted only of those inmates referred by jail staff for mental health evaluations. In these cases, prevalence rates ranging from 24 percent (Nielsen, 1979) to 75 percent (Lamb & Grant, 1982) have been reported. Similar findings were reported by Allodi, Kedward, & Robertson (1977) in a Canadian study.

Tables 18.1 and 18.2 show, as an example, that the prevalence rate of major mental disorders among jail inmates in the lower mainland of British Columbia is significantly higher than would be found in the general population. For example, those inmates who were suffering from a psychotic illness

Table 18.1 Prevalence of DIS/DSM-III Diagnoses Among Admissions to the Vancouver Pretrial Services Centre

DIS/DSM-III Diagnosis	Prevalence (% of total admissions)
Major mental disorders	**15.6**
1. Cognitive impairment (severe)	0.5
2. Schizophrenic disorders	4.9
3. Major affective disorders	10.1
Substance use disorders	**85.9**
1. Alcohol abuse/dependence	77.6
2. Drug use disorders	63.7
Other mental disorders	**88.0**
1. Anxiety disorders	41.1
2. Dysthymic disorders	7.2
3. Somatization disorder	0.7
4. Eating disorders (bulimia)	0.3
5. Sexual disorders	27.0
6. Antisocial personality disorder	64.3

Source: R. Roesch, Mental health intervention in jails, in G. Davies, S. Lloyd-Bostock, M. McMurran, & C. Wilson, eds., *Psychology, law, and criminal justice* (New York: Walter de Gruyter, 1995), pp. 520–531.

Table 18.2 Prevalence of DSM-III-R Diagnoses Among Admissions to the Surrey Pretrial Services Centre

DSM-III-R Diagnosis	Prevalence (% of total admissions)
Major mental disorders	**19.7**
1. Bipolar affective disorder	0.8
2. Major depression	15.7
3. Psychotic disorder NOS	0.8
4. Schizoaffective disorder	2.4
Substance use disorders	**60.9**
1. Alcohol	24.0
2. Cannabis	16.5
3. Cocaine	10.2
4. Hallucinogens	1.6
5. Opioids	5.5
6. Sedative hypnotics	3.1
7. Polydrug	15.0

Source: J. R. P. Ogloff, *The Surrey pretrial mental health program: Community component evaluation* (British Columbia Forensic Psychiatric Services Commission, July 1996). Used by permission of Diane Lamb.

varied from 3 percent to 5 percent —several times higher than in the general population (approximately 1 percent). An additional 10 to 15 percent of inmates suffered from a major affective disorder, such as major depression. Again, this rate is several times higher than that which would be found in the general population. Furthermore, the rate of substance abuse disorders among the inmates is extremely high. (To keep this data in perspective, however, keep in mind that most people with mental disorders do not commit crimes—see Chapter 1.)

While many mentally ill people may enter the jail, apart from receiving some treatment for their mental illness, only those who are seriously ill, and who satisfy certain legal criteria, are typically handled differently by the criminal justice system from other inmates. In particular, the law is concerned that mentally ill people may not be "fit" or competent to participate in the system. Because our system is based on the adversarial process, in which the accused has the right to defend himself or herself against the charges, it is important that the accused have the capacity to participate. Whittemore and Ogloff (1994) identified a number of junctures in the criminal process when an accused's competence or fitness may be called into question (that is, competence to understand their *Charter* cautions, competence to confess, fitness to stand trial, and competence to be sentenced).

The most common concern of the courts is whether the accused is **fit to stand trial**. Moreover, there are cases in which an individual's criminal act is caused by his or her mental illness. In these cases, the accused may be found **not criminally responsible on account of mental disorder (NCRMD)**. Mental health professionals are often called upon to conduct fitness and criminal responsibility assessments. Note that these two concepts are distinct and call for different questions to be answered. An evaluation of competence to participate in the criminal justice system or fitness to stand trial requires the examiner to assess the accused's *present* mental condition and determine whether it interferes with ability to perform the legal tasks related to the trial process (outlined in Section 2 of the *Criminal Code*). In contrast, assessments of criminal responsibility require the examiner to determine the accused's mental state *at the time of the offence* and determine whether it affected the ability to appreciate the offence in question (outlined in Section 16 of the *Criminal Code*).

Competencies in the Criminal Justice System

Central to the Canadian justice system is the right of the accused, as spelled out in Section 11 (d) of the *Charter of Rights and Freedoms,* "to be presumed innocent until proven guilty according to law in a fair and public hearing by an independent and impartial tribunal." Thus, any person charged with an offence has the right to a defence against the charges in court. For an individual accused of an offence to participate in his or her own defence, courts have held that the accused must be "fit to stand trial." The degree of capacity required for *fitness*, however, has been difficult to determine (Whittemore & Ogloff, 1994). It was not until 1992 that the *Criminal Code* (Section 2) specifically defined the standard to be applied:

> *"Unfit to stand trial" means unable on account of mental disorder to conduct a defence at any stage of the proceedings before a verdict is rendered or to instruct counsel to do so, and, in particular, unable on account of mental disorder to: (a) understand the nature or object of the proceedings, (b) understand the possible consequences of the proceedings, or (c) communicate with counsel.*

The *Criminal Code* provides further that an accused is presumed fit to stand trial unless the court is satisfied on a balance of probabilities that the accused is unfit. The party who raises the issue of an accused's fitness has the burden of proving the issue of unfitness.

For an individual to be found unfit, he or she must first have a mental disorder; the *Criminal Code* does not further define disorders. Note that there are three possible ways in which a disorder may render someone unfit.

Case law has subsequently defined more specifically the degree of mental impairment required for ability to communicate with counsel. In *R. v. Taylor* (1992), the Ontario Court of Appeal held that the relevant test is one of "limited cognitive capacity" (p. 567): the accused need only have the ability to recount to the lawyer the facts that would enable the lawyer to properly present the case. The Court stipulated that the accused need not have the ability to act in his or her own best interests, as this was found to be too strict a test.

In 1998, Roesch, Zapf, Webster, and Eaves published the Fitness Interview Test (FIT) to help psychologists and psychiatrists assess whether an individual is fit to stand trial. If an accused is found fit to stand trial, the proceedings continue in the normal manner. An accused found unfit to stand trial,

however, may be ordered detained in custody until the completion of the trial, if there is reason to believe the accused may become unfit if released from hospital. More commonly, though, the Court may remand the accused to a secure psychiatric hospital for treatment to help restore the accused's fitness. If this is done, a review board assumes responsibility for the accused's eventual release. Taking into account public protection, the reintegration of the accused into society, and the accused's mental condition, the review board has three disposition options: (1) conditional discharge, (2) detention in hospital, or (3) a treatment order.

Criminal Responsibility

Why do we need an insanity defence? A simple, compelling answer is offered by Judge Bazelon in *Durham v. United States* (1954):

> *The legal and moral traditions of the western world require that those who, of their own free will and with evil intent (sometimes called* mens rea)*, commit acts which violate the law, shall be criminally responsible for those acts. Our traditions also require that where such acts stem from and are the product of a mental disease or defect as those terms are used herein, moral blame shall not attach, and hence there will not be criminal responsibility. (p. 876)*

The notion of madness can be traced far back in history (see Chapter 1). The ancient Greeks and Romans recognized that some forms of mental illness may affect a person's behaviour. In Roman and in Judaic law there were provisions for exculpating people who committed their acts while mentally ill (that is, for not holding them criminally responsible) (Walker, 1985; Weiner, 1985). However, this principle was not dominant in the ancient world. Plato reported in 350 B.C. that the mentally ill and their families were held responsible for the actions of the mentally ill (Walker, 1985). A widespread practice of exculpating mentally ill people is a relatively recent phenomenon (Perlin, 1989; Walker, 1985).

The first recorded case of an individual being acquitted by reason of insanity in English law occurred in 1505 (Walker, 1968). The modern "insanity test" approach was established in the early part of the nineteenth century by the acquittals, by reason of insanity, of James Hadfield in 1800 and Daniel M'Naghten in 1843 (Moran, 1985). In 1800, James Hadfield tried to shoot King George III and he was charged with high treason. Hadfield suffered from the delusion that King George III's death would cause the world to end with the Second Advent of Christ (Moran, 1985). At trial, Hadfield pleaded insanity and was acquitted (*Rex v. Hadfield*, 1820). The jury's verdict was as follows: "We find the prisoner is not guilty; he being under the influence of insanity at the time the act was committed" (Moran, 1985, p. 35). This phrase became abbreviated into the familiar **not guilty by reason of insanity (NGRI)** verdict that remained in Canadian law until its revision in 1992.

After *Hadfield*, the English parliament passed the *Criminal Lunatics Act* of 1800, which required that people found NGRI be confined to a secure psychiatric hospital (Moran, 1985). From this point on, people acquitted by reason of insanity could be confined in a prison or secure mental hospital for the rest of their lives. It was only in 1991, following the Swain case (see above), that the Supreme Court of Canada held it unconstitutional to automatically confine people acquitted by reason of insanity to secure psychiatric facilities (*R. v. Swain*, 1991).

The insanity defence test used in Canada has its origins in the well-known case *Regina v. M'Naghten* (1843). Daniel M'Naghten attempted to assassinate the Prime Minister of England, Sir Robert Peel, but instead killed the Prime Minister's secretary, Edward Drummond (Moran, 1981, 1985). The jury acquitted M'Naghten because of his insanity (he believed he was being hounded by the Prime Minister and many other enemies). M'Naghten was committed to hospital. where he died approximately twenty years later at the age of 50. (Moran, 1985; Simon & Aaronson, 1988). The case defined a standard of insanity, known appropriately enough as the **M'Naghten standard**, which became the accepted rule in England, the United States, and Canada.

The M'Naghten standard has three elements. First, the accused must have been suffering from "a defect of reason, from disease of the mind" (cited by Moran, 1985, p. 40). Today, these words are interpreted to mean that the accused must have suffered from a mental disorder. Second, the accused must not have known the "nature and quality of the act he was doing," *or*, third, the accused must not have known that "what he was doing was wrong" (cited by Moran, 1985, p. 40). Note the word *or*: inability to understand that an act is wrong can be sufficient even if the accused understands the act itself. Because the final two elements require a subjective exploration of the accused's thinking, the M'Naghten test is referred to as a *cognitive* test of insanity (for example, Low et al., 1986).

The insanity standard remained unchanged for almost a century. In *R. v. Swain* (1991), the insanity defence was challenged on a number of grounds. Following *Swain*, the Supreme Court of Canada gave Parliament six months to change the law. Bill C-30 was passed, changing the legislation governing mentally disordered offenders. The name of the defence was changed from "not guilty by reason of insanity (NGRI)" to "not criminally responsible on account of mental disorder (NCRMD)," and the wording of the standard was revised, but not changed in content. Section 16 of the *Criminal Code* currently outlines the standard as follows:

> *No person is criminally responsible for an act committed or an omission made while suffering from a mental disorder that rendered the person incapable of appreciating the nature and quality of the act or omission or of knowing that it was wrong.*

Although the insanity standard has remained virtually unchanged for a century and a half, its elements are open to more than one interpretation. For example, the meaning of the word "wrong" has been a source of controversy. In 1979, in the case of *R. v. Schwartz*, the Supreme Court determined that "wrong" means wrong according to law and not morally wrong. More recently, however, in *R. v. Chaulk* (1980), the Court decided that the word should be interpreted to include morally wrong.

More significant changes in Bill C-30 relate to who can raise the defence and what happens to people acquitted on these grounds. In the case that opens this chapter, the Crown raised the insanity defence over the objections of Mr. Swain and his counsel. Why would the Crown do this? Perhaps because, until the Swain case, people found NGRI in Canada were automatically confined to a secure psychiatric facility for an indeterminate period. Therefore, having a defendant found NGRI was an effective way of removing him or her from society. The Supreme Court ruled that permitting the Crown to raise the issue of criminal responsibility against the wishes of the accused infringes his or her rights under Section 7 (the right to life, liberty, and security of the person) of the *Charter*. Under current law, the Crown may raise the issue of an accused's mental state only under one of two conditions: after a verdict of guilty has been handed down or if the defence raises the issue of the accused's mental state for any purpose.

Moreover, in *Swain* (1991), the Supreme Court ruled that indeterminate detention infringed the rights of the accused. Currently, under the *Criminal Code*, where a verdict of not criminally responsible on account of mental disorder is rendered, the court may make a disposition in regards to the accused, or the court may defer disposition to the Review Board, which must, as soon as possible and no later than 45 days after the verdict was rendered, hold a hearing and make a disposition. Under exceptional circumstances, the hearing time may be extended to a maximum of 90 days after the verdict.

As with the dispositions for unfit offenders, in making a disposition in respect of an accused found NCRMD, the court or Review Board must take into consideration the need to protect the public from dangerous individuals, the mental condition of the accused, the reintegration of the accused into society, and other needs of the accused. Several disposition options are available to individuals found NCRMD, including: (1) absolute discharge, which is required by law if the accused is found not to be a "significant threat" to the public, (2) conditional discharge, or (3) detention in hospital.

People with mental illnesses also come under control of the law in noncriminal contexts. Later we will discuss other circumstances in which people may be involuntarily admitted to a psychiatric hospital.

Empirical Research and the Insanity Defence

There has been a great deal of controversy over the insanity defence, much of it legal and beyond the realm of empirical research. Some research does exist, though (Ogloff, Schweighofer, Turnbull, & Whittemore, 1992). First, investigators have described the general demographic characteristics of people found NGRI. Second, they have studied detention and release patterns of persons found NGRI. Third, recidivism of NGRI acquittees has been examined. Fourth, researchers have investigated people's attitudes to the insanity defence.

A study by Hodgins (1983) provides some information on Canadian NGRI acquittees. Unfortunately, Hodgins' sample of 225 includes both NGRI acquittees and those found unfit to stand trial. However, she notes that the groups differed very little. Hodgins found that 87 percent of her sample were male, the average age for the men was 32, their average education level was Grade 8, and 78 percent were unemployed. Only 10 percent of the men were married or in common-law relationships. Among the women, the average age was 40, average education level was Grade 7, and 93 percent were unemployed. Thirty-four percent of the women were living as part of a couple. The majority (60 percent) of Hodgins' sample had previously been hospitalized, while a minority (39 percent) had previously been arrested. However, only 19 percent of these earlier crimes were of a violent nature. Of the current crimes, 45 percent were of a violent nature. Given that this figure includes a variety of violent crimes, we can only assume that murder represents some fraction of the 45 percent. Similarly, other studies have found that murderers constitute only a minority of those found NGRI (Ogloff et al., 1992). Of the violent crimes, most of the victims (64 percent) were known by their alleged aggressor. Hodgins found that a majority (76 percent) of her sample were diagnosed as psychotic.

Another study, by Rice and Harris (1990) provides more recent information on Canadian NGRI acquittees. The acquittees' average age was 33 years, the average number of years of schooling was nine, only 42 percent had ever been married and 38 percent were living alone at the time of arrest. A charge of murder had been made against 40 percent of the sample and attempted murder against 34 percent. The majority of the sample (75 percent) were diagnosed as being psychotic; a minority (13 percent) were diagnosed as having a personality disorder. Rice and Harris do not indicate the percentage of NGRI acquittees who had experienced prior hospitalization or arrest. However, their data did allow them to conclude that the NGRI acquittees had less extensive psychiatric and criminal histories than a matched convict group.

The ramifications of the insanity defence in Canada have been detailed by Golding, Eaves, and Kowaz (1989), who obtained outcome information on the 188 persons found NGRI in British Columbia between 1975 and 1983. They reported that the average individual spent slightly over 9 1/2 years in confinement or under supervision after being found NGRI. This figure is even more remarkable given the fact that approximately 30 percent of their sample was found NGRI for minor offences (for example, nuisance crimes). Cases in the sample ranged from minor offences such as nuisance charges and drugs to more serious crimes such as sexual assault and murder. However, Golding et al. concluded that concern for public safety is an insignificant issue in at least 30 percent of cases, and that lengthy detention or supervision is neither humane or pragmatic in these cases. Even for violent offenders, it seems unlikely that those successfully treated with medications required such long time periods to be rendered non-dangerous. Thus, the legally sanctioned reasons for detainment of those found NGRI—treatment and protection—

do not appear to be the only forces operating in release decisions. Unfortunately, little is known about the state of affairs since *Swain* and the resulting changes to the *Criminal Code*. It seems likely that detention times should be reduced by the requirement that criminal review boards absolutely discharge persons found NCRMD when they no longer pose a significant threat of harm to others.

Studies on the recidivism of NGRI acquittees indicate variations across jurisdictions. Overall, however, U.S. data suggest similar rates of recidivism among NGRI acquittees and matched groups of convicted felons (Ogloff et al., 1992).

In her study, Hodgins (1983) found that 36 percent of 176 discharged male NGRI acquittees were arrested on subsequent charges; 80 percent of the charges were for nonviolent crimes. Golding and his colleagues (1989), in the British Columbia study above, also followed NGRI acquittees after their release. They reported, "62.9 percent of the individuals experience a 'failure' of community tenure during outpatient supervision, marked by 2.4 hospitalizations." Golding et al. attributed these results to a natural, phasic recycling of mental disorder, and to the intensive post-release supervision provided in British Columbia. They suggested that expensive criminologically based supervision is probably inappropriate for what is actually a mental health problem.

The public has always seemed troubled by a verdict of NGRI. In 1843, the public rose up in protest of M'Naghten's acquittal (Moran, 1981). More than a century later, in 1982, the verdict of NGRI in the case of John Hinckley, Jr., who attempted to assassinate President Ronald Reagan, resulted in a similar public outcry (Ogloff et al., 1992). The public has long regarded the insanity acquittal as a ticket to freedom (Slovenko, 1983). In fact, far from being a loophole, the insanity defence is "a noose that holds the accused person more tightly than any determinate sentence that might have been imposed" (Coles & Grant, 1990, p. 244).

Recently, public awareness of the NGRI plea has increased. However, media portrayals of the defence are rarely balanced. Media examinations are most likely to focus on the notorious NGRI acquittees who are released and commit subsequent sensational crimes. Although such cases do exist, they represent but a small minority of all NGRI cases (Ogloff et al., 1992). Rather than being "brutal killers," many NGRI acquittees have long histories of serious mental illness, and commit nonviolent crimes. As discussed in Chapter 11, the insanity defence is raised in very few cases, and is successful in even fewer cases. Further, many NGRI acquittees are confined to mental hospitals for long periods—sometimes even longer than if they had been found guilty and sentenced for the crime with which they were charged. And the hospitals where violent acquittees are confined—hospitals specializing in the "criminally insane"—often look more like high-security prisons, with barred cells and armed guards, than like ordinary hospitals. The re-arrest rates of NGRI acquittees do not appear to differ significantly from matched comparison groups of offenders, and the crimes for which they are arrested tend to be nonviolent in nature. There is some evidence that the "failures" in the community are due to the nature of mental disorder as opposed to criminogenic factors. Thus, community mental health support and maintenance may be effective in reducing arrest rates.

INVOLUNTARY CIVIL COMMITMENT

Over the past 30 years, the number of mentally ill people institutionalized in psychiatric hospitals in Canada has decreased dramatically—by about 600 percent. This process has placed considerable stress on the mental health and medical systems, with many general practitioners, hospitals, and community mental health services struggling to provide an acceptable level of care to this population (McCartney, 1994). However, many of the most seriously mentally ill people eventually are involuntarily committed.

People who are civilly committed lose their rights just as those convicted of criminal offences do; however, civil commitment differs in a number of important ways. First, the primary goal is to protect the individual patient (Melton, Petrila, Poythress, & Slobogin, 1997). Second, ironically, involuntarily hospitalized patients tend to have less protection of their rights than those dealt with by criminal law. Third, criminal acts are specifically defined, whereas the terms relevant to civil commitment tend to be vague (for example, "need for treatment"). Fourth, individuals convicted of an offence and incarcerated serve a specific sentence; however, individuals who are civilly committed may remain hospitalized as long as they meet the criteria outlined in the various provincial mental health acts. They also may be recommitted as necessary.

Unlike criminal law, which is under the control of the federal government, mental health acts are legislated by the provinces. Thus, the particular involuntary civil commitment criteria vary across the country. The particular involuntary commitment criteria for each province in Canada are presented in Table 18.3 (see Douglas & Koch, in press). Although legislation differs across provinces, most contain similar elements. First, an individual must be found to be mentally ill. Second, usually there must be a risk of "harm" or "danger" to the mentally ill person or to others. In their review, Douglas and Koch draw a distinction between the "strict definitions of danger" found in legislation in the Yukon, Alberta, Northwest Territories, Manitoba, and Ontario and the broader definitions found in the other provinces. Some provinces have a higher threshold for linking mental disorder to dangerousness; for example, legislation in Ontario requires that "a person's mental disorder likely will result in 'serious bodily harm to another person'" (Douglas & Koch, in press). Some provinces permit mentally ill individuals to be involuntarily committed even without demonstrated danger if they need treatment, or if they will deteriorate mentally or physically if they are not held in hospital.

Under the provincial mental health acts, a physician is required to perform an examination of the patient. The acts do not specify that the physician must be a specialist; therefore, it may be a psychiatrist or some other physician who performs the examination and determines whether the person meets the criteria for civil commitment. Psychologists are not legally qualified to make this determination.

Most mental health legislation also provides for emergency civil commitment. In British Columbia, for example, if there is no other physician qualified to give a second medical certificate, one medical certificate is sufficient to detain an individual for 48 hours. Additionally, a police officer may take an individual into custody and take him or her immediately to a physician. The officer must be satisfied that the individual is suffering from a mental disorder and is acting in a manner dangerous to his or her own safety or that of others. Again, one medical certificate is sufficient to detain the individual for up to 48 hours.

Patient Characteristics

In their forthcoming study Douglas and Koch review the demographic characteristics of people who are civilly committed in Canada, as reported by Statistics Canada (1995). Of the 29,991 patients who were released from psychiatric hospitals in Canada between 1992 and 1993,

> 59% (n = 17,652) were male and 41% (n = 12,339) female (Statistics Canada, 1995). Age was clustered in the 25–34 range. The mean length of stay, in days, was 274. The majority of patients had schizophrenic diagnoses (n = 8,686; 29%), followed by affective diagnoses (n = 5,429; 18%). Other common diagnoses were alcohol dependence (n = 2,215; 7.4%), adjustment reaction (n = 2,034; 6.8%), personality disorders (n = 1,926; 6.4%), neurotic (anxiety) disorders (n = 1,287; 4.3%), and drug abuse (n = 1,067; 3.6%).

Compared to the general population, civilly committed patients in the United States have been found to have lower socioeconomic status and less education, and are more likely to be unemployed or unskilled (Hiday, 1988). Canadian researchers have reported similar demographic and clinical profiles for involuntary patients. For example, Tremblay, King, and Baines, (1994) described 100 patients admitted to hospital in Ontario. The majority of patients were 20 to 39 years of age; 52 percent were male and 48 percent were female; 45.5 percent had never been married; and 31.3 percent were separated, divorced, or widowed at the time of admission. Most had completed secondary school (65.6 percent). Only 23 percent were employed and almost half were supported by Social Services. Sixty-one percent had at least one previous psychiatric admission. Diagnoses, at time of admission, were psychoactive substance abuse (30 percent), mood disorder (27 percent), adjustment disorder (24 percent), schizophrenia (9 percent), and other (10 percent) (psychotic, not classified elsewhere, or organic mental disorder). Similar findings have been obtained by Paredes and his colleagues (Paredes, Kanachowski, Ledwidge, & Stoutenburg, 1990) in British Columbia, and by Harris, Hilton, and Rice (1993) in Ontario except that Harris et al. found that 24 percent of patients were diagnosed with schizophrenia and 8 percent with other psychoses.

Table 18.3 A Comparison of Civil Commitment Legislation Across Canadian Jurisdictions

Specified Statutory Factors	B.C.	Yukon	Alta.	N.W.T.	Sask.	Man.	Ont.	Que.	N.B.	N.S.	P.E.I.	Nfld.
Requirement of mental disorder	Yes	Yes	Yes	Yes	Yes	Yes	Yes	Yes	Yes	Yes	Yes	Yes
Functional definition of mental illness	Yes	Yes	Yes	Yes	Yes	Yes	No	No	Yes	No	Yes	No
Requirement of danger to self or others	Yes	Yes	Yes	Yes	Yes	Yes	Yes	Yes	Yes	Yes	Yes	Yes
Strict definition of danger	No	Yes	Yes	Yes	No	Yes	Yes	No	No	No	No	No
Requirement of need for treatment	Yes	No	No	No	Yes	Yes	No	Yes	No	Yes	No	No
Absolute right to refuse/ consent to treatment	No	No	No	No	No	Yes	Yes	No	No	Yes	No	No
Right to be informed of reasons for detention	Yes	Yes	Yes	Yes	Yes	Yes	Yes	Yes	Yes	No	Yes	No
Right to apply for review panel	Yes	Yes	Yes	No	Yes	Yes	Yes	Yes*	Yes	Yes	Yes	Yes
Specified right to legal counsel	Yes	Yes	No	Yes	No	Yes	Yes	No	Yes	Yes	Yes	No
Provision for apprehension by peace officer	Yes	Yes	Yes	Yes	Yes	Yes	Yes	No	Yes	Yes	Yes	Yes
Length of short-term commitment order	72 hr.	24 hr.	24 hr.	48 hr.	24 hr.	72 hr.	72 hr.	48 hr.	72 hr.	48 hr.	72 hr.	15 days
Length of initial commitment certificate	1 mo.	21 days	1 mo.	14 days	21 days	3 wk.	2 wk.	21 days	1 mo.	7 days	30 days	1 mo.
Length of second commitment certificate	1 mo.	21 days	1 mo.	14 days	21 days	3 mo.	1 mo.	3 mo.	2 mo.	1 mo.	90 days	2 mo.
Length of further commitment certificate	3, 6 mo.	21 days	1, 6 mo.	14 days	21 days	3 mo.	2, 3 mo.	6 mo.	3 mo.	3, 6 mo.	12 mo.	3, 6 mo., 1yr.
Discharge criteria specified	Yes	No	Yes	Yes	Yes	Yes	Yes	No	Yes	No	Yes	No
Statutory presence of review panel	Yes	Yes	Yes	No	Yes	Yes	Yes	Yes*	Yes	Yes	Yes	Yes
Director may give treatment consent	Yes	Yes	Yes	Yes	Yes	Yes	Yes	Yes	Yes	Yes	Yes	Yes
Specified right to appeal to court	Yes	Yes	Yes	Yes	Yes	Yes	Yes	No	No	Yes	No	Yes
Any person may bring issue before court	Yes	Yes	Yes	Yes	Yes	Yes	Yes	Yes	Yes	Yes	Yes	Yes

Source: K. Douglas & W. J. Koch, Civil commitment and civil competence: Psychological issues, in R. Schuller & J. R. P. Ogloff, eds., *An introduction to law and psychology: Canadian perspectives* (Toronto: University of Toronto Press, in press).

Note re Statutes: **B.C.**: *Mental Health Act*, R.S.B.C. 1996, c. 288; **Yukon**: *Mental Health Act*, S.Y.T. 1989–90, c. 28; **Alta.**: *Mental Health Act*, S.A. 1988, c. M-13.1; **NWT.**: *Mental Health Act*, R.S.N.W.T. 1988, c. M-10; **Sask.**: *Mental Health Act*, S.S. 1984–85, c. M-13.1; **Man.**: *Mental Health Act*, R.S.M. 1987, c. M110; **Ont.**: *Mental Health Act*, R.S.O. 1990, c. M.7; **Que.**: *Mental Patients Protection Act*, R.S.Q. 1977, P-41; **N.B.**: *An Act to Amend the Mental Health Act*, R.S.N.B. 1989, c. 23.; **N.S.**: *Hospitals Act*, R.S.N.S. 1989, c. 208; **P.E.I.**: *Mental Health Act*, R.S.P.E.I. 1994, c. 39; **Nfld.**: *Mental Health Act*, R.S.N. 1990, c. M-9.

Some recent research on individuals at a psychiatric hospital in British Columbia who had applied for a review panel to consider their release provides additional and consistent data. Ogloff and Grant (1997; see also Douglas, Ogloff, Nicholls, & Grant, in press; Nicholls, Ogloff, & Douglas, 1997) reported that of 279 psychiatric patients in British Columbia, 167 (59.9 percent) were male. The average age at admission was 38.6, and ranged from 17 to 88. Most patients had been previously admitted to a psychiatric facility ($n = 258$; 91.2 percent), and a majority were diagnosed with a psychotic disorder ($n = 188$; 67.4 percent) at discharge, with over half of the whole sample having a schizophrenic diagnosis ($n = 140$; 50.2 percent).

Consistently with other findings, the people in this sample had difficult histories and were disenfranchised. Very few patients ($n = 12$; 4.2 percent) were employed prior to admission, and almost one-fifth had been living in skid row hotels or were homeless. Approximately one-quarter of patients reported having been physically or sexually abused as children. In addition to these experiences, the group as a whole engaged in a large amount of criminal and suicidal behaviour. More than two-thirds of patients had a history of suicidal or self-injurious behaviour ($n = 191$; 67.5 percent) and approximately one-quarter of patients also engaged in self-harm while hospitalized ($n = 65$; 23.0 percent). The average number of past offences was 4.65, and the average number of violent offences was approximately 1.0. In all, fewer than one-quarter of patients ($n = 65$; 23.3 percent) had prior arrests for violent offences, 137 (49.1 percent) had been violent to others in the two weeks prior to admission, and a surprisingly high number ($n = 179$, 64.2 percent) had a documented history of some sort of violent behaviour to others.

Review Panel Decisions

In most provinces, involuntary patients have the right to apply for release through a review panel (Douglas & Koch, in press). As Table 18.3 shows, the point at which people can apply for a review panel hearing varies significantly across the provinces. In British Columbia, the review panel is composed of a chairperson (a lawyer appointed by the province), a physician (appointed by the hospital), and a patient appointee (not a relative). Regardless of the province, the review panel hears the patient's application for release and makes a legal decision about whether the patient currently meets the criteria, found in the particular mental health act, for involuntary hospitalization. Decisions need not be unanimous; the majority rules.

In British Columbia, where there has been some relevant research, review panels play an increasingly significant role in the discharge process for involuntary patients. Indeed, there were 941 applications for panel hearings in British Columbia in 1994 (Tuokko, 1995). Available research, conducted in that province, identified the "typical" review panel applicant as a male under 30 years of age, transferred from another institution, who was uneducated, unskilled, and unemployed and had problems with work, school, and parents (Gray, Clark, Higenbottam, Ledwidge, & Paredes, 1985). Problems with alcohol abuse were also likely. The applicant tended to be a schizophrenic with normal orientation and memory, and no mental retardation or epilepsy.

Some data are also available on factors that affect the decision-making of a review panel are also available (Higenbottam, Ledwidge, Paredes, Hansen, Kogan, & Lambert, 1985). The "typical" patient who was released by the review panel was represented at the hearing by a lawyer, was unmarried, and was likely to have been deemed capable under the *Patients' Estate Act*. The released patients had typically spent less time in hospital, and had been out of hospital longer since the last admission, than patients who were not released by the panel. Patients who were released were also more likely to be on a waiting list for a boarding home, and were judged by their attending psychiatrist as being less dangerous to self than those who were not released. Finally, released patients typically had a history of drug abuse, but were judged as having less psychopathology than those who were not released.

Despite concerns about deinstitutionalization, surprisingly few studies have explored the rates at which discharged psychiatric patients are rehospitalized. An exception is a study by Goering and Wasylenski (1984) who followed 747 psychiatric patients discharged from a psychiatric hospital in Toronto. Patients were interviewed one month, three months, and two years after discharge. Discharged patients fared poorly; both social isolation and inadequate income persisted throughout the two-year followup period. This is consistent with the findings of Wasylenski (1985) and Harris et al. (1993).

Ledwidge and colleagues (1987) conducted a two-year followup study in British Columbia of 94 patients released by review panels or by an attending physician. There was no significant difference between the two groups. Forty-five percent were readmitted within one year, which is similar to rates reported by other researchers (for example, Mortensen & Eaton, 1994). Schizophrenia was the most common diagnosis. Severity of illness and lack of response to treatment predicted readmission.

Two years after discharge, about 18 percent were in hospital (Ledwidge et al., 1987). On average, adjustment to home life, the workplace, social interaction, and general compliance with followup were poor; however, few incidents of harm to self or others occurred, and legal involvement was minimal.

Rehospitalization studies have produced variable results, partly due to differences in the followup periods. Generally, however, many psychiatric patients are readmitted, the vast majority within the first year following discharge. Released patients tend to experience relationship and financial difficulties, but few contact community mental health services and support agencies.

PROFESSIONAL ETHICS AND REGULATION OF PSYCHOLOGISTS

As a profession, psychology has attempted to ensure that psychologists possess at least minimum qualifications and are competent to perform their duties. There are two general ways in which these goals are met. First, psychologists who practise independently must be registered with the professional regulatory body in their jurisdiction and, in most provinces, the professional designation of "psychologist" may be used only by those registered for practice in that province. Second, registered psychologists are required to abide by professional and ethical standards; and failure to do so can result in some investigation and censure.

Table 18.4 Provincial/Territorial Licensing Requirements for Psychologists

	Academic Entry Requirements	Supervised Experience	Examinations	Exemptions
B.C.	Doc. or equivalent (indep.)	1 year pre-doc.	• EPPP 65% • Oral	University, government, schools
Alta.	Master's (indep.)	1 year (1600 hr.) post-master's	• EPPP 70% • Oral	University
Sask.	Doc. (indep.)	(No experience requirement)	• EPPP 70% • Oral	University, government, health board, schools
Yukon	(No legislation governing practice of psychology)			
Man.	• Doc. (indep.) • Master's (P. Assoc. supervised)	• Doc. (1 pre- and 1 post-year) • Master's (2 years post)	• EPPP (Doc.: 70% Mas.: 65%) • Oral (both)	University, government, schools, hospitals
Ont.	• Doc. (indep.) • Master's (P. Assoc. indep.)	• Doc. (1 pre- and 1 post-year) • Master's (4 years post plus 1 year on supervision register)	• EPPP 70% • Oral jurisprudence	University
Que.	Master's (indep.)	(None)	• No EPPP • No oral • Ethics	(None)
Nfld.	Master's (indep.) (until 2001)	• Doc. (1 pre- and 1 post-year) • Master's (2 years post)	• EPPP (pass score not set) • No oral	University
N.W.T.	Master's in psychology from Canadian university	1 year (1600 hours) while on an intern's registry. Previous supervised experience from another jurisdiction may be considered.	Exam "may" be required	(None)
N.S.	Master's (indep.)	• Doc. (1 pre- and 1 post-year) • Master's (6 years post)	• EPPP 70% • Oral	None
P.E.I.	• Doc. (indep.) • Master's (indep. in inst./agency only)	• Doc. (1 pre- and 1 post-year) • Master's (2 years post)	• No EPPP • Oral	University
N.B.	Master's (indep.)	• Doc. (1 pre- and 1 post-year) • Master's (4 years post)	• EPPP 65% • Oral	University

Source: Lorraine J. Breault, Ph.D., Canadian Psychological Association, March 1998.

Licensure and Competence

All provinces have specific requirements that must be met before applying for licensing as a psychologist. The requirements vary, but generally they consist in academic qualifications, supervised clinical experience, and some form of examination process (see Table 18.4). For example, in some provinces, psychologists may practise independently with a master's degree, but others require a doctorate (usually a Ph.D. in psychology). The required supervised clinical experience varies as well, from none to a range of two to six years (depending on academic credentials). Most provinces require that candidates successfully complete the Examination for Professional Practice in Psychology (EPPP), developed by the Association of State and Provincial Psychology Boards (ASPPB, 1998). Finally, most jurisdictions require successful completion of an oral examination covering stated areas of competence, knowledge of legal, ethical, and professional standards, and overall maturity and professional attitude (Evans, 1997).

Most provinces provide some exemptions to the requirement that the professional title of psychologist be backed up by registration. For example, in most provinces university professors who teach, lecture, or do research in psychology may call themselves psychologists, even if they are not registered with the College of Psychologists.

Once psychologists become licensed to practise, they must maintain high levels of competence. Guidelines instruct psychologists in such areas as the need to recognize limits of expertise, the value of seeking continuing education, and the importance of recognizing personal problems and conflicts that may interfere with their work (for example, CPA, 1991; APA's *Ethical Principles of Psychologists and Code of Conduct*, 1992).

In the *Canadian Code of Ethics for Psychologists* (CPA, 1991), the ethical principle of maintaining a competent practice falls under the general principle of "Responsible Caring," one of four guiding principles. This section directs psychologists to perform only the kinds of activities in which they are competent, and to carry out the activities that they do perform as competently as possible. Although there is a careful attempt to place limitations on psychologists' areas of competence, it should be noted that no province registers psychologists with specialty certification (for example, child psychologists, forensic psychologists).

RELATIONSHIPS WITH CLIENTS

Relationships between psychologist and their clients tend to be very personal. Indeed, as discussed in Chapter 16, this *therapeutic alliance* often provides the very basis for some of the important work done in psychotherapy. It has been suggested that, particularly in the context of psychotherapy, the intimacy of the psychologist-client relationship makes it vulnerable to abuse (Ogloff, 1995). Depending on the context, psychologists may also face other difficulties due to the nature of their professional relationships. For example, when supervising students, employees, or others, the dynamics of their relationships, such as real or perceived differences in power, may contribute to people feeling vulnerable to mistreatment (Sullivan & Ogloff, 1998). For many reasons, therefore, a number of safeguards have been developed to clarify the various roles of psychologists and to ensure the protection of psychologists' clients in various contexts.

Informed Consent

When psychologists engage in professional relationships with clients, they are obligated to inform their clients of the nature and expectations of the relationship being created, and of the details of the procedures that will be administered, such as the assessment, therapy, research protocols, or any other activities that participants will be asked to complete (Evans, 1997; Ogloff, 1995). Most importantly, the process of gaining clients' informed consent must provide a forum in which clients are given all the information they need to make a decision about participating and then allowed to make a real choice on the matter, thereby providing truly informed consent.

Informed consent has been defined in various ways (Ogloff, 1995; Ogloff & Otto, 1991; Roth, Meisel, & Lidz, 1977). For example, Ogloff (1995) states that to meet the requirement of informed consent, clients who consent to participate in treatment or research "must do so voluntarily, knowingly, and intelligently" (p. 352). A decision is considered voluntary if it is made without pressure or coercion, including obvious actions such as manipulation or misrepresentation and less obvious ones such as considerable payment or other significant incentives for participation in research. To make a decision knowingly, participants must be given all relevant information such as the purpose of the research or treatment, risks and benefits, alternatives to the procedures being offered, and consequences of not participating. Finally, the participant or client must have the intelligence or capacity to make an informed decision about the matter.

Evans (1997) described the informed consent process as having four components. Specifically, "[t]he individual from whom the informed consent is obtained must be *competent* to consent, be *informed* by the practitioner, *understand* the information, and the consent must be *voluntary* and not be obtained by misrepresentation or fraud" (p. 86). According to Evans (1997), clients are considered "competent" if they have the cognitive capacity to make a knowledgeable decision. For adults, this capacity is assumed unless there is some reason to suspect otherwise. Even when this assumption is made, however, some basic indicators should be used to try to assure that people meet this requirement. For example, competence can be evaluated by examining their abilities in four areas: understanding relevant information, manipulating it in a rational manner (for example, comparing risks and benefits), appreciating the available options and the likely consequences of exercising them, and communicating their decisions or choices (Appelbaum & Grisso, 1995).

Psychologists must ensure that several specific elements are understood in the process of obtaining informed consent (CPA, 1991). These include the "purpose and nature of the activity; mutual responsibilities; likely benefits and risks; alternatives; the likely consequences of non-action; the option to refuse or withdraw at any time, without prejudice; over what period of time the consent applies; and, how to rescind consent if desired" (ethical principle I.18). The *Code* also recommends that this process include a form to be signed by participants to indicate their understanding. Information should be presented in a manner that clients can understand (CPA, 1991, ethical principle I.17). Researchers have found, however, that informed consent forms used in research tend to be written at a relatively high reading level that many participants might not understand (Ogloff & Otto, 1991).

When psychologists' clients are children (that is, 18 years of age or younger), the requirements for obtaining informed consent may be different, depending on the jurisdiction. In British Columbia, for example, the *Infants Act* (1996) states that a child may give consent to health care if he or she demonstrates an understanding of the nature and consequences as well as the benefits and risks of the procedure, and if the health care provider has determined the procedure to be in the best interests of the child. It seems that the important element, again, is that the child must demonstrate his or her capacity to understand the implications of the decision. This interpretation has been illustrated by the courts in Alberta in a case involving a 16-year-old girl who wanted to obtain a therapeutic abortion, against the wishes of her parents (*C. (J.S.) v. Wren*, 1986). The parents of the girl sought an injunction against the physician who agreed to perform the abortion, but the injunction was denied; this decision was appealed by the parents. The Alberta Court of Appeal agreed with the chambers judge and it was determined that the physician had indeed established the child's capacity: that is, she had sufficient intelligence and understanding to make up her own mind about the abortion.

With older adolescent clients with "sufficient" levels of intelligence and understanding, therefore, it is appropriate to seek informed consent in a manner similar to the procedures followed with adults. If clients are young or if there is reason to believe that they do not have a sufficient understanding of the issue or procedure requiring their consent, informed consent must be sought from the person's parent or guardian. Of course, psychologists then must ensure that the elements of informed consent described above are met for whomever is providing consent.

Confidentiality

Many people who visit psychologists assume that what they say to psychologists is strictly private and confidential, and it is believed that many individuals require an assurance of confidentiality before they are willing to reveal the highly personal things that often are shared with psychologists (Evans, 1997).

Although there has been a movement toward legally protecting confidentiality in psychiatrist- and psychologist-client relationships, these relationships are not considered "privileged"—that is, there is no special legal protection against being required to divulge confidential information in court (Evans, 1997). Canadian law offers such privilege only to the solicitor-client relationship, spousal communications (through statutory law) and, in some jurisdictions, parishioner-clergy relationships.

Yet, for the most part, the content of what is shared in a professional relationship with a psychologist is confidential. Psychologists' ethics codes specifically instruct them to ensure information shared by clients is not released to anyone without the client's consent, except as required by law (APA, 1992; CPA, 1991). There are, however, important exceptions, which should be explained to clients at the beginning of any relationship—ideally during the informed consent process. Such information should be presented in a manner that can be easily understood (Evans, 1997), so that clients can decide what they want to share and, given the limits of confidentiality, whether they wish to engage in the relationship at all.

Evidence of child abuse creates a clear-cut situation in which information must be shared without clients' consent. Similarly, confidentiality must be breached when clients indicate intentions to hurt themselves or others. According to ethics codes, the psychologists may be required to alert appropriate authorities and possibly the identified victims (APA, 1992; CPA, 1991).

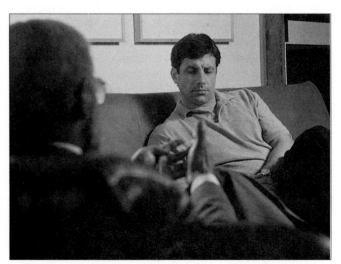

Many people who visit psychologists assume that what they say is strictly private and confidential.

In Ontario, the *Regulated Health Professions Act* (1991) legislation added another justification for breach of confidentiality: a psychologist must report evidence giving reasonable grounds to believe that another health care professional has sexually abused a patient. Finally, in some of the Atlantic provinces, people are obligated to report abuse of elderly people who are unable to care for themselves.

Situations that require reporting are often difficult to predict; a client may be sharing emotions or memories and suddenly reveal information that needs to be reported. This makes it all the more important for psychologists to be clear at the outset of relationships about the limits of confidentiality.

Prohibition Against Sexual Relations with Clients

Because of the personal closeness and intimacy of psychologist-client relationships, the boundaries of personal interactions can sometimes become blurred. Yet crossing boundaries is a serious breach of the professional relationship and often causes significant harm (Keith-Spiegel & Koocher, 1998; Ogloff, 1995).

Psychologists are instructed by their ethics codes about how to avoid dual relationships—that is, relationships with clients outside of the therapeutic relationship—or, when they cannot be avoided, how to manage them. For example, the Canadian *Code* (CPA, 1991) states that psychologists should avoid dual relationships with students, employees, or clients that might affect their ability to be objective and unbiased in determining what is in the best interests of others (ethical principle III.32). Generally, psychologists should not enter into a professional relationship when some other relationship previously exists, and vice versa (Evans, 1997). For example, providing psychotherapy to a friend or a friend's partner would be considered inappropriate, because the therapist may be influenced by other factors related to the friendship, and therefore may not be able to maintain a more objective view of the issues being addressed in therapy. Although it is acknowledged that sometimes dual relationships cannot be foreseen (for example, you may be seeing an acquaintance's partner in therapy without realizing it), psychologists are expected to take all reasonable steps to resolve such situations promptly when they do arise (Keith-Spiegel & Koocher, 1998).

The most serious of all possible dual relationships is the situation in which a psychologist engages in sexual relations with a client. This is an obvious breach in the eyes of psychologists, but complaints of sexually inappropriate behaviours are the most common ethical complaints made against psychologists in many jurisdictions (Borys & Pope, 1989). Although sexual contact with clients is strictly prohibited for psychologists, the specific definitions of such behaviour vary slightly from code to code. For example, the Canadian *Code* (CPA, 1991) states, in a general manner, that psychologists should "not exploit any relationship established as a psychologist to further personal, political, or business interests. … This includes … taking advantage of trust or dependency to engage in sexual activities" (ethical principle III.30).

APA's (1992) ethical principles provide more specific guidelines. This code prohibits psychologists from engaging in sexual intimacies with current clients (ethical standard 4.05) and from accepting as therapy clients anyone with whom they have engaged in sexual intimacies (ethical standard 4.06). In addition, psychologists are not allowed to engage in sexual intimacies with former therapy clients for at least two years following the termination of the professional relationship (ethical standard 4.07), and even then, they may do so only in the "most unusual circumstances" with the burden of proof placed on the psychologist to ensure that there has been no exploitation of the client.

....

RESPONSIBILITIES TO SOCIETY

Duty to Protect Third Parties

The Tarasoff case (*Tarasoff v. Regents of University of California*, 1976) set an important precedent for lawsuits involving mental health professionals. Tatiana Tarasoff was killed by her ex-boyfriend, Prosenjit Poddar, who had earlier been a patient at the University of California–Berkeley Counselling Center. During treatment, he indicated to his psychologist that he planned to harm or kill Ms. Tarasoff. After learning that Mr. Poddar had purchased a gun, the psychologist informed campus police. The psychologist also reported to his supervisor, who did not feel that Mr. Poddar could be involuntarily hospitalized. The police spoke with Mr. Poddar and he assured them he would not hurt Ms. Tarasoff; however, two months later he stabbed her to death. Ms. Tarasoff's parents sued the university and Mr. Poddar's psychologist. In their final ruling, the California Supreme Court stated:

> once a therapist does in fact determine, or under applicable professional standards reasonably should have determined, that a patient poses a serious danger of violence to others, he bears a duty to exercise reasonable care to protect the foreseeable victim of that danger. (Tarasoff, 1976, 551 P.2d at 345)

In this case, the psychologist should have warned Ms. Tarasoff or her parents of the danger. In its ruling, the court noted that confidentiality must be breached to the extent necessary to protect others (Birch, 1992). However, to ensure ethical practice, psychologists must inform their clients about the duty to warn so that the clients can give informed consent for treatment (Birch, 1992). The court acknowledged that dangerousness is difficult to predict and that mental health professionals must exercise "reasonable care," which is based on the current standard of practice.

Since *Tarasoff*, there have been additional cases considered in the United States. In some jurisdictions it was decided that the risk must be immediate and the victim readily identifiable. However, in others *Tarasoff* has been extended to include a duty to protect large groups of people from injury (that is, no identifiable victim), property (for example, arson) and/or negligence on the part of the patient (for example, dangerous driving; see Birch, 1992).

In Canada, there is no legal precedent, but according to the CPA *Code of Ethics* (1991), psychologists have a duty to:

> *do everything reasonably possible to offset the consequences of actions of others when these actions are likely to cause serious physical harm or death. This may include reporting to appropriate authorities (e.g., police) or an intended victim, and would be done even when a confidential relationship is involved. (II.36)*

Birch (1992) suggests that future Canadian rulings will follow the English rather than the U.S. precedent. Birch refers to an article by MacKay (1990) and states, "English courts very rarely hold that one person has a duty to control the actions of another and would be unlikely to extend liability to a *Tarasoff* type case" (1992, p. 99). Alternatively, a court in Alberta held that should a case present itself with facts similar to those found in *Tarasoff*, a psychologist or psychiatrist may be found to have a duty to protect identifiable third parties (see Ogloff & Reaves, 1996b). Should Canada follow English precedent, this would reduce the likelihood that psychologists will be held liable for injuries their clients inflict on others.

Duty to Report Child Abuse

According to Briere (1992, p. xvii), "The majority of adults raised in North America, regardless of gender, age, race, ethnicity, or social class, probably experienced some level of maltreatment as children." Recent estimates of the prevalence of childhood sexual victimization range from 20 to 30 percent for females to 10 to 15 percent for males (Briere, 1992). (See also Chapter 12.) Since 1985, Gelles and Straus (1987) estimated that "severe" parent-child violence (for example, kicking, hitting) occurred in 11 to 14 percent of U.S. families; moreover, 1000 to 5000 children are killed by their parents yearly in America. Not surprisingly, abused children often suffer behavioural and emotional problems (for example, Browne & Finkelhor, 1986). Childhood abuse may also have long-term effects on psychological functioning; for example, adults with a history of abuse may experience posttraumatic stress symptoms, difficulty with interpersonal relationships, and cognitive distortions (Briere, 1992).

Given the prevalence of childhood abuse and the severe ramifications for the victims, it is not surprising that mandatory reporting laws have been instituted in both the United States and Canada (Beck & Ogloff, 1995; Beck, Ogloff, & Corbishley, 1994). These reporting laws apply not only to mental health professionals, but also to anyone who suspects child abuse. However, survey research suggests that although a substantial proportion of practising psychologists have experience with cases of suspected child abuse, not all report suspected abuse (for example, Kalichman & Brosig, 1993; Beck & Ogloff, 1995). This section will briefly review mandatory reporting laws, using British Columbia as an example; then the potential impact of ethical guidelines (APA, 1992; CPA, 1991) on reporting decisions will be discussed.

The legal standard for reporting child abuse exists in every jurisdiction in North America (Beck & Ogloff, 1995; Beck et al., 1994; Ogloff, 1995); however, in the Yukon reporting is not mandatory, but is permitted. The standard for reporting abuse generally includes some statement to the effect that reporting is required if there are *reasonable grounds* to believe that a child has been abused or is in need of protection. This criterion is rather vague, and its terms are not defined. Discretion is therefore required to determine what constitutes abuse or neglect, which introduces subjectivity into the reporting process (Finlayson & Koocher, 1991).

In British Columbia, the *Child, Family and Community Service Act* (1996) outlines situations where child protection is required. Reporting (Section 13 [1]) is required

> *if the child has been, or is likely to be: (a) physically harmed and/or sexually abused or exploited by parent; (b) physically harmed and/or sexually exploited by another person and the parent is unwilling to protect the child; (c) physically harmed because of neglect by the parent; (d) emotionally harmed by the parent's conduct; (e) deprived of necessary health care; or (f) abandoned. (p. 11)*

When the mandatory reporter "has reason to believe that a child needs protection" he or she must promptly report the case to a director (or a person designated by a director) (p. 11). The duty to report applies even if the information on which the suspicion is based was obtained within a confidential relationship (Section 14 [2]). Failure to report suspected abuse is an offence, and may be punishable by a fine and/or imprisonment (Section 14 [3]).

Although the law is quite clear, research shows that psychologists do not always report suspected child abuse (Beck & Ogloff, 1995; Pope & Bajt, 1994). Some psychologists who fail to report suspected abuse consider mandatory reporting of suspected abuse inconsistent with their ethical obligations (for example, confidentiality, respect for the dignity of persons) (see APA, 1992; CPA, 1991). Research also suggests that clinicians are less likely to report emotional and sexual abuse (as opposed to physical abuse) (Beck & Ogloff, 1995) and are less likely to report when they believe it will damage the therapeutic relationship (for example, Brooks, Perry, Starr, & Teply, 1994). Regardless, reporting decisions have important ramifications, and psychologists have a responsibility to make ethically defensible decisions. To ensure they do so, psychologists should be aware of and follow the steps for ethical decision-making outlined in the CPA *Code* (1991).

Duty to Report Elder Abuse

The law is less clear regarding the duty to report elder abuse. Although mandatory reporting laws exist in many of the Atlantic provinces, they are not consistent across Canada. Available research suggests that elder abuse is a problem. For example, Pillemer and Finkelhor (1988) conducted a phone survey of 2020 elderly residents and found that 3 percent of respondents were victims of some form of violence; the majority of victims were assaulted by their partners. On the basis of their literature review, Dutton and McGregor (1992) estimated that all forms of elder abuse (for example, by partner, caretaker) range from 4 percent to 10 percent. These data may actually underestimate prevalence, as elder abuse is often difficult to identify. As is the case with child abuse, psychologists who suspect that their clients may be the victims or perpetrators of elder abuse must make ethically sound decisions about reporting the abuse.

Duty to Abide by the Law

The final area of psychologists' ethics we wish to note here is the requirement that psychologists abide by the law. Ethical principle IV.15 of the CPA *Code* (1991) provides that psychologists

> *Abide by the laws of the society in which they work. If those laws seriously conflict with the ethical principles contained herein, psychologists would do whatever they could to uphold the ethical principles. If upholding the ethical principles could result in serious personal consequences (for example, jail or physical harm), decision for final action would be considered a matter of personal conscience.*

There may be situations in which the legal requirements conflict with the psychologist's ethical obligations. In such cases, psychologists are forced to choose between the law and ethical principles. It must be emphasized that, in such cases, psychologists are not required to uphold their ethical principles at the risk of legal sanction, nor would they be held to have acted unethically if they did not.

SUMMARY

Laws exist in our society to deal with the unique issues that affect people with mental illnesses. The laws include protections and special accommodations in criminal law as well as involuntary hospitalization in the civil context. Accommodations are made to ensure that people with mental illness have the capacity to participate in the legal system. To be found fit to stand trial, an accused must understand the nature of the charges and the purpose, possible outcomes, and effects of the legal proceedings, and must be able to communicate with his or her lawyer. Even if found fit to stand trial, mentally ill accused people who do not understand either the nature and consequences of their actions, or that the actions were wrong, may be found NCRMD.

While it certainly is not illegal to be mentally ill—nor should it be—when mentally ill people pose a risk of harm to themselves or others, they may be involuntarily committed to hospital for treatment. Laws vary from province to province. Taken together, the criminal and civil law emphasize that society has to be prepared to make special provision in law for people with mental illnesses. Unfortunately, society's general lack of understanding of mental illness, as well as the myths surrounding it, sometimes results in the inappropriate treatment of mentally ill people.

Just as mentally ill people exist in the society, and are subject to its laws, the professional behaviour of psychologists and other mental health professionals is subject to legal regulations. The behaviour of psychologists is also governed by ethical standards promulgated by professional associations such as the Canadian Psychological Association. Practising psychol-

ogists must meet the legal and professional standards of their profession. In particular, they must be competent to work in the areas in which they do. Psychologists must obtain informed consent from their clients prior to beginning work with them. Under most circumstances, the identity of their clients and information received from them must remain confidential. Finally, psychologists must refrain from engaging in dual relationships, including, of course, sexual relationships with clients and, under most circumstances, former clients.

While psychologists' primary obligations are to their clients, they also have obligations to third parties and to the society in which they live. For example, psychologists—like all people in Canada—are required to report situations in which they have reason to believe that a child is in need of protection. In some provinces, they must also report suspected elder abuse or situations in which they learn a psychologist may have sexually assaulted clients. In addition, they are ethically obligated to take reasonable steps to protect identifiable third parties when they have reason to believe their clients may seriously harm or kill the third party.

Taken together, the information presented and discussed in this chapter emphasizes the complexities of the society in which we all live. The law must continue to develop appropriate accommodations for people with mental illness whose behaviour results in either legal violations or potential harm to themselves or others. At the same time the law must be sensitive to the unique needs of mentally ill people and to the fact that in many ways they do not differ from people in mainstream society.

KEY TERMS

fit to stand trial (p. 447)

not criminally responsible on account
of mental disorder (NCRMD)
(p. 447)
not guilty by reason of insanity
(NGRI) (p. 448)

M'Naghten standard (p. 449)
informed consent (p. 455)

ADDITIONAL RESOURCES

Bazelon Center for Mental Health Law
1101—15th Street
Suite 1212
Washington, DC 20005-5002
(202) 467-5730
(202) 223-0409 fax
sherryt@bazelon.org

Canadian Psychological Association
151 Slater Street
Suite 205
Ottawa, ON K1P 5H3
(613) 237-2144
(613) 237-1674 fax
iparisien@cpa.ca

Federation of Law Societies of Canada
445—480, boulevard Saint-Laurent
Montreal, QC H2Y 2Y7
(514) 875-6351
(514) 875-6115 fax
pafoley@flsc.ca

www.bazelon.org
This web site of the Bazelon Center for Mental Health Law
addresses issues related to mental health law, including
children's issues, aging issues, fair housing issues, and
advocacy within the legal system for people with mental
illnesses.

www.insight.mcmaster.ca/org/efc/pages/law/charter/
charter.text.html
This site provides an overview of the *Canadian Charter of
Rights and Freedoms*, including the legal rights and proceedings in criminal and penal matters.

www3.sympatico.ca/cmha.toronto.copinge.htm
This site offers a brief overview of Ontario's *Mental Health
Act* and its implications for individuals with mental
illnesses.

www.mhcva.on.ca/MHP/mhpfor5.htm
A discussion of the mental health process in Ontario,
including the role of the Ontario Review Board, an
independent decision-making body that provides a regular
review of persons who are found not criminally responsible
due to mental disorder or unfit to stand trial under the
Criminal Code.

www.cpa.ca
This site provides the text of the *Canadian Code of Ethics
for Psychologists*.

Chapter 19

Prevention and Mental Health Promotion in the Community

Geoffrey Nelson

Isaac Prilleltensky

Ray DeV. Peters

When a spouse dies, grief and a feeling of being adrift are normal. The bereaved person's social world shrinks; physical and mental health often suffer. Sometimes, clinical depression develops. This depression can be treated in various ways: with antidepressants, with ECT, with talk therapies, with social supports. But can some of the far-reaching adverse consequences of bereavement be prevented? In Toronto, Vachon and colleagues (Vachon, Lyall, Rogers, Freedman-Letofsky, & Freeman, 1980) studied Widow to Widow, a prevention program for recently bereaved women. Women were randomly assigned to a control group or to a program in which they were paired with another widow, who provided emotional and practical support. On followup, the women who participated in the program adapted better and more quickly to widowhood than women in the control group. While the authors did not examine clinical depression, programs of this type may have a preventive effect. The intervention was a self-help program, with no professionals involved. Rather, women who had lost their partners offered support to women going through the same life transition. Other interventions use support groups. Whether individually or in groups, people who have been in the same boat can understand what their peers are going through. Furthermore, at the same time that they give support, they are also receiving it; being helpful to others is a key ingredient in the self-help approach.

In the field of abnormal psychology, the dominant emphasis has been on expanding our understanding of the nature and etiology of mental disorders and on developing effective treatments. Throughout this book, we have considered the manifestations and effects of specific disorders on individuals. But people do not live in isolation, but rather as part of families, communities, and societies. In this chapter we consider the mental health not only of individuals but of whole communities. We begin by briefly outlining the field of community psychology, which has highlighted the need for the prevention of mental disorders and the promotion of mental health.

COMMUNITY PSYCHOLOGY

The term **community psychology** was first coined by Canadian psychologist William Line in 1951. In the United States, community psychology had its roots in clinical psychology. Some clinically trained psychologists began to question the appropriateness of an exclusive reliance on treatment approaches. They recognized that the prevalence of mental disorders far outstrips the availability of professional help.

Epidemiological studies have shown that the one-year prevalence rate of mental disorders for adults (Offord et al., 1994) and the six-month prevalence rate for children (Offord et al., 1987) in Ontario is about 18 percent of the population. Using a conservative estimate of the prevalence rate of clinical disorders in children around the world (12 percent), Kramer (1992) argues that "the total number of cases of mental disorders in children under 18 years of age would increase from 237.8 million in 1990 to 261.5 in the year 2000, an increase of 10 percent. In the more developed regions the number of cases would increase from 37.8 million to 38.2 million" (p. 15). What's more, as discussed in Chapter 5, childhood disorders can often set the stage for ongoing problems in adulthood.

There are not, and there never could be, enough trained mental health professionals to provide therapeutic interventions for the large number of children and adults worldwide who are afflicted with mental disorders (Albee, 1990). Moreover, as is clear from Chapter 16, no therapeutic intervention is 100 percent effective. As Offord (1995) states, "the burden of suffering from child psychiatric disorders is extremely high, and one-to-one clinical interventions can never make a large dent in reducing this burden" (p. 287). What can reduce this burden? It seems reasonable to look for the long-term answers at the community level rather than the individual level, and in terms of prevention rather than treatment.

We know that, for health in general, treatment services—despite modern advances in medicine—have not been effective in reducing the rates of disease in a population (Bloom, 1984). Only methods oriented toward disease prevention have been successful in this regard. "[A]s the history of public health methods (that emphasize social change) has clearly established, no mass disease or disorder afflicting humankind has ever been eliminated by attempts at treating affected individuals" (Albee, 1990, p. 370).

In addition to its emphasis on prevention, community psychology has a number of other identifying features that distinguish it from clinical psychology (Prilleltensky & Nelson, 1997). Whereas clinical psychology has historically focussed on the individual or micro level (for example, the family) in diagnosis and treatment, community psychology applies an ecological perspective that stresses the interdependence of the individual, the family, community, and society. Community psychologists believe that interventions for many problems should address multiple levels of analysis. For example, psychotherapy may be somewhat helpful to a family living in poverty, but social policies that reduce poverty may play an even more important role. Sensitivity to a person's social context and appreciation of diversity are key themes of community psychology (Rappaport, 1987).

Another difference is that, in contrast to the clinical psychology focus on deficits and on reducing maladaptive behaviours, community psychology tends to pay more attention to people's strengths and the promotion of wellness (Rappaport, 1987). The community psychologist often functions as an enabler, a consultant, a planner, rather than an expert in diagnosis and treatment. The working style of the community psychologist emphasizes collaboration and participation of diverse groups from the community in planning, implementing, and evaluating interventions.

Community psychologists believe in the importance of informal social supports, rather than an exclusive reliance on professional help. So, for example, community psychologists may help people who are experiencing a problem in living, such as depression, to form self-help or mutual aid groups. Research has shown that this alternative approach of supporting one another can be quite effective (Humphreys & Rappaport, 1994).

Finally, with its U.S. roots in the 1960s, community psychology is oriented to social justice and social change. Community psychologists do not see themselves as value-neutral scientists, because to do so would be to accept the status quo of unjust social conditions. Rather, community psychology has a clear emphasis on values and social ethics (Prilleltensky & Nelson, 1997; Rappaport, 1987). The elimination of racism, sexism, and other forms of social injustice are viewed not only as important in preventing problems, but also as moral imperatives in the work of community psychology.

PREVENTION: SOME DEFINITIONS

Historically, the concept of **prevention** of mental disorders has developed from the fields of physical disease, public health, and epidemiology. The first attempt to identify different categories of prevention activities appeared in a working group report of the Commission on Chronic Illness (1957), which proposed a distinction between **primary prevention**, which is practised prior to the biological origin of the disease (for example, immunization), and **secondary prevention**, which is practised after the disease is identified but before it has caused suffering and disability (for example, the control of blood sugar early in the course of diabetes to prevent systemic damage). Somewhat later, a third class of prevention activities was proposed by Leavell and Clark (1965): **tertiary prevention**, which is practised after suffering or disability from the disease is being experienced, with the goal of preventing further deterioration. Gerald Caplan (1964), a community psychiatrist, played a key role in applying these levels of prevention to mental health problems. (See Chapter 13 for an example of this distinction as applied to suicide prevention.) Graham (1994) comments:

By convention, three types of preventive activity are recognized. Primary prevention involves intervention that reduces the incidence of disorder. Secondary prevention comprises treatment that reduces the duration of the disorder, and tertiary prevention covers rehabilitative activity that reduces the disability arising from an established disorder. (p. 815, emphasis added)

Some argue that the term *prevention* should be reserved for interventions that attempt to reduce the incidence or onset of a disorder and that the term **early intervention** should replace "secondary prevention," and *treatment* or *rehabilitation* replace "tertiary intervention" (Peters, 1990). As Cowen (1977) notes, there is considerable "definitional slippage" in the use of the term *prevention* or *primary prevention*, which can lead to confusion about what constitutes prevention and what constitutes treatment.

In this chapter, we use the term *prevention* to mean primary prevention. There are three key features in our definition of prevention:

1. With successful prevention, new cases of a problem do not occur.
2. Prevention is not aimed at individuals but at populations; the goal is a decline in rates of disorder.
3. Preventive interventions intentionally focus on preventing mental health problems (Cowen, 1980).

Complementary to prevention is the concept of **mental health promotion**. Where prevention, by definition, focusses on reducing problems, promotion focusses on enhancing functioning. Many people think of **mental health** in negative terms, as the absence of disorder. But a broader view defines mental health, or *wellness*, in positive terms, as the *presence* of optimal social, emotional, and cognitive functioning (Peters, 1988). According to the Epp (1988) report *Mental Health for Canadians: Striking a Balance*:

Mental health is the capacity of the individual, the group and the environment to interact with one another in ways that promote subjective well-being, the optimal development and use of mental abilities (cognitive, affective, and relational), the achievement of individual and collective goals consistent with justice and the attainment and preservation of conditions of fundamental equality. (p. 7)

In this report, mental health and mental disorder are viewed as conceptually distinct. There is a mental disorder continuum ranging from severe mental disorder (for example, florid schizophrenia) to the absence of mental disorder, and a mental health continuum ranging from minimal mental health (for example, poor coping skills, low self-esteem) to optimal mental health (for example, good coping skills, high self-esteem).

Cowen (1996) identifies four key characteristics of mental health promotion or wellness enhancement.

1. It is *proactive*; it seeks to promote mental health *before* mental health problems have taken root.
2. It focusses on populations, not individuals.
3. It is multidimensional, focussing on "integrated sets of operations involving individuals, families, settings, community contexts, and macrolevel societal structures and policies" (p. 246).
4. It is ongoing, not a one-shot, time-limited intervention.

In practice, prevention and mental health promotion go together, and a program will normally involve elements of both, inextricably intertwined. Enhancing functioning will often prevent problems, and preventing problems may enhance functioning.

HISTORICAL PERSPECTIVE

Efforts to prevent mental health problems began as early as 1880 in the United States with the formation of a group called the National Association for the Protection of the Insane and the Prevention of Insanity (Spaulding & Balch, 1983). In the early 1900s, Clifford Beers spearheaded the development of the mental hygiene movement in the United States by organizing the National Committee for Mental Hygiene. (See Chapter 1 for the background of this movement.) Influenced by Beers, a Canadian physician named Clarence Hincks founded what is now the Canadian Mental Health Association (CMHA) (Katz, 1954). The prevention of mental health problems was and continues to be one of the goals of the CMHA. Also at the turn of the century a number of helping services were developed designed to promote the mental health of children, such as child guidance clinics, the YWCA, and Girl Scouts (Levine & Levine, 1992).

Over the past century, the thinking underlying prevention has changed. Efforts to prevent mental and emotional problems have been heavily influenced by the field of public health. In the following sections, we trace some of the changes in thinking in the public health field and outline their implications for prevention in mental health.

Pre–Germ Theory Era

In the eighteenth century people believed that disease resulted from "miasmas," or noxious odours, which emanated from soil polluted with waste products. Miasmatists believed that the way to prevent disease was to clean up the environment (Bloom, 1984). Through the development of sewage disposal and sanitation campaigns, the rates of many diseases (for example, typhoid fever, yellow fever, typhus, etc.) dropped dramatically. Some nutritional diseases were reduced without knowledge of the precise cause of the disease. For example, British sailors became known as "limeys" because they learned to prevent scurvy by eating citrus fruits, long before it was known that

VIEWPOINT *No More Rock-Scrubbing*

The following article by G.W. Albee illustrates the opinion that an ounce of prevention is worth a pound of cure.

Most people, if asked to rank-order Albert Schweitzer, Mother Theresa, John Snow, and Ignatz Semmelweiss, would put the first two names at the top and confess ignorance about the latter two. Yet in terms of contributions to humankind, like the number of lives saved, human anguish prevented, and of accomplishments for the betterment of people throughout the world, Snow and Semmelweiss tower over the other two.

It may seem subversive or mean-spirited to fail to praise Schweitzer and Theresa as recent-day saints, but I greatly prefer the canonization of Snow and Semmelweiss.

As B. F. Skinner pointed out at his last public address at the APA Convention in Boston, Schweitzer was trying to save humanity one person at a time. Similarly, Mother Theresa, with a heart full of compassion and kindness, is also trying to save the world one person at a time. It simply can't be done. By way of contrast, John Snow figured out that cholera was a water-borne disease long before the noxious agent causing cholera had

been identified. He observed that the pattern of cholera infection was related to where drinking water came from; in the most famous act in the history of public health he removed the handle from the Broad Street pump and stopped a cholera epidemic.

Semmelweiss puzzled over the high rate of child-bed fever and death in women in the public wards of hospitals in Budapest. (In those days physicians didn't wash their hands, but wiped them dry on the lapels of their frock coats, so the more experienced physicians had stiffer and smellier coats.) Semmelweiss finally decided that somehow medical students and obstetrical trainees were carrying some poison from the dissecting rooms of the anatomy lab to the women giving birth. He ordered all of his medical trainees to wash their hands for ten minutes before they delivered a baby. Suddenly and precipitously the rate of child-bed fever and death dropped to almost nothing. Of course the great experts of the day did not believe either Snow or Semmelweiss. But, fortunately, as Freud was wont to point out, "The captains and the kings depart, truth remains."

The point here is that Snow's and Semmelweiss' work illustrates the

truth of the dictum that "No mass disorder afflicting mankind has ever been eliminated or brought under control by attempts at treating the affected individual." These two public health saints have saved millions of lives while Schweitzer, full of heart and compassion, was treating suffering individuals in his jungle hospital in Africa and while Mother Theresa was administering to the poor and the hopeless in Calcutta. Individual treatment has no effect on incidence.

One cannot help but admire and respect those selfless people who reach out in humanitarian concern to support suffering individuals. But at the same time, if we respect evidence, efforts at primary prevention are even more humane and admirable if our criteria include the reduction of mass human suffering.

All of this is by way of saying that our new AAAPP will pay attention to the critical importance of primary prevention. With the exception of a small number of community psychologists, prevention has not been the focus of current psychological intervention efforts. One need only read the divisional newsletters and the *APA Monitor* to see how important individual psychotherapy, delivered by in-

VIEWPOINT *continued*

dividual practitioners, has become. The mission of this large group of psychologists has changed the structure of APA. While valiant efforts are being made by APA to keep science alive and content, a great many scientists are dissatisfied and the scientific training of applied psychologists has been put on the back burner in a great many clinical programs.

The field of public interest in psychology has also suffered an eclipse. Political conservatives rarely get involved in public interest issues unless they are forced to. Conservatives favor the status quo and resist social change. There has been a major move towards more conservative right-wing explanations of mental and emotional disorders for at least the past ten years. We are told by the American Mental Health fund (founded by Jack Hinckley) that "All mental illness is a medical illness." The Head Guru for psychiatry, E. Fuller Torrey, has said that nearly every mental condition is a brain disease or genetic defect. The American public is being educated to believe that anxiety, phobias, obsessive compulsive behavior, depression, bipolar disorders, schizophrenia, alcohol and other drug abuse, and juvenile delinquency are all caused by bad genes or bad brains. The ad-

vantage of this organic model is that it means that no social changes are required to reduce the stresses of sexism, racism, homophobia, and exploitation of the poor and homeless. Prevention efforts are opposed as wooly-headed idealism. In fact the National Alliance for the Mentally Ill publicly denounces efforts at prevention.

The prevention of mental and emotional disorders must involve social change efforts at creating a more egalitarian and just society. Clearly AAAPP will support the pursuit of social justice. This is not to say that we oppose research into health psychology, biology, physiology, or other organic investigations. What I am talking about is the premature application of preliminary, tentative findings to claim that these have resolved fundamental questions about causation.

I know that not everyone on the AAAPP board, or among the founding members, will agree with the sentiments expressed here. One of the advantages of our new association is that people can be free to disagree, to argue and dispute in the tradition of scientific progress.

Last spring I offered a couple of bright undergraduate students the opportunity to attend our annual confer-

ence on prevention, this one entitled *Improving Children's Lives: Global Perspectives on Prevention.* After some agonizing they both decided that they would rather go to Alaska and volunteer to scrub oil off rocks on the beach. Somehow this symbolized for me one of the critical intellectual conflicts in our society. Should we sit around and scrub oil off rocks after the oil spill or should we demand that safer tankers be require by international law? Treatment or prevention? Schweitzer and Theresa, or Snow and Semmelweiss?

Critical Thinking Questions

1. Why is treatment favoured over prevention in our current health and mental health system?
2. How could our current systems be transformed from their current treatment orientation to more of a prevention orientation?
3. Think of a problem that you or someone you know has experienced during childhood or youth. What could have prevented the problem from occurring?

Source: Albee, G. W. (1991). No more rock-scrubbing, *The Scientist Practitioner*, 1, no. 1.

---

this disease resulted from a deficiency of vitamin C. This is a useful perspective for mental health, a field in which, as we have seen in almost every chapter of this book, etiology is usually complex and impossible to completely pin down.

Public Health Approach

The next major impetus to the field of prevention was the *public health approach*, based on epidemiology (the study of the distribution and determinants of disease in a population—see Chapter 4).

The traditional **public health approach** is characterized by the following steps:

1. identifying a disease and developing a reliable diagnostic method (descriptive epidemiology);
2. developing a theory of the disease's course of development based on laboratory and epidemiological research (analytic epidemiology); and

3. developing and evaluating a disease prevention program (experimental epidemiology) (Bloom, 1984)

Public health researchers tend to focus on three components: (1) characteristics of the host (that is, the person who contracts the disease), (2) characteristics of the environment (that is, stressors), and (3) the agent (that is, the manner in which the disease is transmitted to the host). The thrust of public health prevention is generally twofold: to reduce environmental stressors while enhancing people's capacities to withstand those stressors. In the mental health field, for example, one could attempt to prevent substance abuse problems by strengthening the host (for example, teaching teens how to deal with peer pressure to drink or take drugs), changing the environment (for example, providing good alternative activities in the community for youth), and targeting the agent (for example, regulating sales and reducing access to alcohol and drugs).

The public health approach has been very successful in re-ducing the incidence of many problems, including some men-tal health problems. For example, the incidence of general paresis, an organic psychosis resulting from syphilitic infec-tion, has been greatly reduced as a result of this approach. Yet this approach is effective only with diseases that have a sin-gle identified precursor or cause, be it a vitamin deficiency or a germ. As shown throughout this book, very few mental health problems have a single cause (Albee, 1982).

Many of the initial applications of public health concepts to mental health, in the 1950s and 1960s, focussed on early in-tervention (secondary prevention): programs aimed at peo-ple who were just beginning to experience mental health problems, and striving to nip problems in the bud. Such pro-grams were heavily influenced by the *crisis theory* of two community psychiatrists, Erich Lindemann (1944) and Gerald Caplan (1964). Lindemann and Caplan argued that when peo-ple are in a state of crisis they are very anxious, open to change, and oriented toward help-seeking. Support and guid-ance at this point of crisis can avert prolonged mental health problems can be averted. Thus, mobile crisis intervention teams and suicide prevention hotlines emerged to help people cope with life crises. (See Chapter 13 for examples of sui-cide prevention measures.)

School-based secondary prevention programs were also developed, such as the Primary Mental Health Project (PMHP) which originated in Rochester, New York, in 1957 through the work of Emory Cowen and his colleagues (Cowen et al., 1996). The PMHP staff developed screening instruments for primary-grade children to detect early signs that predicted maladaptation in later grades. Children who showed these early warning signs were paired with nonprofessional helpers trained to develop warm and trusting relationships with the children. Over the years of the PMHP, many evaluations have shown improvements in the identified children's mental health and school adaptation (Cowen et al., 1996). From its begin-nings in a single school, the PMHP has spread to school sys-tems all over North America and abroad. Moreover, as the PMHP has matured, project staff have also implemented a number of successful primary prevention programs (for ex-ample, classroom and school-wide social problem-solving skills curricula, and programs for children who have experi-enced the divorce of their parents).

CURRENT APPROACHES

Two interrelated approaches to prevention are currently pop-ular: one focusses on risk reduction for mental disorders and the other on the promotion of mental health (Cowen, 1996).

Risk Factors

As discussed in Chapter 2, as knowledge grows of any mental disorder, single-factor explanations are generally replaced by interactionist explanations that view behaviour as the product of the interaction of a variety of factors. The health promo-

Table 19.1 Some General Risk Factors

Family circumstances	Low social class
	Family conflict
	Mental illness in the family
	Large family size
	Poor bonding to parents
	Family disorganization
	Communication deviance
Emotional difficulties	Child abuse
	Apathy or emotional blunting
	Emotional immaturity
	Stressful life events
	Low self-esteem
	Emotional dyscontrol
School problems	Academic failure
	Scholastic demoralization
Ecological context	Neighbourhood disorganization
	Racial injustice
	Unemployment
	Extreme poverty
Constitutional handicaps	Perinatal complications
	Sensory disabilities
	Organic handicaps
	Neurochemical imbalance
Interpersonal problems	Peer rejection
	Alienation and isolation
Skill development delays	Subnormal intelligence
	Social incompetence
	Attentional deficits
	Reading disabilities
	Poor work skills and habits

tion approach reflects this complexity, focussing not on single factors but on many risk factors (Rae-Grant, 1994). Over the past 20 years, a substantial amount of research has confirmed that most mental health problems are associated with many different risk factors—most of which are in turn associated with many different types of mental health problems. Moreover, the effects of risk are additive or cumulative. General risk fac-tors for poor mental health are presented in Table 19.1.

The more of these factors are present, the more vulnera-ble a person is to a wide range of mental health problems. At this point in our knowledge, it is difficult to connect specific risk factors with specific forms of abnormal behaviour. (See the discussion of the stress-diathesis and biopsychosocial models in Chapter 2 for an indication of how complex the relationships among factors can be.)

Protective Factors

Some individuals, however, are able to withstand exposure to many risk factors (Hoyt-Meyers et al., 1995). What ac-counts for these "resilient" or "stress-resistant" individuals? Current thinking is that there are **protective factors** that help to offset, or buffer, risk factors. For example, a person with a good social support network or good coping skills may adjust well to a stressful life event such as marital separation or job loss. Albee (1982) views the incidence of mental health problems as an equation:

$$\text{Incidence} = \frac{\text{Risk factors}}{\text{Protective factors}} =$$

$$\frac{\text{Organic causes} + \text{Stress} + \text{Exploitation}}{\text{Coping skills} + \text{Self-esteem} + \text{Support systems}}$$

Prevention can be approached from both sides: by reducing risk factors and by increasing protective factors.

A number of general protective factors for mental health have been identified (Garmezy, 1994). These include:

- Stable care from parents or other caregivers
- Problem-solving abilities
- Attractiveness to peers and adults
- Being and feeling competent
- Identification with competent role models
- Aspirations and an inclination to plan for the future

Risk Reduction

Bloom (1984) outlines the steps in the **risk reduction approach** to health promotion:

1. Identifying a stressful life event or condition that appears to have undesirable consequences for a significant proportion of the population and developing a method to determine who is exposed to the event or condition
2. Developing, through laboratory and epidemiological research, hypotheses about ways to reduce the undesirable consequences
3. Developing and evaluating a prevention program based on the hypotheses

Mental Health Promotion

While the old public health approach begins with a focus on a particular disease, the new health promotion approach begins with a stressful event or situation—a risk factor—that may affect the mental health of a population in various ways. For instance, when a community experiences the closure of a major industry, people who lose their jobs may react with depression, substance abuse, or a variety of other dysfunctional patterns.

In addition to the focus on risk and protective factors, health promotion also uses an **ecological perspective**, which considers multiple levels of analysis. Thus, mental health problems are viewed in the context of characteristics of the *individual* (for example, coping skills, personality traits), the **microsystem** (that is, the family and social network), the **exosystem**, which mediates between the individual, the family, and the larger society (for example, work settings, schools, religious settings, neighbourhoods), and the **macrosystem** (for example, social norms, social class). As shown in

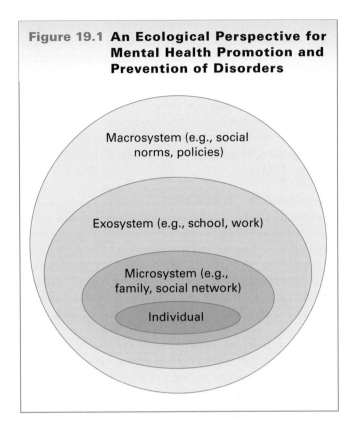

Figure 19.1 An Ecological Perspective for Mental Health Promotion and Prevention of Disorders

Figure 19.1, the levels are seen as nested like Russian dolls: the person in the family in the community in society. Rae-Grant (1994) has shown that both risk factors and protective factors operate at multiple levels of analysis.

Another current approach deemphasizes disorder and emphasizes protective factors toward the enhancement of mental health and wellness (Blanchet, Laurendeau, Paul, & Saucier, 1993; Cowen, 1994; Peters, 1988, 1990). Cowen (1994) argues that there are several key pathways toward mental health promotion:

Attachment. First is the importance of infants and preschool children forming secure attachments to their parents and caregivers. People who have made secure attachments to adults early in life fare well in later life (see Chapters 2 and 5). Moreover, programs that strive to promote attachments yield long-term benefits (Olds, 1988).

Competencies. Second, the development of age-appropriate competencies is critical for the enhancement of wellness. Social competencies (for example, social problem-solving skills, assertiveness, interpersonal skills), academic competencies, and work competencies are all important for psychological well-being. Comprehensive, well-integrated, ongoing programs that are institutionalized in social settings bear the most promise for the promotion of social competence and health (Weissberg & Elias, 1993).

Social environments. Third, healthy and just social environments are important for wellness. One route to the enhancement of psychological well-being is to identify the characteristics of social environments associated with wellness and the processes by which environmental characteristics influence well-being (Moos, 1996). Thus, one strategy to promote wellness is to change social systems toward those characteristics and processes that have been shown to be important for well-being (Cowen, 1977, 1994). Social systems intervention can be aimed at the exosystem level, targeting settings such as schools, neighbourhoods, churches, and workplaces, or at the macrosystem level as attacks on degrading social conditions, including poverty, racism, and sexism (Joffe & Albee, 1981).

Empowerment.   Fourth, psychological and political empowerment is important for wellness. Empowerment refers to perceived and actual control over one's life (Rappaport, 1987—also see Chapter 16 for a discussion of the relationship between stress and control). Empowering interventions are those that enhance participants' "voice and choice" (self-determination and democratic participation) and that are directed and controlled by citizens (Prilleltensky, 1994a).

Resources to cope with stress.   Finally, the ability to cope effectively with stressful life events and conditions is another key pathway to wellness. Throughout life, we face both expected stressors, such as life transitions, and unexpected stressful events. Therefore, skills and resources to meet the challenges posed by stressors are essential for psychological well-being. Research has demonstrated that some individuals are extremely resilient and able to withstand life stressors (for example, Hoyt-Meyers et al., 1995). Moreover, stressors are often seen as presenting an opportunity for growth. Some people, for example, report psychological growth on coming to terms with a marital separation. Therefore, interventions that build up resources to cope with stress can potentially promote well-being.

The Contexts and Processes of Risk and Protective Factors

Researchers have recognized the need to go beyond the identification of general risk and protective factors to understanding *how* these factors operate and how they interact. Neither risk factors nor protective factors affect everyone the same way. Furthermore, not all risk and protective factors have a direct impact on a person's mental health. Some have an immediate impact; others influence functioning indirectly. For instance, it has been suggested that divorce affects young boys more strongly than young girls in the short term, but that girls suffer from "sleeper effects": they feel the consequences of parental divorce later in adolescence (Gore & Eckenrode, 1994). Boys seem to suffer more in the short term, because: (1) parents are more likely to argue in front of boys; (2) boys are more likely than girls to be placed in foster care; and (3) boys respond to family conflict with disruptive behaviour that is more severely punished than girls' behaviour. In the case of girls, the effects of having witnessed a marriage collapse is felt strongly later in adolescence, when close relationships become very important (Rutter, 1987).

Another illustration of the importance of context concerns early parental loss. Losing a parent at a young age has been implicated in vulnerability to later psychiatric disorder. Brown and his colleagues found that girls who lost their mothers before age 11 were likely to experience depression later in life, but only if they did not have adequate care after the loss. This finding suggests that it is not so much the grief of losing a parent that predisposes children to psychiatric illness as the fact that a child who has lost a parent is likely to receive poor care (Brown, Harris, & Bifulco, 1986).

According to Rutter (1987), there are four central mechanisms that can help people cope with adversity and develop positive mental health: (1) reducing risk impact, (2) interrupting unhealthy chain reactions stemming from stressful life events, (3) enhancing self-esteem and self-efficacy, and (4) creating opportunities for personal growth.

Risk impact may be reduced either by altering the *risk* or by altering *exposure* to the risk. Altering the risk means changing it in some way to minimize effects. For instance, for young children to face a separation or new situation without preparation constitutes a risk. The risk for children who need hospitalization can be altered by taking them to visit the hospital before admission and by "practice separations" from parents in secure circumstances. Altering exposure means keeping the person away from the risky situation, or reducing involvement in its riskier aspects. For example, Rutter (1987) found that in high-risk communities, strict parental supervision of children's activities outside the home can reduce the risk for delinquent behaviour. Placing limits on what children can do and how long they can stay out minimizes exposure to the risky environment.

The mechanism of breaking a potentially damaging *chain reaction* can be seen in Brown and colleagues' study of parental loss: ensuring sustained, adequate care breaks the chain of harmful consequences. A nurturing environment can protect children from the consequences of loss, separation, and other risks. *Self-efficacy* can be fostered in children by offering age-appropriate tasks and sufficient rewarding experiences of control. (See Chapter 2 for a fuller discussion of this concept.) Finally, opportunities for personal development may be created by teaching youth social skills they can apply in various settings, and by preventing school dropout. This last mechanism may be conceptualized as promoting beneficial chain reactions. A good education can lead to attractive jobs, a higher income, and the like. Similarly, adequate social skills can lead to friendships, which translate into social supports that have the effect of buffering stress (Gore & Eckenrode, 1994).

TYPES OF PROMOTION/PREVENTION PROGRAMS

Prevention activities may be either biological or psychological. As an example of biological primary prevention, encouraging pregnant women to avoid alcohol can prevent fetal alcohol syndrome (see Chapters 6 and 10). In fact, many prevention programs start with pregnant women, and include counselling on nutrition and substance use. An example of biological secondary prevention is the administration of special diets to children born with PKU. As described in Chapter 6, this diet cannot correct the basic metabolic disorder, but can prevent its most serious consequence, mental retardation. Most prevention and mental health promotion programs, however, are primarily psychological or social in nature, and that is the type of program we will be discussing in this chapter.

Prevention may target children, adolescents, or adults; however, because so many mental health problems have roots in childhood, the majority of prevention programs work with children or youths and their families.

High-Risk Versus Universal Approaches

There are two major types of prevention programs, high-risk and universal. Both types can address the several ecological levels of analysis discussed earlier. The **high-risk approach** is based on the assumption that there are known risk factors for certain mental health problems, and it is most effective to target individuals most exposed to these risk factors.

Recently, a suggestion has been made to divide high-risk programs into two subtypes, selective and indicated (Gordon, 1983; Institute of Medicine, 1994). The former select participants on the basis of characteristics external to the participant (for example, children whose parents have divorced, teenage mothers, adults living on public assistance). The latter select participants on the basis of internal characteristics (for example, low-birth-weight babies, young children experiencing rejection by their peers, high school dropouts).

This distinction, however, is not always clear. High-risk programs often select participants on the basis of multiple risk factors, some internal and some external. Both types of program may use the same intervention activities. Finally, several programs have selected participants who show mild or early-developing mental health problems (for example, young children showing antisocial behaviour). These programs are sometimes referred to as *indicated prevention programs* (Coie, 1996), but might more appropriately be called early intervention programs (Peters, 1990; Peters & McMahon, 1996). In this chapter, we use the more general term *high-risk* to cover both selected and indicated programs.

The **universal approach** is designed to include all individuals in a particular geographical area (for example, neighbourhood, city, province) or particular setting (for example, school, workplace, public housing complex). As you will see from the examples we will discuss, the distinction between high-risk and universal is not always black-and-white; programs may fall along a spectrum in terms of how selective or inclusive participation criteria are.

Narrowly Focussed Versus Comprehensive Ecological Programs

A second important distinction has to do with how broad the focus is in terms of the number of influences and the range of behaviours being addressed. Some programs focus narrowly on a small number of influences on behaviour, or a tightly defined set of target outcome behaviours. Comprehensive programs address a broad range of risk and protective factors as well as a broad range of outcomes. As you read the following section, keep in mind the distinctions between high-risk and universal, narrow and comprehensive ecological programs.

The south side of Ypsilanti, Michigan, in the 1960s was a slum as one probably pictures American slums; in fact, it was described as "one of the most congested slum areas in the State" (Schweinhart & Weikart, 1988). The children of the neighbourhood—black and very poor—had difficulties when they entered school. They grew up to poverty and high rates of unemployment and imprisonment. The Perry Preschool Project set out to see whether the picture could be changed through a preschool educational program designed to give children the intellectual and social skills they needed for school. Selected participants were very poor three- and four-year-old children, with IQs between 60 and 90 (well below average), randomly assigned to experimental and control groups. For two school years, the children in the experimental program had 2 1/2 hours a day of well-organized classroom activities. Each teacher worked with a group of five or six children. Also, every week during the school year, the teacher made a 1 1/2 hour home visit to every mother and child, offering the mothers guidance in child-rearing skills.

What happened when these children started school? Initial results were encouraging; in kindergarten and Grade 1, the children in the experimental group showed more academic readiness and intellectual skills than the control group. Disappointingly, by the time the children had reached Grades 3 and 4, differences in academic performance between the two groups had vanished.

Fortunately, the researchers continued to follow the children through the school age years and into their late teens. It is the long-term effects of the Perry Preschool Project that have been most interesting. At the age of 19, twice as many program participants as control children were employed, attending college or receiving further training. High school graduation rates were 30 percent higher, and arrest and teen pregnancy rates were 40 percent lower.

Moreover, the program was cost-effective. For every dollar invested in the 30-week program, there was a six-dollar return in savings from lower special education, criminal justice, and welfare costs.

PROMOTION/PREVENTION IN PRACTICE

The Perry Preschool Project, described in the case above, is one of the best known of the pioneering "first generation" prevention and mental health promotion programs that began in the

1960s and 1970s. These early programs were often small and poorly funded and rarely evaluated (Price, Cowen, Lorion, & Ramos-McKay, 1989). In 1982, the American Psychological Association established a task force to study these prevention programs. The report of this task force profiled 14 soundly researched programs that had been effective in preventing a number of different problems (Price, Cowen, Lorion, & Ramos-McKay, 1988). These served as models for planning and redesigning "second generation" programs in the 1980s and 1990s.

High-Risk Programs

Like the Perry Preschool Project, most of the early prevention programs—and, in fact, most programs being implemented today—are high-risk programs. The short-term and long-term results of the Perry Preschool Project have received extensive attention over the years and are consistent with several other studies involving enriched preschool experiences for high-risk children. That is, structured preschool experiences can give high-risk disadvantaged children a head start on their early academic performance; these advantages disappear after several years (Consortium for Longitudinal Studies, 1983; Lazar & Darlington, 1982); however, there are long-term benefits (Consortium for Longitudinal Studies, 1983).

Can these benefits be classed as prevention in the field of mental health? There were no specific measures of the incidence of mental disorders in the Perry Preschool Project. However, teen pregnancies, unemployment, arrests, and incarceration are related to a number of mental disorders, including depression and antisocial personality disorder. More generally, if we look at the definition of wellness earlier in the chapter, as not merely the absence of disorder but optimal social, cognitive, and emotional functioning, it seems clear that the measures of life success reflect improved mental health.

On the basis of the Perry Preschool Project and several other demonstration projects started in the early 1960s, the national project Head Start was established in the United States in 1966. This initiative provided one or two years of preschool experiences for nearly one million disadvantaged children. Although overall funding for the Head Start project has decreased over the years, and only one in five eligible disadvantaged children in the United States participates in the program, the long-term prevention effects of the Perry Preschool and other well-researched preschool projects has provided protection for the project through the period of severe social program cuts in the late 1980s and 1990s. In fact, the Head Start program has recently been extended to provide services to high-risk children from birth to three years of age (Ounce of Prevention Fund, 1994).

Another first-generation high-risk prevention project that has been well researched is the Prenatal Early Infancy Project. This project was initiated by David Olds in 1977 in Elmira, New York, a small semi-rural community in upstate New York, which was rated in the 1980 Census as the most economically depressed area in the United States, and which had the highest rates of child abuse and neglect in the state of New York. A major focus of the project was to prevent child abuse and neglect; it consisted of trained registered nurses carrying out home visits with first-time mothers from pregnancy through the child's second year of life (Olds, 1988, 1997).

Four hundred women were enrolled in the project before the 30th week of pregnancy, 85 percent of whom were considered to be high-risk because they were low-income, unmarried, or teenaged. They were randomly assigned to the home visit program or to a control group that received transportation for health care and screening for health problems but no visits.

The home visitation program was designed to improve three aspects of maternal and child functioning: (1) the outcomes of pregnancy, (2) quality of parenting, and (3) the mother's life course development (for example, helping the mothers to return to school, find work, and plan future pregnancies). The nurses completed an average of nine home visits during pregnancy, and 23 visits from birth through the second year of the child's life. Olds attempted to apply the ecological model described in Figure 19.1. Thus, the nurses were trained to attend to the immediate day-to-day needs of the mother and the child, as well as to other family and community concerns. This resulted in a very comprehensive program for fostering maternal and child development: nurses helped mothers learn about pregnancy, infant health, and child-rearing, helped them obtain support from families, friends, and community health and human services, and provided them with direct personal and emotional support.

The results of the evaluation research were striking. During the prenatal period, the nurse-visited women improved the quality of their diets to a greater extent than the women in the non-visited comparison group. By the end of pregnancy, nurse-visited women had fewer kidney infections, experienced greater informal social support, and made better use of formal community services. Two particularly high-risk groups showed especially strong benefits: among women who smoked, those who were nurse-visited had 75 percent fewer preterm deliveries than the control group, and among very young adolescents (aged 14–16) those who were nurse-visited had babies who were nearly 400 grams heavier.

During the first two years after delivery, 14 percent of the poor, unmarried teen mothers in the control group abused or neglected their children, as opposed to only 4 percent of the poor, unmarried teens visited by a nurse. Over a four-year period, the children of nurse-visited women were less likely to visit a physician or emergency department for injuries or ingestions. Among low-income, unmarried women, the rate of subsequent pregnancy was reduced by 42 percent, and the number of months that nurse-visited women participated in the work force was increased by 83 percent. Children born to women who were moderate to heavy smokers when they registered in the program during pregnancy and who received home visits had significantly higher IQ scores at three to four years of age than their counterparts in the control group. Moreover, in a 15-year followup, Olds and colleagues (1997) found that the nurse-visited women had higher rates of employment than the women in the control group, as well as lower rates of substance abuse, verified child abuse or neglect, arrests, convictions, days in jail, use of welfare, and subsequent pregnancies.

In general, the effects of the Prenatal Early Infancy Project on preventing adverse outcomes tended to be concentrated on groups who were at highest risk for these problems, namely poor, unmarried teenaged mothers and their children. The results of this project have fostered great interest in the use of home visiting as an effective prevention approach for high-risk mothers and children. It is important to note that the home visitors in Olds' program were professionally trained registered nurses. Many subsequent home visiting programs are staffed by visitors who often reside in the communities they serve and who have no professional training in health or human services.

Universal Prevention Programs

A good example of a universal program is Botvin's (1996; Botvin et al., 1990) Life Skills Training program, designed to prevent substance abuse, including tobacco, alcohol, and hard drugs, in young adolescents. Beginning in 1980, Botvin and his colleagues developed, evaluated, and refined a school-based prevention program for students in Grades 7 to 9.

The program consists of two general skills training components—personal skills and social skills—and a problem-specific training component relating to drug abuse. The personal skills component is designed to foster a variety of self-management skills, including decision-making and problem-solving, identifying and resisting media influences, and self-control skills for coping with anxiety, anger, and frustration. The social skills component deals with communication, assertiveness, dating relationships, and effective social interaction and conversation. The final component deals with knowledge and attitudes concerning drug use and skills for resisting drug use influences from the media and peers.

The program consists of fifteen class periods (approximately 45 minutes each) for students in Grade 7, with ten "booster" sessions in Grade 8 and five "booster" sessions in Grade 9. The program is offered to all students in a particular classroom or school. Specific teacher and student curriculum materials and exercises have been developed for the program, and it has been successfully implemented by a variety of instructors, including regular classroom teachers, health professionals from outside the school, and older peer leaders from Grades 11 and 12. The instructor acts as skills trainer or coach, with extensive use of instruction, demonstration, rehearsal, feedback, and homework assignments for skill development.

Evaluation studies carried out over the past 15 years have demonstrated the effectiveness of the program in preventing tobacco, alcohol, and drug use/abuse in young adolescents. For example, a large-scale prevention study involving 6000 students in Grade 7 from 56 schools in New York State randomly assigned whole schools to experimental groups, which received Life Skills Training, or control groups (Botvin et al., 1990). Students in the LST program showed significantly less smoking, marijuana use, and problem drinking than control students at the end of Grade 9, significantly less marijuana use and excessive drinking at the end of Grade 10, and less smoking, heavy drinking, or marijuana use at the end of Grade 12.

A more recent example of a universal prevention program is currently being implemented with children and families living in socioeconomically disadvantaged neighbourhoods in eight communities in Ontario. This program, called Better Beginnings, Better Futures, is described in the Focus box.

The project emphasizes the importance of combining community development activities with family and child development. Several similar programs exist in the United States: the Comprehensive Child Development Program (see Pizzolongo, 1996) and the recently announced Early Head Start Project (Ounce of Prevention Fund, 1994), both being implemented nationally and funded by the U.S. government. These two programs are large-scale, involving thousands of children and families, and very comprehensive ecologically in their focus on children, families, and communities. However, they are less universal than the Better Beginnings model, because only families falling below the poverty line qualify.

Growth of the Research and Practice Base

In his review of the literature on mental health promotion and primary prevention 20 years ago, Cowen (1977) referred to progress as being made in "baby steps." In his most recent review, Cowen (1996) speaks of "lengthy strides." Clearly the past two decades have seen tremendous growth in the research and practice bases of mental health promotion/prevention. Recently, two meta-analyses have supported the effectiveness of prevention programs. (See Chapter 17 for a discussion of meta-analysis.) On the basis of a review of 177 evaluations of prevention programs for children and adolescents, Durlak and Wells (1997) report that a number of different types of intervention have proven to be effective in preventing emotional and behavioural problems in children. Similarly, Tobler and Stratton's (1997) meta-analysis of 120 school-based drug abuse prevention programs shows that interactive programs that involve students are effective in preventing drug abuse.

Prevention programs have been applied in a wide variety of settings to address many different problems, including violence against women (Wolfe, Wekerle, & Scott, 1997), criminal behaviour and conduct disorder (Peters & McMahon, 1996), and depression (Muñoz, 1993). In Canada, a number of different types of prevention programs have been developed for children and youth (Prilleltensky & Laurendeau, 1994). In the United States, two influential reports, one by the Institute of Medicine (1994) and one by the National Institute of Mental Health (Reiss & Price, 1996), have outlined how prevention strategies can be applied to a range of mental disorders.

Child sexual abuse is a major risk factor for many mental disorders. If we can effectively prevent child sexual abuse, we may be able to prevent mental disorders. In Calgary, the Who Do You Tell program was started by the Calgary Sexual Assault Centre in 1983 (Tutty, 1997). It has recently been updated and

Focus *Better Beginnings, Better Futures*

The Better Beginnings, Better Futures project is a 25-year longitudinal prevention research project focussing on children from birth to eight years of age and their families. The project began in 1991 and has three major goals:

1. *Prevention.* To prevent serious social, emotional, behavioural, physical, and cognitive problems in young children

2. *Promotion.* To promote the social, emotional, behavioural, physical, and cognitive development of these children

3. *Community development.* To enhance the ability of socioeconomically disadvantaged families and communities to provide for their children

Funding was provided by the Ontario and federal governments to eight communities to provide services tailored to local circumstances for four years of program implementation, from

People participating in the Family Resource Centre, Highfield Community Enrichment Project (Better Beginnings, Better Futures) in Etobicoke, Ontario.

1993 to 1997. To determine both short-term and long-term effects, researchers will follow the progress of the children, their families, and their neighbourhoods until the children reach their mid-twenties. Five communities focussed their programs on children from conception to four years of age, and three concentrated on the four-to-eight-year age range. Children and families from three communities that did not receive program funding are also being evaluated for comparison purposes. All communities offering programs followed the same model, one that is unique in several aspects:

- *A comprehensive ecological model.* An ecological perspective of child development recognizes that children live and grow in families, within neighbourhoods and cultures. Better Beginnings programs attempted to address this broad range of ecological influences on children. Unlike most prevention programs, the project was designed to address child development, parent/family development and community development.

- *Local responsibility and significant parent-community involvement.* In most prevention projects, professionals plan, manage, and deliver services to parents, who are seen as receiving help. In Better Beginnings projects, professionals, parents and other local community members worked collaboratively. Parents and other community members were actively involved in all decisions about the local project, including program development, organization and management, staff hiring, budgets, etc. The transfer of this level of control and responsibility has the potential of empowering community residents, who may have felt little control, individually or collectively, over their own lives and the lives of their children.

Project funding began in 1991, but it took each community at least two and a half years to develop such a comprehensive program, establish organization and management structures, and to hire and train program staff, many of whom were local residents. Although the specific program activities differed somewhat across the eight communities, they generally had the following elements:

- *Home visiting.* All projects for 0-to-4-year-olds included home visiting to families during pregnancy and infancy. Drawing on Olds' work in Elmira, New York (described above), home visitors assisted all families in the neighbourhood with children 4 years of age or under who agreed to participate. Most of the home visitors were residents of the local neighbourhoods and they worked with the families to meet basic needs, provide parent training and child development information, and link families with community health and social services and informal support resources.

- *Classroom enrichment.* The three project sites for the 4-to-8-year-olds enriched children's formal educational experiences with social skills training, academic tutoring, and teacher support.

- *Child care enrichment.* All projects supplemented existing community child care with additional staff, resources, drop-in centres for at-home care providers, toy-lending libraries, etc.

- *Other child-focussed programs.* Other program elements, tailored to needs in each community, included playgroups, breakfast programs, and school-based anti-bullying programs.

- *Family/parent-focussed programs.* Again, a variety of activities were designed to meet community needs, including parent training and parent support groups, cook-

Focus *continued*

ing classes, prenatal programs, and fathers' groups.

- *Community-focussed programs.* A wide range of program activities were designed to create new resources in the community (for example, food banks, crosswalks); activities for community members at large designed to improve the quality of life in the community; and improved cultural awareness, relations, and pride. Included were such activities as neighbourhood safety working groups, cultural workshops and celebrations, and, for aboriginal people, a variety of healing activities and programs.

The Better Beginnings, Better Futures project is considered universal, because it was offered to all children in a given age range and their families. The neighbourhoods selected for the program are "high-risk," because they all have high concentrations of socioeconomically disadvantaged families, but all residents, regardless of their socioeconomic status, were actively encouraged to participate. Of course, not all families chose to do so; an important indicator of success for any program, but particularly for universal programs, is the percentage of potential participants who become actively involved.

To adequately evaluate a program as comprehensive and broad-based as Better Beginnings requires a multidisciplinary approach. Project research includes extensive home interviews with parents, direct assessments of the children's physical, cognitive, social, and mental development, descriptions of program ac-

tivities and costs, and an evaluation of how well the programs were developed and implemented and whether they successfully involved community members as active decision-makers (Peters, 1994; Peters & Russell, 1996).

Since the communities did not complete their four-year implementation phase until late 1997, it is too early to determine short-term effects. However, preliminary reports suggest the successful involvement of parents and community members in the development and organization of the programs (Cameron, Peirson, & Pancer, 1994; Pancer & Cameron, 1994). For current information on the program, see its Web site, listed at the end of this chapter. ▲

implemented by the Calgary Communities Against Sexual Assault in elementary schools where requested by the principal. Parents are invited to an information session and teachers are given in-service training before the program is implemented. The program consists of two one-hour sessions, given in groups of 15 to 20 children, from kindergarten to Grade 6, with somewhat different formats for different age groupings. Children are given information about unwanted touching and, through role-playing, practice in responding to unwanted touch. They also have the opportunity to talk privately with the trainers. This program has been found to enhance children's knowledge about child sexual abuse. While critics argue that such programs place the onus of sexual abuse prevention on children rather than on perpetrators, convicted abusers have stated that strengthening parent-child communication and increasing children's willingness to disclose abuse can act as a deterrent.

PROMOTION/PREVENTION IN CANADA

The Federal Role

Canada has been a leader in promoting the concept of prevention. In 1974, then federal Minister of Health Marc Lalonde released a report entitled *A New Perspective on the Health of Canadians*, which recognized the influence of biological, lifestyle, and environmental factors on disease rates and argued for an increased emphasis on prevention and health promotion. The main message of the report was reemphasized and expanded upon in two reports by the federal Minister of Health, Jake Epp, *Achieving Health for All* (1986) and *Mental Health for Canadians: Striking a Balance* (1988). Both of these reports outlined three health challenges (reducing inequities, increasing prevention, and enhancing coping), three health promotion mechanisms (self-care, mutual aid, and healthy environments), and three implementation strategies (fostering public participation, strengthening community health services, and coordinating healthy public policy). Other national organizations have developed position papers on promotion and prevention. For example, the Canadian Mental Health Association's national office formed a National Primary Prevention Committee in 1977, which produced a volume of working papers (Randall, 1981) and a book on primary prevention programs in Canada (Lumsden, 1984).

However, critics have argued that despite the rhetoric of prevention apparent in federal documents, little has changed in Canadian health systems (Wharf, 1989). Beginning in the late 1980s, the federal government began to drastically reduce transfers to the provinces, which are primarily responsible for health, education, and social services policies and programs.

The Provinces' Role

In 1993, Nelson, Prilleltensky, Laurendeau, and Powell (1996) surveyed mental health promotion/prevention in all the provinces and territories. They obtained information from the departments of children's mental health, adult mental health, and health promotion regarding administrative supports, personnel, policies, budgets, interministerial collaboration, training, and programs. They found a good deal of support on paper for prevention, and many interesting projects. Programs for children, youth, and family include preschool enrichment for high-risk children, youth suicide prevention, and programs aimed at the prevention of physical and/or sexual abuse of children. Programs for adults include those aimed at the prevention of violence against women, support groups for adults experiencing bereavement, and job search programs for people who have lost their jobs.

In spite of these innovations, Nelson et al. (1996) found that health funding has not been reallocated from treatment to prevention, and that, in all provinces and territories, funding for prevention remains very low.

BARRIERS TO PROMOTION/PREVENTION

In spite of the recent groundswell of support for prevention, several obstacles remain (Albee, 1986a; Bloom, 1982; Broskowski & Baker, 1974) that must be overcome if the current prevention movement is to maintain its momentum. These challenges can be grouped into three categories: (1) academic-scientific, (2) professional-organizational, and (3) social-political.

Academic-Scientific

Both critics (Lamb & Zusman, 1979) and proponents of prevention (Cowen, 1977, 1996) have argued that primary prevention has suffered from definitional fuzziness and the lack of a sound research base. There is certainly some merit in these criticisms, given that the field is in its infant stages of development. However, with the growth of the literature in the past two decades, the field is already on stronger conceptual and empirical grounds (Price et al., 1988). More fundamental criticisms such as those of Lamb and Zusman (1979) have been made on two grounds: (1) that emotional problems are genetically caused and thus not preventable and (2) that prevention is not possible without precise knowledge of causation.

Both of these arguments have been largely rebutted. As regards the first argument, almost every chapter in this book has shown the complexity of causation; as discussed in Chapter 2, the balance of research seems to suggest that both nature and nurture exert influences in complex and interacting ways. Even where there is strong evidence for biology as a major etiological factor, social and psychological influences cannot be ignored. As discussed in Chapter 14, for example, it seems likely that a genetic predisposition to schizophrenia exists. Yet there is also strong evidence for the role of social

factors, and it may be possible that a person with a predisposition could be protected from the full development of this devastating disorder by protective factors such as those mentioned earlier in this chapter. Even where the role of biology is clear, prevention and early intervention may provide important benefits. Probably no one would claim that psychological prevention or early intervention would prevent a person with the genetic anomaly called trisomy 21 from developing Down syndrome; yet, as discussed in Chapter 6, the cognitive abilities, emotional well-being, and life course of the person can be significantly improved.

The second argument, that prevention is not possible without a full understanding of causation, would hamstring preventive efforts if accepted, since we can claim a full etiological understanding of few, if any, mental disorders. Yet consider the analogy of public health measures. Should the British navy have refused to issue limes to its sailors until scientists had proposed a causative agent and mechanism for scurvy, backed up by laboratory demonstrations? Should antismoking campaigns have been put on hold until the cellular mechanism by which tobacco leads to cancer could be fully explained? Ultimately, the rebuttal is empirical: many preventive programs have produced good results (Albee, 1986a; Nelson, Potasznik, & Bennett, 1983). Nevertheless, support for further research and development is needed if the field is to grow.

Professional-Organizational

Promotion and prevention have historically received little attention in professional mental health training programs (Iscoe, 1981). Thus, innovations are not disseminated very quickly because so few professionals know about them. Also, practitioners trained in the medical model and one-to-one clinical interventions are often resistant to prevention approaches. Thus, there is a need for continuing education and professional development as well as a shift in emphasis to prevention in professional training schools. Finally, given the breadth of the field of prevention, interdisciplinary cooperation is needed in training programs. Several Canadian universities (for example, the University of Toronto and the University of Waterloo) have in fact recently developed interdisciplinary programs in health promotion.

While many human service organizations in Canada agree that promotion/prevention is important, usually no single organization takes responsibility for its implementation. Overburdened with demands for clinical casework, most local agencies have few or no resources allocated specifically for prevention. Where prevention programs do exist, they are often an added responsibility to an agency with no corresponding reduction in clinical services.

Social-Political

Several writers (Albee, 1986b; Zax & Specter, 1974) have observed that the notions of prevention and systemic change go against the grain of North American society. The values that underlie prevention often conflict with dominant social values in North America. First, Canada is more of an individualist than a collectivist society (Hofstede, 1980); individual liberties, self-determination, and the right to privacy are emphasized over sense of community and felt obligations to others. It is thus natural to many planners to see mental health problems and their solutions as individual rather than community-wide.

A second source of social-political resistance to prevention is societal acceptance of wide differences among people's life circumstances as natural and acceptable. Albee (1986b) has traced this belief to the philosophy of Social Darwinism, which applied the Darwinian concept of "survival of the fittest" to issues of race and social class. According to Social Darwinism, the strong rise to the higher social classes, while the genetically weak and inferior naturally select into the lowest social class. It is a corollary of this viewpoint that cognitive skills and mental health are simply (or at least primarily) a matter of genetic superiority or inferiority. Proponents of this view argue that scarce resources should not be squandered on people who cannot be helped. Some still agree with Jensen (1969), who argued that preschool compensatory education programs for poor, black children should be abandoned because they are ineffective and thus a waste of taxpayers' money.

A third and related source of opposition to prevention is people's beliefs in a just world (Lerner, 1980). Those who believe that the world is just and fair assume that people who live in poverty or women who have been abused have only themselves to blame (Ryan, 1971). If these people had worked harder or shown better judgement, then they would not have suffered. Likewise, people with mental problems are seen as blameworthy rather than in need of help. This belief thus works against the idea that people are entitled to safe, healthy life circumstances and undercuts prevention programs that strive to make such conditions possible.

Fourth, people who have experienced oppressive social conditions or personal life circumstances often do not believe that anything can be done to change such conditions. Internalized feelings of powerlessness often immobilize individuals and groups (Albee, 1986b). Overcoming this inertia to work for change requires a process of personal and political empowerment, which involves anger over injustice, sharing experiences and insights with supportive others, having mentors, and taking concrete steps to effect change in one's personal and social world (Lord & Hutchison, 1993).

A final obstacle to prevention is people's and governments' orientation to the "quick fix"—crisis management rather than long-term planning. Prevention and promotion require a long-term perspective. Planning and implementing prevention programs is quite time-consuming, and the results are often detectable only several years later. Governments are often only in office for a few years, and seldom plan much further.

Probably for the reasons given above, governments are placing little emphasis on prevention. In Canada, provincial ministries of health, welfare, and social services allocate an infinitesimal amount of their budgets to promotion/prevention, usually in the neighbourhood of 0.1 percent (Nelson et al., 1996). The situation in the United States is similar. Goldston

(1991) found that only four states allocated more than $1 million for primary prevention, and no state allocated more than 1 percent of its mental health budget for promotion/prevention. Only seven states had designated prevention units; a followup in 1992 showed that only three still maintained prevention offices (McElhaney, 1992).

CRITIQUES OF PROMOTION/PREVENTION

Person-Centred Rather Than Societal Approaches

When faced with a social or psychological problem, we tend to treat it as a personal problem, not a social one. We define, analyze, research, and treat human problems as if they were all within the individual or the microsystem (Ratcliffe & Wallack, 1986). At best we think also about the exosystem. Rarely do we think about the macrosystem (Prilleltensky, 1994b). Yet there is ample evidence that many social and psychological ills can be traced to the macrosystem, if not as the sole source, at least as a contributing factor.

Pierre Trudeau declared that Canada was, or was to become, a Just Society. Yet three decades later, economic and social differences are marked in Canada (Barlow & Campbell, 1995; Galbraith, 1996; Gil, 1996; Macedo, 1994; Saul, 1995). The richest fifth of the population receive about 44 percent of the nation's income, and the poorest fifth less than 5 percent (Statistics Canada, 1992, p. 151). Moreover, the middle- and lower-income groups are getting an increasingly smaller share of the pie (Barlow & Campbell, 1995). Decision-making power tends to go along with economic resources, a fact reflected in social policies affecting physical and mental health (Ratcliffe & Wallack, 1986). Social and economic class also affects health, both physical and mental. In general, poorer people have worse nutrition, higher infant mortality rates, and shorter life expectancies. As discussed in Chapter 2, people in the lowest income groups are three times as likely to have severe psychological problems (Dohrenwend et al., 1992). Part of the reason is the stress caused by lack of control over work and life circumstances, as discussed in Chapter 16.

Yet the individualistic ideology of our culture means that human problems are most often dealt with in personal rather than social terms. Efforts at promotion/prevention have not escaped this tendency to concentrate on persons and not on systems. Febbraro (1994) detailed how programs designed to prevent child maltreatment, however well-intentioned, end up blaming single mothers for the problems and neglect to challenge social conditions that put the mothers themselves under tremendous stress. According to Febbraro, "the well-being of children in single-mother families is rooted, not within inherent deficits in the mothering skills of single mothers, but within the disadvantaged position of women—and their children—in patriarchal/capitalist societies" (p. 47). Promotion/prevention programs try to teach mothers vital personal skills such as how to play with their children and how to discipline them, but do not address the fundamental societal sources of child abuse, such as child poverty and discrimination against women.

Similarly, Gil (1996) argues that "the futility of violence prevention efforts by government, professional organizations, and social advocacy movements should not be surprising, since the aim of these efforts has been primarily to control, punish, and modify the behaviour of individuals involved in violence, rather than to discern and eliminate its root causes in the fabric of societies" (1996, p. 77). Canadian psychologist and policy analyst Camil Bouchard makes the same point with respect to child poverty. He wrote in 1994 that "Canadian families and children suffering the consequences of poverty are growing in number. In this context, the sole use of preventive psycho-social programs to counter the consequences of poverty without an equally important global strategy to reduce economic inequality or poverty itself seems incomplete, inefficient, and even cynical" (p. 44). Similarly, Albee (1996) has argued that rather than focussing exclusively on the prevention of clinical disorders, prevention programs should also promote competence and address the need for social and political change.

Expert Versus Community-Driven Programs

Both the process and the contents of promotion/prevention programs are typically controlled by health and human service professionals. Although community members increasingly participate in design and implementation, they still take a back seat. Professionals often operate on the basis of an expert model that (1) takes control away from the community, (2) promotes a power imbalance between professionals and citizens, (3) emphasizes deficits instead of strengths, and (4) limits the ability of people to help themselves (Hasenfeld & Chesler, 1989; Hegar, 1989; McKnight, 1995; Reiff, 1974). The expert-driven approach blocks community ownership of problems and solutions and does not encourage self-determination. Yet a sense of ownership is vital for the best outcome (for example, Peirson & Prilleltensky, 1994). Moreover, community members are the experts on their own neighbourhood, and their participation ensures the identification of the most salient risk and protective factors (Pancer & Nelson, 1990).

Planning, Implementation, and Dissemination

While the outcomes of many promotion/prevention programs have been well documented, their planning, implementation, and dissemination have not (Weissberg & Bell, 1997). How to implement and successfully distribute programs is the next frontier in the field. Once we know more about how to implement and disseminate programs we will have a better chance of integrating them into the ongoing plans of schools, communities, and workplaces (Commins & Elias, 1991). It is not enough to do a good thing only once. A successful drug abuse prevention or interpersonal problem-solving program that runs only once helps a very limited number of youth.

The National Mental Health Association in the United States has published guides on how to establish community-based prevention programs and how to communicate their contents to others (NMHA, 1995). Basic program planning and implementation strategies include: (1) open communication between sponsors and participants, (2) participation of all stakeholders in advisory committees, (3) opportunities for sponsors and participants to support each other in their efforts to launch a new program, (4) adequate training for staff and volunteers, (5) exchange of information with similar programs, and (6) inclusive evaluations that take into account multiple viewpoints (NMHA, 1995). Similarly, Bogenschneider (1996) has outlined a set of principles that can guide the planning and implementation of prevention programs.

PANORAMA

Steady progress has been made over the past three decades in developing, evaluating, refining, and expanding prevention programs for mental health problems in children and adults. Early programs tended to concentrate on one or two types of problems in high-risk individuals (the Perry Preschool Project is a good example). Although narrowly focussed, high-risk projects continue to flourish and yield promising results (Institute of Medicine, 1994), the past decade has seen the appearance of more comprehensive ecological and universal programs. These broader approaches have been particularly evident in prevention initiatives with young children living in disadvantaged neighbourhoods and/or families.

Each type of prevention program has advantages and disadvantages. It may turn out that specific approaches fit specific disorders or areas of dysfunction. Discovering which approaches work best for which problems is an exciting challenge for future research.

An even greater challenge for proponents of prevention is to raise its profile and its status among academics, practitioners, and those who hold the purse strings. In concluding their survey of provincial programs, Nelson et al. (1996) recommended:

- that each province develop definitions, standards, and policies for prevention, along with recording systems for budgets, programs, and personnel;

- that each province develop a secretariat for prevention, as it is obvious that prevention is not the unique jurisdiction of any one ministry or department; and

- that the federal government create a national office for prevention, which would develop definitions, standards, and policies, fund demonstration projects, provide technical support, and convene annual meetings of government officials, researchers, professionals, and concerned citizens to discuss progress in the field and plan future directions.

In the United States, the Commission on the Prevention of Mental-Emotional Disabilities recommended in 1987 that "every mental health agency at every level of government allocate a substantial share of its service, education and research budgets to prevention, increasing the allocation to at least 15 percent by 1995" (1987, p. 229). Provincial governments in Canada must also set some goals for the reallocation of funds from treatment to promotion/prevention. At the organization level, prevention needs to be part of organizations' mandates, with earmarked funds.

Education of the public, politicians, government policymakers, and practitioners is needed to develop an appreciation for the promise and potential of prevention.

SUMMARY

Treatment and rehabilitation can never reduce the incidence of psychological disorders in a population. This conclusion provides a strong rationale for the development of strategies that promote mental health and prevent mental disorders. Examples from history show that some health problems can be prevented even without precise scientific knowledge of the causes. Recent advances in the understanding of risk and protective factors for mental health problems have provided direction. Risk and protective factors operate at the level of the individual, the family, the exosystem (for example, school or work), and the macrosystem (society as a whole), suggesting that an ecological perspective is most useful for the development of preventive interventions.

"First generation" prevention programs, developed in the 1960s and 1970s, have already been shown to have long-term benefits in reducing social, emotional, and health problems. More recent programs tend to have a stronger conceptual and empirical foundation than their predecessors. Narrowly focussed programs have given way to more comprehensive, ecologically-oriented promotion/prevention programs, such as the Better Beginnings, Better Futures project in Ontario.

Although several effective promotion/prevention programs have been developed, federal and provincial governments do not currently provide the infrastructure or funding required for widespread promotion/prevention. Additional barriers include a lack of emphasis in professional training, the long-term nature of results, and an individualistic bias in Western culture. Current promotion/prevention programs have been criticized for still being too person-centred, failing to address social causes, and being expert-driven rather than fully collaborating with the community. More study of planning and implementation is needed if successful programs are to be replicated so that they become an integral part of the health and educational system.

KEY TERMS

community psychology (p. 462)
prevention (p. 463)
primary prevention (p. 463)
secondary prevention (p. 463)
tertiary prevention (p. 463)

early intervention (p. 463)
mental health promotion (p. 463)
mental health (p. 463)
public health approach (p. 465)
protective factors (p. 466)
risk reduction approach (p. 467)

ecological perspective (p. 467)
microsystem (p. 467)
exosystem (p. 467)
macrosystem (p. 467)
high-risk approach (p. 469)
universal approach (p. 469)

ADDITIONAL RESOURCES

Canadian Mental Health Association
7000 Minoru Boulevard
Suite 260
Richmond, BC V6Y 3Z5
(604) 279-7110
(604) 279-7118 fax
cmha-rmd@cyberstore.ca

Better Beginnings, Better Futures
Ministry of Community and Social
    Services
4th Floor, Hepburn Block
80 Grosvenor Street
Toronto, ON M7A 1E9
(416) 325-5329
crussell@web.apc.org

Health Canada
Tunney's Pasture
PL 0913A
Ottawa, ON
K1A 0K9
(613) 941-2985
(613) 941-5366 fax
info@www.hc-sc.gc.ca

www.who.int/msa/mnh/mhp/mhp.htm
A discussion of the activities related to the promotion of positive mental health and the influence of psychosocial and behavioural factors on overall health.

www.worldbank.org/children/why/perry.htm
A general discussion and overview of the Perry Preschool Project.

www.opc.on.ca/bbbf/index.html
An overview of the Better Beginnings, Better Futures project currently being implemented in 12 communities across Ontario.

bbbf.queensu.ca
The Better Beginnings, Better Futures Home Page, which contains current information on the program's status and research results.

GLOSSARY

A

ABAB Also called *reversal design*; a nonexperimental investigative method, a variety of ***single-subject design***, that requires the quantification of behaviour in its naturally occurring environment prior to any intervention. This constitutes the A phase or the baseline of the procedure. Next, in the B phase, the treatment is introduced in a controlled manner for a period of time. The next A phase constitutes the reversal, during which time the treatment is not provided, and the subject is exposed to the original baseline conditions. Finally, in the final B phase, the treatment is provided once again.

abstinence syndrome A reaction many individuals experience during treatment for barbiturate abuse. It occurs at the stage at which the user is no longer dependent, and is characterized by insomnia, headaches, aching all over the body, anxiety, and depression, and which can last for months.

acculturation framework A framework used in cross-cultural psychology; as adapted to the field of developmental disabilities, it views people with developmental disabilities as a small subculture within a larger dominant group or culture, a subculture whose goal is integration—a state in which the group participates in the economic, social, and cultural life of the dominant society while maintaining its own identity as a unique cultural entity.

acquired sexual dysfunction Any sexual dysfunction which the sufferer has not always experienced.

activity theory A theory of how to cope with aging that holds the people who age successfully are those who maintain the activity level they had in middle age. More demanding activities can be replaced by less demanding ones. What is important is the amount of activity; if it declines, psychological involvement in life declines with it, and sets the stage for the development of physical and/or mental disorders.

actuarial approach An approach to evaluating and interpreting the data on patients, making predictions, and coming to decisions that relies exclusively on statistical procedures, empirical methods, and formal rules. *See also **clinical approach**.*

addiction model A way of thinking of various psychological problems, such as eating disorders or pathological gambling, that gives them the characteristics of substance dependence.

adjustment disorder In the diathesis-stress perspective, depression that follows exposure to severe stress such as of war, disaster, or prolonged deprivation and resolves when the stressful event has resolved. It can occur in people who are not predisposed to depressive disorder.

affective disorder An altered mood state severe enough to interfere with a person's social and occupational functioning (for example, ability to work or go to school) and whose range of symptoms is not limited to the person's feelings, but affects other bodily and behavioural systems as well. Also called ***mood disorder***.

alarm The first phase of the ***general adaptation syndrome (GAS)***, a concept that was the first formal description and definition of stress as a consequence of adaptation to demands placed on the body. In the alarm phase, the body, faced with an adaptive challenge, mobilizes its defences. *See also **resistance** and **exhaustion**.*

alcohol dehydrogenase An enzyme that helps break down alcohol in the stomach. Women have significantly less of this enzyme than men.

alcohol expectancy theory A theory that proposes drinking behaviour is largely determined by the reinforcement that an individual expects to receive from it. Most of the subjective experiences actually felt are a function of expectation and attitude and not an effect of the drinking.

alter One of two or more unique personalities in a single individual who has ***dissociative identity disorder (DID)***. Alters may be almost polar opposites, requiring different eyeglass prescriptions and having different allergies. Alters may also differ in the age, sex, race, and family history they claim to have.

alternate-form reliability An attribute of a test demonstrated by a high correlation between scores on two versions of a test. To circumvent the problem that one may improve on a test the second time around because of practice, test designers may prepare two forms of the same test—that is, they decide what construct they want their test to measure, think up questions (or items) that would test that construct, and then word those questions in a slightly different way in order to create a second test that measures the same construct as the first.

Alzheimer's disease The most common of the ***primary dementias***. It progresses through three stages: *forgetfulness*, in which there are memory difficulties, problems with concentration, unclear thinking, difficulty finding words, and errors in judgement; *confusion*, in which existing symptoms become more severe and additional symptoms occur such as language difficulties, problems in time and place orientation, sleep difficulties, employment or social difficulties, incontinence, feelings of helplessness, flattening of affect, agitation, irritability, and wandering; and *dementia*, in which the ability to communicate is lost, memory impairment is profound, and a variety of physical symptoms develop such as stooped posture, increasing immobility, total incontinence, increasing vulnerability to pneumonia, congestive heart failure, etc.

amenorrhea Failure to menstruate, a medical effect of ***anorexia nervosa*** and ***bulimia nervosa***.

amniocentesis A procedure for prenatal screening for chromosomal abnormalities conducted between the 11th and 18th weeks of pregnancy. With the assistance of ultrasound, a needle is inserted into the amniotic sac via the abdomen and a small amount of amniotic fluid withdrawn. Cells contained in the fluid are then cultured in the lab.

amotivational syndrome A continuing pattern of apathy, profound self-absorption, detachment from friends and family, and abandonment of career and educational goals evident in some long-term users of *cannabis*.

amphetamines Drugs that have effects on the body similar to those of the naturally occurring hormone adrenaline. Originally developed as a nasal decongestant and asthma treatment in the 1930s. In addition to shrinking mucous membranes and constricting blood vessels, they increase alertness and concentration. Chronic amphetamine use is associated with feelings of fatigue and sadness, as well as periods of social withdrawal and intense anger.

anaclitic depression In the psychodynamic perspective, a type of depressive state that arises from a pattern of interaction of parents with their children that leaves the children feeling deprived, rejected, confused, or overindulged. In anaclitic depression, the child's sense of self may embody conflicts relating to affection, care, and love. When depressed, a person with this background may be demanding of others, exhibit clinging behaviours, seek constant reassurance, and fear the loss of intimate relationships.

anal stage According to Sigmund Freud, a child's age from 18 months to 3 years during which the focus of libidinal pleasure shifts to the anus, with gratification coming from retaining feces (anal retention) or eliminating feces (anal expression).

analogue observational setting An artificial environment set up in an office or laboratory to elicit specific classes of behaviour in individuals. Used when *in vivo observation* in the natural environment is impractical because of time constraints and the unpredictability of modern family life.

anesthesia Sensory symptom of conversion disorder consisting in loss of sensitivity.

anhedonia A loss of pleasure or interest in almost all activities or a lack of reactivity to usually pleasurable events.

anomie A feeling of rootlessness, and lack of norms and a sense of intimate belonging. The word was coined by Émile Durkheim, who believed the division of labour in modern societies undermined the social ties experienced by people in traditional societies, who worked alongside friends and neighbours.

anorexia nervosa An eating disorder characterized by the pursuit of thinness to dangerously low weight levels.

anorgasmia *See female orgasmic disorder.*

Antabuse Disulfiram, a drug that is used to make the experience of drinking extremely aversive. It blocks the action of the metabolizing enzyme acetaldehyde dehydrogenase, resulting in a buildup of acetaldehyde in the body. Like people who naturally lack this enzyme, people who drink alcohol after taking Antabuse experience increased heart rate, nausea, vomiting, and other unpleasant effects.

antagonist drug A neurotransmitter that inhibits the production of acetylcholine, a bodily substance that mediates the transmission of nerve impulses within the brain. Used as a pharmacological agent.

antisocial personality disorder (APD) A personality type in the "Dramatic, Emotional, or Erratic Disorders" cluster characterized by a pervasive pattern of disregard for, and violation of, the rights of others that begins in childhood or early adolescence and continues into adulthood. Also known as *psychopath* and *sociopath*.

anxiety sensitivity The tendency to catastrophically misinterpret arousal-related bodily sensations because one believes the sensations to have harmful consequences, such as death, insanity, or loss of control.

anxious ambivalent The interpersonal style of persons who strongly desire intimacy with others and persistently seek out romantic partners, but who, once they begin to get close to their partner, become anxious and back away; while they desire closeness, they appear to be afraid of it. People are considered to have developed these difficulties as a result of poor parent-child attachments that fail to instill the self-confidence and skills necessary for intimacy. Because this relationship style characterizes *borderline personality disorder (BPD)* patients, the features of borderline disorder may be seen as attempts to adjust to a desire for but distrust of intimacy.

aphonia Symptom of *conversion disorder* consisting in an inability to talk above a whisper.

appraisals In the *transactional model* of stress, evaluations that people constantly make about what is happening to them and its implications for themselves.

approach motivation The ability to seek reward. Depressed people often have a marked deficit in approach motivation, which is related to symptoms such as *anhedonia* and social withdrawal.

aptitude X treatment interaction (ATI) research A line of research that attempts to identify client or therapist characteristics that will pinpoint the best treatment for an individual.

arrhythmias Disturbances in the normal pumping rhythm of the heart. Can result in *myocardial infarction*.

Asperger disorder A developmental disorder similar to *autism* but associated with fewer symptoms, higher functioning, and higher IQ. It is not known whether "core autism" (the full range and severity of symptoms) and Asperger disorder represent points on a continuum of severity, or whether they are related but different disorders.

assessment A procedure in which information is gathered systematically in the evaluation of a condition; it serves as the preliminary to a *diagnosis*. A psychiatric assessment may include interviews with the patient or the patient's family, medical testing, psychophysiological or psychological testing, and the completion of self-report scales or other report rating scales.

asylum A place for treatment of the mentally ill. Units for the mentally ill were established within the great Arab hospitals in Baghdad in A.D. 800 and asylums were created in other Arab cities some 500 years before Europeans built their first asylums. Treatment followed the tradition of care, support, and compassion.

atherogenesis The development of atherosclerosis. Can occur as early as two years of age.

atherosclerosis A buildup of deposits, known as *plaques*, on the walls of the blood vessels. Atherosclerosis can narrow the openings of arteries enough to compromise the blood supply to the heart or the brain, leading to **myocardial infarction** or stroke.

attachment theory A development of the psychoanalytic approach by John Bowlby. According to this view, children form attachments with their parents that become the child's internalized model for all subsequent relationships. Such difficulties form the basis for later problems.

attention deficit hyperactivity disorder (ADHD) A childhood disorder characterized by disruptive behaviour, an inability to control activity levels or impulses, or difficulty concentrating.

attentional deficits Distractibility, poor concentration for an extended period, and a tendency to drift away from ongoing activities, including conversations.

autism The best known of the **pervasive developmental disorders**. Autistic children exhibit a lack of social responsiveness or extreme autistic aloneness; very limited or unusual communication patterns; unusual patterns of behaviour such as a lack of eye contact; self-stimulation including rocking, spinning, or flapping; self-injury including head-banging or hand-biting; an obsessive interest in particular objects; and an obsessive need for sameness. From the Greek *autos*, "self."

autonomic hyperactivity Autonomic arousal. One symptom of panic disorder.

aversion therapy The use of painful or unpleasant stimuli to decrease unwanted behaviours. For example, an alcoholic attempting to stop drinking may be required to drink after being given a drug that causes nausea when mixed with alcohol.

avoidance Escape behaviour by which, in cognitive and behavioural models, anxiety is maintained. It may involve real or imagined danger, and may be physical or cognitive.

avoidance of psychosexual maturity Fears of maturity hypothesized to be the central feature of *anorexia nervosa*. The anorexic's fears are transferred to her body, which can be controlled by deprivation and brought back to a prepubescent state.

avoidant personality disorder A condition in the "Anxious and Fearful Disorders" cluster characterized by pervasive pattern of avoiding interpersonal contacts and an extreme sensitivity to criticism and disapproval. Persons with this disorder clearly desire affection and suffer from loneliness, but they restrict social interactions to those they trust not to criticize them, and even then they keep a certain distance.

avolition A loss of energy, motivation, or interest in activities, including grooming, education, or physical exertion.

B

basal metabolic rate The amount of energy used by a resting person to maintain vital functioning. In *anorexia nervosa*, decreases of more than 30 percent have been observed in basal metabolic rate.

bedlam Any form of rowdy, chaotic behaviour. The noise and disruption among the residents of Bethlem Royal Hospital (as it is now known) prompted the use of the word (the local corruption of "Bethlem"). This asylum was established by Henry VIII in 1547 when he had the monastery of St. Mary of Bethlehem in London converted.

behavioural genetics The study of the way in which inherited features interact with the environment to produce behaviour.

behavioural inhibition A temperament in early childhood that may be related to anxiety disorders later in life, characterized by profound avoidance of others in preschool, and atypical autonomic nervous system responses to novelty.

behavioural medicine Application of the methods of behaviour modification to the treatment or prevention of disease—for example, the use of psychological techniques to control pain in patients undergoing medical procedures, or interventions to improve the diabetics' ability to control their blood glucose.

behaviourism A psychological approach to understanding abnormal behaviour devised by John B. Watson (1858–1935), which declared that psychology must be restricted to the study of observable features, that is, the behaviour of organisms. Watson considered abnormal functioning to be learned and so believed it could be unlearned. His model for learning was derived from Ivan Pavlov's (1849–1936) studies of classical conditioning.

Bender Visual-Motor Gestalt Test is the oldest and most commonly used of neuropsychological assessments often used to screen children for neuropsychological impairment. The test consists of a series of nine cards containing lines and shapes drawn in black on a piece of white cardboard. Children are asked first to copy the images on another card and then to draw them from memory. Errors in reproducing these lines and shapes may indicate neurological problems.

binge eating/purging type A subtype of *anorexia nervosa* in which the afflicted person's dietary restraint breaks down fairly regularly and she binges and/or purges. About half of anorexia nervosa patients are of the binge eating/purging type. *See also* **restricting type**.

binge For purposes of diagnosing *bulimia nervosa*, a period of eating in which (1) the amount of food eaten in a span of time (for example, a one- or two-hour period) is definitely more than most people would consume in a similar period and circumstances and (2) the person feels out of control over what she eats, how much, or whether she can stop.

biological preparedness theory A theory of fear and phobias holding that people and other organisms are biologically prepared to acquire fears of certain stimuli as opposed to otheres. That is, evolution has "hard-wired" organisms to easily learn those associations that facilitate species survival.

Bipolar 1 A subtype of the *bipolar disorders* in which there are one or more manic episodes and usually one or more depressive episodes. *See also* *Bipolar 2*.

Bipolar 2 A subtype of the *bipolar disorders* in which there is at least one hypomanic episode and one or more episodes of major depression. *See also* *Bipolar 1*.

bipolar condition A *mood disorder* in which both *major depressive disorder* and *mania* are exhibited.

bipolar disorders Affective disorders in which the change in mood occurs in both directions, that is, the patient at one time or another experiences both depression (mood lowering) and *mania* (mood elevation).

blood alcohol level (BAL) Alcohol level expressed as a percentage of blood volume. For example, if there are 80 milligrams of alcohol in 100,000 milligrams of blood, (BAL) is 0.08 percent.

body dysmorphic disorder A *somatoform disorder* characterized by an individual's being unusually and excessively preoccupied with some aspect of his or her personal appearance—an imagined defect or an exaggeration of an existing trait.

body image dissatisfaction One of the two main components of body image disturbance, which is a characteristic feature of *bulimia nervosa* and *anorexia nervosa*, consisting in the sufferer's feeling fat and unhappy about her body weight and shape.

body image distortion One of the two main components of body image disturbance, which is a characteristic feature of *bulimia nervosa* and *anorexia nervosa*, consisting in the sufferer's seeing herself as larger than she really is.

body mass index A person's weight in kilograms over his or her height in metres squared, an indicator of how much fat one has on one's body.

borderline personality disorder (BPD) A condition in the "Dramatic, Emotional, or Erratic Disorders" cluster characterized by fluctuations in mood, an unstable sense of one's identity, and instability in one's relationships. This overriding instability makes borderlines unpredictable and impulsive and, along with their irritability and argumentative style, these features tend to seriously interfere with their relationships. However, they seem unable to tolerate being alone and accordingly become desperate about relationships, typically alternating between idealizing and devaluing their partners.

brief psychotic disorder A disorder related to *schizophrenia* characterized by sudden onset of at least one prominent psychotic symptom that lasts for at least one day but less than one month, followed by a full return to premorbid levels of functioning.

bulimia nervosa An eating disorder characterized by a binge-purge syndrome in people who are generally in the normal weight range.

C

cannabis Hashish, which comes from the hemp plant *cannabis sativa*, indigenous to Asia but now grown in many parts of the world. Has psychoactive effects caused primarily by the chemical *THC*.

cardiac output The amount of blood pumped by the heart. One of the two major variables that determine blood pressure. Cardiac output is itself determined by two other variables: the rate at which the heart beats (commonly measured in beats per minute) and the amount of blood ejected from the heart (stroke volume). *See also total peripheral resistance*.

cardiovascular reactivity The degree of change in a cardiovascular function that occurs in response to psychologically significant events.

case study A nonexperimental investigative method resulting in a description of the past and current functioning of a single individual, generally the result of information gathered through intense interactions over long periods. Variables such as family history, education, employment history, medical history, social relationships, and the patient's level of psychological adjustment are described. The goal is a description of an individual's current problem, and its relation to his or her past. A case study seeks to provide a theory concerning the etiology of a patient's problem or psychological makeup, and/or a course of treatment and outcome. The oldest approach to the study of abnormal behaviour.

catatonic subtype One of the five official subtypes of *schizophrenia*, characterized by stupor, rigidity, negativism, odd posturing, excitement, and echopraxia (imitation of someone else's movements) or *echolalia*.

catecholamines A group of molecules that includes neurotransmitters such as serotonin and norepinephrine. Catecholamines have been implicated most directly in models of depression.

categorical Said of an approach to *diagnosis* in which an individual is deemed to either have a disorder or not have a disorder, with no in-between. One of the most frequent criticisms of the DSM is that it is categorical. *See also dimensional*.

cellular immunity One of the three general categories of immune response, based on the action of a class of blood cells called T-lymphocytes. The "T" designation refers to the locus of their production, the thymus gland. Cellular immunity results from a cascade of actions of various types of T-lymphocytes.

child disintegrative disorder (CDD) A developmental disorder evinced by behaviours and deficits in social skill and communication similar to those found in *autism*. The major distinguishing feature is later onset; after a period of several years of normal development, marked deterioration occurs. The ability to speak in sentences is present before onset.

cholecystokinin (CCK) A peptide found in high concentration in the brain stem, the hippocampus, the amygdala, and the cerebral cortex. Induces anxiety in rats, an effect that can be blocked with benzodiazepines. One form of CCK, the tetrapeptide fragment CCK4, induces panic attacks in humans. CCK appears to modulate neurons in the brain, with changes in CCK producing changes in anxiety. Panic and anxiety may involve CCK, and panic disorder may be due to a hypersensitivity to it.

chorionic villus sampling (CVS) A procedure for prenatal screening for chromosomal abnormalities that involves obtaining cells from the vagina and cervix. This test can be carried out earlier than amniocentesis—between the 8th and 12th weeks of pregnancy—but may be less accurate.

circadian rhythms The action of biological cycles occurring at 24-hour intervals.

classical conditioning A type of learning described by the Russian physiologist Ivan Pavlov (1849–1936). In classical conditioning, a response is transferred from one stimulus to another. John B. Watson, an early behaviourist, took the view that **classical conditioning** was the basis for human behaviour, including abnormal behaviour. *See also operant conditioning*.

client-centred therapy A type of therapy developed by Carl Rogers as an alternative to psychoanalysis, based on his belief that psychological problems arose when personal growth was stunted by judgements imposed by others.

clinical approach An approach to evaluating and interpreting the data on patients, making predictions, and coming to decisions that relies on the clinician's experience and personal judgement, guided by intuition honed with professional experience rather than by formal rules. *See also actuarial approach*.

clinical psychologists Persons who are initially trained in general psychology and then receive graduate training in the application of this knowledge to the understanding and amelioration of disorders of thinking and behaviour. They have a thorough grounding in research methods, and some spend their careers doing research on abnormal functioning, although many also provide treatment. The treatment methods of clinical psychologists primarily involve psychological interventions of one kind or another.

clinical significance An attribute of research results, referring to the practical utility of the treatment studied, which does not follow automatically from the results' *statistical significance*.

clusters Groups of personality disorders. DSM-IV lists ten personality disorders in three clusters: (A) odd and eccentric disorders (paranoid, schizoid, and schizotypal); (B) dramatic, emotional, or erratic disorders (antisocial, borderline, histrionic, and narcissistic); and (C) anxious and fearful disorders (avoidant, dependent, and obsessive-compulsive).

coefficient alpha A method for evaluating *internal consistency*, calculated by averaging the intercorrelations of all the items on a given test. The higher the coefficient alpha, the higher the internal consistency.

cognitive contents In the cognitive perspective, the information acquired and stored in *cognitive structures*, which includes images and beliefs about stimuli. Used to assign meaning to events. Cognitive therapists often call cognitive contents cognitive *propositions*, *schemata*, or *core beliefs*.

cognitive errors Errors in reasoning to which eating disorder patients are prone, such as an "all or nothing" thinking style.

cognitive operations In the cognitive perspective, operations performed in order to store, transform, and retrieve information in memory and to process information in general. These processes can be biased and can thus lead to distortions in the appraisal of events, in the estimation of probability, and in the availability of coping strategies.

cognitive products In the cognitive perspective, the conscious products of processing *cognitive contents* from *cognitive structures*. They consist of thoughts or images and are often produced automatically (without efforts or attention).

cognitive restructuring A form of treatment for anxiety disorders based on cognitive therapy that involves three steps: (1) identifying maladaptive cognitive contents (automatic thoughts, beliefs), processes, and products, (2) challenging the maladaptive cognitive contents by helping the client to examine the evidence for or against a belief, and (3) developing more adaptive cognitive contents and processes.

cognitive restructuring One of the cognitive-behavioural approaches to treatment of the personality disorders, directed at challenging the core beliefs thought to underlie the problems and providing skills training and behavioural practices.

cognitive structures In the cognitive perspective, modes of organization according to which information is stored in long-term memory. For example, some theorists hold that the *fear structures* form a network containing three types of information: stimulus, response, and meaning.

cognitive-behavioural theory A psychological theory that reflects the view that both thinking and behaviour are learned and can, therefore, be changed. It assumes that the way people view the world, including their beliefs and attitudes toward the world, themselves, and others, arises out of their experience and that these patterns of thinking and perceiving are maintained by consequences in the same way overt behaviour is maintained. While this treatment approach incorporates some procedures derived from strictly cognitive therapy, it essentially follows the views expressed by Bandura's *social learning theory*.

Community Parent Education Program (COPE) A large-group, community-based version of *parent-training (PT)* programs that works through schools and the community.

community psychology A field of psychology that has highlighted the need for the prevention of mental disorders and the promotion of mental health, as opposed to exclusive reliance on treatment approaches; applies an ecological perspective that stresses the interdependence of the individual, the family, community, and society; embodies sensitivity to a person's social context and appreciation of diversity; pays more attention to people's strengths and the promotion of wellness, in contrast to the clinical psychology focus on deficits and reduction of maladaptive behaviours; stresses the importance of informal social supports, rather than relying solely on professional help; and is oriented to social justice and social change.

comorbidity The common situation in which an individual meets the criteria for more than one diagnostic condition. *See also overlap*.

compulsions Repetitive behaviours (overt actions or cognitive acts) performed in response to an obsession, or according to certain rules or in a stereotyped manner.

computerized axial tomography (CAT) A brain imaging technique in which a narrow band of X-rays is projected through the head. The X-ray source and detector rotate very slightly and project successive images. The exposures are combined by a computer to produce a highly detailed cross-section of the brain.

concordance A concept used in behavioural research into the genetic bases of psychiatric disorders. When the disorder that characterizes one person, called the *index case* or *proband*, also occurs in another person, the two are said to display **concordance**. The degree of concordance is thought to reveal the influence of genetics.

concurrent validity The ability of a diagnostic category to estimate an individual's present standing on factors related to the disorder but not themselves part of the diagnostic criteria. One of the major criticisms of the DSM is that it sheds little light on the non-symptom attributes of people with a given diagnosis.

conduct disorder (CD) A disorder of children who show a pattern of violating the rights of others and major age-appropriate societal norms or rules in a variety of settings.

confound In an experiment, what occurs when two or more variables exert their influence at the same time, making it impossible to accurately establish the causal role of either variable.

congruency hypothesis The hypothesis in the diathesis-stress perspective that distressing life events are more likely to lead to depression when the type of difficulties are in areas of the person's life that he or she feels insecure about. *Congruent* stressful events are those that match the person's specific vulnerability. Thus, neither high levels of stress nor specific personality/constitutional characteristics alone are sufficient causes of depression; it is the interaction between the two factors that creates the risk for depression.

conscious In *psychodynamic* theory, the conscious contains information of which we are currently aware.

constitutional vulnerability model One model of how hostility might lead to health risk, which suggests that the link between hostility and poor health outcomes is the result of a third variable, constitutional vulnerability, with which they are both associated.

construct validity The validity of a test assuming a specific theoretical framework that relates the item the test measures, often rather abstract, to some other item that is more easily assessed. If the two sets of measurements correlate, the test is said to have construct validity.

contact hypothesis The idea that people would grow more comfortable with people of different ethnic groups as they were exposed to them. This hypothesis, applied to disability, suggests that integration into the general population would improve general attitudes toward people with disabilities.

content validity When its content includes a representative sample of behaviours thought to be related to the construct (that is, the concept or entity) the test is designed to measure.

continuous amnesia A subtype of *dissociative amnesia* in which a person can remember nothing following a certain point in time.

control group In an experiment, the group that experiences all aspects of the experiment, including assessments, in a manner identical to the *experimental group*, except for the manipulation of the *independent variable*.

controllable risk factors Factors increasing the likelihood of disease, such as poor diet or smoking, that are under the control of the individual.

conversion disorder A somatoform disorder characterized by motor symptoms or disturbances in sensory functioning that appear to be a result of a neurological problem, but for which no physical cause can be found. Previously known as "hysteria," from the Greek *hystera* ("uterus").

correlational method A nonexperimental investigative method that measures the degree of relationship between two variables; behaviour is not manipulated but quantitatively measured and then analyzed statistically. Following the measurement of the variables, a statistical quantity called a *correlation coefficient* is computed. Generally requires large number of participants.

courtship disorder theory A theory of sexual offending advanced by Kurt Freund that holds it is produced when a person's sexual behaviour becomes fixated at one of the four phases of human sexual interactions: (1) looking for and appraising a potential partner; (2) posturing and displaying oneself to the partner; (3) tactile interaction with the partner; and (4) sexual intercourse. Fixation at stage 1 results in voyeurism; at stage 2 in exhibitionism; at stage 3 in frotteurism; and at stage 4 in rape.

criterion validity An attribute of a test, when it gives higher scores to people already known to have greater ability in the area it tests. The concept arises because some qualities are easier to recognize than to define completely, such as artistic ability.

cross-fostering A type of adoption study in which one group comprises adopted children, whose biological parents have a disorder and whose adoptive parents demonstrate no psychopathology, and the other group comprises adopted children whose biological parents have no disorder but whose adoptive parents develop psychopathology. The comparisons available in this design allow statements concerning the relative impact of genes and environment. Regarded as an improvement on the traditional adoption study.

cultural-familial retardation Also known as *retardation due to psychosocial disadvantage*. Developmental handicaps in which no organic cause or brain dysfunction has been identified. These are found more frequently within lower socioeconomic groups, and commonly at least one parent and possibly one or more siblings have developmental delays or handicaps. Most people within this group function intellectually within the mild range.

cyclothymia *See cyclothymic disorder*.

cyclothymic disorder A less severe form of *bipolar disorder* characterized by a long-standing pattern of alternating mood episodes that do not meet the criteria for *major depressive disorder* or *manic episode*, having a duration of at least two years with recurrent periods of mild depression alternating with *hypomania*. These periods may alternate with other times when the person's mood is normal for up to two months. Also known as *cyclothymia*.

D

defence mechanisms According to Sigmund Freud, mechanisms through which the ego allows the expression of libidinal desires in a distorted or symbolic form.

deinstitutionalization The removal of people with disabilities from institutions and the provision of community-based accommodation and services. The trend to deinstitutionalization has been due to the influence of the *normalization principle*.

delusional disorder A disorder related to *schizophrenia* characterized by the presence of one or more non-bizarre delusions that persist for at least a month. There are no marked impairments in functioning, no evidence to suggest a chemical or medical cause, and no symptoms of schizophrenia. Onset is typically in middle or late life. Subtypes are defined in terms of the content of the delusions: persecutory (the most common), grandiose, jealous, erotomanic, etc. Studies have shown that the majority of people with the disorder would not have been considered normal before the onset of their illness. Often these people have successful work histories, but have had social or interpersonal problems, perhaps appearing aggressive, hostile, withdrawn, or suspicious.

delusions False beliefs that are strongly held, even in the face of solid contradictory evidence.

dementia The most common mental disorder in older adults, in which sufferers lose their memory, judgement, reason, personal dignity, and finally their sense of self.

dependent personality disorder A condition in the "Anxious and Fearful Disorders" cluster characterized by a fear of relying on oneself to make decisions. Dependent people seek advice and direction, need constant reassurance, and seek out relationships where they can adopt a submissive role. They seem to desperately need others to assume responsibility for important aspects of their lives. They also tend to subordinate their needs to those of other people in their lives, even people they hardly know.

dependent variables In an experiment, behavioural responses on measures the researchers hypothesize would be affected by the manipulation of the *independent variable*.

depersonalization A dissociative disorder characterized by the feeling of being unreal and disconnected from the self. It has a sudden onset and is usually confined to adolescence or early adulthood. When such experiences are persistent, recurring, and personally distressing they are considered pathological.

depersonalization The feeling that one is an observer, rather than an initiator, of one's own behaviour.

depressants Drugs that inhibit neurotransmitter activity in the central nervous system. Examples are alcohol, barbiturates ("downers"), and benzodiazepines.

description The specification and classification of clinical phenomena; one of the primary goals of clinical research.

developmental disability Often used interchangeably with *developmental handicap* and in this book synonymous with *mental retardation*.

developmental handicap Often used interchangeably with *developmental disability* and in this book synonymous with *mental retardation*.

developmental psychopathology A field of psychology whose practitioners recognize that the perspectives taken with adults cannot encompass the intricacies of behaviour in an organism undergoing rapid biological, cognitive, and behavioural changes. The field endorses these principles: that behaviour is the result of a complex interplay between genetics, other biological factors, and repeated interpersonal experiences; that the interaction between child and environment is reciprocal; and that a child needs certain experiences to develop normally.

developmental-difference controversy The argument in the field of psychology about whether people near the low end of the normal range of intelligence represent a disorder or merely one extreme of normal human variability.

dextroamphetamine (Dexedrine) Stimulant medication prescribed for children with *attention deficit hyperactivity disorder (ADHD)*.

diagnosis In the realm of medicine and abnormal psychology, a determination or identification of the nature of a person's disease or condition, or a statement of that finding. A diagnosis is made on the basis of a *diagnostic system*.

diagnostic overshadowing The problem of attributing emotional and behavioural difficulties of people with mental retardation to the developmental disorder, causing real psychiatric disorders to be missed. The fact is that such people can develop all types of psychiatric disorders, including less common ones.

diagnostic system A system of rules for recognizing and grouping various types of abnormalities. Forms the basis for *diagnosis*.

dialectical behaviour therapy One of the cognitive-behavioural approaches to treatment of *borderline personality disorder (BPD)*, one of whose main features is the acceptance by the therapist of the patient's demanding and manipulative behaviours. In addition, several standard behavioural procedures are used, such as exposure treatment for the external and internal cues that evoke distress, skills training, contingency management, and cognitive restructuring.

diathesis-stress perspective The view that a predisposition to develop a disorder (the "diathesis"), interacting with the experience of stress, causes mental disorders. According to this perspective, the interaction underlies the onset of all disorders, although either the predisposition or the stress may be more important in a particular disorder, or in a particular person.

dimensional An approach to *diagnosis* based on a continuum for mental disorders from nonexistent or mild to severe. *See also categorical*.

disengagement theory A theory of how to cope with aging that holds as people move into old age, it is normal and natural to slow down as the individual and society begin to separate or *disengage* from each other. From this perspective, aging successfully involves accepting disengagement, and it is the person who refuses to disengage who is at higher risk for mental disorders.

disorganized speech A characteristic of *schizophrenia*. Speech may be disorganized in different ways. For example, in *derailment* the person allows one topic in a conversation to slide into another, loosely related but irrelevant, topic. Often, each phrase may make sense and be related to the next, but the person is soon far from the original topic and seldom returns to it. Sometimes the person will use words that make no sense or create *neologisms* or *word salads*.

disorganized subtype One of the five official subtypes of *schizophrenia*, characterized by disorganized speech, clearly disorganized behaviour, and markedly flat or inappropriate affect. Generally viewed as the most severe subtypes.

disruptions in attachment Failure to form a reliable bond with the parent. In the psychodynamic perspective, attachments can be *secure, avoidant* (being uncomfortable with intimacy), or *anxious/ambivalent* (excessively clinging, feeling that others were not as close as one would wish). The nature of this bond may affect the child's personality.

dissociation The disruption of mental processes involved in memory or consciousness that are normally integrated.

dissociative amnesia Complete memory loss for extensive and important actions and/or personal information. Characterized by a sudden onset, typically in response to a traumatic event or extremely stressful experience, and by an equally sudden return of memory.

dissociative disorders Psychological problems characterized by *dissociation*.

dissociative fugue Loss of memory with the added feature of physical flight. For diagnosis, there must be (1) sudden and unexpected travel away from home or work and (2) an inability to recall one's past and confusion about personal identity. A sufferer leaves the comfort of home and familiar surroundings, and assumes a completely new identity, one that can be quite elaborate and last for years. The person may also display behaviour very different from their previous habits. From the Latin *fugere*, "to flee."

dissociative identity disorder (DID) The most severe and chronic of the dissociative disorders, characterized by the existence of two or more unique personalities in a single individual. Each personality may have its own constellation of behaviour, tone of voice, and physical gestures. *See also alter*.

dizygotic (DZ) twins Non-identical (or fraternal) twins, which result when two independent sperm separately fertilize two independent ova at approximately the same time. DZ twins, like non-twin siblings, have, on average, just 50 percent of their genes in common. From *di* meaning "two."

dopamine A neurotransmitter implicated in *schizophrenia*. There is experimental evidence that symptoms of *schizophrenia* occur when dopamine receptors (particularly the D_2 receptors) are either too numerous or too sensitive.

double-blind A procedure to help ensure that expectations of the subjects of a study do not influence the outcome, according to which neither the subjects nor the experimenters know who is getting the substance in question and who is getting a *placebo*.

Down syndrome The best known chromosomal abnormality associated with mental retardation.

dual diagnosis The co-occurrence of serious behavioural or psychiatric disorders in people with developmental disabilities.

dualistic A view of mind and body as separate entities, subject to different laws. Nowadays avoided in DSM terminology, hence the substitution of the term *psychophysiological* for *psychosomatic*.

dyscalculia A learning disorder that involves problems with recognizing and understanding numerical symbols, sequencing problems, and attention deficits. Also known as *mathematical disorder*.

dysfunctional family According to family systems theory, a kind of family that can give rise to eating disorders by being more conflicted and less expressive, communicative, disclosing, cohesive, and nurturing than other families.

dysgraphia Any of the disorders of written expression, characterized by limited handwriting skills, spelling, grammatical, and punctuation errors. Often co-occurs with dyslexia.

dyslexia A reading disorder that involves difficulties not only in the recognition but also in the comprehension of words. Reading is often very slow and characterized by omitted, substituted, or distorted words. Such difficulties often extend to spelling as well. Also referred to as *reading disorder*.

dyspareunia A sexual dysfunction characterized by genital pain associated with intercourse. Some experts claim lack of lubrication is the most common cause of the problem. Among men, it is rare and usually associated with infections, inflammation, or physical anomalies.

dysthymia *See dysthymic disorder*.

dysthymic disorder A unipolar affective disorder that manifests many of the same symptoms as major depression, except that they are less severe. It persists for at least two years, with only brief interludes of normal mood. Also known as *dysthymia*.

E

early intervention A term that some argue should replace *secondary prevention*, because *prevention* should be reserved for interventions that attempt to reduce the incidence or onset of a disorder.

echolalia One of the common characteristics of speech in autistic children, in which the child repeats another person's words or phrases, using the same or similar intonation.

ecological perspective A perspective on health promotion that considers nested levels of analysis, viewing mental health problems in the context of characteristics of the individual (for example, coping skills, personality traits), the *microsystem* (that is, the family and social network), the *exosystem*, which mediates between the individual, the family, and the larger society (for example, work settings, schools, religious settings, neighbourhoods), and the *macrosystem* (for example, social norms, social class).

effect size A common metric used to summarize the meaning of diverse studies in a *meta-analysis*. It is calculated as the difference between the means of the experimental (that is, the treatment) group and the control group, divided by the standard deviation of either the control group or the pooled sample of both groups.

ego analysts Psychoanalytically oriented therapists who use Freudian techniques to explore the ego rather than the id, and try to help clients understand how they have relied on defence mechanisms to cope with conflicts.

ego In Sigmund Freud's theory, the structure that begins to develop in response to the fact that instinctual demands of the *id* are not always immediately met. The ego develops to curb the desires of id so that the individual does not suffer any unpleasant consequences.

egodystonic homosexuality A type of *gender identity disorder (GID)* in which the afflicted person is attracted to people of the same sex, but experiences conflict with his or her sexual orientation or wishes to change it.

Electra complex The condition in which, according to Sigmund Freud, girls want to seduce their fathers to gain what they truly desire: a penis. By analogy to a character in several Greek tragedies.

electroconvulsive therapy (ECT) The use of electricity to induce a seizure in mental patients by placing electrodes on the skull and administering a convulsive rather than a lethal shock intensity.

electrolyte imbalance A medical effect of the purging characteristic of eating disorders, which can deplete the body of potassium and chloride, resulting in an imbalance of electrolytes (compounds in the body that conduct electricity) that can seriously compromise renal, bowel, and brain functioning. It also affects heart functioning and can lead to cardiac arrest.

emotionally focussed therapy An experiential approach to couples therapy that aims to modify constricted interaction patterns and emotional responses by fostering the development of a secure emotional bond.

empirically supported therapy Psycho-therapeutic intervention that has been demonstrated empirically to be effective.

endogenous opiates The body's natural painkillers. *Opioids* mimic their effects.

epidemiology The study of the *incidence* and *prevalence* of disorders in a population.

estrogen A hormone (the so-called female sex hormone) involved in sexual activity and desire, variations in the level of which can lower or increase sex drive.

ethyl alcohol The effective chemical compound in alcoholic beverages, which reduces anxiety and inhibitions, produces euphoria, and creates a sense of well-being.

etiology Cause or causes, especially of disease.

evidence-based practice Health care based on established scientific findings rather than practitioners' assumptions.

exhaustion The third phase of the *general adaptation syndrome (GAS)*, a concept that was the first formal description and definition of stress as a consequence of adaptation to demands placed on the body. If the challenge persists beyond the *resistance* phase, the body can no longer maintain resistance, and characteristic tissue changes occur. At this point, the organism may succumb to a disease of adaptation, such as an ulcer. *See also alarm.*

exhibitionism A form of *paraphilia* that is also a criminal offence, in which a person exposes his or her genitals to an unsuspecting stranger.

Exner system A way of standardizing the scoring of responses in a Rorschach examination in order to increase its reliability and validity. The Exner system may have greater clinical validity for testing schizophrenia than depressions or personality disorders.

exogenous opiates Narcotics, which bind to receptor sites throughout the body, including the brain, spinal cord, and bloodstream, and reduce the body's production of *endogenous opiates*.

exosystem A level of analysis in the *ecological perspective* that mediates between the individual, the family, and the larger society, consisting in work settings, schools, religious settings, and neighbourhoods.

experiment A scientific procedure in which variables are manipulated and the effects on other variables are gauged. Large groups of subjects are generally used, and the results are analyzed statistically. In a true experiment subjects are randomly assigned to *experimental* and *control groups*.

experimental group In an experiment, the group exposed to a variable that is manipulated, the *independent variable*.

exposure therapy Any therapeutic procedure that repeatedly confronts the person with a stimulus that typically elicits an undesirable behaviour or an unwanted emotional response until the behaviour or response no longer occurs.

expressed emotion (EE) Criticism, hostility, or overinvolvement in one's interpersonal environment. A home in which interactions are characterized by repeated very critical remarks by a spouse, partner, or other family member would be considered to be a high-EE environment. Depressed and schizophrenic patients discharged from hospital into high-EE home environments seem more likely to have relapses.

external locus of control A belief that the determinants of one's life reside outside oneself. People who have an external locus of control see themselves as being buffeted by the random events of the world. *See also internal locus of control.*

external validity The generalizability of the findings in an investigation, or the degree to which the findings apply to other individuals in other settings.

externalizing problems A type of disruptive behaviour disorder under the DSM-IV classification, exhibited by children who behave disruptively, cannot control their activity levels or impulses, or have difficulty concentrating. These behaviours are usually more disturbing to others than to the children themselves.

extrapyramidal effects Severe side-effects of the major tranquillizers.

F

face validity An attribute of a test, when the items on it resemble the characteristics associated with the concept being tested for.

facilitated communication (FC) An alternative approach to teaching people with severe communication impairment, such as low-functioning children with *autism*. In FC, subjects pointed to pictures, letters, or objects while a facilitator provided various types of support to the hand or forearm, on the theory that physical support could overcome neuromotor problems. However, concerns were soon raised about the "ouija board effect"—that is, that facilitators were unintentionally influencing the subject by subtle body movements. Controlled studies confirmed that this was occurring and did not provide support for the emergence of hidden literacy skills.

factitious disorder Faking or bringing on symptoms of illness to gain a doctor's attention and thus satisfy a need to play the role of patient. Not to be considered a *somatoform disorder*, in which the sufferer truly believes there is a serious physical problem.

false memory syndrome Said to be exhibited by persons who claim to remember events that did not really take place, due to the influence of therapists who use leading questions, repeated suggestion, visualization, and hypnosis with the aim of recovering repressed memories.

family therapy A treatment, used for both *anorexia nervosa* and conduct-disordered and oppositional-defiant-disordered children, that revolves around changing the family as a system. Maladaptive behaviour is considered to reflect dysfunction in the family as a whole. Treatment seeks to increase reciprocity and positive reinforcement among family members, establish clear communications, and identify solutions to interpersonal problems. The treatment integrates behavioural social learning, cognitive-behavioural, and family systems perspectives. It is one of the few therapies for anorexia nervosa to receive support in a controlled trial.

fearlessness hypothesis A theory that suggests that a person with *antisocial personality disorder* has a higher threshold for feeling fear than other people. Events that make most people anxious (such as the expectation of being punished) seem to have little or no effect on psychopaths.

female orgasmic disorder A sexual dysfunction characterized by a woman's persistent or recurrent delay in, or absence of, orgasm following normal excitement, causing marked distress or interpersonal difficulty. Also known as **anorgasmia**.

female sexual arousal disorder A sexual dysfunction characterized by a woman's persistent or recurrent inability to attain or maintain arousal until completion of her sexual activity, and the presence of marked distress or difficulty.

fetal alcohol effects (FAE) Defects shown by children who display some of the symptoms of *fetal alcohol syndrome (FAS)* without meeting all diagnostic criteria.

fetal alcohol syndrome (FAS) Prenatal and postnatal growth retardation and central nervous system dysfunction due to alcohol consumption during pregnancy.

fetishisms Sexual behaviours in which the presence of nonliving objects is usually required or strongly preferred for sexual excitement. Most researchers and clinicians also include an excessive attraction to certain parts of the body.

fit to stand trial An attribute of an accused person that qualifies him or her to participate in his or her own defence in court. To be found fit to stand trial, an accused must understand the nature of the charges and the purpose, possible outcomes, and effects of the legal proceedings, and must be able to communicate with his or her lawyer. Under Canada's *Criminal Code* an accused is presumed fit to stand trial unless the court is satisfied on a balance of probabilities that he or she is unfit. The party who raises the issue of fitness has the burden of proving it. In contrast to an evaluation of *not criminally responsible on account of mental disorder (NCRMD)*, an evaluation of fitness to stand trial requires the examiner to assess the accused's *present* mental condition and whether it interferes with ability to perform the legal tasks related to the trial process.

frontal cortex EEG asymmetry Higher EEG alpha readings in the left frontal region of the brain than in the right frontal region (suggesting lower levels of cortical activity in the left frontal cortex). Shown to have an association with depression.

frotteurism A form of *paraphilia* that is also a criminal offence, in which a person touches or rubs against a nonconsenting person for the purpose of sexual pleasure.

functional magnetic resonance imaging (fMRI) A technique that allows observation of neurophysiological activity accompanying specific cognitive tasks.

G

gate control theory An internationally recognized theory of pain developed by Ron Melzack, a psychologist at McGill University in Montreal, and Patrick Wall, a physiologist from the United Kingdom. The theory opens the possibility that a given injury or amount of tissue damage will have different effects on different people at the same time or on the same person at different times.

gender dysphoria Discomfort with one's biologically endowed sex.

gender identity disorder (GID) A condition in which a person experiences strong and persistent identification with the other sex, *gender dysphoria*, and significant distress or impairment in social, occupational, or other important areas of functioning. Previously known as *transsexualism*.

gender identity One of the three aspects of the development of gender identity, referring to a person's basic sense of self as male or female, the first signs of which appear between 18 and 36 months of age. *See also* **sexual orientation** and **gender role**.

gender role One of the three aspects of the development of gender identity, referring to the collection of those characteristics that a society defines as masculine or feminine. Because roles relate to social standards, ideas about gender role change over time and from culture to culture. *See also* **sexual orientation** and **gender identity**.

general adaptation syndrome (GAS) A stereotyped pattern of bodily changes that occur in response to diverse challenges to the organism, first described by Hans Selye. The syndrome comprises three stages: *alarm*, *resistance*, and *exhaustion*. The GAS was the first formal description and definition of stress.

general paresis of the insane (GPI) A disorder evidenced by mania, euphoria, and grandiosity, followed by a progressive deterioration of brain functioning (called *dementia*) and paralysis. Now known to result from untreated infections by the syphilis spirochete.

generalized amnesia A subtype of *dissociative amnesia* in which an individual forgets his or her entire life history.

generalized sexual dysfunctions Any sexual dysfunction which is apparent with all the sufferer's sexual partners and even during solitary sexual activity.

genetic linkage studies Studies in which researchers examine families that have a high incidence of a particular psychiatric disorder. Within these extended families the researchers look for the presence of particular traits (called genetic markers) that can be linked to the occurrence of the disorder.

genital stage According to Sigmund Freud, a period of human development after age 12, during which sexual desires are directed toward involvement with others; it involves the early adolescent shedding the narcissistic qualities of the earlier stages and developing the capacity to become involved in affectionate and romantic relationships with peers.

glove anesthesia A type of *conversion disorder* in which the patient experiences loss of sensation only on the part of the hand that would be covered by a glove. Because the nerve fibres in the hand run all the way up the arm, this loss of sensation cannot have a physical cause, so glove anesthesia is a clear example of conversion disorder.

grossly disorganized behaviour Highly irrational actions or inappropriate emotions. Symptomatic of *schizophrenia*.

H

habituation *See psychological dependence*.

hallucinations False perceptions occurring in the absence of any relevant stimulus. Auditory hallucinations are the most common form, they may occur within any sensory modality.

hallucinogens Drugs that change a person's mental state by inducing perceptual and sensory distortions or hallucinations. Also called *psychedelics*, from the Greek for "soul" and "to make manifest."

health behaviour model One model of how hostility might lead to health risk, which suggests that hostile people may be more likely to engage in unhealthy behaviours (for example, smoking, drug use, high-fat diets) and less likely to have healthy practices, such as exercise.

health psychology Any application of psychological methods and theories to understand the origins of disease, individual responses to disease, and the dimensions and determinants of good health.

hermaphroditism A condition in which a person's reproductive structures are partly female and partly male.

heterosexual gender dysphoria A type of *gender identity disorder (GID)* in which the afflicted person is attracted to people of the opposite sex.

high-risk approach An approach to *prevention* programs based on the assumption that there are known risk factors for certain mental health problems, and that it is most effective to target individuals most exposed to these factors. *See also* **universal approach**.

high-risk studies A research strategy that concentrates on subjects judged to be at high risk for the disorder under investigation. High-risk studies are used as an alternative to *longitudinal studies* of some disorders, which can be prohibitively expensive because of the low incidence of the disorders. They are also often used in conjunction with longitudinal approaches, because the "high-risk status" of the studied sample tends to raise incidence to more economically feasible and scientifically useful levels.

histrionic personality disorder A condition in the "Dramatic, Emotional, or Erratic Disorders" cluster characterized by flamboyant, overly dramatic emotional displays and overresponsiveness to trivial events. These persons are self-centred, demanding, and inconsiderate, and strike others as insincere and shallow, so they cannot hold other people's attention for long and typically have few friends. Though often flirtatious, they seem unable to develop intimacy in relationships.

homosexual gender dysphoria A type of *gender identity disorder (GID)* in which the afflicted person is attracted to people of the same sex.

humoral immunity One of the three general categories of immune response, in which invading antigens are presented by macrophages to B-lymphocytes. ("B" stands for *bursa*, an organ in which such cells are produced in birds. B-lymphocytes derive from the liver and bone marrow in humans.) This causes the B-cells to reproduce—a process reinforced by the lymphokine secretion from the helper T-cells. Some of the activated B-cells remain as memory B-cells. Others go on to be plasma cells, secreting antibodies called immunoglobulins that neutralize antigens in a number of different ways, such as clumping, presenting the antigen to phagocytic cells, or rupturing the antigen.

humours Bodily fluids, disturbances of which, according to Hippocrates, resulted in psychological functioning.

hyperesthesia Sensory symptom of *conversion disorder* consisting in excessive sensitivity.

hypertension A characteristically high level of resting blood pressure (defined as a *systolic blood pressure/diastolic blood pressure* reading of more than 140/80 under precisely defined conditions). Can result from any of variety of causes, but in about 90% of cases it is "essential," meaning a simple cause cannot be identified. Hypertension is a *risk factor* for death due to cardiovascular disease.

hypoactive sexual desire disorder A sexual dysfunction characterized by persistent or recurrent deficiency of sexual fantasies and desire for sex, causing marked distress or interpersonal difficulty.

hypochondriasis A *somatoform disorder* characterized by excessive preoccupation with fears of having a serious illness when there is no underlying illness. The most common diseases people worry about are cancer and heart disease. Often leads to "doctor shopping." From the Greek *hypochondria* for the region below the ribs, thought to be linked to changes in mood and mental functioning.

hypomanic Said of someone having an episode of *mania* that is less severe or briefer than would be considered psychotic, but nevertheless represents significant impairment.

hypoxyphilia The practice heightening the sexual experience by deliberately inducing unconsciousness in oneself by oxygen deprivation, produced by chest compression, strangulation, enclosing the head in a plastic bag, or various other techniques. Also known as *autoerotic asphyxia* and *asphyxiophilia*.

I

id In Sigmund Freud's theory, the structure present at birth that contains, or represents, the biological or instinctual drives that are not constrained at birth, demanding instant gratification without concern for the consequences either to the self or to others.

in vivo observation (*in vivo*, "in the living being") A method used by behaviourally oriented therapists to determine how environmental variables affect a behaviour of concern, in which a clinician may record a running narrative of events, using pencil and paper, video, or still camera, in the client's everyday environment. More commonly, observations are made by *participant observers*, key people in the client's environment, and reported to the clinician. *See also* ***analogue observational setting***.

incidence The number of new cases of a disorder in a particular population over a specified time period, usually a year.

independent variable In an experiment, the variable that is manipulated.

individual psychology Alfred Adler's approach to psychodynamic therapy, which proposes that mental disorders are the consequence of deeply entrenched mistaken beliefs, which lead individuals to develop a maladaptive style of life that protects them from discovering their own imperfections.

inferiority complex A condition we supposedly acquire as children, when we become aware that because we are smaller and less powerful than adults, we are necessarily inferior. Alfred Adler developed the idea that people are driven by this complex.

information processing A type of model explaining how information is processed and stored in memory, based on a computer analogy. The cognitive "hardware" consists of structures to store information (that is, memory structures), which contain information-processing "software" that produce or alter the cognitive contents in memory, and produce thoughts or images in consciousness.

informed consent The type of consent psychologists must obtain from their clients, by informing them of the nature and expectations of the relationship being created, and the details of the procedures that will be administered, such as the assessment, therapy, or research protocols; and by providing a forum in which clients are given all the information they need to make a decision about participating.

intelligence quotient (IQ) A test of judgement, comprehension, and reasoning invented by the French psychologist Alfred Binet (1857–1911), in which a child's mental age, determined by the child's successful performance on age-grouped tests that had been normed, was divided by the child's chronological age, and the quotient multiplied by 100. Theoretically, IQ was a reflection of that person's performance compared with that of others the same age.

interactionist explanation A theory that views behaviour as the product of the interaction of a variety of factors.

internal consistency The degree of reliability within a test—the extent to which different parts of the same test yield the same results.

internal locus of control A belief that the determinants of one's life reside inside oneself. People who have an internal locus of control see themselves as the masters of their own destiny and seem to be protected against the harmful effects of stress on their health. *See also* ***external locus of control***.

internal validity The degree to which the changes in the *dependent variables* of an experiment are a result of the manipulation of the independent variable. If no alternative explanations are possible, the experiment has strong internal validity.

interpersonal psychodynamic psychotherapy A variation of brief psychodynamic therapy that emphasizes the interactions between the client and his or her social environment.

interrater reliability The extent to which two or more clinicians agree on the *diagnosis* of a particular patient.

introjective depression In the psychodynamic perspective, a type of depressive state that arises from a pattern of interaction of parents with their children that is overly critical, controlling, intrusive, and punishing. In introjective depression, the child's sense of self may embody conflicts relating to identity, competition, and aggression. A person with such a background may develop feelings of inferiority, inadequacy, self-criticism, and guilt.

ischemic heart disease A condition in which blood supply to the heart becomes compromised, leading to a *myocardial infarction*. One of the leading causes of death from diseases of the cardiovascular system in Western societies.

L

la belle indifference Surprising unconcern about the severity of their symptoms frequently shown by people with *conversion disorder*.

labelling theory A point of view that suggests that when a person is identified as having a disorder, other people, particularly mental health workers, perceive that person as dysfunctional and different. This perception, which tends to persist even after recovery, results in these people being treated disadvantageously and even disrespectfully.

latency stage According to Sigmund Freud, a period of relative sexual quiescence from age 6 to 12 years, during which the child focusses on developing intellectual and motor skills.

latent task In D. T. Lykken's test of his *fearlessness hypothesis*, the disguised task given to the subjects (the association between particular lever presses and shocks), under cover of the *manifest task*.

late-onset schizophrenia A type of *schizophrenia* that first appears after the age of 45. Diagnostic criteria are the same as those for *early-onset schizophrenia*, the more common type, but late-onset cases are less likely to have disorganized speech, lack of logical thought, and flattened affect, and hallucinations and delusions are likely to be more florid and bizarre. The content of delusions and hallucinations is commonly persecutory, so people with this disorder are most likely to resemble the *paranoid schizophrenia* subtype.

learned helplessness/hopelessness A cognitive approach to the understanding of depression that postulates that a basic cause of depression is the expectation that bad events will occur and there is nothing to be done to prevent them. Depression is seen as arising from people's lack of control over bad events in their lives and the types of explanations they use to understand this lack of control.

learning disorders A group of developmental disorders that include reading disorders, mathematics disorders, and disorders of written expression. Communication disorders and problems related to poor motor skills may also be included. Frequently referred to as *learning disabilities*.

learning In *information processing* models, the development of internal representations of stimuli, actions, outcome, and their interrelationships.

lesions Disruptions of bodily tissue or of the normal function of a bodily system.

libido The energy for *eros*, that is, sexual drives, which in Sigmund Freud's theory are seen as the major life instinct.

lifelong sexual dysfunction Any sexual dysfunction which the sufferer has always experienced.

linkage analysis A method used to isolate the genetic contribution to mental disorder that considers an observable trait that seems linked to an affective disorder to be a genetic marker for the disorder; that is, it is assumed that the same chromosome that carries that trait also carries a gene that increases a person's risk for the disorder.

lithium carbonate Lithium salt, used to treat mania and depression. Has the effect of flattening out the peaks and valleys of the illness, allowing sufferers to achieve some stability in their lives with less disruption for family members. Apparently lithium has preventive effects for both unipolar depression and bipolar disorder, and lithium is considered the treatment of choice for bipolar disorder.

lobotomies Psychosurgery consisting of surgical removal, or disconnection, of the frontal lobes of the brain, intended to relieve all manner of mental and emotional disorders.

localized Said of memory loss in which the person cannot remember some of what happened during a specific period of time, quite often the first few hours after a traumatic experience. Quite often in this condition the memory loss is for a disturbing event.

locus ceruleus A region of the brain that influences arousal and the orienting response toward novel stimuli and is apparently the centre of fear and anxiety.

longitudinal study A scientific study in which a large group of people are evaluated with respect to the existence of psychological or behavioural features and are then followed up, often years or decades later, to determine whether they have developed a disease.

M

M'Naghten standard A standard of insanity defined by the case of *Regina v. M'Naghten* (1843) that became the accepted rule in England, the United States, and Canada. In today's interpretation of the standard, (1) the accused must have been suffering from a mental disorder, and (2) he or she must not have known at least one of two things: the nature and quality of the act and that what he or she was doing was wrong. That is, inability to understand that an act is wrong can be sufficient even if the accused understands the act itself. Because the second element requires determination of the accused's thinking, the M'Naghten standard is referred to as a "cognitive" test of insanity.

macrosystem A level of analysis in the *ecological perspective* that consists in social norms and social class.

magnetic resonance imaging (MRI) Also called nuclear magnetic resonance imaging. A noninvasive technique for examining the structure and the functioning of the brain. A strong homogeneous magnetic field is produced around the head and brief pulses of radio waves are introduced. When the radio waves are turned off, radio waves of a characteristic frequency are emitted from the brain itself, which can be detected. The information gathered is integrated into a computer-generated image of the brain.

major depressive disorder A *mood disorder* in which the person is extremely sad and discouraged and displays a marked loss of pleasure from usual activities. Clinically depressed people often have severe problems sleeping, and experience weight loss and lack of energy.

major depressive disorder A unipolar affective disorder characterized by persistent feelings of sadness, loss of interest or ability to feel pleasure, unexplained weight loss, difficulty sleeping, fatigue, difficulty concentrating, feelings of worthlessness or guilt, suicidal thoughts, and either agitation or slowing down. The person must not be suffering from other disorders that may present as depression, such as *schizoaffective disorder* or a *delusional disorder*.

male erectile disorder A sexual dysfunction characterized by a man's persistent or recurrent inability to reach or sustain an erection until completion of his sexual activity and resultant distress. Also known informally as *impotence*.

male orgasmic disorder A sexual dysfunction characterized by a man's persistent or recurrent delay in, or absence of, orgasm following normal excitement, causing marked distress or interpersonal difficulty. Much less common than *female orgasmic disorder*.

malingering Pretending to be ill in order to achieve some specific objective. Not to be considered a *somatoform disorder*, in which the sufferer truly believes there is a serious physical problem.

mania A bipolar affective disorder characterized by flamboyance and expansiveness. A person experiencing a manic episode may go on shopping sprees, engage in sexually promiscuous behaviour, take on numerous, unrealistic work commitments, brag, and dominate others socially. In general, the person shows intolerance when the world does not cooperate with his or her momentary needs. Extreme or prolonged cases of mania are considered bona fide psychotic states, implying that the person is experiencing a break with reality. From the Greek *mainomai*, "to be mad." *See also hypomanic*.

mania A *mood disorder* in which a person seems extremely elated, more active and in less need of sleep, and displays flights of somewhat disconnected ideas, grandiosity (an illusion of personal importance that can lead to inappropriate behaviour), and impairment in functioning.

manifest task In D. T. Lykken's test of his *fearlessness hypothesis*, the ostensible task given to the subjects (learning a sequence of correct lever presses), which was really a pretext for the *latent task*.

masochist A person who derives sexual pleasure from experiencing his or her own pain or humiliation.

mechanism In *psychophysiological* medicine, a process—an activity of a living system—that mediates the influence of an antecedent factor on disease.

mental health Narrowly, the absence of disorder. In a broader view, the presence of optimal social, emotional, and cognitive functioning—also known as *wellness*.

mental health promotion A concept complementary to the concept of *prevention* in *community psychology* that focusses on the idea of enhancing the functioning of people.

mental hygiene movement A movement started by Dorothea Dix (1802–1877), a Boston schoolteacher, characterized by a desire to protect and provide humane treatment for the mentally ill. Her campaign resulted directly in the opening of 32 state hospitals, including 2 in Canada. Despite the noble aims, the asylums were overcrowded and the staff had no time to do more than warehouse and restrain them.

mental illness Often used to convey the same meaning as *psychological abnormality*, but implies a medical rather than psychological cause.

mental retardation A developmental disorder characterized by significantly subaverage intellectual functioning with onset before the age of 18, accompanied by limitations in two or more areas of adaptive behaviour, such as communication, self-care, academic, domestic, social or community skills, leisure, and work.

mental status examination The most frequently used semistructured interview in psychiatric settings. Screens for patients' emotional, intellectual, and neurological functioning. Used in formal diagnosis or to plan treatment.

meta-analysis A method of quantitatively summing up previous research studies that have used different patient populations and outcome measures. The research results are combined by developing a common metric called an *effect size*.

methadone A heroin replacement used to treat heroin addicts, often to reduce the craving after initial withdrawal symptoms have abated. Methadone therapy appears to work best in conjunction with good individual and group psychological intervention program, as well as ongoing peer support.

methylphenidate (Ritalin) The most frequently prescribed stimulant medication for children with *attention deficit hyperactivity disorder (ADHD)*.

microsystem A level of analysis in the *ecological perspective* that consists in the family and the social network.

Millon Clinical Multiaxial Inventory (MCMI) An objective test of personality developed to help clinicians make diagnostic judgements within the multiaxial DSM system, especially in the personality disorders found on Axis II.

minimal brain dysfunction (MBD) A term common in the 1940s and early 1950s, and the first designation to be accepted by professionals of a pattern of behaviour we now call ADHD. A number of brain pathologies, such as encephalitis, birth trauma, lead toxicities, and head injury, resulted in children showing difficulty with attention, overactivity, and impulse control. It was reasoned, therefore, that children with this combination of behaviours must have some serious but undetectable brain dysfunction. Subsequent research failed to uncover neurological signs in MBD, and the theory fell into disrepute.

Minnesota Multiphasic Personality Inventory (MMPI) The most widely used objective test of personality. The adjective "multiphasic" means that it assesses many aspects of personality. The test contains 567 questions grouped to form ten content scales plus additional scales to detect sources of invalidity such as carelessness, defensiveness, or evasiveness. The revised and updated version, called the MMPI-2, focusses primarily on Axis I disorders.

molecular biology A field in which researchers have been able to compare specific DNA segments, identify the genes that determine individual characteristics, and pinpoint the defective genes that cause various medical and psychological disorders.

monoamine oxidase inhibitors (MAOIs) One of the three known major classes of antidepressants. MAOIs inhibit the release of substances that break down neurotransmitters, allowing them to remain in the synaptic space for longer periods and stimulate greater rates of neuronal firing. Common MAOIs include isocarboxazid (Marplan), phenelzine sulfate (Nardil), and tranylcypromine sulfate (Parnate). *See also **tricyclics** and **selective serotonin reuptake inhibitors (SSRIs)**.*

monozygotic (MZ) twins Identical twins, which result from the fertilization by a single sperm of a single ovum. This is followed by an unusual extra division into exactly matched zygotes, which subsequently develop into genetically identical fetuses. MZ twins have 100 percent of their genes in common. From *mono* meaning "one" and *zygote* meaning "fertilized egg."

mood disorder *See **affective disorder**.*

moral anxiety One of the three types of anxiety that Sigmund Freud thought people expressed. This type develops when people become so afraid of their *id* impulses that they see them as threatening. *See also **realistic anxiety** and **neurotic anxiety**.*

moral therapy A form of treatment advocated by Philippe Pinel and his followers that held that the insane could be controlled without the use of physical or chemical restraints, by means of respect and quiet and peaceful surroundings, plenty of rest, a good diet, moderate exercise, and activities.

mosaicism A cause of ***Down syndrome*** in which cell division occurs unevenly, so that some cells have 45 chromosomes and some have 47. People with mosaic Down syndrome may have fewer physical characteristics, better speech, and higher intellectual functioning, depending upon the numbers of cells affected.

myocardial infarction Heart attack.

N

narcissistic personality disorder A condition in the "Dramatic, Emotional, or Erratic Disorders" cluster characterized by grandiosity, egocentricity, and an exaggerated sense of self-importance with overblown fantasies of success. Narcissistic people typically have difficulty feeling any concern for others, but their own self-esteem is readily shattered by criticism. Their typical behaviour alienates others. When frustrated or slighted, they may become vengeful and aggressive.

natural causes Causes that can be observed and examined. When mental afflictions are seen as being due to natural causes, they are treated in a way that addresses such causes.

negative cognitive triad In the cognitive model, a characteristic outlook of depressed patients in which they see themselves as worthless, helpless to change the events in their lives, and hopeless about the future.

negative schemata In the cognitive model, negatively biased sets of interconnected beliefs, information, and examples applied by depressed patients to the conduct of their lives. These schemata draw them to pessimism, and the patients therefore tend to look for evidence that proves pessimism was justified and to miss information that would disprove it. Negative schemata lead to certain easily observed types of thinking errors or cognitive distortions.

negative symptomatology. Symptoms defined as the absence of normal behaviour, as opposed to the presence of abnormal behaviour. *See also **negative symptomatology**.*

neo-conditioning theories Theories that regard classical and operant conditioning as processes that draw on cognitive mechanisms such as expectations and memory representations of the conditioned stimulus and the unconditioned stimulus.

neologism A newly coined word, usage, or phrase. One manifestation of ***schizophrenia*** is a habit of creating new words.

neuroses A nineteenth-century term for anxiety disorders and several other psychological problems (singular *neurosis*). Still in popular usage.

neurotic anxiety One of the three types of anxiety that Sigmund Freud thought people expressed. This type results from being persistently prevented (usually by parents) from expressing the impulses of the *id*. *See also **realistic anxiety** and **moral anxiety**.*

neurotransmitters The chemical substances that carry the messages from one neuron to the next in the complex pathways of nervous activity within the brain.

neutralize A response to a ***compulsion*** that consists in suppressing the thought or acting to prevent it from coming true.

nicotine An extremely potent central nervous system stimulant related to the amphetamines. The very small amount present in a cigarette is not lethal, and can increase alertness and improve mood. The pleasure centres of the brain seem to have receptors specific to it.

nocturnal myoclonus The second most common sleep disorder in older adults, characterized by periodic leg movement every 20 to 40 seconds for a number of periods throughout the night during sleep. The leg movement may wake the individual, creating insomnia.

nocturnal penile tumescence (NPT) A measure of nighttime erections in which the client sleeps in a laboratory over several nights with a device attached to his penis that records changes in its circumference as a result of blood inflow. The measurement technique is called *phallometry*.

nonpurging type A subtype of *bulimia nervosa* characterized by the afflicted person's compensating for overeating by fasting or exercising to excess. The nonpurging type is encountered far less frequently than the *purging type*.

nonspecific immune responses One of the three general categories of immune response, in which circulating white cells called granulocytes and monocytes identify invading antigens and destroy them by *phagocytosis*: engulfing and digesting them. *See also cellular immunity* and *humoral immunity*.

normal aging A normal process of bodily systems slowing down that ultimately causes some system to stop functioning, so that the person dies of old age rather than of any particular disease.

normalization principle The idea that the lives of individuals with disabilities should be made as normal as possible through their participation in activities common to members of society of similar age.

normative comparison An investigative approach meant to control for the potential irrelevance of statistical significance in research, in which treatment results are compared to those of non-disturbed samples.

not criminally responsible on account of mental disorder (NCRMD) An attribute of an accused person whose criminal act is caused by his or her mental illness. In contrast to *fit to stand trial*, assessments of criminal responsibility require the examiner to determine the accused's mental state *at the time of the offence* and whether it affected the ability to appreciate the offence in question. Formerly known as "not guilty by reason of insanity (NGRI)."

not guilty by reason of insanity (NGRI) *See not criminally responsible on account of mental disorder (NCRMD)*.

nutritional management The first priority in treatment of *anorexia nervosa*, in order to make sure the person gains enough weight for safety, on purely medical grounds. Also, many of the psychological symptoms of the disorder are actually effects of starvation. Eliminating or reducing these effects is often considered a prerequisite to later therapy.

O

obsessions Thoughts, images, or impulses that are persistent, markedly distressing, and egodystonic: that is, they are experienced as intrusive or unacceptable; the person regards them as alien, uncontrollable, and not the kind of thought that he or she would want to have.

Oedipal complex According to Sigmund Freud, a condition that occurs during the *phallic stage*, when boys are presumed to develop sexual desires for their mother and see their father as a competitor for their mother's love. The term is a reference to the character of Oedipus in the play by the Greek tragedian Sophocles.

Ontario Child Health Study (OCHS) A landmark epidemiological study whose primary objective was to estimate the prevalence of various emotional and behavioural disorders among children four to sixteen years of age in Ontario.

operant conditioning Idea developed Burrhus F. Skinner (1904–1990), according to which it is the consequences of behaviour that are important. Some consequences encourage the repetition of the behaviour that produces them, while other consequences result in the opposite effect. *See also classical conditioning*.

opioids Also known as *narcotics*. A class of central nervous system *depressants* whose main effects are the reduction of pain and sleep inducement. Opium, the alkaloid from which opioids are derived, comes from the seeds of the opium poppy, which is indigenous to Asia and the Middle East.

oppositional behaviour Deliberate flouting of the expectations of others, even when it means certain punishment, and perhaps even because of it.

oppositional defiant disorder (ODD) A disorder of children who, more frequently than is usual, refuse to follow instructions, argue apparently just for the sake of arguing, and show hostility toward parents and teachers.

oral stage The first year of life of infants, in which they typically engage in much oral behaviour. Important in Sigmund Freud's theory.

overlap The similarity of symptoms in two or more different disorders (that is, some of the same criteria apply to different diagnoses), which creates problems with diagnosis. *See also comorbidity*.

P

pain disorder A *somatoform disorder* characterized by chronic pain with no known organic cause.

panic attack A discrete period of intense fear or discomfort accompanied by at least four of thirteen specific somatic, behavioural, and cognitive symptoms such as palpitations, shaking, chest pain, and fear of dying, going crazy, or losing control.

paranoid A personality type in the "Odd and Eccentric Disorders" cluster whose primary features are pervasive suspiciousness of other people's motives and a tendency to see everything everyone does as a personal attack.

paranoid schizophrenia The most frequently diagnosed subtype of schizophrenia, in which the patient is preoccupied with one or more *delusions* and/or by frequent auditory *hallucinations* which may be related to the delusional theme. The content of the delusions and hallucinations, though often internally coherent and well integrated, is at considerable variance with the facts, being less organized and elaborate, and more bizarre, than that of delusional disorders.

paranoid subtype One of the five official subtypes of *schizophrenia*, characterized by preoccupation with one or more delusions or by frequent auditory hallucinations, and by an absence of prominent disorganized speech, disorganized behaviour, catatonic behaviour, and flat or inappropriate emotions. Thought to be the least severe of the five subtypes.

paraphilia A redirection of sexual desires toward what is generally considered to be an inappropriate object, or person, or behaviour.

parent training (PT) A treatment for conduct-disordered and oppositional-defiant-disordered children based on a social learning causal model. In PT the immediate goals are to develop certain skills in the parents to promote desirable, prosocial behaviours in the child and at the same time apply disciplinary techniques to minimize undesirable, maladaptive behaviours.

paresthesia Sensory symptom of *conversion disorder* consisting in bizarre sensations.

pedophilia A form of *paraphilia* that is also a criminal offence, in which a person has recurrent fantasies or behaviours involving sexual activity with prepubescent children.

pemoline (Cylert) Stimulant medication prescribed for children with *attention deficit hyperactivity disorder (ADHD)*.

perceived self-efficacy A concept in the social-cognitive perspective denoting a judgement of one's capability to accomplish a certain level of performance. It differs from outcome expectations, which are judgements of the likely consequences behaviours will produce.

performance anxiety The anxiety of dysfunctional people who feel they are expected to perform sexually, and hence do not because they are too busy worrying about and monitoring their own sexual performance and the perceived responses of their partner, and the spontaneous sensory response of sexual arousal is blocked.

person by situation interaction The impact of a person's surroundings on his or her behavioural characteristics, according to Walter Mischel's view that predicting a person's behaviour requires knowledge of both the person's typical behaviour patterns and the characteristics of the setting.

pervasive developmental disorders Developmental disorders whose manifestations are more profound than either mental retardation or learning disorders. *Autism* is the best known pervasive

developmental disorder; others are Asperger Disorder, Rett Disorder, and Child Disintegrative Disorder.

pervasive sense of ineffectiveness An attitude toward life hypothesized to be an underlying vulnerability in eating disorders.

phallic stage In this stage, according to Sigmund Freud, boys become focussed on their penis and girls become aware that they do not have one. Girls are said to develop penis envy (that is, they desire to have a penis and feel cheated).

phenylketonuria (PKU) The best known of several rare metabolic disorders that can cause mental retardation. As a result of a recessive gene passed on from each parent, a liver enzyme is inactive, causing an inability to process or metabolize the amino acid phenylalanine. This substance builds up in the brain to toxic levels, leading to retardation.

physiological dependence A persistent need to administer an intoxicating substance to oneself, with *tolerance* and *withdrawal* symptoms.

placebo A substance that looks and feels like the substance being tested in an experiment, but does not contain the active ingredient.

placebo effect The phenomenon that individuals in treatment programs expect to get better, and as a result may feel an improvement, or that they report improvement to please the experimenter. From the Latin word meaning "I shall please."

point prevalence Attribute of an age group with respect to a disorder—the percentage of people in the group who suffer from it at a given point in time.

polypharmacy Taking multiple medications concurrently, often practised by older adults.

polysubstance abuse The simultaneous misuse or dependence upon two or more substances.

positive symptomatology Symptoms defined as the presence of abnormal behaviour, as opposed to the absence of normal behaviour. *See also negative symptomatology*.

positron emission tomography (PET) is a combination of *computerized axial tomography* and radioisotope imaging. Radiation is generated by injected or inhaled radioisotopes—that is, common elements or substances with the atom altered to be radioactive. As the substance is used in brain activity, radiation is given off and detected, allowing measurement of a variety of biological activities as the processes occur in the living brain.

posttest In an experiment, assessment of the subjects on several dependent variables judged to be important, in order to get a comprehensive picture of the effects of manipulating the *independent variable*.

potential years of life lost (PYLL) A measure of the impact of death on someone's life span calculated by subtracting age of death from his or her life expectancy.

preconscious In *psychodynamic* theory, the preconscious holds information not presently within our awareness but that can readily be brought into awareness.

predictive validity The ability of a test to predict the future course of an individual's development. An essential requirement of a good *diagnostic system*.

premature ejaculation A sexual dysfunction characterized by a man's ejaculating after minimal stimulation and often before or immediately following entry of the penis into the vagina, with marked distress or interpersonal difficulty.

pretest In an experiment, an assessment of subjects on many measures prior to manipulation of the *independent variable*. Done for descriptive purposes.

prevalence The frequency of a disorder in a population at a given point or period of time.

prevention A concept borrowed from the fields of physical disease, public health, and epidemiology and applied to mental disorders by community psychology. There are three categories of prevention activities: *primary*, *secondary*, and *tertiary*.

primary appraisal In the *transactional model* of stress, an *appraisal*, which may occur quite unconsciously, that takes place when a person is faced with an event that may have adaptational significance. It is as if the individual asks: Is this a threat to me? The primary appraisal sets the stage for further events that may or may not lead to stress.

primary dementia A type of *dementia* whose major manifestation is the progressive, irreversible loss of one's former level of cognitive functioning. Can result from Alzheimer's, Picks, and Creutzfeldt-Jakob diseases. *See also secondary dementia.*

primary gain In the psychodynamic view of *somatoform disorders*, a motivation for sickness behaviour consisting in the avoidance of the unresolved conflict.

primary insomnia The most common sleep disorder in older adults, with nocturnal symptoms of difficulty falling asleep, frequent awakenings, shortened sleep, and non-restorative sleep, and daytime symptoms of fatigue, sleepiness, depression, and anxiety. DSM-IV diagnostic criteria require the symptoms to persist for at least one month, to be perceived as stressful, and to not be secondary to any other disorder.

primary prevention A type of *prevention* practised prior to the biological origin of the disease (for example, immunization). *See also secondary prevention and tertiary prevention.*

proband In family studies, the patient, or the person who has come to the attention of the clinician or researcher. Also called the *index case*.

problem-solving A form of cognitive-behavioural treatment for anxiety disorders that consists in training people to divide problems into manageable units that can be systematically analyzed and solved. Rests on the observation that many tend to think of problems in broad, vague, catastrophic ways that allow no solution.

problem-solving skills training A treatment for conduct-disordered and oppositional-defiant-disordered children that usually combines several different procedures including modelling and practice, role-playing, and reinforcement contingencies. It depends upon the observation that ODD and CD children are more inclined to misinterpret others' intentions and actions, have poor social skills, and have a limited repertoire of behavioural responses.

process schizophrenic Schizophrenic patients with a poor history of adjustment prior to being diagnosed with the disorder.

projective test A type of psychological test that reveals information the person being tested cannot or will not report directly. Used to help clinicians form hypotheses about an individual's personality. *See also Rorschach inkblot test.*

prolactin A hormone involved in sexual activity and desire, variations in the level of which can lower or increase sex drive.

pronoun reversal One of the common characteristics of speech in autistic children, in which the child often refers to him- or herself in the third person, perhaps because of trouble shifting reference between speaker and listener or a third party.

protective factor Anything that lessens the likelihood of disease. For example, exercise is thought to be a protective factor for cardiovascular disease.

protective factors Events or circumstances that help to offset, or buffer, *risk factors*.

pseudodementias Cognitive impairment similar to that of *dementia* but reversible. May be brought on by depression, nutritional deficiency, thyroid disorder, or any one of a number of other diseases; symptoms may also occur as side-effects from medications.

psychiatric nurses Persons who have received formal training in nursing before completing a specialization in psychiatric problems and typically work in hospital settings where they manage the day-to-day care of mentally disordered patients.

psychiatric social workers Persons who attend to the influence of the social environment on disordered clients. They usually have a graduate degree in social work and provide assistance to clients in adjusting to life within their families and the community.

psychiatrists Persons trained in medicine prior to doing specialized training in dealing with mental illness. This specialized training focusses on diagnosis and medical treatment that emphasize the use of pharmacological agents in managing mental disorders. Most psychiatrists attend to the medical aspects and biological foundations of these disorders, although they usually also consider psychological and environmental influences.

psychoactive agents Pharmacological agents found to affect the individual's psychological functioning.

psychodynamic Denoting a school of psychology founded by Sigmund Freud. Psychodynamic theories claim that behaviour is controlled by unconscious forces of which the person is unaware.

psychological abnormality Behaviour, speech, or thought that impairs the ability of a person to function in a way generally expected of him or her, in the context in which the unusual functioning occurs.

psychological assessment A systematic gathering and evaluation of information pertaining to an individual with suspected abnormal behaviour.

psychological dependence The state of being psychologically accustomed to a substance or activity as a consequence of regular usage. Also known as *habituation*. Evinced by feelings of restlessness, irritability, and uneasiness when the substance or activity is unavailable.

psychological disorder A specific manifestation of mental illness as described by some set of criteria established by a panel of experts.

psychoneuroimmunology A new field that studies the responsiveness of the immune system to psychosocial influences, and that has shown that the immune system can be affected by learning experiences, emotional states, and personal characteristics.

psychopath *See antisocial personality disorder*.

psychopathology Both the scientific study of psychological abnormality and the problems faced by people who suffer from such disorders.

psychophysiological reactivity model One model of how hostility might lead to health risk, which suggests that hostile people are at higher risk for various diseases because they experience exaggerated autonomic and neuroendocrine responses during stress.

psychosocial vulnerability model One model of how hostility might lead to health risk, which suggests that hostile people experience a more demanding interpersonal life than others.

public health approach An approach to *community psychology* characterized by the following steps: (1) identifying a disease and developing a reliable diagnostic method (descriptive epidemiology); (2) developing a theory of the disease's course of development on the basis of laboratory and epidemiological research (analytic epidemiology); and (3) developing and evaluating a disease prevention program (experimental epidemiology). The thrust of the approach is to reduce environmental stressors while enhancing people's capacities to withstand those stressors.

punishment In *operant conditioning*, what occurs when a behaviour decreases in frequency as a result of its consequences.

purging type A subtype of *bulimia nervosa* characterized by the afflicted person's compensating for overeating, most typically by self-induced vomiting or the use of laxatives, diuretics, or enemas. The purging type is encountered far more frequently than the *non-purging type*.

Q

quality of life A recognized desirable goal in the field of developmental disabilities, about which there is a great deal of disagreement. What constitutes quality of life and how can it be measured? A number of different approaches have been taken. For example, the Quality of Life Interview Schedule (QUOLIS), designed specifically to address the needs of adults with severe and profound disabilities, involves interviews with two informants who know an individual well in different contexts, and quality of life is measured under 12 domains, such as health services and housing and safety. A second approach is reflected in the Quality of Life Project, a conceptual framework that includes three major components of quality of life, each divided into subcomponents.

quasi-experimental study One in which the subjects in the experimental group are not randomly assigned but selected on the basis of certain characteristics, and in which there is no manipulation of *independent variables*.

R

random assignment A procedure that ensures each subject in an experiment has an equal probability of being in either the *experimental* or the *control group*, guaranteeing the equivalence of these groups.

rapid cycling depression/mania A particularly severe type of *bipolar disorder* in which the person moves very quickly in and out of depressive and manic episodes. Its usual progression is toward more frequent episodes of depression and mania.

rational-emotive therapy A form of therapy developed by Albert Ellis that is concerned with how people interpret events and how these interpretations influence their responses. These interpretations, or mediating processes, are cognitive and result from the person's belief systems.

realistic anxiety One of the three types of anxiety that Sigmund Freud thought people expressed. This type occurs when people are faced with a genuinely dangerous situation. *See also neurotic anxiety* and *moral anxiety*.

reframing A strategy in which problems are restated so that they can be more easily dealt with.

reinforcement In *operant conditioning*, what occurs when a behaviour increases in frequency as a result of consistent consequences.

relapse The return of an illness or disorder after a recovery.

reliable Said of a measurement tool when it gives the same measurement for a given thing every time. Its usefulness partly depends on this attribute. *See also valid*.

repressed Said of memories that a person cannot call into awareness, but which remain in the person's subconscious and can be retrieved under certain conditions or with the help of a psychotherapist.

residual schizophrenia A feature of chronic schizophrenia, in which previous prominent *delusions* and *hallucinations* have subsided.

residual subtype One of the five official subtypes of *schizophrenia*, diagnosed when a person who previously met the criteria for one of the other four types has no current *delusions, hallucinations, disorganized speech, grossly disorganized behaviour,* or *catatonic* behaviour, but nevertheless continues to show evidence of disturbance by the continuation of either negative symptoms or very mild levels of earlier positive symptoms, which have lessened either with the passage of time or through treatment.

resistance The second phase of the *general adaptation syndrome (GAS)*, a concept that was the first formal description and definition of stress as a consequence of adaptation to demands placed on the body. In the resistance phase, if the challenge of the *alarm* phase persists, the body actively fights or copes with the challenge through immune and the neuroendocrine changes. These adaptive responses enhance the body's ability to ward off threats in the short term. *See also* **exhaustion**.

response prevention A form of *exposure therapy* that consists in the blocking of ritualistic behaviours observed in obsessive-compulsive disorder.

response shaping A process of shaping behaviour by gradual approximations of what is expected. For example, a mentally retarded child who is unable to get dressed independently can be taught the process gradually by being rewarded for putting on one item at a time until he or she is eventually able to handle the entire task.

responsivity factor The circumstance that treatment must be responsive (or matched) to a particular client's needs and interpersonal style—that is, they must be of sufficient intensity and relevance, and seen by the patient as voluntary. Apparently, in fact treatment programs tend to be determined more by the orientation of the therapist or director.

restrained eaters For most purposes, synonymous with *dieters*. Technically, one who receives a high score on a scale that measures diet and weight history and concerns with food and dieting.

restricting type A subtype of *anorexia nervosa* in which the afflicted person relies on a rigidly controlled, very low intake of food to maintain her low weight. About half of anorexia nervosa patients are of the restricting type. *See also* **binge eating/purging type**.

reversal design *See* **ABAB**.

risk factors Events or circumstances that increase the likelihood of later pathology.

risk reduction approach An approach to health promotion used by community psychology that involves: (1) identifying a stressful life event or condition that appears to have undesirable consequences for a significant proportion of the population and developing a method to determine who is exposed to it; (2) developing, through laboratory and epidemiological research, hypotheses about ways to reduce the undesirable consequences; (3) developing and evaluating a prevention program based on the hypotheses.

role transitions Major life changes, such as leaving home for university, becoming a parent, changing careers, or retiring. May trigger depression if the person does not adapt well.

Rorschach inkblot test The oldest and probably the best known *projective test*. Based on the idea that people see different things in the same inkblot and that what they see reflects their personality. The blots are presented on separate cards and handed to the subject in a particular sequence.

rubella German measles, an infection that can affect infant development and cause mental retardation. Rubella-related problems have declined with routine vaccination.

S

sadist A person who derives sexual pleasure from inflicting pain on or humiliating others. Sadism is considered a sexual variant if it involves cooperative, willing partners and a sexual offence if it involves unwilling partners.

savants Mentally deficient persons who nevertheless display islets of exceptional ability in areas such as mathematics, music, or art, or unusual feats of memory. A small proportion of those persons with *autism* who do not fall within the normal range of intelligence are savants.

scanning behaviours One symptom of generalized anxiety disorder (GAD), consisting in inappropriate watchfulness of one's surroundings for possible threats.

schizoaffective disorder A disorder related to *schizophrenia* characterized by sufficient symptoms for both an affective episode (depression, *mania*, or mixed) and *schizophrenia*.

schizo-aphasia *See* **word salad**.

schizoid A personality type in the "Odd and Eccentric Disorders" cluster whose primary features are a seeming determination to avoid intimate involvement with others and an absence of intense emotions.

schizophrenia One of the most serious psychological disorders, characterized by *delusions, hallucinations,* and *disorganized speech*. There are overall, adverse changes in thought, perception, emotion, and motor behaviour, and a feeling of *depersonalization*. Behaviour in some instances appears to be "autistic," in the sense of being governed by internal stimuli or private events. The individual may be unresponsive to environmental stimuli that would normally prompt reactions, or may respond in a way that suggests a distorted interpretation of the stimuli. Ordinary objects or events seem to take on a marked personal significance. There is pronounced disruption of cognitive transactions: thought and language appear to become loosened from the normal constraints that make for coherent sequences of ideas and distinguish fantasy from reality. Often, some notion or theme involving malevolent forces or inordinate personal power increasingly commands the individual's attention. Many schizophrenics appear to lose their intensity. Language may become impoverished, with little apparent effort or success at communication. They may become withdrawn socially and exhibit little interest in formerly enjoyable pursuits. Attention span may be markedly reduced. From the Greek *schizein*, "to split," and *phrenos*, "mind."

schizophreniform disorder A disorder related to *schizophrenia* with symptomatology similar to that of schizophrenia, but whose duration is between one and six months, the lower limit for a diagnosis of schizophrenia. A somewhat problematic concept, since what distinguishes it from schizophrenia is simply its duration.

schizotypal A personality type in the "Odd and Eccentric Disorders" cluster whose primary features are eccentricity of thought and behaviour and social isolation. The thinking of schizotypal persons tends to be magical and full of odd beliefs. They typically believe in paranormal phenomena, but create odd, idiosyncratic combinations of beliefs or interpret commonplace occurrences in bizarre ways.

science Knowledge obtained by observation and experimentation, critically tested, systematized, and brought under general principles. From the Latin *scientia* ("knowledge").

seasonal affective disorder (SAD) A unipolar affective disorder characterized by a vulnerability to environmental sunlight changes and a pattern of cyclic and time-limited mood problems.

secondary appraisals In the *transactional model* of stress, a set of *appraisals* that occur after a *primary appraisal* if the individual concludes there is an element of threat, equivalent to the question: Is there anything I can do about this?

secondary dementia A *dementia* in which cognitive impairment is the result of a disease whose primary manifestations are physical.

secondary dementia A type of *dementia* in which the symptoms of cognitive loss are secondary to—that is, follow as a result of—other disorders and, although irreversible, are not inherently degenerative. For example, dementia may occur as part of the end stage of a variety of diseases such as Parkinson's, Huntington's, AIDS, and cerebrovascular disease. *See also primary dementia*.

secondary gain In the psychodynamic view of *somatoform disorders*, a motivation for sickness behaviour consisting in the attention and avoidance of responsibility the symptom brings.

secondary prevention A type of *prevention* practised after the disease is identified but before it has caused suffering and disability (for example, the control of blood sugar early in the course of diabetes to prevent systemic damage). *See also primary prevention* and *tertiary prevention*.

selective serotonin reuptake inhibitors (SSRIs) One of the three known major classes of antidepressants. SSRIs, as their name suggests, delay the process of reuptake of neurotransmitters so that they remain available longer to maintain optimal neuronal firing rates. They include fluoxetine (Prozac), sertraline (Zoloft), and paraxetine (Paxil). *See also tricyclics* and *monoamine oxidase inhibitors (MAOIs)*.

self-actualization In Abraham H. Maslow's theory, an actualization of one's potential arrived at by satisfaction of a hierarchy of needs visualized as a pyramid. At the base are biological or survival needs; the next step up is the need for friendship and affiliation; finally, there is an assurance of self-worth, which comes from giving and receiving love and from an internalized sense of self-esteem. In Maslow's view, abnormal or dysfunctional behaviour results from a failure to attain the self-esteem necessary to achieve self-actualization.

self-efficacy A self-perception that results from beliefs people have about their ability to control events that affect their lives.

self-instructional training A cognitive-behavioural approach to therapy that aims to train individuals in effective strategies for talking themselves through difficult challenges (for example, stay calm, focus on the task, don't get carried away by your anger).

sensate focus The final component in sex therapy programs, essentially a form of desensitization applied to sexual fears.

separation anxiety disorder (SAD) A children's disorder characterized by severe and excessive anxiety, even panic, at the prospect of separation from parents or others to whom the child is emotionally attached.

separation-individuation A process identified by Margaret Mahler by which the child learns to distinguish the self from others.

set point A comfortable biological weight range that our bodies seek to maintain, arrived at through a complex interaction between nature and nurture, and in the long run fairly stable and difficult to change. When humans or animals are underfed or overfed, a biological mechanism seeks to maintain weight at the set point by either slowing or speeding up metabolism. Many of the symptoms seen in eating-disordered individuals may be due to the consequences of being significantly below their normal set point.

sexual aversion disorder A sexual dysfunction characterized by persistent or recurrent, extreme aversion to, and avoidance of, almost all genital sex with a partner, causing marked distress or interpersonal difficulty. May also include panic attacks, extreme anxiety, and avoidance of partners.

sexual orientation One of the three aspects of the development of gender identity, referring to the preferred age and sex of one's partner. Gays and lesbians have a same-sex orientation, whereas heterosexuals have an opposite-sex orientation. *See also gender role* and *gender identity*.

sexual response cycle The sequence of changes that occur in the body with increased sexual arousal, orgasm, and the return to the unaroused state, noted by William Masters and Virginia Johnson.

sign A certain feature of a category of abnormal behaviour that a clinician can recognize, although the patient is often unaware of it. *See also symptom*.

single-factor explanation A theory that attributes the supposed causal chain of dysfunctional behaviour to a single factor.

single-subject design A nonexperimental investigative method that, like the case study, is based on the intense investigation of an individual subject, but avoids many criticisms of the case study by using experimentally accepted procedures. It uses observable behaviours that are quantifiable, quantifies the presence of the behaviour prior to any intervention, systematically applies readily observable and quantifiable interventions, and measures the effects of the intervention on the behaviours of the subject.

situational sexual dysfunctions Any sexual dysfunction which is apparent only with a certain sexual partner of the sufferer (for example, the client's spouse).

sleep apnea A sleep disorder characterized by episodes of cessation of breathing (apnea) that last at least ten seconds. Diagnosis requires that there be at least five such episodes per hour of sleep.

sluggish schizophrenia A diagnostic category used in the former USSR whose symptomatology resembles that of *schizophrenia*. However, the category included social maladaptation, defined as illegal acts committed against social institutions, and the so-called delusions of this disorder—which on their own were considered sufficient grounds for a diagnosis—could include ideas about reforming political systems. Thus, this diagnosis appears to have been used as a pretext to incarcerate political dissidents. Also termed *slowly progressive schizophrenia*.

social breakdown A cycle of deterioration of an older person that begins with some circumstance such as loss of mobility or grief, making the person vulnerable and perceived by others as deficient or incompetent; others begin to treat the person in a way that limits his or her opportunities to practice life skills, weakening or eradicating them; this affects the person's self-image, increasing vulnerability and starting the cycle over again. Several passes through this cycle might finally result in a full-blown breakdown. Interventions by family and by society can break the cycle, or even reverse it, starting a cycle of *social reconstruction*. Interventions include counselling, changes in the environment, and education, and can work at any point in the cycle.

social learning theory As originally outlined by Bandura and Walters (1959), a theory that suggested that while *classical* and *operant conditioning* experiences are important, the majority of such experiences are primarily acquired vicariously—that is, by observation of others rather than direct personal experience. This theory has been extended to include not only direct observation of others but also information derived from books, movies, and television.

social reconstruction *See social breakdown*.

social selection theory The theory that people who have *schizophrenia* drift to a lower social status as a result of their symptoms. One of the two explanations offered for the finding that people with schizophrenia are much more likely to come from the lowest socioeconomic class than from any other class. *See also sociogenic theory*.

sociogenic theory The theory that being a member of the lowest social class may result in poorer education, increased stigmatization, and fewer opportunities for economic success, and that to the extent that these factors increase daily stress, social class could contribute to the onset of *schizophrenia*. One of the two explanations offered for the finding that people with schizophrenia are much more likely to come from the lowest socioeconomic class than from any other class. *See also social selection theory*.

sociopath *See antisocial personality disorder*.

somatization disorder A *somatoform disorder* characterized by multiple complaints of physical ailments that do not appear to have any organic basis. These symptoms must cause significant impairment in social and occupational functioning.

somatoform disorders A set of disorders marked by physical symptoms for which there is no known physical cause, excessive preoccupation with minor physical symptoms, or excessive concern about normal bodily functioning.

somatogenesis The idea that psychopathology is caused by biological factors—*soma* meaning "body" in Latin.

SORC Four sets of variables behavioural and cognitively oriented clinicians are concerned with. S stands for *stimuli*, environmental situations that preceded the problem, or in which the problem arose; O stands for *organismic*, factors within the individual that might increase the probability of a behaviour; R stands for overt *responses*—the problem behaviour itself; C stands for *consequences* of the behaviour, particularly those that might reinforce or punish it.

specific phobia A marked and persistent fear and avoidance of specific stimulus or situation. There are four subtypes: (1) animal phobia, (2) environmental phobia (for example, heights, storms), (3) blood-injection-injury phobia, and (4) specific situation phobias (for example, elevators, flying).

specifiers Further descriptors of a patient's condition that capture the natural variation in the expression of affective disturbances, and therefore increase the specificity of diagnoses by conveying important information about salient features that might be otherwise overlooked. For example, one specifier used in conjunction with a diagnosis of *major depressive disorder* is "with melancholic features."

split-half reliability A measure of *internal consistency*, often ascertained by comparing responses on odd-numbered test items with responses on even-numbered test items and seeing if the scores for these responses are correlated.

St. Vitus' Dance An epidemic of mass hysteria, wherein groups of people would suddenly be seized by an irresistible urge to leap about, jumping and dancing, and sometimes convulsing.

Stanford-Binet Scales An intelligence test whose most recent version assesses four general kinds of ability: verbal reasoning, quantitative reasoning, abstract/visual reasoning, and short-term memory. It produces separate scores for each of these functions as well as a global IQ score that summarizes the child's ability. Developed from the work of French psychologist Alfred Binet (1857–1911).

state anxiety A transient emotional experience comprising tension and apprehension (that is, how a person feels right now). *See also trait anxiety*.

statistical significance An attribute of research results when it is extremely unlikely that they could have occurred purely by chance. The standard by which most research is judged as valuable or worthy of being published.

stereotypy The repetition of meaningless gestures or movements. One of the manifestations of a developmental disorder.

stimulants A class of drugs that have a stimulating or arousing effect on the central nervous system, and create their effects by influencing the rate of uptake of the neurotransmitters dopamine and norepinephrine and serotonin at receptor sites in the brain.

stimulus encoding A component of the human brain's information processing that consists in translating sensory stimulation from its raw physical form into a format amenable to higher-order cognitive operations, such as information extraction, taking place in short-term or working memory. For example, in interpreting whether a sentence is a statement or a question, it is first necessary to attach some meaning to its component words or phrases.

stress reactivity paradigm A viewpoint that sees the reaction to stress as important to an understanding of cardiovascular disease.

subject reactivity The change in behaviour often seen when people know they are being observed or filmed. One of the difficulties inherent in *in vivo observation* and *analogue observational settings*.

substance abuse Recurrent substance use that results in significant adverse consequences in social or occupational functioning, or use of a substance that impairs one's performance in hazardous situations, for example drinking and driving.

substance dependence Lack of control over substance use, to the point that a person feels enslaved. Commonly known as *addiction*. *See also* ***physiological dependence*** *and* ***psychological dependence***.

substance intoxication A reversible and temporary condition due to the recent ingestion of, or exposure to, a substance, and characterized by significant maladaptive behavioural or cognitive changes, such as belligerence, disturbed perception, altered mood, and impaired thought processes or motor behaviour.

substance-induced psychotic disorder A disorder related to *schizophrenia* characterized by prominent *hallucinations* and *delusions* that result from the ingestion of a chemical substance (for example, cocaine, marijuana, or an environmental toxin such as carbon monoxide or paint fumes).

superego In Sigmund Freud's theory, the internalization of the moral standards of society inculcated by the child's parents.

supernatural causes Causes beyond the understanding of ordinary mortals, such as the influence of gods, demons, or magic. Psychological dysfunction in various historical periods was thought to result from either possession by demons or the witchcraft of evil people.

switch The transition from one *alter* to another. Occurs suddenly and is often precipitated by stress or some other identifiable cue in the surrounding environment.

symptom A feature of a diagnostic category that a patient recognizes and may find disturbing. *See also* ***sign***.

syndromes Groups of symptoms that tend to occur together.

synergistic Said of drugs whose combined effects exceed or are significantly different from the sum of their individual effects.

systematic desensitization A form of therapy, based on *classical conditioning* processes, that consists in the pairing of anxiety-provoking stimuli with responses incompatible with anxiety.

systolic blood pressure/diastolic blood pressure A measure of the pressure of the blood flowing through the vasculature. It is obtained by finding the number of millimetres of mercury displaced by a sphygmomanometer (blood pressure cuff).

T

temperament An inborn style of interacting with the environment.

tertiary prevention A type of *prevention* practised after suffering or disability from the disease is being experienced, with the goal of preventing further deterioration. *See also* ***primary prevention*** *and* ***secondary prevention***.

testosterone A hormone (the so-called male sex hormone) involved in sexual activity and desire, variations in the level of which can lower or increase sex drive.

test-retest reliability The degree to which a test yields the same results when it is given more than once to the same person. Test-retest reliability can be evaluated by correlating a person's score on a given test with the same person's score on the same test taken at a later time. The higher the correlation between the two scores (as expressed in terms of a correlation coefficient) the more *reliable* it is.

thalidomide A drug prescribed in the 1950s and 60s by European physicians for nausea that was found to cause limb deficiencies or malformations in infants.

THC The chemical delta-9-tetrahydrocannabinol psychoactive effects of *cannabis*. Although the exact mechanisms by which THC exerts its influences is not fully understood, it appears as if it acts upon specific cannabinoid receptors in the body and mimics the effects of naturally occurring substances, including the *endogenous opiates*.

thematic apperception test (TAT) A psychological test using drawings on cards depicting ambiguous social interactions. Those being tested are asked to construct stories about the cards. It is assumed their tales reflect their experiences, outlook on life, and deep-seated needs and conflicts. Validity and reliability of scoring techniques are open to the same criticisms as the those of the Rorschach inkblot test.

therapeutic alliance The relationship between therapist and client, recognized to be a predictor of therapy outcome. Recent research in psychodynamic therapy has underlined its importance.

thought-content symptomatology Psychological symptoms wherein it is the content of thought that is indicative of pathology rather than its manner of expression—for example, *delusions* and *hallucinations*.

thought-form symptomatology Psychological symptoms wherein it is the manner of expression of thought that is indicative of pathology rather than its content—for example, disorganized and incoherent expression of trains of ideas that are loosely connected and subject to irrelevant intrusions.

time-limited dynamic psychotherapy (TLDP) A psychodynamic approach that tends to be brief and involve the client in face-to-face contact with the therapist. The TLDP therapist helps identify patterns of interaction with others that strengthen unhelpful thoughts about oneself and others.

token economy A form of therapy in which appropriate behaviours are rewarded with tokens, which may be exchanged for desired objects or privileges.

tolerance The need of a person for increased amounts of an addictive substance to achieve the desired effect.

total peripheral resistance The resistance of the vasculature (blood vessels) to the flow of blood, affected largely by the degree of constriction of the blood vessels. One of the two major variables that determine blood pressure. *See also cardiac output.*

toxic psychosis Hallucinations, delirium, and paranoia caused by repeated high doses of amphetamines.

trait A personal quality that is characteristic of someone ("generous," "creative," etc.), that is, it is persistently displayed over time and in various situations. Every person manifests several traits, the combination of which makes up his or her personality.

trait anxiety A proneness or tendency to experience state anxiety under stressful or threatening conditions (that is, how an individual generally feels). *See also state anxiety.*

transactional model A model of stress the conceives of stress as a property neither of stimulus nor of response, but rather as an ongoing series of transactions between an individual and his or her environment. Central to this formulation is the idea that people constantly evaluate what is happening to them and its implications for themselves.

transactional model One model of how hostility might lead to health risk, which suggests that the behaviour of hostile individuals constructs, by its natural consequences, a social world that is antagonistic and unsupportive, so that both interpersonal stressors and the lack of social support increase vulnerability. A hybrid of the *psychophysiological reactivity model* and the *psychosocial vulnerability model*.

transference In the psychodynamic approach to therapy, the client's action of responding to the therapist as he or she responded to significant figures from his or her childhood (generally the parents). Considered the core of psychoanalytic therapy.

translocation A cause of *Down syndrome* in which part of the 21st chromosome of the human cell breaks off and attaches to another. Individuals with Down syndrome due to translocation have all of the features found in trisomy 21.

transvestite A person who wears the clothing associated with the opposite sex—in order to produce or enhance sexual excitement.

trephination A prehistoric form of surgery possibly intended to let out evil spirits; it involved chipping a hole into a person's skull.

tricyclics One of the three known major classes of antidepressants. Tricyclics enable more neurotransmitters to be released into the synaptic cleft. They include amoxapine (Asendin), amitriptyline (Elavil), imipramine (Tofranil), and doxepin (Sinequan). *See also monoamine oxidase inhibitors (MAOIs)* and *selective serotonin reuptake inhibitors (SSRIs)*.

trisomy 21 The most common type of Down syndrome, in which there is an extra chromosome on pair 21 of the 23 pairs of chromosomes in the human cell.

two-factor model The most influential theory of fear and phobias during the 1960s and 1970s. The model proposed that fears are acquired by *classical conditioning*, but maintained by *operant conditioning*.

Type I Alcoholics One of two types of alcoholics classified on the basis of drinking history. Type I Alcoholics begin drinking in their mid-twenties to thirties, do not typically develop problems with their drinking until middle age, and tend to have relatively few social and occupational problems but are at risk for developing liver disease. Appear to have a lower heritability component than *Type II Alcoholics*.

Type II Alcoholics One of two types of alcoholics classified on the basis of drinking history. Type II Alcoholics develop drinking problems earlier in life, and show antisocial behaviour that can take the form of fights and arrests, but they experience few medical difficulties. *See also Type I Alcoholics*.

U

unconscious In *psychodynamic* theory, the unconscious contains the majority of our memories and drives, which can only be raised to awareness with great difficulty and typically only in response to special techniques (that is, psychoanalytic procedures).

undifferentiated schizophrenia A subtype of schizophrenia that involves a mixture of symptoms, including *paranoid schizophrenia* symptoms.

undifferentiated subtype One of the five official subtypes of *schizophrenia*, a general category for patients who display prominent symptoms but do not fall easily into the *paranoid*, the *disorganized*, or the *catatonic* category.

unipolar disorders Affective disorders in which the change in mood is only in the direction of depression or lowered mood, followed by a return to normal mood with recovery. *See also bipolar disorders*.

universal approach An approach to *prevention* programs designed to include all individuals in a certain geographical area (for example, the neighbourhood, the city, the province) or a certain setting (for example, school, the workplace, a public housing complex).

V

vaginismus A sexual dysfunction characterized by persistent involuntary contraction of the muscles in the outer third of the vagina upon attempts at penetration by the penis, preventing it from occurring.

valid Said of a measurement tool when it measures what it purports to measure. A rigid ruler would be *reliable*; but it would be useless as a measure of temperature.

vascular disease A condition in which the arteries that supply the brain are partly blocked. By far the most common cause of *secondary dementia*, through stroke.

vigilance One symptom of generalized anxiety disorder (GAD), consisting in excessive fearfulness, anxiety, and cautious withdrawal.

voyeurism A form of *paraphilia* that is also a criminal offence, in which a person secretly looks at naked people.

vulnerability-stress perspective A viewpoint from which our current understanding of schizophrenia derives, according to which certain individuals are vulnerable to schizophrenia and develop symptoms when they are exposed to certain stressors.

W

WAIS-R The most recent version of the *Wechsler Adult Intelligence Scale*, published in 1974. Consists of 11 subscales: 6 verbal tests and 5 performance tests.

Wechsler Adult Intelligence Scale, or WAIS. The most widely used IQ tests, designed to measure diverse aspects of intelligence. Developed by David Wechsler (1896–1981). *See also WAIS-R*.

with melancholic features An important specifier that can be used in conjunction with a diagnosis of *major depressive disorder*. Prominent in this type of depression is *anhedonia*. The depressed mood is worst in the morning. Sleep disturbance featuring early morning awakening, significant weight loss, and psychomotor retardation or agitation are also common.

withdrawal Unpleasant and sometimes dangerous symptoms such as nausea, headache, or tremors experienced when an addictive substance is removed from the body.

word salad Nonsense sounds that result inadvertently when a person's thought patterns are so disorganized that ordinary words become jumbled, as in *schizophrenia*. Also known as *schizo-aphasia*.

REFERENCES

Abe, K., & Masui, T. (1981). Age-sex trends of phobic and anxiety symptoms in adolescents. *British Journal of Psychiatry, 138,* 297–302.

Abel, E. L. (1984). *Fetal alcohol syndrome and fetal alcohol effects.* New York: Plenum Press.

Abel, G. G., Barlow, D., Blanchard, E. B., & Guild, D. (1977). The components of rapists' sexual arousal. *Archives of General Psychiatry, 34,* 895–903.

Abel, G. G., Becker, J. V., Mittelman, M. S., Cunningham-Rathner, J., Rouleau, J. L., & Murphy, W. D. (1987). Self-reported sex crimes of nonincarcerated paraphiliacs. *Journal of Interpersonal Violence, 2,* 3–25.

Abel, G. G., Blanchard, E. B., & Becker, J. V. (1978). An integrated treatment program for rapists. In R. T. Rada (Ed.), *Clinical aspects of the rapist* (pp. 161–214). New York: Grune & Stratton.

Abikoff, H. (1987). *Advances in clinical child psychology.* New York: Plenum.

Abikoff, H., & Klein, R. G. (1992). Attention-deficit/hyperactivity and conduct disorder: Comorbidity and implications for treatment. *Journal of Consulting and Clinical Psychology, 60,* 881–892.

Abraham, J. P., & Crooks, V. J. (Eds.) (1984). *Geriatric mental health.* Toronto, ON: Harcourt Press.

Abraham, S. F., & Beumont, P.J.V. (1982). How patients describe bulimia or binge eating. *Psychological Medicine, 12,* 625–635.

Abrahamson, D. J., Barlow, D. H., & Abrahamson, L. S. (1989). Differential effects of performance demand and distraction on sexually functional and dysfunctional males. *Journal of Abnormal Psychology, 98,* 241–247.

Abramowitz, J. S. (1997). Effectiveness of psychological and pharmacological treatments for obsessive-compulsive disorder: A quantitative review. *Journal of Consulting and Clinical Psychology, 65,* 44–52.

Abramson, L. Y., Metalsky, G. I., & Alloy, L. B. (1989). Hopelessness depression: A theory-based subtype of depression. *Psychological Review, 96,* 358–372.

Achenbach, T. M. (1982). *Developmental Psychopathology.* New York: John Wiley & Sons.

Achenbach, T. M., & Howell, C. T. (1993). Are American children's problems getting worse? A 13 year comparison. *Journal of the American Academy of Child and Adolescent Psychiatry, 32,* 1145–1154.

Ackerknect, E. H. (1968). *Short history of psychiatry.* (S. Wolff, Trans.). New York: Hafner Publishing.

Acklin, M. W., McDowell, C. J., & Orndoff, S. (1992). Statistical power and the Rorschach: 1975–1991. *Journal of Personality Assessment, 59,* 366–379.

Adams, H. E., Lohr, B. A., & Wright, L. W. (1995, March). *Is homophobia associated with homosexual arousal?* Paper presented at the Southeastern Psychological Association Conference, Savannah, GA.

Addiction Research Foundation (1992). Abstinence and reduced drinking: Two approaches to alcohol treatment. *Best advice.* Toronto: Addiction Research Foundation.

Addiction Research Foundation (1997). *Addiction Research Foundation Website.* Available: http://www.arf.org

Adlaf, E. M., Ivis, F. J., Smart, R. G., & Walsh, G. W. (1995). *The Ontario student drug use survey: 1977–1995.* Toronto: Addiction Research Foundation.

Adlaf, E., Ivis, F. J., & Smart, R. (1994). *Alcohol and other drug use among Ontario adults in 1994 and changes since 1977.* Toronto: Addiction Research Foundation.

Adlaf, E., Smart, R., & Walsh, G. (1993). *The Ontario student drug use survey: 1977–1993.* Toronto: Addiction Research Foundation.

Adler, D. A., Drake, R. E., & Teague, G. B. (1990). Clinicians' practices in personality assessment: Does gender influence the use of DSM-III axis II? *Comprehensive Psychiatry, 31,* 125–133.

Adler, N. E., Boyce, T., Chesney, M. A., Cohen, S., Folkman, S., Kahn, R. L., & Syme, S. L. (1994). Socioeconomic status and health: The challenge of the gradient. *American Psychologist, 49,* 15–24.

Agras, W. S., Telch, C. F., Arnow, B., Eldredge, K., Detzer, M. J., Henderson, J., & Marnell, M. (1995). Does interpersonal therapy help patients with binge eating disorder who fail to respond to cognitive-behavioral therapy? *Journal of Consulting and Clinical Psychology, 63,* 356–360.

Ainsworth, M.D.S., & Bowlby, J. (1991). An ethological approach to personality development. *American Psychologist, 46,* 333–341.

Albee, G. W. (1982). Preventing psychopathology and promoting human potential. *American Psychologist, 37,* 1043–1050.

Albee, G. W. (1986a). Advocates and adversaries of prevention. In M. Costlier & S. E. Goldston (Eds.), *A decade of progress in primary prevention* (pp. 309–332). Hanover, NH: University Press of New England.

Albee, G. W. (1986b). Toward a just society: Lessons from observations on the primary prevention of psychopathology. *American Psychologist, 41,* 891–898.

Albee, G. W. (1990). The futility of psychotherapy. *Journal of Mind and Behavior, 11,* 369–384.

Albee, G. W. (1996). Revolutions and counterrevolutions in prevention. *American Psychologist, 51,* 1130–1133.

Alden, L. (1989). Short-term structured treatment for avoidant personality disorder. *Journal of Consulting and Clinical Psychology, 57,* 756–764.

Aldwin, C. (1994). *Stress, coping, and development.* New York: Guilford Press.

Alexander, F. (1950). *Psychosomatic medicine: Its principles and applications.* New York: Norton.

Alexander, J. F., & Parsons, B. V. (1982). *Functional family therapy*. Monterey, CA: Brooks/Cole.

Alford, B. A., & Correia, C. J. (1994). Cognitive therapy for schizophrenia: Theory and empirical status. *Behavioral Therapy, 25,* 17–33.

Al-Issa, I. (1968). Cross-cultural study of symptomatology in schizophrenia. *Canadian Journal of Psychiatry, 13,* 147–156.

Al-Issa, I. (1977). Social and cultural aspects of hallucinations. *Psychological Bulletin, 84,* 570–587.

Allebeck, P. (1989). Schizophrenia: A life-shortening disease. *Schizophrenia Bulletin, 15,* 81–90.

Allen, J. S., & Sarich, V. M. (1988). Schizophrenia in an evolutionary perspective. *Perspectives in Biology and Medicine, 32,* 132–153.

Allodi, F. A., Kedward, H. B., & Robertson, M. (1977). "Insane but guilty": Psychiatric patients in jail. *Canada's Mental Health, 25,* 3–7.

Alterman, A. I., & Cacciola, J. S. (1991). The antisocial personality disorder diagnosis in substance abusers. *Journal of Nervous and Mental Disease, 179,* 401–409.

Althof, S. E., & Seftel, A. D. (1995). The evaluation and management of erectile dysfunction. *Psychiatric Clinics of North America, 18,* 171–192.

Althof, S. E., & Turner, L. A. (1992). Self-injection therapy and external vacuum devices in the treatment of erectile dysfunction: Methods and outcome. In R. C. Rosen & S. R. Leiblum (Eds.), *Erectile disorders: Assessment and treatment* (pp. 283–309). New York: Guilford Press.

Altman, J., Everitt, B. J., Glautier, S., Markou, A., Nutt, D., Oretti, R., Phillips, G. D., & Robbins, T. W. (1996). The biological, social and clinical bases of drug addiction: Commentary and debate. *Psychopharmacology, 125,* 285–345.

Amato, P. R., & Keith, B. (1991). Parental divorce and the well-being of children: A meta-analysis. *Psychological Bulletin, 110,* 26–46.

American Association on Mental Retardation (1992). *Mental retardation: Definition, classification and systems of support.* (9th ed.). Washington, DC: AAMR.

American Psychiatric Association (1952). *Diagnostic and statistical manual of mental disorders.* (1st ed.). Washington, DC: American Psychiatric Association.

American Psychiatric Association (1968). *Diagnostic and statistical manual of mental disorders.* (2nd ed.). Washington, DC: American Psychiatric Association.

American Psychiatric Association (1978). *Electroconvulsive Therapy.* [Task Force Report 14]. Washington, DC: American Psychiatric Association.

American Psychiatric Association (1980). *Diagnostic and statistical manual of mental disorders.* (3rd ed.). Washington, DC: American Psychiatric Association.

American Psychiatric Association (1987). *Diagnostic and statistical manual of mental disorders.* (3rd ed. rev.). Washington, DC: American Psychiatric Association.

American Psychiatric Association (1990). *The practice of ECT: Recommendations for treatment, training, and privileging.* Washington, DC: American Psychiatric Association.

American Psychiatric Association (1994). *Diagnostic and statistical manual of mental disorders.* (4th ed.). Washington, DC: American Psychiatric Association.

American Psychological Association (1992). Ethical principles of psychologists and code of conduct. *American Psychologist, 47,* 1597–1611.

American Psychosomatic Society (1996). Special Issue: Animal models in psychosomatic research. *Psychosomatic Medicine, 58,* 521–632.

Ames, E. (1992). Development of Romanian orphanage children adopted to Canada. *Canadian Psychology, 33,* 503.

Ames, E., Chisholm, K., Fisher, L., Morison, S. J., Thompson, S., Mainemer, H., Carter, M., Ebbern, H., Ellwood, A. L., Ferrari, M., Gilman, L., Lukie, S., & Savoie, L. A. (1997). *The development of Romanian orphanage children adopted to Canada.* [Final report to National Welfare Grants Program, Human Resources Development Canada]. Burnaby, BC: Simon Fraser University.

Amir, V. (1969). Contact hypothesis in ethnic relations. *Psychological Bulletin, 71,* 319–342.

Ancoli-Israel, S. (1989). Epidemiology of sleep disorders. *Clinics in Geriatric Medicine, 5,* 347–362.

Andersen, A. E. (1990). Diagnosis and treatment of males with eating disorders. In A. E. Andersen (Ed.), *Males with eating disorders* (pp. 133–162). New York: Brunner/Mazel.

Andersen, A. E. (1995). Eating disorders in males. In K. D. Brownell & C. G. Fairburn (Eds.), *Eating disorders and obesity: A comprehensive handbook* (pp. 177–182). New York: Guilford Press.

Andersen, A. E., & Mickalide, A. D. (1983). Anorexia nervosa in the male: An underdiagnosed disorder. *Psychosomatics, 24,* 1066–1075.

Anderson, B. J., & Wold, F. M. (1986). Chronic physical illness and sexual behavior. *Journal of Consulting and Clinical Psychology, 54,* 168–175.

Anderson, B. L., Kiecolt-Glaser, J. K., & Glaser, R. (1994). A biobehavioral model of cancer stress and disease course. *American Psychologist, 49,* 389–404.

Anderson, E. M., & Lambert, M. J. (1995). Short-term dynamically oriented psychotherapy: A review and meta-analysis. *Clinical Psychology Review, 15,* 503–514.

Anderson, J. C., Williams, S., McGee, R., & Silva, P. (1987). DSM-III disorders in preadolescent children. *Archives of General Psychiatry, 44,* 69–76.

Anderson, K. E., Lytton, H., & Romney, D. M. (1986). Mothers' interactions with normal and conduct-disordered boys: Who affects whom? *Developmental Psychology, 22,* 604–609.

Andreasen, N. C. (1987). Creativity and mental illness: Prevalence rates in writers and their first degree relatives. *American Journal of Psychiatry, 144,* 1288–1292.

Andreasen, N. C. (1989). Neural mechanisms of negative symptoms. *British Journal of Psychiatry, 155,* 93–98.

Andreasen, N. C., & Black, D. W. (1995). *Introductory text of psychiatry.* Washington, DC: American Psychiatric Press.

Andreasen, N. C., Hoffman, R. E., & Grove, W. M. (1985). Mapping abnormalities in language and cognition. In M. Alpert (Ed.), *Controversies in schizophrenia: Changes and constancies.* New York: Guilford.

Andreason, N. C., & Bardach, J. (1977). Dysmorphobia: Symptom or disease? *American Journal of Psychiatry, 134,* 673–676.

Andrulonis, P. A., Glueck, B. C., Storebel, C. F., Vogel, N. G., Shapiro, A. L., & Aldrige, D. (1981). Organic brain dysfunction and the borderline syndrome. *Psychiatric Clinics of North America, 4,* 47–66.

Anglin, M. D., Almog, I. J., Fisher, D. G., & Peters, K. R. (1989). Alcohol use by heroin addicts. *American Journal of Alcohol & Drug Abuse, 15,* 191–207.

Angst, J., Baastrup, P. C., Grof, P., Hippius, H., Poldinger, W., & Weis, P. (1973). The course of monopolar depression and bipolar psychoses. *Psychiatry, Neurology and Neurosurgery, 76,* 489–500.

Angus, L. E., & Marziali, E. (1988). A comparison of three measures for the diagnosis of borderline personality disorder. *American Journal of Psychiatry, 145,* 1453–1454.

Anonymous (1996). First person account: Social, economic, and medical effects of schizophrenia. *Schizophrenia Bulletin, 22,* 183–185.

Antoni, M. H., Levine, J., Tischer, P., Green, C., & Millon, T. (1986). Refining personality assessments by combining MCMI high-point profiles and MMPI codes: IV. MMPI 89/98. *Journal of Personality Assessment, 50,* 65–72.

Antoni, M. H., Tischer, P., Levine, J., Green, C., & Millon, T. (1985). Refining personality assessments by combining MCMI high-point profiles and MMPI codes: I. MMPI 28/82. *Journal of Personality Assessment, 49,* 392–398.

Antonnucio, D. O., Danton, W. G., & DeNelsky, G. Y. (1995). Psychotherapy versus medication for depression: Challenging the conventional wisdom with data. *Professional Psychology: Research and Practice, 26,* 574–585.

Antonnucio, D. O., Thomas, M., & Danton, W. G. (1997). A cost-effectiveness analysis of cognitive behavior therapy and fluoxetine (Prozac) in the treatment of depression. *Behavior Therapy, 28,* 187–210.

Antony, M. M., & Swinson, R. P. (1996). *The anxiety disorders and their treatment: A critical analysis of the literature on effective treatments.* Ottawa: Health Canada.

APA. See American Psychiatric Association.

Appelbaum, P. S., & Grisso, T. (1995). The MacArthur treatment competence study. I. Mental illness and competency to consent to treatment. *Law and Human Behavior, 19* (2) 105–126.

Arboleda-Florez, J., & Holley, H. L. (1991). Antisocial burnout: An exploratory study. *Bulletin of the American Academy of Psychiatry and Law, 19,* 173–183.

Armbruster, P., & Kazdin, A. E. (1994). Attrition in child psychotherapy. In T. H. Ollendick & R. J. Prinz (Eds.), *Advances in Clinical Child Psychology* (pp. 81–108). New York: Plenum.

Asarnow, J. R., Asarnow, R. F., Hornstein, N., & Russell, A. (1991). Childhood-onset schizophrenia: Developmental perspectives on schziophrenic disorders. In E. F. Walker (Ed.), *Schizophrenia: A life-course developmental perspective* (pp. 95–122). San Diego: Academic Press.

Asayama, S. (1976). Sexual behavior in Japanese students: Comparisons for 1974, 1960, and 1952. *Archives of Sexual Behavior, 5,* 371–390.

Åsberg, M., Thorèn, P., Träskman, L., Bertilsson, L., & Ringberger, V. (1976). Serotonin depression: a biochemical subgroup within affective disorders? *Science, 191,* 478–80.

Ashely, M. J., Ferrence, R., Room, R., Rankin, J., & Single, E. (1994). Moderate drinking and health: Report of an international symposium. *Canadian Medical Association Journal, 151,* 1–20.

Association of State and Provincial Psychology Boards (1998). *Information for candidates: Examination for professional practice in psychology.* Montgomery, AL: Association of State and Provincial Psychology Boards.

Association/Troubles Anxieux du Québec—ATAQ (1996). *Panic disorder: Too often unrecognized. Consensus report.* Montreal: ATAQ.

Atkinson, L., & Feldman, M. (1994). *Survey of aberrant behaviour and its treatment in persons with developmental disabilities in Ontario.* [Report submitted to Ontario Ministry of Community and Social Services]. Toronto: Ontario Mental Health Foundation.

Attie, J., & Brooks-Gunn, F. (1989). Development of eating problems in adolescent girls: A longitudinal study. *Developmental Psychology, 25,* 70–79.

Austad, C. S., & Aronson, H. (1987). The salience of sex role instructions to mental health professionals. *Sex Roles, 16,* 323–333.

Averill, J. R. (1973). Personal control over aversive stimuli and its relationship to stress. *Psychological Bulletin, 80,* 286–303.

Avery, D. H. (1993). Electroconvulsive therapy. In D. L. Dunner (Ed.), *Current psychiatric therapy* (pp. 524–528). Philadelphia: W. B. Saunders.

Awad, G. A., Saunders, E., & Levene, J. (1984). A clinical study of male adolescent sex offenders. *International Journal of Offender Therapy and Comparative Criminology, 28,* 105–116.

Azrin, N. H. (1976). Improvements in the community-reinforcement approach to alcoholism. *Behaviour Research and Therapy, 14,* 339–348.

Bachman, J. G., O'Malley, P. M., & Johnston, J. (1978). *Youth in transition: Adolescence to adulthood.* Ann Arbor: University of Michigan Institute for Social Research.

Backman, J., & Firestone, P. (1979). *Behavior modification or methylphenidate with hyperactive children: A review.* Canadian Psychological Association Conference.

Baekeland, F., & Lundwall, L. (1975). Dropping out of treatment: A critical review. *Psychological Bulletin, 82,* 738–783.

Baer, J. S., Marlatt, G. A., Kivlahan, D. R., Fromme, K., Larimer, M. E., & Williams, E. (1992). An experimental test of three methods of alcohol risk reduction with young adults. *Journal of Consulting and Clinical Psychology, 60,* 974–979.

Baldwin, R. C., & Jolley, D. J. (1986). The prognosis of depression in old age. *British Journal of Psychiatry, 149,* 574–583.

Ballinger, B., & Yalom, I. (1995). Group therapy in practice. In B. Bongar & L. E. Beutler (Eds.), *Comprehensive textbook of psychotherapy: Theory and practice* (pp. 189–204). New York: Oxford University Press.

Baltes, P. B., & Baltes, M. M. (1990). Psychological perspectives on successful aging: The model of selective optimization with compensation. In P. B. Baltes & M. M. Baltes (Eds.), *Successful Aging* (pp. 1–34). Cambridge, UK: Cambridge University Press.

Bancroft, J. (1989). *Human sexuality and its problems.* New York: Churchill Livingstone.

Bandura, A. (1973). *Aggression: A social learning analysis.* Englewood Cliffs, NJ: Prentice Hall.

Bandura, A. (1976). *Social learning theory.* Englewood Cliffs, NJ: Prentice Hall.

Bandura, A. (1977). Self-efficacy: Toward a unifying theory of behavioral change. *Psychological Review, 84,* 191–215.

Bandura, A. (1986). *Social foundations of thought and action: A social cognitive theory.* New Jersey: Prentice-Hall.

Bandura, A. (1988). Self-efficacy conception of anxiety. *Anxiety Research, 1,* 77–98.

Bandura, A. (1989). Human agency in social cognitive theory. *American Psychologist, 44,* 1175–1184.

Bandura, A. (1997). *Self-efficacy: The exercise of control.* New York: W. H. Freeman.

Bandura, A., & Menlove, F. L. (1968). Factors determining vicarious extinction of avoidance behavior through symbolic modelling. *Journal of Personality and Social Psychology, 8,* 99–108.

Bandura, A., & Walters, R. H. (1959). *Adolescent aggression.* New York: Ronald Press.

Bandura, A., & Walters, R. H. (1963). *Social learning and personality development.* New York: Holt, Rinehart & Winston.

Bandura, A., Ross, D., & Ross, S. A. (1961). Transmission of aggression through imitation of aggressive models. *Journal of Abnormal and Social Psychology, 63,* 575–582.

Bandura, A., Ross, D., & Ross, S. A. (1963). Imitation of film-mediated aggressive models. *Journal of Abnormal and Social Psychology, 66,* 3–11.

Barasch, A., Frances, A., Hurt, S., Clarkin, J., & Cohen, S. (1985). Stability and distinctness of borderline personality disorder. *American Journal of Psychiatry, 142,* 1484–1486.

Barbach, L. G., & Levine, L. (1980). *Shared intimacies.* Garden City, NY: Anchor Press/Doubleday.

Barbaree, H. E. (1990). Stimulus control of sexual arousal: Its role in sexual assault. In W. L. Marshall, D. R. Laws, & H. E. Barbaree, *Handbook of sexual assault: Issues, theories, and treatment of the offender* (pp. 115–142). New York: Plenum Press.

Barbaree, H. E., Marshall, W. L., & Lanthier, R. D. (1979). Deviant sexual arousal in rapists. *Behaviour Research and Therapy, 8,* 229–239.

Barbee, J. G., & McLaulin, J. B. (1990). Anxiety disorders: Diagnosis and pharmacotreapy in the elderly. *Psychiatric Annals, 20,* 439–445.

Barefoot, J. C. (1992). Developments in the measurement of hostility. In H. S. Friedman (Ed.), *Hostility, coping and health* (pp.13–31). Washington, DC: American Psychological Association.

Barefoot, J. C., & Schroll, M. (1996). Symptoms of depression, acute myocardial infarction and total mortality in a community sample. *Circulation, 93,* 1976–1980.

Barefoot, J. C., Dodge, K. A., Peterson, B. L., Dahlstrom, W. G., & Williams, R. B. (1989). The Cook-Medley Hostility Scale: Item content and ability to predict survival. *Psychosomatic Medicine, 51,* 46–57.

Barkley, R. A. (1987). *Defiant children: A clinician's manual for parent training.* New York: Guilford.

Barkley, R. A. (1996). Attention-deficit/hyperactivity disorder. In E. J. Mash & R. A. Barkley (Eds.), *Child psychopathology* (pp. 63–112). New York: Guilford Press.

Barkley, R. A., Fischer, M., Edelbrock, C. S., & Smallish, L. (1990). The adolescent outcome of hyperactive children diagnosed by research criteria: I. An 8 year prospective follow-up study. *Journal of the American Academy of Child and Adolescent Psychiatry, 29,* 546–557.

Barloon, T. J., & Noyes, R. (1997). Charles Darwin and panic disorder. *Journal of the American Medical Association, 277* (2), 138–141.

Barlow, D. H. (1988). *Anxiety and its disorders.* New York: Guilford Press.

Barlow, D. H. (1991). The nature of anxiety: Anxiety, depression, and emotional disorders. In R. M. Rapee & D. H. Barlow (Eds.), *Chronic anxiety, generalized anxiety disorder and mixed anxiety-depression.* New York: Guilford Press.

Barlow, D. H. (1994). Psychological interventions in the area of managed competition. *Clinical Psychology, Science and Practice, 1,* 109–122.

Barlow, D. H., & Durand, M. V. (1995). *Abnormal Psychology: An Integrative Approach.* New York: Brooks/Cole.

Barlow, D. H., & Durand, V. M. (1995). *Abnormal psychology: An integrative approach.* New York: Brooks/Cole.

Barlow, D. H., & Durand, V. M. (1995). Substance-related disorders. In *Abnormal psychology: An integrated approach.* New York: Brooks/Cole.

Barlow, M., & Campbell, B. (1995). *Straight through the heart: How the Liberals abandoned the just society.* Toronto: Harper Collins.

Barnard, P. J., & Teasdale, J. D. (1991). Interacting cognitive subsystems: A systematic approach to cognitive-affective interaction and change. *Cognition and Emotion, 5,* 1–39.

Barnes, G. M., Farrell, M. P., & Cairns, A. L. (1986). Parental socialization factors and adolescent drinking behaviors. *Journal of Marriage and the Family, 48,* 27–36.

Barnett, P. A., Spence, J. D., Manuck, S. B., & Jennings, J. R. (1997). Psychological stress and the progression of carotid artery disease. *Journal of Hypertension, 15,* 49–55.

Baroff, G. S. (1986). *Mental retardation: Nature, cause and management.* (2nd ed.). Washington: Hemisphere Publishing Corp.

Baron, M., Risch, N., Levitt, M., & Gruen, R. (1985). Familial transmission of schizotypal and borderline personality disorders. *American Journal of Psychiatry, 142,* 927–934.

Baron, R. A., & Byrne, D. (1977). *Social psychology: Understanding human interaction.* (2nd ed.). Boston: Allyn and Bacon.

Baron, R.A., Earhard, B., & Ozier, M. (1998). *Psychology.* (2nd Canadian ed.) Scarborough: Allyn and Bacon Canada.

Baron-Cohen, S. (1989). The autistic child's theory of mind: A case of specific developmental delay. *Journal of Child Psychology and Psychiatry, 30,* 285–297.

Baron-Cohen, S. (1995). *Mindblindness: An essay on autism and theory.* Cambridge, MA: MIT Press.

Baron-Cohen, S., Leslie, A., & Frith, U. (1985). Does the autistic child have a "theory of mind"? *Cognition, 21,* 37–46.

Barraclough, K. B., Bunch, J., Nelson, B., & Sainsbury, P. (1974). A hundred cases of suicide: clinical aspects. *British Journal of Psychiatry, 125,* 355–373.

Barrera, R. D., Lobato-Barrera, D., & Sulzer-Azaroff, B. (1980). A simultaneous treatment comparison of three expressive language training programs with a mute autistic child. *Journal of Autism and Developmental Disorders, 10,* 21–37.

Barrett, F. M. (1980). Sexual experience, birth control usage, and sex education of unmarried Canadian university students: Changes between 1968 and 1978. *Archives of Sexual Behavior, 9,* 367–390.

Barrett, P. M., Dadds, M. R., & Rapee, R. M. (1996). Family treatment of childhood anxiety: A controlled trial. *Journal of Consulting and Clinical Psychology, 64,* 333–342.

Barsky, A. J., & Klerman, G. L. (1983). Overview: Hypochondriasis, bodily complaints and somatic styles. *American Journal of Psychiatry, 140,* 273–281.

Barsky, A. J., Goodson, J. D., Lane, R. S., & Cleary, P. D. (1988). The amplification of somatic symptoms. *Psychosomatic Medicine, 50,* 510–519.

Barsky, A. J., Wyshak, G., & Klerman, G. L. (1986). Hypochondriasis: An evaluation of the DSM-III criteria in medical outpatients. *Archives of General Psychiatry, 43,* 493–500.

Barsky, A. J., Wyshak, G., & Klerman, G. L. (1992). Psychiatric co-morbidity in DSM-III-R hypochondriasis. *Archives of General Psychiatry, 49,* 101–108.

Barsky, A. J., Wyshak, G., Klerman, G. L., & Latham, K. S. (1990). The prevalence of hypochondriasis in medical outpatients. *Social Psychiatry and Psychiatric Epidemiology, 25,* 89–94.

Barta, P. E., Pearlson, G. D., Powers, R. E., Richards, S. S., & Tune, L. E. (1990). Auditory hallucinations and smaller superior temporal gyral volume in schizophrenia. *American Journal of Psychiatry, 147,* 1457–1462.

Bartholomew, K. (1990). Avoidance of intimacy: An attachment perspective. *Journal of Personal and Social Relationships, 7,* 147–178.

Barton, S. (1994). Chaos, self-organisation, and psychology. *American Psychologist, 49,* 5–14.

Basco, M., & Rush, A. J. (1996). *Cognitive-behavioral therapy for bipolar disorder.* New York: Guilford.

Bassett, A. S. (1989). Chromosome 5 and schizophrenia: Implications for genetic linkage studies. *Schizophrenia Bulletin, 15,* 393–402.

Bassett, A. S., Bury, A., & Honer, W. G. (1994). Testing Liddle's three-syndrome model in families with schizophrenia. *Schizophrenia Research, 12,* 213–221.

Bassett, A. S., Jones, B. D., McGillivray, B. C., & Pantzar, J. T. (1988). Partial trisomy chromosome 5 cosegregating with schizophrenia. *The Lancet, 1,* 799–801.

Bateson, G., Jackson, D. D., Haley, J., & Weakland, J. (1956). Toward a theory of schizophrenia. *Behavioral Science, 1,* 251–264.

Batshaw, M. L., & Perret, Y. M. (1986). *Children with handicaps. A medical primer.* Baltimore: Paul Brookes.

Baumbach, J., & Turner, L. A. (1992). Female gender disorder: A new model and clinical applications. *Journal of Psychology and Human Sexuality, 5,* 107–129.

Baxter, C. (1989). Parent-perceived attitudes of professionals: Implications for service providers. *Disability, Handicap & Society, 4,* 259–269.

Baxter, D. J., Barbaree, H. E., & Marshall, W. L. (1986). Sexual responses to consenting and forced sex in a large sample of rapists and nonrapists. *Behaviour Research and Therapy, 24,* 5513–5520.

Baxter, L. R., Schwartz, J. M., Bergman, K. S., Szuba, M. P., Guze, B. H., Mazziotta, J. C., Alazraki, A., Selin, C. E., Ferng, H. K., Munford, P., & Phelps, M. E. (1992). Caudate glucose metabolic rate changes with both drug and behavior therapy for obsessive-compulsive disorder. *Archives of General Psychiatry, 49,* 681–689.

Beach, S.R.H., & O'Leary, K. D. (1992). Treating depression in the context of marital discord: Outcome and predictors of response of marital therapy versus cognitive therapy. *Behavior Therapy, 23,* 507–528.

Bebko, J. M., Perry, A., & Bryson, S. (1996). Multiple method validation study of Facilitated Communication: II. Individual differences and subgroup results. *Journal of Autism and Developmental Disorders, 26,* 19–42.

Beck, A. T. (1967). *Depression: Causes and treatment.* Philadelphia: University of Pennsylvania Press.

Beck, A. T. (1967). *Depression: Clinical, experimental and theoretical aspects.* New York: Harper and Row.

Beck, A. T. (1976). *Cognitive therapy and the emotional disorders.* New York: International Universities Press.

Beck, A. T. (1996). Beyond belief: A theory of modes, personality, and psychopathology. In P. M. Salkovskis (Ed.), *Frontiers of cognitive therapy* (pp. 1–25). New York: Oxford University Press.

Beck, A. T., & Emery, G. (1985). *Anxiety disorders and phobias: A cognitive perspective.* New York: Basic Books.

Beck, A. T., & Ward, C. H. (1961). Dreams of depressed patients: Characteristic themes in manifest content. *Archives of General Psychiatry, 5,* 462–467.

Beck, A. T., Brown, G., Berchick, R. J., Stewart, B. L., & Steer, R. A. (1990). Relationship between hopelessness and ultimate suicide: A replication with psychiatric outpatients. *American Journal of Psychiatry, 147,* 190–195.

Beck, A. T., Epstein, N., Brown, G., & Steer, R. A. (1988). An inventory for measuring clinical anxiety: Psychometric properties. *Journal of Consulting and Clinical Psychology, 56,* 893–987.

Beck, A. T., Freeman, A., Pretzer, J., Davis, D. D., Fleming, B., Ottaviani, R., Beck, J., Simon, K. M., Padesky, C., Meyer, J., & Trexler, L. (1990). *Cognitive therapy of personality disorders.* New York: Guilford.

Beck, A. T., Rush, P. J., Shaw, B. F., & Emery, G. (1979). *Cognitive therapy of depression.* New York: Guilford.

Beck, A. T., Ward, C. H., Mendelson, M., Mock, J. E., & Erbaugh, J. K. (1962). Reliability of psychiatric diagnosis: II. A study of consistency of clinical judgements and ratings. *American Journal of Psychiatry, 119,* 351–357.

Beck, A. Y., & Beck, R. W. (1972). Screening depressed patients in family practice: A rapid technique. *Postgraduate Medicine, December,* 81–85.

Beck, J. C. (1978). Social influences on the prognosis of schizophrenia. *Schizophrenia Bulletin, 4* (1), 86–90.

Beck, J. G. (1993). Vaginismus. In W. O'Donohue & J. G. Greer (Eds.), *Handbook of sexual dysfunctions: Assessment and treatment* (pp. 381–397). Boston: Allyn and Bacon.

Beck, K. A., & Ogloff, J.R.P. (1995). Child abuse reporting in British Columbia: Psychologists' knowledge of and compliance with the reporting law. *Professional Psychology: Research and Practice, 26* (3), 245–251.

Beck, K., Ogloff, J.R.P., & Corbishley, A. (1994). Teachers' knowledge of, compliance with, and attitudes toward mandatory child abuse reporting. *Canadian Journal of Education, 19,* 15–29.

Beckman, P. J. (1991). Comparison of mothers' and fathers' perceptions of the effect of young children with and without disabilities. *American Journal on Mental Retardation, 95,* 585–595.

Beech, A. R., McManus, D., Baylis, G., Tipper, S. P., et al. (1991). Individual differences in cognitive processes: Towards an explanation of schizophrenic symptomatology. *British Journal of Psychiatry, 82,* 417–426.

Beers, C. (1908). *A mind that found itself.* New York: Doubleday.

Behar, D., & Stewart, M. A. (1982). Aggressive conduct disorder of children: The clinical history and direct observations. *Acta Pscyhiatrica Scandinavica, 65,* 210–220.

Beitcham, J. H., Zucker, K. J., Hood, J. E., DaCosta, G. A., Akman, D., & Cassavia, E. (1992). A review of the longterm effects of child sexual abuse. *Child Abuse and Neglect, 16,* 101–118.

Bellissimo, A., & Steffy, R. A. (1972). Redundancy-associated deficit in schizophrenic reaction time performance. *Journal of Abnormal Psychology, 80,* 299–307.

Bellissimo, A., & Steffy, R. A. (1975). Contextual influences on crossover in the reaction time performance of schizophrenics. *Journal of Abnormal Psychology, 84,* 210–220.

Bender, L. (1938). *A visual motor gestalt test and its clinical use.* New York: American Psychiatric Association.

Bender, L. (1938). The Visual Motor Gestalt Test and its clinical use. *Archives of Neurology and Psychiatry, 30,* 514–537.

Benjamin, L. S. (1979). Use of structural analysis of social behavior (SASB) and Marcov chains to study dyadic interactions. *Journal of Abnormal Psychology, 88* (3), 303–319.

Benjamin, L. T. (1996). Lightner Witmer's legacy to American psychology. *American Psychologist, 51* (3), 235–236.

Benjamin, L. T. (Ed., 1988). *A history of psychology: Critical sources and contemporary research.* New York: McGraw-Hill Books.

Bennett, A. E. (1947). Mad doctors. *Journal of Nervous and Mental Disease, 106,* 11–18.

Benowitz, N. (1990). Clinical pharmacology of caffeine. *Annual Review of Medicine, 41,* 277–288.

Berg, F. M. (1995). *Health risks of weight loss.* (3rd ed.). Hettinger, ND: Healthy Weight Journal.

Berg, I., Butler, A., & Hall, G. (1976). The outcome of adolescent school phobia. *British Journal of Psychiatry, 128,* 80–85.

Bergin, A. E. (1971). The evaluation of therapeutic outcomes. In A. E. Bergin & S. L. Garfield (Eds.), *The evaluation of therapeutic outcomes* (pp. 217–270). New York: Wiley.

Berk, L. E. (1993). *Infants, children and adolescents.* New York: Allyn and Bacon.

Berlin, F. S., Meinecke, C. F. (1981). Treatment of sex offenders with antiandrogenic medication: Conceptualization, review of treatment modalities, and preliminary findings. *American Journal of Psychiatry, 138,* 601–607.

Berlin, I. N. (1987). Suicide among American Indian adolescents: an overview. *Suicide & Life-threatening Behavior, 17* (3), 218–232.

Berman, A. (1994). "To engrave herself on all our memories": The impact of suicide on psychotherapists. In B. L. Mishara (Ed.), *The impact of suicide.* New York: Springer.

Berman, W. H., & Sperling, M. B. (1994). The structure and function of adult attachment. In M. B. Sperling & W. H. Berman (Eds.), *Attachment in adults: Clinical and developmental perspectives* (pp. 3–28). New York: Guilford.

Berney, T., Kolvin, I., Bhate, S. R., Garside, R. F., Jeans, J., Kay, B., & Scarth, L. (1981). School phobia: A therapeutic trial with clomipramine and short-term outcome. *British Journal of Psychiatry, 138,* 110–118.

Bernstein, D. P., Cohen, P., Velez, C. N., Schwab-Stone, M., Siever, L. J., & Shinsato, L. (1993). Prevalence and stability of the DSM-III-R personality disorders in a community-based survey of adolescents. *American Journal of Psychiatry, 50,* 1237–1243.

Bernstein, E. M., & Putnam, F. W. (1986). Development, reliability and validity of a dissociation scale. *Journal of Nervous and Mental Disease, 174,* 727–735.

Bernstein, G. A., & Borchardt, C. M. (1991). Anxiety disorders of childhood and adolescence: A critical review. *Journal of the American Academy of Child and Adolescent Psychiatry, 30,* 519–532.

Bernstein, G. A., Borchardt, C. M., & Perwien, A. R. (1996). Anxiety disorders in children and adolescents: A review of the past 10 years. *Journal of the American Academy of Child and Adolescent Psychiatry, 35* (9), 1110–1119.

Bernstein, G. A., Garfinkel, B. D., & Borchardt, C. M. (1990). Comparative studies of pharmacotherapy for school refusal. *Journal of the American Academy of Child and Adolescent Psychiatry, 29,* 773–781.

Bernstein, S. M., Steiner, B. W., Glaiser, J.T.D., & Muir, C. F. (1981). Changes in patients with gender identity problems after parental death. *American Journal of Psychiatry, 138,* 41–45.

Berrios, G. E. (1987). Commentary on the fundamental symptoms of dementia praecox or the group of schizophrenia. In C. Thompson (Ed.), *The origins of modern psychiatry* (pp. 239–243). New York: Wiley.

Berry, J. W., Kim, U., Power, S., Young, M., & Bujaki, M. (1989). Acculturation attitudes in plural societies. *Applied Psychology: An International Review, 38,* 185–206.

Bertschy, G. (1995). Methadone maintenance treatment: An update. *European Archives of Psychiatry and Clinical Neuroscience, 245* (2), 114–124.

Beskow, J., Gottfires, C. G., Roos, B. E., & Winblad, B. (1996). Determination of monoamine and monoamine metabolites in the human brain: post-mortem studies in a group of suicides and a control group. *Acta Psychiatrica Scandinavica, 53,* 7–20.

Betancourt, H., & Lopez, S. R. (1993). The study of culture, ethnicity, and race in American psychology. *American Psychologist, 48,* 629–637.

Bethell, L. (1984). *The Cambridge history of Latin America. Volume I: Colonial Latin America.* New York: Cambridge University Press.

Bettelheim, B. (1967). *The empty fortress.* New York: Free Press.

Beumont, P.J.V., & Touyz, S. W. (1995). The nutritional management of anorexia and bulimia nervosa. In K. D. Brownell & C. G. Fairburn (Eds.), *Eating disorders and obesity: A comprehensive handbook* (pp. 306–312). New York: Guilford Press.

Beumont, P.J.V., Arthur, B., Russell, J. D., & Touyz, S. W. (1994). Excessive physical activity in dieting disorder patients: Proposals for a supervised exercise programme. *International Journal of Eating Disorders, 15,* 21–36.

Beutler, L. E., Engle, D., Mohr, D., Daldrup, R. J., Bergan, J., Meredith, K., & Merry, W. (1991). Predictors of differential response to cognitive, experiential, and self-directed psychotherapeutic procedures. *Journal of Consulting and Clinical Psychology, 59,* 333–340.

Beutler, L. E., Machado, P.P.P., & Neufeldt, S. A. (1994). Therapist variables. In A. E. Bergin & S. L. Garfield (Eds.), *Handbook of psychotherapy and behavior change* (4th ed., pp. 229–269). New York: Wiley.

Biedel, D. C. (1988). Psychophysiological assessment of anxious emotional states in children. *Journal of Abnormal Psychology, 97,* 80–82.

Biederman, J., Faraone, S. V., Keenan, K., Benjamin, J., Krefcher, B., Moore, C., Sprich-Buckminster, S., Ugaglia, K., Jellinek, M. S., Steingard, R., Spencer, T., Norman, D., Kolodny, R., Kraus, I., Perrin, J., Keller, M. B., & Tsuang, M. T. (1992). Further evidence for family-genetic resk factors in attention-deficit/hyperactivity disorder. *Archives of General Psychiatry, 49,* 728–738.

Biederman, J., Faraone, S. V., Marrs, A., Moore, P., Garcia, J. Ablon, S., Mick, E., Gershon, J., & Kearns, M. E. (1997). Panic disorder and agoraphobia in consecutively referred children and adolescents. *Journal of the American Academy of Child and Adolescent Psychiatry, 36,* 214–223.

Biederman, J., Faraone, S., Keenan, K., & Tsuang, M. T. (1991). Evidence of a familial association between attention deficit disorder and major affective disorders. *Archives of General Psychiatry, 48,* 633–642.

Biederman, J., Rosenbaum, J. F., Bouldoc-Murphy, E. A., Faraone, S., Chaloff, J., Hirshfeld, D. R., & Kagan, J. (1993). A 3-year follow-up of children with and without behavioral inhibition. *Journal of the American Academy of Child and Adolescent Psychiatry, 32* (4), 814–821.

Biederman, J., Rosenbaum, J. F., Hirshfeld, D. R., Faraone, S., Bolduc, E. A., Gersten, M., Meminger, S. R., Kagan, J., Snidman, N., & Reznick, S. (1990). Psychiatric correlates of behavioral inhibition in young children of parents with and without psychiatric disorders. *Archives of General Psychiatry, 47,* 21–26.

Biederman, T., Spencer, T., & Wilens, T. (1997). Psychopharmacology. In J. M. Wiener (Ed.), *Textbook of child and adolescent psychiatry* (2nd ed.) (pp. 779–812).

Billings, J. H., Scherwitz, L. W., Sullivan, R., Sparler, S., & Ornish, D. M. (1996). The Lifestyle Heart Trial: Comprehensive treatment and group support therapy. In R. Allen & S. Scheidt (Eds.), *Heart and mind: The practice of cardiac psychology* (pp. 233–253). Washington, DC: American Psychological Association.

Binder, J. L., Strupp, H. S., & Henry, W. P. (1995). Psychodynamic therapies in practice: Time-limited psychodynamic psychotherapy. In B. Bongar & L. E. Beutler (Eds.), *Comprehensive textbook of psychotherapy: Theory and practice* (pp. 48–63). New York: Oxford University Press.

Birch, D. (1992). Duty to protect: Update and Canadian perspective. *Canadian Psychology, 33,* 94–101.

Birmaher, B., Waterman, G. S., Ryan, N. (1994). Fluoexetene for childhood anxiety disorders. *Journal of the American Academy of Child and Adolesecent Psychiatry 33,* 993–999.

Birnbaum, K. (1914). *Die psychopathischen verbrecker* (2nd ed.). Leipzig: Thième.

Birren, J. E., & Renner, V. J. (1980). Concepts and issues of mental health and aging. In J. E. Birren & R. B. Sloane (Eds.), *Handbook of mental health and aging* (pp. 3–33). Englewood Cliffs, NJ: Prentice-Hall.

Bittman, B. J., & Convit, A. (1993). Competency, civil commitment, and the dangerousness of the mentally ill. *Journal of Forensic Sciences, 38,* 1460–1466.

Black, D. W., Winokur, D. (1990). Suicide and psychiatric diagnosis. In S. J. Blumenthal & D. J. Kupfer (Eds.), *Suicide over the life cycle: Risk factors, assessment and treatment of suicidal patients.* Washington, DC: American Psychiatric Press.

Black, D., Winokur, G., & Nasrallah, A. (1987). The treatment of depression: Electroconvulsive therapy versus antidepressants: A naturalistic evaluation of 1,495 patients. *Comprehensive Psychiatry, 28,* 169–182.

Blackburn, R. (1992). Criminal behavior, personality disorder, and mental confusion: The origins of confusion. *Criminal Behavior and Mental Health, 2,* 66–77.

Blair, D. C., & Lanyon, R. I. (1981). Exhibitionism: Etiology and treatment. *Psychological Bulletin, 89,* 439–463.

Blake, D. D., Weathers, F. W., Nagy, L. M., Kaloupek, D. G., Gusman, F. D., Charney, D. S., & Keane, T. (1995). *Clinician administered PTSD scale (CAPS).* Boston, MA: Behavioral Science Division, National Centre for Post-traumatic Stress Disorder.

Blake, W. (1973). The influence of race on diagnosis. *Smith College Studies in Social Work, 43,* 184–192.

Blanchard, R. (1989). The classification and labeling of nonhomosexual gender dysphorias. *Archives of Sexual Behavior, 18,* 315–334.

Blanchard, R. (1990). Gender identity disorders in adult men. In R. Blanchard & B. W. Steiner (Eds.), *Clinical management of gender identity disorders in children and adults* (pp. 49–76). Washington, DC: American Psychiatry Press.

Blanchard, R. (1993). Partial versus complete autogynephilia and gender dysphoria. *Journal of Sex and Marital Therapy, 19,* 301–307.

Blanchard, R., Steiner, B. W., Clemmensen, L. H., & Dickey, R. (1989). Prediction of regrets in postoperative transsexuals. *Canadian Journal of Psychiatry, 34,* 43–45.

Blanchet, L., Laurendeau, M.-C., Paul, D., & Saucier, J.-F. (1993). *La prévention et la promotion en santé mentale.* Boucherville, Quebec: Gaetan Morin Editeur.

Bland, R. C., Orn, H., & Newman, S. C. (1988). Lifetime prevalence of psychiatric disorders in Edmonton. *Acta Psychiatrica Scandinavica, 77 (Suppl. 338),* 24–32.

Blashfield, R. K., & Davis, R. T. (1993). Dependent and histrionic personality disorders. In P. B. Sutker & H. E. Adams (Eds.), *Comprehensive handbook of psychopathology* (2nd ed.) (pp. 395–409). New York: Plenum Press.

Blatt, B., & Kaplan, F. M. (1966). *Christmas in purgatory: A photographic essay on mental retardation.* Boston: Allyn and Bacon.

Blatt, E. R., & Brown, S. W. (1986). Environmental influences on incidents of alleged child abuse and neglect in New York State psychiatric facilities: Toward an etiology of institutional child maltreatment. *Child Abuse and Neglect, 10* (2), 171–180.

Blatt, S. J. (1974). Levels of object representations in anaclitic and introjective depression. *The Psychoanalytic Study of the Child, 29,* 107–158.

Blazer, D. (1990). *Emotional problems in later life.* New York: Springer.

Blazer, D. G. (1989). Depression in the elderly. *The New England Journal of Medicine, 320,* 164–166.

Blazer, D. G. (1991). Suicide risk factors in the elderly: An epidemiological study. *Journal of Geriatric Psychiary, 24,* 175–190.

Blazer, D. G., George, L., & Hughes, D. (1991). The epidemiology of anxiety: An age comparison. In C. Salzman & B. D. Lebowitz (Eds.), *Anxiety in the elderly.* New York: Springer.

Bleuler, E. (1950). *Dementia preacox of the group of schizophrenias.* New York: International Universities Press. (Originally published 1911.)

Bleuler, M. (1974). The long-term course of the schizophrenic psychoses. *Psychological Medicine, 4,* 244–254.

Bliss, E. L. (1984). A symptom profile of patients with multiple personalities, including MMPI results. *Journal of Nervous and Mental Disease, 172,* 197–202.

Block, J. (1995). On the relationship between I.Q., impulsivity and delinquency: Remarks on the Lynam, Moffitt and Stouthamer-Loeber (1993) interpretation. *Journal of Abnormal Psychology, 104,* 395–398.

Bloom, B. L. (1982). Advances and obstacles in prevention of mental disorders. In H. C. Schulberg & M. Killilea (Eds.), *The modern practice of community mental health* (pp. 126–147). San Francisco: Jossey-Bass.

Bloom, B. L. (1984). *Community mental health* (2nd ed.). Monterey, CA: Brooks/Cole.

Blouin, A. G., & Goldfield, G. S. (1995). Body image and steroid use in male body builders. *International Journal of Eating Disorders, 18,* 159–165.

Blouin, A. G., Blouin, J., Aubin, P., Carter, J., Goldstein, C., Boyer, H., & Perez, E. (1992). Seasonal patterns of bulimia nervosa. *American Journal of Psychiatry, 149,* 73–81.

Blouin, A. G., Zuro, C., & Blouin, J. H. (1990). Family environment in bulimia nervosa: The role of depression. *International Journal of Eating Disorders, 9,* 649–658.

Blum, K., Noble, E. P., Sheridan, P. J., Montgomery, A., Ritchie, T., Jagadeeswaran, P., Nogami, H., Briggs, A. H., & Cohen, J. B. (1990). Allelic association of human dopamine D_2 receptor gene in alcoholism. *Journal of the American Medical Association, 263,* 2055–2060.

Blumenthal, S. J. (1990). An overview and synopsis of risk factors, assessment, and treatment of suicidal patients of the life cycle. *Suicide over the life cycle: Risk factors, assessment and treatment of suicidal patients.* Washington, DC: American Psychiatric Press.

Blumenthal, S. J., & Kupfer, D. J. (1988). Clinical assessment and treatment of youth suicide. *Journal of Youth and Adolescence, 17,* 1–24.

Boffetta, P., & Garfinkel, L. (1990). Alcohol drinking and mortality among men enrolled in an American Cancer Society prospective study. *Epidemiology, 1* (15), 342–348.

Bogen, E. (1932). *The human toxicology of alcohol.* In H. Emerson (Ed.), *Alcohol and man.* New York: MacMillan.

Bogenschneider, K. (1996). Prevention programs: An ecological risk/protective theory for building prevention programs, policies, and community capacity to support youth. *Family Relations, 45,* 127–138.

Bohman, M. (1995). Predisposition to criminality: Swedish adoption studies in retrospect. *Genetics of antisocial behaviour* (Ciba Foundation Symposium 194) (pp. 99–114). Chichester, England: Wiley.

Bohman, M., Cloninger, C. R., von Korring, A. L., & Sigvardsson, S. (1984). Man adoption study of somatoform disorders. III. Cross-fostering analysis and genetic relationship to alcoholism and criminality. *Archives of General Psychiatry, 41,* 872–878.

Bohman, M., Sigvardsson, S., & Cloninger, C. R. (1981). Maternal inheritance of alcohol abuse: Cross-fostering analysis of adopted women. *Archives of General Psychiatry, 38,* 965–969.

Boland, F. J. (1997). Eating disorders and substance abuse. In S. Harrison & V. Carver (Eds.), *Alcohol and drug problems: A practical guide for counsellors* (pp. 473–483). Toronto: ARF Publications.

Boldt, M. (1985). Towards the development of a systematic approach to suicide prevention: The Alberta model. *Canada's Mental Health, 33* (2), 2–4.

Bo-Linn, G. W., Santa Ana, C. A., Morawski, S. G., & Fordtran, J. S. (1983). Purging and calories absorption in bulimic patients and normal women. *Annals of Internal Medicine, 99,* 14–17.

Boll, T. J. (1985). Developing issues in clinical neuropsychology. *Journal of Clinical and Experimental Neuropsychology, 7* (5), 473–485.

Boll, T. J. (1994). Neurologically impaired patients. In M. Hensen & S. M. Turner (Eds.), *Diagnostic interviewing* (2nd ed.) (pp. 345–372). New York: Plenum Press.

Bond, I., & Evans, D. (1967). Avoidance therapy: Its use in two cases of underwear fetishism. *Canadian Medical Association Journal, 96,* 1160–1162.

Boor, M. (1982). The multiple personality epidemic. *Journal of Nervous and Mental Disease, 170,* 302–304.

Booth, D. H., Lewis, V. J., & Blair, A. J. (1990). Dieting restraint and binge eating: Pseudo-quantitative anthropology for a medicalised habit? *Appetite, 43,* 647–660.

Booth-Kewley, S., & Friedman, H. S. (1987). Psychological predictors of heart disease: A quantitative review. *Psychological Bulletin, 101,* 343–362.

Bootzin, R. R., & Perlis, M. L. (1992). Nonpharmacological treatments of insomnia. *Journal of Clinical Psychiatry, 53* (Suppl. 6), 37–41.

Bootzin, R. R., Epstein, D., Engle-Friedman, M., & Salvio, M. (1992). Sleep disturbances. In L. L. Carstensen, B. A. Edelstein, & L. Dornbrand (Eds.), *The practical handbook of clinical gerontology* (pp. 398–420). Thousand Oaks, CA: Sage.

Borduin, C. M., Mann, B. J., Cone, L. T., Henggeler, S. W., Fucci, B. R., Blaske, D. M., & Williams, R. A. (1995). Multisystemic treatment of serious juvenile offenders: Long-term prevention of criminality and violence. *Journal of Consulting and Clinical Psychology, 63,* 569–578.

Borkovec, T. D. (1985). Worry: A potential valuable concept. *Behaviour Research and Therapy, 23,* 481–482.

Borkovec, T. D., & Costello, E. (1993). Efficacy of applied relaxation and cognitive behavioral therapy in the treatment of generalized anxiety disorder. *Journal of Consulting and Clinical Psychology, 61,* 611–619.

Borkovec, T. D., & Inz, J. (1990). The nature of worry in generalized anxiety disorder: A predominance of thought activity. *Behaviour Research and Therapy, 28,* 153–158.

Borkovec, T. D., Abel, J. L., & Newman, H. (1995). Effects of psychotherapy on comorbid conditions in generalized anxiety disorder. *Journal of Consulting and Clinical Psychology, 63,* 479–483.

Borkovec, T. D., Shadick, R. N., & Hopkins, M. C. (1991). The nature of normal and pathological worry. In R. M. Rapee & D. H. Barlow (Eds.), *Chronic anxiety, generalized anxiety disorder and mixed anxiety-depression* (pp. 29–51). New York: Guilford Press.

Borkovec, T. D., Stone, N. M., O'Brien, G. T., & Kaloupek, D. G. (1974). Evaluation of a clinically-relevant target behavior for analog outcome research. *Behavior Therapy, 5,* 503–513.

Bornstein, R. F., Klein, D. N., Mallon, J. C., & Slater, J. F. (1988). Schizotypal personality disorder in an outpatient population: Incidence and clinical characteristics. *Journal of Clinical Psychology, 44,* 322–325.

Bornstein, R. F., Rossner, S. C., & Hill, E. L. (1994). Retest reliability of scores on objective and projective measures of dependency: Relationship to life events and intertest interval. *Journal of Personality Assessment, 62* (3), 398–415.

Borthwick-Duffy, S. A., & Eyman, R. K. (1990). Who are the dually diagnosed? *American Journal on Mental Retardation, 94,* 586–595.

Borys, D. S., & Pope, K. S. (1989). Dual relationships between therapist and client: A national study of psychologists, psychiatrists, and social workers. *Professional Psychology: Research and Practice, 20,* 283–293.

Bos, C. S., & Van Reusen, A. K. (1991). Academic interventions with learning-disabled students. In J. E. Obrzut & G. W. Hynd (Eds.). *Neuropsychological foundations of learning disabilities: A handbook of issues, methods and practices* (pp. 659–683). San Diego, CA: Academic Press.

Boskind-Lodahl, M. (1976). Cinderella's stepsisters: A feminist perspective on anorexia and bulimia. *Signs, the Journal of Women in Culture and Society, 2,* 324–356.

Botvin, G. J. (1996). Substance abuse prevention through life skills training. In R. DeV. Peters & R. J. McMahon (Eds.), *Preventing childhood disorders, substance abuse, and delinquency* (pp. 215–240). Thousand Oaks, CA: Sage.

Botvin, G. J., & Tortu, S. (1988). Preventing substance abuse through life skills training. In R. H. Price, E. L. Cowen, R. P. Lorion, & J. Ramos-McKay (Eds.), *14 ounces of prevention.* Washington, DC: American Psychological Association.

Botvin, G. J., Baker, E., Dusenbury, L., Tortu, S., & Botvin, E. M. (1990). Preventing adolescent drug abuse through a multimodal cognitive-behavioral approach: Results of a three-year study. *Journal of Consulting and Clinical Psychology, 58,* 437–446.

Bouaboula, M., Rinaldi, M., Carayon, P., Carillon, C., Delpech, B., Shire, D., Le-Fur, G., & Casellas, P. (1993). Cannabinoid-receptor expression in human leukocytes. *European Journal of Biochemistry, 214* (1), 173–180.

Bouchard, C. (1994). Discours et parcours de la prévention de la violence: Une réflexion sur les valeurs en jeu. *Canadian Journal of Community Mental Health, 13* (2), 37–46.

Bouchard, S., Bolduc, D., Boisvert, J. M., & Gauthier, J. (1995). Agoraphobia and interpersonal relationships. *Canadian Psychology, 36,* 190–200.

Bouchard, S., Gauthier, J., Laberge, B., Plamondon, J., French, D., Pelletier, M. H., & Godbout, C. (1996). Exposure versus cognitive restructuring in the treatment of panic disorder with agoraphobia. *Behaviour Research and Therapy, 34,* 213–224.

Bouchard, S., Gauthier, J., Nouwen, A., & Ivers, H. (in revision). The role of beliefs in the treatment of panic disorder with agoraphobia. *Behavior Therapy.*

Bouchard, S., Pelletier, M. H., Gauthier, J., Côté, G., & Laberge, B. (1997). Comprehensive review of validated panic measures. *Journal of Anxiety Disorders, 11* (1), 88–111.

Boulenger, J. P., Jerabek, I., Jolicoeur, F. B., & Lavallée, Y. J. (1996). Elevated plasma levels of neuropeptide Y in patients with panic disorder. *American Journal of Psychiatry, 153,* 114–116.

Bowen, R. C., Offord, D. R., & Boyle, M. H. (1990). The prevalence of overanxious disorder and separation anxiety disorder: Results from the Ontario Child Health Study. *Journal of the American Academy of Child and Adolescent Psychiatry, 29,* 753–758.

Bowers, T. G., & Al-Redha, M. R. (1990). A comparison of outcome with group/marital and standard/individual therapies with alcoholics. *Journal of Studies on Alcohol, 51,* 301–309.

Bowlby, J. (1973). *Attachment and loss.* New York: Basic Books.

Bowlby, J. (1977). The making and breaking of affectional bonds: 1. Aetiology and psychopathology in the light of attachment theory. *British Journal of Psychiatry, 30,* 301–210.

Bowlby, J. (1980). *Attachment and loss: III. Loss, sadness and depression.* New York: Basic Books.

Bowlby, J. (1988). *A secure base: Parent-child attachment and health human development.* New York: Basic Books.

Boyle, M. (1991). *Schizophrenia: A scientific delusion?* New York: Routledge.

Boyle, M. H., Offord, D. R., Hofmann, H. G., Catlin, G. P., Byles, J. A., Cadman, D. T., Crawford, J. W., Links, P. S., Rae-Grant, N. I., & Szatmari, P. (1987). Ontario Child Health Study: I. Methodology. *Archives of General Psychiatry, 44,* 826–831.

Braaten, E. B., Otto, S., & Handelsman, M. M. (1993). What do people want to know about psychotherapy? *Psychotherapy, 30,* 565–570.

Braden, M. L. (1989). *Logo reading system.* Obtainable at 219 East St. Vrain, Colorado Springs, CO.

Bradley, R. H., Caldwell, B. M., Rock, S. L., Ramey, C. T., Barnard, K. E., Gray, A., Hammond, M. A., Gottfried, A., Siegel, L. S., & Johnson, D. L. (1989). Home environment and cognitive development in the first three years of life: A collaborative study involving six sites and three ethnic groups in North America. *Developmental Psychology, 25,* 217–235.

Bradley, W. (1937). The behavior of children receiving benzedrine. *American Journal of Psychiatry, 94,* 577–585.

Bradwejn, J., & de Montigny, C. (1984). Benzodiazepines antagonize cholecystokinin-induced activation of rat hippocampal neurons. *Nature, 312,* 363–364.

Bradwejn, J., Koszycki, D., & Shriqui, C. (1991). Enhanced sensitivity to cholecystokinin tetrapeptide in panic disorder. *Archives of General Psychiatry, 48,* 603–610.

Bradwejn, J., Koszycky, D., & Meterissian, G. (1990). Cholecystokinin-tetrapeptide induced panic attacks in patients with panic disorder. *Canadian Journal of Psychiatry, 35,* 83–85.

Brende, J. O., & Rinsley, D. B. (1981). A case of multiple personality with psychological automatisms. *Journal of the American Academy Psychoanalysis, 9* (1), 129–151.

Brenner, H. D., Hodel, B., Roder, V., & Corrigan, P. (1992). Treatment of cognitive dysfunctions and behavioral deficits in schizophrenia. *Schizophrenia bulletin, 18,* 21–26.

Brent, D. A., & Kolko, D. J. (1990). The assessment and treatment of children and adolescents at risk for suicide. In S. J. Blumenthal & D. J. Kupfer (Eds.), *Suicide over the life cycle: Risk factors, assessment and treatment of suicidal patients.* Wahington, DC: American Psychiatric Press.

Breuer, J., & Freud, S. (1974/1893–1895). *Studies on hysteria.* Harmondsworth: Penguin Books.

Bridges, K., Goldberg, O., Evans, B., & Sharpe, T. (1991). Determinants of somatization in primary care. *Psychological Medicine, 21* (2), 473–483.

Briere, J. N. (1992). *Child abuse trauma: Theory and treatment of the lasting effects.* Newbury Park, CA: Sage.

Briere, J., & Runtz, M. (1988). Symptomatology associated with childhood sexual victimization in a nonclinical adult sample. *Child Abuse and Neglect, 12,* 51–59.

Briere, J., & Zaidi, L. Y. (1989). Sexual abuse histories and sequelae in female psychiatric emergency room patients. *American Journal of Psychiatry, 146,* 1602–1606.

Broadhead, J., & Jacoby, R. (1990). Mania in old age: A first prospective study. *International Journal of Geriatric Psychiatry, 5,* 215–222.

Brodaty, H., Harris, L., Peters, K., Wilhelm, K., Hickie, I., Boyce, P., Mitchell, P., Parker, G., & Eyers, K. (1993). Prognosis of depression in the elderly: A comparison with younger patients. *British Journal of Psychiatry, 163,* 589–596.

Brodie, D. A. (1971). Stress ulcer as an experimental model of peptic ulcer disease. In C. J. Pfeiffer (Ed.), *Peptic ulcer* (pp. 71–83). Philadelphia: Lippincott.

Brody, N. (1992). *Intelligence* (2nd ed.). San Diego: Academic Press.

Broga, M. I., & Neufeld, R.W.J. (1981a). Evaluation of information-sequential aspects of schizophrenic performance, I: Framework and current findings. *Journal of Nervous and Mental Disease, 169,* 559–568.

Broga, M. I., & Neufeld, R.W.J. (1981b). Multivariate cognitive performance levels and response styles among paranoid and nonparanoid schizophrenics. *Journal of Abnormal Psychology, 90,* 495–509.

Brooks, C. M., Perry, N. W., Starr, S. D., & Teply, L. L. (1994). Child abuse and neglect reporting laws: Understanding interests, understanding policy. *Behavioral Sciences and the Law, 12,* 49–64.

Broskowski, A., & Baker, F. (1974). Professional, organizational, and social barriers to primary prevention. *American Journal of Orthopsychiatry, 44,* 707–719.

Broverman, I., Broverman, D. M., Clarkson, F. E., Rosenkrantz, P. S., & Vogel, S. R. (1970). Sex-role stereotypes and clinical judgements of mental health. *Journal of Consulting and Clinical Psychology, 34,* 1–7.

Brown, F. W., Golding, J. M., & Smith, G. (1990). Psychiatric comorbidity in primary care somatization disorder. *Psychosomatic Medicine, 52,* 445–451.

Brown, G. L., Ebert, M. H., Goyer, P. F., Jimerson, D. C., Klein, W. J., Bunney, W. E., & Goodwin, F. K. (1982). Aggression, suicide and serotonin: relationship to CSF amine metabolites. *American Journal of Psychiatry, 139,* 741–746.

Brown, G. W., & Harris, T. (1978). *Social origins of depression.* London: Tavistock.

Brown, G. W., Andrews, B., Harris, T., Adler, Z., & Bridge, L. (1986). Social support, self-esteem, and depression. *Psychological Medicine, 16,* 813–831.

Brown, G. W., Carstairs, G. M., & Topping, G. (1958). Post-hospital adjustment of chronic mental patients. *The Lancet, 2,* 685–689.

Brown, G. W., Harris, T. O., & Bifulco, A. (1986). Long-term effects of early loss of parent. In M. Rutter, C. E. Izard, & P. B. Read (Eds.), *Depression in young people: Developmental and clinical perspectives* (pp. 251–298). New York: Guilford Press.

Brown, J. (1985). Historical perspective on child abuse. In A. Downer (Ed.), *Prevention of child sexual abuse: A trainer's manual.* Seattle, WA: Seattle Institute for Child Advocacy Committee for Children.

Brown, T. A., Marten, P. A., & Barlow, D. H. (1995). Discriminant validity of the symptoms constituting the DSM–III-R and DSM–IV associated symptom criterion of generalized anxiety disorder. *Journal of Anxiety Disorders, 9,* 317–318.

Browne, A., & Finkelhor, D. (1986). Impact of child sexual abuse: A review of the literature. *Psychological Bulletin, 99,* 66–77.

Browne, E. G. (1921). *Arabian medicine.* New York: Macmillan.

Brownell, K. D., & Fairburn, C. G. (Eds.) (1995). *Eating disorders and obesity: A comprehensive handbook.* New York: Guilford Press.

Brownell, K. D., & Rodin, J. (1994). The dieting malestorm: Is it possible and advisable to lose weight? *American Psychologist, 49,* 781–791.

Brownmiller, S. (1975). *Against our will: Men, women, and rape.* New York: Bantam Books.

Bruch, H. (1973). *Eating disorders: Obesity, anorexia, and the person within.* New York: Basic Books.

Bruch, H. (1978). *The golden cage.* Cambridge, MA: Harvard University Press.

Bryer, J. B., Nelson, B. A., Miller, J. B., & Krol, P. K. (1987). Childhood sexual and physical abuse as factors in adult psychiatric illness. *American Journal of Psychiatry, 144,* 1426–1430.

Bryson, S. E. (1996). Brief report: Epidemiology of autism. *Journal of Autism and Developmental Disorders, 26,* 165–167.

Bryson, S., Clark, B. S., & Smith, I. M. (1988). First report of a Canadian epidemiological study of autistic syndromes. *Journal of Child Psychology and Psychiatry, 29,* 433–445.

Buchsbaum, M. S. (Ed.) (1990). Frontal lobes, basal ganglia, temporal lobes—Three sites for schizophrenia? *Schizophrenia Bulletin, 16,* 377–452.

Buda, M., & Msuang, M. T. (1990). The epidemiology of suicide: Implications for clinical practice. In S. J. Blumenthal & D. J. Kupfer (Eds.), *Suicide over the life cycle: Risk factors, assessment and treatment of suicidal patients.* Washington, DC: American Psychiatric Press.

Budoff, M., & Siperstein, G. N. (1978). Low-income children's altitudes to mentally retarded children: Effects of labelling and academic behavior. *American Journal of Mental Deficiency, 82,* 474–479.

Buell, M. K., & Minnes, P. M. (1994). An acculturation perspective on deinstitutionalization and service delivery. *Journal of Developmental Disabilities, 3,* 94–107.

Buhrich, N., & McConaghy, N. (1977). Clinical comparison of transvestism and transsexualism. *Australian and New Zealand Journal of Psychiatry, 6,* 83–86.

Bukatko, D., & Daehler, M. W. (1992). *Child development: A topical approach.* Boston: Houghton Mifflin.

Bullough, V. L. (1976). *Sexual variance in society and history.* Chicago: University of Chicago Press.

Burack, J. A., Enns, J. T., Stauder, J.E.A., Mottron, L., & Randolph, B. (1997). In D. J. Cohen & F. R. Volkmar (Eds.), *Handbook of autism and pervasive developmental disorders* (pp. 226–247). New York: Wiley.

Burbach, D., & Borduin, C. (1986). Parent-child relations and the etiology of depression. *Clinical Psychology Review, 6,* 133–153.

Burke, W. J., Rubin, E. H., Zorumski, C. F., & Wetzel, R. D. (1987). The safety of ECT in geriatric psychiatry. *Journal of the American Geriatrics Society, 35,* 516–521.

Burstein, A. G. (1989). *Rorschach's test: Scoring and interpretation.* New York: Hemisphere.

Burton, R. (1977). *The anatomy of melancholy* (reprint ed.). New York: Random House.

Butcher, J. N., Dahlstrom, W. G., Graham, J. R., Tellegen, A., & Kraemer, B. (1989). *Minnesota Multiphasic Personality Inventory. 2: Manual for administration and scoring.* Minneapolis: University of Minnesota Press.

Butler, R. N., & Lewis, M. I. (1982). *Aging and Mental Health.* St. Louis, MO: Mosby.

Buvat, J., Buvat-Herbaut, M., Lemaire, A., Marcolin, G., & Quittelier, E. (1990). Recent developments in the clinical assessment and diagnosis of erectile dysfunction. *Annual Review of Sex Research, 1,* 265–308.

C. (J. S.) v. Wren, 35 D.L.R. (4th) 419 (1986).

Cacioppo, J. T., & Berntson G. G. (1992). Social psychological contributions to the decade of the brain. *American Psychologist, 47,* 1019–1028.

Cadoret, R. J., Yates, W. R., Troughton, E., Woodworth, G., & Stewart, M. A. (1995). Genetic-environment interaction in the genesis of aggressivity and conduct disorders. *Archives of General Psychiatry, 52,* 916–924.

Caldwell, A. (1978). History of psychopharmacology. In W. G. Clark & J. del Giudice (Eds.), *Principles of psychopharmacology* (2nd ed.) (pp. 9–40). New York: Academic Press.

Cambor, R., & Millman, R. B. (1991). Alcohol and drug abuse in adolescence. In M. Lewis (Ed.), *Child and adolescent psychiatry: A comprehensive textbook (pp.* 736–754). Baltimore: Williams & Wilkins.

Cameron, G., Peirson, L., & Pancer, S. M. (1994). Resident participation in the Better Beginnings, Better Futures prevention project: Part II—Factors that facilitate and hinder involvement. *Canadian Journal of Community Mental Health, 13* (2), 213–227.

Campbell, D. (1926). *Arabian medicine and its influences on the Middle Ages.* New York: Dutton.

Campbell, E. (1990). The psychopath and the definition of "mental disease of defect" under the Model Penal Code test of insanity: A question of psychology or a question of law? *Nebraska Law Review, 69,* 190–229.

Campbell, J. L., Thomas, H. M., Gabriellu, W., Liskow, B., & Powell, G. J. (1994). Impact of desipramine or cabamazepine on patient retention in outpatient cocaine treatment: Preliminary findings. *Journal of Addictive Diseases, 13* (4), 191–199.

Campbell, M., & Malone, R. (1991). Mental retardation and psychiatric disorders. *Hospital and Community Psychiatry, 42,* 374–379.

Canadian Committee on Sexual Offences Against Children and Youth (1984). *Report of the Committee.* Ottawa: National Health and Welfare.

Canadian Mental Health Association (1995). *Depression: An overview of the literature.* Ottawa: Health Canada Publications.

Canadian Psychological Association (1991). *Canadian code of ethics for psychologists.* Ottawa: Canadian Psychological Association.

Canadian Study of Health and Aging Working Group (1994). Canadian Study of Health and Aging: Study methods and prevalence of dementia. *Canadian Medical Association Journal, 150,* 899–912.

Canadian Task Force on the Periodic Health Examination (1990). Early detection of depression and prevention of suicide. *Canadian Medical Association Journal, 142,* 1233–1238.

Cannon, T. D., Barr, C. E., & Mednick, S. A. (1991). Genetic and perinatial factors in the etiology of schziophrenia. In E. F. Walker (Ed.), *Schizophrenia: A life-course developmental perspective* (pp. 9–31). San Diego: Academic Press.

Cannon, W. B. (1942). "Voodoo" death. *American Anthropologist, 44,* 169.

Cantwell, D. P., Baker, L., & Rutter, M. (1978). Family factors in the syndrome of infantile autism. In M. Rutter & E. Schopler (Eds.), *Autism: A reappraisal of concepts and treatment.* New York: Plenum Press.

Caplan, G. (1964). *Principles of preventive psychiatry.* New York: Basic Books.

Caplehorn, J. R., & Ross, M. W. (1995). Methadone maintenance and the likelihood of risky needle-sharing. *International Journal of the Addictions, 30,* 685–698.

Carey, G. (1992). Twin imitation for antisocial behaviour: Implications for genetic and family environment research. *Journal of Abnormal Psychology, 101* (1), 18–25.

Carey, G., & DiLalla, D. L. (1994). Personality and psychopathology: Genetic perspective. *Journal of Abnormal Psychology, 103,* 32–43.

Carey, G., & Gottesman, I. I. (1996). Genetics and antisocial behavior: Substance versus sound bytes. *Politics and the Life Sciences, March,* 88–90.

Carey, M. P., Wincze, J. P., & Meisler, A. W. (1993). Sexual dysfunction: Male erectile disorder. In D. H. Barlow (Ed.), *Clinical handbook of psychological disorders: A step-by-step treatment manual* (2nd ed.) (pp. 442–480). New York: Guilford Press.

Carlson, N. R. (1998). *Physiology of behaviour* (6th ed.). Toronto: Allyn and Bacon.

Carlsson, A., Svennerholm, L., & Winblad, B. (1980). Seasonal and circadian monoamine variations in human brains examined post-mortem. *Acta Psychiatrica Scandinavica, 61,* 75–85.

Carlsson, M., & Carlsson, A. (1990). Schizophrenia: A subcortical neurtransmitter imbalance syndrome? *Schizophrenia Bulletin, 16,* 425–432.

Carney, R. M., Freedland, K. E., Rich, M. W., & Jaffe, A. S. (1995). Depression as a risk factor for cardiac events in established coronary heart disease: A review of possible mechanisms. *Annals of Behavioral Medicine, 17,* 142–149.

Carr, E. G., & Kologinsky, E. (1983). Acquisition of sign language by autistic children. II: Spontaneity and generalization effects. *Journal of Applied Behavior Analysis, 16,* 297–314.

Carr, E. G., & Durand, V. M. (1985). Reducing behavior problems through functional communication training. *Journal of Applied Behavior Analysis, 18,* 111–126.

Carr, E. G., Binkoff, J. A., Kologinsky E., & Eddy, M. (1978). Acquisition of sign language by autistic children. I: Expressive labelling. *Journal of Applied Behavior Analysis, 11,* 489–501.

Carson, R. C., & Butcher, J. N. (1992). The schizophrenias and delusional disorders. *Abnormal psychology and modern life* (pp. 426–475). New York: HarperCollins.

Carson, R. C., Butcher, J. N., & Mineka, S. (1998). *Abnormal Psychology and Modern Life* (10th ed.). New York: Longman.

Carter, J. C., Stewart, D. A., Dunn, V. J., & Fairburn, C. G. (1997). Primary prevention of eating disorders: Might it do more harm than good? *International Journal of Eating Disorders, 22,* 167–172.

Carter, J. R., & Neufeld, R.W.J. (in press). Cultural aspects of understanding people with with schizophrenic disorders. In S. S. Kazarian & D. R. Evans (Eds.), *Cultural clinical psychology: Theory, research and practice.* Oxford University Press.

Case, R. B., Moss, A. J., Case, N., et al. (1992). Living alone after myocardial infarction: impact on prognosis. *Journal of the American Medical Association, 267,* 515–519.

Cash, T. F., & Brown, T. A. (1987). Body image in anorexia nervosa and bulimia nervosa: A review of the literature. *Behaviour Modification, 11,* 487–521.

Cash, T. F., & Deagle, E. A. (1997). The nature and extent of body-image disturbances in anorexia nervosa and bulimia nervosa: A meta-analysis. *International Journal of Eating Disorders, 22,* 107–125.

Castellanos, F. X., Giedd, J. N., Marsh, W. L., Hamburger, S. D., Vaituzis, A. C., Dickstein, D. P., Sarfatti, S. E., Vauss, Y. C., Snell, J. W., Lange, N., Kaysen, D., Krain, A. L., Ritchie, G. F., Rajapakse, J. C., & Rapoport, J. L. (1996). Quatitative brain magnetic resonance imaging in attention-deficit hyperactivity disorder. *Archives of General Psychiatry, 53,* 607–616.

Cawley, R. (1974). Psychotherapy and obsessional disorders. In H. R. Beech (Ed.), *Obsessional states* (pp. 259–290). London: Methuen.

Cernovsky, Z. Z., O'Reilly, R. L., & Landmark, J. A. (1994). Birth order, family size, and schizophrenic symptoms. *Social Behavior and Personality, 22,* 291–196.

Chambless, D. L., Caputo, G. C., Bright, P., & Gallagher, R. (1984). Assessment of fear of fear in agoraphobics: The Body Sensations Questionnaire and the Agoraphobic Cognitions Questionnaire. *Journal of Consulting and Clinical Psychology, 52,* 1090–1097.

Chambless, D. L., Caputo, G. C., Jasin, S. E., Gracely, E. J., & Williams, C. (1985). The Mobility Inventory for agoraphobia. *Behaviour Research and Therapy 23,* 35–44.

Chambless, D. L., Sanderson, W. C., Shoham, V., Johnson, S. B., Pope, K. S., Crits-Christoph, P., Baker, M., Johnson, B., Woody, S. R., Sue, S., Beutler, L., Williams, D. A., & McCurry, S. (1996). An update on empirically validated therapies. *The Clinical Psychologist, 49* (2), 5–18.

Chandrasena, R. (1986). Catatonic schizophrenia: An international comparative study. *Canadian Journal of Psychiatry, 31,* 249–252.

Chang, S. C. (1984). Review of I. Yamashita "Tai-jin-kyofu." *Transcultural Psychiatric Research Review, 21,* 283–288.

Channon, S., de Silva, P., Hemsley, D., & Perkins, R. (1989). A controlled trial of cognitive-behavioral and behavioral treatment of anorexia nervosa. *Behaviour Research and Therapy, 27,* 529–535.

Chapman, L. F. (1970). Experimental induction of hangover. *Quarterly Journal of Studies on Alcohol, Suppl. 5,* 67–86.

Chapman, L. J., & Chapman, J. P. (1973). *Disordered thought in schizophrenia.* New York: Appleton Century Crofts.

Chappel, J. (1993). Long term recovery from alcoholism. In N. S. Miller (Ed.), *Psychiatric clinics of North America.* Philadelphia, PA: Saunders.

Cheetam, S. C., Cross, A. J., Crompton, M. R., et al. (1987). Serotonin and GABA function in depressed suicide victims. Abstract of a presentation at the International Conference on New Directions in Affective Disorders, Jerusalem.

Chemtob, C., Roitblat, H. C., Hamada, R. S., Carlson, J. G., & Twentyman, C. T. (1988). A cognitive action theory of post-traumatic stress disorder. *Journal of Anxiety Disorders, 2,* 253–275.

Chesler, P. (1972). *Women and madness.* New York: Avon.

Chesney, M. A., Eagleston, J. E., & Rosenman, R. H. (1981). The Type A structured interview: A behavioral assessment in the rough. *Journal of Behavioral Assessment, 2,* 255–272.

Chesney, M. A., Ekman, P. A., Friesen, W. V., Black, G. W., & Hecker, M.H.L. (1990). Type A behavior pattern: Facial behavior and speech components. *Psychosomatic Medicine, 53,* 307–319.

Cheung, R., & Okazaki, S. (1991). Counseling Americans of Southeast Asian descent: The impact of the refugee experience. In C. C. Lee & B. L. Richardson (Eds.), *Multicultural issues in counseling: New approaches to diversity* (pp. 107–126). Alexandria: American Association for Counseling and Development.

Child, Family and Community Service Act, R.S.B.C., c. 46 (1996).

Chiswick, D. (1992). Compulsory treatment of patients with psychopathic disorder: An abnormally aggressive or seriously irresponsible exercise. *Criminal Behavior and Mental Health, 2,* 106–113.

Christenson, R., & Blazer, D. (1984). Epidemiology of persecutory ideation in an elderly population in the community. *American Journal of Psychiatry, 141,* 1088–1091.

Cicchetti, D., & Beegly, M. (1990). *Children with Down Syndrome: A developmental perspective.* New York: Cambridge University Press.

Cioffi, D. (1991). Beyond attentional strategies: A cognitive-perceptual model of somatic interpretation. *Psychological Bulletin, 109,* 25–41.

Clark, D. A. (1992). Depressive, anxious and intrusive thoughts in psychiatric inpatients and outpatients. *Behaviour Research and Therapy, 30,* 93–102.

Clark, D. M. (1986). A cognitive approach to panic. *Behaviour Research and Therapy, 24,* 461–470.

Clark, D. M. (1996). Panic disorder and social phobia. In D. M. Clark & C. G. Fairburn (Eds.), *Science and practice of cognitive-behaviour therapy* (pp. 119–154). New York: Oxford University Press.

Clark, D. M., & Wells, A. (1995). A cognitive model of social phobia. In R. G. Heimberg, M. R. Liebowitz, D. A. Hope, & F. R. Schneier (Eds.), *Social phobia: Diagnosis, assessment, and treatment* (pp. 69–93). New York: Guilford Press.

Clark, D. M., Salkovskis, P. M., Ost, L. G., Breotholz, E., Koehler, K. A., Westling, B. E., Jeavons, A., & Gelder, M. (1997). Misinterpretation of body sensations in panic disorder. *Journal of Consulting and Clinical Psychology, 65,* 203, 213.

Clark, L., & Lewis, D. (1977). *Rape: The price of coercive sexuality.* Toronto: Women's Educational Press.

Clarke, A. H., & Lewis, M. J. (1982). Fear of crime among the elderly. *British Journal of Criminology, 232,* 49.

Clarkin, J. F., & Carpenter, D. (1995). Family therapy in historical perspective. In B. Bongar & L. E. Beutler (Eds.), *Comprehensive textbook of psychotherapy: Theory and practice* (pp. 205–227). New York: Oxford University Press.

Clarkin, J. F., Koenigsberg, H., Yeomans, F., Selzer, M., Kernberg, P., & Kernberg, O. (1992). Psychodynamic psychotherapy of the borderline patient. In J. F. Clarkin, E. Marziali, & H. Munroe-Blum (Eds.), *Borderline personality disorder* (pp. 268–287). New York: Guilford Press.

Clarkin, J. F., Widiger, T. A., Frances, A. J., Hurt, S. W., & Gilmore, M. (1983). Prototypic typology and the borderline personality disorder. *Journal of Abnormal Psychology, 92,* 263–275.

Claude, D., & Firestone, P. (1995). The development of ADHD boys: A 12-year follow-up. *Canadian Journal of Behavioural Science, 27* (2), 226–249.

Cleckley, H. (1964). *The mask of sanity.* St. Louis, MO: Mosby.

Cleckley, H. (1976). *The mask of sanity* (5th ed.). St. Louis, MO: Mosby.

Clementz, B. A., & Sweeney, J. A. (1990). Is eye movement dysfunction a biological marker for schizophrenia? A methodological review. *Psychological Bulletin, 108,* 77–92.

Clemmensen, L. H. (1990). The "Real-life Test" for surgical candidates. In R. Blanchard & B. W. Steiner (Eds.), *Clinical management of gender identity disorders in children and adults* (pp. 121–135). Washington, DC: American Psychiatric Press.

Cloninger, C. R., & Gottesman, I. I. (1987). Genetic and environmental factors in antisocial behavior disorders. In S.P.A. Mednick, T. E. Moffitt, & S. A. Stack (Eds.), *The causes of crime: New biological approaches* (pp. 92–109). New York: Cambridge University Press.

Cloninger, C. R. (1987). Recent advances in the genetics of anxiety and somatoform disorders. In H. Y. Meltzer (Ed.), *Psychopharmacology: The third generation of progress* (pp. 955–965). New York: Raven Press.

Cloninger, C. R., Martin, R. L., Guze, S. B., & Clayton, P. L. (1986). A prospective follow-up and family study of somatization in men and women. *American Journal of Psychiatry, 143,* 713–714.

Cloninger, C. R., Svrakic, D. M., & Przybeck, T. (1993). Psychobiological model of temperament and character. *Archives of General Psychiatry, 50,* 975–990.

Coccaro, E. F., Siever, L. J., Klar, H. M., et al. (1989). Serotonergic studies in patients with affective and personality disorders: Correlates with suicidal and impulsive aggressive behavior. *Archives of General Psychiatry, 46,* 587–599.

Coffey, G. J., MacKinnon, A., & Minas, I. H. (1993). Interethnic variation in the presence of Schneiderian first rank symptoms. *Australian and New Zealand Journal of Psychiatry, 27,* 219–227.

Cohen, D. (1994). Neuroleptic drug treatment of schizophrenia: The state of the confusion. *Journal of Mind and Behavior, 15* (1–2), 139–156.

Cohen, S., & Herbert, T. B. (1996). Health psychology: Psychological factors and physical disease from the perspective of human psychoneuroimmunology. *Annual Review of Psychology, 47,* 113–142.

Cohen, S., & Wills, T. A. (1985). Stress, social support, and the buffering hypothesis. *Psychological Bulletin, 98,* 310–357.

Cohen, S., Kaplan, J. R., Cunnick, J. E., Manuck, S. B., & Rabin, B. S. (1992). Chronic social stress, affiliation and cellular immune response in nonhuman primates. *Psychological Science, 3,* 301–304.

Cohen, S., Tyrrell, D.A.J., & Smith, A. P. (1993). Negative life events, perceived stress, negative affect and susceptibility to the common cold. *Journal of Personality and Social Psychology, 64,* 131–140.

Coie, J. D. (1996). Prevention of violence and antisocial behavior. In R. DeV. Peters & R. J. McMahon (Eds.), *Preventing childhood disorders, substance abuse, and delinquency* (pp. 1–18). Thousand Oaks, CA: Sage.

Cole, J. D., & Kazarian, S. S. (1988). The Level of Expressed Emotion Scale: A new measure of expressed emotion. *Journal of Consulting and Clinical Psychology, 44,* 392–397.

Cole, J. D., & Kazarian, S. S. (1993). Predictive validity of the Level of Expressed Emotion (LEE) scale: Readmission follow-up data for 1-, 2-, and 5-year periods. *Journal of Clinical Psychology, 49,* 216–218.

Cole, J. O., Saloman, M., Gunderson, J., Sunderland, P., & Simmonds, P. (1984). Drug therapy for borderline patients. *Comprehensive Psychiatry, 25,* 249–254.

Coles, E. M., & Grant, F. (1990). Detention of accused persons found not guilty by reason of insanity: Diversion or preventive treatment. *Health Law in Canada, 11,* 239–254.

Collins, A. (1988). *In the sleep room: The story of the CIA brainwashing experiments in Canada.* Toronto: Lester & Orpen Dennys.

Comer, R. J. (1997). Substance-related disorders. In *Abnormal Psychology* (3rd ed.). New York: Freeman.

Commins, W. W., & Elias, M. J. (1991). Institutionalization of a mental health programs in organizational contexts: The case of elementary schools. *Journal of Community Psychology, 19,* 207–220.

Commission on Chronic Illness (1957). *Chronic illness in the United States* (Vol. 1, published for the Commonwealth Fund). Cambridge, MA: Harvard University Press.

Commission on the Prevention of Mental-Emotional Disabilities (1987). Report of major findings [special issue]. *Journal of Primary Prevention, 7* (4).

Conn, D. K. (1996). Other dementias and disorders due to general medical conditions. In J. Sadavoy, L. W. Lazarus, L. F. Jarvik, & G. T. Grossberg (Eds.), *Comprehensive review of geriatric psychiatry II.* Washington, DC: American Psychiatric Press.

Conners, C. K. (1980). *Food additives and hyperactive children.* New York: Plenum.

Conners, C. K. (1989). *Manual for Conners' Rating Scales.* Tonawanda: Multi-Health Systems.

Connors, M. E., & Morse, W. (1992). Sexual abuse and eating disorders: A review. *International Journal of Eating Disorders, 13,* 1–11.

Consensus Development Panel (1985). NIMH/NIH Consensus Development Conference statement: Mood disorders: Pharmacologic prevention of recurrence. *American Journal of Psychiatry, 142,* 469–476.

Consortium for Longitudinal Studies (1983). *As the twig is bent: Lasting effects of preschool programs.* Hillsdale, NJ: Lawrence Erlbaum.

Constitution Act, Schedule B to the Canada Act, (U. K.) 1982, c. 11.

Consumer Reports (1995, November). Mental health: Does therapy help? Pp. 734–739.

Cook, E. P., Warnke, M., & Dupuy, P. (1993). Gender bias and the DSM-III-R. *Counselor Education and Supervision, 32,* 311–322.

Cook, M., & Mineka, S. (1989). Observational conditioning of fear to fear-relevant versus fear-irrelevant stimuli in rhesus monkeys. *Journal of Abnormal Psychology, 98,* 448–459.

Cook, T. D., & Campbell, D. T. (1979). *Quasi-experimentation: Design and analysis issues for field settings.* Chicago: Rand McNally.

Cook, W., & Medley, D. (1954). Proposed hostility and pharisaic virtue scaled for the MMPI. *Journal of Applied Psychology, 38,* 414–418.

Coons, P. M. (1994). Confirmation of childhood abuse in child and adolescent cases of multiple personality disorder and dissociative disorder not otherwise specified. *Journal of Nervous and Mental Disease, 182,* 461–464.

Coons, P. M., Bowman, E. S., & Milstein, V. (1988). Multiple personality disorder: A clinical investigation of 50 cases. *Journal of Mental and Nervous Disease, 176* (9), 519–527.

Cooper, A. J. (1987). Sadistic homosexual pedophilia treatment with cyproterone acetate. *Canadian Journal of Psychiatry, 32,* 738–740.

Cooper, P. J., & Fairburn, C. G. (1986). The depressive symptoms of bulimia nervosa. *British Journal of Psychiatry, 148,* 268–274.

Cornblatt, B. A., Lenzenweger, M. R., & Erlenmeyer-Kimling, L. (1989). The continuous performance test, identical pairs version (CPT-IP). II. Contrasting attentional profiles in schizophrenic and depressed patients. *Psychiatry Research, 26,* 223–238.

Correctional Services Canada (1992). Violence and suicide in Canadian institutions: Some recent statistics [unsigned article]. *Forum on Corrections Research, 4* (3), 3–5.

Costa, E., & Greengard, P. (1975). *Mechanisms of action of benzodiazopines.* New York: Raven Press.

Costa, P. T., & McCrea, R. R. (1992). The five-factor model of personality and its relevance to personality disorders. *Journal of Personality Disorders, 6,* 343–359.

Costello, C. G. (1982). Fears and phobias in women: A community survey. *Journal of Abnormal Psychology, 91* (4), 280–286.

Costello, C. G. (1994). Two dimensional views of psychopathology. *Behaviour Research and Therapy, 32,* 391–402.

Costello, E. J. (1996). Epidemiology. In M. M. Bristol, D. J. Cohen, E. J. Costello, M. Denckla, T. J. Eckberg, R. Kallen, H. C. Kraemer, C. Lord, R. Maurer, W. J. McIlvane, N. Minshew, M. Sigman, & M. A. Spence, State of the science in autism: Report to the National Institutes of Health. *Journal of Autism and Developmental Disorders, 26,* 121–163.

Costello, E. J., Edelbrock, C. S., Costello, A. J., Dulcan, M. K., Burns, B. J., & Brent, D. (1988). Psychopathology in pediatric primary care: The new hidden morbidity. *Pediatrics, 82,* 415–424.

Costello, R. M. (1975). Alcoholism treatment and evaluation: In search of methods. *International Journal of the Addictions, 10,* 251–275.

Côté, G., & Hodgins, S. (1990). Co-occurring mental disorders among mental disorder among criminal offenders. *Bulletin of the American Academy of Psychiatry and Law, 18,* 271–281.

Côté, G., Gauthier, J., Laberge, B., Cormier, H. J., & Plamondon, J. (1994). Reduced therapist contact in the cognitive-behavioral treatment of panic disorder. *Behavior Therapy, 25,* 123–145.

Cowdry, R. W., & Gardner, D. L. (1988). Pharmacotherapy of borderline personality disorder: Alprazolam, carbamazepine, trifluoperazine, and tranylcypromine. *Archives of General Psychiatry, 45,* 111–119.

Cowen, E. L. (1977). Baby-steps toward primary prevention. *American Journal of Community Psychology, 5,* 1–16.

Cowen, E. L. (1980). The wooing of primary prevention. *American Journal of Community Psychology, 8,* 258–284.

Cowen, E. L. (1994). The enhancement of psychological wellness: Challenges and opportunities. *American Journal of Community Psychology, 22,* 149–179.

Cowen, E. L. (1996). The ontogenesis of primary prevention: Lengthy strides and stubbed toes. *American Journal of Community Psychology, 24,* 235–249.

Cowen, E. L., Hightower, A. D., Pedro-Carroll, J. L., Work, W. C., Wyman, P. A., & Haffey, W. G. (1996). *School-based prevention for children at risk: The Primary Mental Health Project.* Washington, DC: American Psychological Association.

Cox, B. J., & Swinson, R. P. (1995). Assessment and measurement. In M. B. Stein (Ed.), *Social phobia: Clinical and research perspectives* (pp. 261–291). Washington, DC: American Psychiatric Press.

Cox, B. J., & Taylor, S. (1998). Anxiety disorders: Panic and phobias. In T. Millon, P. Blaney, & R. Davis (Eds.), *Oxford textbook of psychopathology* (pp. 000–000). Oxford: Oxford University Press.

Cox, B. J., Swinson, R. P., Morrison, B., & Lee, P. S. (1993). Clomipramine, fluoxetine, and behavior therapy in the treatment of obsessive-compulsive disorder: A meta-analysis. *Journal of Behavior and Experimental Psychiatry, 24,* 149–153.

Cox, B. J., Wessel, I., Norton, R. G., Swinson, R. P., & Direnfeld, D. M. (1995). Publication trends in anxiety disorders research: 1990–1992. *Journal of Anxiety Disorders, 9,* 531–538.

Cox, W. M. (1987). Personality theory and research. In H. T. Blane & K. E. Leonard (Eds.), *Psychological theories of drinking and alcoholism: The Guilford Alcohol Studies Series G* (pp. 55–89). New York: Guilford Press.

Coyne, J. C. (1976). Toward an interactional model of depression. *Psychiatry, 39,* 28–40.

Coyne, J. C., & Calarco, M. M. (1995). Effects of the experience of depression: Application of focus group and survey methodologies. *Psychiatry, 58,* 149–163.

Coyne, J. C., & Gotlib, I. H. (1983). The role of cognition in depression: A critical appraisal. *Psychological Bulletin, 94,* 472–505.

CPA. See Canadian Psychological Association.

Craighead, L. W., & Agras, W. S. (1991). Mechanism of action in cognitive-behavioral and pharmacological interventions for obesity and bulimia nervosa. *Journal of Consulting and Clinical Psychology, 59,* 115–125.

Craighead, W. E., Craighead, L. W., & Ilardi, S. S. (1995). Behavior therapies in historical perspective. In B. Bongar & L. E. Beutler (Eds.), *Comprehensive textbook of psychotherapy: Theory and practice* (pp. 64–83). New York: Oxford University Press.

Craske, M. G., Barlow, D. H., & O'Leary, T. (1992). *Mastery of your anxiety and worry.* Albany: Graywind.

Creese, I., Burt, D. R., & Snyder, S. H. (1976). Dopamine receptor binding predicts clinical and pharmacological potencies of antipsychotic drugs. *Science, 192,* 481–483.

Criminal Code of Canada, R.S.C. 1985, c. C-46.

Crisp, H. H. (1970). Anorexia nervosa: "Feeding disorder," "nervous malnutrition," or "weight phobia"? *World Review of Nutrition and Diet, 12,* 542–544.

Crits-Christoph, P. (1992). The efficacy of brief dynamic psychotherapy: A meta-analysis. *American Journal of Psychiatry, 149,* 151–158.

Crocker, A. C. (1992). Symposium: Prevention of mental retardation and related disabilities. Introduction: Where is the prevention movement? *Mental Retardation, 30,* iii–v.

Cromwell, R. (1975). Assessment of schizophrenia. *Annual Review of Psychology, 26,* 593–619.

Cromwell, R. L. (1993). Schizophrenia research: Things to do before the geneticist arrives. In R. L. Cromwell & C. R. Snyder (Eds.), *Schizophrenia: Origins, processes, treatment, and outcome* (pp. 51–75). New York: Oxford University Press.

Cromwell, R. L., Elkins, I. J., McCarthy, M. E., & O'Neil, T. S. (1994). Searching for the phenotypes of schizophrenia. *Acta Psychiatrica Scandinavica, 90 (Suppl. 384),* 34–39.

Crossley, R. (1992). Getting the words out: Case studies in facilitated communication. *Topics in Language Disorders, 12,* 1–4.

Crow, T. J. (1980). Molecular pathology of schizophrenia: More than one disease process? *British Medical Journal, 280,* 1–9.

Crow, T. J. (1995). A Darwinian approach to the origins of psychosis. *British Journal of Psychiatry, 167,* 12–25.

Cruikshank, W. M. (1972). Some issues facing the field of learning disability. *Journal of Learning Disabilities, 5,* 380–388.

Culbertson, J. L., & Edmonds, J. E. (1996). Learning disabilities. In R. L. Adams, O. A. Parsons, J. L. Culbertson, & S. J. Nixon, *Neuropsychology for Clinical Practice.*

Cumming, E., & Henry, W. E. (1961). *Growing old: The process of disengagement.* New York: Basic Books.

Cummins, R. A. (1988). *The neurologically impaired child: Doman-Delacato techniques reappraised.* New York: Croom Helm.

Cunningham, C. E., & Siegel, L. S. (1987). Peer interactions of normal and attention-deficit disordered disordered boys during free-play, cooperative task, and simulated classroom situations. *Journal of Abnormal Child Psychology and Psychiatry, 15,* 247–268.

Cunningham, C. E., Bremner, R., & Boyle, M. (1995). Large group community-based parenting programs for families of preschoolers at risk for disruptive behaviour disorders: Utilization, cost effectiveness, and outcome. *Journal of Child Psychology & Psychiatry & Allied Disciplines, 36* (7), 1141–1159.

Cunningham, C. E., Davis, J. R., Bremner, R., & Dunn, K. W. (1993). Coping modeling problem solving versus mastery modeling: Effects on adherence, in-session process, and skill acquisition in a residential parent-training program. *Journal of Consulting and Clinical Psychology, 61* (5), 871–877.

Cunningham, S. J., McGrath, P. J., Ferguson, H. B., Humphreys, P., D'Astous, J. D., Latter, J., Goodman, J. T., & Firestone, P. (1987). Personality and behavioural characteristics in pediatric migraine. *Headache, 27,* 16–20.

Cuskelly, M., & Dadds, M. (1992). Behavioural problems in children with Down's Syndrome and their siblings. *Journal of Child Psychology and Psychiatry, 33,* 749–761.

Custer, R. An overview of compulsive gambling. In Carone, P. A., Yoles, S. F., Kiefer, S. N., & Kinsky, L. (Eds.). *Addictive Disorders update: Alcoholism, Drug Abuse, Gambling.* New York: Human Sciences Press, 1982.

DaCosta, M., & Halmi, K. A. (1992). Classification of anorexia nervosa: Question of subtypes. *International Journal of Eating Disorders, 11,* 305–313.

Dadds, M. R., Spence, S. H., Holland, D. E., Barrett, P. M., & Laurens, K. R. (1997). Prevention and early intervention for anxiety disorders: A controlled trial. *Journal of Consulting and Clinical Psychology, 65,* 627–635.

Dahl, A. R. (1986). Some aspects of DSM-III personality disorder illustrated by a consecutive sample of hospitalized patients. *Acta Psychiatrica Scandinavica, 73,* 61–67.

Dalton, A. J., & McLachlan, D. R. (1986). Clinical expression of Alzheimer's disease in Down's syndrome. *Psychiatric Clinics of North America, 9,* 659–670.

Daly, M. (1989). Sleep disorders in the elderly. *Primary Care, 16,* 475–488.

Dana, R. H., & May, W. T. (1986). Health care megatrends and health psychology. *Professional Psychology: Research and Practice, 17,* 251–255.

Dance, K. A., & Neufeld, R. W. (1988). Aptitude-treatment interaction research in clinical settings: A review of attempts to dispel the "patient uniformity" myth. *Psychological Bulletin, 104,* 192–213.

Darke, J. L. (1990). Sexual aggression: Achieving power through humiliation. In W. L. Marshall, D. R. Laws, & H. E. Barbaree (Eds.), *Handbook of sexual assault: Issues, theories and treatment of the offender* (pp. 55–72). New York: Plenum Press.

Darke, S., Ross, J., & Cohen, J. (1994). The use of benzodiazepines among regular amphetamine users. *Addiction, 89,* 1683–1690.

Darling, C. A., Davidson, J. K., Sr., & Cox, R. P. (1991). Female sexual response and the timing of partner orgasm. *Journal of Sex and Marital Therapy, 17,* 3–21.

Dauphinais, P., & King, J. (1992). Psychological assessment with American Indian children. *Applied and Preventive Psychology, 1,* 97–110.

Davey, G.C.L. (1992). Classical conditioning and the acquisition of human fears and phobias: A review and synthesis of the literature. *Advances in Behaviour Research and Therapy, 14,* 29–66.

Davey, G.C.L. (1994). Worrying, social problem-solving abilities, and problem-solving confidence. *Behaviour Research and Therapy, 32,* 327–330.

Davidson, P., Cain, N., Sloane-Reeves, J., Giesow, V. E., Quijano, L. E., Van Heyningen, J., & Shoham, I. (1995). Crisis intervention for community-based individuals with developmental disabilities and behavioral and psychiatric disorders. *Mental Retardation, 33,* 21–30.

Davidson, P., Cain, N., Sloane-Reeves, J., Van Speybroeck, A., Segel, J., Gutkin, J., Quijan., L., Kramer, B., Porter, B., Shoham, I., & Goldstein, E. (1994). Characteristics of community-based individuals with mental retardation and aggressive behavioral disorders. *American Journal on Mental Retardation, 98,* 704–716.

Davies, P. (1988). Alzheimer's disease and related disorders: An overview. In M. K. Aronson (Ed.), *Understanding Alzheimer's disease: What it is, how to cope with it, future directions.* New York: Charles Scribner's Sons.

Davis, M. (1989). Gender and sexual development of women with mental retardation. *The Disabilities Studies Quarterly, 9* (3), 19–20.

Davis, R., Freeman, R. J., & Garner, D. M. (1988). A naturalistic investigation of eating behaviour in bulimia nervosa. *Journal of Consulting and Clinical Psychology, 56,* 273–279.

Davis, R., Freeman, R. J., & Garner, D. M. (1988). A naturalistic investigation of eating behaviour in bulimia nervosa. *Journal of Consulting and Clinical Psychology, 56,* 273–279.

Davison, C. V., & Abramowitz, S. E. (1980). Sex bias in clinical judgement: Later empirical returns. *Psychology of Women Quarterly, 4,* 377–395.

Davison, G. C., & Neale, J. M. (1990). *Abnormal psychology* (5th ed.). New York: Wiley.

Dawson, G. (1996). Grief report: Neuropsychology of autism: A report on the state of the science. *Journal of Autism and Developmental Disorders, 26,* 179–184.

Day, D. (1990). *Young women in Nova Scotia: A study of attitudes, behaviour and aspirations.* Halifax: Nova Scotia Advisory Council on the Status of Women.

Dayan, J., & Minnes, P. (1995). Ethical issues related to the use of Facilitated Communication techniques with persons with autism. *Canadian Psychology, 36,* 183–189.

De Castro, J. (1990). Social facilitation of duration and size but not rate of the spontaneous meal intake of humans. *Physiology and Behavior, 47,* 1129–1135.

De Lacoste, M. C., Horvath, D. S., & Woodward, D. J. (1991). Possible sex differences in the developing human fetal brain. *Journal of Clinical and Experimental Neuropsychology, 13,* 831–846.

De Leo, D., & Ormskerk, S.C.R. (1991). Suicide in the elderly: General characteristics. *Crisis, 12,* 3–17.

Dean, R. R., Kelsey, J. E., Heller, M. R., & Ciaranello, R. D. (1993). Structural foundations of illness and treatment: Receptors. In D. L. Dunner (Ed.), *Current psychiatric theory.* Philadelphia: Saunders.

DeBakey, M. & Gotto, A. (1977). *The living heart* (p. 111). New York: Grosset & Dunlap.

Delacato, C. H. (1966). *Neurological organization and reading.* Springfield, IL: Charles C. Thomas.

Delaney, E. A., & Hopkins, T. F. (1987). *The Stanford-Binet Intelligence Scale: Fourth edition. Examiner's handbook.* Chicago: The Riverside Publishing Co.

DeLeon, P. H., Fox, R. E., & Graham, S. R. (1991). Prescription privileges: Psychology's next frontier? *American Psychologist, 46,* 384–393.

DeLeon, P. H., Sammons, M. T., & Fox, R. E. (1995). A commentary: Canada is not that far north. *Canadian Psychology, 36,* 320–326.

Dell, P. F. (1988). Professional skepticism about multiple personality. *Journal of Nervous & Mental Disease, 176* (9), 528–531.

Dement, W. C., Laughton, E. M., & Carskadon, M. A. (1982). "White paper" on sleep and aging. *Journal of the American Geriatrics Society, 30,* 20–29.

Denckla, M. (1996). Brain mechanisms. In M. M. Bristol, D. J. Cohen, E. J. Costello, M. Denckla, T. J. Eckberg, R. Kallen, H. C. Kraemer, C. Lord, R. Maurer, W. J. McIlvane, N. Minshew, M. Sigman, & M. A. Spence, State of the science in autism: Report to the National Institutes of Health. *Journal of Autism and Developmental Disorders, 26,* 134–140.

Depue, R. A. (in press). *Neurobehavioral systems, personality, and psychopathology.* New York: Springer-Verlag.

Depue, R. A., & Spoont, M. R. (1986). Conceptualizing a serotonin trait: A behavioral dimension of constraint. *Annals of the New York Academy of Sciences, 487,* 47–62.

Depue, R. A., & Zald, D. (1993). Biological and environmental processes in nonpsychotic psychopathology: A neurobehavioral system perspective. In C. Costello (Ed.), *Basic issues in psychopathology*. New York: Guilford Press.

Depue, R. A., Luciana, M., Arbisi, P., Collins, P., & Leon, A. (1994). Dopamine and the structure of personality: Relation of agonist-induced dopamine activity to positive emotionality. *Journal of Personality and Social Psychology, 67*, 485–498.

Derogatis, L. R., Lipman, R. S., & Covi, L. (1973). SCL–90: An out-patient psychiatric rating scale-preliminary report. *Psychopharmacology Bulletin, 9*, 13–27.

DeRyck, B., Gekoski, W. L., Knox, V. J., & Zivian, M. T. (1996, October). *Mental disorders in older adults: The beliefs and attitudes of clinical psychology graduate students*. Quebec: Canadian Association on Gerontology.

Deutsch, S. I., Mastropaolo, J., Schwartz, B. L., Rosse, R. B., Morihisa, J. M. (1989). A "glutamatergic hypothesis" of schizophrenia. *Clinical Neuropharmacology, 12*, 1–13.

Dewey, D., & Hunsley, J. (1990). The effects of marital adjustment and spouse involvement on the behavioral treatment of agoraphobia. *Anxiety Research, 2*, 69–83.

Dhawan, S., & Marshall, W. L. (1995). Sexual abuse histories of sexual offenders. *Sex Abuse: A Journal of Research and Treatment, 8*, 8–15.

Dhawan, S., & Marshall, W. L. (1996). Sexual abuse histories of sexual offenders. *Sexual Abuse: A Journal of Research and Treatment, 8*, 7–15.

Diamond, M. (1982). Sexual identity, monozygotic twins reared in discordant sex roles and a BBC follow-up. *Archives of Sexual Behavior, 11*, 181–186.

Dickens, B. M. (1982). Retardation and sterilization. *International Journal of Law and Psychiatry, 5*, 295–318.

Dickey, R., & Steiner, B. W. (1990). Hormone treatment and surgery. In R. Blanchard & B. W. Steiner (Eds.), *Clinical management of gender identity disorders in children and adults* (pp. 139–158). Washington, DC: American Psychiatric Press.

Dimsdale, J. E., & Ziegler, M. G. (1991). What do plasma and urinary measures of catecholamines tell us about human response to stressors? *Circulation, 83* (Suppl. II), II-36–II-42.

DiNardo, P. A. (1975). Social class and diagnostic suggestion as variables in clinical judgement. *Journal of Consulting and Clinical Psychology, 43*, 363–368.

DiNardo, P. A., O'Brien, G. T., Barlow, D. H., Waddell, M. T., & Blanchard, E. B. (1988). *Anxiety disorders interview schedule-revised (ADIS-R)*. Albany: Phobia and Anxiety Disorders Clinic, State University of New York at Albany.

DiNardo, P., Brown, T. A., & Barlow, D. H. (1994). *Anxiety disorders interview schedule for DSM-IV*. Albany, NY: Graywind.

DiNicola, V. (1990). Overview. Anorexia multiforme: Self-starvation in historical and cultural context. Part I: Self-starvation as a historical chameleon. *Transcultural Psychiatric Research Review, 27*, 165–196.

DiVasto, P. V., Kaufman, L. R., Jackson, R., Christy, J., Pearson, S., & Burgett, T. (1984). The prevalence of sexually stressful events among females in the general population. *Archives of Sexual Behavior, 13*, 59–67.

Dobson, D. J., McDougall, G., Busheikin, J., & Aldous, J. (1995). Effects of social skills training and social milieu treatment on symptoms of schizophrenia. *Psychiatric Services, 46* (4), 376–380.

Dobson, J. C., Kushida, E., Williamson, M., & Friedman, E. G. (1976). Intellectual performances of 36 phenylketonuria patients and their nonaffected siblings. *Pediatrics, 58*, 53–58.

Dobson, K. S. (1989). A meta-analysis of the efficacy of cognitive therapy for depression. *Journal of Consulting and Clinical Psychology, 57*, 414–419.

Dobson, K. S., & Shaw, B. F. (1995). Cognitive therapies in practice. In B. Bongar & L. E. Beutler (Eds.), *Comprehensive textbook of psychotherapy: Theory and practice* (pp. 159–172). New York: Oxford University Press.

Dodge, K. A. (1985). Attributional bias in aggressive children. *Advances in Cognitive Behavioral Research and Therapy, 4*, 34–42.

Dodge, K. A. (1986a). A social information processing model of social competence in children. In M. Perlmutter (Ed.), *Minnesota symposia on child psychology. Vol 18: Cognitive perspectives on children's social and behavioral development*. Hillsdale, NJ: Erlbaum.

Dodge, K. A. (1986b). Social information-processing variables in the development of aggression and altruism in children. In C. Zahn-Waxler, E. M. Cummings, & R. Iannotti (Eds.), *Altruism and aggression: Biological and social origins*. New York: Cambridge University Press.

Dodge, K. A., Price, J. M., Bachorowski, J., & Newman, J. P. (1990). Hostile attributional biases in several aggressive adolescents. *Journal of Abnormal Psychology, 99*, 385–392.

Doherty, K., Dinnunen, T., Militello, F. S., & Garvey, A. J. (1995). Urges to smoke during the first month of abstinence: Relationship to relapse and predictors. *Psychopharmacology, 119* (2), 171–178.

Dohrenwend, B. P., Levav, I., Shrout, P. E., Schwartz, S., Naveh, G., Link, B. G., Skodol, A. B., & Stueve, A. (1992). Socioeconomic status and psychiatric disorders: The causation-selection issue. *Science, 255*, 946–952.

Doman, R. J., Spitz, E. B., Zucman, E., Delacato, C. H., & Doman, G. (1960). Children with severe brain injuries. *JAMA, 174*, 257–262.

Donnellan, A. H., Mirenda, P. L., Mesaros, R. A., & Fassbender, L. L. (1984). Analyzing the communicative functions of aberrant behavior. *Journal of the Association of Persons with Severe Handicaps, 9*, 201–212.

Donwood Problem Gambling Program: Pilot Project (April 1, 1995–March 31, 1996). *Final report*. Unpublished manuscript.

Dorow, R., & Duka, T. (1986). Anxiety: Its generation by drug and by withdrawal. In C. Biggio & E. Costa (Eds.), *GABAergic transmission and anxiety* (pp. 211–225). New York: Raven Press.

Douglas, J. D., & Rice, K. M. (1979). Sex differences in children's anxiety and defensiveness measures. *Developmental Psychology, 15,* 223–224.

Douglas, K. S., Ogloff, J.R.P., Nicholls, T., & Grant, I. (in press). Assessing risk for violence among psychiatric patients: The HCR–20 Violence Risk Assessment Scheme and the Psychopathy Checklist: Screening Version. *Journal of Consulting and Clinical Psychology.*

Douglas, K., & Koch, W. J. (in press). Civil commitment and civil competence: Psychological issues. In R. Schuller & J.R.P. Ogloff (Eds.), *An introduction to law and psychology: Canadian perspectives.* Toronto: University of Toronto Press.

Douglas, V. I. (1972). Stop, look, and listen: The problem of sustained attention and impulse control in hyperactive and normal children. *Canadian Journal of Behavioural Science, 4,* 259–282.

Douville, R., & Casanova, J.-D. (1967). *La vie quotidienne des Indiens du Canada à L'époque de la colonisation Francaise.* Paris: Librarie Hachette.

Downey, G., & Coyne, J. C. (1990). Children of depressed parents: An integrative review. *Psychological Bulletin, 108,* 50–76.

Dozois, D.J.A., & Dobson, K. S. (1995a). Should Canadian psychologists follow the APA trend and seek prescription privileges? A reexamination of the (r)evolution. *Canadian Psychology, 36,* 288–304.

Dozois, D.J.A., & Dobson, K. S. (1995b). Psychology's heritage and prescription privileges: An unconsummatable marriage. *Canadian Psychology, 36,* 327–332.

Drake, R. E., & Vaillant, G. E. (1985). A validity study of axis II of DSM-III. *American Journal of Psychiatry, 142,* 553–558.

Druss, R. G., & Silverman, J. A. (1979). Body image and perfectionism of ballerinas: Comparison and contrast with anorexia nervosa. *General Hospital Psychiatry, 2,* 115–121.

DuBrin, J. R., & Zastowny, T. R. (1988). Predicting early attrition from psychotherapy: An analysis of a large private-practice cohort. *Psychotherapy, 25,* 393–408.

Dugas, M. J., Gagnon, F., Ladouceur, R., & Freeston, M. H. (1998). Generalized anxiety disorder: A preliminary test of a conceptual model. *Behaviour Research and Therapy, 36 (2),* 215–226.

Dugas, M. J., Letarte, H., Rhéaume, J., Freeston, M. H., & Ladouceur, R. (1995). Worry and problem-solving: Evidence of a specific relationship. *Cognitive Therapy and Research, 19,* 109–120.

Dunbar, H. F. (1935). *Emotions and bodily changes.* New York: Columbia University Press.

DuPaul, G. J., & Barkley, R. A. (1990). Medication therapy. In R. A. Barkley (Ed.), *Attention deficit hyperactivity disorder* (pp. 573–612). New York: Guilford Press.

Durand, V. M., & Carr, E. G. (1992). An analysis of maintenance following functional communication training. *Journal of Applied Behavior Analysis, 14,* 345–350.

Durham v. United States, 214 F. 2d 862 (D.C. Cir. 1954).

Durkheim, E. (1951). *Suicide: A study in sociology* (J. A. Spaulding & G. Simpson, Trans.) Glencoe, IL: Free Press. (Original work published 1987.)

Durlak, J. A., & Wells, A. M. (1997). Primary prevention programs for children and adolescents: A meta-analytic review. *American Journal of Community Psychology, 25,* 115–152.

Durrant, J. E., Cunningham, C. E., & Voelker, S. (1990). Academic, social, and general self-concepts of behavioral subgroups of learning disabled children. *Journal of Educational Psychology, 82 (4),* 657–663.

Dutton, D. G., & McGregor, B. (1992). Psychological and legal dimensions of family violence. In D. K. Kagehiro & W. S. Laufer (Eds.), *Handbook of psychology and law* (pp. 318–340). New York: Springer-Verlag.

Dutton, D. G., Saunders, K., Starzomski, A., & Batholomew, K. (1994). Intimacy-anger and insecure attachment as precursors of abuse in intimate relationships. *Journal of Applied Social Psychology, 24,* 1367–1386.

Dykens, E. M., Hodapp, R. M., & Leckman, J. F. (1987). Strengths and weaknesses in the intellectual functioning of males with fragile X syndrome. *American Journal of Mental Deficiency, 92,* 234–236.

Dykens, E. M., Hodapp, R. M., & Leckman, J. F. (1994). *Behavior and development in fragile X syndrome.* London: Sage.

Dykens, E. M., Leckman, J., Paul, R., & Watson, M. (1988). Cognitive, behavioral and adaptive functioning in fragile X and non-fragile X retarded men. *Journal of Autism and Developmental Disorders, 18,* 41–52.

Dykes, M., & McGhie, A. (1976). A comparative study of attentional strategies of schizophrenic and highly creative normal subjects. *British Journal of Psychiatry, 128,* 50–56.

Dyson, L. L. (1991). Families of young children with handicaps: Parental stress and family functioning. *American Journal on Mental Retardation, 95,* 623–629.

Dyson, L., Edgar, E., & Crnic, K. (1989). Psychological predictors of adjustment by siblings of developmentally disabled children. *American Journal on Mental Retardation, 94,* 292–302.

D'Zurilla, T. J. (1988). Problem-solving therapies. In K. S. Dobson (Ed.), *Handbook of cognitive-behavioral therapies* (pp. 85–135). New York: Pergamon Press.

D'Zurilla, T. J., & Goldfried, M. R. (1971). Problem solving and behavior modification. *Journal of Abnormal Psychology, 78,* 107–126.

Eagles, J. M., Hunter, D., & Geddes, J. R. (1992). Gender-specific changes since 1900 in the season-of-birth effect in schizophrenia. *British Journal of Psychiatry, 167,* 469–472.

Eaton, W. W., Anthony, J. C., Tepper, S., & Dryman, A. (1992). Psychopathology and attrition in the Epidemiological Catchment Area study. *American Journal of Epidemiology, 135,* 1051–1059.

Eccles, W. J. (1959). *Frontenac. The courtier Governor.* Toronto: McClelland and Stewart.

Edelbrock, C., & Costello, A. J. (1984). Structured psychiatric interviews for children and adolescents. In G. R. Goldstein & M. Hersen (Eds.), *Handbook of psychological assessment* (pp. 276–290). London: Pergamon.

Edelman, G. M. (1987). *Neural Darwinism: The theory of neuronal group selection.* New York: Basic Books.

Edwards, S., & Dickerson, M. (1987). On the similarity of positive and negative intrusions. *Behaviour Research and Therapy, 25,* 207–211.

Egeland, J., Gerhard, D., Pauls, D., Sussex, J., Kidd, K., Allen, C., Hostetter, A., & Housman, D. (1987). Bipolar affective disorder linked to DNA markers on chromosome 11. *Nature, 325,* 783–787.

Ehlers, C. L., & Schuckit, M. A. (1990). EEG fast frequency activity in sons of alcoholics. *Biological Psychiatry, 27,* 631–641.

Eiler, K., Schafer, M. R., Salstrom, D., & Lowery, R. (1995). Double-blind comparison of monocriptine and placebo in cocaine withdrawal. *American Journal of Drug and Alcohol Abuse, 21* (1), 65–79.

Elkin, I. (1994). The NIMH Treatment of Depression Collaborative Research Program: Where we began and where we are. In A. E. Bergin & S. L. Garfield (Eds.), *Handbook of psychotherapy and behavior change* (4th ed., pp. 114–139). New York: Wiley.

Elkin, I., Shea, M. T., Watkins, J. T., Imber, S. D., Sotsky, S. M., Collins, J. F., Glass, D. R., Pilkonis, P. A., Leber, W. R., Docherty, J. P., Feister, S. J., & Parloff, M. B. (1989). NIMH treatment of depression collaborative research program: General effectiveness of treatments. *Archives of General Psychiatry, 46,* 971–983.

Ellerby, L. (1994). Community based treatment of aboriginal sex offenders: Facing realities and exploring possibilities. *Forum on Corrections Research, 6,* 23–25.

Elliot, M. (1993). *Female sexual abuse of children.* New York: Guilford Press.

Elliot, R., & Greenberg, L. S. (1995). Experiential therapy in practice: The process-experiential approach. In B. M. Bongar & L. E. Beutler (Eds.), *Comprehensive textbook of psychotherapy: Theory and practice* (pp. 123–139). New York: Oxford University Press.

Ellis, A. (1962). *Reason and emotion in psychotherapy.* New York: Lyle Stuart.

Ellis, A., & Grieger, R. (Eds.) (1977). *Handbook of rational-emotive therapy.* New York: Springer.

Ellis, C. R., Singh, N. N., & Landrum, T. J. (1993). Pharmacotherapy: I. *Journal of Developmental and Physical Disabilities, 5,* 1–4.

Emery, R. E. (1982). Interparental conflict and the children of discord and divorce. *Psychological Bulletin, 92,* 310–330.

Emmelkamp, P. M. (1994). Behavior therapy with adults. In A. E. Bergin & S. L. Garlfield (Eds.), *Handbook of psychotherapy and behavior change* (4th ed.) (pp. 379–427). New York: Wiley.

Emrick, C., Tonigan, J. S., Montgomery, H., & Little, L. (1993). Alcoholics Anonymous: What is currently known? In B. S. McCrady & W. R. Miller (Eds.), *Research on Alcoholics Anonymous: Opportunities and alternatives* (pp. 41–76). New Brunswick: Alcohol Research Documentation, Rutgers, State University of New Jersey.

Endler, N. (1982). *Holiday of darkness.* New York: Wiley-Interscience.

Endler, N. S., & Magnusson, D. (1976). *Interactional psychology and personality.* Washington, DC: Hemisphere.

Engel, G. L. (1977). The need for a new medical model: A challenge for biomedicine. *Science, 196,* 129–136.

Enns, M. W., & Reiss, J. P. (1992). Electroconvulsive therapy. *Canadian Journal of Psychiatry, 37,* 671–678.

Epp, J. (1986). Achieving health for all: A framework for health promotion. *Canadian Journal of Public Health, 77,* 393–407.

Epp, J. (1988). *Mental health for Canadians: Striking a balance.* Ottawa: Minister of Supplies and Services.

Erickson, M. F., Sroufe, L. A., & Egeland, B. (1985). The relationship between quality of attachment and behavior problems in preschool in a high-risk sample. In I. Bretherton & E. Waters (Eds.), *Growing points of attachment theory and research. Monographs of the Society for Research in Child Development* (pp. 147–166) Champaign, IL: Research Press.

Erikson, E. (1950). *Childhood and society.* New York: Norton.

Escobar, J. I., Randolf, E. T., & Hill, M. (1986). Symptoms of schizophrenia in Hispanic and Anglo veterans. *Culture, Medicine, and Psychiatry, 10,* 259–276.

Etringer, B. D., Gregory, V. R., & Lando, H. A. (1984). Influence of group cohesion on the behavioral treatment of smoking. *Journal of Consulting and Clinical Psychology, 52,* 1080–1086.

Evans, D. R. (Ed.). (1997). The law, standards of practice, and ethics in the practice of psychology. Toronto, ON: Emond Montgomery Publications Ltd.

Evans, R. G. (1994). Introduction. In R. G. Evans, M. L. Barer, & T. R. Marmor (Eds.), *Why are some people healthy and others not? The determinants of health of populations.* New York: Aldine de Gruyter.

Everaerd, W. (1993). Male erectile disorder. In W. O'Donohue & J. H. Geer (Eds.), *Handbook of sexual dysfunctions. Assessment and treatment* (pp. 201–224).

Ewart, C. K., Taylor, C. B., Kraemer, H. C., & Agras, W. S. (1991). High blood pressure and marital discord: Not being nasty matters more than being nice. *Health Psychology, 10,* 155–163.

Exner, J. E. (1986). *The Rorschach: A comprehensive system* (2nd ed.). New York: Wiley.

Exner, J. E. (1993). *The Rorschach: A comprehensive approach.* New York: Wiley.

Eysenck, H. J. (1952). The effects of psychotherapy: An evaluation. *Journal of Consulting Psychology, 16,* 319–324.

Eysenck, H. J. (1966). *The effects of psychotherapy.* New York: International Science Press.

Eysenck, H. J. (1973). *The inequality of man.* London: Temple South.

Eysenck, H. J. (1977). *Crime and personality* (3rd ed.). London: Routledge & Kegan Paul.

Fairburn, C. G. (1981). A cognitive-behavioral approach to the management of bulimia. *Psychological Medicine, 141,* 707–711.

Fairburn, C. G. (1985). Cognitive-behavioral treatment for bulimia. In D. M. Garner & P. E. Garfinkel (Eds.), *Handbook for psychotherapy for anorexia nervosa and bulimia* (pp. 160–192). New York: Guilford Press.

Fairburn, C. G. (1995a). *Overcoming binge eating.* New York: Guilford Press.

Fairburn, C. G. (1995b). Short-term psychological treatments for bulimia nervosa. In K. D. Brownell & C. G. Fairburn (Eds.), *Eating disorders and obesity: A comprehensive handbook* (pp. 344–348).

Fairburn, C. G., & Beglin, S. J. (1990). Studies of the epidemiology of bulimia nervosa. *American Journal of Psychiatry, 147,* 401–408.

Fairburn, C. G., & Cooper, Z. (1993). The eating disorder examination (12th ed.). In C. G. Fairburn & G. T. Wilson (Eds.), *Binge eating: Nature, assessment, and treatment* (pp. 317–360). New York: Guilford Press.

Fairburn, C. G., & Wilson, G. T. (1993). *Binge eating: Nature, assessment and treatment.* New York: Guilford Press.

Fairburn, C. G., Agras, W. S., & Wilson, G. T. (1992). The research on the treatment of bulimia-nervosa: Practical and theoretical implications. In G. H. Anderson & S. H. Kennedy (Eds.), *The biology of feast and famine: Relevance to eating disorders* (pp. 317–340). San Diego: Academic Press.

Fairburn, C. G., Marcus, M. D., & Wilson, G. T. (1993). Cognitive-behavioral therapy for binge eating and bulimia nervosa: A comprehensive treatment manual. In C. G. Fairburn & G. T. Wilson (Eds.), *Binge eating: Nature, assessment and treatment* (pp. 361–404). New York: Guilford Press.

Fairburn, C. G., Norman, P. A., Welch, S. L., O'Connor, M. E., Doll, H. A., & Peveler, R. C. (1997). A prospective study of outcome in bulimia nervosa and the long-term effects of three psychological treatments. *Archives of General Psychiatry, 52,* 304–312.

Fairburn, C. G., Welch, S. L., Doll, H. A., Davies, B. A., & O'Connor, M. E. (1997). Risk factors for bulimia nervosa. *Archives of General Psychiatry, 54,* 509–517.

Falconer, D. S. (1960). *Introduction to quantitative genetics.* New York: Ronald Press.

Fallon, P., Katzman, M. A., & Wooley, S. C. (1994). *Feminist perspectives on eating disorders.* New York: Guilford Press.

Faraone, S. V., Biederman, J., Keenan, K., & Tsuang, M. T. (1991). Separation of DSM-III attention deficit disorder and conduct disorder: Evidence from a family genetic study of American child psychiatry patients. *Psychological Medicine, 21,* 109–121.

Farrington, D. P. (1978). The family backgrounds of aggressive youths. In L. Hersov, M. Berger, & D. Shaffer (Eds.), *Aggression and antisocial behavior in childhood and adolescence* (pp. 73–93). Oxford: Pergamon.

Farrington, D. P. (1991). Childhood aggression and adult violence: Early precursors and later life outcomes. In D. J. Pepler & K. H. Rubin (Eds.), *The development and treatment of childhood aggression* (pp. 5–30). Hillsdale: Lawrence Erlbaum Associates.

Farrington, D. P., Loeber, R., & Van Kammen, W. B. (1990). Long-term criminal outcomes of hyperactivity-impulsivity-attention deficit and conduct problems in childhood. In L. N. Robins & M. Rutter (Eds.), *Straight and devious pathways from childhood to adulthood* (pp. 62–81). Cambridge: Cambridge University Press.

Fast, G. A., & Preskorn, S. H. (1993). Therapeutic drug monitoring. In D. L. Dunner (Ed.), *Current psychiatric therapy* (pp. 529–534). Philadelphia: Saunders.

Fausto-Sterling, A. (1985). *Myths of gender: Biological theories about women and men.* New York: Basic Books.

Fawcett, J., Scheftner, W. A., Fogg, L., Clarke, D. C., Young, M. A., Hedeker, D., & Gibbons, R. (1990). Time-related predictors of suicide in major affective disorder. *American Journal of Psychiatry, 147* (9), 1189–1194.

Febbraro, A. (1994). Single mothers "at risk" for child maltreatment: An appraisal of person-centred interventions and a call for emancipatory action. *Canadian Journal of Community Mental Health, 13* (2), 47–60.

Feinberg, I. (1982/1983). Schizophrenia: Caused by a fault in programmed synaptic elimination during adolescence? *Journal of Psychiatric Research, 17* (4), 319–334.

Feingold, B. (1975). *Why your child is hyperactive.* New York: Random House.

Feldman, M. A., Case, L., Towns, F., & Betel J. (1985). Parent Education Project I: The development and nurturance of children of mentally retarded parents. *American Journal of Mental Deficiency, 90,* 253–258.

Feldman, M. A., Towns, R., Betel, J., Case, L., Rincover, A., & Rubino, C. A. (1986). Parent Education Project II: Increasing stimulating interactions of developmentally handicapped mothers. *Journal of Applied Behavior Analysis, 19,* 23–27.

Feldman, W., Feldman, E., Goodman, J. T., McGrath, P. J., Pless, R., Corsini, L., & Bennett, S. (1991). Is childhood sexual abuse really increasing in prevalence? An analysis of the evidence. *Pediatrics, 88,* 29–33.

Ferguson, D. M., Horwood, L. J., & Lynskey, M. T. (1993). Prevalence and comorbidity of DSM-III-R disorders in a birth cohort of 15 year olds. *Journal of the American Academy of Child and Adolescent Psychiatry, 32,* 1127–1134.

Ferraro, K. F. (1989). Widowhood and health. In K. S. Markides & C. L. Cooper (Eds.), *Aging, stress, and health* (pp. 69–90). Chichester, England: Wiley.

Finkelhor, D. (1979). *Sexual victimization of children.* New York: Free Press.

Finkelhor, D. (Ed.) (1984). *Child sexual abuse: New theory and research.* New York: Free Press.

Finkelhor, D., & Lewis, I. (1988). An epidemiologic approach to the study of child molestation. *The Annals of the New York Academy of Science, 528,* 64–67.

Finkelhor, D., & Russell, D. (1984). Women as perpetrators. In D. Finkelhor (Ed.), *Child sexual abuse: New theory and research.* New York: Free Press.

Finlayson, L. M., & Koocher, G. P. (1991). Professional judgment and child abuse reporting in sexual abuse cases. *Professional Psychology: Research and Practice, 22* (6), 464–472.

Finn, P. R., Zeitouni, N. C., & Pihl, R. O. (1990). Effects of alcohol on psychophysiological hyper reactivity to non-aversive and aversive stimuli in men at high risk for alcoholism. *Journal of Abnormal Psychology, 99,* 79–85.

Firestone, P. (1976). The effects and side effects of time-out on an aggressive nursery school child. *Journal of Behavior Therapy and Experimental Psychiatry, 21,* 23–26.

Firestone, P. (1982a). Factors associated with children's adherence to stimulant medication. *American Journal of Orthopsychiatry, 52* (3), 447–457.

Firestone, P., & Backman, J. (1979). A review of pharmaological and behavioural approaches to the treatment of hyperactive children. *American Journal of Orthopsychiatry, 49,* 500–504.

Firestone, P., & Peters, S. (1983). Minor physical anomalies and behavior in children: A Review. *Journal of Autism and Development Disorders, 13,* 411–425.

Firestone, P., & Prabhu, A. (1983). Minor physical anomalies and obstretical complications: Their relationship to hyperactive, psychoneurotic and normal children and their families. *Journal of Abnormal Child Psychology, 11* (2), 207–216.

Firestone, P., & Witt, J. E. (1982). Characteristics of families completing and prematurely discontinuing a behavioral parent-training program. *Journal of Pediatric Psychology, 7* (2), 209–222.

Firestone, P., Kelly, J. J., Goodman, J. T., & Davey, J. (1981). Differential effects of parent training and stimulant medication with hyperactives: A progress report. *Journal of the American Academy of Child and Adolescent Psychiatry, 20,* 135–147.

First, M. B., Spitzer, R. L., Gibbon, M., Williams, J.B.W. (1995). *Structured Clinical Interview for DSM-IV–Axis I disorders.* New York: Biometrics Research Department, New York Psychiatric Institute.

First, M. B., Williams, J.B.W., & Spitzer, R. L. (1996). *DTREE: The DSM-IV Expert.* Toronto: MHS.

Fischbach, G. D. (1992). Mind and brain. *Scientific American, 267,* 48–57.

Fischer, M., Barkley, R. A., Edelbrock, C. S., & Smallish, L. (1990). The adolescent outcome of hyperactive children diagnosed by research criteria. *Journal of Consulting and Clinical Psychology, 58* (5), 580–588.

Fishbach, G. D. (1992). Mind and brain. *Scientific American, 267,* 48–57.

Fisher, C., Gross, J., & Zuch, T. (1965). Cycle of penile erection synchronous with dreaming (REM) sleep. *Archives of General Psychiatry, 12,* 29–45.

Fisher, S. (1986). *Stress and strategy.* London: Lawrence Erlbaum Associates.

Fitts, S. N., Gibson, P., Redding, C. A., & Deiter, P. J. (1989). Body dysmorphic disorder: Implications for its validity as a DSM-III-R clinical syndrome. *Psychological Reports, 64,* 655–658.

Fleshner, C. L. (1995). First person account: Insight from a schizophrenia patient with depression. *Schizophrenia Bulletin, 21,* 703–707.

Flynt, S. W., Wood, T. A., & Scott, R. L. (1992). Social support of mothers of children with mental retardation. *American Journal of Mental Retardation, 4,* 233–236.

Foa, E. B., & Kozak, M. J. (1986). Emotional processing of fear: Exposure to corrective information. *Psychological Bulletin, 99,* 20–35.

Foa, E. B., Riggs, D. S., Massie, E. D., & M. Yarczower (1995). The impact of fear activation and anger on the efficacy of exposure treatment for posttraumatic stress disorder. *Behavior Therapy, 26,* 487–499.

Foa, E. B., Steketee, G., & Rothbaum, B. O. (1989). Behavioral/cognitive conceptualizations of post-traumatic stress disorder. *Behavior Therapy, 20,* 155–176.

Foa, E. B., Zinbarg, R., & Rothbaum, B. O. (1992). Uncontrollability and unpredictability in post-traumatic stress disorder: An animal model. *Psychological Bulletin, 112,* 218–238.

Folks, D. G., Ford, C. V., & Regan, W. M. (1984). Conversion symptoms in a general hospital. *Psychosomatics, 25,* 285–295.

Folsom, V., Krahn, D., Nairn, K., Gold, L., Demitrack, M. A., & Silk, K. R. (1993). The impact of alcohol and physical abuse on eating disordered and psychiatric symptoms: A comparison of eating disordered and psychiatric inpatients. *International Journal of Eating Disorders, 13,* 249–257.

Ford, C. S., & Beech, F. A. (1951). *Patterns of sexual behavior.* New York: Ace.

Ford, C. V., & Folks, D. G. (1985). Conversion disorders: An overview. *Psychosomatics, 26,* 371–383.

Ford, D. E., & Kameron, D. (1989). Epidemiologic study of sleep disturbances and psychiatric disorders: An opportunity for prevention? *Journal of the American Medical Association, 262,* 1479–1484.

Ford, D., & Kamerow, D. (1990). Epidemiologic study of sleep disturbances and psychiatric disorders. *Journal of the American Medical Association, 262,* 1479–1484.

Ford, M. R., & Widiger, T. A. (1989). Sex bias in the diagnosis of histrionic and antisocial personality disorders. *Journal of Consulting and Clinical Psychology, 57,* 301–305.

Fordyce, W. E. (1976). *Behavioural methods for chronic pain and illness.* St. Louis, MO: Mosby.

Foster, J. R. (1992). The use of lithium in elderly psychiatric patients: A review of the literature. *Lithium, 3,* 77–93.

Foster, J. R., & Martin, C. C. (1990). Dementia. In D. Bienenfeld (Ed.), *Verwoerdt's clinical geropsychiatry* (3rd ed., pp. 66–84). Baltimore, MD: Williams & Wilkins.

Foulds, G. A. (1965). *Personality and mental illness.* London: Tavistock.

Foy, D. W. (1992). *Treating PTSD: Cognitive-behavioral strategies.* New York: Guilford Press.

Frances, A. (1985). Validating schizotypal personality disorders: Problems with the schizophrenic connection. *Schizophrenia Bulletin, 11,* 595–597.

Frank, E., & Spanier, C. (1995). Interpersonal psychotherapy for depression: Overview, clinical efficacy, and future directions. *Clinical Psychology: Science and Practice, 2,* 349–369.

Frank, E., Anderson, C., & Rubinstein, D. (1978). Frequency of sexual dysfunction in "normal" couples. *The New England Journal of Medicine, 299,* 111–115.

Frank, J. D. (1961). *Persuasion and healing.* Baltimore, MD: Johns Hopkins University Press.

Frankl, V. E. (1962). *Man's search for meaning.* Boston: Beacon Press.

Franklin, D. (1990, November/December). Chap. 12: Hooked–not hooked: Why isn't everyone an addict? *Health* (pp. 39–52).

Frasure-Smith, N., Lesperance, F., & Talajic, M. (1993). Depression following myocardial infarction: Impact on 6-month survival. *Journal of the American Medical Association, 270,* 1819–1825.

Freeston, M. H., Ladouceur, R., Provencher, M., & Blais, F. (1995). Strategies used with intrusive thoughts: Context, appraisal, mood, and efficacy. *Journal of Anxiety Disorders, 9,* 201–205.

Freeston, M. H., Ladouceur, R., Thibodeau, N., & Gagnon, F. (1992). Cognitive intrusions in a non-clinical population. II. Associations with depressive, anxious, and compulsive symptoms. *Behaviour Research and Therapy, 30,* 263–271.

Freeston, M. H., Rhéaume, J., Letarte, H., Dugas, M. J., & Ladouceur, R. (1994). Why do people worry? *Personality and Individual Differences, 17,* 791–802.

Freeston, M., H., Ladouceur, R., Gagnon, F., Thibodeau, N., Rhéaume, J., Letarte, H., & Bujold, A. (1997). Cognitive-behavioral treatment of obsessive thoughts: A controlled study. *Journal of Consulting and Clinical Psychology, 65,* 405–413.

Fremouw, W. J., de Perczel, M., & Ellis, T. E. (1990). *Suicide risk: Assessment and response guidelines.* New York: Pergamon Press.

Frenzel, R. R., & Lang, R. A. (1989). Identifying sexual preferences in intrafamilial and extrafamilial child sexual abusers. *Annals of Sex Research, 2,* 255–275.

Freud, S. (1905). Psychical (or mental) treatment. In J. Strachey (Ed.), *The complete psychological works (Vol. 7).* New York: Norton.

Freud, S. (1917). *A general introduction to psychoanalysis* (J. Rivière, Trans.). New York: Liveright, 1963.

Freud, S. (1917). Mourning and melancholia. In *Collected papers (Vol. 4).* London: Hogarth Press.

Freud, S. (1957). Mourning and melancholia. In J. Strachey (Ed. and Trans.), *The standard edition of the complete psychological works of Sigmund Freud (Vol. 14).* London: Hogarth Press. (Original work published 1917.)

Freund, K. (1990). Courtship disorder. In W. L. Marshall, D. R. Laws, & H. E. Barbaree (Eds.), *Handbook of sexual assault: Issues, theories and treatment of the offender* (pp. 195–207). New York: Plenum Press.

Freund, K., & Watson, R. J. (1991). Assessment of the sensitivity and specificity of a phallometric test: An update of phallometric diagnosis of pedophilia. *Psychological Assessment: A Journal of Consulting and Clinical Psychology, 3,* 254–260.

Freund, K., Watson, R. J., & Dickey, R. (1991a). The types of gender identity disorder. *Annals of Sex Research, 14,* 93–105.

Freund, K., Watson, R. J., & Dickey, R. (1991b). Sex offenses against female children perpetrated by men who are not pedophiles. *Journal of Sex Research, 28,* 409–423.

Frezza, M., Di Padova, C., Pozzato, G., Terpin, M., Baraona, E., & Lieber, C. S. (1990). High blood alcohol levels in women: The role of decreased gastric alcohol dehydrogenase activity and first-pass metabolism. *New England Journal of Medicine, 322* (2), 95–99.

Frick, P. J. (1993). Childhood conduct problems in a family context. *School of Psychology Review, 22,* 376–385.

Frick, P. J., Lahey, B. B., Loeber, R., Stouthamer-Loeber, M., Christ, M.A.G., & Hanson, K. (1992). Familial risk factors to oppositional defiant disorder and conduct disorder: Parental psychopathology and maternal parenting. *Journal of Consulting and Clinical Psychology, 60,* 49–55.

Friedman, H. S., & Booth-Kewley, S. (1987). Personality, Type A behavior, and coronary heart disease: The role of emotional expression. *Journal of Personality and Social Psychology, 53,* 783–792.

Friedman, M., & Rosenman, R. H. (1959). Association of specific behavior pattern with blood and cardiovascular findings. *Journal of the American Medical Association, 169,* 1286–1296.

Friedman, M., & Rosenman, R. H. (1974). *Type A behavior and your heart.* New York: Knopf.

Friedman, M., Thoresen, C. E., Gill, J., Ulmer, D., Powell, L. H., Price, B. A., Brown, B., Thompson, L., Rabin, D., Breall, W. S., Bourg, W., Levy, R., & Dixon, T. (1986). Alteration of Type A behavior and its effect on cardiac recurrences in postmyocardial infarction patients: Summary results of the Recurrent Coronary Prevention Project. *American Heart Journal, 112,* 653–665.

Fries, J. F., & Crapo, L. M. (1981). *Vitality and aging.* San Francisco: Freeman.

Frischolz, E. J., Lipman, L. S., Braun, B. G., & Sachs, R. G. (1992). Psychopathology, hypnotizability, and dissociation. *American Journal of Psychiatry, 149* (11), 1521–1525.

Frith, C. D., Friston, K. J., Herold, S., Silbersweig, D., Fletcher, P., Cahill, C., Dolan, R. J., Frackowiak, R.S.J., & Liddle, P. F. (1995). Regional brain activity in chronic schizophrenic patients during the performance of a verbal fluency task. *British Journal of Psychiatry, 167,* 343–349.

Fromm-Reichmann, F. (1948). Notes on the development of treatment of schizophrenics by psychoanalytic psychotherapy. *Psychiatry, 11,* 263–273.

Frost, R., & Steketee, G. (1997). Perfectionism in obsessive-compulsive patients. *Behaviour Research and Therapy, 35,* 291–296.

Furby, L., Weinrott, M. R., & Blackshaw, L. (1989). Sex offender recidivism: A review. *Psychological Bulletin, 105,* 3–30.

Fyer, A., Liebowitz, M., Gorman, J., Compeas, R., Levine, A., Davie, S., Goetz, D., & Klein, D. (1987). Discontinuation of alpraxolam treatment in panic patients. *American Journal of Psychiatry, 144,* 303–308.

Gabbard, G. O., & Coyne, L. (1987). Predictors of response of antisocial patients to hospital treatment. *Hospital and Community Psychiatry, 38,* 1181–1185.

Gabrielli, W. F., Jr., Mednick, S. A., Volavka, J., Pollock, V. E., Schulsinger, F., & Itil, T. M. (1982). Electroencephalograms in children of alcoholic fathers. *Psychophysiology, 19,* 404–407.

Gaddes, W. H. (1976). Prevalence estimates and the need for definition of learning disabilities. In R. M. Knights & D. J. Bakker (Eds.), *The neuropsychology of learning disorders.* Baltimore, MD: University Park Press.

Gagnon, J., & Simon, W. (1973). *Sexual conduct: The social origins of human sexuality.* Chicago: Aldine.

Gajar, A. (1992). Adults with learning disabilities: Current and future research priorities. *Journal of Learning Disabilities, 25,* 507–519.

Galbraith, J. K. (1996). *The good society.* New York: Houghton Mifflin.

Gallagher, D., & Thompson, L. W. (1982). Treatment of major depressive disorder in older adult outpatients with brief psychotherapies. *Psychotherapy, Theory, Research, and Practice, 19,* 482–490.

Gapstur, S. M., Potter, J. D., Sellers, T. A., & Folson, A. R. (1992). Increased risk of breast cancer with alcohol consumption in postmenopausal women. *American Journal of Epidemiology, 136,* 1221–1231.

Garb, H. (1997). Race bias, social class bias, and gender bias in clinical judgement. *Clinical Psychology, Science and Practice, 4* (2), 99–120.

Gard, M.C.E., & Freeman, C. G. (1996). The dismantling of a myth: A review of eating disorders and socioeconomic status. *International Journal of Eating Disorders, 20,* 1–12.

Garfield, S. L. (1994). Research on client variables in psychotherapy. In A. E. Bergin & S. L. Garfield (Eds.), *Handbook of psychotherapy and behavior change* (4th ed., pp. 190–228). New York: Wiley.

Garfinkel, P. E., & Garner, D. M. (1982). *Anorexia nervosa: A multidimensional perspective.* New York: Brunner/Mazel.

Garfinkel, P. E., Lin, E., Goering, P., Spegg, C., Goldbloom, D. S., Kennedy, S., Kaplan, A. S., & Woodside, D. B. (1995). Bulimia nervosa in a Canadian community sample: Prevalence and comparison of subgroups. *American Journal of Psychiatry, 152,* 1052–1058.

Garfinkel, P. E., Moldofsky, H., & Garner, D. M. (1980). The heterogeneity of anorexia nervosa. *Archives of General Psychiatry, 37,* 1036–1040.

Garland, A., & Zigler, E. (1993). Adolescent suicide prevention: Current research and social policy implications. *American Psychologist, 48,* 169–182.

Garlick, Y., Marshall, W. L., & Thornton, D. (1996). Intimacy deficits and attribution of blame among sex offenders. *Legal and Criminological Psychology, 1,* 251–258.

Garmezy, N. (1985). The NIMH-Israeli high-risk study: Commendation, comments, and cautions. *Schizophrenia Bulletin, 11,* 349–353.

Garmezy, N. (1994). Reflections and commentary on risk, resilience, and development. In R. J. Haggerty, L. R. Sherrod, N. Garmezy, & M. Rutter (Eds.), *Stress, risk, and resilience in children and adolescents: Processes, mechanisms, and interventions* (pp. 1–18). New York: Cambridge University Press.

Garmezy, N. (1996). Stress-resistent children: The search for protective factors. In J. E. Stevenson (Ed.), *Recent research in developmental psychopathology. Journal of child psychology and psychiatry book supplement* (pp. 213–233).

Garner, D. M. (1986). Cognitive therapy for anorexia nervosa. In K. D. Brownell & J. P. Foreyt (Eds.), *Handbook of eating disorders* (pp. 301–327). New York: Basic Books.

Garner, D. M. (1991). *The eating disorder inventory—2 Professional manual.* Odessa, FL: Psychological Assessment Resources.

Garner, D. M. (1997). The 1997 body image survey results. *Psychology Today, 30* (1) 30–44.

Garner, D. M., & Bemis, K. M. (1982). A cognitive-behavioral approach to anorexia nervosa. *Cognitive Therapy and Research, 6,* 123–150.

Garner, D. M., & Bemis, K. M. (1985). Cognitive therapy for anorexia nervosa. In D. M. Garner & P. E. Garfinkel (Eds.), *Handbook of psychotherapy for anorexia nervosa and bulimia* (pp. 107–146). New York: Guilford Press.

Garner, D. M., & Fairburn, C. G. (1988). Relationship between anorexia nervosa and bulimia nervosa: Diagnostic implications. In D. M. Garner & P. E. Garfinkel (Eds.), *Diagnostic issues in anorexia nervosa and bulimia nervosa* (pp. 556–579). New York: Brunner/Mazel.

Garner, D. M., & Garfinkel, P. E. (1978). Sociocultural factors in anorexia nervosa. *The Lancet, 2,* 674.

Garner, D. M., & Garfinkel, P. E. (1980). Socio-cultural factors in the development of anorexia nervosa. *Psychological Medicine, 10,* 647–656.

Garner, D. M., & Rosen, L. W. (1991). Eating disorders in athletes: Research and recommendations. *Journal of Applied Sports Research, 5,* 100–107.

Garner, D. M., & Wooley, S. C. (1991). Confronting the failure of behavioral and dietary treatments of obesity. *Clinical Psychology Review, 11,* 729–780.

Garner, D. M., Garfinkel, P. E., Schwartz, D. M., & Thompson, M. M. (1980). Cultural expectations of thinness of women. *Psychological Reports, 47,* 483–491.

Garner, D. M., Olmstead, M. P., & Polivy, J. (1983). Development and validation of a multidimensional eating disorder inventory for anorexia and bulimia. *International Journal of Eating Disorders, 2,* 15–34.

Garner, D. M., Rockert, W., Davis R., Garner, M. V., Olmstead, M. P., & Eagle, M. (1993). Comparison between cognitive-behavioral and supportive-expressive therapy for bulimia nervosa. *American Journal of Psychiatry, 150,* 37–46.

Garner, D. M., Rockert, W., Olmsted, M. P., Johnson, C. L., & Coscina, D. V. (1985). Psychoeducational principles in the treatment of bulimia and anorexia nervosa. In D. M. Garner & P. E. Garfinkel (Eds.), *Handbook of psychotherapy for anorexia nervosa and bulimia* (pp. 513–572). New York: Guilford Press.

Garner, D. M., Shafer, C., & Rosen, L. (1991). Critical appraisal of the DSM-III-R diagnostic criteria for eating disorders. In S. R. Hooper, G. W. Hynd, & R. E. Mattison (Eds.), *Child psychopathology.* Hillsdale, NJ: Lawrence Erlbaum Associates.

Garrick, T., Minor, R. T., Buack, S., et al. (1989). Predictable and unpredictable shock stimulates gastric contractility and causes mucosal injury in rats. *Behavioural Neuroscience, 103,* 124–130.

Gatz, M., & Smyer, M. A. (1992). The mental health system and older adults in the 1990s. *American Psychologist, 47,* 741–751.

Gatz, M., Kasl-Godley, J. E., & Karel, M. J. (1996). Aging and mental disorders. In J. E. Birren & K. W. Schaie (Eds.),

Handbook of the psychology of aging (pp. 365–382). San Diego, CA: Academic Press.

Gatz, M., Popkin, S. J., Pino, C. P., & Vanden Bos, G. R. (1985). Psychological interventions with older adults. In J. E. Birren & K. W. Schaie (Eds.), *Handbook of the psychology of aging* (2nd ed., pp. 755–785). New York: Van Nostrand Reinhold.

Gawin, F. H., & Kleber, H. D. (1986). Abstinence symptomatology and psychiatric diagnosis in cocaine abusers. *Archives of General Psychiatry, 43,* 107–113.

Gebhard, P. H., & Johnson, A. B. (1979). *The Kinsey data: Marginal tabulations of the 1938–1963 interviews conducted by the Institute for Sex Research.* Philadelphia: Saunders.

Gedye, A. (1995). *The Dementia Scale for Down Syndrome.*

Geen, R. G. (1983). Aggression and television violence. In R. G. Geen & E. I. Donnerstein (Eds.), *Aggression: Theoretical and empirical reviews, Vol. 2: Issues in research* (pp. 103–125). New York: Academic Press.

Geer, J. H. (1965). The development of a scale to measure fear. *Behaviour Research and Therapy, 3,* 45–53.

Geer, J. H., Davison, G. C., & Gatchel, R. I. (1970). Reduction of stress in humans through nonveridical perceived control of aversive stimulation. *Journal of Personality and Social Psychology, 16,* 731–738.

Gelles, R. J., & Straus, M. A. (1987). Is violence toward children increasing? A comparison of 1975 and 1985 survey rates. *Journal of Interpersonal Violence, 2,* 212–222.

Gendreau, P. (1996). The principles of effective intervention with offenders. In A. T. Harland (Ed.), *Choosing correctional options that work: Defining the demand and evaluating the supply* (pp. 117–130). Thousand Oaks, CA: Sage.

George, L. K., Blazer, D. G., & Hughes, D. C. (1989). Social support and the outcome of major depression. *British Journal of Psychiatry, 154,* 478–485.

George, L., & Neufeld, R.W.J. (1985). Cognition and symptomatology in schizophrenia. *Schizophrenia Bulletin, 11,* 264–285.

Gerstley, L. J., McLellan, A. T., Alterman, A. I., Woody, G. E., Luborsky, L., & Prout, M. (1989). Ability to form an alliance with the therapist: A possible marker of prognosis for patients with antisocial personality disorder. *American Journal of Psychiatry, 146,* 508–512.

Gething, L. (1991). Generality vs. specificity of attitudes towards people with disabilities. *British Journal of Medical Psychology, 64,* 55–64.

Gewirtz, G., Squires, E., Sharif, Z., & Honer, W. G. (1994). Results of computerized tomography during first admission for psychosis. *British Journal of Psychiatry, 164* (6), 789–795.

Gfellner, B. M., & Hundelby, J. D. (1995). Patterns of drug use among native and white adolescents: 1990–1993. *Canadian Journal of Public Health, 86* (2), 95–97.

Gibson, P. (1989). Gay male and lesbian youth suicide. In M. R. Feinleib (Ed.), *Report of the Secretary's task force on youth suicide: Vol. 3. Prevention and interventions in youth suicide* (pp. 110–142). Washington, DC: US Government Printing Office.

Gidron, Y., McGrath, P. J., & Goodday, R. (1995). The physical and psychosocial predictors of adolescents' recovery from oral surgery. *Journal of Behavioral Medicine, 18* (4), 385–399.

Giesbrecht, N., Glicksman, L., Douglas, R. R., & Loranger, P. D. (1992). *Questions and answers: Alcohol and other drug use in Ontario.* Toronto: Addiction Research Foundation.

Gil, D. G. (1996). Preventing violence in a violent society: Mission impossible. *American Journal of Orthopsychiatry, 66,* 77–84.

Gilbert, M. (1996, July 27). The movement to break the gender barrier. *The Globe and Mail,* p. C-7.

Gillberg, C. (1991). Outcome in autism and autistic-like conditions. *Journal of the American Academy of Child and Adolescent Psychiatry, 30,* 375–382.

Gillberg, C., & Gillberg, C. (1989). Asperger Syndrome—some epidemiological considerations: A research note. *Journal of Child Psychology and Psychiatry 30,* 631–638.

Gitlin, M. J. (1993). Pharmacotherapy of personality disorders: Conceptual framework and clinical strategies. *Journal of Clinical Psychopharmacology, 13,* 343–353.

Gittelman, R., & Mannuzza, S. (1985). Hyperactive boys almost grow up: I. Psychiatric status. *Archives of General Psychiatry, 42,* 937–947.

Gittelman, R., Abicoff, H., Pollack, E., Klein, D., Katz, S., & Mattes, J. (1980). A controlled trial of behavior modification and methylphenidate in hyperactive children. In C. Whalen & B. Henker (Eds.), *Hyperactive children: The social ecology of identification and treatment* (pp. 221–246). New York: Academic Press.

Gittelman-Klein, R. (1975). Psychiatric characteristics of the relatives of school phobic children. In D.V.S. Sankar (Ed.), *Mental health in children* (pp. 325–334). Westbury, NY: PJD.

Gittelman-Klein, R., & Klein, D. (1980). Separation anxiety in school refusal and its treatment with drugs. In L. Hersov & I. Berg (Eds.), *Out of school* (pp. 321–341). London: Wiley.

Gittelman-Klein, R., & Klein, D. F. (1971). Controlled imipramine treatment of school phobia. *Archives of General Psychiatry, 25,* 204–207.

Glanze, W. D., Anderson, K. E., & Anderson, L. E. (1985). *The Mosby medical encyclopedia.* New York: Plume.

Glaser, R., Pearl, D. K., Kiecolt-Glaser, J. K., & Malarkey, W. B. (1994). Plasma cortisol levels and reactivation of latent Epstein-Barr virus in response to examination stress. *Psychoneuroendocrinology, 19,* 765–772.

Glasgow, R. E., & Rosen, G. M. (1978). Behavioral bibliotherapy: A review of self-help behavior therapy manuals. *Psychological Bulletin, 85,* 1–23.

Glatt, A. E., Zinner, S. H., & McCormack, W. M. (1990). The prevalence of dyspareunia. *Obstetrics & Gynecology, 75,* 433–436.

Glausiusz, J. (1997, January) The genes of 1996. *Discover,* p. 36.

Gleik, J. (1992). *Genius: The life and science of Richard Feynman.* New York: Pantheon.

Glick, I. D., Freund, N. Y., & Olfson, M. (1992). What a psychiatric hospitalization can and cannot do: A review of efficacy studies. In E. Persad, S. S. Kazarian, & L. W. Joseph (Eds.), *The mental hospital in the 21st century* (pp. 191–204). Toronto: Wall & Emerson.

Glicksman, L., Newton-Taylor, B., Adlaf, E., Dewit, D., & Geisbrecht, N. (1995), *University student drug use and lifestyle behaviours—current patterns and lifestyle changes from 1988 to 1993.* Toronto, Addiction Research Foundation.

Glueck, S., & Glueck, E. T. (1950). *Unraveling juvenile delinquency.* Cambridge: Harvard University Press.

Goddard, A. W., & Charney, D. S. (1997). Toward an integrated neurobiology of panic disorder. *Journal of Clinical Psychiatry, 58* (Suppl. 2), 4–12.

Goddard, H. (1912). *The Kallikak family: A study in the heredity of feeblemindedness.* New York: MacMillan.

Goedde, H. W., & Agarwal., D. P. (1987). Polymorphism of aldehyde dehydrogenase and alcohol sensitivity. *Enzyme, 37,* 29–44.

Goering, P., & Wasylenski, D. (1984). From hospital to the community: Six month and two year outcomes for 505 patients. *Journal of Nervous and Mental Disease, 172* (11), 667–673.

Goering, P., Wasylenki, D., & Grisonich, S. (1992). Deinstitutionalization: Its process, history, impact, and implications in the Canada. In E. Persad, S. S. Kazarian, & L. W. Joseph (Eds.), *The mental hospital in the 21st century* (pp. 23–31). Toronto: Wall & Emerson.

Goldberg, R. L., Mann, L. S., Wise, T. N., & Segall, E. R. (1985). Parental qualities as perceived by borderline personality disorder. *Hillside Journal of Clinical Psychiatry, 7,* 134–140.

Goldberg, S. C., Schulz, S. C., Schulz, P. M., Resnick, R. J., Hamer, R. M., & Friedel, R. O. (1986). Borderline and schizotypal personality disorder treated with low-dose thiothixene versus placebo. *Archives of General Psychiatry, 43,* 680–686.

Goldbloom, D. S., & Kennedy, S. H. (1995). Medical complications of anorexia nervosa. In K. D. Brownell & C. G. Fairburn (Eds.), *Eating disorders and obesity: A comprehensive handbook* (pp. 266–270). New York: Guilford Press.

Goldfried, M. R., & Norcross, J. C. (1995). Integrative and eclectic therapies in historical perspective. In B. Bongar & L. E. Beutler (Eds.), *Comprehensive textbook of psychotherapy: Theory and practice* (pp. 254–273). New York: Oxford University Press.

Golding, S. L., Eaves, D., & Kowaz, A. M. (1989). The assessment, treatment and community outcome of insanity acquittees: Forensic history and response to treatment. *International Journal of Law and Psychiatry, 12,* 149–179.

Goldman, M. S., Brown, S. A., & Christiansen, B. A. (1987). Expectancy theory: Thinking about drinking. In H. T. Blane & K. E. Leonard (Eds.), *Psychological theories of drinking and alcoholism* (pp. 181–226). New York: Guilford Press.

Goldman-Rakic, P. S. (1987). Development of cortical circuitry and cognitive function. *Child Development, 58* (3), 601–622.

Goldstein, G. (1990). Neuropsychological heterogeneity in schizophrenia: A consideration of abstraction and problem-solving abilities. *Archives of Clinical Neuropsychology, 5* (3), 251–264.

Goldstein, H., & Wickstrom, S. (1986). Peer intervention effects on communicative interaction among handicapped and non-handicapped preschoolers. *Journal of Applied Behavior Analysis, 19,* 209–214.

Goldstein, M. J., Kant, H. S., & Hartman, J. J. (1973). *Pornography and sexual deviance.* Berkeley: University of California Press.

Goldstein, R. B., Black, D. W., Nasrallah, A., & Winokur, G. (1991). The prediction of suicide. Sensitivity, specificity, and predictive value of a multivariate model applied to suicide among 1906 patients with affective disorders. *Archives of General Psychiatry, 48* (5): 418–422.

Goldstein, T. F., Lue, T. F., Padma-Nathan, H., Rosen, R. C., Steers, W. D., & Wicker, P. A. (1998, May 14). Oral sildenafil in the treatment of erectile dysfunction. *New England Journal of Medicine, 338,* 1397–1404.

Goldston, S. E. (1991). A survey of prevention activities in state mental health authorities. *Professional Psychology: Research and Practice, 22,* 315–321.

Goldstrom, I. P., Burns, B. J., Kessler, L. G., Feverberg, M. A., Larson, D. B., Miller, N. E., & Cromer, W. J. (1987). Mental health service use by elderly adults in a primary care setting. *Journal of Gerontology, 42,* 147–153.

Good, B. J., & Kleinman, A. M. (1985). Culture and anxiety: Cross-cultural evidence for the patterning of anxiety disorders. In A. H. Tumas & J. D. Maser (Eds.), *Anxiety and the anxiety disorders.* Hillsdale: Erlbaum.

Goode, E. (1994, September). Battling deviant behavior. *US News and World Report,* 74–75.

Goodman, R. (1990). Technical note: Are perinatal complications causes or consequences of autism? *Journal of Child Psychology and Psychiatry, 31,* 809–812.

Goodman, R., & Stevenson, J. (1989). A twin study of hyperactivity: I. An examination of hyperactivity scores and categories derived from Rutter teacher and parent questionnaires. *Journal of Child Psychology & Psychiatry & Allied Disciplines, 30,* 671–689.

Goodman, W. K., Rasmussen, S. A., Price, L. H., Mazure, C., Heninger, G. R., & Charney, D. S. (1989). *Manual for the Yale-Brown obsessive compulsive scale (revised).* New Haven: Connecticut Mental Health Centre.

Goodwin, D. W. (1976). *Is alcoholism hereditary?* New York: Oxford University Press.

Goodwin, D. W. (1979). Alcoholism and heredity. *Archives of General Psychiatry, 36,* 57–61.

Goodwin, D. W. (1985). Genetic determinants of alcoholism. In J. H. Mendelson & N. K. Mellow (Eds.), *The diagnosis and treatment of alcoholism* (pp. 65–87). New York: McGraw-Hill.

Goodwin, D. W., & Guze, S. B. (1984). *Psychiatric diagnosis* (3rd ed.). New York: Oxford University Press.

Goodwin, F., & Jamison, K. (1990). *Manic-depressive illness.* Oxford: Oxford University Press.

Gordis, E. (1991). *Alcohol research: Promise for the decade.* Rockville, MD: National Institute of Alcohol Abuse and Alcoholism.

Gordon, R. S. (1983). An operational classification of disease prevention. *Public Health Reports, 98,* 107–109.

Gore, S., & Eckenrode, J. (1994). Context and process in research on risk and resilience. In R. J. Haggerty, L. R. Sherrod, N. Garmezy, & M. Rutter (Eds.), *Stress, risk, and resilience in children and adolescents: Processes, mechanisms, and interventions* (pp. 19–63). New York: Cambridge University Press.

Gortner, E. T., Gollan, J. K., Dobson, K. S., & Jacobson, N. S. (1998). Cognitive-behavioral treatment for depression: Relapse prevention. *Journal of Consulting and Clinical Psychology, 66,* 377–384.

Gorton, G., & Akhtar, S. (1990). The literature on personality disorders, 1985–1988: Trends, issues, and controversies. *Hospital and Community Psychiatry, 41,* 39–51.

Gosselin, C., & Wilson, G. (1980). *Sexual variations.* London: Faber and Faber.

Gotlib, I. H., & Hammen, C. L. (1995). *Psychological aspects of depression: Toward a cognitive-interpersonal integration.* New York: Wiley.

Gottesman, I. I., McGuffin, P., & Farmer, A. E. (1987). Clinical genetics as clues to the "real" genetics of schizophrenia: A decade of modest gains while playing for time. *Schizophrenia Bulletin, 13,* 23–47.

Gottman, J. M. (1981). *Time-series analysis: A comprehensive introduction for social scientists.* New York: Cambridge University Press.

Gould, K. L., Ornish, D., Scherwitz, L., Brown, S., Edens, R. P., Hess, J. J., Mullani, N., Bolomey, L., Dobbs, F., Armstrong, W. T., Merritt, T., Ports, T., Sparler, S., & Billings, J. (1995). Changes in myocardial perfusion abnormalities by positron emission tomography after long-term, intense risk factor modification. *Journal of the American Medical Association, 274,* 894–901.

Gould, M. S. (1990). Suicide clusters and media exposure. In S. J. Blumenthal & D. J. Kupfer (Eds.), *Suicide over the life cycle: Risk factors, assessment and treatment of suicidal patients.* Washington, DC: American Psychiatric Press.

Gould, R. A., & Clum, G. A. (1993). A meta-analysis of self-help treatment approaches. *Clinical Psychology Review, 13,* 169–186.

Gould, R. A., Otto, M. W., & Pollack, M. H. (1995). A meta-analysis of treatment outcome for panic disorder. *Clinical Psychology Review, 15,* 819–844.

Gould, R. A., Otto, M. W., Pollack, M. H., & Yap, L. (1997). Cognitive-behavioral and pharmacological treatment of generalized anxiety disorder: A preliminary meta-analysis. *Behavior Therapy, 28,* 285–305.

Gould, S. J. (1985). *The flamingo's smile: Reflections in natural history.* New York: W. W. Norton.

Graffi, S., & Minnes, P. M. (1988). The attitudes of kindergarten children toward the labels and physical stigmata associated with mental retardation. *American Journal of Mental Deficiency, 93,* 23–35.

Graham, D. Y., Lew, G. M., Klein, P. D., et al. (1992). Effect of treatment of *Helicobacter pylori* infection on long-term recurrence of gastric or duodenal ulcer: A randomized, controlled study. *Annals of Internal Medicine, 116,* 705–708.

Graham, J. R. (1990). *MMPI–2: Assessing personality and psychopathology.* New York: Oxford.

Graham, P. (1994). Prevention. In M. Rutter, E. Taylor, & L. Hersov (Eds.), *Child and adolescent psychiatry* (3rd ed., pp. 815–828). Oxford, UK: Blackwell Scientific Publications.

Graham, P., Rutter, M., & George, P. (1973). Temperamental characteristics as predictors of behavior disorders in children. *American Journal of Orthopsychiatry, 43,* 328–339.

Grant, D. A., & Berg, E. A. (1948). A behavioral analysis of degree of reinforcement and ease of shifting to new responses in a Weigl-type card-sorting problem. *Journal of Experimental Psychology, 38,* 404–411.

Gray, J., Clark, A., Higenbottam, J., Ledwidge, B., & Paredes, J. (1985). Review panels for involuntary psychiatric patients: Which patients apply? *Canadian Journal of Psychiatry, 30,* 573–576.

Gray, P. (1991). *Psychology* (p. 635). New York: Worth. Citing E. P. Bleuler (1911/50), *Dementia praecox, or the group of schizophrenias* (J. Zinkin, Trans.) New York: International Universities Press.

Green, G. (1994). The quality of the evidence. In H. C. Shane (Ed.), *Facilitated Communication: The clinical and social phenomenon.* San Diego, CA: Singular.

Green, R. (1976). One-hundred ten feminine and masculine boys: Behavioral contrasts and demographic similarities. *Archives of Sexual Behavior, 5,* 425–446.

Green, R. (1978). Sexual identity of 37 children raised by homosexual or transsexual parents. *American Journal of Psychiatry, 135,* 692–697.

Green, R. (1987). *The "Sissy Boy Syndrome" and the development of homosexuality.* New Haven, CT: Yale University Press.

Green, R., & Fleming, D. T. (1990). Transsexual surgery follow-up: Status in the 1990s. *Annual Review of Sex Research, 1,* 163–174.

Green, R., Blanchard, R. (1995). Gender identity disorders. In H. I. Kaplan & B. J. Sadock (Eds.), *Comprehensive textbook of psychiatry* (pp. 1345–1360). Baltimore, MD: Williams & Wilkins.

Greenberg, L. S., & Johnson, S. M. (1988). *Emotionally focused therapy for couples.* New York: Guilford.

Greenberg, L., Elliot, R., & Lietaer, G. (1994). Research on experiential therapies. In A. E. Bergin, & S. L. Garlfield, (Eds.), *Handbook of psychotherapy and behavior change* (4th ed.) (pp. 509–539). New York: Wiley.

Greenberg, M. T., Speltz, M. L., & DeKlyen, M. (1993). The role of attachment in the early development of disruptive behavior problems. *Development and Psychopathology, 5,* 191–213.

Greenberg, P., Stiglin, L., Finkelstein, S., & Berndt, E. (1993). The economic burden of depression in 1990. *Journal of Clinical Psychiatry, 54,* 405–426.

Grenier, G., & Byers, E. S. (1995). Rapid ejaculation: A review of conceptual, etiological and treatment issues. *Archives of Sexual Behavior, 24,* 446–472.

Griffin, J. D. (1993, December). An historical oversight. *Newsletter of the Ontario Psychiatric Association,* pp. 9–10.

Grinker, R. R., Werble, B., & Drye, R. C. (1968). *The borderline syndrome.* New York: Basic Books.

Grossman, H. J. (Ed.) (1983). *Classification in mental retardation.* Washington, DC: American Association on Mental Deficiency.

Grove, W. M., Clementz, B. A., Iacono, W. G., & Katsanis, J. (1992). Smooth pursuit ocular motor dysfunction in schizophrenia: Evidence for a major gene. *American Journal of Psychiatry, 149,* 1362–1368.

Grubin, D., & Mason, D. (1997). Medical models of sexual deviance. In D. R. Laws & W. O'Donohue (Eds.), *Sexual deviance: Theory, assessment, and treatment* (pp. 434–448). New York: Guilford Press.

Gunderson, J. G., & Singer, M. T. (1975). Defining borderline patients: An overview. *American Journal of Psychiatry, 132,* 1–10.

Gurian, B. S., Wexler, D., & Baker, E. H. (1992). Late-life paranoia: Possible association with early trauma and infertility. *International Journal of Geriatric Psychiatry, 7,* 277–284.

Gurian, B., & Goisman, R. (1993). Anxiety disorders in the elderly. *Generations, 17,* 39–42.

Guyton, A. C. (1991). *Textbook of medical physiology* (8th ed.) (pp. 365–384). Philadelphia: Saunders.

Guze, S. B., Cloninger, C. R., Martin, R. L., & Clayton, P. J. (1986). A follow-up and family study of Briquet's syndrome. *British Journal of Psychiatry, 149,* 17–23.

Haavik, S. F., & Menninger, K. A. (1981). *Sexuality, law and the developmentally disabled person: Legal and clinical aspects of marriage, parenthood and sterilization.* Baltimore, MD: Paul Brookes.

Hagberg, B., Aicardi, J., Dias, K., & Ramos, O. (1983). A progressive syndrome of autism, dementia, ataxia, and loss of purposeful hand use in girls. Rett's syndrome: Report of 35 cases. *Annals of Neurology, 14,* 471–479.

Hagerman, R. (1987). Fragile X syndrome. *Current Problems in Pediatrics, 17,* 621–674.

Hagerman, R. J., & Boggs, P. M. 1983. *The Fragile X Syndrome.* Dillon, CO: Spectro.

Hahlweg, K., & Markman, H. J. (1988). Effectiveness of behavioral marital therapy: Empirical status of behavioral techniques in preventing and alleviating marital distress. *Journal of Consulting and Clinical Psychology, 56,* 440–447.

Halikas, J. (1993). Treatment of drug abuse syndromes. *Psychiatric Clinics of North America, 16,* 693–702.

Hall, C. S. (1954). *A primer of Freudian psychology.* New York: Menton.

Hall, G.C.N. (1989). Sexual arousal and arousability in a sexual offender population. *Journal of Abnormal Psychology, 98,* 145–149.

Hall, G.C.N., & Hirschman, R. (1991). Toward a theory of sexual aggression: A quadripartite model. *Journal of Consulting and Clinical Psychology, 59,* 662–669.

Hall, S. M., Tunstal, C., Rugg, D., et al. (1985). Nicotine gum and behavioral treatment in smoking cessation. *Journal of Consulting and Clinical Psychology, 53,* 256–258.

Hallahan, D. P. & W. M. Cruikshank (1973). *Psychoeducational foundations of learning disabilities.* Englewood Cliffs, NJ: Prentice-Hall.

Hamilton, M. (1959). The assessment of anxiety states by rating. *British Journal of Medical Psychology, 32,* 50–55.

Hamilton, S., Rothbart, M., & Dawes, R. M. (1986). Sex bias, diagnosis, and DSM-III. *Sex Roles, 15,* 269–274.

Hammen, C. (1991). *Depression runs in families.* New York: Springer.

Hammen, C., Ellicott, A., Gitlin, M., & Jamison, K. (1989). Sociotropy/autonomy and vulnerability to specific life events in unipolar and bipolar patients. *Journal of Abnormal Psychology, 98,* 154–160.

Hanson, D. R., Gottesman, I. I., Heston, L. L. (1990). Long-range schizophrenia forcasting: Many a slip twixt cup and lip. In J. Rolf, A. S. Masten, D. Cicchetti, K. H. Nuechterlein, & S. Weintraub (Eds.), *Risk and protective factors in the development of psychopathology* (pp. 424–444). Cambridge: Cambridge University Press.

Harburg, E., Davis, D. R., & Caplan, R. (1982). Parent and offspring alcohol use. *Journal of Studies oln Alcohol, 43,* 497–516.

Harding, C. M., Brooks, G. W., Ashikaga, T., Strauss, J. S., & Breier, A. (1987). The Vermont longitudinal study of personal with severe mental illness. I. Methodology, study sample, and overall status 32 years later. *American Journal of Psychiatry, 144,* 18–26.

Harding, T. W. (1992). Psychopathic disorder: Time for a decent burial of a bad legal concept? *Criminal Behavior and Mental Health, 2,* vi–ix.

Hardy, J. D., & Smith, T. W. (1988). Cynical hostility and vulnerability to disease: Social support, life stress and physiological response to conflict. *Health Psychology, 7,* 447–459.

Hare, R. D. (1983). Diagnosis of antisocial personality disorder in two prison populations. *American Journal of Abnormal Psychiatry, 140,* 887–890.

Hare, R. D. (1985). A comparison of procedures for the assessment of psychopathy. *Journal of Consulting and Clinical Psychology, 53,* 7–16.

Hare, R. D. (1991). *The Hare Psychopathy Checklist—Revised.* Toronto, Canada: Multihealth Systems.

Hare, R. D. (1996). Psychopathy: A clinical construct whose time has come. *Criminal Justice and Behavior, 23,* 25–54.

Hare, R. D., Hart, S. D., & Harpur, T. J. (1991). Psychopathy and DSM-IV criteria for antisocial personality disorder. *Journal of Abnormal Psychology, 100,* 391–398.

Harmon-Jones, E., & Allen, J. (1997). Behavioural activation sensitivity and resting frontal EEG asymmetry: Covariation of putative indicators related to risk for mood disorders. *Journal of Abnormal Psychology, 106,* 159–163.

Harpur, T. J., & Hare, R. D. (1994). The assessment of psychopathy as a function of age. *Journal of Abnormal Psychology, 103,* 604–609.

Harris, F. C., & Lahey, B. B. (1982). Subject reactivity in direct observation assessment: A review and critical analysis. *Clinical Psychology Review, 2,* 523–538.

Harris, G. T. (1989). The relationship between neuroleptic drug dose and the performance of psychiatric patients in a maximum security token economy program. *Journal of Behavior Therapy and Experimental Psychiatry, 20,* 57–67.

Harris, G., Hilton, N., & Rice, M. (1993). Patients admitted to psychiatric hospital: Problems and resolution at discharge. *Canadian Journal of Behavioural Science, 25,* 267–285.

Harrison, A.G.E. (1992). *A follow-up study of adults identified in childhood as having a learning disability either in reading or arithmetic.* Unpublished doctoral dissertation, Queen's University, Kingston.

Harro, J., Vasar, E., & Bradwejn, J. (1993). Cholecystokinin in animal and human research on anxiety. *Trends in Pharmacological Science, 14,* 244–249.

Harrow, M., & Miller, J. (1980). Schizophrenic thought disorders and impaired perspective. *Journal of Abnormal Psychiatry, 89,* 717–727.

Hart, S. D., & Hare, R. D. (1989). Discriminant validity of the Psychopathy Checklist in a forensic psychiatric population. *Psychological Assessment: A Journal of Consulting and Clinical Psychology, 1,* 211–218.

Hasenfeld, Y., & Chesler, M. A. (1989). Client empowerment in the human services: Personal and professional agenda. *Journal of Applied Behavioral Science, 25,* 499–521.

Hasenfus, N., & Magaro, P. (1976). Creativity and schizophrenia: An equality of empirical constructs. *British Journal of Psychiatry, 129,* 346–349.

Hathaway, S. R., & McKinley, J. C. (1943). *Manual for the Minnesota Multiphasic Personality Inventory.* New York: Psychological Corporation.

Haugaard, J. J., & Repucci, N. D. (1988). *The sexual abuse of children: A comprehensive guide to current knowledge and intervention strategies.* San Francisco: Jossey-Bass.

Hawkins, R. C., & Clement, P. F. (1984). Binge eating syndrome: The measurement problem and a conceptual model. In R. C. Hawkins, W. Fremouw, & P. F. Clement (Eds.). *Binge-eating: Theory, research and treatment* (pp. 229–251). New York: Springer.

Hawkins, R. C., Fremouw, W. J., & Clement, P. F. (1984). *The binge-purge syndrome.* New York: Springer.

Hawton, K., Catalan, J., & Fagg, J. (1992). Sex therapy for erectile dysfunction: Characteristics of couples, treatment outcome, and prognostic factors. *Archives of Sexual Behavior, 21,* 161–176.

Hayes, S. C., Walser, R. D., & Follette, V. M. (1995). Psychology and the temptation of prescription privileges. *Canadian Psychology, 36,* 313–320.

Hayflick, L. (1988). Biological aging theories. In G. Maddox (Ed.), *Encyclopedia of aging* (pp. 64–68). Englewood Cliffs, NJ: Prentice Hall.

Hazelwood, R. R., Dietz, P. E., & Burgess, A. W. (1983). Investigation of autoerotic fatalities. In R. R. Hazelwood, P. E. Dietz, & A. W. Burgess (Eds.), *Autoerotic fatalities* (pp. 121–138). Lexington, NY: D. C. Heath.

Health and Welfare Canada (1988). *The epidemiology of mental retardation.* Report of the Working Group. Ottawa: Ministry of National Health and Welfare.

Health Canada (1995). *Horizons three: Young Canadians' alcohol and other drug use: Increasing our understanding.* Ed. by David Hewitt, Garry Vinje, & Patricia MacNeil. Ottawa: Health Canada.

Health Services and Programs Branch (1994). *Suicide in Canada.* Ministry of National Health and Welfare, Mental Health Division, Health Services Directorate. Toronto: University of Toronto Press.

Heart and Stroke Foundation of Canada (1992). *Cardiovascular disease in Canada, 1991.* Ottawa: Heart and Stroke Foundation of Canada.

Heart and Stroke Foundation of Canada (1998). *Heart disease and stroke in Canada, 1997.* Ottawa: Heart and Stroke Foundation of Canada.

Heatherton, T. F., & Baumeister, R. F. (1991). Binge-eating as escape from self awareness. *Psychological Bulletin, 110,* 86–108.

Heatherton, T. F., & Polivy, J. (1992). Chronic dieting and eating disorders: A spiral model. In J. Crowther, S. E. Hobfall, M.A.P. Stephens, & D. L. Tennenbaum (Eds.), *The etiology of bulimia: The individual and familial context* (pp. 133–155). Washington, DC: Hemisphere.

Heaton, R. K., Baade, L. E., & Johnson, K. L. (1978). Neuropsychological test results associated with psychiatric disorders in adults. *Psychological Bulletin, 85* (1), 141–162.

Heber, R. (1959). A manual on terminology and classification in mental retardation. *American Journal of Mental Deficiency, 56* (Monograph Suppl.).

Hechtman, L. (1991). Resilience and vunerability in long term outcome of attention deficit hyperactive disorder. *Canadian Journal of Psychiatry, 36* (6), 415–421.

Hecker, M.H.L., Chesney, M., Black, G. W., & Frautschi, N. (1988). Coronary-prone behaviors in the Western Collaborative Group Study. *Psychosomatic Medicine, 50,* 153–164.

Hegar, R. (1989). Empowerment-based practice with children. *Social Service Review,* 372–383.

Heidrich, S. M. (1993). The relationship between physical health and psychological well-being in elderly women: A developmental perspective. *Research in Nursing and Health, 16,* 123–130.

Heilbrun, A. B., & Witt, N. (1990). Distorted body image as a risk factor in anorexia nervosa: Replication and clarification. *Psychological Reports, 66,* 407–416.

Heiman, J. R. (1975). The physiology of erotica: Women's sexual arousal. *Psychology Today, 8* (11), 90–94.

Heinrichs, R. W. (1993). Schizophrenia and the brain: Conditions for a neuropsychology of madness. *American Psychologist, 48,* 221–223.

Heinrichs, R. W., & Awad, A. G. (1993). Neurocognitive subtypes of schizophrenia. *Schizophrenia Research, 9,* 49–58.

Helmes, E. (1991). *Subtypes of schizophrenia: Real or apparent?* Paper presnted at the annual meeting of the Canadian Psychological Association, Calgary, Alberta, Canada.

Helms, J. E. (1992). Why is there no study of cultural equivalence of standardized cognitive ability testing? *American Psychologist, 47,* 1083–1101.

Helzer, J. E., Spitznagel, E. L., & McEnvoy, L. (1987). The predictive validity of lay Diagnostic Interview Schedule diagnoses in the general population: A comparison with physician examiners. *Archives of General Psychiatry, 44,* 1069–1077.

Henggeler, S. W., & Schoenwald, S. K. (1993). Multisystemic therapy with juvenile offenders: An effective family-based treatment. *The Family Psychologist, 9,* 24–26.

Henke, P. G. (1988). Recent studies of the central nucleus of the amygdala and stress ulcers. *Neuroscience and Biobehavioral Reviews, 12,* 143–150.

Henke, P. G. (1990). Hippocampal pathway to the amygdala and stress ulcer development. *Brain Research Bulletin, 25,* 691–695.

Henke, P. G. (1992). Stomach pathology and the amygdala. In J. P. Aggleton (Ed.), *The amygdala: Neurobiological aspects of emotion, memory and mental dysfunction* (pp. 323–338). New York: Wiley.

Henriques, J. B., & Davidson, R. J. (1990). Regional brain electrical asymmetries discriminate between previously depressed and healthy control subjects. *Journal of Abnormal Psychology, 99,* 122–31.

Henry, K., & Cohen, C. (1983). The role of labeling in diagnosing borderline personality disorder. *American Journal of Psychiatry, 140,* 1527–1529.

Henry, W. P., Strupp, H. H., Schacht, T. E., & Gaston, L. (1994). Psychodynamic approaches. In A. E. Bergin & S. L. Garfield (Eds.), *Handbook of psychotherapy and behavior change* (4th ed., pp. 467–508). New York: Wiley.

Herman, C. P., & Mack, D. (1975). Restrained and unrestrained eating. *Journal of Personality, 43,* 647–660.

Herman, C. P., & Polivy, J. (1980). Restrained eating. In A. Stunkard (Ed.), *Obesity* (pp. 208–225). Philadelphia: Saunders.

Herman, C. P., & Polivy, J. (1988). Studies of eating in normal dieters. In B. T. Walsh (Ed.), *Eating behavior in eating disorders* (pp. 95–112). Washington, DC: American Psychiatric Association Press.

Herman, C. P., & Polivy, J. (1993). Mental control of eating: Excitatory and inhibitory food thoughts. In D. M. Wegner & J. W. Pennebaker (Eds.), *Handbook of mental control* (pp. 491–505). Englewood Cliffs, NJ: Prentice Hall.

Herman, J. (1981). *Father-daughter incest.* Cambridge (MA): Harvard University Press.

Herman, J. (1992). *Trauma and recovery.* New York: Basic Books.

Herman, J. P., Prewitt, C. M.-F., & Cullinan, W. E. (1996). Neuronal circuit regulation of the hypothalamo-pituitary-adrenocortical stress axis. *Critical Reviews in Neurobiology, 10,* 371–394.

Hershberg, S. G., Carlson, G. A., Cantwell, D. P., & Strober, M. (1982). Anxiety and depressive disorders in psychiatrically disturbed children. *Journal of Clinical Psychiatry, 43,* 358–361.

Hersov, L. (1996). School refusal. In M. Rutter & L. Hersov (Eds.), *Child and adolescent psychiatry: Modern approaches* (pp. 382–399). Oxford: Blackwell.

Hertel, R. K. (1972). Application of stochastic process analyses to the study of psychotherapeutic processes. *Psychological Bulletin, 77,* 421–430.

Herzog, D. B. (1995). Psychodynamic psychotherapy for anorexia nervosa. In K. D. Brownell & C. G. Fairburn (Eds.), *Eating disorders and obesity: A comprehensive handbook* (pp. 330–335). New York: Guilford Press.

Herzog, D. B., Hopkins, J. D., & Burns, C. D. (1993). A follow-up study of 33 subdiagnostic eating disordered women. *International Journal of Eating Disorders, 14,* 261–276.

Herzog, D. B., Norman, D. K., Gordon, C., & Pepose, M. (1984). Sexual conflict and eating disorders in 27 males. *American Journal of Psychiatry, 141,* 989–990.

Heston, L. L. (1966). Psychiatric disorders in foster home reared children of schizophrenic mothers. *British Journal of Psychiatry, 112,* 819–825.

Hetherington, E. M., Cox, M., & Cox, R. (1982). Effects of divorce on parents and children. In M. Lamb (Ed.), *Nontraditional families* (pp. 233–288). Hillsdale: Lawrence Erlbaum.

Hiday, V. A. (1988). Civil commitment: A review of empirical research. *Behavioral Sciences and the Law, 6* (1), 15–43.

Higenbottam, J., Ledwidge, B., Paredes, J., Hansen, M., Kogan, C., & Lambert, L. (1985). Variables affecting the decision making of a review panel. *Canadian Journal of Psychiatry, 30,* 577–581.

Higgins, S. T., Budney, A. J., Bickel, W. K., Foerg, F. E., & Badger, G. J. (1994). Alcohol dependence and simultaneous cocaine and alcohol use in cocaine-dependent patients. *Journal of Addictive Diseases, 13* (4), 177–189.

Higgins, S. T., Budney, A. J., Bickel, W. K., Hughes, J., Foerg, F., & Badger, G. (1993). Achieving cocaine abstinence with a behavioral approach. *American Journal of Psychiatry, 150* (5), 763–769.

Highgate, S., & Neufeld, R.W.J. (1986). Schizophrenic memory-search performance involving nonverbal stimulus properties. *Journal of Abnormal Psychology, 95,* 67–73.

Hill, A. B. (1965). The environment and disease: Association or causation? *Proceedings of the Royal Society of Medicine, 58,* 295–300.

Hill, S. Y., & Steinhauer, S. R. (1993). Assessment of prepubertal and postpubertal boys and girls at risk for developing alcohol with P300 from a visual discrimination task. *Journal of Studies on Alcohol, 54,* 350–358.

Himmelfarb, S., & Murrell, S. A. (1984). The prevalence and correlates of anxiety symptoms in older adults. *Journal of Psychology, 116,* 159–167.

Hindmarsh, K. W., Porter-Serviss, S., & Opheim, E. E. (1994). Alcohol and drug use by students from western Canada in Grades 6 through 12 (1992): Have there been any changes in the past 5 years? *The International Journal of the Addictions, 29* (7), 829–835.

Hingson, R. (1993). Prevention of alcohol impaired driving. *Alcohol Health & Research, 17,* 28–34.

Hinshaw, S. P., & Anderson, C. A. (1996). Conduct and oppositional defiant disorders. In E. J. Mash & R. A. Barkley (Eds.), *Child psychopathology* (pp. 113–149). New York: Guilford Press.

Hinshaw, S. P., & Anderson, C. A. (1996). Conduct and oppositional defiant disorders. In E. J. Mash & R. A. Barkley (Eds.), *Child psychopathology* (pp. 113–149). New York: Guilford Press.

Hinshaw, S. P., & Erhardt, D. (1993). Attention-deficit hyperactiviity disorder: Behavioral interventions. In V. B. Van Hasselt & M. Hersen (Eds.), *Handbook of behavior therapy and pharmacotherapy with children: A comparative analysis* (pp. 233–250). Needham Heights, MA: Allyn and Bacon.

Hirschfeld, R., Klerman, G., Lavori, P., Keller, M. B., Griffith, P., & Coryell, W. (1989). Premorbid personality assessments of first onset of major depression. *Archives of General Psychiatry, 46,* 345–350.

Hirschi, T., & Hidelang, M. J. (1977). Intelligence and delinquency: A revisionist review. *American Sociological Review, 42,* 571–587.

Hoch, P. H. (1909). Constitutional factors in the dementia praecox group. *Review of Neurology and Psychiatry, 8,* 463–475.

Hodgins, S. (1983). A follow-up study of persons found incompetent to stand trial and/or not guilty by reason of insanity in Quebec. *International Journal of Law and Psychiatry, 6,* 399–421.

Hodgson, R. J., & Rachman, S. (1977). Obsessional-compulsive complaints. *Behaviour Research and Therapy, 15,* 389–395.

Hoehn-Saric, R., & Masek, B. J. (1981). Effects of naloxone on normals and chronically anxious patients. *Biological Psychiatry, 16,* 1041–1050.

Hoehn-Saric, R., McLeod, D. R., & Zimmerli, W. D. (1989). Somatic manifestations in women with generalized anxiety disorder: Psychophysiological responses to psychological stress. *Archives of General Psychiatry, 46,* 1113–1119.

Hoek, H. W. (1995). The distribution of eating disorders. In K. D. Brownell & C. G. Fairburn (Eds.), *Eating disorders and obesity: A comprehensive handbook* (pp. 199–206). New York: Guilford Press.

Hoenig, J., (1985). Etiology of transsexualism. In B. W. Steiner (Ed.), *Gender dysphoria: Development, research, and management* (pp. 33–73). New York: Plenum Press.

Hoffman, R. E., Rapaport, J., Ameli, R., McGlashan, T. H., Harcherik, D., & Servan-Schreiber, D. (1995). A neural network simulation of hallucinated "voices" and associated speech perception impairments in schizophrenic patients. *Journal of Cognitive Neuroscience, 7,* 479–496.

Hofstede, G. (1980), *Culture's consequences: International differences in work-related values.* Beverly Hills, CA: Sage.

Hogarty, G. E. (1984). Depot neuroleptics: The relevance of psychosocial factors—A United States perspective. *Journal of Clinical Psychiatry, 45,* 36–42.

Hogarty, G. E. (1993). Prevention of relapse in chronic schizophrenic patients. *Journal of Clinical Psychiatry, 54* (3, Suppl.), 18–23.

Hogarty, G. E., Anderson, C. M., Reiss, D. J., Kornblith, S. J., Greenwald, D. P., Javna, C. D., & Madonia, M. J. (1986). Family psychoeducation, social skills training, and maintenance chemotherapy in the aftercare treatment of schizophrena. I. One year effects of a cotnrolled study on relapse and expressed emotion. *Archives of General Psychiatry, 43,* 633–642.

Holderness, C. C., Brooks-Gunn, J., & Warren, M. P. (1994). Comorbidity of eating disorders and substance abuse review of the literature. *International Journal of Eating Disorders, 16,* 1–34.

Holland, A. J., Hall, A., Murray, R., Russell, G.F.M., & Crisp, A. H. (1984). Anorexia nervosa: A study of 34 twin pairs and one set of triplets. *British Journal of Psychiatry, 145,* 414–419.

Hollander, E., Cohen, L. J., & Simeon, D. (1993). Body dysmorphic disorder. *Psychiatric Annals, 23,* 359–364.

Hollingshead, A. B., & Redlich, F. C. (1958). *Social class and mental illness: A community study.* New York: Wiley.

Hollon, S. D., & Beck, A. T. (1994). Cognitive and cognitive behavioral therapies. In A. E. Bergin & S. L. Garlfield (Eds.), *Handbook of psychotherapy and behavior change* (4th ed.) (pp. 428–466). New York: Wiley.

Holmes, T. H., & Masuda, M. (1974). Life change and illness susceptibility. In B. S. Dohrenwend & B. P. Dohrenwend (Eds.), *Stressful life events: Their nature and effects.* New York: Wiley.

Holmes, T. H., & Rahe, R. H. (1967). The Social Readjustment Rating Scale. *Journal of Psychosomatic Research, 11,* 213–218.

Holt, C. S., Heimberg, R. G., & Hope, D. A. (1992). Avoidant personality disorder and the generalized subtype of social phobia. *Journal of Abnormal Psychology, 101,* 318–325.

Holzman, P. S., Kringlen, E., Matthysse, S., Flanaga, S. D., Lipton, R. B., Cramer, G., Levin, S., Lange, K., & Levy, D. L. (1988). A single dominant gene can account for eye tracking dysfunctions and schizophrenia in offspring of discordant twins. *Archives of General Psychiatry, 45,* 641–647.

Hook, E. B., Cross, P. K., & Regal, R. R. (1990). Factual, statistical and logical issues in the search for a paternal age effect for Down syndrome. *Human Genetics, 85,* 387–388.

Hooley, J. M., & Teasdale, J. D. (1989). Predictors of relapse in unipolar depressives: Expressed emotion, marital distresss, and perceived criticism. *Journal of Abnormal Psychology, 98,* 229–235.

Hoon, E. F., Hoon, P. W., Rand, K. H., Johnson, J., Hall, N. R., & Edwards, N. B. (1991). A psycho-behavioral model of genital herpes recurrence. *Journal of Psychosomatic Research, 35,* 25–36.

Horney, K. (1945). *Our inner conflicts: A constructive theory of neurosis.* New York: Norton.

Horowitz, M. (1986). *Stress response syndromes* (2nd ed.). New York: Jason Aronson.

Horowitz, M. (1993). Stress–response syndromes. In J. P. Wilson & B. Raphael (Eds.), *International Handbook of Traumatic Stress Syndromes* (pp. 49–60). New York: Plenum.

Horowitz, M., Wilner, N., Alvarez, W. (1979). Impact of Event Scale: A measure of subjective stress. *Psychosomatic Medicine, 41,* 209–218.

House, J. S., Landis, K. R., & Umberson, D. (1988). Social relationships and health. *Science, 241,* 540–545.

Houts, A. C., Berman, J. S., & Abramson, H. (1994). Effectiveness of psychological and pharmacological treatments for nocturnal enuresis. *Journal of Consulting and Clinical Psychology, 62,* 737–745.

Howard, K. I., Kopta, S. M., Krause, M. S., & Orlinsky, D. E. (1986). The dose-effect relationship in psychotherapy. *American Psychologist, 41,* 159–164.

Howard, K. I., Lueger, R. J., Maling, M. S., & Martinovich, Z. (1993). A phase model of psychotherapy outcome: Causal mediation of change. *Journal of Consulting and Clinical Psychology, 61,* 678–685.

Howard, R., Castle, D., Wessely, S., & Murray, R. (1993). A comparative study of 470 cases of early-onset and late-onset schizophrenia. *British Journal of Psychiatry, 163,* 352–357.

Howells, K. (1978). Some meanings of children for pedophiles. In M. Cook & G. Wilson (Eds.), *Love and attraction* (pp. 57–82). London: Pergamon Press.

Hoyt-Meyers, L., Cowen, E. L., Work, W. C., Wyman, P. A., Magnus, K., Fagen, D. B., & Lotyczewski, B. S. (1995). Test correlates of resilient outcomes among highly stressed second- and third-grade urban children. *Journal of Community Psychology, 23,* 326–338.

Hsu, L.K.G. (1980). Outcome of anorexia nervosa. *Psychological Medicine, 13,* 231–238.

Hsu, L.K.G. (1988). The outcome of anorexia nervosa: A reappraisal. *Psychological Medicine, 18,* 807–812.

Hubbard, R., & Wald, E. (1993). *Exploding the gene myth.* Boston: Beacon Press.

Hucker, S. J. (1985). Self-harmful sexual behavior. *Psychiatric Clinics of North America, 8,* 323–328.

Hucker, S. J. (1990). Sexual asphyxia. In P. Bowden & R. Buglass (Eds.), *Principles and practice of forensic psychiatry* (pp. 717–721). London: Churchill-Livingstone.

Hucker, S., & Bain, J. (1990). Androgenic hormones and sexual assault. In W. L. Marshall, D. R. Laws, & H. E. Barbaree (Eds.), *Handbook of sexual assault: Issues, theories, and treatment of the offender.* New York: Plenum Press.

Hudson, A., & Clunies-Ross, G. (1978). The Doman-Delacato technique. *Australian Journal of Special Education, 2,* 17–19.

Hudson, A., Melita, B., & Arnold, N. (1993). Assessing the validity of facilitated communication: A case study. *Journal of Autism and Developmental Disorders, 23,* 163–173.

Hudson, J. I., Pope, H. G., & Jonas, J. M. (1984). Treatment of bulimia with anti-depressants: Theoretical considerations and clinical findings. In A. J. Stunkard & E. Steller (Eds.), *Eating and its disorders.* New York: Raven Press.

Huessmann, L. R., Eron, L. D., Lefkowitz, M. M., Walder, L. O., & Leopold, O. (1984). Stability of agression over time and generations. *Developmental Psychology, 20,* 1120–1134.

Hughes, J. R., Gust, S. W., Skoog, K., Keenan, R. M., & Fenwick, J. W. (1991). Symptoms of tobacco withdrawal: A replication and extension. *Archives of General Psychiatry, 48,* 52–61.

Hughes, M. W., Schuster, J. W., & Nelson, C. M. (1993). The acquisition of independent dressing skills by students with multiple disabilities. *Journal of Developmental and Physical Disabilities, 5,* 233–252.

Hull, C. L. (1943). *Principles of behavior.* New York: Appleton-Century-Crofts.

Hull, C. L. (1952). *A behavior system.* New Haven: Yale University Press.

Humphrey, L. L. (1988). Relationships within subtypes of anorexia, bulimia, and normal families. *Journal of the American Academy of Child and Adolescent Psychiatry, 27,* 544–551.

Humphrey, L. L. (1989). Observed family interactions among subtypes of eating disorders using structural analysis of social behavior. *Journal of Consulting and Clinical Psychology, 57,* 206–314.

Humphreys, K., & Rappaport, J. (1994). Researching self-help/mutual aid groups and organizations: Many roads, one journey. *Applied and Preventive Psychology, 3,* 217–231.

Hunsley, J., & Lee, C. M. (1995). The marital effects of individually oriented psychotherapy: Is there evidence for the deterioration hypothesis? *Clinical Psychology Review, 15,* 1–22.

Hunsley, J., & Lefebvre, M. (1990). A survey of the practices and activities of Canadian clinical psychologists. *Canadian Psychology, 31,* 350–358.

Hunsley, J., Aubry, T., & Lee, C. M. (1997). *A profile of Canadian consumers of psychological services.* Ottawa: Canadian Psychological Association and Canadian Register of Health Service Providers in Psychology.

Hunsley, J., Dobson, K., Johnston, C., & Mikail, S. (1998). *Empirically supported treatments in psychology: Recommendations for Canadian professional psychology.* Ottawa: Section on Clinical Psychology, Canadian Psychological Association.

Hurd, H. M., Drewry, W. F., Dewey, R., Pilgrim, C. W., Blumer, G. A., & Burgess, T.J.W. (1916). *The institutional care of the insane in the United States and Canada.* Baltimore, MD: Johns Hopkins Hospital Press.

Hurt, S. W., Clarkin, J. F., Koenigsberg, H. W., Frances, A., & Nurmberg, H. G. (1986). Diagnostic interview for borderlines: Psychometric properties and validity. *Journal of Consulting and Clinical Psychology, 54,* 256–260.

Hurwitz, I., Bibace, R. M., Wolff, P. H., & Rowbotham, B. M. (1972). Neuropsychological function of normal boys, delinquent boys, and boys with learning problems. *Perceptual & Motor Skills, 35,* 387–394.

Hustad, J. A., Beiser, M., & Iacono, W. G. (1992). Negative symptoms and the early course of schizophrenia. *Psychiatry Research, 43,* 215–222.

Huttenlocher, P. R. (1979). Synaptic density in human frontal cortex: Developmental changes and effects of aging. *Brain Research, 163,* 195–205.

Huttenlocher, P. R. (1984). Synapse elimination and plasticity in developing human cerebral cortex. *American Journal of Mental Deficiency, 88* (5), 488–496.

Hynd, G. W., Semrud-Clikeman, M., Lorys, A. R., Novey, E. S., & Eliopulos, P. (1990). Brain morphology in developmental dyslexia and attention deficit disorder/hyperactivity. *Archives of Neurology, 47,* 919–926.

Iacono, W. G., Bassett, A. S., & Jones, B. D. (1988). Eye tracking dysfunction is associated with parital trisomy of chromosome 5 and schizophrenia. *Archives of General Psychiatry, 45,* 1140–1141.

Ialongo, N. S., Horn, W. F., Pascoe, J. M., Greenberg, G., Packard, T., Lopez, M., Wagner, A., & Puttler, L. (1993). The effects of a multimodal intervention with attention-deficit hyperactivity disorder children: A 9-month follow-up. *Journal of the American Academy of Child and Adolescent Psychiatry, 32* (1), 182–189.

Illing, E.M.M., & Kaiserman, M. J. (1995). Mortality attributable to tobacco use in Canada and its regions. *Canadian Journal of Public Health, 86* (4), 257–265.

Infants Act, R.S.B.C. (1996), c. 223.

Inkeles, A. (1983). *Exploring individual modernity.* New York: Guilford Press.

Institute of Law Research & Reform (1988). *Sterilization decisions: Minors & mentally incompetent adults.* Edmonton: University of Alberta.

Institute of Medicine (1994). *Reducing risks for mental disorders: Frontiers for preventive intervention research.* Washington, DC: National Academy Press.

International Association for the Study of Pain, Task Force on Taxonomy (1994). *Classification of chronic pain: Descriptions of chronic pain syndromes and definitions of pain terms* (2nd ed.). Seattle: IASP Press.

International Headache Society (1988). Classification and diagnostic criteria for headache disorders, cranial neuralgias and facial pain. *Cephalalgia, 8* (Suppl. 7): 1–96.

Ironson, G., Taylor, C. B., Boltwood, M., Bartzokis, T., Dennis, C., Chesney, M., Spitzer, S., & Seagall, G. M. (1992). Effects of anger on left ventricular ejection fraction in coronary artery disease. *American Journal of Cardiology, 70,* 281–285.

Iscoe, I. (1981). Conceptual barriers to training for the primary prevention of psychopathology. In J. M. Joffe & G. W. Albee (Eds.), *Prevention through political action and social change* (pp. 110–134). Hanover, New Hampshire: University Press of New England.

Istvan, J., & Matarazzo, J. D. (1984). Tobacco, alcohol and caffeine use: A review of their interrelationship. *Psychological Bulletin, 95,* 301–326.

Izard, C. E. (1977). *Human emotions.* New York: Plenum Press.

Jablensky, A., Sartorius, N., Ernberg, G., Anker, M., et al. (1992). Schizophrenia: Manifestations, incidence, and course in different cultures: A World Health Organization ten-country study. *Psychological Medicine, Mono Suppl. 20,* 97.

Jackson, M., & Cawley, R. (1992). Psychodynamic and psychotherapy on an acute psychiatric ward: The story of an experimental unit. *British Journal of Psychiatry, 160,* 41–50.

Jackson, D. N., & Messick, S. (1961). Acquiescence and desirability as response determinants on the MMPI. *Education and Psychological Measurement, 21,* 771–790.

Jacobs, D. F. (1987). Cost-effectiveness of specialized psychological programs for reducing hospital stays and outpatient visits. *Journal of Clinical Psychology, 43,* 729–735.

Jacobson, N. S. (1995, March/April). The overselling of therapy. *The Family Therapy Networker,* pp. 40–47.

Jacobson, N. S., & Addis, M. E. (1993). Research on couples and couple therapy: What do we know? Where are we going? *Journal of Consulting and Clinical Psychology, 61,* 85–93.

Jacobson, N. S., & Christensen, A. (1996). Studying the effectiveness of psychotherapy: How well can clinical trials do the job? *American Psychologist, 51,* 1031–1039.

Jacobson, N. S., & Margolin, G. (1979). *Marital therapy: Strategies based on social learning and behavior exchange principles.* New York: Brunner/Mazel.

Jacobson, N. S., & Truax, P. (1991). Clinical significance: A statistical approach to defining meaningful change in psychotherapy research. *Journal of Consulting and Clinical Psychology, 59* (1), 12–19.

Jacobson, N. S., Dobson, K. S., Truax, P. A., Addis, M. E., Koerner, K., Gollan, J. K., Gortner, E., & Prince, S. E. (1996). A component analysis of cognitive-behavioral treatment for depression. *Journal of Consulting and Clinical Psychology, 64,* 295–304.

Jaffe, J. H. (1995). Drug addiction and drug abuse. In L. S. Goodman & A. Gilman (Eds.), *The Pharmacological Basis of Therapeutic Behaviour.* New York: Macmillan.

Jamison, K. R. (1995). *An unquiet mind.* New York: Alfred Knopf.

Janicak, P. G., Davis, J. M., Preskorn, S. H., & Ayd, F. J. (1993). *Principles and practice of psychopharmacological therapy.* Baltimore, MD: Williams & Wilkins.

Janicki, M. P. (1989). Aging and persons with mental handicap and developmental disabilities. *Journal of Practical Approaches to Developmental Handicap, 12,* 9–13.

Janoff-Bulman, R. (1992). *Shattered assumptions: Toward a new psychology of trauma.* New York: Free Press.

Jaycox, L., Reivich, K., Gillham, J., & Seligman, M. (1994). Prevention of depressive symptoms in schoolchildren. *Behaviour Research and Therapy, 32,* 801–816.

Jenike, M. A. (1989). Anxiety disorders of old age. In M. A. Jenike (Ed.), *Geriatric psychiatry and psychopharmacology* (pp. 248–271). Chicago: Year Book Medical Publishers.

Jenkins, M. R., & Culbertson, J. L. (1996). Prenatal exposure to alcohol. In R. L. Adams, O. A. Parsons, J. L. Culbertson & S. J. Nixon, *Neuropsychology for Clinical Practice.*

Jenkins-Hall, K., & Sacco, W. P. (1991). Effects of client race and depression on evaluations by white therapists. *Journal of Social and Clinical Psychology, 10,* 322–333.

Jensen, A. R. (1969). How much can we boost I.Q. and scholastic achievement? *Harvard Educational Review, 39,* 1–123.

Jensen, G. B., & Palkenberg, B. (1993). Do alcoholics drink their neurons away? *Lancet, 342,* 1201–1204.

Jeste, D. V., Harris, M. J., & Paulsen, J. S. (1996). Psychosis. In J. Sadavoy, L. W. Lazarus, L. F. Jarvik, & G. T. Grossberg (Eds.), *Comprehensive Review of Geriatric Psychiatry II* (pp. 593–614). Washington, DC: American Psychiatric Press, Inc.

Jeste, D. V., Harris, M. J., Pearlson, G. D., Rabins, P., Lesser, I., Miller, B., Coles, C., & Yassa, R. (1988). Late-onset schizophrenia: Studying clinical validity. *Psychiatric Annals of North America, 11,* 1–13.

Jeste, D. V., Lacro, J. P., Gilbert, P. L., Kline, J., & Kline, N. (1993). Treatment of late-life schizophrenia with neuroleptics. *Schizophrenia Bulletin, 19,* 817–829.

Jeste, D. V., Manley, M., & Harris, M. J., (1991). Psychoses. In J. S. Sadavoy, L. W. Lazarus, & L. F. Jarvik (Eds.), *Comprehensive Review of Geriatric Psychiatry* (pp. 353–368). Washington, DC: American Psychiatric Press, Inc.

Joe, G. W., Dansereau, D. F., & Simpson, D. D. (1994). Node-link mapping for counselling cocaine users in methadone treatment. *Journal of Substance Abuse, 6* (4), 393–406.

Joffe, J. M., & Albee, G. W. (Eds.) (1981). *Prevention through political action and social change.* Hanover, New Hampshire: University Press of New England.

Joffe, R. T., Swinson, R. P., & Regan, J. J. (1988). Personality features of obsessive-compulsive disorder. *American Journal of Psychiatry, 145,* 1127–1129.

Johnson, C., & Connors, M. E. (1987). *The etiology and treatment of bulimia nervosa.* New York: Basic Books.

Johnson, D. J., & Blalock, J. W. (1987). *Adults with learning disabilities: Clinical studies.* New York: Grune & Stratton.

Johnson, J., Weissman, M. M., & Klerman, G. L. (1990). Panic disorder and suicide attempts. *Archives of General Psychiatry, 47,* 805–808.

Johnson, S. L., & Miller, I. (1997). Negative life events and time to recovery from episodes of bipolar disorder. *Journal of Abnormal Psychology, 106,* 449–457.

Johnson, S. M., Hunsley, J., Greenberg, L., & Schindler, D. (in press). Emotionally focused couples therapy: Status and challenges. *Clinical Psychology: Science and Practice.*

Johnson, W. G., Jarrell, M. P., Chupurdia, K. M., & Williamson, D. A. (1994). Repeated binge/purge cycles in bulimia nervosa: Role of glucose and insulin. *International Journal of Eating Disorders, 15,* 331–341.

Johnston, C., & Mash, E. J. (1989). A measure of parenting satisfaction and efficacy. *Journal of Clinical Child Psychology, 18,* 167–175.

Johnstone, T. P. (1968). *Kraepelin, E.: Lectures in clinical psychiatry.* New York: Hafner.

Jones, M. C. (1924). Elimination of children's fears. *Journal of Experimental Psychology, 7,* 382–390.

Jones, R. J. (1983). Cannabis and health. *Annual Review of Medicine, 34,* 247–258.

Jovanovic, V. J. (1969). Der effekt der ersten untersuchungsnacht auf die erektionen in schlaf. *Psychotherapy and Psychosomatics, 17,* 295–308.

Kagan, J. (1982). Heart rate and heart rate variability as signs of a tempermental dimension. In C. E. Izard (Ed.), *Measuring emotions in infants and children.* New York: Cambridge University Press.

Kagan, J., Reznick, S., & Snidman, N. (1988). Biological bases of childhood shyness. *Science, 240,* 167–171.

Kahn, R. S., Westenberg, H.G.M., & Moore, C. (1995). Increased serotonin function and panic disorder. In G. M. Asnis & H. M.

van Praag (Eds.), *Panic disorder: Clinical, biological, and treatment aspects* (pp. 151–180). New York: Wiley Interscience.

Kaiji, L. (1960). Alcoholism in twins. *Studies on the etiology and sequels of abuse of alcohol.* Stockholm: Almquist & Wiksell.

Kalichman, S. C. (1991). Psychopathology and personality characteristics of criminal sexual offenders as a function of victim age. *Archives of Sexual Behavior, 20,* 187–197.

Kalichman, S. C., & Brosig, C. L. (1993). Practicing psychologists' interpretations of and compliance with child abuse reporting laws. *Law and Human Behavior, 17* (1), 83–93.

Kandel, D. B., Simcha-Fagan, O., & Davies, M. (1986). Risk factors for delinquency and illicit drug use from adolescence to young adulthood. *Journal of Drug Issues, 16,* 67–90.

Kanfer, F. H., & Phillips, J. S. (1970). *Learning foundations of behavior therapy.* New York: Wiley.

Kanner, A. D., Coyne, J. C., Schaefer, C., & Lazarus, R. S. (1981). Comparisons of two modes of stress measurement: Daily hassles and uplifts versus major life events. *Journal of Behavioral Medicine, 4,* 1–39.

Kanner, L. (1943). Autistic disturbances of affective contact. *Nervous Child, 2,* 217–250.

Kaplan, A. S., & Woodside, D. B. (1987). Biological aspects of anorexia nervosa and bulimia nervosa. *Journal of Consulting and Clinical Psychology, 55,* 645–653.

Kaplan, H. S. (1974). *The new sex therapy: Active treatment of sexual dysfunctions.* New York: Brunner/Mazel.

Kaplan, H. S. (1979). *Disorders of sexual desire and other new concepts and techniques in sex therapy.* New York: Brunner/Mazel.

Kaplan, J. R., Manuck, S. B., Clarkson, T. B., Lusso, F. M., Taub, D. M., & Miller, E. W. (1983). Social stress and atherosclerosis in normocholesterolemic monkeys. *Science, 220,* 733–735.

Kaplan, M. (1983). A woman's view of DSM-III. *American Psychologist, 38,* 786–792.

Kaplan, M. (1983a). The issue of sex bias in DSM-III. *American Psychologist, 38,* 802–803.

Karacan, I. (1970, April). Clinical evaluation of nocturnal penile tumescence as an objective method for evaluating sexual functioning in ESRD patients. *Dialysis and Transplantation, 7,* 872–876.

Karasek, R. A., Baker, D., Marxer, F., Ahlborn, A., & Theorell, T. (1981). Job decision latitude, job demands and cardiovascular disease: A prospective study of Swedish men. *American Journal of Public Health, 71,* 694–705.

Karasek, R. A., Theorell, T. G., Schwartz, J., Pieper, C., & Alfredsson, L. (1982). Job, psychological factors and coronary heart disease: Swedish prospective findings and U. S. prevalence findings using a new occupational inference method. *Advances in Cardiology, 29,* 62–67.

Karnesh, L. J., & Zucker, E. M. (1945). *Handbook of psychiatry.* St. Louis, MO: Mosby.

Kaschak, E. (1992). *Engendered lives.* New York: Basic Books.

Kastenbaum, R. (1992). Death, suicide and the older adult. *Suicide and Life Threatening Behavior, 22,* 1–14.

Katon, W., Lin, E., von Korff, M., Russo, J., Lipscomb, P., & Bush, T. (1991). Somatization: A spectrum of severity. *American Journal of Psychiatry, 148,* 34–40.

Katz, S. (1954, August 1). The amazing career of Clare Hincks. *Maclean's Magazine.*

Kaufmann, C. A., Delisi, L. E., Lehner, T., & Gilliam, T. C. (1989). Physical mapping, linkage analysis of a putative schizophrenia locus on chromosome 5q. *Schizophrenia Bulletin, 15,* 441–452.

Kaweionnehta Human Resource Group (October, 1993). *First Nations and Inuit community youth solvent abuse survey and study.* Unpublished document, Addiction and Community Funded Programs.

Kay, D.W.K., Cooper, H. F., Garside, R. F., & Roth, M. (1976). The differentiation of paranoid from affective psychoses by patients' premorbid characteristics. *British Journal of Psychiatry, 129,* 207–215.

Kaye, W. H., Weltzin, T. E., McKee, M., McConaha, C., Hansen, D., & Hsu, L.K.G. (1992). Laboratory assessment of feeding behaviour in bulimia nervosa and healthy women: Methods for developing a human feeding laboratory. *American Journal of Clinical Nutrition, 55,* 372–380.

Kazarian, S. S. (1992). The measurement of expressed emotion: A review. *Canadian Journal of Psychiatry, 37,* 51–56.

Kazarian, S. S., & Malla, A. K. (1992). Working with the families of long-term patients: An expressed emotion perspective. In E. Persad, S. S. Kazarian, & L. W. Joseph (Eds.), *The mental hospital in the 21st century* (pp. 91–106). Toronto: Wall & Emerson.

Kazarian, S. S., & Vanderheyden, D. A. (1992). Family education of relatives of people with psychiatric disability: A review. *Psychosocial Rehabilitation Journal, 15* (3), 68–84.

Kazarian, S. S., Malla, A. K., Cole, J. D., & Baker, B. (1990). Comparisons of two expressed emotion scales with the Camberwell Family Interview. *Journal of Clinical Psychology, 46,* 306–309.

Kazarian, S. S., Mazmanian, D. S., McDermott, K., & Olinger, L. J. (1991). *The interrelationship of measures of affective familial climates.* Paper presented at the annual convention of the Canadian Psychological Association, Calgary, Alberta, Canada, June 13–15.

Kazdin, A. E. (1985). *Treatment of antisocial behavior in children and adolescents.* Pacific Grove: Brooks/Cole.

Kazdin, A. E. (1987). Treatment of antisocial behavior in children: Current status and future directions. *Psychological Bulletin, 102,* 187–203.

Kazdin, A. E. (1987a). *Conduct disorders in childhood and adolescence.* Newbury Park, CA: Sage.

Kazdin, A. E. (1992a). Child and adolescent dysfunction and paths towards malajustment: Targets for intervention. *Clinical Psychology Review, 12,* 795–818.

Kazdin, A. E. (1993). Treatment of conduct disorders: progress and directions in psychotherapy research. *Developmental Psychology, 5,* 277–310.

Kazdin, A. E. (1994). Methodology, design, and evaluation in psychotherapy research. In A. E. Bergin & S. L. Garfield (Eds.), *Handbook of psychotherapy and behavior change* (4th ed., pp. 19–71). New York: Wiley.

Kazdin, A. E. (1995). Child, parent and family dysfunction as predictors of outcome in cognitive-behavioral treatment of antisocial children. *Behavioral Research and Therapy, 33* (3), 271–281.

Kazdin, A. E., & Bass, D. (1989). Power to detect differences between alternative treatments in comparative psychotherapy outcome research. *Journal of Consulting and Clinical Psychology, 57,* 138–147.

Kazdin, A. E., Esveldt-Dawson, K., French, N. H., & Unis, A. S. (1987b). Effects of parent management training and problem-solving skills training combined in the treatment of antisocial child behavior. *Journal of the American Academy of Child and Adolescent Psychiatry, 26,* 416–424.

Kazdin, A. E., Mazurick, J. L., & Siegel, T. C. (1994). Treatment outcome among children with externalizing disorder who terminate prematurely versus those who complete psychotherapy. *Journal of the American Academy of Child and Adolescent Psychiatry, 33* (4), 549–557.

Kazdin, A. E., Siegel, T. C., & Bass, D. (1990). Drawing upon clinical practice to inform research on child and adolescent psychotherapy: A survey of practitioners. *Professional Psychology: Research and Practice, 21,* 189–198.

Kazdin, A. E., Siegel, T., & Bass, D. (1992b). Cognitive problem-solving skills training and parent management training in the treatment of antisocial behavior in children. *Journal of Consulting and Clinical Psychology, 60,* 733–747.

Keane, T. M., Caddell, J. M., & Taylor, K. L. (1988). Mississippi scale for combat-related post-traumatic stress disorder: Three studies in reliability and validity. *Journal of Consulting and Clinical Psychology, 56,* 85–90.

Keane, T. M., Zimering, R. T., & Caddell, J. M. (1985). A behavioral formulation of posttraumatic stress disorder. *The Behavior Therapist, 8,* 9–12.

Keck, P. E., & McElroy, S. (1997). The new antipsychotics and their therapeutic potential. *Psychiatric Annals, 27,* 320–331.

Keefler, J., & Koritar, E. (1994). Essential elements of a family psychoeducation program in the aftercare of schizophrenia. Conference: Schizophrenia 1992: Poised for Change, Vancouver, Canada. *Journal of Marital and Family Therapy, 20* (4), 369–380.

Keesey, R. E. (1986). A set-point theory of obesity. In K. D. Brownell & J. P. Foreyt (Eds.), *Handbook of eating disorders* (pp. 63–88). New York: Basic Books.

Keesey, R. E. (1995). A set-point model of body weight regulation. In K. D. Brownell & C. G. Fairburn (Eds.), *Eating disorders and obesity: A comprehensive handbook* (pp. 46–51). New York: Guilford Press.

Keith, S. J. (1997). Pharmacologic advances in the treatment of schizophrenia. *New England Journal of Medicine, 337,* 851–853.

Keith-Spiegel, P., & Koocher, G. P. (1998). *Ethics in psychology: Professional standards and cases, 2nd Ed.* New York: Oxford University Press.

Keller, M. B. (1994). Depression: A long-term illness. *British Journal of Psychiatry, 165,* 9–15.

Kellner, R. (1986). *Somatization and hypochondriasis.* New York: Praeger-Greenwood.

Kelly, G. A. (1955). *A theory of personality.* New York: Norton.

Kelly, T., Soloff, P. H., Cornelius, J., George, A., Lis, J. A., & Ulrich, R. (1992). Can we study (treat) borderline patients? Attrition from research and open treatment. *Journal of Personality Disorders, 6,* 417–433.

Kendall, P. C. (1994). Treating anxiety disorders in children: Results of a randomized clinical trial. *Journal of Consulting and Clinical Psychology, 62,* 100–110.

Kendall, P. C., & Grove, W. M. (1988). Normative comparisons in therapy outcome. *Behavioral Assessment, 10,* 147–158.

Kendall, P. C., & Hammen, C. (1995). *Abnormal psychology.* Boston: Houghton Mifflin.

Kendall, P. C., Reber, M., McLeer, S., Epps, J., & Ronan, K. R. (1990). Cognitive-behavioral treatment of conduct-disordered children. *Cognitive Therapy and Research, 14,* 279–289.

Kendall, P. C., Reber, M., McLeer, S., Epps, J., & Ronan, K. R. (1990). Cognitive-behavioral treatment of conduct-disordered children. *Cognitive Therapy and Research, 14,* 279–289.

Kendler, K. S. (1985). Diagnostic approaches to schizotypal personality disorder: A historical perspective. *Schizophrenia Bulletin, 11,* 538–553.

Kendler, K. S., & Gruenberg, A. M. (1982). Genetic relationship between paranoid personality disorder and the "schizophrenic" spectrum disorders. *American Journal of Psychiatry, 139,* 1185–1186.

Kendler, K. S., Heath, R. C., Neale, M. C., Kessler, R. C., & Eaves, L. J. (1992). A population-based twin study of alcoholism in women. *Journal of the American Medical Association, 268,* 1877–1882.

Kendler, K. S., MacLean, C., Neale, M., Kessler, R., Heath, A., & Eaves, L. (1991). The genetic epidemiology of bulimia nervosa. *American Journal of Psychiatry, 148,* 1627–1637.

Kendler, K. S., Masterson, C. C., & Davis, K. L. (1985). Psychiatric illness in first degree relatives of patients with paranoid psychosis, schizophrenia and medical controls. *British Journal of Psychiatry, 147,* 524–531.

Kendler, K. S., Neale, M. C., Kessler, R. C., Heath, A. C., & Eaves, L. J. (1993). Panic disorder in women: A population-based twin study. *Psychological Medicine, 23,* 397–406.

Kennedy, J. L., et al. (1988). Evidence against linkage of schizophrenia to markers on chromosome 5 in a northern Swedish pedigree. *Nature, 336,* 167–170.

Kennedy, S., Thompson, R., Stancer, H., Roy, A., & Persad, E. (1983). Life events precipitating mania. *British Journal of Psychiatry, 142,* 398–403.

Kermis, M. D. (1984). *The psychology of human aging.* Boston: Allyn and Bacon.

Kernberg, O. F. (1967). Borderline personality organization. *Journal of the American Psychoanalytic Association, 15,* 641–685.

Kernberg, O. F. (1975). *Borderline conditions and pathological narcissism.* New York: Jason Aronson.

Kernberg, O. F. (1985). *Borderline conditions and pathological narcissism.* Northvale, NJ: Jason Aronson.

Kernberg, O., Selzer, M., Koenigsberg, H., Carr, A., & Appelbaum, A. (1989). *Psychodynamic psychotherapy of borderline patients.* New York: Basic Books.

Keso, L., & Salaspuro, M. (1990). Inpatient treatment of employed alcoholics: A randomized clinical trial on Hazelden-type and traditional treatment. *Alcoholism in Clinical and Experimental Research, 14,* 584–598.

Kessler, R. C., McGonagle, K. A., Zhao, S., Nelson, C. B., Hughes, M., Eshleman, S., Wittchen, H.-U., & Kendler, K. S. (1994). Lifetime and 12-month prevalence of *DSM-III-R* psychiatric disorders in the United States. Results from the National Comorbidity Survey. *Archives of General Psychiatry, 51,* 8–19.

Kessler, R. C., Sonnega, A., Bromet, E., Hughes, M., & Nelson, C. B. (1995). Posttraumatic stress disorder in the National Comorbidity Survey. *Archives of General Psychiatry, 52,* 1048–1060.

Keys, A., Brozek, J., Henschel, A., Mickelsen, O., & Taylor, H. L. (1950). *The biology of human starvation (Vols. I, II).* Minneapolis: University of Minnesota Press.

Kihlstrom, J. F. (1984). Conscious, subconscious, unconscious: A cognitive perspective. In K. S. Bowers & D. Meichenbaum (Eds.), *The unconscious reconsidered* (pp. 149–211). New York: Wiley.

Killen, J. D., Fortmann, S. P., & Newman, B. (1990). Evaluation of a treatment approach combining nicotine gum with self-guided behavioural treatments for smoking relapse prevention. *Journal of Consulting and Clinical Psychology, 58,* 85–92.

Kilpatrick, D. G., Best, C. L., Saunders, B. E., & Veronen, L. J. (1988). Rape in marriage and in dating relationships: How bad is it for mental health? *Annals of the New York Academy of Sciences, 528,* 335–344.

King, M. B. (1990). Sneezing as a fetishistic stimulus. *Sexual and Marital Therapy, 5,* 69–72.

King, S. M., Rosenbaum, P., Armstrong R. W., & Milner, R. (1989). An epidemiological study of children's attitudes towards disability. *Developmental Medicine and Child Neurology, 31,* 237–245.

Kingdon, D. G., & Turkington, D. (1991). The use of cognitive therapy with a normalizing rationale in schizophrenia. *Journal of Nervous and Mental Disease, 179,* 207–211.

Kinsey, A. C., Pomeroy, W. B., & Martin, C. E. (1948). *Sexual behavior in the human male.* Philadelphia: Saunders.

Kinsey, A. C., Pomeroy, W. B., Martin, C. E., & Gebhard, P. H. (1953). *Sexual behavior in the human female.* Philadelphia: Saunders.

Kinston, W. (1980). A theoretical and technical approach to narcissistic disturbance. *International Journal of Psychoanalysis, 61,* 383–393.

Kirmayer, L. J., & Robbins, J. M. (1991). Three forms of somatization in primary care: Prevalence, co-occurrence, and sociodemographic characteristics. *Journal of Nervous and Mental Disease, 179* (11), 647–655.

Kirmayer, L. J., Robbins, J. M., & Paris, J. (1994). Somatoform disorders: Personality and social matrix of somatic distress. *Journal of Abnormal Psychology, 103,* 125–136.

Kissen, B., & Kaley, M. M. (1974). Alcohol and cancer. In B. Kissen & H. Begleiter (Eds.), *The biology of alcoholism, Vol. 3* (pp. 481–511). New York: Plenum.

Klein, D. (1992, April 1). The empty pot. *Los Angeles Times.* Pp. A3–14.

Klein, D. F. (1981). Anxiety reconceptualized. In D. F. Klein & J. Rabkin (Eds.), *Psychopharmocology: A generation of research.* New York: Raven.

Klein, D. F. (1993). False suffocation alarms, spontaneous panics, and related conditions: An integrative hypothesis. *Archives of General Psychiatry, 50,* 306–317.

Klein, M. (1932). *The psychoanalysis of children.* London: Hogarth.

Klein, M., et al. (1952). *Developments in psychoanalysis.* London: Hogarth.

Klein, R. G., Koplewicz, H. S., & Kanner, A. (1992). Imipramine treatment of children with separation anxiety disorder. *Journal of the American Academy of Child and Adolescent Psychiatry, 31,* 21–28.

Klerman, G. L., Weissman, M. M., Rounsaville, B. J., & Chevron, E. S. (1984). *Interpersonal psychotherapy of depression.* New York: Basic Books.

Klerman, G., Weissman, M., Rounsaville, B., & Chevron, E. (1984). *Interpersonal psychotherapy for depression.* New York: Basic Books.

Kluft, R. P. (1987). An update on multiple personality disorder. *Hospital and Community Psychiatry, 38,* 363–373.

Klug, W. S., & Cummings, M. R. (1986). *Concepts of genetics.* Glenview, IL: Scott Foresman.

Knight, L. J., & Boland, F. J. (1989). Restrained eating: An experimental disentanglement of the disinhibiting variables of perceived calories and food type. *Journal of Abnormal Psychology, 98,* 412–420.

Knight, R. (1953). Borderline states. *Bulletin of the Menninger Clinic, 17,* 1–12.

Knight, R. A. (1993). Comparing cognitive models of schizophrenics' input dysfunction. In R. L. Cromwell & C. R. Snyder (Eds.), *Schizophrenia: Origins, processes, treatment, and outcome* (pp. 151–175). New York: Oxford University Press.

Knowles, J., Southmayd, S., Delva, N., MacLean, A., Cairns, J., & Letemendia, F. (1979). Five variations of sleep deprivation in a depressed woman. *British Journal of Psychiatry, 135,* 403–410.

Koçak, H. (1989). *Differential and difference equations through computer experiments* (2nd ed.). New York: Springer-Verlag.

Kociol, L., & Schiff, M. (1989). *Alzheimer: A Canadian family resource guide.* Toronto: McGraw-Hill Ryerson.

Kockott, G., & Fahrner, E-M. (1987). Transsexuals who have not undergone surgery: A follow-up study. *Archives of Sexual Behavior, 16,* 511–522.

Koenig, H. G., & Blazer, D. G. (1992a). Epidemiology of geriatric affective disorders. *Clinics in Geriatric Medicine, 8,* 235–251.

Koenig, H. G., & Blazer, D. G. (1992b). Mood disorders and suicide. In J. E. Birren, R. B. Sloane, & G. D. Cohen (Eds.), *Handbook of mental health and aging* (pp. 380–407). San Diego, CA: Academic Press.

Koenig, H. G., & Breitner, J. C. (1990). Use of antidepressants in medically ill older patients. *Psychosomatics, 31,* 22–32.

Kog, E., & Vandereycken, W. (1989). Family interaction in eating disorder patients and normal controls. *International Journal of Eating Disorders, 8,* 11–23.

Koh, S. D. (1978). Remembering in schizophrenia. In S. Schwartz (Ed.), *Language and cognition in schizophrenia.* Hillsdale, NJ: Erlbaum.

Koh, S. D., & Kayton, L. (1974). Memorization of "unrelated" word strings by young nonpsychotic schizophrenics. *Journal of Abnormal Psychology, 83,* 14–22.

Kohn, M. L. (1968). Social class and schizophrenia: A critical review. In D. Rosenthal & S. S. Kety (Eds.), *The transmission of schizophrenia: Proceedings of the second research conference of the Foundations' Fund for Research in Psychiatry, Dorado, Puerto Rico, June 26 to July 1, 1967* (pp. 155–173). London, UK: Pergamon.

Kohut, H. (1977). *The restoration of the self.* New York: International Universities Press.

Kohut, H. (1990). *The search for self: Selected writings of Heinz Kohut: 1978–1981.* (Vol. 3, P. H. Ornstein, Ed.). Madison, WI: International Universities Press.

Kokkinidis, L., & Anisman, H. (1980). Amphetamine models of paranoid schizophrenia: An overview and elaboration of animal experimentation. *Psychological Bulletin, 88,* 551–579.

Kolada, J. L., Bland, R. C., Newman, S. C. (1994). Obsessive-compulsive disorder. *Acta Psychiatrica Scandinavica, 24–35.*

Kopta, S. M., Howard, K. I., Lowry, J. L., & Beutler, L. E. (1994). Patterns of symptomatic recovery in psychotherapy. *Journal of Consulting and Clinical Psychology, 62,* 1009–1016.

Korchin, S. J. (1976). *Modern clinical psychology.* New York: Basic Books.

Korthonen, T. (1988). External validity of subgroups of Finnish learning-disabled children. *Journal of Clinical and Experimental Neuropsychology, 10,* 56.

Koss, M. P. (1985). The hidden rape victim: Personality, attitudinal, and situational characteristics. *Psychology of Women Quarterly, 9,* 193–212.

Koss, M. P. (1988). Stranger and acquaintance rape: Are there differences in the victim's experience? *Psychology of Women Quarterly, 12,* 1–24.

Koss, M. P. (1992). The underdetection of rape: Methodological choices influence incidence estimates. *Journal of Social Issues, 48,* 61–75.

Kosson, D. S., Smith, S. S., & Newman, J. P. (1990). Evaluation of the construct validity of psychopathy in Black and White male inmates: Three preliminary studies. *Journal of Abnormal Psychology, 99,* 250–259.

Kraepelin, E. (1883). *Compendium der psychiatrie.* Leipzig: Abel.

Kraepelin, E. (1913). *Psychiatry: A textbook.* Leipiz: Barth.

Kraepelin, E. (1919). *Dementia praecox* (R. M. Barclay, Trans.). Edinburgh: Livingstone.

Krafft-Ebing, R. V. (1901). *Psychopathia sexualia.* Stuttgart: Ferdinand Enke.

Krahn, D. D. (1991). The relationship of eating disorders and substance abuse. *Journal of Substance Abuse, 3,* 239–254.

Kral, V. A., Eastwood, M. R., Kedward, H. B., McCormak, W. P., & Jones, R. P. (1983). *Mental health care of the elderly: Proceedings of a colloquium on issues in service, assessment, and education.* Ottawa: Health and Welfare Canada.

Kramer, H., & Sprenger, J. (1928/1970). *Malleus maleficarum* [The witches' hammer] (M. Summers, Trans.). New York: Blom. (Original work published in 1487.)

Kramer, M. (1992). Barriers to the primary prevention of mental, neurological, and psychosocial disorders of children: A global perspective. In G. W. Albee, L. A. Bond, & T. V. Cook Monsey (Eds.), *Improving children's lives: Global perspectives on prevention* (pp. 3–36). London: Sage.

Kramer, M., German, P. S., Anthony, J. C. (1985). Patterns of mental disorders among the elderly residents of eastern Baltimore, MD. *Journal of the American Geriatric Society, 33,* 236–245.

Kramer, M., Taube, A., & Redick, R. W. (1973). Patterns of use of psychiatric facilities by the aged: Past, present, and future. In C. Eisdorfer & M. P. Lanton (Eds.), *The psychology of adult development and aging.* Washington, DC: American Psychological Association.

Kramer, P. (1994). *Listening to Prozac.* New York: Viking Press.

Kramer, S. I., & Reifler, B. V. (1992). Depression, dementia, and reversible dementia. *Clinics in Geriatric Medicine, 8,* 289–297.

Krantz, D. S., & Manuck, S. B. (1984). Acute psychophysiologic reactivity and risk of cardiovascular disease: Review and methodologic critique. *Psychological Bulletin, 96,* 435–464.

Kratochwilll, T. R., & Sheridan, S. M. (1990). Advances in behavioral assessment. In T. B. Gutkin & C. R. Reynolds (Eds.), *The handbook of school psychology* (pp. 328–364). New York: Wiley.

Krause, N., & Stryker, S. (1984). Stress and well-being: The buffering role of locus of control beliefs. *Social Science and Medicine, 18,* 783–790.

Kreitman, N. (1976). The coal gas story. United Kingdom suicide rates, 1960–71. *British Journal of Preventive & Social Medicine, 30,* 86–93.

Kresin, D. (1993). Medical aspects of inhibited sexual desire disorder. In W. O'Donohue & J. H. Greer (Eds.), *Handbook of sexual dysfunctions: Assessment and treatment* (pp. 15–52) Boston: Allyn and Bacon.

Kroll, J., & Bachrach, B. (1984). Sin and mental illness in the Middle Ages. *Psychological Medicine, 14,* 507–514.

Krummel, D. A., Seligson, F. H., & Guthrie, H. A. (1996). Hyperactivity—Is candy causal? *Critical Reviews in Food Science & Nutrition, 36* (1–2), 31–47.

Kuch, K., & Cox, B. J. (1992). Symptoms of PTSD in 124 survivors of the Holocaust. *American Journal of Psychiatry, 149,* 337–340.

Kuch, K., Cox, B. J., & Direnfeld, D. M. (1995). A brief self-rating scale for PTSD after road vehicle accidents. *Journal of Anxiety Disorders, 9,* 503–514.

Kuczmarski, R. J. (1992). Prevalence of overweight and weight gain in the United States. *American Journal of Clinical Nutrition, 55,* 495s–502s.

Kuhn, C. M. (1989). Adrenocortical and gonadal steroids in behavioral cardiovascular medicine. In N. Schneiderman, S. M. Weiss, & P. G. Kaufmann. *Handbook of research methods in cardiovascular behavioral medicine.* New York: Plenum.

Kupfer, D. J., Frank, E., Gershon, S., Soares, J. C., Gitlin, M. J., & Altshuler, L. L. (1997). Commentary on forty years of lithium treatment. *Archives of General Psychiatry, 54,* 14–23.

Kuypers, J., & Bengston, V. (1973). Competence and social breakdown: A social-psychological view of aging. *Human Development, 16,* 37–49.

LaCroix, A. Z., & Haynes, S. G. (1987). Gender differences in the stressfulness of workplace roles: A focus on work and health. In R. Barnett, G. Baruch, & L. Biener (Eds.), *Gender and stress* (pp. 96–121). New York: Free Press.

Lader, M. (1982). Differential diagnosis of anxiety in the elderly. *Journal of Clinical Psychiatry, 43,* 4–7.

Lader, M. H., & Wing, L. (1964). Habituation of the psycho-galvanic reflex in patients with anxiety states and in normal subjects. *Journal of Neurology, Neurosurgery, and Psychiatry, 27,* 210–218.

Lader, M., & Sartorius, N. (1968). Anxiety in patients with hysterical conversion symptoms. *Journal of Neurology, Neurosurgery and Psychiatry, 31,* 490–495.

Ladouceur, R., Freeston, M. H., & Rhéaume, J. (1996). Traitement cognitif et comportemental du trouble obsessionnel-compulsif. Partie 1: Modèle explicatif. *Revue Québécoise de Psychologie, 17,* 91–107.

Ladouceur, R., Freeston, M. H., Gagnon, F., Thibodeau, N., & Dumont, J. (1994). Cognitive-behavioral treatment of obsessional ruminations. *Behavior Modification, 19,* 247–257.

Laessle, R. G., Kittle, S., Fichter, M. M., Wittchen, H., & Pirke, K. M. (1987). Major affective disorder in anorexia nervosa and bulimia: A descriptive study. *British Journal of Psychiatry, 151,* 785–789.

Lafave, H., Gerber, G., Pinkney, A., & Beaupre, L. (1992). Psychosocial rehabilitation and the role of the mental hospital in the 21st century. In E. Persad, S. S. Kazarian, & L. W. Joseph (Eds.), *The mental hospital in the 21st century* (pp. 81–90). Toronto: Wall & Emerson.

Lahey, B. B., Hartdagen, S. E., Frick, P. J., McBurnett, K., Connor, R., & Hynd, G. W. (1988). Conduct disorder: Parsing the confounded relationship between parental divorce and antisocial personality. *Journal of Abnormal Psychology, 97,* 334–337.

Lalinec-Michaud, M., Subak, M. E., Ghadirian, A. M., & Kovess, V. (1991). Substance misuse among native and rural high school students in Quebec. *The International Journal of the Addictions, 26* (9), 1003–1012.

Lalonde, M. (1974). *A new perspective on the health of Canadians.* Ottawa: National Health and Welfare.

Lamb, H. R., & Grant, R. W. (1982). The mentally ill in an urban county jail. *Archives of General Psychiatry*, 39, 17–22.

Lamb, H. R., & Zusman, J. (1979). Primary prevention in perspective. *American Journal of Psychiatry, 136,* 12–17.

Lamont, J. A. (1978). Vaginismus. *American Journal of Obstetrics and Gynecology, 131,* 632–636.

Landry, S. H., & Loveland, K. A. (1988). Communication behaviors in autism and developmental language delay. *Journal of Child Psychology and Psychiatry, 29* (5), 621–634.

Lang, A. R., Goeckner, D. J., Adessor, V. J., & Marlatt, G. A. (1975). Effects of alcohol on aggression in male social drinkers. *Journal of Abnormal Psychology, 84,* 508–518.

Lang, R. A., Langevin, R., Checkley, K. L., & Pugh, G. (1987). Genital exhibitionism: Courtship disorder or narcissism? *Canadian Journal of Behavioural Science, 19,* 216–232.

Lang, R., Pugh, G., & Langevin, R. (1988). Treatment of incest and pedophilic offenders: A pilot study. *Behavioral Science and the Law, 6,* 239–255.

Langevin, R. (1983). *Sexual strands: Understanding and treating sexual anomalies in men.* Hillsdale, NJ: Lawrence Erlbaum.

Langevin, R., & Lang, R. A. (1987). The courtship disorders. In G. D. Wilson (Ed.), *Variant sexuality: Research and theory* (pp. 202–228). London: Croom Helm.

Langevin, R., Paitich, D., & Russon, A. E. (1985). Are rapists sexually anomalous, aggressive, or both? In R. Langevin (Ed.), *Erotic preference, gender identity, and aggression in men: New research studies* (pp. 13–38). Hillsdale, NJ: Lawrence Erlbaum.

Langevin, R., Paitich, D., Ramsey, G., Anderson, C., Kamrad, J., Pope, S., Geller, G., & Newman, S. (1979). Experimental studies in the etiology of genital exhibitionism. *Archives of Sexual Behavior, 8,* 307–331.

Langfeldt, T. (1981). Sexual development in children. In M. Cook & K. Howells (Eds.), *Adult sexual interest in children.* New York: Academic Press.

Langner, T. S., et al. (1974). Treatment of psychological disorders among urban children. *Journal of Consulting and Clinical Psychology, 42,* 170–179.

LaRue, A., Dessonville, C., & Jarvik, L. F. (1985). Aging and mental disorders. In J. E. Birren & K. W. Schaie (Eds.), *Handbook of the psychology of aging* (2nd ed.) (pp. 664–702). New York: Van Nostrand Reinhold.

Last, C. G. (1989). Anxiety disorders. In T. H. Ollendick & M. Hersen (Eds.), *Handbook of child psychopathology* (pp. 219–228). New York: Plenum.

Last, C. G., Francis, G., Hersen, M., Kazdin, A. E., & Strauss, C. C. (1987). Separation anxiety and school phobia: A comparison using DSM-III criteria. *American Journal of Psychiatry, 144,* 653–657.

Last, C. G., Strauss, C. C., & Francis, G. (1987). Comorbidity among childhood anxiety disorders. *Journal of Nervous and Mental Disease, 175,* 726–730.

LaVigna, G. W., & Donnellan, A. M. (1986). *Alternatives to punishment: Solving behavior problems with nonaversive strategies.* New York: Irvington.

Lawson, G., Peterson, J. S., & Lawson, A. (1983). *Alcoholism and the family: A guide to treatment and prevention.* Rockville, MD: Aspen.

Lazar, I., & Darlington, R. (1982). Lasting effects of early education: A report from the Consortium for Longitudinal Studies. *Monographs of the Society for Research in Child Development, 47* (2–3, Serial No. 195).

Lazarus, R. S., & Folkman, S. (1984). *Stress, appraisal and coping.* New York: Guilford.

Le Grange, D., Eisler, I., Dare, C., & Russell, G.F.M. (1992). Evaluation of family treatments in adolescent anorexia nervosa: A pilot study. *International Journal of Eating Disorders, 12,* 347–357.

Leavell, H. R., & Clark, E. G. (1965). *Preventive medicine for a doctor in his community: An epimediological approach* (3rd ed.). New York: McGraw-Hill.

LeClair, M. (1996). *A state of aboriginal corrections.* Ottawa: Ministry of the Solicitor General of Canada.

Ledingham, J. E. (1981). Developmental patterns of aggressive and withdrawn behavior in childhood: A possible method for identifying preschizophrenics. *Journal of Abnormal Child Psychology, 9,* 1–22.

Ledingham, J. E. (1990). Recent developments in high risk research. In B. B. Lahey & A. E. Kazdin (Eds.), *Advances in clinical child psychology, Vol. 13* (pp. 91–138). New York: Plenum.

Ledingham, J. E., & Schwartzman, A. E. (1984). A 3-year follow-up of aggressive and withdrawn behaviour in childhood: Preliminary findings. *Journal of Abnormal Child Psychology, 12,* 157–168.

LeDoux, J. E. (1993). Emotional networks in the brain. In M. Lewis & J. M. Haviland (Eds.), *Handbook of emotions* (pp. 109–118). New York: Guilford.

Ledwidge, B., Glackman, W., Paredes, J., Chen, R., Dhami, S., Hansen, M., & Higenbottam, J. (1987). Controlled follow-up of patients released by a review panel at one and two years after separation. *Canadian Journal of Psychiatry, 32,* 448–453.

Lee, S. W., & Piersel, W. C. (1989). Reliability and reactivity of self-recording by preschool children. *Psychological Reports, 64* (3), 747–754.

Leenaars, A. A., & Lester, D. (1992). Comparison of rates and patterns of suicide in Canada and the United States, 1960–1988. *Death Studies, 16,* 417–430.

Lees, M. C., & Neufeld, R.W.J. (1994). Matching the limits of clinical inference to the limits of quantitative methods: A formal appeal to practice what we consistently preach. *Canadian Psychology, 35,* 268–282.

Legault, S. E., Langer, A., Armstrong, P. W., & Freeman, M. R. (1995). Usefulness of ischemic response to mental stress in predicting silent myocardial ischemia during ambulatory monitoring. *American Journal of Cardiology, 75,* 1007–1011.

Lehman, J. F. (1840). *Remarks on insanity and the management of insane persons.* Montreal: John Lovell.

Leichner, P., Arnett, J., Rallo, J. S., Srikomeswaran, S., & Vulcano, B. (1986). An epidemiologic study of maladaptive eating attitudes in a Canadian school age population. *International Journal of Eating Disorders, 5,* 969–982.

Leonard, F. (1991). Using Wechsler data to predict success for learning disabled college students. *Learning Disabilities Research and Practice, 6,* 17–24.

Leonard, H. L., & Rapoport, J. (1991). *Textbook of child and adolescent psychiatry.* Washington, DC: American Psychiatric Press.

Lerner, M. J. (1980). *The belief in a just world: A fundamental delusion.* New York: Plenum.

Letchworth, W. P. (1889). *The insane in foreign countries.* New York: Putnam

Levene, J. E., Newman, F., & Jeffries, J. J. (1989). Focal family therapy outcome study. I. Patient and family functioning. *Canadian Journal of Psychiatry, 34* (7), 641–647.

Levene, J. E., Newman, F., & Jeffries, J. J. (1990). Focal family therapy: Theory and practice. *Family Process, 29,* 73–86.

Levine, E. S., & Padilla, A. M. (1980). *Crossing cultures in therapy: Counseling for the Hispanic.* Monterey: Brooks/Cole.

Levine, M., & Levine, A. (1992). *Helping children: A social history.* Oxford: Oxford University Press.

Levine, S. B. (1989). Comprehensive and sexual health centers: Is it time? *Journal of Sex and Marital Therapy, 15,* 215–224.

Levy, D. L., Holzman, P. S., Matthysse, S., & Mendell, N. R. (1993). Eye tracking dysfunction and schizoprhenia: A critical perspective. *Schizophrenia Bulletin, 19,* 461–536.

Lewinsohn, P. M., & Graf, M. (1973). Pleasant activities and depression. *Journal of Consulting and Clinical Psychology, 41,* 261–268.

Lewis, C. E., & Bucholz, K. K. (1991). Alcoholism, antisocial behaviour and family history. *British Journal of Addiction, 86* (2), 177–194.

Lewis, D. O., Shanok, S. S., Pincus, J. H., & Glaser, G. H. (1979). Violent juvenile delinquents. *Journal of the American Academy of Child and Adolescent Psychiatry, 15,* 307.

Lewis, O. (1961). *The children of Sanchez.* New York: Random House.

Lewis, O. (1969). A Puerto Rican boy. In J. C. Finney (Ed.), *Culture change, mental health, and poverty.* New York: Simon and Schuster.

Lewontin, R. C., Rose, S., & Kamin, L. J. (1984). *Not in our genes: Biology, ideology, and human nature.* New York: Pantheon Books.

Lezak, M. D. (1976). *Neuropsychological assessment.* New York: Oxford University Press.

Liberman, R. P., Eckman T. (1981). Behavior therapy vs. insight oriented therapy for repeated suicide attempters. *Archives of General Psychiatry, 38,* 613–616.

Liddle, P. F. (1987). Schizophrenic syndromes, cognitive performance and neurological dysfunction. *Psychological Medicine, 16,* 49–57.

Liddle, P. F., & Morris, D. L. (1991). Schizophrenic syndromes and frontal lobe performance. *British Journal of Psychiatry, 158,* 340–345.

Liddle, P. F., Barnes, T.R.E., Morris, D., & Haque, S. (1989). Three syndromes in chronic schizophrenia. *British Journal of Psychiatry, 155 (Suppl. 7),* 119–122.

Lieberman, D. A. (1992). *Learning, behavior and cognition* (2nd ed.). Pacific Grove, Brooks/Cole.

Liebert, R. M., & Spiegler, M. D. (1994). *Personality: Strategies and issues.* Pacific Grove, CA: Brooks/Cole.

Lilienfeld, S. O. (1992). The association between antisocial personality and somatization disorders: A review and integration of theoretical models. *Clinical Psychology Review, 12,* 641–662.

Lin, K. M., & Kleinman, A. M. (1988). Psychopathology and clinical course of schizophrenia: A cross-cultural perspective. *Schizophrenia Bulletin, 14,* 555–567.

Lindemann, E. (1944). Symtomatology and management of acute grief. *American Journal of Psychiatry, 101,* 141–148.

Linden, W., & Chambers, L. (1994). Clinical effectiveness of non-drug treatment of hypertension: A meta-analysis. *Annals of Behavioral Medicine, 16,* 35–45.

Lindsley, O. R., Skinner, B. F., & Solomon, R. L. (1954). A method for the experimental analysis of the behavior of psychotic patients. *American Psychologist 9,* 419–420.

Linehan, M. M. (1987). Dialectical behavior therapy for borderline personality disorder. *Bulletin of the Menninger Clinic, 41,* 261–276.

Linehan, M. M. (1993). *Cognitive-behavioral treatment of borderline personality disorder.* New York: Guilford.

Linehan, M. M., & Heard, H. L. (1992). Dialectical behavior therapy for borderline personality disorder. In J. F. Clarkin, E., Marziali, & H. Munroe-Blum (Eds.), *Borderline personality disorder: Clinical and empirical perspectives* (pp. 248–267). New York: Guilford Press.

Linehan, M. M., Armstrong, H. E., Suarez, A., Allmon, D., & Heard, H. L. (1991). Behavioral treatment of chronically parasuicidal borderline patients. *Archives of General Psychiatry, 48,* 1060–1064.

Linehan, M. M., Camper, P., Chiles, J. A., Strosahl, K., & Sherin, E. N. (1987). Interpresonal problem-solving and parasuicide. *Cognitive therpay & Research, 11,* 1–12.

Lingswiler, V. M., Crowther, J. H., & Stephens, M.H.P. (1989). Emotional and somatic consequences of binge episodes. *Addictive Behaviors, 14,* 503–511.

Links, P. S. (1992). Family environment and family psychopathology in the etiology of borderline personality disorder. In J. F. Clarkin, E. Marziali, & H. Munroe-Blum (Eds.), *Borderline personality disorder: Clinical and empirical perspectives* (pp. 45–66). New York: Guilford.

Lipowski, Z. J. (1989). Psychiatry: Mindless, brainless, both or neither? *Canadian Journal of Psychiatry, 34,* 249–254.

Livesley, W. J. (1986). Trait and behavioral prototypes for personality disorder. *American Journal of Psychiatry, 143,* 728–732.

Livesley, W. J., & West, M. (1986). The DSM-III distinction between schizoid and avoidant personalities. *Canadian Journal of Psychiatry, 31,* 59–62.

Livesley, W. J., Schroeder, M. L., Jackson, D. N., & Jang, K. L. (1994). Categorical distinctions in the study of personality disorder: Implications for classification. *Journal of Abnormal Psychology, 103,* 6–17.

Lloyd, K. G., Farley, I. J., Deck, H., et al. (1974). Serotonin and 5 hydrosyindoleaceatic acid in discrete areas of the brainstem of suicide victims and control patients. *Advances in Biochemical Psychopharmcology 11,* 387–397.

LoPiccolo, J. (1978). Direct treatment of sexual dysfunction. In J. LoPiccolo & L. LoPiccolo (Eds.), *Handbook of sex therapy* (pp. 1–17). New York: Plenum Press.

Loeber, R. (1982). The stability of antisocial and delinquent child behavior: A review. *Child Development, 53,* 1431–1446.

Loeber, R. (1988). Natural histories of conduct problems, delinquency, and associated substance use: Evidence for developmental progressions. In B. B. Lahey & A. Kazdin (Eds.), *Advances in clinical child psychology* (pp. 73–124). New York: Plenum.

Loeber, R. (1990). Development and risk factors of juvenile antisocial behavior and delinquency. *Clinical Psychology Review, 10,* 1–42.

Loeber, R., & Dishion, T. (1983). Early predictors of male delinquency: A review. *Psychological Bulletin, 94,* 68–99.

Loeber, R., & Keenan, K. (1994). Interaction between conduct disorder and its comorbid conditions: Effects of age and gender. *Clinical Psychology Review, 14,* 497–523.

Loeber, R., & Stouthamer-Loeber, M. (1986). Family factors as correlates and predictors of juvenile conduct problems and delinquency. In M. Tonry & N. Morris (Eds.), *Crime and justice* (pp. 29–149). Chicago: University of Chicago Press.

Loeber, R., & Stouthamer-Loeber, M. (1987). Predictions. In H. C. Quay (Ed.), *Handbook of juvenile delinquency* (pp. 325–382). New York: Wiley.

Loeber, R., Green, S. M., Keenan, K., & Lahey, B. B. (1995). Which boys will fare worse? Early predictors of the onset of conduct disorder in a six-year longitudinal study. *Journal of the American Academy of Child and Adolescent Psychiatry, 34* (4), 499–509.

Loeber, R., Keenan, K., Lahey, B. B., Green, S. M., & Thomas, C. (1993). Evidence for developmentally based diagnoses of oppositional defiant disorder and conduct disorder. *Journal of Abnormal Child Psychology, 21,* 377–410.

Loewenstein, R. J. (1991). Psychogenic amnesia and psychogenic fugue: A comprehensive review. *Annual Review of Psychiatry, 10,* 223–247.

Loftus, E. F. (1993). When a lie becomes memory's truth: Memory distortion after exposure to misinformation. *Current Directions in Psychological Science, 1,* 121–123.

Loftus, E. F., & Ketcham, K. (1991). *Witness for the defense: The accused, the eyewitness, and the expert who puts memory on trial.* New York: St. Martin's Press.

Logan, A. C., & Goetsch, V. L. (1993). Attention to external threat cues in anxiety states. *Clinical Psychology Review, 13,* 541–559.

Longnecker, M. P. (1994). Alcohol consumption and the risk of cancer in humans: An overview. *Alcohol, 12,* 87–96.

Lopatka, C., & Rachman, S. (1995). Perceived responsibility and compulsive checking: An experimental analysis. *Behaviour Research and Therapy, 33,* 673–684.

Lopez, S. R. (1989). Patient variable biases in clinical judgment: Conceptual overview and methodological considerations. *Psychological Bulletin, 106,* 184–203.

Lopez, S. R., & Hernandez, P. (1986). How culture is considered in evaluations of psychopathology. *Journal of Nervous and Mental Disease, 176,* 598–606.

LoPiccolo, J. (1990). Sexual dysfunction. In A. S. Bellack, M. Hersen, & A. Kazdin (Eds.), *International handbook of behavior therapy and modification* (2nd ed.) (pp. 547–564). New York: Plenum Press.

LoPiccolo, J. (1992). Postmodern sex therapy for erectile failure. In R. C. Rosen & S. R. Leiblum (Eds.), *Erectile disorders: Assessment and treatment* (pp. 171–187). New York: Guilford Press.

Lord, C. (1993). The complexity of social behavior in autism. In S. Baron-Cohen, H. Tager-Flusberg, & D. Cohen (Eds.), *Understanding other minds: Perspectives from autism* (pp. 292–316). Oxford: Oxford University Press.

Lord, C., & Paul, R. (1997). Language and communication in autism. In D. J. Cohen & F. R. Volkmar (Eds), *Handbook of autism and pervasive developmental disorders* (pp. 195–225). New York: Wiley.

Lord, C., & Schopler, E. (1987). Neurobiological implications of sex differences in autism. In E. Schopler & G. B. Mesibov (Eds.), *Neurobiological issues in autism* (pp. 192–211). New York: Plenum.

Lord, J., & Hutchison, P. (1993). The process of empowerment: Implications for theory and practice. *Canadian Journal of Community Mental Health, 12* (1), 5–22.

Lou, H., Henriksen, L., & Bruhn, P. (1990). Dysfunctions in developmental learning disabilities. *The Lancet, 335,* 8–11.

Lovaas, O. I. (1977). *The autistic child: Language development through behavior modification.* New York: Irvington Publishers.

Lovaas, O. I. (1987). Behavioral treatment and normal educational and intellectual functioning in young autistic children. *Journal of Consulting and Clinical Psychology, 55,* 3–9.

Lovaas, O. I., & Smith, T. (1988). Intensive behavioral treatment with young autistic children. In B. B. Lahey & A. E. Kazdin (Eds.), *Advances in clinical child psychology* (Vol. 11, pp. 285–324). New York: Plenum Press.

Lovaas, O. I., Koegel, R. L., Simmons, J. Q., & Long, J. S. (1973). Some generalization and follow-up measures on autistic children in behavior therapy. *Journal of Applied Behavior Analysis, 6,* 131–166.

Low, P. W., Jeffries, J. C., & Bonnie, R. J. (1986). *The trial of John W. Hinckley, Jr.: A case study in the insanity defense.* Mineola, NY: The Foundation Press.

Luborsky, L. (1954). A note on Eysenck's article "The effects of psychotherapy: An evaluation." *British Journal of Psychology, 45,* 129–131.

Luborsky, L., Singer, B., & Luborsky, L. (1975). Comparative studies of psychotherapies: Is it true that "everybody has won and all must have prizes?" *Archives of General Psychiatry, 32,* 995–1008.

Lubs, H. A. (1969). A marker X chromosome. *American Journal of Human Genetics, 21,* 231–244.

Luckey, E. B., & Nass, G. D. (1969). A comparison of sexual attitudes and behavior in an international sample. *Journal of Marriage and the Family, 31,* 364–379.

Lumsden, D. P. (Ed.) (1984). *Community mental health action: Primary prevention programming in Canada.* Ottawa: Canadian Public Health Association.

Lundberg, U., Frankenhaeuser, M. (1980). Pituitary-adrenal and sympathetic-adrenal correlates of distress and effort. *Journal of Psychosomatic Research 24,* 125–133.

Lydiard, R. B., Brawman-Mintzer, O., & Ballenger, J. C. (1996). Recent developments in the psychopharmacology of anxiety disorders. *Journal of Consulting and Clinical Psychology, 64,* 660–668.

Lykken, D. T. (1957). A study of anxiety in the sociopathic personality. *Journal of Abnormal and Social Psychology, 55,* 6–10.

Lykken, D. T. (1995). *The antisocial personalities.* Hillsdale, NJ: Erlbaum.

Lytton, H. (1990). Child and parent effects in boys' conduct disorder: A reinterpretation. *Developmental Psychology, 26,* 683–697.

Macdonald, A.J.D. (1986). Do general practitioners "miss" depression in elderly patients? *British Medical Journal, 292,* 1365–1367.

Mace, N. L. (Ed.) (1990). *Dementia care: Patient, family and community.* Baltimore, MD: John Hopkins University Press.

Macedo, D. (1994). *Literacies of power: What Americans are not allowed to know.* Boulder, CO: Westview.

Mackenzie, C. (1997). *Family physicians' attitudes, beliefs, and clinical behaviours with respect to mental disorders in older adults.* Unpublished Master's thesis, Queen's University, Kingston, Ontario.

MacKay, R. D. (1990). Dangerous patients. Third party safety and psychiatrists' duties—walking the *Tarasoff* tightrope. *Medicine, Science, and the Law,* 30, 52–56.

MacLeod, C., & McLaughlin, K. (1995). Implicit and explicit memory bias in anxiety: A conceptual replication. *Behaviour Research and Therapy, 33,* 1–14.

Maddox, G. L. (1963). Activity and morale: A longitudinal study of selected elderly subjects. *Social Forces, 42,* 195–204.

Magee, W. J., Eaton, W. W., Wittchen, H. U., McGonagle, K. A., & Kessler, R. C. (1996). Agoraphobia, simple phobia, and social phobia in the National Comorbidity Survey. *Archives of General Psychiatry, 53,* 159–168.

Maher, B. (1966). *Principles of psychopathology: An experimental approach.* New York: McGraw-Hill.

Maher, B. (1972). The language of schizophrenia: A review and interpretation. *British Journal of Psychiatry, 120,* 3–15.

Maher, B. A., Manschrek, T. C., Woods, B. T., Yurgelun-Todd, D. A., et al. (1995). Frontal brain volume and context effects in short-term recall in schizophrenia. *Biological Psychiatry, 37,* 144–150.

Maher, W. B., & Maher, B. A. (1985). Psychopathology. 1. From ancient times to the eighteenth century. In G. A. Kimble & K. Schlesinger (Eds.), *Topics in the history of psychology* (Vol. 2). Hillsdale, NJ: Erlbaum.

Mahler, M. S., Pine, F., & Bergman, A. (1975). *The psychological birth of the human infant.* New York: Basic Books.

Mahrer, A. R. (1996). *The complete guide to experiential psychotherapy.* New York: Wiley.

Maier, W., Lichtermann, D., Klingler, T., Heun, R., & Hallmayer, J. (1992). Prevalence of personality disorders (DSM-III-R) in the community. *Journal of Personality Disorders, 6,* 187–196.

Malamuth, N. M. (1986). Predictors of naturalistic sexual aggression. *Journal of Personality and Social Psychology, 50,* 953–962.

Malamuth, N. M., Heavey, C. L., & Linz, D. (1993). Predicting men's antisocial behavior against women: The interactional model of sexual aggression. In G.C.N. Hall, R. Hirschman, J. R. Graham, & M. S. Zaragonzee (Eds.), *Sexual aggression: Issues in etiology, assessment and treatment* (pp. 63–99). Bristol, PA: Taylor & Francis.

Malatesta, V. J., & Adams, H. E. (1984). The sexual dysfunctions. In H. E. Adams & P. B. Sutker (Eds.), *Comprehensive handbook of psychopathology* (pp. 725–775). New York: Plenum Press.

Malla, A. K., Norman, R. M., Williamson, P., Cortese, L., & Diaz, F. (1993). Three syndrome concept of schizophrenia: A factor analytic study. *Schizophrenia Research, 10,* 143–150.

Maller, R. G., & Reiss, S. (1992). Anxiety sensitivity in 1984 and panic attacks in 1987. *Journal of Anxiety Disorders, 6,* 241–247.

Mann, J. J., Stanley, M., McBride, P. A., et al. (1986). Increased serotonin$_2$ and β–adrenergic receptor biding in the frontal cortices of suicide victims. *Archives of General Psychiatry, 43,* 954–959.

Mann, J. J., Arango, V. (1992). Integration of neurobiology and psychopathology in a uinified model of suicidal behavior. *Journal of Clinical Psychopharmacology, 12,* 2S–7S.

Mannuzza, S., & Klein, R. (1992). Predictors of outcome of children with attention-deficit hyperactivity disorder. In G. Weiss (Ed.), *Child and adolescent psychiatric clinics of North America: Attention-deficit hyperactivity disorder* (pp. 567–578). Philadelphia: Saunders.

Mannuzza, S., Klein, R. G., Bonagura, N., Malloy, P., Giampino, T. L., & Addalli, K. A. (1991). Hyperactive boys almost grown up. V. Replication of psychiatric status. *Archives of General Psychiatry, 48,* 77–83.

Mansell, S., Sobsey, D., & Calder, P. (1992). Sexual abuse treatment for persons with developmental disabilities. *Professional Psychology: Research and Practice, 23,* 404–409.

Manson, S. M., Walker, R. D., & Kivlahan, D. R. (1987). Psychiatric assessment and treatment of American Indians and Alaskan natives. *Hospital and Community Psychiatry, 38,* 165–173.

Manuck, S. B., Kaplan, J. R., & Clarkson, T. B. (1983). Behaviorally induced heart rate reactivity and atherosclerosis in cynomolgus monkeys. *Psychosomatic Medicine, 45,* 95–108.

Manuck, S. B., Kaplan, J. R., Adams, M. R., & Clarkson, T. B. (1989). Behaviorally elicited heart rate reactivity and atherosclerosis in female cynomolgus monkeys (*Macaca fascicularis*). *Psychosomatic Medicine, 51,* 306–318.

Marchand, A., Goupil, G., Trudel, G., & Bélanger, L. (1995). Fear and social self-esteem in individuals suffering from panic disorder with agoraphobia. *Scandinavian Journal of Behaviour Therapy, 33,* 163–169.

Marcus, M. D. (1993). Binge eating in obesity. In C. G. Fairburn & G. Terence Wilson (Eds.), *Binge eating: Nature, assessment and treatment* (pp. 77–96). New York: Guilford Press.

Marfo, K., & Kysela, G. M. (1985). Early intervention with mentally handicapped children: A critical appraisal of applied research. *Journal of Pediatric Psychology, 10,* 305–324.

Markovitz, P. J., Calabrese, J. R., Schulz, C. S., & Meltzer, H. Y. (1991). Fluoxetine in the treatment of borderline and schizotypal personality disorders. *American Journal of Psychiatry, 148,* 1067–1076.

Marks, I. M. (1973). Research in neurosis: A selective review. 1. Causes and courses. *Psychological Medicine, 3,* 436–454.

Marks, I. M. (1987). *Fears, phobias, and rituals: Panic, anxiety, and their disorders.* New York: Oxford University Press.

Marks, I. M., & Mathews, A. M. (1979). Brief standard self-rating for phobic patients. *Behaviour Research and Therapy, 17,* 263–267.

Marks, I. M., Birley, J.L.T., & Gelder, M. G. (1966). Modified leucotomy in severe agoraphobia: a controlled serial enquiry. *British Journal of Psychiatry, 112,* 757–769.

Marks, I. M., Swinson, R. P., Basoglu, M., Kuch, K., Noshirvani, H., O'Sullivan, G., Lelliott, P. T., Kirby, M., McNamee, G., Sengun, S., & Wickwire, K. (1993). Alprazolam and exposure alone and combined in panic disorder with agoraphobia: A controlled study in London and Toronto. *British Journal of Psychiatry, 162,* 776–787.

Marlatt, G. A., & Gordon, J. R. (Eds.) (1985). *Relapse prevention maintenance strategies in the treatment of addictive behaviors.* New York: Guilford Press.

Marlatt, G. A., Demming, B., & Reid, J. B. (1973). Loss of control drinking in alcoholics: An experimental analogue. *Journal of Abnormal Psychology, 81,* 233–241.

Marmot, M. G. (1986). Social inequalities in mortality: The social environment. In R. G. Wilkinson (Ed.), *Class and health: Research and longitudinal data.* London: Tavistock.

Marmot, M. G., & Mustard, J. F. (1994). Coronary heart disease from a population perspective. In R. G. Evans, M. L. Barer, & T. R. Marmor (Eds.), *Why are some people healthy and others not?* (pp. 189–216). New York: Aldine de Gruyter.

Marmot, M. G., & Theorell, T. (1988). Social class and cardiovascular disease: The contribution of work. *International Journal of Health Services, 18,* 659–674.

Marmot, M. G., Kogevinas, M., & Elston, M. A. (1987). Social/economic status and disease. *Annual Review of Public Health, 8,* 111–135.

Marques, J. K., Day, D. M., Nelson, C., & West, M. A. (1994). Effects of cognitive-behavioral treatment on sex offender recidivism: Preliminary results of a longitudinal study. *Criminal Justice and Behavior, 21,* 28–54.

Marshall, P., Surridge, D., & Delva, N. (1981). The role of nocturnal penile tumescence in differentiating between organic and psychogenic impotence: The first stage of validation. *Archives of Sexual Behavior, 10,* 1–10.

Marshall, W. L. (1982). A model of dysfunctional behavior. In A. S. Bellack, M. Hersen, & A. E. Kazdin (Eds.), *International handbook of behavior modification and therapy* (pp. 57–78). New York: Plenum Press.

Marshall, W. L. (1985). Exposure. In A. S. Bellack & M. Hersen (Eds.). *Dictionary of behavior therapy techniques* (pp. 121–124). New York: Pergamon Press.

Marshall, W. L. (1989). Intimacy, loneliness and sexual offenders. *Behaviour Research and Therapy, 27,* 491–503.

Marshall, W. L. (1992). The social value of treatment for sexual offenders. *Canadian Journal of Human Sexuality, 1,* 109–114.

Marshall, W. L. (1996). *Phobic disorder and gender.* Unpublished manuscript, Queen's University, Kingston, Ontario.

Marshall, W. L., & Anderson, D. (1996). An evaluation of the benefits of relapse prevention programs with sexual offenders. *Sexual Abuse: A Journal of Research and Treatment, 8,* 209–221.

Marshall, W. L., & Barbaree, H. E. (1984). Disorders of personality, impulse and adjustment. In S. M. Turner & M. Hersen (Eds.), *Adult psychopathology: A behavioral perspective* (pp. 406–449). New York: Wiley.

Marshall, W. L., & Barbaree, H. E. (1988). The long-term evaluation of a behavioral treatment program for child molesters. *Behaviour Research and Therapy, 26,* 499–511.

Marshall, W. L., & Barbaree, H. E. (1990). An integrated theory of sexual offending. In W. L. Marshall, D. R. Laws, & H. E. Barbaree (Eds.), *Handbook of sexual assault: issues, theories, and treatment of the offender* (pp. 257–275). New York: Plenum Press.

Marshall, W. L., & Barbaree, H. E. (1991). Personality, impulse control and adjustment disorders. In M. Hersen & S. M. Turner (Eds.), *Adult psychopathology and diagnosis* (2nd ed.) (pp. 360–391). New York: Wiley.

Marshall, W. L., & Barrett, S. (1990). *Criminal neglect: Why sex offenders go free.* Toronto: Doubleday. (Also reprinted in paperback by Seals/Bantam Books, 1992.)

Marshall, W. L., & Eccles, A. (1993). Pavlovian conditioning processes in adolescent sex offenders. In H. E. Barbaree, W. L. Marshall, & S. M. Hudson (Eds.), *The juvenile sex offender* (pp. 118–142). New York: Guilford Press.

Marshall, W. L., & Gauthier, J. G. (1983). Failures in flooding. In E. B. Foa & P.M.G. Emelkamp (Eds.), *Failures in behavior therapy.* New York: Wiley.

Marshall, W. L., & Hall, G.C.N. (1995). The value of the MMPI in deciding forensic issues in accused sexual offenders. *Sexual Abuse: A Journal of Research and Treatment, 7,* 205–219.

Marshall, W. L., & Hambley, L. S. (1996). Intimacy and loneliness, and their relationship to rape myth acceptance and hostility toward women among rapists. *Journal of Interpersonal Violence, 11,* 586–592.

Marshall, W. L., Barbaree, H. E., & Christophe, D. (1986). Sexual offenders against female children: Sexual preferences for age of victims and type of behaviour. *Canadian Journal of Behavioral Science, 18,* 424–439.

Marshall, W. L., Barbaree, H. E., & Fernandez, Y. M. (1995). Some aspects of social competence in sexual offenders. *Sexual Abuse: A Journal of Research and Treatment, 7,* 113–127.

Marshall, W. L., Bryce, P., Hudson, S. M., Ward, T., & Moth, B. (1996). The enhancement of intimacy and the reduction of loneliness among child molesters. *Journal of Family Violence, 11,* 219–235.

Marshall, W. L., Earls, C. M., Segal, Z. V., & Darke, J. (1983). A behavioral program for the assessment and treatment of sexual aggressors. In K. Craig & R. McMahon (Eds.), *Advances in clinical behavior therapy* (pp. 148–174). New York: Brunner/Mazel.

Marshall, W. L., Eccles, A., & Barbaree, H. E. (1991). Treatment of exhibitionists: A focus on sexual deviance versus cognitive and relationship features. *Behaviour Research and Therapy, 29,* 129–135.

Marshall, W. L., Gauthier, J., & Gordon, A. (1979). Current status of flooding therapy. In M. Hersen, R. M. Eisler, & P. M. Miller (Eds.), *Progress in Behavior Modification,* pp. 205–275. New York: Academic Press.

Marshall, W. L., Hudson, S. M., & Hodkinson, S. (1993). The importance of attachment bonds in the development of juvenile sex offending. In H. E. Barbaree, W. L. Marshall, & S. M. Hudson (Eds.), *The juvenile sex offender* (pp. 164–181). New York: Guilford.

Marshall, W. L., Hudson, S. M., Jones, R., & Fernandez, Y. M. (1995). Empathy in sex offenders. *Clinical Psychology Review, 15,* 99–113.

Marshall, W. L., Jones, R., Ward, T., Johnston, P., & Barbaree, H. E. (1991). Treatment outcome with sex offenders. *Clinical Psychology Review, 11,* 465–485.

Marshall, W. L., Payne, K., Barbaree, H. E., & Eccles, A. (1991). Exhibitionists: Sexual preferences for exposing. *Behaviour Research and Therapy, 29,* 37–40.

Marten, P. A., Brown, T. A., Barlow, D. H., Borkovec, T. D., Shear, M. K., & Lydiard, M. B. (in press). Evaluation of the ratings comprising the associated symptom criterion of DSM-III-R generalized anxiety disorders. *Journal of Nervous and Mental Disease.*

Martin, C., & Tarrier, N. (1992). The importance of cultural factors in the exposure to obsessive ruminations: A case example. *Behaviour Psychotherapy, 2,* 181–184.

Martin, J. P., & Bell, J. (1943). A pedigree of mental defect showing sex-linkage. *Journal of Neurological Psychiatry, 6,* 154–157.

Martin, S. L., Ramey, C. T., & Ramey, S. L. (1990). The prevention of intellectual impairment in children of impoverished families: Findings of a randomized trial of educational daycare. *American Journal of Public Health, 80,* 844–847.

Martinson, F. M. (1976). Eroticism in infancy and childhood. *Journal of Sex Research, 12,* 251–262.

Marx, J. A., Gyorky, Z. K., Royalty, G. M., & Stern, T. E. (1992). Use of self-help books in psychotherapy. *Professional Psychology: Research and Practice, 23,* 300–305.

Marziali, E. (1992). The etiology of borderline personality disorder: Developmental factors. In J. F. Clarkin, E. Marziali, & H. Munroe-Blum (Eds.), *Borderline personality disorder: Clinical and empirical perspectives* (pp. 27–44). New York: Guilford.

Marzuk, P. M., Tierney, H., Tardiff, K., et al. (1988). Increased risk of suicide in persons with AIDS. *Journal of the American Medical Association, 259,* 1333–1337.

Mash, E. J., & Johnston, C. (1983). The prediction of mothers' behavior with their hyperactive children during play and task situations. *Child and Family Behavior Therapy, 5,* 1–14.

Mash, E. J., & Johnston, C. (1990). Determinants of parenting stress: Illustrations from families of hyperactive children and families of physically abused children. *Journal of Clinical Child Psychology, 19,* 313–328.

Maslow, A. H. (1954). *Motivation and personality.* New York: Harper & Row.

Masters, W. H., & Johnson, V. E. (1966). *Human sexual response.* Boston: Little, Brown.

Masters, W. H., & Johnson, V. E. (1970). *Human sexual inadequacy.* Boston: Little, Brown.

Matarazzo, J. D. (1990). Psychological assessment versus psychological testing. *American Psychologist, 45,* 999–1017.

Mather, J. A., Neufeld, R.W.J., Merskey, H., & Russell, N. C. (1992). Disruption of saccade production during oculomotor tracking in schizophrenia and the use of its changes across target velocity as a discriminator of the disorder. *Psychiatry Research, 43,* 93–109.

Mathews, A., Mogg, K., Kentish, J., & Eysenck, M. (1995). Effect of psychological treatment on cognitive bias in generalized anxiety disorder. *Behaviour Research and Therapy, 33,* 293–303.

Matson, J. L., Benavidez, D. A., Compton, L. S., Paclawskyj, T., & Baglio, C. (1996). Behavioral treatment of autistic persons: A review of research from 1980 to the present. *Research in Developmental Disabilities, 17,* 433–465.

Matthysse, S., & Holzman, P. (1989). In reply [to McGue & Gottesman, 1989]. *Archives of General Psychiatry, 46,* 479–480.

Mattick, R. P., & Clarke, J. C. (1988). *Development and validation of measures of social phobia scrutiny fear and social interaction anxiety.* Unpublished manuscript, Sydney, Australia, University of New South Wales.

May, R. (Ed.) (1961). *Existential psychology.* New York: Random House.

Maydeu-Olivares, A., & D'Zurilla, T. J. (1996). A factor analysis of the social problem-solving inventory using polychoric correlations. *European Journal of Psychological Assessment, 11,* 98–107.

Mays, J. B. (1995). *In the jaws of the black dogs.* New York: Viking Press.

McBride, W. G. (1961). Thalidomide and congenital abnormalities. *The Lancet, 2,* 1358.

McBride, W. J., Murphy, J. M., Lumeng, L., & Li, T.-K. (1990). Serotonin, dopamine, and GABA involvement in alcohol drinking of selectively bred rats. *Alcohol, 7,* 199–205.

McCann, D., & Endler, N. (1990). *Depression: New directions in theory, research and practice.* Toronto: Wall & Emerson.

McCartney, P. L. (1994). Does deinstitutionalization cost state mental health authorities more? *Administration and Policy in Mental Health, 21,* 479–486.

McClean, P. D. (1976). Depression as a specific response to stress. In I. G. Sarason & C. D. Spielberger (Eds.), *Stress and anxiety (Vol. 3).* Washington: Hemisphere.

McClellan, A. T., Arndt, I. O., Metzger, D. S., Woody, G. E., & O'Brien, C. P. (1993). The effects of psychosocial services in substance abuse treatment. *Journal of the American Medical Association, 269,* 1953–1959.

McConaghy, N. (1993). *Sexual behavior: Problems and management.* New York: Plenum Press.

McCord, J. (1977). A comparative study of two generations of native Americans. In R. F. Meier (Ed.), *Theories in criminology* (pp. 83–92). Beverly Hill: Sage.

McCord, J. (1983). A longitudinal study of aggression and antisocial behavior. In K. T. Van Dusen & S. A. Mednick (Eds.), *Prospective studies in crime and delinquency* (pp. 269–275). Boston: Kluwer-Nijhoff.

McCord, J. (1988). Identifying developmental paradigms leading to alcololism. *Journal of Studies on Alcohol, 49,* 357–362.

McCord, J., McCord, W., & Howard, A. (1963). Family interaction as antecedent to the direction of male aggressiveness. *Journal of Abnormal and Social Psychology, 66,* 239–242.

McCord, W., & McCord, J. (1964). *The psychopath: An essay on the criminal mind.* New York: Van Nostrand.

McCrady, B. S., Stout, R., Noel, N., Abrams, D., & Nelson, H. F. (1991). Effectiveness of three types of spouse-involved behavioral alcoholism treatments. *British Journal of the Addictions, 86,* 1415–1424.

McCrea, S., Enman, M., & Pettifor, J. (1997). The Canadian Code of Ethics and the prescription privilege debate. *Canadian Psychology, 38,* 49–51.

McDougle, C. J., Price, L. H., and Volkman, F. R. (1994). Recent advances in the pharmacotherapy of autism and related conditions. *Child and Adolescent Psychiatric Clinics of North America, 3,* 71–89.

McEachin, J. J., Smith, T., & Lovaas, O. I. (1993). Long term outcome for children with autism who received early intensive behavioral treatment. *American Journal on Mental Retardation, 97,* 359–372.

McElhaney, S. (1992). From bad to worse … and the light at the end of the tunnel. *The Community Psychologist, 26* (1), 7–8.

McElroy, S. L., Phillips, K. A., Keck, P. E., Hudson, J. I., & Pope, H. G. (1993). Body dysmorphic disorder: Does it have a psychiatric subtype? *Journal of Clinical Psychiatry, 54,* 389–395.

McEwan, B. S., & Stellar, E. (1993). Stress and the individual: Mechanisms leading to disease. *Archives of Internal Medicine, 153,* 2093–2101.

McGee, R., Feehan, M., Williams, S., & Anderson, J. (1992). DSM-III disorders from age 11 to age 15 years. *Journal of the American Academy of Child and Adolescent Psychiatry, 31,* 50–59.

McGlashan, T. H. (1994). What has become of the psychotherapy of schizophrenia? *Acta Psychiatrica Scandinavica, 90 (Suppl. 384),* 147–152.

McGlashan, T. M. (1983). The borderline syndrome. I. Testing three diagnostic systems. *Archives of General Psychiatry, 40,* 1311–1318.

McGrath, P. J., Cunningham, S. J., Lascelles, M. J., & Humphreys, P. (Eds.) (1990). *Help yourself: A program for treating migraine headaches.* [Patient manual and tape]. Ottawa: University of Ottawa Press.

McGrath, P. J., & Goodman, J. E. (1998). Pain in childhood. In J. P. Graham (Ed.), *Cognitive behaviour therapy for children and families* (pp. 143–155). New York: Cambridge University Press.

McGrath, P. J., Humphreys, P., Keene, D., Goodman, J. T., Lascelles, M. A., Cunningham, S. J., & Firestone, P. (1992). The efficacy and efficiency of a self-administered treatment for adolescent migraine. *Pain, 49,* 321–324.

McGreevy, M. A., Steadman, H. J., & Callahan, L. A. (1991). The negligible effects of California's 1982 reform of the insanity defense test. *American Journal of Psychiatry, 148,* 744–750.

McGue, M., & Gottesman, I. I. (1989). A single dominant gene still cannot account for the transmission of schizophrenia. *Archives of General Psychiatry, 46,* 478–479.

McGue, M., Pickens, R. W., & Svikis, D. S. (1992). Sex and age effects on the inheritance of alcohol problems: A twin study. *Journal of Abnormal Psychology, 101,* 3–17.

McGuffin, P. Katz, R., & Rutherford, J. (1991). Nature, nurture and depression: A twin study. *Psychological Medicine, 21,* 329–335.

McGuffin, P. W., & Morrison, R. L. (1994). Schizophrenia. In V. B. Van Hasselt & M. Hersen (Eds.), *Advanced abnormal psychology* (pp. 315–334). New York: Plenum.

McGuffin, P., & O'Donovan, M. C. (1993). Modern diagnostic criteria and models of transmission in schizophrenia. In R. L. Cromwell & C. R. Snyder (Eds.), *Schizophrenia: Origins, processes, treatment, and outcome* (pp. 62–75). New York: Oxford.

McGuire, R. J., Carlisle, J. M., & Young, B. G. (1965). Sexual deviations as conditioned behaviour: A hypothesis. *Behaviour Research and Therapy, 2,* 185–190.

McIntosh, J. L. (1985). Suicide among the elderly: Levels and trends. *American Journal of Orthopsychiatry, 55,* 288–293.

McKim, W. A. (1991). *Drugs and behavior. An introduction to behavioral pharmacology* (2nd ed.). Englewood Cliffs, NJ: Prentice Hall.

McKnight, J. (1995). *The careless society: Community and its counterfeits.* New York: Basic Books.

McLoyd, V. C. (1990). The impact of economic hardship on Black families and children: Psychological distress, parenting, and socioemotional development. *Child Development, 61 (Special issue: Minority children),* 311–346.

McNally, R. J. (1987). Preparedness and phobias: A review. *Psychological Bulletin, 101,* 283–303.

McNally, R. J. (1994). *Panic disorder. A critical analysis.* New York: Guilford Press.

McNally, R. J., Kaspi, S. P., Riemann, B. C., & Zeitlin, S. B. (1990). Selective processing of threat cues in posttraumatic stress disorder. *Journal of Abnormal Psychology, 99,* 398–406.

McNeal, E., & Cimbolic, P. (1986). Antidepressants and biochemical theories of depression. *Psychological Bulletin, 99,* 361–374.

McQueen, P. C., Spence, M. W., Garner, J. B., Pereira, L. H., & Winsor, E.J.T. (1987). Prevalence of major mental retardation and associated disabilities in the Canadian Maritime provinces. *American Journal of Mental Deficiency, 91,* 460–466.

Mealey, L. (1995). The sociobiology of sociopathy: An integrated evolutionary model. *Behavioral and Brain Sciences, 18,* 523–599.

Meana, M., & Binik, Y. M. (1994). Painful coitus: A review of female dyspareunia. *The Journal of Nervous and Mental Disease, 182,* 264–272.

Mechanic, D. (1978). *Medical sociology* (2nd ed.). New York: Free Press.

Mednick, S. A. (1962). Schizophrenia: A learned thought disorder. In G. Neilsen (Ed.), *Clinical Psychology.* Proceedings of XIV International Congress of Applied Psychology. Copenhagen: Munksgaard.

Mednick, S. A., & McNeil, T. F. (1968). Current methodology in research on the etiology of schizophrenia: Serious difficulties which suggest the use of the high-risk-group method. *Psychological Bulletin, 70,* 681–693.

Mednick, S. A., Cudeck, R., Griffith, J. J., Talovic, S. A., & Schulsinger, F. (1984). The Danish High-Risk Project: Recent methods and findings. In N. F. Watt, E. J. Anthony, L. C. Wynne, & J. E. Rolf (Eds.), *Children at risk for schizophrenia: A longitudinal perspective* (pp. 21–42). Cambridge: Cambridge University Press.

Meehl, P. E. (1959). Some ruminations on the validation of clinical procedures. *Canadian Journal of Psychology, 13,* 102–128.

Meehl, P. E. (1962). Schizotaxia, schizotypy, schizophrenia. *American Psychologist, 17,* 827–838.

Meehl, P. E. (1989). Schizotaxia revisited. *Archives of General Psychiatry, 46,* 935–944.

Meehl, P. E. (1995). Bootstraps taxometrics: Solving the classification problem in psychopathology. *American Psychologist, 50,* 266–275.

Meehl, P. E., & Golden, R. R. (1982). Taxometric methods. In P. C. Kendall & J. N. Butcher (Eds.), *Handbook of research methods in clinical psychology.* New York: Wiley.

Meichenbaum, D. (1974). *Cognitive behavior modification.* New York: General Learning Corporation.

Meichenbaum, D. (1985). *Stress inoculation training.* New York: Pergamon Press.

Meichenbaum, D. (1994). *Clinical handbook: Practical therapist manual on treating adults with PTSD.* Waterloo, ON: Institute Press.

Meichenbaum, D. H. (1995). Cognitive behavioral therapy in historical perspective. In B. Bongar & L. E. Beutler (Eds.), *Comprehensive textbook of psychotherapy: Theory and practice* (pp. 140–158). New York: Oxford University Press.

Meichenbaum, D., & Goodman J. (1971). Training impulsive children to talk to themselves: A means of developing self-control. *Journal of Abnormal Psychology, 77,* 115–126.

Meichenbaum, D., & Turk, D. (1976). The cognitive behavioral management of anxiety, anger, and pain. In P. O. Davidson (Ed.), *The behavioral management of anxiety, depression, and pain.* New York: Brunner/Mazel.

Meichenbaum, P. (1977). *Cognitive behaviour modification.* New York: Plenum Press.

Meissner, W. W. (1981). The schizophrenic and the paranoid process. *Schizophrenia Bulletin, 7,* 611–631.

Melton, G. B., Petrila, J., Poythress, N. G., & Slobogin, C. (1997). Civil commitment. In *Psychological evaluations for the courts: A handbook for mental health professionals and lawyers* (pp. 297–336). New York: Guilford Press.

Melzack, R., & Wall, P. D. (1965). Pain mechanisms: A new theory. *Science, 150,* 971–979.

Melzack, R., & Wall, P. D. (1982). *The challenge of pain.* New York: Basic Books.

Mendelson, B. K., & White, D. R. (1985). Development of self-body-esteem in overweight youngsters. *Developmental Psychology, 21,* 90–96.

Mendlewicz, J., & Rainer, J. (1977). Adoption study supporting genetic transmission in manic-depressive illness. *Nature, 268,* 326–329.

Mental Health Act, R.S.B.C. (1996), c. 288.

Menzies, R. G., & Clarke, J. C. (1995). The etiology of phobias: A nonassociative account. *Clinical Psychology Review, 15,* 23–48.

Merikangas, K. R., & Weissman, M. M. (1986). Epidemiology of DSM-III Axis II personality disorders. In A. J. Frances & R. E. Hales (Eds.), *The American Psychiatric Association Annual Review* (pp. 49–74). Washington, DC: American Psychiatric Press.

Merskey, H. (1992). The manufacture of personalities: The production of multiple personality disorder. *British Journal of Psychiatry, 160,* 327–340.

Merskey, H. (1995). *The analysis of hysteria: Understanding conversion and dissociation* (2nd ed.), London, Gaskell.

Merskey, H., & Shafran, B. (1986). Political hazards in the diagnosis of "sluggish schizophrenia." *British Journal of Psychiatry, 148,* 247–256.

Meyer, T. J., Miller, M. L., Metzger, R. L., Borkovec, T. D. (1990). Development and validation of the Penn State Worry Questionnaire. *Behaviour Research and Therapy, 28,* 487–495.

Meyers, W. S., & Keith, C. R. (1991). Homosexual and preoedipal issues in the psychoanalytic psychotherapy of a female-to-male transsexual. In C. W. Socarides & V. D. Volkan (Eds.), *The homosexualities and the therapeutic process* (pp. 75–96). Adison, CT: International Universities Press.

Mezzich, J. E., Good, B. J., Lewis-Frenandez, R., Guarnaccia, P., Lin, K. M., Parron, D., O'Nell, T., Manson, S., Fleming, C., Weiss, M., & Hughes, C. (1993). *Cultural formulation guidelines. Revised cultural proposals for DSM-IV.* Submitted to the DSM-IV Task Force by the Steering Committee, NIMH-Sponsored Group on Culture and Diagnosis.

Michelson, L. K., & Marchione, K. (1991). Behavioral, cognitive, and pharmacological treatments of panic disorder with agoraphobia: Critique and synthesis. *Journal of Consulting and Clinical Psychology, 59,* 100–114.

Miles, C. P. (1977). Conditions predisposing to suicide: A review. *Journal of Nervous and Mental Disease, 164,* 231–246.

Miller, G. E., & Prinz, R. J. (1990). Enhancement of social learning family interventions for childhood conduct disorder. *Psychological Bulletin, 108,* 291–307.

Miller, L. C., Barrett, C. L., Hampe, E., & Noble, H. (1971). Revised anxiety scales for the Louisville Behavior Checklist. *Psychological Reports, 29,* 503–511.

Miller, S. D., et al. (1991). Optical differences in multiple personality disorder: A second look. *Journal of Nervous and Mental Disease, 179,* 132–135.

Miller, W. R. (1983). Motivational interviewing with problem drinkers. *Behavioral Psychotherapy, 11,* 147–172.

Miller, W. R., & Rollnick, S. (1991). *Motivational Interviewing.* New York: Guilford.

Millon, T. (1969). *Modern psychopathology: A biosocial approach to maladaptive learning and functioning.* Philadelphia: Saunders.

Millon, T. (1981). *Disorders of personality: DSM-III: Axis II.* New York: Wiley.

Millon, T. (1983). An integrative theory of personality and psychopathology. In T. Millon (Ed.), *Theories of personality and psychopathology* (pp. 3–19). New York: Holt, Rinehart & Winston.

Millon, T. (1986). Personality prototypes and their diagnostic criteria. In T. Millon & G. L. Klerman (Eds.), *Contemporary directions in psychopathology* (pp. 671–712). New York: Guilford.

Millon, T. (1990). *Toward a new personology.* New York: Wiley.

Millon, T. (1992). The borderline construct: Introductory notes on its history, theory, and empirical grounding. In J. F. Clarkin, E. Marziali & H. Munroe-Blum (Ed.). *Borderline personality disorder: Clinical and empirical perspectives* (pp. 3–23). New York: Guilford.

Millon, T. (1996). *Disorders of personality: DSM-IV and beyond* (2nd ed.). New York: Wiley.

Mills, D. E., & Prkachin, K. M. (1993). Psychological stress reverses antiaggregatory effects of dietary fish oil. *Journal of Behavioral Medicine, 16,* 403–412.

Milner, B. (1963). Effects of different brain lesions on card sorting. *Archives of Neurology, 9,* 90–100.

Milrod, B., & Bush, F. (1997). Long-term outcome of panic disorder treatment. A review of the literature. *Journal of Nervous and Mental Disease, 184,* 723–730.

Minder, B., Das-Smaal, E. A., Brand, E.F.J., & Orlebeke, J. F. (1994). Exposure to lead and specific atttentional problems in schoolchildren. *Journal of Learning Disabilities, 27* (6), 393–399.

Ministry of Education (1978). *Memorandum 14. Re the education of students with learning disabilities: Statement to school boards.* Toronto: Queen's Printer.

Mink, I. T., Blacher, J., & Nihira, K. (1988). Taxonomy of family life styles: III. Replication with families with severely mentally retarded children. *American Journal on Mental Retardation, 93,* 250–264.

Minnes, P. M. (1980). The management of feeding problems. In A. Hudson & M. Griffin (Eds.), *Behaviour analysis and the problems of childhood.* Bundoora, Victoria (Australia): PIT Press.

Minnes, P. M. (1988a). Family resources and stress associated with having a mentally retarded child. *American Journal on Mental Retardation, 93,* 184–192.

Minnes, P. M. (1988b). Family stress associated with a developmentally handicapped child. In N. Ellis, & N. Bray (Eds.), *International Review of Research in Mental Retardation, 15,* 195–226. New York: Academic Press.

Minnes, P. M. (1992). Facilitated Communication: An overview and directions for research. *Journal of Developmental Disabilities, 1,* 57–67.

Minnes, P. M., McShane, J., Forkes, S., Green, S., Clement, B., & Card, L. (1989). Coping resources of parents of developmentally handicapped children living in rural communities. *Australia and New Zealand Journal of Developmental Disabilities, 15,* 109–118.

Mirenda, P., & Schuler, A. (1988). Augmenting communication for persons with autism: Issues and strategies. *Topics in Language Disorders, 9,* 24–43.

Mirsky, A. F., Silberman, E. K., Latz, A., & Nagler, S. (1985). Adult outcomes of high-risk children: Differential effects of town and kibbutz rearing. *Schizophrenia Bulletin, 11,* 150–154.

Mischel, W. (1968). *Personality and Assessment.* New York: Wiley.

Mitchell, J. E. (1986). Anorexia nervosa: Medical and physiological aspects. In K. D. Brownell & J. P. Foreyt (Eds.), *Handbook of eating disorders.* New York: Basic Books.

Mitchell, J. E. (1995). Medical complications of bulimia nervosa. In K. D. Brownell & C. G. Fairburn (Eds.), *Eating disorders and obesity: A comprehensive handbook* (pp. 271–277). New York: Guilford Press.

Mitchell, J. E., & de Zwaan, M. (1993). Pharmacological treatments of binge eating. In C. G. Fairburn & G. T. Wilson (Eds.), *Binge eating: Nature, assessment and treatment* (pp. 250–269). New York: Guilford Press.

Mitchell, J. E., Pyle, R. L., & Eckert, E. D. (1981). Frequency and duration of binge-eating episodes in patients with bulimia. *American Journal of Psychiatry, 138,* 835–836.

Moderate drinking and health (1994). Report of an International Symposium, Toronto, ON, 1993. *Canadian Medical Association Journal, 151,* 79–85.

Moffit, T. E. (1990). Juvenile delinquency and attention deficit disorder: Boys' developmental trajectories from age 3 to age 15. *Child Development, 61,* 893–910.

Moffit, T. E., & Lynam, D. (1994). The neuropsychology of conduct disorder and delinquency: Implications for understanding antisocial behaviour. In D. C. Fowles, P. Sutker, & S. H. Goodman (Eds.), *Progress in experimental personality and psychopathology research* (pp. 233–262). New York: Springer.

Moffitt, T. E. (1993). Adolescence-limited and life-course-persistent antisocial behavior: A developmental taxonomy. *Psychological Review, 100,* 674–701.

Mohr, D. C., & Beutler, L. E. (1990). Erectile dysfunction: A review of diagnostic and treatment procedures. *Clinical Psychology Review, 10,* 123–150.

Monahan, J. (1992). Mental disorder and violent behavior: Perceptions and evidence. *American Psychologist, 47,* 511–521.

Money, J. (1984). Paraphilias: Phenomen-ology and classification. *American Journal of Psychotherapy, 38,* 164–179.

Money, J. (1987). Sin, sickness, or status: Homosexual gender identity and psychoneuroednocrinology. *American Psychologist, 42,* 384–399.

Monroe, S. M., & Simons, A. D. (1991). Diathesis-stress theories in the context of life stress research: Implications for the depressive disorders. *Psychological Bulletin, 110,* 406–425.

Monteiro-Musten, L., Firestone, P., Pisterman, S., Bennet, S., & Mercer, J. (1997). The effects of stimulant medication on preschool ADHD children: Behavioural and cognitive factors. *Journal of the American Academy of Child and Adolescent Psychiatry, 36* (10), 1407–1415.

Moore, E. G., & Rosenberg, M. W. (1997). *Growing old in Canada* (Statistics Canada Census Monograph Series). Toronto: ITP Nelson.

Moos, R. H. (1996). Understanding environments: The key to improving social processes and program outcomes. *American Journal of Community Psychology, 24,* 193–201.

Mora, G. (1967). Paracelsus' psychiatry. *American Journal of Psychiatry, 124,* 803–814.

Morales, A., Condra, M., Owen, J. A., Surridge, D. H., Fenemore, J., & Harris, C. (1987). Is Yohimbine effective in the treatment of organic impotence? Results in a controlled trial. *Journal of Urology, 137,* 1168–1172.

Morales, A., Surridge, D. H., Marshall, P., & Fenemore, J. (1982). Nonhormonal pharmacological treatment of organic impotence. *Journal of Urology, 128,* 45–47.

Moran, R. (1981). *Knowing right from wrong: The insanity defense of Daniel McNaughton.* New York: Macmillan, Free Press.

Moran, R. (1985). The modern foundation for the insanity defense: The cases of James Hadfield (1800) and Daniel M'Naghten (1843). *The Annals of the American Academy of Political and Social Science, 477,* 31–42.

Morey, L. C. (1988). Personality disorders in DSM-III and DSM-III-R: Convergence, coverage, and internal consistency. *American Journal of Psychiatry, 145,* 573–577.

Morey, L. C., & Ochoa, E. S. (1989). An investigation of adherence to diagnostic criteria: Clinical diagnosis of the DSM-III personality disorders. *Journal of Personality Disorders, 3,* 180–192.

Morin, C. M., Kowatch, R. A., Barry, T., & Walton, E. (1993). Cognitive-behavior therapy for late-life insomnia. *Journal of Consulting and Clinical Psychology, 61,* 137–146.

Morison, S. (1997). Resiliency in the aftermath of deprivation: A second look at the development of Romanian orphanage children. Manuscript submitted to *Merrill-Palmer Quarterly.*

Morley, J. E., & Krahn, D. D. (1987). Endocrinology for the psychiatrist. In C. B. Nemeroff & P. T. Loosen (Eds.), *Handbook of clinical psychoneuroendocrinology.* New York: Guilford Press.

Morokoff, P. J. (1993). Female sexual arousal disorder. In W. O'Donohue & J. H. Greer (Eds.), *Handbook of sexual dysfunctions: Assessment and treatment* (pp. 157–199). Boston: Allyn and Bacon.

Morrison, M. S., Neufeld, R.W.J., & Lefebvre, L. A. (1988). The economy of probabilistic stress: Interplay of controlling activity and threat reduction. *British Journal of Mathematical and Statistical Psychology, 41,* 155–177.

Mortensen, P. B., & Eaton, W. W. (1994). Predictors for readmission risk in schizophrenia. *Psychological Medicine, 24,* 223–232.

Moscicki, E. K. (1989). Epidemiology surveys as tools for studying suicidal behavior: A review. *Suicide and Life Threatening Behavior, 19,* 131–146.

Moser, C., & Levitt, E. E. (1987). An exploratory-descriptive study of a sadomasochistically oriented sample. *Journal of Sex Research, 23,* 322–327.

Mosher, L. R., & Keith, S. J. (1980). Psychosocial treatment: Individual, group, family, and community support approaches. *Schizophrenia Bulletin, 6* (1), 10–41.

Moskowitz, D. S., & Schwartzman, A. E. (1988). Life paths of aggressive and withdrawn children. In D. M. Buss & N. Cantor (Eds.), *Personality psychology: Recent trends and emerging directions* (pp. 99–114). New York: Springer-Verlag.

Mowrer, O. H. (1947). On the dual nature of learning—A reinterpretation of "conditioning" and "problem-solving." *Harvard Educational Review, 17,* 102–148.

Mowrer, O. H. (1960). *Learning theory and behavior.* New York: Wiley.

Mulder, R. T., Beautrais, A. L., Joyce, P. R., & Ferguson, D. M. (1998). Relationship between dissociation, childhood sexual abuse, and mental illness in a general population sample. *American Journal of Psychiatry, 155* (6), 806–811.

Mummery, W. K., & Hagen, L. C., (1996). Tobacco pricing, taxation, consumption, and revenue: Alberta 1985–1995. *Canadian Journal of Public Health, 87* (5), 314–316.

Mundy, P., Sigman, M., & Kasari, C. (1990). Joint attention, developmental level and symptom presentation in autism. *Development and Psychopathology, 6,* 389–401.

Muñoz, R. F. (1993). The prevention of depression: Current research and practice. *Applied and Preventive Psychology, 2,* 21–33.

Munro, A. (1986). Folie à deux revisited. *Canadian Journal of Psychiatry, 31,* 233–234.

Munro, A. (1988). Delusional (paranoid) disorders: Etiologic and taxonomic considerations. I. The possible significance of organic brain factors in etiology of delusional disorders. *Canadian Journal of Psychiatry, 33,* 171–174.

Muris, P., Merckelbach, H., & Clavan, M. (1997). Abnormal and normal compulsions. *Behaviour Research and Therapy, 35,* 249–252.

Murray, J. L., & Minnes, P. M. (1994a). Staff attitudes towards the sexuality of persons with intellectual disability. *Australia and New Zealand Journal of Developmental Disabilities, 19,* 45–52.

Murray, J. L., & Minnes, P. M. (1994b). Persons with developmental disabilities who have AIDS: What are the attitudes of those employed in the field? *Journal of Developmental Disabilities, 3,* 734–84.

Murray, M. E. (1979). Minimal brain dysfunction and borderline personality adjustment. *American Journal of Psychotherapy, 33,* 391–403.

Murtagh, D.R.R., & Greenwood, K. M. (1995). Identifying effective psychological treatments for insomnia: A meta-analysis. *Journal of Consulting and Clinical Psychology, 63,* 79–89.

Musto, D. F. (1992). Cocaine's history, especially the American experience. In *Cocaine: Scientific and social dimensions.* Chichester, England: Wiley.

Musty, R. E., & Kabak, L. (1995). Relationships between motivation and depression in chronic marijuana users. *Life Sciences, 56,* 2151–2155.

Myers, J. K., & Bean, L. L. (1968). *A decade later: A follow-up of social class and mental illness.* New York: Wiley.

Myers, J., Weissman, M., Tischler, G., Holzer, C., Leaf, P., Orvaschel, H., Anthony, J., Boyd, J., Burke, J., Kramer, M., & Stoltzman, R. (1984). Six month prevalence of psychiatric disorders in three communities. *Archives of General Psychiatry, 41,* 959–967.

Myklebust, H. R., & Boshes, B. (1960). Psychoneurological learning disorders in children. *Archives of Pediatrics, 77,* 247–256.

Nachshen, J. S., & Minnes, P. M. (in press). The Family Stress and Support Questionnaire: Focussing on the needs of parents. *Journal of Developmental Disabilities.*

Nakdimen, K. A. (1986). A new formulation for borderline personality disorder? *American Journal of Psychiatry, 143,* 1069.

Nakra, B.R.S., & Grossberg, G. T. (1990). Mood disorders. In D. Bienenfeld (Ed.), *Verwoerdt's Clinical Geropsychiatry* (3rd ed., pp. 107–124). Baltimore, MD: Williams & Wilkins.

Nathan, P. E. (1987b). What do behavioral scientists know and what can they do about alcoholism? In C. P. Rivers (Ed.), *Alcohol and addictive behavior: Vol. 34. Nebraska Symposium on Motivation.* Lincoln: University of Nebraska Press.

National Commission on Testing and Public Policy (1990). *From gatekeeper to gateway: Transforming testing in America.* Chestnut Hill, MA: Boston College.

National Institute on Alcohol Abuse and Alcoholism (1990). *Alcohol and health: Seventh special report to the U.S. Congress* (DHHS Publication No. ADM 90-1656). Washington, DC: U.S. Government Printing Office.

National Institute on Drug Abuse (1992a). *Alcohol Alert 15: Alcohol and AIDA.* Washington, DC: U.S. Government Printing Office.

National Institute on Drug Abuse (1992b). *Alcohol Alert 16: Moderate drinking.* Washington, DC: U.S. Government Printing Office.

National Mental Health Association (1995). *Getting started: The NMHA guide to establishing community-based prevention programs.* Alexandria, VA: National Mental Health Association.

Needleman, H. L., Schell, A., Bellinger, D., Leviton, A., & Allred, E. N. (1990). The long term effects of exposure to low dosages of lead in childhood: An 11-year follow-up report. *New England Journal of Medicine, 322,* 83–88.

Neisser, U. (Ed.) (1982). *Memory observed: Remembering in natural contexts.* San Francisco: Freeman.

Nelson, C. A. (1995). The ontogeny of human memory: A cognitive neuroscience perspective. *Developmental Psychology, 31,* 723–738.

Nelson, G., Potasznik, H., & Bennett, E. M. (1983). Primary prevention: Another perspective. *Canadian Journal of Community Mental Health, 2,* 3–12.

Nelson, G., Prilleltensky, I., Laurendeau, M.-C., & Powell, B. (1996). The prevention of mental health problems in Canada: A survey of provincial policies, structures, and programs. *Canadian Psychology, 37,* 161–172.

Nelson, K. B. (1991). Prenatal and perinatal factors in the etiology of autism. *Pediatrics, 87,* 761–766.

Nelson, P. G., Fields, R. D., Yu, C., & Neale, E. A. (1990). Mechanisms involved in activity-dependent synapse formation in mammalian central nervous system cell cultures. *Journal of Neurobiology, 21* (1), 138–156.

Nemroff, C. B., Widerlov, E., Bissette, G., et al. (1984). Elevated oncentration of CSF corticotropin releasing factor–like immunoreactivity in depressed patients. *Science 226,* 1342–1344.

Nestadt, G., Romanoski, A. J., Chahal, R., Merchant, A., Folstein, J. F., Gruenberg, E. M., & McHugh, P. R. (1990). An epidemiological study of histrionic personality disorder. *Psychological Medicine, 20,* 413–422.

Nettelbladt, P., & Uddenberg, N. (1979). Sexual dysfunction and sexual satisfaction in 58 married Swedish men. *Journal of Psychosomatic Medicine, 23,* 141–147.

Neufeld, R.W.J. (1984). Are semantic networks of schizophrenic samples intact? *The Behavioural and Brain Sciences, 7,* 749–750.

Neufeld, R.W.J. (1989). Methodological aspects of laboratory studies of stress. In R.W.J. Neufeld (Ed.), *Advances in the investigation of psychological stress* (pp. 71–132). New York: Wiley.

Neufeld, R.W.J. (1991). Memory in paranoid schizophrenia. In P. A. Magaro (Ed.), *Cognitive bases of mental disorders* (pp. 231–261). Newbury Park, CA: Sage.

Neufeld, R.W.J., & McCarty, T. (1994). A formal analysis of stressor and stress-proneness effects on basic information processing. *British Journal of Mathematical and Statistical Psychology, 47,* 193–226.

Neufeld, R.W.J., & Nicholson, I. R. (1991). *Differential and other equations essential to a servocybernetic (systems) approach to stress-schizophrenia relations.* Department of Psychology Research Bulletin 698. London: University of Western Ontario.

Neufeld, R.W.J., & Williamson, P. (1996, in press). Neuropsychological correlates of positive symptoms. In C. Pantelis, H. Nelson, & T. Barnes (Eds.), *The neuropsychology of schizophrenia.* London: Wiley.

Neufeld, R.W.J., Mather, J. A., Merskey, H., & Russell, N. C. (1995). Multivariate structure of eye movement dysfunction in schizophrenia. *Multivariate Experimental Clinical Research, 11,* 1–21.

Neufeld, R.W.J., Vollick, D., & Highgate, S. (1993). Stochastic modelling of stimulus encoding and memory search in paranoid schizophrenia: Clinical and theoretical implications. In R. L. Cromwell (Ed.), *Schizophrenia: Origins, processes, treatment, and outcome: The second Kansas series in clinical psychology.* Oxford University Press.

Neugarten, B. L., Havighurst, R. J., & Tobin, S. S. (1965). Personality and patterns of aging. In B. L. Neugarten (Ed.), *Middle age and aging* (pp. 173–177). Chicago: University of Chicago Press.

Newcomb, M. D. (1994). Predictors of drug use and implications for the workplace. In S. MacDonald & D. Roman (Eds.), *Research advances in alcohol and drug problems. Vol. II. Drug testing in the workplace.* New York: Plenum Press.

Niccols, G. A. (1994). Fetal alcohol syndrome: Implications for psychologists. *Clinical Psychology Review, 14,* 91–111.

Nicholls, T. L., Ogloff, J.R.P., & Douglas, K. S. (1997). *Comparing risk assessments with female and male psychiatric outpatients: Utility of the HCR-20 and Psychopathy Checklist: Screening Version.* Paper presented at the annual convention of the American Psychological Association, Chicago. Symposium moderator J.R.P. Ogloff.

Nicholson, I. R., & Neufeld, R.W.J. (1989). Forms and mechanisms of susceptibility to stress in schizophrenia. In R.W.J. Neufeld (Ed.), *Advances in the investigation of psychological stress* (pp. 392–420). New York: Wiley.

Nicholson, I. R., & Neufeld, R.W.J. (1992). A dynamic vulnerability perspective on stress and schizophrenia. *American Journal of Orthopsychiatry, 62,* 117–130.

Nicholson, I. R., Chapman, J. E., & Neufeld, R.W.J. (1995). Cautions in the use of the BPRS in schizophrenia research. *Schizophrenia Research, 17,* 177–185.

Nicholson, I., & Neufeld, R.W.J. (1993). A two-dimensional model of paranoid and nonparanoid schizophrenia. *Journal of Abnormal Psychology, 102,* 259–270.

Nicholson, I., & Neufeld, R.W.J. (1995). *The problem of dissecting schizophrenia: Evidence against a mixture of disorders.* Manuscript in submission.

Nielsen, E. D. (1979). Community mental health services in the community jail. *Community Mental Health Journal,* 15, 27–32.

Nietzel, M. T., Speltz, M. L., McCauley, E. A., & Bernstein, D. A. (1998). *Abnormal Psychology.* Boston: Allyn and Bacon.

Nietzel, M. T., Winett, R. A., Macdonald, M. L., & Davidson, W. S. (1977). *Behavioral approaches to community psychology.* New York: Pergamon Press.

Nigg, J. T., & Goldsmith, H. H. (1994). Genetics of personality disorders: Perspectives from personality and psychopathology research. *Psychological Bulletin, 115,* 346–380.

Nirje, B. (1969). The normalization principle and its human management implications. In R. Kugel & W. Wolfensberger (Eds.), *Changing patterns in residential services for the mentally retarded.* Washington, DC: Government Printing Office.

Nolen-Hoeksema, S. (1990). *Sex differences in depression.* Stanford, CA: Stanford University Press.

Norden, M. J. (1989). Fluoxetine in borderline personality disorder. *Progress in Neuropsychopharmacology and Biological Psychiatry 13,* 885–893.

Norman, R. M., & Malla, A. K. (1991). Dysphoric mood and symptomatology in schizophrenia. *Psychological Medicine, 21,* 897–903.

Norman, R.M.G., & Malla, A. (1993a). Stressful life events and schizophrenia. I. A review of the literature. *British Journal of Psychiatry, 162,* 161–166.

Norman, R.M.G., & Malla, A. (1993b). Stressful life events and schizophrenia. II. Conceptual and methodological issues. *British Journal of Psychiatry, 162,* 166–174.

Norman, R.M.G., & Malla, A. K. (1994). A prospective study of daily stressors and symptomatology in schizophrenic patients. *Social Psychiatry and Psychiatric Epidemiology, 29,* 244–249.

Norman, R.M.G., Malla, S. K., Williamson, P. C., Morrison-Stewart, S. L., Helmes, E., & Corteses, L. (in press). EEG coherence and syndromes in schizophrenia. *British Journal of Psychiatry.*

Noyes, R., Kathol, R. G., Fisher, M. M., Phillips, S. B., & Suezer, M. T. (1994). Psychiatric comorbidity among patients with hypochondriasis. *General Hospital Psychiatry, 16,* 78–87.

Nussbaum, N. L., & Bigler, E. D. (1989). Halstead-Reitan neuropsychological test batteries for children. In C. R. Reynolds & E. Fletcher-Janzen (Eds.), *Handbook of clinical child neuropsychology: Critical issues in neuropsychology* (pp. 181–191). New York: Plenum Press.

Nutter, D. E., & Condron, M. K. (1985). Sexual fantasy and activity patterns of males with inhibited sexual desire and males with erectile dysfunction versus normal controls. *Journal of Sex and Marital Therapy, 11,* 91–98.

Oberle, I., Rousseau, F., Heitz, D., Kretz, C., Devys, D., Hanauer, A., Boue, J., Bertheas, M. F., & Mandel., J. L. (1991). Instability of a 550-base pair DNA segment and abnormal methylation in fragile X syndrome. *Science, 252,* 1097–1102.

Obsessive Compulsion Cognitions Working Group (1997). Cognitive assessment of obsessive-compulsive disorder. *Behaviour Research and Therapy, 35,* 667–681.

Ochitil, H. (1982). Conversion disorder. In J. H. Greist, J. W. Jefferson, & R. L. Spitzer (Eds.), *Treatment of mental disorders.* New York: Oxford University Press.

O'Conner, M. C. (1989). Aspects of differential performance by minorites on standardized tests: Linguistic and sociocultural factors. In B. R. Gifford (Ed.), *Test policy and test performance: Education, language, and culture* (pp. 129–181). Boston: Kluwer Academic Publishers.

Offord, D. R. (1995). Child psychiatric epidemiology: Current status and future prospects. *Canadian Journal of Psychiatry, 40,* 284–288.

Offord, D. R., & Bennett, K. J. (1994). Conduct disorder: Long-term outcomes and intervention effectiveness. *Journal of the American Academy of Child and Adolescent Psychiatry, 33* (8), 1069–1078.

Offord, D. R., & Waters, B. G. (1983). Socialization and its failure. In M. D. Levine, W. B. Carey, A. C. Crocker, & R. T. Gross (Eds.), *Developmental-behavioral pediatrics* (pp. 650–682). New York: Wiley.

Offord, D. R., Alder, R. J., & Boyle, M. H. (1986). Prevalence and sociodemographic correlates of conduct disorder. *American Journal of Social Psychiatry, 6* (4), 272–278.

Offord, D. R., Boyle, M. H., Racine, Y. A., Fleming, J. E., Cadman, D. T., Blum, H. M., Byrne, C., Links, P. S., Lipman, E. L., MacMillan, H. L., Grant, M. I., Sanford, M. N., Szatmari, P., Thomas, H., & Woodward, C. A. (1992). Outcome, prognosis, and risk in a longitudinal follow-up study. *Journal of the American Acadamy of Child and Adolescent Psychiatry, 31* (5), 916–923.

Offord, D. R., Boyle, M. H., Szatmari, P., Rae-Grant, N. I., Links, P. S., Cadman, D. T., Byles, J. A., Crawford, J. W., Blum, H. M., Byrne, C., Thomas, H., & Woodward, C. A. (1987). Ontario Child Health Study: II. Six-month prevalence of disorder and rates of service utilization. *Archives of General Psychiatry, 44,* 832–836.

Offord, D., Boyle, M., Campbell, D., Cochrane, J., Goering, P., Lin, E., Rhodes, A., & Wong, M. (1994). *Mental health in Ontario: Selected findings from the Mental Health Supplement to the Ontario Health Survey.* Toronto: Ontario Ministry of Health.

Ogloff, J.R.P. (1995). Navigating the quagmire: Legal and ethical guidelines. In D. Martin & A. Moore (Eds.), *First steps in the art of intervention* (pp. 347–376). Pacific Grove, CA: Brooks/Cole.

Ogloff, J.R.P. (1996, July). *The Surrey Pretrial Mental Health Program: Community component evaluation.* Burnaby, BC: British Columbia Forensic Psychiatric Services Commission.

Ogloff, J.R.P., & Grant, I. (1997, August). *Involuntary committment, review panel decision making, and risk assessment.* Symposium presented at the annual meeting of the American Psychological Association, Chicago. Symposium moderator J.R.P. Ogloff.

Ogloff, J.R.P., & Olley, M. C. (1998). The interaction between ethics and the law: The ongoing refinement of ethical standards for psychologists in Canada. *Canadian Psychology, 39,* 221–230.

Ogloff, J.R.P., & Otto, R. K. (1991). Are research participants truly informed? Readability of informed consent forms used in research. *Ethics and Behavior, 1,* 239–252.

Ogloff, J.R.P., Schweighofer, A., Turnbull, S. D., & Whittemore, K. (1992). Empirical research and the insanity defense: How much do we really know? In J.R.P. Ogloff (Ed.), *Psychology and law: The broadening of the discipline* (pp. 171–210). Durham, NC: Carolina Academic Press.

Olah, A., Stattin, R., & Magnusson, D. (1978). *Comparison of anxiety patterns of Swedish and Hungarian youngsters.* Stockholm: University of Stockholm.

Olds, D. L. (1988). The Prenatal/Early Infancy Project. In R. H. Price, E. L. Cowen, R. P. Lorion, & J. Ramos-McKay (Eds.), *Fourteen ounces of prevention: A casebook for practitioners* (pp. 9–23). Washington, DC: American Psychological Association.

Olds, D. L. (in press). The Prenatal Early Infancy Project: Preventing child abuse and neglect in the context of promoting maternal and child health. In D. A. Wolfe, R. J. McMahon, & R. DeV. Peters (Eds.), *Child abuse: New directions in prevention and treatment across the lifespan.* Thousand Oaks, CA: Sage.

Olds, D. L., Eckenrode, J., Henderson, C. R., Kitzman, H., Powers, J., Cole, R., Sidora, K., Morris, P., Pettitt, L. M., & Luckey, D. (1997). Long-term effects of home visitation on maternal life course and child abuse and neglect: Fifteen year follow-up of a randomized trial. *Journal of the American Medical Association, 278,* 637–643.

O'Leary, K. D., & Kent, R. (1973). Behavior modification for social action: Research tactics and problems. In L. C. Hamerlynck, L. C. Handy, & E. J. Mash (Eds.), *Behavior change: Methodology, concepts, and practice.* Champaign, IL: Research Press.

Ollendick, T. H., King, N. J., & Frary, R. B. (1989). Fears in children and adolescents: Reliability and generalizability across gender, age and nationality. *Behaviour Research and Therapy, 27,* 19–26.

Ollendick, T. H., Matson, J., & Helsel, W. J. (1985). Fears in children and adolescents: Normative data. *Behavioral Research and Therapy, 23,* 465–467.

Ollendick, T. H., Yule, W., & Ollier, K. (1991). Fears in British children and their relationship to manifest anxiety and depression. *Journal of Child Psychology and Psychiatry, 32,* 321–331.

Olmstead, M. P., Davis, R., Rockert, W., Irvine, M. J., Eagle, M., & Garner, D. M. (1991). Efficacy of a brief group psychoeducational intervention for bulimia nervosa. *Behavior Research and Therapy, 29,* 71–83.

Olshansky, S. (1966). Parent responses to a mentally defective child. *Mental Retardation, 4,* 21–23.

Olweus, D. (1979). Stability of aggressive reaction patterns in males: A review. *Psychological Bulletin, 86,* 852–875.

Olweus, D. (1980). Familial and tempermantal determinants of agressive behavior in adolescent boys: A causal analysis. *Developmental Psychology, 16,* 644–660.

O'Malley, S. S., Jaffe, A., Chang, G., Witte, G., Schottenfeld, R. S., & Rousaville, B. J. (1992). Naltrexone in the treatment of alcohol dependence: Preliminary findings. In treatment of alcohol dependence: Preliminary findings. In C. A. Naranjo & E. M. Sellars (Eds.), *Novel pharmacological interventions for alcoholism* (pp. 148–157). New York: Springer-Verlag.

Organista, K. C., & Muñoz, R. F. (1996). Cognitive behavior therapy with Latinos. *Cognitive and Behavioral Practice, 3,* 255–270.

Orlinsky, D. E., & Howard, K. I. (1995). Unity and diversity among psychotherapies: A comparative perspective. In B. Bongar & L. E. Beutler (Eds.), *Comprehensive textbook of psychotherapy: Theory and practice* (pp. 1–23). New York: Oxford University Press.

Ornitz, E. M. (1989). Autism at the interface between sensory and information processing. In G. Dawson (Ed.), *Autism: Nature, diagnosis and treatment* (pp. 174–207). New York: Guilford Press.

O'Rourke, D., Wurtman, J. J., Wurtman, R. J., & Chebli, R. (1987). Serotonin implications in etiology of seasonal affective disorder. *Psychopharmacology Bulletin, 23,* 358–359.

O'Rourke, D., Wurtman, J. J., Wurtman, R. J., Chebli, R., & Gleason, R. (1989). Treatment of seasonal depression with d-fendluramine. *Journal of Clinical Psychology, 50,* 343–347.

Osler, W. (1910). The Lumleian Lectures in angina pectoris. *The Lancet,* 839–844.

Ouellette-Kuntz, H., McCreary, B. D., Minnes, P. M., & Stanton, B. (1994). Evaluating quality of life: The development of the Quality of Life Interview Schedule (QUOLIS). *Journal of Developmental Disabilities, 3,* 17–31.

Ounce of Prevention Fund (1994). *A head start on Head Start: Effective birth-to-three strategies.* Chicago: Ounce of Prevention Fund.

Oyewumi, L. K. (1992). The management of treatment resistant schizophrenic patients. In E. Persad, S. S. Kazarian, & L. W. Joseph (Eds.), *The mental hospital in the 21st century* (pp. 64–80). Toronto: Wall & Emerson.

Ozonoff, S., Pennington, B., & Rogers, S. (1991). Executive function deficits in high-functioning autistic individuals: Relationship to theory of mind. *Journal of Child Psychology and Psychiatry, 32,* 1081–1105.

Palmer, R. L. (1979). The dietary chaos syndrome: A useful new term? *British Journal of Medical Psychology, 52,* 187–190.

Palmer, R. L., & Oppenheimer, R. (1992). Childhood sexual experiences with adults: A comparison of women with eating disorders and those with other diagnoses. *International Journal of Eating Disorders, 12,* 359–364.

Palmour, R. (1989). Genetic counselling for affective disease. *Psychiatric Journal of the University of Ottawa, 14,* 323–328.

Palmour, R. Bradwejn, J., & Ervin, F. (1992). The anxiogenic effects of CCK_4 in monkeys are reduced by CCK-B antagonists, benzodiazepines or adenosine A2 agonists. *Clinical Neuropharmacology, 15* (Suppl. 1), 489B.

Pancer, S. M., & Cameron, G. (1994). Resident participation in the Better Beginnings, Better Futures Prevention Project. Part I. The impacts of involvement. *Canadian Journal of Community Mental Health, 13* (2), 197–211.

Pancer, S. M., & Nelson, G. (1990). Community-based approaches to health promotion: Guidelines for community mobilization. *International Quarterly of Community Health Education, 10,* 91–111.

Pandey, G. N., Pandey, S. C., Janicak, P. G., et al. (1990). Platelet serotonin-2 receptor binding sites in depression and suicide. *Biological Psychiatry, 28,* 215–222.

Pankratz, W. J. (1980). Electroconvulsive therapy: The position of the Canadian Psychiatric Association. *The Canadian Journal of Psychiatry, 25,* 509–514.

Pantony, K., & Caplan, P. J. (1991). Delusional dominating personality disorder: A modest proposal for identifying some consequences of rigid masculine socialization. *Canadian Psychology, 32,* 120–135.

Paradis, C. M., Friedman, S., Hatch, M. L., & Ackerman, R. (1996). Cognitive behavioral treatment of anxiety disorders in Orthodox Jews. *Cognitive and Behavioral Practice, 3,* 271–288.

Paredes, J., Kanachowski, A., Ledwidge, B., & Stoutenburg, K. (1990). The validity of commitment certificates in British Columbia. *Canadian Journal of Psychiatry, 35,* 305–310.

Paredes, J., Ledwidge, B., Beyerstein, D., Cashore, J., & Higenbottam, J. (1987). The review panel process: Interpretations of the findings and recommendations. *Canadian Journal of Psychiatry, 32,* 444–447.

Paris, J. (1996). A critical review or recovered memories in psychotherapy. Part I. Trauma and memory. *Canadian Journal of Psychiatry, 41,* 201–205.

Paris, J., & Frank, H. (1989). Perceptions of parental bonding in borderline patients. *American Journal of Psychiatry, 146,* 1498–1499.

Parke, R. D., & Slaby, R. G. (1993). The development of aggression. In E. M. Hetherington (Ed.), *Handbook of child psychopathology* (pp. 547–641). New York: Wiley.

Parker, K.C.H., Hanson, R. K., & Hinsley, J. (1988). MMPI, Rorschach, and WAIS: A meta-analytic comparison of reliability, stability, and validity. *Psychological Bulletin, 103,* 367–373.

Parmalee, P. A., Katz, I. R., & Lawton, M. P. (1989). Depression among institutionalized aged: Assessment and prevalence estimation. *Journal of Gerontology, 44,* 22–29.

Parry-Jones, B., & Parry-Jones, W. L. (1995). History of bulimia and bulimia nervosa. In K. D. Brownell & C. G. Fairburn (Eds.), *Eating disorders and obesity: A comprehensive handbook* (pp. 145–150). New York: Guilford Press.

Parry-Jones, B., & Parry-Jones, W. L. (1995). History of bulimia and bulimia nervosa. In K. D. Brownell & C. G. Fairburn (Eds.), *Eating disorders and obesity: A comprehensive handbook* (pp. 145–150). New York: Guilford Press.

Pascal, G. R., & Suttell, B. J. (1951). *The Bender-Gestalt Test: Quantification and validity for adults.* New York: Grune & Stratton.

Pasnau, R. O., & Bystritsky, A. (1990). Importance of treating anxiety in the elderly ill patient. *Psychiatric Medicine, 8,* 163–173.

Pate, J. E., Pumariega, A., Hester, C., & Garner, D. M. (1992). Cross-cultural patterns in eating disorders: A review. *Journal of the American Academy of Child and Adolescent Psychiatry, 31,* 802–809.

Patrick, J. (1988). Concordance of the MCMI and the MMPI in the diagnosis of three DSM-III Axis I disorders. *Journal of Clinical Psychology, 44,* 186–190.

Patrick, M., Hobson, R. P., Castle, D., & Howard, R. (1994). Personality disorder and the mental representation of early social experiences. *Development and Psychopathology, 6,* 375–388.

Patterson, G. R. (1974). Interventions for boys with conduct problems: Multiple settings, treatments, and criteria. *Journal of Consulting and Clinical Psychology, 42,* 471–481.

Patterson, G. R. (1982). *Coercive family process.* Eugene, OR: Castalia.

Patterson, G. R. (1986). Performance models for antisocial boys. *American Psychologist, 41,* 432–444.

Patterson, G. R., & Bank, L. (1986). Bootstrapping your way in the nomological thicket. *Behavioral Assessment, 8,* 49–73.

Patterson, G. R., Reid, J. B., & Dishion, T. J. (1992). *Antisocial boys.* Eugene, OR: Castalia.

Pattison, E. M., Sobell, M. B., Sobell, L. C. (1977). *Emerging concepts of alcohol dependence.* New York: Springer.

Patton, G. C., Johnson-Sabine, E., Wood, K., Mann, A. H., & Wakeling, A. (1990). Abnormal eating attitudes in London schoolgirls—A prospective epidemiological study: Outcome at twelve month follow-up. *Psychological Medicine, 20,* 383–394.

Patton, J. R., Payne, J. S., & Beirne-Smith, M. (1986). *Mental retardation* (2nd ed.). Toronto, ON: Merrill.

Paul, S. M., Rehavi, M., Skolnick, P., et al. (1984). High affinity binding of antidepressants to a biogenic amine transport site in human brain and platelet: Studies in depression. In R. M. Post & J. C. Ballenger (Eds.), *Neurobiology of mood disorders.* Baltimore, MD: Williams & Wilkins.

Pavkov, T. W., Lewis, D. A., & Lyons, J. S. (1989). Psychiatric diagnoses and racial bias: An empirical investigation. *Professional Psychology, 20,* 364–368.

Pavlov, I. P. (1928). *Lectures on conditioned reflexes.* New York: International Publishers.

Paxton, S. J. (1993). A prevention program for disturbed eating and body dissatisfaction in adolescent girls: A 1 year follow-up. *Health Education Research, 8,* 43–51.

Paykel, E. S., Ramana, R., Cooper, Z., Hayhurst, H., Kerr, J., & Barocka, A. (1995). Residual symptoms after partial remission: An important outcome in depression. *Psychological Medicine, 25,* 1171–1180.

Pearlson, G. D., Kreger, L., Rabins, P. V., Chase, G. A., Cohen, B., Wirth, J. B., Schlaepfer, T. B., & Tune, L. E. (1989). A chart review study of late-onset and early-onset schizophrenia. *American Journal of Psychiatry, 146,* 1568–1574.

Pecknold, J. C. (1990). Serotonin abnormalities in panic disorder. In J. C. Ballenger (Ed.), *Neurobiology of panic disorder* (pp. 121–142). New York: Wiley.

Peirson, L., & Prilleltensky, I. (1994). Understanding school change to facilitate prevention: A study of change in a secondary school. *Canadian Journal of Community Mental Health, 13* (2), 127–144.

Pekarik, G. (1985). Coping with dropouts. *Professional Psychology: Research and Practice, 16,* 114–123.

Pelham, W. E., & Bender, M. E. (1982). Peer relationships in hyperactive children: Description and treatment. In K. D. Gadow & I. Bialer (Eds.), *Advances in learning and behavioral disabilities* (pp. 365–436). Greenwich, CT: JAI Press.

Pelham, W. E., Schnedler, R., Bologna, N., & Contreras, A. (1980). Behavioral and stimulant treatment of hyperactive children: A therapy study with methylphenidate probes in a within subject design. *Journal of Applied Behavior Analysis, 13* (221), 236.

Pelham, W., Carlson, C., Sams, S., Vallano, G., Dixon, M., & Hoza, B. (1993). Separate and combined effects of methylphenidate and behavior modification on boys with attention-deficit hyperactivity disorder in the classroom. *Journal of Consulting and Clinical Psychology, 61,* 506–515.

Pendery, M. L., Maltzman, I. M., & West, L. J. (1982). Controlled drinking by alcoholics? New findings and reevaluation of a major affirmative study. *Science, 217,* 169–174.

Pennington, B. F., & Smith, S. D. (1988). Genetic influences on learning disabilities: An update. *Journal of Consulting and Clinical Psychology, 56,* 817–823.

Pentalis, C., Barnes, T.R.E., & Nelson, H. E. (1992). Is the concept of frontal-subcortical dementia relevant to schizophrenia? *British Journal of Psychiatry, 160,* 442–460.

Pepler, D. J., & Rubin, K. H. (1991). *The development and treatment of childhood aggression.* Hillsdale, NJ: Erlbaum.

Perfect, W. (1787). *Select cases of different species of insanity.* Rochester, NY: Putnam.

Perkins, K., Grobe, J., DiAmico, D., Fonte, C., Wilson, A., & Stiller, K. (1996). Low-dose nicotine nasal spray use and effects during initial smoking cessation. *Experimental and Clinical Pharmacology, 4* (2), 191–197.

Perley, M., & Guze, S. B. (1962). Hysteria: The stability and usefulness of clinical criteria. *New England Journal of Medicine, 266,* 421–426.

Perlin, M. (1989). *Mental disability law: Civil and criminal.* Charlottesville, VA: Michie.

Perlman, D., & Duck, S. (1987). *Intimate relationships: Development, dynamics, and deterioration.* Newbury Park, CA: Sage.

Perry, A., Bryson, S., & Bebko, J. M. (1993). Multiple method validation study of facilitated communication: Preliminary group results. *Journal of Developmental Disabilities, 2,* 1–19.

Perry, E. K., Marshall, E. F., Blessed, G., et al. (1983). Decreased imipramine binding in the brains of patients with depressive illness. *British Journal of Psychiatry, 142,* 188–192.

Perry, J. C., & Klerman, G. L. (1978). The borderline patient: A comparative analysis of four sets of diagnostic criteria. *Archives of General Psychiatry, 35,* 141–150.

Persons, J. B., Curtis, J. T., & Silberschatz, G. (1991). Psychodynamic and cognitive-behavioral formulations of a single case. *Psychotherapy, 28,* 608–617.

Peters, R. DeV. (1988). Mental health promotion in children and adolescents: An emerging role for psychology. *Canadian Journal of Behavioural Science, 20,* 389–401.

Peters, R. DeV. (1990). Adolescent mental health promotion: Policy and practice. In R. J. McMahon & R. DeV. Peters (Eds.), *Behavior disorders of adolescence* (pp. 207–223). New York: Plenum Press.

Peters, R. DeV. (1994). Better Beginnings, Better Futures: A community-based approach to primary prevention. *Canadian Journal of Community Mental Health, 13* (2), 183–188.

Peters, R. DeV., & McMahon, R. J. (Eds.) (1996). *Preventing childhood disorders, substance abuse, and delinquency.* Thousand Oaks, CA: Sage.

Peters, R. DeV., & Russell, C. C. (1996). Promoting development and preventing disorder: The Better Beginnings, Better Futures Project. In R. DeV. Peters & R. J. McMahon (Eds.), *Preventing childhood disorders, substance abuse, and delinquency* (pp. 19–47). Thousand Oaks, CA: Sage.

Peterson, G. (1991). Children coping with trauma: Diagnosis of "Dissociation Identity Disorder." *Dissociation: Progress in the Dissociation Disorders, 4,* 152–164.

Peterson, R. A., & Reiss, S. (1992). *Anxiety Sensitivity Index revised manual.* Worthington, OH: IDS.

Petrich, J. (1976). Psychiatric treatment in jail: An experiment in healthcare delivery. *American Journal of Psychiatry, 133,* 1439–1440.

Pfiffner, L. J., & Barkley, R. A. (1990). Educational placement and classroom management. In R. A. Barkley (Ed.), *Attention deficit hyperactivity disorder: A handbook for diagnosis and treatment* (pp. 498–539). New York: Guilford Press.

Pfohl, B., Coryell, W., Zimmerman, M., & Stangl, D. (1986). DSM-III personality disorders: Diagnostic overlap and internal consistency of individual DSM-III criteria. *Comprehensive Psychiatry, 27,* 21–34.

Phelps, L., Andrea, R., Rizzo, F. G., Johnston, L., & Main, C. M. (1993). Prevalence of self-induced vomiting and laxative/medication abuse among female adolescents: A longitudinal study. *International Journal of Eating Disorders, 14,* 375–378.

Phifer, J. F., & Murrell, S. A. (1986). Etiologic factors in the onset of depressive symptoms in older adults. *Journal of Abnormal Psychology, 95,* 282–291.

Phillips, D. P. (1979). Suicide, motor vehicle fatalities and the mass media: Evidence toward a theory of suggestion. *American Journal of Sociology, 84* (5), 1150–1174.

Phillips, D. P., & Carstensen, L. L. (1986). Clustering of teenage suicides after television news stories about suicide. *New England Journal of Medicine, 315* (11), 685–689.

Phillips, E. L. (1991). George Washington University's international data on psychotherapy delivery systems: Modeling new approaches to the study of therapy. In L. E. Beutler & M. Crago (Eds.), *Psychotherapy research: An international review of programmatic studies* (pp. 263–273). Washington, DC: American Psychological Association.

Phillips, K. A. (1991). Body dysmorphic disorder: The distress of imagined ugliness. *American Journal of Psychiatry, 148,* 1138–1149.

Phillips, K. A., McElroy, S. L., Keck, P. E., Pope, H. G., & Hudson, J. L. (1993). Body dysmorphic disorder: 30 cases of imagined ugliness. *American Journal of Psychiatry, 150,* 302–308.

Pickens, R. W., Svikis, D. S., McGue, M., Lykken, D. T., Hesten, L. L., & Clayton, P. J. (1991). Heterogeneity in the inheritance of alcoholism. *Archives of General Psychiatry, 47,* 926–932.

Piersma, H. L. (1987). Millon Clinical Multiaxial Inventory computer-generated diagnoses: How do they compare to clinician judgment? *Journal of Psychopathology and Behavioral Assessment, 9,* 305–312.

Pihl, R. O., & Peterson, J. B. (1991). Attention-deficit hyperactivity disorders, childhood conduct disorder and alcoholism: Is there an association? *Alcohol Health Research World, 15,* 25–31.

Pike, K. M., & Rodin, J. (1991). Mothers, daughters, and disordered eating. *Journal of Abnormal Psychology, 100,* 198–204.

Pillemer, K., & Finkelhor, D. (1988). The prevalence of elder abuse: A random sample survey. *Gerontologist, 28* (1), 51–57.

Pincus, H. A., Henderson, B., Blackwood, D., & Dial, T. (1993). Trends in research in two general psychiatric journals in 1969–1990: Research on research. *American Journal of Psychiatry, 150,* 135–142.

Pinel, J.P.J. (1997). *Biopsychology* (3rd ed.). Needham Heights, MA: Allyn and Bacon.

Pinel, P. (1809). *Traite medico-phiosophique sur l'alienation mentale* (2nd ed.). Paris: Chez J. Ant Brosson.

Pisterman, S., Firestone, P., McGrath, P., Goodman, J. T., Webster, I., Mallory, R., & Goffin, B. (1992). The effects of parent training on parenting stress and sense of competence. *Canadian Journal of Behavioural Science, 24* (1), 41–58.

Pithers, W. D., Beal, L. S., Armstrong, J., & Petty, J. (1989). Identification of risk factors through clinical interviews and analysis of records. In D. R. Laws (Ed.), *Relapse prevention with sex offenders* (pp. 77–87). New York: Guilford Press.

Pithers, W. D., Marques, J. K., Gibat, C. C., & Marlatt, G. A. (1983). Relapse prevention with sexual aggressives: A self-control model of treatment and maintenance of change. In J. G. Greer & J. R. Stuart (Eds.), *The sexual aggressor: Current perspectives on treatment* (pp. 214–239). New York: Van Nostrand Reinhold.

Pizzolongo, P. J. (1996). The Comprehensive Child Development Program and other early intervention program models. In R. DeV. Peters & R. J. McMahon (Eds.), *Preventing childhood disorders, substance abuse, and delinquency* (pp. 48–64). Thousand Oaks, CA: Sage.

Plomin, R. (1990). The role of inheritance in behaviour. *Science, 248,* 183–188.

Plomin, R., & Neiderhiser J. M. (1992). Genetics and experience. *Current Directions in Psychological Science, 1,* 160–163.

Pogue-Geile, M. F. (1991). The development of liability to schizophrenia: Early and late developmental models. In E. F. Walker (Ed.), *Schizophrenia: A life-course developmental perspective* (pp. 277–298). San Diego: Academic Press.

Pogue-Geile, M. F., & Oltmanns, T. F. (1980). Sentence-perception and distractibility in schizophrenia. *Journal of Abnormal Psychology, 89,* 115–124.

Polivy, J., & Herman, C. P. (1976a). The effects of alcohol on eating behavior: Disinhibition or sedation. *Addictive Behaviors, I,* 121–125.

Polivy, J., & Herman, C. P. (1976b). Effects of alcohol on eating behavior: Influences of mood and perceived intoxication. *Journal of Abnormal Psychology, 85,* 601–606.

Polivy, J., & Herman, C. P. (1985). Dieting and binging: A causal analysis. *American Psychologist, 40,* 193–201.

Polivy, J., & Herman, C. P. (1987). The diagnosis and treatment of normal eating. *Journal of Consulting and Clinical Psychology, 55,* 635–644.

Polivy, J., & Herman, C. P. (1991). Good and bad dieters: Self-perception and reaction to a dietary challenge. *International Journal of Eating Disorders, 10,* 91–99.

Polivy, J., & Herman, C. P. (1993). Etiology of binge eating: Psychological mechanisms. In C. G. Fairburn & G. T. Wilson (Eds.), *Binge eating: Nature, assessment and treatment* (pp. 173–205). New York: Guilford Press.

Polivy, J., Heatherton, T. F., & Herman, C. P. (1988). Self-esteem, restraint, and eating behavior. *Journal of Abnormal Psychology, 97,* 354–356.

Polvan, N. (1969). Historical aspects of mental ills in Middle East discussed. *Roche Reports, 6,* 3.

Pomerleau, O. F., Colins, A. L., Shiffman, S., & Sanderson, C. S. (1993). Why some people smoke and others do not: New perspectives. *Journal of Consulting and Clinical Psychology, 61,* 723–731.

Pope, H. G., & Hudson, J. I. (1986). Bulimia in men. *Medical Aspects of Human Sexuality, 20,* 1986.

Pope, K. S., & Bajt, T. R. (1994). When laws and values conflict: A dilemma for psychologists. In D. N. Bersoff (Ed.), *Ethical conflicts in psychology* (pp. 99–100). Washington, DC: American Psychological Association.

Porjesz, B., & Begleiter, H. (1983). Brain dysfunction and alcohol. In B. Kissin & H. Begleiter, H. (Eds.), *The pathogenesis of alcoholism* (pp. 415–483). New York: Plenum.

Porporino, F. J., & Motiuk, L. L. (1995). The prison careers of mentally disordered offenders. *International Journal of Law and Psychiatry, 18,* 29–44.

Post, F. (1966). *Persistent persecutory states of the elderly.* Oxford, UK: Pergamon.

Post, R. (1992). Transduction of psychosocial stress into the neurobiology of recurrent affective disorder. *American Journal of Psychiatry, 149,* 999–1010.

Powley, J. (1977). The ventromedial hypothalimic syndrome, satiety and a cephalic phase hypothesis. *Psychological Review, 84,* 89–126.

Prager, S., & Jeste, D. V. (1993). Sensory impairment in late-life schizophrenia. *Schizophrenia Bulletin, 19,* 755–772.

Prentky, R., Burgess, A. W., Rokous, F., Lee, A., Hartman, C., Ressler, R., & Douglas, J. (1989). The presumptive role of fantasy in serial sexual homicide. *The American Journal of Psychiatry, 146,* 887–891.

Preu, P. W. (1944). The concept of psychopathic personality. In J. McV. Hunt (Ed.), *Personality and the behavior disorders* (pp. 63–84). New York: Rowland Press.

Price, R. H., Cowen, E. L., Lorion, R. P., & Ramos-McKay, J. (1989). The search for effective prevention programs: What we learned along the way. *American Journal of Orthopsychiatry, 59,* 49–58.

Price, R. H., Cowen, E. L., Lorion, R. P., & Ramos-McKay, J. (Eds.) (1988). *Fourteen ounces of prevention: A casebook for practitioners.* Washington, DC: American Psychological Association.

Prilleltensky, I. (1994a). Empowerment in mainstream psychology: Legitimacy, obstacles, and possibilities. *Canadian Psychology, 35,* 358–374.

Prilleltensky, I. (1994b). *The morals and politics of psychology: Psychological discourse and the status quo.* Albany: State University of New York Press.

Prilleltensky, I., & Laurendeau, M.-C. (1994). Prevention: Focus on children and youth. *Canadian Journal of Community Mental Health, 13 (Special issue)* (2).

Prilleltensky, I., & Nelson, G. (1997). Community psychology: Reclaiming social justice. In D. Fox & I. Prilleltensky (Eds.), *Critical psychology: An introduction* (pp. 166–184). London: Sage.

Prince, V., & Bentler, P. M. (1972). Survey of 504 cases of transvestism. *Psychological Reports, 32,* 903–917.

Prinz, R. J. (1985). Diet-behavior research with children: Methodological and substantive issues. *Advances in Learning and Behavioral Disabilities, 4,* 181–189.

Prinz, R. J., & Miller, G. E. (1994). Family based treatment for childhood antisocial behavior: Experimental influences on dropout and engagement. *Journal of Consulting and Clinical Psychology, 62,* 645–650.

Prior, M., & Cummins, R. (1992). Questions about facilitated communication and autism. *Journal of autism and Developmental Disorders, 22,* 331–338.

Pritchard, J. C. (1835). *A treatise on insanity and other disorders affecting the mind.* London: Sherwood, Gilbert & Piper.

Prkachin, K. M., Carew, W.L.C., Mills, D. E., & McCarthy, J. L. (Unpublished manuscript, University of Waterloo). Cynical hostility and stress interventions have independent relationships to cardiovascular reactivity.

Prkachin, K. M., Mills, D. E., Kaufman, F. L., & Carew, W.L.C. (1991). Cynical hostility, the perception of contingency and cardiovascular activity. *Canadian Journal of Behavioural Science, 23,* 455–468.

Pueschel, S. M., Tingey, C., Rynders, J. E., Crocker, A. C., & Crutcher, D. M. (1987). *New perspectives on down syndrome.* Baltimore, MD: Paul Brookes.

Purves, D. (1994). *Neural activity and the growth of the brain.* Cambridge, UK: Cambridge University Press.

Putnam, F. W. (1989). *Diagnosis and treatment of multiple personality disorder.* New York: Guilford Press.

Putnam, F. W., Zahn, T. P., & Post, R. M. (1990). Differential autonomic nervous system activity in multiple personality disorder. *Psychiatry Research, 31* (3), 251–260.

Quay, H. C. (1986). Conduct disorders. In H. C. Quay & J. S. Werry (Eds.), *Psychopathological disorders of childhood* (pp. 35–72). New York: Wiley.

Quay, H. C., & Werry, J. S. (1993). *Psychopathological disorders of childhood* (3rd ed.). New York: Wiley.

Quinsey, V. L. (1979). Demographic and clinical variables associated with release from a maximum security psychiatric institution. *Criminal Justice and Behavior, 6,* 390–399.

Quinsey, V. L., & Ambtman, R. (1979). Variables affecting psychiatrists' and teachers' assessments of the dangerousness of mentally ill offenders. *Journal of Consulting and Clinical Psychology, 47,* 353–362.

Quinsey, V. L., & Chaplin, T. C. (1982). Penile responses to nonsexual violence among rapists. *Criminal Justice and Behavior, 9,* 372–381.

Quinsey, V. L., & Cyr, M. (1986). Perceived dangerousness and treatability of offenders: The effects of internal versus external attributions of crime causality. *Journal of Interpersonal Violence, 1,* 458–471.

Quinsey, V. L., & Maguire, A. (1986). Maximum security psychiatric patients: Actuarial and clinical prediction of dangerousness. *Journal of Interpersonal Viol*ence, 1 (2), 143–171.

Quinsey, V. L., & Marshall, W. L. (1983). Procedures for reducing inappropriate sexual arousal: An evaluation review. In J. G. Greer & I. R. Stuart (Eds.), *The sexual aggressor: Current perspectives on treatment.* New York: Van Nostrand Reinhold.

Quinsey, V. L., & Walker, W. D. (1992). Dealing with dangerousness: Community Risk Management Strategies with violent offenders. In R. DeV. Peters, R. J. McMahon, & V. L. Quinsey (Eds.), *Aggression and violence throughout the lifespan* (pp. 244–262). Newbury Park, CA: Sage.

Quinsey, V. L., Chaplin, T. C., & Carrigan, W. F. (1979). Sexual preferences among incestuous and nonincestuous child molesters. *Behavior Therapy, 10,* 562–565.

Quinsey, V. L., Maguire, A., & Varney, G. W. (1981). Assertion and controlled hostility among mentally disordered murderers. *Journal of Consulting and Clinical Psychology, 51,* 550–556.

R. v. Chaulk (1990) 3 S.C.R. 1303.

R. v. M'Naghten, 10 Cl. and F. 200, 8 Eng.Rep. 718 (1843).

R. v. Swain, [1991] 1 S.C.R. 933.

R. v. Taylor (1992) 77 C.C.C.(3d) 551 (Ont. C.A.).

Rabins, P. V. (1992). Schizophrenia and other psychoses. In J. E. Birren, R. B. Sloane, & G. D. Cohen (Eds.), *Handbook of mental health and aging* (2nd ed., pp. 464–475). San Diego: Academic Press Inc.

Rachman, S. (1966). Sexual fetishisms: An experimental analogue. *Psychological Record, 16,* 293–296.

Rachman, S. (1971). *The effects of psychotherapy.* Oxford: Pergamon Press.

Rachman, S. (1990). *Fear and courage* (2nd ed.). New York: Freeman.

Rachman, S. (1991). Neo-conditioning and the classical theory of fear acquisition. *Clinical Psychology Review, 11,* 155–173.

Rachman, S., & de Silva, P. (1978). Abnormal and normal obsessions. *Behaviour Research and Therapy, 16,* 233–248.

Rado, S. (1956). *Psychoanalysis and behaviour II.* New York: Grune & Stratton.

Rae-Grant, N. I. (1994). Preventive interventions for children and adolescents: Where are we now and how far have we come? *Canadian Journal of Community Mental Health, 13* (2), 17–36.

Raine, A. (1993). *The psychopathology of crime: Criminal behavior as a clinical disorder.* San Diego: Academic Press.

Raine, A., Brennan, P., & Mednick, S. A. (1994). Birth complications combined with early maternal rejection at age one year predispose to violent crime at 18 years. *Archives of General Psychiatry, 51,* 984–988.

Raj, B. A., Corvea, M. H., & Dagon, E. M. (1993). The clinical characteristics of panic disorder in the elderly. *Journal of Clinical Psychiatry, 54,* 150–155.

Ramey, C. T., & Ramey, S. L. (1992). Effective early intervention. *Mental Retardation, 30,* 337–345.

Randall, D. (Ed.) (1981). *Contributions to primary prevention in mental health: Working papers.* Toronto: Canadian Mental Health Association/National Office.

Rapee, R. M. (1991). Psychological factors involved in generalized anxiety. In R. M. Rapee & D. H. Barlow (Eds.), *Chronic anxiety: Generalized anxiety disorder and mixed anxiety-depression* (pp. 76–94). New York: Guilford Press.

Rapee, R. M., & Heimberg, R. G. (1997). A cognitive-behavioral model of anxiety in social situations. *Behaviour Research and Therapy, 35,* 741–756.

Rapoport, J. L., & Castellanos, F. X. (1996a). Attention-Deficit/Hyperactivity Disorder. In J. M. Wiener (Ed.), *Diagnosis and Psychopharmacology of Childhood and Adolescent Disorders* (pp. 265–292). New York: Wiley.

Rapoport, J. L., & Ismond, D. R. (1996b). *DSM-IV training guide for diagnosis of childhood disorders.* New York: Brunner/Mazel.

Rapoport, J. L., Buchsbaum, M. S., Zahn, T. P., Weingartner, H., Ludlow, C., & Mikkelsen, E. J. (1978). Dextro-amphetamine: Cognitive and behavioral effects in noermal prepubertal boys. *Science, 199,* 560–563.

Rappaport, J. (1987). Terms of empowerment/exemplars of prevention: Toward a theory for community psychology. *American Journal of Community Psychology, 15,* 121–148.

Raskind, M. A., & Peskind, E. R. (1992). Alzheimer's disease and other dementing disorders. In J. E. Birren, R. B. Sloane, & G. D. Cohen (Eds.), *Handbook of mental health and aging* (2nd ed., pp. 478–513). San Diego, CA: Academic Press.

Ratcliffe, J., & Wallack, L. (1985/86). Primary prevention in public health: An analysis of some basic assumptions. *International Quarterly of Community Health Education, 6,* 216–239.

Rathbone, B. J., & Healey, V. (Eds.) (1989). *Campylobacter pylori and gastroduodenal disease.* Oxford: Blackwell.

Ray, O., & Ksir, C. (1990). *Drugs, society, & human behaviour.* St. Louis, MO: Times Mirror/Mosby College Publishing.

Razay, G., Heaton, K. W., Bolton, C. H., & Hughes, A. O. (1992). Alcohol-consumption and its relation to cardiovascular risk factors in British women. *British Medical Journal, 304* (6819), 80–82.

Read, S. (1996). The dementias. In J. S. Sadavoy, L. W. Lazarus, & L. F. Jarvik (Eds.), *Comprehensive review of geriatric psychiatry* (pp. 287–310). Washington, DC: American Psychiatric Press.

Reaves, R. P., & Ogloff, J.R.P. (1996a). Laws and regulations that affect the practice of psychology. In L. J. Bass, S. T. DeMers, J.R.P. Ogloff, C. Peterson, J. Petifor, R. Reaves, T. Retfalvi, N. Simon, C. Sinclair, & R. Tipton (Eds.), *Professional conduct and discipline in psychology* (pp. 109–116). Washington, DC: American Psychological Association.

Reaves, R. P., & Ogloff, J.R.P. (1996b). Liability for professional misconduct. In L. J. Bass, S. T. DeMers, J.R.P. Ogloff, C. Peterson, J. Petifor, R. Reaves, T. Retfalvi, N. Simon, C. Sinclair, & R. Tipton (Eds.), *Professional conduct and discipline in psychology* (pp. 117–142). Washington, DC: American Psychological Association.

Redman, S., Webb, G. R., Hennrikus, D. J., Gordon, J. J., Sanson-Fisher, R. W., & Robert, W. (1991). The effects of gender upon diagnosis of psychological disturbance. *Journal of Behavioral Medicine, 14,* 527–540.

Redmond, D. E., Jr. (1985). Neurochemical basis for anxiety and anxiety disorders: Evidence from drugs which decrease human fear and anxiety. In A. H. Tuma & J. D. Maser (Eds.), *Anxiety and the anxiety disorders.* Hillsdale, NJ: Erlbaum.

Redmond, D. E., Jr. (1987). Studies of the nucleus locus ceruleus in monkeys and hypotheses for neuropharmacology. In H. Y. Meltzer (Ed.), *Psychopharmacology: The third generation of progress* (pp. 967–976). New York: Raven Press.

Regier, D. A., Myers, J., Kramer, M., Robbins, L. N., Blayer, D., Hough, R., Eaton, W., & Locke, B. Z. (1984). The NIMH Epidemiological Catchment Area program: Historical context, major objectives, and study population characteristics. *Archives of General Psychiatry, 41,* 934–941.

Regulated Health Professions Act, S.O., c. 18 (1991), as amended by S.O., c. 37 (1993).

Reich, J. (1987). Sex distribution of DSM-III personality disorders in psychiatric outpatients. *American Journal of Psychiatry, 144,* 485–488.

Reich, J. (1990). Comparison of males and females with DSM-III dependent personality disorder. *Psychiatry Research, 33,* 207–214.

Reich, J., & Green, A. I. (1991). Effect of personality disorders on outcome of treatment. *Journal of Neurons and Mental Disease, 179,* 74–82.

Reid, D. H. (1983). Trends in training feeding and dressing skills. In J. L. Matson & F. Andrasik (Eds.), *Treatment issues and innovations in mental retardation.* New York: Plenum.

Reid, D. H., Wilson, P. G., & Faw, G. D. (1983). Teaching self-help skills. In J. L. Matson & J. A. Mulick (Eds.), *Handbook of mental retardation.* New York: Pergamon Press.

Reid, K., Morales, A., Harris, C., Surridge, D., Condra, M., & Owen, J. (1987). Double-blind trial of yohimbine in treatment of psychogenic impotence. *The Lancet, 2,* 421–423.

Reiff, R. (1974). The control of knowledge: The power of the helping professions. *Journal of Applied Behavioral Science, 10,* 451–461.

Reisberg, B. (1983). An overview of current concepts of Alzheimer's Disease, senile dementia, and age-associated cognitive decline. In B. Reisberg (Ed.), *Alzheimer's disease: The standard reference* (pp. 3–20). New York: Free Press.

Reiss, D., & Price, R. H. (1996). National research agenda for prevention research: The National Institute of Mental Health Report. *American Psychologist, 51,* 1109–1115.

Reiss, S. (1990). Prevalence of dual diagnosis in community-based day programs in the Chicago metropolitan area. *American Journal on Mental Retardation, 94,* 578–585.

Reiss, S., Levitan, G., & Szyszko, J. (1982). Emotional disturbance and mental retardation: Diagnostic overshadowing. *American Journal of Mental Deficiency, 86,* 567–574.

Reitan, R. M., & Davison, L. A. (1974). *Clinical neuropsychology: Current status and applications.* Washington, DC: V. H. Winston & Sons.

Renken, B., Egeland, B., Marvinney, D., Mangelsdorf, S., & Sroufe, L. A. (1989). Early childhood antecedents of aggression and passive-withdrawal in early elementary school. *Journal of Personality, 57,* 257–281.

Renwick, R., Brown, I., & Raphael, D. (1994). Quality of life: Linking a conceptual approach to service delivery. *Journal of Developmental Disabilities, 3,* 32–44.

Rescorla, R. A. (1988). Pavlovian conditioning. It's not what you think it is. *American Psychologist, 43,* 151–160.

Resick, P. A., Veronen, L. J., Kilpatrick, D. G., Calhoun, K. S., & Atkinson, B. M. (1986). Assessment of fear reactions in sexual assault victims: A factor analytic study of the Veronen-Kilpatrick modified fear survey. *Behavioral Assessment, 8,* 271–283.

Rett Syndrome Diagnostic Criteria Work Group (1988). Diagnostic criteria for Rett syndrome. *Annals of Neurology, 23,* 425–428.

Rex v. Hadfield, 27 St. Tr. 1281, 1312–15 (1820).

Reynolds, C. F. (1996). Sleep disorders. In J. Sadavoy, L. W. Lazarus, L. F. Jarvik, & G. T. Grossberg (Eds.), *Comprehensive Review of Geriatric Psychiatry—II.* Washington, DC: American Psychiatric Press.

Reynolds, C., & Kupfer, D. (1987). Sleep research in affective illness. *Sleep, 10,* 199–215.

Rhéaume, J., Ladouceur, R., Freeston, M. H., & Latarte, H. (1995). Inflated responsibility and its role in OCD: Validation of a theoretical definition of responsibility. *Behaviour Research and Tharapy, 33,* 159–169.

Rice, M. E., & Harris, G. T. (1993). Treatment for prisoners with mental disorder. In J. H. Steadman & Cocozza (Eds.), *Mental illness in America's prisons* (pp. 91–130). Seattle, WA: National Coalition for the Mentally Ill in the Criminal Justice System.

Rice, M. E., Harris, G. T., & Cormier, C. (1992). Evaluation of a maximum security therapeutic community for psychopaths and other mentally disordered offenders. *Law and Human Behavior, 16,* 399–412.

Rice, M. E., Harris, G. T., Lang, C., & Bell, V. (1990). Recidivism among male insanity acquitees. *Journal of Psychiatry and Law, 19,* 379–403.

Rice, M. E., Harris, G. T., Quinsey, V. L. (1996). Treatment of forensic patients. In B. Sales & S. Shah (Eds.), *Mental health and the law: Research, policy, and practice* (pp. 141–190). New York: Carolina Academic Press.

Rice, M. E., Quinsey, V. L., & Harris, G. T. (1991). Predicting sexual recidivism among treated and untreated extrafamilial child molesters from a maximum security psychiatric institution. *Journal of Consulting and Clinical Psychology, 59,* 381–836.

Rice, M., & Harris, G. (1990). The predictors of insanity acquittal. *International Journal of Law and Psychiatry, 14,* 217–234.

Rich, C. L., Fowler, R. C., Fogarty, L. A., & Young, D. (1988). San Diego suicide study. III. Relationship between diagnoses and stressors. *Archives of General Psychiatry, 45,* 589–592.

Rich, C. L., Warsradt, G. M., Nemiroff, R. A., et al. (1991). Suicide, stressors and the life cycle. *American Journal of Psychiatry, 148,* 524–527.

Rich, C. L., Young, D., & Fowler, R. C. (1986). San Diego suicide study. I. Young vs. old subjects. *Archives of General Psychiatry, 43* (6), 577–582.

Richardson, G. M., & McGrath, P. J. (1989). Cognitive-behavioral therapy for migraine headaches: A minimal-therapist-contact approach versus a clinic-based approach. *Headache, 29,* 352–357.

Rickels, K., Schweizer, E., Case, W. G., & Greenblatt, D. J. (1990). Long-term therapeutic use of benzodiazepines. I. Effects of abrupt discontinuation. *Archives of General Psychiatry, 47,* 899–907.

Riefer, D. M., & Batchelder, W. H. (1988). Multinomial modeling and the measurement of cognitive processes. *Psychological Review, 95,* 318–339.

Rimland, B. (1978). Inside the mind of the autistic savant. *Psychology Today, 12,* 68–80.

Rimland, B. (1991). Facilitated communication: Problems, puzzles and paradoxes: Six challenges for researchers. *Autism Research Review International, 5,* 3.

Rimland, B. (1993). Controlled evaluations of facilitated communication. *Autism Research Review International, 7,* 7.

Rimland, B., & Baker, S. M. (1996). Brief report: Alternative approaches to the development of effective treatments for autism. *Journal of Autism and Developmental Disorders, 26,* 237–241.

Rivers, P. C. (1994). *Alcohol and human behavior. Theory, research, and practice.* Englewood Cliffs, NJ: Prentice Hall.

Robbins, T. W. (1990). The case for frontostriatal dysfunction in schizophrenia. *Schizophrenia Bulletin, 16,* 391–402.

Roberts, A. H., Kewman, D. G., Mercier, L., & Hovell, M. (1993). The power of nonspecific effects in healing: Implications for psychosocial and biological treatments. *Clinical Psychology Review, 13,* 375–391.

Robertson, G. B. (1991). *Mental disability and the law in Canada* (2nd ed.). Toronto: Caswell.

Robins, C., Block, P., & Peselow, E. (1989). Relations of sociotropic and autonomous personality characteristics to specific symptoms in depressed patients. *Journal of Abnormal Psychology, 98,* 847–852.

Robins, L. N. (1966). *Deviant children grow up: A sociological and psychiatric study of sociopathic personality.* Baltimore, MD: Williams & Wilkins.

Robins, L. N. (1986). Epidemiology of antisocial personality. In G. L. Klerman, M. M. Weissman, P. S. Appelbaum, & L. H. Roth (Eds.), *Psychiatry: Social, epidemiologic, and legal psychiatry* (pp. 231–244). New York: Basic Books.

Robins, L. N., & Price, R. K. (1991). Adult disorders predicted by childhood conduct problems. Results form thte NIMH Epidemiologic Catchment Area project. *Psychiatry, 54,* 116–132.

Robins, L. N., & Regier, D. A. (1991). *Psychiatric disorders in America.* New York: Free Press.

Robins, L. N., Helzer, J. E., Croughan, J., & Radcliff, K. (1981). National Institute of Mental Health Diagnostic Interview Schedule: Its history, characteristics and validity. Archives of General Psychiatry, 42, 918–924.

Robins, L. N., Helzer, J. E., Croughan, J., & Ratcliff, K. S. (1981). National Institute of Mental Health Diagnostic Interview Schedule. Its history, characteristics, and validity. *Archives of General Psychiatry, 38,* 381–389.

Robins, L. N., Helzer, J. E., Weissman, M. M., Orvaschel, H., Gruenberg, E., Burke, J. D., & Regier, D. A. (1984). Lifetime prevalence of specific psychiatric disorders in three sites. *Archives of General Psychiatry, 41,* 949–958.

Robins, L. N., Locke, B. Z., & Regier, D. A. (1991). An overview of psychiatric disorders in America. In L. N. Robins & D. A. Regier (Eds.), *Psychiatric disorders in America: The Epidemiological Catchment Area study.* New York: Free Press.

Robinson, P. H., Checkley, S. A., & Russell, G.F.M. (1985). Suppression of eating by fenflramine in patients with bulimia nervosa. *British Journal of Psychiatry, 146,* 169–176.

Robinson, R. G., Lipsey, J. R., & Price, T. R. (1985). Diagnosis and clinical management of post-stroke depression. *Psychosomatics, 26,* 769–778.

Rochester, S., & Martin, J. R. (1979). *Crazy talk: A study of the discourse of schizophrenic speakers.* New York: Plenum Press.

Rodin, J. (1985). Insulin levels, hunger, and food intake: An example of feedback loops in body weight regulation. *Health Psychology, 4,* 1–24.

Rodin, J., Silberstein, L. R., & Striegel-Moore, R. H. (1985). Women and weight: A normative discontent. In T. B. Sonderegger (Ed.), *Nebraska Symposium on Motivation. Vol. 32. Psychology and gender* (pp. 267–307). Lincoln: University of Nebraska Press.

Rodnick, E. H., & Shakow, D. (1940). Set in the schizophrenic as measured by a composite reaction time index. *American Journal of Psychiatry, 97,* 214–225.

Roesch, R. (1995). Mental health intervention in jails. In G. Davies, S. Lloyd-Bostock, M. McMurran, & C. Wilson (Eds.), *Psychology, law, and criminal justice* (pp. 520–531). New York: Walter de Gruyter.

Roesch, R., Zapf, P., Webster, C. D., & Eaves, D. (1998). *The Fitness Interview Test.* Burnaby, BC: Mental Health, Law, & Policy Institute, Simon Fraser University.

Rogers, C. R. (1942). *Counselling and psychotherapy: Newer concepts in practice.* Boston: Houghton Mifflin.

Rogers, C. R. (1961). *On becoming a person.* Boston: Houghton Mifflin.

Rogers, C. R. (1966). Client-centered therapy. In S. Arieti et al. (Eds.), *American handbook of psychiatry (Vol. 3).* New York: Basic Books.

Rogers, R., Dion, K. L., & Lynett, E. (1992). Diagnostic validity of antisocial personality disorder. *Law and Human Behavior, 16,* 677–689.

Rogers, R., Duncan, J. C., Lynett, E., & Sewell, K. E. (1994). Prototypical analysis of antisocial personality disorder: DSM-IV and beyond. *Law and Human Behavior, 18,* 471–484.

Rogler, L. H., & Hollingshead, A. B. (1985). *Trapped: Families and schizophrenia* (3rd ed.). Maplewood: Waterfront Press.

Rohrbaugh, M., Shoham, V., Spungen, C., & Steinglass, P. (1995). Family systems therapy in practice. In B. Bongar & L. E. Beutler (Eds.), *Comprehensive textbook of psychotherapy: Theory and practice* (pp. 228–253). New York: Oxford University Press.

Romney, D. M. (1987). A simplex model of the paranoid process: Implications for diagnosis and prognosis. *Acta Psychiatrica Scandinavica, 75,* 651–655.

Romney, D. M. (1990). Thought disorder in the relatives of schizophrenics: A meta-analatyic review of selected published studies. *Journal of Nervous and Mental Disease, 178,* 481–486.

Romney, D. M. (1995). Psychosocial functioning and subjective experience in schizophrenia: A reanalysis. *Schizophrenia Bulletin, 21,* 405–410.

Ronningstan, E., & Gunderson, J. G. (1990). Identifying criteria for narcissistic personality disorder. *American Journal of Psychiatry, 147,* 918–922.

Roose, S. P., Glassman, A. H., Walsh, T., & Cullen, K. (1982). Reversible loss of nocturnal penile tumescence during depression: A preliminary report. *Neuropsychobiology, 8,* 284–288.

Root, M.P.P., Fallon, P., & Friedrich, W. N. (1986). *Bulimia: A systems approach to treatment.* New York: Norton.

Rooth, F. G. (1973). Exhibitionism outside Europe and America. *Archives of Sexual Behavior, 2,* 351–363.

Roper, P. (1990). Changing perceptions through contact. *Disability, Handicap & Society, 5,* 243–255.

Rose, V. G. (in press). An introduction to Canadian law. In R. Schuller & J.R.P. Ogloff (Eds.), *An introduction to law and psychology: Canadian perspectives.* Toronto: University of Toronto Press.

Rosen, G. M. (1993). Self-help or hype? Comments on psychology's failure to advance self-care. *Professional Psychology: Research and Practice, 24,* 340–345.

Rosen, J. C., & Leitenberg, H. (1982). Bulimia nervosa: Treatment with exposure and response prevention. *Behavior Therapy, 13,* 117–124.

Rosen, J. C., & Leitenberg, H. (1985). Exposure plus response prevention treatment of bulimia. In D. M. Garner & P. E. Garfinkel (Eds.), *Handbook of psychotherapy for anorexia nervosa and bulimia* (pp. 193–205). New York: Guilford Press.

Rosen, J. C., Tacy, B., & Howell, D. (1990). Life stress, psychological symptoms and weight reducing behavior in adolescent girls: A prospective analysis. *International Journal of Eating Disorders, 9,* 17–26.

Rosen, R. C., & Beck, J. G. (1988). *Patterns of sexual arousal: Psychophysiological processes and clinical applications.* New York: Guilford Press.

Rosen, R. C., & Leiblum, S. R. (1989). Assessment and treatment of desire disorders. In S. R. Leiblum & R. C. Rosen (Eds.), *Principles and practice of sex therapy* (2nd ed.) (pp. 19–50). New York: Guilford Press.

Rosen, R. C., & Leiblum, S. R. (1995). Treatment of sexual disorders in the 1990s: An integrated approach. *Journal of Consulting and Clinical Psychology, 63,* 877–890.

Rosenbach, A., & Hunot, V. (1995). The introduction of a methadone prescribing programme to a drug-free treatment service: Implications for harm reduction. *Addiction, 90,* 815–821.

Rosenbaum, M., & Patterson, K. M. (1995). Group psychotherapy in historical perspective. In B. Bongar & L. E. Beutler (Eds.), *Comprehensive textbook of psychotherapy: Theory and practice* (pp. 173–188). New York: Oxford University Press.

Rosenberger, P. H., & Miller, G. A. (1989). Comparing borderline definitions: DSM-III borderline and schizotypal disorders. *Journal of Abnormal Psychology, 92,* 161–169.

Rosenhan, D. L. (1973). On being sane in insane places. *Science, 179,* 250–258.

Rosenhan, D. L., & Seligman, M.E.P. (1995). *Abnormal psychology* (3rd ed.). New York: Norton.

Rosenthal, N., Sack, D., Gillin, J., Lewy, A., Goodwin, F., Davenport, Y., Mueller, P., Newson, D., Wehr, T. (1984). Seasonal affective disorder: A description of the syndrome and preliminary findings with light therapy. *Archives of General Psychiatry, 41,* 72–80.

Ross, C. A. (1989). *Multiple personality disorder.* New York: Wiley.

Ross, C. A. (1991). Epidemiology of multiple personality disorder and dissociation. *Psychiatric Clinics of North America, 14,* 503–516.

Ross, C. A., Miller, S. D., Reagor, P., & Bjornson, L., Fraser, G., Anderson, G. (1990). Structured interview data on 102 cases of multiple personality disorder from four centers. *American Journal of Psychiatry, 147* (5), 596–601.

Rossiter, E. M., & Agras, W. S. (1990). An empirical test of the DSM-III-R definition of binge. *International Journal of Eating Disorders, 9,* 513–518.

Rosvold, H. E., Mirsky, A. F., Sarason, I., Bransome, E. D., Jr., Beck, L. H. (1956). A continuous performance test of brain damage. *Journal of Consulting Psychology, 20,* 343–350.

Roth, A., & Fonagy, P. (1996). *What works for whom? A critical review of psychotherapy research.* New York: Guilford.

Roth, L. H., Meisel, A., & Lidz, C. W. (1977). Tests of competency to consent to treatment. *American Journal of Psychiatry, 134,* 279–284.

Rourke, B. P. (1991). *Neuropsychological validation of learning disability subtypes.* New York: Guilford Press.

Routh, D. K., & Ernst, A. R. (1984). Somatization disorder in relatives of children and adolescents with functional abdominal pain. *Journal of Pediatric Psychology, 9,* 427–437.

Roy, A. (1986). Suicide in schizophrenia. In A. Roy (Ed.), *Suicide* (pp. 97–112). Baltimore, MD: Williams & Wilkins.

Roy, A., & Kennedy, S. (1984). Risk factors for depression in Canadians. *Canadian Journal of Psychiatry, 29,* 11–13.

Royal Canadian Mounted Police (1994). *RCMP national drug intelligence estimate, 1993 with trend indicators through 1995.* Ottawa: Minister of Supply and Services.

Rozanski, A., Bairey, C. N., Krantz, D. S., Friedman, J., Resser, K. J., Morell, M., Hilton-Chalfen, S., Hestrin, L., Bietendorf, J., & Berman, D. S. (1988). Mental stress and the induction of silent myocardial ischemia in patients with coronary artery disease. *New England Journal of Medicine, 318,* 1005–1012.

Ruiz, P. (1985). The minority patient. *Community Mental Health Journal, 21,* 208–216.

Ruskin, P. E. (1990). Schizophrenia and delusional disorders. In D. Bienenfeld (Ed.), Verwoerdt's *Clinical geropsychiatry* (3rd ed., pp. 125–136). Baltimore, MD: Williams & Wilkins.

Russell, D.E.H. (1984). *Sexual exploitation: Rape, child sexual abuse, and workplace harassment.* Newbury Park, CA: Sage.

Russell, G.F.M. (1970). Anorexia nervosa: Its identity as an illness and its treatment. In J. H. Price (Ed.). *Modern trends in psychological medicine.* London: Buttersworth (pp. 131–164).

Russell, G.F.M. (1979). Bulimia nervosa: An ominous variant of anorexia nervosa. *Psychological Medicine, 9,* 429–448.

Russell, G.F.M., Szmukler, G. I., Dare, C., & Eiler, I. (1987). An evolution of family therapy in anorexia nervosa and bulimia nervosa. *Archives of General Psychiatry, 44,* 1047–1056.

Rutter, M. (1981). Stress, coping, and development: Some issues and some questions. *Journal of Child Psychology and Psychiatry, 22,* 323–356.

Rutter, M. (1985). Resilience in the face of adversity: Protective factors and resistance to psychiatric disorder. *American Journal of Psychiatry, 122,* 509–522.

Rutter, M. (1987). Psychosocial resilience and protective mechanisms. *American Journal of Orthopsychiatry, 57* (3), 316–331.

Rutter, M., & Giller, H. (1983). *Juvenile delinquency: Trends and perspectives.* New York: Guilford.

Rutter, M., Bailey, A., Simonoff, E., & Pickles, A. (1997). Genetic influences and autism. In D. J. Cohen & F. R. Volkmar (Eds.), *Handbook of autism and pervasive developmental disorders* (pp. 370–387). New York: Wiley.

Rutter, M., Boltin, P., Harrington, R., Le Couteur, A., Macdonald, H., & Simonoff, E. (1990). Genetic factors in child psychiatric disorders. 1. A review of research strategies. *Journal of Child Psychology and Psychiatry, 31,* 5–37.

Rutter, M., Cox, A., Tupling, C., Berger, M., & Yule, W. (1975). Attainment and adjustment in two geographical areas. I. The prevalence of psychiatric disorder. *British Journal of Psychiatry, 126,* 493–509.

Rutter, M., Tizard, J., & Whitmore, K. (1970). *Education, health and behavior.* London: Longman.

Ryan, W. (1971). *Blaming the victim.* New York: Random House.

Sabin, J. E. (1975). Translating despair. *American Journal of Psychiatry, 132,* 197–199.

Sainsbury, P. (1986). The epidemiology of suicide and suicide prevention. In R. A. Baltimore (Ed.), *Suicide.* Williams & Wilkins.

Sakinofsky, I., Roberts, R. S., Brown, Y., Cumming C., & James, P. (1990). Problem resolution and repetition of parasuicide: A prospective study, *British Journal of Psychiatry, 156,* 395–399.

Salekin, R. T., Rogers, R., & Sewell, K. W. (1996). A review and meta-analysis of the Psychopathy Checklist and Psychopathy Checklist—Revised: Predictive validity of dangerousness. *Clinical Psychology: Science and Practice, 3,* 203–215.

Salkovskis, P. M. (1985). Obsessional-compulsive problems: A cognitive–behavioural analysis. *Behaviour Research and Therapy, 23,* 571–583.

Salkovskis, P. M. (1989). Cognitive-behavioural factors and the persistence of intrusive thoughts in obsessional problems. *Behaviour Research and Therapy, 27,* 677–682.

Salkovskis, P. M. (1996). *Frontiers of cognitive therapy.* New York: Oxford University Press.

Salkovskis, P. M. (1996). Understanding of OCD is not improved by redefining it as something else. In R. Rapee (Ed.), *Current controversies in the anxiety disorders* (pp. 191–200). New York: Guilford Press.

Salkovskis, P. M., & Clark, D. M. (1990). Affective response to hyperventilation: A test of the cognitive model of panic. *Behaviour Research and Therapy, 28,* 51–61.

Samelson, F. (1980). J. B. Watson's Little Albert, Curil Burt's twins, and the need for a critical science. *American Psychologist, 35,* 619–625.

Sampson, R. J. (1993). The community context of violent crime. In W. J. Wilson (Ed.), *Sociology in the public agenda.* Newbury Park, CA: Sage.

Sanday, P. R. (1981). The socio-cultural context of rape: A cross-cultural study. *Journal of Social Issues, 37,* 5–27.

Sanders, B., & Giolas, M. (1991). Dissociation and childhood trauma in psychologically disturbed adolescents. *American Journal of Psychiatry, 148,* 50–53.

Sanderson, W. C., & Wetzler, S. (1991). Chronic anxiety and generalized anxiety disorder: Issues in comorbidity. In R. M. Rapee & D. H. Barlow (Eds.), *Chronic anxiety. Generalized anxiety disorder and mixed anxiety-depression* (pp. 119–135). New York: Guilford Press.

Sano, M., Stern, Y., Williams, J. (1989). Coexisting dementia and depression in Parkinson's disease. *Archives of Neurology, 46,* 1284–1286.

Sapolsky, R. M. (1990). Stress in the wild. *Scientific American, 262,* 116–123.

Sapolsky, R. M. (1994). *Why zebras don't get ulcers: A guide to stress, stress–related diseases, and coping.* New York: Freeman.

Sapolsky, R. M. (1995). Social subordinance as a marker of hypercortisolism. Some unexpected subtleties. *Annals of the New York Academy of Sciences,* 626–639.

Sapolsky, R. M. (1996). Why stress is bad for your brain. *Science, 273,* 749–750.

Sarafino, E. P. 1997. *Health psychology: Biopsychosocial interactions.* New York: Wiley.

Sarbin, T. R., & Juhasz, J. B. (1967). The historical background of the concept of hallucination. *Journal of Historical Behavioral Science, 3,* 339–358.

Sass, H. (1987). The classification of schizophrenia in the different diagnostic systems. In H. Hafner, W. F. Gattaz, & W. Janzarik (Eds.), *Search for the causes of schizophrenia* (pp. 19–28). Berlin: Springer-Verlag.

Satterfield, J. H., Hoppe, C. M., & Schell, A. M. (1982). A prospective study of delinquency in 110 adolescent boys with attention deficit disorder and 88 normal adolescent boys. *American Journal of Psychiatry, 139,* 795–798.

Saugstad, L. F. (1989). Social class, marriage, and fertility in schziophrenia. *Schizophrenia Bulletin, 15,* 9–43.

Saul, J. R. (1995). *The unconscious civilization.* Concord, ON: Anansi.

Scarr, S. (1981). *Race, social class and individual differences in IQ. New studies of old issues.* Hillsdale, NJ: Erlbaum.

Scarr, S., & Salapatek, P. (1970). Patterns of fear development during infancy. *Merrill-Palmer Quarterly, 16,* 53–90.

Schachar, R. J., & Logan, G. D. (1990). Impulsivity and inhibitory control in normal development and childhood psychopathology. *Developmental Psychology, 26,* 710–720.

Schachar, R. J., Tannock, R., & Logan, G. (1993). Inhibitory control, impulsiveness, and attention deficit hyperactivity disorder. *Clinical Psychology Review, 13,* 721–740.

Schachter, S., & Latane, B. (1964). Crime, cognition, and the autonomic nervous system. In D. Levine (Ed.), *Nebraska symposium on motivation, Vol. 12.* Lincoln: University of Nebraska Press.

Schalling, D. (1993). Neurochemical correlates of personality, impulsivity, and disinhibitory suicide. In S. Hodgins (Ed.), *Mental disorder and crime* (pp. 208–226). Newbury Park, CA: Sage.

Schalock, R. L., Stark, J. A., Snell, M. E., Coulter, D. L., Polloway, E. A., Luckasson, R., Reiss, S., & Spitalnik, D. M. (1994). The changing conception of mental retardation: Implications for the field. *Mental Retardation, 32,* 181–193.

Scharf, M. B., & Jennings, S. W. (1990). Sleep disorders. In D. Bienenfield (Ed.), *Verwoerdt's clinical geropsychiatry* (3rd ed.) (pp. 178–194). Baltimore, MD: Williams & Wilkins.

Scheff, T. J. (1984). *Being mentally ill: A sociological theory* (2nd ed.). Chicago: Aldine. (Original work published in 1966.)

Schiavi, R. C. (1992). Laboratory methods for evaluating erectile dysfunction. In R. C. Rosen & S. R. Leiblum (Eds.), *Erectile disorders: Assessment and treatment* (pp. 141–170). New York: Guilford Press.

Schildkraut, J. (1965). The catecholamine hypothesis of affective disorder: A review of supporting evidence. *American Journal of Psychiatry, 122,* 509–522.

Schlundt, D. G., & Johnson, W. G. (1990). *Eating disorders: Assessment and treatment.* Boston: Allyn and Bacon.

Schmauk, F. J. (1970). Punishment, arousal, and avoidance learning in sociopaths. *Journal of Abnormal Psychology, 76,* 325–335.

Schmidt, N. B., Lerew, D. R., & Trakowski, J. H. (1997). Body vigilance in panic disorder: Evaluation attention to bodily perturbations. *Journal of Consulting and Clinical Psychology, 65,* 214–220.

Schneider, J. A., & Agras, W. S. (1987). Bulimia in males: A matched comparison with females. *International Journal of Eating Disorders, 6,* 235–242.

Schnurr, P. P., Friedman, M. J., & Rosenberg, S. D. (1993). Premilitary MMPI scores as predictors of combat-related PTSD symptoms. *American Journal of Psychiatry, 150,* 479–483.

Schoenman, T. J. (1984). The mentally ill witch in textbooks of abnormal psychology: Current status and implications of a fallacy. *Professional Psychology, 15,* 299–314.

Schou, M. (1997). Forty years of lithium treatment. *Archives of General Psychiatry, 54,* 9–13.

Schover, L. R. (1981). Male and female therapists' responses to male and female client sexual material: An analogue study. *Archives of Sexual Behavior, 10,* 477–492.

Schreiber, F. R. (1973), *Sybil.* New York: Warner Paperback.

Schreiner-Engel, P., & Schiavi, R. C. (1986). Lifetime psychopathology in individuals with low sexual desire. *Journal of Nervous and Mental Disease, 174,* 646–651.

Schulsinger, F., Kety, S. S., Rosenthal, D., et al. (1979). A family study of suicide. In M. Schon & E. Stromgern (Eds.), *Origin, prevention and treatment of affective disorders.* New York: Acadmic Press.

Schwartz, S. (1982). Is there a schizophrenic language? *The Behavioural and Brain Sciences, 5,* 579–626.

Schwartz, S. (1984). Semantic networks, schizophrenia and language. *The Behavioural and Brain Sciences, 7,* 750–751.

Schweinhart, L. J., & Weikart, D. P. (1988). The High/Scope Perry Preschool Program. In R. H. Price, E. L. Cowen, R. P. Lorion, & J. Ramos-McKay (Eds.), *Fourteen ounces of prevention: A casebook for practitioners* (pp. 53–65). Washington, DC: American Psychological Association.

Schweizer, E., Rickels, K., Case, W. G., & Greenblatt, D. J. (1990). Long-term use of benzodiazepines. II. Effects of gradual taper. *Archives of General Psychiatry, 47,* 908–915.

Scogin, F., & McElreath, L. (1994). Efficacy of psychosocial treatments for geriatric depression: A quantitative review. *Journal of Consulting and Clinical Psychology, 62,* 69–74.

Scogin, F., Bynum, J., Stephens, G., & Calhoon, S. (1990). Efficacy of self-administered treatment programs: Meta-analytic review. *Professional Psychology: Research and Practice, 21,* 42–47.

Scott, K. (1994). Substance use among indigenous Canadians. In D. McKenzie (Ed.), *Research issues: Substance abuse among indigenous Canadians.* Ottawa: Canadian Centre on Substance Abuse.

Scully, D., & Marolla, J. (1983). *Incarcerated rapists: Exploring a sociological model.* Bethesda, MD: National Rape Center.

Seaburn, D., Landau-Stanton, J., & Horwitz, S. (1995). Core techniques in family therapy. In R. H. Mikesell, D. Lusterman, & S. H. McDaniel (Eds.), *Integrating family therapy: Handbook of family psychology and systems theory* (pp. 5–26). Washington, DC: American Psychological Association.

Seeman, M. V., & Seeman, P. (1992). Future schizophrenia medicines. In E. Persad, S. S. Kazarian, & L. W. Joseph (Eds.), *The mental hospital in the 21st century* (pp. 168–172). Toronto: Wall & Emerson.

Seeman, P., & Lee, T. (1975). Antipsychotic drugs: Direct correlation between clinical potency and presynaptic action on dopamine neruons. *Science, 188,* 1217–1219.

Seeman, P., Lee, T., Chau-Wong, M., & Wong, K. (1976). Antipsychotic drug doses and neuroleptic/dopmine receptors. *Nature, 261,* 717–719.

Segal, N. (1988). Freud and the question of women. In E. Timms & N. Segal (Eds.), *Freud in exile: Psychoanalysis and its vicissitudes* (pp. 241–253). New Haven: Yale University Press.

Segal, R., & Sisson, B. V. (1985). Medical complications associated with alcohol use and the assessment of risk of physical damage. In T. E. Bratter & G. G. Forrest (Eds.), *Alcoholism and substance abuse* (pp. 137–175). New York: Free Press.

Segal, Z. V., & Shaw, B. F. (1996). Cognitive therapy. In L. Dickstein, M. Riba, & J. Oldham (Eds.), *Review of Psychiatry* (Vol. 15, pp. 69–90). Washington, DC: American Psychiatric Association Press.

Segal, Z. V., Shaw, B. F., Vella, D. D., & Katz, R. (1992). Cognitive and life stress predictors of relapse in remitted unipolar depressed patients: Test of the congruency hypothesis. *Journal of Abnormal Psychology, 101,* 26–36.

Segger, C. A. (1994). Implicit learning. *Psychological Bulletin, 115,* 163–196.

Segraves, R. T., & Segraves, K. B. (1992). Aging and drug effects on male sexuality. In R. C. Rosen & S. R. Leiblum (Eds.), *Erectile disorders: Assessment and treatment* (pp. 96–138). New York: Guilford Press.

Seidman, B. T., Marshall, W. L., Hudson, S. M., & Robertson, P. J. (1994). An examination of intimacy and loneliness in sex offenders. *Journal of Interpersonal Violence, 9,* 518–534.

Selemon, L. D., Rajkowska, G., Goldman-Rakic, P. S. (1995). Abnormally high neuronal density in the schizophrenic cortex. *Archives of General Psychiatry, 52,* 805–818.

Seligman, M.E.P. (1971). Phobia and preparedness. *Behavior Therapy, 2,* 307–320.

Seligman, M.E.P. (1975). *Helplessness: On depression, development and death.* San Francisco: Freeman.

Seligman, M.E.P. (1995). The effectiveness of psychotherapy: The *Consumer Reports* study. *American Psychologist, 50,* 965–974.

Seligman, M.E.P., Abramson, L., Semmel, A., & Von Beyer, C. (1979). Depressive attributional style. *Journal of Abnormal Psychology, 88,* 242–247.

Seligmann, J., & Gelman, D. (1993, March 15). Is it sadness or madness? Psychiatrists clash over how to classify PMS. *Newsweek,* p. 66.

Selye, H. (1956). *The stress of life.* New York: McGraw-Hill.

Semrud-Clikeman, M., & Hynd, G. W. (1992). Developmental arithmetic disorder. In S. R. Hooper, G. W. Hynd, & R. E. Mattison (Eds.), *Developmental disorders: Diagnostic criteria and clinical assessment* (pp. 97–125). Hillsdale, NJ: Erlbaum.

Serban, G., Conte, H. R., & Plutchik, R. (1987). Borderline and schizotypal personality disorders: Mutually exclusive or overlapping? *Journal of Personality Assessment, 5,* 15–22.

Serin, R. C. (1991). Psychopathy and violence in criminals. *Journal of Interpersonal Violence, 6,* 423–431.

Serin, R. C., & Kuriychuk, M. (1994). Social and cognitive processing deficits in violent offenders: Implications for treatment. *International Journal of Law and Psychiatry, 17,* 431–441.

Sevy, S., Mendlewicz, J., & Mendelbaum, K. (1995). Genetic research in depression. In E. Beckham & W. Leber (Eds.), *Handbook of depression* (pp. 203–212). New York: Guilford Press.

Shadish, W. R., & Sweeney, R. B. (1991). Mediators and moderators in meta-analysis: There is a reason we don't let Dodo birds tell us which psychotherapies should have prizes. *Journal of Consulting and Clinical Psychology, 59,* 883–893.

Shadish, W. R., Matt. G. E., Navarro, A. M., Siegle, G., Crits-Christoph, P., Hazelrigg, M. D., Jorm, A. F., Lyons, L. C., Nietzel, M. T., Prout, H. T., Robinson, L., Smith, M. E., Svartberg, M., & Weiss, B. (1997). Evidence that therapy works in clinically representative conditions. *Journal of Consulting and Clinical Psychology, 65,* 355–365.

Shadish, W. R., Montgomery, L. M., Wilson, P., Wilson, M. R., Bright, I., & Okwumabua, T. (1993). Effects of family and marital psychotherapies: A meta-analysis. *Journal of Consulting and Clinical Psychology, 61,* 992–1002.

Shaffer, D., Garland, A., Gould, M., Fisher, P., & Trautman, P. (1988). Preventing teenage suicide: a critical review. *Journal of the American Academy of Child and Adolescent Psychiatry, 27* (6) 675–687.

Sham, P. C., O'Callaghan, E., Takei, N., Murray, G. K., Hare, E. H., & Murray, R. M. (1992). Schizophrenia following prenatal exposure to influenza epidemics between 1939 and 1960. *British Journal of Psychiatry, 160,* 461–466.

Shapiro, A. K., & Morris, L. A. (1978). The placebo effect in medical and psychological therapies. In S. L. Garfield & A. E. Bergin (Eds.), *Handbook of psychotherapy and behavior change* (pp. 369–410). New York: Wiley.

Shapiro, D. (1981). *Autonomy and rigid character.* New York: Basic Books.

Shapiro, E. S., & Skinner, C. H. (1990). Principles of behavior assessment. In C. R. Reynolds & R. W. Kamphaus (Eds.), *Handbook of psychological and educational assessment of children: Personality, behavior and context* (pp. 343–363). New York: Guilford Press.

Shapiro, F. (1995). *Eye movement desensitization and reprocessing: Basic principles, protocols, and procedures.* New York: Guilford Press.

Shaw, S. F., & Shaw, S. R. (1989). Learning disability college programming: A bibliography. *Journal of Postsecondary Education and Disability, 6,* 77–85.

Shear, M. K. (1988). Cognitive and biological models of panic: Toward an integration. In S. Rachman & J. D. Maser (Eds.), *Panic: Psychological perspectives.*

Sheehan, D. V., Ballenger, J., & Jacobsen, G. (1980). Treatment of endogenous anxiety with phobic, hysterical, and hypochondriacal symptoms. *Archives of General Psychiatry, 37,* 51–59.

Sheikh, J. I. (1992). Anxiety disorders in old age. In J. E. Birren, R. B. Sloan, & G. D. Cohen (Eds.), *Handbook of mental health and aging* (2nd ed., pp. 409–432). San Diego: Academic Press, Inc.

Sherrington, R., et al. (1988). Localization of a susceptibility locus for schizophrenia on chromosome 5. *Nature, 336,* 164–167.

Shiffman, S. (1993). Smoking cessation treatment: Any progress? *Journal of Consulting and Clinical Psychology, 61,* 718–722.

Shneidman, E. S. (1987). A psychological approach to suicide. In G. R. Vanden Bos & B. K. Bryant (Eds.), *Cataclysms, crises, and catastrophes: Psychology in action.* Washington, DC: American Psychologial Association.

Shorter, E. (1992). *From paralysis to fatigue: A history of psychosomatic illness in the modern era.* New York: Free Press.

Shorter, E. (1997). *A history of psychiatry: From the era of the asylum to the age of Prozac.* New York: Wiley.

Shuchter, S., Downs, N., & Zisook, S. (1997). *Biologically informed treatment for depression.* New York: Guilford.

Shuwall, M., & Siris, S. G. (1994). Suicidal ideation in postpsychotic depression. *Comprehensive Psychiatry, 35,* 132–134.

Sieber, J. E. (1994). Issues presented by mandatory reporting requirements to researchers of child abuse and neglect. *Ethics and Behavior, 4* (1), 1–22.

Siegel, L. S., & Cunningham, C. E. (1984). Social interactions: A transactional approach with illustrations from children with development problems. *New Directions for Child Development, 24,* 85–98.

Siegleman, M. (1979). Adjustment of homosexual and heterosexual women: A cross-national replication. *Archives of Sexual Behavior, 8,* 121–126.

Siever, L. J. (1985). Biological markers in schizotypal personality disorders. *Schizophrenia Bulletin, 11,* 564–575.

Siever, L. J., & Davis, K. L. (1991). A psychobiological perspective on the personality disorders. *American Journal of Psychiatry, 148,* 1647–1658.

Sigman, M., & Mundy, P. (1989). Social attachments in autistic children. *Journal of Child Psychiatry, 28,* 74–81.

Sigmundson, H. K. (1994). Pharmacotherapy of schizophrenia: A review. *Canadian Journal of Psychiatry, 39* (9 Suppl. 2), S70–S75.

Sigvardsson, S., von Korring, A. L., Bohman, M., & Cloninger, C. R. (1984). An adoption study of somatoform disorders. *Archives of General Psychiatry, 41,* 853–859.

Silberstein, L. R., Mishkind, M. E., Streigel-Moore, R. H., Timko, C., & Rodin, J. (1989). Men and their bodies: A comparison of homosexual and heterosexual men. *Psychosomatic Medicine, 51,* 337–346.

Silver, L. B. (1979). The minimal brain dysfunction syndrome. In J. D. Noshpitz (Ed.), *Basic handbook of child psychiatry* (Vol. 2, pp. 416–439). New York: Basic Books.

Silverman, J. A. (1995). History of anorexia nervosa. In K. D. Brownell & C. G. Fairburn (Eds.), *Eating disorders and obesity: A comprehensive handbook* (pp. 141–144). New York: Guilford Press.

Silverman, K., Evans, S. M., Strain, E. C., & Griffiths, R. R. (1992). Withdrawal syndrome after the double-blind cessation of caffeine consumption. *New England Journal of Medicine, 327* (16), 1109–1114.

Silverstein, B., Feld, S., & Kozlowski, L. T. (1980). The availability of low-nicotine cigarettes as a cause of cigarette smoking among teenage females. *Journal of Health and Social Behavior, 21,* 383–388.

Silverstone, T., & Goodall, E. (1986). A pharmacological analysis of human feeding: Its contribution to the understanding of affective disorders. In M. O. Carruba & J. E. Blundell (Eds.), *Pharmacology of eating disorders: Theoretical and clinical developments* (pp. 141–150). New York: Raven Press.

Simeon, J. G., & Ferguson, H. B. (1992). Clinical, cognitive, and neurophysiological effects of alprazolam in children and adolescents with overanxious and avoidant disorders. *Journal of the American Academy of Child and Adolescent Psychiatry, 31,* 29–33.

Simmons, H. G. (1987). Psychosurgery and the abuse of psychiatric authority in Ontario. *Journal of Health Politics, Policy and Law, 12,* 537–550.

Simon, G. E., & von Korff, M. (1991). Somatization and psychiatric disorder in the NIMH Epidemiologic Catchment Area study. *American Journal of Psychiatry, 148,* 1494–1500.

Simon, R. J., & Aaronson, D. E. (1988). *The insanity defense: A critical assessment of law and policy in the post-Hinckley era.* New York: Praeger.

Simon, R. J., Fleiss, J. L., Gurland, B. J., Stiller, P. R., & Sharpe, L. (1973). Depression and schizophrenia in hospitalized black and white mental patients. *Archives of General Psychiatry, 28,* 509–512.

Singer, J. (1990). *Repression and dissociation: Implications for personality theory, psychopathology and health.* Chicago: University of Chicago Press.

Singer, J. A., & Salovey, P. (1988). Mood and memory: Evaluating the network theory of affect. *Clinical Psychology Review, 8,* 211–225.

Single, E. W., Brewster, J. M., MacNeil, P., Hatcher, J., & Trainor, C. (1995). The 1993 general social survey. I. Alcohol use in Canada. *Canadian Journal of Public Health, 86,* 397–401.

Single, E. W., Brewster, J. M., MacNeil, P., Hatcher, J., & Trainor, C. (1995). The 1993 general social survey. II. Alcohol problems in Canada. *Canadian Journal of Public Health, 86,* 402–407.

Single, E., MacLennan, A., & MacNeil, P. (1994). *Horizons, 1994.* Ottawa: Canadian Centre on Substance Abuse.

Single, E., Robson, L., Xie, X., & Rehm, J. (1997). *The costs of substance abuse in Canada.* Ottawa: Canadian Centre on Substance Abuse.

Skelton, J. A. (1995). How much better is clozapine? A meta-analytic review and critical appraisal. *Experimental and Clinical Pharmacology, 3,* 270–279.

Skinner, B. F. (1953). *Science and human behavior.* New York: Macmillan.

Sklar, L. S., & Anisman, H. (1979). Stress and coping factors influence tumor growth. *Science, 205,* 513–515.

Skrtic, T. M., Summers, J. A., Brotherson, M. J., & Turnbull, A. P. (1984). Severely handicapped children and their brothers and sisters. In J. Blacher (Ed.), *Severely handicapped young children and their families. Research in review* (pp. 215–246). New York: Academic Press.

Slade, P. D. (1974). Psychometric studies of obsessional illness and obsessional personality. In H. R. Beech (Ed.), *Obsessional states* (pp. 95–112). London: Methuen.

Slater, E., & Glithero, E. (1965). A follow-up of patients diagnosed as suffering from hysteria. *Journal of Psychosomatic Research, 9,* 9–13.

Slater, E., & Shields, J. (1969). Genetical aspects of anxiety. In M. H. Lader (Ed.), *Studies of Anxiety.* Ashford, England: Headley.

Slovenko, R. (1983). Disposition of the insanity acquittee. *Journal Psychiatry and Law, 11,* 97–112.

Small, R. D., & Sudar, M. (1995). Islands of brilliance. *Psychosocial-Rehabilitation—Journal, 18* (3), 37–50.

Smallbone, S. W., & Dadds, M. R. (1997). *Childhood attachment and adult attachment in incarcerated adult male sex offenders.* Submitted.

Smalley, S. L., & Collins, F. (1996). In M. M. Bristol, D. J. Cohen, E. J. Costello, M. Denckla, T. J. Eckberg, R. Kallen, H. C. Kraemer, C. Lord, R. Maurer, W. J. McIlvane, N. Minshew,

M. Sigman, & M. A. Spence, State of the science in autism: Report to the National Institutes of Health. *Journal of Autism and Developmental Disorders, 26,* 195–198.

Smith, B., & Sechrest, L. (1991). Treatment of aptitude X treatment interactions. *Journal of Consulting and Clinical Psychology, 59,* 233–244.

Smith, D., Carroll, J. L., & Fuller, G. B. (1988). The relationship between the Millon Clinical Multiaxial Inventory and the MMPI in a private outpatient mental health clinic population. *Journal of Clinical Psychology, 44,* 165–174.

Smith, G. R., Monson, R. A., & Ray, D. B. (1986). Psychiatric consultation in somatization disorder. *New England Journal of Medicine, 314,* 1407–1413.

Smith, G. T., Goldman, M., Greenbaum, P. E., Christiansen, B. A. (1995). Expectancy for social facilitation from drinking: The divergent paths of high-expectancy and low-expectancy adolescents. *Journal of Abnormal Psychology, 104,* 32–40.

Smith, M. L., Glass, G. V., & Miller, T. I. (1980). *The benefits of psychotherapy.* Baltimore, MD: The John Hopkins University Press.

Smith, P. L. (1995). Psychophysically principled models of visual simple reaction time. *Psychological Review, 102,* 567–593.

Smith, T. W. (1992). Hostility and health: Current status of a psychosomatic hypothesis. *Health Psychology, 11,* 139–150.

Smith, T. W., & Frohm, K. D. (1985). What's so unhealthy about hostility? Construct validity and psychosocial correlates of the Cook and Medley Ho scale. *Health Psychology, 4,* 503–520.

Smith, W. H. (1993). Incorporating hypnosis into the psychotherapy of patients with multiple personality disorder. *Bulletin of the Menninger Clinic, 57* (3), 344–354.

Smukler, A. J., & Schiebel, D. (1975). Personality characteristics of exhibitionism. *Diseases of the Nervous System, 36,* 600–603.

Smyer, M. A., Zarit, S. H., & Qualls, S. H. (1990). Psychological intervention with the aging individual. In J. E. Birren, & K. W. Schaie (Eds.), *Handbook of the psychology of aging* (3rd ed., pp. 375–404). San Diego, CA: Academic Press.

Snyder, J. J. (1977). Reinforcement and analysis of interaction in problem and nonproblem families. *Journal of Abnormal Psychology, 86,* 528–535.

Sobell, L. C., Toneatto, A., & Sobell, M. B. (1990). Behavior therapy. In A. S. Bellack and M. Hersen (Eds.), *Handbook of comparative treatments for adult disorders* (pp. 479–505). New York: Brunner/Mazel.

Sobell, M. B., & Sobell, L. C. (1973). Alcoholics treated by individualized behavior therapy: One year treatment outcome. *Behaviour Research and Therapy, 11,* 599–618.

Sobell, M. B., & Sobell, L. C. (1976). Second year treatment outcome of alcoholics treated by individualized behavior therapy: Results. *Behaviour Research and Therapy, 14,* 195–215.

Sobin, C., Sackeim, H. A., Prudic, J., Devanand, D. P., Moody, B. J., & McElhiney, M. C. (1995). Predictors of retrograde amnesia following ECT. *American Journal of Psychiatry, 152,* 995–1001.

Sobsey, D., Gray, S., Wells, D., Pyper D., & Reimer-Heck, B. (1991). *Disability, sexuality and abuse: An annotated bibliography.* Baltimore, MD: Paul H. Brookes.

Solnit, A. J., & Stark, M. H. (1961). Mourning and the birth of a defective child. *Psychoanalytic Study of the Child, 16,* 523–527.

Sommers-Flanagan, J., & Sommers-Flanagan, R. (1996). Efficacy of antidepressant medication with depressed youth: What psychologists should know. *Professional Psycholology: Research and Practice, 27,* 145–153.

Sovner, R., & Hurley, A. D. (1989). Ten diagnostic principles for recognizing psychiatric disorders in mentally retarded persons. *Psychiatric Aspects of Mental Retardation Reviews, 8,* 9–13.

Spanos, N. (1994). Multiple identity enactments and multiple personality disorder: A sociocognitive perspective. *Psychological Bulletin, 116* (1), 143–165.

Spanos, N. (1996). *Multiple identities and false memories.* Washington, DC: American Psychiatric Press.

Spanos, N., Weekes, J., & Bertrand, L. (1985). Multiple personality: A social psychological perspective. *Journal of Abnormal Psychology, 94,* 362–376.

Spark, R. F. (1991). *Male sexual health: A couples' guide.* Mount Vernon, NY: Consumer Reports Books.

Spaulding, J., & Balch, P. (1983). A brief history of primary prevention in the 20th century: 1908 to 1980. *American Journal of Community Psychology, 11,* 59–80.

Spector, I. P., & Carey, M. P. (1990). Incidence and prevalence of the sexual dysfunctions: A critical review of the literature. *Archives of Sexual Behavior, 19,* 389–408.

Speisman, J., Lazarus, R. S., Mordkoff, A., & Davidson, L. (1964). Experimental reduction of stress based on ego defense theory. *Journal of Abnormal and Social Psychology, 68,* 367–380.

Spence, M. A. (1996). Pathophysiology of autism: Etiology and brain mechanisms. In M. M. Bristol, D. J. Cohen, E. J. Costello, M. Denckla, T. J. Eckberg, R. Kallen, H. C. Kraemer, C. Lord, R. Maurer, W. J. McIlvane, N. Minshew, M. Sigman, & M. A. Spence, State of the science in autism: Report to the National Institutes of Health. *Journal of Autism and Developmental Disorders, 26,* 129–134.

Spencer, T., Biederman, J., Wilens, T., Harding, M., O'Donnell, D., & Griffin, S. (1996). Pharmacotherapy of attention-deficit hyperactivity disorder across the lifecycle: A literature review. *Journal of the American Academy of Child and Adolescent Psychiatry, 35,* 409–432.

Spengler, A. (1977). Manifest sadomasochism of males: Results of an empirical study. *Archives of Sexual Behavior, 6,* 441–456.

Spiegel, D. (1994). Dissociative disorders. In R. E. Hales, S. C. Yudofsky, & J. A. Talbott (Eds.), *The American Psychiatric Press textbook of psychiatry* (2nd ed.). Washington, DC: American Psychiatric Press.

Spiegel, D., & Cardena, E. (1991). Disintegrated experience: The dissociative disorders revisited. *Journal of Abnormal Psychology, 100,* 366–378.

Spiegel, D., & Kato, P. M. (1996). Psychosocial influences on cancer incidence and progression. *Harvard Review of Psychiatry, 4,* 10–26.

Spielberger, C. D. (1983). *Manual for the State-Trait Anxiety Inventory (Form Y) (Self-Evaluation Questionnaire).* Palo Alto: Consulting Psychologist Press.

Spitz, R. A. (1945). Hospitalism: An inquiry into the genesis of psychiatric conditions in early childhood. *Psychoanalytic study of the child. (Vol. 2).* New York: International Universities Press.

Spitzer, L., & Rodin, J. (1987). Effects of fructose and glucose preloads on subsequent food intake. *Appetite, 8,* 135–145.

Spitzer, R. L., & Williams, J.D.W. (1985). *Structured clinical interview for DSM-IIIR: Patient version.* New York: New York State Psychiatric Institute, Biometrics Research Division.

Spitzer, R. L., Devlin, M. J., Walsh, B. T., Hasin, D., Wing, R. R., Marcus, M. D., Stunkard, A., Wadden, T. A., Yanovski, S., Agras, W. S., Mitchell, J., & Nonas, C. (1992). Binge eating disorder: A multisite field trial for the diagnostic criteria. *International Journal of Eating Disorders, 11,* 191–203.

Spitzer, R. L., Endicott, J., & Gibbon, M. (1979). Crossing the border into borderline personality and borderline schizophrenia. *Archives of General Psychiatry, 36,* 17–24.

Spitzer, R. L., Endicott, J., & Robins, E. (1978). Research diagnosis criteria: Rationale and reliability. *Archives of General Psychiatry, 75,* 773–782.

Spitzer, R. L., Skodol, A. E., Gibbon, M., & Williams, J.B.W. (1983). *Psychopathology: A Case Book.* New York: McGraw Hill.

Spitzer, R. L., Williams, J.B.W., Gibbon, M., & First, M. B. (1992). The structured clinical interview for DSM-III-R (SCID). I. History, rationale, and description. *Archives of General Psychiatry, 49,* 624–629.

Spoont, M. R. (1992). Modulatory role of serotonin in neural information processing: Implication for human psychopathology. *Psychological Bulletin, 112* (2), 330–350.

Spring, B. (1981). Stress and schizophrenia: Some definition issues. *Schizophrenia Bulletin, 7,* 24–23.

Spring, B., & Coons, H. (1982). Stress as a precursor of schizophrenic episode. In R.W.J. Neufeld (Ed.), *Psychological stress and psychopathology.* New York: McGraw-Hill.

Sprock, J., Blashfield, R. K., & Smith, B. (1990). Gender weighting of DSM-III-R personality disorder criteria. *American Journal of Psychiatry, 147,* 586–590.

Squire, L. R., & Zola-Morgan, S. (1988). Memory: Brain and behavior. *Trends in Neurosciences,* 170–175.

Srole, L., Langner, T. S., Michael, S. T., Opler, M. K., & Rennie, T.A.C. (1962). *Mental health in the metropolis: The midtown Manhattan study.* New York: McGraw-Hill.

Staddon, J.E.R. (1984). Social learning theory and the dynamics of interaction. *Psychological Review, 91,* 502–507.

Starker, S. (1988). Do-it-yourself therapy: The prescription of self-help books by psychologists. *Psychotherapy, 25,* 142–146.

Statistics Canada (1992), *Income distributions by size in Canada, 1991.* Cat. 13-207. Ottawa: Ministry of Industry, Science, and Technology, 1992.

Statistics Canada (1993). *Languange, tradition, lifestyle and social issues: 1991 Aboriginal peoples survey.* Cat. 89-533. Ottawa: Statistics Canada.

Statistics Canada (1994), Census Analysis Division. *Population projections 1993–2041: Canada, provinces and territories.* Ottawa: Minister of Industry, Science, and Technology.

Statistics Canada (1995, March), Health Sciences Division. *Mental health statistics, 1992–93.* Ottawa: Statistics Canada.

Steele, N. (1993). Cost effectiveness of treatment. In B. K. Schwartz & H. R. Cellini (Eds.), *The sex offender: Corrections, treatment and legal practice* (pp. 4.1–4.19). Kingston, NJ: Civic Research Institute.

Steffy, R. A., & Galbraith, K. (1980). Relation between latency and redundancy-associated deficit in schizophrenic reaction time performance. *Journal of Abnormal Psychology, 89,* 419–427.

Steffy, R. A., & Waldman, I. (1993). Schizophrenics' reaction time: North star or shooting star? In R. L. Cromwell & C. R. Snyder (Eds.), *Schizophrenia: Origins, processes, treatment, and outcome* (pp. 111–134). New York: Oxford University Press.

Steffy, R. A., Asarnow, R. F., Asarnow, J. R., MacCrimmon, D. J., & Cleghorn, J. M. (1984). The McMaster-Waterloo High-Risk Project: Multifaceted strategy for high-risk research. In N. F. Watt, E. J. Anthony, L. C. Wynne, & J. E. Rolf (Eds.), *Children at risk for schizophrenia: A longitudinal perspective* (pp. 401–413). Cambridge: Cambridge University Press.

Steiger, H. (1989). Anorexia nervosa and bulimia in males: Lessons from a low-risk population. *Canadian Journal of Psychiatry, 34,* 419–424.

Steiger, H., Goldstein, C., Mongrain, M., & Van der Feen, J. (1990). Description of eating-disordered, psychiatric, and normal women along cognitive and psychodynamic dimensions. *International Journal of Eating Disorders, 9,* 129–140.

Steiger, H., Van der Feen, J., Goldstein, C., & Leichner, P. (1989). Defense styles and parental bonding in eating-disordered women. *International Journal of Eating Disorders, 8,* 131–140.

Stein, M., Walker, J., & Ford, D. (1994). Setting diagnostic thresholds for social phobia. *American Journal of Psychiatry, 101,* 408–412.

Stein, R. M., & Ellinwood, E. H. (1993). Stimulant use: Cocaine and amphetamine. In D. L. Dunner (Ed.), *Current psychiatric therapy* (pp. 98–105). Philadelphia: Saunders.

Steinhauer, S. R., & Hill, S. Y. (1993). Auditory event-related potentials in children at high risk for alcoholism. *Journal of Studies on Alcohol, 54,* 408–421.

Steinhausen, C. H., Rauss-Mason, C., & Seidel, R. (1991). Follow-up studies of anorexia nervosa: A review of four decades of outcome research. *Psychological Medicine, 21,* 447–451.

Steinhausen, H. C. (1995). The course and outcome of anorexia nervosa. In K. D. Brownell & C. G. Fairburn (Eds.), *Eating disorders and obesity: A comprehensive handbook* (pp. 234–237). New York: Guilford Press.

Stephenson, P. S., & Walker, G. A. (1979). The psychiatrist-woman patient relationship. *Canadian Journal of Psychiatry, 24,* 5–16.

Stevenson, J., & Meares, R. (1992). An outcome study of psychotherapy for patients with borderline personality disorder. *American Journal of Psychiatry, 149,* 358–362.

Stewart, D. J. (1972). Effects of social reinforcement on dependency and aggressive responses of psychopathic, neurotic, and subculture delinquents. *Journal of Abnormal Psychology, 79,* 76–83.

Stewart, M. A. (1970). Hyperactive children. *Scientific American, 222,* 94–98.

Stewart, P. J., Potter, J., Dulber, C., Niday, P., Nimrod, C., Tawagi, G. (1995). Change in smoking prevalence among pregnant women 1982–93. *Canadian Journal of Public Health, 86* (1), 37–41.

Stewart, S. H., & Zeitlin, S. B. (1995). Anxiety sensitivity and alcohol use motives. *Journal of Anxiety Disorders, 9,* 229–240.

Stine, O. C., Xu-J., Koskela, R. McMahon, F. J., Gschwend, M., Friddle, C., Clark, C. D., McInnis, M. G., Simpson, S. G., Breschel, T. S., Vishio, E., Riskin, K., Feilotter, H., Chen, E., Shen, S., Folstein, S., Meyers, D. A., Botsein, D., Marr, T. G., & DePaulo, J. R. (1995). Evidence for linkage of bipolar disorder to chromosome 18 with a parent of origin effect. *American Journal of Human Genetics, 57,* 1384–1394.

Stirpe, T. (1994). *Problem and compulsive gambling workshop: Literature review.* Toronto: Addiction Research Foundation, 1994.

Stone, M. (1993). Long-term outcome in personality disorders. *British Journal of Psychiatry, 162,* 299–313.

Stone, W. L., Lemanek, K. L., Fishel, P. T., Fernandez, M. C., & Altemeier, W. A. (1990). Play and imitation skills in the diagnosis of autism in young children. *Pediatrics, 86,* 267–272.

Storandt, M., & Vanden Bos, G. (Eds.) (1994). *Neurophsychological assessment of dementia and depression in older adults.* Washington, DC: American Psychological Association.

Stratton, H. G., Hobbs, G. E., & Carscallen, H. B. (1947). Subcoma insulin and pentothal sodium as aids to psychotherapy. *American Journal of Psychiatry, 104,* 56–59.

Strauss, C. C., Forehand, K., & Frame, C. (1986). The association between social withdrawal and internalizing problems of children. *Journal of Abnormal Child Psychology, 22,* 525–535.

Stravynski, A., Lesage, A., Marcouiller, M., & Elie, R. (1989). A test of the therapeutic mechanism in social skills training with avoidant personality disorder. *Journal of Nervous and Mental Disease, 177,* 739–744.

Stravynsky, A., Greenberg, D. (1989). Behavioural psychotherapy for social phobia and dysfunction. *International Review of Psychiatry, 1,* 207–217.

Stravynsky, A., Marks, I., & Yule, W. (1982). Social skills problems in neurotic outpatients: Social skills training with and without cognitive modification. *Archives of General Psychiatry, 39,* 1378–1385.

Streissguth, A. P., & LaDue, R. A. (1987). *Fetal alcohol: Teratogenic causes of developmental disabilities.* Washington, DC: American Association on Mental Deficiency Monograph.

Streissguth, A. P., Barr, H. M., & Sampson, P. D. (1990). Moderate prenatal alcohol exposure: Effects on child IQ and learning problems at age 7 1/2 years. *Alcoholism: Clinical and Experimental Research, 14,* 662–669.

Striegel-Moore, R. H. (1993). Etiology of binge eating: A developmental perspective. In C. G. Fairburn & G. T. Wilson (Eds.), *Binge eating: Nature, assessment and treatment* (pp. 144–172). New York: Guilford Press.

Striegel-Moore, R. H. (1995). A feminist perspective on the etiology of eating disorders. In K. D. Brownell & C. G. Fairburn (Eds.), *Eating disorders and obesity: A comprehensive handbook* (pp. 224–225). New York: Guilford Press.

Striegel-Moore, R. H., Silberstein, L. R., & Rodin, J. (1986). Towards an understanding of risk factors for bulimia. *American Psychologist, 41,* 246–263.

Strober, M. (1995). Family-genetic perspectives on anorexia nervosa and bulimia nervosa. In K. D. Brownell & C. G. Fairburn (Eds.), *Eating disorders and obesity: A comprehensive handbook* (pp. 212–218). New York: Guilford Press.

Strober, M. (1995). Family-genetic perspectives on anorexia nervosa and bulimia nervosa. In K. D. Brownell & C. G. Fairburn (Eds.), *Eating disorders and obesity: A comprehensive handbook* (pp. 212–218). New York: Guilford Press.

Strober, M., & Katz, J. L. (1987). Do eating disorders and affective disorders share a common etiology? A dissenting opinion. *International Journal of Eating Disorders, 6,* 111–122.

Strober, M., Morrell, W., Burroughs, J., Salkin, B., & Jacobs, C. (1985). A controlled family study of anorexia nervosa. *Journal of Psychiatric Research, 19,* 239–246.

Stuart, G. W., Laraia, M. T., Ballenger, J. C., & Lydiard, R. B. (1990). Early family experiences of women with bulimia and depression. *Archives of Psychiatric Nursing, IV* (1), 43–52.

Stunkard, A. J., Foch, T. T., & Hrubec, Z. (1986). A twin study of human obesity. *Journal of the American Medical Association, 256,* 51–54.

Sturge, C. (1982). Reading retardation and antisocial behaviour. *Journal of Child Psychology & Psychiatry & Allied Disciplines, 23,* 21–31.

Suarez, E., & Williams, R. B. (1989). Situational determinants of cardiovascular and emotional reactivity in high and low hostile men. *Psychosomatic Medicine, 51,* 404–418.

Suddath, R. L., Casanova, M. R., Goldberg, T. E., Daniel, D. G., Kelsoe, J. R., Jr., Weinberger, D. R. (1989). Temporal lobe pathology in schizophrenia: A quantitative magnetic resonance imaging study. *American Journal of Psychiatry, 146,* 646–472.

Sue, S. (1991). Ethnicity and culture in psychological research and practice. In L. Garnets, J. M. Jones, D. Kimmel, S. Sue, & C. Travis (Eds.), *Psychological perspectives on human diversity in America.* Washington, DC: American Psychological Association.

Suedfeld, P., & Landon, P. B. (1978). Approaches to treatment. In R. D. Hare & D. Schalling (Eds.), *Psychopathic behavior: Approaches to research* (pp. 347–276). Chichester, England: Wiley.

Sugarmon, P. A., & Crawford, D. (1994). Schizophrenia in the Afro-Caribbean community. *British Journal of Psychiatry, 164,* 474–480.

Sullivan, E. V., Mathalon, D. H., Zipurshky, R. B., Kersteen-Tucker, Z., Knight, R. T., & Pfefferbaum, A. (1993). Factors of the Wisconsin Card Sorting Test as measures of frontal-lobe dysfunction in schizophrenia and in chronic alcoholism. *Psychiatry Research, 46,* 175–199.

Sullivan, L., & Ogloff, J.R.P. (1998). Appropriate supervisor–graduate students relationships. *Ethics and Behavior, 8,* 229–248.

Sundgot-Borgen, J. (1993). Prevalence of eating disorders in elite female athletes. *International Journal of Sports Nutrition, 3,* 29–40.

Suomi, S. J. (1987). Perinatal development: A psychobiological approach. In N. A. Krasnegor, E. M. Blass, M. A. Hofer, & W. P. Smotherman (Eds.) *Behavioural Biology* (pp. 397–420). New York: Academic Press.

Suomi, S. J., Kraemer, G. U., Baysinger, C. M., & Delizio, R. D. (1981). Inherited and experiential factors associated with individual differences in anxious behavior displayed by rhesus monkeys. In D. Klein & J. Rabkin (Eds.), *Anxiety: New research and changing concepts.* New York: Raven Press.

Surwit, R. S., & Williams, P. G. (1996). Animal models provide insight into psychosomatic factors in diabetes. *Psychosomatic Medicine, 58,* 582–589.

Sussman, S. (1992). *From institution to community: An historical and evaluative study of services for mentally ill people in Ontario, Canada.* Unpublished doctoral dissertation, Loughborough University of Technology.

Sutcliffe, J. P., & Jones, J. (1962). Personal identity, multiple personality, and hypnosis. *International Journal of Clinical and Experimental Hypnosis, 10,* 231–269.

Svartberg, M., & Stiles, T. C. (1991). Comparative effects of short-term psychodynamic psychotherapy: A meta-analysis. *Journal of Consulting and Clinical Psychology, 59,* 704–714.

Swanson, J., Holzer, C., Ganju, V., & Jono, R. (1990). Violence and psychiatric disorder in the community: Evidence from the Epidemiologic Catchment Area surveys. *Hospital and Community Psychiatry, 41,* 761–770.

Swartz, M., Blazer, D., George, L., & Landerman, R. (1986). Somatization disorder in a community population. *American Journal of Psychiatry, 143,* 1403–1408.

Swartz, M., Landerman, R., George, L. K., Blazer, D. G., & Escobar, J. (1991). Somatization disorder. In L. N. Robins & D. A. Regier (Eds.), *Psychiatric disorders in America: The Epidemiologic Catchment Area study* (pp. 220–257). New York: Free Press.

Sweeney, J. A., Clementz, B. A., Haas, G. L., Escobar, M. D., Drake, K., & Frances, A. J. (1994). Eye tracking dysfunction in schizophrenia: Characterization of component eye movement abnormalities, diagnositic specificity, and the role of attention. *Journal of Abnormal Psychology, 103,* 222–230.

Swinson, R. P., Cox, B. J., Kerr, S. A., Kuch, K., & Fergus, K. (1992). A survey of anxiety disorders clinics in Canadian hospitals. *Canadian Journal of Psychiatry, 37,* 188–191.

Swinson, R. P., Fergus, K. D., Cox, B. J., & Wiskwire, K. (1995). Efficacy of telephone-administered behavioral therapy for panic disorder with agoraphobia. *Behaviour Research and Therapy, 33,* 465–469.

Swinson, R. P., Soulios, C., Cox, B. J., & Kuch, K. (1992). Brief treatment of emergency room patients with panic attacks. *American Journal of Psychiatry, 149,* 944–946.

Szab'o, G., Tabakoff, B., & Hoffman, P. L. (1994). The NDMA receptor antagonist dizocilpine differentially affects environment-dependent and environment-independent ethanol tolerance. *Psychopharmacology, 113* (3–4), 511–517.

Szasz, T. S. (1960). The myth of mental illness. *American Psychologist, 15,* 113–118.

Szasz, T. S. (1961). *The myth of mental illness.* New York: Harper & Row.

Szasz, T. S. (1974). *The age of madness: The history of involuntary hospitalization.* New York: Jason Aronson.

Szasz, T. S. (1985). Psychiatry: Rhetoric and reality. *The Lancet, 2,* 711–712.

Szatmari, P. (1992). The epidemiology of attention-deficit hyperactivity disorders. In G. Weiss (Ed.), *Child and adolescent psychiatric clinics of North America: Attention-deficit hyperactivity disorder* (pp. 361–372). Philadelphia: Saunders.

Szatmari, P., & Mahoney, W. (1993). The genetics of autism and pervasive developmental disorders: A review of the evidence. *Journal of Developmental Disabilities, 2,* 39–55.

Szatmari, P., Boyle, M. H., & Offord, D. R. (1989a). ADDH and conduct disorder: Degree of diagnostic overlap and differences among correlates. *Journal of the American Academy of Child and Adolescent Psychiatry, 28* (6), 865–872.

Szatmari, P., Offord, D. R., & Boyle, M. H. (1989b). Correlates, associated impairments and patterns of service utilization of children with attention deficit disorder: Findings from the Ontario Child Health Study. *Journal of Child Psychology & Psychiatry & Allied Disciplines, 30* (2), 205–217.

Tabakoff, B., & Hoffman, P. L. (1991). Neurochemical effects of alcohol. In R. J. Frances & S. I. Muller (Eds.), *Clinical textbook of addictive disorders* (pp. 501–525). New York: Guilford Press.

Takei, N., Sham, P., O'Callaghan, E., Murray, G. K., Glover, G., & Murray, R. M. (1994). Prenatal expose to influenza and the development of schizophrenia: Is the effect confined to females? *American Journal of Psychiatry, 151,* 117–119.

Tallis, F., & Eysenck, M. W. (1994). Worry: Mechanisms and modulating influences. *Behavioural and Cognitive Psychotherapy, 22,* 37–56.

Tannahill, R. (1980). *Sex in history.* New York: Stein and Day.

Tanney, B. L. (1992). Mental disorders, psychiatric patients and suicide. In R. Maris, A. Berman, J. Maltsberger, & R. Yufit (Eds.), *Assessment and prediction of suicide* (pp. 277–320). New York: Guilford Press.

Tarasoff v. Regents of University of California, 17 Cal. 3d 425, 131 Cal. Rptr. 14, 551 P. 2d 334 (1976).

Tausig, H. B. (1962). Thalidomide: A lesson in remote effects of drugs. *American Journal of Diseases of Children, 104,* 111–113.

Tavris, C. (1992). *The mismeasure of women.* New York: Simon and Schuster.

Taylor, G. J., Parker, J.D.A., Bagby, R. M., & Acklin, M. W. (1992). Alexithymia and somatic complaints in psychiatric outpatients. *Journal of Psychosomatic Research, 36* (5), 417–424.

Taylor, H. G. (1989). Learning disabilities. In E. J. Mash & R. A. Barkley (Eds.), *Treatment of childhood disorders.* New York: Guilford Press.

Taylor, S. (1995). Assessment of obsessions and compulsions: Reliability, validity, and sensitivity to treatment effects. *Clinical Psychology Review, 15,* 261–296.

Taylor, S. (1996). Meta-analysis of cognitive-behavioral treatments for social phobia. *Journal of Behavior Therapy and Experimental Psychiatry, 27,* 1–9.

Taylor, S. (1999). *Anxiety sensitivity: Theory, research, and treatment of the fear of anxiety.* Mahwah, NJ: Lawrence Erlbaum.

Taylor, S., Woody, S., Koch, W. J., McLean, P., Paterson, R., & Anderson, K. (1997). Cognitive restructuring in the treatment of social phobia: Efficacy and mode of action. *Behavior Modification, 21,* 487–511.

Taylor, S., Woody, S., McLean, P., & Koch, W. J. (1997). Sensitivity of outcome measures for treatments of generalized social phobia. *Assessment, 4,* 193–203.

Teasdale, J. D. (1996). The relationship between cognition and emotion: The mind-in-place in mood disorders. In D. M. Clark & C. G. Fairburn (Eds.), *Science and practice of cognitive-behaviour therapy* (pp. 67–94). New York: Oxford University Press.

Teasell, R. W., & Merskey, H. (1997). Chronic pain disability in the workplace. *Pain Forum, 6,* 228–238.

Tennent, G., Tennent, D., Prins, H., & Bedford, A. (1993). Is psychopathic disorder a treatable condition? *Medicine, Science, and the Law, 33,* 63–66.

Test, M. A., & Stein, L. L. (1978). Community treatment of the chronic patient: Research overview. *Schizophrenia Bulletin, 4* (3), 350–364.

Thase, M. E., & Kupfer, D. J. (1996). Recent developments in pharmacotherapy of mood disorders. *Journal of Consulting and Clinical Psychology, 64,* 646–659.

Thase, M., & Howland, R. (1995). Biological processes in depression. In E. Beckham & W. Leber (Eds.), *Handbook of depression* (pp. 213–279). New York: Guilford Press.

Thase, M., & Kupfer, D. (1987). Current status of EEG sleep in the assessment and treatment of depression. In G. Burrows & J. Werry (Eds.), *Advances in human psychopharmacology* (Vol. 4, pp. 93–148). Greenwich, CT: JAI Press.

Theander, S. (1985). Outcome and prognosis in anorexia nervosa and bulimia: Some results of previous investigations compared with those of a Swedish long-term study. *Journal of Psychiatric Research, 19,* 493–508.

Thigpen, C. H., & Cleckley, H. M. (1957). *The three faces of Eve.* New York: Fawcett.

Thomas, A. M., & LoPiccolo, J. (1994). Sexual functioning in persons with diabetes: Issues in research, treatment, and education. *Clinical Psychology Review, 14,* 61–86.

Thomas, A., & Chess, S. (1977). *Temperament and development.* New York: Brunner/Mazel.

Thombs, D. L. (1993). The differentially discriminating properties of alcohol expectancies for female and male drinkers. *Journal of Counseling and Development, 71,* 321–325.

Thompson, L. W., Gallagher, D., & Breckenridge, J. S. (1987). Comparative effectiveness of psychotherapies for depressed elders. *Journal of Consulting and Clinical Psychology, 55,* 385–390.

Thompson-Pope, S. K., & Turkat, I. D. (1988). Reactions to ambiguous stimuli among paranoid personalities. *Journal of Psychopathology and Behavioral Assessment, 10,* 21–32.

Thorndike, R. L., Hagen, E. P., & Sattler, J. M. (1986). *The Stanford-Binet Intelligence Scale, 4th Ed.: Guide for administering and scoring.* Chicago: Riverside.

Thyer, B. A. (1993). Childhood separation anxiety disorder and adult-onset agoraphobia: Review of evidence. In C. G. Last (Ed.), *Anxiety across the lifespan: A developmental perspective* (pp. 128–147). New York: Springer.

Tiefer, L., & Melman, A. (1989). Comprehensive evaluation of erectile dysfunction and medical treatments. In S. R. Leiblum & R. C. Rosen (Eds.), *Principles and practice of sex therapy, 2nd Ed.: Update for the 1990s* (pp. 207–236). New York: Guilford Press.

Tillich, R. (1952). *Courage to be.* New Haven, CT: Yale University Press.

Timmreck, T. C. (1994). *An introduction to epidemiology.* Boston: Jones & Bartlett.

Tobler, N. S., & Stratton, H. H. (1997). Effectiveness of school-based drug prevention programs: A meta analysis of the research. *Journal of Primary Prevention, 18,* 71–128.

Toch, H. (1971). *The social psychology of social movements.* London: Methuen.

Tomasulo, D. (1994). Action techniques in group counseling: The double. *Habilitative Mental Healthcare Newsletter, 13,* 41–45.

Tomasulo, D., Keller, E., & Pfadt, A. (1995). The healing crowd: Process, content and technique issues in group counseling for people with mental retardation. *Habilitative Mental Healthcare Newsletter, 14,* 43–49.

Torgersen, S. (1976). The nature and origin of common phobic fears. *British Journal of Psychiatry, 134,* 343–351.

Torgersen, S. (1983). Genetic factors in anxiety disorders. *Archives of General Psychiatry, 40,* 1085–1089.

Torgersen, S. (1984). Genetic and nosological aspects of schizotypal and borderline personality disorders. *Archives of General Psychiatry, 41,* 546–554.

Torgersen, S. (1986). Genetic factors in moderately severe and mild affective disorders. *Archives of General Psychiatry, 43,* 222–226.

Torgersen, S., & Alnaes, R. (1992). Differential perception of parental bonding in schizotypal and borderline personality disorder patients. *Comprehensive Psychiatry, 33,* 34–88.

Tousignant, M., & Hanigan, D. (1993). Suicidal behavior and depression in youth. In P. Cappeliez & R. S. Flynn (Eds.), *Depression and the social environment* (pp. 93–120). Montreal: McGill, Queen's University Press.

Trautman, P. D. (1989). Specific treatment modalities for adolescent suicide attempters. In M. R. Feinleib (Ed.), *Report of the Secretary's Task Force on Youth Suicide. Vol. 3. Prevention and Intervention in Youth Suicide* (pp. 253–263). Washington, DC: U.S. Government Printing Office.

Tremblay, P., King, P., & Baines, G. (1994). Clinical and demographic characteristics of voluntary and involuntary psychiatric inpatients. *Canadian Journal of Psychiatry, 39,* 297–299.

Tremblay, R. E., Masse, B., Perron, D., Leblanc, M., Schwartzman, A. E., & Ledingham, J. E. (1992). Early disruptive behavior, poor school achievement, delinquent behavior and delinquent personality. *Journal of Consulting and Clinical Psychology, 60,* 64–72.

Tremblay, R. E., Pihl, R. O., Vitaro, F., & Dobkin, P. L. (1994). Predicting early onset of male antisocial behavior from preschool behavior. *Archives of General Psychiatry, 51,* 732–739.

Trull, T. J., Widiger, T. A., & Frances, A. (1987). Covariation of criteria for avoidant, schizoid, and dependent personality disorders. *American Journal of Psychiatry, 144,* 767–771.

Tryon, W. W. (1993). Neural networks. II. Unified learning theory and behavioral psychotherapy. *Clinical Psychology Review, 13,* 353–371.

Tsoi, W. F. (1990). Developmental profile of 200 male and 100 female transsexuals in Singapore. *Archives of Sexual Behavior, 19,* 595–605.

Tsuang, M. T., & Faraone, S. V. (1994). Schizophrenia. In G. Winokur & P. J. Clayton (Eds.), *The medical basis of psychiatry* (2nd ed., pp. 87–114). Philadelphia: Saunders.

Tunnell, G. B. (1977). Three dimensions of naturalness: An expanded definition of field research. *Psychology Bulletin, 84* (3), 426–437.

Tuokko, A. (1995, April 12). *1994 annual report from the British Columbia Review Panel Office.* Report available from the first author.

Turk, D. C. (1996). Biopsychosocial perspective on chronic pain. In R. J. Gatchel & D. C. Turk (Eds.), *Psychological approaches to pain management: A practitioner's handbook* (pp. 3–32). New York: Guilford.

Turk, D., & Okifuji, A. (1998). Interdisciplinary approach to pain management: Philosophy, operations and efficacy. In M. A. Ashburn & L. J. Rice (Eds.), *The management of pain* (pp. 235–248). New York: Churchill Livingstone.

Turkat, I. D., & Banks, D. S. (1987). Paranoid personality and its disorder. *Journal of Psychopathology and Behavioral Assessment, 9,* 295–304.

Turkat, I. D., & Levin, R. A. (1984). Formulation of personality disorders. In H. E. Adams & P. B. Sutker (Eds.), *Comprehensive handbook of psychotherapy* (pp. 495–522). New York: Plenum.

Turkat, I. D., Keane, S. P., & Thompson-Pope, S. K. (1990). Social processing in paranoid personalities. *Journal of Psychopathology and Behavioral Assessment, 12,* 263–269.

Turnbull, A. P., Summers, J. A., & Brotherson, M. J. (1986). Family life cycle: Theoretical and empirical implications and future directions for families with mentally retarded members. In J. J. Gallagher, & P. M. Vietze (Eds.), *Families of handicapped persons: Research, programs and policy issues* (pp. 45–65). Baltimore, MD: Brookes.

Turnbull, J. M. (1989). Anxiety and physical illness in the elderly. *Journal of Clinical Psychiatry, 50,* 40–45.

Turnbull, J., Freeman, C. P., Barry, F., & Henderson, A. (1989). The clinical characteristics of bulimic women. *International Journal of Eating Disorders, 8,* 399–409.

Turner, J. R. (1994). *Cardiovascular reactivity and stress: Patterns of physiological response.* New York: Plenum.

Turner, R. J., & Wagonfield, M. O. (1967). Occupational mobility and schizophrenia. *American Sociological Review, 32,* 104–113.

Turner, S. M., Beidel, D. C., Dancu, C. V., & Keys, D. J. (1991). Social Phobia: Axis I and II correlates. *Journal of Abnormal Psychology, 100,* 102–106.

Turner, S. M., Beidel, D. C., Dancu, C. V., & Stanley, M. A. (1989). An empirically derived inventory to measure social fears and anxiety: The Social Phobia and Anxiety Inventory. *Psychological Assessment, 1,* 35–40.

Tutkun, H., Sar, V., Yargic, L., Ozpulat, T., Yanik, M., & Kiziltan, E. (1998). Frequency of dissociative disorders among psychiatric patients in a Turkish university clinic. *American Journal of Psychiatry, 155* (6), 800–806.

Tutty, L. M. (1997). Child sexual abuse prevention programs: Evaluating Who Do You Tell. *Child Abuse and Neglect, 21,* 869–881.

Tymchuk, A., & Andron, L., & Tymchuk, M. (1990). Training mothers with mental handicaps to understand behavioral and developmental principles. *Mental Handicap Research, 3,* 51–59.

Tymchuk, A., & Feldman, M. A. (1991). Parents with mental retardation and their children: Review of research relevant to professional practice. *Canadian Psychology, 32,* 486–494.

Udry, J. R. (1993). The politics of sex research. *Journal of Sex Research, 30,* 103–110.

Ullman, L., & Krasner, L. (1975). *A psychological approach to abnormal behavior* (2nd ed.). Englewood Cliffs, NJ: Prentice-Hall.

United States Department of Health and Human Services (1993). *Depression in primary care. Vol. 1. Detection and diagnosis.* Baltimore, MD: Agency for Health Care Policy and Research.

Vachon, M.L.S., Lyall, W.A.L., Rogers, J., Freedman-Letofsky, K., & Freeman, S.J.J. (1980). A controlled study of self-help intervention for widows. *American Journal of Psychiatry, 137,* 1380–1384.

Valdes, M., Garcia, L., Treserra, J., et al. (1986). Psychogenic pain and depressive disorders: An empirical study. *Journal of Affective Disorders, 16,* 21–25.

Van Ameringen, M., Mancini, C., Styan, D., Donison, D. (1991). Relationship of social phobia with other psychiatric illness. *Journal of Affective Disorders, 21,* 93–99.

Van der Molen, G. M., Van den Hout, M. A., Vroemen, J., Lousberg, H., & Griez, E. (1986). Cognitive determinants of lactate-induced anxiety. *Behaviour Research and Therapy, 24,* 677–680.

Van Etten, M. L., & Taylor, S. (1997). Comparative efficacy of treatments for posttraumatic stress disorder: A meta-analysis. *Behavior Therapy.* Under review.

Vanderheyden, D. A., & Boland, F. J. (1987). A comparison of normal, mild, moderate and severe binge-eaters and binge-vomiters using discriminant function analysis. *International Journal of Eating Disorders, 6,* 331–337.

Vaughn, C. E., & Leff, J. P. (1976). The influence of family and social factors on the course of psychiatric illness: A comparison of schizophrenic and depressed neurotic patients. *British Journal of Psychiatry,* 129, 125–137.

Venter, A., Lord, C., & Schopler, E. (1992). A follow-up study of high-functioning autistic children. *Journal of Child Psychology and Psychiatry, 33,* 489–507.

Vessey, J. T., & Howard, K. I. (1993). Who seeks psychotherapy? *Psychotherapy, 30,* 546–553.

Vincent, K. R., & Harman, M. J. (1991). Exner Rorschach: An analysis of its clinical validity. *Journal of Clinical Psychology, 47,* 596–599.

Virkkunen, M., & Linnoila, M. (1993). Serotonin in personality disorders with habitual violence and impulsivity. In S. Hodgins (Ed.), *Mental disorder and crime* (pp. 194–207). Newbury Park, CA: Sage.

Vitiello, M. V., & Prinz, P. N. (1994). Sleep disturbances in the elderly. In M. L. Albert, & J. E. Knoefel (Eds.), *Clinical neurology of aging,* New York: Oxford University Press.

Vitousek, K. B., & Manke, F. (1994). Personality variables and diagnosis in anorexia nervosa and bulimia nervosa. *Journal of Abnormal Psychology, 103,* 137–148.

Vogel, P. (1987). The right to parent. *Entourage, 2,* 33–39.

Volkmar, F. R., & Schwab-Stone, M. (1996). Childhood disorders in DSM-IV. *Journal of Child Psychology and Psychiatry, 37,* 779–784.

Volkmar, F., Carter, A., Grossman, J., & Klin, A. (1997). Social development in autism. In D. J. Cohen & F. R. Volkmar (Eds.), *Handbook of autism and pervasive developmental disorders* (pp. 173–194). New York: Wiley.

Volpicelli, J. R., Alterman, A. I., Hayashida., M., & O'Brien, C. P. (1992). Naltrexone in the treatment of alcohol dependence. *Archives of General Psychiatry, 49,* 876–880.

Wachtel, P. L. (1982). What can dynamic therapies contribute to behavior therapy? *Behavior Therapy, 13,* 594–609.

Wagner, P. S. (1996). First person account: A voice from another closet. *Schizophrenia Bulletin, 22,* 399–401.

Wahler, R. G., & Dumas, J. E. (1989). Attentional problems in dysfunctional mother-child interactions: An interbehavioral model. *Psychological Bulletin, 105,* 116–130.

Wakefield, J. (1992). Disorder as dysfunction: A conceptual critique of DSM-III-R's definition of mental disorder. *Psychological Review, 99,* 232–247.

Wakefield, J. C. (1987). Sex bias in the diagnosis of primary orgasmic dysfunction. *American Psychologist, 42,* 464–471.

Waldinger, R. J., & Frank, A. F. (1989). Transference and the vicissitudes of medication use by borderline patients. *Psychiatry, 52,* 416–427.

Walker, E. F. (1994). Neurodevelopmental precursors of schizophrenia. In A. S. David & J. C. Cutting (Eds.), *The neuropsychology of schizophrenia* (pp. 119–129). Hove, UK: Erlbaum.

Walker, L. S., Garber, J., & Greene, J. W. (1991). Somatization symptoms in pediatric abdominal pain patients: Relation to chronicity of abdominal pain and parent somatization. *Journal of Abnormal Child Psychology, 19,* 379–394.

Walker, N. (1968). *Crime and insanity in England. Vol. 1.* The historical perspective. Edinburgh: Edinburgh University Press.

Walker, N. (1985). The insanity defense before 1800. *The Annals of the American Academy of Political and Social Science, 477,* 25–30.

Wallace, J., & Pfohl, B. (1995). Age-related differences in the symptomatic expression of major depression. *Journal of Nervous and Mental Disease, 183,* 99–102.

Wallace, S. T., & Alden, L. E. (1991). A comparison of social standards and perceived ability in anxious and nonanxious men. *Cognitive Therapy & Research, 15,* 237–254.

Wallach, M. A., & Kogan, N. (1965). *Modes of thinking in young children: A study of the creativity-intelligence distinction.* New York: Holt, Rinehart & Winston.

Waller, G. (1991). Sexual abuse as a factor in eating disorders. *British Journal of Psychiatry, 159,* 664–671.

Wallgren, H., & Barry, H. (1971). *Actions of alcohol.* Amsterdam: Elsevier.

Walsh, B. T. (1995). Pharmacotherapy of eating disorders. In K. D. Brownell & C. G. Fairburn (Eds.), *Eating disorders and obesity: A comprehensive handbook* (pp. 313–317). New York: Guilford Press.

Walsh, B. T., & Devlin, M. J. (1992). Pharmacological treatment of eating disorders. In D. Shaffer (Ed.), *Psychiatric clinics of North America* (pp. 149–160). Philadelphia: Saunders.

Walsh, B. T., Hadigan, C. M., Kissileff, H. R., & LaChaussée, J. L. (1992). Bulimia nervosa: A syndrome of feast and famine. In G. H. Anderson & S. H. Kennedy (Eds.), *The biology of feast and famine* (pp. 3–20). New York: Academic Press.

Walsh, G., & Adlaf, E. (1995). A profile of student cannabis users: Preliminary results. In *Epidemiological trends in drug abuse.* Washington, DC: U.S. Department of Health and Human Services.

Walsh, J. (1990). Assessment and treatment of the schizotypal personality disorder. *Journal of Independent Social Work, 4,* 41–59.

Ward, T., Hudson, S. M., Marshall, W. L., & Siegert, R. (1995). Attachment style and intimacy deficits in sex offenders: A theoretical framework. *Sexual Abuse: A Journal of Research and Treatment, 7,* 317–335.

Warner, R. (1978). The diagnosis of antisocial and hysterical personality disorders: An example of sex bias. *Journal of Nervous and Mental Disease, 166,* 839–845.

Warsh, C. K. (1989). *Moments of unreason: The practice of Canadian psychiatry and the Homewood Retreat, 1883–1923.* Montreal: McGill Queen's University Press.

Wartenberg, A. A., Nirenberg, T. D., Liepman, M. R., Silvia, L. Y., Begin, A. M., & Monti, P. M. (1990). Detoxification of alcoholics: Improving care by symptom-triggered sedation. *Alcoholism in Clinical and Experimental Research, 14,* 71–75.

Wasik, B. H., Ramey, C. T., Bryant, D. M., & Sparling, J. J. (1990). A longitudinal study of two early intervention strategies: Project CARE. *Child Development, 61,* 1682–1692.

Wasylenki, D. A. (1990). Psychotherapy of schizophrenia revisited. Annual meeting of the Canadian Psychiatric Association, Toronto, Canada. *Hospital and Community Psychiatry, 43* (2), 123–127.

Wasylenski, D. (1985). Psychiatric aftercare in a metropolitan setting. *Canadian Journal of Psychiatry, 30* (5), 329–336.

Waterhouse, L., Morris, R., Allen, D., Dunn, M., Fein, D., Feinstein, C., Rapin, I., & Wing, L. (1996). Diagnosis and classification in autism. *Journal of Autism and Developmental Disorders, 26,* 59–86.

Watson, D., & Friend, R. (1969). Measurement of social-evaluative anxiety. *Journal of Consulting and Clinical Psychology, 33,* 448–457.

Watson, J. B. (1913). Psychology as the behaviorist views it. *Psychological Review, 20,* 158–177.

Watson, J. B. (1924). *Behaviorism.* New York: Norton.

Watson, J. B., & Rayner, R. (1920). Conditioned emotional reactions. *Journal of Experimental Psychology, 3,* 1–14.

Waxman, H. M., & Carner, E. A. (1984). Physicians' recognition, diagnosis, and treatment of mental disorders in elderly patients. *The Gerontologist, 24,* 593–597.

Webster, C. D., Harris, G. T., Rice, M. E., Cormier, C., & Quinsey, V. L. (1994). *The violence prediction scheme: Assessing dangerousness in high risk men.* Toronto: Centre of Criminology, University of Toronto.

Webster-Stratton, C. (1994). Advancing videotape parent training: A comparison study. *Journal of Consulting and Clinical Psychology, 62,* 583–593.

Webster-Stratton, C., & Hammond, M. (1997). Treating children with early-onset conduct problems: A comparison of child and parent training interventions. *Journal of Consulting and Clinical Psychology, 65,* 93–109.

Wechsler, D. (1967). *Manual: Wechsler Preschool and Primary Scale of Intelligence.* New York: Psychological Corporation.

Wechsler, D. (1974). *The Measurement of Adult Intelligence Scale.* Baltimore, MD: Williams & Wilkins.

Wechsler, D. (1991). *Wechsler Intelligence Scale for Children: Third Ed.* San Antonio: Psychological Corporation.

Weddington, W. W., Brown, B. S., Haertzen, M. H., Cone, E. J., Dax, E. M., Herning, R. I., & Michaelson, B. S. (1990). Changes in mood, craving, and sleep during short term abstinence reported by male cocaine addicts. *Archives of General Psychiatry, 47,* 861–868.

Wegner, D. M. (1989). *White bears and other unwanted thoughts.* New York: Viking.

Wehr, T., & Rosenthal, N. (1989). Seasonality and affective illness. *American Journal of Psychiatry, 146,* 829–839.

Weinberger, D. R. (1987). Implications of normal brain development for the pathogenesis of schizophrenia. *Archives of General Psychiatry, 44,* 660–670.

Weinberger, D. R., Wagner, R. L., & Wyatt, R. J. (1983). Neuropathological studies of schizophrenia: A selective review. *Schizophrenia Bulletin, 9,* 193–212.

Weinberger, J. (1995). Common factors aren't so common: The common factors dilemma. *Clinical Psychology: Science and Practice, 2,* 45–69.

Weinberger, M., Hiner, S. L., & Tierney, W. M. (1987). In support of hassles as a measure of stress in predicting health outcomes. *Journal of Behavioral Medicine, 10,* 19–31.

Weiner, B. (1985). Mental disability and criminal law. In S. Brakel, J. Parry, & B. Weiner (Eds.), *The mentally disabled and the law.* (3rd ed.). (pp. 763–773). Washington, DC: American Bar Foundation.

Weiner, D. B. (1979). The apprenticeship of Philippe Pinel: A new document, "Observations of Citizen Pussin on the insane." *American Journal of Psychiatry, 136,* 1128–1134.

Weiner, H. (1996). Use of animal models in peptic ulcer disease. *Psychosomatic Medicine, 58,* 524–545.

Weiner, R. D., & Coffey, C. E. (1991). Electroconvulsive therapy in the United States. *Psychopharmacology Bulletin, 27,* 9–15.

Weisman, A., Beck, A. T., & Kovacs, M. (1979). Drug abuse, hoplessness and suicidal behavior. *International Journal of the Addictions, 14,* 451–464.

Weiss, B., & Weisz, J. R. (1995). Relative effectiveness of behavioral and nonbehavioral child psychotherapy. *Journal of Consulting and Clinical Psychology, 63,* 317–320.

Weiss, G., & Hechtman, L. (1986). *Hyperactive children grown up.* New York: Guilford Press.

Weiss, G., & Hechtman, L. (1993). *Hyperactive children grown up: ADHD in children, adolescents, and adults* (2nd ed.). New York: Guilford Press.

Weiss, J. (1972). Psychological factors in stress and disease. *Scientific American, 226,* 104–113.

Weiss, J. M. (1970). Somatic effects of predictable and unpredictable shock. *Psychosomatic Medicine, 32,* 397–408.

Weiss, J. M. (1971). Effects of coping behavior with and without a feedback signal on stress pathology in rats. *Journal of Comparative and Physiological Psychology, 77,* 22–30.

Weiss, R. D., & Stephens, P. S. (1992), Substance abuse and suicide. In D. Jacobs (Ed.), *Suicide and clinical practice.* Washington, DC: American Psychiatric Press.

Weissberg, R. P., & Bell, D. N. (1997). A meta-analytic review of primary prevention programs for children and adolescents: Contributions and caveats. *American Journal of Community Psychology, 25,* 207–214.

Weissberg, R. P., & Elias, M. J. (1993). Enhancing young people's social competence and health behavior: An important challenge for educators, scientists, policymakers, and funders. *Applied and Preventive Psychology, 2,* 179–190.

Weissman, M. M., Leaf, P. J., Tischler, G. L., Blazer, D. G., Karno, M., Bruce, M. L., & Florio, L. P. (1988). Affective disorders in five United States communities. *Psychological Medicine, 18,* 141–153.

Weissman, M. M., Leckman, J. F., Merikangas, K. R., Gammon, G. B., & Prusoff, B. A. (1984). Depression and anxiety disorders in parents and children. *Archives of General Psychiatry, 41,* 845–852.

Weisz, J. R., Weiss, B., & Donenberg, G. R. (1992). The lab versus the clinic: Effects of child and adolescent psychotherapy. *American Psychologist, 47,* 1578–1585.

Wells, K. B., & Sturm, R. (1996). Informing the policy process: From efficacy to effectiveness data on pharmacotherapy. *Journal of Consulting and Clinical Psychology, 64,* 638–645.

Wells, K., Sturm, R., Sherbourne, C., & Meredith, L. (1996). *Caring for depression.* Cambridge, MA: Harvard University Press.

Werner, E. E. (1992). *Overcoming the odds: High risk children from birth to adulthood.* Ithaca, NY: Cornell University Press.

Werry, J. S. (1992). Child psychiatric disorders: Are they classifiable? *British Journal of Psychiatry, 161,* 472–480.

West, M., Keller, A., Links, P. S., & Patrick, J. (1993). Borderline disorder and attachment pathology. *Canadian Journal of Psychiatry, 38,* 16–22.

Whalen, C. K., & Henker, B. (1985). The social worlds of hyperactive (ADDH) children. *Clinical Psychology Review, 5,* 447–478.

Whalen, C. K., Henker, B., & Dotemoto, S. (1980). Methylphenidate and hyperactivity: Effects on teacher behaviors. *Science, 208,* 1280–1282.

Whalley, L. J. (1989). Drug treatments of dementia. *British Journal of Psychiatry, 155,* 595–611.

Wharf, B. (1989). Implementing "Achieving health for all." *Canadian Review of Social Policy, 24,* 42–48.

Wheeler, D. L., Jacobson, J. W., Paglieri, R. A., & Schwartz, A. A. (1993). An experimental assessment of facilitated communication. *Mental Retardation, 31,* 49–60.

White, J. (1983). Christianity and mental illness. In *Masks of melancholy: A Christian physician looks at depression and suicide* (pp. 11–54). Downers Grove, IL: InterVarsity.

Whittemore, K. E., & Ogloff, J.R.P. (1994). Fitness and competency issues in Canadian criminal courts: Elucidating the standards for mental health professionals. *Canadian Journal of Psychiatry, 39,* 198–210.

Widiger, T. A., & Corbitt, E. M. (1993). Antisocial personality disorder: Proposals for DSM-IV. *Journal of Personality Disorders, 7,* 63–77.

Widiger, T. A., & Costa, P. T. (1994). Personality and personality disorders. *Journal of Abnormal Psychology, 103,* 78–91.

Widiger, T. A., & Frances, A. (1985). The DSM-III personality disorders: Perspectives from psychology. *Archives of General Psychiatry, 42,* 615–623.

Widiger, T. A., & Frances, A. J. (1989). Epidemiology, diagnosis, and comorbidity of borderline personality disorder. In A. Tasman, R. E. Hales, & A. J. Frances (Eds.), *Review of Psychiatry* (Vol. 8, pp. 8–24). Washington, DC: American Psychiatric Press.

Widiger, T. A., & Rogers, J. H. (1989). Prevalence and comorbidity of personality disorders. *Psychiatric Annals, 19,* 132–136.

Widiger, T. A., & Shea, T. (1991). Differentiation of Axis I and Axis II disorders. *Journal of Abnormal Psychology, 100,* 399–406.

Widiger, T. A., & Spitzer, R. L. (1991). Sex bias in the diagnosis of personality disorders: Conceptual and methodological issues. *Clinical Psychology Review, 11,* 1–22.

Widiger, T. A., & Trull, T. J. (1991). Diagnosis and clinical assessment. *Annual Review of Psychology, 41,* 109–135.

Widiger, T. A., & Trull, T. J. (1992). Personality and psychopathology: An application of the five-factor model. *Journal of Personality, 60,* 363–393.

Widiger, T. A., & Trull, T. J. (1993). Borderline and narcissistic personality disorders. In P. B. Sutker & H. E. Adams (Eds.), *Comprehensive handbook of psychopathology* (2nd ed.) (pp. 371–397). New York: Plenum Press.

Widiger, T. A., Frances, A. J., & Trull, T. J. (1987). A psychometric analysis of the social-interpersonal and cognitive-perceptual items for the schizotypal personality disorder. *Archives of General Psychiatry, 44,* 741–745.

Widiger, T. A., Frances, A. J., Spitzer, R. L., & Williams, J.B.W. (1988). The DSM-III personality disorder: An overview. *American Journal of Psychiatry, 145,* 786–795.

Widiger, T. A., Freeman, K., & Bailey, B. (1990). Convergent and discriminant validity of personality disorder prototypic acts. *Psychological Assessment: A Journal of Consulting and Clinical Psychology, 2,* 107–113.

Widiger, T. A., Miele, G. M., & Tilly, S. M. (1992). Alternative perspectives on the diagnosis of borderline personality disorder. In J. F. Carkin, E. Marziali, & H. Munroe-Blum (Eds.), *Borderline personality disorder: Clinical and empirical perspectives* (pp. 89–115). New York: Guilford.

Wikler, L., M., Wasow, M., & Hatfield, E. (1981). Chronic sorrow revisited: Parents vs. professional depiction of the adjustment of parents of mentally retarded children. *American Journal of Orthopsychiatry, 51,* 63–70.

Wilfley, D. E., & Rodin, J. (1995). Cultural influences on eating disorders. In K. D. Brownell & C. G. Fairburn (Eds.), *Eating disorders and obesity: A comprehensive handbook.* New York: Guilford Press.

Wilfley, D. E., Agras, W. S., Telch, C. F., Rossiter, E. M., Schneider, J. A., Cole, A. G., Sifford, L. A., & Raeburn, S. D. (1993). Group cognitive-behavioral therapy and group interpersonal psychotherapy for the nonpurging bulimic individual: A controlled comparison. *Journal of Consulting and Clinical Psychology, 61,* 296–305.

Wilkins, J. A., Boland, F. J., & Albinson, J. (1990). A comparison of male and female university athletes and nonathletes on eating disorder indices: Are athletes protected? *Journal of Sport Behavior, 14,* 129–143.

Williams, G., Chamove, A. S., & Miller, H. R. (1990). Eating disorders, perceived control, assertiveness and hostility. *British Journal of Clinical Psychology, 29,* 327–335.

Williams, J.M.G. (1997). *Cry of pain: Understanding suicidice and self harm.* London: Penguin.

Williams, J.M.G., & Broadbent, K. (1986). Autobiographical memory in attempted suicide patients. *Journal of Abnormal Psychology, 95,* 144–149.

Williams, J.M.R. (1992). *The psychological treatment of depression.* New York: Routledge.

Williams, L., Ellis, C. R., Ickowicz, A., Singh, N. N., & Singh, Y. N. (1993). Pharmacotherapy of aggressive behavior in individuals with mental retardation and mental illness. *Journal of Developmental and Physical Disabilities, 5,* 87–94.

Williams, R. B., Barefoot, J. C., Califf, R. M., et al. (1992). Prognostic importance of social and economic resources among medically treated patients with angiographically documented coronary artery disease. *Journal of the American Medical Association, 267,* 520–524.

Williamson, D. F., Kahn, H. S., Remington, P. L., & Anda, R. F. (1990). The 10-year incidence of overweight and major weight gain in US adults. *Archives of Internal Medicine, 150,* 665–672.

Wilmer, H. A. (1976). Origins of a Jungian-oriented therapeutic community for schizophrenic patients. *Hospital & Community Psychiatry, 27* (5) 338–342.

Wilson, E. O. (1994). *Naturalist.* Washington, DC: Island Press.

Wilson, G. I., Nathan, P. E., O'Leary, K. O., & Clark, L. A. (1996). Substance-related disorders. In *Abnormal Psychology: Integrated Perspectives.* Needham Heights, MA: Allyn and Bacon.

Wilson, G. T. (1993). Binge eating and addictive disorders. In C. G. Fairburn & G. T. Wilson (Eds.), *Binge eating: Nature, assessment and treatment* (pp. 97–120). New York: Guilford Press.

Wilson, G. T. (1995). Eating disorders and addictive disorders. In K. D. Brownell & C. G. Fairburn (Eds.), *Eating disorders and obesity: A comprehensive handbook* (pp. 165–170). New York: Guilford Press.

Wilson, G. T. (1996). Treatment of bulimia nervosa: When CBT fails. *Behavior Research and Therapy, 34,* 295–315.

Wilson, G. T., & Fairburn, C. G. (1993). Cognitive treatments for eating disorders. *Journal of Consulting and Clinical Pscyhology, 61,* 261–269.

Wilson, G. T., & Lawson, D. M. (1976). Effects of alcohol on sexual arousal in women. *Journal of Abnormal Psychology, 85,* 489–497.

Wilson, W. H., Ellinwood, E. H., Mathew, R. J., & Johnson, K. (1994). Effects of marijuana on performance of a computerized cognitive-neurological test battery. *Psychiatry Research, 51,* 115–125.

Winnicott, D. W. (1965). *The maturation process and the facilitating environment.* London: Hogarth.

Winokur, G. (1977). Delusional disorder (paranoia). *Comprehensive Psychiatry, 18,* 511–521.

Winokur, G., & Clayton, P., & Reich, T. (1969). *Manic depressive illness.* St. Louis, MO: Mosby.

Wise, R. A., & Bozarth, M. A. (1987). A psychomotor stimulant theory of addiction. *Psychological Review, 94,* 469–492.

Wise, T. N., Fagan, P. J., Schmidt, C. W., Ponticas, Y., et al. (1991). Personality and sexual functioning of transvestic fetishists and other paraphilias. *Journal of Nervous and Mental Disease, 179,* 694–698.

Wiseman, C. V., Gray, J. J., Mosimann, J. E., & Ahrens, A. H. (1992). Cultural expectations of thinness in women: An update. *International Journal of Eating Disorders, 11,* 85–89.

Wolf, M. M. (1978). Social validity: the case for subjective measurement or how applied behaviour analysis is finding its heart. *Journal of Applied Behaviour Analysis, 11,* 203–214.

Wolfe, D. A., & Wekerle, C. (1993). Treatment strategies for child physical abuse and neglect: A critical progress report. *Clinical Psychology Review, 13,* 473–500.

Wolfe, D. A., Wekerle, C., & Scott, K. (1997). *Alternatives to violence: Empowering youth to develop healthy relationships.* Thousand Oaks, CA: Sage.

Wolfe, R., Morrow, J., & Fredrickson, B. L. (1996). Mood disorders in older adults. In L. L. Carstensen, B. A. Edelstein, & L. Dornbrand (Eds.), *The practical handbook of clinical gerontology* (pp. 274–303). Thousand Oaks, CA: Sage.

Wolfensberger, W. (1972). *The principle of normalization in human services.* Toronto: Leonard Crainford.

Wolfensberger, W. (1975). *The origin and nature of our institutional models.* Syracuse, NY: Human Policy Press.

Wolff, P. H., Waber, D., Bauermeister, M., Cohen, C., & Ferber, R. (1982). The neuropsychological status of adolescent delinquent boys. *Journal of Child Psychology & Psychiatry, 23,* 267–279.

Wolpe, J. (1958). *Psychotherapy by reciprocal inhibition.* Stanford, CA: Stanford University Press.

Wolpe, J., & Lang, P. J. (1964). A fear survey schedule for use in behavior therapy. *Behaviour Research and Therapy, 2,* 27–30.

Wolpe, J., & Rachman, S. (1960). Psychoanalytic evidence: A critique based on Freud's case of Little Hans. *Journal of Nervous and Mental Disease, 131,* 135–145.

Wong, D. F., Wagner, H. N., Jr., Tune, L. E., Dannals, R. F., Pearlson, G. D., Links, J. M., Tamminga, C. A., Broussoule, E. P., Ravert, H. T., Wilson, A. A., Toung, J.K.T., Malat, J., Williams, J. A., O'Tuama, L. A., Snyder, S. H., Kuhar, M. J., Gjedde, A. (1986). Positron emission tomography reveals elevated D$_2$ dopamine receptors in drug-naive schizophrenics. *Science, 234,* 1558–1562.

Wong, F. (1984). *The criminal and institutional behaviors of psychopaths.* Programs Branch Users Report. Ottawa: Ministry of the Solicitor General of Canada.

Wong, S., & Elek, D. (1990). *The treatment of psychopaths: A review.* Unpublished manuscript, University of Saskatchewan, Saskatoon, Saskatchewan.

Woodford, L., & Minnes, P. M. (1997). Well-being in older parents of adults with developmental disabilities. Paper presented at Ontario Association on Developmental Disabilities conference, Toronto, Ontario.

Woodhouse, K. W. (1993). Sleep disorders in the elderly. In R. Levy, R. Howard, & A. Burns (Eds.), *Treatment and care in old age psychiatry.* Petersfield, UK: Wrightson Biomedical Publishing.

Woodill, G. (1992). Controlling the sexuality of developmentally disabled persons: Historical perspectives. *Journal of Developmental Disabilities, 1,* 1–14.

Woody, S. R., Chambless, D. L., & Glass, C. R. (1997). Self-focused attention in the treatment of social phobia. *Behaviour Research and Therapy, 35,* 117–129.

Wooley, O. W., & Wooley, S. C. (1982). The Beverly Hills eating disorder: The mass marketing of anorexia nervosa. *International Journal of Eating Disorders, 1,* 57–69.

World Health Organization (1948). *Manual of the international statistical classification of diseases, injuries, and cause of death.* Geneva: WHO.

World Health Organization (1973). *Report of the International Pilot Study of Schizophrenia. Vol. 1. Results of the initial evaluation phase.* Geneva: WHO.

World Health Organization (1992). *International classification of diseases and related health problems* (10th rev.). Geneva: WHO.

Wormith, J. S., Bradford, J.M.W., Pawlak, A., Borzecki, M., & Zohar, A. (1988). The assessment of deviant sexual arousal as a function of intelligence, instructional set and alcohol ingestion. *Canadian Journal of Psychiatry, 33,* 800–808.

Wright, L. S. (1985). High school polydrug users and abusers. *Adolescence, 20* (80), 852–861.

Wu, J., & Bunney, W. (1990). The biological basis of an antidepressant response to sleep deprivation and relapse: Review and hypothesis. *American Journal of Psychiatry, 147,* 14–21.

Wurtman, R. J., & Wurtman, J. J. (1984). Nutrients, neurotransmitter synthesis, and the control of food intake. In A. J. Stunkard & E. Stellar (Eds.), *Eating and its disorders* (pp. 77–86). New York: Raven Press.

Wyatt, G. E. (1985). The sexual abuse of Afro-American and white American women in childhood. *Child Abuse and Neglect, 9,* 507–519.

Wyngaarden, M. (1981). Interviewing mentally retarded persons: Issues and strategies. In R. Bruininks, C. E. Meyers, B. B. Sigford, & K. C. Lakin (Eds.), *Deinstitutionalization and community adjustment of mentally retarded people.* Monograph No. 4 (pp. 107–113). Washington, DC: American Association on Mental Deficiency.

Yalom, I. D., Green, R., & Fisk, N. (1973). Prenatal exposure to female hormones: Effect on psychosexual development in boys. *Archives of General Psychiatry, 28,* 554–561.

Yassa, R., Dastoor, D., Nastase, C., Camille, Y., & Belzile, L. (1993). The prevalence of late-onset schizophrenia in a psychogeriatric population. *Journal of Geriatric Psychiatry and Neurology, 6,* 120–125.

Yassa, R., Nair, N.P.V., & Iskandar, H. (1988). Late onset bipolar disorder in psychosis and depression in the elderly. *Psychiatry Clinics of North America, 11,* 117–131.

Yates, A. (1973). Abnormalities of psychomotor functions. In H. J. Eysenck (Ed.), *Handbook of abnormal psychology* (pp. 261–283). San Diego: R. R. Knapp.

Yoshida, A., Huang, I-Y., & Ikawa, M. (1984). Molecular abnormality of an inactive aldehyde dehydrogenase variant commonly found in Orientals. *Proceedings of the National Academy of Sciences, 81,* 258–261.

Yu, S., Pritchard, M. D., Kremer, E., Lynch, M., Nancarrow, J., Baker, E., Holman, K., Mulley, J. C., Warren, S. T., Schlessinger, D., Sutherland, G. R., & Richards, R. I. (1991). Fragile X genotype characterized by an unstable region of DNA. *Science, 252,* 1179–1181.

Yukon Bureau of Statistics (1990). *Yukon alcohol and drug survey, 1990. Vol. I. Technical report.* Whitehorse: Yukon Executive Office.

Zametkin, A. J., Nordahl, T. E., Gross, M., King, A. C., Semple, W. E., Rumsey, J., Hamburger, S., & Cohen, R. M. (1990). Cerebral glucose metabolism in adults with hyperactivity of childhood onset. *New England Journal of Medicine, 323,* 1361–1366.

Zane, G., & Williams, S. L. (1993). Performance-related anxiety in agoraphobia: Treatment procedures and cognitive mechanisms of change. *Behavior Therapy, 24,* 625–644.

Zarit, S. H. (1980). Depression. In *Aging and mental disorders* (pp. 184–195). New York: Free Press.

Zax, M., & Specter, G. A. (1974). *An introduction to community psychology.* New York: Wiley.

Zeck, P. M., Tierney, H., Tardiff, K., et al. (1988). Increased risk of suicide in persons with AIDS. *Journal of the American Medical Association, 259,* 1333–7.

Zemishlany, Z., Siever, L. J., & Coccuro, E. F. (1988). Biological factors in personality disorders. *Israel Journal of Psychiatry and Related Sciences, 25,* 12–23.

Zigler, E. (1967). Familial mental retardation: A continuing dilemma. *Science, 155,* 292–298.

Zigler, E., & Balla, D. (Eds.) (1982). *Mental retardation: The developmental-difference controversy.* Hillsdale, NJ: Erlbaum.

Zigler, E., & Hodapp, R. M. (1991). *Understanding mental retardation.* Cambridge: Cambridge University Press.

Zigler, E., Hodapp, R., & Edison, M. (1990). From theory to practice in the care and education of mentally retarded individuals. *American Journal on Mental Retardation, 95,* 1–12.

Zigman, W. B., Schupf, N., Lubin, R. A., & Silverman, W. P. (1987). Premature regression of adults with Down syndrome. *American Journal of Mental Deficiency, 92,* 161–168.

Zilboorg, G., & Henry, G. W. (1941). *A history of medical psychology.* New York: Norton.

Zimmerman, M., & Coryell, W. (1989). DSM-III personality disorder diagnoses in a nonpatient sample. *Archives of General Psychiatry, 46,* 682–689.

Zimmerman, M., & Coryell, W. H. (1990). Diagnosing personality disorders in the community: A comparison of self-report and interview measures. *Archives of General Psychiatry, 47,* 527–531.

Zipurski, R. B., Marsh, L., Lim, K. O., Dement, S., Shear, P. K., Sullivan, E. V., Murphy, G. M., Cseransky, J. G., & Pfefferbaum, A. (1994). Volumetric MRI assessment of temporal lobe structures in schizophrenia. *Biological Psychiatry, 35,* 501–516.

Ziv, A., & Luz, M. (1973). Manifest anxiety in children of different socioeconomic levels. *Human Development, 16,* 224–232.

Zivian, M. T., Larsen, W., Gekoski, W. L., Knox, V. J., & Hatchette, V. (1994). Psychotherapy for the elderly: Public opinion. *Psychotherapy, 31,* 492–502.

Zivian, M. T., Larsen, W., Knox, V. J., Gekoski, W. L., & Hatchette, V. (1992). Psychotherapy for the elderly: Psychotherapists' preferences. *Psychotherapy, 29,* 668–674.

Zoccolillo, M., Pickles, A., Quinton, D., & Rutter, M. (1992). The outcome of childhood conduct disorder: Implications for defining adult personality disorder and conduct disorder. *Psychological Medicine, 22,* 971–986.

Zubin, J. (1978, April). *Progress in the biometrics of schizophrenia.* Invited address, Department of Psychology, University of Waterloo, Waterloo, ON.

Zubin, J., & Spring, B. J. (1977). Vulnerability: A new view of schizophrenia. *Journal of Abnormal Psychology, 86,* 103–126.

Zucker, K. J. (1990a). Gender identity disorders in children: Clinical descriptions and natural history. In R. Blanchard & B. W. Steiner (Eds.), *Clinical management of gender identity disorders in children and adults* (pp. 3–23). Washington, DC: American Psychiatry Press.

Zucker, K. J. (1990b). Gender identity disorders in children. In R. Blanchard & B. W. Steiner (Eds.), *Clinical management of gender identity disorders in children and adults* (pp. 27–45). Washington, DC: American Psychiatry Press.

Zucker, K. J., Finegan, J. K., Deering, R. W., & Bradley, S. J. (1984). Two subgroups of gender-problem children. *Archives of Sexual Behavior, 13,* 27–29.

NAME INDEX

SUBJECT INDEX

PHOTO CREDITS

DSM-IV Multiaxial Classification System, First Four Axes

Axis I Clinical Syndromes	Axis II Personality Disorders	Axis III General Medical Conditions
Disorders usually first diagnosed in infancy, adolescence	Paranoid	Infectious and parasitic diseases
Delirium, dementia, amnesia, and other cognitive disorders	Schizoid	Neoplasms
Substance-related disorders	Schizotypal	Endocrine, nutritional, and metabolic diseases
Schizophrenia and other psychotic disorders	Antisocial	Diseases of the blood and blood-forming organs
Mood disorders	Borderline	Diseases of the nervous system and sense organs
Anxiety disorders	Histrionic	
Somatoform disorders	Narcissistic	Diseases of the circulatory system
Factitious disorder	Avoidant	Diseases of the respiratory system
Dissociative disorders	Dependent	Diseases of the digestive system
Sexual and gender identity disorders	Obsessive-compulsive	Diseases of the genitourinary system
Eating disorders		
Sleep disorders		
Impulse control disorders not elsewhere classified		
Adjustment disorders		

Axis IV
Psychosocial and Environmental Problems

Check:

_____ Problems with primary support group (Childhood, Adult, Parent-Child). Specify: _____

_____ Problems related to the social environment. Specify: _____

_____ Educational problem. Specify: _____

_____ Occupational problem. Specify: _____

_____ Housing problem. Specify: _____

_____ Economic problem. Specify: _____

_____ Problems with access to health care services. Specify: _____

_____ Problems related to interaction with the legal system/crime. Specify: _____

_____ Other psychosocial problem. Specify: _____

Source: Reprinted with permission from the *Diagnostic and Statistical Manual of Mental Disorders*, Fourth Edition. Copyright 1994 American Psychiatric Association.